The SportingNews

HOCKEY GUIDE

2001-2002 EDITION

Editor/Hockey Guide
CRAIG CARTER

CONTENTS

2001-2002 NHL Season......................................3
  National Hockey League directory 4
  Individual teams section
    (schedules, directories, rosters, etc.) 5
  Mighty Ducks of Anaheim................................5
  Atlanta Thrashers..8
  Boston Bruins 11
  Buffalo Sabres 14
  Calgary Flames 17
  Carolina Hurricanes 20
  Chicago Blackhawks 23
  Colorado Avalanche 26
  Columbus Blue Jackets..................................29
  Dallas Stars 32
  Detroit Red Wings 35
  Edmonton Oilers 38
  Florida Panthers 41
  Los Angeles Kings 44
  Minnesota Wild 47
  Montreal Canadiens 50
  Nashville Predators 53
  New Jersey Devils.......................................56
  New York Islanders 59
  New York Rangers 62
  Ottawa Senators..65
  Philadelphia Flyers 68
  Phoenix Coyotes 71
  Pittsburgh Penguins 74
  St. Louis Blues 77
  San Jose Sharks 80
  Tampa Bay Lightning 83
  Toronto Maple Leafs 86
  Vancouver Canucks 89
  Washington Capitals 92
  Schedule, day by day 95
2000-01 NHL Review...................................103
  Regular season 104
    Final standings.......................................104
    Individual leaders....................................104
    Statistics of players with two or more teams 105
    Miscellaneous 111

Stanley Cup playoffs 115
  Results, round by round 115
  Game summaries, Stanley Cup finals 116
  Individual leaders......................................117
  Individual statistics 118
  Miscellaneous 121
All-Star Game..123
  Awards 124
  Player draft 125
NHL History..131
  Stanley Cup champions 132
  All-Star Games 133
  Year-by-year standings 135
  Records 152
  Statistical leaders 155
  Award winners 172
  The Sporting News awards 181
  Hall of Fame 185
  Milestones 193
  Team by team 200
Minor Leagues 255
  American Hockey League...............................256
  International Hockey League............................277
  East Coast Hockey League.............................288
  Central Hockey League 308
  United Hockey League 319
Major Junior Leagues..................................333
  Canadian Hockey League 334
  Ontario Hockey League 337
  Quebec Major Junior Hockey League 354
  Western Hockey League 369
College Hockey 385
  NCAA Division I 386
  Central Collegiate Hockey Association 389
  Eastern College Athletic Conference 393
  Hockey East 397
  Western Collegiate Hockey Association 400
  Canadian Interuniversity Athletic Union 404
  Canadian colleges 405
Index of teams 408

ON THE COVER: Ray Bourque of the Colorado Avalanche hoists the Stanley Cup (Photo by Dilip Vishwanat/THE SPORTING NEWS.).

Spine photo: Mario Lemieux (File photo).

Copyright © 2001 by The Sporting News, a division of Vulcan Sports Media; 10176 Corporate Square Drive, Suite 200, St. Louis, MO 63132. All rights reserved. Printed in the U.S.A.

No part of the *Hockey Guide* may be reproduced or transmitted in any form or by any means, electronic or mechanical, including photocopy, recording or any information storage and retrieval system now known or to be invented, without permission in writing from the publisher, except by a reviewer who wishes to quote brief passages in connection with a review written for inclusion in a magazine, newspaper or broadcast.

ISBN: 0-89204-653-8

10 9 8 7 6 5 4 3 2 1

2001-02 NHL SEASON

NHL directory

Team information

Schedule

GV
847.5
.S67
2001/02

NATIONAL HOCKEY LEAGUE
DIRECTORY

LEAGUE OFFICES

OFFICERS
Commissioner
Gary B. Bettman
Director, administration & executive assistant to the commissioner
Debbie Jordan
Exec. vice president & chief legal officer
William Daly
Exec. v.p. and dir. of hockey operations
Colin Campbell
Exec. v.p. and chief operating officer
Jon Litner
Exec. v.p. and chief financial officer
Craig Hartnett
Senior vice president, hockey operations
Jim Gregory (Toronto)
Senior vice president, general counsel
David Zimmerman
Senior vice president, finance
Joseph DeSousa

NHL ENTERPRISES
President, NHL Enterprises
Ed Horne
Sr. vice president & general counsel
Richard Zahnd
Group v.p., consumer products marketing
Brian Jennings
Group vice president & managing dir., NHL International
Ken Yaffe
Sr. v.p., television & media ventures
Doug Perlman
Pres., NHL ICE and Sr. v.p., new bus. dev.
Keith Ritter

NHL COMMUNICATIONS STAFF
Group vice president, communications
Bernadette Mansur
Vice president, media relations
Frank Brown

V.p., public relations & media services
Gary Meagher (Toronto)
Chief statistician
Benny Ercolani (Toronto)
Director, media relations
Amy Early
Director, communications
Jamey Horan
Director, news services
Greg Inglis
Manager, public relations
David Keon (Toronto)
Manager, news services
Adam Schwartz
Manager, p.r. & editorial services
Chris Tredree (Toronto)
Coordinator, public relations
Jennifer Perkinson
Associate, public relations
Julie Young (Toronto)
Assistant
Mary Kay Wright

CORPORATE COMMUNICATIONS
Director, community relations
Ken Martin
Manager, corporate communications & player publicity
Sandra Carreon
Manager, corporate communications
Brian Walker
Manager, diversity task force
Nirva Milord
Associate, community relations
Ann Marie Lynch
Assistant
Myrna Mollison
Assistant, diversity task force
Jessica Murray

NEW YORK OFFICE
Address
1251 Avenue of the Americas
47th Floor
New York, NY 10020
Phone
212-789-2000
FAX
212-789-2020

TAPPAN OFFICE (NHL PRODUCTIONS)
Address
183 Oak Tree Road
Tappan, NY 10983
Phone
845-365-6701
FAX
845-365-6010

TORONTO OFFICE
Address
50 Bay Street, 11th Floor
Toronto, Ont. M5J 2X8
Phone
416-981-2777
FAX
416-981-2779

MONTREAL OFFICE
Address
1800 McGill College Avenue
Suite 2600
Montreal, Que., Canada H3A 3J6
Phone
514-841-9220
FAX
514-841-1070

DIVISIONAL ALIGNMENT

EASTERN CONFERENCE

ATLANTIC DIVISION
New Jersey Devils
New York Islanders
New York Rangers
Philadelphia Flyers
Pittsburgh Penguins

NORTHEAST DIVISION
Boston Bruins
Buffalo Sabres
Montreal Canadiens
Ottawa Senators
Toronto Maple Leafs

SOUTHEAST DIVISION
Atlanta Thrashers
Carolina Hurricanes
Florida Panthers
Tampa Bay Lightning
Washington Capitals

WESTERN CONFERENCE

CENTRAL DIVISION
Chicago Blackhawks
Columbus Blue Jackets
Detroit Red Wings
Nashville Predators
St. Louis Blues

NORTHWEST DIVISION
Calgary Flames
Colorado Avalanche
Edmonton Oilers
Minnesota Wild
Vancouver Canucks

PACIFIC DIVISION
Mighty Ducks of Anaheim
Dallas Stars
Los Angeles Kings
Phoenix Coyotes
San Jose Sharks

MIGHTY DUCKS OF ANAHEIM
WESTERN CONFERENCE/PACIFIC DIVISION

Ducks' Schedule
Home games shaded; D—Day game; *—All-Star Game at Los Angeles

October
SUN	MON	TUE	WED	THU	FRI	SAT
	1	2	3	4 BOS	5	6 PIT
7	8 TOR	9 MON	10	11	12 WAS	13
14 TB	15	16	17 BOS	18 LA	19	20
21 VAN	22	23	24 PHO	25	26	27
28 COL	29	30	31 SJ			

November
SUN	MON	TUE	WED	THU	FRI	SAT
				1	2 CHI	3
4 ATL	5	6	7 CAL	8	9 DET	10
11 DAL	12	13	14 SJ	15	16 CBJ	17 WAS
18	19	20 TB	21 FLA	22	23	24 NYI
25 NYR	26	27	28 EDM	29	30 SJ	

December
SUN	MON	TUE	WED	THU	FRI	SAT
						1
2 NAS	3	4	5 EDM	6 VAN	7	8 CAL
9	10 COL	11	12 VAN	13	14 CBJ	15
16 LA	17	18 MIN	19 COL	20	21 PHO	22
23 PHO	24	25	26 SJ	27 LA	28	29
30 CHI	31 CBJ					

January
SUN	MON	TUE	WED	THU	FRI	SAT
		1	2 DET	3	4 FLA	5
6	7	8	9 STL	10	11 MIN	12 NAS
13 NAS	14	15	16 BUF	17	18 EDM	19 CAL
20	21 LA	22	23 MIN	24	25 DAL	26 NAS
27	28 STL	29	30 CBJ	31		

February
SUN	MON	TUE	WED	THU	FRI	SAT
					1	2 *
3	4	5	6 PHI	7	8 CAR	9
10 DAL	11	12	13 CAL	14	15	16
17	18	19	20	21	22	23
24	25	26	27 MIN	28		

March
SUN	MON	TUE	WED	THU	FRI	SAT
					1	2
3 D CHI	4	5	6 ATL	7	8 NJ	9
10 OTT	11	12	13 PIT	14	15 CHI	16
17 STL	18	19 DET	20	21 PHI	22 STL	23
24 D DAL	25	26	27 PHO	28 PHO	29	30 VAN
31						

April
SUN	MON	TUE	WED	THU	FRI	SAT
	1	2 SJ	3 DET	4	5 EDM	6
7 DAL	8	9	10	11	12 COL	13
14 D LA	15	16	17	18	19	20

2001-02 SEASON
CLUB DIRECTORY

Chairman and governor
Tony Tavares
President and general manager
Pierre Gauthier
Assistant general manager
David McNab
Director of scouting
Alain Chainey
Pro scout
Lucien DeBlois
Head coach
Bryan Murray
Assistant coach
Guy Charron

Mgr. of communications/team services
Alex Gilchrist
Media relations coordinator
Merit Tully
Media relations intern
Carlos Porras III
Head athletic trainer
Chris Phillips
Assistant athletic trainer
Greg Thayer
Equipment manager
Mark O'Neill
Assistant equipment manager
John Allaway

DRAFT CHOICES

Rd.— Player	Ht./Wt.	Overall	Pos.	Last team
1— Stanislav Chistov	5-9/169	5	C/RW	OMSK, Russia
2— Mark Popovic	6-1/194	35	D	Toronto (OHL)
3— Joel Stepp	6-0/185	69	C/LW	Red Deer (WHL)
4— Timo Parssinen	5-10/176	102	F	HPK (Finland)
4— Vladimir Korsunov	6-2/202	105	D	Spartak Jr., Russia
4— Brandon Rogers	6-1/190	118	D	Hotchkiss (USHSE)
5— Joel Perreault	6-2/165	137	C	B.-Comeau (QMJHL)
6— Jan Tabacek	5-11/169	170		Martin (SVK)
7— Tony Martensson	6-0/189	224	C	Brynas, Sweden
8— Martin Gerber		232	G	Langnau, Switzerland
9— Pierre Parenteau	5-11/165	264	C	Chicoutimi (QMJHL)

MISCELLANEOUS DATA

Home ice (capacity)
The Arrowhead Pond of Anaheim
(17,174)
Address
2695 E. Katella Avenue
P.O. Box 61077
Anaheim, CA 92803-6177
Business phone
714-940-2900
Ticket information
714-940-2143

Website
www.mightyducks.com
Training site
Anaheim
Club colors
Purple, jade, silver and white
Radio affiliation
To be announced
TV affiliation
KCAL (Channel 9), FOX Sports West 2
(Cable)

TRAINING CAMP ROSTER

No.	FORWARDS	Ht./Wt.	Place (BORN)	Date	NHL exp.	2000-01 clubs
	Maxim Balmochnykh	6-1/200	Lipetsk, U.S.S.R.	3-7-79	0	Cincinnati (AHL)
42	Dan Bylsma (RW)	6-2/212	Grand Haven, Mich.	9-19-70	6	Anaheim
	Alexander Chagodayev	6-1/180	Moscow, U.S.S.R.	1-15-81	0	Lokomotiv Yaroslavl (Russian), SKA St. Petersburg (Russian)
	Stanislav Chistov	5-9/169	Cheljabinsk, U.S.S.R.	4-17-83	0	Avangard Omsk (Russian)
	Marc Chouinard (C)	6-5/204	Charlesbourg, Ont.	5-5-77	1	Cincinnati (AHL), Anaheim
17	Matt Cullen (C)	6-0/195	Virginia, Minn.	11-2-76	4	Anaheim
	Jim Cummins (RW)	6-2/219	Dearborn, Mich.	5-17-70	10	Anaheim
	Torrey DiRoberto (C)	5-11/186	New York	4-17-78	0	Cincinnati (AHL), Baton Rouge (ECHL)
39	Jeff Friesen (LW)	6-0/205	Meadow Lake, Sask.	8-5-76	7	San Jose, Anaheim
	Tobias Johansson (LW)	5-11/180	Malmo, Sweden	10-22-77	0	
9	Paul Kariya (LW)	5-10/180	Vancouver	10-16-74	7	Anaheim
27	Denny Lambert (LW)	5-10/215	Wawa, Ont.	1-7-70	7	Atlanta
12	Mike LeClerc (LW)	6-1/205	Winnipeg	11-10-76	5	Anaheim
	Jay Legault (LW)	6-4/217	Peterborough, Ont.	5-15-79	0	Cincinnati (AHL), Baton Rouge (ECHL)
	Andy McDonald (C)	5-10/192	Strathroy, Ont.	8-25-77	1	Cincinnati (AHL), Anaheim
16	Marty McInnis (LW)	5-11/190	Weymouth, Mass.	6-2-70	10	Anaheim
	Tommi Miettinen (C/LW)	5-10/165	Kuopio, Finland	12-3-75	0	Ilves Tampere (Finland)
	Samuel Pahlsson (C)	5-11/190	Ornskoldsvik, Sweden	12-17-77	1	Boston, Anaheim
	Timo Parssinen (LW)	5-10/176	Lohja, Finland	1-19-77	0	HPK Hameenlinna (Finland)
	Joel Perreault (C)	6-2/165	Montreal	4-6-83	0	Baie-Comeau (QMJHL)
	Jonas Ronnqvist (LW)	6-1/200	Sweden	8-22-73	1	Bjorkloven (Sweden), Anaheim, Cincinnati (AHL)
20	Steve Rucchin (C)	6-2/212	Thunder Bay, Ont.	7-4-71	7	Anaheim
	Maxim Rybin (RW)	5-9/176	Moscow, U.S.S.R.	6-15-81	0	Sarnia (OHL)
	Kevin Sawyer (LW)	6-2/205	Christina Lake, B.C.	2-18-74	4	Cincinnati (AHL), Anaheim
	Alexei Smirnov (LW)	6-3/211	Tver, U.S.S.R.	1-28-82	0	Dynamo Moscow (Russian)
	Jarrett Smith (C)	6-1/190	Edmonton	6-15-79	0	Cincinnati (AHL), Baton Rouge (ECHL)
	Joel Stepp (C/LW)	6-1/185	Estevan, Sask.	2-11-83	0	Red Deer (WHL)
	Petr Tenkrat (RW)	6-1/185	Kladno, Czechoslovakia	5-31-77	1	Cincinnati (AHL), Anaheim
13	German Titov (C)	6-1/201	Moscow, U.S.S.R.	10-15-65	8	Anaheim
	Bob Wren (C)	5-10/182	Preston, Ont.	9-16-74	2	Cincinnati (AHL), Anaheim

No.	DEFENSEMEN	Ht./Wt.	Place	Date	NHL exp.	2000-01 clubs
3	Keith Carney	6-2/211	Providence, R.I.	2-3-70	10	Phoenix
	Bill Cass	5-11/217	Boston	9-30-80	0	Boston College (Hockey East)
28	Niclas Havelid	5-11/200	Enkoping, Sweden	4-12-73	2	Anaheim
	Vladimir Korsunov	6-2/202	Moscow, U.S.S.R.	3-16-83	0	Spartak (Russian Jr.)
	Antti-Jussi Niemi	6-1/183	Vantaa, Finland	9-22-77	1	Cincinnati (AHL), Anaheim
19	Chris O'Sullivan	6-2/205	Dorchester, Mass.	5-15-74	4	Cincinnati (AHL)
	Peter Podhradsky	6-1/185	Bratislava, Czechoslovakia	12-10-79	0	Cincinnati (AHL)
	Mark Popovic	6-1/194	Stoney Creek, Ont.	10-11-82	0	Toronto St. Michael's (OHL)
	Brandon Rogers	6-1/190	Rochester, N.H.	2-27-82	0	Hotchkiss (USHS (East))
24	Ruslan Salei	6-1/206	Minsk, U.S.S.R.	11-2-74	5	Anaheim
4	Alexei Tezikov	6-1/198	Togliatti, U.S.S.R.	6-22-78	2	Portland (AHL), Cincinnati (AHL)
7	Pavel Trnka	6-3/200	Plzen, Czechoslovakia	7-27-76	4	Anaheim
10	Oleg Tverdovsky	6-0/200	Donetsk, U.S.S.R.	5-18-76	7	Anaheim
6	Vitali Vishnevski	6-2/190	Kharkov, U.S.S.R.	3-18-80	2	Anaheim
3	Sergei Vyshedkevich	6-0/195	Moscow, U.S.S.R.	1-3-75	2	Atlanta, Orlando (IHL), Cincinnati (AHL)
33	Jason York	6-1/200	Nepean, Ont.	5-20-70	9	Ottawa

No.	GOALTENDERS	Ht./Wt.	Place	Date	NHL exp.	2000-01 clubs
	Ilja Bryzgalov	6-3/196	Togliatti, U.S.S.R.	6-22-80	0	Lada Togliatti (Russian)
47	Jean-Sebastien Giguere	6-0/185	Montreal	6-16-77	4	Cincinnati (AHL), Anaheim
	Gregg Naumenko	6-1/201	Chicago	3-30-77	1	Cincinnati (AHL), Anaheim
31	Steve Shields	6-3/215	Toronto	7-19-72	6	San Jose

2000-01 REVIEW
INDIVIDUAL STATISTICS

SCORING

	Games	G	A	Pts.	PIM	+/-	PPG	SHG	Shots	Shooting Pct.
Paul Kariya	66	33	34	67	20	-9	18	3	230	14.3
Teemu Selanne*	61	26	33	59	36	-8	10	0	202	12.9
Oleg Tverdovsky	82	14	39	53	32	-11	8	0	188	7.4
Marty McInnis	75	20	22	42	40	-21	10	0	136	14.7
Matt Cullen	82	10	30	40	38	-23	4	0	159	6.3
Tony Hrkac	80	13	25	38	29	0	0	0	88	14.8
Mike Leclerc	54	15	20	35	26	-1	3	0	130	11.5
German Titov	71	9	11	20	61	-21	1	0	78	11.5
Petr Tenkrat	46	5	9	14	16	-11	0	0	79	6.3
Niclas Havelid	47	4	10	14	34	-6	2	0	69	5.8

	Games	G	A	Pts.	PIM	+/-	PPG	SHG	Shots	Shooting Pct.
Jeff Friesen*	15	2	10	12	10	-2	2	0	29	6.9
Jim Cummins	79	5	6	11	167	-11	0	0	45	11.1
Mike Crowley	39	1	10	11	20	-16	0	0	45	2.2
Vitaly Vishnevski	76	1	10	11	99	-1	0	0	49	2.0
Pascal Trepanier	57	6	4	10	73	-12	3	0	86	7.0
Dan Bylsma	82	1	9	10	22	-12	0	0	50	2.0
Steve Rucchin	16	3	5	8	0	-5	2	0	19	15.8
Pavel Trnka	59	1	7	8	42	-12	0	0	59	1.7
Ladislav Kohn*	51	4	3	7	42	-15	0	1	86	4.7
Marc Chouinard	44	3	4	7	12	-5	0	0	26	11.5
Jason Marshall*	50	3	4	7	105	-12	2	1	38	7.9
Samuel Pahlsson*	59	3	4	7	14	-9	1	1	46	6.5
Ruslan Salei	50	1	5	6	70	-14	0	0	73	1.4
Jonas Ronnqvist	38	0	4	4	14	-7	0	0	30	0.0
Antti Aalto	12	1	1	2	2	1	0	0	18	5.6
Antti-Jussl Niemi	28	1	1	2	22	-6	0	0	18	5.6
Jean-Sebastien Giguere (goalie)	34	0	2	2	8	0	0	0	0	0.0
Patrick Traverse*	15	1	0	1	6	-6	0	0	7	14.3
Andrei Nazarov*	16	1	0	1	29	-9	0	0	13	7.7
Andy McDonald	16	1	0	1	6	0	0	0	21	4.8
Kevin Sawyer	9	0	1	1	27	-1	0	0	6	0.0
Bob Wren	1	0	0	0	0	-1	0	0	0	0.0
Gregg Naumenko (goalie)	2	0	0	0	2	0	0	0	0	0.0
Dominic Roussel (goalie)*	13	0	0	0	0	0	0	0	0	0.0
Guy Hebert (goalie)*	41	0	0	0	0	0	0	0	0	0.0

GOALTENDING

	Games	Min.	Goals	SO	Avg.	W	L	T	ENG	Shots	Sv. Pct.
Jean-Sebastien Giguere	34	2031	87	4	2.57	11	17	5	3	976	.911
Dominic Roussel*	13	653	31	0	2.85	2	5	2	2	295	.895
Guy Hebert*	41	2215	115	2	3.12	12	23	4	0	1112	.897
Gregg Naumenko	2	70	7	0	6.00	0	1	0	0	29	.759

*Played with two or more NHL teams.

RESULTS

OCTOBER
6— Minnesota ....W 3-1
8— St. Louis ....L.......1-5
11— Boston ....L.....*2-3
14— At New Jersey ....L.......2-4
16— At N.Y. Rangers ....W.....4-3
17— At N.Y. Islanders ....W.....4-3
20— At Buffalo........................T.....*2-2
21— At Philadelphia ....W.....4-3
23— Los Angeles....................L....*4-5
25— At Los Angeles ....L.......2-6
27— Edmonton ....W.....3-2
29— At Calgary ....W.....6-3
30— At Edmonton ....L.......3-5

NOVEMBER
1— Phoenix ....T....*1-1
4— At Nashville ....T....*3-3
5— At Chicago ....L.......2-4
8— Vancouver ....L.......2-7
11— At Colorado ....L.......1-3
12— Detroit ....L.......2-3
15— Colorado ....L.......0-3
18— At Phoenix........................W.....6-2
19— N.Y. Islanders ....W.....2-1
22— New Jersey ....L.......2-5
24— At Calgary ....T....*2-2
25— At Edmonton ....L.......2-3
28— At Vancouver ....L.......1-4
30— At San Jose ....L....*2-3

DECEMBER
3— Los Angeles ....W.....4-0
5— At St. Louis........................L.......0-1
6— At Columbus......................L.......2-5
8— At Minnesota ....W....*1-0
10— Dallas ....L.......0-1
13— Columbus ....W....*5-4
15— N.Y. Rangers ....W.....6-4
17— Tampa Bay ....W.....3-1
20— Atlanta ....L.......2-4
22— At Detroit ....L....*1-2
23— At St. Louis........................L.......2-5
27— At Dallas ....L.......1-3
28— At Nashville ....T....*2-2
31— At Minnesota ....L.......2-3

JANUARY
3— Florida ....W....*3-2
5— Calgary ....T....*4-4
10— St. Louis ....L.......2-4
12— Buffalo ....L.......0-4
14— At Carolina ....L.......0-4
15— At Pittsburgh ....L.......2-3
17— At Atlanta ....W.....5-2
19— Phoenix ....L.......3-4
21— Colorado ....L.......2-4
24— Minnesota ....L.......0-5
26— At Detroit ....L.......2-3
27— At Columbus......................L.......1-2
31— Nashville............................L.......0-3

FEBRUARY
1— At Phoenix.........................W.....4-2
7— Chicago ....L.......2-3
9— Washington ....L.......3-4
11— Carolina ....T....*2-2
14— Edmonton ....T....*3-3
16— At Dallas ....L....*2-3
19— Calgary ....W.....6-2
21— San Jose ....W.....1-0
23— At San Jose ....L.......1-3
25— Columbus ....L.......2-5
28— Detroit ....L.......1-3

MARCH
2— Dallas ....L.......2-5
4— Los Angeles ....W.....4-0
7— Montreal ....W.....4-2
9— Chicago ....W.....3-1
11— Nashville...........................W....*1-0
13— At Washington ....W.....2-0
14— At Toronto ....L.......2-3
16— At Ottawa ....L.......1-4
18— At Chicago.........................W.....4-1
21— At Dallas ....L.......0-8
24— At Los Angeles ....T....*3-3
29— At San Jose ....L.......4-7
30— At Vancouver ....T....*2-2

APRIL
1— Vancouver ....W.....2-1
4— At Colorado ....T....*1-1
6— Phoenix ....L.......2-5
8— San Jose...........................L.......1-4
*Denotes overtime game.

– 7 –

ATLANTA THRASHERS
EASTERN CONFERENCE/SOUTHEAST DIVISION

Thrashers' Schedule
Home games shaded; D—Day game; *—All-Star Game at Los Angeles

October

SUN	MON	TUE	WED	THU	FRI	SAT
	1	2	3	4 BUF	5	6 BOS
7	8	9	10	11	12	13 CAR
14	15	16 PHI	17	18	19 NYR	20 CAR
21	22	23 PIT	24	25	26 WAS	27 TB
28	29	30 OTT	31			

November

SUN	MON	TUE	WED	THU	FRI	SAT
				1 SJ	2	3 D LA
4 ANA	5	6	7 NJ	8 BUF	9	10 WAS
11	12	13 MIN	14	15	16 NAS	17
18 NYR	19 BUF	20	21	22 MON	23	24 OTT
25	26	27 MON	28	29 TB	30	

December

SUN	MON	TUE	WED	THU	FRI	SAT
						1 D FLA
2	3	4 BOS	5	6 WAS	7	8 PIT
9	10 PHI	11	12 MON	13	14 CHI	15 WAS
16	17	18 BOS	19 SJ	20	21 CAR	22
23 DAL	24	25	26 FLA	27	28 TOR	29
30	31 D FLA					

January

SUN	MON	TUE	WED	THU	FRI	SAT
		1	2 DAL	3 PHO	4	5
6 NYI	7	8 PHI	9 OTT	10	11 CAL	12
13 TB	14	15 TOR	16	17 PHI	18	19 FLA
20	21	22 WAS	23	24 NJ	25	26 D PIT
27 PHO	28	29	30 TOR	31		

February

SUN	MON	TUE	WED	THU	FRI	SAT
					1	2 *
3	4	5 EDM	6	7 NJ	8 NYR	9
10	11 TOR	12	13	14	15	16
17	18	19	20	21	22	23
24	25	26 BUF	27	28		

March

SUN	MON	TUE	WED	THU	FRI	SAT
					1 NYI	2 NYI
3	4 MON	5	6 ANA	7	8 BOS	9
10 D NYI	11	12 TB	13	14 COL	15	16 VAN
17	18 PIT	19	20 TB	21	22 NYR	23 OTT
24	25	26	27 MIN	28	29	30 DET
31						

April

SUN	MON	TUE	WED	THU	FRI	SAT
	1	2 CAL	3 COL	4	5 NJ	6
7 D CAR	8	9	10 FLA	11	12 CBJ	13
14 D CAR	15	16	17	18	19	20

2001-02 SEASON
CLUB DIRECTORY

President and governor
Stan Kasten

Vice president and general manager
Dave Waddell

Vice president of sales and marketing
Derek Schiller

Vice president of public relations
Greg Hughes

Director of player personnel
Jack Ferriera

Dir. of player evaluation and dev.
Bob Owen

Director of marketing
Jim Pfeifer

Director of media relations
Tom Hughes

Multimedia specialist
John Heid

Junior publicist
Susan Sanderman

Director of team services
Michele Zarzaca

Director of ticket sales
Dan Froehlich

Manager of hockey administration
Larry Simmons

Manager of community relations
Terry Hickman

Senior manager of marketing
Rob Preiditsch

Manager of media relations
Rob Koch

Senior manager of ticket sales
Keith Brennan

Manager of ticket operations
Wendell Byrne

Head coach
Curt Fraser

Assistant coaches
Tim Bothwell
Steve Weeks

Head trainer
Scott Green

Assistant trainer
Craig Brewer

Equipment manager
Bobby Stewart

Assistant equipment managers
Joe Guilmet
Rob Thomson

Strength & conditioning coach
Chris Reichert

Massage therapist
Inar Treiguts

DRAFT CHOICES

Rd.— Player	Ht./Wt.	Overall	Pos.	Last team
1— Ilja Kovalchuk	6-2/207	1	F	Spartak Jr., Russia
3— Michael Garnett	6-1/185	80	G	Saskatoon (WHL)
4— Brian Sipotz	6-6/225	100	D	Miami Univ. (CCHA)
4— Milan Gajic	5-11/182	112	C	Burnaby (BCJHL)
5— Colin Stuart	6-1/195	135	C	Colorado Col. (WCHA)
6— Pasi Nurminen	5-10/187	189	G	Jokerit, Finland
7— Matt Suderman	6-2/224	199	D	Saskatoon (WHL)
7— Colin Fitzrandolph	6-3/195	201	C	Phillips-Exeter (USHSE)
9— Mario Cartelli	6-1/196	262	D	Trinec, Czech.

MISCELLANEOUS DATA

Home ice (capacity)
Philips Arena (18,545)

Address
1 CNN Center, Box 105583
Atlanta, GA 30348-5583

Business phone
404-827-5300

Ticket information
404-584-7825

Website
www.atlantathrashers.com

Training site
Duluth, GA

Club colors
Navy, blue, copper, bronze and gold

Radio affiliation
WQXI (790 AM)

TV affiliation
Turner South, WUPA/WPN (Channel 69)

TRAINING CAMP ROSTER

No.	FORWARDS	Ht./Wt.	Place (BORN)	Date (BORN)	NHL exp.	2000-01 clubs
	Bryan Adams (LW)	6-0/185	Fort St. James, B.C.	3-20-77	2	Atlanta, Orlando (IHL)
23	Lubos Bartecko (LW)	6-1/195	Kezmarok, Czechoslovakia	7-14-76	3	St. Louis
	Zdenek Blatny (C/LW)	6-1/187	Brno, Czechoslovakia	1-14-81	0	Kootenay (WHL)
19	Bob Corkum (C)	6-0/222	Salisbury, Mass.	12-18-67	11	Los Angeles, New Jersey
9	Hnat Domenichelli (LW)	6-0/194	Edmonton	2-17-76	5	Atlanta
22	Shean Donovan (RW)	6-3/210	Timmins, Ont.	1-22-75	7	Atlanta
21	Ray Ferraro (C)	5-9/200	Trail, B.C.	8-23-64	17	Atlanta
	Milan Gajic (C)	5-11/182	Vancouver	6-1-81	0	Burnaby (BCJHL)
	Simon Gamache (LW)	5-10/185	Thetford Mines, Que.	1-3-81	0	Val-d'Or (QMJHL)
	Dany Heatley (LW)	6-1/200	Freibourg, Germany	1-21-81	0	Univ. of Wisconsin (WCHA)
	Darcy Hordichuk (LW)	6-1/200	Kamsack, Sask.	8-10-80	1	Orlando (IHL), Atlanta
15	Tony Hrkac (C)	5-11/170	Thunder Bay, Ont.	7-7-66	11	Anaheim
	David Kaczowka (LW)	6-2/208	Regina, Sask.	7-5-81	0	Regina (WHL)
	Tomi Kallio (LW)	6-1/180	Turku, Finland	1-27-77	1	Atlanta
24	Andreas Karlsson (C)	6-3/195	Leksand, Sweden	8-19-75	2	Atlanta
	Ilya Kovalchuk (RW)	6-2/207	Tver, U.S.S.R.	4-15-83	0	Spartak (Russian Div. 1)
	Derek MacKenzie (C)	5-11/169	Sudbury, Ont.	6-11-81	0	Sudbury (OHL)
	Wes Mason (LW)	6-2/190	Windsor, Ont.	12-12-77	0	Orlando (IHL)
36	Jeff Odgers (RW)	6-0/200	Spy Hill, Sask.	5-31-69	10	Atlanta
65	Kamil Piros (C)	6-1/183	Most, Czechoslovakia	11-20-78	0	Chem. Litvinov (Czech Republic)
8	Jarrod Skalde (C)	6-0/185	Niagara Falls, Ont.	2-26-71	8	Atlanta, Orlando (IHL)
	Dan Snyder (C)	6-0/185	Elmira, Ont.	2-23-78	1	Orlando (IHL), Atlanta
13	Patrik Stefan (C)	6-3/200	Pribram, Czechoslovakia	9-16-80	2	Atlanta
	Colin Stuart (C)	6-1/195	Rochester, Minn.	7-8-82	0	Colorado College (WCHA)
	Per Svartvadet (LW)	6-1/190	Solleftea, Sweden	5-17-75	2	Atlanta
	Brad Tapper (RW)	6-0/175	Scarborough, Ont.	4-28-78	1	Atlanta, Orlando (IHL)
	J.P. Vigier (RW)	6-0/200	Notre Dame de Lourdes, Man.	8-11-76	1	Orlando (IHL), Atlanta
	Dmitri Vlasenkov (LW)	5-11/183	Safonovo, U.S.S.R.	1-1-78	0	Orlando (IHL)

DEFENSEMEN

No.	DEFENSEMEN	Ht./Wt.	Place (BORN)	Date (BORN)	NHL exp.	2000-01 clubs
2	Adam Burt	6-2/205	Detroit	1-15-69	13	Atlanta
2	Petr Buzek	6-0/215	Jihlava, Czechoslovakia	4-26-77	4	Atlanta
29	Brett Clark	6-1/185	Wapella, Sask.	12-23-76	4	Atlanta, Orlando (IHL)
	Jeff Dessner	6-2/177	Glenview, Ill.	4-16-77	0	Univ. of Wisconsin (WCHA)
6	David Harlock	6-2/220	Toronto	3-16-71	7	Atlanta
8	Frantisek Kaberle	6-0/185	Kladno, Czechoslovakia	11-8-73	2	Atlanta
	Ilja Nikulin	6-3/211	Moscow, U.S.S.R.	3-12-82	0	Dynamo Moscow (Russian)
28	Todd Reirden	6-5/220	Deerfield, Ill.	6-25-71	3	St. Louis, Worcester (AHL)
	Luke Sellars	6-1/195	Toronto	5-21-81	0	Ottawa (OHL)
	Vladimir Sicak	5-11/192	Jindrichuv Hradec, Czech.	1-12-80	0	Orlando (IHL), Greenville (ECHL)
	Brian Sipotz	6-6/225	South Bend, Ind.	9-16-81	0	Miami of Ohio (CCHA)
71	Jiri Slegr	6-0/206	Jihlava, Czechoslovakia	5-30-71	8	Pittsburgh, Atlanta
4	Chris Tamer	6-2/208	Dearborn, Mich.	11-17-70	8	Atlanta
	Daniel Tjarnqvist	6-2/180	Umea, Sweden	10-14-76	0	Djurgarden Stockholm (Sweden)
38	Yannick Tremblay	6-2/200	Pointe-aux-Trembles, Que.	11-15-75	5	Atlanta
	Libor Ustrnul	6-5/228	Olomouc, Czechoslovakia	2-20-82	0	Plymouth (OHL)
	Mike Weaver	5-9/185	Bramalea, Ont.	5-2-78	0	Orlando (IHL)

GOALTENDERS

No.	GOALTENDERS	Ht./Wt.	Place (BORN)	Date (BORN)	NHL exp.	2000-01 clubs
	Scott Fankhouser	6-2/206	Bismark, N.D.	7-1-75	2	Orlando (IHL), Atlanta
	Michael Garnett	6-1/185	Saskatoon, Sask.	11-25-82	0	Saskatoon (WHL)
	Milan Hnilicka	6-0/180	Kladno, Czechoslovakia	6-24-73	2	Atlanta
34	Norm Maracle	5-9/195	Belleville, Ont.	10-2-74	4	Atlanta, Orlando (IHL)
1	Damian Rhodes	6-0/180	St. Paul, Minn.	5-28-69	9	Atlanta
	Rob Zepp	6-1/160	Scarborough, Ont.	9-7-81	0	Plymouth (OHL)

2000-01 REVIEW
INDIVIDUAL STATISTICS

SCORING

	Games	G	A	Pts.	PIM	+/-	PPG	SHG	Shots	Shooting Pct.
Ray Ferraro	81	29	47	76	91	-11	11	0	172	16.9
Donald Audette*	64	32	39	71	64	-3	13	1	187	17.1
Andrew Brunette	77	15	44	59	26	-5	6	0	104	14.4
Patrik Stefan	66	10	21	31	22	-3	0	0	93	10.8
Stephen Guolla	63	12	16	28	23	-6	2	0	96	12.5
Hnat Domenichelli	63	15	12	27	18	-9	4	0	150	10.0
Tomi Kallio	56	14	13	27	22	-3	2	0	115	12.2
Shean Donovan	63	12	11	23	47	-14	1	3	93	12.9
Steve Staios	70	9	13	22	137	-23	4	0	156	5.8
Per Svartvadet	69	10	11	21	20	-6	0	2	98	10.2

	Games	G	A	Pts.	PIM	+/-	PPG	SHG	Shots	Shooting Pct.
Jiri Slegr*	33	3	16	19	36	-1	2	0	78	3.8
Chris Tamer	82	4	13	17	128	-1	0	1	90	4.4
Andreas Karlsson	60	5	11	16	16	-2	0	1	83	6.0
Frantisek Kaberle	51	4	11	15	18	11	1	0	99	4.0
Gord Murphy	27	3	11	14	12	-11	2	0	44	6.8
Jeff Odgers	82	6	7	13	226	-8	0	0	67	9.0
Yannick Tremblay	46	4	8	12	30	-6	1	0	102	3.9
Dean Sylvester	43	5	6	11	8	-16	1	0	82	6.1
Yves Sarault	20	5	4	9	26	-9	2	0	44	11.4
Herbert Vasiljevs	21	4	5	9	14	-11	2	0	41	9.8
Denny Lambert	67	1	7	8	215	-5	0	0	44	2.3
Ladislav Kohn*	26	3	4	7	44	-12	0	1	43	7.0
Brad Tapper	16	2	3	5	6	1	0	0	21	9.5
Andrei Skopintsev	17	1	3	4	16	-7	0	0	10	10.0
Jarrod Skalde	19	1	2	3	20	-8	0	0	24	4.2
Sergei Vyshedkevich	23	1	2	3	14	-7	0	0	28	3.6
Brett Clark	28	1	2	3	14	-12	0	0	35	2.9
Chris Joseph*	19	0	3	3	20	-7	0	0	25	0.0
Adam Burt	27	0	2	2	27	2	0	0	18	0.0
Bryan Adams	9	0	1	1	2	-4	0	0	3	0.0
David Harlock	65	0	1	1	62	-28	0	0	26	0.0
Dan Snyder	2	0	0	0	0	0	0	0	2	0.0
Jean-Pierre Vigier	2	0	0	0	0	-2	0	0	1	0.0
Brian Pothier	3	0	0	0	2	4	0	0	0	0.0
Petr Buzek	5	0	0	0	8	2	0	0	11	0.0
Scott Fankhouser (goalie)	7	0	0	0	2	0	0	0	0	0.0
Darcy Hordichuk	11	0	0	0	38	-3	0	0	6	0.0
Norm Maracle (goalie)	13	0	0	0	0	0	0	0	0	0.0
Milan Hnilicka (goalie)	36	0	0	0	4	0	0	0	0	0.0
Damian Rhodes (goalie)	38	0	0	0	16	0	0	0	0	0.0

GOALTENDING

	Games	Min.	Goals	SO	Avg.	W	L	T	ENG	Shots	Sv. Pct.
Milan Hnilicka	36	1879	105	2	3.35	12	19	2	1	951	.890
Damian Rhodes	38	2072	116	0	3.36	7	19	7	5	1129	.897
Norm Maracle	13	753	43	0	3.43	2	8	3	3	406	.894
Scott Fankhouser	7	260	16	0	3.69	2	1	0	0	160	.900

*Played with two or more NHL teams.

RESULTS

OCTOBER
7— N.Y. Rangers .... L 1-2
11— Washington .... T *3-3
15— At Tampa Bay .... L 2-5
17— New Jersey .... T *3-3
20— N.Y. Islanders .... L 3-5
21— At Ottawa .... T *6-6
25— At Edmonton .... W 3-1
27— At Vancouver .... T *1-1
28— At San Jose .... T *2-2

NOVEMBER
2— Los Angeles .... L 2-5
4— At Boston .... W 8-3
6— Ottawa .... L 2-3
12— At Washington .... T *2-2
13— At Florida .... W 4-1
15— Nashville .... W 1-0
17— Philadelphia .... L *2-3
18— At Pittsburgh .... L 1-3
22— At Tampa Bay .... L 2-8
23— Montreal .... L 0-6
25— Washington .... W 2-1
27— At Montreal .... L 2-3
29— Detroit .... L 4-6

DECEMBER
1— Tampa Bay .... W 5-3
2— At Columbus .... W 2-1
4— Boston .... W 5-4
6— Carolina .... L 3-5
8— Florida .... W *4-3

RESULTS (continued)
9— At N.Y. Islanders .... W 5-2
11— At New Jersey .... L 0-4
13— Chicago .... W 3-1
15— St. Louis .... L 3-6
19— At Los Angeles .... W *7-6
20— At Anaheim .... W 4-2
22— At Phoenix .... L 1-5
26— Toronto .... W 5-3
28— At N.Y. Rangers .... W 4-1
29— At N.Y. Islanders .... L 2-5

JANUARY
1— At Washington .... L 2-4
3— At Minnesota .... T *1-1
5— Philadelphia .... L 4-6
6— At Philadelphia .... T *2-2
10— Dallas .... L 2-3
12— Montreal .... L 0-3
13— At Washington .... L 1-4
17— Anaheim .... L 2-5
20— At New Jersey .... L 2-3
21— N.Y. Islanders .... T *4-4
23— At Nashville .... L 3-4
25— Toronto .... L *1-2
27— At Pittsburgh .... L 1-5
29— At N.Y. Rangers .... W 7-2
30— Pittsburgh .... L 3-6

FEBRUARY
1— Carolina .... L 1-3
7— At Toronto .... L 1-7
9— Boston .... W 5-1

(February continued)
10— Florida .... L 3-7
13— Buffalo .... W 5-4
15— At Buffalo .... L 1-3
17— At Philadelphia .... L 1-5
21— At Carolina .... L 3-6
23— At Chicago .... L 0-1
25— At Colorado .... L 2-5
27— Carolina .... T *1-1

MARCH
2— At Florida .... W 4-3
3— Florida .... T *2-2
6— Colorado .... L 2-4
8— Pittsburgh .... L 3-5
10— At Boston .... W 7-5
11— Calgary .... T *3-3
14— At Ottawa .... L 1-8
16— Columbus .... L 0-3
18— Vancouver .... L 3-5
21— Tampa Bay .... L 3-4
22— At Tampa Bay .... W 2-0
24— At Montreal .... W 3-2
26— Buffalo .... L 0-4
28— New Jersey .... L 2-4
30— At Buffalo .... L 0-4

APRIL
1— N.Y. Rangers .... L 2-4
3— Ottawa .... W 5-2
5— At Detroit .... L 0-4
6— At Carolina .... L 2-3
*Denotes overtime game.

BOSTON BRUINS
EASTERN CONFERENCE/NORTHEAST DIVISION

Bruins' Schedule
Home games shaded; D—Day game; *—All-Star Game at Los Angeles

October

SUN	MON	TUE	WED	THU	FRI	SAT
	1	2	3	4 ANA	5	6 ATL
7	8 D WAS	9	10 MIN	11	12	13 SJ
14	15	16 PHO	17 ANA	18	19	20 NAS
21	22	23 TOR	24	25 TOR	26	27 NYR
28 CHI	29	30 NJ	31			

November

SUN	MON	TUE	WED	THU	FRI	SAT
				1	2	3 D NJ
4	5	6 EDM	7	8 MIN	9	10 CBJ
11	12	13 MON	14	15 NJ	16	17 BUF
18	19	20 MON	21	22	23 D VAN	24 TOR
25	26	27 TB	28	29 PHI	30	

December

SUN	MON	TUE	WED	THU	FRI	SAT
						1 OTT
2	3	4 ATL	5	6 PIT	7	8 BUF
9	10	11	12 PIT	13 WAS	14	15 PHI
16	17	18 ATL	19	20 MON	21	22 NYI
23	24	25	26 OTT	27	28 FLA	29 TB
30	31 UAL					

January

SUN	MON	TUE	WED	THU	FRI	SAT
		1	2 CAR	3 TOR	4	5 WAS
6	7	8 PIT	9	10 LA	11	12 NYI
13 WAS	14	15	16	17 OTT	18	19 STL
20 STL	21 D	22	23 NYR	24 OTT	25	26 FLA
27	28 CHI	29	30 MON	31		

February

SUN	MON	TUE	WED	THU	FRI	SAT
					1	2 *
3	4 CBJ	5 BUF	6	7	8	9 D FLA
10	11 COL	12 VAN	13	14	15	16
17	18	19	20	21	22	23
24	25	26 NYI	27	28 CAR		

March

SUN	MON	TUE	WED	THU	FRI	SAT
					1 BUF	2
3	4 PHI	5	6 MON	7	8 ATL	9 CAL
10	11	12	13 NYR	14 TOR	15	16 D DET
17	18	19 PHO	20	21 BUF	22	23 FLA
24 TB	25	26 CAR	27	28	29	30 D CAR
31						

April

SUN	MON	TUE	WED	THU	FRI	SAT
	1	2 PHI	3	4 NYI	5	6 D NYR
7 NJ	D 8	9 TB	10	11 OTT	12	13 PIT
14	15	16	17	18	19	20

2001-02 SEASON
CLUB DIRECTORY

Owner and governor
Jeremy M. Jacobs
Alternative governor
Louis Jacobs
President and alternate governor
Harry Sinden
Senior assistant to the president
Nate Greenberg
V.p., g.m. and alternate govorner
Mike O'Connell
Assistant general manager
Jeff Gorton
Executive vice president
Richard Krezwick
Chief legal officer
Michael Wall
Director of administration
Dale Hamilton-Powers
Assistant to the president
Joe Curnane
Team travel coordinator/admin. asst.
Carol Gould
Coach
Robbie Ftorek
Assistant coaches
Wayne Cashman
Jim Hughes

Director of pro scouting & player dev.
Sean Coady
Director of amateur scouting
Scott Bradley
Scouting staff
Gerry Cheevers, Adam Creighton, Daniel Dore, Yuri Karmanov, Don Matheson, David McNamara, Tom McVie, Don Saatzer, Tom Songin, Svenake Svensson
Director of media relations
Heidi Holland
Media relations manager
Mark Awdycki
Dir. of marketing and community rel.
Sue Byrne
Strength & conditioning coach
John Whitesides
Athletic trainer
Don Del Negro
Physical therapist
Scott Waugh
Equipment manager
Peter Henderson
Assistant equipment managers
Chris "Muggsy" Aldrich
Keith Robinson

DRAFT CHOICES

Rd.— Player	Ht./Wt.	Overall	Pos.	Last team
1— Shaone Morrisonn	6-3/182	19	D	Kamloops (WHL)
3— Darren McLachlan	6-1/230	77	LW	Seattle (WHL)
4— Matti Kaltiainen	6-2/218	111	G	Blues Jr., Finland
5— Jiri Jakes	6-4/225	147	RW	Brandon (WHL)
6— Andrew Alberts	6-4/218	179	D	Waterloo (USHL)
7— Jordan Sigalet	6-1/180	209	G	Victoria (BCJHL)
8— Milan Jurcina	6-4/190	241	D	Halifax (QMJHL)
9— Marcel Rodman	6-0/183	282	RW	Peterborough (OHL)

MISCELLANEOUS DATA

Home ice (capacity)
FleetCenter (17,565)
Address
One FleetCenter, Suite 250
Boston, MA 02114-1303
Business phone
617-624-1900
Ticket information
617-931-2222
Website
www.bostonbruins.com

Training site
Wilmington, MA
Club colors
Gold, black and white
Radio affiliation
WBZ (1030 AM) & Bruins Radio Network
TV affiliation
UPN38 (Channel 38) & NESN (New England Sports Network)

BOSTON BRUINS

No.	FORWARDS	Ht./Wt.	Place	BORN Date	NHL exp.	2000-01 clubs
41	Jason Allison (C)	6-4/205	North York, Ont.	5-29-75	8	Boston
11	P.J. Axelsson (RW)	6-1/174	Kungalv, Sweden	2-26-75	4	Boston
	Chris Berti (C)	6-5/206	Scarborough, Ont.	10-6-81	0	Sarnia (OHL), Erie (OHL)
22	Mikko Eloranta (C/LW)	6-0/185	Turku, Finland	8-24-72	2	Boston
	Lee Goren (RW)	6-3/190	Winnipeg	12-26-77	1	Providence (AHL), Boston
9	Bill Guerin (RW)	6-2/210	Wilbraham, Mass.	11-9-70	10	Edmonton, Boston
51	Jay Henderson (LW)	5-11/188	Edmonton	9-17-78	3	Boston, Providence (AHL)
	Andy Hilbert (C)	5-11/190	Howell, Mich.	2-6-81	0	Univ. of Michigan (CCHA)
	Ivan Huml (LW)	6-2/183	Kladno, Czechoslovakia	9-6-81	0	Providence (AHL)
	Jiri Jakes (RW)	6-4/225	Prague, Czechoslovakia	10-4-82	0	Brandon (WHL)
26	Mike Knuble (LW)	6-3/222	Toronto	7-4-72	5	Boston
20	Martin Lapointe (RW)	5-11/215	Lachine, Que.	9-12-73	10	Detroit
	Eric Manlow (C)	6-0/190	Belleville, Ont.	4-7-75	1	Providence (AHL), Boston
	Darren McLachlan (LW)	6-1/230	Penticton, B.C.	2-16-83	0	Seattle (WHL)
62	Andrei Nazarov (LW)	6-5/234	Chelyabinsk, U.S.S.R.	4-22-74	8	Anaheim, Boston
12	Brian Rolston (C/LW)	6-2/205	Flint, Mich.	2-21-73	7	Boston
14	Sergei Samsonov (LW)	5-8/184	Moscow, U.S.S.R.	10-27-78	4	Boston
	Martin Samuelsson (RW)	6-2/189	Upperlands Vasby, Sweden	1-25-82	0	
6	Joe Thornton (C)	6-4/225	London, Ont.	7-2-79	4	Boston
7	Rob Zamuner (LW)	6-3/203	Oakville, Ont.	9-17-69	10	Ottawa
54	Jeff Zehr (LW)	6-3/195	Woodstock, Ont.	12-10-78	1	Greenville (ECHL)

DEFENSEMEN

No.		Ht./Wt.	Place	Date	exp.	2000-01 clubs
49	Johnathan Aitken	6-4/210	Edmonton	5-24-78	1	Sparta Praha (Czech Republic)
	Bobby Allen	6-1/198	Braintree, Mass.	11-14-78	0	Boston College (Hockey East)
44	Nick Boynton	6-2/210	Etobicoke, Ont.	1-14-79	2	Providence (AHL), Boston
62	Vratislav Cech	6-3/196	Tabor, Czechoslovakia	1-28-79	0	Providence (AHL), Greenville (ECHL)
77	Paul Coffey	6-0/200	Weston, Ont.	6-1-61	21	Boston
25	Hal Gill	6-7/240	Concord, Mass.	4-6-75	4	Boston
55	Jonathan Girard	5-11/192	Joliette, Que.	5-27-80	3	Boston, Providence (AHL)
	Richard Jackman	6-2/192	Toronto	6-28-78	2	Dallas, Utah (IHL)
	Lars Jonsson	6-1/198	Borlange, Sweden	1-2-82	0	Leksand (Sweden)
	Pavel Kolarik	6-1/207	Czechoslovakia	10-24-72	1	Providence (AHL), Boston
	Jamo Kultanen	6-2/198	Finland	1-8-73	1	Boston
39	Zdenek Kutlak	6-3/207	Budejovice, Czech Republic	2-13-80	1	Providence (AHL), Boston
	Tuukka Makela	6-3/202	Helsinki, Finland	5-24-82	0	Montreal (QMJHL)
18	Kyle McLaren	6-4/219	Humboldt, Sask.	6-18-77	6	Boston
	Shaone Morrisonn	6-3/182	Vancouver	12-23-82	0	Kamloops (WHL)
6	Sean O'Donnell	6-3/230	Ottawa	9-13-71	7	Minnesota, New Jersey
32	Don Sweeney	5-10/184	St. Stephen, N.B.	8-17-66	13	Boston
66	Eric Van Acker	6-5/220	St. Jean, Que.	3-1-79	0	Greenville (ECHL)
20	Darren Van Impe	6-1/205	Saskatoon, Sask.	5-18-73	7	Boston

GOALTENDERS

No.		Ht./Wt.	Place	Date	exp.	2000-01 clubs
34	Byron Dafoe	5-11/190	Sussex, England.	2-25-71	9	Boston
47	John Grahame	6-2/210	Denver	8-31-75	2	Boston, Providence (AHL)
	Matti Kaltiainen	6-2/218	Espoo, Finland	4-30-82	0	Espoo (Finland Jr.)
	Andrew Raycroft	6-0/150	Belleville, Ont.	5-4-80	1	Boston, Providence (AHL)
1	Peter Skudra	6-1/189	Riga, U.S.S.R.	4-24-73	4	Buffalo, Rochester (AHL), Boston, Providence (AHL)

2000-01 REVIEW
INDIVIDUAL STATISTICS

SCORING

	Games	G	A	Pts.	PIM	+/-	PPG	SHG	Shots	Shooting Pct.
Jason Allison	82	36	59	95	85	-8	11	3	185	19.5
Sergei Samsonov	82	29	46	75	18	6	3	0	215	13.5
Joe Thornton	72	37	34	71	107	-4	19	1	181	20.4
Bill Guerin*	64	28	35	63	122	-4	7	1	225	12.4
Brian Rolston	77	19	39	58	28	6	5	0	286	6.6
Andrei Kovalenko	76	16	21	37	27	-14	7	1	119	13.4
Mikko Eloranta	62	12	11	23	38	2	1	1	89	13.5
P.J. Axelsson	81	8	15	23	27	-12	0	0	146	5.5
Mike Knuble	82	7	13	20	37	0	0	1	92	7.6
Dixon Ward	63	5	13	18	65	-1	0	0	88	5.7
Kyle McLaren	58	5	12	17	53	-5	2	0	91	5.5
Jonathan Girard	31	3	13	16	14	2	2	0	42	7.1
Darren Van Impe	31	3	10	13	41	-9	2	0	40	7.5
Don Sweeney	72	2	10	12	26	-1	1	0	60	3.3

	Games	G	A	Pts.	PIM	+/-	PPG	SHG	Shots	Shooting Pct.
Hal Gill	80	1	10	11	71	-2	0	0	79	1.3
Jarno Kultanen	62	2	8	10	26	-3	0	0	76	2.6
Patrick Traverse*	37	2	6	8	14	4	1	0	39	5.1
Peter Popovic	60	1	6	7	48	-5	0	0	34	2.9
Eric Weinrich*	22	1	5	6	10	-8	1	0	28	3.6
Shawn Bates	45	2	3	5	26	-12	0	0	59	3.4
Andrei Nazarov*	63	1	4	5	200	-14	0	0	50	2.0
Ken Belanger	40	2	2	4	121	-6	0	0	35	5.7
Cameron Mann	15	1	3	4	6	0	0	0	17	5.9
Paul Coffey	18	0	4	4	30	-6	0	0	28	0.0
Lee Goren	21	2	0	2	7	-3	1	0	9	22.2
Samuel Pahlsson*	17	1	1	2	6	-5	0	0	13	7.7
Zdenek Kutlak	10	0	2	2	4	-3	0	0	7	0.0
Byron Dafoe (goalie)	45	0	2	2	6	0	0	0	0	0.0
Brandon Smith	3	1	0	1	0	-1	1	0	2	50.0
Eric Manlow	8	0	1	1	2	0	0	0	3	0.0
Andre Savage	1	0	0	0	0	0	0	0	1	0.0
Marquis Mathieu	1	0	0	0	2	0	0	0	0	0.0
Nicholas Boynton	1	0	0	0	0	-1	0	0	1	0.0
Kay Whitmore (goalie)	5	0	0	0	0	0	0	0	0	0.0
Eric Nickulas	7	0	0	0	4	-2	0	0	6	0.0
Joe Hulbig	7	0	0	0	4	-3	0	0	0	0.0
John Grahame (goalie)	10	0	0	0	2	0	0	0	0	0.0
Pavel Kolarik	10	0	0	0	4	-2	0	0	1	0.0
Jay Henderson	13	0	0	0	26	-1	0	0	12	0.0
Andrew Raycroft (goalie)	15	0	0	0	0	0	0	0	0	0.0
Peter Skudra (goalie)*	25	0	0	0	0	0	0	0	0	0.0

GOALTENDING

	Games	Min.	Goals	SO	Avg.	W	L	T	ENG	Shots	Sv. Pct.
Byron Dafoe	45	2536	101	2	2.39	22	14	7	1	1076	.906
Andrew Raycroft	15	649	32	0	2.96	4	6	0	3	291	.890
Peter Skudra*	25	1116	62	0	3.33	6	12	1	1	511	.879
John Grahame	10	471	28	0	3.57	3	4	0	3	211	.867
Kay Whitmore	5	203	18	0	5.32	1	2	0	0	94	.809

*Played with two or more NHL teams.

RESULTS

OCTOBER

5— Ottawa .... T.... *4-4
7— At Philadelphia .... W.....5-1
9— Florida .... W.....4-2
11— At Anaheim .... W.... *3-2
13— At Los Angeles .... L.....0-5
14— At San Jose .... L.....2-5
17— At Edmonton .... L.....1-6
20— At Calgary .... L.....2-3
26— Washington .... W.....4-1
28— Toronto .... L.... *1-2
29— At N.Y. Rangers .... L.....1-5
31— At N.Y. Islanders .... L.....2-4

NOVEMBER

2— Chicago .... W.....5-4
4— Atlanta .... L.....3-8
5— At Toronto .... L.....1-7
9— Ottawa .... W.....2-1
11— Nashville .... T.... *2-2
16— New Jersey .... L.... *2-3
18— Minnesota .... L.....1-6
21— At Ottawa .... L.....1-2
22— At Detroit .... W.....5-4
24— Carolina .... L.....1-3
26— Los Angeles .... T.... *4-4
28— Pittsburgh .... W.....3-1

DECEMBER

1— At Washington .... L.....2-3
2— Washington .... L.....0-2
4— At Atlanta .... L.....4-5

6— At Pittsburgh .... W.....3-2
8— At Columbus .... L.... *2-3
9— N.Y. Rangers .... W.....6-4
12— Buffalo .... L.....0-3
16— Carolina .... W.....4-1
19— Philadelphia .... T.... *4-4
21— Toronto .... W.....4-0
23— Detroit .... L.... *1-2
27— At N.Y. Islanders .... W.....5-2
29— At Florida .... L.....0-3
30— At Tampa Bay .... T.... *1-1

JANUARY

1— At Buffalo .... W.....4-3
5— At Washington .... T.... *1-1
6— Dallas .... L.....0-4
9— Pittsburgh .... W.....5-2
10— At Montreal .... W.....2-1
13— N.Y. Rangers .... W.....4-1
16— At New Jersey .... W.....5-4
18— At Carolina .... L.....2-4
19— At Nashville .... L.... *0-1
22— Florida .... L.....2-3
24— At Toronto .... W.....2-1
26— At Buffalo .... W.....2-1
27— New Jersey .... W.... *4-3
30— St. Louis .... W.....5-1

FEBRUARY

1— Montreal .... L.....0-3
6— Philadelphia .... W.....4-3
9— At Atlanta .... L.....1-5

10— Tampa Bay .... W.....6-2
15— At Tampa Bay .... W.....6-3
16— At Florida .... L.....1-2
18— At Carolina .... L.....4-5
21— At Colorado .... L.....2-8
23— At Dallas .... L.... *4-5
24— At St. Louis .... L.... *2-3
27— Phoenix .... W.....7-4

MARCH

1— Tampa Bay .... W.....3-1
3— San Jose .... W.....3-2
5— At Philadelphia .... L.....4-6
6— Buffalo .... L.....1-3
8— Ottawa .... L.....3-5
10— Atlanta .... L.....5-7
15— Vancouver .... T.... *2-2
17— At Montreal .... W.....3-2
20— At Pittsburgh .... T.... *2-2
22— Montreal .... W.... *3-2
24— Colorado .... L.....2-4
25— At N.Y. Rangers .... W.....3-2
28— At Toronto .... W.....3-0
30— At Ottawa .... L.... *4-5
31— N.Y. Islanders .... W.....4-2

APRIL

2— Montreal .... W.... *3-2
4— At Buffalo .... W.....3-2
6— At New Jersey .... L.....2-5
7— N.Y. Islanders .... W.....4-2

*Denotes overtime game.

BUFFALO SABRES
EASTERN CONFERENCE/NORTHEAST DIVISION

BUFFALO SABRES

Sabres' Schedule
Home games shaded: D—Day game; *—All-Star Game at Los Angeles

October

SUN	MON	TUE	WED	THU	FRI	SAT
	1	2	3	4 ATL	5	6 OTT
7 NYR	8	9	10 PHI	11	12 DET	13
14 D PIT	15	16 NAS	17	18	19 CBJ	20 MON
21	22	23 SJ	24	25	26 MON	27 NJ
28	29	30 PHO	31			

November

SUN	MON	TUE	WED	THU	FRI	SAT
				1	2 TB	3 OTT
4	5	6	7	8 ATL	9	10 NYR
11 FLA	12	13 NAS	14	15	16 FLA	17 BOS
18 ATL	19	20	21 TOR	22	23 CAL	24 PIT
25	26	27 NYR	28 WAS	29	30	

December

SUN	MON	TUE	WED	THU	FRI	SAT
						1 NYI
2	3	4 CAR	5	6	7 COL	8 BOS
9	10	11	12 DAL	13	14 CAR	15 NYR
16	17	18	19 CHI	20	21 TOR	22 TOR
23	24	25	26 MON	27	28	29 CBJ
30	31 CAR					

January

SUN	MON	TUE	WED	THU	FRI	SAT
		1	2	3 CAL	4	5
6 MIN	7	8 VAN	9	10 PIT	11	12 NJ
13	14	15	16 ANA	17 LA	18	19 PHO
20	21 COL	22	23 STL	24	25 TB	26
27 D WAS	28	29 CAR	30	31		

February

SUN	MON	TUE	WED	THU	FRI	SAT
					1	2 *
3	4	5 BOS	6	7	8 OTT	9
10 NJ	11	12 NJ	13	14	15	16
17	18	19	20	21	22	23
24	25	26 ATL	27	28		

March

SUN	MON	TUE	WED	THU	FRI	SAT
					1 BOS	2 TOR
3	4 EDM	5	6	7 NYI	8 MON	9
10 D DET	11	12 NYI	13	14 PHI	15 FLA	16
17 TB	18	19 OTT	20	21 BOS	22	23 TOR
24 OTT	25	26 WAS	27	28 STL	29	30 D PHI
31						

April

SUN	MON	TUE	WED	THU	FRI	SAT
	1 PHI	2	3 NYI	4	5 FLA	6
7 TB	8	9	10 PIT	11	12 WAS	13 MON
14	15	16	17	18	19	20

2001-02 SEASON
CLUB DIRECTORY

Chairman of the board
John J. Rigas

Vice chairman of the board and counsel
Robert O. Swados

Vice chairman of the board
Robert E. Rich Jr.

Chief executive officer
Timothy J. Rigas

Executive vice president/administration
Ron Bertovich

Exec. v.p./finance & bus. development
Ed Hartman

Exec. v.p./integrated marketing
John Cimperman

Senior v.p./corporate sales
Kerry Atkinson

Senior v.p./legal and business affairs
Kevin Billet

Senior vice president/marketing
Christye Peterson

Vice president/communications
Michael Gilbert

Vice president/corporate relations
Seymour H. Knox IV

V.p./ticket sales and operations
John Sinclair

General manager
Darcy Regier

Assistant to the general manager
Larry Carriere

Director of communications
Gregg Huller

Communications coordinator
Kevin Wiles

Director of player personnel
Don Luce

Professional scouts
Kevin Devine, Terry Martin

Scouting staff
Don Barrie, Jim Benning, Bo Berglund, Paul Merritt, Darryl Plandowski, Mike Racicot, Rudy Migay, David Volek

Head coach
Lindy Ruff

Associate coach
Don Lever

Assistant coach
Brian McCutcheon

Strength and conditioning coach
Doug McKenney

Assistant strength coach
Dennis Cole

Goaltender coach
Jim Corsi

Administrative assistant coach
Jeff Holbrook

Head trainer/massage therapist
Jim Pizzutelli

Head equipment manager
Rip Simonick

Assistant equipment manager
George Babcock

On-site travel coordinator
Kim Christiano

Club doctor
Dr. John Marzo

DRAFT CHOICES

Rd.— Player	Ht./Wt.	Overall	Pos.	Last team
1— Jiri Novotny	6-2/194	22	C	Budejovice, Czech.
2— Derek Roy	5-8/187	32	C	Kitchener (OHL)
2— Chris Thorburn	6-2/190	50	C	North Bay (OHL)
2— Jason Pominville	5-11/174	55	RW	Shawinigan (QMJHL)
5— Michal Vondrka	6-0/178	155	LW	Budejovice, Czech.
8— Calle Aslund	6-2/194	234	D	Huddinge, Sweden
8— Marek Dubec	6-1/191	247	D	Vsetin Jr., Czech.
9— Ryan Jorde	6-2/210	279	D	Tri-City (WHL)

MISCELLANEOUS DATA

Home ice (capacity)
HSBC Arena (18,690)

Address
HSBC Arena
One Seymour H. Knox III Plaza
Buffalo, NY 14203

Business phone
716-855-4100

Ticket information
888-223-6000

Website
www.sabres.com

Training site
Buffalo, NY

Club colors
Black, white, red, gray and silver

Radio affiliation
WNSA (107.7 FM)

TV affiliation
Empire Sports Network

No.	FORWARDS	Ht./Wt.	Place	BORN Date	NHL exp.	2000-01 clubs
	Jeremy Adduono (RW)....	6-0/182	Thunder Bay, Ont.	8-4-79	0	Rochester (AHL)
61	Maxim Afinogenov (RW).	5-11/176	Moscow, U.S.S.R.	9-4-79	2	Buffalo
41	Stu Barnes (C)	5-11/186	Spruce Grove, Alta.	12-25-70	10	Buffalo
	Eric Boulton (LW)	6-0/201	Halifax, Nova Scotia	8-17-76	1	Buffalo
37	Curtis Brown (C/LW)	6-0/190	Unity, Sask.	2-12-76	7	Buffalo
18	Tim Connolly (C)	6-0/186	Baldwinsville, N.Y.	5-7-81	2	New York Islanders
17	J.P. Dumont (RW)	6-1/187	Montreal	5-1-78	3	Buffalo
77	Chris Gratton (C)	6-4/219	Brantford, Ont.	7-5-75	8	Buffalo
55	Denis Hamel (RW)	6-2/200	Lachute, Que.	5-10-77	2	Buffalo
13	Slava Kozlov (LW)	5-10/195	Voskresensk, U.S.S.R.	5-3-72	10	Detroit
	Jaroslav Kristek (RW)	6-0/183	Zlin, Czechoslovakia	3-16-80	0	Rochester (AHL)
	Artem Kriukov (C)..........	6-3/180	U.S.S.R.	3-5-82	0	Lokomotiv Yaroslavl (Russian)
40	Francois Methot (C)........	6-0/175	Montreal	4-26-78	0	Rochester (AHL)
	Norm Milley (RW)	5-11/175	Toronto	2-14-80	0	Rochester (AHL)
	David Moravec (RW)	6-0/180	Czech Republic	3-24-73	1	HC Vitkovice (Czech Republic)
	Jiri Novotny (C)	6-2/187	Pelhrimov, Czechoslavakia	8-12-83	0	Budejovice (Czechoslavakia Jrs.), HC Ceske Budejovice (Czech Republic)
26	Andrew Peters (LW)	6-4/195	St. Catharines, Ont.	5-5-80	0	Rochester (AHL)
	Jason Pominville (RW)....	5-11/174	Repentigny, Que.	11-30-82	0	Shawinigan (QMJHL)
	Taylor Pyatt (LW)............	6-4/220	Thunder Bay, Ont.	8-19-81	1	New York Islanders
9	Erik Rasmussen (LW/C)...	6-2/205	Minneapolis	3-28-77	4	Buffalo
32	Rob Ray (RW)	6-0/215	Stirling, Ont.	6-8-68	12	Buffalo
	Derek Roy (C)	5-8/187	Ottawa	5-4-83	0	Kitchener (OHL)
81	Miroslav Satan (RW)	6-1/195	Topolcany, Czechoslavakia	10-22-74	6	Buffalo
16	Chris Taylor (C)	6-0/189	Stratford, Ont.	3-6-72	6	Rochester (AHL), Buffalo
	Chris Thorburn (C)	6-2/190	Sault Ste. Marie, Ont.	5-3-83	0	North Bay (OHL)
23	Darren Van Oene (LW).....	6-3/207	Edmonton	1-18-78	0	Rochester (AHL)
25	Vaclav Varada (RW)........	6-0/200	Vsetin, Czechoslavakia	4-26-76	6	Buffalo
	Michal Vondrka (LW).......	6-0/178	Ces Budejovice, Czech.	5-17-83	0	HC Ceske Budejovice (Czech Republic)
	DEFENSEMEN					
51	Brian Campbell	5-11/185	Strathroy, Ont.	5-23-79	2	Rochester (AHL), Buffalo
	Gerard Dicaire...............	6-2/190	Faro, Yukon	9-14-82	0	Seattle (WHL)
29	Jason Holland...............	6-2/193	Morinville, Alta.	4-30-76	4	Rochester (AHL)
10	Doug Houda	6-2/190	Blairmore, Alta.	6-3-66	14	Rochester (AHL)
21	Mike Hurlbut.................	6-2/200	Massena, N.Y.	7-10-66	5	Rochester (AHL)
45	Dmitri Kalinin.................	6-2/198	Chelyabinsk, U.S.S.R.	7-22-80	2	Buffalo
74	Jay McKee...................	6-3/205	Kingston, Ont.	9-8-77	6	Buffalo
3	James Patrick	6-2/200	Winnipeg	6-14-63	18	Buffalo
42	Richard Smehlik	6-3/222	Ostrava, Czechoslavakia	1-23-70	9	Buffalo
	Henrik Tallinder.............	6-3/194	Stockholm, Sweden	1-10-79	0	TPS Turku (Finland)
4	Rhett Warrener	6-1/210	Shaunavon, Sask.	1-27-76	6	Buffalo
5	Jason Woolley	6-1/207	Toronto	7-27-69	10	Buffalo
44	Alexei Zhitnik	5-11/215	Kiev, U.S.S.R.	10-10-72	9	Buffalo
	GOALTENDERS					
43	Martin Biron	6-1/154	Lac St. Charles, Que.	8-15-77	4	Buffalo, Rochester (AHL)
	Ryan Miller	6-1/150	East Lansing, Mich.	7-17-80	0	Michigan State (CCHA)
35	Mika Noronen	6-1/191	Tampere, Finland	6-17-79	1	Rochester (AHL), Buffalo

SCORING

	Games	G	A	Pts.	PIM	+/-	PPG	SHG	Shots	Shooting Pct.
Miroslav Satan...	82	29	33	62	36	5	8	2	206	14.1
Jean-Pierre Dumont	79	23	28	51	54	1	9	0	156	14.7
Stu Barnes..	75	19	24	43	26	-2	3	2	160	11.9
Chris Gratton...	82	19	21	40	102	0	5	0	156	12.2
Doug Gilmour...	71	7	31	38	70	3	4	0	91	7.7
Alexei Zhitnik..	78	8	29	37	75	-3	5	0	149	5.4
Maxim Afinogenov...	78	14	22	36	40	1	3	0	190	7.4
Dave Andreychuk..	74	20	13	33	32	0	8	0	119	16.8
Curtis Brown...	70	10	22	32	34	15	2	1	105	9.5
Erik Rasmussen..	82	12	19	31	51	0	1	0	95	12.6
Vaclav Varada..	75	10	21	31	81	-2	2	0	112	8.9
Jason Woolley..	67	5	18	23	46	0	4	0	92	5.4
Dimitri Kalinin..	79	4	18	22	38	-2	2	0	88	4.5
Rhett Warrener...	77	3	16	19	78	10	0	0	103	2.9
Richard Smehlik..	56	3	12	15	4	6	0	0	40	7.5
Vladimir Tsyplakov..	36	7	7	14	10	2	0	0	39	17.9

	Games	G	A	Pts.	PIM	+/-	PPG	SHG	Shots	Shooting Pct.
James Patrick	54	4	9	13	12	9	1	0	48	8.3
Steve Heinze*	14	5	7	12	8	6	1	0	19	26.3
Denis Hamel	41	8	3	11	22	-2	1	1	55	14.5
Jay McKee	74	1	10	11	76	9	0	0	62	1.6
Rob Ray	63	4	6	10	210	2	0	0	33	12.1
Donald Audette*	12	2	6	8	12	1	1	0	38	5.3
Eric Boulton	35	1	2	3	94	-1	0	0	20	5.0
Dominik Hasek (goalie)	67	0	3	3	22	0	0	0	0	0.0
Chris Taylor	14	0	2	2	6	1	0	0	21	0.0
Peter Skudra (goalie)*	1	0	0	0	0	0	0	0	0	0.0
Mika Noronen (goalie)	2	0	0	0	0	0	0	0	0	0.0
Brian Campbell	8	0	0	0	2	-2	0	0	7	0.0
Martin Biron (goalie)	18	0	0	0	0	0	0	0	0	0.0

GOALTENDING

	Games	Min.	Goals	SO	Avg.	W	L	T	ENG	Shots	Sv. Pct.
Peter Skudra*	1	0	0	0	0.00	0	0	0	0	0	.000
Dominik Hasek	67	3904	137	11	2.11	37	24	4	2	1726	.921
Martin Biron	18	918	39	2	2.55	7	7	1	1	427	.909
Mika Noronen	2	108	5	0	2.78	2	0	0	0	39	.872

*Played with two or more NHL teams.

RESULTS

OCTOBER
5— Chicago ....W 4-2
7— Los Angeles ....W 5-3
13— At Edmonton ....L 2-3
14— At Vancouver ....L 0-4
17— At Montreal ....L 3-4
20— Anaheim ....T *2-2
21— At Detroit ....L ...*4-5
25— Carolina............................W 4-1
27— Toronto..............................W 2-1
28— At Chicago........................W 3-1

NOVEMBER
3— Montreal ....W 5-4
4— At Philadelphia.................L 0-3
9— N.Y. Islanders ....W 3-0
11— At New Jersey ....W 4-0
13— Calgary ....W *3-2
15— Dallas ....T *2-2
17— Minnesota ....W 3-1
18— At St. Louis ....L 1-4
22— Philadelphia ....L 1-3
24— N.Y. Rangers ....W 3-2
25— At Montreal ....W 5-3
28— At Ottawa ....L 1-3

DECEMBER
1— Pittsburgh..........................L 4-6
2— At Pittsburgh ....W 3-2
5— At Montreal ....W 3-2
7— New Jersey.......................W 5-2
8— At N.Y. Rangers ....L 2-5

12— At Boston ....W 3-0
15— At Carolina........................L 3-5
16— Florida ....W 3-2
20— At Washington ....T *2-2
21— Washington ....L 1-3
23— San Jose ....W 5-2
26— Pittsburgh.........................L 3-5
29— Ottawa ....W 2-0
30— At N.Y. Islanders...............W 2-0

JANUARY
1— Boston ....L 3-4
3— At Toronto ....T *1-1
5— Toronto ....T *3-3
6— At Nashville ....W 2-0
9— At San Jose ....L 1-2
11— At Los Angeles ....L 2-3
12— At Anaheim ....W 4-0
16— Tampa Bay ....W 3-1
19— Florida ....W 1-0
20— At Toronto ....L 0-2
23— Columbus ....L 1-2
26— Boston ....L 1-2
27— At N.Y. Islanders...............W 2-1
31— At Florida ....L 2-5

FEBRUARY
1— At Tampa Bay ....L 2-4
6— At N.Y. Rangers ....W 6-3
7— N.Y. Islanders ....W *2-1
10— At Ottawa ....W *2-1
11— Montreal ....L 3-4

13— At Atlanta...........................L 4-5
15— Atlanta ....W 3-1
17— New Jersey ....W 5-1
19— Ottawa ....W 2-0
22— At New Jersey ....W 1-0
23— Phoenix ....L 3-7
25— Tampa Bay ....W 5-4
27— At Ottawa ....W 4-1

MARCH
1— At Philadelphia...................L 0-2
3— At Colorado ....W *3-2
4— At Dallas ....L 1-4
6— At Boston ....W 3-1
9— Edmonton...........................L 0-4
14— N.Y. Rangers ....W 6-3
16— Vancouver ....W 4-2
17— At Washington ....W 3-2
20— Toronto..............................W 3-0
21— At Carolina.........................L 0-1
24— Carolina.............................W 3-1
26— At Atlanta...........................W 4-0
27— At Pittsburgh ....L 1-4
30— Atlanta ....W 4-0

APRIL
1— At Tampa Bay ....W 4-2
2— At Florida............................W 5-3
4— Boston ....L 2-3
6— Washington ....W 2-1
8— Philadelphia ....L 1-2

*Denotes overtime game.

CALGARY FLAMES
WESTERN CONFERENCE/NORTHWEST DIVISION

CALGARY FLAMES

Flames' Schedule
Home games shaded; D—Day game; *—All-Star Game at Los Angeles

October

SUN	MON	TUE	WED	THU	FRI	SAT
	1	2	3 EDM	4	5	6 CHI
7	8 PHO	9	10 DET	11 NAS	12	13 DAL
14	15	16	17	18 FLA	19	20 TOR
21	22 STL	23 CHI	24	25 NAS	26	27 MIN
28	29	30	31			

November

SUN	MON	TUE	WED	THU	FRI	SAT
				1 CBJ	2	3 MON
4	5	6	7 ANA	8 LA	9	10 COL
11	12	13	14	15 CHI	16	17 STL
18	19	20 LA	21	22 OTT	23 BUF	24
25 CBJ	D 26	27 DET	28	29 DAL	30	

December

SUN	MON	TUE	WED	THU	FRI	SAT
						1 COL
2	3 LA	4 SJ	5	6 SJ	7	8 ANA
9	10 DET	11	12 TB	13	14 DAL	15 STL
16	17	18	19 PHO	20	21 COL	22
23	24	25	26 EDM	27 VAN	28	29 MIN
30	31 EDM					

January

SUN	MON	TUE	WED	THU	FRI	SAT
		1	2	3 BUF	4	5 MON
6	7	8 NYI	9 NJ	10	11 ATL	12
13	14	15 NYI	16	17 PIT	18	19 ANA
20	21	22 TOR	23	24 COL	25	26 VAN
27	28 MIN	29	30 DET	31		

February

SUN	MON	TUE	WED	THU	FRI	SAT
					1	2 *
3	4	5	6 SJ	7	8 VAN	9 VAN
10	11	12 PHO	13 ANA	14	15	16
17	18	19	20	21	22	23
24	25	26 COL	27	28 STL		

March

SUN	MON	TUE	WED	THU	FRI	SAT
					1	2 NAS
3	4 NYR	5	6 WAS	7 PHI	8	9 BOS
10	11 CAR	12	13 FLA	14 TB	15	16 CBJ
17	18 MIN	19	20	21 SJ	22	23 EDM
24	25 CBJ	26	27	28 DAL	29	30 LA
31						

April

SUN	MON	TUE	WED	THU	FRI	SAT
	1	2 ATL	3	4 MIN	5	6 NAS
7 CHI	8	9 PHO	10	11	12 EDM	13 VAN
14	15	16	17	18	19	20

2001-02 SEASON
CLUB DIRECTORY

Co-owners
N. Murray Edwards, Harley N. Hotchkiss, Alvin G. Libin, Allan P. Markin, J.R. (Bud) McCaig, Byron J. Seaman, Daryl K. Seaman

President & chief executive officer
Ron Bremner

Vice president/general manager
Craig Button

V.p., finance & administration
Michael Holditch

Vice president, marketing & sales
Garry McKenzie

Assistant to the general manager
Dan Stuchal

Head coach
Greg Gilbert

Assistant coaches
Rob Cookson, Brad McCrimmon, Brian Scrudland

Development coach
Jamie Hislop

Goaltending consultant
Grant Fuhr

Director, hockey administration
Mike Burke

Pro scout
Tod Button

Scouts
Mike Sands, Bob Atrill, Jeff Crisp, Tomas Jelinek, Larry Johnston, Pertii Hasahen, Bob Richardson

Physical therapist
Morris Boyer

Athletic therapist
To be announced

Equipment manager
Gus Thorson

Strength & conditioning
Rich Hesketh

Assistant equipment manager
Les Jarvis

Head physician-sport medicine
Dr. Willem Meeuwisse

Orthopedic surgeon
Dr. Nicholas Mohtadi

Internal medicine
Dr. Terry Groves

Team Dentist
Dr. Bill Blair

Director, communications
Peter Hanlon

Manager, media relations
Sean O'Brien

Admin. assistant, communications
Bernie Hargrave

Director, community relations
Holly Brown

Controller
Jackie Manwaring

Director, human resources
Eleanor Culver

Director of marketing
Al Molnar

Director, advertising and publishing
Pat Halls

Director, executive suites
Bob White

Business development manager
Kevin Gross

Director, game presentation
Dave Imbach

Director, sales & customer care
Dave Sclanders

DRAFT CHOICES

Rd.— Player	Ht./Wt.	Overall	Pos.	Last team
1— Chuck Kobasew	5-11/195	14	RW	Boston Col. (H. East)
2— Andrei Taratukhin	6-0/198	41	C/F	OMSK, Russia
2— Andrei Medvedev	6-0/202	56	G	Spartak Jr., Russia
4— Tomi Maki	5-11/172	108	RW	Jokerit, Finland
4— Egor Shastin	5-9/172	124	F	OMSK, Russia
5— James Hakewill	6-3/205	145	D	Westminster (USHSE)
5— Yuri Trubachev	5-9/187	164	C	St. Petersburg, Russia
7— Garett Bembridge	6-0/180	207	RW	Saskatoon (WHL)
7— David Moss	6-3/185	220	LW	Cedar Rapids (USHL)
8— Joe Campbell	6-4/172	233	D	Des Moines (USHL)
8— Ville Hamalainen	5-11/187	251	F	Saipa, Finland

MISCELLANEOUS DATA

Home ice (capacity)
Pengrowth Saddledome (17,158)

Address
P.O. Box 1540
Station M
Calgary, Alta. T2P 3B9

Business phone
403-777-2177

Ticket information
403-777-0000

Website
www.calgaryflames.com

Training site
Calgary

Club colors
Red, white, gold and black

Radio affiliation
The Team 920 (920 AM)

TV affiliation
CTV Sportsnet, CBC-TV

TRAINING CAMP ROSTER

No.	FORWARDS	Ht./Wt.	Place	Born Date	NHL exp.	2000-01 clubs
26	Steve Begin (LW)	5-11/190	Trois-Rivieres, Que.	6-14-78	3	Saint John (AHL), Calgary
	Blair Betts (C)	6-1/183	Edmonton	2-16-80	0	Saint John (AHL)
17	Chris Clark (RW)	6-0/202	South Windsor, Conn.	3-8-76	2	Saint John (AHL), Calgary
22	Craig Conroy (C)	6-2/193	Potsdam, N.Y.	9-4-71	7	St. Louis, Calgary
38	Jeff Cowan (LW)	6-2/192	Scarborough, Ont.	9-27-76	2	Calgary
23	Miikka Elomo (LW)	6-0/198	Turku, Finland	4-21-77	1	Saint John (AHL)
44	Rico Fata (RW)	5-11/197	Sault Ste. Marie, Ont.	2-12-80	3	Saint John (AHL), Calgary
25	Dwayne Hay (LW)	6-1/183	London, Ont.	2-11-77	4	Calgary
	Jukka Hentunen (LW)	5-10/187	Finland	5-3-74	0	Jokerit Helsinki (Finland)
12	Jarome Iginla (RW)	6-1/202	Edmonton	7-1-77	6	Calgary
	Chuck Kobasew (RW)	5-11/195	Osoyoos, B.C.	4-17-82	0	Boston College (Hockey East)
26	Dave Lowry (LW)	6-1/200	Sudbury, Ont.	2-14-65	16	Calgary
	Tomi Maki (RW)	5-11/172	Helsinki, Finland	8-19-83	0	Jokerit Helsinki (Finland Jr.)
19	Dean McAmmond (LW)	5-11/195	Grand Cache, Alta.	6-15-73	9	Chicago, Philadelphia
44	Rob Niedermayer (C)	6-2/204	Cassiar, B.C.	12-28-74	8	Florida
	Ronald Petrovicky (RW)	5-11/188	Zlina, Czechoslovakia	2-15-77	1	Calgary
	Oleg Saprykin (C/LW)	6-0/187	Moscow, U.S.S.R.	2-12-81	2	Calgary
27	Marc Savard (C)	5-10/184	Ottawa	7-17-77	4	Essen (Germany), Calgary
11	Jeff Shantz (C)	6-0/195	Edmonton	10-10-73	8	Calgary
	Egor Shastin (LW)	5-9/172	Kiev, U.S.S.R.	9-10-82	0	Avangard Omsk (Russian)
	Jarrett Stoll (C)	6-1/199	Melville, Sask.	6-24-82	0	Kootenay (WHL)
	Shaun Sutter (C)	5-11/160	Red Deer, Alta.	6-2-80	0	Calgary (WHL), Saint John (AHL)
	Andrei Taratukhin (C)	6-0/198	Omsk, U.S.S.R.	2-22-83	0	Avangard Omsk (Russian Div. II)
	Yuri Trubachev (C)	5-9/187	Cherepovets, U.S.S.R.	3-9-83	0	SKA St. Petersburg (Russian)
23	Clarke Wilm (C)	6-0/202	Central Butte, Sask.	10-24-76	3	Calgary

No.	DEFENSEMEN	Ht./Wt.	Place	Born Date	NHL exp.	2000-01 clubs
6	Bob Boughner	6-0/203	Windsor, Ont.	3-8-71	6	Pittsburgh
	Micki Dupont				0	Saint John (AHL)
7	Dallas Eakins	6-1/198	Dade City, Fla.	1-20-67	9	Chicago (IHL), Calgary
	Kurtis Foster	6-5/205	Carp, Ont.	11-24-81	0	Peterborough (OHL)
3	Denis Gauthier	6-2/210	Montreal	10-1-76	4	Calgary
	James Hakewill	6-3/205	Wilmette, Ill.	6-7-82	0	Westminster Prep (USHS (East))
6	Phil Housley	5-10/185	St. Paul, Minn.	3-9-64	19	Calgary
29	Igor Kravchuk	6-1/218	Ufa, U.S.S.R.	9-13-66	10	Ottawa, Calgary
	Jordan Leopold	6-0/193	Golden Valley, Minn.	8-3-80	0	Univ. of Minnesota (WCHA)
	Toni Lydman	6-1/183	Lahti, Finland	9-25-77	1	Calgary
53	Derek Morris	5-11/200	Edmonton	8-24-78	4	Calgary, Saint John (AHL)
28	Robyn Regehr	6-2/225	Recife, Brazil	4-19-80	2	Calgary
	Chris St. Croix	6-0/199	Voorhees, N.J.	5-2-79	0	Saint John (AHL)
33	Brad Werenka	6-1/218	Two Hills, Alta.	2-12-69	7	Calgary

No.	GOALTENDERS	Ht./Wt.	Place	Born Date	NHL exp.	2000-01 clubs
	Brent Krahn	6-4/200	Winnipeg	4-2-82	0	Calgary (WHL)
	Andrei Medvedev	6-0/202	Moscow, U.S.S.R.	4-1-83	0	Spartak (Russian Div. 1)
	Lavente Szuper	5-11/178	Budapest, Hungary	6-11-80	0	Saint John (AHL)
1	Roman Turek	6-3/200	Pisek, Czechoslovakia	5-21-70	5	St. Louis
29	Mike Vernon	5-9/180	Calgary	2-24-63	18	Calgary
35	Kay Whitmore	5-11/180	Sudbury, Ont.	4-10-67	8	Providence (AHL), Boston

2000-01 REVIEW

INDIVIDUAL STATISTICS

SCORING

	Games	G	A	Pts.	PIM	+/-	PPG	SHG	Shots	Shooting Pct.
Jarome Iginla	77	31	40	71	62	-2	10	0	229	13.5
Marc Savard	77	23	42	65	46	-12	10	1	197	11.7
Valeri Bure	78	27	28	55	26	-21	16	0	276	9.8
Cory Stillman*	66	21	24	45	45	-6	7	0	148	14.2
Dave Lowry	79	18	17	35	47	-2	5	0	108	16.7
Phil Housley	69	4	30	34	24	-15	0	0	115	3.5
Derek Morris	51	5	23	28	56	-15	3	1	142	3.5
Oleg Saprykin	59	9	14	23	43	4	2	0	95	9.5
Jeff Shantz	73	5	15	20	58	-7	0	0	88	5.7
Tommy Albelin	77	1	19	20	22	2	1	0	69	1.4
Toni Lydman	62	3	16	19	30	-7	1	0	80	3.8
Jason Wiemer	65	10	5	15	177	-15	3	0	76	13.2
Clarke Wilm	81	7	8	15	69	-11	2	0	85	8.2
Jeff Cowan	51	9	4	13	74	-8	2	0	48	18.8
Daniel Tkaczuk	19	4	7	11	14	1	1	0	34	11.8

	Games	G	A	Pts.	PIM	+/-	PPG	SHG	Shots	Shooting Pct.
Bill Lindsay*	52	1	9	10	97	-8	0	0	57	1.8
Ronald Petrovicky	30	4	5	9	54	0	1	0	30	13.3
Denis Gauthier	62	2	6	8	78	3	0	0	33	6.1
Igor Kravchuk*	37	0	8	8	4	-12	0	0	54	0.0
Craig Conroy*	14	3	4	7	14	0	0	1	32	9.4
Chris Clark	29	5	1	6	38	0	1	0	43	11.6
Brad Werenka	33	1	4	5	16	-3	0	0	23	4.3
Benoit Gratton	14	1	3	4	14	0	0	0	13	7.7
Ron Sutter	21	1	3	4	12	4	0	0	16	6.3
Dwayne Hay	49	1	3	4	16	-4	0	0	39	2.6
Robyn Regehr	71	1	3	4	70	-7	0	0	62	1.6
Steve Smith	13	0	2	2	17	-2	0	0	3	0.0
Niklas Andersson	11	0	1	1	4	0	0	0	8	0.0
Dallas Eakins	17	0	1	1	11	-1	0	0	4	0.0
Mike Vernon (goalie)	41	0	1	1	16	0	0	0	0	0.0
Fred Brathwaite (goalie)	49	0	1	1	2	0	0	0	0	0.0
Steve Begin	4	0	0	0	21	0	0	0	3	0.0
Rico Fata	5	0	0	0	6	-3	0	0	6	0.0
Marty Murray	7	0	0	0	0	-2	0	0	6	0.0
Wade Belak*	23	0	0	0	79	-2	0	0	8	0.0

GOALTENDING

	Games	Min.	Goals	SO	Avg.	W	L	T	ENG	Shots	Sv. Pct.
Fred Brathwaite	49	2742	106	5	2.32	15	17	10	6	1181	.910
Mike Vernon	41	2246	121	3	3.23	12	23	5	3	1034	.883

*Played with two or more NHL teams.

RESULTS

OCTOBER
5— Detroit ....L.....3-4
10—Colorado ....L.....1-3
12—Columbus ....L.....2-3
14—At N.Y. Islanders...............W.....2-0
15—At Detroit ....W.....4-2
18—At Vancouver......................L.....1-4
20—Boston................................W.....3-2
21—Toronto...............................L.....1-2
24—Phoenix ....T....*2-2
26—At St. Louis........................L.....3-4
27—At Minnesota ....L.....1-3
29—Anaheim ....L.....3-6

NOVEMBER
1— At Edmonton ....L.....2-3
4— Pittsburgh...........................T....*1-1
5— Minnesota...........................L....*2-3
8— At Minnesota ....W.....1-0
10—At Florida............................T....*3-3
11—At Tampa Bay ....W.....4-3
13—At Buffalo............................L....*2-3
16—Chicago...............................L.....2-5
18—N.Y. Rangers......................L....*4-5
19—At Edmonton ....L.....0-2
22—At Minnesota ....T....*1-1
24—Anaheim ....T....*2-2
25—At Colorado ....T....*2-3
28—At Nashville ....L.....1-6
29—At Dallas.............................W.....4-3

DECEMBER
2— Montreal..............................T....*1-1
4— San Jose.............................L.....0-8
7— Nashville.............................W.....3-0
9— Carolina...............................W.....7-2
13—At Montreal ....W.....3-1
14—At Ottawa ....L.....2-4
16—At Toronto ....W...*6-5
19—At Colorado ....W.....3-0
20—At Phoenix ....L.....2-4
22—Edmonton ....T....*1-1
29—Vancouver ....W.....5-0
31—Montreal ....W...*5-4

JANUARY
3— At San Jose........................W.....1-0
5— At Anaheim ....T....*4-4
6— At Los Angeles ....L.....0-5
11—Nashville..............................W.....2-1
13—Ottawa ....L.....2-5
14—At Vancouver.......................L.....1-5
17—At San Jose ....T....*4-4
21—Detroit ....W.....4-2
23—Phoenix ....L.....2-4
25—At Los Angeles ....W.....3-0
27—Vancouver ....L.....3-5
30—Edmonton ....L.....3-5

FEBRUARY
1— Chicago ....W.....5-3
6— San Jose.............................T....*1-1
9— At Colorado ....W.....5-3

[March column]
10—At Vancouver.......................W.....4-1
13—Washington ....T....*4-4
15—At St. Louis.........................L.....1-4
18—At Phoenix...........................W.....4-1
19—At Anaheim ....L.....2-6
22—Los Angeles ....L.....0-2
24—Edmonton ....L.....1-3
26—Dallas ....W.....3-2

MARCH
1— Minnesota............................T....*1-1
3— St. Louis..............................W...*3-2
6— Toronto ....L.....1-3
8— At Philadelphia.....................L.....2-5
10—At Pittsburgh ....L.....3-6
11—At Atlanta ....T....*3-3
14—At Columbus ....L.....0-3
15—At Detroit ....L.....2-5
17—St. Louis ....T....*2-2
19—New Jersey ....L.....2-4
22—Philadelphia ....W.....3-1
24—At Columbus ....L.....4-6
25—At Chicago ....W.....3-1
27—Columbus ....W.....3-0
29—Colorado ....L.....0-1
31—Dallas ....L.....0-2

APRIL
2— At Dallas ....T....*4-4
4— At Chicago............................W.....5-2
5— At Nashville ....L.....0-4
7— Los Angeles ....L.....2-3

*Denotes overtime game.

CAROLINA HURRICANES
EASTERN CONFERENCE/SOUTHEAST DIVISION

CAROLINA HURRICANES

Hurricanes' Schedule
Home games shaded; D—Day game; *—All-Star Game at Los Angeles

October

SUN	MON	TUE	WED	THU	FRI	SAT
	1	2	3	4	5 NYR	6
7 D DAL	8	9 OTT	10	11 TOR	12	13 ATL
14	15	16	17 NYI	18 NYI	19	20 ATL
21	22	23 COL	24 MIN	25	26 NYI	27
28 D LA	29	30 DET	31			

November

SUN	MON	TUE	WED	THU	FRI	SAT
				1 STL	2 NYR	3
4 D PHO	5	6	7	8 WAS	9 SJ	10
11 D EDM	12	13 DET	14	15 OTT	16	17 TB
18	19 CBJ	20	21 DAL	22	23	24
25 D TB	26	27 TOR	28 NYR	29	30 WAS	

December

SUN	MON	TUE	WED	THU	FRI	SAT
						1
2 D WAS	3	4 BUF	5	6	7	8 FLA
9	10 NYR	11	12 FLA	13	14 BUF	15
16 PIT	17	18 OTT	19	20	21 ATL	22 PHI
23	24	25	26 TOR	27 TB	28	29
30 WAS	31 BUF					

January

SUN	MON	TUE	WED	THU	FRI	SAT
		1	2 BOS	3	4	5 NJ
6 PHI	7	8	9	10 EDM	11	12 VAN
13	14	15 MIN	16	17 MON	18	19 D NJ
20	21 VAN	22	23 NAS	24	25 FLA	26 PHI
27	28	29 BUF	30 TB	31		

February

SUN	MON	TUE	WED	THU	FRI	SAT
					1	2 *
3	4	5 PIT	6	7 LA	8 ANA	9
10 SJ	11	12	13	14	15	16
17	18	19	20	21	22	23
24	25	26 TOR	27	28 BOS		

March

SUN	MON	TUE	WED	THU	FRI	SAT
					1	2 MON
3	4	5 CHI	6	7 PIT	8 WAS	9
10	11 CAL	12	13	14	15	16 MON
17	18 MON	19	20	21 FLA	22	23 D NJ
24	25	26 BOS	27	28 PHI	29	30 D BOS
31						

April

SUN	MON	TUE	WED	THU	FRI	SAT
	1	2 OTT	3 NJ	4	5	6
7 D ATL	8 NYI	9	10 TB	11	12 FLA	13
14 D ATL	15	16	17	18	19	20

2001-02 SEASON
CLUB DIRECTORY

Owner/governor
Peter Karmanos Jr.
General partner
Thomas Thewes
Chief executive officer/general manager
Jim Rutherford
President/chief operating officer
Jim Cain
Vice president/asst. general manager
Jason Karmanos
Chief financial officer
Mike Amendola
Head coach
Paul Maurice
Assistant coaches
Randy Ladouceur
Kevin McCarthy
Director of amateur scouting
Sheldon Ferguson
Amateur scouts
Willy Langer
Willy Lindstrom
Tony MacDonald
Bert Marshall
Terry E. McDonnell

Pro scout
Claude Larose
Video coordinator
Chris Huffine
Head athletic therapist/strength and conditioning coach
Peter Friesen
Assistant athletic therapist
Stu Lempke
Equipment managers
Skip Cunningham
Bob Gorman
Wally Tatomir
Executive assistants, hockey operations
Kelly Kirwin
Debbie Shannon
Director of public/media relations
Jerry Higgins
Media relations manager
Mike Sundheim

DRAFT CHOICES

Rd.— Player	Ht./Wt.	Overall	Pos.	Last team
1— Igor Knyazev	6-0/180	15	D	Spartak Jr., Russia
2— Michael Zigomanis	6-0/190	46	C	Kingston (OHL)
3— Kevin Estrada	5-10/180	91	LW	Chilliwack (BCJHL)
4— Rob Zepp	6-0/181	110	G	Plymouth (OHL)
6— Daniel Boisclair	6-2/185	181	G	Cape Breton (QMJHL)
7— Sean Curry	6-4/230	211	D	Tri-City (WHL)
8— Carter Trevisani	6-1/185	244	D	Ottawa (OHL)
9— Peter Reynolds	6-3/195	274	D	North Bay (OHL)

MISCELLANEOUS DATA

Home ice (capacity)
Entertainment & Sports Arena (18,730)
Address
1400 Edwards Mill Road
Raleigh, NC 27607
Business phone
919-467-7825
Ticket information
1-888-645-8491
Website
www.carolinahurricanes.com

Training site
Fort Myers, FL & Raleigh
Club colors
Red, black and silver
Radio affiliation
WRBZ (850 AM)
TV affiliation
FOX Sports South, Comcast Sports Net
(Cable)

No.	FORWARDS	Ht./Wt.	Place	BORN Date	NHL exp.	2000-01 clubs
	Craig Adams (RW)	6-0/200	Calgary	4-26-77	1	Carolina, Cincinnati (IHL)
13	Bates Battaglia (LW)	6-2/205	Chicago	12-13-75	4	Carolina
27	Rod Brind'Amour (C)	6-1/200	Ottawa	8-9-70	13	Carolina
	Erik Cole (LW)	6-0/185	Oswego, N.Y.	11-6-78	0	Cincinnati (IHL)
17	Jeff Daniels (LW)	6-1/200	Oshawa, Ont.	6-24-68	10	Carolina
	Brad DeFauw (LW)	6-2/210	Edina, Minn.	11-10-77	0	Cincinnati (IHL)
11	Chris Dingman (LW)	6-4/245	Edmonton	7-6-76	4	Colorado
	Kevin Estrada (LW)	5-10/180	Surrey, B.C.	5-28-82	0	Chilliwack (BCJHL)
44	Brian Felsner (C/LW)	5-10/183	Mt. Clemens, Mich.	11-11-72	1	Cincinnati (IHL)
21	Ron Francis (C)	6-3/200	Sault Ste. Marie, Ont.	3-1-63	20	Carolina
23	Martin Gelinas (LW)	5-11/195	Shawinigan, Que.	6-5-70	13	Carolina
	Jeff Heerema (RW)	6-1/184	Thunder Bay, Ont.	1-17-80	0	Cincinnati (IHL)
24	Sami Kapanen (RW)	5-10/175	Helsinki, Finland	6-14-73	6	Carolina
36	Greg Koehler (C)	6-2/195	Scarborough, Ont.	2-27-75	1	Cincinnati (IHL), Carolina
	Tomas Kurka (LW)	5-11/190	Litvinov, Czechoslovakia	12-14-81	0	Plymouth (OHL)
19	Darren Langdon (LW)	6-1/210	Deer Lake, Nfld.	1-8-71	7	Carolina
12	Craig MacDonald (C)	6-2/185	Antigonish, Nova Scotia.	4-7-77	1	Cincinnati (IHL)
	Ian MacNeil (C)	6-2/178	Halifax, Nova Scotia.	4-27-77	0	Cincinnati (IHL)
92	Jeff O'Neill (C)	6-0/195	King City, Ont.	2-23-76	6	Carolina
15	Byron Ritchie (C)	5-10/185	Burnaby, B.C.	4-24-77	2	Cincinnati (IHL)
	Jarslav Svoboda (RW)	6-1/174	Cervenka, Czechoslovakia	6-1-80	0	Cincinnati (IHL)
	Josef Vasicek (C)	6-4/196	Havlickuv Brod, Czech.	9-12-80	1	Carolina, Cincinnati (IHL)
16	Tommy Westlund (RW)	6-0/202	Fors, Sweden	12-29-74	2	Carolina
25	Shane Willis (RW)	6-0/176	Edmonton	6-13-77	3	Carolina
	Mike Zigomanis (C)	6-0/183	North York, Ont.	1-17-81	0	Kingston (OHL)
	DEFENSEMEN					
14	Steve Halko	6-1/190	Etobicoke, Ont.	3-8-74	4	Carolina
	Igor Knyazev	6-0/183	Elektrosal, U.S.S.R.	1-27-83	0	Spartak (Russian Div. 1)
53	Greg Kuznik	6-0/182	Prince George, B.C.	6-12-78	1	Cincinnati (IHL), Carolina
5	Marek Malik	6-5/210	Ostrava, Czechoslovakia	6-24-75	6	Carolina
8	Sandis Ozolinsh	6-3/205	Riga, U.S.S.R.	8-3-72	9	Carolina
	Harlan Pratt	6-2/191	Fort McMurray, Alta.	12-10-78	0	Cincinnati (IHL)
19	Mike Rucinski	5-11/188	Trenton, Mich.	3-30-75	3	Cincinnati (IHL), Carolina
45	David Tanabe	6-1/195	Minneapolis	7-19-80	2	Carolina
	Nikos Tselios	6-4/187	Oak Park, Ill.	1-20-79	0	Cincinnati (IHL)
	Niclas Wallin	6-2/207	Sweden	2-20-75	1	Carolina, Cincinnati (IHL)
27	Aaron Ward	6-2/225	Windsor, Ont.	1-17-73	7	Detroit
2	Glen Wesley	6-1/201	Red Deer, Alta.	10-2-68	14	Carolina
	GOALTENDERS					
1	Arturs Irbe	5-8/190	Riga, U.S.S.R.	2-2-67	10	Carolina
	Tyler Moss	6-0/185	Ottawa	6-29-75	3	Carolina, Cincinnati (IHL)
	Jean-Marc Pelletier	6-3/195	Atlanta	3-4-78	1	Cincinnati (IHL)

2000-01 REVIEW
INDIVIDUAL STATISTICS

SCORING

	Games	G	A	Pts.	PIM	+/-	PPG	SHG	Shots	Shooting Pct.
Jeff O'Neill	82	41	26	67	106	-18	17	0	242	16.9
Ron Francis	82	15	50	65	32	-15	7	0	130	11.5
Sami Kapanen	82	20	37	57	24	-12	7	0	223	9.0
Rod Brind'Amour	79	20	36	56	47	-7	5	1	163	12.3
Martin Gelinas	79	23	29	52	59	-4	6	1	170	13.5
Shane Willis	73	20	24	44	45	-6	9	0	172	11.6
Sandis Ozolinsh	72	12	32	44	71	-25	4	2	145	8.3
David Tanabe	74	7	22	29	42	-9	5	0	130	5.4
Bates Battaglia	80	12	15	27	76	-14	2	0	133	9.0
Rob DiMaio	74	6	18	24	54	-14	0	2	99	6.1
Josef Vasicek	76	8	13	21	53	-8	1	0	103	7.8
Glen Wesley	71	5	16	21	42	-2	3	0	92	5.4
Marek Malik	61	6	14	20	34	-4	1	0	72	8.3
Kevin Hatcher	57	4	14	18	38	2	3	0	98	4.1
Dave Karpa	80	4	6	10	159	-19	2	0	69	5.8
Tommy Westlund	79	5	3	8	23	-9	0	0	47	10.6
Niclas Wallin	37	2	3	5	21	-11	0	0	19	10.5
Scott Pellerin*	19	0	5	5	6	-4	0	0	21	0.0
Jeff Daniels	67	1	1	2	15	-3	0	0	42	2.4
Darren Langdon	54	0	2	2	94	-4	0	0	6	0.0

	Games	G	A	Pts.	PIM	+/-	PPG	SHG	Shots	Shooting Pct.
Arturs Irbe (goalie)	77	0	2	2	6	0	0	0	0	0.0
Craig Adams	44	1	0	1	20	-7	0	0	15	6.7
Steven Halko	48	0	1	1	6	-10	0	0	24	0.0
Greg Koehler	1	0	0	0	0	0	0	0	0	0.0
Greg Kuznik	1	0	0	0	0	0	0	0	0	0.0
Mike Rucinski	2	0	0	0	0	0	0	0	2	0.0
Tyler Moss (goalie)	12	0	0	0	0	0	0	0	0	0.0

GOALTENDING

	Games	Min.	Goals	SO	Avg.	W	L	T	ENG	Shots	Sv. Pct.
Arturs Irbe	77	4406	180	6	2.45	37	29	9	7	1947	.908
Tyler Moss	12	557	37	0	3.99	1	6	0	1	251	.853

*Played with two or more NHL teams.

RESULTS

OCTOBER

7— Washington ....T....*3-3
10— Dallas ....W....5-2
13— At Florida ....T....*2-2
14— At Nashville ....L....1-2
18— At Pittsburgh ....W....3-2
21— At Montreal ....L....2-5
24— San Jose......................L....2-3
25— At Buffalo.....................L....1-4
27— New Jersey ....T....*3-3
29— St. Louis.......................L....1-4
31— Tampa Bay ....W....*6-5

NOVEMBER

3— At Colorado ....L....3-5
4— At San Jose ....L....1-4
8— At Toronto.....................L....0-5
10— Toronto..........................W....3-1
12— Ottawa...........................W....4-0
15— Florida ....L....1-4
16— At Ottawa ....W....1-0
18— At New Jersey ....L....*2-3
22— At Pittsburgh ....W....3-1
24— At Boston ....W....3-1
26— Nashville........................L....4-7
29— At Florida........................W....*2-1
30— Philadelphia ....W....2-0

DECEMBER

3— Ottawa ....L....0-2
6— At Atlanta ....W....5-3
9— At Calgary.......................L....2-7

13— At Minnesota ....T....*1-1
15— Buffalo.............................W....5-3
16— At Boston.........................L....1-4
19— At N.Y. Islanders ....L....1-2
23— At Philadelphia................L....*1-2
26— At Tampa Bay ....L....2-3
27— N.Y. Rangers ....W....4-3
29— At Columbus ....L....1-3
31— Chicago ....W....2-1

JANUARY

3— Tampa Bay ....W....3-2
6— Colorado ....T....*2-2
7— N.Y. Islanders ....W....5-2
9— Florida ....W....7-3
12— At Florida...........................T....*2-2
14— Anaheim ....W....4-0
16— At Montreal ....W....*3-2
18— Boston................................W....4-2
20— Los Angeles.......................L....3-6
22— N.Y. Rangers ....L....2-5
24— At N.Y. Rangers ....W....3-2
27— Philadelphia ....L....3-4
29— Tampa Bay ....W....5-2
31— Toronto ....L....3-4

FEBRUARY

1— At Atlanta ....W....3-1
7— At Phoenix............................W....*2-1
8— At Los Angeles ....L....2-4
11— At Anaheim ....T....*2-2
14— At Detroit ....L....*3-4

16— Phoenix ....L.....0-2
18— Boston................................W....5-4
19— At Philadelphia....................L.....0-4
21— Atlanta................................W....6-3
23— New Jersey ....W....3-2
24— Washington ....L.....1-2
27— At Atlanta............................T....*1-1

MARCH

1— At N.Y. Islanders................W....3-1
2— At New Jersey ....L....3-7
4— At Chicago...........................W....6-3
7— Columbus.............................W....2-1
8— At Tampa Bay ....L....0-1
11— Edmonton ....L....2-3
14— Montreal ....L....3-6
15— At Washington ....W....3-0
18— N.Y. Islanders ....W....2-1
21— Buffalo.................................W....1-0
23— Pittsburgh ....W....5-3
24— At Buffalo.............................L....1-3
26— Montreal ....L....2-4
28— At Washington......................L.....0-7
30— Washington ....W....*4-3

APRIL

1— At Ottawa ....W....*3-2
3— At St. Louis.........................T....*2-2
4— At N.Y. Rangers ....W....3-1
6— Atlanta................................W....3-2
8— Pittsburgh...........................L....4-6

*Denotes overtime game.

CHICAGO BLACKHAWKS
WESTERN CONFERENCE/CENTRAL DIVISION

Blackhawks' Schedule
Home games shaded; D—Day game; *—All-Star Game at Los Angeles

October

SUN	MON	TUE	WED	THU	FRI	SAT
	1	2	3	4 VAN	5	6 CAL
7	8	9 EDM	10	11 PHO	12 MIN	13
14 CBJ	15	16	17	18 NAS	19	20 DAL
21 COL	22	23 CAL	24	25 SJ	26	27
28 BOS	29	30 LA	31			

November

SUN	MON	TUE	WED	THU	FRI	SAT
				1 LA	2 ANA	3
4 DET	5	6 PHI	7	8	9 VAN	10
11 SJ	12	13 VAN	14	15 CAL	16 EDM	17
18	19	20	21 NAS	22	23 CBJ	24
25 DET	26	27	28 VAN	29	30 TOR	

December

SUN	MON	TUE	WED	THU	FRI	SAT
						1 TOR
2	3 MON	4	5 MIN	6	7 NYI	8
9 LA	10	11	12 STL	13	14 ATL	15 NAS
16	17 DET	18	19 BUF	20	21 EDM	22
23 DET	24	25	26 STL	27 COL	28	29
30 ANA	31 OTT					

January

SUN	MON	TUE	WED	THU	FRI	SAT
		1	2	3	4 TB	5
6 PIT	7	8	9 COL	10 CBJ	11	12 CBJ
13	14 EDM	15	16 FLA	17	18 TB	19
20 DAL	21	22	23 STL	24	25 STL	26
27	28 BOS	29	30 NJ	31		

February

SUN	MON	TUE	WED	THU	FRI	SAT
					1	2 *
3	4	5	6 PHO	7	8 3J	9 OOL
10	11	12	13 FLA	14	15	16
17	18	19	20	21	22	23
24	25	26 PHI	27 MON	28		

March

SUN	MON	TUE	WED	THU	FRI	SAT
					1	2
3 ANA	D 4	5 CAR	6	7 NYR	8	9
10	11 LA	12 PHO	13	14	15 ANA	16 SJ
17	18 DAL	19	20 NJ	21	22	23
24 STL	D 25	26	27 NAS	28	29 MIN	30
31 MIN	D					

April

SUN	MON	TUE	WED	THU	FRI	SAT
	1	2	3 NAS	4	5 STL	6
7 CAL	8	9 WAS	10 DET	11	12 DAL	13
14 CBJ	D 15	16	17	18	19	20

2001-02 SEASON
CLUB DIRECTORY

President
William W. Wirtz
Senior vice president/general manager
Robert J. Pulford
Vice president
Peter R. Wirtz
General manager
Mike Smith
Assistant general manager
Nick Beverley
Director of player personnel
Dale Tallon
Head coach
Brian Sutter
Assistant coaches
Al MacAdam
Denis Savard
Goaltending consultant
Vladislav Tretiak
Scouts
Ron Anderson, Michel Dumas, Bruce
Franklin, Tim Higgins, Sakari Pietela
Manager of team services
Matt Colleran
Head trainers
Michael Gapski

Equipment manager
Troy Parchman
Assistant equipment managers
Bill Stehle
Lou Varga
Massage therapist
Pawel Prylinski
Exec. director of communications
Jim De Maria
Dir. of community relations/p.r. asst.
Barbara Davidson
Manager of public relations
Tony Ommen
Exec. dir. of marketing/merchandising
Jim Sofranko
Manager, special events
Drew Stevenson
Manager, game operations
Mike Sullivan
Director of ticket operations
James K. Bare
Sales manager
Doug Ryan

DRAFT CHOICES

Rd.— Player	Ht./Wt.	Overall	Pos.	Last team
1— Tuomo Ruutu	6-2/196	9	C/LW	Jokerit, Finland
1— Adam Munro	6-1/187	29	G	Erie (OHL)
2— Matt Keith	6-1/190	59	RW	Spokane (WHL)
3— Craig Andersson	6-1/170	73	G	Guelph (OHL)
4— Brent MacLellan	6-3/211	104	D	Rimouski (QMJHL)
4— Vladimir Gusev	6-1/189	115	D	Khabarovsk, Russia
4— Aleksey Zotkin	6-0/200	119		Magnitogorsk, Russia
5— Tommi Jaminki	6-0/183	142	LW	Blues Jr , Finland
6— Alexander Golvin	5-11/192	174	LW	OMSK, Russia
6— Petr Puncochar	6-1/202	186	D	Karlovy Vary, Czech.
7— Teemu Jaaskelainen	6-0/198	205	D	Ilves, Finland
7— Oleg Minakov	6-2/183	216	RW	Elektrostal Jr., Russia
9— Jeff Miles	5-11/188	268	C	U. of Vermont (ECAC)

MISCELLANEOUS DATA

Home ice (capacity)
United Center (20,500)
Address
1901 W. Madison Street
Chicago, IL 60612
Business phone
312-455-7000
Ticket information
312-943-7000
Website
www.chicagoblackhawks.com

Training site
Chicago
Club colors
Red, black and white
Radio affiliation
WSCR (670 AM)
TV affiliation
FOX Sports Chicago

TRAINING CAMP ROSTER

No.	FORWARDS	Ht./Wt.	Place	Date	NHL exp.	2000-01 clubs
			—BORN—			
10	Tony Amonte (RW)	6-0/190	Hingham, Mass.	8-2-70	11	Chicago
	Mark Bell (C/LW)	6-3/198	St. Paul's, Ont.	8-5-80	1	Norfolk (AHL), Chicago
	Kyle Calder (C)	5-11/180	Mannville, Alta.	1-5-79	2	Norfolk (AHL), Chicago
55	Eric Daze (RW)	6-6/234	Montreal	7-2-75	7	Chicago
45	Aaron Downey (RW)	6-0/210	Shelburne, Ontario	9-27-74	2	Norfolk (AHL), Chicago
	Casey Hankinson (LW)	6-1/187	Edina, Minn.	5-8-76	1	Norfolk (AHL), Chicago
	Tommi Jaminki (LW)	6-0/183	Turku, Finland	2-11-83	0	Espoo (Finland Jr.)
27	Ty Jones (RW)	6-3/218	Richland, Wash.	2-22-79	1	Norfolk (AHL)
	Matt Keith (RW)	6-1/190	Edmonton	4-11-83	0	Spokane (WHL)
22	Igor Korolev (C)	6-1/190	Moscow, U.S.S.R.	9-6-70	9	Toronto
11	Josef Marha (C)	6-0/176	Havlickov Brod, Czech.	6-2-76	6	Chicago, Norfolk (AHL)
	Jonas Nordqvist (C)	6-2/191	Leksand, Sweden	4-26-82	0	Leksand (Sweden)
92	Michael Nylander (C)	6-1/195	Stockholm, Sweden	10-3-72	8	Chicago
	Nathan Perrott (RW)	6-0/215	Owen Sound, Ont.	12-8-76	0	Norfolk (AHL)
24	Bob Probert (LW)	6-3/225	Windsor, Ont.	6-5-65	16	Chicago
	Igor Radulov (LW)	6-0/176	U.S.S.R.	8-23-82	0	SKA St. Petersburg (Russian)
	Tuomo Ruutu (C/RW)	6-2/196	Vantaa, Finland	2-16-83	0	Jokerit (Finland)
	Mike Souza (LW/C)	6-1/190	Melrose, Mass.	1-28-78	0	Norfolk (AHL)
26	Steve Sullivan (RW)	5-9/160	Timmins, Ont.	7-6-74	6	Chicago
32	Steve Thomas (RW)	5-10/185	Stockport, England	7-15-63	17	Toronto
14	Ryan VandenBussche	6-0/200	Simcoe, Ontario	2-28-73	5	Chicago
17	Reto Von Arx (LW)	5-10/176	Egerkingen, Switzerland	5-5-82	1	Chicago, Norfolk (AHL)
	Pavel Vorobiev (RW)	6-0/183	Karaganda, U.S.S.R.	5-5-82	0	Lokomotiv Yaroslavl (Russian)
	Mikhail Yakubov (C)	6-3/185	Bamaul, U.S.S.R.	2-16-82	0	Lada Togliatti (Russian)
26	Valeri Zelepukin (LW)	6-1/200	Voskresensk, U.S.S.R.	9-17-68	10	Chicago, Norfolk (AHL)
13	Alex Zhamnov (C)	6-1/200	Moscow, U.S.S.R.	10-1-70	9	Chicago
	Aleksey Zotkin (LW)	6-0/200	U.S.S.R.	2-5-82	0	Metal. Magnitogorsk (Russian)
	DEFENSEMEN					
33	Jamie Allison	6-1/195	Lindsay, Ont.	5-13-75	6	Chicago
	Alexander Barkunov	6-1/190	Novosibirsk, U.S.S.R.	5-13-81	0	Lokomotiv Yaroslavl (Russian)
38	Nolan Baumgartner	6-1/195	Calgary	3-23-76	5	Norfolk (AHL), Chicago
6	Kevin Dean	6-3/210	Madison, Wis.	4-1-69	7	Chicago
	Vladimir Gusev	6-1/189	U.S.S.R.	11-24-82	0	Khabarovsk (Russian)
	Kent Huskins	6-2/190	Ottawa	5-4-79	0	Clarkson (ECAC)
52	Alexander Karpovtsev	6-3/215	Moscow, U.S.S.R.	4-7-70	8	Dynamo Moscow (Russian), Chicago
24	Jon Klemm	6-3/200	Cranbrook, B.C.	1-8-70	9	Colorado
	Brent MacLellan	6-3/211	Halifax, Nova Scotia	3-23-83	0	Rimouski (QMJHL)
19	Chris McAlpine	6-0/210	Roseville, Minn.	12-1-71	6	Norfolk (AHL), Chicago
	Steve McCarthy	6-0/197	Trail, B.C.	2-3-81	2	Chicago, Norfolk (AHL)
2	Boris Mironov	6-3/223	Moscow, U.S.S.R.	3-21-72	8	Chicago
33	Steve Poapst	5-11/199	Cornwall, Ont.	1-3-69	3	Norfolk (AHL), Chicago
28	Jaroslav Spacek	5-11/198	Rokycany, Czechoslovakia	2-11-74	3	Florida, Chicago
	Dmitri Tolkunov	6-2/191	Kiev, U.S.S.R.	5-5-79	0	Norfolk (AHL)
	Marty Wilford	6-0/216	Cobourg, Ont.	4-17-77	0	Norfolk (AHL)
	GOALTENDERS					
	Craig Andersson	6-2/170	Park Ridge, Ill.	5-21-81	0	Guelph (OHL)
	Mike Leighton	6-2/175	Petrolia, Ont.	5-18-81	0	Windsor (OHL)
	Adam Munro	6-1/187	Burlington, Ont.	11-12-82	0	Erie (OHL)
29	Steve Passmore	5-9/165	Thunder Bay, Ont.	1-29-73	3	Lowell (AHL), Los Angeles, Chicago (IHL), Chicago
41	Jocelyn Thibault	5-11/170	Montreal	1-12-75	8	Chicago

2000-01 REVIEW

INDIVIDUAL STATISTICS

SCORING

	Games	G	A	Pts.	PIM	+/-	PPG	SHG	Shots	Shooting Pct.
Steve Sullivan	81	34	41	75	54	3	6	8	204	16.7
Tony Amonte	82	35	29	64	54	-22	9	1	256	13.7
Michael Nylander	82	25	39	64	32	7	4	0	176	14.2
Eric Daze	79	33	24	57	16	1	9	1	205	16.1
Alexei Zhamnov	63	13	36	49	40	-12	3	1	117	11.1
Dean McAmmond*	61	10	16	26	43	4	1	0	95	10.5
Chris Herperger	61	10	15	25	20	0	0	1	76	13.2
Jaroslav Spacek*	50	5	18	23	20	7	2	0	85	5.9
Boris Mironov	66	5	17	22	42	-14	3	0	143	3.5
Bob Probert	79	7	12	19	103	-13	1	0	45	15.6
Stephane Quintal	72	1	18	19	60	-9	0	0	109	0.9
Kyle Calder	43	5	10	15	14	-4	0	0	63	7.9

	Games	G	A	Pts.	PIM	+/-	PPG	SHG	Shots	Shooting Pct.
Alexander Karpovtsev	53	2	13	15	39	-4	1	0	52	3.8
Kevin Dean	69	0	11	11	30	-16	0	0	75	0.0
Steve Dubinsky	60	6	4	10	33	-4	0	1	70	8.6
Jean-Yves Leroux	59	4	4	8	22	-9	1	0	60	6.7
Valeri Zelepukin	36	3	4	7	18	-14	0	2	38	7.9
Ryan Vandenbussche	64	2	5	7	146	-8	0	0	24	8.3
Chris McAlpine	50	0	6	6	32	5	0	0	61	0.0
Anders Eriksson*	13	2	3	5	2	-4	1	0	19	10.5
Steve Poapst	36	2	3	5	12	3	0	0	27	7.4
Steve McCarthy	44	0	5	5	8	-7	0	0	32	0.0
Reto Von Arx	19	3	1	4	4	-4	0	0	12	25.0
Jamie Allison	44	1	3	4	53	7	0	0	16	6.3
Blair Atcheynum	19	1	2	3	2	-7	0	0	18	5.6
Josef Marha	15	0	3	3	6	-4	0	0	17	0.0
Jocelyn Thibault (goalie)	66	0	3	3	2	0	0	0	0	0.0
Kris King	13	1	0	1	8	-3	0	0	12	8.3
Casey Hankinson	11	0	1	1	9	-3	0	0	15	0.0
Mark Bell	13	0	1	1	4	0	0	0	14	0.0
Aaron Downey	3	0	0	0	6	-1	0	0	2	0.0
Michel Larocque (goalie)	3	0	0	0	0	0	0	0	0	0.0
Steve Passmore (goalie)*	6	0	0	0	4	0	0	0	0	0.0
Nolan Baumgartner	8	0	0	0	6	-4	0	0	7	0.0
Robbie Tallas (goalie)	12	0	0	0	0	0	0	0	0	0.0
Mark Janssens	28	0	0	0	33	-8	0	0	15	0.0

GOALTENDING

	Games	Min.	Goals	SO	Avg.	W	L	T	ENG	Shots	Sv. Pct.
Steve Passmore*	6	340	14	0	2.47	0	4	1	0	147	.905
Jocelyn Thibault	66	3844	180	6	2.81	27	32	7	7	1711	.895
Robbie Tallas	12	627	35	0	3.35	2	7	0	1	265	.868
Michel Larocque	3	152	9	0	3.55	0	2	0	0	59	.847

*Played with two or more NHL teams.

RESULTS

OCTOBER

5— At Buffalo	L	2-4
7— At Columbus	W	5-3
12— Detroit	L	0-4
14— At Montreal	L	*4-5
15— Columbus	W	2-1
18— N.Y. Rangers	L	2-4
20— Dallas	L	1-5
21— At St. Louis	L	0-1
26— Colorado	L	0-2
28— Buffalo	L	1-3
29— At Minnesota	W	3-2

NOVEMBER

2— At Boston	L	4-5
3— At Detroit	W	6-1
5— Anaheim	W	4-2
8— San Jose	L	*2-3
10— Minnesota	L	2-5
11— At Toronto	T	*3-3
14— At Vancouver	L	2-4
16— At Calgary	W	5-2
17— At Edmonton	T	*3-3
21— At Phoenix	W	4-1
22— At San Jose	L	1-4
24— At Minnesota	L	0-2
27— At Detroit	W	*6-5
30— Nashville	L	0-3

DECEMBER

1— At Nashville	W	2-1
3— Columbus	W	5-0
7— Minnesota	L	2-4
9— At St. Louis	L	4-6
10— St. Louis	L	1-6
13— At Atlanta	L	1-3
15— At Dallas	L	1-4
16— At Nashville	W	3-0
21— Vancouver	W	6-4
23— At Ottawa	W	3-2
27— Phoenix	T	*1-1
29— Detroit	W	*3-2
31— At Carolina	L	1-2

JANUARY

3— Vancouver	W	6-0
5— Edmonton	L	1-2
7— Tampa Bay	W	7-4
9— At N.Y. Islanders	W	6-3
12— At Columbus	W	3-1
14— Colorado	T	*2-2
17— Florida	W	5-0
19— Washington	W	3-1
21— Pittsburgh	L	0-4
25— Philadelphia	L	1-5
26— At Colorado	L	2-5
28— At Vancouver	W	6-2
31— At Edmonton	L	2-3

FEBRUARY

1— At Calgary	L	3-5
6— At Los Angeles	T	*3-3
7— At Anaheim	W	3-2
10— At San Jose	L	*2-3
11— At Phoenix	L	2-3
14— San Jose	L	0-7
16— St. Louis	W	6-2
18— Los Angeles	W	3-0
19— At N.Y. Rangers	L	2-4
21— Detroit	L	3-7
23— Atlanta	W	1-0
25— Toronto	W	6-4
27— At Washington	W	3-2

MARCH

1— Los Angeles	T	*2-2
4— Carolina	L	3-6
7— At Dallas	W	4-1
9— At Anaheim	L	1-3
10— At Los Angeles	T	*2-2
13— Dallas	L	0-3
15— Nashville	W	3-2
18— Anaheim	L	1-4
22— Nashville	L	*1-2
24— At St. Louis	L	1-5
25— Calgary	L	1-3
28— Ottawa	L	2-5
29— At Pittsburgh	L	2-5

APRIL

1— Edmonton	T	*3-3
2— At New Jersey	L	3-4
4— Calgary	L	2-5
6— Toronto	L	0-1
8— At Columbus	L	*3-4

*Denotes overtime game.

COLORADO AVALANCHE
WESTERN CONFERENCE/NORTHWEST DIVISION

Avalanche Schedule
Home games shaded; D—Day game; *—All-Star Game at Los Angeles

October

SUN	MON	TUE	WED	THU	FRI	SAT
	1	2	3 PIT	4	5	6
7	8	9 VAN	10	11 EDM	12	13 VAN
14	15	16 TB	17	18 EDM	19	20 CBJ
21 CHI	22	23 CAR	24	25 VAN	26	27 PHO
28 ANA	29	30	31 STL			

November

SUN	MON	TUE	WED	THU	FRI	SAT
				1	2 MIN	3 TOR
4	5	6 MON	7	8 OTT	9	10 CAL
11	12	13 MIN	14	15	16 NYI	17
18 D NJ	19	20 NYR	21 NYI	22	23	24 EDM
25	26	27 FLA	28	29	30 VAN	

December

SUN	MON	TUE	WED	THU	FRI	SAT
						1 CAL
2	3 OTT	4	5 DET	6	7 BUF	8 CBJ
9	10 ANA	11	12 CBJ	13	14 SJ	15
16 MIN	17	18	19 ANA	20	21 CAL	22
23 MIN	24	25	26 DAL	27 CHI	28	29 PHI
30	31					

January

SUN	MON	TUE	WED	THU	FRI	SAT
		1 D NAS	2	3 NYR	4	5 D DET
6	7	8	9 CHI	10	11	12 EDM
13	14	15 SJ	16	17 PHO	18	19 SJ
20	21 BUF	22	23 EDM	24 CAL	25	26 D LA
27	28 LA	29	30 NAS	31		

February

SUN	MON	TUE	WED	THU	FRI	SAT
					1	2 *
3	4 DET	5	6	7	8 MIN	9 CHI
10	11 BOS	12	13 STL	14	15	16
17	18	19	20	21	22	23
24	25	26 CAL	27	28 PHO		

March

SUN	MON	TUE	WED	THU	FRI	SAT
					1	2 D DAL
3	4 NJ	5	6 CBJ	7	8	9 D LA
10	11 STL	12	13	14 ATL	15	16 D PHI
17 D NAS	18	19 WAS	20	21 LA	22	23 D DET
24	25	26	27	28 SJ	29	30 PHO
31						

April

SUN	MON	TUE	WED	THU	FRI	SAT
	1 NAS	2	3 ATL	4	5 DAL	6
7 STL	8	9 VAN	10	11	12 ANA	13
14 D DAL	15	16	17	18	19	20

2001-02 SEASON
CLUB DIRECTORY

Owner & Governor
E. Stanley Kroenke

Alternate governor, president and g.m.
Pierre Lacroix

Assistant general manager
Brian MacDonald

Head coach
Bob Hartley

Assistant coaches
Jacques Cloutier
Bryan Trottier

Vice president of player personnel
Michel Goulet

Director of hockey administration
Charlotte Grahame

Team services assistant
Ronnie Jameson

Chief scout
Jim Hammett

Pro scout
Brad Smith

Scouts
Yvon Gendron, Garth Joy, Steve Lyons,
Don Paarup, Orval Tessier

European scout
Joni Lehto

Computer research consultant
John Donohue

Strength & conditioning coach
Paul Goldberg

Head athletic trainer
Pat Karns

Kinesiologist
Matt Sokolowski

Massage Therapist
Gregorio Pradera

Equipment managers
Wayne Flemming
Mark Miller

Assistant equipment manager
Dave Randolph

V.p. of communications & team services
Jean Martineau

Dir. of special projects/communications
Hayne Ellis

Assistant director of communications
Damen Zier

DRAFT CHOICES

Rd.— Player	Ht./Wt.	Overall	Pos.	Last team
2— Peter Budaj	6-0/200	63	G	Toronto (OHL)
3— Danny Bois	6-0/192	97	RW	London (OHL)
4— Colt King	6-2/221	130	LW	Guelph (OHL)
5— Frantisek Skladany	6-0/183	143	LW	Boston Univ. (H. East)
5— Cody McCormick	6-2/200	144	C/RW	Belleville (OHL)
5— Mikko Viitanen	6-3/218	149	D	Ahmat, Finland
5— Pierre-Luc Emond	6-0/193	165	C	Drummondville (QMJHL)
6— Scott Horvath	6-3/228	184	RW	Mass.-Amherst (H. East)
6— Charlie Stephens	6-3/225	196	C/RW	Guelph (OHL)
7— M0arek Svatos	5-9/170	227	RW	Kootenay (WHL)

MISCELLANEOUS DATA

Home ice (capacity)
Pepsi Center (18,007)

Address
1000 Chopper Cr.
Denver, CO 80204

Business phone
303-405-1100

Ticket information
303-405-1111

Website
www.coloradoavalanche.com

Training site
Denver, Sweden & Finland

Club colors
Burgundy, steel blue, black, white and
silver

Radio affiliation
KKFN (950 AM)

TV affiliation
FOX Sports Net (Cable)

COLORADO AVALANCHE

No.	FORWARDS	Ht./Wt.	Place	BORN Date	NHL exp.	2000-01 clubs
	Yuri Babenko (C)	6-0/185	Penza, U.S.S.R.	1-2-78	1	Hershey (AHL), Colorado
	Danny Bois (RW)	6-0/192	Thunder Bay, Ont.	6-1-83	0	London (OHL)
37	Chris Drury (C)	5-10/180	Trumbull, Conn.	8-20-76	3	Colorado
	Pierre-Luc Emond (C)	6-0/193	Valleyfield, Que.	10-10-82	0	Drummondville (QMJHL)
21	Peter Forsberg (C)	6-0/190	Ornskoldsvik, Sweden	7-20-73	7	Colorado
23	Milan Hejduk (RW)	5-11/185	Sstnad-Laberm, Czech.	2-14-76	3	Colorado
	Dan Hinote (RW)	6-0/190	Leesburg, Fla.	1-30-77	2	Colorado
	Colt King (LW)	6-2/221	Thunder Bay, Ont.	3-4-83	0	Guelph (OHL)
	Jordan Krestanovich	6-0/170	Langley, B.C.	6-14-81	0	Hershey (AHL), Calgary (WHL)
	Mikhail Kuleshov (LW)	6-2/200	Perm, U.S.S.R.	1-7-81	0	SKA St. Petersburg (Russian), Hershey (AHL)
	Brad Larsen (LW)	6-0/210	Nakusp, B.C.	6-28-77	2	Hershey (AHL), Colorado
	Yevgeny Lazarev (LW)	6-2/215	Kharkov, U.S.S.R.	4-25-80	0	Hershey (AHL)
	Cody McCormick (C/RW)	6-2/200	London, Ont.	4-18-83	0	Belleville (OHL)
	Vaclav Nedorost (C)	6-1/187	Budejovice, Czechoslovakia	3-16-82	0	HC Ceske Budejovice (Czech Republic)
	Ville Nieminen (LW)	5-11/205	Tampere, Finland	4-6-77	2	Hershey (AHL), Colorado
27	Scott Parker (RW)	6-4/220	Hanford, Calif.	1-29-78	2	Colorado
25	Shjon Podein (LW)	6-2/200	Eden Prairie, Minn.	3-5-68	9	Colorado
39	Joel Prpic (C)	6-7/225	Sudbury, Ont.	9-25-74	3	Hershey (AHL), Colorado
	Steve Reinprecht (C)	6-1/195	Edmonton	5-7-76	2	Los Angeles, Colorado
19	Joe Sakic (C)	5-11/190	Burnaby, B.C.	7-7-69	13	Colorado
	Rob Shearer (C)	5-10/190	Kitchener, Ont.	10-19-76	1	Hershey (AHL), Colorado
	Frantisek Skladany (LW)	6-0/183	Martin, Czechoslovakia	4-22-82	0	Boston University (Hockey East)
	Charlie Stephens (C/RW)	6-2/205	Nilestown, Ont.	4-5-81	0	Guelph (OHL)
40	Alex Tanguay (LW)	6-0/190	Ste.-Justine, Que.	11-21-79	2	Colorado
	Radim Vrbata (RW)	6-1/185	Mlada Boleslav, Czech.	6-13-81	0	Shawinigan (QMJHL), Hershey (AHL)
26	Stephane Yelle (C)	6-1/190	Ottawa	5-9-74	6	Colorado
	DEFENSEMEN					
	Rick Berry	6-1/190	Brandon, Man.	11-4-78	1	Hershey (AHL), Colorado
4	Rob Blake	6-4/220	Simcoe, Ont.	12-10-69	12	Los Angeles, Colorado
7	Greg de Vries	6-3/215	Sundridge, Ont.	1-4-73	6	Colorado
52	Adam Foote	6-1/202	Toronto	7-10-71	10	Colorado
29	Eric Messier	6-2/200	Drummondville, Que.	10-29-73	5	Colorado
6	Bryan Muir	6-4/220	Winnipeg	6-8-73	6	Tampa Bay, Detroit (IHL), Hershey (AHL), Colorado
	Alex Riazantsev	5-11/200	Moscow, U.S.S.R.	3-15-80	0	Hershey (AHL)
	Argis Saviels	6-1/192	Riga, U.S.S.R.	1-15-82	0	Owen Sound (OHL), Hershey (AHL)
55	Martin Skoula	6-3/218	Litvinov, Czechoslovakia	10-28-79	2	Colorado
43	Dan Smith	6-2/195	Fernie, B.C.	10-19-76	2	Hershey (AHL)
	Ben Storey	6-2/180	Ottawa	6-22-77	0	Hershey (AHL)
	Mikko Vitanen	6-3/218	Rajamaki, Finland	2-18-82	0	Ahmat (Finland Div. 1)
	GOALTENDERS					
1	David Aebischer	6-1/185	Fribourg, Switzerland	2-7-78	1	Colorado
	Peter Budaj	6-0/200	Banska Bystrica, Czech.	9-18-82	0	Toronto St. Michael's (OHL)
	Frederic Cassivi	6-4/220	Sorel, Que.	6-12-75	0	Hershey (AHL)
33	Patrick Roy	6-0/192	Quebec City	10-5-65	17	Colorado
	Philippe Sauve	6-0/175	Buffalo	2-27-80	0	Hershey (AHL)

2000-01 REVIEW
INDIVIDUAL STATISTICS

SCORING

	Games	G	A	Pts.	PIM	+/-	PPG	SHG	Shots	Shooting Pct.
Joe Sakic	82	54	64	118	30	45	19	3	332	16.3
Peter Forsberg	73	27	62	89	54	23	12	2	178	15.2
Milan Hejduk	80	41	38	79	36	32	12	1	213	19.2
Alex Tanguay	82	27	50	77	37	35	7	1	135	20.0
Chris Drury	71	24	41	65	47	6	11	0	204	11.8
Ray Bourque	80	7	52	59	48	25	2	2	216	3.2
Shjon Podein	82	15	17	32	68	7	0	0	137	10.9
Adam Deadmarsh*	39	13	13	26	59	-2	7	0	86	15.1
Martin Skoula	82	8	17	25	38	8	3	0	108	7.4
Ville Nieminen	50	14	8	22	38	8	2	0	68	20.6
Greg De Vries	79	5	12	17	51	23	0	0	76	6.6
Dan Hinote	76	5	10	15	51	1	1	0	69	7.2
Jon Klemm	78	4	11	15	54	22	2	0	97	4.1
Adam Foote	35	3	12	15	42	6	1	1	59	5.1
Stephane Yelle	50	4	10	14	20	-3	0	1	54	7.4

	Games	G	A	Pts.	PIM	+/-	PPG	SHG	Shots	Shooting Pct.
Aaron Miller*	56	4	9	13	29	19	0	0	49	8.2
Eric Messier	64	5	7	12	26	-3	0	0	60	8.3
Rob Blake*	13	2	8	10	8	11	1	0	44	4.5
Dave Reid	73	1	9	10	21	1	0	0	66	1.5
Steven Reinprecht*	21	3	4	7	2	-1	0	0	28	10.7
Scott Parker	69	2	3	5	155	-2	0	0	35	5.7
Patrick Roy (goalie)	62	0	5	5	10	0	0	0	0	0.0
Rick Berry	19	0	4	4	38	5	0	0	10	0.0
Nolan Pratt	46	1	2	3	40	2	0	0	26	3.8
Chris Dingman	41	1	1	2	108	-3	0	0	33	3.0
Alexei Gusarov*	9	0	1	1	6	2	0	0	4	0.0
David Aebischer (goalie)	26	0	1	1	0	0	0	0	0	0.0
Rob Shearer	2	0	0	0	0	-2	0	0	0	0.0
Yuri Babenko	3	0	0	0	0	0	0	0	2	0.0
Joel Prpic	3	0	0	0	2	0	0	0	0	0.0
Bryan Muir*	8	0	0	0	4	0	0	0	3	0.0
Brad Larsen	9	0	0	0	0	1	0	0	3	0.0

GOALTENDING

	Games	Min.	Goals	SO	Avg.	W	L	T	ENG	Shots	Sv. Pct.
Patrick Roy	62	3585	132	4	2.21	40	13	7	5	1513	.913
David Aebischer	26	1393	52	3	2.24	12	7	3	3	538	.903

*Played with two or more NHL teams.

RESULTS

OCTOBER
4— At Dallas ....T....*2-2
7— At Edmonton ....T....*1-1
10— At Calgary ....W.....3-1
12— At Vancouver ....W.....5-2
14— Columbus ....W.....3-1
17— At Washington ....W....*4-3
18— At Columbus ....W.....5-1
20— Florida ....W.....5-1
25— Nashville..............................W...*2-1
26— At Chicago..........................W.....2-0
28— Edmonton..........................W.....4-2
30— Phoenix ....L.....0-4

NOVEMBER
1— At Vancouver ....L.....3-4
3— Carolina.................................W.....5-3
7— Minnesota ....W.....2-0
9— St. Louis ....T....*3-3
11— Anaheim ....W.....3-1
13— Pittsburgh ....W....*3-2
15— At Anaheim ....W.....3-0
16— At Phoenix...........................L.....3-6
18— At Los Angeles ....L.....4-6
22— Columbus.............................W.....5-2
25— Calgary..................................W....*3-2
29— Phoenix.................................W.....2-1

DECEMBER
1— Dallas.....................................W.....4-2
3— At N.Y. Rangers ....W.....6-3
5— At New Jersey ....L.....1-6

JANUARY
2— Los Angeles ....W.....6-2
4— San Jose..............................T....*2-2
6— At Carolina...........................T....*2-2
7— At Detroit ....L....*3-4
10— At Columbus ....W.....4-2
12— At Minnesota ....W.....5-0
14— At Chicago...........................T....*2-2
16— N.Y. Islanders ....W.....4-1
18— Vancouver ....W.....7-3
20— At San Jose ....W.....2-1
21— At Anaheim ....W.....4-2
26— Chicago ....W.....5-2
27— At Nashville ....W.....5-1
30— At San Jose ....W.....3-1

FEBRUARY
1— At Vancouver ....L.....3-5
7— Washington ....L.....1-3
9— Calgary ....L.....3-5
8— At Tampa Bay ....W.....2-0
9— At Florida ....W.....4-2
11— Tampa Bay ....T....*2-2
13— Philadelphia ....T....*3-3
15— Detroit ....L.....3-5
19— Calgary ....L.....0-3
21— Los Angeles ....W.....5-2
23— Vancouver ....W....*3-2
26— At Nashville ....L.....2-5
27— Edmonton............................W.....3-2
29— Nashville................................W.....3-1

10— St. Louis ....L....*3-4
13— At Montreal ....W....*3-2
15— At Ottawa ....L.....1-4
17— At Toronto ....T....*5-5
19— At Pittsburgh ....W.....5-1
21— Boston ....W.....8-2
23— Minnesota ....W.....4-1
25— Atlanta ....W.....5-2

MARCH
3— Buffalo.....................................L...*2-3
4— At Phoenix............................W.....5-0
6— At Atlanta ....W.....4-2
8— At St. Louis ....W.....5-2
10— At Dallas ....L...*2-3
11— Dallas ....W.....3-2
13— New Jersey ....L.....3-6
17— Detroit ....W.....5-3
18— Minnesota ....W.....4-3
20— San Jose...............................W.....4-1
22— At St. Louis ....W.....3-1
24— At Boston ....W.....4-2
28— At Edmonton ....L.....1-4
29— At Calgary ....W.....1-0
31— At Los Angeles ....L.....0-4

APRIL
2— Edmonton.............................W.....5-3
4— Anaheim ....T....*1-1
7— At Detroit ....L.....3-4
8— At Minnesota.......................W.....4-2
*Denotes overtime game.

COLUMBUS BLUE JACKETS
WESTERN CONFERENCE/CENTRAL DIVISION

Blue Jackets' Schedule
Home games shaded; D—Day game; *—All-Star Game at Los Angeles

October
SUN	MON	TUE	WED	THU	FRI	SAT
	1	2	3	4 STL	5	6 PHI
7	8 PHI	9	10	11	12 MON	13
14 CHI	15	16 DET	17	18	19 BUF	20 COL
21	22	23 LA	24	25 EDM	26	27 SJ
28	29	30 VAN	31			

November
SUN	MON	TUE	WED	THU	FRI	SAT
				1 CAL	2 EDM	3
4	5	6 VAN	7	8	9 EDM	10 BOS
11	12	13 STL	14	15	16 ANA	17 NAS
18	19 CAR	20	21 DET	22	23 CHI	24
25 CAL	D 26	27 PHO	28	29 STL	30	

December
SUN	MON	TUE	WED	THU	FRI	SAT
						1 STL
2	3	4	5 FLA	6 TB	7	8 COL
9	10 NJ	11	12 COL	13	14 ANA	15 LA
16	17 PHO	18	19	20	21	22 DAL
23	24	25	26	27 DET	28	29 BUF
30	31 ANA					

January
SUN	MON	TUE	WED	THU	FRI	SAT
		1	2	3 STL	4	5
6	D 7 NAS	8	9 WAS	10 CHI	11	12 CHI
13	14 NYR	15	16 NYR	17	18 MIN	19 NAS
20	21 DAL	22	23	24 SJ	25	26 PHO
27	28 DAL	29	30 ANA	31		

February
SUN	MON	TUE	WED	THU	FRI	SAT
					1	2 *
3	4 BOS	5	6 OTT	7	8 DET	9 NAS
10	11	12 MIN	13	14	15	16
17	18	19	20	21	22	23
24	25	26 LA	27	28 PIT		

March
SUN	MON	TUE	WED	THU	FRI	SAT
				1	2 LA	D
3 PHO	4	5	6 COL	7	8 NYI	9
10 MIN	11 PIT	12	13	14 VAN	15	16 CAL
17	18	19	20 MIN	21 DET	22	23 WAS
24	25 CAL	26 EDM	27	28 VAN	29	30 SJ
31						

April
SUN	MON	TUE	WED	THU	FRI	SAT
	1 DAL	2	3	4 NAS	5	6 MON
7	8 TOR	9	10 SJ	11	12 ATL	13
14 CHI	D 15	16	17	18	19	20

2001-02 SEASON
CLUB DIRECTORY

Owner/governor
John H. McConnell

Alternate governor
John P. McConnell

President/g.m./alternate governor
Doug MacLean

Exec. v.p./assistant general manager
Jim Clark

Head coach
Dave King

Associate coach
Newell Brown

Assistant coach
Gerard Gallant

Goaltending coach
Rick Wamsley

Director of amateur scouting
Don Boyd

Asst. director of amateur scouting
Paul Castron

Director of pro scouting
Bob Strumm

Hockey operations manager
Chris MacFarland

Strength and conditioning coach
Mark Casterline

Athletic trainer
Chris Mizer

Equipment manager
Tim LeRoy

Assistant equipment manager
Jamie Healy

Director of communications
Todd Sharrock

Assistant director of communications
Jason Rothwell

Manager, multimedia and publications
Steve Ostaszewicz

DRAFT CHOICES
Rd.— Player	Ht./Wt.	Overall	Pos.	Last team
1— Pascal LeClaire	6-1/185	8	G	Halifax (QMJHL)
2— Tim Jackman	6-2/190	38	RW	Mankato State (WCHA)
2— Kiel McLeod	6-5/211	53	C	Kelowna (WHL)
3— Aaron Johnson	6-0/186	85	D	Rimouski (QMJHL)
3— Per Mars		87		Brynas, Sweden
5— Cole Jarrett	5-10/200	141	D	Plymouth (OHL)
6— Justin Aikins	6-0/177	173	C	Langley (BCJHL)
6— Artem Vostrikov	6-1/172	187		Togliatti Jr., Russia
7— Raffaele Sannitz	5-11/183	204	F	Lugano, Switzerland
8— Ryan Bowness	6-2/198	236	RW	Brampton (OHL)
8— Andrew Murray	6-2/210	242	C	Selkirk (MJHL)

MISCELLANEOUS DATA

Home ice (capacity)
Nationwide Arena (18,136)

Office address
Nationwide Arena
200 W. Nationwide Blvd.
Columbus, OH 43215

Business phone
614-246-4625

Ticket information
1-800-645-2657

Website
www.bluejackets.com

Training site
Columbus

Club colors
Red, white, blue, silver and electric green

Radio affiliation
WBNS (1460 AM), WWCD (101.1 FM)

TV affiliation
Fox Sports Net Ohio

TRAINING CAMP ROSTER

No.	FORWARDS	Ht./Wt.	Place	Date	NHL exp.	2000-01 clubs
49	Serge Aubin (C)	6-0/190	Val d'Or, Que.	2-15-75	3	Columbus
	Blake Bellefeuille (C)	5-10/208	Framingham, Mass.	12-27-77	0	Syracuse (AHL)
	Jan Caloun (RW)	5-10/190	Usti-nad-Labem, Czech.	12-20-72	3	Columbus, HIFK Helsinki (Finland)
	Mathieu Darche (LW)	6-1/225	St. Laurent, Que.	11-26-76	1	Syracuse (AHL), Columbus
49	Matt Davidson (RW)	6-2/190	Flin Flon, Man.	8-9-77	1	Syracuse (AHL), Columbus
9	Kevin Dineen (RW)	5-11/189	Quebec City	10-28-63	17	Columbus
17	Ted Drury (C/LW)	6-0/204	Boston	9-13-71	8	Columbus, Chicago (IHL)
5	Bruce Gardiner (C)	6-1/193	North York, Ont.	2-11-72	5	Columbus
	Brett Harkins (LW)	6-1/185	North Ridgefield, Ohio	7-2-70	3	Houston (IHL)
	Tim Jackman (RW)	6-2/190	Minot, N.D.	11-14-81	0	Minnesota-Mankato (WCHA)
	Janne Jokila (LW)	5-9/174	Turkum, Finland	4-22-82	0	TPS Turku (Finland)
	Ben Knopp (RW)	6-0/185	Calgary	4-8-82	0	Moose Jaw (WHL)
	Espen Knutsen (C)	5-11/180	Oslo, Norway	1-12-72	2	Columbus
	Tyler Kolarik (C)	5-10/190	Philadelphia	1-26-81	0	Harvard University (ECAC)
18	Robert Kron (LW)	5-11/182	Brno, Czechoslovakia	2-27-67	11	Columbus
	Per Mars (C/RW)	6-3/215	Sweden	10-23-82	0	Brynas Gavle (Sweden)
	Kiel McLeod (C)	6-5/211	Fort Saskatchewan, Alta.	12-30-82	0	Kelowna (WHL)
	Brad Moran (C)	5-11/180	Abbotsford, B.C.	3-20-79	0	Syracuse (AHL)
	Andrej Nedorost (C)	6-1/198	Trencin, Czechoslovakia	4-30-80	0	HC Keramika Plzen (Czech Republic)
	Chris Nielsen (RW)	6-1/190	Moshi, Tanzania.	2-16-80	1	Syracuse (AHL), Columbus
	Martin Paroulek (LW)	5-11/187	Uherske Hradisti, Czech.	11-4-79	0	Vsetin (Czech Republic)
46	Sean Pronger (C)	6-3/210	Dryden, Ont.	11-30-72	5	Manitoba (IHL)
80	Geoff Sanderson (LW)	6-0/190	Hay River, Northwest Terr.	2-1-72	11	Columbus
	Sean Selmser (LW)	6-1/180	Calgary	11-10-74	1	Syracuse (AHL), Columbus
	Jody Shelley (LW)	6-3/230	Yarmouth, Nova Scotia	2-6-76	1	Syracuse (AHL), Columbus
16	Mike Sillinger (C)	5-11/191	Regina, Sask.	6-29-71	11	Florida, Ottawa
11	Blake Sloan (RW)	5-10/196	Park Ridge, Ill.	7-27-75	3	Dallas, Houston (IHL), Columbus
	Martin Spanhel (LW)	6-2/202	Gottwaldov, Czechoslovakia	7-1-77	1	Syracuse (AHL), Columbus
	David Vyborny (C)	5-10/183	Jihlava, Czechoslovakia	1-22-75	1	Columbus
14	Ray Whitney (LW)	5-10/175	Fort Saskatchewan, Alta.	5-8-72	10	Florida, Columbus
29	Tyler Wright (C)	5-11/187	Canora, Sask.	4-6-73	9	Columbus

DEFENSEMEN

No.	DEFENSEMEN	Ht./Wt.	Place	Date	NHL exp.	2000-01 clubs
	Jonas Andersson-Junkka	6-2/165	Kiruna, Sweden	5-4-75	0	
32	Radim Bicanek	6-1/195	Uherske Hradiste, Czech.	1-18-75	6	Syracuse (AHL), Columbus
34	Jean-Luc Grand-Pierre	6-3/207	Montreal	2-2-77	3	Columbus
6	Jamie Heward	6-2/207	Regina, Sask.	3-30-71	5	Columbus
	Cole Jarrett	5-10/200	Sault Ste. Marie, Ont.	1-4-83	0	Plymouth (OHL)
	Aaron Johnson	6-0/186	Point Hawksbury, Nova Scotia	4-30-83	0	Rimouski (QMJHL)
	Rostislav Klesla	6-2/198	Novy Jicin, Czechoslovakia	3-21-82	1	Columbus, Brampton (OHL)
	Petteri Nummelin	5-10/183	Turku, Finland	11-25-72	1	Columbus
4	Lyle Odelein	6-0/210	Quill Lake, Sask.	7-21-68	12	Columbus
4	Jamie Pushor	6-3/220	Lethbridge, Alta.	2-11-73	6	Columbus
5	Deron Quint	6-2/209	Durham, N.H.	3-12-76	6	Syracuse (AHL), Columbus
37	Mattias Timander	6-3/215	Solleftea, Sweden	4-16-74	5	Columbus

GOALTENDERS

No.	GOALTENDERS	Ht./Wt.	Place	Date	NHL exp.	2000-01 clubs
30	Marc Denis	6-0/190	Montreal	8-1-77	4	Columbus
	Jean-Francois Labbe	5-10/172	Sherbrooke, Que.	6-15-72	1	Hartford (AHL), Syracuse (AHL)
	Pascal Leclaire	6-1/185	Repentigny, Que.	11-7-82	0	Halifax (QMJHL)
31	Ron Tugnutt	5-11/160	Scarborough, Ont.	10-22-67	13	Columbus

2000-01 REVIEW
INDIVIDUAL STATISTICS

SCORING

	Games	G	A	Pts.	PIM	+/-	PPG	SHG	Shots	Shooting Pct.
Geoff Sanderson	68	30	26	56	46	4	9	0	199	15.1
Espen Knutsen	66	11	42	53	30	-3	2	0	62	17.7
Steve Heinze*	65	22	20	42	38	-19	14	0	125	17.6
Tyler Wright	76	16	16	32	140	-9	4	1	141	11.3
David Vyborny	79	13	19	32	22	-9	5	0	125	10.4
Serge Aubin	81	13	17	30	107	-20	0	0	110	11.8
Jamie Heward	69	11	16	27	33	3	9	0	108	10.2
Deron Quint	57	7	16	23	16	-19	3	0	148	4.7
Bruce Gardiner	73	7	15	22	78	-1	0	0	60	11.7
Kevyn Adams*	66	8	12	20	52	-4	0	0	84	9.5
Alex Selivanov	59	8	11	19	38	-11	5	0	104	7.7
Robert Kron	59	8	11	19	10	4	0	1	134	6.0
Lyle Odelein	81	3	14	17	118	-16	1	0	104	2.9

	Games	G	A	Pts.	PIM	+/-	PPG	SHG	Shots	Shooting Pct.
Petteri Nummelin	61	4	12	16	10	-11	2	0	99	4.0
Kevin Dineen	66	8	7	15	126	2	0	0	74	10.8
Jamie Pushor	75	3	10	13	94	7	0	1	64	4.7
Mattias Timander	76	2	9	11	24	-8	0	0	68	2.9
Chris Nielsen	29	4	5	9	4	4	0	0	36	11.1
Frantisek Kucera*	48	2	5	7	12	-5	0	0	51	3.9
Mike Maneluk*	39	5	1	6	33	-11	2	0	31	16.1
Jean-Luc Grand-Pierre	64	1	4	5	73	-6	0	0	33	3.0
Ray Whitney*	3	0	3	3	2	-1	0	0	3	0.0
Jan Caloun	11	0	3	3	2	-8	0	0	14	0.0
Steve Maltais	26	0	3	3	12	-9	0	0	30	0.0
Rostislav Klesla	8	2	0	2	6	-1	0	0	10	20.0
Bill Bowler	9	0	2	2	8	-3	0	0	3	0.0
Radim Bicanek	9	0	2	2	6	1	0	0	11	0.0
Krzysztof Oliwa*	10	0	2	2	34	1	0	0	5	0.0
Martin Spanhel	6	1	0	1	2	-1	0	0	8	12.5
Blake Sloan*	14	1	0	1	13	-2	0	0	16	6.3
Ron Tugnutt (goalie)	53	0	1	1	2	0	0	0	0	0.0
Jody Shelley	1	0	0	0	10	0	0	0	0	0.0
Sean Selmser	1	0	0	0	5	0	0	0	2	0.0
Ted Drury	1	0	0	0	0	-3	0	0	3	0.0
Michael Gaul	2	0	0	0	4	0	0	0	3	0.0
Kevin Dahl	4	0	0	0	2	1	0	0	3	0.0
Matt Davidson	5	0	0	0	0	2	0	0	2	0.0
Mathieu Darche	9	0	0	0	0	-4	0	0	9	0.0
Marc Denis (goalie)	32	0	0	0	2	0	0	0	0	0.0

GOALTENDING

	Games	Min.	Goals	SO	Avg.	W	L	T	ENG	Shots	Sv. Pct.
Ron Tugnutt	53	3129	127	4	2.44	22	25	5	5	1528	.917
Marc Denis	32	1830	99	0	3.25	6	20	4	2	940	.895

*Played with two or more NHL teams.

RESULTS

OCTOBER
7— Chicago .... L 3-5
9— Los Angeles .... L 1-7
12— At Calgary .... W 3-2
14— At Colorado .... L 1-3
15— At Chicago .... L 1-2
18— Colorado .... L 1-5
21— At Pittsburgh .... L 2-5
22— Detroit .... L ...*1-2
25— San Jose .... L 1-3
27— Washington .... W 3-1
28— At Detroit .... L 1-4
31— Los Angeles .... W 4-1

NOVEMBER
1— At Dallas .... L 0-4
4— At Ottawa .... T ...*2-2
5— Edmonton .... L 2-4
9— San Jose .... W 5-2
11— Phoenix .... W 2-1
14— Dallas .... W 3-2
16— At Nashville .... W 5-1
17— Florida .... L 0-3
19— Vancouver .... L 1-6
22— At Colorado .... L 2-5
24— At Dallas .... L 0-3
25— Dallas .... L 2-4
29— Philadelphia .... L 3-4

DECEMBER
2— Atlanta .... L 1-2
3— At Chicago .... L 0-5

6— Anaheim .... W 5-2
8— Boston .... W ...*3-2
10— At Phoenix .... T ...*1-1
13— At Anaheim .... L ...*4-5
14— At San Jose .... L 1-2
16— At Vancouver .... L 3-4
18— At Montreal .... W 2-0
21— Ottawa .... T ...*3-3
23— At N.Y. Islanders ...... W 7-5
26— At St. Louis .... L 0-5
27— At New Jersey .... T ...*2-2
29— Carolina .... W 3-1
31— New Jersey .... L 3-6

JANUARY
3— Edmonton .... W 5-2
6— At Vancouver .... L 3-4
7— At Edmonton .... L 2-4
10— Colorado .... L 2-4
12— Chicago .... L 1-3
15— Minnesota .... W 3-0
17— At Minnesota .... L ...*2-3
21— Tampa Bay .... W 3-1
23— At Buffalo .... W 2-1
27— Anaheim .... W 2-1
31— Detroit .... L ...*2-3

FEBRUARY
1— At St. Louis .... T ...*2-2
6— St. Louis .... T ...*2-2
8— At Nashville .... L 1-3
10— Nashville .... W 3-2

12— N.Y. Rangers .... L 3-4
14— At Toronto .... T ...*2-2
16— At Detroit .... L 2-4
17— Pittsburgh .... L ...*2-3
20— At San Jose .... L ...*2-3
21— At Phoenix .... L 2-3
24— At Los Angeles .... L 1-3
25— At Anaheim .... W 5-2
28— Phoenix .... W 5-2

MARCH
1— At Nashville .... W 5-2
7— At Carolina .... L 1-2
9— At Florida .... W ...*7-6
10— At Tampa Bay .... L 1-4
14— Calgary .... W 3-0
16— At Atlanta .... W 3-0
17— N.Y. Islanders .... T ...*3-3
19— Nashville .... L 1-2
21— Vancouver .... T ...*1-1
24— Calgary .... W 6-4
26— At Edmonton .... L 2-4
27— At Calgary .... L 0-3
29— At Los Angeles .... L 0-3

APRIL
1— St. Louis .... W 2-1
3— Detroit .... W 2-1
5— At St. Louis .... L 1-4
6— At Minnesota .... L 2-3
8— Chicago .... W ...*4-3

*Denotes overtime game.

COLUMBUS BLUE JACKETS

DALLAS STARS
WESTERN CONFERENCE/PACIFIC DIVISION

DALLAS STARS

Stars' Schedule
Home games shaded; D—Day game; *—All-Star Game at Los Angeles

October

SUN	MON	TUE	WED	THU	FRI	SAT
	1	2	3	4	5 NAS	6
7 D CAR	8	9 LA	10	11 VAN	12	13 CAL
14	15	16	17 STL	18 PHO	19	20 CHI
21	22	23	24 PIT	25	26 DET	27
28 D NYI	29 NYR	30	31 DET			

November

SUN	MON	TUE	WED	THU	FRI	SAT
				1	2 NAS	3 NAS
4	5	6	7 SJ	8	9 PHO	10
11 ANA	12	13	14	15 LA	16	17 SJ
18	19 NYI	20	21 CAR	22	23 PHI	24
25 D MIN	26	27	28	29 CAL	30	

December

SUN	MON	TUE	WED	THU	FRI	SAT
						1 EDM
2 VAN	3	4	5 OTT	6	7 EDM	8
9	10	11	12 BUF	13	14 CAL	15 PHO
16	17 SJ	18	19	20 PHI	21	22 CBJ
23 ATL	24	25	26 COL	27	28 WAS	29
30	31 BOS					

January

SUN	MON	TUE	WED	THU	FRI	SAT
		1	2 ATL	3	4	5 D STL
6	7	8 TB	9 FLA	10	11	12 D DET
13 MIN	14	15	16 DET	17	18 FLA	19
20 CHI	21 CBJ	22	23 VAN	24	25 ANA	26
27	28 CBJ	29	30	31		

February

SUN	MON	TUE	WED	THU	FRI	SAT
					1	2 *
3	4	5	6 NAS	7	8 EDM	9
10 ANA	11 LA	12	13 NYR	14	15	16
17	18	19	20	21	22	23
24	25	26 PHO	27	28 VAN		

March

SUN	MON	TUE	WED	THU	FRI	SAT
					1	2 D COL
3 D SJ	4	5	6 LA	7	8 MIN	9
10 NJ	11	12 WAS	13	14 MON	15	16 TOR
17	18 CHI	19	20 STL	21	22 PHO	23
24 D ANA	25	26 SJ	27	28 CAL	29	30 EDM
31						

April

SUN	MON	TUE	WED	THU	FRI	SAT
	1 CBJ	2	3 STL	4	5 COL	6
7 ANA	8 LA	9	10 MIN	11	12 CHI	13
14 D COL	15	16	17	18	19	20

2001-02 SEASON
CLUB DIRECTORY

Chairman of the board and owner
Thomas O. Hicks
President and alternate governor
James R. Lites
V.p. hockey operations & g.m.
Bob Gainey
Assistant general manager
Doug Armstrong
Director, hockey operations
Les Jackson
Head coach
Ken Hitchcock
Assistant coaches
Doug Jarvis
Craig Ludwig
Rick Wilson

Director, media relations
Larry Kelly
Manager, media relations
Mark Janko
Head athletic trainer
Dave Surprenant
Head equipment manager
Dave Smith
Assistant equipment manager
Steve Sumner
Strength and conditioning coach
J.J. McQueen
Coaching assistant/video coordinator
Leon Friedrich
Equipment assistant
Mike Wroblewski

DRAFT CHOICES

Rd.— Player	Ht./Wt.	Overall	Pos.	Last team
1— Jason Bacashihua	5-11/167	26	G	Chicago (NAHL)
3— Yared Hagos	6-1/202	70	C	AIK, Sweden
3— Anthony Aquino	5-10/180	92	RW	Merrimack (H. East)
4— Daniel Volrab	6-0/180	126	C	Sparta, Czech.
5— Mike Smith	6-3/189	161	G	Sudbury (OHL)
6— Michal Blazek	6-2/187	167	D	Vsetin Jr., Czech.
6— Jussi Jokinen	5-11/183	192	F	Karpat, Finland
8— Marco Rosa	6-0/170	255	C	Merrimack (H. East)
9— Dale Sullivan	5-11/170	265	RW	Hull (QMJHL)
9— Marek Tomica	6-0/172	285	W	Slavia, Czech.

MISCELLANEOUS DATA

Home ice (capacity)
American Airlines Center (18,500)
Address
211 Cowboys Parkway
Irving, TX 75063
Business phone
972-831-2401
Ticket information
214-467-8277
Website
www.dallasstars.com

Training site
Dallas and Irving, TX
Club colors
Green, black, gold and white
Radio affiliation
WBAP (820 AM)
TV affiliation
FOX Sports Southwest (Cable), KDFI
(Channel 27)

TRAINING CAMP ROSTER

No.	FORWARDS	Ht./Wt.	Place	Date	NHL exp.	2000-01 clubs
	Anthony Aquino (RW)	5-10/180	Toronto	8-1-82	0	Merrimack College (Hockey East)
28	Donald Audette (RW)	5-8/184	Laval, Que.	9-23-69	12	Atlanta, Buffalo
	Jeff Bateman (C)	5-11/165	Belleville, Ont.	8-29-81	0	Brampton (OHL)
	Gregor Baumgartner (C)	6-2/185	Leoben, Austria.	7-13-79	0	Utah (IHL)
	Justin Cox (RW)	6-0/160	Merritt, B.C.	3-13-81	0	Prince George (WHL)
19	Rob DiMaio (RW)	5-10/190	Calgary	2-19-68	13	Carolina
	Brett Draney (LW)	6-1/179	Merritt, B.C.	3-12-81	0	Medicine Hat (WHL)
	Teemu Elomo (LW)	5-11/176	Turku, Finland	1-13-79	0	TPS Turku (Finland)
	Steve Gainey (LW)	6-0/180	Montreal	1-26-79	1	Utah (IHL), Dallas
	Yared Hagos (C)	6-1/202	Stockholm, Sweden	3-27-83	0	AIK Solna (Sweden Jr.), AIK Solna (Sweden)
12	Benoit Hogue (C)	5-10/194	Repentigny, Que.	10-28-66	14	Dallas
13	Valeri Kamensky (LW)	6-2/202	Voskresensk, U.S.S.R.	4-18-66	10	New York Rangers
	Niko Kapanen (C)	5-9/180	Hameenlinna, Finland	4-29-78	0	TPS Turku (Finland)
15	Jamie Langenbrunner	6-1/200	Duluth, Minn.	7-24-75	7	Dallas
26	Jere Lehtinen (LW)	6-0/192	Espoo, Finland	6-24-73	6	Dallas
36	Roman Lyashenko (C)	6-0/188	Murmansk, U.S.S.R.	5-2-79	2	Dallas, Utah (IHL)
10	Cameron Mann (RW)	6-0/194	Thompson, Man.	4-20-77	4	Boston, Providence (AHL)
29	Grant Marshall (RW)	6-1/193	Mississauga, Ont.	6-9-73	7	Dallas
	Antti Miettinen (RW)	5-11/176	Hameenlinna, Finland	7-3-80	0	Hameenlinna (Finland)
9	Mike Modano (C)	6-3/205	Livonia, Mich.	6-7-70	13	Dallas
	Jim Montgomery (C)	5-9/180	Montreal	6-30-69	4	Kentucky (AHL), San Jose
45	Brenden Morrow (LW)	5-11/200	Carlisle, Sask.	1-16-79	2	Dallas
22	Kirk Muller (C)	6-0/205	Kingston, Ont.	2-8-66	17	Dallas
25	Joe Nieuwendyk (C)	6-1/205	Oshawa, Ont.	9-10-66	15	Dallas
	Steve Ott (C/LW)	5-11/160	Stoney Point, Ont.	8-19-82	0	Windsor (OHL)
	Mike Ryan (C)	6-1/170	Milton, Mass.	5-16-80	0	Northeastern Univ. (Hockey East)
49	Jon Sim (LW)	5-10/184	New Glasgow, Nova Scotia	9-29-77	3	Dallas, Utah (IHL)
	Mathias Tjarnqvist (C)	6-1/183	Umea, Sweden	4-15-79	0	Djurgarden Stockholm (Sweden)
	Marco Tuokko (LW)	5-11/172	Turku, Finland	3-27-79	0	TPS Turku (Finland)
77	Pierre Turgeon (C)	6-1/199	Rouyn, Que.	8-28-69	14	St. Louis
22	Shaun Van Allen (C)	6-1/204	Calgary	8-29-67	10	Dallas
	Ladislav Vlcek (LW/RW)	5-11/172	Czechoslovakia	9-26-81	0	Kladno (Czechoslovakia Jrs.)
	Daniel Volrab (C)	6-0/180	Decin, Czechoslovakia	3-11-83	0	Sparta Praha (Czech Republic)

DEFENSEMEN

No.	DEFENSEMEN	Ht./Wt.	Place	Date	NHL exp.	2000-01 clubs
4	Gerald Diduck	6-2/220	Edmonton	4-6-65	17	Dallas
	John Erskine	6-4/197	Kingston, Ont.	6-26-80	0	Utah (IHL)
2	Derian Hatcher	6-5/230	Sterling Heights, Mich.	6-4-72	10	Dallas
4	Greg Hawgood	5-10/190	St. Albert, Alta.	8-10-68	11	Vancouver, Kansas City (IHL)
44	Sami Helenius	6-5/225	Helsinki, Finland	1-22-74	4	Dallas
	Dan Jancevski	6-3/208	Windsor, Ont.	6-15-81	0	London (OHL), Sudbury (OHL)
37	Brad Lukowich	6-1/200	Cranbrook, B.C.	8-12-76	4	Dallas
21	Jyrki Lumme	6-1/209	Tampere, Finland	7-16-66	13	Phoenix
	Jeff MacMillan	6-3/202	Durham, Ontario	3-30-79	0	Utah (IHL)
24	Richard Matvichuk	6-2/215	Edmonton	2-5-73	9	Dallas
5	Darryl Sydor	6-1/205	Edmonton	5-13-72	10	Dallas
4	Mark Wotton	6-1/195	Foxwarren, Man.	11-16-73	4	Utah (IHL), Dallas
56	Sergei Zubov	6-1/200	Moscow, U.S.S.R.	7-22-70	9	Dallas

GOALTENDERS

No.	GOALTENDERS	Ht./Wt.	Place	Date	NHL exp.	2000-01 clubs
	Chad Alban	5-9/165	Kalamazoo, Mich.	4-27-76	0	Grand Rapids (IHL), Utah (IHL)
	Jason Bacashihua	5-11/167	Garden City, Mich.	9-20-82	0	Chicago (NAHL)
20	Ed Belfour	5-11/192	Carman, Man.	4-21-65	13	Dallas
	Dan Ellis	6-0/180	Saskatoon, Sask.	6-19-80	0	University of Nebraska-Omaha (NCAA)
	Mike Smith	6-3/189	Kingston, Ont.	3-22-82	0	Sudbury (OHL)
	Marty Turco	5-11/183	Sault Ste. Marie, Ont.	8-13-75	1	Dallas

2000-01 REVIEW
INDIVIDUAL STATISTICS

SCORING

	Games	G	A	Pts.	PIM	+/-	PPG	SHG	Shots	Shooting Pct.
Mike Modano	81	33	51	84	52	26	8	3	208	15.9
Brett Hull	79	39	40	79	18	10	11	0	219	17.8
Joe Nieuwendyk	69	29	23	52	30	5	12	0	166	17.5
Sergei Zubov	79	10	41	51	24	22	6	0	173	5.8
Darryl Sydor	81	10	37	47	34	5	8	0	140	7.1
Jere Lehtinen	74	20	25	45	24	14	7	0	148	13.5
Brenden Morrow	82	20	24	44	128	18	7	0	121	16.5
Grant Marshall	75	13	24	37	64	1	4	0	93	14.0

	Games	G	A	Pts.	PIM	+/-	PPG	SHG	Shots	Shooting Pct.
Jamie Langenbrunner	53	12	18	30	57	4	3	2	104	11.5
Ted Donato	65	8	17	25	26	6	1	0	71	11.3
Mike Keane	67	10	14	24	35	4	1	0	64	15.6
Shaun Van Allen	59	7	16	23	16	5	0	2	51	13.7
Derian Hatcher	80	2	21	23	77	5	1	0	97	2.1
Richard Matvichuk	78	4	16	20	62	5	2	0	85	4.7
Brad Lukowich	80	4	10	14	76	28	0	0	43	9.3
Benoit Hogue	34	3	7	10	26	-1	0	0	35	8.6
Kirk Muller	55	1	9	10	26	-4	0	0	54	1.9
Roman Lyashenko	60	6	3	9	45	-1	0	0	48	12.5
Tyler Bouck	48	2	5	7	29	-3	0	0	41	4.9
John MacLean*	28	4	2	6	17	0	1	0	41	9.8
Blake Sloan*	33	2	2	4	4	-2	0	0	29	6.9
Sami Helenius	57	1	2	3	99	1	0	0	18	5.6
Jonathan Sim	15	0	3	3	6	-2	0	0	18	0.0
Jamie Wright	2	1	0	1	0	-3	0	0	4	25.0
Grant Ledyard*	8	0	1	1	4	3	0	0	7	0.0
Ed Belfour (goalie)	63	0	1	1	4	0	0	0	0	0.0
Mark Wotton	1	0	0	0	0	0	0	0	0	0.0
Steve Gainey	1	0	0	0	0	0	0	0	0	0.0
Greg Leeb	2	0	0	0	0	-1	0	0	4	0.0
Gerald Diduck	14	0	0	0	18	4	0	0	8	0.0
Richard Jackman	16	0	0	0	18	-6	0	0	10	0.0
Marty Turco (goalie)	26	0	0	0	12	0	0	0	0	0.0

GOALTENDING

	Games	Min.	Goals	SO	Avg.	W	L	T	ENG	Shots	Sv. Pct.
Marty Turco	26	1266	40	3	1.90	13	6	1	1	532	.925
Ed Belfour	63	3687	144	8	2.34	35	20	7	2	1508	.905

*Played with two or more NHL teams.

RESULTS

OCTOBER
4— Colorado ....T...*2-2
7— At Ottawa ....L....1-3
9— At Toronto ....W....3-1
10— At Carolina ....L....2-5
12— Philadelphia ....W....4-1
14— Washington ....W....3-0
18— San Jose ....W....2-1
20— At Chicago ....W....5-1
21— Los Angeles ....W....4-3
25— Vancouver ....L....2-6
27— Phoenix ....L....2-4
28— At St. Louis ....L....*3-4

NOVEMBER
1— Columbus ....W....4-0
3— At Phoenix ....T...*2-2
11— Montreal ....W....2-0
14— At Columbus ....L....2-3
15— At Buffalo ....T...*2-2
17— At Detroit ....W....1-0
20— Tampa Bay ....W....6-2
22— At Nashville ....W....1-0
24— Columbus ....W....3-0
25— At Columbus ....W....4-2
29— Calgary ....L....3-4

DECEMBER
1— At Colorado ....L....2-4
2— At Phoenix ....W....5-2
6— At San Jose ....T...*2-2
7— At Los Angeles ....L....2-5

10— At Anaheim ....W....1-0
13— Edmonton ....W....5-2
15— Chicago ....W....4-1
17— At Minnesota ....L....0-6
20— At New Jersey ....L....1-4
21— At N.Y. Islanders ....W....3-1
23— At Pittsburgh ....W....8-2
27— Anaheim ....W....3-1
29— Los Angeles ....L....1-4
31— N.Y. Rangers ....W....6-1

JANUARY
4— At Detroit ....L....2-4
6— At Boston ....W....4-0
8— At N.Y. Rangers ....W....2-1
10— At Atlanta ....W....3-2
12— Detroit ....L....2-3
14— At Tampa Bay ....W....3-2
15— At Florida ....L....0-2
17— Nashville ....W...*4-3
19— Pittsburgh ....W...*6-5
21— At Phoenix ....L....2-5
22— Vancouver ....W....2-1
24— New Jersey ....L....1-4
26— San Jose ....L....1-2
30— At Los Angeles ....L....0-8

FEBRUARY
1— At San Jose ....W....4-2
7— Edmonton ....W....3-2
9— Minnesota ....L....1-2
11— St. Louis ....T...*3-3

13— At Nashville ....W....2-1
14— Los Angeles ....W....4-2
16— Anaheim ....W...*3-2
18— Detroit ....L....1-2
21— Minnesota ....W....6-2
23— Boston ....W...*5-4
25— At Edmonton ....L....*2-3
26— At Calgary ....L....2-3
28— At Vancouver ....L....4-5

MARCH
2— At Anaheim ....W....5-2
4— Buffalo ....W....4-1
7— Chicago ....L....1-4
10— Colorado ....W...*3-2
11— At Colorado ....L....2-3
13— At Chicago ....W....3-0
16— Phoenix ....T...*1-1
18— Ottawa ....W....5-1
19— At Minnesota ....W....4-1
21— Anaheim ....W....8-0
23— N.Y. Islanders ....W....2-1
25— St. Louis ....T...*1-1
28— At Vancouver ....W....3-1
30— At Edmonton ....W....5-4
31— At Calgary ....W....2-0

APRIL
2— Calgary ....T...*4-4
4— Nashville ....W....5-1
7— At San Jose ....W...*5-4
*Denotes overtime game.

DETROIT RED WINGS
WESTERN CONFERENCE/CENTRAL DIVISION

Red Wings' Schedule
Home games shaded; D—Day game; *—All-Star Game at Los Angeles

October

SUN	MON	TUE	WED	THU	FRI	SAT
	1	2	3	4 SJ	5	6 VAN
7	8	9	10 CAL	11	12 BUF	13 NYI
14	15	16 CBJ	17	18 PHI	19	20 LA
21	22	23	24 EDM	25	26 DAL	27 NAS
28	29	30 CAR	31 DAL			

November

SUN	MON	TUE	WED	THU	FRI	SAT
				1	2 NYI	3
4 CHI	5	6	7 PHO	8	9 ANA	10 LA
11	12	13 CAR	14	15	16 MIN	17 LA
18	19	20 NAS	21 CBJ	22	23 STL	24
25 CHI	26	27 CAL	28	29	30 NJ	

December

SUN	MON	TUE	WED	THU	FRI	SAT
						1 NJ
2	3	4	5 COL	6	7 PHO	8
9	10 CAL	11	12	13 EDM	14	15 VAN
16	17 CHI	18	19 VAN	20	21 SJ	22
23 CHI	24	25	26 MIN	27 CBJ	28	29 NAS
30	31 MIN					

January

SUN	MON	TUE	WED	THU	FRI	SAT
		1	2 ANA	3	4	5 D COL
6	7	8	9 VAN	10	11	12 D DAL
13	14	15 PHO	16 DAL	17	18 WAS	19
20 OTT	21	22	23 SJ	24	25 PHO	26 STL
27	28 EDM	29	30 CAL	31		

February

SUN	MON	TUE	WED	THU	FRI	SAT
					1	2 *
3	4 COL	5	6 NYR	7	8 CBJ	9 OTT
10	11 MON	12	13 MIN	14	15	16
17	18	19	20	21	22	23
24	25	26 TB	27 FLA	28		

March

SUN	MON	TUE	WED	THU	FRI	SAT
				1	2 D PIT	
3	4	5	6 TOR	7	8	9 D STL
10 D BUF	11	12	13 EDM	14	15	16 D BOS
17 D NYR	18	19 ANA	20	21 CBJ	22	23 D COL
24	25 NAS	26	27	28 NAS	29	30 ATL
31						

April

SUN	MON	TUE	WED	THU	FRI	SAT
	1 TOR	2	3 ANA	4 LA	5	6 SJ
7	8	9	10 CHI	11	12	13 D STL
14 D STL	15	16	17	18	19	20

2001-02 SEASON
CLUB DIRECTORY

Owner/governor
Mike Ilitch

Owner/secretary-treasurer
Marian Ilitch

Vice president/alternate governor
Christopher Ilitch

Sr. vice president/alternate governor
Jim Devellano

General manager
Ken Holland

Assistant general manager
Jim Nill

Head coach
Scotty Bowman

Associate coaches
Dave Lewis
Barry Smith

Goaltending consultant
Jim Bedard

NHL scout
Dan Belisle

Pro scouts
Mark Howe
Glenn Merkosky

Scouts
Hakan Andersson, Bruce Haralson,
Vladimir Havluj, Mark Leach, Joe
McDonnell, Bruce Southern, Marty
Stein

Athletic trainer
John Wharton

Equipment manager
Paul Boyer

Assistant equipment manager
Tim Abbott

Assistant athletic trainer
Piet Van Zant

Masseurs
Daryl Pittman
Sergei Tchekmarev

Team physicians
Dr. John Finley
Dr. David Collon

Team dentist
C.J. Regula

DRAFT CHOICES

Rd.— Player	Ht./Wt.	Overall	Pos.	Last team
2— Igor Grigorenko	5-11/183	62	RW	Togliatti Jr., Russia
4— Drew MacIntyre	6-0/173	121	G	Sherbrooke (QMJHL)
4— Miroslav Blatak	5-11/172	129	D	Zlin, Czechoslovakia
5— Andreas Jamtin	5-11/185	157	RW	Farjestad, Sweden
6— Nick Pannoni	5-11/155	195	G	Seattle (WHL)
8— Dmitri Bykov	5-10/169	258	D	Kazan, Russia
9— Francois Senez	6-3/215	288	D	Rensselaer (ECAC)

MISCELLANEOUS DATA

Home ice (capacity)
Joe Louis Arena (19,983)

Address
600 Civic Center Drive
Detroit, MI 48226

Business phone
313-396-7544

Ticket information
248-645-6666

Website
www.detroitredwings.com

Training site
Traverse City, Mich.

Club colors
Red and white

Radio affiliation
WXYT (1270 AM)

TV affiliation
WKBD (Channel 50), FOX Sports
Detroit (Cable)

TRAINING CAMP ROSTER

DETROIT RED WINGS

No.	FORWARDS	Ht./Wt.	Place	Born Date	NHL exp.	2000-01 clubs
	Sean Avery (C/LW)	5-10/188		4-10-80	0	Cincinnati (AHL)
	Per Backer (RW/LW)		Sweden	1-4-82	0	Grums (Sweden)
	Ryan Barnes (LW)	6-1/201	Dunnville, Ont.	1-30-80	0	Cincinnati (AHL), Toledo (ECHL)
	Steve Brule (RW)	6-0/200	Montreal	1-15-75	1	Manitoba (IHL)
	Yuri Butsayev (C)	6-1/183	Togliatti, U.S.S.R.	10-11-78	2	Detroit, Cincinnati (AHL)
11	Mathieu Dandenault	6-1/196	Magog, Que.	2-3-76	6	Detroit
	Pavel Datsyuk (C)	5-11/180	Sverdlovsk, U.S.S.R.	7-20-78	0	Ak Bars Kazan (Russian)
	Adam DeLeeuw (LW)	6-0/206	Brampton, Ont.	2-29-80	0	Toronto (OHL)
19	Boyd Devereaux (C)	6-2/195	Seaforth, Ont.	4-16-78	4	Detroit
33	Kris Draper (C)	5-10/190	Toronto	5-24-71	11	Detroit
91	Sergei Fedorov (C)	6-2/200	Pskov, U.S.S.R.	12-13-69	11	Detroit
41	Brent Gilchrist (LW)	5-11/180	Moose Jaw, Sask.	4-3-67	13	Detroit
	Igor Grigorenko (RW)	5-11/183	Samara, U.S.S.R.	4-9-83	0	Lada Togliatti (Russian)
96	Tomas Holmstrom (LW)	6-0/198	Pieta, Sweden	1-23-73	5	Detroit
	Andreas Jamtin (RW)	5-11/185	Stockholm, Sweden	5-4-83	0	Farjestad Karlstad (Sweden)
	Tomas Kopecky (C/LW)	6-3/187	Ilava, Czechoslovakia	2-2-82	0	Lethbridge (WHL), Cincinnati (AHL)
8	Igor Larionov (C)	5-10/170	Voskresensk, U.S.S.R.	12-3-60	11	Florida, Detroit
18	Kirk Maltby (RW)	6-0/190	Guelph, Ont.	12-22-72	8	Detroit
25	Darren McCarty (RW)	6-1/215	Burnaby, B.C.	4-1-72	8	Detroit
20	Luc Robitaille (LW)	6-1/205	Montreal	2-17-66	15	Los Angeles
37	Marc Rodgers (RW)	5-9/185	Shawville, Que.	3-16-72	1	Cincinnati (AHL)
14	Brendan Shanahan (LW)	6-3/215	Mimico, Ont.	1-23-69	14	Detroit
	Tomek Valtonen (LW)	6-1/198	Piotrkow Trybunalski, Poland	1-8-80	0	Jokerit (Finland)
	Jason Williams (C)	5-11/185	London, Ont.	8-11-80	1	Cincinnati (AHL), Detroit
19	Steve Yzerman (C)	5-10/185	Cranbrook, B.C.	5-9-65	18	Detroit
	Henrik Zetterberg (C)	5-11/180	Njurunda, Sweden	10-9-80	0	Timra (Sweden)
	DEFENSEMEN					
	Miroslav Blatak	5-11/172	Zlin, Czechoslovakia	5-25-82	0	HC Continental Zlin (Czech Republic)
24	Chris Chelios	6-1/190	Chicago	1-25-62	18	Detroit
28	Steve Duchesne	5-11/195	Sept-Iles, Que.	6-30-65	15	Detroit
2	Jiri Fischer	6-5/210	Horovice, Czechoslovakia	7-31-80	2	Detroit, Cincinnati (AHL)
	Niklas Kronvall	5-11/165	Stockholm, Sweden	1-12-81	0	
4	Uwe Krupp	6-6/233	Cologne, West Germany	6-24-65	13	
32	Maxim Kuznetsov	6-5/198	Pavlodar, U.S.S.R.	3-24-77	1	Detroit
5	Nicklas Lidstrom	6-2/190	Vasteras, Sweden	4-28-70	10	Detroit
2	Fredrik Olausson	6-0/199	Dadesjo, Sweden	10-5-66	14	Bern (Switzerland)
3	Jesse Wallin	6-2/190	Saskatoon, Sask.	3-10-78	2	Cincinnati (AHL), Detroit
	GOALTENDERS					
39	Dominik Hasek	5-11/168	Pardubice, Czechoslovakia	1-29-65	11	Buffalo
34	Manny Legace	5-9/165	Toronto	2-4-73	3	Detroit
	Stefan Liv	6-0/172	Sweden	12-21-80	0	HV 71 Jonkoping (Sweden)
	Drew MacIntyre	6-0/173	Charlottetown, P.E.I.	6-24-83	0	Sherbrooke (QMJHL)
30	Chris Osgood	5-10/181	Peace River, Alta.	11-26-72	8	Detroit

2000-01 REVIEW
INDIVIDUAL STATISTICS

SCORING

	Games	G	A	Pts.	PIM	+/-	PPG	SHG	Shots	Shooting Pct.
Brendan Shanahan	81	31	45	76	81	9	15	1	278	11.2
Nicklas Lidstrom	82	15	56	71	18	9	8	0	272	5.5
Sergei Fedorov	75	32	37	69	40	12	14	2	268	11.9
Martin Lapointe	82	27	30	57	127	3	13	0	181	14.9
Steve Yzerman	54	18	34	52	18	4	5	0	155	11.6
Tomas Holmstrom	73	16	24	40	40	-12	9	0	74	21.6
Vyacheslav Kozlov	72	20	18	38	30	9	4	0	187	10.7
Pat Verbeek	67	15	15	30	73	0	7	0	113	13.3
Igor Larionov*	39	4	25	29	28	6	2	0	31	12.9
Mathieu Dandenault	73	10	15	25	38	11	2	0	95	10.5
Kris Draper	75	8	17	25	38	17	0	1	123	6.5
Steve Duchesne	54	6	19	25	48	9	2	0	76	7.9
Darren McCarty	72	12	10	22	123	-5	1	1	118	10.2
Doug Brown	60	9	13	22	14	0	2	1	91	9.9
Larry Murphy	57	2	19	21	12	-6	0	0	81	2.5
Kirk Maltby	79	12	7	19	22	16	1	3	119	10.1
Boyd Devereaux	55	5	6	11	14	1	0	0	66	7.6
Todd Gill	68	3	8	11	53	17	0	1	66	4.5
Aaron Ward	73	4	5	9	57	-4	0	0	48	8.3

	Games	G	A	Pts.	PIM	+/-	PPG	SHG	Shots	Shooting Pct.
Jiri Fischer	55	1	8	9	59	3	0	0	64	1.6
Brent Gilchrist	60	1	8	9	41	-8	0	0	75	1.3
Maxim Kuznetsov	25	1	2	3	23	-1	0	0	17	5.9
Jason Williams	5	0	3	3	2	1	0	0	7	0.0
Chris Chelios	24	0	3	3	45	4	0	0	26	0.0
Yuri Butsayev	15	1	1	2	4	-2	0	0	18	5.6
Manny Legace (goalie)	39	0	2	2	4	0	0	0	0	0.0
Jesse Wallin	1	0	0	0	2	0	0	0	1	0.0
Chris Osgood (goalie)	52	0	0	0	8	0	0	0	0	0.0

GOALTENDING

	Games	Min.	Goals	SO	Avg.	W	L	T	ENG	Shots	Sv. Pct.
Manny Legace	39	2136	73	2	2.05	24	5	5	1	909	.920
Chris Osgood	52	2834	127	1	2.69	25	19	4	1	1310	.903

*Played with two or more NHL teams.

RESULTS

OCTOBER
5— At Calgary ....W.....4-3
6— At Edmonton ....L......1-2
11—Edmonton ....L......3-4
12—At Chicago...................W.....4-0
15—Calgary......................L......2-4
17—St. Louis....................W.....2-1
19—Nashville....................L.....*1-2
21—Buffalo......................W.....*5-4
22—At Columbus ....W.....*2-1
25—Tampa Bay ....W.....5-1
28—Columbus.....................W.....4-1
31—At Washington................L......2-6

NOVEMBER
1— At Montreal ....W.....4-2
3— Chicago ....L......1-6
8— At Phoenix.....................W.....4-2
11—At Los Angeles ....T....*2-2
12—At Anaheim.....................W.....3-2
15—San Jose ....W.....4-1
17—Dallas.........................L......0-1
18—At Nashville...................L......2-3
20—Nashville......................W.....6-3
22—Boston.........................L......4-5
24—Vancouver ....W.....3-2
25—At N.Y. Islanders..............W.....4-3
27—Chicago ....L.....*5-6
29—At Atlanta.....................W.....6-4

DECEMBER
1— At Florida.....................W.....3-1
2— At Tampa Bay ....L......0-3

6— Toronto ....L......0-3
8— Philadelphia...................W.....5-1
10—Pittsburgh.....................L......3-4
13—Florida ....T.....*3-3
15—At Colorado....................W.....5-3
16—At St. Louis...................T.....*2-2
18—Edmonton.......................W.....*4-3
20—San Jose ....L......0-2
22—Anaheim........................W.....*2-1
23—At Boston ....W.....*2-1
27—Minnesota......................L......3-5
29—At Chicago.....................L.....*2-3
31—Los Angeles ....W.....2-1

JANUARY
4— Dallas ....W.....4-2
5— At Minnesota ....L.....*2-3
7— Colorado.......................W.....*4-3
9— Phoenix........................T.....*2-2
12—At Dallas......................W.....3-2
15—At San Jose....................W.....3-2
16—At Vancouver...................W.....4-2
20—At Edmonton....................L......1-2
21—At Calgary.....................L......2-4
24—Nashville......................W.....4-3
26—Anaheim........................W.....3-2
30—At New Jersey..................L......1-3
31—At Columbus....................W.....*3-2

FEBRUARY
6— Ottawa.........................W.....4-2
8— Toronto........................W.....2-1
10—At Toronto ....T.....*3-3

14—Carolina.......................W....*4-3
16—Columbus.......................W.....4-2
18—At Dallas......................W.....2-1
20—At Nashville...................T.....*3-3
21—At Chicago.....................W.....7-3
23—St. Louis......................W.....4-2
25—Phoenix........................W.....6-3
28—At Anaheim.....................W.....3-1

MARCH
2— At Phoenix.....................T.....*2-2
3— At Los Angeles ....L......3-6
6— Al Vancouver...................W.....4-3
10—At St. Louis...................T.....*2-2
11—At Minnesota...................W....*3-2
13—Vancouver ....T....*2-2
15—Calgary........................W.....5-2
17—At Colorado ....L......3-5
18—At San Jose....................W.....6-4
22—Minnesota......................W.....4-2
24—At N.Y. Rangers................W.....6-0
28—St. Louis......................W.....5-2
31—At Philadelphia................L......0-1

APRIL
1— Washington.....................W....*2-1
3— At Columbus....................L......1-2
5— Atlanta........................W.....4-0
7— Colorado.......................W.....4-3

*Denotes overtime game.

DETROIT RED WINGS

EDMONTON OILERS
WESTERN CONFERENCE/NORTHWEST DIVISION

EDMONTON OILERS

Oilers' Schedule
Home games shaded; D—Day game; *—All-Star Game at Los Angeles

October

SUN	MON	TUE	WED	THU	FRI	SAT
	1	2	3 CAL	4	5	6 PHO
7	8	9 CHI	10	11 COL	12	13 NAS
14 MIN	15	16 TOR	17	18 COL	19	20 FLA
21 NAS	22	23	24 DET	25 CBJ	26	27 VAN
28	29	30 MON	31			

November

SUN	MON	TUE	WED	THU	FRI	SAT
				1	2 CBJ	3
4 D MIN	5	6 BOS	7	8	9 CBJ	10
11 D CAR	12	13 PHO	14	15	16 CHI	17 VAN
18	19	20 STL	21	22 LA	23	24 COL
25	26	27	28 ANA	29 LA	30	

December

SUN	MON	TUE	WED	THU	FRI	SAT
						1 DAL
2	3	4	5 ANA	6	7 DAL	8 NAS
9	10	11 SJ	12	13 DET	14 TB	15
16 PHI	17	18 NYI	19	20 NJ	21 CHI	22
23	24	25	26 CAL	27	28 MIN	29
30 NJ	31 CAL					

January

SUN	MON	TUE	WED	THU	FRI	SAT
		1	2 NYR	3	4	5 VAN
6 MON	7	8	9	10 CAR	11	12 COL
13	14 CHI	15 STL	16	17	18 ANA	19 PIT
20	21 SJ	22	23 COL	24	25	26 TOR
27	28 DET	29	30 VAN	31		

February

SUN	MON	TUE	WED	THU	FRI	SAT
					1	2 *
3	4	5 ATL	6	7 STL	8 DAL	9
10 PHO	11	12 SJ	13	14	15	16
17	18	19	20	21	22	23
24	25	26	27	28 NAS		

March

SUN	MON	TUE	WED	THU	FRI	SAT
					1	2 STL
3	4 BUF	5	6 TB	7	8 FLA	9
10 D WAS	11	12	13 DET	14 OTT	15	16 WAS
17	18	19	20 SJ	21	22	23 CAL
24 VAN	25	26 CBJ	27	28 LA	29	30 DAL
31						

April

SUN	MON	TUE	WED	THU	FRI	SAT
	1	2 MIN	3	4	5 ANA	6 LA
7	8	9	10 PHO	11	12 CAL	13
14 MIN	D 15	16	17	18	19	20

2001-02 SEASON
CLUB DIRECTORY

Owner
Edmonton Investors Group, Ltd.
Governor
Cal Nichols
Alternate governors
Kevin Lowe, Gordon Buchanan
President & chief executive officer
Patrick LaForge
General manager
Kevin Lowe
Assistant general manager
Scott Howson
V.p. of player personnel/hockey ops.
Kevin Prendergast
Head coach
Craig MacTavish
Assistant coaches
Charlie Huddy
Mark Lamb
Bill Moores
Video coordinator
Brian Ross
Scouting staff
Bill Dandy, Brad Davis, Lorne Davis,
Morey Gare, Stu MacGregor, Bob
Mancini, Chris McCarthy, Kent
Nilsson, Gord Pell, Dave Semenko

Athletic trainer/therapist
Ken Lowe
Equipment manager
Barrie Stafford
Assistant equipment manager
Lyle Kulchisky
Massage therapist
Stewart Poirier
Team physicians
Dr. David C. Reid, Dr. Boris Boyko
Vice president, public relations
Bill Tuele
Information coordinator
Steve Knowles
Public relations coordinator
Warren Suitor
Vice president, finance
Darryl Boessenkool
Vice president, sponsorships, sales & services
Allan Watt
Vice president, properties
Darrell Holowaychuk
Director of ticketing
John Yeomans
Director of broadcast
Don Metz

DRAFT CHOICES

Rd.— Player	Ht./Wt.	Overall	Pos.	Last team
1— Ales Hemsky	6-0/170	13	RW	Hull (QMJHL)
2— Doug Lynch	6-3/205	43	D	Red Deer (WHL)
2— Edward Caron	6-2/214	52	LW	Phillips-Exeter (USHSE)
3— Kenny Smith	6-2/209	84	D	Harvard (ECAC)
5— Jussi Markkanen	5-11/183	133	G	Tappara, Finland
5— Jake Brenk	6-2/187	154	C	Breck, Min. (USHSW)
6— Mikael Svensk	6-2/191	185	D	Frolunda, Sweden
7— Dan Baum	6-0/169	215	C/LW	Prince George (WHL)
8— Kari Haakana	6-1/222	248	D	Jokerit, Finland
9— Ales Pisa	6-0/194	272	D	Pardubice, Czech.
9— Shay Stephenson	6-2/180	278	LW	Red Deer (WHL)

MISCELLANEOUS DATA

Home ice (capacity)
Skyreach Centre (16,839)
Address
11230 110 Street
Edmonton, Alta. T5G 3H7
Business phone
780-414-4000
Ticket information
780-414-4000
Website
www.edmontonoilers.com

Training site
Sherwood Park, Alberta
Club colors
White, midnight blue, metallic copper and red
Radio affiliation
CHED (630 AM)
TV affiliation
SportsNet & CBXT-TV

TRAINING CAMP ROSTER

EDMONTON OILERS

No.	FORWARDS	Ht./Wt.	Place	BORN — Date	NHL exp.	2000-01 clubs
	Jake Brenk (C)	6-2/187	Detroit Lakes, Minn.	4-16-82	0	Breck (USHS (West))
	Ed Caron (LW)	6-2/214	Nashua, N.H.	4-30-82	0	Phillips-Exeter (USHS (East))
33	Anson Carter (C)	6-1/175	Toronto	6-6-74	5	Edmonton
	Jason Chimera (C)	6-0/180	Edmonton	5-2-79	1	Hamilton (AHL), Edmonton
37	Dan Cleary (LW)	6-0/203	Carbonear, Nfld.	12-18-78	4	Edmonton
	Mike Comrie (C)	5-9/172	Edmonton	9-11-80	1	Kootenay (WHL), Edmonton
25	Josh Green (LW)	6-4/213	Camrose, Alta.	11-16-77	3	Edmonton, Hamilton (AHL)
25	Mike Grier (RW)	6-1/227	Detroit	1-5-75	5	Edmonton
	Paul Healey (RW)	6-2/200	Edmonton	3-20-75	2	Hamilton (AHL)
17	Jochen Hecht (C)	6-3/196	Mannheim, West Germany	6-21-77	3	St. Louis
	Ales Hemsky (RW)	6-0/170	Pardubice, Czechoslovakia	8-13-83	0	Hull (QMJHL)
	Michael Henrich (RW)	6-2/206	Thornhill, Ont.	3-3-80	0	Hamilton (AHL), Tallahassee (ECHL)
	Shawn Horcoff (C)	6-1/194	Trail, B.C.	9-17-78	1	Hamilton (AHL), Edmonton
27	Georges Laraque (RW)	6-3/240	Montreal	12-7-76	4	Edmonton
	Greg Leeb (C)	5-9/160	Red Deer, Alta.	5-31-77	1	Utah (IHL), Dallas
	Matthew Lombardi (C)	5-11/191	Montreal	3-18-82	0	Victoriaville (QMJHL)
26	Todd Marchant (LW)	5-10/178	Buffalo	8-12-73	8	Edmonton
	Alexei Mikhnov (LW)	6-5/194	U.S.S.R.	8-31-82	0	
18	Ethan Moreau (LW)	6-2/205	Orillia, Ont.	9-22-75	6	Edmonton
17	Rem Murray (LW)	6-2/195	Stratford, Ont.	10-9-72	5	Edmonton
	Fernando Pisani (C/LW)	6-1/185	Edmonton	12-27-76	0	Hamilton (AHL)
28	Domenic Pittis (LW)	5-11/190	Calgary	10-1-74	4	Edmonton
15	Marty Reasoner (C)	6-0/203	Rochester, N.Y.	2-26-77	3	St. Louis, Worcester (AHL)
	Craig Reichert (RW)	6-1/200	Winnipeg	5-11-74	1	Dusseldorf (Germany)
	Jani Rita (LW/RW)	6-1/206	Helsinki, Finland	7-25-81	0	Jokerit Helsinki (Finland)
	Peter Sarno (C)	5-11/185	Toronto	7-26-79	0	Hamilton (AHL)
94	Ryan Smyth (LW)	6-1/195	Banff, Alta.	2-21-76	7	Edmonton
25	Steve Staios (RW/D)	6-1/200	Hamilton, Ont.	7-28-73	6	Atlanta
	Brian Swanson (C)	5-10/185	Eagle River, Alaska	3-24-76	1	Edmonton, Hamilton (AHL)
	DEFENSEMEN					
	Marc-Andre Bergeron	5-10/190	St. Louis de France, Que.		0	Shawinigan (QMJHL)
34	Eric Brewer	6-3/220	Verona, B.C.	4-17-79	3	Edmonton
23	Sean Brown	6-3/205	Oshawa, Ont.	11-5-76	5	Edmonton
22	Sven Butenschon	6-4/215	Itzehoe, West Germany	3-22-76	4	Wilkes-Barre/Scranton (AHL), Pittsburgh, Edmonton
21	Scott Ferguson	6-1/202	Camrose, Alta.	1-6-73	3	Hamilton (AHL), Edmonton
	Paul Flache	6-5/195	Toronto	3-4-82	0	Brampton (OHL)
	Chris Hajt	6-3/206	Amherst, N.Y.	7-5-78	1	Hamilton (AHL), Edmonton
	Alex Henry	6-5/220	Elliot Lake, Ont.	10-18-79	0	Hamilton (AHL)
	Jan Horacek	6-4/206	Benesov, Czechoslovakia	5-22-79	0	Worcester (AHL), Peoria (ECHL)
	Alexander Ljubimov	6-3/190	Togliatti, U.S.S.R.	2-15-80	0	
	Doug Lynch	6-3/205	North Vancouver	4-4-83	0	Red Deer (WHL)
	Alain Nasreddine	6-1/203	Montreal	7-10-75	1	Hamilton (AHL)
44	Janne Niinimaa	6-2/220	Raahe, Finland	5-22-75	5	Edmonton
5	Tom Poti	6-3/215	Worcester, Mass.	3-22-77	3	Edmonton
	Alexei Semenov	6-6/210	Murmansk, U.S.S.R.	4-10-81	0	Sudbury (OHL)
21	Jason Smith	6-3/208	Calgary	11-2-73	8	Edmonton
	Kenny Smith	6-2/209	Stoneham, Mass.	12-31-81	0	Harvard University (ECAC)
	GOALTENDERS					
	Ty Conklin	6-0/180	Anchorage, Alaska	3-30-76	0	Univ. of New Hamp. (Hockey East)
	Jussi Markkanen	5-11/183	Imatra, Finland	5-8-75	0	Tappara Tampere (Finland)
35	Tommy Salo	5-11/173	Surahammar, Sweden	2-1-71	7	Edmonton

2000-01 REVIEW
INDIVIDUAL STATISTICS

SCORING

	Games	G	A	Pts.	PIM	+/-	PPG	SHG	Shots	Shooting Pct.
Doug Weight	82	25	65	90	91	12	8	0	188	13.3
Ryan Smyth	82	31	39	70	58	10	11	0	245	12.7
Janne Niinimaa	82	12	34	46	90	6	8	0	122	9.8
Anson Carter	61	16	26	42	23	1	7	1	102	15.7
Todd Marchant	71	13	26	39	51	1	0	4	113	11.5
Mike Grier	74	20	16	36	20	11	2	3	124	16.1
Rem Murray	82	15	21	36	24	5	1	3	122	12.3
Daniel Cleary	81	14	21	35	37	5	2	0	107	13.1
Tom Poti	81	12	20	32	60	-4	6	0	161	7.5
Georges Laraque	82	13	16	29	148	5	1	0	73	17.8
Igor Ulanov	67	3	20	23	90	15	1	0	74	4.1

	Games	G	A	Pts.	PIM	+/-	PPG	SHG	Shots	Shooting Pct.
Bill Guerin*	21	12	10	22	18	11	4	0	64	18.8
Mike Comrie	41	8	14	22	14	6	3	0	62	12.9
Eric Brewer	77	7	14	21	53	15	2	0	91	7.7
Jason Smith	82	5	15	20	120	14	1	1	140	3.6
Sergei Zholtok*	37	4	16	20	22	8	1	0	61	6.6
Ethan Moreau	68	9	10	19	90	-6	0	1	97	9.3
Shawn Horcoff	49	9	7	16	10	8	0	0	42	21.4
Domenic Pittis	47	4	5	9	49	-5	0	0	42	9.5
Chad Kilger*	34	5	2	7	17	-7	1	0	28	17.9
Dan LaCouture*	37	2	4	6	29	-2	0	0	22	9.1
Sean Brown	62	2	3	5	110	2	0	0	30	6.7
Sven Butenschon*	7	1	1	2	2	2	0	0	3	33.3
Brian Swanson	16	1	1	2	6	-1	0	0	8	12.5
Frank Musil	13	0	2	2	4	-2	0	0	0	0.0
Michel Riesen	12	0	1	1	4	2	0	0	16	0.0
Scott Ferguson	20	0	1	1	13	2	0	0	8	0.0
Tommy Salo (goalie)	73	0	1	1	4	0	0	0	0	0.0
Chris Hajt	1	0	0	0	0	-1	0	0	0	0.0
Jason Chimera	1	0	0	0	0	0	0	0	0	0.0
Joaquin Gage (goalie)	5	0	0	0	0	0	0	0	0	0.0
Patrick Cote	6	0	0	0	18	-2	0	0	0	0.0
Dominic Roussel (goalie)*	8	0	0	0	2	0	0	0	0	0.0

GOALTENDING

	Games	Min.	Goals	SO	Avg.	W	L	T	ENG	Shots	Sv. Pct.
Tommy Salo	73	4364	179	8	2.46	36	25	12	5	1856	.904
Joaquin Gage	5	260	15	0	3.46	2	2	0	1	125	.880
Dominic Roussel*	8	348	21	0	3.62	1	4	0	1	151	.861

*Played with two or more NHL teams.

RESULTS

OCTOBER

6— Detroit .... W 2-1
7— Colorado .... T *1-1
10— At Montreal .... L 2-5
11— At Detroit .... W 4-3
13— Buffalo .... W 3-2
15— At Minnesota .... W 5-3
17— Boston .... W 6-1
19— Toronto .... L 1-4
22— Phoenix .... T *3-3
25— Atlanta .... L 1-3
27— At Anaheim .... L 2-3
28— At Colorado .... L 2-4
30— Anaheim .... W 5-3

NOVEMBER

1— Calgary .... W 3-2
3— Minnesota .... W 3-0
5— At Columbus .... W 4-2
7— At N.Y. Rangers ...... L 3-4
9— At Philadelphia .... L 0-2
11— At Pittsburgh .... L 2-5
12— At Minnesota .... W ...*5-4
14— St. Louis .... W 3-0
17— Chicago .... T *3-3
19— Calgary .... W 2-0
22— At Toronto .... L 3-4
23— At Ottawa .... W 5-3
25— Anaheim .... W 3-2
29— Montreal .... L 2-3

DECEMBER

2— At Vancouver ....L 2-5
3— San Jose ....T *3-3
6— Nashville ....W 4-0
9— Los Angeles ....L 2-4
13— At Dallas ....L 2-5
14— At Nashville ....W 6-2
16— At Washington ....L 0-4
18— At Detroit ....L *3-4
20— Vancouver ....W *3-2
22— At Calgary ....T *1-1
27— At Colorado ....L 2-3
28— At San Jose ....T *2-2
30— Montreal ....W *3-2

JANUARY

1— At St. Louis ....L 2-5
3— At Columbus ....L 2-5
5— At Chicago ....W 2-1
7— Columbus ....W 4-2
10— Nashville ....L 2-5
12— Vancouver ....L 2-3
14— Ottawa ....W 4-1
16— At Nashville ....W 2-1
18— At St. Louis ....L 1-4
20— Detroit ....W 2-1
22— San Jose ....T *2-2
24— At San Jose ....L 1-6
26— Phoenix ....T *1-1
30— At Calgary ....W 5-3
31— Chicago ....W 3-2

FEBRUARY

7— At Dallas ....L 2-3
9— At Phoenix ....L 0-2
12— At Los Angeles ....W 6-3
14— At Anaheim ....T *3-3
16— N.Y. Islanders ....L 2-4
17— Vancouver ....L *5-6
20— Los Angeles ....W 5-0
24— At Calgary ....W 3-1
25— Dallas ....W *3-2
28— St. Louis ....W 5-3

MARCH

2— Minnesota ....W 3-1
7— Toronto ....W 4-0
9— At Buffalo ....W 4-0
11— At Carolina ....W 3-2
13— At Tampa Bay ....W ...*5-4
14— At Florida ....T *2-2
17— New Jersey ....L *5-6
19— Philadelphia ....L 2-4
21— At Los Angeles ....W 7-0
24— At Phoenix ....L 4-7
26— Columbus ....W 4-2
28— Colorado ....W 4-1
30— Dallas ....L 4-5

APRIL

1— At Chicago ....T *3-3
2— At Colorado ....L 3-5
4— Minnesota ....T *2-2
7— At Vancouver ....W 4-2

*Denotes overtime game.

FLORIDA PANTHERS
EASTERN CONFERENCE/SOUTHEAST DIVISION

Panthers' Schedule
Home games shaded; D—Day game; *—All-Star Game at Los Angeles

October
SUN	MON	TUE	WED	THU	FRI	SAT
	1	2	3	4 PHI	5	6 NYI
7 TB	8	9	10 OTT	11	12	13 PHI
14	15	16 VAN	17	18 CAL	19	20 EDM
21	22	23	24 WAS	25	26 LA	27
28 PIT	29	30 NYI	31 NYR			

November
SUN	MON	TUE	WED	THU	FRI	SAT
				1	2	3 NYR
4	5	6	7 PIT	8	9	10 PHI
11	12 BUF	13	14 TOR	15	16 BUF	17 MON
18	19 TOR	20	21 ANA	22	23	24 NJ
25	26	27 COL	28	29 MIN	30	

December
SUN	MON	TUE	WED	THU	FRI	SAT
						1 ATL
2	3	4	5 CBJ	6	7	8 CAR
9	10	11	12 CAR	13	14 NJ	15 NYI
16	17 NYR	18	19 WAS	20	21	22 STL
23	24	25	26 ATL	27	28 BOS	29 TOR
30	31 D ATL					

January
SUN	MON	TUE	WED	THU	FRI	SAT
		1	2 LA	3	4 ANA	5 SJ
6	7 WAS	8	9 DAL	10	11 OTT	12 WAS
13	14	15	16 CHI	17	18 DAL	19 ATL
20	21 D MON	22	23 NJ	24	25 CAR	26 BOS
27	28	29	30 PHO	31		

February
SUN	MON	TUE	WED	THU	FRI	SAT
					1	2 *
3	4 NYI	5	6 TB	7 TB	8	9 BOS D
10	11	12 NAS	13 CHI	14	15	16
17	18	19	20	21	22	23
24	25	26 WAS	27 DET	28		

March
SUN	MON	TUE	WED	THU	FRI	SAT
					1	2 TB
3	4	5 PIT	6	7	8 EDM	9 NAS
10	11	12	13 CAL	14	15 BUF	16
17 OTT	18	19	20 MON	21 CAR	22	23 BOS
24 NJ	25 MON	26	27	28 OTT	29	30 NYR
31						

April
SUN	MON	TUE	WED	THU	FRI	SAT
	1	2	3 PIT	4	5 BUF	6 TOR
7	8 PHI	9	10 ATL	11	12 CAR	13
14 D TB	15	16	17	18	19	20

2001-02 SEASON
CLUB DIRECTORY

Owners
Alan Cohen, David Epstein, Bernie Kosar, Mike Maroone, Jordan Zimmerman, Steve Cohen, Al Maroone, Dr. Elliott Hahn, H. Wayne Huizenga

President & general manager
William A. Torrey

Chief operating officer
Jeff Cogen

Chief financial officer
Bill Duffy

Senior vice president
Steve Dangerfield

V.p., corporate sales & client services
Kimberly Terranova Sciarretta

Assistant general manager
Chuck Fletcher

Head coach
Duane Sutter

Assistant coaches
Paul Baxter
George Kingston

Director of amateur scouting
Tim Murray

Amateur scouts
Wayne Meier, Darwin Bennett, Ron Harris, Todd Hearty, Marty Nanne

Pro scouts
Michael Abbamont, Billy Dea, Joe Paterson

European scouts
Pavel Routa
Slavomir Lener

Head medical trainer
Stan Wong

Strength & conditioning coach
Ian Pyka

Head equipment manager
Mark Brennan

Dir. of broadcasting & communications
Mike Hanson

Media relations manager
Randy Sieminski

Director of finance/controller
Evelyn Lopez

DRAFT CHOICES

Rd.— Player	Ht./Wt.	Overall	Pos.	Last team
1— Stephen Weiss	5-11/178	4	C	Plymouth (OHL)
1— Lukas Krajicek	6-1/183	24	D	Peterborough (OHL)
2— Greg Watson	6-1/177	34	C/LW	Prince Albert (WHL)
3— Tomas Malec	6-1/185	64	D	Rimouski (QMJHL)
3— Grant McNeill	6-2/196	68	D	Prince Albert (WHL)
4— Michael Woodford	5-11/185	117	RW	Cushing Acad. (USHSE)
5— Billy Thompson	6-2/180	136	G	Prince George (WHL)
6— Dustin Johner	5-10/168	169	C	Seattle (WHL)
7— Toni Koivisto	6-0/189	200	F	Lukko, Finland
8— Kyle Bruce	6-0/181	231	RW	Prince Albert (WHL)
9— Jan Blanar	6-3/183	263	D	Trencin Jr., Slovakia
9— Ivan Majesky	6-5/224	267	D	Ilves, Finland

MISCELLANEOUS DATA

Home ice (capacity)
National Car Rental Center (19,250)

Address
One Panther Parkway
Sunrise, FL 33323

Business phone
954-835-7000

Ticket information
954-835-7000

Website
www.floridapanthers.com

Training site
Hull, Quebec and Sunrise, FL

Club colors
Red, navy blue, yellow and gold

Radio affiliation
WQAM (560 AM)

TV affiliation
FOX SportsNet

TRAINING CAMP ROSTER

No.	FORWARDS	Ht./Wt.	Place — BORN	Date	NHL exp.	2000-01 clubs
42	Kevyn Adams (C)	6-1/195	Washington, D.C.	10-8-74	4	Columbus, Florida
	Eric Beaudoin (LW)	6-2/202	Ottawa	5-3-80	0	Louisville (AHL)
	Paul Brousseau (RW)	6-2/200	Pierrefonds, Que.	9-18-73	4	Louisville (AHL), Florida
10	Pavel Bure (RW)	5-10/189	Moscow, U.S.S.R.	3-31-71	10	Florida
8	Valeri Bure (RW)	5-10/185	Moscow, U.S.S.R.	6-13-74	7	Calgary
	Robert Fried (RW)	6-3/210	Philadelphia	3-8-81	0	Harvard University (ECAC)
	Eric Godard (RW)	6-4/215	Vernon, B.C.	3-7-80	0	Louisville (AHL)
	Mike Green (C)	5-11/192	Victoria, B.C.	8-23-79	0	Saskatoon (WHL), Louisville (AHL)
	Niklas Hagman (LW)	5-11/183	Espoo, Finland	12-5-79	0	Karpat (Finland)
	Paul Harvey (RW)	6-4/196	South Boston, Mass.	8-8-78	0	Louisville (AHL), Port Huron (UHL)
	Kristian Huselius (LW)	6-1/183	Stockholm, Sweden	11-10-78	0	Vastra Frolunda (Sweden)
	Ryan Jardine (LW)	6-3/190	Ottawa	3-15-80	0	Louisville (AHL)
17	Ryan Johnson (C)	6-1/200	Thunder Bay, Ont.	6-14-76	4	Tampa Bay
62	Olli Jokinen (C)	6-3/218	Kuopio, Finland	12-5-78	4	Florida
25	Viktor Kozlov (C)	6-5/232	Togliatti, U.S.S.R.	2-14-75	7	Florida
3	Paul Laus (RW)	6-1/212	Beamsville, Ont.	9-26-70	8	Florida
	David Morisset (RW)	6-2/193	Langley, B.C.	4-6-81	0	Seattle (WHL)
48	Marcus Nilson (C)	6-2/193	Balsta, Sweden	3-1-78	3	Florida
39	Ivan Novoseltsev (C)	6-1/183	Golitsino, U.S.S.R.	1-23-79	2	Louisville (AHL), Florida
	Sean O'Connor (RW)	6-2/211	Victoria, B.C.	10-19-81	0	Moose Jaw (WHL)
	Josh Olson (LW)	6-5/220	Grand Forks, N.D.	7-13-81	0	Portland (WHL)
	Serge Payer (C)	5-11/175	Rockland, Ont.	5-7-79	1	Louisville (AHL), Florida
	Denis Shvidki (RW)	6-0/205	Kharkov, U.S.S.R.	11-21-80	1	Florida, Louisville (AHL)
	Nick Smith (C)	6-2/194	Hamilton, Ont.	3-23-79	0	Louisville (AHL)
	Janis Sprukts (C)	6-3/224	Aiga, Latvia	1-31-82	0	Lukko Rauma (Finland Jr.)
22	Rocky Thompson (RW)	6-2/205	Calgary	8-8-77	3	Louisville (AHL), Florida
	Greg Watson (C)	6-1/177	Eastend, Sask.	3-2-83	0	Prince Albert (WHL)
	Stephen Weiss (C)	5-11/178	Toronto	4-3-83	0	Plymouth (OHL)
24	Jason Wiemer (C)	6-1/220	Kimberley, B.C.	4-14-76	7	Calgary
	Michael Woodford (RW)	5-11/185	Boston	10-4-81	0	Cushing Academy (USHS (East))
8	Peter Worrell (LW)	6-6/235	Pierrefonds, Que.	8-18-77	4	Florida

No.	DEFENSEMEN	Ht./Wt.	Place	Date	NHL exp.	2000-01 clubs
6	Dan Boyle	5-11/190	Ottawa	7-12-76	3	Florida, Louisville (AHL)
	Joe DiPenta	6-2/220	Barrie, Ont.	2-25-79	0	Philadelphia (AHL)
	Chris Eade	6-1/191	Etobicoke, Ont.	4-20-82	0	North Bay (OHL), Louisville (AHL)
45	Brad Ference	6-3/196	Calgary	4-2-79	2	Florida, Louisville (AHL)
4	Bret Hedican	6-2/205	St. Paul, Minn.	8-10-70	10	Florida
15	John Jakopin	6-5/239	Toronto	5-16-75	4	Louisville (AHL), Florida
	Lukas Krajicek	6-1/183	Prostejov, Czechoslovakia	3-11-83	0	Peterborough (OHL)
	Tomas Malec	6-1/185	Skalica, Czechoslovakia	5-3-82	0	Rimouski (QMJHL)
	Grant McNeill	6-2/196	Vermilion, Alta.	6-8-83	0	Prince Albert (WHL)
5	Jeff Norton	6-2/195	Acton, Mass.	11-25-65	14	Pittsburgh, San Jose
2	Lance Pitlick	5-11/211	Fridley, Minn.	11-5-67	7	Florida
	Kyle Rossiter	6-3/218	Edmonton	6-9-80	0	Louisville (AHL)
	Vladimir Sapozhnikov	6-3/205	Seversk, Russia	8-2-82	0	North Bay (OHL)
24	Robert Svehla	6-1/210	Martin, Czechoslovakia	1-2-69	7	Florida
	Joey Tetarenko	6-2/212	Prince Albert, Sask.	3-3-78	1	Florida
	Lance Ward	6-3/215	Lloydminster, Alta.	6-2-78	1	Louisville (AHL), Florida

No.	GOALTENDERS	Ht./Wt.	Place	Date	NHL exp.	2000-01 clubs
37	Trevor Kidd	6-2/190	Dugald, Man.	3-29-72	9	Florida
1	Roberto Luongo	6-3/175	St. Leonard, Que.	4-4-79	2	Florida, Louisville (AHL)
	Davis Parley	6-1/164	Grenfell, Sask.	9-4-82	0	Kamloops (WHL)
	Billy Thompson	6-2/180	Saskatoon, Sask.	9-24-82	0	Prince George (WHL)

2000-01 REVIEW
INDIVIDUAL STATISTICS

SCORING

	Games	G	A	Pts.	PIM	+/-	PPG	SHG	Shots	Shooting Pct.
Pavel Bure	82	59	33	92	58	-2	19	5	384	15.4
Viktor Kozlov	51	14	23	37	10	-4	6	0	139	10.1
Marcus Nilson	78	12	24	36	74	-3	0	0	141	8.5
Mike Sillinger*	55	13	21	34	44	-12	1	0	100	13.0
Rob Niedermayer	67	12	20	32	50	-12	3	1	115	10.4
Ray Whitney*	43	10	21	31	28	-16	5	0	117	8.5
Robert Svehla	82	6	22	28	76	-8	0	0	121	5.0
Greg Adams	60	11	12	23	10	-3	2	0	66	16.7
Len Barrie	60	5	18	23	135	4	0	1	48	10.4
Dan Boyle	69	4	18	22	28	-14	1	0	83	4.8

	Games	G	A	Pts.	PIM	+/-	PPG	SHG	Shots	Shooting Pct.
Anders Eriksson*	60	0	21	21	28	2	0	0	80	0.0
Bret Hedican	70	5	15	20	72	-7	4	0	104	4.8
Denis Shvidki	43	6	10	16	16	6	0	0	28	21.4
Olli Jokinen	78	6	10	16	106	-22	0	0	121	5.0
Vaclav Prospal*	34	4	12	16	10	-2	1	0	68	5.9
Scott Mellanby*	40	4	9	13	46	-13	1	0	58	6.9
Igor Larionov*	26	5	6	11	10	-11	2	0	15	33.3
Peter Worrell	71	3	7	10	248	-10	0	0	86	3.5
Kevyn Adams*	12	3	6	9	2	7	0	0	21	14.3
Ivan Novoseltsev	38	3	6	9	16	-5	0	0	34	8.8
Serge Payer	43	5	1	6	21	0	0	1	34	14.7
Joey Tetarenko	29	3	1	4	44	-1	0	0	21	14.3
Todd Simpson*	25	1	3	4	74	0	0	0	26	3.8
Jaroslav Spacek*	12	2	1	3	8	-4	1	0	21	9.5
Paul Laus	25	1	2	3	66	5	0	0	18	5.6
John Jakopin	60	1	2	3	62	-4	0	0	23	4.3
Lance Pitlick	68	1	2	3	42	-5	0	0	24	4.2
Yan Golubovsky	6	0	2	2	2	3	0	0	4	0.0
Lance Ward	30	0	2	2	45	-3	0	0	17	0.0
Andrej Podkonicky	6	1	0	1	2	0	0	0	5	20.0
Brad Ference	14	0	1	1	14	-10	0	0	5	0.0
Mike Wilson	19	0	1	1	25	-7	0	0	26	0.0
Trevor Kidd (goalie)	42	0	1	1	6	0	0	0	0	0.0
Paul Brousseau	1	0	0	0	0	0	0	0	0	0.0
Rocky Thompson	4	0	0	0	19	0	0	0	0	0.0
David Emma	6	0	0	0	0	-1	0	0	6	0.0
Peter Ratchuk	8	0	0	0	0	-1	0	0	11	0.0
Roberto Luongo (goalie)	47	0	0	0	2	0	0	0	0	0.0

GOALTENDING

	Games	Min.	Goals	SO	Avg.	W	L	T	ENG	Shots	Sv. Pct.
Roberto Luongo	47	2628	107	5	2.44	12	24	7	6	1333	.920
Trevor Kidd	42	2354	130	1	3.31	10	23	6	3	1217	.893

*Played with two or more NHL teams.

RESULTS

OCTOBER

6— Vancouver ....L....*3-4
9— At Boston ....L......2-4
13— Carolina ....T....*2-2
18— At Phoenix ....L...*1-2
20— At Colorado ....L......1-5
22— At Minnesota ....T...*0-0
25— New Jersey ....L......1-2
27— At Nashville ....T...*3-3
28— Ottawa ....W......3-1
30— At New Jersey ....L....*5-6

NOVEMBER

1— N.Y. Islanders ....L......0-3
4— Washington ....L......2-3
8— Montreal ....L......2-4
10— Calgary ....T...*3-3
13— Atlanta ....L......1-4
15— At Carolina ....W......4-1
17— At Columbus ....W......3-0
18— At Ottawa ....L......2-5
21— At Montreal ....W......4-1
24— At Tampa Bay ....L......1-2
25— Tampa Bay ....W..*2-1
29— Carolina ....L...*1-2

DECEMBER

1— Detroit ....L......1-3
2— At St. Louis......................L......2-5
4— At Toronto ....T....*4-4
6— N.Y. Islanders ....L......1-4
8— At Atlanta ....L...*3-4
9— Colorado ....L......2-4

JANUARY

3— At Anaheim ....L...*2-3
4— At Los Angeles ....W......4-3
6— At San Jose ....L......1-3
9— At Carolina ....L......3-7
12— Carolina ....T...*2-2
13— Philadelphia ....L......1-4
15— Dallas ....W......2-0
17— At Chicago ....L......0-5
19— At Buffalo ....L......0-1
20— At Philadelphia ....L......3-5
22— At Boston ....W......3-2
24— At Washington ....L......1-2
26— Ottawa ....L...*4-5
27— Tampa Bay ....W..*3-2
30— At Tampa Bay ....L......3-4
31— Buffalo ....W......5-2

FEBRUARY

7— Minnesota ....W......2-1
9— N.Y. Rangers ....L......2-4
10— At Atlanta ....W......7-3

13— At Detroit ....T....*3-3
15— At Pittsburgh ....W......4-1
16— At Buffalo ....L......2-3
18— At N.Y. Rangers ....L......3-6
20— Pittsburgh ....T....*2-2
22— New Jersey ....L......0-2
23— At Washington ....L......3-5
27— Philadelphia ....L......2-5
29— Boston ....W......3-0
30— Toronto ....L......1-4

14— Phoenix ....W......4-3
16— Boston ....W......2-1
19— St. Louis ....W......3-0
21— At Pittsburgh ....L...*2-3
22— At Ottawa ....L......2-4
24— At N.Y. Islanders ....L......4-5
26— At New Jersey ....L......3-5
28— At N.Y. Rangers ....L......2-4

MARCH

2— Atlanta ....L......3-4
3— At Atlanta ....T...*2-2
7— San Jose ....T...*3-3
9— Columbus ....L...*6-7
11— At N.Y. Islanders............W......4-1
14— Edmonton ....T...*2-2
16— Pittsburgh ....L......3-6
17— Toronto ....L......3-5
20— At Montreal ....T...*3-3
21— At Toronto ....W......3-1
23— Washington ....W......4-1
28— Montreal ....T...*2-2
30— Tampa Bay ....L......2-4

APRIL

2— Buffalo ....L......3-5
3— At Philadelphia ....W......2-1
5— At Washington ....L......0-3
7— N.Y. Rangers ....W......3-0

*Denotes overtime game.

LOS ANGELES KINGS
WESTERN CONFERENCE/PACIFIC DIVISION

Kings' Schedule
Home games shaded; D—Day game; *—All-Star Game at Los Angeles

October
SUN	MON	TUE	WED	THU	FRI	SAT
1	2	3	4 PHO	5	6	
7 MIN	8	9 DAL	10	11 STL	12	13 TB
14	15	16 WAS	17	18 ANA	19	20 DET
21	22	23 CBJ	24	25 TB	26 FLA	27
28 D CAR	29	30 CHI	31			

November
SUN	MON	TUE	WED	THU	FRI	SAT
				1 CHI	2	3 D ATL
4	5	6	7	8 CAL	9	10 DET
11	12	13	14	15 DAL	16	17 DET
18 MIN	19	20 CAL	21	22 EDM	23	24 D SJ
25	26	27	28	29 EDM	30	

December
SUN	MON	TUE	WED	THU	FRI	SAT
						1 D NAS
2	3 CAL	4	5	6 STL	7	8 STL
9 CHI	10	11 NAS	12	13 VAN	14	15 CBJ
16 ANA	17	18 TOR	19	20 OTT	21	22 MON
23	24	25	26 PHO	27 ANA	28	29 NYR
30	31					

January
SUN	MON	TUE	WED	THU	FRI	SAT
		1	2 FLA	3	4	5 NYI
6	7 NJ	8	9 NYR	10 BOS	11	12 D SJ
13	14	15 NAS	16	17 BUF	18	19 D NYI
20	21 ANA	22	23	24 MIN	25	26 D COL
27	28 COL	29	30 MIN	31		

February
SUN	MON	TUE	WED	THU	FRI	SAT
					1	2 *
3	4 PHI	5	6	7 CAR	8 PHO	9
10	11 DAL	12	13 PHO	14	15	16
17	18	19	20	21	22	23
24	25	26 CBJ	27 PIT	28		

March
SUN	MON	TUE	WED	THU	FRI	SAT
					1	2 D CBJ
3	4 OTT	5	6 DAL	7 NAS	8	9 D COL
10	11 CHI	12	13	14 STL	15	16 D PIT
17 SJ	18	19	20	21 COL	22	23 D SJ
24 PHO	25	26 VAN	27	28 EDM	29	30 CAL
31						

April
SUN	MON	TUE	WED	THU	FRI	SAT
	1	2 VAN	3	4 DET	5	6 EDM
7	8 DAL	9	10	11 VAN	12	13 D SJ
14 D ANA	15	16	17	18	19	20

2001-02 SEASON
CLUB DIRECTORY

Owners
Philip F. Anschutz
Edward P. Roski, Jr.
President
Tim Leiweke
Sr. vice president, general manager
Dave Taylor
Coach
Andy Murray
Assistant coaches
Ray Bennett
Mark Hardy
Dave Tippett
Assistant general manager
Kevin Gilmore
Director of player personnel
Bill O'Flaherty
Assistant to general manager
John Wolf
Director of amateur scouting
Al Murray

Director of pro scouting
Ace Bailey
Scouting staff
Serge Aubry, Michel Boucher, Mark
Davis, Greg Drechsel, Gary Harker,
Rob Laird, Vaclav Nedomansky,
Parry Shockey, John Stanton, Victor
Tjumenev, Ari Vuori
Vice president of sales and marketing
Kurt Schwartzkopf
Dir., media relations and team services
Mike Altieri
Mgr., media relations and team services
Jeff Moeller
Media relations assistant
Lee Callans
Trainers
Rick Burrill, Grady Clark, Pete Demers,
Rick Garcia, Dave Good, Joe
Horrigan, Peter Millar, Robert Zolg

DRAFT CHOICES
Rd.— Player	Ht./Wt.	Overall	Pos.	Last team
1— Jens Karlsson	6-3/200	18	F	Frolunda, Sweden
1— David Steckel	6-5/200	30	LW/C	Ohio State (CCHA)
2— Mike Cammalleri	5-8/175	49	C	U. of Michigan (CCHA)
2— Jaroslav Bednar	5-11/198	51	C	IFK, Finland
3— Henrik Juntunen	6-2/185	83	RW	Karpat, Finland
4— Richard Petiot	6-2/190	116	D	Camrose (AJHL)
5— Terry Denike	6-2/190	152	G	Weyburn (SJHL)
5— Tuukka Mantyla	5-9/176	153	D	Tappara, Finland
7— Cristobal Huet	6-0/190	214	G	Lugano, Switzerland
8— Mike Gavinet	6-3/180	237	D	Neb.-Omaha (CCHA)
9— Sebastien LaPlante	5-11/170	277	G	Rayside-Balfour (NOJHL)

MISCELLANEOUS DATA

Home ice (capacity)
STAPLES Center (18,118)
Address
555 N. Nash Street
El Segundo, CA 90245
Business phone
213-742-7100
Ticket information
888-546-4752
Website
www.lakings.com

Training site
El Segundo, CA
Club colors
Purple, silver, black and white
Radio affiliation
KSPN (1110 AM)
TV affiliation
FOX Sports Net

LOS ANGELES KINGS

No.	FORWARDS	Ht./Wt.	Place (BORN)	Date	NHL exp.	2000-01 clubs
	Jared Aulin (C)	5-11/175	Calgary	3-15-82	0	Kamloops (WHL)
	Jaroslav Bednar (C)	5-11/198	Prague, Czechoslovakia	11-8-76	0	HIFK Helsinki (Finland)
	Eric Belanger (LW/C)	6-0/177	Sherbrooke, Que.	12-16-77	1	Los Angeles, Lowell (AHL)
16	Ken Belanger (LW)	6-4/225	Sault Ste. Marie, Ont.	5-14-74	7	Boston, Providence (AHL)
9	Kelly Buchberger (RW)	6-2/210	Langenburg, Sask.	12-2-66	15	Los Angeles
	Mike Cammalleri (C)	5-8/175	Richmond Hill, Ont.	6-8-82	0	Univ. of Michigan (CCHA)
29	Brad Chartrand (RW)	5-11/191	Winnipeg	12-14-74	2	Lowell (AHL), Los Angeles
18	Adam Deadmarsh (RW)	6-0/195	Trail, B.C.	5-10-75	7	Colorado, Los Angeles
17	Nelson Emerson (RW)	5-10/180	Hamilton, Ont.	8-17-67	11	Los Angeles
	Alexander Frolov (LW)	6-3/191	Moscow, U.S.S.R.	6-19-82	0	
23	Steve Heinze (RW)	5-11/193	Lawrence, Mass.	1-30-70	10	Columbus, Buffalo
23	Craig Johnson (LW)	6-2/197	St. Paul, Minn.	3-8-72	7	Los Angeles
	Henrik Juntunen (RW)	6-2/185	Goteburg, Sweden	4-24-83	0	Karpat Oulu (Finland Jr.), Karpat (Finland)
	Jens Karlsson (RW/LW)	6-3/200	Goteburg, Sweden	11-7-82	0	Vastra Frolunda (Sweden)
11	Steve Kelly (C)	6-2/211	Vancouver	10-26-76	5	New Jersey, Los Angeles
22	Ian Laperriere (C/RW)	6-1/197	Montreal	1-19-74	8	Los Angeles
	Yanick Lehoux (C)	5-11/170	Montreal	4-8-82	0	Baie-Comeau (QMJHL)
21	Adam Mair (C)	6-2/194	Hamilton, Ont.	2-15-79	3	St. John's (AHL), Toronto, Los Angeles
27	Glen Murray (RW)	6-3/222	Halifax, Nova Scotia	11-1-72	10	Los Angeles
33	Ziggy Palffy (RW)	5-10/180	Skalica, Czechoslovakia	5-5-72	8	Los Angeles
27	Randy Robitaille (C)	5-11/198	Ottawa	10-12-75	5	Milwaukee (IHL), Nashville
	Andrei Shefer (LW)	6-1/180	Sverdlovsk, U.S.S.R.	7-26-81	0	SKA-2 St. Petersburg (Russian Div. III), Severstal Cherepovets (Russian)
21	Bryan Smolinski (C)	6-1/208	Toledo, Ohio	12-27-71	9	Los Angeles
	David Steckel (C)	6-5/200	Milwaukee.	3-15-82	0	Ohio State (CCHA)
15	Jozef Stumpel (C)	6-3/216	Nitra, Czechoslovakia	7-20-72	10	Slovan Bratislava (Slovakia), Los Angeles
21	Scott Thomas (LW)	6-2/200	Buffalo	1-18-70	3	Manitoba (IHL), Los Angeles
	DEFENSEMEN					
43	Philippe Boucher	6-3/221	St. Apollnaire, Que.	3-24-73	9	Manitoba (IHL), Los Angeles
12	Rich Brennan	6-2/205	Schenectady, N.Y.	11-26-72	4	Lowell (AHL), Los Angeles
	Joe Corvo	6-1/205	Oak Park, Ill.	6-20-77	1	Lowell (AHL)
	Brett Hauer	6-2/180	Richfield, Minn.	7-11-71	2	Manitoba (IHL)
8	Jere Karalahti	6-2/210	Helsinki, Finland	3-25-75	2	Los Angeles
	Andreas Lilja	6-3/220	Sweden	7-13-75	1	Lowell (AHL), Los Angeles
	Tuukka Mantyla	5-9/176	Tampere, Finland	5-25-81	0	Tappara Tampere (Finland)
3	Aaron Miller	6-3/205	Buffalo	8-11-71	8	Colorado, Los Angeles
44	Jaroslav Modry	6-2/219	Ceske-Budejovice, Czech.	2-27-71	7	Los Angeles
14	Mattias Norstrom	6-2/201	Stockholm, Sweden	1-2-72	8	Los Angeles
	Richard Petiot	6-2/190	Daysland, Alta.	8-20-82	0	Camrose (AJHL)
	Mike Pudlick	6-3/192	Fridley, Minn.	2-24-78	0	Lowell (AHL)
21	Mathieu Schneider	5-10/192	New York	6-12-69	13	Los Angeles
	Lubomir Visnovsky	5-10/172	Czechoslovakia	8-11-76	1	Los Angeles
	Tomas Zizka	6-1/198	Sternberk, Czechoslovakia	10-10-79	0	HC Continental Zlin (Czech Republic)
	GOALTENDERS					
34	Marcel Cousineau	5-9/180	Delson, Que.	4-30-73	4	Lowell (AHL)
	Terry Denike	6-2/190	Burlington, Ont.	4-16-81	0	Weyburn (SJHL)
35	Stephane Fiset	6-1/198	Montreal	6-17-70	12	Los Angeles, Lowell (AHL)
29	Felix Potvin	6-1/190	Anjou, Que.	6-23-71	10	Vancouver, Los Angeles
	Travis Scott	6-2/185	Ottawa	9-14-75	1	Lowell (AHL), Los Angeles
1	Jamie Storr	6-2/198	Brampton, Ont.	12-28-75	7	Los Angeles
	Alexey Volkov	6-1/185	Yekaterinburg, U.S.S.R.	3-15-80	0	Lowell (AHL), New Orleans (ECHL)

2000-01 REVIEW
INDIVIDUAL STATISTICS

SCORING

	Games	G	A	Pts.	PIM	+/-	PPG	SHG	Shots	Shooting Pct.
Zigmund Palffy	73	38	51	89	20	22	12	4	217	17.5
Luc Robitaille	82	37	51	88	66	10	16	1	235	15.7
Bryan Smolinski	78	27	32	59	40	10	5	3	183	14.8
Jozef Stumpel	63	16	39	55	14	20	9	0	95	16.8
Mathieu Schneider	73	16	35	51	56	0	7	1	183	8.7
Rob Blake*	54	17	32	49	69	-8	9	0	223	7.6
Glen Murray	64	18	21	39	32	9	3	0	138	13.0
Lubomir Visnovsky	81	7	32	39	36	16	3	0	105	6.7
Steven Reinprecht*	59	12	17	29	12	11	3	2	72	16.7
Nelson Emerson	78	11	11	22	54	-13	0	0	157	7.0

	Games	G	A	Pts.	PIM	+/-	PPG	SHG	Shots	Shooting Pct.
Eric Belanger	62	9	12	21	16	14	1	2	80	11.3
Kelly Buchberger	82	6	14	20	75	-10	0	0	66	9.1
Jaroslav Modry	63	4	15	19	48	16	0	0	72	5.6
Ian Laperriere	79	8	10	18	141	5	0	0	60	13.3
Mattias Norstrom	82	0	18	18	60	10	0	0	59	0.0
Bob Corkum*	58	4	6	10	18	-12	1	0	47	8.5
Craig Johnson	26	4	5	9	16	0	0	0	36	11.1
Jere Karalahti	56	2	7	9	38	8	0	0	26	7.7
Adam Deadmarsh*	18	4	2	6	4	3	0	0	40	10.0
Philippe Boucher	22	2	4	6	20	4	2	0	40	5.0
Stu Grimson	72	3	2	5	235	-2	0	0	26	11.5
Aaron Miller*	13	0	5	5	14	3	0	0	10	0.0
Scott Thomas	24	3	1	4	9	0	0	0	16	18.8
Tomas Vlasak	10	1	3	4	2	4	0	0	15	6.7
Jason Blake*	17	1	3	4	10	-8	0	0	27	3.7
Aki Berg*	47	0	4	4	43	3	0	0	31	0.0
Felix Potvin (goalie)*	23	0	3	3	2	0	0	0	0	0.0
Brad Chartrand	4	1	0	1	2	-2	0	0	6	16.7
Steve Kelly*	11	1	0	1	4	0	0	0	4	25.0
Marko Tuomainen	11	0	1	1	4	1	0	0	12	0.0
Travis Scott (goalie)	1	0	0	0	0	0	0	0	0	0.0
Andreas Lilja	2	0	0	0	4	-2	0	0	1	0.0
Richard Brennan	2	0	0	0	0	-3	0	0	1	0.0
Stephane Fiset (goalie)	7	0	0	0	2	0	0	0	0	0.0
Adam Mair*	10	0	0	0	6	-3	0	0	5	0.0
Steve Passmore (goalie)*	14	0	0	0	0	0	0	0	0	0.0
Jamie Storr (goalie)	45	0	0	0	4	0	0	0	0	0.0

GOALTENDING

	Games	Min.	Goals	SO	Avg.	W	L	T	ENG	Shots	Sv. Pct.
Felix Potvin*	23	1410	46	5	1.96	13	5	5	0	571	.919
Jamie Storr	45	2498	114	4	2.74	19	18	6	7	1131	.899
Steve Passmore*	14	718	37	1	3.09	3	8	1	2	310	.881
Stephane Fiset	7	318	19	0	3.58	3	0	1	0	129	.853
Travis Scott	1	25	3	0	7.20	0	0	0	0	10	.700

*Played with two or more NHL teams.

RESULTS

OCTOBER

6— At Washington ....W.....4-1
7— At Buffalo.........................L.....3-5
9— At Columbus ....W.....7-1
11— St. Louis ....T....*4-4
13— Boston ....W.....5-0
15— Phoenix ....L.....5-6
17— At Nashville ....T....*1-1
19— At St. Louis....................L.....1-7
21— At Dallas ....L.....3-4
23— At Anaheim ....W...*5-4
25— Anaheim ....W.....6-2
28— At Phoenix ....L.....1-3
31— At Columbus...................L.....1-4

NOVEMBER

2— At Atlanta ....W.....5-2
4— At New Jersey ....W.....2-1
5— At N.Y. Islanders.............W.....4-1
7— Phoenix ....T....*3-3
9— Vancouver ....W.....2-0
11— Detroit ....T....*2-2
16— N.Y. Islanders ....W.....5-1
18— Colorado.........................W.....6-4
23— New Jersey......................L.....1-6
25— At Pittsburgh ....T....*2-2
26— At Boston.........................T...*4-4
28— At N.Y. Rangers ....L.....6-7

DECEMBER

2— Minnesota ....W.....3-2
3— At Anaheim ....L.....0-4

7— Dallas ....W.....5-2
9— At Edmonton ....W.....4-2
10— At Vancouver..................W.....2-1
14— N.Y. Rangers..................T....*5-5
16— Tampa Bay ....L.....3-4
19— Atlanta ....L...*6-7
21— At Colorado.....................L.....2-5
22— At Minnesota ....L.....3-4
26— San Jose ....L.....1-2
28— At St. Louis ....W.....5-2
29— At Dallas ....W.....4-1
31— At Detroit ....L.....1-2

JANUARY

2— At Colorado ....L.....2-6
4— Florida ....L.....3-4
6— Calgary ....W.....5-0
11— Buffalo ....W.....3-2
13— St. Louis ....L.....2-4
16— At Ottawa ....W....*7-6
17— At Toronto ....W.....2-1
20— At Carolina ....W.....6-3
22— At Philadelphia.................L.....0-3
25— Calgary ....L.....0-3
27— Minnesota ....L.....1-4
30— Dallas ....W.....8-0

FEBRUARY

1— Nashville ....L.....4-6
6— Chicago ....T....*3-3
8— Carolina ....W.....4-2
10— Washington ....L.....3-4

12—Edmonton ....L.....3-6
14— At Dallas ....L.....2-4
16— At Minnesota ....W.....4-0
18— At Chicago ....L.....0-3
20— At Edmonton ....L.....0-5
22— At Calgary ....W.....2-0
24— Columbus ....W.....3-1
27— At Nashville ....W.....2-1

MARCH

1— At Chicago ....T....*2-2
3— Detroit ....W.....6-3
4— At Anaheim ....L.....0-4
6— Montreal ....W.....4-3
8— Nashville ....W.....4-1
10— Chicago ....T....*2-2
14— At San Jose ....W.....4-1
17— San Jose ....W....*1-0
19— Phoenix ....W.....6-2
21— Edmonton ....L.....0-7
24— Anaheim ....T....*3-3
26— San Jose ....T....*0-0
27— At San Jose ....L...*2-3
29— Columbus ....W.....3-0
31— Colorado ....W.....4-0

APRIL

2— Vancouver ....W.....3-1
3— At Phoenix ....T....*2-2
5— At Vancouver......................L...*2-3
7— At Calgary ....W.....3-2
*Denotes overtime game.

Wild Schedule
Home games shaded; D—Day game; *—All-Star Game at Los Angeles

October
SUN	MON	TUE	WED	THU	FRI	SAT
	1	2	3	4	5	6 D SJ
7 LA	8	9	10 BOS	11	12 CHI	13
14 EDM	15	16 SJ	17	18	19 STL	20
21	22	23	24 CAR	25	26	27 CAL
28	29	30 NAS	31 NAS			

November
SUN	MON	TUE	WED	THU	FRI	SAT
				1	2 COL	3
4 D EDM	5	6 NYR	7	8 BOS	9	10
11 D VAN	12	13 ATL	14 COL	15	16 DET	17
18 LA	19	20 PHO	21 SJ	22	23 D PHO	24
25 D DAL	26	27 VAN	28	29 FLA	30	

December
SUN	MON	TUE	WED	THU	FRI	SAT
						1
2 STL	3	4	5 CHI	6	7	8 D PHI
9	10 MON	11	12	13	14 PIT	15
16 COL	17	18 ANA	19	20	21	22 VAN
23 COL	24	25	26 DET	27	28 EDM	29 CAL
30	31 DET					

January
SUN	MON	TUE	WED	THU	FRI	SAT
		1	2 TB	3	4 NAS	5
6 BUF	7	8 MON	9	10 NAS	11 ANA	12
13 DAL	14	15 CAR	16	17	18 CBJ	19 OTT
20	21	22	23 ANA	24 LA	25	26 NJ
27	28 CAL	29	30 LA	31		

February
SUN	MON	TUE	WED	THU	FRI	SAT
					1	2 *
3	4	5 TOR	6 WAS	7	8 COL	9
10 D NYI	11	12 CBJ	13 DET	14	15	16
17	18	19	20	21	22	23
24	25	26	27 ANA	28		

March
SUN	MON	TUE	WED	THU	FRI	SAT
					1	2 VAN
3	4	5 NYR	6	7 STL	8 DAL	9
10 CBJ	11	12 OTT	13	14	15	16
17 D PHO	18 CAL	19	20 CBJ	21	22	23 D NYI
24	25	26 STL	27 ATL	28	29 CHI	30
31 D CHI						

April
SUN	MON	TUE	WED	THU	FRI	SAT
	1	2 EDM	3	4 CAL	5 VAN	6
7	8 SJ	9	10 DAL	11	12 PHO	13
14 D EDM	15	16	17	18	19	20

2001-02 SEASON
CLUB DIRECTORY

Owner
Bob Naegele Jr.
Chief executive officer
Jac Sperling
President
Tod Leiweke
Exec. vice president/general manager
Doug Risebrough
Chief amateur scout
Tom Thompson
Head coach
Jacques Lemaire

Assistant coaches
Mike Ramsey
Mario Tremblay
Dir. of hockey operations and legal affairs
Tom Lynn
V.p. of communications and broadcasting
Bill Robertson
Mgr. of media relations/team services
Brad Smith
Head athletic therapist
Don Fuller

DRAFT CHOICES

Rd.— Player	Ht./Wt.	Overall	Pos.	Last team
1— Mikko Koivu	6-2/183	6	C	TPS, Finland
2— Kyle Wanvig	6-2/210	36	RW	Red Deer (WHL)
3— Chris Heid	6-1/205	74	D	Spokane (WHL)
3— Stephane Veilleux	6-1/187	93	C	Val-d'Or (QMJHL)
4— Tony Virta	5-10/187	103	RW	TPS, Finland
7— Derek Boogaard	6-6/249	202	F	Prince George (WHL)
8— Jake Riddle	6-1/210	239	LW	Seattle (WHL)

MISCELLANEOUS DATA

Home ice (capacity)
Xcel Energy Center (18,064)
Office address
317 Washington Street
St. Paul, MN 55102
Business phone
651-602-6000
Ticket information
651-222-9453
Website
www.wild.com

Training site
Minneapolis
Club colors
Red, green, gold and wheat
Radio affiliation
WCCO (830 AM)
TV affiliation
FOX Sports Net (Cable), KMSP UPN
(Channel 9)

TRAINING CAMP ROSTER

No.	FORWARDS	Ht./Wt.	Place	Date	NHL exp.	2000-01 clubs
	Steve Aronson (RW)	6-1/205	Minnetonka, Minn.	7-15-78	0	Cleveland (IHL), Jackson (ECHL)
	Peter Bartos (LW)	6-0/185	Martin, Czechoslovakia	9-15-73	1	Cleveland (IHL), Minnesota
	Sylvain Blouin (RW)	6-2/222	Montreal	5-21-74	4	Minnesota
15	Andrew Brunette (LW)	6-1/210	Sudbury, Ont.	8-24-73	6	Atlanta
34	Jim Dowd (C)	6-1/190	Brick, N.J.	12-25-68	10	Minnesota
	Pascal Dupuis (LW)	6-0/196	Laval, Que.	4-7-79	1	Cleveland (IHL), Minnesota
	Marian Gaborik (LW)	6-1/183	Trencin, Czechoslovakia	2-14-82	1	Minnesota
44	Aaron Gavey (LW)	6-2/200	Sudbury, Ont.	2-22-74	6	Minnesota
43	Ravil Gusmanov (RW)	6-3/185	Naberezhnye Chelny, U.S.S.R.	7-22-72	1	Metal. Magnitogorsk (Russian)
14	Darby Hendrickson (LW)	6-1/195	Richfield, Minn.	8-28-72	8	Minnesota
17	Matt Johnson (LW)	6-5/235	Welland, Ont.	11-23-75	7	Minnesota
	Mikko Koivu (C)	6-2/183	Turku, Finland	3-12-83	0	TPS Turku (Finland Jr.), TPS Turku (Finland)
57	Antti Laaksonen (LW)	6-0/180	Tammela, Finland	10-3-73	3	Minnesota
21	Darryl Laplante (LW)	6-0/198	Calgary	3-28-77	3	Cleveland (IHL)
22	Pavel Patera (C)	6-1/172	Kladno, Czechoslovakia	9-6-71	2	Cleveland (IHL), Minnesota
39	Stacy Roest (C)	5-9/185	Lethbridge, Alta.	3-15-74	3	Minnesota
	Roman Simicek (C)	6-1/190	Ostrava, Czechoslovakia	11-4-71	1	Pittsburgh, Minnesota
	Cam Stewart (LW)	5-11/196	Kitchener, Ont.	9-18-71	6	Minnesota
	Maxim Sushinsky (LW)	5-8/158	U.S.S.R.	7-1-74	1	Avangard Omsk (Russian), Minnesota
	Stephane Veilleux (C)	6-1/187	Beaureville, Que.	11-16-81	0	Val-d'Or (QMJHL)
	Toni Virta (RW)	5-10/187	Hameenlinna, Finland	6-28-72	0	TPS Turku (Finland)
17	Wes Walz (C)	5-10/185	Calgary	5-15-70	7	Minnesota
	Kyle Wanvig (RW)	6-2/197	Calgary	1-29-81	0	Red Deer (WHL)
34	Sergei Zholtok (C)	6-1/191	Riga, U.S.S.R.	12-2-72	7	Montreal, Edmonton
	DEFENSEMEN					
	Ladislav Benysek	6-2/190	Olomouc, Czechoslavakia	3-24-75	2	Minnesota
5	Brad Bombardir	6-1/205	Powell River, B.C.	5-5-72	4	Minnesota
33	J.J. Daigneault	5-11/192	Montreal	10-12-65	16	Cleveland (IHL), Minnesota
	Chris Heid	6-1/205	Langley, B.C.	3-14-83	0	Spokane (WHL)
33	Filip Kuba	6-3/205	Ostrava, Czechoslovakia	12-29-76	3	Minnesota
23	Jason Marshall	6-2/200	Cranbrook, B.C.	2-22-71	8	Anaheim, Washington
	Mike Matteucci	6-3/225	Trail, B.C.	12-12-71	1	Cleveland (IHL), Minnesota
	Willie Mitchell	6-3/205	Port McNeill, B.C.	4-23-77	2	Albany (AHL), New Jersey, Minnesota
	Eric Reitz	6-0/192	Detroit	8-29-82	0	Barrie (OHL)
	Travis Roche	6-1/190	Whitecourt, Alta.	6-17-78	1	Univ. of North Dakota (WCHA), Minnesota
	Nick Schultz	6-0/187	Strasbourg, Sask.	8-25-82	0	Prince Albert (WHL), Cleveland (IHL)
	Lubomir Sekeras	6-0//176	Trencin, Czechoslovakia	11-18-68	1	Minnesota
42	Andy Sutton	6-6/245	Kingston, Ont.	3-10-75	3	Minnesota
	GOALTENDERS					
1	Martin Brochu	6-0/199	Anjou, Que.	3-10-73	1	Saint John (AHL)
35	Manny Fernandez	6-0/185	Etobicoke, Ont.	8-27-74	6	Minnesota
	Derek Gustafson	5-11/210	Gresham, Ore.	6-21-79	1	Jackson (ECHL), Cleveland (IHL),
29	Jamie McLennan	6-0/190	Edmonton	6-30-71	7	Minnesota
30	Dwayne Roloson	6-1/190	Simcoe, Ont.	10-12-69	4	Worcester (AHL)

2000-01 REVIEW
INDIVIDUAL STATISTICS

SCORING

	Games	G	A	Pts.	PIM	+/-	PPG	SHG	Shots	Shooting Pct.
Scott Pellerin*	58	11	28	39	45	6	2	2	117	9.4
Marian Gaborik	71	18	18	36	32	-6	6	0	179	10.1
Lubomir Sekeras	80	11	23	34	52	-8	4	0	102	10.8
Wes Walz	82	18	12	30	37	-8	0	7	152	11.8
Filip Kuba	75	9	21	30	28	-6	4	0	141	6.4
Darby Hendrickson	72	18	11	29	36	1	3	1	114	15.8
Jim Dowd	68	7	22	29	80	-6	0	0	92	7.6
Antti Laaksonen	82	12	16	28	24	-7	0	2	129	9.3
Stacy Roest	76	7	20	27	20	3	1	0	125	5.6
Aaron Gavey	75	10	14	24	52	-8	1	0	100	10.0
Sergei Krivokrasov	54	7	15	22	20	-1	2	0	107	6.5
Sean O'Donnell*	63	4	12	16	128	-2	1	0	58	6.9
Brad Bombardir	70	0	15	15	42	-6	0	0	81	0.0
Cameron Stewart	54	4	9	13	18	-3	0	1	61	6.6
Maxim Sushinsky	30	7	4	11	29	-7	3	0	62	11.3

	Games	G	A	Pts.	PIM	+/-	PPG	SHG	Shots	Shooting Pct.
Jeff Nielsen	59	3	8	11	4	-16	1	0	82	3.7
Willie Mitchell*	17	1	7	8	11	4	0	0	16	6.3
Andy Sutton	69	3	4	7	131	-11	2	0	64	4.7
Ladislav Benysek	71	2	5	7	38	-11	1	0	48	4.2
Peter Bartos	13	4	2	6	6	2	1	0	18	22.2
Roman Simicek*	28	2	4	6	21	-4	2	0	14	14.3
Sylvain Blouin	41	3	2	5	117	-5	0	0	37	8.1
Curtis Leschyshyn*	54	2	3	5	19	-2	1	0	43	4.7
Pavel Patera	20	1	3	4	4	-8	0	0	14	7.1
Steve McKenna*	20	1	1	2	19	0	0	0	12	8.3
Matt Johnson	50	1	1	2	137	-6	0	0	21	4.8
Kai Nurminen	2	1	0	1	2	-1	0	0	1	100.0
Pascal Dupuis	4	1	0	1	4	0	1	0	8	12.5
Jamie McLennan (goalie)	38	0	1	1	4	0	0	0	0	0.0
J.J. Daigneault	1	0	0	0	2	-1	0	0	0	0.0
Travis Roche	1	0	0	0	0	0	0	0	0	0.0
Zac Bierk (goalie)	1	0	0	0	2	0	0	0	0	0.0
Chris Armstrong	3	0	0	0	0	-3	0	0	4	0.0
Christian Matte	3	0	0	0	2	0	0	0	8	0.0
Mike Matteucci	3	0	0	0	2	-2	0	0	3	0.0
Derek Gustafson (goalie)	4	0	0	0	0	0	0	0	0	0.0
Brian Bonin	7	0	0	0	0	-3	0	0	7	0.0
Manny Fernandez (goalie)	42	0	0	0	6	0	0	0	0	0.0

MINNESOTA WILD

GOALTENDING

	Games	Min.	Goals	SO	Avg.	W	L	T	ENG	Shots	Sv. Pct.
Manny Fernandez	42	2461	92	4	2.24	19	17	4	1	1147	.920
Derek Gustafson	4	239	10	0	2.51	1	3	0	1	97	.897
Jamie McLennan	38	2230	98	2	2.64	5	23	9	2	1032	.905
Zac Bierk	1	60	6	0	6.00	0	1	0	0	27	.778

*Played with two or more NHL teams.

RESULTS

OCTOBER
6— At Anaheim ....L......1-3
7— At Phoenix ....L......1-4
11—Philadelphia ....T....*3-3
13—At St. Louis.....................L......0-2
15—Edmonton ....L......3-5
18—Tampa Bay ....W......6-5
20— San Jose........................L......1-3
22—Florida ....T....*0-0
24—At Montreal....................T....*2-2
25—At Toronto........................L......1-6
27—Calgary ....W......3-1
29— Chicago ....L......2-3

NOVEMBER
3— At Edmonton ....L......0-3
5— At Calgary ....W....*3-2
7— At Colorado ....L......0-2
8— Calgary ....L......0-1
10—At Chicago ....W......5-2
12—Edmonton ....L....*4-5
15—N.Y. Rangers ....L......2-3
17—At Buffalo.........................L......1-3
18—At Boston ....W......6-1
22—Calgary ....T....*1-1
24—Chicago ....W......2-0
26—Vancouver ....W......4-2
28—At San Jose ....L......1-4
30—At Phoenix......................L......0-2

DECEMBER
2— At Los Angeles ....L......2-3
7— At Chicago......................W......4-2

8— Anahcim ....L....*0-1
10—Nashville.........................L......1-2
13—Carolina ....T...*1-1
14—At Washington ....L......1-2
17—Dallas ....W......6-0
20— Ottawa ....T...*2-2
22—Los Angeles ....W......4-3
27—At Detroit ....W......5-3
29—Phoenix ....T...*2-2
31—Anahcim ....W......3-2

JANUARY
3— Atlanta ....T...*1-1
5— Detroit ....W....*3-2
6— At St. Louis.....................L......1-5
10—Washington ....W......3-0
12—Colorado ....L......0-5
14—At N.Y. Rangers ....L......2-4
15—At Columbus ....L......0-3
17—Columbus ....W....*3-2
19—N.Y. Islanders ....W......3-2
21—New Jersey ....L......2-4
24—At Anaheim ....W......5-0
27—At Los Angeles ....W......4-1
30—At Vancouver ....L....*2-3

FEBRUARY
6— At Tampa Bay ....W......4-2
7— At Florida ....L......1-2
9— At Dallas ....W......2-1
11—Pittsburgh ....W......4-2
14—At Pittsburgh ....L......1-2
16—Los Angeles ....L......0-4

18—San Jose ....W......3-1
21—At Dallas ....L......2-6
23—At Colorado ....L......1-4
24—At Nashville ....L......1-2
26—Vancouver ....L......2-5

MARCH
1— At Calgary.................T....*1-1
2— At Edmonton ....L......1-3
4— At Vancouver................W....*4-3
6— St. Louis ....T...*3-3
8— At New Jersey ....L......2-6
9— At N.Y. Islanders............W......4-1
11—Detroit ....L....*2-3
14—St. Louis ....L....*0-1
15—At Philadelphia..............L......0-3
18—At Colorado ....L......3-4
19—Dallas............................L......1-4
21—Nashville ....T....*0-0
22—At Detroit ....L......2-4
25—Vancouver ....T....*2-2
28—Phoenix ....L......0-2
31—At Nashville ....L......1-4

APRIL
2— At San Jose ....L......2-4
4— At Edmonton ....T....*2-2
6— Columbus.....................W......3-2
8— Colorado.......................L......2-4
*Denotes overtime game.

MONTREAL CANADIENS
EASTERN CONFERENCE/NORTHEAST DIVISION

Canadiens' Schedule
Home games shaded; D—Day game; *—All-Star Game at Los Angeles

October

SUN	MON	TUE	WED	THU	FRI	SAT
	1	2	3	4 OTT	5	6 TOR
7	8	9 ANA	10	11	12 CBJ	13 NJ
14	15 NYR	16	17	18	19 WAS	20 BUF
21	22	23	24	25	26 BUF	27 PHI
28	29	30 EDM	31			

November

SUN	MON	TUE	WED	THU	FRI	SAT
				1 VAN	2	3 CAL
4	5	6 COL	7	8 NAS	9	10 NYI
11 NYR	12	13 BOS	14	15	16	17 FLA
18	19	20 BOS	21	22 ATL	23	24 WAS
25	26	27 ATL	28	29 NYI	30	

December

SUN	MON	TUE	WED	THU	FRI	SAT
						1 NYR
2	3 CHI	4	5 NJ	6	7	8 PHO
9	10 MIN	11	12 ATL	13 PHI	14	15 TOR
16	17 TB	18	19 PIT	20 BOS	21	22 LA
23	24	25	26 BUF	27	28 STL	29 NYI
30	31					

January

SUN	MON	TUE	WED	THU	FRI	SAT
		1	2	3 VAN	4	5 CAL
6 EDM	7	8 MIN	9	10 NYI	11	12 TOR
13	14 PHI	15	16 WAS	17 CAR	18	19 TB
20	21 D FLA	22	23 WAS	24	25	26 D OTT
27 D SJ	28	29	30 BOS	31		

February

SUN	MON	TUE	WED	THU	FRI	SAT
					1	2 *
3	4	5 NJ	6	7 PIT	8	9 D TOR
10	11 DET	12	13	14	15	16
17	18	19	20	21	22	23
24	25	26 OTT	27 CHI	28		

March

SUN	MON	TUE	WED	THU	FRI	SAT
					1	2 CAR
3	4 ATL	5	6 BOS	7	8 BUF	9 TOR
10	11 NYR	12	13	14 DAL	15	16 CAR
17	18 CAR	19	20 FLA	21	22 TB	23 NAS
24	25	26 FLA	27	28 TB	29	30 PIT
31						

April

SUN	MON	TUE	WED	THU	FRI	SAT
	1 PIT	2	3	4 PHI	5	6 CBJ
7 OTT	8	9 OTT	10	11	12 NJ	13 BUF
14	15	16	17	18	19	20

2001-02 SEASON
CLUB DIRECTORY

President
Pierre Boivin
General manager
Andre Savard
Assistant general manager
Martin Madden
Vice president, finance and admin.
Fred Steer
Exec. vice president & g.m. events
Aldo Giampaolo
Advertising, sponsorship & publications
Francois-Xavier Seigneur
Coach
Michel Therrien
Assistant coaches
Guy Carbonneau
Rick Green
Roland Melanson
Pro scout
Pierre Mondou
Supervisor of prospect development
Clement Jodoin
Professional scout
Doug Robinson
Chief scout
Pierre Dorion
Scouts
Neil Armstrong, Bred Bandel, Elmer Benning, Frederick Corey, Hannu Laine, Mats Naslund, Gerry O'Flaherty, Antonin Routa, Claude Ruel, Richard Scammell, Nikolai Vakourov
Director of team services
Michele Lapointe
Chief surgeon
Dr. David Mulder
Club physician
Dr. Vincent Lacroix
Senior medical advisor
Dr. D.G. Kinnear
Orthopedist
Dr. Eric Lenczner
Ophthalmologist
Dr. John Little
Dentist
Dr. Pierre Desautels
Athletic trainer
Gaetan Lefebvre
Athletic therapist
Graham Rynbend
Assistant to the athletic therapist
Jon Armano
Strength and conditioning coach
Stephane Dube
Equipment manager
Pierre Gervais
Assistants to the equipment manager
Robert Boulanger
Pierre Ouellette
Video coordinator
Mario Leblanc

DRAFT CHOICES

Rd.— Player	Ht./Wt.	Overall	Pos.	Last team
1— Michael Komisarek	6-4/225	7	D	U. of Michigan (CCHA)
1— Alexander Perezhogin ..	5-11/185	25	C	OMSK, Russia
2— Duncan Milroy	6-0/180	37	RW	Swift Current (WHL)
3— Tomas Plekanec	5-10/189	71	LW	Kladno, Czechoslovakia
4— Martti Jarventie............	5-11/185	109	D	TPS, Finland
6— Eric Himelfarb.............	5-9/161	171	C	Sarnia (OHL)
7— Andrew Archer.............	6-4/194	203	D	Guelph (OHL)
9— Viktor Ujcik..................	5-10/194	266	F	Slavia Praha, Czech.

MISCELLANEOUS DATA

Home ice (capacity)
Molson Centre (21,273)
Address
1260 rue de la Gauchetiere Ouest
Montreal, Que. H3B 5E8
Business phone
514-932-2582
Ticket information
514-932-2582
Website
www.canadiens.com
Training site
Montreal
Club colors
Red, white and blue
Radio affiliation
CJAD (800 AM), CKAC (730 AM)
TV affiliation
TQS (Cable), RDS (Cable), CBST, TSN

TRAINING CAMP ROSTER

No.	FORWARDS	Ht./Wt.	Place	BORN Date	NHL exp.	2000-01 clubs
	Arron Asham (RW/C)	5-11/195	Portage-La-Prairie, Man.	4-13-78	3	Quebec (AHL), Montreal
	Jozef Balej (RW)	5-11/170	Ilava, Czechoslovakia	2-22-82	0	Portland (WHL)
	Francis Belanger (LW)	6-2/216	Bellefeuille, Que.	1-15-78	1	Philadelphia (AHL), Montreal, Quebec (AHL)
17	Benoit Brunet (LW)	5-11/198	Montreal	8-24-68	12	Montreal
8	Jan Bulis (C)	6-1/201	Pardubice, Czechoslovakia	3-18-78	4	Washington, Portland (AHL), Montreal
	Alexander Buturlin (LW) ..	5-11/183	Moscow, U.S.S.R.	9-3-81	0	Sarnia (OHL)
	Eric Chouinard (C)	6-2/195	Atlanta	7-8-80	1	Quebec (AHL), Montreal
10	Andreas Dackell (RW)	5-10/195	Gavle, Sweden	12-29-72	5	Ottawa
63	Craig Darby (C)	6-3/200	Oneida, N.Y.	9-26-72	6	Montreal
43	Xavier Delisle (RW)	5-11/200	Quebec City	5-24-77	2	Montreal, Quebec (AHL)
39	Benoit Gratton (C)	5-11/194	Montreal	12-28-76	4	Saint John (AHL), Calgary
	Marcel Hossa (C)	6-1/200	Ilava, Czechoslovakia	10-12-81	0	Portland (WHL)
39	Joe Juneau (LW)	6-0/199	Pont-Rouge, Que.	1-5-68	10	Phoenix
15	Chad Kilger (C)	6-4/215	Cornwall, Ont.	11-27-76	6	Edmonton, Montreal
11	Saku Koivu (C)	5-10/181	Turku, Finland	11-23-74	6	Montreal
26	Eric Landry (C)	5-11/185	Gatineau, Que.	1-20-75	3	Quebec (AHL), Montreal
	Jerome Marois (LW)	6-0/188	Quebec	1-27-81	0	Rouyn-Noranda (QMJHL)
	Duncan Milroy (RW)	6-0/180	Edmonton	2-8-83	0	Swift Current (WHL)
29	Gino Odjick (LW)	6-3/227	Maniwaki, Que.	9-7-70	11	Philadelphia, Montreal
	Alexander Perezhogin (C)	5-11/185	Ust-Kamenogorsk, U.S.S.R.	8-10-83	0	Avangard (Russian Div. II)
44	Yanic Perreault (C)	5-10/185	Sherbrooke, Que.	4-4-71	8	Toronto
32	Oleg Petrov (RW)	5-8/175	Moscow, U.S.S.R.	4-18-71	6	Montreal
	Tomas Plekanec (LW)	5-10/189	Kladno, Czechoslovakia	10-31-82	0	HC Kladno (Czech Republic)
37	Patrick Poulin (C)	6-1/216	Vanier, Que.	4-23-73	10	Montreal
	Mike Ribeiro (C)	5-11/150	Montreal	2-10-80	2	Quebec (AHL), Montreal
26	Martin Rucinsky (LW)......	6-1/205	Most, Czechoslovakia	3-11-71	10	Montreal
49	Brian Savage (RW)	6-2/192	Sudbury, Ont.	2-24-71	8	Montreal
	Marc-Andre Thinel (RW) .	5-11/158	St. Jerome, Que.	3-24-81	0	Victoriaville (QMJHL)
	Jason Ward (RW/C)........	6-2/193	Chapleau, Ont.	1-16-79	2	Quebec (AHL), Montreal
44	Richard Zednik (RW)	6-0/199	Bystrica, Czechoslovakia	1-6-76	6	Washington, Montreal
	DEFENSEMEN					
51	Francis Bouillon	5-8/189	New York	10-17-75	2	Montreal, Quebec (AHL)
43	Patrice Brisebois.............	6-1/203	Montreal	1-27-71	11	Montreal
	Mathieu Descoteaux	6-3/220	Pierreville, Que.	9-23-77	1	Quebec (AHL), Montreal
28	Karl Dykhuis	6-3/214	Sept-Iles, Que.	7-8-72	9	Montreal
	Miroslav Guren	6-2/213	Uherske Hradiste, Czech.	9-24-76	2	Quebec (AHL)
	Ron Hainsey	6-2/187	Bolton, Conn.	3-24-81	0	Mass.-Lowell (Hockey East), Quebec (AHL)
	Martti Jarventie	5-11/185	Tampere, Finland	4-4-76	0	TPS Turku (Finland)
	Mike Komisarek	6-4/225	Islip Terrace, N.Y.	1-19-82	0	Univ. of Michigan (CCHA)
24	Christian Laflamme..........	6-1/210	St. Charles, Que.	11-24-76	5	Montreal
	Andrei Markov	6-0/185	Voskresensk, U.S.S.R.	12-20-78	1	Montreal, Quebec (AHL)
5	Stephane Quintal	6-3/234	Boucherville, Que.	10-22-68	13	Chicago
	Gennady Razin	6-4/200	Kharkov, U.S.S.R.	2-3-78	0	Quebec (AHL)
52	Craig Rivet......................	6-2/207	North Bay, Ont.	9-13-74	7	Montreal
	Stephane Robidas............	5-11/180	Sherbrooke, Que.	3-3-73	2	Montreal
2	Darryl Shannon	6-2/208	Barrie, Ont.	6-21-68	13	Montreal, Quebec (AHL)
44	Sheldon Souray	6-4/230	Elk Point, Alta.	7-13-76	4	Montreal
3	Patrick Traverse	6-4/200	Montreal	3-14-74	4	Anaheim, Boston, Montreal
	GOALTENDERS					
	Mathieu Garon	G-2/182	Chandler, Que.	1-9-78	1	Montreal, Quebec (AHL)
31	Jeff Hackett.....................	6-1/198	London, Ont.	6-1-68	12	Montreal
	Vadim Tarasov	5-11/158	Ust-Kamenogorsk, U.S.S.R.	12-31-76	0	Metallurg Novokuznetsk (Russian)
60	Jose Theodore	5-11/185	Laval, Que.	9-13-76	6	Quebec (AHL), Montreal

MONTREAL CANADIENS

2000-01 REVIEW
INDIVIDUAL STATISTICS

SCORING

	Games	G	A	Pts.	PIM	+/-	PPG	SHG	Shots	Shooting Pct.
Saku Koivu	54	17	30	47	40	2	7	0	113	15.0
Oleg Petrov..............................	81	17	30	47	24	-11	4	2	158	10.8
Brian Savage............................	62	21	24	45	26	-13	12	0	172	12.2
Martin Rucinsky........................	57	16	22	38	66	-5	5	1	141	11.3
Patrice Brisebois.......................	77	15	21	36	28	-31	11	0	178	8.4
Trevor Linden*..........................	57	12	21	33	52	-2	6	0	96	12.5
Craig Darby..............................	78	12	16	28	16	-17	0	1	97	12.4
Chad Kilger*............................	43	9	16	25	34	-1	1	1	75	12.0
Eric Weinrich*..........................	60	6	19	25	34	-1	2	0	81	7.4
Dainius Zubrus*........................	49	12	12	24	30	-7	3	0	70	17.1
Andrei Markov..........................	63	6	17	23	18	-6	2	0	82	7.3
Patrick Poulin...........................	52	9	11	20	13	1	0	0	65	13.8
Jim Campbell............................	57	9	11	20	53	-3	6	0	81	11.1

	Games	G	A	Pts.	PIM	+/-	PPG	SHG	Shots	Shooting Pct.
Karl Dykhuis	67	8	9	17	44	9	2	0	66	12.1
Benoit Brunet	35	3	11	14	12	-4	0	0	61	4.9
Stephane Robidas	65	6	6	12	14	0	1	0	77	7.8
Eric Landry	51	4	7	11	43	-9	2	0	54	7.4
Sheldon Souray	52	3	8	11	95	-11	0	0	103	2.9
Sergei Zholtok*	32	1	10	11	8	-15	0	0	78	1.3
Richard Zednik*	12	3	6	9	10	-2	1	0	23	13.0
Juha Lind	47	3	4	7	4	-4	0	0	36	8.3
Francis Bouillon	29	0	6	6	26	3	0	0	24	0.0
Xavier Delisle	14	3	2	5	6	-5	1	0	15	20.0
Patrick Traverse*	19	2	3	5	10	-8	0	0	16	12.5
Arron Asham	46	2	3	5	59	-9	0	0	32	6.3
Jan Bulis*	12	0	5	5	0	-1	0	0	20	0.0
Eric Chouinard	13	1	3	4	0	1	1	0	11	9.1
P.J. Stock*	20	1	2	3	32	-1	0	0	9	11.1
Craig Rivet	26	1	2	3	36	-8	0	0	22	4.5
Andrei Bashkirov	18	0	3	3	0	-2	0	0	22	0.0
Christian Laflamme	39	0	3	3	42	-11	0	0	16	0.0
Matthieu Descoteaux	5	1	1	2	4	-2	1	0	6	16.7
Johan Witehall*	26	1	1	2	6	0	0	0	18	5.6
Gino Odjick*	13	1	0	1	44	0	0	0	11	9.1
Jose Theodore (goalie)	59	1	0	1	6	0	0	0	1	100.0
Darryl Shannon	7	0	1	1	6	-4	0	0	6	0.0
Jeff Hackett (goalie)	19	0	1	1	0	0	0	0	0	0.0
Barry Richter	2	0	0	0	2	-1	0	0	0	0.0
Eric Fichaud (goalie)	2	0	0	0	0	0	0	0	0	0.0
Mike Ribeiro	2	0	0	0	2	0	0	0	3	0.0
Enrico Ciccone	3	0	0	0	14	-1	0	0	0	0.0
Eric Bertrand	3	0	0	0	0	0	0	0	0	0.0
Matt Higgins	6	0	0	0	2	-2	0	0	3	0.0
Francis Belanger	10	0	0	0	29	-3	0	0	2	0.0
Mathieu Garon (goalie)	11	0	0	0	0	0	0	0	0	0.0
Jason Ward	12	0	0	0	12	3	0	0	4	0.0

GOALTENDING

	Games	Min.	Goals	SO	Avg.	W	L	T	ENG	Shots	Sv. Pct.
Mathieu Garon	11	589	24	2	2.44	4	5	1	1	233	.897
Jose Theodore	59	3298	141	2	2.57	20	29	5	6	1546	.909
Jeff Hackett	19	998	54	0	3.25	4	10	2	2	477	.887
Eric Fichaud	2	62	4	0	3.87	0	2	0	2	32	.875

*Played with two or more NHL teams.

RESULTS

OCTOBER

6— At New Jersey ....L.....4-8
7— At Toronto ....L.....0-2
10— Edmonton ....W.....5-2
11— At N.Y. Rangers ....L.....1-3
14— Chicago ....W...*5-4
17— Buffalo ....W.....4-3
19— At Philadelphia................T....*3-3
21— Carolina ....W.....5-2
24— Minnesota ....T....*2-2
27— At N.Y. Islanders ....L.....1-2
28— N.Y. Islanders ....L.....1-2

NOVEMBER

1— Detroit ....L.....2-4
3— At Buffalo ....L.....4-5
4— N.Y. Rangers ....L.....2-5
8— At Florida ....W.....4-2
10— At Tampa Bay ....L.....1-3
11— At Dallas ....L.....0-2
14— Tampa Bay ....L.....0-1
17— At Washington ....L.....3-4
18— Toronto ....L.....1-6
21— Florida ....L.....1-4
23— At Atlanta ....W.....6-0
25— Buffalo ....L.....3-5
27— Atlanta ....W.....3-2
29— At Edmonton ....W.....3-2
30— At Vancouver ....W.....4-3

DECEMBER

2— At Calgary ....T....*1-1
5— Buffalo ....L.....2-3

8— At Ottawa...........................L.....0-1
9— Ottawa ....L.....2-4
13— Calgary ....L.....1-3
15— At New Jersey ....L.....1-2
16— Pittsburgh ....T...*4-4
18— Columbus ....L.....0-2
21— Nashville ....W.....4-2
23— Toronto ....L.....2-5
27— At Vancouver ....L.....2-3
30— At Edmonton ....L...*2-3
31— At Calgary ....L...*4-5

JANUARY

2— At N.Y. Islanders...............W.....3-0
5— At Pittsburgh ....W.....4-3
6— At Ottawa ....L.....3-4
10— Boston ....L.....1-2
12— At Atlanta ....W.....3-0
13— Phoenix ....W.....5-2
16— Carolina ....L...*2-3
18— Tampa Bay ....W.....3-1
20— N.Y. Rangers ....T...*2-2
23— St. Louis ....L.....2-5
24— At Pittsburgh ....L.....1-3
27— Washington ....W.....4-2
28— Ottawa ....W.....4-1
31— At N.Y. Rangers ....L.....2-4

FEBRUARY

1— At Boston ....W.....3-0
6— New Jersey ....L.....0-4
10— N.Y. Islanders ....W.....5-3
11— At Buffalo ....W.....4-3

13— Colorado ....L...*2-3
17— Washington ....L.....3-6
18— At Ottawa ....L.....0-4
21— Vancouver ....L.....1-2
23— At Washington ....L.....1-3
24— At Toronto ....L.....1-5
27— At Philadelphia ....W.....3-2
28— Pittsburgh ....W.....4-2

MARCH

3— Philadelphia ....W.....3-1
6— At Los Angeles ....L.....3-4
7— At Anaheim ....L.....2-4
10— At Phoenix ....T...*3-3
12— At San Jose ....L.....0-3
14— At Carolina ....W.....6-3
17— Boston ....L.....2-3
20— Florida ....T...*3-3
22— At Boston ....L...*2-3
24— Atlanta ....L.....2-3
26— At Carolina ....W.....4-2
28— At Florida ....T...*2-2
29— At Tampa Bay ....W.....6-2
31— Toronto ....W.....4-1

APRIL

2— At Boston ....L...*2-3
5— Philadelphia ....W...*3-2
7— New Jersey ....L.....0-2
*Denotes overtime game.

NASHVILLE PREDATORS
WESTERN CONFERENCE/CENTRAL DIVISION

Predators' Schedule
Home games shaded; D—Day game; *—All-Star Game at Los Angeles

October

SUN	MON	TUE	WED	THU	FRI	SAT
	1	2	3	4	5 DAL	6 STL
7	8	9	10	11 CAL	12	13 EDM
14	15	16 BUF	17	18 CHI	19	20 BOS
21	22 EDM	23 VAN	24	25 CAL	26	27 DET
28	29	30 MIN	31 MIN			

November

SUN	MON	TUE	WED	THU	FRI	SAT
				1	2 DAL	3 DAL
4	5	6	7	8 MON	9	10 OTT
11	12	13 BUF	14	15	16 ATL	17 CBJ
18	19	20 DET	21 CHI	22	23 PIT	24
25	26	27 SJ	28	29 PHO	30	

December

SUN	MON	TUE	WED	THU	FRI	SAT
					1	D LA
2 ANA	3	4	5	6 OTT	7	8 EDM
9	10	11 LA	12 NYR	13	14	15 CHI
16	17	18	19	20 VAN	21	22 SJ
23	24	25	26 TB	27	28	29 DET
30 STL	31					

January

SUN	MON	TUE	WED	THU	FRI	SAT
		1 D COL	2	3 NJ	4 MIN	5
6 D	7	8 TOR	9	10 MIN	11	12 ANA
13 CBJ	14 ANA	15 LA	16	17 TOR	18	19 CBJ
20	21 PHO	22	23 CAR	24 PHI	25	26 ANA
27	28 VAN	29	30 COL	31		

February

SUN	MON	TUE	WED	THU	FRI	SAT
					1	2 *
3	4	5	6 DAL	7	8 WAS	9 CBJ
10	11	12 FLA	13	14	15	16
17	18	19	20	21	22	23
24	25	26 SJ	27	28 EDM		

March

SUN	MON	TUE	WED	THU	FRI	SAT
					1	2 CAL
3	4	5 SJ	6	7 LA	8	9 FLA
10 TB	11	12 VAN	13	14	15 PHO	16
17 D COL	18	19 STL	20	21 NJ	22	23 MON
24	25 DET	26	27 CHI	28 DET	29	30 STL
31						

April

SUN	MON	TUE	WED	THU	FRI	SAT
	1 COL	2	3 CHI	4 CBJ	5	6 CAL
7	8	9 STL	10	11 NYI	12	13
14 D PHO	15	16	17	18	19	20

2001-02 SEASON
CLUB DIRECTORY

Owner, chairman and governor
Craig Leipold
President, COO and alternate governor
Jack Diller
Exec. v.p./g.m. and alternate governor
David Poile
Assistant general manager
Ray Shero
Communications manager
Ken Anderson
Communications coordinator
Greg Harvey
Head coach
Barry Trotz
Assistant coaches
Paul Gardner
Brent Peterson
Chief amateur scout
Craig Channell

Director of player personnel
Paul Fenton
Strength and conditioning coach
Mark Nemish
Goaltending coach
Mitch Korn
Head athletic trainer
Dan Redmond
Equipment manager
Pete Rogers
Assistant equipment manager
Chris Scoppetto
Massage therapist
Anthony Garrett
Video coach
Robert Bouchard

DRAFT CHOICES

Rd.— Player	Ht./Wt.	Overall	Pos.	Last team
1— Dan Hamhuis	6-0/195	12	D	Prince George (WHL)
2— Timofei Shiskanov	6-0/183	33	F	Spartak Jr., Russia
2— Tomas Slovak	6-1/191	42	D	Kosice, Slovakia
3— Denis Platonov	6-1/194	75		Saratov, Russia
3— Oliver Setzinger	6-0/180	76	C	Ilves, Finland
4— Jordin Tootoo	5-8/185	98	RW	Brandon (WHL)
6— Anton Lavrentiev	6-4/183	178	D	Kazan, Russia
8— Gustav Grasberg	5-11/183	240	C	Mora Jr., Sweden
9— Mikko Lehtonen	6-1/194	271	D	Karpat, Finland

MISCELLANEOUS DATA

Home ice (capacity)
Gaylord Entertainment Center (17,113)
Address
501 Broadway
Nashville, TN 37203
Business phone
615-770-2300
Ticket information
615-770-7825
Website
www.nashvillepredators.com

Training site
Nashville
Club colors
Blue, gold, silver, steel and orange
Radio affiliation
WTN (99.7 FM)
TV affiliation
FOX Sports Net

TRAINING CAMP ROSTER

No.	FORWARDS	Ht./Wt.	Place	BORN Date	NHL exp.	2000-01 clubs
	Jonas Andersson (RW) ...	6-2/189	Lidingo, Sweden	2-24-81	0	Milwaukee (IHL)
	Denis Arkhipov (RW/LW).	6-3/195	Kazan, U.S.S.R.	5-19-79	1	Milwaukee (IHL), Nashville
	Bill Bowler (C)	5-9/180	Toronto	9-25-74	1	Syracuse (AHL), Columbus
	Marian Cisar (RW)..........	6-0/192	Bratislava, Czechoslovakia	2-25-78	2	Milwaukee (IHL), Nashville
	Greg Classen (C)	6-1/194	Aylsham, Saskatoon	8-24-77	1	Nashville, Milwaukee (IHL)
	Martin Erat (LW)	6-0/197	Trebic, Czechoslovakia	8-28-81	0	Saskatoon (WHL), Red Deer (WHL)
21	Tom Fitzgerald (RW)........	6-0/196	Billerica, Mass.	8-28-68	13	Nashville
40	David Gosselin (C).........	6-1/197	Levis, Que.	6-22-77	1	Milwaukee (IHL)
32	Stu Grimson (LW)	6-5/239	Kamloops, B.C.	5-20-65	13	Los Angeles
	Scott Hartnell (RW)	6-2/192	Regina, Sask.	4-18-82	1	Nashville
22	Greg Johnson (C)..........	5-10/202	Thunder Bay, Ont.	3-16-71	8	Nashville
10	Patric Kjellberg (LW)	6-2/208	Trelleborg, Sweden	6-17-69	4	Nashville
11	David Legwand (C).........	6-2/185	Detroit	8-17-80	3	Nashville
	Bryan Lundbohm (C).......	5-11/190	Roseau, Minn.	8-24-77	0	Univ. of North Dakota (WCHA)
18	Mark Mowers (C)	5-11/184	Whitesboro, N.Y.	2-16-74	2	Milwaukee (IHL)
16	Vladimir Orszagh (RW)....	5-11/173	Banska Bystrica, Czech.	5-24-77	3	Djurgarden Stockholm (Sweden)
	Denis Platonov (C/LW)	6-1/194	U.S.S.R.	11-6-81	0	Saratov (Russian Div. II)
7	Cliff Ronning (C).............	5-8/165	Vancouver	10-1-65	15	Nashville
23	Yves Sarault (LW)..........	6-1/183	Valleyfield, Que.	12-23-72	7	Orlando (IHL), Atlanta
	Oliver Setzinger (C)	6-0/180	Horn, Austria	7-11-83	0	Ilves Tampere (Finland)
	Timofei Shiskanov (RW)..	6-0/183	Moscow, U.S.S.R.	6-10-83	0	Spartak (Russian Jr.)
40	Jeremy Stevenson (LW) ..	6-2/217	San Bernardino, Calif.	7-28-74	5	Milwaukee (IHL), Nashville
50	Petr Sykora (C).............	6-2/180	Pardubice, Czechoslovakia	12-21-78	1	
	Jordan Tootoo (RW)........	5-8/185	Churchill, Man.	2-2-83	0	Brandon (WHL)
24	Scott Walker (RW)..........	5-10/190	Cambridge, Ont.	7-19-73	7	Nashville
43	Vitali Yachmenev (RW)....	5-9/190	Chelyabinsk, U.S.S.R.	1-8-75	6	Nashville
	DEFENSEMEN					
26	Bubba Berenzweig	6-2/218	Arlington Heights, Ill.	8-8-77	2	Milwaukee (IHL), Nashville
38	Alexandre Boikov.............	6-0/198	Chelyabinsk, U.S.S.R.	2-7-75	2	CSKA (Russian), Milwaukee (IHL), Nashville
	Mikhail Chernov..............	6-2/196	Prokopjevsk, U.S.S.R.	11-11-78	0	Philadelphia (AHL)
44	Mark Eaton	6-2/205	Wilmington, Del.	5-6-77	2	Milwaukee (IHL), Nashville
	Dan Hamhuis..................	6-0/195	Smithers, B.C.	12-13-82	0	Prince George (WHL)
23	Bill Houlder...................	6-2/211	Thunder Bay, Ont.	3-11-67	14	Nashville
32	Cale Hulse.....................	6-3/215	Edmonton	11-10-73	6	Nashville
	Andrew Hutchinson	6-2/186	Evanston, Ill.	3-24-80	0	Michigan State (CCHA)
41	Richard Lintner................	6-3/214	Trencin, Czechoslovakia	11-15-77	2	Nashville
	Marc Moro......................	6-1/215	Toronto	7-17-77	3	Milwaukee (IHL), Nashville
14	Bert Robertsson	6-3/210	Sodertalje, Sweden	6-30-74	4	Houston (IHL), New York Rangers, Hartford (AHL), Milwaukee (IHL)
3	Karlis Skrastins..............	6-1/205	Riga, U.S.S.R.	7-9-74	3	Nashville
46	Pavel Skrbek..................	6-3/213	Kladno, Czechoslovakia	8-9-78	2	Milwaukee (IHL), Nashville
	Tomas Slovak	6-1/191	Kosice, Czechoslovakia	4-5-83	0	HC Kosice (Slovakia)
44	Kimmo Timonen	5-10/196	Kuopio, Finland	3-18-75	3	Nashville
	Alexei Vasiliev	6-1/192	Yaroslavl, U.S.S.R.	9-1-77	1	Milwaukee (IHL)
	GOALTENDERS					
1	Mike Dunham	6-3/200	Johnson City, N.Y.	6-1-72	5	Nashville
	Brian Finley....................	6-2/180	Sault Ste. Marie, Ont.	7-3-81	0	Barrie (OHL), Brampton (OHL)
	Jan Lasak	6-0/204	Zvolen, Czechoslovakia	4-10-79	0	Milwaukee (IHL)
30	Chris Mason	6-0/189	Red Deer, Alta.	4-20-76	2	Nashville, Milwaukee (IHL)
29	Tomas Vokoun................	6-3/183	Karlovy Vary, Czechoslovakia	7-2-76	4	Nashville

2000-01 REVIEW
INDIVIDUAL STATISTICS

SCORING

	Games	G	A	Pts.	PIM	+/-	PPG	SHG	Shots	Shooting Pct.
Cliff Ronning....................................	80	19	43	62	28	4	6	0	237	8.0
Scott Walker.....................................	74	25	29	54	66	-2	9	3	159	15.7
Patric Kjellberg	81	14	31	45	12	-2	5	0	139	10.1
David Legwand	81	13	28	41	38	1	3	0	172	7.6
Vitali Yachmenev	78	15	19	34	10	-5	4	1	123	12.2
Greg Johnson...................................	82	15	17	32	46	-6	1	0	97	15.5
Marian Cisar	60	12	15	27	45	-7	5	0	97	12.4
Randy Robitaille	62	9	17	26	12	-11	5	0	121	7.4
Kimmo Timonen	82	12	13	25	50	-6	6	0	151	7.9
Drake Berehowsky*	66	6	18	24	100	-9	3	0	94	6.4
Tom Fitzgerald	82	9	9	18	71	-5	0	2	135	6.7

	Games	G	A	Pts.	PIM	+/-	PPG	SHG	Shots	Shooting Pct.
Bill Houlder	81	4	12	16	40	-7	0	1	78	5.1
Scott Hartnell	75	2	14	16	48	-8	0	0	92	2.2
Robert Valicevic	60	8	6	14	26	-2	1	0	62	12.9
Denis Arkhipov	40	6	7	13	4	0	0	0	42	14.3
Karlis Skrastins	82	1	11	12	30	-12	0	0	66	1.5
Mark Eaton	34	3	8	11	14	7	1	0	32	9.4
Richard Lintner	50	3	5	8	22	2	1	0	81	3.7
Cale Hulse	82	1	7	8	128	-5	0	0	93	1.1
Greg Classen	27	2	4	6	14	-4	1	0	18	11.1
Sebastien Bordeleau	14	2	3	5	14	-4	0	0	20	10.0
Ville Peltonen	23	3	1	4	2	-7	0	0	38	7.9
Mike Watt	18	1	1	2	8	-2	0	0	18	5.6
Jeremy Stevenson	8	1	0	1	39	-1	0	0	6	16.7
Sean Haggerty	3	0	1	1	0	1	0	0	2	0.0
Chris Mason (goalie)	1	0	0	0	0	0	0	0	0	0.0
Rory Fitzpatrick	2	0	0	0	2	-2	0	0	0	0.0
Andy Berenzweig	5	0	0	0	0	0	0	0	0	0.0
Craig Millar*	5	0	0	0	6	1	0	0	2	0.0
Pavel Skrbek	5	0	0	0	4	1	0	0	2	0.0
Marc Moro	6	0	0	0	12	1	0	0	1	0.0
Alexandre Boikov	8	0	0	0	13	-1	0	0	3	0.0
Brantt Myhres*	20	0	0	0	28	-5	0	0	1	0.0
Tomas Vokoun (goalie)	37	0	0	0	2	0	0	0	0	0.0
Mike Dunham (goalie)	48	0	0	0	2	0	0	0	0	0.0

GOALTENDING

	Games	Min.	Goals	SO	Avg.	W	L	T	ENG	Shots	Sv. Pct.
Chris Mason	1	59	2	0	2.03	0	1	0	0	20	.900
Mike Dunham	48	2810	107	4	2.28	21	21	4	2	1381	.923
Tomas Vokoun	37	2088	85	2	2.44	13	17	5	4	940	.910

*Played with two or more NHL teams.

RESULTS

OCTOBER
6— At Pittsburgh .... W 3-1
7— Pittsburgh .... L 1-3
13— Washington .... W 3-1
14— Carolina .... W 2-1
17— Los Angeles .... T *1-1
19— At Detroit .... W ... *2-1
21— San Jose .... L 3-5
24— Vancouver .... T *4-4
25— At Colorado .... L *1-2
27— Florida .... T *3-3
31— St. Louis .... L 2-4

NOVEMBER
2— At Philadelphia .... W 3-1
4— Anaheim .... T *3-3
7— At N.Y. Islanders .... L 1-2
8— At New Jersey .... W 4-3
11— At Boston .... T .. *2-2
15— At Atlanta .... L 0-1
16— Columbus .... L 1-5
18— Detroit .... W 3-2
20— At Detroit .... L 3-6
22— Dallas .... L 0-1
24— St. Louis .... L 0-4
26— At Carolina .... W 7-4
28— Calgary .... W 6-1
30— At Chicago .... W 3-0

DECEMBER
1— Chicago .... L 1-2
4— At Vancouver .... L 3-6
6— At Edmonton .... L 0-4
7— At Calgary .... L 0-3
10— At Minnesota .... W 2-1
12— Philadelphia .... T *2-2
14— Edmonton .... L 2-6
16— Chicago .... L 0-3
20— At Toronto .... W 3-1
21— At Montreal .... L 2-4
23— At N.Y. Rangers .... W ... *3-2
26— Colorado .... W 5-2
28— Anaheim .... T ... *2-2
29— At Colorado .... L 1-3

JANUARY
1— Vancouver .... L 2-5
4— At St. Louis .... W 4-2
6— Buffalo .... L 0-2
8— At Vancouver .... L 1-2
10— At Edmonton .... W 5-2
11— At Calgary .... L 1-2
13— At San Jose .... W 3-3
16— Edmonton .... L 1-2
17— At Dallas .... L ... *3-4
19— Boston .... W ... *1-0
21— St. Louis .... W 3-1
23— Atlanta .... W 4-3
24— At Detroit .... L 3-4
27— Colorado .... L 1-5
29— At Phoenix .... W 5-2
31— At Anaheim .... W 3-0

FEBRUARY
1— At Los Angeles .... W 6-4
8— Columbus .... W 3-1

10— At Columbus .... L 2-3
13— Dallas .... L 1-2
16— San Jose .... L 0-2
18— Tampa Bay .... W 3-2
20— Detroit .... T *3-3
21— At Washington .... L 1-2
24— Minnesota .... W 2-1
27— Los Angeles .... L 1-2

MARCH
1— Columbus .... L 2-5
4— N.Y. Rangers .... W 5-2
6— At Phoenix .... L 1-5
8— At Los Angeles .... L 1-4
10— At San Jose .... W 3-0
11— At Anaheim .... L ... *0-1
15— At Chicago .... L 2-3
17— Phoenix .... W 4-1
19— At Columbus .... W 2-1
21— At Minnesota .... T ... *0-0
22— At Chicago .... W ... *2-1
24— Ottawa .... L 0-4
29— Phoenix .... W ... *4-3
31— Minnesota .... W 4-1

APRIL
4— At Dallas .... L 1-5
5— Calgary .... W 4-0
7— At St. Louis .... L 0-1
*Denotes overtime game.

NEW JERSEY DEVILS
EASTERN CONFERENCE/ATLANTIC DIVISION

Devils' Schedule
Home games shaded; D—Day game; *—All-Star Game at Los Angeles

October

SUN	MON	TUE	WED	THU	FRI	SAT
	1	2	3	4	5	6 WAS
7	8	9	10	11 NYI	12	13 MON
14	15	16	17 NYR	18 SJ	19	20 OTT
21	22	23 OTT	24	25	26	27 BUF
28	29	30 BOS	31			

November

SUN	MON	TUE	WED	THU	FRI	SAT
				1 PHO	2	3 D BOS
4	5	6	7 ATL	8	9 TOR	10 TOR
11	12	13 PIT	14	15 BOS	16	17 D
18 D COL	19	20 PHI	21	22	23 TB	24 FLA
25	26	27 PIT	28	29	30 DET	

December

SUN	MON	TUE	WED	THU	FRI	SAT
						1 DET
2	3	4 TB	5 MON	6	7	8 D WAS
9	10 CBJ	11	12 NYI	13	14 FLA	15 OTT
16	17	18	19 NYR	20 EDM	21	22 D OTT
23	24	25	26 PIT	27	28	29 VAN
30 EDM	31					

January

SUN	MON	TUE	WED	THU	FRI	SAT
		1 STL	2	3 NAS	4	5 CAR
6	7 LA	8	9 CAL	10 PHI	11	12 BUF
13	14	15 TB	16	17 NYR	18	19 D CAR
20 TB	21	22 FLA	23 ATL	24	25	26 MIN
27	28	29 NYI	30 CHI	31		

February

SUN	MON	TUE	WED	THU	FRI	SAT
					1	2 *
3	4	5 MON	6	7 ATL	8	9 D PIT
10 BUF	11	12 BUF	13	14	15	16
17	18	19	20	21	22	23
24	25	26 NYR	27 PHI	28		

March

SUN	MON	TUE	WED	THU	FRI	SAT
					1 TOR	2
3	4 COL	5 PHO	6	7	8 ANA	9
10 DAL	11	12	13 NYI	14	15	16 D NYR
17 VAN	18	19	20 CHI	21 NAS	22	23 D CAR
24	25 FLA	26	27 PIT	28	29 WAS	30 TOR
31						

April

SUN	MON	TUE	WED	THU	FRI	SAT
	1 NYI	2	3 CAR	4	5 ATL	6
7 D BOS	8	9	10 PHI	11	12 MON	13 WAS
14	15	16	17	18	19	20

2001-02 SEASON
CLUB DIRECTORY

CEO/president and general manager
Louis A. Lamoriello
Head coach
Larry Robinson
Assistant coaches
Viacheslav Fetisov
Kurt Kleinendorst
Goaltending coach
Jacques Caron
Medical trainer
Bill Murray

Strength & conditioning coordinator
Michael Vasalani
Equipment manager
Rich Matthews
Assistant equipment managers
Alex Abasto
Lou Centanni
Director, public relations
Jeff Altstadter
Director, information & publications
Mike Levine

DRAFT CHOICES

Rd.— Player	Ht./Wt.	Overall	Pos.	Last team
1— Adrian Foster	6-1/200	28	LW	Saskatoon (WHL)
2— Igor Pohanka	6-3/185	44	C	Prince Albert (WHL)
2— Thomas Pihlman	6-2/205	48	F	Jyvaskyla, Finland
2— Victor Uchevatov	6-4/205	60	D	Yaroslavl, Russia
3— Robin Leblanc	6-1/177	67	RW	Baie-Comeau (QMJHL)
3— Brandon Nolan	6-0/177	72	C/LW	Oshawa (OHL)
4— Andrei Posnov		128		Krylja, Russia
5— Andreas Salomonsson	6-0/185	163		Djurgarden, Sweden
6— James Massen	6-1/218	194	RW	Sioux Falls (USHL)
8— Aaron Voros	6-3/178	229	C	Victoria (BCJHL)
8— Evgeny Gamalej		257	D	Dyn. Moscow 2, Russia

MISCELLANEOUS DATA

Home ice (capacity)
Continental Airlines Arena (19,040)
Address
P.O. Box 504
50 Route 120 North
East Rutherford, N.J. 07073
Business phone
201-935-6050
Ticket information
201-935-3900

Website
www.newjerseydevils.com
Training site
West Orange, NJ
Club colors
Red, black and white
Radio affiliation
WABC (770 AM)
TV affiliation
FOX Sports Net New York

No.	FORWARDS	Ht./Wt.	Place	BORN Date	NHL exp.	2000-01 clubs
25	Jason Arnott (C)	6-4/225	Collingwood, Ont.	10-11-74	8	New Jersey
	Christian Berglund (C)	5-11/185	Orebro, Sweden	3-12-80	0	
	Jiri Bicek (LW)	5-10/195	Kosice, Czechoslovakia	12-3-78	1	Albany (AHL), New Jersey
18	Sergei Brylin (C)	5-10/190	Moscow, U.S.S.R.	1-13-74	7	New Jersey
14	Sylvain Cloutier (C)	6-0/195	Mont-Laurier, Que.	2-13-74	1	Albany (AHL)
	Pierre Dagenais (LW)	6-4/210	Blainville, Que.	3-4-78	1	Albany (AHL), New Jersey
26	Patrik Elias (LW)	6-1/200	Trebic, Czechoslovakia	4-13-76	6	New Jersey
	Adrian Foster (LW)	6-1/200	Lethbridge, Alta.	1-15-82	0	Saskatoon (WHL)
	Brian Gionta (RW)	5-7/160	Rochester, N.Y.	1-18-79	0	Boston College (Hockey East)
23	Scott Gomez (C)	5-11/200	Anchorage, Alaska	12-23-79	2	New Jersey
	Stanislav Gron (C)	6-2/210	Bratislava, Czechoslovakia	10-28-78	1	Albany (AHL), New Jersey
16	Bobby Holik (C)	6-4/230	Jihlava, Czechoslovakia	1-1-71	11	New Jersey
	Mike Jefferson (C)	5-9/190	Brampton, Ont.	10-21-80	1	Albany (AHL), New Jersey
	Robin Leblanc (RW)	6-1/177	Chur, Switzerland	1-11-83	0	Baie-Comeau (QMJHL)
11	John Madden (C)	5-11/195	Barrie, Ont.	5-4-73	3	New Jersey
21	Randy McKay (RW)	6-2/210	Montreal	1-25-67	13	New Jersey
33	Jim McKenzie (RW)	6-4/227	Gull Lake, Sask.	11-3-69	12	New Jersey
12	Sergei Nemchinov (C)	6-0/205	Moscow, U.S.S.R.	1-14-64	10	New Jersey
	Brandon Nolan (C/LW)	6-0/177	Sault Ste. Marie, Ont.	7-18-83	0	Oshawa (OHL)
20	Jay Pandolfo (LW)	6-1/190	Winchester, Mass.	12-27-74	5	New Jersey
	Thomas Pihlman (LW)	6-2/205	Espoo, Finland	11-13-82	0	JyP Jyvaskyla (Finland)
	Igor Pohanka (C)	6-3/185	Plestany, Czechoslovakia	7-5-83	0	Prince Albert (WHL)
	Andrei Posnov (C)		U.S.S.R.	11-19-81	0	Krylja Sovetov Moscow (Russian Div. 1)
	Andreas Salomonsson	6-1/185	Sweden	12-19-73	0	Djurgarden Stockholm (Sweden)
23	Turner Stevenson (RW)	6-3/226	Port Alberni, B.C.	5-18-72	9	New Jersey
17	Petr Sykora (RW)	6-0/190	Plzen, Czechoslovakia	11-19-76	6	New Jersey
42	Ed Ward (RW)	6-3/220	Edmonton	11-10-69	8	New Jersey, Albany (AHL)
	DEFENSEMEN					
5	Tommy Albelin	6-1/194	Stockholm, Sweden	5-21-64	14	Calgary
	Josef Boumedienne	6-1/190	Stockholm, Sweden	1-12-78	0	Albany (AHL)
	Mike Commodore	6-4/225	Fort Saskatchewan, Alta.	11-4-79	1	Albany (AHL), New Jersey
3	Ken Daneyko	6-1/215	Windsor, Ont.	4-17-64	18	New Jersey
	Sascha Goc	6-2/220	Schwenningen, W. Germany	4-17-79	1	Albany (AHL), New Jersey
	Andre Lakos	6-6/230	Vienna, Austria	7-29-79	0	Albany (AHL)
27	Scott Niedermayer	6-1/200	Edmonton	8-31-73	10	New Jersey
28	Brian Rafalski	5-9/200	Dearborn, Mich.	9-28-73	2	New Jersey
	Henrik Rehnberg	6-2/195	Grava, Sweden	7-20-77	0	Albany (AHL)
4	Scott Stevens	6-1/215	Kitchener, Ont.	4-1-64	19	New Jersey
	Victor Uchevatov	6-4/205	Angarsk, U.S.S.R.	2-10-83	0	Torpedo Yaroslavl (Russian)
5	Colin White	6-4/210	New Glasgow, Nova Scotia	12-12-77	2	New Jersey
	GOALTENDERS					
	Ari Ahonen	6-2/170	Jyvaskyla, Finland	2-6-81	0	HIFK Helsinki (Finland Jr.)
30	Martin Brodeur	6-2/205	Montreal	5-6-72	9	New Jersey
	J.F. Damphousse	6-0/175	St. Alexis-des-Monts, Que.	7-21-79	0	Albany (AHL)
	Frederic Henry	5-11/180	Cap Rouge, Que.	8-9-77	0	Albany (AHL)

NEW JERSEY DEVILS

2000-01 REVIEW
INDIVIDUAL STATISTICS

SCORING

	Games	G	A	Pts.	PIM	+/-	PPG	SHG	Shots	Shooting Pct.
Patrik Elias	82	40	56	96	51	45	8	3	220	18.2
Alexander Mogilny	75	43	40	83	43	10	12	0	240	17.9
Petr Sykora	73	35	46	81	32	36	9	2	249	14.1
Scott Gomez	76	14	49	63	46	-1	2	0	155	9.0
Jason Arnott	54	21	34	55	75	23	8	0	138	15.2
Sergei Brylin	75	23	29	52	24	25	3	1	130	17.7
Brian Rafalski	78	9	43	52	26	36	6	0	142	6.3
Bobby Holik	80	15	35	50	97	19	3	0	206	7.3
Randy McKay	77	23	20	43	50	3	12	0	120	19.2
John Madden	80	23	15	38	12	24	0	3	163	14.1
Scott Niedermayer	57	6	29	35	22	14	1	0	87	6.9
Scott Stevens	81	9	22	31	71	40	3	0	171	5.3
Sergei Nemchinov	65	8	22	30	16	11	1	0	70	11.4
Turner Stevenson	69	8	18	26	97	11	2	0	92	8.7
Colin White	82	1	19	20	155	32	0	0	114	0.9
Jay Pandolfo	63	4	12	16	16	3	0	0	57	7.0
Ken Sutton	53	1	7	8	37	9	0	0	35	2.9

	Games	G	A	Pts.	PIM	+/-	PPG	SHG	Shots	Shooting Pct.
Pierre Dagenais	9	3	2	5	6	1	1	0	20	15.0
Mike Commodore	20	1	4	5	14	5	0	0	11	9.1
Bob Corkum*	17	3	1	4	4	4	0	0	19	15.8
Steve Kelly*	24	2	2	4	21	0	0	0	18	11.1
Jim McKenzie	53	2	2	4	119	0	0	0	32	6.3
Ken Daneyko	77	0	4	4	87	8	0	0	50	0.0
Willie Mitchell*	16	0	2	2	29	0	0	0	14	0.0
Jiri Bicek	5	1	0	1	4	0	0	0	10	10.0
Ed Ward	4	0	1	1	6	2	0	0	4	0.0
Sean O'Donnell*	17	0	1	1	33	2	0	0	9	0.0
Martin Brodeur (goalie)	72	0	1	1	14	0	0	0	2	0.0
Stanislav Gron	1	0	0	0	0	1	0	0	2	0.0
Mike Jefferson	2	0	0	0	6	0	0	0	3	0.0
John Vanbiesbrouck (goalie)*	4	0	0	0	0	0	0	0	0	0.0
Chris Terreri (goalie)*	10	0	0	0	0	0	0	0	0	0.0
Sasha Goc	11	0	0	0	4	7	0	0	7	0.0

GOALTENDING

	Games	Min.	Goals	SO	Avg.	W	L	T	ENG	Shots	Sv. Pct.
John Vanbiesbrouck*	4	240	6	1	1.50	4	0	0	0	93	.935
Martin Brodeur	72	4297	166	9	2.32	42	17	11	2	1762	.906
Chris Terreri*	10	453	21	0	2.78	2	5	1	0	167	.874

*Played with two or more NHL teams.

RESULTS

OCTOBER
6— Montreal .... W 8-4
13— At Ottawa .... L 1-3
14— Anaheim .... W 4-2
17— At Atlanta .... T *3-3
19— At Washington .... L 2-5
21— Tampa Bay .... W 7-2
25— At Florida .... W 2-1
27— At Carolina .... T *3-3
28— At Pittsburgh .... W 9-0
30— Florida .... W ... *6-5

NOVEMBER
1— Philadelphia .... T *1-1
2— At Toronto .... L 3-5
4— Los Angeles .... L 1-2
8— Nashville .... L 3-4
10— Pittsburgh .... L 2-4
11— Buffalo .... L 0-4
14— San Jose .... L 2-3
16— At Boston .... W ... *3-2
18— Carolina .... W ... *3-2
22— At Anaheim .... W 5-2
23— At Los Angeles .... W 6-1
25— At San Jose .... W 3-2
29— N.Y. Rangers .... W 5-2

DECEMBER
1— N.Y. Islanders .... T *0-0
3— At N.Y. Islanders .... T *1-1
5— Colorado .... W 6-1
7— At Buffalo .... L 2-5

JANUARY
9— Washington .... L 2-3
11— Atlanta .... W 4-0
15— Montreal .... W 2-1
16— At Philadelphia .... L 3-6
20— Dallas .... W 4-1
22— At Florida .... W 2-0
23— At Tampa Bay .... W 5-1
27— Columbus .... T *2-2
29— Washington .... W 4-2
31— At Columbus .... W 6-3

JANUARY
2— Philadelphia .... T *1-1
4— N.Y. Islanders .... W 4-2
6— At N.Y. Rangers .... T *5-5
10— Phoenix .... W 5-1
13— Toronto .... T *4-4
16— Boston .... L 4-5
18— At Philadelphia .... W 7-1
20— Atlanta .... W 3-2
21— At Minnesota .... W 4-2
24— At Dallas .... W 4-1
25— At St. Louis .... L *3-4
27— At Boston .... T *3-4
30— Detroit .... W 3-1
31— At N.Y. Islanders .... L 2-3

FEBRUARY
6— At Montreal .... W 4-0
8— At Ottawa .... T *4-4
10— At Pittsburgh .... L *4-5
11— At N.Y. Rangers .... T *1-1

FEBRUARY
14— Ottawa .... L 2-3
16— Pittsburgh .... T *4-4
17— At Buffalo .... L 1-5
19— At Toronto .... W 2-0
22— Buffalo .... L 0-1
23— At Carolina .... L 2-3
26— Florida .... W 5-3
27— At N.Y. Islanders .... W 4-1

MARCH
2— Carolina .... W 7-3
4— Tampa Bay .... W 6-0
6— Ottawa .... W ... *3-2
8— Minnesota .... W 6-2
10— At Philadelphia .... W 3-2
13— At Colorado .... W 6-3
14— At Phoenix .... W 3-2
17— At Edmonton .... W ... *6-5
19— At Calgary .... W 4-2
21— N.Y. Rangers .... W 4-0
23— Vancouver .... W 4-0
25— Pittsburgh .... L 2-4
27— At Tampa Bay .... W 7-1
28— At Atlanta .... W 4-2
31— N.Y. Rangers .... L 3-4

APRIL
2— Chicago .... W 4-3
3— At Washington .... W 6-4
6— Boston .... W 5-2
7— At Montreal .... W 2-0

*Denotes overtime game.

NEW YORK ISLANDERS
EASTERN CONFERENCE/ATLANTIC DIVISION

Islanders' Schedule
Home games shaded; D—Day game; *—All-Star Game at Los Angeles

October

SUN	MON	TUE	WED	THU	FRI	SAT
	1	2	3	4	5 TB	6 FLA
7	8	9	10 PIT	11 NJ	12	13 DET
14	15	16	17 CAR	18 CAR	19	20 SJ
21	22	23	24	25	26 CAR	27
28 D DAL	29	30 FLA	31			

November

SUN	MON	TUE	WED	THU	FRI	SAT
				1	2 DET	3 PHI
4	5	6 TB	7	8 NYR	9	10 MON
11	12	13	14 PIT	15	16 COL	17 PHO
18	19 DAL	20	21 COL	22	23 TOR	24 ANA
25	26	27 WAS	28	29 MON	30	

December

SUN	MON	TUE	WED	THU	FRI	SAT
						1 BUF
2	3	4 PHI	5	6 PHI	7 CHI	8
9	10	11 OTT	12 NJ	13	14	15 FLA
16	17	18 EDM	19	20	21 NYR	22 BOS
23	24	25	26	27 OTT	28	29 MON
30	31					

January

SUN	MON	TUE	WED	THU	FRI	SAT
		1 WAS	D 2	3 PIT	4	5 LA
6 ATL	7	8 CAL	9	10 MON	11	12 BOS
13	14	15 CAL	16	17 SJ	18	19 D LA
20	21	22 NYR	23 PIT	24	25	26 TB
27	28	29 NJ	30 NYR	31		

February

SUN	MON	TUE	WED	THU	FRI	SAT
					1	2 *
3	4	5 FLA	6 STL	7 TOR	8	9
10 D MIN	11	12 PHI	13	14	15	16
17	18	19	20	21	22	23
24	25	26 BOS	27	28		

March

SUN	MON	TUE	WED	THU	FRI	SAT
					1 ATL	2 ATL
3	4 PIT	5	6	7 BUF	8 CBJ	9
10 D ATL	11	12 BUF	13 NJ	14	15	16 OTT
17	18	19 TOR	20	21 VAN	22	23 D MIN
24	25 NYR	26	27 OTT	28 TOR	29	30 WAS
31						

April

SUN	MON	TUE	WED	THU	FRI	SAT
	1 NJ	2	3 BUF	4 BOS	5	6 WAS
7	8 CAR	9	10	11 NAS	12 TB	13
14 D PHI	15	16	17	18	19	20

2001-02 SEASON
CLUB DIRECTORY

Owner and governor
Charles B. Wang
Owner and alternate governor
Sanjay Kumar
Sr. v.p. of operations and alt. governor
Michael J. Picker
Sr. v.p. of sales and marketing
Paul Lancey
Alternate governor and general counsel
Roy E. Reichbach
Alternate governor
William M. Skehan
General manager
Mike Milbury
Assistant g.m./dir. of player personnel
Gordie Clark
Assistant g.m./dir. of hockey operations
Mike Santos, Esq.
Manager, hockey administration
Joanne Holewa
Head coach
Peter Laviolette
Assistant coaches
Greg Cronin, Jacques Laperriere, Kelly Miller
Head amateur scout
Tony Feltrin
Western scout
Earl Ingarfield
Director of European scouting
Anders Kallur
Director of pro scouting
Ken Morrow
Assistant director of pro scouting
Kevin Maxwell
Scouting staff
Jim Madigan, Mario Saraceno, Karel Pavlik, Doug Gibson, Brian Hunter, Harri Rindell, Harkie Singh, Nikolai Ladygin
Video coordinator
Bob Smith
Director of medical services
Dr. Elliot Pellman
Internist
Dr. Clifford Cooper

Team orthopedists
Dr. Elliott Hershman, Dr. Kenneth Montgomery, Dr. David Gazzaniga
Team dentists
Dr. Bruce Michnick, Dr. Jan Sherman
Head trainer
Rich Campbell
Strength & conditioning coach
Sean Donellan
Head equipment manager
Joe McMahon
Equipment assistant
Bill Nichols
Senior vice president/CFO
Arthur McCarthy
Vice president of administration
Janet L. Kask
Vice president of communications
Chris Botta
V.p. of corporate and community relations
Bill Kain
Director of corporate relations
Bob Nystrom
Director of merchandise
Chris DiPierri
Director of ticket sales
Larry Fitzpatrick
Director of game operations
Tim Beach
Controller
Ralph Sellitti
Creative services manager
Mauricio Acosta
Manager of multimedia and team services
Kerry Gwydir
Manager of game operations and events
Brad Preston
Internet and publications coordinator
Nancy Koenig
Special events coordinator
Kevin Schwab
Media relations coordinator
Jamie Fabos
Community relations coordinator
Heather Cozzens

DRAFT CHOICES

Rd.— Player	Ht./Wt.	Overall	Pos.	Last team
4— Cory Stillman	6-2/204	101	C	Kingston (OHL)
5— Dusan Salficky	6-1/185	132	G	Plzen, Czechoslovakia
6— Andy Chiodo	5-11/201	166	G	Toronto (OHL)
7— Jan Hulub	6-3/185	197	D	Liberec Jr., Czech.
8— Mike Bray	6-3/208	228	RW	Quebec (QMJHL)
9— Bryan Perez	6-1/198	260	F	Des Moines (USHL)
9— Roman Kuhtinov	6-1/207	280	D	Novokuznetsk, Russia
9— Juha-Pekka Ketola	6-1/178	287	C	Lukko, Finland

MISCELLANEOUS DATA

Home ice (capacity)
Nassau Veterans Memorial Coliseum (16,297)
Address
Uniondale, NY 11553
Business phone
516-501-6700
Ticket information
1-800-882-4753
Website
www.newyorkislanders.com

Training site
Syosset, NY
Club colors
Blue and orange
Radio affiliation
WJWR (620 AM)
TV affiliation
FOX Sports New York

NEW YORK ISLANDERS

No.	FORWARDS	Ht./Wt.	Place (BORN)	Date	NHL exp.	2000-01 clubs
17	Shawn Bates (C)	5-11/190	Melrose, Mass.	4-3-75	4	Boston, Providence (AHL)
11	Jason Blake (C)	5-10/180	Moorhead, Minn.	9-2-73	3	Los Angeles, Lowell (AHL), New York Islanders
	Brian Collins (C)	6-1/190	Worcester, Mass.	9-13-80	0	Boston University (Hockey East)
21	Mariusz Czerkawski (RW)	6-0/199	Radomski, Poland	4-13-72	8	New York Islanders
	Trent Hunter (C/RW)	6-3/194	Red Deer, Alta.	7-5-80	0	Springfield (AHL)
15	Brad Isbister (RW)	6-4/228	Edmonton	5-7-77	4	New York Islanders
	Alexandre Kharitonov	5-8/150	U.S.S.R.	3-30-76	1	Tampa Bay
	Juraj Kolnik (RW)	5-10/182	Nitra, Czechoslovakia	11-13-80	1	Lowell (AHL), Springfield (AHL), New York Islanders
28	Jason Krog (C)	5-11/191	Fernie, B.C.	10-9-75	2	Lowell (AHL), Springfield (AHL), New York Islanders
13	Oleg Kvasha (C)	6-5/216	Moscow, U.S.S.R.	7-26-78	3	New York Islanders
13	Claude Lapointe (C)	5-9/183	Lachine, Que.	10-11-68	11	New York Islanders
10	Mats Lindgren (C)	6-2/202	Skelleftea, Sweden	10-1-74	5	New York Islanders
	Justin Mapletoft (C)	6-1/180	Lloydminster, Sask.	6-11-81	0	Red Deer (WHL)
	Radek Martinek (RW/LW)	6-1/200	Havlicko Brod, Czech.	8-31-76	0	HC Ceske Budejovice (Czechoslovakia)
32	Petr Mika (C)	6-4/195	Prague, Czechoslovakia	2-12-79	1	Lowell (AHL), Springfield (AHL)
	Kristofer Ottoson (RW)	5-10/187	Sweden	1-9-76	0	Djurgarden Stockholm (Sweden)
21	Mark Parrish (RW)	5-11/191	Edina, Minn.	2-2-77	3	New York Islanders
27	Michael Peca (C)	5-11/181	Toronto	3-26-74	7	
38	Dave Scatchard (C)	6-2/220	Hinton, Alta.	2-20-76	4	New York Islanders
	Cory Stillman (C)	6-2/204	Lindsay, Ont.	3-2-83	0	Kingston (OHL)
	Raffi Torres (LW)	6-0/207	Toronto	10-8-81	0	Brampton (OHL)
	Dimitri Upper (C)	6-0/176	U.S.S.R.	8-27-78	0	Tor. Nichny Nov. (Russian), Ak Bars Kazan (Russian)
8	Steve Webb (RW)	6-0/208	Peterborough, Ont.	4-30-75	5	New York Islanders
	Mattias Weinhandl (RW)	6-0/183	Ljungby, Sweden	6-1-80	0	MoDo Ornskoldsvik (Sweden)
19	Alexei Yashin (C)	6-3/225	Sverdlovsk, U.S.S.R.	11-5-73	8	Ottawa
	DEFENSEMEN					
6	Adrian Aucoin	6-2/210	Ottawa	7-3-73	7	Vancouver, Tampa Bay
33	Eric Cairns	6-6/235	Oakville, Ont.	6-27-74	5	New York Islanders
41	Ray Giroux	5-11/185	North Bay, Ont.	7-20-76	1	AIK Solna (Sweden), HIFK Helsinki (Finland), Jokerit Helsinki (Finland)
5	Kevin Haller	6-2/199	Trochu, Alta.	12-5-70	12	New York Islanders
22	Roman Hamrlik	6-2/215	Gottwaldov, Czechoslovakia	4-12-74	9	New York Islanders
29	Kenny Jonsson	6-3/211	Angelholm, Sweden	10-6-74	7	New York Islanders
	Marko Kiprusoff	6-0/194	Turku, Finland	6-6-72	1	Kloten (Switzerland)
36	Evgeny Korolev	6-1/186	Moscow, U.S.S.R.	7-24-78	2	New York Islanders, Louisville (AHL)
	Branislav Mezei	6-5/221	Nitra, Czechoslovakia	10-8-80	1	Lowell (AHL), New York Islanders
	Anders Myrvold	6-2/200	Lorenskog, Norway	8-12-75	3	Springfield (AHL), New York Islanders
7	Ray Schultz	6-2/200	Red Deer, Alta.	11-14-76	4	Lowell (AHL), Cleveland (IHL), New York Islanders
2	Ken Sutton	6-1/205	Edmonton	11-5-69	10	New Jersey
	Dick Tarnstrom	6-0/180	Sundbyberg, Sweden	1-20-75	0	AIK Solna (Sweden)
	Arto Tukio	6-0/189	Tampere, Finland	4-4-81	0	Ilves Tampere (Finland)
	GOALTENDERS					
	Andy Chiodo	5-11/201	Toronto	4-25-83	0	Toronto (OHL)
	Rick DiPietro	6-0/185	Lewiston, Me.	9-19-81	1	Chicago (IHL), New York Islanders
	Dusan Salficky	6-1/185	Czechoslovakia	3-28-72	0	HC Keramika Plzen (Czech Republic)
30	Garth Snow	6-3/210	Wrentham, Mass.	7-28-69	8	Wilkes-Barre/Scranton (AHL), Pittsburgh
35	Stephen Valiquette	6-5/205	Etobicoke, Ont.	8-20-77	1	Springfield (AHL)

2000-01 REVIEW
INDIVIDUAL STATISTICS

SCORING

	Games	G	A	Pts.	PIM	+/-	PPG	SHG	Shots	Shooting Pct.
Mariusz Czerkawski	82	30	32	62	48	-24	10	1	287	10.5
Roman Hamrlik	76	16	30	46	92	-20	5	1	232	6.9
Dave Scatchard	81	21	24	45	114	-9	4	0	176	11.9
Tim Connolly	82	10	31	41	42	-14	5	0	171	5.8
Brad Isbister	51	18	14	32	59	-19	7	1	129	14.0
Claude Lapointe	80	9	23	32	56	-2	1	1	94	9.6
Mark Parrish	70	17	13	30	28	-27	6	0	123	13.8
Kenny Jonsson	65	8	21	29	30	-22	5	0	91	8.8
Bill Muckalt	60	11	15	26	33	-4	1	0	90	12.2
Oleg Kvasha	62	11	9	20	46	-15	0	0	118	9.3
Garry Galley	56	6	14	20	59	-4	4	0	94	6.4

	Games	G	A	Pts.	PIM	+/-	PPG	SHG	Shots	Shooting Pct.
Taylor Pyatt	78	4	14	18	39	-17	1	0	86	4.7
Jason Blake*	30	4	8	12	24	-12	1	1	73	5.5
Zdeno Chara	82	2	7	9	157	-27	0	1	83	2.4
Aris Brimanis	56	0	8	8	26	-12	0	0	66	0.0
Juraj Kolnik	29	4	3	7	12	-8	0	0	38	10.5
Mats Lindgren	20	3	4	7	10	4	0	2	34	8.8
Mark Lawrence	36	3	4	7	32	-9	1	0	32	9.4
Jeff Toms*	39	2	4	6	10	-7	0	0	37	5.4
Kevin Haller	30	1	5	6	56	5	0	0	19	5.3
Mike Stapleton*	34	1	4	5	2	-5	0	0	22	4.5
Branislav Mezei	42	1	4	5	53	-5	0	0	29	3.4
Eric Cairns	45	2	2	4	106	-18	0	0	21	9.5
Steve Martins*	39	1	3	4	20	-7	0	1	28	3.6
Jason Krog	9	0	3	3	0	4	0	0	7	0.0
Ray Schultz	13	0	2	2	40	-1	0	0	3	0.0
Rick DiPietro (goalie)	20	0	2	2	6	0	0	0	0	0.0
Steve Webb	31	0	2	2	35	1	0	0	8	0.0
Craig Berube*	38	0	2	2	54	-5	0	0	27	0.0
Anders Myrvold	12	0	1	1	0	-2	0	0	8	0.0
Mathieu Biron	14	0	1	1	12	2	0	0	10	0.0
Chris Terreri (goalie)*	8	0	0	0	2	0	0	0	0	0.0
Evgeny Korolev	8	0	0	0	6	0	0	0	11	0.0
Robert Petrovicky	11	0	0	0	4	-1	0	0	3	0.0
Jesse Belanger	12	0	0	0	2	-5	0	0	7	0.0
Wade Flaherty (goalie)*	20	0	0	0	2	0	0	0	0	0.0
John Vanbiesbrouck (goalie)*	44	0	0	0	8	0	0	0	0	0.0

GOALTENDING

	Games	Min.	Goals	SO	Avg.	W	L	T	ENG	Shots	Sv. Pct.
Chris Terreri*	8	443	18	0	2.44	2	4	1	2	205	.912
John Vanbiesbrouck*	44	2390	120	1	3.01	10	25	5	4	1177	.898
Wade Flaherty*	20	1017	56	1	3.30	6	10	0	3	470	.881
Rick DiPietro	20	1083	63	0	3.49	3	15	1	2	515	.878

*Played with two or more NHL teams.

RESULTS

OCTOBER
6— At Tampa Bay ....T....*3-3
11—At Toronto ....L.....2-3
14—Calgary ....L.....0-2
17—Anaheim ....L.....3-4
20—At Atlanta ....W....5-3
21—At Washington.................T....*4-4
27—Montreal ....W....2-1
28—At Montreal ....W....2-1
31—Boston ....W....4-2

NOVEMBER
1— At Florida............................W.....3-0
3— At Tampa Bay ....L....*3-4
5— Los Angeles ....L.....1-4
7— Nashville.............................W.....2-1
9— At Buffalo.............................L.....0-3
11—San Jose ....L.....0-4
16—At Los Angeles ....L.....1-5
18—At San Jose ....L.....3-5
19—At Anaheim ....L.....1-2
22—N.Y. Rangers ....L....*3-4
24—At Washington....................L.....0-1
25—Detroit ....L.....3-4
27—Tampa Bay ....W.....7-4
30—Toronto ....L.....4-6

DECEMBER
1— At New Jersey ....T....*0-0
3— New Jersey ....T....*1-1
6— At Florida............................W.....4-1
9— Atlanta ....L.....2-5

(continued)
10—At Philadelphia...................L.....2-5
12—Washington ....L.....2-3
15—Toronto ....W.....3-2
16—At Ottawa ....L.....0-6
19—Carolina ....W.....2-1
21—Dallas ....L.....1-3
23—Columbus ....L.....5-7
27—Boston ....L.....2-5
29—Atlanta ....W.....5-2
30—Buffalo ....L.....0-2

JANUARY
2— Montreal ....L.....0-3
4— At New Jersey ....L.....2-4
6— Phoenix ....L.....1-2
7— At Carolina ....L.....2-5
9— Chicago ....L.....3-6
12—At Pittsburgh ....L.....3-4
13—Pittsburgh ....W.....6-5
16—At Colorado ....L.....1-4
19—At Minnesota ....L.....2-3
21—At Atlanta ....T....*4-4
23—Ottawa ....L.....2-3
26—At N.Y. Rangers ....W.....3-2
27—Buffalo ....L.....1-2
31—New Jersey ....W.....3-2

FEBRUARY
1— At Philadelphia....................L.....0-2
7— At Buffalo..............................L....*1-2
9— Philadelphia ....L.....2-5
10—At Montreal ....L.....3-5

(continued)
12—At Ottawa ....L.....1-3
14—Philadelphia ....L.....1-3
16—At Edmonton ....W....4-2
18—At Vancouver ....L.....2-3
22—Philadelphia ....W....*4-3
24—Florida ....W.....5-4
25—At Pittsburgh ....L.....1-6
27—New Jersey ....L.....1-4

MARCH
1— Carolina ....L.....1-3
3— Tampa Bay ....L.....0-6
5— At N.Y. Rangers ....W.....5-2
6— Washington ....L.....1-5
9— Minnesota ....L.....1-4
11—Florida ....L.....1-4
14—At Pittsburgh ....W.....3-1
17—At Columbus........................T....*3-3
18—At Carolina ....L.....1-2
20—At St. Louis ....W....*4-3
23—At Dallas ....L.....1-4
25—At Phoenix ....T....*2-2
28—At N.Y. Rangers ....L.....2-4
29—N.Y. Rangers ....L.....4-6
31—At Boston ....L.....2-4

APRIL
2— Pittsburgh ....W.....4-1
4— At Toronto ....L.....2-4
6— Ottawa ....L.....3-4
7— At Boston..............................L.....2-4

*Denotes overtime game.

Rangers' Schedule
Home games shaded; D—Day game; *—All-Star Game at Los Angeles

October
SUN	MON	TUE	WED	THU	FRI	SAT
	1	2	3	4	5 CAR	6
7 BUF	8	9	10 WAS	11	12	13 OTT
14	15 MON	16	17 NJ	18	19 ATL	20 TB
21 SJ	22	23	24	25 STL	26	27 BOS
28	29 DAL	30	31 FLA			

November
SUN	MON	TUE	WED	THU	FRI	SAT
				1	2 CAR	3 FLA
4	5	6 MIN	7	8 NYI	9	10 BUF
11 MON	12	13	14 PHI	15	16	17 PIT
18 ATL	19	20 COL	21	22	23 WAS	24
25 ANA	26	27 BUF	28 CAR	29	30	

December
SUN	MON	TUE	WED	THU	FRI	SAT
						1 MON
2 TB	3	4 WAS	5	6 TOR	7	8 TOR
9	10 CAR	11	12 NAS	13	14	15 BUF
16	17 FLA	18	19 NJ	20	21 NYI	22
23 D OTT	24	25	26	27	28 SJ	29 LA
30	31 PHO					

January
SUN	MON	TUE	WED	THU	FRI	SAT
		1	2 EDM	3 COL	4	5 D PIT
6	7	8	9 LA	10	11	12 D PHI
13	14 CBJ	15	16 CBJ	17 NJ	18	19
20	21	22 NYI	23 BOS	24	25	26 D WAS
27	28 TB	29	30 NYI	31		

February
SUN	MON	TUE	WED	THU	FRI	SAT
					1	2 *
3	4	5	6 DET	7	8 ATL	9
10 D PIT	11	12	13 DAL	14	15	16
17	18	19	20	21	22	23
24	25	26 NJ	27	28 OTT		

March
SUN	MON	TUE	WED	THU	FRI	SAT
					1	2 D PHI
3	4 CAL	5 MIN	6	7 CHI	8	9 D PIT
10	11 MON	12	13 BOS	14	15	16 D NJ
17 D DET	18	19 VAN	20	21 OTT	22 ATL	23
24 NYI	25	26	27 PHI	28	29	30 FLA
31						

April
SUN	MON	TUE	WED	THU	FRI	SAT
	1 TB	2	3	4 TOR	5	6 D BOS
7	8 PIT	9	10 TOR	11	12	13 D PHI
14	15	16	17	18	19	20

2001-02 SEASON
CLUB DIRECTORY

Chairman, MSG/president and CEO, Cablevision Systems Corporation
James L. Dolan

Vice chairman, MSG/vice chairman, general counsel and secretary, Cablevision Systems Corporation
Robert S. Lemle

President, sports team operations
Steve Mills

President and g.m./alternate governor
Glen Sather

Exec. v.p. and general counsel/alt. gov.
Kenneth W. Munoz

V.p., player development and asst. g.m.
Don Maloney

Director, player personnel
Tom Renney

Dir., hockey administration and scouting
Peter Stephan

Head coach
Ron Low

Assistant coaches
Ted Green
Walt Kyle

Goaltending analyst
Sam St. Laurent

Amateur scouting staff
Ray Clearwater, Rich Brown, Andre Beaulieu, Bob Crocker, Jan Gajdosik, Ernie Gare, Martin Madden Jr., Christer Rockstom

Professional scouting staff
Dave Brown, Harry Howell, Gilles Leger

Scouting manager
Bill Short

Video analyst
Jerry Dineen

Vice president, operations
Mark Piazza

Vice president, public relations
John Rosasco

Director, public relations
Jason Vogel

Public relations coordinators
Jennifer Schoenfeld
Keith Soutar

Vice president, marketing
Jeanie Baumgartner

V.p., business and community dev.
Patricia Kerr

Medical trainer
Jim Ramsay

Equipment manager
Acacio Marques

Assistant equipment manager
James Johnson

Massage therapist
Bruce Lifrieri

Coaching staff assistant
Pat Boller

DRAFT CHOICES

Rd.— Player	Ht./Wt.	Overall	Pos.	Last team
1— Daniel Blackburn	6-0/180	10	G	Kootenay (WHL)
2— Fedor Tjutin	6-3/202	40	D	St. Petersburg, Russia
3— Garth Murray	6-1/205	79	C/LW	Regina (WHL)
4— Bryce Lampman	6-1/193	113	D	Omaha (USHL)
5— Shawn Collymore	5-11/180	139	RW	Quebec (QMJHL)
6— Marek Zidlicky	5-11/180	176	D	IFK, Finland
7— Petr Preucil	6-1/168	206	C	Quebec (QMJHL)
7— Pontus Petterstrom	6-0/180	226	F	Tingsryd Jr., Sweden
8— Leonid Zhvachin	6-0/185	230	D	Podolsk, Russia
8— Ryan Hollweg	5-9/201	238	C	Medicine Hat (WHL)
9— Juris Stals	6-0/185	269	C	Lukko, Finland

MISCELLANEOUS DATA

Home ice (capacity)
Madison Square Garden (18,200)

Address
2 Pennsylvania Plaza
New York, NY 10121

Business phone
212-465-6486

Ticket information
212-307-7171

Website
www.newyorkrangers.com

Training site
New York

Club colors
Blue, red and white

Radio affiliation
MSG Radio

TV affiliation
MSG Network

NEW YORK RANGERS

No.	FORWARDS	Ht./Wt.	Place	BORN Date	NHL exp.	2000-01 clubs
38	Derek Armstrong (C)	6-0/193	Ottawa	4-23-73	6	Hartford (AHL), New York Rangers
8	Pavel Brendl (RW)	6-1/197	Opocno, Czechoslovakia	3-23-81	0	Calgary (WHL)
8	Zdeno Ciger (LW)	6-1/190	Martin, Czechoslovakia	10-19-69	6	Slovan Bratislava (Slovakia)
	Shawn Collymore (RW)	5-11/180	Lasalle, Que.	5-2-83	0	Quebec (QMJHL)
10	Jason Dawe (LW)	5-10/190	North York, Ont.	5-29-73	7	Hartford (AHL)
20	Radek Dvorak (RW)	6-1/194	Tabor, Czechoslovakia	3-9-77	6	New York Rangers
28	Nils Ekman (LW)	5-11/182	Stockholm, Sweden	3-11-76	2	Detroit (IHL), Tampa Bay
14	Theo Fleury (RW)	5-6/180	Oxbow, Sask.	6-29-68	13	New York Rangers
17	Colin Forbes (LW)	6-3/205	New Westminister, B.C.	2-16-76	5	Ottawa, New York Rangers
43	Kyle Freadrich (LW)	6-5/231	Edmonton	12-28-78	2	Detroit (IHL), Tampa Bay
	Ken Gernander (C/LW)	5-10/175	Grand Rapids, Minn.	6-30-69	2	Hartford (AHL)
17	Michal Grosek (LW)	6-2/216	Vyskov, Czechoslovakia	6-1-75	8	New York Rangers, Hartford (AHL)
	Mike Harder (RW)	6-0/185	Winnipeg	2-8-73	0	Hartford (AHL), Louisville (AHL)
	Barrett Heisten (LW)	6-1/189	Anchorage, Alaska	3-19-80	0	Seattle (WHL)
27	Jan Hlavac (LW)	6-0/183	Prague, Czechoslovakia	9-20-76	2	New York Rangers
21	Andreas Johansson (C)	6-2/202	Hofors, Sweden	5-19-73	5	Bern (Switzerland)
16	Jamie Lundmark (C)	6-0/174	Edmonton	1-16-81	0	Seattle (WHL)
6	Manny Malhotra (C)	6-2/210	Mississauga, Ont.	5-18-80	3	Hartford (AHL), New York Rangers
20	Sandy McCarthy (RW)	6-3/225	Toronto	6-15-72	8	New York Rangers
11	Mark Messier (C)	6-1/205	Edmonton	1-18-61	22	New York Rangers
	Dominic Moore (C)	6-0/180	Thornhill, Ont.	8-3-80	0	Harvard University (ECAC)
	Garth Murray (C/LW)	6-1/205	Regina, Sask.	9-17-82	0	Regina (WHL)
93	Petr Nedved (C)	6-3/195	Liberec, Czechoslovakia	12-9-71	10	New York Rangers
	Mikael Samuelsson (C)	6-1/195	Mariefred, Sweden	12-23-76	1	San Jose, Kentucky (AHL)
	Brad Smyth (RW)	6-0/195	Ottawa	3-13-73	5	Hartford (AHL), New York Rangers
21	Jeff Toms (LW)	6-5/213	Swift Current, Sask.	6-4-74	6	New York Islanders, Springfield (AHL), New York Rangers, Hartford (AHL)
18	Mike York (C)	5-10/185	Pontiac, Mich.	1-3-78	2	New York Rangers
	DEFENSEMEN					
	Pat Aufiero	6-2/186	Winchester, Mass.	7-1-80	0	Boston University (Hockey East)
55	Drew Bannister	6-2/208	Belleville, Ont.	9-4-74	5	Hartford (AHL), New York Rangers
3	Brad Brown	6-4/218	Baie Verte, Ont.	12-27-75	4	New York Rangers
48	Sean Gagnon	6-2/210	Sault Ste. Marie, Ont.	9-11-73	3	Ottawa, Grand Rapids (IHL)
	Christian Gosselin	6-5/235	Laval, Que.	8-21-76	0	Kentucky (AHL)
3	Kim Johnsson	6-2/189	Malmo, Sweden	3-16-76	2	New York Rangers
33	Dave Karpa	6-1/210	Regina, Sask.	5-7-71	10	Carolina
	Matt Kinch	5-11/189	Red Deer, Alta.	2-17-80	0	Calgary (WHL)
	Tomas Kloucek	6-3/203	Prague, Czechoslovakia	3-7-80	1	Hartford (AHL), New York Rangers
	Bryce Lampman	6-1/193	Rochester, Minn.	8-31-82	0	Omaha (USHL)
2	Brian Leetch	6-0/185	Corpus Christi, Tex.	3-3-68	14	New York Rangers
24	Sylvain Lefebvre	6-3/205	Richmond, Que.	10-14-67	12	New York Rangers
7	Vladimir Malakhov	6-4/230	Sverdlovsk, U.S.S.R.	8-30-68	9	New York Rangers
	Mike Mottau	6-0/192	Quincy, Mass.	3-19-78	1	Hartford (AHL), New York Rangers
	Filip Novak	6-0/174	Ceske Budejovice, Czech.	5-7-82	0	Regina (WHL)
	Dale Purinton	6-3/214	Fort Wayne, Ind.	10-11-76	2	Hartford (AHL), New York Rangers
	Peter Smrek	6-1/194	Martin, Czechoslovakia	2-16-79	1	Worcester (AHL), St. Louis, New York Rangers, Hartford (AHL)
	Fedor Tjutin	6-3/202	Izhevsk, U.S.S.R.	7-19-83	0	SKA St. Petersburg (Russian)
55	Igor Ulanov	6-3/211	Kraskokamsk, U.S.S.R.	10-1-69	10	Edmonton
49	David Wilkie	6-2/210	Ellensburg, Wash.	5-30-74	6	Houston (IHL), New York Rangers
	GOALTENDERS					
	Dan Blackburn	6-0/180	Montreal	5-20-83	0	Kootenay (WHL)
31	Guy Hebert	5-11/185	Troy, N.Y.	1-7-67	10	Anaheim, New York Rangers
	Johan Holmqvist	6-1/200	Tierp, Sweden	5-24-78	1	Hartford (AHL), New York Rangers
	Jason Labarbera	6-2/205	Burnaby, B.C.	1-18-80	1	Hartford (AHL), New York Rangers, Charlotte (ECHL)
35	Mike Richter	5-11/185	Philadelphia	9-22-66	13	New York Rangers
	Vitali Yeremeyev	5-10/167	Ust-Kamenogorsk, U.S.S.R.	9-23-75	1	Charlotte (ECHL), Hartford (AHL), New York Rangers

2000-01 REVIEW
INDIVIDUAL STATISTICS

SCORING

	Games	G	A	Pts.	PIM	+/-	PPG	SHG	Shots	Shooting Pct.
Brian Leetch	82	21	58	79	34	-18	10	1	241	8.7
Petr Nedved	79	32	46	78	54	10	9	1	230	13.9
Theoren Fleury	62	30	44	74	122	0	8	7	238	12.6
Radek Dvorak	82	31	36	67	20	9	5	2	230	13.5
Mark Messier	82	24	43	67	89	-25	12	3	131	18.3
Jan Hlavac	79	28	36	64	20	3	5	0	195	14.4
Valeri Kamensky	65	14	20	34	36	-18	6	0	129	10.9
Michael York	79	14	17	31	20	1	3	2	171	8.2
Adam Graves	82	10	16	26	77	-16	1	0	136	7.4

	Games	G	A	Pts.	PIM	+/-	PPG	SHG	Shots	Shooting Pct.
Kim Johnsson	75	5	21	26	40	-3	4	0	104	4.8
Sandy McCarthy	81	11	10	21	171	3	0	0	95	11.6
Michal Grosek	65	9	11	20	61	-10	2	0	84	10.7
Sylvain Lefebvre	71	2	13	15	55	3	0	0	39	5.1
Manny Malhotra	50	4	8	12	31	-10	0	0	46	8.7
Richard Pilon	69	2	9	11	175	-2	0	0	24	8.3
Tim Taylor	38	2	5	7	16	-6	0	0	34	5.9
Eric Lacroix*	46	2	3	5	39	-6	0	0	22	9.1
Colin Forbes*	19	1	4	5	15	-3	0	0	20	5.0
Tomas Kloucek	43	1	4	5	74	-3	0	0	22	4.5
Alexei Gusarov*	26	1	3	4	6	-2	0	0	21	4.8
Brad Brown	48	1	3	4	107	0	0	0	14	7.1
Jeff Ulmer	21	3	0	3	8	-6	0	0	22	13.6
Peter Smrek*	14	0	3	3	12	1	0	0	9	0.0
Johan Witehall*	15	0	3	3	8	-5	0	0	16	0.0
Mike Mottau	18	0	3	3	13	-6	0	0	17	0.0
Jeff Toms*	15	1	1	2	0	-3	0	0	12	8.3
Vladimir Malakhov	3	0	2	2	4	0	0	0	6	0.0
Dale Purinton	42	0	2	2	180	5	0	0	13	0.0
Brad Smyth	4	1	0	1	4	0	0	0	10	10.0
David Wilkie	1	0	0	0	2	-2	0	0	1	0.0
Jason Labarbera (goalie)	1	0	0	0	0	0	0	0	0	0.0
Bert Robertsson	2	0	0	0	4	-1	0	0	0	0.0
Johan Holmqvist (goalie)	2	0	0	0	2	0	0	0	0	0.0
John MacLean*	2	0	0	0	0	-2	0	0	0	0.0
Derek Armstrong	3	0	0	0	0	0	0	0	6	0.0
Drew Bannister	3	0	0	0	0	-1	0	0	3	0.0
Jason Doig	3	0	0	0	0	0	0	0	1	0.0
Vitali Yeremeyev (goalie)	4	0	0	0	0	0	0	0	0	0.0
Tony Tuzzolino	6	0	0	0	5	-1	0	0	3	0.0
Guy Hebert (goalie)*	13	0	0	0	0	0	0	0	0	0.0
Kirk McLean (goalie)	23	0	0	0	0	0	0	0	0	0.0
Mike Richter (goalie)	45	0	0	0	0	0	0	0	0	0.0

GOALTENDING

	Games	Min.	Goals	SO	Avg.	W	L	T	ENG	Shots	Sv. Pct.
Jason Labarbera	1	10	0	0	0.00	0	0	0	0	2	1.000
Mike Richter	45	2635	144	0	3.28	20	21	3	5	1343	.893
Guy Hebert*	13	735	42	0	3.43	5	7	1	2	409	.897
Kirk McLean	23	1220	71	0	3.49	8	10	1	0	639	.889
Vitali Yeremeyev	4	212	16	0	4.53	0	4	0	0	104	.846
Johan Holmqvist	2	119	10	0	5.04	0	2	0	0	71	.859

*Played with two or more NHL teams.

RESULTS

OCTOBER
7— At Atlanta ....W....2-1
11—Montreal....................W....3-1
14—At Pittsburgh ....L....6-8
16—Anaheim ....L....3-4
18—At Chicago................W....4-2
22—Tampa Bay ....L....2-4
24—Philadelphia ....L....4-5
26—At Philadelphia...........L....0-3
27—Pittsburgh ....L....1-4
29—Boston ....W....5-1

NOVEMBER
1— Tampa Bay ....W....6-1
2— At Ottawa ....L....5-6
4— At Montreal ....W....5-2
7— Edmonton.................W....4-3
9— At Washington ....W....5-3
12—Phoenix ....L....0-2
15—At Minnesota ....W....3-2
17—At Vancouver ....L....3-4
18—At Calgary ....W...*5-4
21—Toronto ....L....1-3
22—At N.Y. Islanders........W...*4-3
24—At Buffalo ....L....2-3
26—Ottawa ....W....3-2
28—Los Angeles ....W....7-6
29—At New Jersey ....L....2-5

DECEMBER
2— At Toronto ....L....2-8
3— Colorado...................L....3-6

6— Washington................W....3-2
8—Buffalo.......................W....5-2
9—At Boston...................L....4-6
12—At San Jose ....L....2-3
14—At Los Angeles ....T....*5-5
15—At Anaheim ....L....4-6
18—Florida ....W....6-3
20—St. Louis ....L....3-6
23—Nashville ....L....*2-3
27—At Carolina ....L....3-4
28—Atlanta ....L....1-4
31—At Dallas ....L....1-6

JANUARY
4— At Phoenix ....L....1-3
6— New Jersey ....T....*5-5
8—Dallas........................L....1-2
13—At Boston..................L....1-4
14—Minnesota ....W....4-2
16—Philadelphia ....W...*4-3
18—Toronto ....W....*2-1
20—At Montreal ....T....*2-2
22—At Carolina ....W....5-2
24—Carolina ....L....2-3
26—N.Y. Islanders ....L....2-3
27—At Toronto ....L....1-3
29—Atlanta ....L....2-7
31—Montreal ....W....4-2

FEBRUARY
6—Buffalo.......................L....3-6
9—At Florida...................W....4-2

11—New Jersey ....T....*1-1
12—At Columbus ....W....4-3
17—At Tampa Bay ....W....5-4
19—Chicago ....W....4-2
23—At Pittsburgh ....L....4-6
25—At Philadelphia ....L....1-2
26—Ottawa ....L....2-3
28—Florida ....W....4-2

MARCH
2— Pittsburgh..................L....5-7
4— At Nashville ....L....2-5
5— N.Y. Islanders ....L....2-5
9—At Washington.............L....3-5
10—At Ottawa ....W....3-2
12—Pittsburgh..................T....*3-3
14—At Buffalo ....L....3-6
17—At Philadelphia ....L....1-2
19—Washington ....W....6-3
21—At New Jersey ....L....0-4
24—Detroit ....L....0-6
25—Boston ....L....2-3
28—N.Y. Islanders ....W....4-2
29—At N.Y. Islanders ....W....6-4
31—At New Jersey ....W....4-3

APRIL
1— At Atlanta ....W....4-2
4— Carolina ....L....1-3
5— At Tampa Bay ....W...*4-3
7— At Florida ....L....0-3

*Denotes overtime game.

OTTAWA SENATORS
EASTERN CONFERENCE/NORTHEAST DIVISION

Senators' Schedule
Home games shaded; D—Day game; *—All-Star Game at Los Angeles

October
SUN	MON	TUE	WED	THU	FRI	SAT
	1	2	3 TOR	4 MON	5	6 BUF
7	8	9 CAR	10 FLA	11	12	13 NYR
14	15	16 PIT	17	18 PIT	19	20 NJ
21	22	23 NJ	24	25 PHI	26	27 STL
28	29	30 ATL	31			

November
SUN	MON	TUE	WED	THU	FRI	SAT
				1	2	3 BUF
4	5	6	7	8 COL	9	10 NAS
11	12	13 WAS	14	15 CAR	16	17 TOR
18	19	20 VAN	21	22 CAL	23	24 ATL
25	26	27 STL	28	29	30	

December
SUN	MON	TUE	WED	THU	FRI	SAT
						1 BOS
2	3 COL	4	5 DAL	6 NAS	7	8 TB
9	10 NYI	11	12	13 PHO	14	15 NJ
16	17	18 CAR	19	20 LA	21	22 D NJ
23 D NYR	24	25	26 BOS	27 NYI	28	29 PIT
30	31 CHI					

January
SUN	MON	TUE	WED	THU	FRI	SAT
		1	2	3 WAS	4	5 D TOR
6	7 TOR	8	9 ATL	10	11 FLA	12 TB
13	14	15 PHI	16	17 BOS	18	19 MIN
20 DET	21	22 PHI	23	24 BOS	25	26 D MON
27	28	29	30 PHI	31		

February
SUN	MON	TUE	WED	THU	FRI	SAT
					1	2 *
3	4 TB	5	6 CBJ	7	8 BUF	9 DET
10	11	12 PIT	13	14	15	16
17	18	19	20	21	22	23
24	25	26 MON	27	28 NYR		

March
SUN	MON	TUE	WED	THU	FRI	SAT
					1	2 WAS
3	4 LA	5	6	7 SJ	8	9 PHO
10	11	12 MIN	13	14 EDM	15	16 NYI
17 FLA	18	19 BUF	20	21 NYR	22	23 ATL
24 BUF	25	26	27 NYI	28 FLA	29	30 TB
31						

April
SUN	MON	TUE	WED	THU	FRI	SAT
	1	2 CAR	3	4	5 WAS	6
7 MON	8	9 MON	10	11 BOS	12	13 TOR
14	15	16	17	18	19	20

2001-02 SEASON
CLUB DIRECTORY

Chairman, governor
Rod Bryden
President and CEO & alt. governor
Roy Mlakar
General manager
Marshall Johnston
Executive vice president
Steve Violetta
COO & alternate governor
Cyril Leeder
Head coach
Jacques Martin
Assistant coaches
Don Jackson
Roger Neilson
Perry Pearn
Director of hockey operations
Trevor Timmins
Director of legal relations
Peter Chiarelli
Director of player personnel
Jarmo Kekalainen
Vice president, broadcast
Jim Steel
Vice president, communications
Phil Legault

Director, communications
Steve Keogh
Manager, media relations
Ian Mendes
Media relations assistant
Jen Eves
Video coordinator & conditioning coach
Randy Lee
Head equipment manager
John Gervais
Assistant equipment manager
Chris Cook
Head athletic trainer
Kevin Wagner
Massage therapist
Brad Joyal
Team doctor
Jamie Kissick, M.D.
Scouts
Dale Engel, George Fargher, Bob Janecyk, Frank Jay, Lewis Mangelluzzo, Phil Myre, John Phelan, Boris Shagus, Ken Williamson

DRAFT CHOICES

Rd.— Player	Ht./Wt.	Overall	Pos.	Last team
1— Jason Spezza	6-2/214	2	C	Windsor (OHL)
1— Tim Gleason	6-0/199	23	D	Windsor (OHL)
3— Neil Komadoski	6-1/212	81	D	Notre Dame (CCHA)
4— Ray Emery	6-2/187	99	G	Sault Ste. Marie (OHL)
4— Christoph Schubert	6-1/186	127		Munchen, Germany
5— Stefan Schauer	6-1/193	162		Riebersee, Germany
6— Brooks Laich	6-0/184	193	C	Moose Jaw (WHL)
7— Jan Platil	6-1/193	218	D	Barrie (OHL)
7— Brandon Bochenski	6-0/180	223	RW	Lincoln, Min. (USHL)
8— Neil Petruic	6-1/183	235	D	Kindersley, Sask. (SJHL)
8— Gregg Johnson	5-10/183	256	C	Boston Univ. (H. East)
9— Tony Dahlman	5-11/194	286	RW	Ilves, Finland

MISCELLANEOUS DATA

Home ice (capacity)
Corel Centre (18,500)
Address
1000 Palladium Drive
Ottawa, Ont. K2VIA5
Business phone
613-599-0250
Ticket information
613-599-0103
Website
www.ottawasenators.com

Training site
Ottawa
Club colors
Black, red and gold
Radio affiliation
Team 1200 (1200 AM)
TV affiliation
CHRO TV, CTV Sportsnet

OTTAWA SENATORS

No.	FORWARDS	Ht./Wt.	Place	Date	NHL exp.	2000-01 clubs
11	Daniel Alfredsson (RW)...	5-11/195	Partille, Sweden	12-11-72	6	Ottawa
20	Magnus Arvedson (LW)...	6-2/198	Karlstad, Sweden	11-25-71	4	Ottawa
	Chris Bala (LW)	6-1/180	Alexandria, Va.	9-24-78	0	Harvard University (ECAC)
14	Radek Bonk (C)	6-3/210	Koprivnice, Czechoslovakia	1-9-76	7	Ottawa
	Ivan Ciernik (RW)	6-1/234	Levice, Czechoslovakia	10-30-77	2	Grand Rapids (IHL), Ottawa
12	Mike Fisher (C)	6-1/193	Peterborough, Ont.	6-5-80	2	Ottawa
	Alexandre Giroux (C/LW) .	6-2/165	Quebec	6-16-81	0	Hull (QMJHL), Rouyn-Noranda (QMJHL)
	Konstantin Gorovikov	5-11/172	Novosibirsk, Russia	8-31-77	0	Grand Rapids (IHL)
	Martin Havlat (C/LW)	6-1/178	Brno, Czechoslovakia	4-19-81	1	Ottawa
	Chris Herperger (LW)	6-0/190	Esterhazy, Sask.	2-24-74	2	Norfolk (AHL), Chicago
18	Marian Hossa (LW)	6-1/199	Stara Lubovna, Czech.	1-12-79	4	Ottawa
28	Eric Lacroix (LW)	6-1/207	Montreal	7-15-71	8	New York Rangers, Ottawa
	Josh Langfeld (RW)	6-3/205	Fridley, Minn.	7-17-77	0	Univ. of Michigan (CCHA)
15	Shawn McEachern (LW) ..	5-11/193	Waltham, Mass.	2-28-69	10	Ottawa
11	Bill Muckalt (RW)	6-1/200	Surrey, B.C.	7-15-74	3	New York Islanders
	Chris Neil (RW)	6-0/210	Markdale, Ont.	6-18-79	0	Grand Rapids (IHL)
26	Andre Roy (RW)	6-4/213	Port Chester, N.Y.	2-8-75	4	Ottawa
56	Petr Schastlivy (LW)	6-1/204	Angarsk, U.S.S.R.	4-18-79	2	Grand Rapids (IHL), Ottawa
	Jason Spezza (C)	6-2/214	Mississauga, Ont.	6-13-83	0	Mississauga Icedogs (OHL), Windsor (OHL)
	Chris Szysky (RW)	5-11/205	White City, Sask.	6-8-76	0	Grand Rapids (IHL)
	Jeff Ulmer (RW)	5-11/190	Wilcox, Sask.	4-27-77	1	Hartford (AHL), New York Rangers
	Antoine Vermette (C)	6-0/184	St. Agapit, Que.	7-20-82	0	Victoriaville (QMJHL)
26	Todd White (C)	5-10/180	Kanata, Ont.	5-21-75	4	Grand Rapids (IHL), Ottawa

No.	DEFENSEMEN	Ht./Wt.	Place	Date	NHL exp.	2000-01 clubs
3	Zdeno Chara	6-9/246	Trencin, Czechoslovakia	3-18-77	4	New York Islanders
25	Jason Doig	6-3/228	Montreal	1-29-77	5	New York Rangers, Hartford (AHL)
	Tim Gleason	6-0/199	Southfield, Mich.	1-29-83	0	Windsor (OHL)
24	John Gruden	6-0/203	Virginia, Minn.	6-4-70	5	Grand Rapids (IHL)
	Shane Hnidy	6-1/200	Brandon, Man.	11-8-75	1	Ottawa, Grand Rapids (IHL)
	Neil Komadoski	6-1/212	St. Louis	2-10-82	0	Univ. of Notre Dame (CCHA)
	Joel Kwiatkowski	6-2/201	Kendersley, Sask.	3-22-77	1	Grand Rapids (IHL), Ottawa
4	Curtis Leschyshyn	6-1/205	Thompson, Man.	9-21-69	13	Minnesota, Ottawa
7	Ricard Persson	6-1/201	Ostersund, Sweden	8-24-69	6	Ottawa
4	Chris Phillips	6-3/215	Fort McMurray, Alta.	3-9-78	4	Ottawa
	Karel Rachunek	6-1/191	Gottwaldov, Czechoslovakia	8-27-79	2	Ottawa
6	Wade Redden	6-2/205	Lloydminster, Sask.	6-12-77	5	Ottawa
20	Jamie Rivers	6-0/197	Ottawa	3-16-75	6	Ottawa, Grand Rapids (IHL)
5	Sami Salo	6-3/192	Turku, Finland	9-2-74	3	Ottawa
	Stefan Schauer	6-1/193	Scongau, West Germany	1-12-83	0	Riebersee (Germany Div. 1)
	Christoph Schubert	6-1/186	Germany	2-5-82	0	Munchen (Germany Div. II)
	Julien Vauclair	6-0/200	Delemont, Switzerland	10-2-79	0	Lugano (Switzerland)
	Anton Volchenkov	6-0/209	Moscow, U.S.S.R.	2-25-82	0	

No.	GOALTENDERS	Ht./Wt.	Place	Date	NHL exp.	2000-01 clubs
	Mathieu Chouinard	6-1/209	Laval, Que.	4-11-80	0	Grand Rapids (IHL)
	Ray Emery	6-2/187	Hamilton, Ont.	9-28-82	0	Sault Ste. Marie (OHL)
30	Mike Fountain	6-1/180	North York, Ont.	1-26-72	4	Grand Rapids (IHL), Ottawa
1	Jani Hurme	6-0/187	Turku, Finland	1-7-75	2	Ottawa
	Simon Lajeunesse	6-0/170	Quebec City	1-22-81	0	Val-d'Or (QMJHL)
40	Patrick Lalime	6-3/185	St. Bonaventure, Que.	7-7-74	3	Ottawa

2000-01 REVIEW

INDIVIDUAL STATISTICS

SCORING

	Games	G	A	Pts.	PIM	+/-	PPG	SHG	Shots	Shooting Pct.
Alexei Yashin	82	40	48	88	30	10	13	2	263	15.2
Marian Hossa	81	32	43	75	44	19	11	2	249	12.9
Shawn McEachern	82	32	40	72	62	10	9	0	231	13.9
Daniel Alfredsson	68	24	46	70	30	11	10	0	206	11.7
Radek Bonk	74	23	36	59	52	27	5	2	139	16.5
Wade Redden	78	10	37	47	49	22	4	0	159	6.3
Martin Havlat	73	19	23	42	20	8	7	0	133	14.3
Rob Zamuner	79	19	18	37	52	7	1	2	123	15.4
Magnus Arvedson	51	17	16	33	24	23	1	2	79	21.5
Karel Rachunek	71	3	30	33	60	17	3	0	77	3.9
Andreas Dackell	81	13	18	31	24	7	1	0	72	18.1
Jason York	74	6	16	22	72	7	3	0	133	4.5

	Games	G	A	Pts.	PIM	+/-	PPG	SHG	Shots	Shooting Pct.
Mike Fisher	60	7	12	19	46	-1	0	0	83	8.4
Sami Salo	31	2	16	18	10	9	1	0	61	3.3
Chris Phillips	73	2	12	14	31	8	2	0	77	2.6
Vaclav Prospal*	40	1	12	13	12	1	0	0	68	1.5
Ricard Persson	33	1	8	9	35	8	0	0	43	2.3
Andre Roy	64	3	5	8	169	1	0	0	33	9.1
Mike Sillinger*	13	3	4	7	4	1	0	0	19	15.8
Jamie Rivers	45	2	4	6	44	6	0	0	41	4.9
Igor Kravchuk*	15	1	5	6	14	4	0	0	13	7.7
Todd White	16	4	1	5	4	5	0	0	12	33.3
Petr Schastlivy	17	3	2	5	6	-1	0	0	32	9.4
Shane Hnidy	52	3	2	5	84	8	0	0	47	6.4
Curtis Leschyshyn*	11	0	4	4	0	7	0	0	8	0.0
Ivan Ciernik	4	2	0	2	2	2	0	0	7	28.6
John Emmons*	41	1	1	2	20	-5	0	0	28	3.6
Joel Kwiatkowski	4	1	0	1	0	1	0	0	2	50.0
Eric Lacroix*	9	0	1	1	4	0	0	0	10	0.0
Colin Forbes*	39	0	1	1	31	-3	0	0	26	0.0
Patrick Lalime (goalie)	60	0	1	1	2	0	0	0	0	0.0
Michael Fountain (goalie)	1	0	0	0	0	0	0	0	0	0.0
Sean Gagnon	5	0	0	0	13	0	0	0	0	0.0
David Oliver	7	0	0	0	2	0	0	0	2	0.0
Jani Hurme (goalie)	22	0	0	0	0	0	0	0	0	0.0

GOALTENDING

	Games	Min.	Goals	SO	Avg.	W	L	T	ENG	Shots	Sv. Pct.
Patrick Lalime	60	3607	141	7	2.35	36	19	5	3	1640	.914
Jani Hurme	22	1296	54	2	2.50	12	5	4	4	563	.904
Michael Fountain	1	59	3	0	3.05	0	1	0	0	25	.880

*Played with two or more NHL teams.

RESULTS

OCTOBER
5— At Boston .... T ... *4-4
7— Dallas .... W 3-1
13— New Jersey .... W 3-1
14— At Toronto .... W 4-0
17— At Philadelphia .... W 6-1
19— Pittsburgh .... T ... *3-3
21— Atlanta .... T ... *6-6
25— At Pittsburgh .... W 3-2
27— At Tampa Bay .... W 6-0
28— At Florida .... L 1-3
31— Toronto .... W 4-3

NOVEMBER
2— N.Y. Rangers .... W 6-5
4— Columbus .... T ... *2-2
6— At Atlanta .... W 3-2
9— At Boston .... L 1-2
11— At Philadelphia .... L 3-4
12— At Carolina .... L 0-4
16— Carolina .... L 0-1
18— Florida .... W 5-2
21— Boston .... W 2-1
23— Edmonton .... L 3-5
25— At Toronto .... W 4-2
26— At N.Y. Rangers .... L 2-3
28— Buffalo .... W 3-1

DECEMBER
2— Philadelphia .... W 5-3
3— At Carolina .... W 2-0
5— Pittsburgh .... L 2-4

8— Montreal .... W 1-0
9— At Montreal .... W 4-2
14— At Calgary .... W 4-2
16— N.Y. Islanders .... W 6-0
20— At Minnesota .... T ... *2-2
21— At Columbus .... T ... *3-3
23— Chicago .... L 2-3
27— Washington .... L 1-5
29— At Buffalo .... L 0-2
30— At Pittsburgh .... L 3-5

JANUARY
2— St. Louis .... W 3-1
4— Tampa Bay .... W 8-3
6— Montreal .... W 4-3
10— At Vancouver .... W 5-1
13— At Calgary .... W 5-2
14— At Edmonton .... L 1-4
16— Los Angeles .... L ... *6-7
18— Washington .... W 5-4
20— Tampa Bay .... W 3-0
23— At N.Y. Islanders ...... W 3-2
25— At Tampa Bay .... W 5-2
26— At Florida .... W 5-4
28— At Montreal .... L 1-4
30— At Washington .... T ... *1-1

FEBRUARY
6— At Detroit .... L 2-4
8— New Jersey .... T ... *4-4
10— Buffalo .... L ... *1-2
12— N.Y. Islanders .... W 3-1

14— At New Jersey .... W 3-2
15— Colorado .... W 4-1
18— Montreal .... W 4-0
19— At Buffalo .... L 0-2
22— Florida .... W 4-2
24— Vancouver .... W 3-0
26— At N.Y. Rangers .... W 3-2
27— Buffalo .... L 1-4

MARCH
1— San Jose .... W 8-4
3— At Toronto .... W ... *3-2
6— At New Jersey .... L ... *2-3
8— At Boston .... W 5-3
10— N.Y. Rangers .... L 2-3
11— At Washington .... L 5-6
14— Atlanta .... W 8-1
16— Anaheim .... W 4-1
18— At Dallas .... L 1-5
21— At Phoenix .... W 5-2
22— At San Jose .... W 2-1
24— At Nashville .... W 4-0
26— Philadelphia .... T ... *3-3
28— At Chicago .... W 5-2
30— Boston .... W ... *5-4

APRIL
1— Carolina .... L ... *2-3
3— At Atlanta .... L 2-5
6— At N.Y. Islanders .... W 4-3
7— Toronto .... W 5-3

*Denotes overtime game.

PHILADELPHIA FLYERS
EASTERN CONFERENCE/ATLANTIC DIVISION

Flyers' Schedule
Home games shaded; D—Day game; *—All-Star Game at Los Angeles

October

SUN	MON	TUE	WED	THU	FRI	SAT
	1	2	3	4 FLA	5	6 CBJ
7	8 CBJ	9	10 BUF	11	12	13 FLA
14	15	16 ATL	17	18 DET	19	20 WAS
21	22	23	24	25 OTT	26	27 MON
28	29	30 WAS	31 PIT			

November

SUN	MON	TUE	WED	THU	FRI	SAT
				1	2	3 NYI
4	5	6 CHI	7	8 TB	9	10 FLA
11	12	13	14 NYR	15 WAS	16	17 D NJ
18	19	20 NJ	21	22	23 DAL	24
25 VAN	26	27	28	29 BOS	30	

December

SUN	MON	TUE	WED	THU	FRI	SAT
						1 TB
2	3	4 NYI	5	6 NYI	7	8 D MIN
9	10 ATL	11	12	13 MON	14	15 BOS
16 EDM	17	18 STL	19	20 DAL	21	22 CAR
23	24	25	26 WAS	27	28 PHO	29 COL
30	31 VAN					

January

SUN	MON	TUE	WED	THU	FRI	SAT
		1	2 SJ	3	4	5
6 CAR	7	8 ATL	9	10 NJ	11	12 D NYR
13	14 MON	15 OTT	16	17 ATL	18	19 TOR
20	21 PIT	22 OTT	23	24 NAS	25	26 CAR
27	28	29 PIT	30 OTT	31		

February

SUN	MON	TUE	WED	THU	FRI	SAT
					1	2 *
3	4 LA	5	6 ANA	7	8	9 STL
10	11	12 NYI	13	14	15	16
17	18	19	20	21	22	23
24	25	26 CHI	27 NJ	28		

March

SUN	MON	TUE	WED	THU	FRI	SAT
					1	2 D NYR
3	4 BOS	5	6	7 CAL	8 TB	9
10 TOR	11	12 TOR	13	14 BUF	15	16 D COL
17	18 TB	19	20	21 ANA	22	23 D PIT
24	25 TOR	26	27 NYR	28 CAR	29	30 D BUF
31						

April

SUN	MON	TUE	WED	THU	FRI	SAT
	1 BUF	2 BOS	3	4 MON	5	6 PIT
7	8 FLA	9	10 NJ	11	12	13 D NYR
14 D NYI	15	16	17	18	19	20

Chairman
Edward M. Snider

President and general manager
Bob Clarke

Chairman of the board emeritus
Joseph C. Scott

Executive vice president
Keith Allen

Exec. v.p. and chief operating officer
Ron Ryan

Assistant general manager
Paul Holmgren

Head coach
Bill Barber

Assistant coaches
E.J. McGuire
Mike Stothers

Goaltending coach
Rejean Lemelin

Pro scouts
Al Hill
Ron Hextall
Terry Murray

Chief scout
Dennis Patterson

Scouts
Serge Boudreault, John Chapman, Inge Hammarstrom, Vaclav Slansky, Simon Nolet, Chris Pryor, Evgeny Zimin

Director of ticket operations
Cecilia Baker

Vice president, sales
Jack Betson

Vice president, sales and marketing
Kathi Gillin

Manager, sales and services
Nicole Allison

Assistant manager, sales and services
Diane Smith

Marketing assistant
Kevin Morley

Asst. to the v.p., sales and marketing
Debbie Brown

Director of public relations
Zack Hill

Dir. of media services and publications
Joe Klueg

Manager of game presentation and special events
Linda Held

Assistant director, public relations
Jill Lipson

Director, community relations
Linda Panasci

Director, fan services
Joe Kadlec

Public relations assistant
Kristin Lewandowski

Medical trainer
John Worley

Head equipment manager
Jim Evers

Equipment managers
Harry Bricker
Anthony Oratorio

Orthopedic surgeon
Arthur Bartolozzi

DRAFT CHOICES

Rd.— Player	Ht./Wt.	Overall	Pos.	Last team
1— Jeff Woywitka	6-2/197	27	D	Red Deer (WHL)
3— Patrick Sharp	6-0/188	95	C	U. of Vermont (ECAC)
5— Jussi Timonen	6-0/200	146	D	Kalpa Jr., Finland
5— Berend Bruckler	6-1/180	150	G	Tri-Cities (USHL)
5— Roman Malek	5-11/161	158	G	Slavia, Czech.
6— Dennis Seidenberg	6-0/180	172		Mannheim, Germany
6— Andrei Razin	5-11/177	177		Magnitogorsk, Russia
7— Thierry Douville	6-4/212	208	D	Baie-Comeau (QMJHL)
7— David Printz	6-5/220	225	D	Great Falls (AWHL)

MISCELLANEOUS DATA

Home ice (capacity)
First Union Center (19,519)

Address
First Union Center
3601 South Broad Street
Philadelphia, PA 19148

Business phone
215-465-4500

Ticket information
215-336-2000

Website
www.philadelphiaflyers.com

Training site
Flyers Skate Zone, Voorhees, NJ

Club colors
Orange, white and black

Radio affiliation
WIP (610 AM)

TV affiliation
Comcast SportsNet (cable); UPN 57
WPSG-TV

PHILADELPHIA FLYERS

No.	FORWARDS	Ht./Wt.	Place	BORN Date	NHL exp.	2000-01 clubs
	Jesse Boulerice (LW)	6-1/200	Plattsburgh, N.Y.	8-10-78	0	Philadelphia (AHL)
	Tomas Divisek (C)	6-2/194	Most, Czechoslovakia	7-17-79	1	Philadelphia (AHL), Philadelphia
	Jiri Dopita (C)	6-3/209	Sumperk, Czechoslovakia	12-2-68	0	Vsetin (Czech Republic)
	Todd Fedoruk (LW)	6-1/205	Redwater, Alba.	2-13-79	1	Philadelphia (AHL), Philadelphia
	Ruslan Fedotenko (RW)	6-2/190	Kiev, U.S.S.R.	1-18-79	1	Philadelphia (AHL), Philadelphia
11	Mark Freer (C)	5-10/180	Peterborough, Ont.	7-14-68	7	Philadelphia (AHL)
12	Simon Gagne (C)	6-0/175	Ste. Foy, Que.	2-29-80	2	Philadelphia
	Mark Greig (RW)	5-11/190	High River, Alta.	1-25-70	8	Philadelphia, Philadelphia (AHL)
26	Matt Herr (LW)	6-2/203	Hackensack, N.J.	5-26-76	2	Portland (AHL), Washington, Philadelphia (AHL)
	Petr Hubacek (C)	6-2/183	Brno, Czechoslovakia	9-2-79	1	Philadelphia
	Kirby Law (RW)	6-0/180	McCreary, Man.	3-11-77	1	Philadelphia (AHL), Philadelphia
10	John LeClair (LW)	6-3/226	St. Albans, Vt.	7-5-69	11	Philadelphia
28	Kent Manderville (C)	6-3/200	Edmonton	4-12-71	10	Philadelphia
28	Marty Murray (C)	5-9/178	Deloraine, Man.	2-16-75	4	Calgary, Saint John (AHL)
	Vaclav Pletka (RW)	5-10/176	Mlada Boleslav, Czech.	6-8-79	0	Philadelphia (AHL)
25	Keith Primeau (C)	6-5/220	Toronto	11-24-71	11	Philadelphia
	Paul Ranheim (LW)	6-1/210	St. Louis	1-25-66	13	Philadelphia
8	Mark Recchi (RW)	5-10/185	Kamloops, B.C.	2-1-68	13	Philadelphia
97	Jeremy Roenick (C)	6-0/207	Boston	1-17-70	13	Phoenix
	Patrick Sharp (C)	6-0/188	Thunder Bay, Ont.	12-27-81	0	Univ. of Vermont (ECAC)
	Radovan Somik (LW)	6-2/194	Martin, Czechoslovakia	5-5-77	0	HC Continental Zlin (Czech Republic)
92	Rick Tocchet (RW)	6-0/210	Scarborough, Ont.	4-9-64	17	Philadelphia
12	Mike Watt (LW/C)	6-2/208	Seaforth, Ont.	3-31-76	4	Milwaukee (IHL), Nashville
15	Peter White (C)	5-11/200	Montreal	3-15-69	6	Philadelphia
	Justin Williams (RW)	6-1/176	Cobourg, Ont.	10-4-81	1	Philadelphia
58	Matt Zultek (LW)	6-3/218	Windsor, Ont.	3-12-79	0	Philadelphia (AHL)
	DEFENSEMEN					
	Jason Beckett	6-3/203	Lethbridge, Alta.	7-23-80	0	Philadelphia (AHL), Trenton (ECHL)
43	Andy Delmore	6-1/192	Windsor, Ont.	12-26-76	3	Philadelphia
37	Eric Desjardins	6-1/205	Rouyn, Que.	6-14-69	13	Philadelphia
	Francis Lessard	6-2/184	Montreal	5-30-79	0	Philadelphia (AHL)
33	Chris McAllister	6-8/225	Saskatoon, Sask.	6-16-75	4	Philadelphia
3	Dan McGillis	6-2/225	Hawkesbury, Ont.	7-1-72	5	Philadelphia
22	Luke Richardson	6-3/210	Kanata, Ont.	3-26-69	14	Philadelphia
	Sergei Skrobot	6-3/191	Most, Czechoslovakia	3-9-80	0	Philadelphia (AHL), Trenton (ECHL)
32	John Slaney	6-0/185	St. John's, Nfld.	2-7-72	7	Wilkes-Barre/Scranton (AHL), Philadelphia (AHL)
	Bruno St. Jacques	6-2/204	Montreal	8-22-80	0	Philadelphia (AHL)
23	Michal Sykora	6-5/225	Pardubice, Czechoslovakia	7-5-73	7	Philadelphia
6	Chris Therien	6-4/230	Ottawa	12-14-71	7	Philadelphia
39	Brad Tiley	6-1/185	Markdale, Ont.	7-5-71	3	Philadelphia (AHL), Philadelphia
	Jussi Timonen	6-0/200	Kuopio, Finland	6-29-83	0	KalPa Kuopio (Finland Jr.)
22	Eric Weinrich	6-1/213	Roanoke, Va.	12-19-66	13	Montreal, Boston
	Jeff Woywitka	6-2/197	Vermillion, Alta.	9-1-83	0	Red Deer (WHL)
	GOALTENDERS					
33	Brian Boucher	6-1/190	Woonsocket, R.I.	8-1-77	2	Philadelphia
	Berend Bruckler	6-1/180	Graz, Austria	9-26-81	0	Tri-Cities (USHL)
	Roman Cechmanck	6-3/187	Czechoslovakia	3-2-71	1	Philadelphia (AHL), Philadelphia
35	Neil Little	6-1/193	Medicine Hat, Alta.	12-18-71	0	Philadelphia (AHL)
	Roman Malek	5-11/161	Czechoslovakia	9-25-77	0	Slavia Praha (Czech Republic)
	Antero Niittymaki	6-0/176	Turku, Finland	6-18-80	0	TPS Turku (Finland)
	Maxime Ouellet	6-0/180	Beauport, Que.	6-17-81	1	Philadelphia, Philadelphia (AHL), Rouyn-Noranda (QMJHL)
	Brian Regan	6-0/175	New Haven, Conn.	9-23-75	0	Trenton (ECHL), Philadelphia (AHL)

2000-01 REVIEW

INDIVIDUAL STATISTICS

SCORING

	Games	G	A	Pts.	PIM	+/-	PPG	SHG	Shots	Shooting Pct.
Mark Recchi	69	27	50	77	33	15	7	1	191	14.1
Keith Primeau	71	34	39	73	76	17	11	0	165	20.6
Simon Gagne	69	27	32	59	18	24	6	0	191	14.1
Daymond Langkow	71	13	41	54	50	12	3	0	190	6.8
Daniel McGillis	82	14	35	49	86	13	4	0	207	6.8
Eric Desjardins	79	15	33	48	50	-3	6	1	187	8.0
Ruslan Fedotenko	74	16	20	36	72	8	3	0	119	13.4
Rick Tocchet	60	14	22	36	83	10	5	0	76	18.4

	Games	G	A	Pts.	PIM	+/-	PPG	SHG	Shots	Shooting Pct.
Justin Williams	63	12	13	25	22	6	0	0	99	12.1
Peter White	77	9	16	25	16	1	1	0	68	13.2
Paul Ranheim	80	10	7	17	14	2	0	2	123	8.1
Michal Sykora	49	5	11	16	26	9	1	1	71	7.0
Jody Hull	71	7	8	15	10	-1	0	2	78	9.0
Kent Manderville	82	5	10	15	47	-2	0	3	136	3.7
Andy Delmore	66	5	9	14	16	2	2	0	119	4.2
Chris Therien	73	2	12	14	48	22	1	0	103	1.9
John LeClair	16	7	5	12	0	2	3	0	48	14.6
Todd Fedoruk	53	5	5	10	109	0	0	0	28	17.9
Kevin Stevens*	23	2	7	9	18	-2	0	0	31	6.5
Luke Richardson	82	2	6	8	131	23	0	1	75	2.7
Michel Picard	7	1	4	5	0	6	1	0	12	8.3
Chris McAllister	60	2	2	4	124	1	0	0	33	6.1
Gino Odjick*	17	1	3	4	28	0	0	0	21	4.8
P.J. Stock*	31	1	3	4	78	-2	0	0	18	5.6
Derek Plante	12	1	2	3	4	0	0	0	20	5.0
Mark Greig	7	1	1	2	4	-2	0	0	7	14.3
Dean McAmmond*	10	1	1	2	0	-1	1	0	17	5.9
Petr Hubacek	6	1	0	1	2	-1	0	0	5	20.0
Roman Cechmanek (goalie)	59	0	1	1	4	0	0	0	0	0.0
Kirby Law	1	0	0	0	0	-1	0	0	0	0.0
Brad Tiley	2	0	0	0	0	-1	0	0	1	0.0
Maxime Ouellet (goalie)	2	0	0	0	0	0	0	0	0	0.0
Tomas Divisek	2	0	0	0	0	-1	0	0	2	0.0
Steve Washburn	3	0	0	0	0	0	0	0	0	0.0
Keith Jones	8	0	0	0	4	-5	0	0	11	0.0
Brian Boucher (goalie)	27	0	0	0	2	0	0	0	0	0.0

GOALTENDING

	Games	Min.	Goals	SO	Avg.	W	L	T	ENG	Shots	Sv. Pct.
Roman Cechmanek	59	3431	115	10	2.01	35	15	6	2	1464	.921
Maxime Ouellet	2	76	3	0	2.37	0	1	0	1	27	.889
Brian Boucher	27	1470	80	1	3.27	8	12	5	6	644	.876

*Played with two or more NHL teams.

RESULTS

OCTOBER
5— Vancouver ....W.....6-3
7— Boston ....L.....1-5
11—At Minnesota ....T....*3-3
12— At Dallas ....L.....1-4
14— At Phoenix......................L.....3-6
17—Ottawa ....L.....1-6
19—Montreal ....T....*3-3
21—Anaheim ....L.....3-4
24— At N.Y. Rangers ....W.....5-4
26—N.Y. Rangers ....W.....3-0
29—Washington ....T....*1-1

NOVEMBER
1— At New Jersey ....T....*1-1
2— Nashville ....L.....1-3
4— Buffalo ....W.....3-0
8— At Pittsburgh ....L.....2-5
9— Edmonton....................W.....2-0
11—Ottawa ....W.....4-3
15—At Toronto ....W....*2-1
17—At Atlanta ....W....*3-2
18—Washington ....W.....5-3
22— At Buffalo ....W.....3-1
24—Pittsburgh ....L.....0-1
26—Phoenix ....L.....1-2
29—At Columbus ....W.....4-3
30—At Carolina ....L.....0-2

DECEMBER
2— At Ottawa.....................L.....3-5
6— Tampa Bay ....W.....6-3

8— At Detroit.....................L......1-5
10—N.Y. Islanders ....W.....5-2
12—At Nashville ....T....*2-2
13—At Colorado ....T....*3-3
16—New Jersey ....W.....6-3
19—At Boston....................T....*4-4
21—San Jose ....W.....4-3
23—Carolina ....W....*2-1
27—At Florida ....W.....5-2
28—At Tampa Bay ....L.....3-4
30—At Washington ....L.....3-6

JANUARY
2— At New Jersey ....T....*1-1
5— At Atlanta ....W.....6-4
6— Atlanta ....T....*2-2
8— At St. Louis ....W....*2-1
12—At Tampa Bay ....W.....3-0
13—At Florida ....W.....4-1
16—At N.Y. Rangers ....L....*3-4
18—New Jersey ....L.....1-7
20—Florida ....W.....5-3
22—Los Angeles ....W.....3-0
25—At Chicago ....W.....5-1
27—At Carolina ....W.....4-3
28—At Washington ....L.....2-4
31—At Pittsburgh ....W.....5-1

FEBRUARY
1— N.Y. Islanders ....W.....2-0
6— At Boston....................L.....3-4
7— At Pittsburgh ....L.....4-9

9— At N.Y. Islanders..............W.....5-2
14—At N.Y. Islanders...........W.....3-1
15—Toronto ....W.....5-2
17—Atlanta ....W.....5-1
19—Carolina ....W.....4-0
22—At N.Y. Islanders ....L....*3-4
24—Tampa Bay ....T....*0-0
25—N.Y. Rangers ....W.....2-1
27—Montreal ....L.....2-3

MARCH
1— Buffalo........................W.....2-0
3— At Montreal..................L.....1-3
5— Boston........................W.....6-4
8— Calgary......................W.....5-2
10—New Jersey ....L.....2-3
13—St. Louis ....W.....5-2
15—Minnesota ....W.....3-0
17—N.Y. Rangers ....W.....2-1
19—At Edmonton ....W.....4-2
22—At Calgary ....L.....1-3
24—At Toronto ....L.....3-5
26—At Ottawa ....T....*3-3
29—Toronto ....L.....1-2
31—Detroit ....W.....1-0

APRIL
3— Florida ....L.....1-2
5— At Montreal..................L....*2-3
7— Pittsburgh ....W....*4-3
8— At Buffalo ....W.....2-1
*Denotes overtime game.

PHOENIX COYOTES
WESTERN CONFERENCE/PACIFIC DIVISION

Coyotes' Schedule
Home games shaded; D—Day game; *—All-Star Game at Los Angeles

October

SUN	MON	TUE	WED	THU	FRI	SAT
	1	2	3	4 LA	5	6 EDM
7	8 CAL	9	10	11 CHI	12	13 WAS
14	15	16 BOS	17	18 DAL	19	20 VAN
21	22	23	24 ANA	25	26	27 COL
28	29	30 BUF	31			

November

SUN	MON	TUE	WED	THU	FRI	SAT
				1 NJ	2 WAS	3
4 D	5 CAR	6	7 DET	8	9 DAL	10 STL
11	12	13 EDM	14	15 SJ	16	17 NYI
18	19	20 MIN	21	22	23 D MIN	24 STL
25	26	27 CBJ	28	29 NAS	30	

December

SUN	MON	TUE	WED	THU	FRI	SAT
						1 PIT
2	3	4	5 STL	6	7 DET	8 MON
9	10	11 TOR	12	13 OTT	14	15 DAL
16	17 CBJ	18	19 CAL	20	21 ANA	22
23 ANA	24	25	26 LA	27	28 PHI	29
30 SJ	31 NYR					

January

SUN	MON	TUE	WED	THU	FRI	SAT
		1	2	3 ATL	4 SJ	5
6 TB	7	8	9 SJ	10	11	12
13	14	15 DET	16	17 COL	18	19 BUF
20	21 NAS	22	23 CHI	24	25 DET	26 CBJ
27	28 ATL	29	30 FLA	31		

February

SUN	MON	TUE	WED	THU	FRI	SAT
					1	2 *
3	4 VAN	5	6 CHI	7	8 LA	9
10 EDM	11	12 CAL	13 LA	14	15	16
17	18	19	20	21	22	23
24	25	26 DAL	27	28 COL		

March

SUN	MON	TUE	WED	THU	FRI	SAT
					1	2
3 CBJ	4	5 NJ	6	7 VAN	8	9 OTT
10	11	12 CHI	13	14	15 NAS	16
17 D MIN	18	19 BOS	20 PIT	21	22 DAL	23
24 LA	25	26	27 ANA	28 ANA	29	30 COL
31						

April

SUN	MON	TUE	WED	THU	FRI	SAT
	1 STL	2	3	4 SJ	5	6
7 VAN	8	9 CAL	10 EDM	11	12 MIN	13
14 D NAS	15	16	17	18	19	20

2001-02 SEASON
CLUB DIRECTORY

Chairman and CEO
Steve Ellman
Managing partner
Wayne Gretzky
President and partner
Shawn Hunter
Executive v.p. and general manager
Cliff Fletcher
Assistant general manager
Laurence Gilman
Head coach
Bob Francis
Assistant coaches
Rick Bowness
Pat Conacher
Goaltending coach
Benoit Allaire
Strength & conditioning coach
Stieg Theander

Video coordinator
Steve Peters
Athletic therapist
Gord Hart
Massage therapist
Jukka Nieminen
Equipment manager
Stan Wilson
Assistant equipment managers
Tony Silva
Jason Rudee
V.p. of media & player relations
Richard Nairn
Director of media relations
Rick Braunstein
Publications & media relations coord.
Ryan Lichtenfels

DRAFT CHOICES

Rd.— Player	Ht./Wt.	Overall	Pos.	Last team
1— Fredrik Sjostrom	6-0/194	11	RW	Frolunda, Sweden
2— Matthew Spiller	6-5/210	31	D	Seattle (WHL)
2— Martin Podlesak	6-6/200	45	C	Lethbridge (WHL)
3— Beat Schiess-Forster	6-1/209	78	D	Davos, Switzerland
5— David Klema	6-0/178	148	C	Des Moines (USHL)
6— Scott Polaski	6-2/182	180	RW	Sioux City (USHL)
7— Steve Belanger	6-1/198	210	G	Kamloops (WHL)
8— Frantisek Lukes	5-9/162	243	LW	Toronto (OHL)
9— Severin Blindenbacher	5-11/183	273	D	Kloten, Switzerland

MISCELLANEOUS DATA

Home ice (capacity)
America West Arena (16,210)
Address
Alltel Ice Den
9375 E. Bell Road
Scottsdale, AZ 85260
Business phone
480-473-5600
Ticket information
480-563-7825
Website
www.phoenixcoyotes.com

Training site
Scottsdale, AZ
Club colors
Red, green, sand, sienna and purple
Radio affiliation
KDUS (1060 AM) and KDKB (93.3 FM)
TV affiliation
FOX Sports Arizona, WB 61, KTVK
(Channel 3)

TRAINING CAMP ROSTER

No.	FORWARDS	Ht./Wt.	BORN Place	Date	NHL exp.	2000-01 clubs
	Ramzi Abid (LW)	6-2/195	Montreal	3-24-80	0	Springfield (AHL)
94	Sergei Berezin (LW)	5-10/200	Voskresensk, U.S.S.R.	11-5-71	5	Toronto
	Tyler Bouck (RW)	6-0/185	Camrose, Alta.	1-13-80	1	Dallas, Utah (IHL)
8	Daniel Briere (C)	5-10/181	Gatineau, Que.	10-6-77	4	Phoenix, Springfield (AHL)
19	Shane Doan (RW)	6-2/218	Halkirk, Alta.	10-10-76	6	Phoenix
26	Michal Handzus (C)	6-5/210	Banska Bystrica, Czech.	3-11-77	3	St. Louis, Phoenix
	Jason Jaspers (C/LW)	6-0/185	Thunder Bay, Ont.	4-8-81	0	Sudbury (OHL)
10	Mike Johnson (RW)	6-2/200	Scarborough, Ont.	10-3-74	5	Tampa Bay, Phoenix
	David Klema (C)	6-0/178	Roseau, Minn.	4-3-82	0	Des Moines (USHL)
	Krys Kolanos (C)	6-2/196	Calgary	7-27-81	0	Boston College (Hockey East)
18	Daymond Langkow (C)	5-11/180	Edmonton	9-27-76	6	Philadelphia
	Ryan Lauzon (C)	5-10/185	Halifax, Nova Scotia	10-8-80	0	Springfield (AHL)
22	Claude Lemieux (RW)	6-1/215	Buckingham, Que.	7-16-65	18	Phoenix
10	Trevor Letowski (C)	5-10/176	Thunder Bay, Ont.	4-5-77	3	Phoenix
9	Brad May (LW)	6-1/210	Toronto	11-29-71	10	Phoenix
47	Ladislav Nagy (C)	5-11/183	Presov, Yugoslavia	6-1-79	2	St. Louis, Worcester (AHL), Phoenix
	Martin Podlesak (C)	6-6/200	Melnik, Czechoslovakia	9-26-82	0	Tri-City (WHL), Lethbridge (WHL)
	Branko Radivojevic (RW)	6-1/185	Piestany, Czechoslovakia	11-24-80	0	Belleville (OHL)
	Brad Ralph (LW)	6-2/198	Ottawa	10-17-80	1	Phoenix, Springfield (AHL)
	Fredrik Sjostrom (RW)	6-0/194	Fargelanda, Sweden	5-6-83	0	V. Frolunda Goteborg (Sweden Jr.), Vastra Frolunda (Sweden)
	Wyatt Smith (C)	5-11/200	Thief River Falls, Minn.	2-13-77	2	Phoenix, Springfield (AHL)
26	Mike Sullivan (C)	6-2/201	Marshfield, Mass.	2-28-68	10	Phoenix
	Jeff Taffe (C)	6-1/180	Hastings, Minn.	2-19-81	0	Univ. of Minnesota (WCHA)
	Jean-Guy Trudel (RW)	6-0/190	Cadillac, Que.	10-18-75	1	Springfield (AHL)
8	Todd Warriner (LW)	6-1/200	Blenheim, Ont.	1-3-74	7	Tampa Bay
27	Landon Wilson (RW)	6-2/216	St. Louis	3-15-75	6	Phoenix
	Ruslan Zainullin (RW)	6-2/202	Kazan, U.S.S.R.	2-14-82	0	Ak Bars Kazan (Russian)
	DEFENSEMEN					
	Goran Bezina	6-3/203	Split, Yugoslavia	3-21-80	0	Fribourg-Gotteron (Switzerland)
18	Joel Bouchard	6-0/200	Montreal	1-23-74	7	Grand Rapids (IHL), Phoenix
	David Cullen	6-1/195	St. Catherine's, Ont.	12-30-76	1	Springfield (AHL), Phoenix
	Martin Grenier	6-5/230	Laval, Que.	11-2-80	0	Quebec (QMJHL), Victoriaville (QMJHL)
2	Paul Mara	6-4/210	Ridgewood, N.J.	9-7-79	3	Tampa Bay, Detroit (IHL), Phoenix
55	Danny Markov	6-1/190	Moscow, U.S.S.R.	7-11-76	4	Toronto
27	Teppo Numminen	6-2/199	Tampere, Finland	7-3-68	13	Phoenix
	Kirill Safronov	6-2/196	Leningrad, U.S.S.R.	2-26-81	0	Springfield (AHL)
	Beat Scheiss-Forster	6-1/209	Herisau, Switzerland	2-2-83	0	Davos (Switzerland Jr.), Davos (Switzerland)
22	Todd Simpson	6-3/215	Edmonton	5-28-73	6	Florida, Phoenix
	Matthew Spiller	6-5/210	Daysland, Alta.	2-7-83	0	Seattle (WHL)
15	Radoslav Suchy	6-1/191	Poprad, Czechoslovakia	4-7-76	2	Phoenix
	Ossi Vaananen	6-3/200	Vantaa, Finland	8-18-80	1	Phoenix
	GOALTENDERS					
	Josh Blackburn	6-0/185	Del Rio, Tex.	11-13-78	0	Univ. of Michigan (CCHA)
1	Sean Burke	6-4/210	Windsor, Ont.	1-29-67	13	Phoenix
	Patrick DesRochers	6-3/195	Penetang, Ont.	10-27-79	0	Springfield (AHL)
42	Robert Esche	6-0/188	Utica, N.Y.	1-22-78	3	Phoenix

2000-01 REVIEW

INDIVIDUAL STATISTICS

SCORING

	Games	G	A	Pts.	PIM	+/-	PPG	SHG	Shots	Shooting Pct.
Jeremy Roenick	80	30	46	76	114	-1	13	0	192	15.6
Keith Tkachuk*	64	29	42	71	108	6	15	0	230	12.6
Shane Doan	76	26	37	63	89	0	6	1	220	11.8
Joe Juneau	69	10	23	33	28	-2	5	0	100	10.0
Landon Wilson	70	18	13	31	92	3	2	0	123	14.6
Teppo Numminen	72	5	26	31	36	9	1	0	109	4.6
Travis Green	69	13	15	28	63	-11	3	0	113	11.5
Claude Lemieux	46	10	16	26	58	1	2	0	99	10.1
Brad May	62	11	14	25	107	10	0	0	83	13.3
Jyrki Lumme	58	4	21	25	44	3	0	0	77	5.2
Juha Ylonen	69	9	14	23	38	10	0	1	72	12.5
Trevor Letowski	77	7	15	22	32	-2	0	1	110	6.4
Mika Alatalo	70	7	12	19	22	1	0	0	64	10.9
Ossi Vaananen	81	4	12	16	90	9	0	0	69	5.8

	Games	G	A	Pts.	PIM	+/-	PPG	SHG	Shots	Shooting Pct.
Keith Carney	82	2	14	16	86	15	0	0	65	3.1
Daniel Briere	30	11	4	15	12	-2	9	0	43	25.6
Wyatt Smith	42	3	7	10	13	7	0	1	40	7.5
Radoslav Suchy	72	0	10	10	22	1	0	0	33	0.0
Mike Sullivan	72	5	4	9	16	-6	0	3	59	8.5
Michal Handzus*	10	4	4	8	21	5	0	1	14	28.6
Mike Johnson*	12	2	3	5	4	0	1	0	17	11.8
Stan Neckar*	53	2	2	4	63	-2	0	0	16	12.5
Paul Mara*	16	0	4	4	14	1	0	0	20	0.0
Joel Bouchard	32	1	2	3	22	-8	0	0	26	3.8
Robert Esche (goalie)	25	0	3	3	2	0	0	0	0	0.0
Chris Joseph*	24	1	1	2	16	-4	0	1	33	3.0
Ladislav Nagy*	6	0	1	1	2	0	0	0	5	0.0
Todd Simpson*	13	0	1	1	12	-4	0	0	9	0.0
Sean Burke (goalie)	62	0	1	1	16	0	0	0	0	0.0
Brad Ralph	1	0	0	0	0	0	0	0	0	0.0
David Cullen	2	0	0	0	0	1	0	0	0	0.0
Tavis Hansen	7	0	0	0	4	-1	0	0	2	0.0
Louie Debrusk	39	0	0	0	79	-5	0	0	12	0.0

GOALTENDING

	Games	Min.	Goals	SO	Avg.	W	L	T	ENG	Shots	Sv. Pct.
Sean Burke	62	3644	138	4	2.27	25	22	13	5	1766	.922
Robert Esche	25	1350	68	2	3.02	10	8	4	1	657	.896

*Played with two or more NHL teams.

RESULTS

OCTOBER

5— St. Louis	W	4-1
7— Minnesota	W	4-1
12— At San Jose	L	1-2
14— Philadelphia	W	6-3
15— At Los Angeles	W	6-5
18— Florida	W	*2-1
21— At Vancouver	W	*3-2
22— At Edmonton	T	*3-3
24— At Calgary	T	*2-2
27— At Dallas	W	4-2
28— Los Angeles	W	3-1
30— At Colorado	W	4-0

NOVEMBER

1— At Anaheim	T	*1-1
3— Dallas	T	*2-2
7— At Los Angeles	T	*3-3
8— Detroit	L	2-4
11—At Columbus	L	1-2
12— At N.Y. Rangers	W	2-0
14— At Washington	T	*2-2
16— Colorado	W	6-3
18— Anaheim	L	2-6
21— Chicago	L	1-4
25— At St. Louis	L	1-5
26— At Philadelphia	W	2-1
29— At Colorado	L	1-2
30— Minnesota	W	2-0

DECEMBER

2— Dallas	L	2-5
6— Vancouver	T	*1-1
10— Columbus	T	*1-1
14— Tampa Bay	W	3-2
16— San Jose	L	*1-2
20— Calgary	W	4-2
22— Atlanta	W	5-1
27— At Chicago	T	*1-1
29— At Minnesota	T	*2-2
30— At St. Louis	L	1-2

JANUARY

1— San Jose	L	2-3
4— N.Y. Rangers	W	3-1
6— At N.Y. Islanders	W	2-1
9— At Detroit	T	*2-2
10— At New Jersey	L	1-5
12— At Toronto	L	2-3
13— At Montreal	L	2-5
15— St. Louis	W	3-1
17— Pittsburgh	W	5-4
19— At Anaheim	W	4-3
21— Dallas	W	5-2
23— At Calgary	W	4-2
24— At Vancouver	L	2-6
26— At Edmonton	T	*1-1
29— Nashville	L	2-5

FEBRUARY

1— Anaheim	L	2-4
7— Carolina	L	*1-2
9— Edmonton	W	2-0
11— Chicago	W	3-2
13— At Tampa Bay	W	5-2
14— At Florida	L	3-4

16— At Carolina	W	2-0
18— Calgary	L	1-4
21— Columbus	W	3-2
23— At Buffalo	W	7-3
25— At Detroit	L	3-6
27— At Boston	I	4-7
28— At Columbus	L	2-5

MARCH

2— Detroit	T	*2-2
4— Colorado	L	0-5
6— Nashville	W	5-1
8— Vancouver	W	*3-2
10— Montreal	T	*3-3
14— New Jersey	L	2-3
16— At Dallas	T	*1-1
17— At Nashville	L	1-4
19— At Los Angeles	L	2-6
21— Ottawa	L	2-5
24— Edmonton	W	7-4
25— N.Y. Islanders	T	*2-2
28— At Minnesota	W	2-0
29— At Nashville	L	*3-4
31— San Jose	W	3-1

APRIL

3— Los Angeles	T	*2-2
5— At San Jose	L	0-3
6— At Anaheim	W	5-2

*Denotes overtime game.

PITTSBURGH PENGUINS
EASTERN CONFERENCE/ATLANTIC DIVISION

Penguins' Schedule
Home games shaded; D—Day game; *—All-Star Game at Los Angeles

October

SUN	MON	TUE	WED	THU	FRI	SAT
	1	2	3 COL	4	5	6 ANA
7	8	9	10 NYI	11	12	13
14 D BUF	15	16 OTT	17	18 OTT	19	20 STL
21	22	23 ATL	24 DAL	25	26	27 TOR
28 FLA	29	30	31 PHI			

November

SUN	MON	TUE	WED	THU	FRI	SAT
				1 TOR	2	3 TB
4	5	6 CAR	7 FLA	8	9	10 TB
11	12	13 NJ	14 NYI	15	16	17 NYR
18	19	20	21 VAN	22	23 NAS	24 BUF
25	26	27 NJ	28	29 SJ	30	

December

SUN	MON	TUE	WED	THU	FRI	SAT
						1 PHO
2	3	4 TOR	5	6 BOS	7	8 ATL
9	10	11 WAS	12 BOS	13	14 MIN	15
16 CAR	17	18	19 MON	20	21 WAS	22 WAS
23	24	25	26 NJ	27	28	29 OTT
30	31					

January

SUN	MON	TUE	WED	THU	FRI	SAT
		1	2	3 NYI	4	5 D NYR
6 CHI	7	8 BOS	9	10 BUF	11	12 D STL
13	14	15 VAN	16	17 CAL	18	19 EDM
20	21 PHI	22	23 TB	24 NYI	25	26 D ATL
27	28	29 PHI	30 SJ	31		

February

SUN	MON	TUE	WED	THU	FRI	SAT
					1	2 *
3	4	5 CAR	6	7 MON	8	9 D NJ
10 D NYR	11	12 OTT	13	14	15	16
17	18	19	20	21	22	23
24	25	26	27 LA	28 CBJ		

March

SUN	MON	TUE	WED	THU	FRI	SAT
					1	2 D DET
3	4 NYI	5 FLA	6	7 CAR	8	9 D NYR
10	11 CBJ	12	13 ANA	14	15	16 D LA
17	18 ATL	19	20 PHO	21	22	23 D PHI
24 WAS	25	26	27 NJ	28	29	30 MON
31						

April

SUN	MON	TUE	WED	THU	FRI	SAT
	1 MON	2	3 FLA	4 TB	5	6 PHI
7	8 NYR	9	10 BUF	11	12 TOR	13 BOS
14	15	16	17	18	19	20

2001-02 SEASON
CLUB DIRECTORY

Ownership
Mario Lemieux and the Lemieux Group

Executive v.p./general manager
Craig Patrick

Executive vice president/COO
Tom Rooney

Executive vice president/CFO
Ken Sawyer

Assistant general manager
Ed Johnston

Head coach
Ivan Hlinka

Assistant coaches
Randy Hillier
Rick Kehoe
Joe Mullen

Goaltending coach and scout
Gilles Meloche

Head scout
Greg Malone

Scouts
Herb Brooks
Wayne Daniels
Charlie Hodge
Mark Kelley
Neil Shea

Vice president, general counsel
Ted Black

Vice president, corporate sales
David Soltesz

Vice president/controller
Kevin Hart

V.p./communications/marketing
Tom McMillan

Director of media relations
Steve Bovino

Manager, media relations
Keith Wehner

Vice president, ticket sales
Mark Anderson

Strength and conditioning coach
John Welday

Equipment manager
Steve Latin

Assistant equipment manager
Paul Flati

Trainers
Mark Mortland
Scott Johnson

Team physician
Dr. Charles Burke

DRAFT CHOICES

Rd.— Player	Ht./Wt.	Overall	Pos.	Last team
1— Colby Armstrong	6-1/180	21	RW	Red Deer (WHL)
2— Noah Welch	6-3/212	54	D	St. Sebastian's (USHSE)
3— Drew Fata	6-1/211	86	D	Toronto (OHL)
3— Alexandre Rouleau	6-1/180	96	D	Val-d'Or (QMJHL)
4— Tomas Surovy	6-0/191	120	F	Poprad, Slovakia
4— Ben Eaves	5-8/174	131	C	Boston Col. (H. East)
5— Andy Schneider	6-0/220	156	D	Lincoln, N.D. (USHL)
7— Tomas Duba	6-0/176	217	G	Sparta, Czech.
8— Brandon Crawford-West	5-11/185	250	G	Texas Tornado (NAHL)

MISCELLANEOUS DATA

Home ice (capacity)
Mellon Arena (16,958)

Address
Mellon Arena
66 Mario Lemieux Place
Pittsburgh, PA 15219

Business phone
412-642-1300

Ticket information
412-642-7367 and 1-800-642-7367

Website
www.pittsburghpenguins.com

Training site
Canonsburg, PA

Club colors
Black, gold and white

Radio affiliation
3WS (94.5 FM and 970 AM)

TV affiliation
Fox Sports Net Pittsburgh

TRAINING CAMP ROSTER

No.	FORWARDS	Ht./Wt.	Place	Date	NHL exp.	2000-01 clubs
	Colby Armstrong (RW)....	6-1/180	Lloydminster, Sask.	11-23-82	0	Red Deer (WHL)
	Kris Beech (C)	6-2/178	Salmon Arm, B.C.	2-5-81	1	Calgary (WHL), Washington
	Greg Crozier (LW)..........	6-3/199	Williamsville, N.Y.	7-6-76	1	Wilkes-Barre/Scranton (AHL), Pittsburgh
	Ben Eaves (C)	5-8/174	Minneapolis	3-27-82	0	Boston College (Hockey East)
	Shane Endicott (C)	6-4/200	Saskatoon, Sask.	12-21-81	0	Seattle (WHL)
38	Jan Hrdina (C)	6-0/200	Hradec Kralove, Czech.	2-5-76	3	Pittsburgh
	Konstantin Koltsov (LW)...	6-0/187	Minsk, U.S.S.R.	4-17-81	0	Ak Bars Kazan (Russian)
	Tom Kostopoulos (RW)...	6-0/205	Mississauga, Ont.	1-24-79	0	Wilkes-Barre/Scranton (AHL)
27	Alexei Kovalev (C)..........	6-1/215	Moscow, U.S.S.R.	2-24-73	9	Pittsburgh
	Milan Kraft (C)	6-3/191	Plzen, Czechoslovakia	1-17-80	1	Pittsburgh, Wilkes-Barre/Scranton (AHL)
33	Dan LaCouture (LW)........	6-1/201	Hyannis, Mass.	4-13-77	3	Edmonton, Pittsburgh
20	Robert Lang (C)	6-2/216	Teplice, Czechoslovakia	12-19-70	8	Pittsburgh
66	Mario Lemieux (C)..........	6-4/200	Montreal	10-5-65	17	Pittsburgh
	Alexandre Mathieu (C).....	6-2/177	Repentigny, Que.	2-12-79	0	Wilkes-Barre/Scranton (AHL)
	Eric Meloche (RW)	5-11/195	Montreal	5-1-76	0	Wilkes-Barre/Scranton (AHL)
24	Ian Moran (RW/D)...........	6-0/206	Cleveland	8-24-72	7	Pittsburgh
95	Aleksey Morozov (RW)....	6-1/196	Moscow, U.S.S.R.	2-16-77	4	Pittsburgh
	Matt Murley (LW)	6-1/192	Troy, N.Y.	12-17-79	0	Rensselaer Poly. Inst. (ECAC)
29	Krzysztof Oliwa (RW)	6-5/235	Tychy, Poland	4-12-73	5	Columbus, Pittsburgh
	Michel Ouellet (RW)	6-1/182	Rimouski, Que.	3-5-82	0	Rimouski (QMJHL)
	Toby Petersen (C)..........	5-10/196	Minneapolis	10-27-78	1	Wilkes-Barre/Scranton (AHL), Pittsburgh
22	Wayne Primeau (C)	6-3/225	Scarborough, Ont.	6-4-76	7	Tampa Bay, Pittsburgh
	Michal Sivek (C)	6-3/209	Nachod, Czechoslovakia	1-21-81	0	Sparta Praha (Czech Republic)
	Tomas Skvaridlo (C/LW)..	6-1/180	Zvolen, Czechoslovakia	6-19-81	0	Kingston (OHL)
12	Martin Sonnenberg (LW).	6-0/184	Wetaskiwin, Alta.	1-23-78	2	Wilkes-Barre/Scranton (AHL)
17	Kevin Stevens (LW)	6-3/230	Brockton, Mass.	4-15-65	14	Philadelphia, Pittsburgh
82	Martin Straka (C)	5-9/176	Plzen, Czechoslovakia	9-3-72	9	Pittsburgh
	Tomas Surovy (RW/LW)..	6-0/191	Banska Bystrica, Czech.	9-24-81	0	HC SKP Poprad (Slovakia)
	Billy Tibbetts (RW)	6-2/215	Boston	10-14-74	1	Wilkes-Barre/Scranton (AHL), Pittsburgh
	Darcy Verot (LW)	6-0/190	Radville, Sask.	7-13-76	0	Wilkes-Barre/Scranton (AHL)
	Alexander Zevakhin (C)....	6-0/187	Perm, U.S.S.R.	6-4-80	0	Wilkes-Barre/Scranton (AHL)
	DEFENSEMEN					
	Drew Fata	6-1/211	Sault Ste. Marie, Ont.	7-28-83	0	Toronto St. Michael's (OHL)
7	Andrew Ference..............	5-10/190	Edmonton	3-17-79	2	Wilkes-Barre/Scranton (AHL), Pittsburgh
	Brian Gaffaney	6-5/205	Alexandria, Minn.	10-4-77	0	St. Cloud State (WCHA), Wilkes-Barre/Scranton (AHL)
8	Hans Jonsson.................	6-1/202	Jarved, Sweden	8-2-73	2	Pittsburgh
11	Darius Kasparaitis...........	5-11/212	Elektrenai, U.S.S.R.	10-16-72	9	Pittsburgh
	David Koci	6-6/216	Prague, Czechoslovakia	5-12-81	0	Prince George (WHL)
5	Janne Laukkanen............	6-1/194	Lahti, Finland	3-19-70	7	Pittsburgh
	Ross Lupaschuk	6-1/211	Edmonton	1-19-81	0	Red Deer (WHL)
	Josef Melichar	6-2/214	Ceske Budejovice, Czech.	1-20-79	1	Wilkes-Barre/Scranton (AHL), Pittsburgh
	Brooks Orpik...................	6-3/217	Amherst, N.Y.	9-26-80	0	Boston College (Hockey East)
	Darcy Robinson	6-3/229	Kamloops, B.C.	5-3-81	0	Saskatoon (WHL), Red Deer (WHL)
	Alexandre Rouleau..........	6-1/180	Mont-Laurier, Que.	7-29-83	0	Val-d'Or (QMJHL)
28	Michal Rozsival	6-1/208	Vlasim, Czechoslovakia	9-3-78	2	Pittsburgh, Wilkes-Barre/Scranton (AHL)
	Andy Schneider	6-0/220	Grand Forks, N.D.	7-31-81	0	Lincoln (USHL)
	Robert Scuderi	6-1/194	Syosset, N.Y.	12-30-78	0	Boston College (Hockey East)
	Noah Welch	6-3/212	Brighton, Mass.	8-26-82	0	St. Sebastian's (USHS (East))
7	Mike Wilson	6-6/212	Brampton, Ont.	2-26-75	6	Florida, Louisville (AHL)
	GOALTENDERS					
30	Jean-Sebastien Aubin	5-11/176	Montreal	7-19-77	3	Pittsburgh
	Sebastien Caron	6-1/150	Amqui, Que.	6-25-80	0	Wilkes-Barre/Scranton (AHL)
	Johan Hedberg	5-11/185	Leksand, Sweden	5-5-73	2	Manitoba (IHL), Pittsburgh
	Joel Laing	5-10/185	Mayfield, Sask.	11-3-75	0	Wilkes-Barre/Scranton (AHL), Wheeling (ECHL)
	Mark Scally....................	5-10/165	Coraopolis, Pa.	6-29-77	0	Wheeling (ECHL), Wilkes-Barre/Scranton (AHL)

2000-01 REVIEW

INDIVIDUAL STATISTICS

SCORING

	Games	G	A	Pts.	PIM	+/-	PPG	SHG	Shots	Shooting Pct.
Jaromir Jagr	81	52	69	121	42	19	14	1	317	16.4
Alexei Kovalev	79	44	51	95	96	12	12	2	307	14.3
Martin Straka	82	27	68	95	38	19	7	1	185	14.6
Robert Lang	82	32	48	80	28	20	10	0	177	18.1
Mario Lemieux	43	35	41	76	18	15	16	1	171	20.5
Jan Hrdina	78	15	28	43	48	19	3	0	89	16.9
Josef Beranek	70	9	14	23	43	-7	2	0	152	5.9
Kevin Stevens*	32	8	15	23	55	-4	2	0	76	10.5
Hans Jonsson	58	4	18	22	22	11	2	0	44	9.1

	Games	G	A	Pts.	PIM	+/-	PPG	SHG	Shots	Shooting Pct.
Janne Laukkanen	50	3	17	20	34	9	0	0	58	5.2
Alexei Morozov	66	5	14	19	6	-8	0	0	72	6.9
Darius Kasparaitis	77	3	16	19	111	11	1	0	81	3.7
Rene Corbet	43	8	9	17	57	-3	2	0	85	9.4
Jiri Slegr*	42	5	10	15	60	-9	0	1	67	7.5
Andrew Ference	36	4	11	15	28	6	1	0	47	8.5
Milan Kraft	42	7	7	14	8	-6	1	1	63	11.1
Jeff Norton*	32	2	10	12	20	8	1	0	17	11.8
Kip Miller	33	3	8	11	6	0	1	0	38	7.9
Roman Simicek*	29	3	6	9	30	-5	1	0	19	15.8
Toby Petersen	12	2	6	8	4	3	0	0	25	8.0
Ian Moran	40	3	4	7	28	5	0	0	73	4.1
Wayne Primeau*	28	1	6	7	54	0	0	0	30	3.3
Michal Rozsival	30	1	4	5	26	3	0	0	17	5.9
Marc Bergevin*	36	1	4	5	26	5	0	0	11	9.1
Matthew Barnaby*	47	1	4	5	168	-7	0	0	38	2.6
Bob Boughner	58	1	3	4	147	18	0	0	46	2.2
Krzysztof Oliwa*	26	1	2	3	131	-4	0	0	17	5.9
William Tibbetts*	29	1	2	3	79	-2	0	0	16	6.3
Frantisek Kucera*	7	0	2	2	0	-2	0	0	9	0.0
Josef Melichar	18	0	2	2	21	-5	0	0	9	0.0
Sven Butenschon*	5	0	1	1	2	1	0	0	6	0.0
Jean-Sebastien Aubin (goalie)	36	0	1	1	4	0	0	0	0	0.0
Greg Crozier	1	0	0	0	0	0	0	0	0	0.0
Dennis Bonvie	3	0	0	0	0	-1	0	0	1	0.0
Bobby Dollas*	5	0	0	0	4	0	0	0	6	0.0
Rich Parent (goalie)	7	0	0	0	0	0	0	0	0	0.0
Johan Hedberg (goalie)	9	0	0	0	0	0	0	0	0	0.0
Dan LaCouture*	11	0	0	0	14	0	0	0	1	0.0
Daniel Trebil*	16	0	0	0	7	-1	0	0	17	0.0
Steve McKenna*	34	0	0	0	100	-4	0	0	7	0.0
Garth Snow (goalie)	35	0	0	0	8	0	0	0	0	0.0

GOALTENDING

	Games	Min.	Goals	SO	Avg.	W	L	T	ENG	Shots	Sv. Pct.
Johan Hedberg	9	545	24	0	2.64	7	1	1	0	253	.905
Garth Snow	35	2032	101	3	2.98	14	15	4	1	1014	.900
Rich Parent	7	332	17	0	3.07	1	1	3	1	150	.887
Jean-Sebastien Aubin	36	2050	107	0	3.13	20	14	1	5	973	.890

*Played with two or more NHL teams.

RESULTS

OCTOBER

6— Nashville	L	1-3
7— At Nashville	W	3-1
13— Tampa Bay	W	3-2
14— N.Y. Rangers	W	8-6
18— Carolina	L	2-3
19— At Ottawa	T	*3-3
21— Columbus	W	5-2
25— Ottawa	L	2-3
27— At N.Y. Rangers	W	4-1
28— New Jersey	L	0-9

NOVEMBER

1— At San Jose	L	2-3
3— At Vancouver	W	4-2
4— At Calgary	T	*1-1
8— Philadelphia	W	5-2
10— At New Jersey	W	4-2
11— Edmonton	W	5-2
13— At Colorado	L	*2-3
16— At St. Louis	L	3-4
18— Atlanta	W	3-1
22— Carolina	L	1-3
24— At Philadelphia	W	1-0
25— Los Angeles	T	*2-2
28— At Boston	L	1-3

DECEMBER

1— At Buffalo	W	6-4
2— Buffalo	L	2-3
5— At Ottawa	W	4-2
6— Boston	L	2-3
9— At Toronto	L	1-5
10— At Detroit	W	4-3
13— Toronto	L	4-7
15— Florida	L	1-4
16— At Montreal	T	*4-4
20— At Florida	T	*2-2
21— At Tampa Bay	T	*1-1
23— Dallas	L	2-8
26— At Buffalo	W	5-3
27— Toronto	W	5-0
30— Ottawa	W	5-3

JANUARY

3— Washington	W	3-2
5— Montreal	L	3-4
8— At Washington	W	5-3
9— At Boston	L	2-5
12— N.Y. Islanders	W	4-3
13— At N.Y. Islanders	L	5-6
15— Anaheim	W	3-2
17— At Phoenix	L	4-5
19— At Dallas	L	*5-6
21— At Chicago	W	4-0
24— Montreal	W	3-1
27— Atlanta	W	5-1
30— At Atlanta	W	6-3
31— Philadelphia	L	1-5

FEBRUARY

7— Philadelphia	W	9-4
10— New Jersey	W	*5-4
11— At Minnesota	L	2-4
14— Minnesota	W	2-1
16— At New Jersey	T	*4-4
17— At Columbus	W	*3-2
19— Colorado	L	1-5
21— Florida	W	*3-2
23— N.Y. Rangers	W	6-4
25— N.Y. Islanders	W	6-1
28— At Montreal	L	2-4

MARCH

2— At N.Y. Rangers	W	7-5
3— At Washington	L	3-4
7— Washington	L	3-4
8— At Atlanta	W	5-3
10— Calgary	W	6-3
12— At N.Y. Rangers	T	*3-3
14— N.Y. Islanders	L	1-3
16— At Florida	W	6-3
17— At Tampa Bay	L	1-5
20— Boston	T	*2-2
23— At Carolina	L	3-5
25— At New Jersey	W	4-2
27— Buffalo	W	4-1
29— Chicago	W	5-2
31— St. Louis	W	5-3

APRIL

2— At N.Y. Islanders	L	1-4
4— Tampa Bay	W	4-2
7— At Philadelphia	L	*3-4
8— At Carolina	W	6-4

*Denotes overtime game.

ST. LOUIS BLUES
WESTERN CONFERENCE/CENTRAL DIVISION

Blues' Schedule
Home games shaded; D—Day game; *—All-Star Game at Los Angeles

October

SUN	MON	TUE	WED	THU	FRI	SAT
	1	2	3	4 CBJ	5	6 NAS
7	8	9	10	11 LA	12	13 TOR
14	15	16	17 DAL	18	19 MIN	20 PIT
21	22 CAL	23	24	25 NYR	26	27 OTT
28	29	30	31 COL			

November

SUN	MON	TUE	WED	THU	FRI	SAT
				1 CAR	2	3 WAS
4	5	6 SJ	7	8 VAN	9	10 PHO
11	12	13 CBJ	14	15 VAN	16	17 CAL
18	19	20 EDM	21	22	23 PHO	24
25	26	27 OTT	28	29 CBJ	30	

December

SUN	MON	TUE	WED	THU	FRI	SAT
						1 CBJ
2 MIN	3	4	5 PHO	6 LA	7	8 LA
9	10	11	12 CHI	13 TOR	14	15 CAL
16	17	18 PHI	19	20	21 TB	22 FLA
23	24	25	26 CHI	27	28 MON	29
30 NAS	31					

January

SUN	MON	TUE	WED	THU	FRI	SAT
		1 NJ	2	3 CBJ	4	5 D DAL
6	7	8 SJ	9 ANA	10	11	12 D PIT
13	14	15 EDM	16	17 VAN	18	19 BOS
20	21 D BOS	22	23 BUF	24	25 CHI	26 DET
27	28 ANA	29	30 WAS	31		

February

SUN	MON	TUE	WED	THU	FRI	SAT
					1	2 *
3	4	5 NYI	6	7 EDM	8	9 PHI
10	11	12 ATL	13 COL	14	15	16
17	18	19	20	21	22	23
24	25	26 VAN	27	28 CAL		

March

SUN	MON	TUE	WED	THU	FRI	SAT
					1	2 EDM
3	4	5	6	7 MIN	8	9 D DET
10	11 COL	12	13 SJ	14 LA	15	16
17 ANA	18	19 NAS	20 DAL	21	22 ANA	23
24 D CHI	25	26 MIN	27	28 BUF	29	30 NAS
31						

April

SUN	MON	TUE	WED	THU	FRI	SAT
	1 PHO	2	3 DAL	4	5 CHI	6
7 COL	8	9 NAS	10	11 SJ	12	13 D DET
14 D DET	15	16	17	18	19	20

2001-02 SEASON
CLUB DIRECTORY

Chairman of the board and owner
Bill Laurie
President & chief executive officer
Mark Sauer
Sr. vice president and general manager
Larry Pleau
Sr. v.p., marketing and communications
Jim Woodcock
V.p./director of hockey operations
John Ferguson Jr.
Head coach
Joel Quenneville
Assistant coaches
Jim Roberts
Mike Kitchen
Goaltending coach
Keith Allain

Athletic trainer
Ray Barile
Strength and conditioning coach
To be announced
Video coach
Jamie Kompon
Equipment manager
Bert Godin
Assistant equipment manager
Eric Bechtol
Director of communications
Frank Buonomo
Assistant director of communications
Greg Franklin
Communications manager
Stan Richardson

DRAFT CHOICES

Rd.— Player	Ht./Wt.	Overall	Pos.	Last team
2— Jay McClement	6-1/193	57	C	Brampton (OHL)
3— Tuomas Nissinen	6-0/176	89	G	Kalpa Jr., Finland
4— Igor Valeev	5-11/203	122	RW	North Bay (OHL)
5— Dimitri Semin	5-10/165	159	F	Spartak Jr., Russia
6— Brett Scheffelmaier	6-5/204	190	D	Medicine Hat (WHL)
8— Petr Cajanek	5-11/176	253	F	Zlin, Czechoslovakia
9— Grant Jacobsen	6-2/201	270	C	Regina (WHL)
9— Simon Skoog	6-2/218	283	D	Morrum, Sweden

MISCELLANEOUS DATA

Home ice (capacity)
Savvis Center (19,022)
Address
1401 Clark
St. Louis, MO 63103
Business phone
314-622-2500
Ticket information
314-241-1888
Website
www.stlouisblues.com

Training site
Chesterfield, MO
Club colors
Blue, gold, navy and white
Radio affiliation
KTRS (550 AM)
TV affiliation
KPLR (Channel 11) & FOX Sports
Midwest

ST. LOUIS BLUES

No.	FORWARDS	Ht./Wt.	Place	BORN Date	NHL exp.	2000-01 clubs
40	Eric Boguniecki (C)	5-8/192	New Haven, Conn.	5-6-75	2	Louisville (AHL), Worcester (AHL), St. Louis
71	Sebastien Bordeleau (C)	5-11/185	Vancouver	2-15-75	6	Nashville, Worcester (AHL)
	Petr Cajanek (C)	5-11/176	Czech Republic	8-18-75	0	Zlin (Czechoslovakia)
	Daniel Corso (C)	5-10/184	St. Hubert, Que.	4-3-78	1	Worcester (AHL), St. Louis
38	Pavol Demitra (RW)	6-0/190	Dubnica, Czechoslovakia	11-29-74	8	St. Louis
	Dallas Drake (RW)	6-1/190	Trail, B.C.	2-4-69	9	St. Louis
32	Mike Eastwood (C)	6-3/209	Cornwall, Ont.	7-1-67	10	St. Louis
12	Mike Keane (RW)	6-0/185	Winnipeg	5-29-67	13	Dallas
	Reed Low (RW)	6-5/228	Moose Jaw, Sask.	6-26-76	1	St. Louis
21	Jamal Mayers (RW)	6-2/212	Toronto	10-24-74	4	St. Louis
	Jay McClement (C)	6-1/193	Kingston, Ont.	3-2-83	0	Brampton (OHL)
27	Scott Mellanby (RW)	6-1/205	Montreal	6-11-66	16	Florida, St. Louis
9	Tyson Nash (LW)	5-11/195	Edmonton	3-11-75	3	St. Louis
	Jeff Panzer (C)	5-10/160	Grand Forks, N.D.	4-7-78	0	Univ. of North Dakota (WCHA), Worcester (AHL)
	Justin Papineau (C)	5-10/160	Ottawa	1-15-80	0	Worcester (AHL)
	Mike Peluso (C)	6-1/208	Denver	9-2-74	0	Portland (AHL), Worcester (AHL)
	Michel Riesen (LW)	6-2/190	Oberbalm, Switzerland	4-11-79	1	Edmonton, Hamilton (AHL)
	Mark Rycroft (RW)	5-11/197	Nanaimo, B.C.	7-12-78	0	Worcester (AHL)
	Dimitri Semin (C)	5-10/165	Moscow, U.S.S.R.	8-14-83	0	Spartak (Russian Div. 1)
16	Cory Stillman (LW)	6-0/194	Peterborough, Ont.	12-20-73	7	Calgary, St. Louis
7	Keith Tkachuk (LW)	6-2/225	Melrose, Mass.	3-28-72	10	Phoenix, St. Louis
	Daniel Tkaczuk (C)	6-1/197	Toronto	6-10-79	1	Saint John (AHL), Calgary
	Andrei Troschinsky (C)	6-5/187	Ust-Kamenogorsk, U.S.S.R.	2-14-78	0	Worcester (AHL)
	Igor Valeev (C)	5-11/203	Chelyabinsk, U.S.S.R.	1-9-81	0	North Bay (OHL)
37	Sergei Varlamov (RW)	5-11/195	Kiev, U.S.S.R.	7-21-78	2	Saint John (AHL)
39	Doug Weight (C)	5-11/200	Warren, Mich.	1-21-71	11	Edmonton
48	Scott Young (RW)	6-1/200	Clinton, Mass.	10-1-67	13	St. Louis
	DEFENSEMEN					
	Ed Campbell	6-2/200	Worcester, Mass.	11-26-74	0	Worcester (AHL)
55	Vladimir Chebaturkin	6-2/212	Tyumen, U.S.S.R.	4-23-75	4	St. Louis, Worcester (AHL)
	Dale Clarke	6-1/193	Belleville, Ont.	3-23-78	1	Worcester (AHL), Peoria (ECHL), St. Louis
37	Jeff Finley	6-2/205	Edmonton	4-14-67	12	St. Louis
	Sean Hill	6-0/203	Duluth, Minn.	2-14-70	11	St. Louis
	Barret Jackman	6-1/200	Trail, B.C.	3-5-81	0	Regina (WHL)
	Alexander Khavanov	6-2/190	Dynamo, U.S.S.R.	1-30-72	1	St. Louis
2	Al MacInnis	6-2/208	Inverness, Nova Scotia	7-11-63	20	St. Louis
47	Rich Pilon	6-2/220	Saskatoon, Sask.	4-30-68	13	New York Rangers
44	Chris Pronger	6-6/220	Dryden, Ont.	10-10-74	8	St. Louis
34	Darren Rumble	6-1/200	Barrie, Ont.	1-23-69	6	Worcester (AHL), St. Louis
	Bryce Salvador	6-1/194	Brandon, Man.	2-11-76	1	St. Louis
	Brett Scheffelmaier	6-5/202	Coronation, Alta.	3-31-81	0	Medicine Hat (WHL)
	Mike Van Ryn	6-1/190	London, Ont.	5-14-79	1	St. Louis, Worcester (AHL)
	Matt Walker	6-2/212	Beaverlodge, Alta.	4-7-80	0	Worcester (AHL), Peoria (ECHL)
	GOALTENDERS					
40	Fred Brathwaite	5-7/175	Ottawa	11-24-72	6	Calgary
35	Brent Johnson	6-2/200	Farmington, Mich.	3-12-77	2	St. Louis
	Tuomas Nissinen	6-0/176	Kuopio, Finland	7-17-83	0	KalPa Kuopio (Finland Jr.)
	Cody Rudkowsky	6-1/200	Willingdon, Alta.	7-21-78	0	Worcester (AHL)

2000-01 REVIEW
INDIVIDUAL STATISTICS

SCORING

	Games	G	A	Pts.	PIM	+/-	PPG	SHG	Shots	Shooting Pct.
Pierre Turgeon	79	30	52	82	37	14	11	0	171	17.5
Scott Young	81	40	33	73	30	15	14	3	321	12.5
Al MacInnis	59	12	42	54	52	23	6	1	218	5.5
Chris Pronger	51	8	39	47	75	21	4	0	121	6.6
Pavol Demitra	44	20	25	45	16	27	5	0	124	16.1
Jochen Hecht	72	19	25	44	48	11	8	3	208	9.1
Dallas Drake	82	12	29	41	71	18	2	0	142	8.5
Craig Conroy*	69	11	14	25	46	2	0	3	101	10.9
Michal Handzus*	36	10	14	24	12	11	3	2	58	17.2
Alexander Khavanov	74	7	16	23	52	16	2	0	92	7.6
Mike Eastwood	77	6	17	23	28	4	0	2	51	11.8
Jamal Mayers	77	8	13	21	117	-3	0	0	132	6.1

	Games	G	A	Pts.	PIM	+/-	PPG	SHG	Shots	Shooting Pct.
Ladislav Nagy*	40	8	8	16	20	-2	2	0	59	13.6
Tyson Nash	57	8	7	15	110	8	0	1	113	7.1
Daniel Corso	28	10	3	13	14	0	5	0	42	23.8
Lubos Bartecko	50	5	8	13	12	-1	0	0	51	9.8
Marty Reasoner	41	4	9	13	14	-5	0	0	65	6.2
Sean Hill	48	1	10	11	51	5	0	0	47	2.1
Jeff Finley	72	2	8	10	38	7	0	0	35	5.7
Bryce Salvador	75	2	8	10	69	-4	0	0	60	3.3
Scott Mellanby*	23	7	1	8	25	0	2	0	37	18.9
Keith Tkachuk*	12	6	2	8	14	-3	2	0	41	14.6
Cory Stillman*	12	3	4	7	6	-2	3	0	26	11.5
Todd Reirden	38	2	4	6	43	-2	1	0	58	3.4
Reed Low	56	1	5	6	159	4	0	0	31	3.2
Darren Rumble	12	0	4	4	27	7	0	0	11	0.0
Alexei Gusarov*	16	0	4	4	6	-3	0	0	10	0.0
Reid Simpson	38	2	1	3	96	-3	0	0	23	8.7
Vlad Chebaturkin	22	1	2	3	26	5	0	0	5	20.0
Peter Smrek*	6	2	0	2	2	1	0	0	5	40.0
Pascal Rheaume	8	2	0	2	5	-1	2	0	16	12.5
Roman Turek (goalie)	54	0	1	1	6	0	0	0	0	0.0
Eric Boguniecki	1	0	0	0	0	-1	0	0	1	0.0
Mike Van Ryn	1	0	0	0	0	-2	0	0	1	0.0
Marc Bergevin*	2	0	0	0	0	1	0	0	1	0.0
Dale Clarke	3	0	0	0	0	1	0	0	5	0.0
Jaroslav Obsut	4	0	0	0	2	1	0	0	3	0.0
Daniel Trebil*	10	0	0	0	0	1	0	0	9	0.0
Brent Johnson (goalie)	31	0	0	0	2	0	0	0	0	0.0

GOALTENDING

	Games	Min.	Goals	SO	Avg.	W	L	T	ENG	Shots	Sv. Pct.
Brent Johnson	31	1744	63	4	2.17	19	9	2	2	676	.907
Roman Turek	54	3232	123	6	2.28	24	18	10	7	1248	.901

*Played with two or more NHL teams.

RESULTS

OCTOBER
5— At Phoenix ....L.....1-4
6— At San Jose ....W.....4-1
8— At Anaheim ....W.....5-1
11— At Los Angeles ....T....*4-4
13— Minnesota ....W.....2-0
17— At Detroit ....L.....1-2
19— Los Angeles ....W.....7-1
21— Chicago ....W.....1-0
26— Calgary ....W.....4-3
28— Dallas ....W....*4-3
29— At Carolina ....W.....4-1
31— At Nashville ....W.....4-2

NOVEMBER
2— Washington ....W.....2-0
4— Toronto ....T....*0-0
9— At Colorado ....T....*3-3
11— At Vancouver ....W.....5-2
14— At Edmonton ....L.....0-3
16— Pittsburgh ....W.....4-3
18— Buffalo ....W.....4-1
21— Vancouver ....L.....3-4
24— At Nashville ....W.....4-0
25— Phoenix ....W.....5-1
29— At Toronto ....W....*6-5

DECEMBER
2— Florida ....W.....5-2
5— Anaheim ....W.....1-0
9— Chicago ....W.....6-4
10— At Chicago ....W.....6-1

15— At Atlanta ....W.....6-3
16— Detroit ....T....*2-2
20— At N.Y. Rangers ....W.....6-3
23— Anaheim ....W.....5-2
26— Columbus ....W.....5-0
28— Los Angeles ....L.....2-5
30— Phoenix ....W.....2-1

JANUARY
1— Edmonton ....W.....5-2
2— At Ottawa ....L.....1-3
4— Nashville ....L.....2-4
6— Minnesota ....W.....5-1
8— Philadelphia ....L....*1-2
10— At Anaheim ....W.....4-2
11— At San Jose ....L.....3-6
13— At Los Angeles ....W.....4-2
15— At Phoenix ....L.....1-3
18— Edmonton ....W.....4-1
20— Vancouver ....W.....3-0
21— At Nashville ....L.....1-3
23— At Montreal ....W.....5-2
25— New Jersey ....W....*4-3
27— San Jose ....L....*3-4
29— Toronto ....W.....2-1
30— At Boston ....L.....1-5

FEBRUARY
1— Columbus ....T....*2-2
6— At Columbus ....T....*2-2
8— Tampa Bay ....W.....4-1
10— At Colorado ....W....*4-3

11— At Dallas ....T....*3-3
15— Calgary ....W.....4-1
16— At Chicago ....L.....2-6
19— At Florida ....L.....0-3
20— At Tampa Bay ....L.....2-3
23— At Detroit ....L.....2-4
24— Boston ....W....*3-2
26— San Jose ....W.....7-2
28— At Edmonton ....L.....3-5

MARCH
2— At Vancouver ....L....*2-3
3— At Calgary ....L....*2-3
6— At Minnesota ....T....*3-3
8— Colorado ....L.....2-5
10— Detroit ....T....*2-2
13— At Philadelphia ....L.....2-5
14— At Minnesota ....W....*1-0
17— At Calgary ....T....*2-2
20— N.Y. Islanders ....L....*3-4
22— Colorado ....L.....1-3
24— Chicago ....W.....5-1
25— At Dallas ....T....*1-1
28— At Detroit ....L.....2-5
31— At Pittsburgh ....L.....3-5

APRIL
1— At Columbus ....L.....1-2
3— Carolina ....T....*2-2
5— Columbus ....W.....4-1
7— Nashville ....W.....1-0
*Denotes overtime game.

SAN JOSE SHARKS
WESTERN CONFERENCE/PACIFIC DIVISION

Sharks' Schedule
Home games shaded; D—Day game; *—All-Star Game at Los Angeles

October

SUN	MON	TUE	WED	THU	FRI	SAT
	1	2	3	4 DET	5	6 D MIN
7	8	9	10	11 TB	12	13 BOS
14	15	16 MIN	17	18 NJ	19	20 NYI
21	22 NYR	23 BUF	24	25 CHI	26	27 CBJ
28	29	30	31 ANA			

November

SUN	MON	TUE	WED	THU	FRI	SAT
				1 ATL	2	3 VAN
4	5	6 STL	7 DAL	8	9 CAR	10
11 CHI	12	13	14 ANA	15 PHO	16	17 DAL
18	19	20	21 MIN	22	23	24 D LA
25	26	27 NAS	28	29 PIT	30 ANA	

December

SUN	MON	TUE	WED	THU	FRI	SAT
						1
2	3	4 CAL	5	6 CAL	7	8 VAN
9	10	11 EDM	12	13	14 COL	15
16	17 DAL	18	19 ATL	20	21 DET	22 NAS
23	24	25	26 ANA	27	28 NYR	29
30 PHO	31					

January

SUN	MON	TUE	WED	THU	FRI	SAT
		1	2 PHI	3	4 PHO	5 FLA
6	7	8 STL	9 PHO	10	11	12 D LA
13	14	15 COL	16	17 NYI	18	19 COL
20	21 EDM	22	23 DET	24 CBJ	25	26
27 MON	D 28	29 TOR	30 PIT	31		

February

SUN	MON	TUE	WED	THU	FRI	SAT
					1	2 *
3	4	5	6 CAL	7	8 CHI	9
10 CAR	11	12 EDM	13	14	15	16
17	18	19	20	21	22	23
24	25	26 NAS	27	28 WAS		

March

SUN	MON	TUE	WED	THU	FRI	SAT
					1 TB	2
3 DAL	D 4	5 NAS	6	7 OTT	8	9 VAN
10 VAN	11	12	13 STL	14	15 WAS	16 CHI
17 LA	18	19	20 EDM	21 CAL	22	23 D LA
24	25	26 DAL	27	28 COL	29	30 CBJ
31						

April

SUN	MON	TUE	WED	THU	FRI	SAT
	1	2 ANA	3	4 PHO	5	6 DET
7	8 MIN	9	10 CBJ	11 STL	12	13 D LA
14	15	16	17	18	19	20

2001-02 SEASON
CLUB DIRECTORY

Owner & chairman
George Gund III
Co-owner
Gordon Gund
President & chief executive officer
Greg Jamison
Exec. v.p. and general manager
Dean Lombardi
Vice president & chief financial officer
Gregg Olson
VVice president & assistant g.m.
Wayne Thomas
Head coach
Darryl Sutter
Assistant coaches
Rich Preston
To be announced
Strength & conditioning coach
Mac Read
Assistant to the general manager
Joe Will

Executive assistant
Brenda Will
Director of media relations
Ken Arnold
Media relations manager
Scott Emmert
Media relations coordinator
Ben Stephenson
Director of pro development
Doug Wilson
Head trainer
Ray Tufts
Equipment manager
Mike Aldrich
Assistant equipment manager
Kurt Harvey
Team physician
Dr. Arthur J. Ting
Director of advertising and publicity
Beth Brigino

DRAFT CHOICES

Rd.— Player	Ht./Wt.	Overall	Pos.	Last team
1— Marcel Goc	6-1/187	20	C	Schwennigen, Ger.
4— Christian Ehrhoff	6-2/183	106	D	Krefeld, Germany
4— Dimitri Patzold	6-0/183	107	G	Erding Jr., Germany
5— Tomas Plihal	6-1/180	140	F	Liberec Jr., Czech.
6— Ryan Clowe	6-2/190	175	RW	Rimouski (QMJHL)
6— Tom Cavanagh	5-10/178	182	RW	Phillips-Exeter (USHSE)

MISCELLANEOUS DATA

Home ice (capacity)
Compaq Center at San Jose (17,496)
Address
525 West Santa Clara Street
San Jose, CA 95113
Business phone
408-287-7070
Ticket information
408-287-7070
Website
www.sjsharks.com

Training site
San Jose
Club colors
Deep pacific teal, shimmering gray,
burnt orange and black
Radio affiliation
KFOX (98.5 FM)
TV affiliation
FOX Sports Net

SAN JOSE SHARKS

No.	FORWARDS	Ht./Wt.	Place	Date	NHL exp.	2000-01 clubs
	Matt Bradley (RW)	6-2/195	Stittsville, Ont.	6-13-78	1	Kentucky (AHL), San Jose
	Jonathan Cheechoo (RW)	6-0/205	Moose Factory, Ont.	7-15-80	0	Kentucky (AHL)
25	Vincent Damphousse (C)	6-1/200	Montreal	12-17-67	15	San Jose
	Niko Dimitrakos (RW)	5-11/200	Somerville, Mass.	5-21-79	0	Univ. of Maine (Hockey East)
	Jon DiSalvatore (RW)	6-1/180	Bangor, Me.	3-30-81	0	Providence College (Hockey East)
	Marcel Goc (C)	6-1/187	Calv, West Germany	8-24-83	0	Schwenningen (Germany)
9	Adam Graves (LW)	6-0/200	Tecumseh, Ont.	4-12-68	14	New York Rangers
9	Todd Harvey (RW)	6-0/205	Hamilton, Ont.	2-17-75	7	San Jose
15	Alex Korolyuk (RW)	5-9/195	Moscow, U.S.S.R.	1-15-76	4	Ak Bars Kazan (Russian), San Jose
	Ryan Kraft (C)	5-9/181	Bottineau, N.D.	11-7-75	0	Kentucky (AHL)
	Eric LaPlante (LW)	6-0/185	St. Maurice, Que.	12-1-79	0	Kentucky (AHL)
	Willie Levesque (RW)	6-0/195	Oak Bluffs, Mass.	1-22-80	0	Northeastern Univ. (Hockey East)
14	Patrick Marleau (C)	6-2/210	Swift Current, Sask.	9-15-79	4	San Jose
37	Stephane Matteau (LW)	6-4/220	Rouyn-Noranda, Que.	9-2-69	11	San Jose
	Graig Mischler (C)	6-3/174	Holbrook, N.Y.	9-15-78	0	Northeastern Univ. (Hockey East)
11	Owen Nolan (RW)	6-1/210	Belfast, Northern Ireland	2-12-72	11	San Jose
	Tomas Plihal (LW/RW)	6-1/180	Frydlant, Czechoslovakia	3-28-83	0	Liberic (Czechoslovakia Jrs.)
18	Mike Ricci (C)	6-0/190	Scarborough, Ont.	10-27-71	11	San Jose
8	Teemu Selanne (RW)	6-0/200	Helsinki, Finland	7-3-70	9	Anaheim, San Jose
	Mark Smith (C)	5-10/200	Eyebrow, Sask.	10-24-77	1	San Jose, Kentucky (AHL)
19	Marco Sturm (LW)	6-0/195	Dingolfing, West Germany	9-8-78	4	San Jose
24	Niklas Sundstrom (LW)	6-0/195	Ornskoldsvik, Sweden	1-6-75	6	San Jose
17	Scott Thornton (LW)	6-3/216	London, Ont.	1-9-71	11	San Jose
	Miroslav Zalesak (RW)	6-0/185	Skalica, Czechoslovakia	1-2-80	0	Kentucky (AHL)
	DEFENSEMEN					
42	Steve Bancroft	6-1/214	Toronto	10-6-70	1	Kentucky (AHL)
	Matt Carkner	6-4/222	Winchester, Ont.	11-3-80	0	Peterborough (OHL)
	Rob Davison	6-2/210	St. Catharine's, Ont.	5-1-80	0	Kentucky (AHL)
	Christian Ehrhoff	6-2/183	Moers, West Germany	7-6-82	0	Krefeld Pinguine (Germany)
	Jim Fahey	6-0/215	Boston	5-11-79	0	Northeastern Univ. (Hockey East)
43	Scott Hannan	6-2/220	Richmond, B.C.	1-23-79	3	San Jose
	Jeff Jillson	6-3/219	North Smithfield, R.I.	7-24-80	0	Univ. of Michigan (CCHA)
	Robert Jindrich	5-11/190	Plezn, Czechoslovakia	11-14-76	0	Kentucky (AHL)
	Tero Maatta	6-1/205	Vantaa, Finland	1-2-82	0	Blues Espoo (Finland)
27	Bryan Marchment	6-1/185	Scarborough, Ont.	5-1-69	13	San Jose
	Angel Nikolov	6-1/185	Most, Czechoslovakia	11-18-75	0	Litvinov (Czech Republic)
10	Marcus Ragnarsson	6-1/215	Ostervala, Sweden	8-13-71	6	San Jose
40	Mike Rathje	6-5/235	Mannville, Alta.	5-11-74	8	San Jose
	Pasi Saarinen	5-11/194	Tamperi, Finland	4-17-77	0	Jokerit Helsinki (Finland)
7	Brad Stuart	6-2/210	Rocky Mountain House, Alta.	11-6-79	2	San Jose
20	Gary Suter	6-0/215	Madison, Wis.	6-24-64	16	San Jose
	GOALTENDERS					
	Miikka Kiprusoff	6-2/190	Turku, Finland	10-26-76	1	Kentucky (AHL), San Jose
35	Evgeni Nabokov	6-0/200	Ust-Kamenogorsk, U.S.S.R.	7-25-75	2	San Jose
	Dimitri Patzold	6-0/183	Germany	2-3-83	0	Erding (German Jr.)
	Nolan Schaefer	6-1/175	Regina, Sask.	1-15-80	0	Providence College (Hockey East)
	Vesa Toskala	5-9/172	Tampere, Finland	5-20-77	0	Kentucky (AHL)

2000-01 REVIEW
INDIVIDUAL STATISTICS
SCORING

	Games	G	A	Pts.	PIM	+/-	PPG	SHG	Shots	Shooting Pct.
Patrick Marleau	81	25	27	52	22	7	5	0	146	17.1
Owen Nolan	57	24	25	49	75	0	10	1	191	12.6
Niklas Sundstrom	82	10	39	49	28	10	4	1	100	10.0
Vincent Damphousse	45	9	37	46	62	17	4	0	101	8.9
Mike Ricci	81	22	22	44	60	3	9	2	141	15.6
Scott Thornton	73	19	17	36	114	4	4	0	159	11.9
Jeff Friesen*	64	12	24	36	56	7	2	0	120	10.0
Gary Suter	68	10	24	34	84	8	4	0	157	6.4
Marco Sturm	81	14	18	32	28	9	2	3	153	9.2
Stephane Matteau	80	13	19	32	32	5	1	0	81	16.0
Alexander Korolyuk	70	12	13	25	41	2	3	0	140	8.6
Brad Stuart	77	5	18	23	56	10	1	0	119	4.2
Todd Harvey	69	10	11	21	72	6	1	0	66	15.2
Bryan Marchment	75	7	11	18	204	15	0	1	73	9.6
Scott Hannan	75	3	14	17	51	10	0	0	96	3.1

	Games	G	A	Pts.	PIM	+/-	PPG	SHG	Shots	Shooting Pct.
Marcus Ragnarsson	68	3	12	15	44	2	1	0	74	4.1
Teemu Selanne*	12	7	6	13	0	1	2	0	31	22.6
Mike Rathje	81	0	11	11	48	7	0	0	89	0.0
Tony Granato	60	4	5	9	65	-1	1	0	85	4.7
Shawn Heins	38	3	4	7	57	2	2	0	45	6.7
Jim Montgomery	28	1	6	7	19	-1	1	0	17	5.9
Mark Smith	42	2	2	4	51	2	0	0	39	5.1
Bill Lindsay*	16	0	4	4	29	2	0	0	14	0.0
Bobby Dollas*	16	1	1	2	14	4	0	0	5	20.0
Matt Bradley	21	1	1	2	19	0	0	0	16	6.3
Evgeni Nabokov (goalie)	66	0	2	2	8	0	0	0	1	0.0
Jeff Norton*	10	0	1	1	8	4	0	0	5	0.0
Paul Kruse	1	0	0	0	5	0	0	0	0	0.0
Mikael Samuelsson	4	0	0	0	0	0	0	0	3	0.0
Miikka Kiprusoff (goalie)	5	0	0	0	0	0	0	0	0	0.0
Steve Shields (goalie)	21	0	0	0	2	0	0	0	0	0.0

GOALTENDING

	Games	Min.	Goals	SO	Avg.	W	L	T	ENG	Shots	Sv. Pct.
Miikka Kiprusoff	5	154	5	0	1.95	2	1	0	1	51	.902
Evgeni Nabokov	66	3700	135	6	2.19	32	21	7	3	1582	.915
Steve Shields	21	1135	47	2	2.48	6	8	5	1	531	.911

Combination shutout: Nabokov and Kiprusoff.
*Played with two or more NHL teams.

RESULTS

OCTOBER

6— St. Louis	L	1-4
12—Phoenix	W	2-1
14—Boston	W	5-2
18—At Dallas	L	1-2
20—At Minnesota	W	3-1
21—At Nashville	W	5-3
24—At Carolina	W	3-2
25—At Columbus	W	3-1
28—Atlanta	T	*2-2

NOVEMBER

1— Pittsburgh	W	3-2
4— Carolina	W	4-1
5— At Vancouver	T	*2-2
8— At Chicago	W	*3-2
9— At Columbus	L	2-5
11—At N.Y. Islanders	W	4-0
14—At New Jersey	W	3-2
15—At Detroit	L	1-4
18—N.Y. Islanders	W	5-3
22—Chicago	W	4-1
25—New Jersey	L	2-3
28—Minnesota	W	4-1
30—Anaheim	W	*3-2

DECEMBER

3— At Edmonton	T	*3-3
4— At Calgary	W	8-0
6— Dallas	T	*2-2
8— Vancouver	L	1-6
12—N.Y. Rangers	W	3-2

14—Columbus	W	2-1
16—At Phoenix	W	*2-1
18—At Washington	W	5-3
20—At Detroit	W	2-0
21—At Philadelphia	L	3-4
23—At Buffalo	L	2-5
26—At Los Angeles	W	2-1
28—Edmonton	T	*2-2
30—Vancouver	L	3-6

JANUARY

1— At Phoenix	W	3-2
3— Calgary	L	0-1
4— At Colorado	T	*2-2
6— Florida	W	3-1
9— Buffalo	W	2-1
11—St. Louis	W	6-3
13—Nashville	L	3-5
15—Detroit	L	2-3
17—Calgary	T	*4-4
20—Colorado	L	1-2
22—At Edmonton	T	*2-2
24—Edmonton	W	6-1
26—At Dallas	W	2-1
27—At St. Louis	W	*4-3
30—Colorado	L	1-3

FEBRUARY

1— Dallas	L	2-4
6— At Calgary	T	*1-1
8— At Vancouver	T	*0-0
10—Chicago	W	*3-2

14—At Chicago	W	7-0
16—At Nashville	W	2-0
18—At Minnesota	L	1-3
20—Columbus	W	*3-2
21—At Anaheim	L	0-1
23—Anaheim	L	3-1
26—At St. Louis	L	2-7
28—At Toronto	L	1-2

MARCH

1— At Ottawa	L	4-8
3— At Boston	L	2-3
6— At Tampa Bay	L	*1-2
7— At Florida	T	*3-3
10—Nashville	L	0-3
12—Montreal	W	3-0
14—Los Angeles	L	1-4
17—At Los Angeles	L	*0-1
18—Detroit	L	4-6
20—At Colorado	L	1-4
22—Ottawa	L	1-2
26—At Los Angeles	T	*0-0
27—Los Angeles	W	*3-2
29—Anaheim	W	7-4
31—At Phoenix	L	1-3

APRIL

2— Minnesota	W	4-2
5— Phoenix	W	3-0
7— Dallas	L	*4-5
8— At Anaheim	W	4-1

*Denotes overtime game.

TAMPA BAY LIGHTNING
EASTERN CONFERENCE/SOUTHEAST DIVISION

Lightning Schedule
Home games shaded; D—Day game; *—All-Star Game at Los Angeles

October
SUN	MON	TUE	WED	THU	FRI	SAT
	1	2	3	4	5 NYI	6
7 FLA	8	9	10	11 SJ	12	13 LA
14 ANA	15	16 COL	17	18	19	20 NYR
21	22	23 WAS	24	25 LA	26	27 ATL
28	29	30 TOR	31			

November
SUN	MON	TUE	WED	THU	FRI	SAT
				1	2 BUF	3 PIT
4	5	6 NYI	7	8 PHI	9	10 PIT
11	12	13	14	15 TOR	16	17 CAR
18	19	20 ANA	21 WAS	22	23 NJ	24
25 D CAR	26	27 BOS	28	29 ATL	30	

December
SUN	MON	TUE	WED	THU	FRI	SAT
						1 PHI
2 NYR	3	4 NJ	5	6 CBJ	7	8 OTT
9	10 VAN	11	12 CAL	13	14 EDM	15
16	17 MON	18	19	20	21 STL	22
23	24	25	26 NAS	27 CAR	28	29 BOS
30	31 TOR					

January
SUN	MON	TUE	WED	THU	FRI	SAT
		1	2 MIN	3	4 CHI	5
6 PHO	7	8 DAL	9	10	11	12 OTT
13 ATL	14	15 NJ	16	17	18 CHI	19 MON
20	21 NJ	22	23 PIT	24	25 BUF	26 NYI
27	28 NYR	29	30 CAR	31		

February
SUN	MON	TUE	WED	THU	FRI	SAT
					1	2 *
3	4 OTT	5	6 FLA	7 FLA	8	9 WAS
10	11 WAS	12	13	14	15	16
17	18	19	20	21	22	23
24	25	26 DET	27	28		

March
SUN	MON	TUE	WED	THU	FRI	SAT
					1 SJ	2 FLA
3	4	5	6 EDM	7	8 PHI	9
10 NAS	11	12 ATL	13	14 CAL	15	16
17 BUF	18 PHI	19	20 ATL	21	22 MON	23
24 BOS	25	26 TOR	27	28 MON	29	30 OTT
31						

April
SUN	MON	TUE	WED	THU	FRI	SAT
	1 NYR	2	3 WAS	4 PIT	5	6
7 BUF	8	9	10 BOS	11 CAR	12 NYI	13
14 D FLA	15	16	17	18	19	20

2001-02 SEASON
CLUB DIRECTORY

Chief executive officer & governor
Tom Wilson
President
Ron Campbell
Senior v.p. & general manager
Rick Dudley
Assistant general manager
Jay Feaster
Head coach
John Tortorella

Associate coach
Craig Ramsay
Goaltending coach
Jeff Reese
Vice president of public relations
Bill Wickett
Director of public relations
Jay Preble
Media relations manager
Jay Levin

DRAFT CHOICES

Rd.— Player	Ht./Wt.	Overall	Pos.	Last team
1— Alexander Svitov	6-3/198	3	C	OMSK, Russia
2— Alexander Polushin	6-3/198	47	C/LW	Tver, Russia
2— Andreas Holmqvist	6-3/187	61	D	Hammarby Jr., Sweden
3— Eugeni Artukhin	6-4/213	94	RW	Podolsk, Russia
4— Aaron Lobb	6-4/193	123	RW	London (OHL)
5— Paul Lynch	6-3/195	138	D	Valley Jr., Mass. (EJHL)
6— Art Femenella	6-7/234	188	D	Sioux City (USHL)
7— Dennis Packard	6-5/214	219	LW	Harvard (ECAC)
7— Jeremy Van Hoof	6-2/200	222	D	Ottawa (OHL)
8— J.F. Soucy	6-3/180	252	C	Montreal (QMJHL)
8— Dimitri Bezrukov	6-3/196	259	LW	Nizhnekamsk, Russia
9— Vitali Smolyninov		261		Neftechimik Jr., Russia
9— Ilja Solarev	6-3/176	281	LW	Perm, Russia
9— Henrik Bergfors	6-4/225	289	D	Sodertalje Jr., Sweden

MISCELLANEOUS DATA

Home ice (capacity)
Ice Palace (19,758)
Address
401 Channelside Drive
Tampa, Fla. 33602
Business phone
813-301-6500
Ticket information
813-301-6600
Website
www.tampabaylightning.com

Training site
Brandon, FL
Club colors
Black, blue, silver and white
Radio affiliation
WDAE (620 AM)
TV affiliation
Sunshine Network (Cable)

TRAINING CAMP ROSTER

No.	FORWARDS	Ht./Wt.	Place	BORN Date	NHL exp.	2000-01 clubs
	Dmitry Afanasenkov (LW)	6-2/200	Arkhangelsk, U.S.S.R.	5-12-80	1	Detroit (IHL), Tampa Bay
	Nikita Alexeev (RW)	6-5/215	Murmansk, U.S.S.R.	12-27-81	0	Erie (OHL)
38	Dave Andreychuk (LW)	6-4/220	Hamilton, Ont.	9-29-63	19	Buffalo
	Yevgeny Artukhin (RW)	6-4/213	Moscow, U.S.S.R.	4-4-83	0	Podolsk (Russian)
36	Matthew Barnaby (LW)	6-0/189	Ottawa.	5-4-73	9	Pittsburgh, Tampa Bay
	Martin Cibak (C)	6-1/195	Liptovmikulas, Czech.	5-17-80	0	Detroit (IHL)
34	Gordie Dwyer (LW)	6-2/216	Dalhousie, N.B.	1-25-78	2	Tampa Bay, Detroit (IHL)
	Matt Elich (RW)	6-3/196	Detroit	9-22-79	2	Detroit (IHL), Tampa Bay
	Johan Hagglund (C)	6-2/194	Ornskoldsvik, Sweden	6-9-82	0	
9	Brian Holzinger (C/RW)	5-11/190	Parma, Ohio.	10-10-72	7	Tampa Bay
	Sheldon Keefe (RW)	5-11/185	Brampton, Ont.	9-17-80	1	Detroit (IHL), Tampa Bay
4	Vincent Lecavalier (C)	6-4/205	Ile-Bizard, Que.	4-21-80	3	Tampa Bay
	Aaron Lobb (RW)	6-4/193	Brucefield, Ont.	6-10-83	0	London (OHL)
33	Fredrik Modin (LW)	6-4/220	Sundsvall, Sweden	10-8-74	5	Tampa Bay
	Jimmie Olvestad (LW)	6-1/194	Stockholm, Sweden	2-16-80	0	Djurgarden Stockholm (Sweden)
	Alexander Polushin (C)	6-3/198	Kirov, U.S.S.R.	5-8-83	0	Tver (Russian Div. 1)
13	Vaclav Prospal (C)	6-2/195	Ceske-Budejovice, Czech.	2-17-75	5	Ottawa, Florida
	Brad Richards (LW)	6-1/187	Montague, P.E.I.	5-2-80	1	Tampa Bay
	Pavel Sedov (RW)	6-3/200	Voskresensk, U.S.S.R.	1-12-82	0	
15	Martin St. Louis (RW)	5-9/185	Laval, Que.	9-8-71	3	Tampa Bay
	Samuel St. Pierre (RW)	6-2/201	Laurierville, Que.	6-28-79	0	Detroit (IHL), Johnstown (ECHL)
	Alexander Svitov (C)	6-3/198	Omsk, U.S.S.R.	11-3-82	0	Avangard Omsk (Russian)
26	Tim Taylor (C)	6-1/188	Stratford, Ont.	2-6-69	8	New York Rangers
36	Juha Ylonen (C)	6-1/189	Helsinki, Finland	2-13-72	5	Phoenix
	Thomas Ziegler (RW)	5-11/174	Zurich, Switzerland	6-9-78	1	Detroit (IHL), Tampa Bay
	DEFENSEMEN					
49	Kaspars Astashenko	6-2/183	Riga, U.S.S.R.	2-7-75	2	Detroit (IHL), Tampa Bay
34	Mathieu Biron	6-6/212	Lac St. Charles, Que.	4-29-80	2	Lowell (AHL), New York Islanders, Springfield (AHL)
7	Ben Clymer	6-1/195	Edina, Minn.	4-11-78	2	Detroit (IHL), Tampa Bay
27	Jassen Cullimore	6-5/220	Simcoe, Ont.	12-4-72	7	Tampa Bay
3	Sergey Gusev	6-1/205	Nizhny Tagil, U.S.S.R.	7-31-75	4	Tampa Bay, Detroit (IHL)
	Andreas Holmqvist	6-3/187	Stockholm, Sweden	7-23-81	0	Hammarby (Sweden Jr.)
	Mike Jones	6-4/195	Toledo, Ohio	5-18-76	0	Detroit (IHL)
	Kyle Kos	6-3/207	Hope, B.C.	5-25-79	0	Detroit (IHL)
13	Pavel Kubina	6-4/230	Caledna, Czechoslovakia	4-15-77	4	Tampa Bay
	Kristian Kudroc	6-6/229	Michalovce, Czechoslovakia	5-21-81	1	Detroit (IHL), Tampa Bay
	Mikko Kuparinen	6-4/218	Hameenlinna, Finland	3-29-77	0	Detroit (IHL), Johnstown (ECHL)
2	Grant Ledyard	6-2/195	Winnipeg	11-19-61	17	Tampa Bay, Dallas
	Paul Lynch	6-3/195	Salem, Mass.	4-23-82	0	Valley Junior Warriors (EJHL)
24	Stan Neckar	6-1/207	Ceske-Budejovice, Czech.	12-22-75	7	Phoenix, Tampa Bay
18	Marek Posmyk	6-5/209	Jihlava, Czechoslovakia	9-15-78	2	Tampa Bay, Detroit (IHL)
4	Nolan Pratt	6-2/208	Fort McMurray, Alta.	8-14-75	5	Colorado
	Marek Priechodsky	6-2/194	Obranca, Slovakia	10-24-79	0	Bratislava (Slovakia)
21	Cory Sarich	6-3/193	Saskatoon, Sask.	8-16-78	3	Tampa Bay, Detroit (IHL)
	Kenton Smith	5-11/177	Edmonton	9-10-79	0	Detroit (IHL), Johnstown (ECHL)
23	Petr Svoboda	6-2/198	Most, Czechoslovakia	2-14-66	17	Tampa Bay
	Jeremy Van Hoof	6-3/200	Lindsay, Ont.	8-12-81	0	Ottawa (OHL)
30	Andrei Zyuzin	6-1/210	Ufa, U.S.S.R.	1-21-78	4	Tampa Bay, Detroit (IHL)
	GOALTENDERS					
35	Nikolai Khabibulin	6-1/195	Sverdlovsk, U.S.S.R.	1-13-73	6	Tampa Bay
35	Dieter Kochan	6-1/165	Saskatoon, Sask.	11-5-74	2	Detroit (IHL), Tampa Bay
	Evgeny Konstantinov	6-0/167	Kazan, U.S.S.R.	3-29-81	1	Tampa Bay, Detroit (IHL), Louisiana (ECHL)
80	Kevin Weekes	6-0/195	Toronto	4-4-75	4	Tampa Bay

2000-01 REVIEW

INDIVIDUAL STATISTICS

SCORING

	Games	G	A	Pts.	PIM	+/-	PPG	SHG	Shots	Shooting Pct.
Brad Richards	82	21	41	62	14	-10	7	0	179	11.7
Fredrik Modin	76	32	24	56	48	-1	8	0	217	14.7
Vincent Lecavalier	68	23	28	51	66	-26	7	0	165	13.9
Martin St. Louis	78	18	22	40	12	-4	3	3	141	12.8
Mike Johnson*	64	11	27	38	38	-10	3	1	107	10.3
Brian Holzinger	70	11	25	36	64	-9	3	0	87	12.6
Pavel Kubina	70	11	19	30	103	-14	6	1	128	8.6
Alexander Kharitonov	66	7	15	22	8	-9	0	0	103	6.8
Todd Warriner	64	10	11	21	46	-13	3	2	99	10.1
Ryan Johnson	80	7	14	21	44	-20	1	0	71	9.9
Nils Ekman	43	9	11	20	40	-15	2	1	72	12.5
Andrei Zyuzin	64	4	16	20	76	-8	2	1	92	4.3
Paul Mara*	46	6	10	16	40	-17	2	0	58	10.3

	Games	G	A	Pts.	PIM	+/-	PPG	SHG	Shots	Shooting Pct.
Wayne Primeau*	47	2	13	15	77	-17	0	0	47	4.3
Adrian Aucoin*	26	1	11	12	25	-8	1	0	60	1.7
Cory Sarich	73	1	8	9	106	-25	0	0	66	1.5
Matthew Barnaby*	29	4	4	8	97	-3	1	0	29	13.8
Jassen Cullimore	74	1	6	7	80	-6	0	0	56	1.8
Ben Clymer	23	5	1	6	21	-7	3	0	25	20.0
Stan Drulia	34	2	4	6	18	-11	1	0	20	10.0
Maxim Galanov	25	0	5	5	8	-5	0	0	10	0.0
Sheldon Keefe	49	4	0	4	38	-13	0	0	32	12.5
Grant Ledyard*	14	2	2	4	12	-5	0	0	12	16.7
Kristian Kudroc	22	2	2	4	36	0	0	0	12	16.7
Petr Svoboda	19	1	3	4	41	-4	0	0	16	6.3
Bryan Muir*	10	0	3	3	15	-7	0	0	14	0.0
Dimitry Afanasenkov	9	1	1	2	4	1	0	0	8	12.5
John Emmons*	12	1	1	2	22	0	0	0	9	11.1
Kaspars Astashenko	15	1	1	2	4	-4	0	0	4	25.0
Craig Millar*	16	1	1	2	10	-8	0	0	10	10.0
Steve Martins*	20	1	1	2	13	-9	0	0	18	5.6
Stan Neckar*	16	0	2	2	8	-1	0	0	10	0.0
Sergey Gusev	16	1	0	1	10	-3	0	0	13	7.7
Kyle Freadrich	13	0	1	1	36	-1	0	0	3	0.0
Gordie Dwyer	28	0	1	1	96	-7	0	0	12	0.0
Kevin Weekes (goalie)	61	0	1	1	4	0	0	0	0	0.0
Evgeny Konstantinov (goalie)	1	0	0	0	0	0	0	0	0	0.0
Marek Posmyk	1	0	0	0	0	-1	0	0	0	0.0
Nikolai Khabibulin (goalie)	2	0	0	0	0	0	0	0	0	0.0
Wade Flaherty (goalie)*	2	0	0	0	0	0	0	0	0	0.0
Thomas Ziegler	5	0	0	0	0	-2	0	0	2	0.0
Matt Elich	8	0	0	0	0	-5	0	0	7	0.0
Dieter Kochan (goalie)	10	0	0	0	0	0	0	0	0	0.0
Dan Cloutier (goalie)*	24	0	0	0	4	0	0	0	0	0.0

GOALTENDING

	Games	Min.	Goals	SO	Avg.	W	L	T	ENG	Shots	Sv. Pct.
Evgeny Konstantin	1	0	0	0	0.00	0	0	0	0	0	.000
Nikolai Khabibulin	2	123	6	0	2.93	1	1	0	0	69	.913
Kevin Weekes	61	3378	177	4	3.14	20	33	3	8	1742	.898
Dieter Kochan	10	314	18	0	3.44	0	3	0	1	138	.870
Dan Cloutier*	24	1005	59	1	3.52	3	13	3	3	541	.891
Wade Flaherty*	2	118	8	0	4.07	0	2	0	0	55	.855

*Played with two or more NHL teams.

RESULTS

OCTOBER
6— N.Y. Islanders .... T ... *3-3
8— Vancouver .... L 4-5
13— At Pittsburgh ....L 2-3
15— Atlanta ....W 5-2
18— At Minnesota ....L 5-6
21— At New Jersey ....L 2-7
22— At N.Y. Rangers ....W 4-2
25— At Detroit ....L 1-5
27— Ottawa ....L 0-6
31— At Carolina ....L *5-6

NOVEMBER
1— At N.Y. Rangers ....L 1-6
3— N.Y. Islanders ....W *4-3
5— Washington ....W 5-2
10— Montreal ....W 3-1
11— Calgary ....L 3-4
14— At Montreal ....W 1-0
17— At Toronto ....T *2-2
20— At Dallas ....L 2-6
22— Atlanta ....W 8-2
24— Florida ....W 2-1
25— At Florida ....L *1-2
27— At N.Y. Islanders ....L 4-7
29— At Washington ....L 1-4

DECEMBER
1— At Atlanta ....L 3-5
2— Detroit ....W 3-0
6— At Philadelphia ....L 3-6
8— Colorado ....L 0-2

JANUARY
3— At Carolina ....L 2-3
4— At Ottawa ....L 3-8
7— At Chicago ....L 4-7
10— At Toronto ....W 3-1
12— Philadelphia ....L 0-3
14— Dallas ....L 2-3
16— At Buffalo ....L 1-3
18— At Montreal ....L 1-3
20— At Ottawa ....L 0-3
21— At Columbus ....L 1-3
23— Washington ....L 2-5
25— Ottawa ....L 2-5
27— At Florida ....L *2-3
29— At Carolina ....L 2-5
30— Florida ....W 4-3

FEBRUARY
1— Buffalo ....W 4-2
6— Minnesota ....L 2-4
8— At St. Louis ....L 1-4

11— At Colorado ....T ...*2-2
14— At Phoenix ....L 2-3
16— At Los Angeles ....W 4-3
17— At Anaheim ....L 1-3
21— Pittsburgh ....T ...*1-1
23— New Jersey ....L 1-5
26— Carolina ....W 3-2
28— Philadelphia ....W 4-3
30— Boston ....T ...*1-1
31— Toronto ....L 2-3

MARCH
1— At Boston ....L 1-3
3— At N.Y. Islanders ....W 6-0
4— At New Jersey ....L 0-6
6— San Jose ....W *2-1
8— Carolina ....W 1-0
10— Columbus ....W 4-1
13— Edmonton ....L *4-5
15— Toronto ....W 3-2
17— Pittsburgh ....W 5-1
21— At Atlanta ....W 4-3
22— Atlanta ....L 0-2
24— Washington ....L 2-3
27— New Jersey ....L 1-7
29— Montreal ....L 2-6
30— At Florida ....W 4-2

10— At Boston ....L 2-6
13— Phoenix ....L 2-5
15— Boston ....L 3-6
17— N.Y. Rangers ....L 4-5
18— At Nashville ....L 2-3
20— St. Louis ....W 3-2
24— At Philadelphia ....T ...*0-0
25— At Buffalo ....L 4-5

APRIL
1— Buffalo ....L 2-4
4— At Pittsburgh ....L 2-4
5— N.Y. Rangers ....L *3-4
8— At Washington ....L 1-2

*Denotes overtime game.

– 85 –

TORONTO MAPLE LEAFS
EASTERN CONFERENCE/NORTHEAST DIVISION

Maple Leafs' Schedule
Home games shaded; D—Day game; *—All-Star Game at Los Angeles

October
SUN	MON	TUE	WED	THU	FRI	SAT
	1	2	3 OTT	4	5	6 MON
7	8 ANA	9	10	11 CAR	12	13 STL
14	15	16 EDM	17	18 VAN	19	20 CAL
21	22	23 BOS	24	25 BOS	26	27 PIT
28	29	30 TB	31			

November
SUN	MON	TUE	WED	THU	FRI	SAT
				1 PIT	2	3 COL
4	5	6 WAS	7	8	9 NJ	10 NJ
11	12	13	14 FLA	15 TB	16	17 OTT
18	19 FLA	20	21 BUF	22	23 NYI	24 BOS
25	26	27 CAR	28	29	30 CHI	

December
SUN	MON	TUE	WED	THU	FRI	SAT
						1 CHI
2	3	4 PIT	5	6 NYR	7	8 NYR
9	10	11 PHO	12	13 STL	14	15 MON
16	17	18 LA	19	20	21 BUF	22 BUF
23	24	25	26 CAR	27	28 ATL	29 FLA
30	31 TB					

January
SUN	MON	TUE	WED	THU	FRI	SAT
		1	2	3 BOS	4	5 D OTT
6	7 OTT	8 NAS	9	10	11 WAS	12 MON
13	14	15 ATL	16	17 NAS	18	19 PHI
20	21	22 CAL	23	24	25 VAN	26 EDM
27	28	29 SJ	30 ATL	31		

February
SUN	MON	TUE	WED	THU	FRI	SAT
					1	2 *
3	4	5 MIN	6	7 NYI	8	9 D MON
10	11 ATL	12	13	14	15	16
17	18	19	20	21	22	23
24	25	26 CAR	27	28		

March
SUN	MON	TUE	WED	THU	FRI	SAT
					1 NJ	2 BUF
3	4 WAS	5	6 DET	7	8	9 MON
10 PHI	11	12 PHI	13	14 BOS	15	16 DAL
17	18	19 NYI	20	21 WAS	22	23 BUF
24	25 PHI	26 TB	27	28 NYI	29	30 NJ
31						

April
SUN	MON	TUE	WED	THU	FRI	SAT
	1 DET	2	3	4 NYR	5	6 FLA
7	8 CBJ	9	10 NYR	11	12 PIT	13 OTT
14	15	16	17	18	19	20

2001-02 SEASON
CLUB DIRECTORY

Chairman of the board and governor
Steve A. Stavro
Alternate governor
Brian P. Bellmore
President, CEO and alt. governor
Richard Peddie
Exec. v.p. and alternate governor
Ken Dryden
Sr. v.p. and g.m., Air Canada Centre
Bob Hunter
Senior vice president, business
Tom Anselmi
Senior vice president, CFO
Ian Clarke
Vice president, sports communications & community development
John Lashway
Vice president, people
Mardi Walker
V.p., regulatory affairs and gen. counsel
Robin Brudner
Vice president, sales and service
Chris Overholt
General manager and head coach
Pat Quinn
Assistant to the president
Bill Watters
Director of player personnel
Mike Penny
Assistant coaches
Keith Acton, Rick Ley
Development coach
Paul Dennis
Community representatives
Wendel Clark, Darryl Sittler
Chief European scout
Thommie Bergman
Director, amateur scouting
Mark Hillier

Scouts
George Armstrong, Bob Johnson, Garth Malarchuk, Murray Oliver, Mark Yannetti
European scouts
Leonid Vaysfeld, Jan Kovac
Director, hockey operations
Casey Vanden Heuvel
Travel coordinator
Mary Speck
Director, media relations
Pat Park
Coordinators, media relations
Dave Griffiths, Reid Mitchell
Manager, corporate communications
Tara McCarthy
Director, community relations
Kristy Fletcher
Coordinators, community relations
Sefu Bernard, Paulette Minard
Manager, game presentation
Mike Ferriman
Manager, game operations
Nancy Gilks
Head athletic therapist
Chris Broadhurst
Athletic therapist
Brent Smith
Equipment manager
Brian Papineau
Assistant equipment managers
Bobby Hastings, Scott McKay
Team doctors
Dr. Michael Clarfield, Dr. Darrell Ogilvie-Harris, Dr. Leith Douglas, Dr. Rob Devenyi, Dr. Simon McGrail
Team dentist
Dr. Ernie Lewis
Team psychologist
Robert Offenberger

DRAFT CHOICES

Rd.— Player	Ht./Wt.	Overall	Pos.	Last team
1— Carlo Colaiacovo	6-1/184	17	D	Erie (OHL)
2— Karel Pilar	6-3/207	39	D	Litvinov, Czech.
3— Brendan Bell	6-1/198	65	D	Ottawa (OHL)
3— Jay Harrison	6-3/200	82	D	Brampton (OHL)
3— Nicolas Corbeil	5-10/177	88	C	Sherbrooke (QMJHL)
5— Kyle Wellwood	5-9/190	134	C	Belleville (OHL)
6— Max Kondratiev	6-1/176	168	D	Togliatti Jr., Russia
6— Jaroslav Sklenar	6-1/169	183	F	Brno Jr., Czech.
7— Ivan Kolozvary	6-0/169	198	F	Trencin Jr., Slovakia
7— Jan Chovan	5-11/178	213	G	Belleville (OHL)
8— Tomas Mojzis	6-1/186	246	D	Moose Jaw (WHL)
9— Mike Knoepfli	6-1/185	276	LW	Georgetown, Ont. (OPJA)

MISCELLANEOUS DATA

Home ice (capacity)
Air Canada Centre (18,819)
Address
Air Canada Centre
40 Bay Street
Toronto, Ont. M5J 2X2
Business phone
416-815-5700
Ticket information
416-815-5700
Website
www.torontomapleleafs.com

Training site
Toronto
Club colors
Blue and white
Radio affiliation
Mojo Radio (640 AM)
TV affiliation
CBC, CTV, CTV Sportsnet

No.	FORWARDS	Ht./Wt.	Place (BORN)	Date	NHL exp.	2000-01 clubs
	Nik Antropov (C)	6-5/203	Vost, U.S.S.R.	2-18-80	2	Toronto
	Brad Boyes (C)	6-0/181	Mississaugua, Ont.	4-17-82	0	Erie (OHL)
	Luca Cereda (C)	6-2/203	Lugano, Switzerland	9-7-81	0	
	Nicolas Corbeil (C)	5-10/177	Laval, Que.	3-30-83	0	Sherbrooke (QMJHL)
27	Shayne Corson (LW)	6-1/198	Barrie, Ont.	8-13-66	16	Toronto
28	Tie Domi (RW)	5-10/200	Windsor, Ont.	11-1-69	12	Toronto
	Jeff Farkas (C)	6-0/185	Amherst, Mass.	1-24-78	2	St. John's (AHL), Toronto
39	Travis Green (C)	6-2/200	Castlegar, B.C.	12-20-70	9	Phoenix
	Mikael Hakansson (C)	6-1/196	Stockholm, Sweden	3-31-74	0	St. John's (AHL)
14	Jonas Hoglund (LW)	6-3/215	Karlstad, Sweden	8-29-72	5	Toronto
	Bobby House (RW)	6-1/210	Whitehorse, Yukon.	1-7-73	0	St. John's (AHL)
	Don MacLean (C)	6-2/199	Sydney, Nova Scotia.	1-14-77	2	Toronto, St. John's (AHL)
18	Alyn McCauley (C)	5-11/190	Brockville, Ont.	5-29-77	4	Toronto, St. John's (AHL)
39	Craig Mills (RW)	6-0/195	Toronto	8-27-76	3	Springfield (AHL)
89	Alexander Mogilny (RW) .	5-11/200	Khabarovsk, U.S.S.R.	2-18-69	12	New Jersey
	Alexei Ponikarovksy	6-4/196	Kiev, U.S.S.R.	4-9-80	1	St. John's (AHL), Toronto
16	Robert Reichel (C)	5-10/186	Litvinov, Czechoslovakia	6-25-71	8	Litvinov (Czech Republic)
20	Mikael Renberg (RW)	6-2/218	Pitea, Sweden	5-5-72	7	Lulea (Sweden)
10	Gary Roberts (LW)	6-1/190	North York, Ont.	5-23-66	15	Toronto
13	Mats Sundin (C)	6-5/220	Bromma, Sweden	2-13-71	11	Toronto
	Michal Travnicek (RW)	6-1/198		3-14-80	0	St. John's (AHL)
16	Darcy Tucker (C)	5-11/185	Castor, Alta.	3-15-75	6	Toronto
10	Garry Valk (LW)	6-1/200	Edmonton	11-27-67	11	Toronto
	Kyle Wellwood (C)	5-9/190	Windsor, Ont.	5-16-83	0	Belleville (OHL)

DEFENSEMEN

No.	DEFENSEMEN	Ht./Wt.	Place	Date	NHL exp.	2000-01 clubs
29	Wade Belak	6-4/222	Saskatoon, Sask.	3-7-76	5	Calgary, Toronto
	Brendan Bell	6-1/198	Ottawa	3-31-83	0	Ottawa (OHL)
5	Aki Berg	6-3/220	Turku, Finland	7-28-77	5	Los Angeles, Toronto
	Christian Chartier	6-0/219	Russel, Man.	10-29-80	0	Prince George (WHL)
	Carlo Colaiacovo	6-1/184	Toronto	1-27-83	0	Erie (OHL)
33	David Cooper	6-2/204	Ottawa	11-2-73	3	St. John's (AHL), Toronto
4	Cory Cross	6-5/219	Lloydminster, Alta.	7-31-75	8	Toronto
	Nathan Dempsey	6-0/190	Spruce Grove, Alta.	7-14-74	3	St. John's (AHL), Toronto
8	Anders Eriksson	6-2/220	Bollnas, Sweden	1-9-75	6	Chicago, Florida
33	Maxim Galanov	6-1/210	Krasnoyarsk, U.S.S.R.	3-13-74	4	Louisville (AHL), Tampa Bay, Detroit (IHL)
	Jay Harrison	6-3/200	Oshawa, Ont.	11-3-82	0	Brampton (OHL)
15	Tomas Kaberle	6-2/200	Rakovnik, Czechoslovakia	3-2-78	3	Toronto
6	Dave Manson	6-2/220	Prince Albert, Sask.	1-27-67	15	Toronto
44	Bryan McCabe	6-1/210	Toronto	6-8-75	6	Toronto
	Karel Pilar	6-3/207	Prague, Czechoslovakia	12-23-77	0	Litvinov (Czech Republic)
	Allan Rourke	6-2/210	Mississauga, Ont.	3-6-80	0	St. John's (AHL)
	D.J. Smith	6-2/205	Windsor, Ont.	5-13-77	2	St. John's (AHL)
	Petr Svoboda	6-2/200	Jihlava, Czechoslovakia	6-20-80	1	St. John's (AHL), Toronto
	Lubos Velebny	6-1/189	Zvolen, Slovakia	2-9-82	0	
	Dmitri Yakushin	6-0/200	Kharkov, Ukraine	1-21-78	1	St. John's (AHL)
36	Dmitry Yushkevich	5-11/208	Yaroslavl, U.S.S.R.	11-19-71	9	Toronto
	Jon Zion	6-0/187	Nepean, Ont.	5-21-81	0	Ottawa (OHL)

GOALTENDERS

No.	GOALTENDERS	Ht./Wt.	Place	Date	NHL exp.	2000-01 clubs
	Jamie Hodson	6-2/192	Brandon, Man.	4-8-80	0	Brandon (WHL), St. John's (AHL)
31	Curtis Joseph	5-11/190	Keswick, Ont.	4-29-67	12	Toronto
1	Mike Minard	6-3/205	Owen Sound, Ont.	11-1-76	1	St. John's (AHL)
	Mikael Tellqvist	5-11/174	Sweden	9-19-79	0	Djurgarden Stockholm (Sweden)
29	Jimmy Waite	6-1/190	Sherbrooke, Que.	4-15-69	11	St. John's (AHL)

2000-01 REVIEW
INDIVIDUAL STATISTICS

SCORING

	Games	G	A	Pts.	PIM	+/-	PPG	SHG	Shots	Shooting Pct.
Mats Sundin	82	28	46	74	76	15	9	0	226	12.4
Gary Roberts	82	29	24	53	109	16	8	2	138	21.0
Yanic Perreault	76	24	28	52	52	0	5	0	134	17.9
Sergei Berezin	79	22	28	50	8	2	10	0	256	8.6
Jonas Hoglund	82	23	26	49	14	1	5	0	196	11.7
Tomas Kaberle	82	6	39	45	24	10	0	0	96	6.3
Darcy Tucker	82	16	21	37	141	6	2	0	122	13.1
Steve Thomas	57	8	26	34	46	0	1	0	140	5.7
Igor Korolev	73	10	19	29	28	3	2	0	78	12.8

	Games	G	A	Pts.	PIM	+/-	PPG	SHG	Shots	Shooting Pct.
Bryan McCabe	82	5	24	29	123	16	3	0	159	3.1
Garry Valk	74	8	18	26	46	4	1	0	87	9.2
Shayne Corson	77	8	18	26	189	1	0	0	102	7.8
Dmitry Yushkevich	81	5	19	24	52	-2	1	0	110	4.5
Tie Domi	82	13	7	20	214	2	1	0	60	21.7
Nik Antropov	52	6	11	17	30	5	0	0	71	8.5
Danny Markov	59	3	13	16	34	6	1	0	49	6.1
Dave Manson	74	4	7	11	93	13	0	0	70	5.7
Nathan Dempsey	25	1	9	10	4	13	1	0	31	3.2
Dmitri Khristich*	27	3	6	9	8	8	2	0	23	13.0
Cory Cross	41	3	5	8	50	7	1	0	34	8.8
Alexei Ponikarovsky	22	1	3	4	14	-1	0	0	21	4.8
Aki Berg*	12	3	0	3	2	-6	3	0	12	25.0
Petr Svoboda	18	1	2	3	10	-5	1	0	17	5.9
Wade Belak*	16	1	1	2	31	-4	0	0	8	12.5
Adam Mair*	16	0	2	2	14	3	0	0	17	0.0
Alyn McCauley	14	1	0	1	0	0	0	0	13	7.7
Donald MacLean	3	0	1	1	2	-2	0	0	2	0.0
Curtis Joseph (goalie)	68	0	1	1	8	0	0	0	0	0.0
David Cooper	2	0	0	0	0	-1	0	0	3	0.0
Jeff Farkas	2	0	0	0	2	-1	0	0	1	0.0
Glenn Healy (goalie)	15	0	0	0	0	0	0	0	0	0.0

GOALTENDING

	Games	Min.	Goals	SO	Avg.	W	L	T	ENG	Shots	Sv. Pct.
Curtis Joseph	68	4100	163	6	2.39	33	27	8	5	1907	.915
Glenn Healy	15	871	38	0	2.62	4	7	3	1	331	.885

*Played with two or more NHL teams.

RESULTS

OCTOBER
7— Montreal .... W 2-0
9— Dallas .... L 1-3
11— N.Y. Islanders .... W 3-2
14— Ottawa .... L 0-4
16— At Vancouver .... L 2-5
19— At Edmonton .... W 4-1
21— At Calgary .... W 2-1
25— Minnesota .... W 6-1
27— At Buffalo .... L 1-2
28— At Boston .... W ... *2-1
31— At Ottawa .... L 3-4

NOVEMBER
2— New Jersey .... W 5-3
4— At St. Louis .... T ... *0-0
5— Boston .... W 7-1
8— Carolina .... W 5-0
10— At Carolina .... L 1-3
11— Chicago .... T ... *3-3
15— Philadelphia .... L ... *1-2
17— Tampa Bay .... T ... *2-2
18— At Montreal .... W 6-1
21— At N.Y. Rangers .... W 3-1
22— Edmonton .... W 4-3
25— Ottawa .... L 2-4
29— St. Louis .... L ... *5-6
30— At N.Y. Islanders .... W 6-4

DECEMBER
2— N.Y. Rangers .... W 8-2
4— Florida .... T ... *4-4

6— At Detroit .... W 3-0
9— Pittsburgh .... W 5-1
13— At Pittsburgh .... W 7-4
15— At N.Y. Islanders .... L 2-3
16— Calgary .... L ... *5-6
20— Nashville .... L 1-3
21— At Boston .... L 0-4
23— At Montreal .... W 5-2
26— At Atlanta .... L 3-5
27— At Pittsburgh .... L 0-5
30— At Florida .... W 4-1
31— At Tampa Bay .... W 3-2

JANUARY
3— Buffalo .... T ... *1-1
5— At Buffalo .... T ... *3-3
6— Washington .... L 2-3
10— Tampa Bay .... L 1-3
12— Phoenix .... W 3-2
13— At New Jersey .... T ... *4-4
17— Los Angeles .... L 1-2
18— At N.Y. Rangers .... L ... *1-2
20— Buffalo .... W 2-0
24— Boston .... L 1-2
25— At Atlanta .... W ... *2-1
27— N.Y. Rangers .... W 3-1
29— At St. Louis .... L 1-2
31— At Carolina .... W 4-3

FEBRUARY
1— At Washington .... L 4-5
7— Atlanta .... W 7-1

8— At Detroit .... L 1-2
10— Detroit .... T ... *3-3
14— Columbus .... T ... *2-2
15— At Philadelphia .... L 2-5
17— Colorado .... T ... *5-5
19— New Jersey .... L 0-2
22— Vancouver .... W 4-1
24— Montreal .... W 5-1
25— At Chicago .... L 4-6
28— San Jose .... W 2-1

MARCH
1— At Washington .... W ... *3-2
3— Ottawa .... L ... *2-3
6— At Calgary .... W 3-1
7— At Edmonton .... L 0-4
10— At Vancouver .... T ... *3-3
14— Anaheim .... W 3-2
15— At Tampa Bay .... L 2-3
17— At Florida .... W 5-3
20— At Buffalo .... L 0-3
21— Florida .... L 1-3
24— Philadelphia .... W 5-3
28— Boston .... L 0-3
29— At Philadelphia .... W 2-1
31— At Montreal .... L 1-4

APRIL
4— N.Y. Islanders .... W 4-2
6— At Chicago .... W 1-0
7— At Ottawa .... L 3-5

*Denotes overtime game.

VANCOUVER CANUCKS
WESTERN CONFERENCE/NORTHWEST DIVISION

Canucks' Schedule
Home games shaded; D—Day game; *—All-Star Game at Los Angeles

October

SUN	MON	TUE	WED	THU	FRI	SAT
	1	2	3	4 CHI	5	6 DET
7	8	9 COL	10	11 DAL	12	13 COL
14	15	16 FLA	17	18 TOR	19	20 PHO
21 ANA	22	23 NAS	24	25 COL	26	27 EDM
28	29	30 CBJ	31			

November

SUN	MON	TUE	WED	THU	FRI	SAT
				1 MON	2	3 SJ
4	5	6 CBJ	7	8 STL	9 CHI	10
11 D MIN	12	13 CHI	14	15 STL	16	17 EDM
18	19	20 OTT	21 PIT	22	23 D BOS	24
25 PHI	26	27 MIN	28 CHI	29	30 COL	

December

SUN	MON	TUE	WED	THU	FRI	SAT
						1
2 DAL	3	4	5	6 ANA	7	8 SJ
9	10 TB	11	12 ANA	13 LA	14	15 DET
16	17	18	19 DET	20 NAS	21	22 MIN
23	24	25	26	27 CAL	28	29 NJ
30	31 PHI					

January

SUN	MON	TUE	WED	THU	FRI	SAT
		1	2	3 MON	4	5 EDM
6	7	8 BUF	9 DET	10	11	12 CAR
13	14	15 PIT	16	17 STL	18	19 WAS
20	21 CAR	22	23 DAL	24	25 TOR	26 CAL
27	28 NAS	29	30 EDM	31		

February

SUN	MON	TUE	WED	THU	FRI	SAT
					1	2 *
3	4 PHO	5	6	7	8 CAL	9 CAL
10	11	12 BOS	13	14	15	16
17	18	19	20	21	22	23
24	25	26 STL	27	28 DAL		

March

SUN	MON	TUE	WED	THU	FRI	SAT
					1	2 MIN
3	4	5	6	7 PHO	8	9 SJ
10 SJ	11	12 NAS	13	14 CBJ	15	16 ATL
17 NJ	18	19 NYR	20	21 NYI	22	23
24 EDM	25	26 LA	27	28 CBJ	29	30 ANA
31						

April

SUN	MON	TUE	WED	THU	FRI	SAT
	1	2 LA	3	4	5 MIN	6
7 PHO	8	9 COL	10	11 LA	12	13 CAL
14	15	16	17	18	19	20

2001-02 SEASON
CLUB DIRECTORY

Chairman & governor
John E. McCaw Jr.
President, chief executive officer
Stanley B. McCammon
President & general manager, alt. gov.
Brian P. Burke
Chief operating officer, alternate gov.
David Cobb
Senior v.p., sales and marketing
John Rizzardini
V.p. and g.m., arena operations
Harvey Jones
Vice president, finance & CFO
Victor de Bonis
V.p., broadcast and new media
Chris Hebb
Sr. v.p., director of hockey operations
David M. Nonis
Vice president, player personnel
Steve Tambellini
Head coach
Marc Crawford
Assistant coaches
Jack McIlhargey
Mike Johnston
Strength & conditioning coach
Peter Twist
Goaltending consultant
Andy Moog
Assistant coach, video
Eric Crawford
Senior editor, alumni liaison
Norm Jewison
Manager, media relations
Chris Brumwell
Coordinator, media relations
T.C. Carling
Assistant, media relations
Rob Viccars

Director, community relations
Veronica Varhaug
Coordinator, community relations
Allanah Mooney
Assistant, community relations
Regan McDonald
Professional scouts
Bob Murray, Shawn Dineen
European scouts
Thomas Gradin
Russian scouts
Sergei Chibisov
Amateur scouts
Barry Dean, Ron Delorme, Jim Eagle,
Tim Lenardon, Mario Marois, Jack
McCartan, Mike McHugh, Dave
Morrison, Ken Slater, Daryl Stanley
Scouting information coordinator
Jonathan Wall
Medical trainer
Mike Bernstein
Assistant medical trainers
Jon Sanderson, Marty Dudgeon
Equipment manager
Pat O'Neill
Assistant equipment manager
Darren Granger
Assistant equipment trainer
Jamie Hendricks
Team doctors
Dr. Rui Avelar, Dr. Bill Regan
Team dentist
Dr. David Lawson
Team chiropractor
Dr. Sid Sheard
Team optometrist
Dr. Alan R. Boyco

DRAFT CHOICES

Rd.— Player	Ht./Wt.	Overall	Pos.	Last team
1— R.J. Umberger	6-2/200	16	C	Ohio State (CCHA)
3— Fedor Fedorov..............	6-3/202	66	LW	Sudbury (OHL)
4— Evgeny Gladskikh.........	6-0/176	114	LW	Magnitogorsk, Russia
5— Kevin Bieksa	6-1/180	151	D	Bowling Green (CCHA)
7— Jason King...................	6-0/194	212	RW	Halifax (QMJHL)
8— Konstantin Mihailov	6-0/176	245	C	Nizhnekamsk, Russia

MISCELLANEOUS DATA

Home ice (capacity)
General Motors Place (18,422)
Address
800 Griffiths Way
Vancouver, B.C. V6B 6G1
Business phone
604-899-7400
Ticket information
604-280-4400
Website
www.canucks.com

Training site
Burnaby, B.C.
Club colors
Deep blue, sky blue, deep red, white and
silver
Radio affiliation
CKNW (980 AM)
TV affiliation
Sportsnet (Cable)

TRAINING CAMP ROSTER

No.	FORWARDS	Ht./Wt.	Place	BORN Date	NHL exp.	2000-01 clubs
	Nathan Barrett (C)	5-11/192	Vancouver	8-3-81	0	Lethbridge (WHL)
	Thatcher Bell (C)..............	6-0/172	Charlottetown, P.E.I.	2-1-82	0	Rimouski (QMJHL)
44	Todd Bertuzzi (LW)	6-3/230	Sudbury, Ont.	2-2-75	6	Vancouver
8	Donald Brashear (LW)	6-2/230	Bedford, Ind.	1-7-72	8	Vancouver
	Mike Brown (LW)............	6-4/205	Surrey, B.C.	4-27-79	1	Kansas City (IHL), Vancouver
25	Andrew Cassels (C)	6-1/185	Bramalea, Ont.	7-23-69	12	Vancouver
	Artem Chubarov (C)	6-1/189	Gorky, U.S.S.R.	12-12-79	2	Vancouver, Kansas City (IHL)
24	Matt Cooke (C)	5-11/205	Belleville, Ont.	9-7-78	3	Vancouver
22	Johan Davidsson (C/RW)	6-1/181	Jonkoping, Sweden	1-6-76	2	Blues Espoo (Finland)
15	Harold Druken (C)	6-0/200	St. John's, Nfld.	1-26-79	2	Kansas City (IHL), Vancouver
	Fedor Fedorov (C)...........	6-3/187	Moscow, U.S.S.R.	6-11-81	0	Sudbury (OHL)
	Evgeny Gladskikh (LW)....	6-0/176	U.S.S.R.	4-24-82	0	Metal. Magnitogorsk (Russian)
21	Josh Holden (C)	6-1/190	Calgary	1-18-78	3	Kansas City (IHL), Vancouver
	Steve Kariya (LW)	5-7/170	Vancouver	12-22-77	2	Vancouver, Kansas City (IHL)
	Pat Kavanagh (RW)	6-3/192	Ottawa	3-14-79	1	Kansas City (IHL), Vancouver
26	Trent Klatt (RW).............	6-1/210	Minneapolis	1-30-71	10	Vancouver
	Brad Leeb (LW)	5-11/180	Red Deer, Alta.	8-27-79	1	Kansas City (IHL)
7	Brendan Morrison (C)......	5-11/190	Pitt Meadows, B.C.	8-12-75	4	Vancouver
19	Markus Naslund (LW).....	6-0/186	Ornskoldsvik, Sweden	7-30-73	8	Vancouver
20	Denis Pederson (C)	6-2/205	Prince Albert, Sask.	9-10-75	6	Vancouver
	Ryan Ready (LW)............	6-0/195	Peterborough, Ont.	11-7-78	0	Kansas City (IHL)
	Brandon Reid (C)............	5-9/170	Kirkland, Que.	3-9-81	0	Val-d'Or (QMJHL)
	Jarkko Ruutu (RW).........	6-2/194	Vantaa, Finland	8-23-75	2	Kansas City (IHL), Vancouver
72	Peter Schaefer (LW)	5-11/195	Yellow Grass, Sask.	7-12-77	3	Vancouver
	Daniel Sedin (LW)...........	6-1/194	Ornskoldsvik, Sweden	9-26-80	1	Vancouver
	Henrik Sedin (C).............	6-2/196	Ornskoldsvik, Sweden	9-26-80	1	Vancouver
17	Vadim Sharifijanov (RW) .	6-0/205	Ufa, U.S.S.R.	12-23-75	3	Kansas City (IHL)
	Nathan Smith (C)............	6-1/192	Strathcona, Alta.	2-9-82	0	Swift Current (WHL)
14	Mike Stapleton (C)	5-10/185	Sarnia, Ont.	5-5-66	14	New York Islanders, Vancouver
	R.J. Umberger (C)	6-2/200	Pittsburgh	5-3-82	0	Ohio State (CCHA)
	DEFENSEMEN					
7	Bryan Allen	6-4/210	Kingston, Ont.	8-21-80	1	Vancouver
23	Murray Baron	6-3/225	Prince George, B.C.	6-1-67	12	Vancouver
15	Drake Berehowsky	6-2/212	Toronto	1-3-72	10	Nashville, Vancouver
	Kevin Bieska	6-1/180	Grimsby, Ont.	5-16-81	0	Bowling Green (CCHA)
	Ryan Bonni	6-4/190	Winnipeg	2-18-79	1	Kansas City (IHL)
	Tim Branham	6-2/185	Minoqua, Wis.	5-10-81	0	Barrie (OHL)
	Darrell Hay.....................	6-0/190	Kamloops, B.C.	4-2-80	0	Kansas City (IHL), Florida (ECHL)
36	Bryan Helmer..................	6-1/190	Sault Ste. Marie, Ont.	7-15-72	3	Kansas City (IHL), Vancouver
55	Ed Jovanovski.................	6-2/210	Windsor, Ont.	6-26-76	6	Vancouver
	Zenith Komarniski...........	6-0/200	Edmonton	8-13-78	1	Kansas City (IHL)
20	Scott Lachance	6-1/212	Charlottesville, Va.	10-22-72	10	Vancouver
2	Mattias Ohlund	6-3/210	Pitea, Sweden	9-9-76	4	Vancouver
3	Brent Sopel....................	6-1/205	Saskatoon, Sask.	1-7-77	3	Vancouver, Kansas City (IHL)
34	Jason Strudwick..............	6-3/220	Edmonton	7-17-75	5	Vancouver
	Rene Vydareny	6-1/198	Bratislava, Czechoslovakia	5-6-81	0	Kansas City (IHL)
	David Ytfeldt..................	6-0/187	Ornskoldsvik, Sweden	9-29-79	0	JyP Jyvaskyla (Finland), Vastra Frolunda (Sweden)
	GOALTENDERS					
	Alex Auld	6-4/196	Cold Lake, Alta.	1-7-81	0	North Bay (OHL)
39	Dan Cloutier...................	6-1/182	Mont-Laurier, Que.	4-22-76	4	Detroit (IHL), Tampa Bay, Vancouver
	Alfie Michaud..................	5-10/177	Selkirk, Man.	11-6-76	1	Kansas City (IHL)

2000-01 REVIEW
INDIVIDUAL STATISTICS

SCORING

	Games	G	A	Pts.	PIM	+/-	PPG	SHG	Shots	Shooting Pct.
Markus Naslund	72	41	34	75	58	-2	18	1	277	14.8
Andrew Cassels	66	12	44	56	10	1	2	0	104	11.5
Todd Bertuzzi..	79	25	30	55	93	-18	14	0	203	12.3
Brendan Morrison..	82	16	38	54	42	2	3	2	179	8.9
Ed Jovanovski...	79	12	35	47	102	-1	4	0	193	6.2
Peter Schaefer..	82	16	20	36	22	4	3	4	163	9.8
Daniel Sedin	75	20	14	34	24	-3	10	0	127	15.7
Trent Klatt	77	13	20	33	31	8	3	0	140	9.3
Harold Druken	55	15	15	30	14	2	6	0	82	18.3
Henrik Sedin..	82	9	20	29	38	-2	2	0	98	9.2
Donald Brashear..	79	9	19	28	145	0	0	0	127	7.1

	Games	G	A	Pts.	PIM	+/-	PPG	SHG	Shots	Shooting Pct.
Mattias Ohlund	65	8	20	28	46	-16	1	1	136	5.9
Matt Cooke	81	14	13	27	94	5	0	2	121	11.6
Adrian Aucoin*	47	3	13	16	20	13	1	0	99	3.0
Brent Sopel	52	4	10	14	10	4	0	0	57	7.0
Scott Lachance	76	3	11	14	46	5	0	0	55	5.5
Denis Pederson	61	4	8	12	65	0	0	1	70	5.7
Murray Baron	82	3	8	11	63	-13	0	0	56	5.4
Greg Hawgood	16	2	5	7	6	8	1	0	16	12.5
Steve Kariya	17	1	6	7	8	-1	1	0	22	4.5
Jarkko Ruutu	21	3	3	6	32	1	0	1	23	13.0
Bryan Helmer	20	2	4	6	18	0	0	0	28	7.1
Jason Strudwick*	60	1	4	5	64	16	0	0	21	4.8
Mike Stapleton*	18	1	2	3	8	-6	1	0	9	11.1
Drake Berehowsky*	14	1	1	2	21	0	1	0	13	7.7
Felix Potvin (goalie)*	35	0	2	2	2	0	0	0	0	0.0
Josh Holden	10	1	0	1	0	0	0	0	12	8.3
Artem Chubarov	1	0	0	0	0	-1	0	0	0	0.0
Mike Brown	1	0	0	0	5	0	0	0	1	0.0
Bryan Allen	6	0	0	0	0	0	0	0	2	0.0
Dan Cloutier (goalie)*	16	0	0	0	0	0	0	0	0	0.0
Bob Essensa (goalie)	39	0	0	0	4	0	0	0	0	0.0

GOALTENDING

	Games	Min.	Goals	SO	Avg.	W	L	T	ENG	Shots	Sv. Pct.
Dan Cloutier*	16	914	37	0	2.43	4	6	5	0	348	.894
Bob Essensa	39	2059	92	1	2.68	18	12	3	4	854	.892
Felix Potvin*	35	2006	103	1	3.08	14	17	3	2	914	.887

*Played with two or more NHL teams.

RESULTS

OCTOBER
5— At Philadelphia............L....3-6
6— At Florida........................W....*4-3
8— At Tampa Bay...............W....5-4
12—Colorado.........................L....2-5
14—Buffalo..............................W....4-0
16—Toronto............................W....5-2
18—Calgary.............................W....4-1
21—Phoenix.............................L....*2-3
24—At Nashville ....T....*4-4
25—At Dallas...........................W....6-2
27—Atlanta...............................T....*1-1

NOVEMBER
1— Colorado............................W....4-3
3— Pittsburgh...........................L....2-4
5— San Jose............................T....*2-2
8— At Anaheim.........................W....7-2
9— At Los Angeles ....L....0-2
11—St. Louis.............................L....2-5
14—Chicago ....W....4-2
17—N.Y. Rangers ....W....4-3
19—At Columbus......................W....6-1
21—At St. Louis ....W....4-3
22—At Washington....................L....*2-3
24—At Detroit............................L....2-3
26—At Minnesota......................L....2-4
28—Anaheim.............................W....4-1
30—Montreal.............................L....3-4

DECEMBER
2— Edmonton...........................W....5-2
4— Nashville............................W....6-3

6— At Phoenix.........................T....*1-1
8— At San Jose........................W....6-1
10—Los Angeles ....L....1-2
16—Columbus...........................W....4-3
20—At Edmonton ....L....*2-3
21—At Chicago..........................L....4-6
23—At Colorado ....L....*2-3
27—Montreal.............................W....3-2
29—At Calgary...........................L....0-5
30—At San Jose.........................W....6-3

JANUARY
1— At Nashville ....W....5-2
3— At Chicago...........................L....0-6
6— Columbus............................W....4-3
8— Nashville..............................W....2-1
10—Ottawa.................................L....1-5
12—At Edmonton ....W....3-2
14—Calgary................................W....5-1
16—Detroit..................................L....2-4
18—At Colorado ....L....3-7
20—At St. Louis..........................L....0-3
22—At Dallas..............................L....1-2
24—Phoenix...............................W....6-2
27—At Calgary............................W....5-3
28—Chicago ....L....2-6
30—Minnesota............................W....*3-2

FEBRUARY
1— Colorado..............................W....5-3
8— San Jose..............................T....*0-0
10—Calgary ....L....1-4
14—Washington ....L....*3-4

17—At Edmonton ....W....*6-5
18—N.Y. Islanders ....W....3-2
21—At Montreal ....W....2-1
22—At Toronto ....L....1-4
24—At Ottawa.............................L....0-3
26—At Minnesota.......................W....5-2
28—Dallas..................................W....5-4

MARCH
2— St. Louis..............................W....*3-2
4— Minnesota............................L....*3-4
6— Detroit..................................L....3-4
8— At Phoenix...........................L....*2-3
10—Toronto................................T....*3-3
13—At Detroit.............................T....*2-2
15—At Boston............................T....*2-2
16—At Buffalo.............................L....2-4
18—At Atlanta............................W....5-3
21—At Columbus........................T....*1-1
23—At New Jersey ....L....0-4
25—At Minnesota........................T....*2-2
28—Dallas..................................L....1-3
30—Anaheim ....T....*2-2

APRIL
1— At Anaheim..........................L....1-2
2— At Los Angeles ....L....1-3
5— Los Angeles ....W....*3-2
7— Edmonton............................L....2-4
*Denotes overtime game.

VANCOUVER CANUCKS

WASHINGTON CAPITALS
EASTERN CONFERENCE/SOUTHEAST DIVISION

Capitals' Schedule
Home games shaded; D—Day game; *—All-Star Game at Los Angeles

October
SUN	MON	TUE	WED	THU	FRI	SAT
	1	2	3	4	5	6 NJ
7	8 D BOS	9	10 NYR	11	12 ANA	13 PHO
14	15	16 LA	17	18	19 MON	20 PHI
21	22	23 TB	24 FLA	25	26 ATL	27
28	29	30 PHI	31			

November
SUN	MON	TUE	WED	THU	FRI	SAT
				1	2 PHO	3 STL
4	5	6 TOR	7	8 CAR	9	10 ATL
11	12	13 OTT	14	15 PHI	16	17 ANA
18	19	20	21 TB	22	23 NYR	24 MON
25	26	27 NYI	28 BUF	29	30 CAR	

December
SUN	MON	TUE	WED	THU	FRI	SAT
						1
2 D CAR	3	4 NYR	5	6 ATL	7	8 D NJ
9	10	11 PIT	12	13 BOS	14	15 ATL
16	17	18	19 FLA	20	21 PIT	22 PIT
23	24	25	26 PHI	27	28 DAL	29
30 CAR	31					

January
SUN	MON	TUE	WED	THU	FRI	SAT
		1 NYI	D 2	3 OTT	4	5 BOS
6	7 FLA	8	9 CBJ	10	11 TOR	12 FLA
13	14 BOS	15	16 MON	17	18 DET	19 VAN
20	21	22 ATL	23 MON	24	25	26 D NYR
27 BUF	D 28	29	30 STL	31		

February
SUN	MON	TUE	WED	THU	FRI	SAT
					1	2 *
3	4	5	6 MIN	7	8 NAS	9 TB
10	11 TB	12	13	14	15	16
17	18	19	20	21	22	23
24	25	26 FLA	27	28 SJ		

March
SUN	MON	TUE	WED	THU	FRI	SAT
					1	2 OTT
3	4 TOR	5	6 CAL	7	8 CAR	9
10 D EDM	11	12 DAL	13	14	15 SJ	16 EDM
17	18	19 COL	20	21 TOR	22	23 CBJ
24 PIT	25	26 BUF	27	28	29 NJ	30 NYI
31						

April
SUN	MON	TUE	WED	THU	FRI	SAT
	1	2	3 TB	4	5 OTT	6 NYI
7	8	9 CHI	10	11	12 BUF	13 NJ
14	15	16	17	18	19	20

2001-02 SEASON
CLUB DIRECTORY

Owners
Ted Leonsis
Raul Fernandez
Michael Jordan
Dick Patrick
President and governor
Dick Patrick
Senior v.p. of business operations
Declan J. Bolger
Vice president/general manager
George McPhee
Director of hockey operations
Shawn Simpson
Assistant to the general manager
Frank Provenzano
Director of amateur scouting
Ross Mahoney
Head coach
Ron Wilson
Assistant coaches
Tim Army
Tim Hunter

Goaltending coach
Dave Prior
Team physician
Dr. Ben Shaffer
Trainer
Greg Smith
Assistant trainer
Tim Clark
Equipment manager
Doug Shearer
Assistant equipment manager
Craig Leydig
Equipment assistant
Brian Metzger
Strength and conditioning coach
Frank Costello
Massage therapist
Curt Millar
Manager, media relations
Brian Potter
Manager, information
Nate Ewell

DRAFT CHOICES

Rd.— Player	Ht./Wt.	Overall	Pos.	Last team
2— Nathan Paetsch	6-0/195	58	D	Moose Jaw (WHL)
3— Owen Fussey	6-0/185	90	RW	Calgary (WHL)
4— Jeff Lucky	6-1/193	125	RW	Spokane (WHL)
5— Artem Ternavsky	6-2/208	160	D	Sherbrooke (QMJHL)
6— Zbynek Novak	6-2/192	191	F	Slavia, Czech.
7— John Oduya	5-11/200	221	D	Victoriaville (QMJHL)
8— Matt Maglione	6-1/185	249	D	Princeton (ECAC)
8— Peter Polcik	6-4/187	254	LW	Nitra Jr., Slovakia
9— Robert Muller	5-7/163	275	G	Mannheim, Germany
9— Viktor Hubl	6-0/176	284	W	Slavia, Czech.

MISCELLANEOUS DATA

Home ice (capacity)
MCI Center (18,672)
Address
MCI Center
601 F St., NW
Washington, DC 20004
Business phone
202-266-2200
Ticket information
202-266-2277
Website
www.washingtoncaps.com

Training site
Odenton, MD
Club colors
Bronze, blue and black
Radio affiliation
WTEM (980 AM)
TV affiliation
Comcast SportsNet, WBDC (Channel 50)

TRAINING CAMP ROSTER

No.	FORWARDS	Ht./Wt.	Place	BORN Date	NHL exp.	2000-01 clubs
	Krys Barch (LW)	6-2/199	Guelph, Ont.	3-26-80	0	Portland (AHL)
	Derek Bekar (LW/C)	6-3/194	Burnaby, B.C.	9-15-75	1	Worcester (AHL), Portland (AHL)
12	Peter Bondra (LW)	6-1/205	Luck, Ukraine	2-7-68	11	Washington
	Chris Corrinet (RW)	6-3/220	Derby, Conn.	10-29-78	0	Princeton University (ECAC), Portland (AHL)
10	Ulf Dahlen (RW)	6-3/191	Ostersund, Sweden	1-12-67	12	Washington
	Owen Fussey (RW)	6-0/185	Winnipeg	4-2-83	0	Calgary (WHL)
11	Jeff Halpern (C)	5-11/198	Potomac, Md.	5-3-76	2	Washington
68	Jaromir Jagr (RW)	6-2/235	Kladno, Czechoslovakia	2-15-72	11	Pittsburgh
12	Dmitri Khristich (RW)	6-2/195	Kiev, U.S.S.R.	7-23-69	11	Toronto, Washington
22	Steve Konowalchuk (RW)	6-2/210	Salt Lake City	11-11-72	10	Washington
14	Trevor Linden (C)	6-4/211	Medicine Hat, Alta.	4-11-70	13	Montreal, Washington
	Jeff Lucky (RW)	6-1/193	Regina, Sask.	3-17-83	0	Spokane (WHL)
20	Glen Metropolit (C)	5-11/196	Toronto	6-25-74	2	Washington, Portland (AHL)
13	Andrei Nikolishin (C)	6-0/214	Vorkuta, U.S.S.R.	3-25-73	7	Washington
77	Adam Oates (C)	5-10/180	Weston, Ont.	8-27-62	16	Washington
	Matt Pettinger (LW)	6-0/205	Victoria, B.C.	10-22-80	1	Portland (AHL), Washington
14	Joe Sacco (RW)	6-1/190	Medford, Mass.	2-4-69	11	Washington
17	Chris Simon (LW)	6-4/231	Wawa, Ont.	1-30-72	9	Washington
	Brian Sutherby (C)	6-2/180	Edmonton	3-1-82	0	Moose Jaw (WHL)
	Trent Whitfield (C)	5-11/199	Estevan, Sask.	6-17-77	2	Portland (AHL), Washington
	Nolan Yonkman (RW)	6-5/218	Punnichy, Sask.	4-1-81	0	Kelowna (WHL), Brandon (WHL)
15	Dainius Zubrus (RW)	6-4/224	Elektrenai, U.S.S.R.	6-16-78	5	Montreal, Washington

DEFENSEMEN

No.	DEFENSEMEN	Ht./Wt.	Place	BORN Date	NHL exp.	2000-01 clubs
3	Sylvain Cote	6-0/190	Quebec City	1-19-66	17	Washington
	Jakub Cutta	6-3/195	Yablonec, Czechoslovakia	12-29-81	1	Washington, Swift Current (WHL)
	Mike Farrell	6-1/205	Edina, Minn.	10-20-78	0	Portland (AHL)
55	Sergei Gonchar	6-2/208	Chelyabinsk, U.S.S.R.	4-13-74	7	Washington
6	Calle Johansson	5-11/203	Goteborg, Sweden	2-14-67	14	Washington
2	Ken Klee	6-1/211	Indianapolis	4-24-71	7	Washington
4	Frantisek Kucera	6-2/205	Prague, Czechoslovakia	2-3-68	8	Columbus, Pittsburgh
15	Dmitri Mironov	6-4/229	Moscow, U.S.S.R.	12-25-65	10	Washington, Houston (IHL)
	Nathan Paetsch	6-0/195	Humboldt, Sask.	3-30-83	0	Moose Jaw (WHL)
	Stephen Peat	6-2/205	Princeton, B.C.	3-10-80	0	Portland (AHL)
29	Joe Reekie	6-3/225	Victoria, B.C.	2-22-65	16	Washington
	Artem Ternavski	6-2/208	Magnitagorsk, U.S.S.R.	6-2-83	0	Sherbrooke (QMJHL)
45	Ryan Vanbuskirk	6-2/207	Sault Ste. Marie, Mich.	1-12-80	0	Portland (AHL), Richmond (ECHL)
19	Brendan Witt	6-2/224	Humboldt, Sask.	2-20-75	7	Washington
24	Rob Zettler	6-3/197	Sept-Iles, Que.	3-8-68	13	Portland (AHL), Washington

GOALTENDERS

No.	GOALTENDERS	Ht./Wt.	Place	BORN Date	NHL exp.	2000-01 clubs
1	Craig Billington	5-10/166	London, Ont.	9-11-66	13	Washington
	Sebastien Charpentier	5-9/173	Drummondville, Que.	4-18-77	0	Portland (AHL)
	Curtis Cruickshank	6-3/220	Ottawa	3-21-79	0	Portland (AHL)
37	Olaf Kolzig	6-3/226	Johannesburg, South Africa	4-6-70	10	Washington

2000-01 REVIEW
INDIVIDUAL STATISTICS

SCORING

	Games	G	A	Pts.	PIM	+/-	PPG	SHG	Shots	Shooting Pct.
Adam Oates	81	13	69	82	28	-9	5	0	72	18.1
Peter Bondra	82	45	36	81	60	8	22	4	305	14.8
Sergei Gonchar	76	19	38	57	70	12	8	0	241	7.9
Ulf Dahlen	73	15	33	48	6	11	6	0	145	10.3
Steve Konowalchuk	82	24	23	47	87	8	6	0	163	14.7
Jeff Halpern	80	21	21	42	60	13	2	1	110	19.1
Andrei Nikolishin	81	13	25	38	34	9	4	0	145	9.0
Calle Johansson	76	7	29	36	26	11	5	0	154	4.5
Richard Zednik*	62	16	19	35	61	-2	4	0	155	10.3
Dmitri Khristich*	43	10	19	29	8	-8	4	0	54	18.5
Chris Simon	60	10	10	20	109	-12	4	0	123	8.1
Sylvain Cote	68	7	11	18	18	-3	1	1	86	8.1
Jan Bulis*	39	5	13	18	26	0	1	0	41	12.2
Joe Sacco	69	7	7	14	48	4	0	0	81	8.6
Joe Reekie	74	2	9	11	77	14	0	0	59	3.4
Dmitri Mironov	36	3	5	8	6	-7	1	0	33	9.1
Brendan Witt	72	3	3	6	101	2	0	0	87	3.4
Ken Klee	54	2	4	6	60	-5	0	0	58	3.4

	Games	G	A	Pts.	PIM	+/-	PPG	SHG	Shots	Shooting Pct.
Trent Whitfield	61	2	4	6	35	3	0	0	47	4.3
Joe Murphy	14	1	5	6	20	-5	1	0	22	4.5
Glen Metropolit	15	1	5	6	10	-2	0	0	20	5.0
James Black	42	1	5	6	4	-3	0	0	34	2.9
Matthew Herr	22	2	3	5	17	3	0	0	20	10.0
Trevor Linden*	12	3	1	4	8	2	0	0	30	10.0
Rob Zettler	29	0	4	4	55	0	0	0	17	0.0
Terry Yake	12	0	3	3	8	0	0	0	13	0.0
Dainius Zubrus*	12	1	1	2	7	-4	1	0	13	7.7
Olaf Kolzig (goalie)	72	0	2	2	14	0	0	0	0	0.0
Craig Billington (goalie)	12	0	1	1	0	0	0	0	0	0.0
Craig Berube*	22	0	1	1	18	-3	0	0	8	0.0
Corey Hirsch (goalie)	1	0	0	0	0	0	0	0	0	0.0
Jakub Cutta	3	0	0	0	0	-1	0	0	1	0.0
Kris Beech	4	0	0	0	2	-2	0	0	0	0.0
Brantt Myhres*	5	0	0	0	29	0	0	0	0	0.0
Jason Marshall*	5	0	0	0	17	-1	0	0	5	0.0
Matt Pettinger	10	0	0	0	2	-1	0	0	6	0.0

GOALTENDING

	Games	Min.	Goals	SO	Avg.	W	L	T	ENG	Shots	Sv. Pct.
Corey Hirsch	1	20	0	0	0.00	1	0	0	0	8	1.000
Craig Billington	12	660	27	0	2.45	3	5	2	0	317	.915
Olaf Kolzig	72	4279	177	5	2.48	37	26	8	7	1941	.909

*Played with two or more NHL teams.

RESULTS

OCTOBER
6— Los Angeles ....L.....1-4
7— At Carolina ....T....*3-3
11— At Atlanta ....T....*3-3
13— At Nashville ....L.....1-3
14— At Dallas ....L.....0-3
17— Colorado ....L....*3-4
19— New Jersey ....W....5-2
21— N.Y. Islanders ....T....*4-4
26— At Boston ....L.....1-4
27— At Columbus ....L.....1-3
29— At Philadelphia.................T....*1-1
31— Detroit ....W....6-2

NOVEMBER
2— At St. Louis.......................L.....0-2
4— At Florida ....W....3-2
5— At Tampa Bay ....L.....2-5
9— N.Y. Rangers ....L.....3-5
12— Atlanta ....T....*2-2
14— Phoenix ....T....*2-2
17— Montreal ....W....4-3
18— At Philadelphia.................L.....3-5
22— Vancouver ....W...*3-2
24— N.Y. Islanders ....W....1-0
25— At Atlanta ....L.....1-2
29— Tampa Bay ....W....4-1

DECEMBER
1— Boston ....W....3-2
2— At Boston ....W....2-0
6— At N.Y. Rangers ....L.....2-3

9— At New Jersey ....W...3-2
12— At N.Y. Islanders...............W...3-2
14— Minnesota ....W...2-1
16— Edmonton ....W...4-0
18— San Jose ....L.....3-5
20— Buffalo ....T....*2-2
21— At Buffalo ....W...3-1
23— Florida ....W...5-3
27— At Ottawa ....W...5-1
29— At New Jersey ....L.....2-4
30— Philadelphia......................W...6-3

JANUARY
1— Atlanta ....W....4-2
3— At Pittsburgh ....L.....2-3
5— Boston ....T....*1-1
6— At Toronto ....W...3-2
8— Pittsburgh..........................L.....3-5
10— At Minnesota ....L.....0-3
13— Atlanta ....W....4-1
18— At Ottawa ....L.....4-5
19— At Chicago ....L.....1-3
23— At Tampa Bay ....W...5-2
24— Florida ....W...2-1
27— At Montreal ....L.....2-4
28— Philadelphia......................W....4-2
30— Ottawa ....T....*1-1

FEBRUARY
1— Toronto ....W....5-4
7— At Colorado ....W....3-1
9— At Anaheim ....W....4-3

10— At Los Angeles ....W.....4-3
13— At Calgary ....T....*4-4
14— At Vancouver ....W...*4-3
17— At Montreal ....W....6-3
21— Nashville...........................W...2-1
23— Montreal ....W...3-1
24— At Carolina ....W...2-1
27— Chicago ....L.....2-3

MARCH
1— Toronto ....L....*2-3
3— Pittsburgh ....W....4-3
6— At N.Y. Islanders...............W.....5-1
7— At Pittsburgh ....W....4-3
9— N.Y. Rangers ....W....5-3
11— Ottawa ....W....6-5
13— Anaheim ....L.....0-2
15— Carolina ....L.....0-3
17— Buffalo ....L.....2-3
19— At N.Y. Rangers ....L.....3-6
23— At Florida ....L.....1-4
24— At Tampa Bay ....W...3-2
28— Carolina ....W...7-0
30— At Carolina........................L....*3-4

APRIL
1— At Detroit...........................L....*1-2
3— New Jersey ....L.....4-6
5— Florida ....W....3-0
6— At Buffalo............................L.....1-2
8— Tampa Bay ....W...2-1

*Denotes overtime game.

SCHEDULE

DAY BY DAY

*Denotes afternoon game.

WEDNESDAY, OCTOBER 3
Ottawa at Toronto
Colorado at Pittsburgh
Edmonton at Calgary

THURSDAY, OCTOBER 4
Anaheim at Boston
Atlanta at Buffalo
Montreal at Ottawa
Florida at Philadelphia
St. Louis at Columbus
Chicago at Vancouver
Detroit at San Jose
Phoenix at Los Angeles

FRIDAY, OCTOBER 5
N.Y. Rangers at Carolina
N.Y. Islanders at Tampa Bay
Nashville at Dallas

SATURDAY, OCTOBER 6
Minnesota at San Jose*
Atlanta at Boston
Ottawa at Buffalo
Toronto at Montreal
Columbus at Philadelphia
New Jersey at Washington
Anaheim at Pittsburgh
N.Y. Islanders at Florida
St. Louis at Nashville
Chicago at Calgary
Phoenix at Edmonton
Detroit at Vancouver

SUNDAY, OCTOBER 7
Dallas at Carolina*
Buffalo at N.Y. Rangers
Florida at Tampa Bay
Minnesota at Los Angeles

MONDAY, OCTOBER 8
Washington at Boston*
Philadelphia at Columbus
Anaheim at Toronto
Phoenix at Calgary

TUESDAY, OCTOBER 9
Ottawa at Carolina
Anaheim at Montreal
Vancouver at Colorado
Los Angeles at Dallas
Chicago at Edmonton

WEDNESDAY, OCTOBER 10
Washington at N.Y. Rangers
N.Y. Islanders at Pittsburgh
Ottawa at Florida
Calgary at Detroit
Philadelphia at Buffalo
Boston at Minnesota

THURSDAY, OCTOBER 11
Toronto at Carolina
N.Y. Islanders at New Jersey
Los Angeles at St. Louis
Calgary at Nashville
Phoenix at Chicago
Vancouver at Dallas
Colorado at Edmonton
Tampa Bay at San Jose

FRIDAY, OCTOBER 12
Montreal at Columbus
Buffalo at Detroit
Chicago at Minnesota
Washington at Anaheim

SATURDAY, OCTOBER 13
St. Louis at Toronto
New Jersey at Montreal
N.Y. Rangers at Ottawa
Detroit at N.Y. Islanders
Carolina at Atlanta
Philadelphia at Florida
Edmonton at Nashville
Calgary at Dallas
Colorado at Vancouver
Washington at Phoenix
Tampa Bay at Los Angeles
Boston at San Jose

SUNDAY, OCTOBER 14
Pittsburgh at Buffalo*
Edmonton at Minnesota
Columbus at Chicago
Tampa Bay at Anaheim

MONDAY, OCTOBER 15
N.Y. Rangers at Montreal

TUESDAY, OCTOBER 16
Nashville at Buffalo
Ottawa at Pittsburgh
Philadelphia at Atlanta
Columbus at Detroit
San Jose at Minnesota
Tampa Bay at Colorado
Toronto at Edmonton
Florida at Vancouver
Boston at Phoenix
Washington at Los Angeles

WEDNESDAY, OCTOBER 17
N.Y. Islanders at Carolina
New Jersey at N.Y. Rangers
Dallas at St. Louis
Boston at Anaheim

THURSDAY, OCTOBER 18
Pittsburgh at Ottawa
Carolina at N.Y. Islanders
San Jose at New Jersey
Philadelphia at Detroit
Chicago at Nashville
Phoenix at Dallas
Edmonton at Colorado
Florida at Calgary
Toronto at Vancouver
Anaheim at Los Angeles

FRIDAY, OCTOBER 19
Columbus at Buffalo
Montreal at Washington
N.Y. Rangers at Atlanta
St. Louis at Minnesota

SATURDAY, OCTOBER 20
Buffalo at Montreal
San Jose at N.Y. Islanders
Washington at Philadelphia
Atlanta at Carolina
Colorado at Columbus
Toronto at Calgary

Ottawa at New Jersey
N.Y. Rangers at Tampa Bay
Los Angeles at Detroit
Pittsburgh at St. Louis
Boston at Nashville
Chicago at Dallas
Florida at Edmonton
Vancouver at Phoenix

SUNDAY, OCTOBER 21
Colorado at Chicago
Vancouver at Anaheim

MONDAY, OCTOBER 22
San Jose at N.Y. Rangers
Calgary at St. Louis
Nashville at Edmonton

TUESDAY, OCTOBER 23
New Jersey at Ottawa
Los Angeles at Columbus
Boston at Toronto
Pittsburgh at Atlanta
Washington at Tampa Bay
San Jose at Buffalo
Calgary at Chicago
Carolina at Colorado
Nashville at Vancouver

WEDNESDAY, OCTOBER 24
Dallas at Pittsburgh
Washington at Florida
Edmonton at Detroit
Carolina at Minnesota
Anaheim at Phoenix

THURSDAY, OCTOBER 25
Toronto at Boston
Ottawa at Philadelphia
Edmonton at Columbus
Los Angeles at Tampa Bay
N.Y. Rangers at St. Louis
San Jose at Chicago
Nashville at Calgary
Vancouver at Colorado

FRIDAY, OCTOBER 26
Montreal at Buffalo
N.Y. Islanders at Carolina
Washington at Atlanta
Los Angeles at Florida
Dallas at Detroit

SATURDAY, OCTOBER 27
N.Y. Rangers at Boston
Pittsburgh at Toronto
Philadelphia at Montreal
St. Louis at Ottawa
Tampa Bay at Atlanta
Buffalo at New Jersey
Detroit at Nashville
Colorado at Phoenix
Minnesota at Calgary
Vancouver at Edmonton
Columbus at San Jose

SUNDAY, OCTOBER 28
Dallas at N.Y. Islanders*
Los Angeles at Carolina*
Florida at Pittsburgh
Boston at Chicago
Colorado at Anaheim

– 95 –

MONDAY, OCTOBER 29
Dallas at N.Y. Rangers

TUESDAY, OCTOBER 30
New Jersey at Boston
Phoenix at Buffalo
Florida at N.Y. Islanders
Philadelphia at Washington
Detroit at Carolina
Tampa Bay at Toronto
Ottawa at Atlanta
Minnesota at Nashville
Los Angeles at Chicago
Montreal at Edmonton
Columbus at Vancouver

WEDNESDAY, OCTOBER 31
Florida at N.Y. Rangers
Pittsburgh at Philadelphia
Nashville at Minnesota
St. Louis at Colorado
Detroit at Dallas
San Jose at Anaheim

THURSDAY, NOVEMBER 1
Toronto at Pittsburgh
Phoenix at New Jersey
Carolina at St. Louis
Columbus at Calgary
Montreal at Vancouver
Chicago at Los Angeles
Atlanta at San Jose

FRIDAY, NOVEMBER 2
Tampa Bay at Buffalo
Phoenix at Washington
N.Y. Rangers at Carolina
N.Y. Islanders at Detroit
Colorado at Minnesota
Nashville at Dallas
Columbus at Edmonton
Chicago at Anaheim

SATURDAY, NOVEMBER 3
Boston at New Jersey*
Atlanta at Los Angeles*
Colorado at Toronto
Buffalo at Ottawa
N.Y. Islanders at Philadelphia
Montreal at Calgary
Tampa Bay at Pittsburgh
N.Y. Rangers at Florida
Washington at St. Louis
Dallas at Nashville
Vancouver at San Jose

SUNDAY, NOVEMBER 4
Phoenix at Carolina*
Edmonton at Minnesota*
Detroit at Chicago
Atlanta at Anaheim

TUESDAY, NOVEMBER 6
Edmonton at Boston
Tampa Bay at N.Y. Islanders
Minnesota at N.Y. Rangers
Pittsburgh at Carolina
Vancouver at Columbus
Washington at Toronto
Colorado at Montreal
Philadelphia at Chicago
San Jose at St. Louis

WEDNESDAY, NOVEMBER 7
Atlanta at New Jersey
Pittsburgh at Florida
San Jose at Dallas
Detroit at Phoenix
Calgary at Anaheim

THURSDAY, NOVEMBER 8
Minnesota at Boston
Atlanta at Buffalo
N.Y. Rangers at N.Y. Islanders
Carolina at Washington
Nashville at Montreal
Colorado at Ottawa
Philadelphia at Tampa Bay
Vancouver at St. Louis
Calgary at Los Angeles

FRIDAY, NOVEMBER 9
San Jose at Carolina
Edmonton at Columbus
Toronto at New Jersey
Vancouver at Chicago
Phoenix at Dallas
Detroit at Anaheim

SATURDAY, NOVEMBER 10
Columbus at Boston
N.Y. Rangers at Buffalo
New Jersey at Toronto
N.Y. Islanders at Montreal
Nashville at Ottawa
Atlanta at Washington
Pittsburgh at Tampa Bay
Philadelphia at Florida
Phoenix at St. Louis
Colorado at Calgary
Detroit at Los Angeles

SUNDAY, NOVEMBER 11
Edmonton at Carolina*
Vancouver at Minnesota*
Montreal at N.Y. Rangers
San Jose at Chicago
Dallas at Anaheim

MONDAY, NOVEMBER 12
Buffalo at Florida

TUESDAY, NOVEMBER 13
Montreal at Boston
Ottawa at Washington
St. Louis at Columbus
Carolina at Detroit
Pittsburgh at New Jersey
Buffalo at Nashville
Atlanta at Minnesota
Edmonton at Phoenix
Chicago at Vancouver

WEDNESDAY, NOVEMBER 14
N.Y. Islanders at Pittsburgh
Toronto at Florida
Philadelphia at N.Y. Rangers
Minnesota at Colorado
San Jose at Anaheim

THURSDAY, NOVEMBER 15
New Jersey at Boston
Carolina at Ottawa
Washington at Philadelphia
Toronto at Tampa Bay
Chicago at Calgary
San Jose at Phoenix
St. Louis at Vancouver
Dallas at Los Angeles

FRIDAY, NOVEMBER 16
Florida at Buffalo
Anaheim at Columbus
Nashville at Atlanta
Minnesota at Detroit
N.Y. Islanders at Colorado
Chicago at Edmonton

SATURDAY, NOVEMBER 17
Philadelphia at New Jersey*
Buffalo at Boston
Florida at Montreal
Toronto at Ottawa
Anaheim at Washington
N.Y. Rangers at Pittsburgh
Carolina at Tampa Bay
Los Angeles at Detroit
Columbus at Nashville
St. Louis at Calgary
N.Y. Islanders at Phoenix
Edmonton at Vancouver
Dallas at San Jose

SUNDAY, NOVEMBER 18
Colorado at New Jersey*
Los Angeles at Minnesota
Atlanta at N.Y. Rangers

MONDAY, NOVEMBER 19
Columbus at Carolina
Florida at Toronto
Buffalo at Atlanta
N.Y. Islanders at Dallas

TUESDAY, NOVEMBER 20
Vancouver at Ottawa
New Jersey at Philadelphia
Boston at Montreal
Anaheim at Tampa Bay
Nashville at Detroit
Colorado at N.Y. Rangers
St. Louis at Edmonton
Los Angeles at Calgary
Minnesota at Phoenix

WEDNESDAY, NOVEMBER 21
Colorado at N.Y. Islanders
Tampa Bay at Washington
Detroit at Columbus
Toronto at Buffalo
Vancouver at Pittsburgh
Anaheim at Florida
Chicago at Nashville
Carolina at Dallas
Minnesota at San Jose

THURSDAY, NOVEMBER 22
Calgary at Ottawa
Montreal at Atlanta
Los Angeles at Edmonton

FRIDAY, NOVEMBER 23
Vancouver at Boston*
Phoenix at Minnesota*
Calgary at Buffalo
Toronto at N.Y. Islanders
N.Y. Rangers at Washington
Chicago at Columbus
New Jersey at Tampa Bay
St. Louis at Detroit
Pittsburgh at Nashville
Philadelphia at Dallas

SATURDAY, NOVEMBER 24
San Jose at Los Angeles*
Atlanta at Ottawa
Boston at Toronto
Washington at Montreal
Anaheim at N.Y. Islanders
Buffalo at Pittsburgh
New Jersey at Florida
Phoenix at St. Louis
Edmonton at Colorado

SUNDAY, NOVEMBER 25
Tampa Bay at Carolina*
Calgary at Columbus*
Dallas at Minnesota*
Anaheim at N.Y. Rangers
Chicago at Detroit
Vancouver at Philadelphia

TUESDAY, NOVEMBER 27
Tampa Bay at Boston
N.Y. Rangers at Buffalo
Washington at N.Y. Islanders
Phoenix at Columbus
Carolina at Toronto
Atlanta at Montreal
New Jersey at Pittsburgh
Calgary at Detroit
Ottawa at St. Louis
Vancouver at Minnesota
Florida at Colorado
Nashville at San Jose

WEDNESDAY, NOVEMBER 28
Carolina at N.Y. Rangers
Buffalo at Washington
Vancouver at Chicago
Edmonton at Anaheim

THURSDAY, NOVEMBER 29
Montreal at N.Y. Islanders
St. Louis at Columbus
Boston at Philadelphia
Atlanta at Tampa Bay
Florida at Minnesota
Dallas at Calgary
Nashville at Phoenix
Edmonton at Los Angeles
Pittsburgh at San Jose

FRIDAY, NOVEMBER 30
Carolina at Washington
New Jersey at Detroit
Toronto at Chicago
Colorado at Vancouver
San Jose at Anaheim

SATURDAY, DECEMBER 1
Atlanta at Florida*
Nashville at Los Angeles*
Chicago at Toronto
N.Y. Rangers at Montreal
Boston at Ottawa
Buffalo at N.Y. Islanders
Tampa Bay at Philadelphia
Detroit at New Jersey
Columbus at St. Louis
Colorado at Calgary
Pittsburgh at Phoenix
Dallas at Edmonton

SUNDAY, DECEMBER 2
Washington at Carolina*
Tampa Bay at N.Y. Rangers
St. Louis at Minnesota
Nashville at Anaheim
Dallas at Vancouver

MONDAY, DECEMBER 3
Chicago at Montreal
Ottawa at Colorado
Calgary at Los Angeles

TUESDAY, DECEMBER 4
N.Y. Rangers at Washington
Buffalo at Carolina
Pittsburgh at Toronto
Tampa Bay at New Jersey

Boston at Atlanta
Philadelphia at N.Y. Islanders
Calgary at San Jose

WEDNESDAY, DECEMBER 5
New Jersey at Montreal
Columbus at Florida
Colorado at Detroit
Minnesota at Chicago
Ottawa at Dallas
Anaheim at Edmonton
St. Louis at Phoenix

THURSDAY, DECEMBER 6
Toronto at N.Y. Rangers
N.Y. Islanders at Philadelphia
Pittsburgh at Boston
Washington at Atlanta
Columbus at Tampa Bay
Ottawa at Nashville
San Jose at Calgary
Anaheim at Vancouver
St. Louis at Los Angeles

FRIDAY, DECEMBER 7
Colorado at Buffalo
Phoenix at Detroit
N.Y. Islanders at Chicago
Edmonton at Dallas

SATURDAY, DECEMBER 8
Washington at New Jersey*
Minnesota at Philadelphia*
Buffalo at Boston
N.Y. Rangers at Toronto
Phoenix at Montreal
Tampa Bay at Ottawa
Colorado at Columbus
Atlanta at Pittsburgh
Carolina at Florida
Los Angeles at St. Louis
Edmonton at Nashville
Anaheim at Calgary
San Jose at Vancouver

SUNDAY, DECEMBER 9
Los Angeles at Chicago

MONDAY, DECEMBER 10
Carolina at N.Y. Rangers
New Jersey at Columbus
Minnesota at Montreal
Philadelphia at Atlanta
Anaheim at Colorado
Detroit at Calgary
Tampa Bay at Vancouver

TUESDAY, DECEMBER 11
Ottawa at N.Y. Islanders
Phoenix at Toronto
Pittsburgh at Washington
Los Angeles at Nashville
Edmonton at San Jose

WEDNESDAY, DECEMBER 12
Nashville at N.Y. Rangers
Florida at Carolina
Boston at Pittsburgh
Montreal at Atlanta
Buffalo at Dallas
N.Y. Islanders at New Jersey
St. Louis at Chicago
Columbus at Colorado
Tampa Bay at Calgary
Vancouver at Anaheim

THURSDAY, DECEMBER 13
Phoenix at Ottawa
Montreal at Philadelphia

Boston at Washington
Toronto at St. Louis
Detroit at Edmonton
Vancouver at Los Angeles

FRIDAY, DECEMBER 14
Carolina at Buffalo
Florida at New Jersey
Minnesota at Pittsburgh
Chicago at Atlanta
Calgary at Dallas
San Jose at Colorado
Tampa Bay at Edmonton
Columbus at Anaheim

SATURDAY, DECEMBER 15
Philadelphia at Boston
Montreal at Toronto
New Jersey at Ottawa
Florida at N.Y. Islanders
Buffalo at N.Y. Rangers
Atlanta at Washington
Calgary at St. Louis
Chicago at Nashville
Dallas at Phoenix
Detroit at Vancouver
Columbus at Los Angeles

SUNDAY, DECEMBER 16
Colorado at Minnesota
Edmonton at Philadelphia
Carolina at Pittsburgh
Los Angeles at Anaheim

MONDAY, DECEMBER 17
Florida at N.Y. Rangers
Tampa Bay at Montreal
Chicago at Detroit
San Jose at Dallas
Columbus at Phoenix

TUESDAY, DECEMBER 18
Atlanta at Boston
Edmonton at N.Y. Islanders
St. Louis at Philadelphia
Ottawa at Carolina
Los Angeles at Toronto
Anaheim at Minnesota

WEDNESDAY, DECEMBER 19
Chicago at Buffalo
Montreal at Pittsburgh
San Jose at Atlanta
Washington at Florida
Vancouver at Detroit
New Jersey at N.Y. Rangers
Anaheim at Colorado
Calgary at Phoenix

THURSDAY, DECEMBER 20
Montreal at Boston
Los Angeles at Ottawa
Dallas at Philadelphia
Edmonton at New Jersey
Vancouver at Nashville

FRIDAY, DECEMBER 21
Toronto at Buffalo
N.Y. Islanders at N.Y. Rangers
Atlanta at Carolina
Washington at Pittsburgh
St. Louis at Tampa Bay
San Jose at Detroit
Edmonton at Chicago
Calgary at Colorado
Phoenix at Anaheim

SATURDAY, DECEMBER 22
Ottawa at New Jersey*
Buffalo at Toronto

Los Angeles at Montreal
Boston at N.Y. Islanders
Carolina at Philadelphia
Pittsburgh at Washington
Dallas at Columbus
St. Louis at Florida
San Jose at Nashville
Minnesota at Vancouver

SUNDAY, DECEMBER 23
Ottawa at N.Y. Rangers*
Dallas at Atlanta
Detroit at Chicago
Anaheim at Phoenix
Minnesota at Colorado

WEDNESDAY, DECEMBER 26
Ottawa at Boston
Montreal at Buffalo
Philadelphia at Washington
Toronto at Carolina
Calgary at Edmonton
Pittsburgh at New Jersey
Florida at Atlanta
Chicago at St. Louis
Tampa Bay at Nashville
Detroit at Minnesota
Colorado at Dallas
Los Angeles at Phoenix
Anaheim at San Jose

THURSDAY, DECEMBER 27
N.Y. Islanders at Ottawa
Carolina at Tampa Bay
Columbus at Detroit
Colorado at Chicago
Calgary at Vancouver
Anaheim at Los Angeles

FRIDAY, DECEMBER 28
Toronto at Atlanta
Boston at Florida
Montreal at St. Louis
Washington at Dallas
Minnesota at Edmonton
Philadelphia at Phoenix
N.Y. Rangers at San Jose

SATURDAY, DECEMBER 29
Montreal at N.Y. Islanders
Ottawa at Pittsburgh
Boston at Tampa Bay
Toronto at Florida
Buffalo at Columbus
Detroit at Nashville
Philadelphia at Colorado
Minnesota at Calgary
New Jersey at Vancouver
N.Y. Rangers at Los Angeles

SUNDAY, DECEMBER 30
Carolina at Washington
Nashville at St. Louis
Anaheim at Chicago
New Jersey at Edmonton
Phoenix at San Jose

MONDAY, DECEMBER 31
Atlanta at Florida*
Chicago at Ottawa
Carolina at Buffalo
Minnesota at Detroit
Anaheim at Columbus
Toronto at Tampa Bay
N.Y. Rangers at Phoenix
Boston at Dallas
Edmonton at Calgary
Philadelphia at Vancouver

TUESDAY, JANUARY 1
N.Y. Islanders at Washington*
Colorado at Nashville*
St. Louis at New Jersey

WEDNESDAY, JANUARY 2
Boston at Carolina
Anaheim at Detroit
Tampa Bay at Minnesota
N.Y. Rangers at Edmonton
Atlanta at Dallas
Florida at Los Angeles
Philadelphia at San Jose

THURSDAY, JANUARY 3
Toronto at Boston
Washington at Ottawa
Nashville at New Jersey
Pittsburgh at N.Y. Islanders
Columbus at St. Louis
Buffalo at Calgary
Atlanta at Phoenix
N.Y. Rangers at Colorado
Montreal at Vancouver

FRIDAY, JANUARY 4
Nashville at Minnesota
Tampa Bay at Chicago
Florida at Anaheim
Phoenix at San Jose

SATURDAY, JANUARY 5
N.Y. Rangers at Pittsburgh*
Colorado at Detroit*
Dallas at St. Louis*
Ottawa at Toronto*
Washington at Boston
Los Angeles at N.Y. Islanders
New Jersey at Carolina
Montreal at Calgary
Florida at San Jose

SUNDAY, JANUARY 6
Nashville at Columbus*
Philadelphia at Carolina
Buffalo at Minnesota
N.Y. Islanders at Atlanta
Pittsburgh at Chicago
Montreal at Edmonton
Tampa Bay at Phoenix

MONDAY, JANUARY 7
Toronto at Ottawa
Florida at Washington
Los Angeles at New Jersey

TUESDAY, JANUARY 8
Vancouver at Buffalo
Calgary at N.Y. Islanders
Atlanta at Philadelphia
Nashville at Toronto
Boston at Pittsburgh
Dallas at Tampa Bay
Montreal at Minnesota
St. Louis at San Jose

WEDNESDAY, JANUARY 9
Columbus at Washington
Calgary at New Jersey
Ottawa at Atlanta
Dallas at Florida
Vancouver at Detroit
Los Angeles at N.Y. Rangers
Chicago at Colorado
San Jose at Phoenix
St. Louis at Anaheim

THURSDAY, JANUARY 10
Los Angeles at Boston
Pittsburgh at Buffalo
N.Y. Islanders at Montreal
New Jersey at Philadelphia
Minnesota at Nashville
Columbus at Chicago
Carolina at Edmonton

FRIDAY, JANUARY 11
Toronto at Washington
Calgary at Atlanta
Ottawa at Florida
Anaheim at Minnesota

SATURDAY, JANUARY 12
N.Y. Rangers at Philadelphia*
St. Louis at Pittsburgh*
Dallas at Detroit*
Los Angeles at San Jose*
N.Y. Islanders at Boston
New Jersey at Buffalo
Montreal at Toronto
Chicago at Columbus
Ottawa at Tampa Bay
Washington at Florida
Anaheim at Nashville
Colorado at Edmonton
Carolina at Vancouver

SUNDAY, JANUARY 13
Tampa Bay at Atlanta
Dallas at Minnesota

MONDAY, JANUARY 14
Columbus at N.Y. Rangers
Boston at Washington
Philadelphia at Montreal
Edmonton at Chicago
Nashville at Anaheim

TUESDAY, JANUARY 15
Philadelphia at Ottawa
Minnesota at Carolina
Atlanta at Toronto
Tampa Bay at New Jersey
Edmonton at St. Louis
San Jose at Colorado
N.Y. Islanders at Calgary
Detroit at Phoenix
Pittsburgh at Vancouver
Nashville at Los Angeles

WEDNESDAY, JANUARY 16
N.Y. Rangers at Columbus
Washington at Montreal
Chicago at Florida
Detroit at Dallas
Buffalo at Anaheim

THURSDAY, JANUARY 17
Ottawa at Boston
Atlanta at Philadelphia
Montreal at Carolina
N.Y. Rangers at New Jersey
Vancouver at St. Louis
Toronto at Nashville
Phoenix at Colorado
Pittsburgh at Calgary
Buffalo at Los Angeles
N.Y. Islanders at San Jose

FRIDAY, JANUARY 18
Minnesota at Columbus
Chicago at Tampa Bay
Washington at Detroit
Florida at Dallas
Anaheim at Edmonton

SATURDAY, JANUARY 19
Carolina at New Jersey*
N.Y. Islanders at Los Angeles*
Philadelphia at Toronto
Minnesota at Ottawa
Vancouver at Washington
Montreal at Tampa Bay
Atlanta at Florida
Boston at St. Louis
Columbus at Nashville
Anaheim at Calgary
Buffalo at Phoenix
Pittsburgh at Edmonton
Colorado at San Jose

SUNDAY, JANUARY 20
Ottawa at Detroit
Dallas at Chicago

MONDAY, JANUARY 21
St. Louis at Boston*
Montreal at Florida*
Vancouver at Carolina
Dallas at Columbus
Philadelphia at Pittsburgh
New Jersey at Tampa Bay
Phoenix at Nashville
Edmonton at San Jose
Buffalo at Colorado
Los Angeles at Anaheim

TUESDAY, JANUARY 22
N.Y. Rangers at N.Y. Islanders
Ottawa at Philadelphia
Washington at Atlanta
Toronto at Calgary

WEDNESDAY, JANUARY 23
St. Louis at Buffalo
Boston at N.Y. Rangers
Montreal at Washington
Nashville at Carolina
Tampa Bay at Pittsburgh
New Jersey at Florida
San Jose at Detroit
Colorado at Edmonton
Phoenix at Chicago
Vancouver at Dallas
Minnesota at Anaheim

THURSDAY, JANUARY 24
Boston at Ottawa
Nashville at Philadelphia
San Jose at Columbus
Pittsburgh at N.Y. Islanders
New Jersey at Atlanta
Colorado at Calgary
Minnesota at Los Angeles

FRIDAY, JANUARY 25
Tampa Bay at Buffalo
Florida at Carolina
Phoenix at Detroit
St. Louis at Chicago
Anaheim at Dallas
Toronto at Vancouver

SATURDAY, JANUARY 26
Ottawa at Montreal*
Washington at N.Y. Rangers*
Atlanta at Pittsburgh*
Colorado at Los Angeles*
New Jersey at Minnesota
Florida at Boston
Tampa Bay at N.Y. Islanders
Carolina at Philadelphia
Phoenix at Columbus

Toronto at Edmonton
Detroit at St. Louis
Anaheim at Nashville
Vancouver at Calgary

SUNDAY, JANUARY 27
San Jose at Montreal*
Buffalo at Washington*

MONDAY, JANUARY 28
Chicago at Boston
Tampa Bay at N.Y. Rangers
Phoenix at Atlanta
Anaheim at St. Louis
Calgary at Minnesota
Detroit at Edmonton
Columbus at Dallas
Los Angeles at Colorado
Nashville at Vancouver

TUESDAY, JANUARY 29
New Jersey at N.Y. Islanders
Pittsburgh at Philadelphia
Buffalo at Carolina
San Jose at Toronto

WEDNESDAY, JANUARY 30
Philadelphia at Ottawa
N.Y. Islanders at N.Y. Rangers
St. Louis at Washington
Boston at Montreal
Chicago at New Jersey
Toronto at Atlanta
Carolina at Tampa Bay
Phoenix at Florida
San Jose at Pittsburgh
Los Angeles at Minnesota
Nashville at Colorado
Detroit at Calgary
Edmonton at Vancouver
Columbus at Anaheim

SATURDAY, FEBRUARY 2
All-Star Game at Los Angeles*

MONDAY, FEBRUARY 4
Boston at Columbus
Ottawa at Tampa Bay
N.Y. Islanders at Florida
Detroit at Colorado
Phoenix at Vancouver
Philadelphia at Los Angeles

TUESDAY, FEBRUARY 5
Buffalo at Boston
St. Louis at N.Y. Islanders
Pittsburgh at Carolina
Minnesota at Toronto
Montreal at New Jersey
Edmonton at Atlanta

WEDNESDAY, FEBRUARY 6
Minnesota at Washington
Ottawa at Columbus
Tampa Bay at Florida
N.Y. Rangers at Detroit
Dallas at Nashville
Chicago at Phoenix
Philadelphia at Anaheim
Calgary at San Jose

THURSDAY, FEBRUARY 7
Toronto at N.Y. Islanders
Pittsburgh at Montreal
Atlanta at New Jersey
Florida at Tampa Bay
Edmonton at St. Louis
Carolina at Los Angeles

FRIDAY, FEBRUARY 8
Ottawa at Buffalo
N.Y. Rangers at Atlanta
Columbus at Detroit
Washington at Nashville
Colorado at Minnesota
Edmonton at Dallas
Vancouver at Calgary
Los Angeles at Phoenix
Carolina at Anaheim
Chicago at San Jose

SATURDAY, FEBRUARY 9
Florida at Boston*
New Jersey at Pittsburgh*
Montreal at Toronto*
Detroit at Ottawa
Nashville at Columbus
Philadelphia at St. Louis
Washington at Tampa Bay
Chicago at Colorado
Calgary at Vancouver

SUNDAY, FEBRUARY 10
Pittsburgh at N.Y. Rangers*
N.Y. Islanders at Minnesota*
Buffalo at New Jersey
Edmonton at Phoenix
Dallas at Anaheim
Carolina at San Jose

MONDAY, FEBRUARY 11
Tampa Bay at Washington
Atlanta at Toronto
Detroit at Montreal
Boston at Colorado
Dallas at Los Angeles

TUESDAY, FEBRUARY 12
New Jersey at Buffalo
Pittsburgh at Ottawa
N.Y. Islanders at Philadelphia
Minnesota at Columbus
Atlanta at St. Louis
Florida at Nashville
Calgary at Phoenix
San Jose at Edmonton
Boston at Vancouver

WEDNESDAY, FEBRUARY 13
Detroit at Minnesota
St. Louis at Colorado
Florida at Chicago
N.Y. Rangers at Dallas
Calgary at Anaheim
Phoenix at Los Angeles

FRI., FEB. 15-SUN., FEB. 24
NHL players will participate in 2002
Olympic Winter Games at Salt Lake City,
Utah.

TUESDAY, FEBRUARY 26
Boston at N.Y. Islanders
New Jersey at N.Y. Rangers
Chicago at Philadelphia
Florida at Washington
Los Angeles at Columbus
Carolina at Toronto
Ottawa at Montreal
Buffalo at Atlanta
Detroit at Tampa Bay
San Jose at Nashville
Calgary at Colorado
Dallas at Phoenix
St. Louis at Vancouver

WEDNESDAY, FEBRUARY 27
Los Angeles at Pittsburgh
Detroit at Florida
Philadelphia at New Jersey
Montreal at Chicago
Minnesota at Anaheim

THURSDAY, FEBRUARY 28
Carolina at Boston
Ottawa at N.Y. Rangers
Pittsburgh at Columbus
San Jose at Washington
St. Louis at Calgary
Nashville at Edmonton
Phoenix at Colorado
Dallas at Vancouver

FRIDAY, MARCH 1
Boston at Buffalo
Toronto at New Jersey
N.Y. Islanders at Atlanta
San Jose at Tampa Bay

SATURDAY, MARCH 2
Philadelphia at N.Y. Rangers*
Detroit at Pittsburgh*
Dallas at Colorado*
Columbus at Los Angeles*
Buffalo at Toronto
Carolina at Montreal
Washington at Ottawa
Atlanta at N.Y. Islanders
Florida at Tampa Bay
Nashville at Calgary
St. Louis at Edmonton
Minnesota at Vancouver

SUNDAY, MARCH 3
Anaheim at Chicago*
San Jose at Dallas*
Columbus at Phoenix

MONDAY, MARCH 4
Philadelphia at Boston
Edmonton at Buffalo
Pittsburgh at N.Y. Islanders
Calgary at N.Y. Rangers
Toronto at Washington
Atlanta at Montreal
New Jersey at Colorado
Ottawa at Los Angeles

TUESDAY, MARCH 5
Florida at Pittsburgh
N.Y. Rangers at Minnesota
Carolina at Chicago
New Jersey at Phoenix
Nashville at San Jose

WEDNESDAY, MARCH 6
Calgary at Washington
Boston at Montreal
Anaheim at Atlanta
Edmonton at Tampa Bay
Toronto at Detroit
Los Angeles at Dallas
Columbus at Colorado

THURSDAY, MARCH 7
Buffalo at N.Y. Islanders
Calgary at Philadelphia
Carolina at Pittsburgh
Minnesota at St. Louis
Los Angeles at Nashville
N.Y. Rangers at Chicago
Vancouver at Phoenix
Ottawa at San Jose

FRIDAY, MARCH 8
Montreal at Buffalo
Washington at Carolina
N.Y. Islanders at Columbus
Boston at Atlanta
Philadelphia at Tampa Bay
Edmonton at Florida
Minnesota at Dallas
New Jersey at Anaheim

SATURDAY, MARCH 9
N.Y. Rangers at Pittsburgh*
Detroit at St. Louis*
Los Angeles at Colorado*
Calgary at Boston
Toronto at Montreal
Ottawa at Phoenix
Nashville at Florida
Vancouver at San Jose

SUNDAY, MARCH 10
Atlanta at N.Y. Islanders*
Detroit at Buffalo*
Edmonton at Washington*
Columbus at Minnesota
Toronto at Philadelphia
Nashville at Tampa Bay
New Jersey at Dallas
Ottawa at Anaheim
San Jose at Vancouver

MONDAY, MARCH 11
Montreal at N.Y. Rangers
Calgary at Carolina
Columbus at Pittsburgh
Colorado at St. Louis
Chicago at Los Angeles

TUESDAY, MARCH 12
N.Y. Islanders at Buffalo
Dallas at Washington
Philadelphia at Toronto
Tampa Bay at Atlanta
Vancouver at Nashville
Ottawa at Minnesota
Chicago at Phoenix

WEDNESDAY, MARCH 13
N.Y. Islanders at New Jersey
Calgary at Florida
Edmonton at Detroit
Boston at N.Y. Rangers
Pittsburgh at Anaheim
St. Louis at San Jose

THURSDAY, MARCH 14
Toronto at Boston
Edmonton at Ottawa
Vancouver at Columbus
Dallas at Montreal
Buffalo at Philadelphia
Colorado at Atlanta
Calgary at Tampa Bay
St. Louis at Los Angeles

FRIDAY, MARCH 15
Buffalo at Florida
Phoenix at Nashville
Chicago at Anaheim
Washington at San Jose

SATURDAY, MARCH 16
Detroit at Boston*
N.Y. Rangers at New Jersey*
Colorado at Philadelphia*
Pittsburgh at Los Angeles*
Dallas at Toronto
Carolina at Montreal
N.Y. Islanders at Ottawa

Vancouver at Atlanta
Calgary at Columbus
Washington at Edmonton
Chicago at San Jose

SUNDAY, MARCH 17
Phoenix at Minnesota*
Detroit at N.Y. Rangers*
Colorado at Nashville*
Florida at Ottawa
Buffalo at Tampa Bay
Vancouver at New Jersey
St. Louis at Anaheim

MONDAY, MARCH 18
Tampa Bay at Philadelphia
Montreal at Carolina
Pittsburgh at Atlanta
Calgary at Minnesota
Dallas at Chicago
Los Angeles at San Jose

TUESDAY, MARCH 19
Phoenix at Boston
Ottawa at Buffalo
Vancouver at N.Y. Rangers
N.Y. Islanders at Toronto
Anaheim at Detroit
Nashville at St. Louis
Washington at Colorado

WEDNESDAY, MARCH 20
Phoenix at Pittsburgh
Atlanta at Tampa Bay
Montreal at Florida
Columbus at Minnesota
St. Louis at Dallas
New Jersey at Chicago
San Jose at Edmonton

THURSDAY, MARCH 21
N.Y. Rangers at Ottawa
Vancouver at N.Y. Islanders
Anaheim at Philadelphia
Florida at Carolina
Detroit at Columbus
Boston at Buffalo
Washington at Toronto
New Jersey at Nashville
San Jose at Calgary
Colorado at Los Angeles

FRIDAY, MARCH 22
Atlanta at N.Y. Rangers
Montreal at Tampa Bay
Anaheim at St. Louis
Phoenix at Dallas

SATURDAY, MARCH 23
Carolina at New Jersey*
Minnesota at N.Y. Islanders*
Philadelphia at Pittsburgh*
Detroit at Colorado*
San Jose at Los Angeles*
Buffalo at Toronto
Atlanta at Ottawa
Washington at Columbus
Montreal at Nashville
Boston at Florida
Calgary at Edmonton

SUNDAY, MARCH 24
St. Louis at Chicago*
Anaheim at Dallas*
Buffalo at Ottawa
Washington at Pittsburgh
Boston at Tampa Bay
Los Angeles at Phoenix
Edmonton at Vancouver

MONDAY, MARCH 25

N.Y. Rangers at N.Y. Islanders
Toronto at Philadelphia
Florida at New Jersey
Detroit at Nashville
Columbus at Calgary

TUESDAY, MARCH 26

Washington at Buffalo
Boston at Carolina
Tampa Bay at Toronto
Florida at Montreal
Minnesota at St. Louis
Columbus at Edmonton
Los Angeles at Vancouver
Dallas at San Jose

WEDNESDAY, MARCH 27

Ottawa at N.Y. Islanders
New Jersey at Pittsburgh
Minnesota at Atlanta
Philadelphia at N.Y. Rangers
Nashville at Chicago
Phoenix at Anaheim

THURSDAY, MARCH 28

Florida at Ottawa
Philadelphia at Carolina
N.Y. Islanders at Toronto
Tampa Bay at Montreal
Nashville at Detroit
Buffalo at St. Louis
Dallas at Calgary
Los Angeles at Edmonton
Anaheim at Phoenix
Columbus at Vancouver
Colorado at San Jose

FRIDAY, MARCH 29

Washington at New Jersey
Chicago at Minnesota

SATURDAY, MARCH 30

Carolina at Boston*
Buffalo at Philadelphia*
New Jersey at Toronto
Pittsburgh at Montreal
Tampa Bay at Ottawa
N.Y. Islanders at Washington
N.Y. Rangers at Florida
Atlanta at Detroit
St. Louis at Nashville
Los Angeles at Calgary
Colorado at Phoenix
Dallas at Edmonton
Anaheim at Vancouver
Columbus at San Jose

SUNDAY, MARCH 31

Minnesota at Chicago*

MONDAY, APRIL 1

Philadelphia at Buffalo
New Jersey at N.Y. Islanders
Montreal at Pittsburgh
N.Y. Rangers at Tampa Bay

Toronto at Detroit
Columbus at Dallas
Nashville at Colorado
St. Louis at Phoenix

TUESDAY, APRIL 2

Carolina at Ottawa
Boston at Philadelphia
Atlanta at Calgary
Minnesota at Edmonton
Vancouver at Los Angeles
Anaheim at San Jose

WEDNESDAY, APRIL 3

Tampa Bay at Washington
New Jersey at Carolina
Pittsburgh at Florida
N.Y. Islanders at Buffalo
St. Louis at Dallas
Nashville at Chicago
Atlanta at Colorado
Detroit at Anaheim

THURSDAY, APRIL 4

N.Y. Islanders at Boston
Montreal at Philadelphia
Nashville at Columbus
N.Y. Rangers at Toronto
Pittsburgh at Tampa Bay
Minnesota at Calgary
Detroit at Los Angeles
Phoenix at San Jose

FRIDAY, APRIL 5

Florida at Buffalo
Ottawa at Washington
Colorado at Dallas
New Jersey at Atlanta
Chicago at St. Louis
Minnesota at Vancouver
Edmonton at Anaheim

SATURDAY, APRIL 6

N.Y. Rangers at Boston*
Florida at Toronto
Columbus at Montreal
Washington at N.Y. Islanders
Pittsburgh at Philadelphia
Calgary at Nashville
Edmonton at Los Angeles
Detroit at San Jose

SUNDAY, APRIL 7

Boston at New Jersey*
Atlanta at Carolina*
Buffalo at Tampa Bay
Montreal at Ottawa
Colorado at St. Louis
Calgary at Chicago
Dallas at Anaheim
Phoenix at Vancouver

MONDAY, APRIL 8

Carolina at N.Y. Islanders
Pittsburgh at N.Y. Rangers
Florida at Philadelphia

Columbus at Toronto
San Jose at Minnesota
Dallas at Los Angeles

TUESDAY, APRIL 9

Tampa Bay at Boston
Chicago at Washington
Ottawa at Montreal
Nashville at St. Louis
Vancouver at Colorado
Phoenix at Calgary

WEDNESDAY, APRIL 10

Philadelphia at New Jersey
Toronto at N.Y. Rangers
Tampa Bay at Carolina
San Jose at Columbus
Buffalo at Pittsburgh
Florida at Atlanta
Chicago at Detroit
Minnesota at Dallas
Phoenix at Edmonton

THURSDAY, APRIL 11

Boston at Ottawa
San Jose at St. Louis
N.Y. Islanders at Nashville
Los Angeles at Vancouver

FRIDAY, APRIL 12

Washington at Buffalo
Atlanta at Columbus
Chicago at Dallas
Montreal at New Jersey
Toronto at Pittsburgh
N.Y. Islanders at Tampa Bay
Carolina at Florida
Calgary at Edmonton
Minnesota at Phoenix
Colorado at Anaheim

SATURDAY, APRIL 13

N.Y. Rangers at Philadelphia*
Detroit at St. Louis*
Los Angeles at San Jose*
Pittsburgh at Boston
Buffalo at Montreal
Toronto at Ottawa
New Jersey at Washington
Vancouver at Calgary

SUNDAY, APRIL 14

Philadelphia at N.Y. Islanders*
Edmonton at Minnesota*
Carolina at Atlanta*
Tampa Bay at Florida*
Columbus at Chicago*
Dallas at Colorado*
St. Louis at Detroit*
Anaheim at Los Angeles*
Nashville at Phoenix*

2001-02 NHL SEASON *Schedule*

2000-01 NHL REVIEW

Regular season

Stanley Cup playoffs

All-Star Game

Awards

Player draft

REGULAR SEASON

FINAL STANDINGS

EASTERN CONFERENCE

NORTHEAST DIVISION

	G	W	L	T	RT	Pts.	GF	GA	Home	Away	Div. Rec.
Ottawa Senators	82	48	21	9	4	109	274	205	26-7-5-3	22-14-4-1	13-5-1-1
Buffalo Sabres	82	46	30	5	1	98	218	184	26-12-3-0	20-18-2-1	11-7-2-0
Toronto Maple Leafs	82	37	29	11	5	90	232	207	19-11-7-4	18-18-4-1	7-10-2-1
Boston Bruins	82	36	30	8	8	88	227	249	21-12-5-3	15-18-3-5	11-6-1-2
Montreal Canadiens	82	28	40	8	6	70	206	232	15-20-4-2	13-20-4-4	5-13-0-2

ATLANTIC DIVISION

	G	W	L	T	RT	Pts.	GF	GA	Home	Away	Div. Rec.
New Jersey Devils	82	48	19	12	3	111	295	195	24-11-6-0	24-8-6-3	7-5-7-1
Philadelphia Flyers	82	43	25	11	3	100	240	207	26-11-4-0	17-14-7-3	11-5-2-2
Pittsburgh Penguins	82	42	28	9	3	96	281	256	24-15-2-0	18-13-7-3	12-5-2-1
New York Rangers	82	33	43	5	1	72	250	290	17-20-3-1	16-23-2-0	5-12-3-0
New York Islanders	82	21	51	7	3	52	185	268	12-27-1-1	9-24-6-2	7-10-2-1

SOUTHEAST DIVISION

	G	W	L	T	RT	Pts.	GF	GA	Home	Away	Div. Rec.
Washington Capitals	82	41	27	10	4	96	233	211	24-9-6-2	17-18-4-2	12-4-3-1
Carolina Hurricanes	82	38	32	9	3	88	212	225	23-15-3-0	15-17-6-3	11-5-4-0
Florida Panthers	82	22	38	13	9	66	200	246	12-18-7-4	10-20-6-5	5-10-3-2
Atlanta Thrashers	82	23	45	12	2	60	211	289	10-23-6-2	13-22-6-0	6-10-4-0
Tampa Bay Lightning	82	24	47	6	5	59	201	280	17-19-3-2	7-28-3-3	9-8-0-3

WESTERN CONFERENCE

CENTRAL DIVISION

	G	W	L	T	RT	Pts.	GF	GA	Home	Away	Div. Rec.
Detroit Red Wings	82	49	20	9	4	111	253	202	27-9-3-2	22-11-6-2	11-3-3-3
St. Louis Blues	82	43	22	12	5	103	249	195	28-5-5-3	15-17-7-2	9-7-4-0
Nashville Predators	82	34	36	9	3	80	186	200	16-18-7-0	18-18-2-3	8-11-1-0
Chicago Blackhawks	82	29	40	8	5	71	210	246	14-21-4-2	15-19-4-3	11-7-0-2
Columbus Blue Jackets	82	28	39	9	6	71	190	233	19-15-4-3	9-24-5-3	6-10-2-2

PACIFIC DIVISION

	G	W	L	T	RT	Pts.	GF	GA	Home	Away	Div. Rec.
Dallas Stars	82	48	24	8	2	106	241	187	26-10-5-0	22-14-3-2	11-6-3-0
San Jose Sharks	82	40	27	12	3	95	217	192	22-14-4-1	18-13-8-2	11-5-2-2
Los Angeles Kings	82	38	28	13	3	92	252	228	20-12-8-1	18-16-5-2	8-7-4-1
Phoenix Coyotes	82	35	27	17	3	90	214	212	21-11-7-2	14-16-10-1	7-7-5-1
Mighty Ducks of Anaheim	82	25	41	11	5	66	188	245	15-20-4-2	10-21-7-3	5-10-2-3

NORTHWEST DIVISION

	G	W	L	T	RT	Pts.	GF	GA	Home	Away	Div. Rec.
Colorado Rockies	82	52	16	10	4	118	270	192	28-6-5-2	24-10-5-2	14-5-1-0
Edmonton Oilers	82	39	28	12	3	93	243	222	23-9-7-2	16-19-5-1	11-5-3-1
Vancouver Canucks	82	36	28	11	7	90	239	238	21-12-5-3	15-16-6-4	10-6-1-3
Calgary Flames	82	27	36	15	4	73	197	236	12-18-9-2	15-18-6-2	5-10-3-2
Minnesota Wild	82	25	39	13	5	68	168	210	14-13-10-4	11-26-3-1	4-10-4-2

Note: RT denotes games in which the team is tied after regulation time, but loses in overtime; teams receive two points for each victory, one for each tie and one for each overtime loss.

INDIVIDUAL LEADERS

SCORING

TOP SCORERS

	Games	G	A	Pts.	PIM	+/-	PPG	SHG	Shots	Shooting Pct.
Jaromir Jagr, Pittsburgh	81	52	*69	*121	42	19	14	1	317	16.4
Joe Sakic, Colorado	82	54	64	118	30	†45	19	3	332	16.3
Patrik Elias, New Jersey	82	40	56	96	51	†45	8	3	220	18.2
Alexei Kovalev, Pittsburgh	79	44	51	95	96	12	12	2	307	14.3
Jason Allison, Boston	82	36	59	95	85	-8	11	3	185	19.5

	Games	G	A	Pts.	PIM	+/-	PPG	SHG	Shots	Shooting Pct.
Martin Straka, Pittsburgh	82	27	68	95	38	19	7	1	185	14.6
Pavel Bure, Florida	82	*59	33	92	58	-2	19	5	*384	15.4
Doug Weight, Edmonton	82	25	65	90	91	12	8	0	188	13.3
Zigmund Palffy, Los Angeles	73	38	51	89	20	22	12	4	217	17.5
Peter Forsberg, Colorado	73	27	62	89	54	23	12	2	178	15.2
Alexei Yashin, Ottawa	82	40	48	88	30	10	13	2	263	15.2
Luc Robitaille, Los Angeles	82	37	51	88	66	10	16	1	235	15.7
Bill Guerin, Edmonton-Boston	85	40	45	85	140	7	11	1	289	13.8
Mike Modano, Dallas	81	33	51	84	52	26	8	3	208	15.9
Alexander Mogilny, New Jersey	75	43	40	83	43	10	12	0	240	17.9
Pierre Turgeon, St. Louis	79	30	52	82	37	14	11	0	171	17.5
Adam Oates, Washington	81	13	69	82	28	-9	5	0	72	18.1
Peter Bondra, Washington	82	45	36	81	60	8	*22	4	305	14.8
Petr Sykora, New Jersey	73	35	46	81	32	36	9	2	249	14.1
Robert Lang, Pittsburgh	82	32	48	80	28	20	10	0	177	18.1

The scoring leader is awarded the Art Ross Memorial Trophy.
*Led league.
†Tied for league lead.

Games
Bill Guerin, Edm.-Bos. 85
Craig Conroy, St.L.-Cal. 83
75 players with 82

Points
Jaromir Jagr, Pittsburgh 121
Joe Sakic, Colorado 118
Patrik Elias, New Jersey 96
Jason Allison, Boston 95
Alexei Kovalev, Pittsburgh 95
Martin Straka, Pittsburgh 95
Pavel Bure, Florida 92
Doug Weight, Edmonton............90
Peter Forsberg, Colorado 89
Zigmund Palffy, Los Angeles 89

Points by a defenseman
Brian Leetch, N.Y. Rangers 79
Nicklas Lidstrom, Detroit 71
Rob Blake, L.A.-Colo. 59
Ray Bourque, Colorado 59
Sergei Gonchar, Washington 57

Goals
Pavel Bure, Florida 59
Joe Sakic, Colorado 54
Jaromir Jagr, Pittsburgh 52
Peter Bondra, Washington 45
Alexei Kovalev, Pittsburgh 44
Alexander Mogilny, New Jersey ..43
Milan Hejduk, Colorado 41
Markus Naslund, Vancouver 41
Jeff O'Neill, Carolina 41
Patrik Elias, New Jersey 40
Bill Guerin, Edm.-Bos. 40
Alexei Yashin, Ottawa 40
Scott Young, St. Louis 40

Assists
Jaromir Jagr, Pittsburgh 69
Adam Oates, Washington 69
Martin Straka, Pittsburgh 68
Doug Weight, Edmonton............65
Joe Sakic, Colorado 64
Peter Forsberg, Colorado 62
Jason Allison, Boston 59
Brian Leetch, N.Y. Rangers 58
Patrik Elias, New Jersey 56
Nicklas Lidstrom, Detroit 56

Power-play goals
Peter Bondra, Washington 22
Pavel Bure, Florida 19
Joe Sakic, Colorado 19

Joe Thornton, Boston 19
Paul Kariya, Anaheim 18
Markus Naslund, Vancouver 18
Jeff O'Neill, Carolina 17
Keith Tkachuk, Pho.-St.L. 17
Valeri Bure, Calgary 16
Mario Lemieux, Pittsburgh 16
Luc Robitaille, Los Angeles 16

Shorthanded goals
Steve Sullivan, Chicago 8
Theoren Fleury, N.Y. Rangers 7
Wes Walz, Minnesota 7
Pavel Bure, Florida 5
Peter Bondra, Washington 4
Craig Conroy, St.L.-Cal. 4
Todd Marchant, Edmonton 4
Zigmund Palffy, Los Angeles 4
Peter Schaefer, Vancouver 4
20 players with 3

Game-winning goals
Joe Sakic, Colorado 12
Jaromir Jagr, Pittsburgh 10
Alexei Yashin, Ottawa 10
Milan Hejduk, Colorado 9
Alexei Kovalev, Pittsburgh 9
Peter Bondra, Washington 8
Pavel Bure, Florida 8
Eric Daze, Chicago 8
Brett Hull, Dallas 8
Martin Lapointe, Detroit 8
Zigmund Palffy, Los Angeles 8
Mark Recchi, Philadelphia 8

Game-tying goals
Pavel Bure, Florida 3
Jarome Iginla, Calgary 3
Brendan Morrison, Vancouver 3
21 players with 2

Shots
Pavel Bure, Florida 384
Joe Sakic, Colorado 332
Scott Young, St. Louis 321
Jaromir Jagr, Pittsburgh 317
Alexei Kovalev, Pittsburgh 307

Shooting percentage (82 shots minimum)
Gary Roberts, Toronto 21.0
Keith Primeau, Philadelphia 20.6
Mario Lemieux, Pittsburgh 20.5
Joe Thornton, Boston 20.4
Alex Tanguay, Colorado 20.0

Plus/minus
Patrik Elias, New Jersey 45
Joe Sakic, Colorado 45
Scott Stevens, New Jersey 40
Brian Rafalski, New Jersey 36
Petr Sykora, New Jersey............36
Alex Tanguay, Colorado.............35
Milan Hejduk, Colorado 32
Colin White, New Jersey 32
Radek Bonk, Ottawa 27
Pavol Demitra, St. Louis 27

Penalty minutes
Peter Worrell, Florida 248
Shayne Corson, Toronto 189
Sandy McCarthy, N.Y. Rangers ..171
Zdeno Chara, N.Y. Islanders 157
Colin White, New Jersey 155
Donald Brashear, Vancouver 145
Darcy Tucker, Toronto 141
Bill Guerin, Edm.-Bos. 140
Tyler Wright, Columbus 140
Steve Staios, Atlanta 137

Consecutive-game point streaks
Jaromir Jagr, Pittsburgh 16
Theoren Fleury, N.Y. Rangers 14
Patrik Elias, New Jersey 13
Petr Sykora, New Jersey............13
Pavel Bure, Florida 11
Adam Oates, Washington 11
Mark Recchi, Philadelphia 11
Alex Tanguay, Colorado.............11
Joe Thornton, Boston 11

Consecutive-game goal streaks
Pavel Bure, Florida 7
Daniel Briere, Phoenix 6
Jaromir Jagr, Pittsburgh 6
Joe Sakic, Colorado 6
10 players with 5

Consecutive-game assist streaks
Jaromir Jagr, Pittsburgh 16
Petr Sykora, New Jersey..............9
Jaromir Jagr, Pittsburgh 9
Rod Brind'Amour, Carolina 8
Patrik Elias, New Jersey 8
Alex Tanguay, Colorado................8

Most games scoring three or more goals
Pavel Bure, Florida 4
Alexei Kovalev, Pittsburgh 4
Peter Bondra, Washington 3
Patrik Elias, New Jersey 3
Jaromir Jagr, Pittsburgh 3

Points by a rookie

Brad Richards, Tampa Bay	62
Shane Willis, Carolina	44
Martin Havlat, Ottawa	42
Lubomir Visnovsky, Los Angeles	39
Marian Gaborik, Minnesota	36
Ruslan Fedotenko, Philadelphia	36
Steven Reinprecht, L.A.-Colo.	36

Goals by a rookie

Brad Richards, Tampa Bay	21
Daniel Sedin, Vancouver	20
Shane Willis, Carolina	20
Martin Havlat, Ottawa	19
Marian Gaborik, Minnesota	18

Assists by a rookie

Brad Richards, Tampa Bay	41
Lubomir Visnovsky, Los Angeles	32
Karel Rachunek, Ottawa	30
Shane Willis, Carolina	24
Martin Havlat, Ottawa	23

GOALTENDING

Games

Arturs Irbe, Carolina	77
Tommy Salo, Edmonton	73
Olaf Kolzig, Washington	72
Martin Brodeur, New Jersey	72
Curtis Joseph, Toronto	68

Minutes

Arturs Irbe, Carolina	4406
Tommy Salo, Edmonton	4364
Martin Brodeur, New Jersey	4297
Olaf Kolzig, Washington	4279
Curtis Joseph, Toronto	4100

Goals allowed

Arturs Irbe, Carolina	180
Jocelyn Thibault, Chicago	180
Tommy Salo, Edmonton	179
Olaf Kolzig, Washington	177
Kevin Weekes, Tampa Bay	177

Shutouts

Dominik Hasek, Buffalo	11
Roman Cechmanek, Philadelphia	10
Martin Brodeur, New Jersey	9
Tommy Salo, Edmonton	8
Ed Belfour, Dallas	8

Lowest goals-against average
(25 games played minimum)

Marty Turco, Dallas	1.90
Roman Cechmanek, Philadelphia	2.01
Manny Legace, Detroit	2.05
Dominik Hasek, Buffalo	2.11
Brent Johnson, St. Louis	2.17

Highest goals-against average
(25 games played minimum)

Damian Rhodes, Atlanta	3.36
Milan Hnilicka, Atlanta	3.35
Peter Skudra, Buf.-Bos.	3.33
Trevor Kidd, Florida	3.31
Mike Richter, N.Y. Rangers	3.28

Games won

Martin Brodeur, New Jersey	42
Patrick Roy, Colorado	40
Dominik Hasek, Buffalo	37
Arturs Irbe, Carolina	37
Olaf Kolzig, Washington	37

Best winning percentage
(25 games played minimum)

Manny Legace, Detroit (24-5-5)	.779
Patrick Roy, Colorado (40-13-7)	.725
Martin Brodeur, N.J. (42-17-11)	.679
Roman Cechmanek, Phil. (35-15-6)	.679
Marty Turco, Dallas (13-6-1)	.675

Worst winning percentage
(25 games played minimum)

Jamie McLennan, Min. (5-23-9)	.257
Marc Denis, Columbus (6-20-4)	.267
Damian Rhodes, Atlanta (7-19-7)	.318
Dan Cloutier, T.B.-Van. (7-19-8)	.324
Trevor Kidd, Florida (10-23-6)	.333

Games lost

Kevin Weekes, Tampa Bay	33
Jocelyn Thibault, Chicago	32
Guy Hebert, Ana.-NYR	30
Arturs Irbe, Carolina	29
Jose Theodore, Montreal	29

Tie games

Sean Burke, Phoenix	13
Tommy Salo, Edmonton	12
Martin Brodeur, New Jersey	11
Fred Brathwaite, Calgary	10
Roman Turek, St. Louis	10

Shots against

Arturs Irbe, Carolina	1947
Olaf Kolzig, Washington	1941
Curtis Joseph, Toronto	1907
Tommy Salo, Edmonton	1856
Sean Burke, Phoenix	1766

Saves

Arturs Irbe, Carolina	1767
Olaf Kolzig, Washington	1764
Curtis Joseph, Toronto	1744
Tommy Salo, Edmonton	1677
Sean Burke, Phoenix	1628

Highest save percentage
(25 games played minimum)

Marty Turco, Dallas	.925
Mike Dunham, Nashville	.923
Sean Burke, Phoenix	.922
Dominik Hasek, Buffalo	.9214
Roman Cechmanek, Philadelphia	.9206

Lowest save percentage
(25 games played minimum)

Brian Boucher, Philadelphia	.876
Peter Skudra, Buf.-Bos.	.879
Mike Vernon, Calgary	.883
Jean-Sebastien Aubin, Pittsburgh	.8896
Milan Hnilicka, Atlanta	.8900

STATISTICS OF PLAYERS WITH TWO OR MORE TEAMS
SCORING

	Games	G	A	Pts.	PIM	+/–	PPG	SHG	Shots	Shooting Pct.
Kevyn Adams, Columbus	66	8	12	20	52	-4	0	0	84	9.5
Kevyn Adams, Florida	12	3	6	9	2	7	0	0	21	14.3
Totals	78	11	18	29	54	3	0	0	105	10.5
Adrian Aucoin, Vancouver	47	3	13	16	20	13	1	0	99	3.0
Adrian Aucoin, Tampa Bay	26	1	11	12	25	-8	1	0	60	1.7
Totals	73	4	24	28	45	5	2	0	159	2.5
Donald Audette, Atlanta	64	32	39	71	64	-3	13	1	187	17.1
Donald Audette, Buffalo	12	2	6	8	12	1	1	0	38	5.3
Totals	76	34	45	79	76	-2	14	1	225	15.1
Matthew Barnaby, Pittsburgh	47	1	4	5	168	-7	0	0	38	2.6
Matthew Barnaby, Tampa Bay	29	4	4	8	97	-3	1	0	29	13.8
Totals	76	5	8	13	265	-10	1	0	67	7.5
Wade Belak, Calgary	23	0	0	0	79	-2	0	0	8	0.0
Wade Belak, Toronto	16	1	1	2	31	-4	0	0	8	12.5
Totals	39	1	1	2	110	-6	0	0	16	6.3
Drake Berehowsky, Nashville	66	6	18	24	100	-9	3	0	94	6.4
Drake Berehowsky, Vancouver	14	1	1	2	21	0	1	0	13	7.7
Totals	80	7	19	26	121	-9	4	0	107	6.5
Aki Berg, Los Angeles	47	0	4	4	43	3	0	0	31	0.0
Aki Berg, Toronto	12	3	0	3	2	-6	3	0	12	25.0
Totals	59	3	4	7	45	-3	3	0	43	7.0
Marc Bergevin, St. Louis	2	0	0	0	0	1	0	0	1	0.0
Marc Bergevin, Pittsburgh	36	1	4	5	26	5	0	0	11	9.1

	Games	G	A	Pts.	PIM	+/-	PPG	SHG	Shots	Shooting Pct.
Totals..........	38	1	4	5	26	6	0	0	12	8.3
Craig Berube, Washington..........	22	0	1	1	18	-3	0	0	8	0.0
Craig Berube, N.Y. Islanders..........	38	0	2	2	54	-5	0	0	27	0.0
Totals..........	60	0	3	3	72	-8	0	0	35	0.0
Jason Blake, Los Angeles..........	17	1	3	4	10	-8	0	0	27	3.7
Jason Blake, N.Y. Islanders..........	30	4	8	12	24	-12	1	1	73	5.5
Totals..........	47	5	11	16	34	-20	1	1	100	5.0
Rob Blake, Los Angeles..........	54	17	32	49	69	-8	9	0	223	7.6
Rob Blake, Colorado..........	13	2	8	10	8	11	1	0	44	4.5
Totals..........	67	19	40	59	77	3	10	0	267	7.1
Jan Bulis, Washington..........	39	5	13	18	26	0	1	0	41	12.2
Jan Bulis, Montreal..........	12	0	5	5	0	-1	0	0	20	0.0
Totals..........	51	5	18	23	26	-1	1	0	61	8.2
Sven Butenschon, Pittsburgh..........	5	0	1	1	2	1	0	0	6	0.0
Sven Butenschon, Edmonton..........	7	1	1	2	2	2	0	0	3	33.3
Totals..........	12	1	2	3	4	3	0	0	9	11.1
Dan Cloutier, Tampa Bay (goalie)..........	24	0	0	0	4	0	0	0	0	0.0
Dan Cloutier, Vancouver (goalie)..........	16	0	0	0	0	0	0	0	0	0.0
Totals..........	40	0	0	0	4	0	0	0	0	0.0
Craig Conroy, St. Louis..........	69	11	14	25	46	2	0	3	101	10.9
Craig Conroy, Calgary..........	14	3	4	7	14	0	0	1	32	9.4
Totals..........	83	14	18	32	60	2	0	4	133	10.5
Bob Corkum, Los Angeles..........	58	4	6	10	18	-12	1	0	47	8.5
Bob Corkum, New Jersey..........	17	3	1	4	4	4	0	0	19	15.8
Totals..........	75	7	7	14	22	-8	1	0	66	10.6
Adam Deadmarsh, Colorado..........	39	13	13	26	59	-2	7	0	86	15.1
Adam Deadmarsh, Los Angeles..........	18	4	2	6	4	3	0	0	40	10.0
Totals..........	57	17	15	32	63	1	7	0	126	13.5
Bobby Dollas, San Jose..........	16	1	1	2	14	4	0	0	5	20.0
Bobby Dollas, Pittsburgh..........	5	0	0	0	4	0	0	0	6	0.0
Totals..........	21	1	1	2	18	4	0	0	11	9.1
John Emmons, Ottawa..........	41	1	1	2	20	-5	0	0	28	3.6
John Emmons, Tampa Bay..........	12	1	1	2	22	0	0	0	9	11.1
Totals..........	53	2	2	4	42	-5	0	0	37	5.4
Anders Eriksson, Chicago..........	13	2	3	5	2	-4	1	0	19	10.5
Anders Eriksson, Florida..........	60	0	21	21	28	2	0	0	80	0.0
Totals..........	73	2	24	26	30	-2	1	0	99	2.0
Wade Flaherty, N.Y. Islanders (goalie)..........	20	0	0	0	2	0	0	0	0	0.0
Wade Flaherty, Tampa Bay (goalie)..........	2	0	0	0	0	0	0	0	0	0.0
Totals..........	22	0	0	0	2	0	0	0	0	0.0
Colin Forbes, Ottawa..........	39	0	1	1	31	-3	0	0	26	0.0
Colin Forbes, N.Y. Rangers..........	19	1	4	5	15	-3	0	0	20	5.0
Totals..........	58	1	5	6	46	-6	0	0	46	2.2
Jeff Friesen, San Jose..........	64	12	24	36	56	7	2	0	120	10.0
Jeff Friesen, Anaheim..........	15	2	10	12	10	-2	2	0	29	6.9
Totals..........	79	14	34	48	66	5	4	0	149	9.4
Bill Guerin, Edmonton..........	21	12	10	22	18	11	4	0	64	18.8
Bill Guerin, Boston..........	64	28	35	63	122	-4	7	1	225	12.4
Totals..........	85	40	45	85	140	7	11	1	289	13.8
Alexei Gusarov, Colorado..........	9	0	1	1	6	2	0	0	4	0.0
Alexei Gusarov, N.Y. Rangers..........	26	1	3	4	6	-2	0	0	21	4.8
Alexei Gusarov, St. Louis..........	16	0	4	4	6	-3	0	0	10	0.0
Totals..........	51	1	8	9	18	-3	0	0	35	2.9
Michal Handzus, St. Louis..........	36	10	14	24	12	11	3	2	58	17.2
Michal Handzus, Phoenix..........	10	4	4	8	21	5	0	1	14	28.6
Totals..........	46	14	18	32	33	16	3	3	72	19.4
Guy Hebert, Anaheim (goalie)..........	41	0	0	0	0	0	0	0	0	0.0
Guy Hebert, N.Y. Rangers (goalie)..........	13	0	0	0	0	0	0	0	0	0.0
Totals..........	54	0	0	0	0	0	0	0	0	0.0
Steve Heinze, Columbus..........	65	22	20	42	38	-19	14	0	125	17.6
Steve Heinze, Buffalo..........	14	5	7	12	8	6	1	0	19	26.3
Totals..........	79	27	27	54	46	-13	15	0	144	18.8
Mike Johnson, Tampa Bay..........	64	11	27	38	38	-10	3	1	107	10.3
Mike Johnson, Phoenix..........	12	2	3	5	4	0	1	0	17	11.8
Totals..........	76	13	30	43	42	-10	4	1	124	10.5
Chris Joseph, Phoenix..........	24	1	1	2	16	-4	0	1	33	3.0
Chris Joseph, Atlanta..........	19	0	3	3	20	-7	0	0	25	0.0
Totals..........	43	1	4	5	36	-11	0	1	58	1.7
Steve Kelly, New Jersey..........	24	2	2	4	21	0	0	0	18	11.1
Steve Kelly, Los Angeles..........	11	1	0	1	4	0	0	0	4	25.0
Totals..........	35	3	2	5	25	0	0	0	22	13.6

	Games	G	A	Pts.	PIM	+/–	PPG	SHG	Shots	Shooting Pct.
Dmitri Khristich, Toronto	27	3	6	9	8	8	2	0	23	13.0
Dmitri Khristich, Washington	43	10	19	29	8	-8	4	0	54	18.5
Totals	70	13	25	38	16	0	6	0	77	16.9
Chad Kilger, Edmonton	34	5	2	7	17	-7	1	0	28	17.9
Chad Kilger, Montreal	43	9	16	25	34	-1	1	1	75	12.0
Totals	77	14	18	32	51	-8	2	1	103	13.6
Ladislav Kohn, Anaheim	51	4	3	7	42	-15	0	1	86	4.7
Ladislav Kohn, Atlanta	26	3	4	7	44	-12	0	1	43	7.0
Totals	77	7	7	14	86	-27	0	2	129	5.4
Igor Kravchuk, Ottawa	15	1	5	6	14	4	0	0	13	7.7
Igor Kravchuk, Calgary	37	0	8	8	4	-12	0	0	54	0.0
Totals	52	1	13	14	18	-8	0	0	67	1.5
Frantisek Kucera, Columbus	48	2	5	7	12	-5	0	0	51	3.9
Frantisek Kucera, Pittsburgh	7	0	2	2	0	-2	0	0	9	0.0
Totals	55	2	7	9	12	-7	0	0	60	3.3
Dan LaCouture, Edmonton	37	2	4	6	29	-2	0	0	22	9.1
Dan LaCouture, Pittsburgh	11	0	0	0	14	0	0	0	1	0.0
Totals	48	2	4	6	43	-2	0	0	23	8.7
Eric Lacroix, N.Y. Rangers	46	2	3	5	39	-6	0	0	22	9.1
Eric Lacroix, Ottawa	9	0	1	1	4	0	0	0	10	0.0
Totals	55	2	4	6	43	-6	0	0	32	6.3
Igor Larionov, Florida	26	5	6	11	10	-11	2	0	15	33.3
Igor Larionov, Detroit	39	4	25	29	28	6	2	0	31	12.9
Totals	65	9	31	40	38	-5	4	0	46	19.6
Grant Ledyard, Tampa Bay	14	2	2	4	12	-5	0	0	12	16.7
Grant Ledyard, Dallas	8	0	1	1	4	3	0	0	7	0.0
Totals	22	2	3	5	16	-2	0	0	19	10.5
Curtis Leschyshyn, Minnesota	54	2	3	5	19	-2	1	0	43	4.7
Curtis Leschyshyn, Ottawa	11	0	4	4	0	7	0	0	8	0.0
Totals	65	2	7	9	19	5	1	0	51	3.9
Trevor Linden, Montreal	57	12	21	33	52	-2	6	0	96	12.5
Trevor Linden, Washington	12	3	1	4	8	2	0	0	30	10.0
Totals	69	15	22	37	60	0	6	0	126	11.9
Bill Lindsay, Calgary	52	1	9	10	97	-8	0	0	57	1.8
Bill Lindsay, San Jose	16	0	4	4	29	2	0	0	14	0.0
Totals	68	1	13	14	126	-6	0	0	71	1.4
John MacLean, N.Y. Rangers	2	0	0	0	0	-2	0	0	0	0.0
John MacLean, Dallas	28	4	2	6	17	0	1	0	41	9.8
Totals	30	4	2	6	17	-2	1	0	41	9.8
Adam Mair, Toronto	16	0	2	2	14	3	0	0	17	0.0
Adam Mair, Los Angeles	10	0	0	0	6	-3	0	0	5	0.0
Totals	26	0	2	2	20	0	0	0	22	0.0
Paul Mara, Tampa Bay	46	6	10	16	40	-17	2	0	58	10.3
Paul Mara, Phoenix	16	0	4	4	14	1	0	0	20	0.0
Totals	62	6	14	20	54	-16	2	0	78	7.7
Jason Marshall, Anaheim	50	3	4	7	105	-12	2	1	38	7.9
Jason Marshall, Washington	5	0	0	0	17	-1	0	0	5	0.0
Totals	55	3	4	7	122	-13	2	1	43	7.0
Steve Martins, Tampa Bay	20	1	1	2	13	-9	0	0	18	5.6
Steve Martins, N.Y. Islanders	39	1	3	4	20	-7	0	1	28	3.6
Totals	59	2	4	6	33	-16	0	1	46	4.3
Dean McAmmond, Chicago	61	10	16	26	43	4	1	0	95	10.5
Dean McAmmond, Philadelphia	10	1	1	2	0	-1	1	0	17	5.9
Totals	71	11	17	28	43	3	2	0	112	9.8
Steve McKenna, Minnesota	20	1	1	2	19	0	0	0	12	8.3
Steve McKenna, Pittsburgh	34	0	0	0	100	-4	0	0	7	0.0
Totals	54	1	1	2	119	-4	0	0	19	5.3
Scott Mellanby, Florida	40	4	9	13	46	-13	1	0	58	6.9
Scott Mellanby, St. Louis	23	7	1	8	25	0	2	0	37	18.9
Totals	63	11	10	21	71	-13	3	0	95	11.6
Craig Millar, Nashville	5	0	0	0	6	1	0	0	2	0.0
Craig Millar, Tampa Bay	16	1	1	2	10	-8	0	0	10	10.0
Totals	21	1	1	2	16	-7	0	0	12	8.3
Aaron Miller, Colorado	56	4	9	13	29	19	0	0	49	8.2
Aaron Miller, Los Angeles	13	0	5	5	14	3	0	0	10	0.0
Totals	69	4	14	18	43	22	0	0	59	6.8
Willie Mitchell, New Jersey	16	0	2	2	29	0	0	0	14	0.0
Willie Mitchell, Minnesota	17	1	7	8	11	4	0	0	16	6.3
Totals	33	1	9	10	40	4	0	0	30	3.3
Bryan Muir, Tampa Bay	10	0	3	3	15	-7	0	0	14	0.0
Bryan Muir, Colorado	8	0	0	0	4	0	0	0	3	0.0
Totals	18	0	3	3	19	-7	0	0	17	0.0

	Games	G	A	Pts.	PIM	+/–	PPG	SHG	Shots	Shooting Pct.
Brantt Myhres, Nashville	20	0	0	0	28	-5	0	0	1	0.0
Brantt Myhres, Washington	5	0	0	0	29	0	0	0	0	0.0
Totals	25	0	0	0	57	-5	0	0	1	0.0
Ladislav Nagy, St. Louis	40	8	8	16	20	-2	2	0	59	13.6
Ladislav Nagy, Phoenix	6	0	1	1	2	0	0	0	5	0.0
Totals	46	8	9	17	22	-2	2	0	64	12.5
Andrei Nazarov, Anaheim	16	1	0	1	29	-9	0	0	13	7.7
Andrei Nazarov, Boston	63	1	4	5	200	-14	0	0	50	2.0
Totals	79	2	4	6	229	-23	0	0	63	3.2
Stan Neckar, Phoenix	53	2	2	4	63	-2	0	0	16	12.5
Stan Neckar, Tampa Bay	16	0	2	2	8	-1	0	0	10	0.0
Totals	69	2	4	6	71	-3	0	0	26	7.7
Jeff Norton, Pittsburgh	32	2	10	12	20	8	1	0	17	11.8
Jeff Norton, San Jose	10	0	1	1	8	4	0	0	5	0.0
Totals	42	2	11	13	28	12	1	0	22	9.1
Sean O'Donnell, Minnesota	63	4	12	16	128	-2	1	0	58	6.9
Sean O'Donnell, New Jersey	17	0	1	1	33	2	0	0	9	0.0
Totals	80	4	13	17	161	0	1	0	67	6.0
Gino Odjick, Philadelphia	17	1	3	4	28	0	0	0	21	4.8
Gino Odjick, Montreal	13	1	0	1	44	0	0	0	11	9.1
Totals	30	2	3	5	72	0	0	0	32	6.3
Krzysztof Oliwa, Columbus	10	0	2	2	34	1	0	0	5	0.0
Krzysztof Oliwa, Pittsburgh	26	1	2	3	131	-4	0	0	17	5.9
Totals	36	1	4	5	165	-3	0	0	22	4.5
Samuel Pahlsson, Boston	17	1	1	2	6	-5	0	0	13	7.7
Samuel Pahlsson, Anaheim	59	3	4	7	14	-9	1	1	46	6.5
Totals	76	4	5	9	20	-14	1	1	59	6.8
Steve Passmore, Los Angeles (goalie)	14	0	0	0	0	0	0	0	0	0.0
Steve Passmore, Chicago (goalie)	6	0	0	0	4	0	0	0	0	0.0
Totals	20	0	0	0	4	0	0	0	0	0.0
Scott Pellerin, Minnesota	58	11	28	39	45	6	2	2	117	9.4
Scott Pellerin, Carolina	19	0	5	5	6	-4	0	0	21	0.0
Totals	77	11	33	44	51	2	2	2	138	8.0
Felix Potvin, Vancouver (goalie)	35	0	2	2	2	0	0	0	0	0.0
Felix Potvin, Los Angeles (goalie)	23	0	3	3	2	0	0	0	0	0.0
Totals	58	0	5	5	4	0	0	0	0	0.0
Wayne Primeau, Tampa Bay	47	2	13	15	77	-17	0	0	47	4.3
Wayne Primeau, Pittsburgh	28	1	6	7	54	0	0	0	30	3.3
Totals	75	3	19	22	131	-17	0	0	77	3.9
Vaclav Prospal, Ottawa	40	1	12	13	12	1	0	0	68	1.5
Vaclav Prospal, Florida	34	4	12	16	10	-2	1	0	68	5.9
Totals	74	5	24	29	22	-1	1	0	136	3.7
Steven Reinprecht, Los Angeles	59	12	17	29	12	11	3	2	72	16.7
Steven Reinprecht, Colorado	21	3	4	7	2	-1	0	0	28	10.7
Totals	80	15	21	36	14	10	3	2	100	15.0
Dominic Roussel, Anaheim (goalie)	13	0	0	0	0	0	0	0	0	0.0
Dominic Roussel, Edmonton (goalie)	8	0	0	0	2	0	0	0	0	0.0
Totals	21	0	0	0	2	0	0	0	0	0.0
Teemu Selanne, Anaheim	61	26	33	59	36	-8	10	0	202	12.9
Teemu Selanne, San Jose	12	7	6	13	0	1	2	0	31	22.6
Totals	73	33	39	72	36	-7	12	0	233	14.2
Mike Sillinger, Florida	55	13	21	34	44	-12	1	0	100	13.0
Mike Sillinger, Ottawa	13	3	4	7	4	1	0	0	19	15.8
Totals	68	16	25	41	48	-11	1	0	119	13.4
Roman Simicek, Pittsburgh	29	3	6	9	30	-5	1	0	19	15.8
Roman Simicek, Minnesota	28	2	4	6	21	-4	2	0	14	14.3
Totals	57	5	10	15	51	-9	3	0	33	15.2
Todd Simpson, Florida	25	1	3	4	74	0	0	0	26	3.8
Todd Simpson, Phoenix	13	0	1	1	12	-4	0	0	9	0.0
Totals	38	1	4	5	86	-4	0	0	35	2.9
Peter Skudra, Buffalo (goalie)	1	0	0	0	0	0	0	0	0	0.0
Peter Skudra, Boston (goalie)	25	0	0	0	0	0	0	0	0	0.0
Totals	26	0	0	0	0	0	0	0	0	0.0
Jiri Slegr, Pittsburgh	42	5	10	15	60	-9	0	1	67	7.5
Jiri Slegr, Atlanta	33	3	16	19	36	-1	2	0	78	3.8
Totals	75	8	26	34	96	-10	2	1	145	5.5
Blake Sloan, Dallas	33	2	2	4	4	-2	0	0	29	6.9
Blake Sloan, Columbus	14	1	0	1	13	-2	0	0	16	6.3
Totals	47	3	2	5	17	-4	0	0	45	6.7
Peter Smrek, St. Louis	6	2	0	2	2	1	0	0	5	40.0
Peter Smrek, N.Y. Rangers	14	0	3	3	12	1	0	0	9	0.0
Totals	20	2	3	5	14	2	0	0	14	14.3

	Games	G	A	Pts.	PIM	+/–	PPG	SHG	Shots	Shooting Pct.
Jaroslav Spacek, Florida	12	2	1	3	8	-4	1	0	21	9.5
Jaroslav Spacek, Chicago	50	5	18	23	20	7	2	0	85	5.9
Totals	62	7	19	26	28	3	3	0	106	6.6
Mike Stapleton, N.Y. Islanders	34	1	4	5	2	-5	0	0	22	4.5
Mike Stapleton, Vancouver	18	1	2	3	8	-6	1	0	9	11.1
Totals	52	2	6	8	10	-11	1	0	31	6.5
Kevin Stevens, Philadelphia	23	2	7	9	18	-2	0	0	31	6.5
Kevin Stevens, Pittsburgh	32	8	15	23	55	-4	2	0	76	10.5
Totals	55	10	22	32	73	-6	2	0	107	9.3
Cory Stillman, Calgary	66	21	24	45	45	-6	7	0	148	14.2
Cory Stillman, St. Louis	12	3	4	7	6	-2	3	0	26	11.5
Totals	78	24	28	52	51	-8	10	0	174	13.8
P.J. Stock, Montreal	20	1	2	3	32	-1	0	0	9	11.1
P.J. Stock, Philadelphia	31	1	3	4	78	-2	0	0	18	5.6
Totals	51	2	5	7	110	-3	0	0	27	7.4
Chris Terreri, New Jersey (goalie)	10	0	0	0	0	0	0	0	0	0.0
Chris Terreri, N.Y. Islanders (goalie)	8	0	0	0	2	0	0	0	0	0.0
Totals	18	0	0	0	2	0	0	0	0	0.0
Keith Tkachuk, Phoenix	64	29	42	71	108	6	15	0	230	12.6
Keith Tkachuk, St. Louis	12	6	2	8	14	-3	2	0	41	14.6
Totals	76	35	44	79	122	3	17	0	271	12.9
Jeff Toms, N.Y. Islanders	39	2	4	6	10	-7	0	0	37	5.4
Jeff Toms, N.Y. Rangers	15	1	1	2	0	-3	0	0	12	8.3
Totals	54	3	5	8	10	-10	0	0	49	6.1
Patrick Traverse, Anaheim	15	1	0	1	6	-6	0	0	7	14.3
Patrick Traverse, Boston	37	2	6	8	14	4	1	0	39	5.1
Patrick Traverse, Montreal	19	2	3	5	10	-8	0	0	16	12.5
Totals	71	5	9	14	30	-10	1	0	62	8.1
Daniel Trebil, Pittsburgh	16	0	0	0	7	-1	0	0	17	0.0
Daniel Trebil, St. Louis	10	0	0	0	0	1	0	0	9	0.0
Totals	26	0	0	0	7	0	0	0	26	0.0
John Vanbiesbrouck, N.Y. Islanders (goalie)	44	0	0	0	8	0	0	0	0	0.0
John Vanbiesbrouck, New Jersey (goalie)	4	0	0	0	0	0	0	0	0	0.0
Totals	48	0	0	0	8	0	0	0	0	0.0
Eric Weinrich, Montreal	60	6	19	25	34	-1	2	0	81	7.4
Eric Weinrich, Boston	22	1	5	6	10	-8	1	0	28	3.6
Totals	82	7	24	31	44	-9	3	0	109	6.4
Ray Whitney, Florida	43	10	21	31	28	-16	5	0	117	8.5
Ray Whitney, Columbus	3	0	3	3	2	-1	0	0	3	0.0
Totals	46	10	24	34	30	-17	5	0	120	8.3
Johan Witehall, N.Y. Rangers	15	0	3	3	8	-5	0	0	16	0.0
Johan Witehall, Montreal	26	1	1	2	6	0	0	0	18	5.6
Totals	41	1	4	5	14	-5	0	0	34	2.9
Richard Zednik, Washington	62	16	19	35	61	-2	4	0	155	10.3
Richard Zednik, Montreal	12	3	6	9	10	-2	1	0	23	13.0
Totals	74	19	25	44	71	-4	5	0	178	10.7
Sergei Zholtok, Montreal	32	1	10	11	8	-15	0	0	78	1.3
Sergei Zholtok, Edmonton	37	4	16	20	22	8	1	0	61	6.6
Totals	69	5	26	31	30	-7	1	0	139	3.6
Dainius Zubrus, Montreal	49	12	12	24	30	-7	3	0	70	17.1
Dainius Zubrus, Washington	12	1	1	2	7	-4	1	0	13	7.7
Totals	61	13	13	26	37	-11	4	0	83	15.7

GOALTENDING

	Games	Min.	Goals	SO	Avg.	W	L	T	ENG	Shots	Sv. Pct.
Dan Cloutier, Tampa Bay	24	1005	59	1	3.52	3	13	3	3	541	.891
Dan Cloutier, Vancouver	16	914	37	0	2.43	4	6	5	0	348	.894
Totals	40	1919	96	1	3.00	7	19	8	3	889	.892
Wade Flaherty, N.Y. Islanders	20	1017	56	1	3.30	6	10	0	3	470	.881
Wade Flaherty, Tampa Bay	2	118	8	0	4.07	0	2	0	0	55	.855
Totals	22	1135	64	1	3.38	6	12	0	3	525	.878
Guy Hebert, Anaheim	41	2215	115	2	3.12	12	23	4	0	1112	.897
Guy Hebert, N.Y. Rangers	13	735	42	0	3.43	5	7	1	2	409	.897
Totals	54	2950	157	2	3.19	17	30	5	2	1521	.897
Steve Passmore, Los Angeles	14	718	37	1	3.09	3	8	1	2	310	.881
Steve Passmore, Chicago	6	340	14	0	2.47	0	4	1	0	147	.905
Totals	20	1058	51	1	2.89	3	12	2	2	457	.888
Felix Potvin, Vancouver	35	2006	103	1	3.08	14	17	3	2	914	.887
Felix Potvin, Los Angeles	23	1410	46	5	1.96	13	5	5	0	571	.919
Totals	58	3416	149	6	2.62	27	22	8	2	1485	.900
Dominic Roussel, Anaheim	13	653	31	0	2.85	2	5	2	2	295	.895

	Games	Min.	Goals	SO	Avg.	W	L	T	ENG	Shots	Sv. Pct.
Dominic Roussel, Edmonton	8	348	21	0	3.62	1	4	0	1	151	.861
Totals.............................	21	1001	52	0	3.12	3	9	2	3	446	.883
Peter Skudra, Buffalo....................	1	0	0	0	0.00	0	0	0	0	0	.000
Peter Skudra, Boston....................	25	1116	62	0	3.33	6	12	1	1	511	.879
Totals.............................	26	1116	62	0	3.33	6	12	1	1	511	.879
Chris Terreri, New Jersey	10	453	21	0	2.78	2	5	1	0	167	.874
Chris Terreri, N.Y. Islanders...........	8	443	18	0	2.44	2	4	1	2	205	.912
Totals.............................	18	896	39	0	2.61	4	9	2	2	372	.895
John Vanbiesbrouck, N.Y. Islanders.	44	2390	120	1	3.01	10	25	5	4	1177	.898
John Vanbiesbrouck, New Jersey...	4	240	6	1	1.50	4	0	0	0	93	.935
Totals.............................	48	2630	126	2	2.87	14	25	5	4	1270	.901

MISCELLANEOUS

HAT TRICKS

(Players scoring three or more goals in a game)

Date	Player, Team	Opp.	Goals
10-13-00—	Ian Laperriere, Los Angeles	Bos.	3
10-14-00—	Jaromir Jagr, Pittsburgh	NYR	4
10-14-00—	Dainius Zubrus, Montreal	Chi.	3
10-21-00—	Donald Audette, Atlanta	Ott.	3
10-21-00—	Andreas Dackell, Ottawa	Atl.	3
10-21-00—	Brian Savage, Montreal	Car.	3
10-22-00—	Fredrik Modin, Tampa Bay	NYR	3
10-23-00—	Marty McInnis, Anaheim	L.A.	3
10-28-00—	John Madden, New Jersey	Pit.	4
10-28-00—	Randy McKay, New Jersey	Pit.	4
10-31-00—	Richard Zednik, Washington	Det.	3
11-1-00—	Theoren Fleury, N.Y. Rangers	T.B.	3
11-4-00—	Tomi Kallio, Atlanta	Bos.	3
11-8-00—	Andrew Cassels, Vancouver	Ana.	3
11-8-00—	Alexei Kovalev, Pittsburgh	Phil.	3
11-14-00—	Ryan Smyth, Edmonton	St.L.	3
11-18-00—	Jonas Hoglund, Toronto	Mon.	3
11-18-00—	Marian Hossa, Ottawa	Fla.	3
11-18-00—	Steve Konowalchuk, Washington	Phil.	3
11-22-00—	Sergei Fedorov, Detroit	Bos.	3
11-26-00—	Antti Laaksonen, Minnesota	Van.	3
11-28-00—	Zigmund Palffy, Los Angeles	NYR	3
11-29-00—	Shean Donovan, Atlanta	Det.	3
11-29-00—	Cory Stillman, Calgary	Dal.	3
12-4-00—	Ray Ferraro, Atlanta	Bos.	3
12-5-00—	Patrik Elias, New Jersey	Colo.	3
12-6-00—	John LeClair, Philadelphia	T.B.	3
12-8-00—	Harold Druken, Vancouver	S.J.	3
12-9-00—	Donald Audette, Atlanta	NYI	3
12-12-00—	Jean-Pierre Dumont, Buffalo	Bos.	3
12-14-00—	Rob Blake, Los Angeles	NYR	3
12-15-00—	Pierre Turgeon, St Louis	Atl.	3
12-16-00—	Jaromir Jagr, Pittsburgh	Mon.	3
12-18-00—	Todd Harvey, San Jose	Wash.	3
12-20-00—	Pavol Demitra, St Louis	NYR	3
12-20-00—	Keith Tkachuk, Phoenix	Cal.	3
12-21-00—	Joe Sakic, Colorado	L.A.	3
12-21-00—	Steve Sullivan, Chicago	Van.	3
12-23-00—	Michal Handzus, St Louis	Ana.	3
12-26-00—	Scott Walker, Nashville	Colo.	3
12-27-00—	Peter Bondra, Washington	Ott.	4
12-30-00—	Todd Bertuzzi, Vancouver	S.J.	3
12-31-00—	Joe Nieuwendyk, Dallas	NYR	3
1-4-01—	Radek Bonk, Ottawa	T.B.	3
1-4-01—	Alexander Mogilny, New Jersey	NYI	3
1-6-01—	Jan Hlavac, N.Y. Rangers	N.J.	3
1-6-01—	Alexei Yashin, Ottawa	Mon.	3

Date	Player, Team	Opp.	Goals
1-7-01—	Rod Brind'Amour, Carolina	NYI	3
1-8-01—	Martin Straka, Pittsburgh	Wash.	3
1-9-01—	Andrei Kovalenko, Boston	Pit.	3
1-14-01—	Markus Naslund, Vancouver	Cal.	3
1-14-01—	Ryan Smyth, Edmonton	Ott.	3
1-16-01—	Bryan Smolinski, Los Angeles	Ott.	3
1-17-01—	Jere Lehtinen, Dallas	Nash.	3
1-24-01—	Mario Lemieux, Pittsburgh	Mon.	3
2-1-01—	Peter Bondra, Washington	Tor.	3
2-1-01—	Teemu Selanne, Anaheim	Pho.	3
2-7-01—	Alexei Kovalev, Pittsburgh	Phil.	3
2-10-01—	Pavel Bure, Florida	Atl.	4
2-10-01—	Alexei Kovalev, Pittsburgh	N.J.	3
2-10-01—	Geoff Sanderson, Columbus	Nash	3
2-13-01—	Ray Ferraro, Atlanta	Buf.	3
2-14-01—	Pavel Bure, Florida	Pho.	3
2-17-01—	Petr Nedved, N.Y. Rangers	T.B.	3
2-19-01—	Paul Kariya, Anaheim	Cal.	3
2-21-01—	Shane Willis, Carolina	Atl.	3
2-23-01—	Alexei Kovalev, Pittsburgh	NYR	3
2-23-01—	Jeremy Roenick, Phoenix	Buf.	3
3-1-01—	Daniel Alfredsson, Ottawa	S.J.	3
3-1-01—	Joe Thornton, Boston	T.B.	3
3-4-01—	Sandis Ozolinsh, Carolina	Chi.	3
3-7-01—	Scott Thornton, San Jose	Fla.	3
3-8-01—	Keith Primeau, Philadelphia	Cal.	3
3-9-01—	Peter Bondra, Washington	NYR	3
3-9-01—	Deron Quint, Columbus	Fla.	3
3-10-01—	Jaromir Jagr, Pittsburgh	Cal.	3
3-11-01—	Pavel Bure, Florida	NYI	3
3-14-01—	Martin Havlat, Ottawa	Atl.	3
3-15-01—	Brendan Shanahan, Detroit	Cal.	4
3-16-01—	Steve Heinze, Buffalo	Van.	3
3-16-01—	Tyler Wright, Columbus	Atl.	3
3-17-01—	Pavel Bure, Florida	Tor.	3
3-17-01—	Patrik Elias, New Jersey	Edm.	3
3-18-01—	Tomas Holmstrom, Detroit	S.J.	3
3-18-01—	Brett Hull, Dallas	Ott.	3
3-21-01—	Brett Hull, Dallas	Ana.	4
3-29-01—	Radek Dvorak, N.Y. Rangers	NYI	4
3-29-01—	Paul Kariya, Anaheim	S.J.	3
3-29-01—	Teemu Selanne, San Jose	Ana.	3
3-31-01—	Jason Allison, Boston	NYI	3
4-2-01—	Joe Sakic, Colorado	Edm.	3
4-3-01—	Patrik Elias, New Jersey	Wash.	3
4-7-01—	Mike Ricci, San Jose	Dal.	3

OVERTIME GOALS

Date	Player, Team	Opponent	Time	Final score
10-6-00—	Ed Jovanovski, Vancouver	Florida	2:20	Vancouver 4, Florida 3
10-11-00—	Joe Thornton, Boston	Anaheim	2:03	Boston 3, Anaheim 2
10-14-00—	Patrice Brisebois, Montreal	Chicago	2:39	Montreal 5, Chicago 4
10-17-00—	Peter Forsberg, Colorado	Washington	2:37	Colorado 4, Washington 3
10-18-00—	Joe Juneau, Phoenix	Florida	1:15	Phoenix 2, Florida 1
10-19-00—	Cliff Ronning, Nashville	Detroit	1:51	Nashville 2, Detroit 1
10-21-00—	Brendan Shanahan, Detroit	Buffalo	4:27	Detroit 5, Buffalo 4
10-21-00—	Jeremy Roenick, Phoenix	Vancouver	0:16	Phoenix 3, Vancouver 2
10-22-00—	Kirk Maltby, Detroit	Columbus	2:01	Detroit 2, Columbus 1
10-23-00—	Zigmund Palffy, Los Angeles	Anaheim	1:04	Los Angeles 5, Anaheim 4
10-25-00—	Peter Forsberg, Colorado	Nashville	3:58	Colorado 2, Nashville 1
10-28-00—	Mats Sundin, Toronto	Boston	3:36	Toronto 2, Boston 1
10-28-00—	Al MacInnis, St Louis	Dallas	0:15	St. Louis 4, Dallas 3
10-30-00—	Bobby Holik, New Jersey	Florida	1:55	New Jersey 6, Florida 5
10-31-00—	Sandis Ozolinsh, Carolina	Tampa Bay	2:35	Carolina 6, Tampa Bay 5
11-3-00—	Craig Millar, Tampa Bay	N.Y. Islanders	2:46	Tampa Bay 4, N.Y. Islanders 3
11-5-00—	Antti Laaksonen, Minnesota	Calgary	3:11	Minnesota 3, Calgary 2
11-8-00—	Marco Sturm, San Jose	Chicago	4:44	San Jose 3, Chicago 2
11-12-00—	Doug Weight, Edmonton	Minnesota	1:24	Edmonton 5, Minnesota 4
11-13-00—	Jean-Pierre Dumont, Buffalo	Calgary	1:29	Buffalo 3, Calgary 2
11-13-00—	Joe Sakic, Colorado	Pittsburgh	3:56	Colorado 3, Pittsburgh 2
11-15-00—	Mark Recchi, Philadelphia	Toronto	3:26	Philadelphia 2, Toronto 1
11-16-00—	Scott Gomez, New Jersey	Boston	4:58	New Jersey 3, Boston 2
11-17-00—	Daniel McGillis, Philadelphia	Atlanta	1:01	Philadelphia 3, Atlanta 2
11-18-00—	Patrik Elias, New Jersey	Carolina	4:20	New Jersey 3, Carolina 2
11-18-00—	Valeri Kamensky, N.Y. Rangers	Calgary	2:44	N.Y. Rangers 5, Calgary 4
11-22-00—	Theoren Fleury, N.Y. Rangers	N.Y. Islanders	4:25	N.Y. Rangers 4, N.Y. Islanders 3
11-22-00—	Andrei Nikolishin, Washington	Vancouver	4:17	Washington 3, Vancouver 2
11-25-00—	Pavel Bure, Florida	Tampa Bay	2:47	Florida 2, Tampa Bay 1
11-25-00—	Milan Hejduk, Colorado	Calgary	0:39	Colorado 3, Calgary 2
11-27-00—	Steve Sullivan, Chicago	Detroit	4:32	Chicago 6, Detroit 5
11-29-00—	Jochen Hecht, St Louis	Toronto	0:18	St. Louis 6, Toronto 5
11-29-00—	Bates Battaglia, Carolina	Florida	1:41	Carolina 2, Florida 1
11-30-00—	Scott Hannan, San Jose	Anaheim	4:50	San Jose 3, Anaheim 2
12-8-00—	Ray Ferraro, Atlanta	Florida	0:22	Atlanta 4, Florida 3
12-8-00—	Geoff Sanderson, Columbus	Boston	4:51	Columbus 3, Boston 2
12-8-00—	Oleg Tverdovsky, Anaheim	Minnesota	0:21	Anaheim 1, Minnesota 0
12-13-00—	Niclas Havelid, Anaheim	Columbus	2:13	Anaheim 5, Columbus 4
12-16-00—	Valeri Bure, Calgary	Toronto	0:34	Calgary 6, Toronto 5
12-16-00—	Gary Suter, San Jose	Phoenix	1:53	San Jose 2, Phoenix 1
12-18-00—	Larry Murphy, Detroit	Edmonton	3:05	Detroit 4, Edmonton 3
12-19-00—	Frantisek Kaberle, Atlanta	Los Angeles	1:20	Atlanta 7, Los Angeles 6
12-20-00—	Anson Carter, Edmonton	Vancouver	2:41	Edmonton 3, Vancouver 2
12-22-00—	Sergei Fedorov, Detroit	Anaheim	0:19	Detroit 2, Anaheim 1
12-23-00—	Mathieu Dandenault, Detroit	Boston	1:30	Detroit 2, Boston 1
12-23-00—	David Legwand, Nashville	N.Y. Rangers	3:17	Nashville 3, N.Y. Rangers 2
12-23-00—	Daniel McGillis, Philadelphia	Carolina	3:50	Philadelphia 2, Carolina 1
12-23-00—	Milan Hejduk, Colorado	Vancouver	3:59	Colorado 3, Vancouver 2
12-29-00—	Jaroslav Spacek, Chicago	Detroit	2:25	Chicago 3, Detroit 2
12-30-00—	Doug Weight, Edmonton	Montreal	1:49	Edmonton 3, Montreal 2
12-31-00—	Derek Morris, Calgary	Montreal	1:34	Calgary 5, Montreal 4
1-3-01—	Petr Tenkrat, Anaheim	Florida	4:01	Anaheim 3, Florida 2
1-5-01—	Filip Kuba, Minnesota	Detroit	2:58	Minnesota 3, Detroit 2
1-7-01—	Steve Yzerman, Detroit	Colorado	1:08	Detroit 4, Colorado 3
1-8-01—	Keith Primeau, Philadelphia	St. Louis	1:59	Philadelphia 2, St. Louis 1
1-16-01—	Ron Francis, Carolina	Montreal	0:33	Carolina 3, Montreal 2
1-16-01—	Bryan Smolinski, Los Angeles	Ottawa	2:01	Los Angeles 7, Ottawa 6
1-16-01—	Theoren Fleury, N.Y. Rangers	Philadelphia	2:46	N.Y. Rangers 4, Philadelphia 3
1-17-01—	Brett Hull, Dallas	Nashville	1:41	Dallas 4, Nashville 3
1-17-01—	Sean O'Donnell, Minnesota	Columbus	3:53	Minnesota 3, Columbus 2
1-18-01—	Brian Leetch, N.Y. Rangers	Toronto	4:33	N.Y. Rangers 2, Toronto 1
1-19-01—	Darryl Sydor, Dallas	Pittsburgh	0:42	Dallas 6, Pittsburgh 5
1-19-01—	Cale Hulse, Nashville	Boston	2:24	Nashville 1, Boston 0
1-25-01—	Bryan McCabe, Toronto	Atlanta	0:39	Toronto 2, Atlanta 1
1-25-01—	Pierre Turgeon, St Louis	New Jersey	3:17	St. Louis 4, New Jersey 3
1-26-01—	Marian Hossa, Ottawa	Florida	2:54	Ottawa 5, Florida 4
1-27-01—	Sergei Samsonov, Boston	New Jersey	1:14	Boston 4, New Jersey 3
1-27-01—	Pavel Bure, Florida	Tampa Bay	0:59	Florida 3, Tampa Bay 2
1-27-01—	Brad Stuart, San Jose	St. Louis	1:51	San Jose 4, St. Louis 3
1-30-01—	Mattias Ohlund, Vancouver	Minnesota	1:43	Vancouver 3, Minnesota 2

Date	Player, Team	Opponent	Time	Final score
1-31-01—	Steve Yzerman, Detroit	Columbus	1:00	Detroit 3, Columbus 2
2-7-01—	Maxim Afinogenov, Buffalo	N.Y. Islanders	0:42	Buffalo 2, N.Y. Islanders 1
2-7-01—	Jeff O'Neill, Carolina	Phoenix	0:25	Carolina 2, Phoenix 1
2-10-01—	Maxim Afinogenov, Buffalo	Ottawa	1:52	Buffalo 2, Ottawa 1
2-10-01—	Alexei Kovalev, Pittsburgh	New Jersey	0:18	Pittsburgh 5, New Jersey 4
2-10-01—	Daniel Corso, St Louis	Colorado	0:50	St. Louis 4, Colorado 3
2-10-01—	Bryan Marchment, San Jose	Chicago	2:07	San Jose 3, Chicago 2
2-13-01—	Joe Sakic, Colorado	Montreal	2:21	Colorado 3, Montreal 2
2-14-01—	Sergei Fedorov, Detroit	Carolina	2:51	Detroit 4, Carolina 3
2-14-01—	Adam Oates, Washington	Vancouver	4:19	Washington 4, Vancouver 3
2-16-01—	Derian Hatcher, Dallas	Anaheim	1:35	Dallas 3, Anaheim 2
2-17-01—	Alexei Kovalev, Pittsburgh	Columbus	1:19	Pittsburgh 3, Columbus 2
2-17-01—	Brendan Morrison, Vancouver	Edmonton	0:58	Vancouver 6, Edmonton 5
2-20-01—	Marco Sturm, San Jose	Columbus	4:18	San Jose 3, Columbus 2
2-21-01—	Mario Lemieux, Pittsburgh	Florida	2:10	Pittsburgh 3, Florida 2
2-22-01—	Roman Hamrlik, N.Y. Islanders	Philadelphia	4:42	N.Y. Islanders 4, Philadelphia 3
2-23-01—	Joe Nieuwendyk, Dallas	Boston	1:00	Dallas 5, Boston 4
2-24-01—	Pierre Turgeon, St Louis	Boston	1:20	St. Louis 3, Boston 2
2-25-01—	Todd Marchant, Edmonton	Dallas	0:31	Edmonton 3, Dallas 2
3-1-01—	Gary Roberts, Toronto	Washington	1:21	Toronto 3, Washington 2
3-2-01—	Mattias Ohlund, Vancouver	St. Louis	3:40	Vancouver 3, St. Louis 2
3-3-01—	Alexei Yashin, Ottawa	Toronto	0:42	Ottawa 3, Toronto 2
3-3-01—	Stu Barnes, Buffalo	Colorado	2:08	Buffalo 3, Colorado 2
3-3-01—	Marc Savard, Calgary	St. Louis	4:01	Calgary 3, St. Louis 2
3-4-01—	Aaron Gavey, Minnesota	Vancouver	2:26	Minnesota 4, Vancouver 3
3-6-01—	Patrik Elias, New Jersey	Ottawa	0:28	New Jersey 3, Ottawa 2
3-8-01—	Brad Richards, Tampa Bay	San Jose	4:02	Tampa Bay 2, San Jose 1
3-8-01—	Shane Doan, Phoenix	Vancouver	0:38	Phoenix 3, Vancouver 2
3-9-01—	Robert Kron, Columbus	Florida	0:43	Columbus 7, Florida 6
3-10-01—	Brad Lukowich, Dallas	Colorado	1:47	Dallas 3, Colorado 2
3-11-01—	Brendan Shanahan, Detroit	Minnesota	0:37	Detroit 3, Minnesota 2
3-11-01—	Mike Crowley, Anaheim	Nashville	3:40	Anaheim 1, Nashville 0
3-13-01—	Eric Brewer, Edmonton	Tampa Bay	1:17	Edmonton 5, Tampa Bay 4
3-14-01—	Scott Young, St Louis	Minnesota	3:09	St. Louis 1, Minnesota 0
3-17-01—	Patrik Elias, New Jersey	Edmonton	4:51	New Jersey 6, Edmonton 5
3-17-01—	Bryan Smolinski, Los Angeles	San Jose	0:40	Los Angeles 1, San Jose 0
3-20-01—	Roman Hamrlik, N.Y. Islanders	St. Louis	0:23	N.Y. Islanders 4, St. Louis 3
3-22-01—	Brian Rolston, Boston	Montreal	2:49	Boston 3, Montreal 2
3-22-01—	Mark Eaton, Nashville	Chicago	1:54	Nashville 2, Chicago 1
3-27-01—	Mike Ricci, San Jose	Los Angeles	1:53	San Jose 3, Los Angeles 2
3-29-01—	David Legwand, Nashville	Phoenix	0:36	Nashville 4, Phoenix 3
3-30-01—	Martin Havlat, Ottawa	Boston	2:26	Ottawa 5, Boston 4
3-30-01—	Rod Brind'Amour, Carolina	Washington	3:07	Carolina 4, Washington 3
4-1-01—	Shane Willis, Carolina	Ottawa	1:18	Carolina 3, Ottawa 2
4-1-01—	Steve Yzerman, Detroit	Washington	0:11	Detroit 2, Washington 1
4-2-01—	Andrei Kovalenko, Boston	Montreal	2:53	Boston 3, Montreal 2
4-5-01—	Brian Savage, Montreal	Philadelphia	3:49	Montreal 3, Philadelphia 2
4-5-01—	Manny Malhotra, N.Y. Rangers	Tampa Bay	3:23	N.Y. Rangers 4, Tampa Bay 3
4-5-01—	Harold Druken, Vancouver	Los Angeles	3:19	Vancouver 3, Los Angeles 2
4-7-01—	John LeClair, Philadelphia	Pittsburgh	4:39	Philadelphia 4, Pittsburgh 3
4-7-01—	Mike Modano, Dallas	San Jose	2:10	Dallas 5, San Jose 4
4-8-01—	Tyler Wright, Columbus	Chicago	2:41	Columbus 4, Chicago 3

PENALTY-SHOT INFORMATION

Date	Shooter, Team	Goaltender, Team	Scored	Final score
10-11-00—	Brad Isbister, N.Y. Islanders	Glenn Healy, Toronto	No	Toronto 3, N.Y. Islanders 2
10-15-00—	David Vyborny, Columbus	Robbie Tallas, Chicago	Yes	Chicago 2, Columbus 1
10-15-00—	Scott Pellerin, Minnesota	Joaquin Gage, Edmonton	No	Edmonton 5, Minnesota 3
11-1-00—	Martin Straka, Pittsburgh	Evgeni Nabokov, San Jose	No	San Jose 3, Pittsburgh 2
11-3-00—	Dainius Zubrus, Montreal	Dominik Hasek, Buffalo	No	Buffalo 5, Montreal 4
11-9-00—	Robert Kron, Columbus	Steve Shields, San Jose	No	Columbus 5, San Jose 2
11-26-00—	Maxim Sushinsky, Minnesota	Felix Potvin, Vancouver	No	Minnesota 4, Vancouver 2
12-1-00—	Patrik Elias, New Jersey	John Vanbiesbrouck, NYI	No	New York Islanders 0, New Jersey 0
12-1-00—	Alex Tanguay, Colorado	Ed Belfour, Dallas	No	Colorado 4, Dallas 2
12-20-00—	Gary Roberts, Toronto	Mike Dunham, Nashville	No	Nashville 3, Toronto 1
12-20-00—	Antti Laaksonen, Minnesota	Patrick Lalime, Ottawa	No	Ottawa 2, Minnesota 2
12-23-00—	David Legwand, Nashville	Kirk McLean, N.Y. Rangers	Yes	Nashville 3, N.Y. Rangers 2
1-4-01—	Marian Hossa, Ottawa	Dan Cloutier, Tampa Bay	No	Ottawa 8, Tampa Bay 3
1-9-01—	Martin Straka, Pittsburgh	Byron Dafoe, Boston	No	Boston 5, Pittsburgh 2
1-20-01—	Daniel Alfredsson, Ottawa	Dan Cloutier, Tampa Bay	No	Ottawa 3, Tampa Bay 0
1-21-01—	Petr Sykora, New Jersey	Manny Fernandez, Minnesota	No	New Jersey 4, Minnesota 2

Date	Shooter, Team	Goaltender, Team	Scored	Final score
1-22-01—	Brett Hull, Dallas	Felix Potvin, Vancouver	No	Dallas 2, Vancouver 1
1-24-01—	Jeff Friesen, San Jose	Dominic Roussel, Edmonton	No	San Jose 6, Edmonton 1
1-30-01—	Martin Straka, Pittsburgh	Damian Rhodes, Atlanta	Yes	Pittsburgh 6, Atlanta 3
2-1-01—	Mike Johnson, Tampa Bay	Martin Biron, Buffalo	No	Tampa Bay 4, Buffalo 2
2-18-01—	Joe Nieuwendyk, Dallas	Chris Osgood, Detroit	Yes	Detroit 2, Dallas 1
2-21-01—	Ray Ferraro, Atlanta	Arturs Irbe, Carolina	Yes	Carolina 6, Atlanta 3
2-26-01—	Marty Reasoner, St. Louis	Evgeni Nabokov, San Jose	Yes	St. Louis 7, San Jose 2
2-27-01—	Dave Scatchard, N.Y. Islanders	Martin Brodeur, New Jersey	No	New Jersey 4, N.Y. Islanders 1
2-28-01—	Martin Rucinsky, Montreal	Jean-Sebastien Aubin, Pittsburgh	No	Montreal 4, Pittsburgh 2
2-28-01—	Jeremy Roenick, Phoenix	Marc Denis, Columbus	No	Columbus 5, Phoenix 2
3-18-01—	Andrew Cassels, Vancouver	Norm Maracle, Atlanta	No	Vancouver 5, Atlanta 3
3-19-01—	David Vyborny, Columbus	Tomas Vokoun, Nashville	Yes	Nashville 2, Columbus 1
3-22-01—	Alexei Zhamnov, Chicago	Tomas Vokoun, Nashville	No	Nashville 2, Chicago 1
3-29-01—	Martin Rucinsky, Montreal	Kevin Weekes, Tampa Bay	Yes	Montreal 6, Tampa Bay 2
3-30-01—	Joe Sacco, Washington	Arturs Irbe, Carolina	Yes	Carolina 4, Washington 3
4-7-01—	Zigmund Palffy, Los Angeles	Fred Brathwaite, Calgary	No	Los Angeles 3, Calgary 2

TEAM STREAKS

Most consecutive games won
New Jersey, Feb. 26-Mar. 23 13
Colorado, Oct. 10-28 9
Edmonton, Feb. 20-Mar. 13 9
St. Louis, Nov. 24-Dec. 15 8
St. Louis, Oct. 19-Nov. 2 7
Colorado, Jan. 16-30 7

Most consecutive games undefeated
Detroit, Jan 31-Mar. 2...........................13
New Jersey, Feb. 26-Mar. 23 13
Dallas, Mar. 13-Apr. 7 13
Phoenix, Oct. 14-Nov. 7 12
St. Louis, Nov. 24-Dec. 26 12
Washington, Jan. 28-Feb. 24 12

Most consecutive home games won
Detroit, Jan. 24-Feb. 25 8
Washington, Nov. 17-Dec. 16...............7
New Jersey, Feb. 26-Mar. 23 7
St. Louis, Oct. 13-Nov. 2 6
Colorado, Nov. 11-Dec. 1 6
Philadelphia, Jan. 20-Feb. 19 6
Detroit, Mar. 15-Apr. 7 6

Most consecutive home games undefeated
Detroit, Dec. 31-Apr. 7 19
Colorado, Nov. 3-Dec. 13 11
Buffalo, Oct. 5-Nov. 17 10
Six streaks of 9

Most consecutive road games won
New Jersey, Feb. 27-Apr. 7 10
Dallas, Mar. 13-Apr. 7 6
Colorado, Oct. 10-26 5
Toronto, Nov. 18-Dec. 13 5
St. Louis, Nov. 24-Dec. 20 5
Washington, Feb. 14-Mar. 7 5

Most consecutive road games undefeated
San Jose, Dec. 26-Feb. 16 10
New Jersey, Feb. 27-Apr. 7...................10
Washington, Feb. 7-Mar. 7 9
Phoenix, Oct. 15-Nov. 7 8
Edmonton, Feb. 12-Mar. 21 8

TEAM OVERTIME GAMES

Team	OVERALL					HOME					AWAY				
	G	W	L	T	Pct.	G	W	L	T	Pct.	G	W	L	T	Pct.
N.Y. Rangers	11	5	1	5	.682	6	2	1	3	.583	5	3	0	2	.800
Buffalo	10	4	1	5	.650	5	2	0	3	.700	5	2	1	2	.600
Detroit	23	10	4	9	.630	11	6	2	3	.682	12	4	2	6	.583
Dallas	16	6	2	8	.625	10	5	0	5	.750	6	1	2	3	.417
San Jose	22	7	3	12	.591	9	4	1	4	.667	13	3	2	8	.538
Carolina	18	6	3	9	.583	5	2	0	3	.700	13	4	3	6	.538
Nashville	17	5	3	9	.559	9	2	0	7	.611	8	3	3	2	.500
Philadelphia	19	5	3	11	.553	6	2	0	4	.667	13	3	3	7	.500
Colorado	20	6	4	10	.550	11	4	2	5	.591	9	2	2	5	.500
Edmonton	20	5	3	12	.550	12	3	2	7	.542	8	2	1	5	.563
New Jersey	20	5	3	12	.550	9	3	0	6	.667	11	2	3	6	.455
St. Louis	23	6	5	12	.522	11	3	3	5	.500	12	3	2	7	.542
Phoenix	23	3	3	17	.500	11	2	2	7	.500	12	1	1	10	.500
Los Angeles	19	3	3	13	.500	10	1	1	8	.500	9	2	2	5	.500
Atlanta	16	2	2	12	.500	9	1	2	6	.444	7	1	0	6	.571
Pittsburgh	15	3	3	9	.500	4	2	0	2	.750	11	1	3	7	.409
Minnesota	22	4	5	13	.477	16	2	4	10	.438	6	2	1	3	.583
Calgary	22	3	4	15	.477	13	2	2	9	.500	9	1	2	6	.444
Anaheim	20	4	5	11	.475	9	3	2	4	.556	11	1	3	7	.409
Ottawa	16	3	4	9	.469	9	1	3	5	.389	7	2	1	4	.571
N.Y. Islanders	12	2	3	7	.458	3	1	1	1	.500	9	1	2	6	.444
Vancouver	23	5	7	11	.457	11	3	3	5	.500	12	2	4	6	.417
Toronto	19	3	5	11	.447	11	0	4	7	.318	8	3	1	4	.625
Washington	16	2	4	10	.438	9	1	2	6	.444	7	1	2	4	.429
Columbus	18	3	6	9	.417	9	2	3	4	.444	9	1	3	5	.389
Boston	20	4	8	8	.400	11	3	3	5	.500	9	1	5	3	.278
Chicago	15	2	5	8	.400	7	1	2	4	.429	8	1	3	4	.375
Tampa Bay	13	2	5	6	.385	7	2	2	3	.500	6	0	3	3	.250
Montreal	16	2	6	8	.375	8	2	2	4	.500	8	0	4	4	.250
Florida	24	2	9	13	.354	13	2	4	7	.423	11	0	5	6	.273
Totals	274	122	122	152	.500	274	69	53	152	.529	274	53	69	152	.471

STANLEY CUP PLAYOFFS

CONFERENCE QUARTERFINALS

EASTERN CONFERENCE

	W	L	Pts.	GF	GA
New Jersey Devils	4	2	8	20	8
Carolina Hurricanes	2	4	4	8	20

(New Jersey won Eastern Conference quarterfinals, 4-2)
Thur. April 12—Carolina 1, at New Jersey 5
Sun. April 15—Carolina 0, at New Jersey 2
Tue. April 17—New Jersey 4, at Carolina 0
Wed. April 18—New Jersey 2, at Carolina 3 (a)
Fri. April 20—Carolina 3, at New Jersey 2
Sun. April 22—New Jersey 5, at Carolina 1
(a)—Rod Brind'Amour scored at 0:46 (OT) for Carolina.

	W	L	Pts.	GF	GA
Toronto Maple Leafs	4	0	8	10	3
Ottawa Senators	0	4	0	3	10

(Toronto won Eastern Conference quarterfinals, 4-0)
Fri. April 13—Toronto 1, at Ottawa 0 (b)
Sat. April 14—Toronto 3, at Ottawa 0
Mon. April 16—Ottawa 2, at Toronto 3 (c)
Wed. April 18—Ottawa 1, at Toronto 3
(b)—Mats Sundin scored at 10:49 (OT) for Toronto.
(c)—Cory Cross scored at 2:16 (OT) for Toronto.

	W	L	Pts.	GF	GA
Pittsburgh Penguins	4	2	8	14	10
Washington Capitals	2	4	4	10	14

(Pittsburgh won Eastern Conference quarterfinals, 4-2)
Thur. April 12—Pittsburgh 0, at Washington 1
Sat. April 14—Pittsburgh 2, at Washington 1
Mon. April 16—Washington 0, at Pittsburgh 3
Wed. April 18—Washington 4, at Pittsburgh 3 (d)
Sat. April 21—Pittsburgh 2, at Washington 1
Mon. April 23—Washington 3, at Pittsburgh 4 (e)
(d)—Jeff Halpern scored at 4:01 (OT) for Washington.
(e)—Martin Straka scored at 13:04 (OT) for Pittsburgh.

	W	L	Pts.	GF	GA
Buffalo Sabres	4	2	8	21	13
Philadelphia Flyers	2	4	4	13	21

(Buffalo won Eastern Conference quarterfinals, 4-2)
Wed. April 11—Buffalo 2, at Philadelphia 1
Sat. April 14—Buffalo 4, at Philadelphia 3 (f)
Mon. April 16—Philadelphia 3, at Buffalo 2
Tue. April 17—Philadelphia 3, at Buffalo 4 (g)
Thur. April 19—Buffalo 1, at Philadelphia 3
Sat. April 21—Philadelphia 0, at Buffalo 8
(f)—Jay McKee scored at 18:02 (OT) for Buffalo.
(g)—Curtis Brown scored at 6:13 (OT) for Buffalo.

WESTERN CONFERENCE

	W	L	Pts.	GF	GA
Colorado Avalanche	4	0	8	16	9
Vancouver Canucks	0	4	0	9	16

(Colorado won Western Conference quarterfinals, 4-0)
Thur. April 12—Vancouver 4, at Colorado 5
Sat. April 14—Vancouver 1, at Colorado 2
Mon. April 16—Colorado 4, at Vancouver 3 (h)
Wed. April 18—Colorado 5, at Vancouver 1
(h)—Peter Forsberg scored at 2:50 (OT) for Colorado.

	W	L	Pts.	GF	GA
Los Angeles Kings	4	2	8	15	17
Detroit Red Wings	2	4	4	17	15

(Los Angeles won Western Conference quarterfinals, 4-2)
Wed. April 11—Los Angeles 3, at Detroit 5

Sat. April 14—Los Angeles 0, at Detroit 4
Sun. April 15—Detroit 1, at Los Angeles 2
Wed. April 18—Detroit 3, at Los Angeles 4 (i)
Sat. April 21—Los Angeles 3, at Detroit 2
Mon. April 23—Detroit 2, at Los Angeles 3 (j)
(i)—Eric Belanger scored at 2:36 (OT) for Los Angeles.
(j)—Adam Deadmarsh scored at 4:48 (OT) for Los Angeles.

	W	L	Pts.	GF	GA
Dallas Stars	4	2	8	16	13
Edmonton Oilers	2	4	4	13	16

(Dallas won Western Conference quarterfinals, 4-2)
Wed. April 11—Edmonton 1, at Dallas 2 (k)
Sat. April 14—Edmonton 4, at Dallas 3
Sun. April 15—Dallas 3, at Edmonton 2 (l)
Tue. April 17—Dallas 1, at Edmonton 2 (m)
Thur. April 19—Edmonton 3, at Dallas 4 (n)
Sat. April 21—Dallas 3, at Edmonton 1
(k)—Jamie Langenbrunner scored at 2:08 (OT) for Dallas.
(l)—Benoit Hogue scored at 19:48 (OT) for Dallas.
(m)—Mike Comrie scored at 17:19 (OT) for Edmonton.
(n)—Kirk Muller scored at 8:01 (OT) for Dallas.

	W	L	Pts.	GF	GA
St. Louis Blues	4	2	8	16	11
San Jose Sharks	2	4	4	11	16

(St. Louis won Western Conference quarterfinals, 4-2)
Thur. April 12—San Jose 1, at St. Louis 3
Sat. April 14—San Jose 1, at St. Louis 0
Mon. April 16—St. Louis 6, at San Jose 3
Tue. April 17—St. Louis 2, at San Jose 3
Thur. April 19—San Jose 3, at St. Louis 3 (o)
Sat. April 21—St. Louis 2, at San Jose 1
(o)—Bryce Salvador scored at 9:54 (OT) for St. Louis.

CONFERENCE SEMIFINALS

EASTERN CONFERENCE

	W	L	Pts.	GF	GA
New Jersey Devils	4	3	8	21	18
Toronto Maple Leafs	3	4	6	18	21

(New Jersey won Eastern Conference semifinals, 4-3)
Thur. April 26—Toronto 2, at New Jersey 0
Sat. April 28—Toronto 5, at New Jersey 6 (p)
Tue. May 1—New Jersey 3, at Toronto 2 (q)
Thur. May 3—New Jersey 1, at Toronto 3
Sat. May 5—Toronto 3, at New Jersey 2
Mon. May 7—New Jersey 4, at Toronto 2
Wed. May 9—Toronto 1, at New Jersey 5
(p)—Randy McKay scored at 5:31 (OT) for New Jersey.
(q)—Brian Rafalski scored at 7:00 (OT) for New Jersey.

	W	L	Pts.	GF	GA
Pittsburgh Penguins	4	3	8	17	17
Buffalo Sabres	3	4	6	17	17

(Pittsburgh won Eastern Conference semifinals, 4-3)
Thur. April 26—Pittsburgh 3, at Buffalo 0
Sat. April 28—Pittsburgh 3, at Buffalo 1
Mon. April 30—Buffalo 4, at Pittsburgh 1
Wed. May 2—Buffalo 5, at Pittsburgh 2
Sat. May 5—Pittsburgh 2, at Buffalo 3 (r)
Tue. May 8—Buffalo 2, at Pittsburgh 3 (s)
Thur. May 10—Pittsburgh 3, at Buffalo 2 (t)
(r)—Stu Barnes scored at 8:34 (OT) for Buffalo.
(s)—Martin Straka scored at 11:29 (OT) for Pittsburgh.
(t)—Darius Kasparaitis scored at 13:01 (OT) for Pittsburgh.

WESTERN CONFERENCE

	W	L	Pts.	GF	GA
Colorado Avalanche	4	3	8	17	10
Los Angeles Kings	3	4	6	10	17

(Colorado won Western Conference semifinals, 4-3)

Thur. April 26—Los Angeles 4, at Colorado 3 (u)
Sat. April 28—Los Angeles 0, at Colorado 2
Mon. April 30—Colorado 4, at Los Angeles 3
Wed. May 2—Colorado 3, at Los Angeles 0
Fri. May 4—Los Angeles 1, at Colorado 0
Sun. May 6—Colorado 0, at Los Angeles 1 (v)
Wed. May 9—Los Angeles 1, at Colorado 5

(u)—Jaroslav Modry scored at 14:23 (OT) for Los Angeles.
(v)—Glen Murray scored at 2:41 (2OT) for Los Angeles.

	W	L	Pts.	GF	GA
St. Louis Blues	4	0	8	13	6
Dallas Stars	0	4	0	6	13

(St. Louis won Western Conference semifinals, 4-0)

Fri. April 27—St. Louis 4, at Dallas 2
Sun. April 29—St. Louis 2, at Dallas 1
Tue. May 1—Dallas 2, at St. Louis 3 (w)
Thur. May 3—Dallas 1, at St. Louis 4

(w)—Cory Stillman scored at 9:26 (2OT) for St. Louis.

CONFERENCE FINALS

EASTERN CONFERENCE

	W	L	Pts.	GF	GA
New Jersey Devils	4	1	8	17	7
Pittsburgh Penguins	1	4	2	7	17

(New Jersey won Eastern Conference finals, 4-1)

Sat. May 12—Pittsburgh 1, at New Jersey 3
Tue. May 15—Pittsburgh 4, at New Jersey 2
Thur. May 17—New Jersey 3, at Pittsburgh 0
Sat. May 19—New Jersey 5, at Pittsburgh 0
Tue. May 22—Pittsburgh 2, at New Jersey 4

WESTERN CONFERENCE

	W	L	Pts.	GF	GA
Colorado Avalanche	4	1	8	17	11
St. Louis Blues	1	4	2	11	17

(Colorado won Western Conference finals, 4-1)

Sat. May 12—St. Louis 1, at Colorado 4
Mon. May 14—St. Louis 2, at Colorado 4
Wed. May 16—Colorado 3, at St. Louis 4 (x)
Fri. May 18—Colorado 4, at St. Louis 3 (y)
Mon. May 21—St. Louis 1, at Colorado 2 (z)

(x)—Scott Young scored at 10:27 (2OT) for St. Louis.
(y)—Stephane Yelle scored at 4:23 (OT) for Colorado.
(z)—Joe Sakic scored at 0:24 (OT) for Colorado.

STANLEY CUP FINALS

	W	L	Pts.	GF	GA
Colorado Rockies	4	3	8	19	11
New Jersey Devils	3	4	6	11	19

(Colorado won on Stanley Cup championship, 4-3)

Sat. May 26—New Jersey 0, at Colorado 5
Tue. May 29—New Jersey 2, at Colorado 1
Thur. May 31—Colorado 3, at New Jersey 1
Sat. June 2—Colorado 2, at New Jersey 3
Mon. June 4—New Jersey 4, at Colorado 1
Thur. June 7—Colorado 4, at New Jersey 0
Sat. June 9—New Jersey 1, at Colorado 3

GAME SUMMARIES, STANLEY CUP FINALS

GAME 1

AT COLORADO, MAY 26

Colorado 5, New Jersey 0

New Jersey	0	0	0	—	0
Colorado	1	2	2	—	5

FIRST PERIOD—1. Colorado, Sakic 10 (Hejduk, Blake), 11:07. Penalties—White, New Jersey (holding), 4:28; Podein, Colorado (elbowing), 13:46.

SECOND PERIOD—2. Colorado, Drury 9 (Hinote, Nieminen), 9:35. 3. Colorado, Sakic 11 (Blake, Skoula), 15:06. Penalties—De Vries, Colorado (boarding), 7:01; Tanguay, Colorado (tripping), 10:46; Daneyko, New Jersey (boarding), 14:16; Nieminen, Colorado (goalie interference), 14:16.

THIRD PERIOD—4. Colorado, Blake 5 (Tanguay, Sakic), 5:36 (pp). 5. Colorado, Reinprecht 2 (Dingman, Reid), 17:36. Penalties—Hinote, Colorado (holding), 3:30; Stevenson, New Jersey (goalie interference), 4:45; White, New Jersey (roughing), 8:04; Sykora, New Jersey (charging), 8:04; Foote, Colorado (double roughing minor), 8:04; Daneyko, New Jersey (slashing, roughing), 9:43; O'Donnell, New Jersey (roughing), 11:34; Podein, Colorado (tripping), 11:34; De Vries, Colorado (tripping), 13:20; O'Donnell, New Jersey served by Gomez (instigator, fighting major, game misconduct), 17:36; Dingman, Colorado (fighting major), 17:36; Hinote, Colorado (roughing), 18:20.

Shots on goal—New Jersey 7-11-7-25; Colorado 14-7-9-30. Power-play opportunities—New Jersey 0 of 6; Colorado 1 of 5. Goalies—New Jersey, Brodeur 12-7 (30 shots-25 saves); Colorado, Roy 13-4 (25-25). A—18,007. Referees—Paul Devorski, Dan Marouelli. Linesmen—Brad Lazarowich, Dan Schachte.

GAME 2

AT COLORADO, MAY 29

New Jersey 2, Colorado 1

New Jersey	2	0	0	—	2
Colorado	1	0	0	—	1

FIRST PERIOD—1. Colorado, Sakic 12 (Hejduk, Blake), 5:58 (pp). 2. New Jersey, Corkum 1 (Rafalski), 14:29. 3. New Jersey, Stevenson 1 (Niedermayer, Mogilny), 17:20. Penalties—Niedermayer, New Jersey (cross-checking), 1:43; Brylin, New Jersey (interference), 4:53; Elias, New Jersey (slashing), 12:28; Messier, Colorado (roughing), 14:46; Foote, Colorado (holding stick), 15:17; Holik, New Jersey (slashing), 19:39.

SECOND PERIOD—No scoring. Penalties—DeVries, Colorado (interference), 9:11; Madden, New Jersey (diving), 9:11; Skoula, Colorado (holding), 14:47.

THIRD PERIOD—No scoring. Penalties—Daneyko, New Jersey (cross-checking), 1:28; White, New Jersey (roughing), 2:58; Nieminen, Colorado (roughing), 2:58; Mogilny, New Jersey (high-sticking), 4:26.

Shots on goal—New Jersey 12-6-2-20; Colorado 8-4-8-20. Power-play opportunities—New Jersey 0 of 3; Colorado 1 of 6. Goalies—New Jersey, Brodeur 13-7 (20 shots-19 saves); Colorado, Roy 13-5 (20-18). A—18,007. Referees—Bill McCreary, Rob Shick. Linesmen—Brad Lazarowich, Mark Wheler.

GAME 3

AT NEW JERSEY, MAY 31

Colorado 3, New Jersey 1

Colorado	1	0	2	—	3
New Jersey	1	0	0	—	1

FIRST PERIOD—1. New Jersey, Arnott 8 (Holik, Elias), 3:16 (pp). 2. Colorado, Skoula 1 (Podein, Messier), 10:38. Penalties—Foote, Colorado (tripping), 1:29; Yelle, Colorado (interference), 6:28; Brylin, New Jersey (interference), 14:29; Tanguay, Colorado (hooking), 15:03; Nieminen, Colorado (boarding), 16:29.

SECOND PERIOD—No scoring. Penalties—O'Donnell, New Jersey (cross-checking), 2:40; O'Donnell, New Jersey (holding), 8:25; Foote, Colorado (tripping), 14:52; Arnott, New Jersey (boarding), 19:02.

THIRD PERIOD—3. Colorado, Bourque 4 (Sakic), 0:31 (pp). 4. Colorado, Hinote 2 (Nieminen, Drury), 6:28. Penalties—Klemm, Colorado (holding), 8:22.

Shots on goal—Colorado 5-11-5-21; New Jersey 8-3-11-22. Power-play opportunities—Colorado 1 of 4; New Jersey 1 of 6. Goalies—Colorado, Roy 14-5 (22 shots-21 saves); New Jersey, Brodeur 13-8 (21-19). A—19,040. Referees—Kerry Fraser, Dan Marouelli. Linesmen—Kevin Collins, Dan Schachte.

GAME 4

AT NEW JERSEY, JUNE 2

New Jersey 3, Colorado 2

| Colorado | 1 | 1 | 0 | — | 2 |
| New Jersey | 0 | 1 | 2 | — | 3 |

FIRST PERIOD—1. Colorado, Blake 6 (Tanguay), 3:58. Penalties—Stevenson, New Jersey (interference) 1:36; Gomez, New Jersey (goalie interference), 4:42; Yelle, Colorado (diving), 7:15; Sykora, New Jersey (hooking), 7:15; Stevens, New Jersey (hooking), 7:42; Sakic, Colorado (hooking), 8:26.

SECOND PERIOD—2. New Jersey, Elias 8 (Sykora), 3:42 (sh). 3. Colorado, Drury 10 (Dingman, Hinote), 13:54. Penalties—White, New Jersey (roughing), 2:18; Skoula, Colorado (interference), 10:16; Stevenson, New Jersey (tripping), 16:42.

THIRD PERIOD—4. New Jersey, Gomez 5 (Pandolfo, Corkum), 8:09. 5. New Jersey, Sykora 9 (Elias, Holik), 17:23.

Shots on goal—Colorado 4-4-4-12; New Jersey 8-11-16-35. Power-play opportunities—Colorado 0 of 5; New Jersey 0 of 2. Goalies—Colorado, Roy 14-6 (35 shots-32 saves); New Jersey, Brodeur 14-8 (12-10). A—19,040. Referees—Paul Devorski, Bill McCreary. Linesmen—Kevin Collins, Dan Schachte.

GAME 5

AT COLORADO, JUNE 4

New Jersey 4, Colorado 1

| New Jersey | 2 | 1 | 1 | — | 4 |
| Colorado | 1 | 0 | 0 | — | 1 |

FIRST PERIOD—1. New Jersey, Elias 9 (Sykora, Rafalski), 3:09. 2. Colorado, Tanguay 3 (Sakic, Bourque), 10:09 (pp). 3. New Jersey, Mogilny 5 (Gomez, Rafalski), 18:47. Penalties—Holik, New Jersey (tripping), 8:56; New Jersey bench, served by Gomez (too many men on the ice), 19:24.

SECOND PERIOD—4. New Jersey, Brylin 3 (Mogilny, Niedermayer), 4:39 (pp). Penalties—Blake, Colorado (interference), 3:53; Niedermayer, New Jersey (interference), 16:33.

THIRD PERIOD—5. New Jersey, Madden 4 (Stevenson, Brylin), 18:05. Penalties—McKenzie, New Jersey (holding), 12:54; Sutton, New Jersey (roughing), 20:00; Hinote, Colorado (roughing), 20:00.

Shots on goal—New Jersey 6-10-10-26; Colorado 6-9-8-23. Power-play opportunities—New Jersey 1 of 1; Colorado 1 of 4. Goalies—New Jersey, Brodeur 15-8 (23 shots-22 saves); Colorado, Roy 14-7 (26-22). A—18,007. Referees—Kerry Fraser, Rob Shick. Linesmen—Brad Lazarowich, Mark Wheler.

GAME 6

AT NEW JERSEY, JUNE 7

Colorado 4, New Jersey 0

| Colorado | 1 | 2 | 1 | — | 4 |
| New Jersey | 0 | 0 | 0 | — | 0 |

FIRST PERIOD—1. Colorado, Foote 3 (unassisted), 18:02. Penalties—Reid, Colorado (obstruction-holding stick), 5:22; Foote, Colorado (high-sticking), 7:20; Mogilny, New Jersey (hooking), 9:12; Skoula, Colorado (hooking), 11:08.

SECOND PERIOD—2. Colorado, Nieminen 4 (Skoula, Foote), 2:26 (pp). 3. Colorado, Drury 11 (Reinprecht, Foote), 18:27. Penalties—Holik, New Jersey (roughing), 0:29; Colorado bench, served by Nieminen (too many men on the ice), 8:35; Niedermayer, New Jersey (holding), 11:10; Bourque, Colorado (obstruction-hooking), 13:01.

THIRD PERIOD—4. Colorado, Tanguay 4 (Reid, Sakic), 13:46. Penalties—Podein, Colorado (interference), 3:24; Niedermayer, New Jersey (slashing), 8:26; White, New Jersey (slashing), 17:27; Hinote, Colorado (fighting major), 18:19; Sutton, New Jersey (roughing, fighting major), 18:19; White, New Jersey (high sticking), 19:43; Dingman, Colorado (fighting major), 19:48; Daneyko, New Jersey (fighting major), 19:48.

Shots on goal—Colorado 5-7-6-18; New Jersey 12-7-5-24. Power-play opportunities—Colorado 1 of 7; New Jersey 0 of 6. Goalies—Colorado, Roy 15-7 (24 shots-24 saves); New Jersey, Brodeur 15-9 (18-14). A—19,040. Referees—Dan Marouelli, Bill McCreary. Linesmen—Kevin Collins, Brad Lazarowich.

GAME 7

AT COLORADO, JUNE 9

Colorado 3, New Jersey 1

| New Jersey | 0 | 1 | 0 | — | 1 |
| Colorado | 1 | 2 | 0 | — | 3 |

FIRST PERIOD—1. Colorado, Tanguay 5 (Hinote), 7:58. Penalties—Brylin, New Jersey (boarding), 3:20; Gomez, New Jersey (holding), 16:06.

SECOND PERIOD—2. Colorado, Tanguay 6 (Sakic, Foote), 4:57. 3. Colorado, Sakic 13 (Hejduk, Tanguay), 6:16 (pp). 4. New Jersey, Sykora 10 (Elias, Arnott), 9:33 (pp). Penalties—O'Donnell, New Jersey (high sticking), 5:51; Messier, Colorado (high sticking), 9:22; Messier, Colorado (holding), 12:23; Arnott, New Jersey (tripping), 12:23.

THIRD PERIOD—No scoring. Penalties—Blake, Colorado (interference), 4:59; White, New Jersey (high-sticking), 10:32; Foote, Colorado (holding stick), 12:11; Stevens, New Jersey (tripping), 14:46.

Shots on goal—New Jersey 9-12-5-26; Colorado 10-7-5-22. Power-play opportunities—New Jersey 1 of 3; Colorado 1 of 5. Goalies—New Jersey, Brodeur 15-10 (22 shots-19 saves); Colorado, Roy 16-7 (26-25). A—18,007. Referees—Kerry Fraser, Dan Marouelli. Linesmen—Kevin Collins, Dan Schachte.

INDIVIDUAL LEADERS

Goals: Joe Sakic, Colorado (13)
Assists: Milan Hejduk, Colorado (16)
Points: Joe Sakic, Colorado (26)
Penalty minutes: Adam Foote, Colorado (47)
Goaltending average: Patrick Roy, Colorado (1.70)
Shutouts: Martin Brodeur, New Jersey (4)
Patrick Roy, Colorado (4)

TOP SCORERS

	Games	G	A	Pts.	PIM
Joe Sakic, Colorado	21	13	13	26	6
Patrik Elias, New Jersey	25	9	14	23	10
Milan Hejduk, Colorado	23	7	16	23	6
Petr Sykora, New Jersey	25	10	12	22	12
Alex Tanguay, Colorado	23	6	15	21	8
Rob Blake, Colorado	23	6	13	19	16
Brian Rafalski, New Jersey	25	7	11	18	7
Mario Lemieux, Pittsburgh	18	6	11	17	4
Chris Drury, Colorado	23	11	5	16	4
Bobby Holik, New Jersey	25	6	10	16	37
Alexander Mogilny, New Jersey	25	5	11	16	8

BUFFALO SABRES

(Lost Eastern Conference semifinals to Pittsburgh, 4-3)

SCORING

	Games	G	A	Pts.	PIM
Miroslav Satan	13	3	10	13	8
Chris Gratton	13	6	4	10	14
Donald Audette	13	3	6	9	4
Stu Barnes	13	4	4	8	2
Jean-Pierre Dumont	13	4	3	7	8
Steve Heinze	13	3	4	7	10
Alexei Zhitnik	13	1	6	7	12
Doug Gilmour	13	2	4	6	12
Jason Woolley	8	1	5	6	2
Curtis Brown	13	5	0	5	8
Maxim Afinogenov	11	2	3	5	4
Vaclav Varada	13	0	4	4	8
Dave Andreychuk	13	1	2	3	4
James Patrick	13	1	2	3	2
Dimitri Kalinin	13	0	2	2	4
Rhett Warrener	13	0	2	2	4
Jay McKee	8	1	0	1	6
Vladimir Tsyplakov	9	1	0	1	4
Erik Rasmussen	3	0	1	1	0
Richard Smehlik	10	0	1	1	4
Rob Ray	3	0	0	0	2
Dominik Hasek (goalie)	13	0	0	0	14

GOALTENDING

	Gms.	Min.	W	L	T	G	SO	Avg.
Dominik Hasek	13	833	7	6	0	29	1	2.09

CAROLINA HURRICANES

(Lost Eastern Conference quarterfinals to New Jersey, 4-2)

SCORING

	Games	G	A	Pts.	PIM
Sami Kapanen	6	2	3	5	0
Rod Brind'Amour	6	1	3	4	6
Jeff O'Neill	6	1	2	3	10
David Tanabe	6	2	0	2	12
Josef Vasicek	6	2	0	2	0
Bates Battaglia	6	0	2	2	2
Jeff Daniels	6	0	2	2	2
Sandis Ozolinsh	6	0	2	2	5
Martin Gelinas	6	0	1	1	6
Shane Willis	2	0	0	0	0
Craig Adams	3	0	0	0	0
Ron Francis	3	0	0	0	0
Marek Malik	3	0	0	0	6
Niclas Wallin	3	0	0	0	0
Darren Langdon	4	0	0	0	12
Rob DiMaio	6	0	0	0	4
Kevin Hatcher	6	0	0	0	6
Arturs Irbe (goalie)	6	0	0	0	4
Dave Karpa	6	0	0	0	17
Scott Pellerin	6	0	0	0	4
Glen Wesley	6	0	0	0	0
Tommy Westlund	6	0	0	0	17

GOALTENDING

	Gms.	Min.	W	L	T	G	SO	Avg.
Arturs Irbe	6	360	2	4	0	20	0	3.33

COLORADO AVALANCHE

(Winner of 2001 Stanley Cup)

SCORING

	Games	G	A	Pts.	PIM
Joe Sakic	21	13	13	26	6
Milan Hejduk	23	7	16	23	6
Alex Tanguay	23	6	15	21	8
Rob Blake	23	6	13	19	16
Chris Drury	23	11	5	16	4
Peter Forsberg	11	4	10	14	6
Ray Bourque	21	4	6	10	12
Ville Nieminen	23	4	6	10	20
Adam Foote	23	3	4	7	47
Dan Hinote	23	2	4	6	21
Steven Reinprecht	22	2	3	5	2
Shjon Podein	23	2	3	5	14
Martin Skoula	23	1	4	5	8
Eric Messier	23	2	2	4	14
Chris Dingman	16	0	4	4	14
Dave Reid	18	0	4	4	6
Jon Klemm	22	1	2	3	16
Stephane Yelle	23	1	2	3	8
Greg De Vries	23	0	1	1	20
Patrick Roy (goalie)	23	0	1	1	0
David Aebischer (goalie)	1	0	0	0	0
Bryan Muir	3	0	0	0	0
Scott Parker	4	0	0	0	2

GOALTENDING

	Gms.	Min.	W	L	T	G	SO	Avg.
David Aebischer	1	1	0	0	0	0	0	0.00
Patrick Roy	23	1451	16	7	0	41	4	1.70

DALLAS STARS

(Lost Western Conference semifinals to St. Louis, 4-0)

SCORING

	Games	G	A	Pts.	PIM
Mike Modano	9	3	4	7	0
Brett Hull	10	2	5	7	6
Sergei Zubov	10	1	5	6	4
Mike Keane	10	3	2	5	4
Joe Nieuwendyk	7	4	0	4	4
Jamie Langenbrunner	10	2	2	4	6
Kirk Muller	10	1	3	4	12
Darryl Sydor	10	1	3	4	0
John Maclean	10	2	1	3	6
Brenden Morrow	10	0	3	3	12
Shaun Van Allen	8	0	2	2	8
Benoit Hogue	7	1	0	1	6
Jere Lehtinen	10	1	0	1	2
Brad Lukowich	10	1	0	1	0
Ted Donato	8	0	1	1	0
Grant Ledyard	9	0	1	1	4
Derian Hatcher	10	0	1	1	16
Tyler Bouck	1	0	0	0	0
Sami Helenius	1	0	0	0	0
Roman Lyashenko	1	0	0	0	0
Grant Marshall	9	0	0	0	0
Ed Belfour (goalie)	10	0	0	0	6
Richard Matvichuk	10	0	0	0	14

GOALTENDING

	Gms.	Min.	W	L	T	G	SO	Avg.
Ed Belfour	10	671	4	6	0	25	0	2.24

DETROIT RED WINGS

(Lost Western Conference quarterfinals to Los Angeles, 4-2)

SCORING

	Games	G	A	Pts.	PIM
Nicklas Lidstrom	6	1	7	8	0
Sergei Fedorov	6	2	5	7	0
Steve Duchesne	6	2	4	6	0
Vyacheslav Kozlov	6	4	1	5	2
Brendan Shanahan	2	2	2	4	0
Tomas Holmstrom	6	1	3	4	8
Igor Larionov	6	1	3	4	0
Pat Verbeek	5	2	0	2	6
Chris Chelios	5	1	0	1	2
Darren McCarty	6	1	0	1	2
Brent Gilchrist	5	0	1	1	0
Mathieu Dandenault	6	0	1	1	0
Kris Draper	6	0	1	1	2
Martin Lapointe	6	0	1	1	8
Larry Murphy	6	0	1	1	0
Steve Yzerman	1	0	0	0	0
Boyd Devereaux	2	0	0	0	0
Jason Williams	2	0	0	0	0
Doug Brown	4	0	0	0	2
Jiri Fischer	5	0	0	0	9
Todd Gill	5	0	0	0	8
Kirk Maltby	6	0	0	0	6
Chris Osgood (goalie)	6	0	0	0	0

GOALTENDING

	Gms.	Min.	W	L	T	G	SO	Avg.
Chris Osgood	6	365	2	4	0	15	1	2.47

EDMONTON OILERS

(Lost Western Conference quarterfinals to Dallas, 4-2)

SCORING

	Games	G	A	Pts.	PIM
Ryan Smyth	6	3	4	7	4
Eric Brewer	6	1	5	6	2
Doug Weight	6	1	5	6	17
Anson Carter	6	3	1	4	4
Mike Comrie	6	1	2	3	0
Rem Murray	6	2	0	2	6
Daniel Cleary	6	1	1	2	8
Georges Laraque	6	1	1	2	8
Janne Niinimaa	6	0	2	2	6
Tom Poti	6	0	2	2	2
Jason Smith	6	0	2	2	6
Josh Green	3	0	0	0	0
Domenic Pittis	3	0	0	0	0
Sergei Zholtok	3	0	0	0	2
Ethan Moreau	4	0	0	0	2
Shawn Horcoff	5	0	0	0	0
Scott Ferguson	6	0	0	0	0
Mike Grier	6	0	0	0	8
Todd Marchant	6	0	0	0	4
Tommy Salo (goalie)	6	0	0	0	0
Igor Ulanov	6	0	0	0	4

GOALTENDING

	Gms.	Min.	W	L	T	G	SO	Avg.
Tommy Salo	6	406	2	4	0	15	0	2.22

LOS ANGELES KINGS

(Lost Western Conference semifinals to Colorado, 4-3)

SCORING

	Games	G	A	Pts.	PIM
Mathieu Schneider	13	0	9	9	10
Zigmund Palffy	13	3	5	8	8
Jozef Stumpel	13	3	5	8	10
Glen Murray	13	4	3	7	4
Luc Robitaille	13	4	3	7	10
Adam Deadmarsh	13	3	3	6	4
Bryan Smolinski	13	1	5	6	14
Eric Belanger	13	1	4	5	2
Nelson Emerson	13	2	2	4	4
Ian Laperriere	13	1	2	3	12
Mattias Norstrom	13	0	2	2	18
Kelly Buchberger	8	1	0	1	2
Jaroslav Modry	10	1	0	1	4
Scott Thomas	12	1	0	1	4
Philippe Boucher	13	0	1	1	2
Aaron Miller	13	0	1	1	6
Stephane Fiset (goalie)	1	0	0	0	0
Andreas Lilja	1	0	0	0	0
Stu Grimson	5	0	0	0	4
Steve Kelly	8	0	0	0	2
Lubomir Visnovsky	8	0	0	0	0
Jere Karalahti	13	0	0	0	18
Felix Potvin (goalie)	13	0	0	0	4

GOALTENDING

	Gms.	Min.	W	L	T	G	SO	Avg.
Stephane Fiset	1	0	0	0	0	0	0	0.00
Felix Potvin	13	812	7	6	0	33	2	2.44

NEW JERSEY DEVILS

(Lost Stanley Cup finals to Colorado, 4-3)

SCORING

	Games	G	A	Pts.	PIM
Patrik Elias	25	9	14	23	10
Petr Sykora	25	10	12	22	12
Brian Rafalski	25	7	11	18	7
Bobby Holik	25	6	10	16	37
Alexander Mogilny	25	5	11	16	8
Jason Arnott	23	8	7	15	16
Scott Gomez	25	5	9	14	24
Randy McKay	19	6	3	9	8
Scott Stevens	25	1	7	8	37
John Madden	25	4	3	7	6
Sergei Brylin	20	3	4	7	6
Scott Niedermayer	21	0	6	6	14
Jay Pandolfo	25	1	4	5	4
Turner Stevenson	23	1	3	4	20
Sergei Nemchinov	25	1	3	4	4
Bob Corkum	12	1	2	3	0
Sean O'Donnell	23	1	2	3	41
Ken Daneyko	25	0	3	3	21
Colin White	25	0	3	3	42
Martin Brodeur (goalie)	25	0	1	1	0
Jim McKenzie	3	0	0	0	2
Ken Sutton	6	0	0	0	13

GOALTENDING

	Gms.	Min.	W	L	T	G	SO	Avg.
Martin Brodeur	25	1505	15	10	0	52	4	2.07

OTTAWA SENATORS

(Lost Eastern Conference quarterfinals to Toronto, 4-0)

SCORING

	Games	G	A	Pts.	PIM
Marian Hossa	4	1	1	2	4
Shawn McEachern	4	0	2	2	2
Chris Phillips	1	1	0	1	0
Daniel Alfredsson	4	1	0	1	2
Mike Fisher	4	0	1	1	4
Eric Lacroix	4	0	1	1	0
Alexei Yashin	4	0	1	1	0

	Games	G	A	Pts.	PIM
Shane Hnidy	1	0	0	0	0
Jamie Rivers	1	0	0	0	4
Magnus Arvedson	2	0	0	0	0
Radek Bonk	2	0	0	0	2
Ricard Persson	2	0	0	0	0
Andre Roy	2	0	0	0	16
Todd White	2	0	0	0	0
Karel Rachunek	3	0	0	0	0
Andreas Dackell	4	0	0	0	0
Martin Havlat	4	0	0	0	2
Patrick Lalime (goalie)	4	0	0	0	0
Curtis Leschyshyn	4	0	0	0	0
Wade Redden	4	0	0	0	0
Sami Salo	4	0	0	0	0
Mike Sillinger	4	0	0	0	2
Jason York	4	0	0	0	4
Rob Zamuner	4	0	0	0	6

GOALTENDING

	Gms.	Min.	W	L	T	G	SO	Avg.
Patrick Lalime	4	251	0	4	0	10	0	2.39

PHILADELPHIA FLYERS

(Lost Eastern Conference quarterfinals to Buffalo, 4-2)

SCORING

	Games	G	A	Pts.	PIM
Daymond Langkow	6	2	4	6	2
Mark Recchi	6	2	2	4	2
Simon Gagne	6	3	0	3	0
John Leclair	6	1	2	3	2
Kent Manderville	6	1	2	3	2
Keith Primeau	4	0	3	3	8
Eric Desjardins	6	1	1	2	0
Paul Ranheim	6	0	2	2	2
Andy Delmore	2	1	0	1	2
Daniel McGillis	6	1	0	1	6
Chris Therien	6	1	0	1	8
Derek Plante	5	0	1	1	0
Ruslan Fedotenko	6	0	1	1	4
Michal Sykora	6	0	1	1	0
Rick Tocchet	6	0	1	1	6
Brian Boucher (goalie)	1	0	0	0	0
Todd Fedoruk	2	0	0	0	20
Chris McAllister	2	0	0	0	0
P.J. Stock	2	0	0	0	0
Peter White	3	0	0	0	0
Dean McAmmond	4	0	0	0	2
Roman Cechmanek (goalie)	6	0	0	0	0
Jody Hull	6	0	0	0	4
Luke Richardson	6	0	0	0	4

GOALTENDING

	Gms.	Min.	W	L	T	G	SO	Avg.
Roman Cechmanek	6	347	2	4	0	18	0	3.11
Brian Boucher	1	37	0	0	0	3	0	4.86

PITTSBURGH PENGUINS

(Lost Eastern Conference finals to New Jersey, 4-1)

SCORING

	Games	G	A	Pts.	PIM
Mario Lemieux	18	6	11	17	4
Martin Straka	18	5	8	13	8
Jaromir Jagr	16	2	10	12	18
Alexei Kovalev	18	5	5	10	16
Andrew Ference	18	3	7	10	16
Robert Lang	16	4	4	8	4
Jan Hrdina	18	2	5	7	8
Kevin Stevens	17	3	3	6	20
Alexei Morozov	18	3	3	6	6

	Games	G	A	Pts.	PIM
Janne Laukkanen	18	2	2	4	14
Wayne Primeau	18	1	3	4	2
Darius Kasparaitis	17	1	1	2	26
Josef Beranek	13	0	2	2	2
Rene Corbet	17	1	0	1	12
Marc Bergevin	12	0	1	1	2
Bob Boughner	18	0	1	1	22
Ian Moran	18	0	1	1	4
J-Sebastien Aubin (goalie)	1	0	0	0	0
Dan Lacouture	5	0	0	0	0
Krzysztof Oliwa	5	0	0	0	16
Milan Kraft	8	0	0	0	2
Hans Jonsson	16	0	0	0	8
Johan Hedberg (goalie)	18	0	0	0	0

GOALTENDING

	Gms.	Min.	W	L	T	G	SO	Avg.
J.-Sebastien Aubin	1	1	0	0	0	0	0	0.00
Johan Hedberg	18	1123	9	9	0	43	2	2.30

ST. LOUIS BLUES

(Lost Western Conference finals to Colorado, 4-1)

SCORING

	Games	G	A	Pts.	PIM
Pierre Turgeon	15	5	10	15	2
Scott Young	15	6	7	13	2
Al MacInnis	15	2	8	10	18
Keith Tkachuk	15	2	7	9	20
Cory Stillman	15	3	5	8	8
Chris Pronger	15	1	7	8	32
Dallas Drake	15	4	2	6	16
Scott Mellanby	15	3	3	6	17
Pavol Demitra	15	2	4	6	2
Jochen Hecht	15	2	4	6	4
Alexander Khavanov	15	3	2	5	14
Jamal Mayers	15	2	3	5	8
Marty Reasoner	10	3	1	4	0
Bryce Salvador	14	2	0	2	18
Mike Eastwood	15	0	2	2	2
Pascal Rheaume	3	0	1	1	0
Daniel Corso	12	0	1	1	0
Sean Hill	15	0	1	1	12
Todd Reirden	1	0	0	0	0
Jeff Finley	2	0	0	0	0
Brent Johnson (goalie)	2	0	0	0	0
Reid Simpson	5	0	0	0	2
Alexei Gusarov	13	0	0	0	4
Roman Turek (goalie)	14	0	0	0	2

GOALTENDING

	Gms.	Min.	W	L	T	G	SO	Avg.
Brent Johnson	2	62	0	1	0	2	0	1.94
Roman Turek	14	908	9	5	0	31	0	2.05

SAN JOSE SHARKS

(Lost Western Conference quarterfinals to St. Louis, 4-2)

SCORING

	Games	G	A	Pts.	PIM
Stephane Matteau	6	1	3	4	0
Scott Thornton	6	3	0	3	8
Vincent Damphousse	6	2	1	3	14
Mike Ricci	6	0	3	3	0
Niklas Sundstrom	6	0	3	3	2
Patrick Marleau	6	2	0	2	4
Owen Nolan	6	1	1	2	8
Teemu Selanne	6	0	2	2	2
Marco Sturm	6	0	2	2	0
Tony Granato	4	1	0	1	4
Brad Stuart	5	1	0	1	0

	Games	G	A	Pts.	PIM
Bryan Marchment	5	0	1	1	2
Marcus Ragnarsson	5	0	1	1	8
Scott Hannan	6	0	1	1	6
Jeff Norton	6	0	1	1	2
Mike Rathje	6	0	1	1	4
Gary Suter	1	0	0	0	0
Shawn Heins	2	0	0	0	0
Alexander Korolyuk	2	0	0	0	0
Miikka Kiprusoff (goalie)	3	0	0	0	0
Evgeni Nabokov (goalie)	4	0	0	0	0
Todd Harvey	6	0	0	0	8
Bill Lindsay	6	0	0	0	16

GOALTENDING

	Gms.	Min.	W	L	T	G	SO	Avg.
Miikka Kiprusoff	3	149	1	1	0	5	0	2.01
Evgeni Nabokov	4	218	1	3	0	10	1	2.75

TORONTO MAPLE LEAFS

(Lost Eastern Conference semifinals to New Jersey, 4-3)

SCORING

	Games	G	A	Pts.	PIM
Mats Sundin	11	6	7	13	14
Gary Roberts	11	2	9	11	0
Steve Thomas	11	6	3	9	4
Sergel Berezln	11	2	5	7	2
Bryan McCabe	11	2	3	5	16
Yanic Perreault	11	2	3	5	4
Tomas Kaberle	11	1	3	4	0
Dmitry Yushkevich	11	0	4	4	12
Nik Antropov	9	2	1	3	12
Cory Cross	11	2	1	3	10
Shayne Corson	11	1	1	2	14
Danny Markov	11	1	1	2	12
Aki Berg	11	0	2	2	4
Darcy Tucker	11	0	2	2	6
Garry Valk	5	1	0	1	2
Tie Domi	8	0	1	1	20
Dave Manson	2	0	0	0	2
Jonas Hoglund	10	0	0	0	4
Alyn McCauley	10	0	0	0	2
Curtis Joseph (goalie)	11	0	0	0	4
Igor Korolev	11	0	0	0	0

GOALTENDING

	Gms.	Min.	W	L	T	G	SO	Avg.
Curtis Joseph	11	685	7	4	0	24	3	2.10

VANCOUVER CANUCKS

(Lost Western Conference quarterfinals to Colorado, 4-0)

SCORING

	Games	G	A	Pts.	PIM
Todd Bertuzzi	4	2	2	4	8
Mattias Ohlund	4	1	3	4	6

	Games	G	A	Pts.	PIM
Henrik Sedin	4	0	4	4	0
Trent Klatt	4	3	0	3	0
Brendan Morrison	4	1	2	3	0
Daniel Sedin	4	1	2	3	0
Ed Jovanovski	4	1	1	2	0
Scott Lachance	2	0	1	1	2
Harold Druken	4	0	1	1	0
Denis Pederson	4	0	1	1	4
Jarkko Ruutu	4	0	1	1	8
Bryan Allen	2	0	0	0	2
Dan Cloutier (goalie)	2	0	0	0	0
Bob Essensa (goalie)	2	0	0	0	0
Jason Strudwick	2	0	0	0	0
Pat Kavanagh	3	0	0	0	2
Peter Schaefer	3	0	0	0	0
Murray Baron	4	0	0	0	0
Drake Berehowsky	4	0	0	0	12
Donald Brashear	4	0	0	0	0
Matt Cooke	4	0	0	0	4
Brent Sopel	4	0	0	0	2

GOALTENDING

	Gms.	Min.	W	L	T	G	SO	Avg.
Bob Essensa	2	122	0	2	0	6	0	2.95
Dan Cloutier	2	117	0	2	0	9	0	4.62

WASHINGTON CAPITALS

(Lost Eastern Conference quarterfinals to Pittsburgh, 4-2)

SCORING

	Games	G	A	Pts.	PIM
Jeff Halpern	6	2	3	5	17
Steve Konowalchuk	6	2	3	5	14
Sergei Gonchar	6	1	3	4	2
Trevor Linden	6	0	4	4	14
Calle Johansson	6	1	2	3	2
Peter Bondra	6	2	0	2	2
Brendan Witt	6	2	0	2	12
Ulf Dahlen	6	0	1	1	2
Ken Klee	6	0	1	1	8
Chris Simon	6	0	1	1	4
Glen Metropolit	1	0	0	0	0
Dmitri Khristich	3	0	0	0	0
Joe Reekie	4	0	0	0	4
Sylvain Cote	5	0	0	0	2
Trent Whitfield	5	0	0	0	2
Olaf Kolzig (goalie)	6	0	0	0	0
Andrei Nikolishin	6	0	0	0	2
Adam Oates	6	0	0	0	0
Joe Sacco	6	0	0	0	2
Rob Zettler	6	0	0	0	0
Dainius Zubrus	6	0	0	0	2

GOALTENDING

	Gms.	Min.	W	L	T	G	SO	Avg.
Olaf Kolzig	6	375	2	4	0	14	1	2.24

MISCELLANEOUS

HAT TRICKS

(Players scoring three or more goals in a game)

No player scored more than two in a game during 2001 playoffs.

OVERTIME GOALS

Date	Player, Team	Opponent	Time	Final score
4-11-01—	Jamie Langenbrunner, Dallas	Edmonton	2:08	Dallas 2, Edmonton 1
4-13-01—	Mats Sundin, Toronto	Ottawa	10:49	Toronto 1, Ottawa 0
4-14-01—	Jay McKee, Buffalo	Philadelphia	18:02	Buffalo 4, Philadelphia 3
4-15-01—	Benoit Hogue, Dallas	Edmonton	19:48	Dallas 3, Edmonton 2
4-16-01—	Cory Cross, Toronto	Ottawa	2:16	Toronto 3, Ottawa 2
4-16-01—	Peter Forsberg, Colorado	Vancouver	2:50	Colorado 4, Vancouver 3
4-17-01—	Curtis Brown, Buffalo	Philadelphia	6:13	Buffalo 4, Philadelphia 3
4-17-01—	Mike Comrie, Edmonton	Dallas	17:19	Edmonton 2, Dallas 1
4-18-01—	Eric Belanger, Los Angeles	Detroit	2:36	Los Angeles 4, Detroit 3
4-18-01—	Rod Brind'Amour, Carolina	New Jersey	0:46	Carolina 3, New Jersey 2
4-18-01—	Jeff Halpern, Washington	Pittsburgh	4:01	Washington 4, Pittsburgh 3
4-19-01—	Kirk Muller, Dallas	Edmonton	8:01	Dallas 4, Edmonton 3
4-19-01—	Bryce Salvador, St. Louis	San Jose	9:54	St. Louis 3, San Jose 2
4-23-01—	Adam Deadmarsh, Los Angeles	Detroit	4:48	Los Angeles 3, Detroit 2
4-23-01—	Martin Straka, Pittsburgh	Washington	13:04	Pittsburgh 4, Washington 3
4-26-01—	Jaroslav Modry, Los Angeles	Colorado	14:23	Los Angeles 4, Colorado 3
4-28-01—	Randy McKay, New Jersey	Toronto	5:31	New Jersey 6, Toronto 5
5-1-01—	Brian Rafalski, New Jersey	Toronto	7:00	New Jersey 3, Toronto 2
5-1-01—	Cory Stillman, St. Louis	Dallas	*9:26	St. Louis 3, Dallas 2
5-5-01—	Stu Barnes, Buffalo	Pittsburgh	8:34	Buffalo 3, Pittsburgh 2
5-6-01—	Glen Murray, Los Angeles	Colorado	*2:41	Los Angeles 1, Colorado 0
5-8-01—	Martin Straka, Pittsburgh	Buffalo	11:29	Pittsburgh 3, Buffalo 2
5-10-01—	Darius Kasparaitis, Pittsburgh	Buffalo	13:01	Pittsburgh 3, Buffalo 2
5-16-01—	Scott Young, St. Louis	Colorado	*10:27	St. Louis 4, Colorado 3
5-18-01—	Stephane Yelle, Colorado	St. Louis	4:23	Colorado 4, St. Louis 3
5-21-01—	Joe Sakic, Colorado	St. Louis	0:24	Colorado 2, St. Louis 1

*Goal scored in second overtime.

PENALTY-SHOT INFORMATION

Date	Shooter	Goaltender	Scored	Final score
4-11-01—	Mark Recchi, Philadelphia	Dominik Hasek, Buffalo	No	Buffalo 2, Philadelphia 1
5-2-01—	Martin Straka, Pittsburgh	Dominik Hasek, Buffalo	No	Buffalo 5, Pittsburgh 2
5-12-01—	Joe Sakic, Colorado	Roman Turek, St. Louis	Yes	Colorado 4, St. Louis 1

ALL-STAR GAME

ROSTERS

NORTH AMERICA

Coach: Jacques Martin, Ottawa Senators
Assistant coach: Larry Robinson, New Jersey Devils

Forwards (Pos.)	Club	Country
Jason Allison (C)	Boston Bruins	Canada
Tony Amonte (RW)	Chicago Blackhawks	U.S.A.
Donald Audette (RW)	Atlanta Thrashers	Canada
Theo Fleury (RW)*	New York Rangers	Canada
Simon Gagne (C)	Philadelphia Flyers	Canada
Bill Guerin (RW)	Boston Bruins	U.S.A.
Brett Hull (RW)	Dallas Stars	U.S.A.
Paul Kariya (LW)*	Mighty Ducks of Anaheim	Canada
Mario Lemieux (C)	Pittsburgh Penguins	Canada
Luc Robitaille (LW)	Los Angeles Kings	Canada
Joe Sakic (C)*	Colorado Avalanche	Canada
Doug Weight (C)	Edmonton Oilers	U.S.A.
Defensemen		
Rob Blake*	Los Angeles Kings	Canada
Ray Bourque*	Colorado Avalanche	Canada
Brian Leetch	New York Rangers	U.S.A.
Ed Jovanovski	Vancouver Canucks	Canada
Scott Niedermayer	New Jersey Devils	Canada
Scott Stevens	New Jersey Devils	Canada
Goaltenders		
Martin Brodeur	New Jersey Devils	Canada
Sean Burke	Phoenix Coyotes	Canada
Patrick Roy*	Colorado Avalanche	Canada

*In starting lineup.

†Gagne replaced injured Vincent Damphousse (San Jose), Niedermayer replaced injured Al MacInnis (St. Louis), Jovanovski replaced injured Chris Pronger (St. Louis).

WORLD

Coach: Joel Quenneville, St. Louis Blues
Assistant coach: Bob Hartley, Colorado Avalanche

Forwards (Pos.)	Club	Country
Radek Bonk (C)	Ottawa Senators	Czech Rep.
Pavel Bure (RW)*	Florida Panthers	Russia
Sergei Fedorov (C)	Detroit Red Wings	Russia
Peter Forsberg (C)*	Colorado Avalanche	Sweden
Milan Hejduk (RW)	Colorado Avalanche	Czech Rep.
Marian Hossa (RW)	Ottawa Senators	Slovakia
Jaromir Jagr (RW)*	Pittsburgh Penguins	Czech Rep.
Alexei Kovalev (C)	Pittsburgh Penguins	Russia
Fredrik Modin (LW)	Tampa Bay Lightning	Sweden
Marcus Naslund (LW)	Vancouver Canucks	Sweden
Ziggy Palffy (RW)	Los Angeles Kings	Slovakia
Mats Sundin (C)	Toronto Maple Leafs	Sweden
Defensemen		
Sergei Gonchar	Washington Capitals	Russia
Nicklas Lidstrom*	Detroit Red Wings	Sweden
Janne Niinimaa	Edmonton Oilers	Finland
Teppo Numminen	Phoenix Coyotes	Finland
Sandis Ozolinsh*	Carolina Hurricanes	Latvia
Marcus Ragnarsson	San Jose Sharks	Sweden
Goaltenders		
Roman Cechmanek	Philadelphia Flyers	Czech Rep.
Dominik Hasek*	Buffalo Sabres	Czech Rep.
Evgeni Nabokov	San Jose Sharks	Kazakhstan

*In starting lineup.

†Hejduk replaced injured Alexander Mogilny (New Jersey).

GAME SUMMARY

North America 14, World 12

North America	3	6	5	—	14
World	3	4	5	—	12

FIRST PERIOD—1. North America, Fleury 1 (Kariya, Stevens), 0:49. 2. World, Sundin 1 (Modin, Lidstrom), 8:01. 3. North America, Amonte 1 (Weight, Guerin), 11:22. 4. North America, Robitaille 1 (Allison, Blake), 12:00. 5. World, Sundin 2 (Modin, Numminen), 17:05. 6. World, Forsberg 1 (Samsonov), 17:26.

SECOND PERIOD—7. World, Naslund 1 (Gonchar, Hossa), 2:40. 8. North America, Amonte 1 (Weight), 3:25. 9. North America, Lemieux 1 (Stevens), 4:53. 10. North America, Sakic 1 (Kariya, Fleury), 6:59. 11. World, Samsonov 1 (Forsberg, Lidstrom), 8:08. 12. North America, Amonte 2 (Guerin, Leetch), 8:36. 13. North America, Guerin 2 (Amonte), 14:36. 14. World, Palffy 1 (Modin, Sundin), 17:01. 15. North America, Robitaille 2 (Audette), 18:13. 16. World, Fedorov 1 (Bure, Kovalev), 19:35.

THIRD PERIOD—17. World, Hejduk 1 (Ozolinsh, Forsberg), 1:05. 18. North America, Weight 1 (Amonte, Guerin), 2:56. 19. North America, Gagne 1 (Naslund, Hossa), 5:50. 21. World, Fedorov 2 (Bure, Numminen), 8:55. 22. North America, Fleury 2 (Kariya), 12:03. 23. World, Kovalev 1 (Sundin, Gonchar), 13:57. 24. North America, Gagne 2 (unassisted) 17:07. 25. North America, Guerin 3 (Jovanovski, Weight) 17:58. 26. World, Lidstrom 1 (Palffy, Modin) 19:59.

Shots on goal—North America 17-20-16-53; World 11-11-23-45. Power-play opportunities—North America 0 of 0; World 0 of 0. Goalies—North America, Roy (11 shots, 8 saves), Burke (0:00 second, 11-7), Brodeur W (0:00 third, 23-18); World, Hasek (17-14), Cechmanek (0:00 second, 20-14), Nabokov L (0:00 third, 16-11). A—18,646. Referees—Mick McGeough, Richard Trottier. Linesmen—Randy Mitton, Mark Wheler.

2000-01 NHL REVIEW   All-Star Game

AWARDS

2000-01 NHL REVIEW *Awards*

THE SPORTING NEWS
ALL-STAR TEAM

First team	Position	Second team
Martin Brodeur, New Jersey	Goaltender	Sean Burke, Phoenix
Rob Blake, Los Angeles-Colorado	Defense	Brian Leetch, N.Y. Rangers
Nicklas Lidstrom, Detroit	Defense	Chris Pronger, St. Louis
Alexei Kovalev, Pittsburgh	Left wing	Patrik Elias, New Jersey
Joe Sakic, Colorado	Center	Mario Lemieux, Pittsburgh
Jaromir Jagr, Pittsburgh	Right wing	Pavel Bure, Florida

Note: THE SPORTING NEWS All-Star Team is selected by the NHL players.

AWARD WINNERS

Player of the Year: Joe Sakic, Colorado
Coach of the Year: Scotty Bowman, Detroit
Rookie of the Year: Evgeni Nabokov, San Jose
Executive of the Year: Brian Burke, Vancouver

Note: THE SPORTING NEWS player and rookie awards are selected by the NHL players, the coaches award by the NHL coaches and the executive award by NHL executives.

NATIONAL HOCKEY LEAGUE
ALL-STAR TEAMS

First team	Position	Second team
Dominik Hasek, Buffalo	Goaltender	Roman Cechmanek, Philadelphia
Ray Bourque, Colorado	Defense	Rob Blake, Los Angeles
Nicklas Lidstrom, Detroit	Defense	Scott Stevens, New Jersey
Patrik Elias, New Jersey	Left wing	Luc Robitaille, Los Angeles
Joe Sakic, Colorado	Center	Mario Lemieux, Pittsburgh
Jaromir Jagr, Pittsburgh	Right wing	Pavel Bure, Florida

AWARD WINNERS

Art Ross Trophy: Jaromir Jagr, Pittsburgh
Maurice Richard Trophy: Pavel Bure, Florida
Hart Memorial Trophy: Joe Sakic, Colorado
James Norris Memorial Trophy: Nicklas Lidstrom, Detroit
Vezina Trophy: Dominik Hasek, Buffalo
Bill Jennings Trophy: Dominik Hasek, Buffalo
Calder Memorial Trophy: Evgeni Nabokov, San Jose

Lady Byng Memorial Trophy: Joe Sakic, Colorado
Conn Smythe Trophy: Patrick Roy, Colorado
Bill Masterton Memorial Trophy: Adam Graves, N.Y. Rangers
Frank J. Selke Trophy: John Madden, New Jersey
Jack Adams Award: Bill Barber, Philadelphia
King Clancy Trophy: Shjon Podein, Colorado

PLAYER DRAFT

FIRST ROUND

No.— Selecting club	Player	Pos.	Previous team (league)
1— Atlanta	Ilja Kovalchuk	F	Spartak Jr., Russia
2— Ottawa (from N.Y. Islanders)	Jason Spezza	C	Windsor (OHL)
3— Tampa Bay	Alexander Svitov	C	OMSK, Russia
4— Florida	Stephen Weiss	C	Plymouth (OHL)
5— Anaheim	Stanislav Chistov	C/RW	OMSK, Russia
6— Minnesota	Mikko Koivu	C	TPS, Finland
7— Montreal	Michael Komisarek	D	U. of Michigan (CCHA)
8— Columbus	Pascal LeClaire	G	Halifax (QMJHL)
9— Chicago	Tuomo Ruutu	C/LW	Jokerit, Finland
10— N.Y. Rangers	Daniel Blackburn	G	Kootenay (WHL)
11— Phoenix (from Calgary)	Fredrik Sjostrom	RW	Frolunda, Sweden
12— Nashville	Dan Hamhuis	D	Prince George (WHL)
13— Edmonton (from Boston)	Ales Hemsky	RW	Hull (QMJHL)
14— Calgary (from Phoenix)	Chuck Kobasew	RW	Boston College (H. East)
15— Carolina	Igor Knyazev	D	Spartak Jr., Russia
16— Vancouver	R.J. Umberger	C	Ohio State (CCHA)
17— Toronto	Carlo Colaiacovo	D	Erie (OHL)
18— Los Angeles	Jens Karlsson	F	Frolunda, Sweden
19— Boston (from Edmonton)	Shaone Morrisonn	D	Kamloops (WHL)
20— San Jose	Marcel Goc	C	Schwennigen, Germany
21— Pittsburgh	Colby Armstrong	RW	Red Deer (WHL)
22— Buffalo	Jlrl Novotny	C	Budejovice, Czech.
23— Ottawa (from Philadelphia)	Tim Gleason	D	Windsor (OHL)
24— Florida (from St. Louis)	Lukas Krajicek	D	Peterborough (OHL)
25— Montreal (from Washington)	Alexander Perezhogin	C	OMSK, Russia
26— Dallas	Jason Bacashihua	G	Chicago (NAHL)
27— Philadelphia (from Ottawa)	Jeff Woywitka	D	Red Deer (WHL)
28— New Jersey	Adrian Foster	LW	Saskatoon (WHL)
29— Chicago (from Detroit)	Adam Munro	G	Erie (OHL)
30— Los Angeles (from Colorado)	David Steckel	LW/C	Ohio State (CCHA)

SECOND ROUND

No.— Selecting club	Player	Pos.	Previous team (league)
31— Phoenix (from N.Y. Islanders)	Matthew Spiller	D	Seattle (WHL)
32— Buffalo (from Tampa Bay)	Derek Roy	C	Kitchener (OHL)
33— Nashville (from Atlanta)	Timofei Shiskanov	F	Spartak Jr., Russia
34— Florida	Greg Watson	C/LW	Prince Albert (WHL)
35— Anaheim	Mark Popovic	D	Toronto (OHL)
36— Minnesota	Kyle Wanvig	RW	Red Deer (WHL)
37— Montreal	Duncan Milroy	RW	Swift Current (WHL)
38— Columbus	Tim Jackman	RW	Mankato State (WCHA)
39— Toronto (from Chicago)	Karel Pilar	D	Litvinov, Czech.
40— N.Y. Rangers	Fedor Tjutin	D	St. Petersburg, Russia
41— Calgary	Andrei Taratukhin	C/F	OMSK, Russia
42— Nashville	Tomas Slovak	D	Kosice, Slovakia
43— Edmonton (from Boston)	Doug Lynch	D	Red Deer (WHL)
44— New Jersey (from Phoenix)	Igor Pohanka	C	Prince Albert (WHL)
45— Phoenix	Martin Podlesak	C	Lethbridge (WHL)
46— Carolina	Michael Zigomanis	C	Kingston (OHL)
47— Tampa Bay (from Vancouver)	Alexander Polushin	C/LW	Tver, Russia
48— New Jersey (from Vancouver)	Thomas Pihlman	F	Jyvaskyla, Finland
49— Los Angeles (from Toronto)	Mike Cammalleri	C	U. of Michigan (CCHA)
50— Buffalo	Chris Thorburn	C	North Bay (OHL)
51— Los Angeles	Jaroslav Bednar	C	IFK, Finland
52— Edmonton	Edward Caron	LW	Phillips-Exeter (USHSE)
53— Columbus (from San Jose)	Kiel McLeod	C	Kelowna (WHL)
54— Pittsburgh	Noah Welch	D	St. Sebastian's (USHSE)
55— Buffalo	Jason Pominville	RW	Shawinigan (QMJHL)
56— Calgary (from Philadelphia)	Andrei Medvedev	G	Spartak Jr., Russia
57— St. Louis	Jay McClement	C	Brampton (OHL)
58— Washington	Nathan Paetsch	D	Moose Jaw (WHL)
59— Chicago (from Dallas)	Matt Keith	RW	Spokane (WHL)
60— New Jersey (from Ottawa)	Victor Uchevatov	D	Yaroslavl, Russia

No.—Selecting club	Player	Pos.	Previous team (league)
61— Tampa Bay (from New Jersey)	Andreas Holmqvist	D	Hammarby Jr., Sweden
62— Detroit	Igor Grigorenko	RW	Togliatti Jr., Russia
63— Colorado	Peter Budaj	G	Toronto (OHL)

THIRD ROUND

No.—Selecting club	Player	Pos.	Previous team (league)
64— Florida (from N.Y. Islanders)	Tomas Malec	D	Rimouski (QMJHL)
65— Toronto (from Tampa Bay)	Brendan Bell	D	Ottawa (OHL)
66— Vancouver (from Atlanta)	Fedor Fedorov	LW	Sudbury (OHL)
67— New Jersey	Robin Leblanc	RW	Baie-Comeau (QMJHL)
68— Florida	Grant McNeill	D	Prince Albert (WHL)
69— Anaheim	Joel Stepp	C/LW	Red Deer (WHL)
70— Dallas (from Minnesota)	Yared Hagos	C	AIK, Sweden
71— Montreal	Tomas Plekanec	LW	Kladno, Czechoslovakia
72— New Jersey (from Columbus)	Brandon Nolan	C/LW	Oshawa (OHL)
73— Chicago	Craig Andersson	G	Guelph (OHL)
74— Minnesota (from N.Y. Rangers)	Chris Heid	D	Spokane (WHL)
75— Nashville (from Calgary)	Denis Platonov		Saratov, Russia
76— Nashville	Oliver Setzinger	C	Ilves, Finland
77— Boston	Darren McLachlan	LW	Seattle (WHL)
78— Phoenix	Beat Schiess-Forster	D	Davos, Switzerland
79— N.Y. Rangers (from Carolina)	Garth Murray	C/LW	Regina (WHL)
80— Atlanta (from Vancouver)	Michael Garnett	G	Saskatoon (WHL)
81— Ottawa (from New Jersey)	Neil Komadoski	D	U. of Notre Dame (CCHA)
82— Toronto	Jay Harrison	D	Brampton (OHL)
83— Los Angeles	Henrik Juntunen	RW	Karpat, Finland
84— Edmonton	Kenny Smith	D	Harvard (ECAC)
85— Columbus (from San Jose)	Aaron Johnson	D	Rimouski (QMJHL)
86— Pittsburgh	Drew Fata	D	Toronto (OHL)
87— Columbus (from Buffalo)	Per Mars		Brynas, Sweden
88— Toronto (from Philadelphia)	Nicolas Corbeil	C	Sherbrooke (QMJHL)
89— St. Louis	Tuomas Nissinen	G	Kalpa Jr., Finland
90— Washington	Owen Fussey	RW	Calgary (WHL)
91— Carolina	Kevin Estrada	LW	Chilliwack (BCJHL)
92— Dallas	Anthony Aquino	RW	Merrimack (H. East)
93— Minnesota (from Ottawa)	Stephane Veilleux	C	Val-d'Or (QMJHL)
94— Tampa Bay (from New Jersey)	Eugeni Artukhin	RW	Podolsk, Russia
95— Philadelphia (from Detroit)	Patrick Sharp	C	U. of Vermont (ECAC)
96— Pittsburgh	Alexandre Rouleau	D	Val-d'Or (QMJHL)
97— Colorado	Danny Bois	RW	London (OHL)

FOURTH ROUND

No.—Selecting club	Player	Pos.	Previous team (league)
98— Nashville (from N.Y. Islanders)	Jordin Tootoo	RW	Brandon (WHL)
99— Ottawa (from Tampa Bay)	Ray Emery	G	Sault Ste. Marie (OHL)
100— Atlanta	Brian Sipotz	D	Miami Univ. (CCHA)
101— N.Y. Islanders (from Florida)	Cory Stillman	C	Kingston (OHL)
102— Anaheim	Timo Parssinen	F	HPK (Finland)
103— Minnesota	Tony Virta	RW	TPS, Finland
104— Chicago (from Montreal)	Brent MacLellan	D	Rimouski (QMJHL)
105— Anaheim (from Columbus)	Vladimir Korsunov	D	Spartak Jr., Russia
106— San Jose (from Chicago)	Christian Ehrhoff	D	Krefeld, Germany
107— San Jose (from N.Y. Rangers)	Dimitri Patzold	G	Erding Jr., Germany
108— Calgary	Tomi Maki	RW	Jokerit, Finland
109— Montreal	Martti Jarventie	D	TPS, Finland
110— Carolina (from Nashville)	Rob Zepp	G	Plymouth (OHL)
111— Boston	Matti Kaltiainen	G	Blues Jr., Finland
112— Atlanta (from Phoenix)	Milan Gajic	C	Burnaby (BCJHL)
113— N.Y. Rangers (from Carolina)	Bryce Lampman	D	Omaha (USHL)
114— Vancouver	Evgeny Gladskikh	LW	Magnitogorsk, Russia
115— Chicago (from Toronto)	Vladimir Gusev	D	Khabarovsk, Russia
116— Los Angeles	Richard Petiot	D	Camrose (AJHL)
117— Florida (from Columbus)	Michael Woodford	RW	Cushing Academy (USHSE)
118— Anaheim (from Edmonton)	Brandon Rogers	D	Hotchkiss (USHSE)
119— Chicago (from San Jose)	Aleksey Zotkin		Magnitogorsk, Russia
120— Pittsburgh	Tomas Surovy	F	Poprad, Slovakia
121— Detroit	Drew MacIntyre	G	Sherbrooke (QMJHL)
122— St. Louis (from Buffalo)	Igor Valeev	RW	North Bay (OHL)
123— Tampa Bay (from Philadelphia)	Aaron Lobb	RW	London (OHL)
124— Calgary (from St. Louis)	Egor Shastin	F	OMSK, Russia

No.—Selecting club	Player	Pos.	Previous team (league)
125—Washington	Jeff Lucky	RW	Spokane (WHL)
126—Dallas	Daniel Volrab	C	Sparta, Czech.
127—Ottawa	Christoph Schubert		Munchen, Germany
128—New Jersey	Andrei Posnov		Krylja, Russia
129—Detroit	Miroslav Blatak	D	Zlin, Czechoslovakia
130—Colorado	Colt King	LW	Guelph (OHL)
131—Pittsburgh	Ben Eaves	C	Boston College (H. East)

FIFTH ROUND

No.—Selecting club	Player	Pos.	Previous team (league)
132—N.Y. Islanders	Dusan Salficky	G	Plzen, Czechoslovakia
133—Edmonton	Jussi Markkanen	G	Tappara, Finland
134—Toronto (from Tampa Bay)	Kyle Wellwood	C	Belleville (OHL)
135—Atlanta	Colin Stuart	C	Colorado College (WCHA)
136—Florida	Billy Thompson	G	Prince George (WHL)
137—Anaheim	Joel Perreault	C	Baie-Comeau (QMJHL)
138—Tampa Bay (from Philadelphia)	Paul Lynch	D	Valley Jr., Mass. (EJHL)
139—N.Y. Rangers (from Minnesota)	Shawn Collymore	RW	Quebec (QMJHL)
140—San Jose (from Montreal)	Tomas Plihal	F	Liberec Jr., Czech.
141—Columbus	Cole Jarrett	D	Plymouth (OHL)
142—Chicago	Tommi Jaminki	LW	Blues Jr., Finland
143—Colorado (from N.Y. Rangers)	Frantisek Skladany	LW	Boston Univ. (H. East)
144—Colorado	Cody McCormick	C/RW	Belleville (OHL)
145—Calgary	James Hakewill	D	Westminster (USHSE)
146—Philadelphia (from Nashville)	Jussi Timonen	D	Kalpa Jr., Finland
147—Boston	Jiri Jakes	RW	Brandon (WHL)
148—Phoenix	David Klema	C	Des Moines (USHL)
149—Colorado (from Carolina)	Mikko Viitanen	D	Ahmat, Finland
150—Philadelphia	Berend Bruckler	G	Tri-Cities (USHL)
151—Vancouver	Kevin Bieksa	D	Bowling Green (CCHA)
152—Los Angeles (from Toronto)	Terry Denike	G	Weyburn (SJHL)
153—Los Angeles	Tuukka Mantyla	D	Tappara, Finland
154—Edmonton	Jake Brenk	C	Breck, Min. (USHSW)
155—Buffalo (from San Jose)	Michal Vondrka	LW	Budejovice, Czech.
156—Pittsburgh	Andy Schneider	D	Lincoln, N.D. (USHL)
157—Detroit (from Buffalo)	Andreas Jamtin	RW	Farjestad, Sweden
158—Philadelphia	Roman Malek	G	Slavia, Czech.
159—St. Louis	Dimitri Semin	F	Spartak Jr., Russia
160—Washington	Artem Ternavsky	D	Sherbrooke (QMJHL)
161—Dallas	Mike Smith	G	Sudbury (OHL)
162—Ottawa	Stefan Schauer		Riebersee, Germany
163—New Jersey	Andreas Salomonsson		Djurgarden, Sweden
164—Calgary (from Detroit)	Yuri Trubachev	C	St. Petersburg, Russia
165—Colorado	Pierre-Luc Emond	C	Drummondville (QMJHL)

SIXTH ROUND

No.—Selecting club	Player	Pos.	Previous team (league)
166—N.Y. Islanders	Andy Chiodo	G	Toronto (OHL)
167—Dallas (from Tampa Bay)	Michal Blazek	D	Vsetin Jr., Czech.
168—Toronto (from Atlanta)	Max Kondratiev	D	Togliatti Jr., Russia
169—Florida	Dustin Johner	C	Seattle (WHL)
170—Anaheim	Jan Tabacek		Martin (SVK)
171—Montreal (from Minnesota)	Eric Himelfarb	C	Sarnia (OHL)
172—Philadelphia (from Montreal)	Dennis Seidenberg		Mannheim, Germany
173—Columbus	Justin Aikins	C	Langley (BCJHL)
174—Chicago	Alexander Golvin	LW	OMSK, Russia
175—San Jose	Ryan Clowe	RW	Rimouski (QMJHL)
176—N.Y. Rangers	Marek Zidlicky	D	IFK, Finland
177—Philadelphia (from Calgary)	Andrei Razin		Magnitogorsk, Russia
178—Nashville	Anton Lavrentiev	D	Kazan, Russia
179—Boston	Andrew Alberts	D	Waterloo (USHL)
180—Phoenix	Scott Polaski	RW	Sioux City (USHL)
181—Carolina	Daniel Boisclair	G	Cape Breton (QMJHL)
182—San Jose (from Vancouver)	Tom Cavanagh	RW	Phillips-Exeter (USHSE)
183—Toronto	Jaroslav Sklenar	F	Brno Jr., Czech.
184—Colorado (from Los Angeles)	Scott Horvath	RW	Mass.-Amherst (H. East)
185—Edmonton	Mikael Svensk	D	Frolunda, Sweden
186—Chicago (from San Jose)	Petr Puncochar	D	Karlovy Vary, Czech.
187—Columbus (from Pittsburgh)	Artem Vostrikov		Togliatti Jr., Russia
188—Tampa Bay (from Buffalo)	Art Femenella	D	Sioux City (USHL)

No.— Selecting club	Player	Pos.	Previous team (league)
189—Atlanta (from Philadelphia)	Pasi Nurminen	G	Jokerit, Finland
190—St. Louis	Brett Scheffelmaier	D	Medicine Hat (WHL)
191—Washington	Zbynek Novak	F	Slavia, Czech.
192—Dallas	Jussi Jokinen	F	Karpat, Finland
193—Ottawa	Brooks Laich	C	Moose Jaw (WHL)
194—New Jersey	James Massen	RW	Sioux Falls (USHL)
195—Detroit	Nick Pannoni	G	Seattle (WHL)
196—Colorado	Charlie Stephens	C/RW	Guelph (OHL)

SEVENTH ROUND

No.— Selecting club	Player	Pos.	Previous team (league)
197—N.Y. Islanders	Jan Hulub	D	Liberec Jr., Czech.
198—Toronto (from Tampa Bay)	Ivan Kolozvary	F	Trencin Jr., Slovakia
199—Atlanta	Matt Suderman	D	Saskatoon (WHL)
200—Florida	Toni Koivisto	F	Lukko, Finland
201—Atlanta (from Anaheim)	Colin Fitzrandolph	C	Phillips-Exeter (USHSE)
202—Minnesota	Derek Boogaard	F	Prince George (WHL)
203—Montreal	Andrew Archer	D	Guelph (OHL)
204—Columbus	Raffaele Sannitz	F	Lugano, Switzerland
205—Chicago	Teemu Jaaskelainen	D	Ilves, Finland
206—N.Y. Rangers	Petr Preucil	C	Quebec (QMJHL)
207—Calgary	Garett Bembridge	RW	Saskatoon (WHL)
208—Philadelphia (from Nashville)	Thierry Douville	D	Baie-Comeau (QMJHL)
209—Boston	Jordan Sigalet	G	Victoria (BCJHL)
210—Phoenix	Steve Belanger	G	Kamloops (WHL)
211—Carolina	Sean Curry	D	Tri-City (WHL)
212—Vancouver	Jason King	RW	Halifax (QMJHL)
213—Toronto	Jan Chovan	G	Belleville (OHL)
214—Los Angeles	Cristobal Huet	G	Lugano, Switzerland
215—Edmonton	Dan Baum	C/LW	Prince George (WHL)
216—Chicago (from San Jose)	Oleg Minakov	RW	Elektrostal Jr., Russia
217—Pittsburgh	Tomas Duba	G	Sparta, Czech.
218—Ottawa (from Buffalo)	Jan Platil	D	Barrie (OHL)
219—Tampa Bay (from Philadelphia)	Dennis Packard	LW	Harvard (ECAC)
220—Calgary (from St. Louis)	David Moss	LW	Cedar Rapids (USHL)
221—Washington	John Oduya	D	Victoriaville (QMJHL)
222—Tampa Bay (from Dallas)	Jeremy Van Hoof	D	Ottawa (OHL)
223—Ottawa	Brandon Bochenski	RW	Lincoln, Min. (USHL)
224—Anaheim (from New Jersey)	Tony Martensson	C	Brynas, Sweden
225—Philadelphia (from Ottawa)	David Printz	D	Great Falls (AWHL)
226—N.Y. Rangers (from Detroit)	Pontus Petterstrom	F	Tingsryd Jr., Sweden
227—Colorado	Marek Svatos	RW	Kootenay (WHL)

EIGHTH ROUND

No.— Selecting club	Player	Pos.	Previous team (league)
228—N.Y. Islanders	Mike Bray	RW	Quebec (QMJHL)
229—New Jersey (from Tampa Bay)	Aaron Voros	C	Victoria (BCJHL)
230—N.Y. Rangers (from Atlanta)	Leonid Zhvachin	D	Podolsk, Russia
231—Florida	Kyle Bruce	RW	Prince Albert (WHL)
232—Anaheim	Martin Gerber	G	Langnau, Switzerland
233—Calgary (from Minnesota)	Joe Campbell	D	Des Moines (USHL)
234—Buffalo (from San Jose)	Calle Aslund	D	Huddinge, Sweden
235—Ottawa (from Montreal)	Neil Petruic	D	Kindersley, Sask. (SJHL)
236—Columbus	Ryan Bowness	RW	Brampton (OHL)
237—Los Angeles (from Chicago)	Mike Gavinet	D	Nebraska-Omaha (CCHA)
238—N.Y. Rangers	Ryan Hollweg	C	Medicine Hat (WHL)
239—Minnesota (from Calgary)	Jake Riddle	LW	Seattle (WHL)
240—Nashville	Gustav Grasberg	C	Mora Jr., Sweden
241—Boston	Milan Jurcina	D	Halifax (QMJHL)
242—Columbus	Andrew Murray	C	Selkirk (MJHL)
243—Phoenix	Frantisek Lukes	LW	Toronto (OHL)
244—Carolina	Carter Trevisani	D	Ottawa (OHL)
245—Vancouver	Konstantin Mihailov	C	Nizhnekamsk, Russia
246—Toronto	Tomas Mojzis	D	Moose Jaw (WHL)
247—Buffalo (from Los Angeles)	Marek Dubec	D	Vsetin Jr., Czech.
248—Edmonton	Kari Haakana	D	Jokerit, Finland
249—Washington (from San Jose)	Matt Maglione	D	Princeton (ECAC)
250—Pittsburgh	Brandon Crawford-West	G	Texas Tornado (NAHL)
251—Calgary (from Buffalo)	Ville Hamalainen	F	Saipa, Finland
252—Tampa Bay (from Philadelphia)	J.F. Soucy	C	Montreal (QMJHL)

No.—Selecting club	Player	Pos.	Previous team (league)
253—St. Louis	Petr Cajanek	F	Zlin, Czechoslovakia
254—Washington	Peter Polcik	LW	Nitra Jr., Slovakia
255—Dallas	Marco Rosa	C	Merrimack (H. East)
256—Ottawa	Gregg Johnson	C	Boston Univ. (H. East)
257—New Jersey	Evgeny Gamalej	D	Dynamo Moscow 2, Russia
258—Detroit	Dmitri Bykov	D	Kazan, Russia
259—Tampa Bay (from Colorado)	Dimitri Bezrukov	LW	Nizhnekamsk, Russia

NINTH ROUND

No.—Selecting club	Player	Pos.	Previous team (league)
260—N.Y. Islanders	Bryan Perez	F	Des Moines (USHL)
261—Tampa Bay	Vitali Smolyninov		Neftechimik Jr., Russia
262—Atlanta	Mario Cartelli	D	Trinec, Czech.
263—Florida	Jan Blanar	D	Trencin Jr., Slovakia
264—Anaheim	Pierre Parenteau	C	Chicoutimi (QMJHL)
265—Dallas (from Minnesota)	Dale Sullivan	RW	Hull (QMJHL)
266—Montreal	Viktor Ujcik	F	Slavia Praha, Czech.
267—Florida (from Columbus)	Ivan Majesky	D	Ilves, Finland
268—Chicago	Jeff Miles	C	U. of Vermont (ECAC)
269—N.Y. Rangers	Juris Stals	C	Lukko, Finland
270—St. Louis (from Calgary)	Grant Jacobsen	C	Regina (WHL)
271—Nashville	Mikko Lehtonen	D	Karpat, Finland
272—Edmonton (from Boston)	Ales Pisa	D	Pardubice, Czech.
273—Phoenix	Severin Blindenbacher	D	Kloten, Switzerland
274—Carolina	Peter Reynolds	D	North Bay (OHL)
275—Washington (from Vancouver)	Robert Muller	G	Mannheim, Germany
276—Toronto	Mike Knoepfli	LW	Georgetown, Ont. (OPJA)
277—Los Angeles	Sebastien LaPlante	G	Rayside-Balfour (NOJHL)
278—Edmonton	Shay Stephenson	LW	Red Deer (WHL)
279—Buffalo (from San Jose)	Ryan Jorde	D	Tri-City (WHL)
280—N.Y. Islanders (from Pittsburgh)	Roman Kuhtinov	D	Novokuznetsk, Russia
281—Tampa Bay (from Buffalo)	Ilja Solarev	LW	Perm, Russia
282—Boston (from Philadelphia)	Marcel Rodman	RW	Peterborough (OHL)
283—St. Louis	Simon Skoog	D	Morrum, Sweden
284—Washington	Viktor Huhl	W	Slavia, Czech.
285—Dallas	Marek Tomica	W	Slavia, Czech.
286—Ottawa	Tony Dahlman	RW	Ilves, Finland
287—N.Y. Islanders (from New Jersey)	Juha-Pekka Ketola	C	Lukko, Finland
288—Detroit	Francois Senez	D	Rensselaer (ECAC)
289—Tampa Bay (from Colorado)	Henrik Bergfors	D	Sodertalje Jr., Sweden

NHL HISTORY

Stanley Cup champions

All-Star Games

Year-by-year standings

Records

Statistical leaders

Award winners

The Sporting News awards

Hall of Fame

Milestones

Team by team

STANLEY CUP CHAMPIONS

The Stanley Cup was donated in 1893 to be awarded to signify supremacy in Canadian amateur hockey. Eventually, other teams, including professional clubs and clubs outside of Canada, began vying for the trophy. Since 1926 only NHL clubs have competed for the Stanley Cup.

Season Club	Coach	Season Club	Coach
1892-93—Montreal Am. Ath. Assn.*		1948-49—Toronto Maple Leafs	Hap Day
1893-94—Montreal Am. Ath. Assn.*		1949-50—Detroit Red Wings	Tommy Ivan
1894-95—Montreal Victorias*	Mike Grant†	1950-51—Toronto Maple Leafs	Joe Primeau
1895-96—(Feb. '96) Winnipeg Victorias*	J. Armitage	1951-52—Detroit Red Wings	Tommy Ivan
1895-96—(Dec. '96) Montreal Victorias*	Mike Grant†	1952-53—Montreal Canadiens	Dick Irvin
1896-97—Montreal Victorias*	Mike Grant†	1953-54—Detroit Red Wings	Tommy Ivan
1897-98—Montreal Victorias*	F. Richardson	1954-55—Detroit Red Wings	Jimmy Skinner
1898-99—Montreal Shamrocks*	H.J. Trihey†	1955-56—Montreal Canadiens	Toe Blake
1899-1900—Montreal Shamrocks*	H.J. Trihey†	1956-57—Montreal Canadiens	Toe Blake
1900-01—Winnipeg Victorias*	D.H. Bain	1957-58—Montreal Canadiens	Toe Blake
1901-02—Montreal Am. Ath. Assn.*	C. McKerrow	1958-59—Montreal Canadiens	Toe Blake
1902-03—Ottawa Silver Seven*	A.T. Smith	1959-60—Montreal Canadiens	Toe Blake
1903-04—Ottawa Silver Seven*	A.T. Smith	1960-61—Chicago Black Hawks	Rudy Pilous
1904-05—Ottawa Silver Seven*	A.T. Smith†	1961-62—Toronto Maple Leafs	Punch Imlach
1905-06—Montreal Wanderers*	Cecil Blachford†	1962-63—Toronto Maple Leafs	Punch Imlach
1906-07—(Jan. '07) Kenora Thistles*	Tommy Phillips†	1963-64—Toronto Maple Leafs	Punch Imlach
1906-07—(Mar. '07) Montreal Wanderers*	Cecil Blachford	1964-65—Montreal Canadiens	Toe Blake
1907-08—Montreal Wanderers*	Cecil Blachford	1965-66—Montreal Canadiens	Toe Blake
1908-09—Ottawa Senators*	Bruce Stuart†	1966-67—Toronto Maple Leafs	Punch Imlach
1909-10—Montreal Wanderers*	Pud Glass†	1967-68—Montreal Canadiens	Toe Blake
1910-11—Ottawa Senators*	Bruce Stuart†	1968-69—Montreal Canadiens	Claude Ruel
1911-12—Quebec Bulldogs*	C. Nolan	1969-70—Boston Bruins	Harry Sinden
1912-13—Quebec Bulldogs*	Joe Malone†	1970-71—Montreal Canadiens	Al MacNeil
1913-14—Toronto Blueshirts*	Scotty Davidson†	1971-72—Boston Bruins	Tom Johnson
1914-15—Vancouver Millionaires*	Frank Patrick	1972-73—Montreal Canadiens	Scotty Bowman
1915-16—Montreal Canadiens*	George Kennedy	1973-74—Philadelphia Flyers	Fred Shero
1916-17—Seattle Metropolitans*	Pete Muldoon	1974-75—Philadelphia Flyers	Fred Shero
1917-18—Toronto Arenas	Dick Carroll	1975-76—Montreal Canadiens	Scotty Bowman
1919-20—Ottawa Senators	Pete Green	1976-77—Montreal Canadiens	Scotty Bowman
1920-21—Ottawa Senators	Pete Green	1977-78—Montreal Canadiens	Scotty Bowman
1921-22—Toronto St. Pats	Eddie Powers	1978-79—Montreal Canadiens	Scotty Bowman
1922-23—Ottawa Senators	Pete Green	1979-80—New York Islanders	Al Arbour
1923-24—Montreal Canadiens	Leo Dandurand	1980-81—New York Islanders	Al Arbour
1924-25—Victoria Cougars*	Lester Patrick	1981-82—New York Islanders	Al Arbour
1925-26—Montreal Maroons	Eddie Gerard	1982-83—New York Islanders	Al Arbour
1926-27—Ottawa Senators	Dave Gill	1983-84—Edmonton Oilers	Glen Sather
1927-28—New York Rangers	Lester Patrick	1984-85—Edmonton Oilers	Glen Sather
1928-29—Boston Bruins	Cy Denneny	1985-86—Montreal Canadiens	Jean Perron
1929-30—Montreal Canadiens	Cecil Hart	1986-87—Edmonton Oilers	Glen Sather
1930-31—Montreal Canadiens	Cecil Hart	1987-88—Edmonton Oilers	Glen Sather
1931-32—Toronto Maple Leafs	Dick Irvin	1988-89—Calgary Flames	Terry Crisp
1932-33—New York Rangers	Lester Patrick	1989-90—Edmonton Oilers	John Muckler
1933-34—Chicago Black Hawks	Tommy Gorman	1990-91—Pittsburgh Penguins	Bob Johnson
1934-35—Montreal Maroons	Tommy Gorman	1991-92—Pittsburgh Penguins	Scotty Bowman
1935-36—Detroit Red Wings	Jack Adams	1992-93—Montreal Canadiens	Jacques Demers
1936-37—Detroit Red Wings	Jack Adams	1993-94—New York Rangers	Mike Keenan
1937-38—Chicago Black Hawks	Bill Stewart	1994-95—New Jersey Devils	Jacques Lemaire
1938-39—Boston Bruins	Art Ross	1995-96—Colorado Avalanche	Marc Crawford
1939-40—New York Rangers	Frank Boucher	1996-97—Detroit Red Wings	Scotty Bowman
1940-41—Boston Bruins	Cooney Weiland	1997-98—Detroit Red Wings	Scotty Bowman
1941-42—Toronto Maple Leafs	Hap Day	1998-99—Dallas Stars	Ken Hitchcock
1942-43—Detroit Red Wings	Jack Adams	1999-00—New Jersey Devils	Larry Robinson
1943-44—Montreal Canadiens	Dick Irvin	2000-01—Colorado Rockies	Bob Hartley
1944-45—Toronto Maple Leafs	Hap Day		
1945-46—Montreal Canadiens	Dick Irvin		
1946-47—Toronto Maple Leafs	Hap Day		
1947-48—Toronto Maple Leafs	Hap Day		

NOTE: 1918-19 series between Montreal and Seattle cancelled after five games because of influenza epidemic.

*Stanley Cups won by non-NHL clubs.

†Team captain.

ALL-STAR GAMES

RESULTS

Date	Site	Winning team, score	Losing team, score	Att.
2-14-34†	Maple Leaf Gardens, Toronto	Toronto Maple Leafs, 7	NHL All-Stars, 3	*14,000
11-3-37‡	Montreal Forum	NHL All-Stars, 6	Montreal All-Stars§, 5	8,683
10-29-39∞	Montreal Forum	NHL All-Stars, 5	Montreal Canadiens, 2	*6,000
10-13-47	Maple Leaf Gardens, Toronto	NHL All-Stars, 4	Toronto Maple Leafs, 3	14,169
11-3-48	Chicago Stadium	NHL All-Stars, 3	Toronto Maple Leafs, 1	12,794
10-10-49	Maple Leaf Gardens, Toronto	NHL All-Stars, 3	Toronto Maple Leafs, 1	13,541
10-8-50	Olympia Stadium, Detroit	Detroit Red Wings, 7	NHL All-Stars, 1	9,166
10-9-51	Maple Leaf Gardens, Toronto	First Team▲, 2	Second Team▲, 2	11,469
10-5-52	Olympia Stadium, Detroit	First Team▲, 1	Second Team▲, 1	10,680
10-3-53	Montreal Forum	NHL All-Stars, 3	Montreal Canadiens, 1	14,153
10-2-54	Olympia Stadium, Detroit	NHL All-Stars, 2	Detroit Red Wings, 2	10,689
10-2-55	Olympia Stadium, Detroit	Detroit Red Wings, 3	NHL All-Stars, 1	10,111
10-9-56	Montreal Forum	NHL All-Stars, 1	Montreal Canadiens, 1	13,095
10-5-57	Montreal Forum	NHL All-Stars, 5	Montreal Canadiens, 3	13,095
10-4-58	Montreal Forum	Montreal Canadiens, 6	NHL All-Stars, 3	13,989
10-3-59	Montreal Forum	Montreal Canadiens, 6	NHL All-Stars, 1	13,818
10-1-60	Montreal Forum	NHL All-Stars, 2	Montreal Canadiens, 1	13,949
10-7-61	Chicago Stadium	NHL All-Stars, 3	Chicago Blackhawks, 1	14,534
10-6-62	Maple Leaf Gardens, Toronto	Toronto Maple Leafs, 4	NHL All-Stars, 1	14,236
10-5-63	Maple Leaf Gardens, Toronto	NHL All-Stars, 3	Toronto Maple Leafs, 3	14,034
10-10-64	Maple Leaf Gardens, Toronto	NHL All-Stars, 3	Toronto Maple Leafs, 2	14,232
10-20-65	Montreal Forum	NHL All-Stars, 5	Montreal Canadiens, 2	14,284
1-18-67	Montreal Forum	Montreal Canadiens, 3	NHL All-Stars, 0	14,284
1-16-68	Maple Leaf Gardens, Toronto	Toronto Maple Leafs, 4	NHL All-Stars, 3	15,753
1-21-69	Montreal Forum	West Division, 3	East Division, 3	16,260
1-20-70	St. Louis Arena	East Division, 4	West Division, 1	16,587
1-19-71	Boston Garden	West Division, 2	East Division, 1	14,790
1-25-72	Met Sports Center, Bloomington, Minn.	East Division, 3	West Division, 2	15,423
1-30-73	Madison Square Garden, New York	East Division, 5	West Division, 4	16,986
1-29-74	Chicago Stadium	West Division, 6	East Division, 4	16,426
1-21-75	Montreal Forum	Wales Conference, 7	Campbell Conference, 1	16,080
1-20-76	The Spectrum, Philadelphia	Wales Conference, 7	Campbell Conference, 5	16,436
1-25-77	Pacific Coliseum, Vancouver	Wales Conference, 4	Campbell Conference, 3	15,607
1-24-78	Buffalo Memorial Auditorium	Wales Conference, 3	Campbell Conference, 2 (OT)	16,433
	1979 All-Star Game replaced by Challenge Cup series between Team NHL and Soviet Union			
2-5-80	Joe Louis Arena, Detroit	Wales Conference, 6	Campbell Conference, 3	21,002
2-10-81	The Forum, Los Angeles	Campbell Conference, 4	Wales Conference, 1	15,761
2-9-82	Capital Centre, Landover, Md.	Wales Conference, 4	Campbell Conference, 2	18,130
2-8-83	Nassau Coliseum, Long Island, N.Y.	Campbell Conference, 9	Wales Conference, 3	15,230
1-31-84	Meadowlands Arena, East Rutherford, N.J.	Wales Conference, 7	Campbell Conference, 6	18,939
2-12-85	Olympic Saddledome, Calgary	Wales Conference, 6	Campbell Conference, 4	16,683
2-4-86	Hartford Civic Center	Wales Conference, 4	Campbell Conference, 3 (OT)	15,126
	1987 All-Star Game replaced by Rendez-Vous '87 between Team NHL and Soviet Union			
2-9-88	St. Louis Arena	Wales Conference, 6	Campbell Conference, 5 (OT)	17,878
2-7-89	Northlands Coliseum, Edmonton	Campbell Conference, 9	Wales Conference, 5	17,503
1-21-90	Pittsburgh Civic Arena	Wales Conference, 12	Campbell Conference, 7	17,503
1-19-91	Chicago Stadium	Campbell Conference, 11	Wales Conference, 5	18,472
1-18-92	The Spectrum, Philadelphia	Campbell Conference, 10	Wales Conference, 6	17,380
2-6-93	Montreal Forum	Wales Conference, 16	Campbell Conference, 6	17,137
1-22-94	Madison Square Garden, New York	Eastern Conference, 9	Western Conference, 8	18,200
	1995 All-Star Game canceled because of NHL lockout			
1-20-96	FleetCenter, Boston	Eastern Conference 5	Western Conference 4	17,565
1-18-97	San Jose Arena	Eastern Conference 11	Western Conference 7	17,442
1-18-98	General Motors Place, Vancouver	North America 8	World 7	18,422
1-24-99	Ice Palace, Tampa	North America 8	World 6	19,758
2-6-00	Air Canada Centre, Toronto	World 9	North America 4	19,300
2-4-01	Pepsi Center, Denver	North America 14	World 12	18,646

*Estimated figure.
†Benefit game for Toronto Maple Leafs left wing Ace Bailey, who suffered a career-ending skull injury earlier in the season.
‡Benefit game for the family of Montreal Canadiens center Howie Morenz, who died of a heart attack earlier in the year.
§Montreal All-Star roster made up of players from Montreal Canadiens and Maroons.
∞Benefit game for the family of Montreal Canadiens defenseman Babe Siebert, who drowned earlier in the year.
▲First Team roster supplemented by players from the four American clubs and Second Team roster supplemented by players from the two Canadian clubs.

MOST VALUABLE PLAYERS

Date	Player, All-Star Game team (regular-season team)	Date	Player, All-Star Game team (regular-season team)
10-6-62	Eddie Shack, Toronto Maple Leafs	2-9-82	Mike Bossy, Wales Conf. (New York Islanders)
10-5-63	Frank Mahovlich, Toronto Maple Leafs	2-8-83	Wayne Gretzky, Campbell Conf. (Edmonton Oilers)
10-10-64	Jean Beliveau, All-Stars (Montreal Canadiens)	1-31-84	Don Maloney, Wales Conf. (New York Rangers)
10-20-65	Gordie Howe, All-Stars (Detroit Red Wings)	2-12-85	Mario Lemieux, Wales Conf. (Pittsburgh Penguins)
1-18-67	Henri Richard, Montreal Canadiens	2-4-86	Grant Fuhr, Campbell Conf. (Edmonton Oilers)
1-16-68	Bruce Gamble, Toronto Maple Leafs	2-9-88	Mario Lemieux, Wales Conf. (Pittsburgh Penguins)
1-21-69	Frank Mahovlich, East Div. (Detroit Red Wings)	2-7-89	Wayne Gretzky, Campbell Conf. (Los Angeles Kings)
1-20-70	Bobby Hull, East Div. (Chicago Blackhawks)	1-21-90	Mario Lemieux, Wales Conf. (Pittsburgh Penguins)
1-19-71	Bobby Hull, West Div. (Chicago Blackhawks)	1-19-91	Vincent Damphousse, Camp. Conf. (Tor. Maple Leafs)
1-25-72	Bobby Orr, East Division (Boston Bruins)	1-18-92	Brett Hull, Campbell Conf. (St. Louis Blues)
1-30-73	Greg Polis, West Division (Pittsburgh Penguins)	2-6-93	Mike Gartner, Wales Conf. (New York Rangers)
1-29-74	Garry Unger, West Division (St. Louis Blues)	1-22-94	Mike Richter, Eastern Conf. (New York Rangers)
1-21-75	Syl Apps Jr., Wales Conf. (Pittsburgh Penguins)	1-20-96	Ray Bourque, Eastern Conf. (Boston Bruins)
1-20-76	Peter Mahovlich, Wales Conf. (Montreal Canadiens)	1-18-97	Mark Recchi, Eastern Conf. (Montreal Canadiens)
1-25-77	Rick Martin, Wales Conference (Buffalo Sabres)	1-18-98	Teemu Selanne, North America (Ana. Mighty Ducks)
1-24-78	Billy Smith, Campbell Conf. (New York Islanders)	1-24-99	Wayne Gretzky, North America (New York Rangers)
2-5-80	Reggie Leach, Campbell Conf. (Philadelphia Flyers)	2-6-00	Pavel Bure, World (Florida Panthers)
2-10-81	Mike Liut, Campbell Conf. (St. Louis Blues)	2-4-01	Bill Guerin, North America (Boston Bruins)

YEAR-BY-YEAR STANDINGS

Note: Prior to 1926-27 season, clubs outside the NHL also competed for the Stanley Cup. Non-NHL clubs are denoted in parentheses. Sometimes playoff rounds were decided by total goals scored, rather than by games won.

1917-18

Team	W	L	T	Pts.	GF	GA
Montreal Canadiens	13	9	0	26	115	84
Toronto Arenas	13	9	0	26	108	109
Ottawa Senators	9	13	0	18	102	114
Montreal Wanderers	1	5	0	2	17	35

PLAYOFFS

Semifinals: Toronto 10 goals, Montreal Canadiens 7 goals (2-game series); Vancouver (PCHL) 3 goals, Seattle (PCHL) 2 goals (2-game series).
Stanley Cup finals: Toronto 3, Vancouver (PCHL) 2.

1918-19

Team	W	L	T	Pts.	GF	GA
Ottawa Senators	12	6	0	24	71	54
Montreal Canadiens	10	8	0	20	88	78
Toronto Arenas	5	13	0	10	65	92

PLAYOFFS

Semifinals: Seattle (PCHL) 7 goals, Vancouver 5 goals (2-game series); Montreal Canadiens 3, Ottawa 1.
Stanley Cup finals: Series between Montreal Canadiens and Seattle (PCHL) abandoned (with each team winning two games and one game tied) due to influenza epidemic.

1919-20

Team	W	L	T	Pts.	GF	GA
Ottawa Senators	19	5	0	38	121	64
Montreal Canadiens	13	11	0	26	129	113
Toronto St. Patricks	12	12	0	24	119	106
Quebec Bulldogs	4	20	0	8	91	177

PLAYOFFS

Semifinals: Seattle (PCHL) 7 goals, Vancouver (PCHL) 3 goals (2-game series).
Stanley Cup finals: Ottawa 3, Seattle (PCHL) 2.

1920-21

Team	W	L	T	Pts.	GF	GA
Toronto St. Patricks	15	9	0	30	105	100
Ottawa Senators	14	10	0	28	97	75
Montreal Canadiens	13	11	0	26	112	99
Hamilton Tigers	6	18	0	12	92	132

PLAYOFFS

Semifinals: Vancouver (PCHL) 2, Seattle (PCHL) 0; Ottawa 2, Toronto 0.
Stanley Cup finals: Ottawa 3, Vancouver (PCHL) 2.

1921-22

Team	W	L	T	Pts.	GF	GA
Ottawa Senators	14	8	2	30	106	84
Toronto St. Patricks	13	10	1	27	98	97
Montreal Canadiens	12	11	1	25	88	94
Hamilton Tigers	7	17	0	14	88	105

PLAYOFFS

Preliminaries: Regina (WCHL) 2 goals, Calgary (WCHL) 1 goal (2-game series); Regina (WCHL) 3, Edmonton (WCHL) 2; Vancouver (PCHL) 2, Seattle (PCHL) 0; Vancouver (PCHL) 5 goals, Regina (WCHL) 2 goals (2-game series); Toronto 5 goals, Ottawa 4 goals (2-game series).
Stanley Cup finals: Toronto 3, Vancouver (PCHL) 2.

1922-23

Team	W	L	T	Pts.	GF	GA
Ottawa Senators	14	9	1	29	77	54
Montreal Canadiens	13	9	2	28	73	61
Toronto St. Patricks	13	10	1	27	82	88
Hamilton Tigers	6	18	0	12	81	110

PLAYOFFS

Quarterfinals: Ottawa 3 goals, Montreal Canadiens 2 goals (2-game series); Vancouver (PCHL) 5 goals, Victoria (PCHL) 3 goals (2-game series). **Semifinals:** Ottawa 3, Vancouver (PCHL) 1; Edmonton (WCHL) 4 goals, Regina (WCHL) 3 goals (2-game series).
Stanley Cup finals: Ottawa 2, Edmonton (WCHL) 0.

1923-24

Team	W	L	T	Pts.	GF	GA
Ottawa Senators	16	8	0	32	74	54
Montreal Canadiens	13	11	0	26	59	48
Toronto St. Patricks	10	14	0	20	59	85
Hamilton Tigers	9	15	0	18	63	68

PLAYOFFS

First round: Vancouver (PCHL) 4 goals, Seattle (PCHL) 3 goals (2-game series); Calgary (WCHL) 4 goals, Regina (WCHL) 2 goals (2-game series). **Second round:** Montreal Canadiens 2, Ottawa 0; Calgary (WCHL) 2, Vancouver (PCHL) 1. **Third round:** Montreal Canadiens 2, Vancouver (PCHL) 0.
Stanley Cup finals: Montreal Canadiens 2, Calgary (WCHL) 0.

1924-25

Team	W	L	T	Pts.	GF	GA
Hamilton Tigers	19	10	1	39	90	60
Toronto St. Patricks	19	11	0	38	90	84
Montreal Canadiens	17	11	2	36	93	56
Ottawa Senators	17	12	1	35	83	66
Montreal Maroons	9	19	2	20	45	65
Boston Bruins	6	24	0	12	49	119

PLAYOFFS

Quarterfinals: Victoria (WCHL) 6 goals, Saskatoon (WCHL) 4 goals (2-game series). **Semifinals:** Montreal Canadiens 2, Toronto 0; Victoria (WCHL) 3 goals, Calgary (WCHL) 1 goal (2-game series).
Stanley Cup finals: Victoria (WCHL) 3, Montreal Canadiens 1.

1925-26

Team	W	L	T	Pts.	GF	GA
Ottawa Senators	24	8	4	52	77	42
Montreal Maroons	20	11	5	45	91	73
Pittsburgh Pirates	19	16	1	39	82	70
Boston Bruins	17	15	4	38	92	85
New York Americans	12	20	4	28	68	89
Toronto St. Patricks	12	21	3	27	92	114
Montreal Canadiens	11	24	1	23	79	108

PLAYOFFS

Quarterfinals: Victoria (WHL) 4 goals, Saskatoon (WHL) 3 goals (2-game series); Montreal Maroons 6 goals, Pittsburgh 4 goals (2-game series). **Semifinals:** Victoria (WHL) 5 goals, Edmonton (WHL) 3 goals (2-game series); Montreal Maroons 2 goals, Ottawa 1 goal (2-game series).
Stanley Cup finals: Montreal Maroons 3, Victoria (WHL) 1.

NHL HISTORY *Year-by-year standings*

1926-27

AMERICAN DIVISION

Team	W	L	T	Pts.	GF	GA
New York Rangers	25	13	6	56	95	27
Boston Bruins	21	20	3	45	97	89
Chicago Blackhawks	19	22	3	41	115	116
Pittsburgh Pirates	15	26	3	33	79	108
Detroit Cougars	12	28	4	28	76	105

CANADIAN DIVISION

Team	W	L	T	Pts.	GF	GA
Ottawa Senators	30	10	4	64	89	69
Montreal Canadiens	28	14	2	58	99	67
Montreal Maroons	20	20	4	44	71	68
New York Americans	17	25	2	36	82	91
Toronto St. Patricks	15	24	5	35	79	94

PLAYOFFS

League quarterfinals: Montreal Canadiens 2 goals, Montreal Maroons 1 goal (2-game series); Boston 10 goals, Chicago 5 goals (2-game series). **Semifinals:** Ottawa 5 goals, Montreal Canadiens 1 goal (2-game series); Boston 3 goals, N.Y. Rangers 1 goal (2-game series).
Stanley Cup finals: Ottawa 2, Boston 0.

1927-28

AMERICAN DIVISION

Team	W	L	T	Pts.	GF	GA
Boston Bruins	20	13	11	51	77	70
New York Rangers	19	16	9	47	94	79
Pittsburgh Pirates	19	17	8	46	67	76
Detroit Cougars	19	19	6	44	88	79
Chicago Blackhawks	7	34	3	17	68	134

CANADIAN DIVISION

Team	W	L	T	Pts.	GF	GA
Montreal Canadiens	26	11	7	59	116	48
Montreal Maroons	24	14	6	54	96	77
Ottawa Senators	20	14	10	50	78	57
Toronto Maple Leafs	18	18	8	44	89	88
New York Americans	11	27	6	28	63	128

PLAYOFFS

League quarterfinals: Montreal Maroons 3 goals, Ottawa 1 goal (2-game series); N.Y. Rangers 6 goals, Pittsburgh 4 goals (2-game series). **Semifinals:** Montreal Maroons 3 goals, Montreal Canadiens 2 goals (2-game series); N.Y. Rangers 5 goals, Boston 2 goals (2-game series).
Stanley Cup finals: N.Y. Rangers 3, Montreal Maroons 2.

1928-29

AMERICAN DIVISION

Team	W	L	T	Pts.	GF	GA
Boston Bruins	26	13	5	57	89	52
New York Rangers	21	13	10	52	72	65
Detroit Cougars	19	16	9	47	72	63
Pittsburgh Pirates	9	27	8	26	46	80
Chicago Blackhawks	7	29	8	22	33	85

CANADIAN DIVISION

Team	W	L	T	Pts.	GF	GA
Montreal Canadiens	22	7	15	59	71	43
New York Americans	19	13	12	50	53	53
Toronto Maple Leafs	21	18	5	47	85	69
Ottawa Senators	14	17	13	41	54	67
Montreal Maroons	15	20	9	39	67	65

PLAYOFFS

League quarterfinals: N.Y. Rangers 1 goal, N.Y. Americans 0 goals (2-game series); Toronto 7 goals, Detroit 2 goals (2-game series). **Semifinals:** Boston 3, Montreal Canadiens 0; N.Y. Rangers 2, Toronto 0.
Stanley Cup finals: Boston 2, N.Y. Rangers 0.

1929-30

AMERICAN DIVISION

Team	W	L	T	Pts.	GF	GA
Boston Bruins	38	5	1	77	179	98
Chicago Blackhawks	21	18	5	47	117	111
New York Rangers	17	17	10	44	136	143
Detroit Cougars	14	24	6	34	117	133
Pittsburgh Pirates	5	36	3	13	102	185

CANADIAN DIVISION

Team	W	L	T	Pts.	GF	GA
Montreal Maroons	23	16	5	51	141	114
Montreal Canadiens	21	14	9	51	142	114
Ottawa Senators	21	15	8	50	138	118
Toronto Maple Leafs	17	21	6	40	116	124
New York Americans	14	25	5	33	113	161

PLAYOFFS

League quarterfinals: Montreal Canadiens 3 goals, Chicago 2 goals (2-game series); N.Y. Rangers 6 goals, Ottawa 3 goals (2-game series). **Semifinals:** Boston 3, Montreal Maroons 1; Montreal Canadiens 2, N.Y. Rangers 0.
Stanley Cup finals: Montreal Canadiens 2, Boston 0.

1930-31

AMERICAN DIVISION

Team	W	L	T	Pts.	GF	GA
Boston Bruins	28	10	6	62	143	90
Chicago Blackhawks	24	17	3	51	108	78
New York Rangers	19	16	9	47	106	87
Detroit Falcons	16	21	7	39	102	105
Philadelphia Quakers	4	36	4	12	76	184

CANADIAN DIVISION

Team	W	L	T	Pts.	GF	GA
Montreal Canadiens	26	10	8	60	89	60
Toronto Maple Leafs	22	13	9	53	99	53
Montreal Maroons	20	18	6	46	106	46
New York Americans	18	16	10	46	76	74
Ottawa Senators	10	30	4	24	91	142

PLAYOFFS

League quarterfinals: Chicago 4 goals, Toronto 3 goals (2-game series); N.Y. Rangers 8 goals, Montreal Maroons 1 goal (2-game series). **Semifinals:** Montreal Canadiens 3, Boston 2; Chicago 2, N.Y. Rangers 0.
Stanley Cup finals: Montreal Canadiens 3, Chicago 2.

1931-32

AMERICAN DIVISION

Team	W	L	T	Pts.	GF	GA
New York Rangers	23	17	8	54	134	112
Chicago Blackhawks	18	19	11	47	86	101
Detroit Falcons	18	20	10	46	95	108
Boston Bruins	15	21	12	42	122	117

CANADIAN DIVISION

Team	W	L	T	Pts.	GF	GA
Montreal Canadiens	25	16	7	57	128	111
Toronto Maple Leafs	23	18	7	53	155	127
Montreal Maroons	19	22	7	45	142	139
New York Americans	16	24	8	40	95	142

PLAYOFFS

League quarterfinals: Toronto 6 goals, Chicago 2 goals (2-game series); Montreal Maroons 3 goals, Detroit 1 goal (2-game series). **Semifinals:** N.Y. Rangers 3, Montreal Canadiens 1; Toronto 4 goals, Montreal Maroons 3 (2-game series). **Stanley Cup finals:** Toronto 3, N.Y. Rangers 0.

1932-33

AMERICAN DIVISION

Team	W	L	T	Pts.	GF	GA
Boston Bruins	25	15	8	58	124	88
Detroit Red Wings	25	15	8	58	111	93
New York Rangers	23	17	8	54	135	107
Chicago Blackhawks	16	20	12	44	88	101

CANADIAN DIVISION

Team	W	L	T	Pts.	GF	GA
Toronto Maple Leafs	24	18	6	54	119	111
Montreal Maroons	22	20	6	50	135	119
Montreal Canadiens	18	25	5	41	92	115
New York Americans	15	22	11	41	91	118
Ottawa Senators	11	27	10	32	88	131

PLAYOFFS

League quarterfinals: Detroit 5 goals, Montreal Maroons 2 goals (2-game series); N.Y. Rangers 8 goals, Montreal Canadiens 5 goals (2-game series). **Semifinals:** Toronto 3, Boston 2; N.Y. Rangers 6 goals, Detroit 3 goals (2-game series). **Stanley Cup finals:** N.Y. Rangers 3, Toronto 1.

1933-34

AMERICAN DIVISION

Team	W	L	T	Pts.	GF	GA
Detroit Red Wings	24	14	10	58	113	98
Chicago Blackhawks	20	17	11	51	88	83
New York Rangers	21	19	8	50	120	113
Boston Bruins	18	25	5	41	111	130

CANADIAN DIVISION

Team	W	L	T	Pts.	GF	GA
Toronto Maple Leafs	26	13	9	61	174	119
Montreal Canadiens	22	20	6	50	99	101
Montreal Maroons	19	18	11	49	117	122
New York Americans	15	23	10	40	104	132
Ottawa Senators	13	29	6	32	115	143

PLAYOFFS

League quarterfinals: Chicago 4 goals, Montreal Canadiens 3 goals (2-game series); Montreal Maroons 2 goals, N.Y. Rangers 1 goal (2-game series). **Semifinals:** Detroit 3, Toronto 2; Chicago 6 goals, Montreal Maroons 2 goals (2-game series). **Stanley Cup finals:** Chicago 3, Detroit 1.

1934-35

AMERICAN DIVISION

Team	W	L	T	Pts.	GF	GA
Boston Bruins	26	16	6	58	129	112
Chicago Blackhawks	26	17	5	57	118	88
New York Rangers	22	20	6	50	137	139
Detroit Red Wings	19	22	7	45	127	114

CANADIAN DIVISION

Team	W	L	T	Pts.	GF	GA
Toronto Maple Leafs	30	14	4	64	157	111
Montreal Maroons	24	19	5	53	123	92
Montreal Canadiens	19	23	6	44	110	145
New York Americans	12	27	9	33	100	142
St. Louis Eagles	11	31	6	28	86	144

PLAYOFFS

League quarterfinals: Montreal Maroons 1 goal, Chicago 0 goals (2-game series); N.Y. Rangers 6 goals, Montreal Canadiens 5 goals (2-game series). **Semifinals:** Toronto 3, Boston 1; Montreal Maroons 5 goals, N.Y. Rangers 4 (2-game series). **Stanley Cup finals:** Montreal Maroons 3, Toronto 0.

1935-36

AMERICAN DIVISION

Team	W	L	T	Pts.	GF	GA
Detroit Red Wings	24	16	8	56	124	103
Boston Bruins	22	20	6	50	92	83
Chicago Blackhawks	21	19	8	50	93	92
New York Rangers	19	17	12	50	96	50

CANADIAN DIVISION

Team	W	L	T	Pts.	GF	GA
Montreal Maroons	22	16	10	54	114	106
Toronto Maple Leafs	23	19	6	52	126	106
New York Americans	16	25	7	39	109	122
Montreal Canadiens	11	26	11	33	82	123

PLAYOFFS

League quarterfinals: Toronto 8 goals, Boston 6 goals (2-game series); N.Y. Americans 7 goals, Chicago 5 goals (2-game series). **Semifinals:** Detroit 3, Montreal Maroons 0; Toronto 2, N.Y. Americans 1. **Stanley Cup finals:** Detroit 3, Toronto 1.

1936-37

AMERICAN DIVISION

Team	W	L	T	Pts.	GF	GA
Detroit Red Wings	25	14	9	59	128	102
Boston Bruins	23	18	7	53	120	110
New York Rangers	19	20	9	47	117	106
Chicago Blackhawks	14	27	7	35	99	131

CANADIAN DIVISION

Team	W	L	T	Pts.	GF	GA
Montreal Canadiens	24	18	6	54	115	111
Montreal Maroons	22	17	9	53	126	110
Toronto Maple Leafs	22	21	5	49	119	115
New York Americans	15	29	4	34	122	161

PLAYOFFS

League quarterfinals: Montreal Maroons 2, Boston 1; N.Y. Rangers 2, Toronto 0. **Semifinals:** Detroit 3, Montreal Canadiens 2; N.Y. Rangers 2, Montreal Maroons 0. **Stanley Cup finals:** Detroit 3, N.Y. Rangers 2.

1937-38

AMERICAN DIVISION

Team	W	L	T	Pts.	GF	GA
Boston Bruins	30	11	7	67	142	89
New York Rangers	27	15	6	60	149	96
Chicago Blackhawks	14	25	9	37	97	139
Detroit Red Wings	12	25	11	35	99	133

CANADIAN DIVISION

Team	W	L	T	Pts.	GF	GA
Toronto Maple Leafs	24	15	9	57	151	127
New York Americans	19	18	11	49	110	111
Montreal Canadiens	18	17	13	49	123	128
Montreal Maroons	12	30	6	30	101	149

PLAYOFFS

League quarterfinals: N.Y. Americans 2, N.Y. Rangers 1; Chicago 2, Montreal Canadiens 1. **Semifinals:** Toronto 3, Boston 0; Chicago 2, N.Y. Americans 1. **Stanley Cup finals:** Chicago 3, Toronto 1.

1938-39

Team	W	L	T	Pts.	GF	GA
Boston Bruins	36	10	2	74	156	76
New York Rangers	26	16	6	58	149	105
Toronto Maple Leafs	19	20	9	47	114	107
New York Americans	17	21	10	44	119	157
Detroit Red Wings	18	24	6	42	107	128
Montreal Canadiens	15	24	9	39	115	146
Chicago Blackhawks	12	28	8	32	91	132

PLAYOFFS

League quarterfinals: Toronto 2, N.Y. Americans 0; Detroit 2, Montreal 1. **Semifinals:** Boston 4, N.Y. Rangers 3; Toronto 2, Detroit 1.
Stanley Cup finals: Boston 4, Toronto 1.

1939-40

Team	W	L	T	Pts.	GF	GA
Boston Bruins	31	12	5	67	170	98
New York Rangers	27	11	10	64	136	77
Toronto Maple Leafs	25	17	6	56	134	110
Chicago Blackhawks	23	19	6	52	112	120
Detroit Red Wings	16	26	6	38	90	126
New York Americans	15	29	4	34	106	140
Montreal Canadiens	10	33	5	25	90	167

PLAYOFFS

League quarterfinals: Toronto 2, Chicago 0; Detroit 2, N.Y. Americans 1. **Semifinals:** N.Y. Rangers 4, Boston 2; Toronto 2, Detroit 0.
Stanley Cup finals: N.Y. Rangers 4, Toronto 2.

1940-41

Team	W	L	T	Pts.	GF	GA
Boston Bruins	27	8	13	67	168	102
Toronto Maple Leafs	28	14	6	62	145	99
Detroit Red Wings	21	16	11	53	112	102
New York Rangers	21	19	8	50	143	125
Chicago Blackhawks	16	25	7	39	112	139
Montreal Canadiens	16	26	6	38	121	147
New York Americans	8	29	11	27	99	186

PLAYOFFS

League quarterfinals: Detroit 2, N.Y. Rangers 1; Chicago 2, Montreal 1. **Semifinals:** Boston 4, Toronto 3; Detroit 2, Chicago 0.
Stanley Cup finals: Boston 4, Detroit 0.

1941-42

Team	W	L	T	Pts.	GF	GA
New York Rangers	29	17	2	60	177	143
Toronto Maple Leafs	27	18	3	57	158	136
Boston Bruins	25	17	6	56	160	118
Chicago Blackhawks	22	23	3	47	145	155
Detroit Red Wings	19	25	4	42	140	147
Montreal Canadiens	18	27	3	39	134	173
Brooklyn Americans	16	29	3	35	133	175

PLAYOFFS

League quarterfinals: Boston 2, Chicago 1; Detroit 2, Montreal 1. **Semifinals:** Toronto 4, New York 2; Detroit 2, Boston 0.
Stanley Cup finals: Toronto 4, Detroit 3.

1942-43

Team	W	L	T	Pts.	GF	GA
Detroit Red Wings	25	14	11	61	169	124
Boston Bruins	24	17	9	57	195	176
Toronto Maple Leafs	22	19	9	53	198	159
Montreal Canadiens	19	19	12	50	181	191
Chicago Blackhawks	17	18	15	49	179	180
New York Rangers	11	31	8	30	161	253

PLAYOFFS

League semifinals: Detroit 4, Toronto 2; Boston 4, Montreal 1.
Stanley Cup finals: Detroit 4, Boston 0.

1943-44

Team	W	L	T	Pts.	GF	GA
Montreal Canadiens	38	5	7	83	234	109
Detroit Red Wings	26	18	6	58	214	177
Toronto Maple Leafs	23	23	4	50	214	174
Chicago Blackhawks	22	23	5	49	178	187
Boston Bruins	19	26	5	43	223	268
New York Rangers	6	39	5	17	162	310

PLAYOFFS

League semifinals: Montreal 4, Toronto 1; Chicago 4, Detroit 1.
Stanley Cup finals: Montreal 4, Chicago 0.

1944-45

Team	W	L	T	Pts.	GF	GA
Montreal Canadiens	38	8	4	80	228	121
Detroit Red Wings	31	14	5	67	218	161
Toronto Maple Leafs	24	22	4	52	183	161
Boston Bruins	16	30	4	36	179	219
Chicago Blackhawks	13	30	7	33	141	194
New York Rangers	11	29	10	32	154	247

PLAYOFFS

League semifinals: Toronto 4, Montreal 2; Detroit 4, Boston 3.
Stanley Cup finals: Toronto 4, Detroit 3.

1945-46

Team	W	L	T	Pts.	GF	GA
Montreal Canadiens	28	17	5	61	172	134
Boston Bruins	24	18	8	56	167	156
Chicago Blackhawks	23	20	7	53	200	178
Detroit Red Wings	20	20	10	50	146	159
Toronto Maple Leafs	19	24	7	45	174	185
New York Rangers	13	28	9	35	144	191

PLAYOFFS

League semifinals: Montreal 4, Chicago 0; Boston 4, Detroit 1.
Stanley Cup finals: Montreal 4, Boston 1.

1946-47

Team	W	L	T	Pts.	GF	GA
Montreal Canadiens	34	16	10	78	189	138
Toronto Maple Leafs	31	19	10	72	209	172
Boston Bruins	26	23	11	63	190	175
Detroit Red Wings	22	27	11	55	190	193
New York Rangers	22	32	6	50	167	186
Chicago Blackhawks	19	37	4	42	193	274

PLAYOFFS

League semifinals: Montreal 4, Boston 1; Toronto 4, Detroit 1.
Stanley Cup finals: Toronto 4, Montreal 2.

1947-48

Team	W	L	T	Pts.	GF	GA
Toronto Maple Leafs	32	15	13	77	182	143
Detroit Red Wings	30	18	12	72	187	148
Boston Bruins	23	24	13	59	167	168
New York Rangers	21	26	13	55	176	201
Montreal Canadiens	20	29	11	51	147	169
Chicago Blackhawks	20	34	6	46	195	225

PLAYOFFS

League semifinals: Toronto 4, Boston 1; Detroit 4, New York 2.
Stanley Cup finals: Toronto 4, Detroit 0.

1948-49

Team	W	L	T	Pts.	GF	GA
Detroit Red Wings	34	19	7	75	195	145
Boston Bruins	29	23	8	66	178	163
Montreal Canadiens	28	23	9	65	152	126
Toronto Maple Leafs	22	25	13	57	147	161
Chicago Blackhawks	21	31	8	50	173	211
New York Rangers	18	31	11	47	133	172

PLAYOFFS

League semifinals: Detroit 4, Montreal 3; Toronto 4, Boston 1.
Stanley Cup finals: Toronto 4, Detroit 0.

1949-50

Team	W	L	T	Pts.	GF	GA
Detroit Red Wings	37	19	14	88	229	164
Montreal Canadiens	29	22	19	77	172	150
Toronto Maple Leafs	31	27	12	74	176	173
New York Rangers	28	31	11	67	170	189
Boston Bruins	22	32	16	60	198	228
Chicago Blackhawks	22	38	10	54	203	244

PLAYOFFS

League semifinals: Detroit 4, Toronto 3; New York 4, Montreal 1.
Stanley Cup finals: Detroit 4, New York 3.

1950-51

Team	W	L	T	Pts.	GF	GA
Detroit Red Wings	44	13	13	101	236	139
Toronto Maple Leafs	41	16	13	95	212	138
Montreal Canadiens	25	30	15	65	173	184
Boston Bruins	22	30	18	62	178	197
New York Rangers	20	29	21	61	169	201
Chicago Blackhawks	13	47	10	36	171	280

PLAYOFFS

League semifinals: Montreal 4, Detroit 2; Toronto 4, Boston 1.
Stanley Cup finals: Toronto 4, Montreal 1.

1951-52

Team	W	L	T	Pts.	GF	GA
Detroit Red Wings	44	14	12	100	215	133
Montreal Canadiens	34	26	10	78	195	164
Toronto Maple Leafs	29	25	16	74	168	157
Boston Bruins	25	29	16	66	162	176
New York Rangers	23	34	13	59	192	219
Chicago Blackhawks	17	4	9	43	158	241

PLAYOFFS

League semifinals: Detroit 4, Toronto 0; Montreal 4, Boston 3.
Stanley Cup finals: Detroit 4, Montreal 0.

1952-53

Team	W	L	T	Pts.	GF	GA
Detroit Red Wings	36	16	18	90	222	133
Montreal Canadiens	28	23	19	75	155	148
Boston Bruins	28	29	13	69	152	172
Chicago Blackhawks	27	28	15	69	169	175
Toronto Maple Leafs	27	30	13	67	156	167
New York Rangers	17	37	16	50	152	211

PLAYOFFS

League semifinals: Boston 4, Detroit 2; Montreal 4, Chicago 3.
Stanley Cup finals: Montreal 4, Boston 1.

1953-54

Team	W	L	T	Pts.	GF	GA
Detroit Red Wings	37	19	14	88	191	132
Montreal Canadiens	35	24	11	81	195	141
Toronto Maple Leafs	32	24	14	78	152	131
Boston Bruins	32	28	10	74	177	181
New York Rangers	29	31	10	68	161	182
Chicago Blackhawks	12	51	7	31	133	242

PLAYOFFS

League semifinals: Detroit 4, Toronto 1; Montreal 4, Boston 0.
Stanley Cup finals: Detroit 4, Montreal 3.

1954-55

Team	W	L	T	Pts.	GF	GA
Detroit Red Wings	42	17	11	95	204	134
Montreal Canadiens	41	18	11	93	228	157
Toronto Maple Leafs	24	24	22	70	147	135
Boston Bruins	23	26	21	67	169	188
New York Rangers	17	35	18	52	150	210
Chicago Blackhawks	13	40	17	43	161	235

PLAYOFFS

League semifinals: Detroit 4, Toronto 0; Montreal 4, Boston 1.
Stanley Cup finals: Detroit 4, Montreal 3.

1955-56

Team	W	L	T	Pts.	GF	GA
Montreal Canadiens	45	15	10	100	222	131
Detroit Red Wings	30	24	16	76	183	148
New York Rangers	32	28	10	74	204	203
Toronto Maple Leafs	24	33	13	61	153	181
Boston Bruins	23	34	13	59	147	185
Chicago Blackhawks	19	39	12	50	155	216

PLAYOFFS

League semifinals: Montreal 4, New York 1; Detroit 4, Toronto 1.
Stanley Cup finals: Montreal 4, Detroit 1.

1956-57

Team	W	L	T	Pts.	GF	GA
Detroit Red Wings	38	20	12	88	198	157
Montreal Canadiens	35	23	12	82	210	155
Boston Bruins	34	24	12	80	195	174
New York Rangers	26	30	14	66	184	227
Toronto Maple Leafs	21	34	15	57	174	192
Chicago Blackhawks	16	39	15	47	169	225

PLAYOFFS

League semifinals: Boston 4, Detroit 1; Montreal 4, New York 1.
Stanley Cup finals: Montreal 4, Boston 1.

1957-58

Team	W	L	T	Pts.	GF	GA
Montreal Canadiens	43	17	10	96	250	158
New York Rangers	32	25	13	77	195	188
Detroit Red Wings	29	29	12	70	176	207
Boston Bruins	27	28	15	69	199	194
Chicago Blackhawks	24	39	7	55	163	202
Toronto Maple Leafs	21	38	11	53	192	226

PLAYOFFS

League semifinals: Montreal 4, Detroit 0; Boston 4, New York 2.
Stanley Cup finals: Montreal 4, Boston 2.

1958-59

Team	W	L	T	Pts.	GF	GA
Montreal Canadiens	39	18	13	91	258	158
Boston Bruins	32	29	9	73	205	215
Chicago Blackhawks	28	29	13	69	197	208
Toronto Maple Leafs	27	32	11	65	189	201
New York Rangers	26	32	12	64	201	217
Detroit Red Wings	25	37	8	58	167	218

PLAYOFFS

League semifinals: Montreal 4, Chicago 2; Toronto 4, Boston 3.
Stanley Cup finals: Montreal 4, Toronto 1.

1959-60

Team	W	L	T	Pts.	GF	GA
Montreal Canadiens	40	18	12	92	255	178
Toronto Maple Leafs	35	26	9	79	199	195
Chicago Blackhawks	28	29	13	69	191	180
Detroit Red Wings	26	29	15	67	186	197
Boston Bruins	28	34	8	64	220	241
New York Rangers	17	38	15	49	187	247

PLAYOFFS

League semifinals: Montreal 4, Chicago 0; Toronto 4, Detroit 2.
Stanley Cup finals: Montreal 4, Toronto 0.

1960-61

Team	W	L	T	Pts.	GF	GA
Montreal Canadiens	41	19	10	92	254	188
Toronto Maple Leafs	39	19	12	90	234	176
Chicago Blackhawks	29	24	17	75	198	180
Detroit Red Wings	25	29	16	66	195	215
New York Rangers	22	38	10	54	204	248
Boston Bruins	15	42	13	43	176	254

PLAYOFFS

League semifinals: Chicago 4, Montreal 2; Detroit 4, Toronto 1.
Stanley Cup finals: Chicago 4, Detroit 2.

1961-62

Team	W	L	T	Pts.	GF	GA
Montreal Canadiens	42	14	14	98	259	166
Toronto Maple Leafs	37	22	11	85	232	180
Chicago Blackhawks	31	26	13	75	217	186
New York Rangers	26	32	12	64	195	207
Detroit Red Wings	23	33	14	60	184	219
Boston Bruins	15	47	8	38	177	306

PLAYOFFS

League semifinals: Chicago 4, Montreal 2; Toronto 4, New York 2.
Stanley Cup finals: Toronto 4, Chicago 2.

1962-63

Team	W	L	T	Pts.	GF	GA
Toronto Maple Leafs	35	23	12	82	221	180
Chicago Blackhawks	32	21	17	81	194	178
Montreal Canadiens	28	19	23	79	225	183
Detroit Red Wings	32	25	13	77	200	194
New York Rangers	22	36	12	56	211	233
Boston Bruins	14	39	17	45	198	281

PLAYOFFS

League semifinals: Toronto 4, Montreal 1; Detroit 4, Chicago 2.
Stanley Cup finals: Toronto 4, Detroit 1.

1963-64

Team	W	L	T	Pts.	GF	GA
Montreal Canadiens	36	21	13	85	209	167
Chicago Blackhawks	36	22	12	84	218	169
Toronto Maple Leafs	33	25	12	78	192	172
Detroit Red Wings	30	29	11	71	191	204
New York Rangers	22	38	10	54	186	242
Boston Bruins	18	40	12	48	170	212

PLAYOFFS

League semifinals: Toronto 4, Montreal 3; Detroit 4, Chicago 3.
Stanley Cup finals: Toronto 4, Detroit 3.

1964-65

Team	W	L	T	Pts.	GF	GA
Detroit Red Wings	40	23	7	87	224	175
Montreal Canadiens	36	23	11	83	211	185
Chicago Blackhawks	34	28	8	76	224	176
Toronto Maple Leafs	30	26	14	74	204	173
New York Rangers	20	38	12	52	179	246
Boston Bruins	21	43	6	48	166	253

PLAYOFFS

League semifinals: Chicago 4, Detroit 3; Montreal 4, Toronto 2.
Stanley Cup finals: Montreal 4, Chicago 3.

1965-66

Team	W	L	T	Pts.	GF	GA
Montreal Canadiens	41	21	8	90	239	173
Chicago Blackhawks	37	25	8	82	240	187
Toronto Maple Leafs	34	25	11	79	208	187
Detroit Red Wings	31	27	12	74	221	194
Boston Bruins	21	43	6	48	174	275
New York Rangers	18	41	11	47	195	261

PLAYOFFS

League semifinals: Montreal 4, Toronto 0; Detroit 4, Chicago 2.
Stanley Cup finals: Montreal 4, Detroit 2.

1966-67

Team	W	L	T	Pts.	GF	GA
Chicago Blackhawks	41	17	12	94	264	170
Montreal Canadiens	32	25	13	77	202	188
Toronto Maple Leafs	32	27	11	75	204	211
New York Rangers	30	28	12	72	188	189
Detroit Red Wings	27	39	4	58	212	241
Boston Bruins	17	43	10	44	182	253

PLAYOFFS

League semifinals: Toronto 4, Chicago 2; Montreal 4, New York 0.
Stanley Cup finals: Toronto 4, Montreal 2.

1967-68

EAST DIVISION

Team	W	L	T	Pts.	GF	GA
Montreal Canadiens	42	22	10	94	236	167
New York Rangers	39	23	12	90	226	183
Boston Bruins	37	27	10	84	259	216
Chicago Blackhawks	32	26	16	80	212	222
Toronto Maple Leafs	33	31	10	76	209	176
Detroit Red Wings	27	35	12	66	245	257

WEST DIVISION

Team	W	L	T	Pts.	GF	GA
Philadelphia Flyers	31	32	11	73	173	179
Los Angeles Kings	31	33	10	72	200	224

Team	W	L	T	Pts.	GF	GA
St. Louis Blues	27	31	16	70	177	191
Minnesota North Stars	27	32	15	69	191	226
Pittsburgh Penguins	27	34	13	67	195	216
Oakland Seals	15	42	17	42	153	219

PLAYOFFS

Division semifinals: Montreal 4, Boston 0; Chicago 4, New York 2; St. Louis 4, Philadelphia 3; Minnesota 4, Los Angeles 3. **Division finals:** Montreal 4, Chicago 1; St. Louis 4, Minnesota 3. **Stanley Cup finals:** Montreal 4, St. Louis 0.

1968-69

EAST DIVISION

Team	W	L	T	Pts.	GF	GA
Montreal Canadiens	46	19	11	103	271	202
Boston Bruins	42	18	16	100	303	221
New York Rangers	41	26	9	91	231	196
Toronto Maple Leafs	35	26	15	85	234	217
Detroit Red Wings	33	31	12	78	239	221
Chicago Blackhawks	34	33	9	77	280	246

WEST DIVISION

Team	W	L	T	Pts.	GF	GA
St. Louis Blues	37	25	14	88	204	157
Oakland Seals	29	36	11	69	219	251
Philadelphia Flyers	20	35	21	61	174	225
Los Angeles Kings	24	42	10	58	185	260
Pittsburgh Penguins	20	45	11	51	189	270
Minnesota North Stars	18	43	15	51	189	252

PLAYOFFS

Division semifinals: Montreal 4, New York 0; Boston 4, Toronto 0; St. Louis 4, Philadelphia 0; Los Angeles 4, Oakland 3. **Division finals:** Montreal 4, Boston 2; St. Louis 4, Los Angeles 0. **Stanley Cup finals:** Montreal 4, St. Louis 0.

1969-70

EAST DIVISION

Team	W	L	T	Pts.	GF	GA
Chicago Blackhawks	45	22	9	99	250	170
Boston Bruins	40	17	19	99	277	216
Detroit Red Wings	40	21	15	95	246	199
New York Rangers	38	22	16	92	246	189
Montreal Canadiens	38	22	16	92	244	201
Toronto Maple Leafs	29	34	13	71	222	242

WEST DIVISION

Team	W	L	T	Pts.	GF	GA
St. Louis Blues	37	27	12	86	224	179
Pittsburgh Penguins	26	38	12	64	182	238
Minnesota North Stars	19	35	22	60	224	257
Oakland Seals	22	40	14	58	169	243
Philadelphia Flyers	17	35	24	58	197	225
Los Angeles Kings	14	52	10	38	168	290

PLAYOFFS

Division semifinals: Chicago 4, Detroit 0; Boston 4, N.Y. Rangers 2; St. Louis 4, Minnesota 2; Pittsburgh 4, Oakland 0. **Division finals:** Boston 4, Chicago 0; St. Louis 4, Pittsburgh 2. **Stanley Cup finals:** Boston 4, St. Louis 0.

1970-71

EAST DIVISION

Team	W	L	T	Pts.	GF	GA
Boston Bruins	57	14	7	121	399	207
New York Rangers	49	18	11	109	259	177

Team	W	L	T	Pts.	GF	GA
Montreal Canadiens	42	23	13	97	291	216
Toronto Maple Leafs	37	33	8	82	248	211
Buffalo Sabres	24	39	15	63	217	291
Vancouver Canucks	24	46	8	56	229	296
Detroit Red Wings	22	45	11	55	209	308

WEST DIVISION

Team	W	L	T	Pts.	GF	GA
Chicago Blackhawks	49	20	9	107	277	184
St. Louis Blues	34	25	19	87	223	208
Philadelphia Flyers	28	33	17	73	207	225
Minnesota North Stars	28	34	16	72	191	223
Los Angeles Kings	25	40	13	63	239	303
Pittsburgh Penguins	21	37	20	62	221	240
California Golden Seals	20	53	5	45	199	320

PLAYOFFS

Division semifinals: Montreal 4, Boston 3; N.Y. Rangers 4, Toronto 2; Chicago 4, Philadelphia 0; Minnesota 4, St. Louis 2. **Division finals:** Montreal 4, Minnesota 2; Chicago 4, N.Y. Rangers 3. **Stanley Cup finals:** Montreal 4, Chicago 3.

1971-72

EAST DIVISION

Team	W	L	T	Pts.	GF	GA
Boston Bruins	54	13	11	119	330	204
New York Rangers	48	17	13	109	317	192
Montreal Canadiens	46	16	16	108	307	205
Toronto Maple Leafs	33	31	14	80	209	208
Detroit Red Wings	33	35	10	76	261	262
Buffalo Sabres	16	43	19	51	203	289
Vancouver Canucks	20	50	8	48	203	297

WEST DIVISION

Team	W	L	T	Pts.	GF	GA
Chicago Blackhawks	46	17	15	107	256	166
Minnesota North Stars	37	29	12	86	212	191
St. Louis Blues	28	39	11	67	208	247
Philadelphia Flyers	26	38	14	66	220	258
Pittsburgh Penguins	26	38	14	66	200	236
California Golden Seals	21	39	18	60	216	288
Los Angeles Kings	20	49	9	49	206	305

PLAYOFFS

Division semifinals: Boston 4, Toronto 1; N.Y. Rangers 4, Montreal 2; Chicago 4, Pittsburgh 0; St. Louis 4, Minnesota 3. **Division finals:** N.Y. Rangers 4, Chicago 0; Boston 4, St. Louis 0. **Stanley Cup finals:** Boston 4, N.Y. Rangers 2.

1972-73

EAST DIVISION

Team	W	L	T	Pts.	GF	GA
Montreal Canadiens	52	10	16	120	329	184
Boston Bruins	51	22	5	107	330	235
New York Rangers	47	23	8	102	297	208
Buffalo Sabres	37	27	14	88	257	219
Detroit Red Wings	37	29	12	86	265	243
Toronto Maple Leafs	27	41	10	64	247	279
Vancouver Canucks	22	47	9	53	233	339
New York Islanders	12	60	6	30	170	347

WEST DIVISION

Team	W	L	T	Pts.	GF	GA
Chicago Blackhawks	42	27	9	93	284	225
Philadelphia Flyers	37	30	11	85	296	256
Minnesota North Stars	37	30	11	85	254	230
St. Louis Blues	32	34	12	76	233	251
Pittsburgh Penguins	32	37	9	73	257	265

Team	W	L	T	Pts.	GF	GA
Los Angeles Kings	31	36	11	73	232	245
Atlanta Flames	25	38	15	65	191	239
California Golden Seals	16	46	16	48	213	323

PLAYOFFS

Division semifinals: Montreal 4, Buffalo 2; N.Y. Rangers 4, Boston 1; Chicago 4, St. Louis 1; Philadelphia 4, Minnesota 2. **Division finals:** Montreal 4, Philadelphia 1; Chicago 4, N.Y. Rangers 1.
Stanley Cup finals: Montreal 4, Chicago 2.

1973-74

EAST DIVISION

Team	W	L	T	Pts.	GF	GA
Boston Bruins	52	17	9	113	349	221
Montreal Canadiens	45	42	9	99	293	240
New York Rangers	40	24	14	94	300	251
Toronto Maple Leafs	35	27	16	86	274	230
Buffalo Sabres	32	34	12	76	242	250
Detroit Red Wings	29	39	10	68	255	319
Vancouver Canucks	24	43	11	59	224	296
New York Islanders	19	41	18	56	182	247

WEST DIVISION

Team	W	L	T	Pts.	GF	GA
Philadelphia Flyers	50	16	12	112	273	164
Chicago Blackhawks	41	14	23	105	272	164
Los Angeles Kings	33	33	12	78	233	231
Atlanta Flames	30	34	14	74	214	238
Pittsburgh Penguins	28	41	9	65	242	273
St. Louis Blues	26	40	12	64	206	248
Minnesota North Stars	23	38	17	63	235	275
California Golden Seals	13	55	10	36	195	342

PLAYOFFS

Division semifinals: Boston 4, Toronto 0; N.Y. Rangers 4, Montreal 2; Philadelphia 4, Atlanta 0; Chicago 4, Los Angeles 1. **Division finals:** Boston 4, Chicago 2; Philadelphia 4, N.Y. Rangers 3.
Stanley Cup finals: Philadelphia 4, Boston 2.

1974-75

PRINCE OF WALES CONFERENCE

ADAMS DIVISION

Team	W	L	T	Pts.	GF	GA
Buffalo Sabres	49	16	15	113	354	240
Boston Bruins	40	26	14	94	345	245
Toronto Maple Leafs	31	33	16	78	280	309
California Golden Seals	19	48	13	51	212	316

NORRIS DIVISION

Team	W	L	T	Pts.	GF	GA
Montreal Canadiens	47	14	19	113	374	225
Los Angeles Kings	42	17	21	105	269	185
Pittsburgh Penguins	37	28	15	89	326	289
Detroit Red Wings	23	45	12	58	259	335
Washington Capitals	8	67	5	21	181	446

CLARENCE CAMPBELL CONFERENCE

PATRICK DIVISION

Team	W	L	T	Pts.	GF	GA
Philadelphia Flyers	51	18	11	113	293	181
New York Rangers	37	29	14	88	319	276
New York Islanders	33	25	22	88	264	221
Atlanta Flames	34	31	15	83	243	233

SMYTHE DIVISION

Team	W	L	T	Pts.	GF	GA
Vancouver Canucks	38	32	10	86	271	254
St. Louis Blues	35	31	14	84	269	267
Chicago Blackhawks	37	35	8	82	268	241
Minnesota North Stars	23	50	7	53	221	341
Kansas City Scouts	15	54	11	41	184	328

PLAYOFFS

Preliminaries: Toronto 2, Los Angeles 1; Chicago 2, Boston 1; Pittsburgh 2, St. Louis 0; N.Y. Islanders 2, N.Y. Rangers 1. **Quarterfinals:** Philadelphia 4, Toronto 0; Buffalo 4, Chicago 1; Montreal 4, Vancouver 1; N.Y. Islanders 4, Pittsburgh 3. **Semifinals:** Philadelphia 4, N.Y. Islanders 3; Buffalo 4, Montreal 2.
Stanley Cup finals: Philadelphia 4, Buffalo 2.

1975-76

PRINCE OF WALES CONFERENCE

ADAMS DIVISION

Team	W	L	T	Pts.	GF	GA
Boston Bruins	48	15	17	113	313	237
Buffalo Sabres	46	21	13	105	339	240
Toronto Maple Leafs	34	31	15	83	294	276
California Golden Seals	27	42	11	65	250	278

NORRIS DIVISION

Team	W	L	T	Pts.	GF	GA
Montreal Canadiens	58	11	11	127	337	174
Los Angeles Kings	38	33	9	85	263	265
Pittsburgh Penguins	35	33	12	82	339	303
Detroit Red Wings	26	44	10	62	226	300
Washington Capitals	11	59	10	32	224	394

CLARENCE CAMPBELL CONFERENCE

PATRICK DIVISION

Team	W	L	T	Pts.	GF	GA
Philadelphia Flyers	51	13	16	118	348	209
New York Islanders	42	21	17	101	297	190
Atlanta Flames	35	33	12	82	262	237
New York Rangers	29	42	9	67	262	333

SMYTHE DIVISION

Team	W	L	T	Pts.	GF	GA
Chicago Blackhawks	32	30	18	82	254	261
Vancouver Canucks	33	32	15	81	271	272
St. Louis Blues	29	37	14	72	249	290
Minnesota North Stars	20	53	7	47	195	303
Kansas City Scouts	12	56	12	36	190	351

PLAYOFFS

Preliminaries: Buffalo 2, St. Louis 1; N.Y. Islanders 2, Vancouver 0; Los Angeles 2, Atlanta 0; Toronto 2, Pittsburgh 1. **Quarterfinals:** Montreal 4, Chicago 0; Philadelphia 4, Toronto 3; Boston 4, Los Angeles 3; N.Y. Islanders 4, Buffalo 2. **Semifinals:** Montreal 4, N.Y. Islanders 1; Philadelphia 4, Boston 1.
Stanley Cup finals: Montreal 4, Philadelphia 0.

1976-77

PRINCE OF WALES CONFERENCE

ADAMS DIVISION

Team	W	L	T	Pts.	GF	GA
Boston Bruins	49	23	8	106	312	240
Buffalo Sabres	48	24	8	104	301	220
Toronto Maple Leafs	33	32	15	81	301	285
Cleveland Barons	25	42	13	63	240	292

NORRIS DIVISION

Team	W	L	T	Pts.	GF	GA
Montreal Canadiens	60	8	12	132	387	171
Los Angeles Kings	34	31	15	83	271	241
Pittsburgh Penguins	34	33	13	81	240	252
Washington Capitals	24	42	14	62	221	307
Detroit Red Wings	16	55	9	41	183	309

CLARENCE CAMPBELL CONFERENCE

PATRICK DIVISION

Team	W	L	T	Pts.	GF	GA
Philadelphia Flyers	48	16	16	112	323	213
New York Islanders	47	21	12	106	288	193
Atlanta Flames	34	34	12	80	264	265
New York Rangers	29	37	14	72	272	310

SMYTHE DIVISION

Team	W	L	T	Pts.	GF	GA
St. Louis Blues	32	39	9	73	239	276
Minnesota North Stars	23	39	18	64	240	310
Chicago Blackhawks	26	43	11	63	240	298
Vancouver Canucks	25	42	13	63	235	294
Colorado Rockies	20	46	14	54	226	307

PLAYOFFS

Preliminaries: N.Y. Islanders 2, Chicago 0; Buffalo 2, Minnesota 0; Los Angeles 2, Atlanta 1; Toronto 2, Pittsburgh 1. **Quarterfinals:** Montreal 4, St. Louis 0; Philadelphia 4, Toronto 2; Boston 4, Los Angeles 2; N.Y. Islanders 4, Buffalo 0. **Semifinals:** Montreal 4, N.Y. Islanders 2; Boston 4, Philadelphia 0.
Stanley Cup finals: Montreal 4, Boston 0.

1977-78

PRINCE OF WALES CONFERENCE

ADAMS DIVISION

Team	W	L	T	Pts.	GF	GA
Boston Bruins	51	18	11	113	333	218
Buffalo Sabres	44	19	17	105	288	215
Toronto Maple Leafs	41	29	10	92	271	237
Cleveland Barons	22	45	13	57	230	325

NORRIS DIVISION

Team	W	L	T	Pts.	GF	GA
Montreal Canadiens	59	10	11	129	359	183
Detroit Red Wings	32	34	14	78	252	266
Los Angeles Kings	31	34	15	77	243	245
Pittsburgh Penguins	25	37	18	68	254	321
Washington Capitals	17	49	14	48	195	321

CLARENCE CAMPBELL CONFERENCE

PATRICK DIVISION

Team	W	L	T	Pts.	GF	GA
New York Islanders	48	17	15	111	334	210
Philadelphia Flyers	45	20	15	105	296	200
Atlanta Flames	34	27	19	87	274	252
New York Rangers	30	37	13	73	279	280

SMYTHE DIVISION

Team	W	L	T	Pts.	GF	GA
Chicago Blackhawks	32	29	19	83	230	220
Colorado Rockies	19	40	21	59	257	305
Vancouver Canucks	20	43	17	57	239	320
St. Louis Blues	20	47	13	53	195	304
Minnesota North Stars	18	53	9	45	218	325

PLAYOFFS

Preliminaries: Philadelphia 2, Colorado 0; Buffalo 2, N.Y. Rangers 1; Toronto 2, Los Angeles 0; Detroit 2, Atlanta 0. **Quarterfinals:** Montreal 4, Detroit 1; Boston 4, Chicago 0; Toronto 4, N.Y.

Islanders 3; Philadelphia 4, Buffalo 1. **Semifinals:** Montreal 4, Toronto 0; Boston 4, Philadelphia 1.
Stanley Cup finals: Montreal 4, Boston 2.

1978-79

PRINCE OF WALES CONFERENCE

ADAMS DIVISION

Team	W	L	T	Pts.	GF	GA
Boston Bruins	43	23	14	100	316	270
Buffalo Sabres	36	28	16	88	280	263
Toronto Maple Leafs	34	33	13	81	267	252
Minnesota North Stars	28	40	12	68	257	289

NORRIS DIVISION

Team	W	L	T	Pts.	GF	GA
Montreal Canadiens	52	17	11	115	337	204
Pittsburgh Penguins	36	31	13	85	281	279
Los Angeles Kings	34	34	12	80	292	286
Washington Capitals	24	41	15	63	273	338
Detroit Red Wings	23	41	16	62	252	295

CLARENCE CAMPBELL CONFERENCE

PATRICK DIVISION

Team	W	L	T	Pts.	GF	GA
New York Islanders	51	15	14	116	358	214
Philadelphia Flyers	40	25	15	95	281	248
New York Rangers	40	29	11	91	316	292
Atlanta Flames	41	31	8	90	327	280

SMYTHE DIVISION

Team	W	L	T	Pts.	GF	GA
Chicago Blackhawks	29	36	15	73	244	277
Vancouver Canucks	25	42	13	63	217	291
St. Louis Blues	18	50	12	48	249	348
Colorado Rockies	15	53	12	42	210	331

PLAYOFFS

Preliminaries: Philadelphia 2, Vancouver 1; N.Y. Rangers 2, Los Angeles 0; Toronto 2, Atlanta 0; Pittsburgh 2, Buffalo 1. **Quarterfinals:** N.Y. Islanders 4, Chicago 0; Montreal 4, Toronto 0; Boston 4, Pittsburgh 0; N.Y. Rangers 4, Philadelphia 1. **Semifinals:** N.Y. Rangers 4, N.Y. Islanders 2; Montreal 4, Boston 3.
Stanley Cup finals: Montreal 4, N.Y. Rangers 1.

1979-80

PRINCE OF WALES CONFERENCE

ADAMS DIVISION

Team	W	L	T	Pts.	GF	GA
Buffalo Sabres	47	17	16	110	318	201
Boston Bruins	46	21	13	105	310	234
Minnesota North Stars	36	28	16	88	311	253
Toronto Maple Leafs	35	40	5	75	304	327
Quebec Nordiques	25	44	11	61	248	313

NORRIS DIVISION

Team	W	L	T	Pts.	GF	GA
Montreal Canadiens	47	20	13	107	328	240
Los Angeles Kings	30	36	14	74	290	313
Pittsburgh Penguins	30	37	13	73	251	303
Hartford Whalers	27	34	19	73	303	312
Detroit Red Wings	26	43	11	63	268	306

CLARENCE CAMPBELL CONFERENCE

PATRICK DIVISION

Team	W	L	T	Pts.	GF	GA
Philadelphia Flyers	48	12	20	116	327	254
New York Islanders	39	28	13	91	281	247

Team	W	L	T	Pts.	GF	GA
New York Rangers	38	32	10	86	308	284
Atlanta Flames	35	32	13	83	282	269
Washington Capitals	27	40	13	67	261	293

SMYTHE DIVISION

Team	W	L	T	Pts.	GF	GA
Chicago Blackhawks	34	27	19	87	241	250
St. Louis Blues	34	34	12	80	266	278
Vancouver Canucks	27	37	16	70	256	281
Edmonton Oilers	28	39	13	69	301	322
Winnipeg Jets	20	49	11	51	214	314
Colorado Rockies	19	48	13	51	234	308

PLAYOFFS

Preliminaries: Philadelphia 3, Edmonton 0; Buffalo 3, Vancouver 1; Montreal 3, Hartford 0; Boston 3, Pittsburgh 2; N.Y. Islanders 3, Los Angeles 1; Minnesota 3, Toronto 0; Chicago 3, St. Louis 0; N.Y. Rangers 3, Atlanta 1. **Quarterfinals:** Philadelphia 4, N.Y. Rangers 1; Buffalo 4, Chicago 0; Minnesota 4, Montreal 3; N.Y. Islanders 4, Boston 1. **Semifinals:** Philadelphia 4, Minnesota 1; N.Y. Islanders 4, Buffalo 2. **Stanley Cup finals:** N.Y. Islanders 4, Philadelphia 2.

1980-81

PRINCE OF WALES CONFERENCE

ADAMS DIVISION

Team	W	L	T	Pts.	GF	GA
Buffalo Sabres	39	20	21	99	327	250
Boston Bruins	37	30	13	87	316	272
Minnesota North Stars	35	28	17	87	291	263
Quebec Nordiques	30	32	18	78	314	318
Toronto Maple Leafs	28	37	15	71	322	367

NORRIS DIVISION

Team	W	L	T	Pts.	GF	GA
Montreal Canadiens	45	22	13	103	332	232
Los Angeles Kings	43	24	13	99	337	290
Pittsburgh Penguins	30	37	13	73	302	345
Hartford Whalers	21	41	18	60	292	372
Detroit Red Wings	19	43	18	56	252	339

CLARENCE CAMPBELL CONFERENCE

PATRICK DIVISION

Team	W	L	T	Pts.	GF	GA
New York Islanders	48	18	14	110	355	260
Philadelphia Flyers	41	24	15	97	313	249
Calgary Flames	39	27	14	92	329	298
New York Rangers	30	36	14	74	312	317
Washington Capitals	26	36	18	70	286	317

SMYTHE DIVISION

Team	W	L	T	Pts.	GF	GA
St. Louis Blues	45	18	17	107	352	281
Chicago Blackhawks	31	33	16	78	304	315
Vancouver Canucks	28	32	20	76	289	301
Edmonton Oilers	29	35	16	74	328	327
Colorado Rockies	22	45	13	57	258	344
Winnipeg Jets	9	57	14	32	246	400

PLAYOFFS

Preliminaries: N.Y. Islanders 3, Toronto 0; St. Louis 3, Pittsburgh 2; Edmonton 3, Montreal 0; N.Y. Rangers 3, Los Angeles 1; Buffalo 3, Vancouver 0; Philadelphia 3, Quebec 2; Calgary 3, Chicago 0; Minnesota 3, Boston 0. **Quarterfinals:** N.Y. Islanders 4, Edmonton 2; N.Y. Rangers 4, St. Louis 2; Minnesota 4, Buffalo 1; Calgary 4, Philadelphia 3. **Semifinals:** N.Y. Islanders 4, N.Y. Rangers 0; Minnesota 4, Calgary 2. **Stanley Cup finals:** N.Y. Islanders 4, Minnesota 1.

1981-82

PRINCE OF WALES CONFERENCE

ADAMS DIVISION

Team	W	L	T	Pts.	GF	GA
Montreal Canadiens	46	17	17	109	360	223
Boston Bruins	43	27	10	96	323	285
Buffalo Sabres	39	26	15	93	307	273
Quebec Nordiques	33	31	16	82	356	345
Hartford Whalers	21	41	18	60	264	351

PATRICK DIVISION

Team	W	L	T	Pts.	GF	GA
New York Islanders	54	16	10	118	385	250
New York Rangers	39	27	14	92	316	306
Philadelphia Flyers	38	31	11	87	325	313
Pittsburgh Penguins	31	36	13	75	310	337
Washington Capitals	26	41	13	65	319	338

CLARENCE CAMPBELL CONFERENCE

NORRIS DIVISION

Team	W	L	T	Pts.	GF	GA
Minnesota North Stars	37	23	20	94	346	288
Winnipeg Jets	33	33	14	80	319	332
St. Louis Blues	32	40	8	72	315	349
Chicago Blackhawks	30	38	12	72	332	363
Toronto Maple Leafs	20	44	16	56	298	380
Detroit Red Wings	21	47	12	54	270	351

SMYTHE DIVISION

Team	W	L	T	Pts.	GF	GA
Edmonton Oilers	48	17	15	111	417	295
Vancouver Canucks	30	33	17	77	290	286
Calgary Flames	29	34	17	75	334	345
Los Angeles Kings	24	41	15	63	314	369
Colorado Rockies	18	49	13	49	241	362

PLAYOFFS

Wales Conference division semifinals: Quebec 3, Montreal 2; Boston 3, Buffalo 1; N.Y. Islanders 3, Pittsburgh 2; N.Y. Rangers 3, Philadelphia 1. **Division finals:** Quebec 4, Boston 3; N.Y. Islanders 4, N.Y. Rangers 2. **Conference finals:** N.Y. Islanders 4, Quebec 0.
Campbell Conference division semifinals: Chicago 3, Minnesota 1; St. Louis 3, Winnipeg 1; Los Angeles 3, Edmonton 2; Vancouver 3, Calgary 0. **Division finals:** Chicago 4, St. Louis 2; Vancouver 4, Los Angeles 1. **Conference finals:** Vancouver 4, Chicago 1.
Stanley Cup finals: N.Y. Islanders 4, Vancouver 0.

1982-83

PRINCE OF WALES CONFERENCE

ADAMS DIVISION

Team	W	L	T	Pts.	GF	GA
Boston Bruins	50	20	10	110	327	228
Montreal Canadiens	42	24	14	98	350	286
Buffalo Sabres	38	29	13	89	318	285
Quebec Nordiques	34	34	12	80	343	336
Hartford Whalers	19	54	7	45	261	403

PATRICK DIVISION

Team	W	L	T	Pts.	GF	GA
Philadelphia Flyers	49	23	8	106	326	240
New York Islanders	42	26	12	96	302	226
Washington Capitals	39	25	16	94	306	283
New York Rangers	35	35	10	80	306	287
New Jersey Devils	17	49	14	48	230	338
Pittsburgh Penguins	18	53	9	45	257	394

CLARENCE CAMPBELL CONFERENCE

NORRIS DIVISION

Team	W	L	T	Pts.	GF	GA
Chicago Blackhawks	47	23	10	104	338	268
Minnesota North Stars	40	24	16	96	321	290
Toronto Maple Leafs	28	40	12	68	293	330
St. Louis Blues	25	40	15	65	285	316
Detroit Red Wings	21	44	15	57	263	344

SMYTHE DIVISION

Team	W	L	T	Pts.	GF	GA
Edmonton Oilers	47	21	12	106	424	315
Calgary Flames	32	34	14	78	321	317
Vancouver Canucks	30	35	15	75	303	309
Winnipeg Jets	33	39	8	74	311	333
Los Angeles Kings	27	41	12	66	308	365

PLAYOFFS

Wales Conference division semifinals: Boston 3, Quebec 1; Buffalo 3, Montreal 0; N.Y. Rangers 3, Philadelphia 0; N.Y. Islanders 3, Washington 1. **Division finals:** Boston 4, Buffalo 3; N.Y. Islanders 4, N.Y. Rangers 2. **Conference finals:** N.Y. Islanders 4, Boston 2. **Campbell Conference division semifinals:** Chicago 3, St. Louis 1; Minnesota 3, Toronto 1; Edmonton 3, Winnipeg 0; Calgary 3, Vancouver 1. **Division finals:** Chicago 4, Minnesota 1; Edmonton 4, Calgary 1. **Conference finals:** Edmonton 4, Chicago 0. **Stanley Cup finals:** N.Y. Islanders 4, Edmonton 0.

1983-84

PRINCE OF WALES CONFERENCE

ADAMS DIVISION

Team	W	L	T	Pts.	GF	GA
Boston Bruins	49	25	6	104	336	261
Buffalo Sabres	48	25	7	103	315	257
Quebec Nordiques	42	28	10	94	360	278
Montreal Canadiens	35	40	5	75	286	295
Hartford Whalers	28	42	10	66	288	320

PATRICK DIVISION

Team	W	L	T	Pts.	GF	GA
New York Islanders	50	26	4	104	357	269
Washington Capitals	48	27	5	101	308	226
Philadelphia Flyers	44	26	10	98	350	290
New York Rangers	42	29	9	93	314	304
New Jersey Devils	17	56	7	41	231	350
Pittsburgh Penguins	16	58	6	38	254	390

CLARENCE CAMPBELL CONFERENCE

NORRIS DIVISION

Team	W	L	T	Pts.	GF	GA
Minnesota North Stars	39	31	10	88	345	344
St. Louis Blues	32	41	7	71	293	316
Detroit Red Wings	31	42	7	69	298	323
Chicago Blackhawks	30	42	8	68	277	311
Toronto Maple Leafs	26	45	9	61	303	387

SMYTHE DIVISION

Team	W	L	T	Pts.	GF	GA
Edmonton Oilers	57	18	5	119	446	314
Calgary Flames	34	32	14	82	311	314
Vancouver Canucks	32	39	9	73	306	328
Winnipeg Jets	31	38	11	73	340	374
Los Angeles Kings	23	44	13	59	309	376

PLAYOFFS

Wales Conference division semifinals: Montreal 3, Boston 0; Quebec 3, Buffalo 0; N.Y. Islanders 3, N.Y. Rangers 2; Washington 3, Philadelphia 0. **Division finals:** Montreal 4, Quebec 2; N.Y. Islanders 4, Washington 1. **Conference finals:** N.Y. Islanders 4, Montreal 2. **Campbell Conference division semifinals:** Minnesota 3, Chicago 2; St. Louis 3, Detroit 1; Edmonton 3, Winnipeg 0; Calgary 3, Vancouver 1. **Division finals:** Minnesota 4, St. Louis 3; Edmonton 4, Calgary 3. **Conference finals:** Edmonton 4, Minnesota 0. **Stanley Cup finals:** Edmonton 4, N.Y. Islanders 1.

1984-85

PRINCE OF WALES CONFERENCE

ADAMS DIVISION

Team	W	L	T	Pts.	GF	GA
Montreal Canadiens	41	27	12	94	309	262
Quebec Nordiques	41	30	9	91	323	275
Buffalo Sabres	38	28	14	90	290	237
Boston Bruins	36	34	10	82	303	287
Hartford Whalers	30	41	9	69	268	318

PATRICK DIVISION

Team	W	L	T	Pts.	GF	GA
Philadelphia Flyers	53	20	7	113	348	241
Washington Capitals	46	25	9	101	322	240
New York Islanders	40	34	6	86	345	312
New York Rangers	26	44	10	62	295	345
New Jersey Devils	22	48	10	54	264	346
Pittsburgh Penguins	24	51	5	53	276	385

CLARENCE CAMPBELL CONFERENCE

NORRIS DIVISION

Team	W	L	T	Pts.	GF	GA
St. Louis Blues	37	31	12	86	299	288
Chicago Blackhawks	38	35	7	83	309	299
Detroit Red Wings	27	41	12	66	313	357
Minnesota North Stars	25	43	12	62	268	321
Toronto Maple Leafs	20	52	8	48	253	358

SMYTHE DIVISION

Team	W	L	T	Pts.	GF	GA
Edmonton Oilers	49	20	11	109	401	298
Winnipeg Jets	43	27	10	96	358	332
Calgary Flames	41	27	12	94	363	302
Los Angeles Kings	34	32	14	82	339	326
Vancouver Canucks	25	46	9	59	284	401

PLAYOFFS

Wales Conference division semifinals: Montreal 3, Boston 2; Quebec 3, Buffalo 2; Philadelphia 3, N.Y. Rangers 0; N.Y. Islanders 3, Washington 2. **Division finals:** Quebec 4, Montreal 3; Philadelphia 4, N.Y. Islanders 1. **Conference finals:** Philadelphia 4, Quebec 2. **Campbell Conference division semifinals:** Minnesota 3, St. Louis 0; Chicago 3, Detroit 0; Edmonton 3, Los Angeles 0; Winnipeg 3, Calgary 1. **Division finals:** Chicago 4, Minnesota 2; Edmonton 4, Winnipeg 0. **Conference finals:** Edmonton 4, Chicago 2. **Stanley Cup finals:** Edmonton 4, Philadelphia 1.

1985-86

PRINCE OF WALES CONFERENCE

ADAMS DIVISION

Team	W	L	T	Pts.	GF	GA
Quebec Nordiques	43	31	6	92	330	289
Montreal Canadiens	40	33	7	87	330	280
Boston Bruins	37	31	12	86	311	288
Hartford Whalers	40	36	4	84	332	302
Buffalo Sabres	37	37	6	80	296	291

PATRICK DIVISION

Team	W	L	T	Pts.	GF	GA
Philadelphia Flyers	53	23	4	110	335	241
Washington Capitals	50	23	7	107	315	272
New York Islanders	39	29	12	90	327	284
New York Rangers	36	38	6	78	280	276
Pittsburgh Penguins	34	38	8	76	313	305
New Jersey Devils	28	49	3	59	300	374

CLARENCE CAMPBELL CONFERENCE

NORRIS DIVISION

Team	W	L	T	Pts.	GF	GA
Chicago Blackhawks	39	33	8	86	351	349
Minnesota North Stars	38	33	9	85	327	305
St. Louis Blues	37	34	9	83	302	291
Toronto Maple Leafs	25	48	7	57	311	386
Detroit Red Wings	17	57	6	40	266	415

SMYTHE DIVISION

Team	W	L	T	Pts.	GF	GA
Edmonton Oilers	56	17	7	119	426	310
Calgary Flames	40	31	9	89	354	315
Winnipeg Jets	26	47	7	59	295	372
Vancouver Canucks	23	44	13	59	282	333
Los Angeles Kings	23	49	8	54	284	389

PLAYOFFS

Wales Conference division semifinals: Hartford 3, Quebec 0; Montreal 3, Boston 0; N.Y. Rangers 3, Philadelphia 2; Washington 3, N.Y. Rangers 0. **Division finals:** Montreal 4, Hartford 3; N.Y. Rangers 4, Washington 2. **Conference finals:** Montreal 4, N.Y. Rangers 1.
Campbell Conference division semifinals: Toronto 3, Chicago 0; St. Louis 3, Minnesota 2; Edmonton 3, Vancouver 0; Calgary 3, Winnipeg 0. **Division finals:** St. Louis 4, Toronto 3; Calgary 4, Edmonton 3. **Conference finals:** Calgary 4, St. Louis 3. **Stanley Cup finals:** Montreal 4, Calgary 1.

1986-87

PRINCE OF WALES CONFERENCE

ADAMS DIVISION

Team	W	L	T	Pts.	GF	GA
Hartford Whalers	43	30	7	93	287	270
Montreal Canadiens	41	29	10	92	277	241
Boston Bruins	39	34	7	85	301	276
Quebec Nordiques	31	39	10	72	267	276
Buffalo Sabres	28	44	8	64	280	308

PATRICK DIVISION

Team	W	L	T	Pts.	GF	GA
Philadelphia Flyers	46	26	8	100	310	245
Washington Capitals	38	32	10	86	285	278
New York Islanders	35	33	12	82	279	281
New York Rangers	34	38	8	76	307	323
Pittsburgh Penguins	30	38	12	72	297	290
New Jersey Devils	29	45	6	64	293	368

CLARENCE CAMPBELL CONFERENCE

NORRIS DIVISION

Team	W	L	T	Pts.	GF	GA
St. Louis Blues	32	33	15	79	281	293
Detroit Red Wings	34	36	10	78	260	274
Chicago Blackhawks	29	37	14	72	290	310
Toronto Maple Leafs	32	42	6	70	286	319
Minnesota North Stars	30	40	10	70	296	314

SMYTHE DIVISION

Team	W	L	T	Pts.	GF	GA
Edmonton Oilers	50	24	6	106	372	284
Calgary Flames	46	31	3	95	318	289

PLAYOFFS

Wales Conference division semifinals: Quebec 4, Hartford 2; Montreal 4, Boston 0; Philadelphia 4, N.Y. Rangers 2; N.Y. Islanders 4, Washington 3. **Division finals:** Montreal 4, Quebec 3; Philadelphia 4, N.Y. Islanders 3. **Conference finals:** Philadelphia 4, Montreal 2.
Campbell Conference division semifinals: Toronto 4, St. Louis 2; Detroit 4, Chicago 0; Edmonton 4, Los Angeles 1; Winnipeg 4, Calgary 2. **Division finals:** Detroit 4, Toronto 3; Edmonton 4, Winnipeg 0. **Conference finals:** Edmonton 4, Detroit 1.
Stanley Cup finals: Edmonton 4, Philadelphia 3.

1987-88

PRINCE OF WALES CONFERENCE

ADAMS DIVISION

Team	W	L	T	Pts.	GF	GA
Montreal Canadiens	45	22	13	103	298	238
Boston Bruins	44	30	6	94	300	251
Buffalo Sabres	37	32	11	85	283	305
Hartford Whalers	35	38	7	77	249	267
Quebec Nordiques	32	43	5	69	271	306

PATRICK DIVISION

Team	W	L	T	Pts.	GF	GA
New York Islanders	39	31	10	88	308	267
Philadelphia Flyers	38	33	9	85	292	282
Washington Capitals	38	33	9	85	281	249
New Jersey Devils	38	36	6	82	295	296
New York Rangers	36	34	10	82	300	283
Pittsburgh Penguins	36	35	9	81	319	316

CLARENCE CAMPBELL CONFERENCE

NORRIS DIVISION

Team	W	L	T	Pts.	GF	GA
Detroit Red Wings	41	28	11	93	322	269
St. Louis Blues	34	38	8	76	278	294
Chicago Blackhawks	30	41	9	69	284	326
Toronto Maple Leafs	21	49	10	52	273	345
Minnesota North Stars	19	48	13	51	242	349

SMYTHE DIVISION

Team	W	L	T	Pts.	GF	GA
Calgary Flames	48	23	9	105	397	305
Edmonton Oilers	44	25	11	99	363	288
Winnipeg Jets	33	36	11	77	292	310
Los Angeles Kings	30	42	8	68	318	359
Vancouver Canucks	25	46	9	59	272	320

PLAYOFFS

Wales Conference division semifinals: Montreal 4, Hartford 2; Boston 4, Buffalo 2; New Jersey 4, N.Y. Islanders 2; Washington 4, Philadelphia 3. **Division finals:** Boston 4, Montreal 1; New Jersey 4, Washington 3. **Conference finals:** Boston 4, New Jersey 3.
Campbell Conference division semifinals: Detroit 4, Toronto 2; St. Louis 4, Chicago 1; Calgary 4, Los Angeles 1; Edmonton 4, Winnipeg 1. **Division finals:** Detroit 4, St. Louis 1; Edmonton 4, Calgary 0. **Conference finals:** Edmonton 4, Detroit 1.
Stanley Cup finals: Edmonton 4, Boston 0.

1988-89

PRINCE OF WALES CONFERENCE

ADAMS DIVISION

Team	W	L	T	Pts.	GF	GA
Montreal Canadiens	53	18	9	115	315	218
Boston Bruins	37	29	14	88	289	256
Buffalo Sabres	38	35	7	83	291	299
Hartford Whalers	37	38	5	79	299	290
Quebec Nordiques	27	46	7	61	269	342

PATRICK DIVISION

Team	W	L	T	Pts.	GF	GA
Washington Capitals	41	29	10	92	305	259
Pittsburgh Penguins	40	33	7	87	347	349
New York Rangers	37	35	8	82	310	307
Philadelphia Flyers	36	36	8	80	307	285
New Jersey Devils	27	41	12	66	281	325
New York Islanders	28	47	5	61	265	325

CLARENCE CAMPBELL CONFERENCE

NORRIS DIVISION

Team	W	L	T	Pts.	GF	GA
Detroit Red Wings	34	34	12	80	313	316
St. Louis Blues	33	35	12	78	275	285
Minnesota North Stars	27	37	16	70	258	278
Chicago Blackhawks	27	41	12	66	297	335
Toronto Maple Leafs	28	46	6	62	259	342

SMYTHE DIVISION

Team	W	L	T	Pts.	GF	GA
Calgary Flames	54	17	9	117	354	226
Los Angeles Kings	42	31	7	91	376	335
Edmonton Oilers	38	34	8	84	325	306
Vancouver Canucks	33	39	8	74	251	253
Winnipeg Jets	26	42	12	64	300	355

PLAYOFFS

Wales Conference division semifinals: Montreal 4, Hartford 0; Boston 4, Buffalo 1; Philadelphia 4, Washington 2; Pittsburgh 4, N.Y. Rangers 0. **Division finals:** Montreal 4, Boston 1; Philadelphia 4, Pittsburgh 3. **Conference finals:** Montreal 4, Philadelphia 2.
Campbell Conference division semifinals: Chicago 4, Detroit 2; St. Louis 4, Minnesota 1; Calgary 4, Vancouver 3; Los Angeles 4, Edmonton 3. **Division finals:** Chicago 4, St. Louis 1; Calgary 4, Los Angeles 0. **Conference finals:** Calgary 4, Chicago 1.
Stanley Cup finals: Calgary 4, Montreal 2.

1989-90

PRINCE OF WALES CONFERENCE

ADAMS DIVISION

Team	W	L	T	Pts.	GF	GA
Boston Bruins	46	25	9	101	289	232
Buffalo Sabres	45	27	8	98	286	248
Montreal Canadiens	41	28	11	93	288	234
Hartford Whalers	38	33	9	85	275	268
Quebec Nordiques	12	61	7	31	240	407

PATRICK DIVISION

Team	W	L	T	Pts.	GF	GA
New York Rangers	36	31	13	85	279	267
New Jersey Devils	37	34	9	83	295	288
Washington Capitals	36	38	6	78	284	275
New York Islanders	31	38	11	73	281	288
Pittsburgh Penguins	32	40	8	72	318	359
Philadelphia Flyers	30	39	11	71	290	297

CLARENCE CAMPBELL CONFERENCE

NORRIS DIVISION

Team	W	L	T	Pts.	GF	GA
Chicago Blackhawks	41	33	6	88	316	294
St. Louis Blues	37	34	9	83	295	279
Toronto Maple Leafs	38	38	4	80	337	358
Minnesota North Stars	36	40	4	76	284	291
Detroit Red Wings	28	38	14	70	288	323

SMYTHE DIVISION

Team	W	L	T	Pts.	GF	GA
Calgary Flames	42	23	15	99	348	265
Edmonton Oilers	38	28	14	90	315	283
Winnipeg Jets	37	32	11	85	298	290
Los Angeles Kings	34	39	7	75	338	337
Vancouver Canucks	25	41	14	64	245	306

PLAYOFFS

Wales Conference division semifinals: Boston 4, Hartford 3; Montreal 4, Buffalo 3; N.Y. Rangers 4, N.Y. Islanders 1; Washington 4, New Jersey 2. **Division finals:** Boston 4, Montreal 1; Washington 4, N.Y. Rangers 1. **Conference finals:** Boston 4, Washington 0.
Campbell Conference division semifinals: Chicago 4, Minnesota 3; St. Louis 4, Toronto 1; Los Angeles 4, Calgary 2; Edmonton 4, Winnipeg 3. **Division finals:** Chicago 4, St. Louis 3; Edmonton 4, Los Angeles 0. **Conference finals:** Edmonton 4, Chicago 2.
Stanley Cup finals: Edmonton 4, Boston 1.

1990-91

PRINCE OF WALES CONFERENCE

ADAMS DIVISION

Team	W	L	T	Pts.	GF	GA
Boston Bruins	44	24	12	100	299	264
Montreal Canadiens	39	30	11	89	273	249
Buffalo Sabres	31	30	19	81	292	278
Hartford Whalers	31	38	11	73	238	276
Quebec Nordiques	16	50	14	46	236	354

PATRICK DIVISION

Team	W	L	T	Pts.	GF	GA
Pittsburgh Penguins	41	33	6	88	342	305
New York Rangers	36	31	13	85	297	265
Washington Capitals	37	36	7	81	258	258
New Jersey Devils	32	33	15	79	272	264
Philadelphia Flyers	33	37	10	76	252	267
New York Islanders	25	45	10	60	223	290

CLARENCE CAMPBELL CONFERENCE

NORRIS DIVISION

Team	W	L	T	Pts.	GF	GA
Chicago Blackhawks	49	23	8	106	284	211
St. Louis Blues	47	22	11	105	310	250
Detroit Red Wings	34	38	8	76	273	298
Minnesota North Stars	27	39	14	68	256	266
Toronto Maple Leafs	23	46	11	57	241	318

SMYTHE DIVISION

Team	W	L	T	Pts.	GF	GA
Los Angeles Kings	46	24	10	102	340	254
Calgary Flames	46	26	8	100	344	263
Edmonton Oilers	37	37	6	80	272	272
Vancouver Canucks	28	43	9	65	243	315
Winnipeg Jets	26	43	11	63	260	288

PLAYOFFS

Wales Conference division semifinals: Boston 4, Hartford 2; Montreal 4, Buffalo 2; Pittsburgh 4, New Jersey 3; Washington

4, N.Y. Rangers 2. **Division finals:** Boston 4, Montreal 3; Pittsburgh 4, Washington 1. **Conference finals:** Pittsburgh 4, Boston 2.

Campbell Conference division semifinals: Minnesota 4, Chicago 2; St. Louis 4, Detroit 3; Los Angeles 4, Vancouver 2; Edmonton 4, Calgary 3. **Division finals:** Minnesota 4, St. Louis 2; Edmonton 4, Los Angeles 2. **Conference finals:** Minnesota 4, Edmonton 1.

Stanley Cup finals: Pittsburgh 4, Minnesota 2.

1991-92

PRINCE OF WALES CONFERENCE

ADAMS DIVISION

Team	W	L	T	Pts.	GF	GA
Montreal Canadiens	41	28	11	93	267	207
Boston Bruins	36	32	12	84	270	275
Buffalo Sabres	31	37	12	74	289	299
Hartford Whalers	26	41	13	65	247	283
Quebec Nordiques	20	48	12	52	255	318

PATRICK DIVISION

Team	W	L	T	Pts.	GF	GA
New York Rangers	50	25	5	105	321	246
Washington Capitals	45	27	8	98	330	275
Pittsburgh Penguins	39	32	9	87	343	308
New Jersey Devils	38	31	11	87	289	259
New York Islanders	34	35	11	79	291	299
Philadelphia Flyers	32	37	11	75	252	273

CLARENCE CAMPBELL CONFERENCE

NORRIS DIVISION

Team	W	L	T	Pts.	GF	GA
Detroit Red Wings	43	25	12	98	320	256
Chicago Blackhawks	36	29	15	87	257	236
St. Louis Blues	36	33	11	83	279	266
Minnesota North Stars	32	42	6	70	246	278
Toronto Maple Leafs	30	43	7	67	234	294

SMYTHE DIVISION

Team	W	L	T	Pts.	GF	GA
Vancouver Canucks	42	26	12	96	285	250
Los Angeles Kings	35	31	14	84	287	296
Edmonton Oilers	36	34	10	82	295	297
Winnipeg Jets	33	32	15	81	251	244
Calgary Flames	31	37	12	74	296	305
San Jose Sharks	17	58	5	39	219	359

PLAYOFFS

Wales Conference division semifinals: Montreal 4, Hartford 3; Boston 4, Buffalo 3; N.Y. Rangers 4, New Jersey 3; Pittsburgh 4, Washington 3. **Division finals:** Boston 4, Montreal 0; Pittsburgh 4, N.Y. Rangers 2. **Conference finals:** Pittsburgh 4, Boston 0.

Campbell Conference division semifinals: Detroit 4, Minnesota 3; Chicago 4, St. Louis 2; Vancouver 4, Winnipeg 3; Edmonton 4, Los Angeles 2. **Division finals:** Chicago 4, Detroit 0; Edmonton 4, Vancouver 2. **Conference finals:** Chicago 4, Edmonton 0.

Stanley Cup finals: Pittsburgh 4, Chicago 0.

1992-93

PRINCE OF WALES CONFERENCE

ADAMS DIVISION

Team	W	L	T	Pts.	GF	GA
Boston Bruins	51	26	7	109	332	268
Quebec Nordiques	47	27	10	104	351	300
Montreal Canadiens	48	30	6	102	326	280

Team	W	L	T	Pts.	GF	GA
Buffalo Sabres	38	36	10	86	335	297
Hartford Whalers	26	52	6	58	284	369
Ottawa Senators	10	70	4	24	202	395

PATRICK DIVISION

Team	W	L	T	Pts.	GF	GA
Pittsburgh Penguins	56	21	7	119	367	268
Washington Capitals	43	34	7	93	325	286
New York Islanders	40	37	7	87	308	299
New Jersey Devils	40	37	7	87	335	297
Philadelphia Flyers	36	37	11	83	319	319
New York Rangers	34	39	11	79	304	308

CLARENCE CAMPBELL CONFERENCE

NORRIS DIVISION

Team	W	L	T	Pts.	GF	GA
Chicago Blackhawks	47	25	12	106	279	230
Detroit Red Wings	47	28	9	103	369	280
Toronto Maple Leafs	44	29	11	99	288	241
St. Louis Blues	37	36	11	85	282	278
Minnesota North Stars	36	38	10	82	272	293
Tampa Bay Lightning	23	54	7	53	245	332

SMYTHE DIVISION

Team	W	L	T	Pts.	GF	GA
Vancouver Canucks	46	29	9	101	346	278
Calgary Flames	43	30	11	97	322	282
Los Angeles Kings	39	35	10	88	338	340
Winnipeg Jets	40	37	7	87	322	320
Edmonton Oilers	26	50	8	60	242	337
San Jose Sharks	11	71	2	24	218	414

PLAYOFFS

Wales Conference division semifinals: Buffalo 4, Boston 0; Montreal 4, Quebec 2; Pittsburgh 4, New Jersey 1; N.Y. Islanders 4, Washington 2. **Division finals:** Montreal 4, Buffalo 0; N.Y. Islanders 4, Pittsburgh 3. **Conference finals:** Montreal 4, N.Y. Islanders 1.

Campbell Conference division semifinals: St. Louis 4, Chicago 0; Toronto 4, Detroit 3; Vancouver 4, Winnipeg 2; Los Angeles 4, Calgary 2. **Division finals:** Toronto 4, St. Louis 3; Los Angeles 4, Vancouver 2. **Conference finals:** Los Angeles 4, Toronto 3.

Stanley Cup finals: Montreal 4, Los Angeles 1.

1993-94

EASTERN CONFERENCE

ATLANTIC DIVISION

Team	W	L	T	Pts.	GF	GA
New York Rangers	52	24	8	112	299	231
New Jersey Devils	47	25	12	106	306	220
Washington Capitals	39	35	10	88	277	263
New York Islanders	36	36	12	84	282	264
Florida Panthers	33	34	17	83	233	233
Philadelphia Flyers	35	39	10	80	294	314
Tampa Bay Lightning	30	43	11	71	224	251

NORTHEAST DIVISION

Team	W	L	T	Pts.	GF	GA
Pittsburgh Penguins	44	27	13	101	299	285
Boston Bruins	42	29	13	97	289	252
Montreal Canadiens	41	29	14	96	283	248
Buffalo Sabres	43	32	9	95	282	218
Quebec Nordiques	34	42	8	76	277	292
Hartford Whalers	27	48	9	63	227	288
Ottawa Senators	14	61	9	37	201	397

WESTERN CONFERENCE

CENTRAL DIVISION

Team	W	L	T	Pts.	GF	GA
Detroit Red Wings	46	30	8	100	356	275
Toronto Maple Leafs	43	29	12	98	280	243
Dallas Stars	42	29	13	97	286	265
St. Louis Blues	40	33	11	91	270	283
Chicago Blackhawks	39	36	9	87	254	240
Winnipeg Jets	24	51	9	57	245	344

PACIFIC DIVISION

Team	W	L	T	Pts.	GF	GA
Calgary Flames	42	29	13	97	302	256
Vancouver Canucks	41	40	3	85	279	276
San Jose Sharks	33	35	16	82	252	265
Mighty Ducks of Anaheim	33	46	5	71	229	251
Los Angeles Kings	27	45	12	66	294	322
Edmonton Oilers	25	45	14	64	261	305

PLAYOFFS

Eastern Conference quarterfinals: N.Y. Rangers 4, N.Y. Islanders 0; Washington 4, Pittsburgh 2; New Jersey 4, Buffalo 3; Boston 4, Montreal 3. **Semifinals:** N.Y. Rangers 4, Washington 1; New Jersey 4, Boston 2. **Finals:** N.Y. Rangers 4, New Jersey 3.
Western Conference quarterfinals: San Jose 4, Detroit 3; Vancouver 4, Calgary 3; Toronto 4, Chicago 2; Dallas 4, St. Louis 0. **Semifinals:** Toronto 4, San Jose 3; Vancouver 4, Dallas 1. **Finals:** Vancouver 4, Toronto 1.
Stanley Cup finals: N.Y. Rangers 4, Vancouver 3.

1994-95

EASTERN CONFERENCE

ATLANTIC DIVISION

Team	W	L	T	Pts.	GF	GA
Philadelphia Flyers	28	16	4	60	150	132
New Jersey Devils	22	18	8	52	136	121
Washington Capitals	22	18	8	52	136	120
New York Rangers	22	23	3	47	139	134
Florida Panthers	20	22	6	46	115	127
Tampa Bay Lightning	17	28	3	37	120	144
New York Islanders	15	28	5	35	126	158

NORTHEAST DIVISION

Team	W	L	T	Pts.	GF	GA
Quebec Nordiques	30	13	5	65	185	134
Pittsburgh Penguins	29	16	3	61	181	158
Boston Bruins	27	18	3	57	150	127
Buffalo Sabres	22	19	7	51	130	119
Hartford Whalers	19	24	5	43	127	141
Montreal Canadiens	18	23	7	43	125	148
Ottawa Senators	9	34	5	23	117	174

WESTERN CONFERENCE

CENTRAL DIVISION

Team	W	L	T	Pts.	GF	GA
Detroit Red Wings	33	11	4	70	180	117
St. Louis Blues	28	15	5	61	178	135
Chicago Blackhawks	24	19	5	53	156	115
Toronto Maple Leafs	21	19	8	50	135	146
Dallas Stars	17	23	8	42	136	135
Winnipeg Jets	16	25	7	39	157	177

PACIFIC DIVISION

Team	W	L	T	Pts.	GF	GA
Calgary Flames	24	17	7	55	163	135
Vancouver Canucks	18	18	12	48	153	148
San Jose Sharks	19	25	4	42	129	161
Los Angeles Kings	16	23	9	41	142	174

Team	W	L	T	Pts.	GF	GA
Edmonton Oilers	17	27	4	38	136	183
Mighty Ducks of Anaheim	16	27	5	37	125	164

PLAYOFFS

Eastern Conference quarterfinals: N.Y. Rangers 4, Quebec 2; Pittsburgh 4, Washington 3; Philadelphia 4, Buffalo 1; New Jersey 4, Boston 1. **Semifinals:** New Jersey 4, Pittsburgh 1; Philadelphia 4, N.Y. Rangers 0. **Finals:** New Jersey 4, Philadelphia 2.
Western Conference quarterfinals: Detroit 4, Dallas 1; Vancouver 4, St. Louis 3; Chicago 4, Toronto 3; San Jose 4, Calgary 3. **Semifinals:** Detroit 4, San Jose 0; Chicago 4, Vancouver 0. **Finals:** Detroit 4, Chicago 1.
Stanley Cup finals: New Jersey 4, Detroit 0.

1995-96

EASTERN CONFERENCE

ATLANTIC DIVISION

Team	W	L	T	Pts.	GF	GA
Philadelphia Flyers	45	24	13	103	282	208
New York Rangers	41	27	14	96	272	237
Florida Panthers	41	31	10	92	254	234
Washington Capitals	39	32	11	89	234	204
Tampa Bay Lightning	38	32	12	88	238	248
New Jersey Devils	37	33	12	86	215	202
New York Islanders	22	50	10	54	229	315

NORTHEAST DIVISION

Team	W	L	T	Pts.	GF	GA
Pittsburgh Penguins	49	29	4	102	362	284
Boston Bruins	40	31	11	91	282	269
Montreal Canadiens	40	32	10	90	265	248
Hartford Whalers	34	39	9	77	237	259
Buffalo Sabres	33	42	7	73	247	262
Ottawa Senators	18	59	5	41	191	291

WESTERN CONFERENCE

CENTRAL DIVISION

Team	W	L	T	Pts.	GF	GA
Detroit Red Wings	62	13	7	131	325	181
Chicago Blackhawks	40	28	14	94	273	220
Toronto Maple Leafs	34	36	12	80	247	252
St. Louis Blues	32	34	16	80	219	248
Winnipeg Jets	36	40	6	78	275	291
Dallas Stars	26	42	14	66	227	280

PACIFIC DIVISION

Team	W	L	T	Pts.	GF	GA
Colorado Avalanche	47	25	10	104	326	240
Calgary Flames	34	37	11	79	241	240
Vancouver Canucks	32	35	15	79	278	278
Mighty Ducks of Anaheim	35	39	8	78	234	247
Edmonton Oilers	30	44	8	68	240	304
Los Angeles Kings	24	40	18	66	256	302
San Jose Sharks	20	55	7	47	252	357

PLAYOFFS

Eastern Conference quarterfinals: Philadelphia 4, Tampa Bay 2; Pittsburgh 4, Washington 2; N.Y. Rangers 4, Montreal 2; Florida 4, Boston 1. **Semifinals:** Florida 4, Philadelphia 2; Pittsburgh 4, N.Y. Rangers 1. **Finals:** Florida 4, Pittsburgh 3.
Western Conference quarterfinals: Detroit 4, Winnipeg 2; Colorado 4, Vancouver 2; Chicago 4, Calgary 0; St. Louis 4, Toronto 2. **Semifinals:** Detroit 4, St. Louis 3; Colorado 4, Chicago 2. **Finals:** Colorado 4, Detroit 2.
Stanley Cup finals: Colorado 4, Florida 0.

1996-97

EASTERN CONFERENCE

ATLANTIC DIVISION

Team	W	L	T	Pts.	GF	GA
New Jersey Devils	45	23	14	104	231	182
Philadelphia Flyers	45	24	13	103	274	217
Florida Panthers	35	28	19	89	221	201
New York Rangers	38	34	10	86	258	231
Washington Capitals	33	40	9	75	214	231
Tampa Bay Lightning	32	40	10	74	217	247
New York Islanders	29	41	12	70	240	250

NORTHEAST DIVISION

Team	W	L	T	Pts.	GF	GA
Buffalo Sabres	40	30	12	92	237	208
Pittsburgh Penguins	38	36	8	84	285	280
Ottawa Senators	31	36	15	77	226	234
Montreal Canadiens	31	36	15	77	249	276
Hartford Whalers	32	39	11	75	226	256
Boston Bruins	26	47	9	61	234	300

WESTERN CONFERENCE

CENTRAL DIVISION

Team	W	L	T	Pts.	GF	GA
Dallas Stars	48	26	8	104	252	198
Detroit Red Wings	38	26	18	94	253	197
Phoenix Coyotes	38	37	7	83	240	243
St. Louis Blues	36	35	11	83	236	239
Chicago Blackhawks	34	35	13	81	223	210
Toronto Maple Leafs	30	44	8	68	230	273

PACIFIC DIVISION

Team	W	L	T	Pts.	GF	GA
Colorado Avalanche	49	24	9	107	277	205
Mighty Ducks of Anaheim	36	33	13	85	245	233
Edmonton Oilers	36	37	9	81	252	247
Vancouver Canucks	35	40	7	77	257	273
Calgary Flames	32	41	9	73	214	239
Los Angeles Kings	28	43	11	67	214	268
San Jose Sharks	27	47	8	62	211	278

PLAYOFFS

Eastern Conference quarterfinals: New Jersey 4, Montreal 1; Buffalo 4, Ottawa 3; Philadelphia 4, Pittsburgh 1; N.Y. Rangers 4, Florida 1. **Semifinals:** N.Y. Rangers 4, New Jersey 1; Philadelphia 4, Buffalo 1. **Finals:** Philadelphia 4, N.Y. Rangers 1.
Western Conference quarterfinals: Colorado 4, Chicago 2; Edmonton 4, Dallas 3; Detroit 4, St. Louis 2; Anaheim 4, Phoenix 3. **Semifinals:** Colorado 4, Edmonton 1; Detroit 4, Anaheim 0. **Finals:** Detroit 4, Colorado 2.
Stanley Cup finals: Detroit 4, Philadelphia 0.

1997-98

EASTERN CONFERENCE

ATLANTIC DIVISION

Team	W	L	T	Pts.	GF	GA
New Jersey Devils	48	23	11	107	225	166
Philadelphia Flyers	42	29	11	95	242	193
Washington Capitals	40	30	12	92	219	202
New York Islanders	30	41	11	71	212	225
New York Rangers	25	39	18	68	197	231
Florida Panthers	24	43	15	63	203	256
Tampa Bay Lightning	17	55	10	44	151	269

NORTHEAST DIVISION

Team	W	L	T	Pts.	GF	GA
Pittsburgh Penguins	40	24	18	98	228	188
Boston Bruins	39	30	13	91	221	194
Buffalo Sabres	36	29	17	89	211	187
Montreal Canadiens	37	32	13	87	235	208
Ottawa Senators	34	33	15	83	193	200
Carolina Hurricanes	33	41	8	74	200	219

WESTERN CONFERENCE

CENTRAL DIVISION

Team	W	L	T	Pts.	GF	GA
Dallas Stars	49	22	11	109	242	167
Detroit Red Wings	44	23	15	103	250	196
St. Louis Blues	45	29	8	98	256	204
Phoenix Coyotes	35	35	12	82	224	227
Chicago Blackhawks	30	39	13	73	192	199
Toronto Maple Leafs	30	43	9	69	194	237

PACIFIC DIVISION

Team	W	L	T	Pts.	GF	GA
Colorado Avalanche	39	26	17	95	231	205
Los Angeles Kings	38	33	11	87	227	225
Edmonton Oilers	35	37	10	80	215	224
San Jose Sharks	34	38	10	78	210	216
Calgary Flames	26	41	15	67	217	252
Mighty Ducks of Anaheim	26	43	13	65	205	261
Vancouver Canucks	25	43	14	64	224	273

PLAYOFFS

Eastern Conference quarterfinals: Ottawa 4, New Jersey 2; Washington 4, Boston 2; Buffalo 4, Philadelphia 1; Montreal 4, Pittsburgh 2. **Semifinals:** Washington 4, Ottawa 1; Buffalo 4, Montreal 0. **Finals:** Washington 4, Buffalo 2.
Western Conference quarterfinals: Edmonton 4, Colorado 3; Dallas 4, San Jose 2; Detroit 4, Phoenix 2; St. Louis 4, Los Angeles 0. **Semifinals:** Dallas 4, Edmonton 1; Detroit 4, St. Louis 2. **Finals:** Detroit 4, Dallas 2.
Stanley Cup finals: Detroit 4, Washington 0.

1998-99

EASTERN CONFERENCE

ATLANTIC DIVISION

Team	W	L	T	Pts.	GF	GA
New Jersey Devils	47	24	11	105	248	196
Philadelphia Flyers	37	26	19	93	231	196
Pittsburgh Penguins	38	30	14	90	242	225
New York Rangers	33	38	11	77	217	227
New York Islanders	24	48	10	58	194	244

NORTHEAST DIVISION

Team	W	L	T	Pts.	GF	GA
Ottawa Senators	44	23	15	103	239	179
Toronto Maple Leafs	45	30	7	97	268	231
Boston Bruins	39	30	13	91	214	181
Buffalo Sabres	37	28	17	91	207	175
Montreal Canadiens	32	39	11	75	184	209

SOUTHEAST DIVISION

Team	W	L	T	Pts.	GF	GA
Carolina Hurricanes	34	30	18	86	210	202
Florida Panthers	30	34	18	78	210	228
Washington Capitals	31	45	6	68	200	218
Tampa Bay Lightning	19	54	9	47	179	292

WESTERN CONFERENCE

CENTRAL DIVISION

Team	W	L	T	Pts.	GF	GA
Detroit Red Wings	43	32	7	93	245	202
St. Louis Blues	37	32	13	87	237	209
Chicago Blackhawks	29	41	12	70	202	248
Nashville Predators	28	47	7	63	190	261

PACIFIC DIVISION

Team	W	L	T	Pts.	GF	GA
Dallas Stars	51	19	12	114	236	168
Phoenix Coyotes	39	31	12	90	205	197
Anaheim Mighty Ducks	35	34	13	83	215	206
San Jose Sharks	31	33	18	80	196	191
Los Angeles Kings	32	45	5	69	189	222

NORTHWEST DIVISION

Team	W	L	T	Pts.	GF	GA
Colorado Avalanche	44	28	10	98	239	205
Edmonton Oilers	33	37	12	78	230	226
Calgary Flames	30	40	12	72	211	234
Vancouver Canucks	23	47	12	58	192	258

PLAYOFFS

Eastern Conference quarterfinals: Pittsburgh 4, New Jersey 3; Buffalo 4, Ottawa 0; Boston 4, Carolina 2; Toronto 4, Philadelphia 2. **Semifinals:** Toronto 4, Pittsburgh 2; Buffalo 4, Boston 2. **Finals:** Buffalo 4, Toronto 1.
Western Conference quarterfinals: Dallas 4, Edmonton 0; Colorado 4, San Jose 2; Detroit 4, Anaheim 0; St. Louis 4, Phoenix 3. **Semifinals:** Dallas 4, St. Louis 2; Colorado 4, Detroit 2. **Finals:** Dallas 4, Colorado 3.
Stanley Cup finals: Dallas 4, Buffalo 2.

1999-2000

EASTERN CONFERENCE

ATLANTIC DIVISION

Team	W	L	T	RT	Pts.	GF	GA
Philadelphia Flyers	45	25	12	3	105	237	179
New Jersey Devils	45	29	8	5	103	251	203
Pittsburgh Penguins	37	37	8	6	88	241	236
New York Rangers	29	41	12	3	73	218	246
New York Islanders	24	49	9	1	58	194	275

NORTHEAST DIVISION

Team	W	L	T	RT	Pts.	GF	GA
Toronto Maple Leafs	45	30	7	3	100	246	222
Ottawa Senators	41	30	11	2	95	244	210
Buffalo Sabres	35	36	11	4	85	213	204
Montreal Canadiens	35	38	9	4	83	196	194
Boston Bruins	24	39	19	6	73	210	248

SOUTHEAST DIVISION

Team	W	L	T	RT	Pts.	GF	GA
Washington Capitals	44	26	12	2	102	227	194
Florida Panthers	43	33	6	6	98	244	209
Carolina Hurricanes	37	35	10	0	84	217	216
Tampa Bay Lightning	19	54	9	7	54	204	310
Atlanta Thrashers	14	61	7	4	39	170	313

WESTERN CONFERENCE

CENTRAL DIVISION

Team	W	L	T	RT	Pts.	GF	GA
St. Louis Blues	51	20	11	1	114	248	165
Detroit Red Wings	48	24	10	2	108	278	210
Chicago Blackhawks	33	39	10	2	78	242	245
Nashville Predators	28	47	7	7	70	199	240

PACIFIC DIVISION

Team	W	L	T	RT	Pts.	GF	GA
Dallas Stars	43	29	10	6	102	211	184
Los Angeles Kings	39	31	12	4	94	245	228
Phoenix Coyotes	39	35	8	4	90	232	228
San Jose Sharks	35	37	10	7	87	225	214
Mighty Ducks of Anaheim .	34	36	12	3	83	217	227

NORTHWEST DIVISION

Team	W	L	T	RT	Pts.	GF	GA
Colorado Avalanche	42	29	11	1	96	233	201
Edmonton Oilers	32	34	16	8	88	226	212
Vancouver Canucks	30	37	15	8	83	227	237
Calgary Flames	31	41	10	5	77	211	256

Note: RT denotes games in which the team is tied after regulation time, but loses in overtime; teams receive two points for each victory, one for each tie and one for each overtime loss.

PLAYOFFS

Eastern Conference quarterfinals: Philadelphia 4, Buffalo 1; Pittsburgh 4, Washington 1; Toronto 4, Ottawa 2; New Jersey 4, Florida 0; **Semifinals:** Philadelphia 4, Pittsburgh 2; New Jersey 4, Toronto 2. **Finals:** New Jersey 4, Philadelphia 3.
Western Conference quarterfinals: San Jose 4, St. Louis 3; Dallas 4, Edmonton 1; Colorado 4, Phoenix 1; Detroit 4, Los Angeles 0. **Semifinals:** Dallas 4, San Jose 1; Colorado 4, Detroit 1. **Finals:** Dallas 4, Colorado 3.
Stanley Cup finals: New Jersey 4, Dallas 2.

RECORDS

Most seasons
- NHL: 26—Gordie Howe, Detroit Red Wings and Hartford Whalers, 1946-47 through 1970-71 and 1979-80.
- CHL: 9—Richie Hansen, Fort Worth Texans, Salt Lake Golden Eagles, Wichita Wind, 1975-76 through 1983-84.
- AHL: 20—Fred Glover, Indianapolis Caps, St. Louis Flyers, Cleveland Barons.
   Willie Marshall, Pittsburgh Hornets, Rochester Americans, Hershey Bears, Providence Reds, Baltimore Clippers.
- IHL: 18—Glenn Ramsay, Cincinnati Mohawks, Fort Wayne Komets, Troy Bruins, Toledo Blades, St. Paul Saints, Omaha Knights, Des Moines Oak Leafs, Toledo Hornets, Port Huron Flags, 1956-57 through 1973-74.

Most games played
- NHL: 1,767—Gordie Howe, Detroit Red Wings and Hartford Whalers (26 seasons).
- AHL: 1,205—Willie Marshall, Pittsburgh Hornets, Rochester Americans, Hershey Bears, Providence Reds, Baltimore Clippers (20 seasons).
- IHL: 1,054—Jock Callander, Toledo Goaldiggers, Muskegon Lumberjacks, Atlanta Knights and Cleveland Lumberjacks (17 seasons).
- CHL: 575—Richie Hansen, Fort Worth Texans, Salt Lake Golden Eagles, Wichita Wind (9 seasons).
- WHA: 551—Andre Lacroix, Philadelphia Blazers, New York Golden Blades, Jersey Knights, San Diego Mariners, Houston Aeros and New England Whalers (7 seasons).

Most goals
- NHL: 894—Wayne Gretzky, Edmonton Oilers, Los Angeles Kings, St. Louis Blues, New York Rangers (20 seasons).
- IHL: 547—Dave Michayluk, Kalamazoo Wings, Muskegon Lumberjacks, Cleveland Lumberjacks (13 seasons).
- AHL: 523—Willie Marshall, Pittsburgh Hornets, Rochester Americans, Hershey Bears, Providence Reds, Baltimore Clippers (20 seasons).
- WHA: 316—Marc Tardif, Quebec Nordiques (6 seasons).
- CHL: 204—Richie Hansen, Fort Worth Texans, Salt Lake Golden Eagles, Wichita Wind (9 seasons).

Most assists
- NHL: 1,963—Wayne Gretzky, Edmonton Oilers, Los Angeles Kings, St. Louis Blues, New York Rangers (20 seasons).
- AHL: 852—Willie Marshall, Pittsburgh Hornets, Hershey Bears, Rochester Americans, Providence Reds, Baltimore Clippers (20 seasons).
- IHL: 826—Len Thornson, Huntington Hornets, Indianapolis Chiefs, Fort Wayne Komets (13 seasons).
- WHA: 547—Andre Lacroix, Philadelphia Blazers, Jersey Knights, San Diego Mariners, Houston Aeros, New England Whalers (7 seasons).
- CHL: 374—Richie Hansen, Fort Worth Texans, Salt Lake Golden Eagles, Wichita Wind (9 seasons).

Most points
- NHL: 2,857—Wayne Gretzky, Edmonton Oilers, Los Angeles Kings, St. Louis Blues, New York Rangers (20 seasons).
- AHL: 1,375—Willie Marshall, Pittsburgh Hornets, Hershey Bears, Rochester Americans, Providence Reds, Baltimore Clippers (20 seasons).
- IHL: 1,252—Len Thornson, Huntington Hornets, Indianapolis Chiefs, Fort Wayne Komets (13 seasons).
- WHA: 798—Andre Lacroix, Philadelphia Blazers, Jersey Knights, San Diego Mariners, Houston Aeros, New England Whalers (7 seasons).
- CHL: 578—Richie Hansen, Fort Worth Texans, Salt Lake Golden Eagles, Wichita Wind (9 seasons).

Most penalty minutes
- NHL: 3,966—Dave "Tiger" Williams, Toronto Maple Leafs, Vancouver Canucks, Detroit Red Wings, Los Angeles Kings, Hartford Whalers (13 seasons).
- AHL: 2,402—Fred Glover, Indianapolis Caps, St. Louis Flyers, Cleveland Barons (20 seasons).
- IHL: 2,175—Gord Malinoski, Dayton Gems, Saginaw Gears (9 seasons).
- WHA: 962—Paul Baxter, Cleveland Crusaders, Quebec Nordiques (5 seasons).
- CHL: 899—Brad Gassoff, Tulsa Oilers, Dallas Black Hawks (5 seasons).

Most shutouts
- NHL: 103—Terry Sawchuk, Detroit Red Wings, Boston Bruins, Los Angeles Kings, New York Rangers, Toronto Maple Leafs (20 seasons).
- AHL: 45—Johnny Bower, Cleveland Barons, Providence Reds (11 seasons).
- IHL: 45—Glenn Ramsay, Cincinnati Mohawks, Fort Wayne Komets, Troy Bruins, Toledo Blades, St. Paul Saints, Omaha Knights, Des Moines Oak Leafs, Toledo Hornets, Port Huron Flags (18 seasons).
- WHA: 16—Ernie Wakely, Winnipeg Jets, San Diego Mariners, Houston Aeros (6 seasons).
- CHL: 12—Michel Dumas, Dallas Black Hawks (4 seasons).
   Mike Veisor, Dallas Black Hawks (5 seasons).

Most goals
- NHL: 92—Wayne Gretzky, Edmonton Oilers, 1981-82 season.
- WHA: 77—Bobby Hull, Winnipeg Jets, 1974-75 season.
- CHL: 77—Alain Caron, St. Louis Braves, 1963-64 season.
- IHL: 75—Dan Lecours, Milwaukee Admirals, 1982-83 season.
- AHL: 70—Stephan Lebeau, Sherbrooke Canadiens, 1988-89 season.

Most goals by a defenseman
- NHL: 48—Paul Coffey, Edmonton Oilers, 1985-86 season.
- IHL: 34—Roly McLenahan, Cincinnati Mohawks, 1955-56 season.

NHL HISTORY *Records*

CHL: 29—Dan Poulin, Nashville South Stars, 1981-82 season.
AHL: 28—Greg Tebbutt, Baltimore Skipjacks, 1982-83 season.
WHA: 24—Kevin Morrison, Jersey Knights, 1973-74 season.

Most assists
NHL: 163—Wayne Gretzky, Edmonton Oilers, 1985-86 season.
IHL: 109—John Cullen, Flint Spirits, 1987-88 season.
WHA: 106—Andre Lacroix, San Diego Mariners, 1974-75 season.
AHL: 89—George "Red" Sullivan, Hershey Bears, 1953-54 season.
CHL: 81—Richie Hansen, Salt Lake Golden Eagles, 1981-82 season.

Most assists by a defenseman
NHL: 102—Bobby Orr, Boston Bruins, 1970-71 season.
IHL: 86—Gerry Glaude, Muskegon Zephyrs, 1962-63 season.
WHA: 77—J. C. Tremblay, Quebec Nordiques, 1975-76 season.
AHL: 62—Craig Levie, Nova Scotia Voyageurs, 1980-81 season.
        Shawn Evans, Nova Scotia Oilers, 1987-88 season.
CHL: 61—Barclay Plager, Omaha Knights, 1963-64 season.

Most points
NHL: 215—Wayne Gretzky, Edmonton Oilers, 1985-86 season.
IHL: 157—John Cullen, Flint Spirits, 1987-88 season.
WHA: 154—Marc Tardif, Quebec Nordiques, 1977-78 season.
AHL: 138—Don Biggs, Binghamton Rangers, 1992-93 season.
CHL: 125—Alain Caron, St. Louis Braves, 1963-64 season.

Most points by a defenseman
NHL: 139—Bobby Orr, Boston Bruins, 1970-71 season.
IHL: 101—Gerry Glaude, Muskegon Zephyrs, 1962-63 season.
WHA: 89—J. C. Tremblay, Quebec Nordiques, 1972-73 and 1975-76 seasons.
CHL: 85—Dan Poulin, Nashville South Stars, 1981-82 season.
AHL: 84—Greg Tebbutt, Baltimore Skipjacks, 1982-83 season.

Most penalty minutes
IIL: 640—Kevin Evans, Kalamazoo, 1986-87 season.
NHL: 472—Dave Schultz, Philadelphia Flyers, 1974-75 season.
AHL: 446—Robert Ray, Rochester Americans, 1988-89 season.
CHL: 411—Randy Holt, Dallas Black Hawks, 1974-75 season.
WHA: 365—Curt Brackenbury, Minnesota Fighting Saints and Quebec Nordiques, 1975-76 season.

Most shutouts
NHL: 22—George Hainsworth, Montreal Canadiens, 1928-29 season.
NHL: 15—(modern era) Tony Esposito, Chicago Black Hawks, 1969-70 season.
IHL: 10—Charlie Hodge, Cincinnati Mohawks, 1953-54 season.
        Joe Daley, Winnipeg Jets, 1975-76 season.
CHL: 9—Marcel Pelletier, St. Paul Rangers, 1963-64 season.
AHL: 9—Gordie Bell, Buffalo Bisons, 1942-43 season.
WHA: 5—Gerry Cheevers, Cleveland Crusaders, 1972-73 season.

Lowest goals against average
NHL: 0.98—George Hainsworth, Montreal Canadiens, 1928-29 season.
AHL: 1.79—Frank Brimsek, Providence Reds, 1937-38 season.
IHL: 1.88—Glenn Ramsay, Cincinnati Mohawks, 1956-57 season.
CHL: 2.16—Russ Gillow, Oklahoma City Blazers, 1967-68 season.
WHA: 2.57—Don McLeod, Houston Aeros, 1973-74 season.

INDIVIDUAL—GAME

Most goals
NHL: 7—Joe Malone, Quebec Bulldogs vs. Toronto St. Pats, January 31, 1920.
NHL: 6—(modern era) Syd Howe, Detroit Red Wings vs. N.Y. Rangers, Feb. 3, 1944.
        Gordon "Red" Berenson, St. Louis Blues vs. Philadelphia, Nov. 7, 1968.
        Darryl Sittler, Toronto Maple Leafs vs. Boston, Feb. 7, 1976.
CHL: 6—Jim Mayer, Dallas Black Hawks, February 23, 1979.
AHL: 6—Bob Heron, Pittsburgh Hornets, 1941-42.
        Harry Pidhirny, Springfield Indians, 1953-54.
        Camille Henry, Providence Reds, 1955-56.
        Patrick Lebeau, Fredericton Canadiens, Feb. 1, 1991.
IHL: 6—Pierre Brillant, Indianapolis Chiefs, Feb. 18, 1959.
        Bryan McLay, Muskegon Zephyrs, Mar. 8, 1961.
        Elliott Chorley, St. Paul Saints, Jan. 17, 1962.
        Joe Kastelic, Muskegon Zephyrs, Mar. 1, 1962.
        Tom St. James, Flint Generals, Mar. 15, 1985.
WHA: 5—Ron Ward, New York Raiders vs. Ottawa, January 4, 1973.
        Ron Climie, Edmonton Oilers vs. N.Y. Golden Blades, November 6, 1973.
        Andre Hinse, Houston Aeros vs. Edmonton, Jan. 16, 1975.
        Vaclav Nedomansky, Toronto Toros vs. Denver Spurs, Nov. 13, 1975.
        Wayne Connelly, Minnesota Fighting Saints vs. Cincinnati Stingers, Nov. 27, 1975.
        Ron Ward, Cleveland Crusaders vs. Toronto Toros, Nov. 30, 1975.
        Real Cloutier, Quebec Nordiques fs. Phoenix Roadrunners, Oct. 26, 1976.

Most assists
AHL: 9—Art Stratton, Buffalo Bisons vs. Pittsburgh, Mar. 17, 1963.
IHL: 9—Jean-Paul Denis, St. Paul Saints, Jan. 17, 1962.
NHL: 7—Billy Taylor, Detroit Red Wings vs. Chicago, Mar. 16, 1947.
     Wayne Gretzky, Edmonton Oilers vs. Washington, Feb. 15, 1980.
WHA: 7—Jim Harrison, Alberta Oilers vs. New York, January 30, 1973.
     Jim Harrison, Cleveland Crusaders vs. Toronto, Nov. 30, 1975.
CHL: 6—Art Stratton, St. Louis Braves, 1966-67.
     Ron Ward, Tulsa Oilers, 1967-68.
     Bill Hogaboam, Omaha Knights, January 15, 1972.
     Jim Wiley, Tulsa Oilers, 1974-75.

Most points
IHL: 11—Elliott Chorley, St. Paul Saints, Jan. 17, 1962.
     Jean-Paul Denis, St. Paul Saints, Jan. 17, 1962.
NHL: 10—Darryl Sittler, Toronto Maple Leafs vs. Boston, Feb. 7, 1976.
WHA: 10—Jim Harrison, Alberta Oilers vs. New York, January 30, 1973.
AHL: 9—Art Stratton, Buffalo Bisons vs Pittsburgh, Mar. 17, 1963.
CHL: 8—Steve Vickers, Omaha Knights vs. Kansas City, Jan. 15, 1972.

Most penalty minutes
NHL: 67—Randy Holt, Los Angeles Kings vs. Philadelphia, March 11, 1979.
IHL: 63—Willie Trognitz, Dayton Gems, Oct. 29, 1977.
AHL: 54—Wally Weir, Rochester Americans vs. New Brunswick, Jan. 16, 1981.
CHL: 49—Gary Rissling, Birmingham Bulls vs. Salt Lake, Dec. 5, 1980.
WHA: 46—Dave Hanson, Birmingham Bulls vs. Indianapolis, Feb. 5, 1978.

STANLEY CUP PLAYOFFS

INDIVIDUAL—CAREER

Most years in playoffs: 21—Ray Bourque, Boston, Colorado.
Most consecutive years in playoffs: 20—Larry Robinson, Montreal, Los Angeles.
Most games: 236—Mark Messier, Edmonton, New York Rangers.
Most games by goaltender: 196—Patrick Roy, Montreal, Colorado.
Most goals: 122—Wayne Gretzky, Edmonton, Los Angeles, St. Louis, New York Rangers.
Most assists: 260—Wayne Gretzky, Edmonton, Los Angeles, St. Louis, New York Rangers.
Most points: 382—Wayne Gretzky, Edmonton, Los Angeles, St. Louis, New York Rangers.
Most penalty minutes: 729—Dale Hunter, Quebec, Washington, Colorado.
Most shutouts: 19—Patrick Roy, Montreal, Colorado.

INDIVIDUAL—SEASON

Most goals: 19—Reggie Leach, Philadelphia (1975-76).
     Jari Kurri, Edmonton (1984-85).
Most goals by a defenseman: 12—Paul Coffey, Edmonton (1984-85).
Most assists: 31—Wayne Gretzky, Edmonton (1987-88).
Most assists by a defenseman: 25—Paul Coffey, Edmonton (1984-85).
Most points: 47—Wayne Gretzky, Edmonton (1984-85).
Most points by a defenseman: 37—Paul Coffey, Edmonton (1984-85).
Most penalty minutes: 141—Chris Nilan, Montreal (1985-86).
Most shutouts: 4—Clint Benedict, Montreal Maroons (1927-28); Dave Kerr, N.Y. Rangers (1936-37); Frank McCool, Toronto (1944-45); Terry Sawchuk, Detroit (1951-52); Bernie Parent, Philadelphia (1974-75); Ken Dryden, Montreal (1976-77); Ed Belfour, Dallas (1999-2000).
Most consecutive shutouts: 3—Frank McCool, Toronto (1944-45).

INDIVIDUAL—GAME

Most goals: 5—Maurice Richard, Montreal vs. Toronto, March 23, 1944.
     Darryl Sittler, Toronto vs. Philadelphia, April 22, 1976.
     Reggie Leach, Philadelphia vs. Boston, May 6, 1976.
     Mario Lemieux, Pittsburgh vs. Philadelphia, April 25, 1989.
Most assists: 6—Mikko Leinonen, N.Y. Rangers vs. Philadelphia, April 8, 1982.
     Wayne Gretzky, Edmonton vs. Los Angeles, April 9, 1987.
Most points: 8—Patrik Sundstrom, New Jersey vs. Washington, April 22, 1988.
     Mario Lemieux, Pittsburgh vs. Philadelphia, April 25, 1989.

CLUB

Most Stanley Cup championships: 24—Montreal Canadiens.
Most consecutive Stanley Cup championships: 5—Montreal Canadiens.
Most final series apperances: 32—Montreal Canadiens.
Most years in playoffs: 72—Montreal Canadiens.
Most consecutive playoff appearances: 29—Boston Bruins.
Most consecutive playoff game victories: 12—Edmonton Oilers.
Most goals, one team, one game: 13—Edmonton vs. Los Angeles, April 9, 1987.
Most goals, one team, one period: 7—Montreal Canadiens vs. Toronto, March 30, 1944, 3rd period.

STATISTICAL LEADERS

1917-18

Goals
Joe Malone, Mon. Canadiens 44
Cy Denneny, Ottawa 36
Reg Noble, Toronto 28
Newsy Lalonde, Mon. Canadiens 23
Corbett Denneny, Toronto 20

Lowest goals-against average
(Min. 15 games)
Georges Vezina, Mon. Canadiens 3.82
Hap Holmes, Toronto 4.75
Clint Benedict, Ottawa 5.18

Shutouts
Clint Benedict, Ottawa 1
Georges Vezina, Mon. Canadiens 1

1918-19

Goals
Odie Cleghorn, Montreal 24
Newsy Lalonde, Montreal.....................21
Cy Denneny, Ottawa 18
Frank Nighbor, Ottawa.........................17
Didier Pitre, Montreal 15

Lowest goals-against average
(Min. 15 games)
Clint Benedict, Ottawa 2.94
Georges Vezina, Montreal 4.33
Bert Lindsay, Toronto 5.19

Shutouts
Clint Benedict, Ottawa 2
Georges Vezina, Montreal 1

1919-20

Goals
Joe Malone, Quebec.............................39
Newsy Lalonde, Montreal.....................36
Frank Nighbor, Ottawa.........................26
Corbett Denneny, Toronto 23
Reg Noble, Toronto 24

Lowest goals-against average
(Min. 15 games)
Clint Benedict, Ottawa 2.67
Georges Vezina, Montreal 4.71
Frank Brophy, Quebec 7.05

Shutouts
Clint Benedict, Ottawa 5

1920-21

Goals
Cecil Dye, Tor.-Ham.............................35
Cy Denneny, Ottawa 34
Newsy Lalonde, Montreal.....................32
Joe Malone, Hamilton 28
Three players tied with 19

Lowest goals-against average
(Min. 15 games)
Clint Benedict, Ottawa 3.13
Jake Forbes, Toronto 3.90

Georges Vezina, Montreal 4.13
Howard Lockhart, Hamilton 5.50

Shutouts
Clint Benedict, Ottawa 2
Howard Lockhart, Hamilton 1
Georges Vezina, Montreal 1

1921-22

Goals
Harry Broadbent, Ottawa.....................30
Cecil Dye, Toronto 30
Cy Denneny, Ottawa 28
Joe Malone, Hamilton 23
Odie Cleghorn, Montreal 21

Lowest goals-against average
(Min. 15 games)
Clint Benedict, Ottawa 3.50
Georges Vezina, Montreal 3.92
John Roach, Toronto...........................4.14
Howard Lockhart, Hamilton 4.29

Shutouts
Clint Benedict, Ottawa 2

1922-23

Goals
Cecil Dye, Toronto 26
Billy Boucher, Montreal 25
Cy Denneny, Ottawa 23
Odie Cleghorn, Montreal 18
Jack Adams, Toronto 18

Lowest goals-against average
(Min. 15 games)
Clint Benedict, Ottawa 2.25
Georges Vezina, Montreal 2.54
John Roach, Toronto...........................3.67
Jake Forbes, Hamilton........................4.58

Shutouts
Clint Benedict, Ottawa 4
Georges Vezina, Montreal 2
John Roach, Toronto..............................1

1923-24

Goals
Cy Denneny, Ottawa 22
Billy Burch, Hamilton...........................16
Billy Boucher, Montreal 16
Cecil Dye, Toronto 16
Aurel Joliat, Montreal 15

Lowest goals-against average
(Min. 15 games)
Georges Vezina, Montreal 2.00
Clint Benedict, Ottawa 2.05
Jake Forbes, Hamilton........................2.83
John Roach, Toronto...........................3.48

Shutouts
Clint Benedict, Ottawa 3
Georges Vezina, Montreal 3
Jake Forbes, Hamilton...........................1
John Roach, Toronto..............................1

1924-25

Goals
Cecil Dye, Toronto 38
Howie Morenz, Mon. Canadiens..........30
Aurel Joliat, Mon. Canadiens...............29
Cy Denneny, Ottawa 28
Jack Adams, Toronto 21
Billy Burch, Hamilton............................21

Points
Cecil Dye, Toronto 44
Cy Denneny, Ottawa 42
Aurel Joliat, Mon. Canadiens...............40
Howie Morenz, Mon. Canadiens..........34
Billy Boucher, Mon. Canadiens............31

Lowest goals-against average
(Min. 15 games)
Georges Vezina, Mon. Canadiens 1.87
Jake Forbes, Hamilton........................2.00
Clint Benedict, Mon. Maroons...........2.17
Alex Connell, Ottawa 2.20
John Roach, Toronto...........................2.80

Shutouts
Alex Connell, Ottawa 7
Jake Forbes, Hamilton............................6
Georges Vezina, Mon. Canadiens 5
Clint Benedict, Mon. Maroons................2
Charles Stewart, Boston.........................2

1925-26

Goals
Nels Stewart, Mon. Maroons................34
Carson Cooper, Boston 28
Jimmy Herberts, Boston 26
Cy Denneny, Ottawa 24
Howie Morenz, Mon. Canadiens..........23

Points
Nels Stewart, Mon. Maroons................42
Cy Denneny, Ottawa 36
Carson Cooper, Boston 31
Jimmy Heberts, Boston.........................31
Three players tied with 26

Lowest goals-against average
(Min. 15 games)
Alex Connell, Ottawa 1.17
Roy Worters, Pittsburgh 1.94
Clint Benedict, Mon. Maroons...........2.03
Charles Stewart, Boston.....................2.29
Jake Forbes, New York........................2.39

Shutouts
Alex Connell, Ottawa 15
Roy Worters, Pittsburgh 7
Clint Benedict, Mon. Maroons................6
Charles Stewart, Boston.........................6
Jake Forbes, New York...........................2
John Roach, Toronto..............................2

1926-27

Goals
Bill Cook, N.Y. Rangers 33
Cecil Dye, Chicago 25

Howie Morenz, Mon. Canadiens..........25
Billy Burch, N.Y. Americans................19
Three players tied with 18

Assists

Dick Irvine, Chicago 18
Frank Boucher, N.Y. Rangers................15
Irvine Bailey, Toronto 13
Frank Fredrickson, Bos.-Det. 13
Frank Clancy, Ottawa 10

Points

Bill Cook, N.Y. Rangers 37
Dick Irvin, Chicago..............................36
Howie Morenz, Mon. Canadiens........32
Frank Fredrickson, Det.-Bos. 31
Babe Dye, Chicago 30

Penalty minutes

Nels Stewart, Mon. Maroons.............133
Eddie Shore, Boston...........................130
Reginald Smith, Ottawa 125
Albert Siebert, Mon. Maroons 116
George Boucher, Ottawa.....................115

Lowest goals-against average
(Min. 25 games)

Clint Benedict, Mon. Maroons............1.51
George Hainsworth, Mon. Canadiens..1.52
Lorne Chabot, N.Y. Rangers 1.56
Alex Connell, Ottawa 1.57
Hal Winkler, NYR-Bos. 1.81

Shutouts

George Hainsworth, Mon. Canadiens...14
Clint Benedict, Mon. Maroons............13
Alex Connell, Ottawa 12
Lorne Chabot, N.Y. Rangers 10
Jake Forbes, N.Y. Americans 8

1927-28

Goals

Howie Morenz, Mon. Canadiens..........33
Aurel Joliat, Mon. Canadiens..............28
Nels Stewart, Mon. Maroons..............27
Frank Boucher, N.Y. Rangers..............23
George Hay, Detroit 22

Assists

Howie Morenz, Mon. Canadiens..........18
Fred Cook, N.Y. Rangers 14
George Hay, Detroit 13
Frank Boucher, N.Y. Rangers..............12
Aurel Joliat, Mon. Canadiens..............11
Sylvio Mantha, Mon. Canadiens..........11

Points

Howie Morenz, Mon. Canadiens..........51
Aurel Joliat, Mon. Canadiens..............39
Frank Boucher, N.Y. Rangers..............35
George Hay, Detroit 35
Nels Stewart, Mon. Maroons..............34

Penalty minutes

Eddie Shore, Boston...........................165
Ivan Johnson, N.Y. Rangers 146
Clarence Boucher, N.Y. Americans 129
Albert Siebert, Mon. Maroons 109
Aurel Joliat, Mon. Canadiens.............105

Lowest goals-against average
(Min. 25 games)

George Hainsworth, Mon. Canadiens...1.09
Alex Connell, Ottawa 1.29
Hal Winkler, Boston............................1.59
Roy Worters, Pittsburgh 1.73
Clint Benedict, Mon. Maroons............1.75

Shutouts

Alex Connell, Ottawa 15
Hal Winkler, Boston.............................15
George Hainsworth, Mon. Canadiens...13
Lorne Chabot, N.Y. Rangers 11
Harry Holmes, Detroit 11

1928-29

Goals

Irvine Bailey, Toronto 22
Nels Stewart, Mon. Maroons..............21
Carson Cooper, Detroit 18
Howie Morenz, Mon. Canadiens..........17
Harry Oliver, Boston.............................17

Assists

Frank Boucher, N.Y. Rangers..............16
Andy Blair, Toronto 15
Gerald Lowrey, Pit.-Tor. 12
Irvine Bailey, Toronto 10
Howie Morenz, Mon. Canadiens..........10

Points

Irvine Bailey, Toronto 32
Nels Stewart, Mon. Maroons..............29
Carson Cooper, Detroit 27
Howie Morenz, Mon. Canadiens..........27
Andy Blair, Toronto 27

Penalty minutes

Mervyn Dutton, Mon. Maroons..........139
Lionel Conacher, N.Y. Americans........132
Reginald Smith, Mon. Maroons 120
Eddie Shore, Boston..............................96
Alex Smith, Ottawa...............................96

Lowest goals-against average
(Min. 25 games)

George Hainsworth, Mon. Canadiens..0.98
Tiny Thompson, Boston 1.18
Roy Worters, N.Y. Americans.............1.21
Clarence Dolson, Detroit 1.43
John Roach, N.Y. Rangers 1.48

Shutouts

George Hainsworth, Mon. Canadiens.....22
John Roach, N.Y. Rangers 13
Roy Worters, N.Y. Americans..............13
Lorne Chabot, Toronto 12
Tiny Thompson, Boston 12

1929-30

Goals

Ralph Weiland, Boston.........................43
Aubrey Clapper, Boston.......................41
Howie Morenz, Mon. Canadiens..........40
Nels Stewart, Mon. Maroons..............39
Hec Kilrea, Ottawa...............................36

Assists

Frank Boucher, N.Y. Rangers..............36
Norman Gainor, Boston........................31
Bill Cook, N.Y. Rangers 30
Ralph Weiland, Boston.........................30
Frank Clancy, Ottawa...........................23

Points

Ralph Weiland, Boston.........................73
Frank Boucher, N.Y. Rangers..............62
Aubrey Clapper, Boston.......................61
Bill Cook, N.Y. Rangers 59
Hec Kilrea, Ottawa...............................58

Penalty minutes

Joe Lamb, Ottawa 119
Sylvio Mantha, Mon. Canadiens.........108

Eddie Shore, Boston............................105
Mervyn Dutton, Mon. Maroons...........98
Harvey Rockburn, Detroit......................97

Lowest goals-against average
(Min. 25 games)

Tiny Thompson, Boston 2.23
Charles Gardiner, Chicago 2.52
James Walsh, Mon. Maroons...............2.55
George Hainsworth, Mon. Canadiens..2.57
Alex Connell, Ottawa 2.68

Shutouts

Lorne Chabot, Toronto 6
George Hainsworth, Mon. Canadiens......4
Alex Connell, Ottawa 3
Charles Gardiner, Chicago 3
Tiny Thompson, Boston 3

1930-31

Goals

Charlie Conacher, Toronto 31
Bill Cook, N.Y. Rangers 30
Howie Morenz, Mon. Canadiens..........28
Ebbie Goodfellow, Detroit....................25
Nels Stewart, Mon. Maroons..............25
Ralph Weiland, Boston.........................25

Assists

Joe Primeau, Toronto...........................32
Frank Boucher, N.Y. Rangers..............27
Ebbie Goodfellow, Detroit....................23
Howie Morenz, Mon. Canadiens..........23
Aurel Joliat, Mon. Canadiens..............22

Points

Howie Morenz, Mon. Canadiens..........51
Ebbie Goodfellow, Detroit....................48
Charlie Conacher, Toronto 43
Bill Cook, N.Y. Rangers 42
Ace Bailey, Toronto..............................42

Penalty minutes

Harvey Rockburn, Detroit....................118
Eddie Shore, Boston............................105
Darcy Coulson, Philadelphia...............103
Allan Shields, Philadelphia 98
Marty Burke, Mon. Canadiens.............91
Joe Lamb, Ottawa................................91

Lowest goals-against average
(Min. 25 games)

Roy Worters, N.Y. Americans.............1.68
Charles Gardiner, Chicago 1.77
John Roach, N.Y. Rangers 1.98
George Hainsworth, Mon. Canadiens..2.02
Tiny Thompson, Boston 2.05

Shutouts

Charles Gardiner, Chicago 12
George Hainsworth, Mon. Canadiens......8
Roy Worters, N.Y. Americans.................8
John Roach, N.Y. Rangers 7
Lorne Chabot, Toronto 6
Clarence Dolson, Detroit 6

1931-32

Goals

Charles Conacher, Toronto 34
Bill Cook, N.Y. Rangers 34
Harvey Jackson, Toronto......................28
Dave Trottier, Mon. Maroons...............26
Howie Morenz, Mon. Canadiens..........24

Assists

Joe Primeau, Toronto...........................37
Reginald Smith, Mon. Maroons 33

Harvey Jackson, Toronto.....................25
Howie Morenz, Mon. Canadiens..........25
Aurel Joliat, Mon. Canadiens................24

Points

Harvey Jackson, Toronto.....................53
Joe Primeau, Toronto.........................50
Howie Morenz, Mon. Canadiens..........49
Charlie Conacher, Toronto..................48
Bill Cook, N.Y. Rangers......................48

Penalty minutes

Georges Mantha, N.Y. Americans......107
Nick Wasnie, N.Y. Rangers................106
Reginald Horner, Toronto.....................97
Dave Trottier, Mon. Maroons...............94
Alex Levinsky, N.Y. Rangers................88

Lowest goals-against average
(Min. 25 games)

Charles Gardiner, Chicago.................2.10
Alex Connell, Detroit..........................2.25
George Hainsworth, Mon. Canadiens..2.32
John Roach, N.Y. Rangers.................2.34
Tiny Thompson, Boston......................2.42

Shutouts

John Roach, N.Y. Rangers.....................9
Tiny Thompson, Boston...........................9
Alex Connell, Detroit................................6
George Hainsworth, Mon. Canadiens......6
Roy Worters, N.Y. Americans..................5

Goals

Bill Cook, N.Y. Rangers.......................28
Harvey Jackson, Toronto.....................27
Martin Barry, Boston...........................24
Fred Cook, N.Y. Rangers.....................22
Lawrence Northcott, Mon. Maroons....22

Assists

Frank Boucher, N.Y. Rangers.............28
Eddie Shore, Boston...........................27
Paul Haynes, Mon. Maroons...............25
Norman Himes, N.Y. Americans..........25
Johnny Gagnon, Mon. Canadiens.......23

Points

Bill Cook, N.Y. Rangers.......................50
Harvey Jackson, Toronto.....................44
Lawrence Northcott, Mon. Maroons....43
Reg Smith, Mon. Maroons...................41
Paul Haynes, Mon. Maroons...............41

Penalty minutes

Reginald Horner, Toronto...................144
Ivan Johnson, N.Y. Rangers..............127
Allan Shields, Ottawa........................119
Eddie Shore, Boston..........................102
Vern Ayres, N.Y. Americans.................97

Lowest goals-against average
(Min. 25 games)

Tiny Thompson, Boston......................1.83
John Roach, Detroit............................1.93
Charles Gardiner, Chicago.................2.10
Dave Kerr, Mon. Maroons...................2.20
Andy Aitkenhead, N.Y. Rangers........2.23

Shutouts

Tiny Thompson, Boston.........................11
John Roach, Detroit...............................10
George Hainsworth, Mon. Canadiens.....8
Bill Beveridge, Ottawa............................5
Lorne Chabot, Toronto............................5
Charles Gardiner, Chicago......................5
Roy Worters, N.Y. Americans..................5

Goals

Charlie Conacher, Toronto...................32
Marty Barry, Boston.............................27
Aurel Joliat, Mon. Canadiens...............22
Nels Stewart, Boston............................22
Johnny Sorrell, Detroit..........................21

Assists

Joe Primeau, Toronto...........................32
Frank Boucher, N.Y. Rangers..............30
Cecil Dillon, N.Y. Rangers....................26
Elwyn Romnes, Chicago.......................21
Charlie Conacher, Toronto....................20

Points

Charlie Conacher, Toronto...................52
Joe Primeau, Toronto...........................46
Frank Boucher, N.Y. Rangers..............44
Marty Barry, Boston.............................39
Cecil Dillon, N.Y. Rangers....................39

Penalty minutes

Reginald Horner, Toronto....................146
Lionel Conacher, Chicago.....................87
Ivan Johnson, N.Y. Rangers.................86
Nels Stewart, Boston............................68
Earl Seibert, N.Y. Rangers...................66

Lowest goals-against average
(Min. 25 games)

Charles Gardiner, Chicago..................1.73
Wilfred Cude, Det.-Mon. C..................1.57
Roy Worters, N.Y. Americans.............2.14
Lorne Chabot, Mon. Canadiens..........2.15
Andy Aitkenhead, N.Y. Rangers........2.35

Shutouts

Charles Gardiner, Chicago....................10
Lorne Chabot, Mtl Canadiens..................8
Andy Aitkenhead, N.Y. Rangers.............7
Dave Kerr, Mon. Maroons........................6
Wilfred Cude, Det.-Mon. C.......................5
Tiny Thompson, Boston............................5

Goals

Charlie Conacher, Toronto...................36
Cecil Dillon, N.Y. Rangers....................25
Syd Howe, St.L.-Det..............................22
Harvey Jackson, Toronto.......................22
Three players tied with..........................21

Assists

Art Chapman, N.Y. Americans..............34
Frank Boucher, N.Y. Rangers...............32
Larry Aurie, Detroit...............................29
Herb Lewis, Detroit...............................27
Howie Morenz, Chicago........................26
Eddie Shore, Boston.............................26

Points

Charlie Conacher, Toronto....................57
Syd Howe, St. Louis-Detroit..................47
Larry Aurie, Detroit...............................46
Frank Boucher, N.Y. Rangers...............45
Harvey Jackson, Toronto.......................44

Penalty minutes

Reginald Horner, Toronto....................125
Irvine Frew, St. Louis............................89
Earl Seibert, N.Y. Rangers...................86
Albert Siebert, Boston...........................80
Ralph Bowman, St.L.-Det......................72

Lowest goals-against average
(Min. 25 games)

Lorne Chabot, Chicago........................1.83
Alex Connell, Mon. Maroons...............1.92
Norman Smith, Detroit..........................2.08
George Hainsworth, Toronto................2.28
Tiny Thompson, Boston........................2.33

Shutouts

Alex Connell, Mon. Maroons...................9
Lorne Chabot, Chicago............................8
George Hainsworth, Toronto....................8
Tiny Thompson, Boston...........................8
Dave Kerr, N.Y. Rangers.........................4
John Roach, Det.-Tor...............................4

Goals

Charlie Conacher, Toronto...................23
Bill Thoms, Toronto...............................23
Marty Barry, Detroit...............................21
David Schriner, N.Y. Americans............19
Reginald Smith, Mon. Maroons............19

Assists

Art Chapman, N.Y. Americans..............28
David Schriner, N.Y. Americans............26
Elwyn Romnes, Chicago.......................25
Herb Lewis, Detroit...............................23
Paul Thompson, Chicago......................23

Points

David Schriner, N.Y. Americans............45
Marty Barry, Detroit...............................40
Paul Thompson, Chicago......................40
Five players tied with.............................38

Penalty minutes

Reginald Horner, Toronto....................167
Allan Shields, Mon. Maroons................81
Reginald Smith, Mon. Maroons............75
Charlie Conacher, Toronto....................74
Three players tied with..........................69

Lowest goals-against average
(Min. 25 games)

Tiny Thompson, Boston........................1.73
Mike Karakas, Chicago........................1.92
Dave Kerr, N.Y. Rangers......................2.02
Norman Smith, Detroit..........................2.14
Bill Beveridge, Mon. Maroons.............2.22

Shutouts

Tiny Thompson, Boston.........................10
Mike Karakas, Chicago............................9
George Hainsworth, Toronto....................8
Dave Kerr, N.Y. Rangers.........................8
Wilfred Cude, Mon. Canadiens................6
Norman Smith, Detroit.............................6

Goals

Larry Aurie, Detroit................................23
Nels Stewart, Bos.-NYA........................23
Mehlville Keeling, N.Y. Rangers...........22
Harvey Jackson, Toronto.......................21
David Schriner, N.Y. Americans............21

Assists

Syl Apps, Toronto..................................29
Marty Barry, Detroit...............................27
Bob Gracie, Mon. Maroons...................25
David Schriner, N.Y. Americans............25
Art Chapman, N.Y. Americans..............23

Points

David Schriner, N.Y. Americans 46
Syl Apps, Toronto 45
Marty Barry, Detroit 44
Larry Aurie, Detroit 43
Harvey Jackson, Toronto 40

Penalty minutes

Reginald Horner, Toronto 124
Allan Shields, NYA-Bos. 94
Lionel Conacher, Mon. Maroons 64
Jack Portland, Boston 58
Joe Jerwa, Bos.-NYA 57

Lowest goals-against average
(Min. 25 games)

Norman Smith, Detroit 2.13
Dave Kerr, N.Y. Rangers 2.21
Wilfred Cude, Mon. Canadiens 2.24
Tiny Thompson, Boston 2.29
Turk Broda, Toronto 2.32

Shutouts

Norman Smith, Detroit 6
Tiny Thompson, Boston 6
Wilfred Cude, Mon. Canadiens 5
Mike Karakas, Chicago 5
Dave Kerr, N.Y. Rangers 4

1937-38

Goals

Gord Drillon, Toronto 26
Georges Mantha, Mon. Canadiens 23
Paul Thompson, Chicago 22
Syl Apps, Toronto 21
Cecil Dillon, N.Y. Rangers 21
David Schriner, N.Y. Americans 21

Assists

Syl Apps, Toronto 29
Art Chapman, N.Y. Americans 27
Gord Drillon, Toronto 26
Phil Watson, N.Y. Rangers 25
Bill Thoms, Toronto 24

Points

Gord Drillon, Toronto 52
Syl Apps, Toronto 50
Paul Thompson, Chicago 44
Georges Mantha, Mon. Canadiens 42
Cecil Dillon, N.Y. Rangers 39
Bill Cowley, Boston 39

Penalty minutes

Reginald Horner, Toronto 82
Art Coulter, N.Y. Rangers 80
Ott Heller, N.Y. Rangers 68
Stew Evans, Mon. Maroons 59
Four players tied with 56

Lowest goals-against average
(Min. 25 games)

Tiny Thompson, Boston 1.85
Dave Kerr, N.Y. Rangers 2.00
Earl Robertson, N.Y. Americans 2.31
Turk Broda, Toronto 2.64
Wilfred, Cude, Mon. Canadiens 2.68

Shutouts

Dave Kerr, N.Y. Rangers 8
Tiny Thompson, Boston 7
Turk Broda, Toronto 6
Earl Robertson, N.Y. Americans 6
Wilfred Cude, Mon. Canadiens 3
Norman Smith, Detroit 3

1938-39

Goals

Roy Conacher, Boston 26
Toe Blake, Montreal 24
Alex Shibicky, N.Y. Rangers 24
Clint Smith, N.Y. Rangers 21
Brian Hextall, N.Y. Rangers 20

Assists

Bill Cowley, Boston 34
Paul Haynes, Montreal 33
David Schriner, N.Y. Americans 31
Marty Barry, Detroit 28
Tom Anderson, N.Y. Americans 27

Points

Toe Blake, Montreal 47
David Schriner, N.Y. Americans 44
Bill Cowley, Boston 42
Clint Smith, N.Y. Rangers 41
Marty Barry, Detroit 41

Penalty minutes

Reginald Horner, Toronto 85
Murray Patrick, N.Y. Rangers 64
Art Coulter, N.Y. Rangers 58
Stew Evans, Montreal 58
Earl Seibert, Chicago 57

Lowest goals-against average
(Min. 25 games)

Frank Brimsek, Boston 1.59
Dave Kerr, N.Y. Rangers 2.18
Turk Broda, Toronto 2.23
Tiny Thompson, Bos.-Det. 2.49
Mike Karakas, Chicago 2.75

Shutouts

Frank Brimsek, Boston 10
Turk Broda, Toronto 8
Dave Kerr, N.Y. Rangers 6
Mike Karakas, Chicago 5
Tiny Thompson, Bos.-Det. 4

1939-40

Goals

Brian Hextall, N.Y. Rangers 24
Woody Dumart, Boston 22
Milt Schmidt, Boston 22
Herb Cain, Boston 21
Gord Drillon, Toronto 21

Assists

Milt Schmidt, Boston 30
Phil Watson, N.Y. Rangers 28
Bill Cowley, Boston 27
Bob Bauer, Boston 26
Syd Howe, Detroit 23

Points

Milt Schmidt, Boston 52
Woody Dumart, Boston 43
Bob Bauer, Boston 43
Gord Drillon, Toronto 40
Bill Cowley, Boston 40

Penalty minutes

Reginald Horner, Toronto 87
Art Coulter, N.Y. Rangers 68
Erwin Chamberlain, Toronto 63
Jack Church, Toronto 62
Walter Pratt, N.Y. Rangers 61

Lowest goals-against average
(Min. 25 games)

Dave Kerr, N.Y. Rangers 1.60
Paul Goodman, Chicago 2.00

Frank Brimsek, Boston 2.04
Turk Broda, Toronto 2.30
Tiny Thompson, Detroit 2.61

Shutouts

Dave Kerr, N.Y. Rangers 8
Frank Brimsek, Boston 6
Earl Robertson, N.Y. Americans 6
Turk Broda, Toronto 4
Paul Goodman, Chicago 4

1940-41

Goals

Brian Hextall, N.Y. Rangers 26
Roy Conacher, Boston 24
David Schriner, Toronto 24
Gord Drillon, Toronto 23
Three players tied with 20

Assists

Bill Cowley, Boston 45
Neil Colville, N.Y. Rangers 28
Bill Taylor, Toronto 26
Milton Schmidt, Boston 25
Phil Watson, N.Y. Rangers 25

Points

Bill Cowley, Boston 62
Brian Hextall, N.Y. Rangers 44
Gord Drillon, Toronto 44
Syl Apps, Toronto 44
Lynn Patrick, N.Y. Rangers 44
Syd Howe, Detroit 44

Penalty minutes

Jimmy Orlando, Detroit 99
Clifford Goupille, Montreal 81
Erwin Chamberlain, Montreal 75
Joe Cooper, Chicago 66
Des Smith, Boston 61

Lowest goals-against average
(Min. 25 games)

Turk Broda, Toronto 2.06
Frank Brimsek, Boston 2.12
John Mowers, Detroit 2.12
Dave Kerr, N.Y. Rangers 2.60
Bert Gardiner, Montreal 2.84

Shutouts

Frank Brimsek, Boston 6
Turk Broda, Toronto 5
John Mowers, Detroit 4
Bert Gardiner, Montreal 2
Paul Goodman, Chicago 2
Dave Kerr, N.Y. Rangers 2

1941-42

Goals

Lynn Patrick, New York 32
Roy Conacher, Boston 24
Robert Hamill, Bos.-Chi. 24
Brian Hextall, New York 24
Gord Drillon, Toronto 23
Don Grosso, Detroit 23

Assists

Phil Watson, New York 37
Brian Hextall, New York 32
Syd Abel, Detroit 31
Don Grosso, Detroit 30
Bill Thoms, Chicago 30

Points

Brian Hextall, New York 56
Lynn Patrick, New York 54
Don Grosso, Detroit 53

Phil Watson, New York..........................52
Syd Abel, Detroit...................................49

Penalty minutes
Pat Egan, Brooklyn.............................104
Jack Stewart, Detroit............................93
Ken Reardon, Montreal.........................83
Jimmy Orlando, Detroit.........................81
Bingo Kampman, Toronto.....................67

Lowest goals-against average
(Min. 25 games)
Frank Brimsek, Boston.......................2.44
Turk Broda, Toronto...........................2.83
Jim Henry, New York...........................2.98
John Mowers, Detroit..........................3.06
Sam LoPresti, Chicago.......................3.23

Shutouts
Turk Broda, Toronto................................6
John Mowers, Detroit..............................5
Frank Brimsek, Boston............................3
Sam LoPresti, Chicago............................3
Three players tied with............................1

1942-43

Goals
Doug Bentley, Chicago...........................33
Joseph Benoit, Montreal........................30
Gord Drillon, Montreal...........................28
Lorne Carr, Toronto...............................27
Bill Cowley, Boston................................27
Brian Hextall, New York.........................27

Assists
Bill Cowley, Boston................................45
Max Bentley, Chicago............................44
Herbert O'Connor, Montreal...................43
Billy Taylor, Toronto...............................42
Doug Bentley, Chicago...........................40
Elmer Lach, Montreal.............................40

Points
Doug Bentley, Chicago...........................73
Bill Cowley, Boston................................72
Max Bentley, Chicago............................70
Lynn Patrick, New York..........................61
Lorne Carr, Toronto...............................60
Billy Taylor, Toronto...............................60

Penalty minutes
James Orlando, Detroit..........................89
Reginald Hamilton, Toronto...................68
Jack Stewart, Detroit.............................68
Erwin Chamberlain, Boston...................67
Victor Myles, New York..........................57

Lowest goals-against average
(Min. 25 games)
John Mowers, Detroit..........................2.48
Turk Broda, Toronto...........................3.18
Frank Brimsek, Boston.......................3.52
Bert Gardiner, Chicago.......................3.60
Paul Bibeault, Montreal......................3.82

Shutouts
John Mowers, Detroit..............................6
Bill Beveridge, New York.........................1
Paul Bibeault, Montreal...........................1
Frank Brimsek, Boston............................1
Turk Broda, Toronto................................1
Bert Gardiner, Chicago............................1

1943-44

Goals
Doug Bentley, Chicago...........................38
Herb Cain, Boston.................................36

Lorne Carr, Toronto...............................36
Carl Liscombe, Detroit...........................36
Moderre Bruneteau, Detroit...................35

Assists
Clint Smith, Chicago..............................49
Elmer Lach, Montreal.............................48
Herb Cain, Boston.................................46
Herbert O'Connor, Montreal...................42
Bill Cowley, Boston................................41
Art Jackson, Boston...............................41

Points
Herb Cain, Boston.................................82
Doug Bentley, Chicago...........................77
Lorne Carr, Toronto...............................74
Carl Liscombe, Detroit...........................73
Elmer Lach, Montreal.............................72
Clint Smith, Chicago..............................72

Penalty minutes
Mike McMahon, Montreal.......................78
Harold Jackson, Detroit.........................76
Pat Egan Det.-Bos................................75
Bob Dill, New York.................................66
Erwin Chamberlain, Montreal.................65

Lowest goals-against average
(Min. 25 games)
Bill Durnan, Montreal..........................2.18
Paul Bibeault, Toronto........................3.00
Connie Dion, Detroit...........................3.08
Mike Karakas, Chicago.......................3.04
Bert Gardiner, Boston.........................5.17

Shutouts
Paul Bibeault, Toronto.............................5
Mike Karakas, Chicago............................3
Bill Durnan, Montreal..............................2
Connie Dion, Detroit................................1
Jim Franks, Bos.-Det...............................1
Bert Gardiner, Boston..............................1

1944-45

Goals
Maurice Richard, Montreal.....................50
Herb Cain, Boston.................................32
Toe Blake, Montreal...............................29
Ted Kennedy, Toronto............................29
Bill Mosienko, Chicago..........................28

Assists
Elmer Lach, Montreal.............................54
Bill Cowley, Boston................................40
Toe Blake, Montreal...............................38
Gus Bodnar, Toronto.............................36
Syd Howe, Detroit..................................36

Points
Elmer Lach, Montreal.............................80
Maurice Richard, Montreal.....................73
Toe Blake, Montreal...............................67
Bill Cowley, Boston................................65
Five players tied with.............................54

Penalty minutes
Bob Dill, New York.................................59
Joe Cooper, Chicago.............................50
Hal Jackson, Detroit..............................45
Pete Horeck, Chicago............................44
Ted Lindsay, Detroit..............................43

Lowest goals-against average
(Min. 25 games)
Bill Durnan, Montreal..........................2.42
Harry Lumley, Detroit..........................3.22
Frank McCool, Toronto........................3.22

Mike Karakas, Chicago.......................3.90
Paul Bibeault, Boston..........................4.46

Shutouts
Mike Karakas, Chicago............................4
Frank McCool, Toronto............................4
Bill Durnan, Montreal..............................1
Harry Lumley, Detroit..............................1
Ken McAuley, New York...........................1

1945-46

Goals
Gaye Stewart, Toronto...........................37
Max Bentley, Chicago............................31
Toe Blake, Montreal...............................29
Maurice Richard, Montreal.....................27
Clint Smith, Chicago..............................26

Assists
Elmer Lach, Montreal.............................34
Max Bentley, Chicago............................30
Bill Mosienko, Chicago..........................30
Albert DeMarco, New York.....................27
Alex Kaleta, Chicago.............................27

Points
Max Bentley, Chicago............................61
Gaye Stewart, Toronto...........................52
Toe Blake, Montreal...............................50
Clint Smith, Chicago..............................50
Maurice Richard, Montreal.....................48
Bill Mosienko, Chicago..........................48

Penalty minutes
Jack Stewart, Detroit.............................73
Armand Guidolin, Boston.......................62
John Mariucci, Chicago.........................58
Emile Bouchard, Montreal......................52
Maurice Richard, Montreal.....................50

Lowest goals-against average
(Min. 25 games)
Bill Durnan, Montreal..........................2.60
Paul Bibeault, Bos.-Mon......................2.88
Harry Lumley, Detroit..........................3.18
Frank Brimsek, Boston.......................3.26
Mike Karakas, Chicago.......................3.46

Shutouts
Bill Durnan, Montreal..............................4
Paul Bibeault, Bos.-Mon..........................2
Frank Brimsek, Boston............................2
Harry Lumley, Detroit..............................2
Three players tied with............................1

1946-47

Goals
Maurice Richard, Montreal.....................45
Bobby Bauer, Boston.............................30
Roy Conacher, Detroit...........................30
Max Bentley, Chicago............................29
Ted Kennedy, Toronto............................28

Assists
Billy Taylor, Detroit................................46
Max Bentley, Chicago............................43
Milt Schmidt, Boston..............................35
Doug Bentley, Chicago...........................34
Ted Kennedy, Toronto............................32

Points
Max Bentley, Chicago............................72
Maurice Richard, Montreal.....................71
Billy Taylor, Detroit................................63
Milt Schmidt, Boston..............................62
Ted Kennedy, Toronto............................60

Penalty minutes

Gus Mortson, Toronto........................133
Johnny Mariucci, Chicago..................110
Murph Chamberlain, Montreal 97
Jimmy Thomson, Toronto...................97
Bill Ezinicki, Toronto...........................93

Lowest goals-against average
(Min. 25 games)

Bill Durnan, Montreal........................2.30
Turk Broda, Toronto 2.86
Frank Brimsek, Boston......................2.91
Charlie Rayner, New York..................3.05
Harry Lumley, Detroit........................3.05

Shutouts

Charlie Rayner, New York.......................5
Turk Broda, Toronto 4
Bill Durnan, Montreal.............................4
Frank Brimsek, Boston...........................3
Harry Lumley, Detroit.............................3

1947-48

Goals

Ted Lindsay, Detroit 33
Elmer Lach, Montreal 30
Maurice Richard, Montreal...................28
Gaye Stewart, Tor.-Chi........................27
Syl Apps, Toronto................................26
Max Bentley, Chi.-Tor..........................26

Assists

Doug Bentley, Chicago 37
Buddy O'Connor, New York...................36
Edgar Laprade, New York.....................34
Elmer Lach, Montreal 31
Sid Abel, Detroit..................................30

Points

Elmer Lach, Montreal 61
Buddy O'Connor, New York...................60
Doug Bentley, Chicago 57
Gaye Stewart, Tor.-Chi........................56
Max Bentley, Chi.-Tor..........................54
Bud Poile, Tor.-Chi..............................54

Penalty minutes

Bill Barilko, Toronto............................147
Ken Reardon, Montreal 129
Gus Mortson, Toronto 118
Bill Ezinicki, Toronto.............................97
Ted Lindsay, Detroit 95

Lowest goals-against average
(Min. 25 games)

Turk Broda, Toronto 2.38
Harry Lumley, Detroit........................2.45
Bill Durnan, Montreal 2.74
Frank Brimsek, Boston.......................2.82
Jim Henry, New York..........................3.19

Shutouts

Harry Lumley, Detroit.............................7
Turk Broda, Toronto 5
Bill Durnan, Montreal.............................5
Frank Brimsek, Boston...........................3
Jim Henry, New York..............................2

1948-49

Goals

Sid Abel, Detroit..................................28
Doug Bentley, Chicago 28
Jim Conacher, Det.-Chi. 26
Roy Conacher, Chicago 26
Ted Lindsay, Detroit 26
Harry Watson, Toronto..........................26

Assists

Doug Bentley, Chicago 43
Roy Conacher, Chicago 42
Paul Ronty, Boston...............................29
Ted Lindsay, Detroit 28
Sid Abel, Detroit..................................26
Gus Bodnar, Chicago............................26

Points

Roy Conacher, Chicago 68
Doug Bentley, Chicago 66
Sid Abel, Detroit..................................54
Ted Lindsay, Detroit 54
Jim Conacher, Det.-Chi. 49
Paul Ronty, Boston...............................49

Penalty minutes

Bill Ezinicki, Toronto...........................145
Bep Guidolin, Det.-Chi.........................116
Erwin Chamberlain, Montreal...............111
Maurice Richard, Montreal...................110
Ken Reardon, Montreal 103

Lowest goals-against average
(Min. 25 games)

Bill Durnan, Montreal........................2.10
Harry Lumley, Detroit........................2.42
Turk Broda, Toronto 2.68
Frank Brimsek, Boston.......................2.72
Claude Rayner, New York 2.90

Shutouts

Bill Durnan, Montreal...........................10
Claude Rayner, New York 7
Harry Lumley, Detroit.............................6
Turk Broda, Toronto 5
Frank Brimsek, Boston...........................1
Gordon Henry, Boston............................1

1949-50

Goals

Maurice Richard, Montreal....................43
Gordie Howe, Detroit............................35
Sid Abel, Detroit..................................34
Gordie Howe, Detroit............................35
Metro Prystai, Chicago.........................29
John Peirson, Boston............................27

Assists

Ted Lindsay, Detroit 55
Paul Ronty, Boston...............................36
Sid Abel, Detroit..................................35
Bep Guidolin, Chicago..........................34
Doug Bentley, Chicago 33
Gordie Howe, Detroit............................33
Elmer Lach, Montreal 33

Points

Ted Lindsay, Detroit 78
Sid Abel, Detroit..................................69
Gordie Howe, Detroit............................68
Maurice Richard, Montreal....................65
Paul Ronty, Boston...............................59

Penalty minutes

Bill Ezinicki, Toronto...........................144
Gus Kyle, New York.............................143
Ted Lindsay, Detroit 141
Bill Gadsby, Chicago...........................138
Gus Mortson, Toronto 125

Lowest goals-against average
(Min. 25 games)

Bill Durnan, Montreal........................2.20
Harry Lumley, Detroit........................2.35
Turk Broda, Toronto 2.45
Chuck Rayner, New York....................2.62
Jack Gelineau, Boston........................3.28

Shutouts

Tuck Broda, Toronto 9
Bill Durnan, Montreal.............................8
Harry Lumley, Detroit.............................7
Chuck Rayner, New York........................6
Frank Brimsek, Chicago 5

1950-51

Goals

Gordie Howe, Detroit............................43
Maurice Richard, Montreal....................42
Tod Sloan, Toronto...............................31
Sid Smith, Toronto 30
Roy Conacher, Chicago 26

Assists

Gordie Howe, Detroit............................43
Ted Kennedy Toronto 43
Max Bentley, Toronto 41
Milton Schmidt, Boston 39
Sid Abel, Detroit..................................38

Points

Gordie Howe, Detroit............................86
Maurice Richard, Montreal....................66
Max Bentley, Toronto 62
Sid Abel, Detroit..................................61
Milt Schmidt, Boston 61
Ted Kennedy, Toronto...........................61

Penalty minutes

Gus Mortson, Toronto 142
Tom Johnson, Montreal 128
Bill Ezinicki, Boston.............................119
Tony Leswick, New York 112
Ted Lindsay, Detroit 110

Lowest goals-against average
(Min. 25 games)

Al Rollins, Toronto 1.75
Terry Sawchuk, Detroit......................1.98
Turk Broda, Toronto 2.19
Gerry McNeil, Montreal 2.63
Jack Gelineau, Boston........................2.81

Shutouts

Terry Sawchuk, Detroit.........................11
Turk Broda, Toronto 6
Gerry McNeil, Montreal 6
Al Rollins, Toronto 5
Jack Gelineau, Boston............................4

1951-52

Goals

Gordie Howe, Detroit............................47
Bill Mosienko, Chicago..........................31
Bernie Geoffrion, Montreal 30
Ted Lindsay, Detroit 30
Maurice Richard, Montreal....................27
Sid Smith, Toronto 27

Assists

Elmer Lach, Montreal 50
Don Raleigh, New York 42
Gordie Howe, Detroit............................39
Ted Lindsay, Detroit 39
Sid Abel, Detroit..................................36

Points

Gordie Howe, Detroit............................86
Ted Lindsay, Detroit 69
Elmer Lach, Montreal 65
Don Raleigh, New York 61
Sid Smith, Toronto 57

Penalty minutes

Gus Kyle, Boston	127
Ted Lindsay, Detroit	123
Fern Flaman, Toronto	110
Gus Mortson, Toronto	106
Al Dewsbury, Chicago	99

Lowest goals-against average
(Min. 25 games)

Terry Sawchuk, Detroit	1.90
Al Rollins, Toronto	2.20
Gerry McNeil, Montreal	2.34
Jim Henry, Boston	2.51
Claude Rayner, New York	3.00

Shutouts

Terry Sawchuk, Detroit	12
Jim Henry, Boston	7
Gerry McNeil, Montreal	5
Al Rollins, Toronto	5
Harry Lumley, Chicago	2
Claude Rayner, New York	2

1952-53

Goals

Gordie Howe, Detroit	49
Ted Lindsay, Detroit	32
Wally Hergesheimer, New York	30
Maurice Richard, Montreal	28
Fleming Mackell, Boston	27

Assists

Gordie Howe, Detroit	46
Alex Delvecchio, Detroit	43
Ted Lindsay, Detroit	39
Paul Ronty, New York	38
Metro Prystai, Detroit	34

Points

Gordie Howe, Detroit	95
Ted Lindsay, Detroit	71
Maurice Richard, Montreal	61
Wally Hergesheimer, New York	59
Alex Delvecchio, Detroit	59

Penalty minutes

Maurice Richard, Montreal	112
Ted Lindsay, Detroit	111
Fern Flaman, Toronto	110
George Gee, Chicago	99
Leo Boivin, Toronto	97
Al Dewsbury, Chicago	97

Lowest goals-against average
(Min. 25 games)

Terry Sawchuk, Detroit	1.90
Gerry McNeil, Montreal	2.12
Harry Lumley, Toronto	2.38
Jim Henry, Boston	2.46
Al Rollins, Chicago	2.50

Shutouts

Harry Lumley, Toronto	10
Gerry McNeil, Montreal	10
Terry Sawchuk, Detroit	9
Jim Henry, Boston	7
Al Rollins, Chicago	6

1953-54

Goals

Maurice Richard, Montreal	37
Gordie Howe, Detroit	33
Bernie Geoffrion, Montreal	29
Wally Hergesheimer, New York	27
Ted Lindsay, Detroit	26

Assists

Gordie Howe, Detroit	48
Bert Olmstead, Montreal	37
Ted Lindsay, Detroit	36
Four players tied with	33

Points

Gordie Howe, Detroit	81
Maurice Richard, Montreal	67
Ted Lindsay, Detroit	62
Bernie Geoffrion, Montreal	54
Bert Olmstead, Montreal	52

Penalty minutes

Gus Mortson, Chicago	132
Maurice Richard, Montreal	112
Douglas Harvey, Montreal	110
Ted Lindsay, Detroit	110
Gordie Howe, Detroit	109
Ivan Irwin, New York	109

Lowest goals-against average
(Min. 25 games)

Harry Lumley, Toronto	1.85
Terry Sawchuk, Detroit	1.92
Gerry McNeil, Montreal	2.15
Jim Henry, Boston	2.58
John Bower, New York	2.60

Shutouts

Harry Lumley, Toronto	13
Terry Sawchuk, Detroit	12
Jim Henry, Boston	8
Gerry McNeil, Montreal	6
John Bower, New York	5
Jacques Plante, Montreal	5

1954-55

Goals

Bernie Geoffrion, Montreal	38
Maurice Richard, Montreal	38
Jean Beliveau, Montreal	37
Sid Smith, Toronto	33
Gordie Howe, Detroit	29
Danny Lewicki, New York	29

Assists

Bert Olmstead, Montreal	48
Doug Harvey, Montreal	43
Ted Kennedy, Toronto	42
George Sullivan, Chicago	42
Earl Reibel, Detroit	41

Points

Bernie Geoffrion, Montreal	75
Maurice Richard, Montreal	74
Jean Beliveau, Montreal	73
Earl Reibel, Detroit	66
Gordie Howe, Detroit	62

Penalty minutes

Fern Flaman, Boston	150
Tony Leswick, Detroit	137
Bucky Hollingworth, Chicago	135
Gus Mortson, Chicago	133
Jean Beliveau, Montreal	125

Lowest goals-against average
(Min. 25 games)

Terry Sawchuk, Detroit	1.94
Harry Lumley, Toronto	1.94
Jacques Plante, Montreal	2.11
John Henderson, Boston	2.40
Jim Henry, Boston	3.00

Shutouts

Terry Sawchuk, Detroit	12
Harry Lumley, Toronto	8

John Henderson, Boston	5
Jacques Plante, Montreal	5
Gump Worsley, New York	4

1955-56

Goals

Jean Beliveau, Montreal	47
Gordie Howe, Detroit	38
Maurice Richard, Montreal	38
Tod Sloan, Toronto	37
Bernie Goeffrion, Montreal	29

Assists

Bert Olmstead, Montreal	56
Andy Bathgate, New York	47
Bill Gadsby, New York	42
Jean Beliveau, Montreal	41
Gordie Howe, Detroit	41

Points

Jean Beliveau, Montreal	88
Gordie Howe, Detroit	79
Maurice Richard, Montreal	71
Bert Olmstead, Montreal	70
Tod Sloan, Toronto	66
Andy Bathgate, New York	66

Penalty minutes

Lou Fontinato, New York	202
Ted Lindsay, Detroit	161
Jean Beliveau, Montreal	143
Bob Armstrong, Boston	122
Vic Stasiuk, Boston	118

Lowest goals-against average
(Min. 25 games)

Jacques Plante, Montreal	1.86
Glenn Hall, Detroit	2.11
Terry Sawchuk, Boston	2.66
Harry Lumley, Toronto	2.69
Gump Worsley, New York	2.90

Shutouts

Glenn Hall, Detroit	12
Terry Sawchuk, Boston	9
Jacques Plante, Montreal	7
Gump Worsley, New York	4
Harry Lumley, Toronto	3
Al Rollins, Chicago	3

1956-57

Goals

Gordie Howe, Detroit	44
Jean Beliveau, Montreal	33
Maurice Richard, Montreal	33
Ed Litzenberger, Chicago	32
Real Chevrefils, Boston	31

Assists

Ted Lindsay, Detroit	55
Jean Beliveau, Montreal	51
Andy Bathgate, New York	50
Gordie Howe, Detroit	45
Doug Harvey, Montreal	44

Points

Gordie Howe, Detroit	89
Ted Lindsay, Detroit	85
Jean Beliveau, Montreal	84
Andy Bathgate, New York	77
Ed Litzenberger, Chicago	64

Penalty minutes

Gus Mortson, Chicago	147
Lou Fontinato, New York	139

Leo LaBine, Boston 128
Pierre Pilote, Chicago.....................117
Jack Evans, New York 110

Lowest goals-against average
(Min. 25 games)

Jacques Plante, Montreal 2.02
Glenn Hall, Detroit............................2.24
Terry Sawchuk, Boston 2.38
Don Simmons, Boston 2.42
Ed Chadwich, Toronto 2.74

Shutouts

Jacques Plante, Montreal 9
Ed Chadwick, Toronto 5
Glenn Hall, Detroit..................................4
Don Simmons, Boston 4
Al Rollins, Chicago 3
Gump Worsley, New York 3

1957-58

Goals

Dickie Moore, Montreal 36
Gordie Howe, Detroit.............................33
Camille Henry, New York.......................32
Fleming Mackell, Boston 32
Andy Bathgate, New York......................30
Bronco Horvath, Boston 30

Assists

Henri Richard, Montreal 52
Andy Bathgate, New York.......................48
Dickie Moore, Montreal 48
Gordie Howe, Detroit..............................44
Fleming Mackell, Boston 40

Points

Dickie Moore, Montreal 84
Henri Richard, Montreal 80
Andy Bathgate, New York........................78
Gordie Howe, Detroit...............................77
Bronco Horvath, Boston 66

Penalty minutes

Lou Fontinato, New York.......................152
Forbes Kennedy, Detroit 135
Doug Harvey, Montreal 131
Ted Lindsay, Chicago 110
Jack Evans, New York 108

Lowest goals-against average
(Min. 25 games)

Jacques Plante, Montreal 2.09
Gump Worsley, New York 2.32
Don Simmons, Boston 2.45
Harry Lumley, Boston 2.84
Glenn Hall, Chicago 2.88

Shutouts

Jacques Plante, Montreal 9
Glenn Hall, Chicago 7
Don Simmons, Boston 5
Gump Worsley, New York 4
Ed Chadwick, Toronto 4

1958-59

Goals

Jean Beliveau, Montreal 45
Dickie Moore, Montreal 41
Andy Bathgate, N.Y Rangers 40
Ed Litzenberger, Chicago.......................33
Andy Hebenton, New York 33

Assists

Dickie Moore, Montreal 55
Andy Bathgate, New York.......................48

Jean Beliveau, Montreal 46
Bill Gadsby, New York 46
Gordie Howe, Detroit..............................46

Points

Dickie Moore, Montreal 96
Jean Beliveau, Montreal 91
Andy Bathgate, New York.......................88
Gordie Howe, Detroit...............................78
Ed Litzenberger, Chicago........................77

Penalty minutes

Ted Lindsay, Chicago 184
Lou Fontinato, New York.......................149
Carl Brewer, Toronto 125
Jim Bartlett, New York 118
Pete Goegan, Detroit 109
Eddie Shack, New York 109

Lowest goals-against average
(Min. 25 games)

Jacques Plante, Montreal 2.15
Johnny Bower, Toronto 2.74
Glenn Hall, Chicago..........................2.97
Eddie Chadwick, Toronto 3.00
Gump Worsley, New York 3.06

Shutouts

Jacques Plante, Montreal 9
Terry Sawchuk, Detroit 5
Johnny Bower, Toronto 3
Eddie Chadwick, Toronto 3
Don Simmons, Boston 3

1959-60

Goals

Bobby Hull, Chicago...............................39
Bronco Horvath, Boston..........................39
Jean Beliveau, Montreal 34
Dean Prentice, New York.........................32
Bernie Geoffrion, Montreal 30
Henri Richard, Montreal 30

Assists

Don McKenney, Boston...........................49
Andy Bathgate, New York........................48
Gordie Howe, Detroit...............................45
Henri Richard, Montreal 43
Bobby Hull, Chicago................................42

Points

Bobby Hull, Chicago................................81
Bronco Horvath, Boston...........................80
Jean Beliveau, Montreal 74
Andy Bathgate, New York.........................74
Henri Richard, Montreal 73
Gordie Howe, Detroit................................73

Penalty minutes

Carl Brewer, Toronto 150
Lou Fontinato, New York........................137
Vic Stasiuk, Boston 121
Stan Mikita, Chicago...............................119
Fern Flamen, Boston 112

Lowest goals-against average
(Min. 25 games)

Jacques Plante, Montreal 2.54
Glenn Hall, Chicago 2.57
Terry Sawchuk, Detroit......................2.69
Johnny Bower, Toronto 2.73
Don Simmons, Boston 3.36

Shutouts

Glenn Hall, Chicago 6
Johnny Bower, Toronto 5
Terry Sawchuk, Detroit............................5
Jacques Plante, Montreal 3

Harry Lumley, Boston 2
Don Simmons, Boston 2

1960-61

Goals

Bernie Geoffrion, Montreal 50
Frank Mahovlich, Toronto......................48
Dickie Moore, Montreal 35
Jean Beliveau, Montreal 32
Bobby Hull, Chicago..............................31

Assists

Jean Beliveau, Montreal 58
Red Kelly, Toronto.................................50
Gordie Howe, Detroit.............................49
Andy Bathgate, New York......................48
Bill Hay, Chicago 48

Points

Bernie Geoffrion, Montreal 95
Jean Beliveau, Montreal 90
Frank Mahovlich, Toronto......................84
Andy Bathgate, New York......................77
Gordie Howe, Detroit.............................72

Penalty minutes

Pierre Pilote, Chicago..........................165
Reg Fleming, Chicago 145
Jean Guy Talbot, Montreal 143
Frank Mahovlich, Toronto......................131
Eric Nesterenko, Chicago 125

Lowest goals-against average
(Min. 25 games)

Johnny Bower, Toronto 2.50
Charlie Hodge, Montreal....................2.53
Jacques Plante, Montreal 2.80
Hank Bassen, Detroit........................2.97
Terry Sawchuk, Detroit......................3.17

Shutouts

Glenn Hall, Chicago 6
Charlie Hodge, Montreal..........................4
Johnny Bower, Toronto 2
Jacques Plante, Montreal 2
Terry Sawchuk, Detroit............................2

1961-62

Goals

Bobby Hull, Chicago..............................50
Gordie Howe, Detroit.............................33
Frank Mahovlich, Toronto......................33
Claude Provost, Montreal 33
Gilles Tremblay, Montreal 32

Assists

Andy Bathgate, New York......................56
Bill Hay, Chicago 52
Stan Mikita, Chicago..............................52
Gordie Howe, Detroit.............................44
Alex Delvecchio, Detroit 43

Points

Bobby Hull, Chicago..............................84
Andy Bathgate, New York......................84
Gordie Howe, Detroit.............................77
Stan Mikita, Chicago..............................77
Frank Mahovlich, Toronto......................71

Penalty minutes

Lou Fontinato, Montreal 167
Ted Green, Boston................................116
Bob Pulford, Toronto 98
Stan Mikita, Chicago 97
Eric Nesterenko, Chicago 97
Pierre Pilote, Chicago.............................97

Lowest goals-against average
(Min. 25 games)

Jacques Plante, Montreal	2.37
John Bower, Toronto	2.58
Glenn Hall, Chicago	2.66
Henry Bassen, Detroit	2.81
Gump Worsley, New York	2.90

Shutouts

Glenn Hall, Chicago	9
Terry Sawchuk, Detroit	5
Jacques Plante, Montreal	4
Henry Bassen, Detroit	3
Three players tied with	2

1962-63

Goals

Gordie Howe, Detroit	38
Camille Henry, New York	37
Frank Mahovlich, Toronto	36
Andy Bathgate, New York	35
Parker MacDonald, Detroit	33

Assists

Henri Richard, Montreal	50
Jean Beliveau, Montreal	49
Gordie Howe, Detroit	48
Andy Bathgate, New York	46
Stan Mikita, Chicago	45

Points

Gordie Howe, Detroit	86
Andy Bathgate, New York	81
Stan Mikita, Chicago	76
Frank Mahovlich, Toronto	73
Henri Richard, Montreal	73

Penalty minutes

Howie Young, Detroit	273
Carl Brewer, Tornoto	168
Lou Fontinato, Montreal	141
Ted Green, Boston	117
Bill Gladsby, Detroit	116

Lowest goals-against average
(Min. 25 games)

Jacques Plante, Montreal	2.46
Terry Sawchuk, Detroit	2.48
Don Simmons, Toronto	2.50
Glenn Hall, Chicago	2.51
Johnny Bower, Toronto	2.62

Shutouts

Glenn Hall, Chicago	5
Jacques Plante, Montreal	5
Terry Sawchuk, Detroit	3
Gump Worsley, New York	2
Four players tied with	1

1963-64

Goals

Bobby Hull, Chicago	43
Stan Mikita, Chicago	39
Ken Wharram, Chicago	39
Camille Henry, New York	29
Jean Beliveau, Montreal	28

Assists

Andy Bathgate, N.Y.-Tor.	58
Jean Beliveau, Montreal	50
Stan Mikita, Chicago	50
Gordie Howe, Detroit	47
Pierre Pilote, Chicago	46

Points

Stan Mikita, Chicago	89
Bobby Hull, Chicago	87
Jean Beliveau, Montreal	78

Andy Bathgate, N.Y.-Tor.	77
Gordie Howe, Detroit	73

Penalty minutes

Vic Hadfield, New York	151
Terry Harper, Montreal	149
Stan Mikita, Chicago	146
Ted Green, Boston	145
Reg Fleming, Chicago	140

Lowest goals-against average
(Min. 25 games)

Johnny Bower, Toronto	2.12
Charlie Hodge, Montreal	2.26
Glenn Hall, Chicago	2.30
Terry Sawchuk, Detroit	2.70
Eddie Johnston, Boston	3.01

Shutouts

Charlie Hodge, Montreal	8
Glenn Hall, Chicago	7
Ed Johnston, Boston	6
Johnny Bower, Toronto	5
Terry Sawchuk, Detroit	5

1964-65

Goals

Norm Ullman, Detroit	42
Bobby Hull, Chicago	39
Gordie Howe, Detroit	29
Stan Mikita, Chicago	28
Claude Provost, Montreal	27

Assists

Stan Mikita, Chicago	59
Gordie Howe, Detroit	47
Pierre Pilote, Chicago	45
Alex Delvecchio, Detroit	42
Norm Ullman, Detroit	41

Points

Stan Mikita, Chicago	87
Norm Ullman, Detroit	83
Gordie Howe, Detroit	76
Bobby Hull, Chicago	71
Alex Delvecchio, Detroit	67

Penalty minutes

Carl Brewer, Toronto	177
Ted Lindsay, Detroit	173
Pierre Pilote, Chicago	162
Bob Baun, Toronto	160
John Ferguson, Montreal	156
Ted Green, Boston	156

Lowest goals-against average
(Min. 25 games)

Johnny Bower, Toronto	2.38
Roger Crozier, Detroit	2.42
Glenn Hall, Chicago	2.43
Denis DeJordy, Chicago	2.52
Terry Sawchuk, Toronto	2.56

Shutouts

Roger Crozier, Detroit	6
Glenn Hall, Chicago	4
Johnny Bower, Toronto	3
Denis DeJordy, Chicago	3
Charlie Hodge, Montreal	3
Ed Johnston, Boston	3

1965-66

Goals

Bobby Hull, Chicago	54
Frank Mahovlich, Toronto	32
Alex Delvecchio, Detroit	31
Norm Ullman, Detroit	31

Stan Mikita, Chicago	30
Bobby Rousseau, Montreal	30

Assists

Jean Beliveau, Montreal	48
Stan Mikita, Chicago	48
Bobby Rousseau, Montreal	48
Gordie Howe, Detroit	46
Bobby Hull, Chicago	43

Points

Bobby Hull, Chicago	97
Stan Mikita, Chicago	78
Bobby Rousseau, Montreal	78
Jean Beliveau, Montreal	77
Gordie Howe, Detroit	75

Penalty minutes

Reg Fleming, Bos.-N.Y.	166
John Ferguson, Montreal	153
Bryan Watson, Detroit	133
Ted Green, Boston	113
Vic Hadfield, New York	112

Lowest goals-against average
(Min. 25 games)

Johnny Bower, Toronto	2.25
Gump Worsley, Montreal	2.36
Charlie Hodge, Montreal	2.58
Glenn Hall, Chicago	2.63
Roger Crozier, Detroit	2.78

Shutouts

Roger Crozier, Detroit	7
Bruce Gamble, Toronto	4
Glenn Hall, Chicago	4
Johnny Bower, Toronto	3
Cesare Maniago, New York	2
Gump Worsley, Montreal	2

1966-67

Goals

Bobby Hull, Chicago	52
Stan Mikita, Chicago	35
Ken Wharram, Chicago	31
Rod Gilbert, New York	28
Bruce MacGregor, Detroit	28

Assists

Stan Mikita, Chicago	62
Phil Goyette, New York	49
Pierre Pilote, Chicago	46
Bobby Rousseau, Montreal	44
Norm Ullman, Detroit	44

Points

Stan Mikita, Chicago	97
Bobby Hull, Chicago	80
Norm Ullman, Detroit	70
Ken Wharram, Chicago	65
Gordie Howe, Detroit	65

Penalty minutes

John Ferguson, Montreal	177
Reg Fleming, New York	146
Gary Bergman, Detroit	129
Gilles Marotte, Boston	112
Ed Van Impe, Chicago	111

Lowest goals-against average
(Min. 25 games)

Glenn Hall, Chicago	2.38
Denis DeJordy, Chicago	2.46
Charlie Hodge, Montreal	2.60
Ed Giacomin, New York	2.61
Johnny Bower, Toronto	2.64

Shutouts

Ed Giacomin, New York	9
Roger Crozier, Detroit	4

Denis DeJordy, Chicago 4
Charlie Hodge, Montreal.......................3
Three players tied with...........................2

1967-68

Goals
Bobby Hull, Chicago.............................44
Stan Mikita, Chicago 40
Gordie Howe, Detroit............................39
Phil Esposito, Boston 35
Wayne Connelly, Minnesota 35

Assists
Phil Esposito, Boston 49
Alex Delvecchio, Detroit 48
Rod Gilbert, New York..........................48
Stan Mikita, Chicago 47
Jean Ratelle, New York.........................46

Points
Stan Mikita, Chicago 87
Phil Esposito, Boston 84
Gordie Howe, Detroit............................82
Jean Ratelle, New York.........................78
Rod Gilbert, New York...........................77

Penalty minutes
Gary Dornhoefer, Philadelphia............134
Ted Green, Boston..............................133
Reg Fleming, New York 132
Forbes Kennedy, Philadelphia.............130
Kent Douglas, Oak.-Det. 126

Lowest goals-against average
(Min. 25 games)
Gump Worsley, Montreal 1.98
Johnny Bower, Toronto 2.25
Boug Favell, Philadelphia 2.27
Bruce Gamble, Toronto 2.31
Ed Giacomin, New York.....................2.44

Shutouts
Ed Giacomin, New York..........................8
Les Binkley, Pittburgh 6
Cesare Maniago, Minnesota 6
Lorn Worsley, Montreal 6
Bruce Gamble, Toronto 5
Glen Hall, St. Louis 5

1968-69

Goals
Bobby Hull, Chicago.............................58
Phil Esposito, Boston 49
Frank Mahovlich, Detroit 49
Ken Hodge, Boston 45
Gordie Howe, Detroit............................44

Assists
Phil Esposito, Boston 77
Stan Mikita, Chicago 67
Gordie Howe, Detroit............................59
Alex Delvecchio, Detroit 58
Four players tied with............................49

Points
Phil Esposito, Boston 126
Bobby Hull, Chicago...........................107
Gordie Howe, Detroit..........................103
Stan Mikita, Chicago 97
Ken Hodge, Boston 90

Penalty minutes
Forbes Kennedy, Phi.-Tor. 219
Jim Dorey, Toronto.............................200
John Ferguson, Montreal 185
Carol Vadnais, Oakland 151
Don Awrey, Bosotn..............................149

Lowest goals-against average
(Min. 25 games)
Jacques Plante, St. Louis.................1.96
Glenn Hall, St. Louis 2.17
Gump Worsley, Montreal 2.26
Ron Edwards, Detroit 2.54
Ed Giacomin, New York.....................2.55

Shutouts
Ed Giacomin, New York...........................7
Jaques Plante, St. Louis.........................5
Gump Worsley, Montreal 5
Roy Edwards, Detroit 4
Gary Smith, Oakland 4
Gerry Desjardins, Los Angeles..............4

1969-70

Goals
Phil Esposito, Boston 43
Garry Unger, Detroit.............................42
Stan Mikita, Chicago 39
Bobby Hull, Chicago.............................38
Frank Mahovlich, Detroit 38

Assists
Bobby Orr, Boston................................87
Phil Esposito, Boston 56
Tommy Williams, Minnesota 52
Walt Tkaczuk, New York.......................50
Phil Goyette, St. Louis..........................49

Points
Bobby Orr, Boston..............................120
Phil Esposito, Boston 99
Stan Mikita, Chicago 86
Phil Goyette, St. Louis..........................78
Walt Tkaczuk, New York.......................77

Penalty minutes
Keith Magnuson, Chicago 213
Carol Vadnais, California 212
Bryan Watson, Pittsburgh 189
Barry Gibbs, Minnesota.......................182
Earl Heiskala, Philadelphia 171

Lowest goals-against average
(Min. 25 games)
Ernie Wakely, St. Louis......................2.11
Tony Esposito, Chicago......................2.17
Jacques Plante St. Louis 2.19
Ed Giacomin, New York......................2.36
Roy Edwards, Detroit 2.59

Shutouts
Tony Esposito, Chicago..........................15
Ed Giacomin, New York...........................6
Bruce Gambel, Toronto 5
Jacques Plante, St. Louis.......................5
Gerry Cheevers, Boston 4
Rogie Vachon, Montreal 4
Ernie Wakely, St. Louis...........................4

Wins by goaltenders
Tony Esposito, Chicago..........................38
Ed Giacomin, New York...........................35
Rogie Vachon, Montreal 31
Gerry Cheevers, Boston 24
Roy Edwards, Detroit 24

1970-71

Goals
Phil Esposito, Boston 76
John Bucyk, Boston 51
Bobby Hull, Chicago.............................44
Ken Hodge, Boston 43
Dennis Hull, Chicago............................40

Assists
Bobby Orr, Boston..............................102
Phil Esposito, Boston 76
John Bucyk, Boston 65
Ken Hodge, Boston 62
Wayne Cashman, Boston 58

Points
Phil Esposito, Boston 152
Bobby Orr, Boston..............................139
John Bucyk, Boston 116
Ken Hodge, Boston 105
Bobby Hull, Chicago.............................96

Penalty minutes
Keith Magnuson, Chicago 291
Dennis Hextall, California 217
Jim Dorey, Toronto.............................198
Pete Mahovlich, Montreal....................181
Tracy Pratt, Buffalo.............................179

Lowest goals-against average
(Min. 25 games)
Jacques Plante, Toronto.....................1.88
Ed Giacomin, New York......................2.15
Tony Esposito, Chicago......................2.27
Gilles Villemure, New York 2.29
Glenn Hall, St. Louis 2.41

Shutouts
Ed Giacomin, New York...........................8
Tony Esposito, Chicago...........................6
Cesare Maniago, Minnesota 5
Jacques Plante, Toronto 4
Ed Johnston, Boston 4
Gilles Villemure, New York 4

Wins by goaltenders
Tony Esposito, Chicago..........................35
Ed Johnston, Boston 30
Gerry Cheevers, Boston 27
Ed Giacomin, New York...........................27
Jacques Plante, Toronto 24

1971-72

Goals
Phil Esposito, Boston 66
Vic Hadfield, New York..........................50
Bobby Hull, Chicago.............................50
Yvan Cournoyer, Montreal....................47
Jean Ratelle, New York.........................46

Assists
Bobby Orr, Boston................................80
Phil Esposito, Boston 67
Jean Ratelle, New York.........................63
Vic Hadfield, New York..........................56
Fred Stanfield, Boston..........................56

Points
Phil Esposito, Boston 133
Bobby Orr, Boston..............................117
Jean Ratelle, New York.......................109
Vic Hadfield, New York........................106
Rod Gilbert, New York...........................97

Penalty minutes
Bryan Watson, Pittsburgh 212
Keith Magnuson, Chicago 199
Gary Dornhoefer, Philadelphia.............183
Barclay Plager, St. Louis 176
Rick Floey, Philadelphia......................168

Lowest goals-against average
(Min. 25 games)
Tony Esposito, Chicago......................1.76
Gilles Villemure, New York 2.08

Lorne Worsley, Minnesota..............2.12
Ken Dryden, Montreal 2.34
Gary Smith, Chicago 2.41

Shutouts
Tony Esposito, Chicago 9
Ken Dryden, Montreal 8
Gary Smith, Chicago 5
Doug Favell, Philadelphia 5
Al Smith, Detroit.................................4
Gilles Meloche, California......................4

Wins by goaltenders
Tony Esposito, Chicago 31
Gerry Cheevers, Boston 27
Ed Johnston, Boston 27
Ed Giacomin, New York.......................24
Gilles Villemure, New York 24

1972-73

Goals
Phil Esposito, Boston..........................55
Mickey Redmond, Detroit....................52
Rick McLeish, Philadelphia 50
Jacques Lemaire, Montreal 44
Three players tied with 41

Assists
Phil Esposito, Boston..........................75
Bobby Orr, Boston.............................72
Bobby Clarke, Philadelphia..................67
Pit Martin, Chicago............................61
Gilbert Perreault, Buffalo 60

Points
Phil Esposito, Boston 130
Bobby Clarke, Philadelphia..................104
Bobby Orr, Boston............................101
Rick MacLeish, Philadelphia................100
Jacques Lemaire, Montreal 95

Penalty minutes
Dave Shultz, Philadelphia 259
Bob Kelly, Philadelphia 238
Steve Durbano, St. Louis 231
Andre Dupont, St.L.-Phi. 215
Don Saleski, Philadelphia 205

Lowest goals-against average
(Min. 25 games)
Ken Dryden, Montreal 2.26
Gilles Villemure, N.Y. Rangers..........2.29
Tony Esposito, Chicago 2.51
Roy Edwards, Detroit 2.63
Dave Dryden, Buffalo 2.68

Shutouts
Ken Dryden, Montreal 6
Roy Edwards, Detroit 6
Tony Esposito, Chicago 4
Cesare Maniago, Minnesota 4
Rogie Vachon, Los Angeles...................4

Wins by goaltenders
Ken Dryden, Montreal 33
Tony Esposito, Chicago 32
Roy Edwards, Detroit 27
Ed Giacomin, N.Y. Rangers 26
Ed Johnston, Boston 24

1973-74

Goals
Phil Esposito, Boston..........................61
Ken Hodge, Boston 50

Richard Martin, Buffalo 52
Mickey Redmond, Detroit....................51
Bill Goldsworthy, Minnesota................48

Assists
Bobby Orr, Boston.............................90
Phil Esposito, Boston..........................77
Dennis Hextall, Minnesota..................62
Syl Apps, Pittsburgh 61
Andre Boudrias, Vancouver..................59
Wayne Cashman, Boston 59

Points
Phil Esposito, Boston 145
Bobby Orr, Boston............................122
Ken Hodge, Boston 105
Wayne Cashman, Boston 89
Bobby Clarke, Philadelphia..................87

Penalty minutes
Dave Schultz, Philadelphia 348
Steve Durbano, St.L.-Pit. 284
Bryan Watson, Pit.-St.L.-Det. 255
Andre Dupont, Philadelphia................216
Gary Howatt, N.Y. Islanders 204

Lowest goals-against average
(Min. 25 games)
Bernie Parent, Philadelphia 1.89
Tony Esposito, Chicago 2.04
Doug Favell, Toronto 2.71
Wayne Thomas, Montreal 2.76
Dan Bouchard, Atlanta 2.77

Shutouts
Bernie Parent, Philadelphia 12
Tony Esposito, Chicago 10
Gilles Gilbert, Boston 6
Dan Bouchard, Atlanta 5
Ed Giacomin, N.Y. Rangers 5
Rogie Vachon, Los Angeles...................5

Wins by goaltenders
Bernie Parent, Philadelphia 47
Tony Esposito, Chicago 34
Gilles Gilbert, Boston 34
Ed Giacomin, N.Y. Rangers 30
Rogie Vachon, Los Angeles..................28

1974-75

Goals
Phil Esposito, Boston..........................61
Guy Lafleur, Montreal 53
Rick Martin, Buffalo 52
Danny Grant, Detroit 50
Marcel Dionne, Detroit 47

Assists
Bobby Clarke, Philadelphia..................89
Bobby Orr, Boston.............................89
Pete Mahovlich, Montreal....................82
Marcel Dionne, Detroit 74
Phil Esposito, Boston..........................66
Guy Lafleur, Montreal 66

Points
Bobby Orr, Boston............................135
Phil Esposito, Boston 127
Marcel Dionne, Detroit 121
Guy Lafleur, Montreal 119
Pete Mahovlich, Montreal...................117

Penalty minutes
Dave Schultz, Philadelphia 472
Andre Dupont, Philadelphia................276
Phil Russell, Chicago 260
Bryan Watson, Detroit 238
Bob Gassoff, St. Louis 222

Lowest goals-against average
(Min. 25 games)
Bernie Parent, Philadelphia 2.03
Rogie Vachon, Los Angeles................2.24
Gary Edwards, Los Angeles 2.34
Chico Resch, N.Y. Islanders 2.47
Ken Dryden, Montreal 2.69

Shutouts
Bernie Parent, Philadelphia 12
Tony Esposito, Chicago 6
Gary Smith, Vancouver 6
Rogie Vachon, Los Angeles...................6
Phil Myre, Atlanta...............................5

Wins by goaltenders
Bernie Parent, Philadelphia 44
Tony Esposito, Chicago 34
Gary Smith, Vancouver 32
Ken Dryden, Montreal 30
Rogie Vachon, Los Angeles.................27

1975-76

Goals
Reggie Leach, Philadelphia 61
Guy Lafleur, Montreal 56
Pierre Larouche, Pittsburgh 53
Jean Pronovost, Pittsburgh..................52
Bill Barber, Philadelphia 50
Danny Gare, Buffalo 50

Assists
Bobby Clarke, Philadelphia..................89
Pete Mahovlich, Montreal....................71
Guy Lafleur, Montreal 69
Gilbert Perreault, Buffalo 69
Jean Ratelle, NYR-Bos. 69

Points
Guy Lafleur, Montreal 125
Bobby Clarke, Philadelphia..................119
Gilbert Perreault, Buffalo 113
Bill Barber, Philadelphia 112
Pierre Larouche, Pittsburgh 111

Penalty minutes
Steve Durbano, Pit.-K.C. 370
Bryan Watson, Detroit 322
Dave Schultz, Philadelphia 307
Bob Gassoff, St. Louis 306
Dave Williams, Toronto 306

Lowest goals-against average
(Min. 25 games)
Ken Dryden, Montreal 2.03
Chico Resch, N.Y. Islanders 2.07
Dan Bouchard, Atlanta 2.54
Wayne Stephenson, Philadelphia 2.58
Billy Smith, N.Y. Islanders.................2.61

Shutouts
Ken Dryden, Montreal 8
Chico Resch, N.Y. Islanders 7
Rogie Vachon, Los Angeles...................5
Tony Esposito, Chicago 4
Jim Rutherford, Detroit 4

Wins by goaltenders
Ken Dryden, Montreal 42
Wayne Stephenson, Philadelphia 40
Gilles Gilbert, Boston 33
Tony Esposito, Chicago 30
Gerry Desjardins, Buffalo 29

1976-77

Goals
Steve Shutt, Montreal.........................60
Guy Lafleur, Montreal 56

Marcel Dionne, Los Angeles................53
Rick MacLeish, Philadelphia................49
Wilf Paiement, Colorado.....................41

Assists

Guy Lafleur, Montreal 80
Marcel Dionne, Los Angeles................69
Larry Robinson, Montreal 66
Borje Salming, Toronto 66
Tim Young, Minnesota 66

Points

Guy Lafleur, Montreal 136
Marcel Dionne, Los Angeles..............122
Steve Shutt, Montreal........................105
Rick MacLeish, Philadelphia................97
Gilbert Perreault, Buffalo 95
Tim Young, Minnesota 95

Penalty minutes

Dave Williams, Toronto 338
Dennis Polonich, Detroit 274
Bob Gassoff, St. Louis 254
Phil Russell, Chicago 233
Dave Schultz, Los Angeles 232

Lowest goals-against average
(Min. 25 games)

Michel Larocque, Montreal................2.09
Ken Dryden, Montreal 2.14
Chico Resch, N.Y. Islanders 2.28
Billy Smith, N.Y. Islanders 2.50
Don Edwards, Buffalo........................2.51

Shutouts

Ken Dryden, Montreal 10
Rogie Vachon, Los Angeles...................8
Bernie Parent, Philadelphia 5
Dunc Wilson, Pittsburgh 5
Michel Larocque, Montreal.....................4
Mike Palmateer, Toronto 4

Wins by goaltenders

Ken Dryden, Montreal 41
Bernie Parent, Philadelphia 35
Rogie Vachon, Los Angeles.................33
Gerry Desjardins, Buffalo 31
Gerry Cheevers, Boston 30

1977-78

Goals

Guy Lafleur, Montreal 60
Mike Bossy, N.Y. Islanders 53
Steve Shutt, Montreal..........................49
Lanny McDonald, Toronto 47
Bryan Trottier, N.Y. Islanders...............46

Assists

Bryan Trottier, N.Y. Islanders...............77
Guy Lafleur, Montreal 72
Darryl Sittler, Toronto..........................72
Bobby Clarke, Philadelphia..................68
Denis Potvin, N.Y. Islanders 64

Points

Guy Lafleur, Montreal 132
Bryan Trottier, N.Y. Islanders.............123
Darryl Sittler, Toronto........................117
Jacques Lemaire, Montreal 97
Denis Potvin, N.Y. Islanders 94

Penalty minutes

Dave Schultz, L.A.-Pit........................405
Dave Williams, Toronto 351
Dennis Polonich, Detroit 254
Randy Holt, Chi.-Cle. 249
Andre Dupont, Philadelphia...............225

Lowest goals-against average
(Min. 25 games)

Ken Dryden, Montreal 2.05
Bernie Parent, Philadelphia 2.22
Gilles Gilbert, Boston 2.53
Chico Resch, N.Y. Islanders 2.55
Tony Esposito, Chicago 2.63

Shutouts

Bernie Parent, Philadelphia 7
Ken Dryden, Montreal 5
Don Edwards, Buffalo............................5
Tony Esposito, Chicago 5
Mike Palmateer, Toronto 5

Wins by goaltenders

Don Edwards, Buffalo..........................38
Ken Dryden, Montreal 37
Mike Palmateer, Toronto 34
Bernie Parent, Philadelphia 29
Rogie Vachon, Los Angeles.................29

1978-79

Goals

Mike Bossy, N.Y. Islanders 69
Marcel Dionne, Los Angeles................59
Guy Lafleur, Montreal 52
Guy Chouinard, Atlanta 50
Bryan Trottier, N.Y. Islanders...............47

Assists

Bryan Trottier, N.Y. Islanders...............87
Guy Lafleur, Montreal 77
Marcel Dionne, Los Angeles................71
Bob MacMillan, Atlanta 71
Denis Potvin, N.Y. Islanders 70

Points

Bryan Trottier, N.Y. Islanders.............134
Marcel Dionne, Los Angeles..............130
Guy Lafleur, Montreal 129
Mike Bossy, N.Y. Islanders 126
Bob MacMillan, Atlanta 108

Penalty minutes

Dave Williams, Toronto 298
Randy Holt, Van.-L.A..........................282
Dave Schultz, Pit.-Buf. 243
Dave Hutchison, Toronto...................235
Willi Plett, Atlanta..............................213

Lowest goals-against average
(Min. 25 games)

Ken Dryden, Montreal 2.30
Chico Resch, N.Y. Islanders 2.50
Bernie Parent, Philadelphia 2.70
Michel Larocque, Montreal................2.84
Billy Smith, N.Y. Islanders 2.87

Shutouts

Ken Dryden, Montreal 5
Tony Esposito, Chicago 4
Mario Lessard, Los Angeles..................4
Mike Palmateer, Toronto 4
Bernie Parent, Philadelphia 4

Wins by goaltenders

Dan Bouchard, Atlanta 32
Ken Dryden, Montreal 30
Don Edwards, Buffalo..........................26
Mike Palmateer, Toronto 26
Chico Resch, N.Y. Islanders 26

1979-80

Goals

Charlie Simmer, Los Angeles 56
Blaine Stoughton, Hartford..................56

Danny Gare, Buffalo 56
Marcel Dionne, Los Angeles................53
Mike Bossy, N.Y. Islanders 51
Wayne Gretzky, Edmonton 51

Assists

Wayne Gretzky, Edmonton 86
Marcel Dionne, Los Angeles................84
Guy Lafleur, Montreal 75
Gil Perreault, Buffalo...........................66
Bryan Trottier, N.Y. Islanders...............62

Points

Marcel Dionne, Los Angeles..............137
Wayne Gretzky, Edmonton 137
Guy Lafleur, Montreal 125
Gil Perreault, Buffalo.........................106
Mike Rogers, Hartford.......................105

Penalty minutes

Jimmy Mann, Winnipeg 287
Paul Holmgren, Philadelphia...............267
Terry O'Reilly, Boston........................265
Terry Ruskowski, Chicago..................252
Paul Mulvey, Washington...................240

Lowest goals-against average
(Min. 25 games)

Bob Sauve, Buffalo............................2.36
Denis Herron, Montreal 2.51
Don Edwards, Buffalo........................2.57
Gilles Gilbert, Boston 2.73
Pete Peeters, Philadelphia.................2.73

Shutouts

Tony Esposito, Chicago 6
Gerry Cheevers, Boston 4
Bob Sauve, Buffalo................................4
Rogie Vachon, Detroit 4
Michel Larocque, Montreal.....................3
Chico Resch, N.Y. Islanders 3

Wins by goaltenders

Mike Liut, St. Louis 32
Tony Esposito, Chicago 31
Pete Peeters, Philadelphia..................29
Gilles Meloche, Minnesota 27
Denis Herron, Montreal 25

1980-81

Goals

Mike Bossy, N.Y. Islanders 68
Marcel Dionne, Los Angeles................58
Charlie Simmer, Los Angeles 56
Wayne Gretzky, Edmonton 55
Rick Kehoe, Pittsburgh........................55

Assists

Wayne Gretzky, Edmonton 109
Kent Nilsson, Calgary 82
Marcel Dionne, Los Angeles................77
Bernie Federko, St. Louis 73
Bryan Trottier, N.Y. Islanders...............72

Points

Wayne Gretzky, Edmonton 164
Marcel Dionne, Los Angeles..............135
Kent Nilsson, Calgary 131
Mike Bossy, N.Y. Islanders 119
Dave Taylor, Los Angeles 112

Penalty minutes

Dave Williams, Vancouver..................333
Paul Holmgren, Philadelphia...............306
Chris Nilan, Montreal 262
Jim Korn, Detroit................................246
Willi Plett, Calgary 237
Behn Wilson, Philadelphia..................237

Lowest goals-against average
(Min. 25 games)

Richard Sevigny, Montreal 2.40
Rick St. Croix, Philadelphia 2.49
Don Edwards, Buffalo.....................2.96
Pete Peeters, Philadelphia.............2.96
Michel Larocque, Montreal.............3.03

Shutouts

Don Edwards, Buffalo...........................3
Chico Resch, N.Y. Islanders 3
11 goalies tied with 2

Wins by goaltenders

Mario Lessard, Los Angeles...............35
Mike Liut, St. Louis...........................33
Tony Esposito, Chicago......................29
Greg Millen, Pittsburgh......................25
Rogie Vachon, Boston.......................25

1981-82

Goals

Wayne Gretzky, Edmonton 92
Mike Bossy, N.Y. Islanders.............64
Dennis Maruk, Washington 60
Dino Ciccarelli, Minnesota.................55
Rick Vaive, Toronto 54

Assists

Wayne Gretzky, Edmonton 120
Peter Stastny, Quebec......................93
Denis Savard, Chicago 87
Mike Bossy, N.Y. Islanders.............83
Bryan Trottier, N.Y. Islanders...........79

Points

Wayne Gretzky, Edmonton 212
Mike Bossy, N.Y. Islanders...........147
Peter Stastny, Quebec....................139
Dennis Maruk, Washington 136
Bryan Trottier, N.Y. Islanders...........129

Penalty minutes

Paul Baxter, Pittsburgh....................407
Dave Williams, Toronto 341
Glen Cochrane, Philadelphia.............329
Pat Price, Pittsburgh 322
Al Secord, Chicago 303

Lowest goals-against average
(Min. 25 games)

Denis Herron, Montreal 2.64
Rick Wamsley, Montreal...................2.75
Bill Smith, N.Y.Islanders..................2.97
Roland Melanson, N.Y. Islanders 3.23
Grant Fuhr, Edmonton 3.31

Shutouts

Denis Herron, Montreal 3
Richard Brodeur, Vancouver 2
Mario Lessard, Los Angeles................2
Mike Liut, St. Louis...........................2
Pat Riggin, Calgary 2
Doug Soetaert, Winnipeg 2
Rick Wamsley, Montreal.....................2

Wins by goaltenders

Billy Smith, N.Y. Islanders...............32
Grant Fuhr, Edmonton 28
Mike Liut, St. Louis...........................28
Dan Bouchard, Quebec......................27
Don Edwards, Buffalo.........................26
Gilles Meloche, Minnesota 26

1982-83

Goals

Wayne Gretzky, Edmonton 71
Lanny McDonald, Calgary 66

Mike Bossy, N.Y. Islanders.............60
Michel Goulet, Quebec 57
Marcel Dionne, Los Angeles...............56

Assists

Wayne Gretzky, Edmonton 125
Denis Savard, Chicago 85
Peter Stastny, Quebec.......................77
Paul Coffey, Edmonton.......................67
Bobby Clarke, Philadelphia.................62

Points

Wayne Gretzky, Edmonton 196
Peter Stastny, Quebec....................124
Denis Savard, Chicago 120
Mike Bossy, N.Y. Islanders...........118
Marcel Dionne, Los Angeles..............107
Barry Pederson, Boston 107

Penalty minutes

Randy Holt, Washington 275
Dave Williams, Vancouver.................265
Brian Sutter, St. Louis 254
Paul Baxter, Pittsburgh.....................238
Jim Korn, Toronto 238

Lowest goals-against average
(Min. 25 games)

Pete Peeters, Boston.......................2.36
Roland Melanson, N.Y. Islanders 2.66
Billy Smith, N.Y. Islanders................2.87
Pelle Lindbergh, Philadelphia 2.98
Murray Bannerman, Chicago.............3.10

Shutouts

Pete Peeters, Boston............................8
Murray Bannerman, Chicago...............4
Bob Froese, Philadelphia 4
Pelle Lindbergh, Philadelphia 3
Corrado Micalef, Detroit 2
Ed Mio, N.Y. Rangers 2

Wins by goaltenders

Pete Peeters, Boston..........................40
Andy Moog, Edmonton 33
Rick Wamsley, Montreal......................27
Bob Sauve, Buffalo.............................25
Murray Bannerman, Chicago...............24
Roland Melanson, N.Y. Islanders 24

1983-84

Goals

Wayne Gretzky, Edmonton 87
Michel Goulet, Quebec 56
Glenn Anderson, Edmonton 54
Tim Kerr, Philadelphia 54
Jari Kurri, Edmonton 52
Rick Vaive, Toronto 52

Assists

Wayne Gretzky, Edmonton 118
Paul Coffey, Edmonton.......................86
Barry Pederson, Boston 77
Peter Stastny, Quebec.......................73
Bryan Trottier, N.Y. Islanders...........71

Points

Wayne Gretzky, Edmonton 205
Paul Coffey, Edmonton.....................126
Michel Goulet, Quebec 121
Peter Stastny, Quebec....................119
Mike Bossy, N.Y. Islanders...........118

Penalty minutes

Chris Nilan, Montreal 338
Willie Plett, Minnesota 316
Gary Rissling, Pittsburgh 297

Dave Williams, Vancouver.................294
Jim Korn, Toronto 257

Lowest goals-against average
(Min. 25 games)

Pat Riggin, Washington 2.66
Tom Barrasso, Buffalo.......................2.84
Al Jensen, Washington......................2.91
Doug Keans, Boston..........................2.84
Bob Froese, Philadelphia...................3.14

Shutouts

Pat Riggin, Washington 4
Al Jensen, Washington........................4
Mike Liut, St. Louis...........................3
Nine goalies tied with 2

Wins by goaltenders

Grant Fuhr, Edmonton 30
Peter Peeters, Boston........................29
Dan Bouchard, Quebec......................29
Bob Froese, Philadelphia...................28
Glen Hanlon, N.Y. Rangers................28

1984-85

Goals

Wayne Gretzky, Edmonton 73
Jari Kurri, Edmonton 71
Mike Bossy, N.Y. Islanders.............58
Michel Goulet, Quebec 55
John Ogrodnick, Detroit 55

Assists

Wayne Gretzky, Edmonton 135
Paul Coffey, Edmonton.......................84
Marcel Dionne, Los Angeles...............80
Dale Hawerchuk, Winnipeg.................77
Bernie Federko, St. Louis 73

Points

Wayne Gretzky, Edmonton 208
Jari Kurri, Edmonton 135
Dale Hawerchuk, Winnipeg...............130
Marcel Dionne, Los Angeles..............126
Paul Coffey, Edmonton.....................121

Penalty minutes

Chris Nilan, Montreal 358
Torrie Robertson, Hartford 337
John Blum, Boston............................263
Tim Hunter, Calgary 259
Bob McGill, Toronto 250

Lowest goals-against average
(Min. 25 games)

Tom Barrasso, Buffalo.......................2.66
Pat Riggin, Washington 2.98
Pelle Lindbergh, Philadelphia 3.02
Steve Penney, Montreal....................3.08
Bob Sauve, Buffalo............................3.22
Warren Skorodenski, Chicago 3.22

Shutouts

Tom Barrasso, Buffalo...........................5
Kelly Hrudey, N.Y. Islanders 2
Bob Janecyk, Los Angeles 2
Pelle Lindbergh, Philadelphia 2
Pat Riggin, Washington 2
Warren Skorodenski, Chicago 2
Steve Weeks, Hartford.......................2

Wins by goaltenders

Pelle Lindbergh, Philadelphia 40
Brian Hayward, Winnipeg...................33
Reggie Lemelin, Calgary 30
Pat Riggin, Washington 28
Murray Bannerman, Chicago...............27

1985-86

Goals
Jari Kurri, Edmonton 68
Mike Bossy, N.Y. Islanders 61
Tim Kerr, Philadelphia 58
Glenn Anderson, Edmonton 54
Michel Goulet, Quebec 53

Assists
Wayne Gretzky, Edmonton 163
Mario Lemieux, Pittsburgh...................93
Paul Coffey, Edmonton.........................90
Peter Stastny, Quebec 81
Neal Broten, Minnesota........................76

Points
Wayne Gretzky, Edmonton 215
Mario Lemieux, Pittsburgh..................141
Paul Coffey, Edmonton........................138
Jari Kurri, Edmonton 131
Mike Bossy, N.Y. Islanders 123

Penalty minutes
Joey Kocur, Detroit..............................377
Torrie Robertson, Hartford 358
Dave Williams, Los Angeles 320
Tim Hunter, Calgary 291
Dave Brown, Philadelphia....................277

Lowest goals-against average
(Min. 25 games)
Bob Froese, Philadelphia...................2.55
Al Jensen, Washington.......................3.18
Kelly Hrudey, N.Y. Islanders 3.21
Clint Malarchuk, Quebec 3.21
John Vanbiesbrouck, N.Y. Rangers ...3.32

Shutouts
Bob Froese, Philadelphia.........................5
Clint Malarchuk, Quebec 4
Doug Soetaert, Montreal 3
John Vanbiesbrouck, N.Y. Rangers 3

Wins by goaltenders
Bob Froese, Philadelphia......................31
John Vanbiesbrouck, N.Y. Rangers 31
Tom Barrasso, Buffalo...........................29
Rejean Lemelin, Calgary.......................29
Grant Fuhr, Edmonton 29

1986-87

Goals
Wayne Gretzky, Edmonton 62
Tim Kerr, Philadelphia 58
Mario Lemieux, Pittsburgh....................54
Jari Kurri, Edmonton 54
Dino Ciccarelli, Minnesota....................52

Assists
Wayne Gretzky, Edmonton 121
Ray Bourque, Boston.............................72
Mark Messier, Edmonton 70
Kevin Dineen, Hartford 69
Bryan Trottier, N.Y. Islanders...............64

Points
Wayne Gretzky, Edmonton 183
Jari Kurri, Edmonton 108
Mario Lemieux, Pittsburgh..................107
Mark Messier, Edmonton 107
Doug Gilmour, St. Louis.......................105

Penalty minutes
Dave Williams, Los Angeles 358
Tim Hunter, Calgary 357
Brian Curran, N.Y. Islanders 356

Basil McRae, Det.-Que. 342
Rick Tocchet, Philadelphia..................286

Lowest goals-against average
(Min. 25 games)
Brian Hayward, Montreal...................2.81
Patrick Roy, Montreal 2.93
Ron Hextall, Philadelphia 3.00
Daniel Berthiaume, Winnipeg............3.17
Mario Gosselin, Quebec 3.18
Glen Hanlon, Detroit..........................3.18

Shutouts
Mike Liut, Hartford 4
Bill Ranford, Boston 3
Rejean Lemelin, Calgary 2
Allan Bester, Toronto 2
Tom Barrasso, Buffalo...........................2

Wins by goaltenders
Ron Hextall, Philadelphia 37
Mike Liut, Hartford 31
Mike Vernon, Calgary 30
Andy Moog, Edmonton 28
Alain Chevrier, New Jersey...................24

1987-88

Goals
Mario Lemieux, Pittsburgh....................70
Craig Simpson, Pit.-Edm......................56
Jimmy Carson, Los Angeles.................55
Luc Robitaille, Los Angeles..................53
Joe Nieuwendyk, Calgary 51

Assists
Wayne Gretzky, Edmonton 109
Mario Lemieux, Pittsburgh....................98
Denis Savard, Chicago 87
Dale Hawerchuk, Winnipeg...................77
Mark Messier, Edmonton 74

Points
Mario Lemieux, Pittsburgh..................168
Wayne Gretzky, Edmonton 149
Denis Savard, Chicago 131
Dale Hawerchuk, Winnipeg.................121
Luc Robitaille, Los Angeles 111
Peter Stastny, Quebec 111
Mark Messier, Edmonton 111

Penalty minutes
Bob Probert, Detroit.............................398
Basil McRae, Minnesota......................378
Tim Hunter, Calgary 337
Richard Zemlak, Minnesota.................307
Jay Miller, Boston................................304

Lowest goals-against average
(Min. 25 games)
Pete Peeters, Washington 2.78
Brian Hayward, Montreal...................2.86
Patrick Roy, Montreal 2.90
Rejean Lemelin, Boston......................2.93
Greg Stefan, Detroit 3.11

Shutouts
Grant Fuhr, Edmonton 4
Glen Hanlon, Detroit...............................4
Clint Malarchuk, Washington 4
Kelly Hrudey, N.Y. Islanders 3
Rejean Lemelin, Boston 3
Patrick Roy, Montreal 3

Wins by goaltenders
Grant Fuhr, Edmonton 40
Mike Vernon, Calgary 39
Ron Hextall, Philadelphia 30

John Vanbiesbrouck, N.Y. Rangers 27
Tom Barrasso, Buffalo...........................25
Mike Liut, Hartford 25

1988-89

Goals
Mario Lemieux, Pittsburgh....................85
Bernie Nicholls, Los Angeles................70
Steve Yzerman, Detroit.........................65
Wayne Gretzky, Los Angeles 54
Joe Nieuwendyk, Calgary 51
Joe Mullen, Calgary..............................51

Assists
Mario Lemieux, Pittsburgh..................114
Wayne Gretzky, Los Angeles 114
Steve Yzerman, Detroit.........................90
Paul Coffey, Pittsburgh.........................83
Bernie Nicholls, Los Angeles................80

Points
Mario Lemieux, Pittsburgh..................199
Wayne Gretzky, Los Angeles 168
Steve Yzerman, Detroit.......................155
Bernie Nicholls, Los Angeles..............150
Rob Brown, Pittsburgh.........................115

Penalty minutes
Tim Hunter, Calgary 375
Basil McRae, Minnesota......................365
Dave Manson, Chicago........................352
Marty McSorley, Los Angeles..............350
Mike Hartman, Buffalo 316

Lowest goals-against average
(Min. 25 games)
Patrick Roy, Montreal 2.47
Mike Vernon, Calgary 2.65
Pete Peeters, Washington 2.85
Brian Hayward, Montreal...................2.90
Rick Wamsley, Calgary.......................2.96

Shutouts
Greg Millen, St. Louis 6
Pete Peeters, Washington 4
Kirk McLean, Vancouver.........................4
Peter Sidorkiewicz, Hartford 4
Patrick Roy, Montreal 4

Wins by goaltenders
Mike Vernon, Calgary 37
Patrick Roy, Montreal 33
Ron Hextall, Philadelphia 30
John Vanbiesbrouck, N.Y. Rangers 28
Kelly Hrudey, NYI-L.A...........................28

1989-90

Goals
Brett Hull, St. Louis...............................72
Steve Yzerman, Detroit.........................62
Cam Neely, Boston...............................55
Brian Bellows, Minnesota.....................55
Pat LaFontaine, N.Y. Islanders.............54

Assists
Wayne Gretzky, Los Angeles 102
Mark Messier, Edmonton 84
Adam Oates, St. Louis..........................79
Mario Lemieux, Pittsburgh...................78
Paul Coffey, Pittsburgh.........................74

Points
Wayne Gretzky, Los Angeles 142
Mark Messier, Edmonton 129
Steve Yzerman, Detroit.......................127
Mario Lemieux, Pittsburgh..................123
Brett Hull, St. Louis.............................113

Penalty minutes

Basil McRae, Minnesota....................351
Alan May, Washington 339
Marty McSorley, Los Angeles............322
Troy Mallette, N.Y. Rangers 305
Wayne Van Dorp, Chicago.................303

Lowest goals-against average
(Min. 25 games)

Mike Liut, Har.-Was..........................2.527
Patrick Roy, Montreal........................2.534
Rejean Lemelin, Boston 2.805
Andy Moog, Boston 2.886
Daren Puppa, Buffalo 2.888

Shutouts

Mike Liut, Har.-Was..............................4
Andy Moog, Boston 3
Mike Fitzpatrick, N.Y. Islanders 3
Patrick Roy, Montreal............................3
Jon Casey, Minnesota 3

Wins by goaltenders

Patrick Roy, Montreal...........................31
Daren Puppa, Buffalo 31
Jon Casey, Minnesota 31
Andy Moog, Boston 24
Bill Ranford, Edmonton 24

1990-91

Goals

Brett Hull, St. Louis..............................86
Cam Neely, Boston 51
Theo Fleury, Calgary.............................51
Steve Yzerman, Detroit..........................51
Mike Gartner, N.Y. Rangers 49

Assists

Wayne Gretzky, Los Angeles 122
Adam Oates, St. Louis..........................90
Al MacInnis, Calgary 75
Ray Bourque, Boston 73
Mark Recchi, Pittsburgh........................73

Points

Wayne Gretzky, Los Angeles 163
Brett Hull, St. Louis............................131
Adam Oates, St. Louis........................115
Mark Recchi, Pittsburgh......................113
John Cullen, Pit.-Har. 110

Penalty minutes

Rob Ray, Buffalo 350
Mike Peluso, Chicago.........................320
Bob Probert, Detroit............................315
Craig Berube, Philadelphia 293
Gino Odjick, Vancouver.......................296

Lowest goals-against average
(Min. 25 games)

Ed Belfour, Chicago 2.47
Don Beaupre, Washington 2.64
Patrick Roy, Montreal.........................2.71
Andy Moog, Boston 2.87
Pete Peters, Philadelphia....................2.88

Shutouts

Don Beaupre, Washington 5
Andy Moog, Boston 4
Bob Essesna, Winnipeg.........................4
Ed Belfour, Chicago 4
John Vanbiesbrouck, N.Y. Rangers 3
Jon Casey, Minnesota 3
Kelly Hrudey, Los Angeles.....................3
Vincent Riendeau, St. Louis...................3

Wins by goaltenders

Ed Belfour, Chicago 43
Mike Vernon, Calgary...........................31
Tim Cheveldae, Detroit 30
Vincent Riendeau, St. Louis 29
Tom Barrasso, Pittsburgh.....................27
Bill Ranford, Edmonton.........................27

1991-92

Goals

Brett Hull, St. Louis..............................70
Kevin Stephens, Pittsburgh...................54
Gary Roberts, Calgary 53
Jeremy Roenick, Chicago......................53
Pat LaFontaine, Buffalo 46

Assists

Wayne Gretzky, Los Angeles 90
Mario Lemieux, Pittsburgh....................87
Brian Leech, N.Y. Rangers 80
Adam Oates, St.L.-Bos.........................79
Dale Hawerchuck, Buffalo 75

Points

Mario Lemieux, Pittsburgh..................131
Kevin Stephens, Pittsburgh.................123
Wayne Gretzky, Los Angeles 121
Brett Hull, St. Louis............................109
Luc Robitaille, Los Angeles.................107
Mark Messier, N.Y. Rangers 107

Penalty minutes

Mike Peluso, Chicago.........................408
Rob Ray, Buffalo 354
Gino Odjick, Vancouver 348
Ronnie Stern, Calgary 338
Link Gaetz, San Jose 326

Lowest goals-against average
(Min. 25 games)

Patrick Roy, Montreal.........................2.36
Ed Belfour, Chicago 2.70
Kirk McLean, Vancouver 2.74
John Vanbiesbrouck, N.Y Rangers....2.85
Bob Essensa, Winnipeg......................2.88

Shutouts

Ed Belfour, Chicago 5
Bob Essesna, Winnipeg.........................5
Kirk McLean, Vancouver 5
Patrick Roy, Montreal.............................5
Ron Hextall, Philadelphia 3
Mike Richter, N.Y Rangers 3
Kay Whitmore, Hartford 3

Wins by goaltenders

Tim Cheveldae, Detroit 38
Kirk McLean, Vancouver 38
Patrick Roy, Montreal............................36
Don Beaupre, Washington 29
Andy Moog, Boston 28

1992-93

Goals

Alexander Mogilny, Buffalo....................76
Teemu Selanne, Winnipeg.....................76
Mario Lemieux, Pittsburgh....................69
Luc Robitaille, Los Angeles...................63
Pavel Bure, Vancouver 60

Assists

Adam Oates, Boston 97
Doug Gilmour, Toronto..........................95
Pat LaFontaine, Buffalo 95
Mario Lemieux, Pittsburgh....................91
Craig Janney, St. Louis 82

Points

Mario Lemieux, Pittsburgh..................160
Pat LaFontaine, Buffalo 148
Adam Oates, Boston...........................142
Steve Yzerman, Detroit........................137
Teemu Selanne, Winnipeg....................137

Penalty minutes

Marty McSorley, Los Angeles............399
Gino Odjick, Vancouver 370
Tie Domi, NYR-Win..............................344
Nick Kypreos, Hartford 325
Mike Peluso, Ottawa............................318

Lowest goals-against average
(Min. 25 games)

Felix Potvin, Toronto 2.50
Ed Belfour, Chicago 2.59
Tom Barrasso, Pittsburgh 3.01
Curtis Joseph, St. Louis......................3.02
Kay Whitmore, Vancouver..................3.10

Shutouts

Ed Belfour, Chicago 7
Tommy Soderstrom, Philadelphia 5
Tom Barrasso, Pittsburgh 4
Tim Cheveldae, Detroit..........................4
John Vanbiesbrouck, N.Y. Rangers 4

Wins by goaltenders

Tom Barrasso, Pittsburgh.....................43
Ed Belfour, Chicago 41
Andy Moog, Boston 37
Tim Cheveldae, Detroit.........................34
Bob Essensa, Winnipeg........................33

1993-94

Goals

Pavel Bure, Vancouver 60
Brett Hull, St. Louis..............................57
Sergei Federov, Detroit.........................56
Dave Andreychuk, Toronto 53
Adam Graves, N.Y. Rangers 52
Brendan Shannahan, St. Louis 52
Ray Sheppard, Detroit..........................52

Assists

Wayne Gretzky, Los Angeles 92
Doug Gilmour, Toronto..........................84
Adam Oates, Boston.............................80
Sergei Zubov, N.Y. Rangers..................77
Ray Bourque, Boston............................71

Points

Wayne Gretzky, Los Angeles 130
Segei Fedorov, Detroit.........................120
Adam Oates, Boston...........................112
Doug Gilmour, Toronto........................111
Pavel Bure, Vancouver 107
Mike Recchi, Philadelphia 107
Jeremy Roenick, Chicago....................107

Penalty minutes

Tie Domi, Winnipeg.............................347
Shane Churla, Dallas 333
Warren Rychel, Los Angeles 322
Craig Berube, Washington 305
Kelly Chase, St. Louis 278

Lowest goals-against average
(Min. 27 games)

Dominik Hasek, Buffalo.......................1.95
Martin Brodeur, New Jersey 2.40
Patrick Roy, Montreal..........................2.50
John Vanbiesbrouck, Florida..............2.53
Mike Richter, N.Y. Rangers................2.57

Shutouts

Ed Belfour, Chicago 7
Dominik Hasek, Buffalo 7
Patrick Roy, Montreal 7
Ron Hextall, N.Y. Islanders 5
Mike Richter, N.Y. Rangers 5

Wins by goaltenders

Mike Richter, N.Y. Rangers 42
Ed Belfour, Chicago 37
Curtis Joseph, St. Louis 36
Patrick Roy, Montreal 35
Felix Potvin, Toronto 34

1994-95

Goals

Peter Bondra, Washington 34
Jaromir Jagr, Pittsburgh 32
Owen Nolan, Quebec 30
Ray Sheppard, Detroit 30
Alexei Zhamnov, Winnipeg 30

Assists

Ron Francis, Pittsburgh 48
Paul Coffey, Detroit 44
Joe Sakic, Quebec 43
Eric Lindros, Philadelphia 41
Adam Oates, Boston 41

Points

Jaromir Jagr, Pittsburgh 70
Eric Lindros, Philadelphia 70
Alexei Zhamnov, Winnipeg 65
Joe Sakic, Quebec 62
Ron Francis, Pittsburgh 59

Penalty minutes

Enrico Ciccone, Tampa Bay 225
Shane Churla, Dallas 186
Bryan Marchment, Edmonton 184
Craig Berube, Washington 173
Rob Ray, Buffalo 173

**Lowest goals-against average
(Min. 13 games)**

Dominik Hasek, Buffalo 2.111
Rick Tabaracci, Was.-Cal. 2.114
Jim Carey, Washington 2.13
Chris Osgood, Detroit............................2.26
Ed Belfour, Chicago 2.28

Shutouts

Ed Belfour, Chicago 5
Dominik Hasek, Buffalo 5
Jim Carey, Washington 4
Arturs Irbe, San Jose 4
Blaine Lacher, Boston 4
John Vanbiesbrouck, Florida 4

Wins by goaltenders

Ken Wregget, Pittsburgh 25
Ed Belfour, Chicago 22
Trevor Kidd, Calgary 22
Curtis Joseph, St. Louis 20
Martin Broduer, New Jersey 19
Dominik Hasek, Buffalo 19
Blaine Lacher, Boston 19
Mike Vernon, Detroit 19

1995-96

Goals

Mario Lemieux, Pittsburgh.....................69
Jaromir Jagr, Pittsburgh 62
Alexander Mogilny, Vancouver 55
Peter Bondra, Washington 52
John LeClair, Philadelphia 51
Joe Sakic, Colorado 51

Assists

Ron Francis, Pittsburgh 92
Mario Lemieux, Pittsburgh....................92
Jaromir Jagr, Pittsburgh 87
Peter Forsberg, Colorado 86
Wayne Gretzky, L.A.-St.L. 79
Doug Weight, Edmonton 79

Points

Mario Lemieux, Pittsburgh....................161
Jaromir Jagr, Pittsburgh 149
Joe Sakic, Colorado 120
Ron Francis, Pittsburgh 119
Peter Forsberg, Colorado 116

Penalty minutes

Matthew Barnaby, Buffalo 335
Enrico Ciccone, T.B.-Chi. 306
Tie Domi, Toronto 297
Brad May, Buffalo 295
Rob Ray, Buffalo 287

**Lowest goals-against average
(Min. 25 games)**

Ron Hextall, Philadelphia 2.176
Chris Osgood, Detroit...........................2.178
Jim Carey, Washington 2.256
Mike Vernon, Detroit 2.264
Martin Brodeur, New Jersey 2.34

Shutouts

Jim Carey, Washington 9
Martin Brodeur, New Jersey 6
Chris Osgood, Detroit..............................5
Daren Puppa, Tampa Bay 5
Sean Burke, Hartford 4
Jeff Hackett, Chicago 4
Guy Hebert, Anaheim 4
Ron Hextall, Philadelphia 4

Wins by goaltenders

Chris Osgood, Detroit.............................39
Jim Carey, Washington 35
Martin Brodeur, New Jersey 34
Bill Ranford, Edm.-Bos. 34
Patrick Roy, Mon.-Col. 34

1996-97

Goals

Keith Tkachuk, Phoenix..........................52
Teemu Selanne, Anaheim 51
John LeClair, Philadelphia 50
Mario Lemieux, Pittsburgh.....................50
Zigmund Pfaffy, N.Y. Islanders 48

Assists

Wayne Gretzky, N.Y. Rangers 72
Mario Lemieux, Pittsburgh.....................72
Ron Francis, Pittsburgh 63
Steve Yzerman, Detroit 63
Doug Weight, Edmonton 61

Points

Mario Lemieux, Pittsburgh....................122
Teemu Selanne, Anaheim 109
Paul Kariya, Anaheim 99
Wayne Gretzky, N.Y. Rangers 97
John LeClair, Philadelphia 97

Penalty minutes

Gino Odjick, Vancouver 371
Bob Probert, Chicago 326
Paul Laus, Florida..................................313
Rob Ray, Buffalo 286
Tie Domi, Toronto 275

**Lowest goals-against average
(Min. 25 games)**

Martin Brodeur, New Jersey 1.88
Andy Moog, Dallas 2.15
Jeff Hackett, Chicago 2.16
Dominik Hasek, Buffalo 2.27
John Vanbiesbrouck, Florida 2.29

Shutouts

Martin Brodeur, New Jersey 10
Nikolai Khabibulin, Phoenix....................7
Patrick Roy, Colorado 7
Curtis Joseph, Edmonton........................6
Chris Osgood, Detroit..............................6

Wins by goaltenders

Patrick Roy, Colorado 38
Martin Brodeur, New Jersey 37
Dominik Hasek, Buffalo 37
Grant Fuhr, St. Louis 33
Mike Richter, N.Y. Rangers 33

1997-98

Goals

Peter Bondra, Washington 52
Teemu Selanne, Anaheim 52
Pavel Bure, Vancouver 51
John LeClair, Philadelphia 51
Zigmund Palffy, N.Y. Islanders 45

Assists

Wayne Gretzky, N.Y. Rangers 67
Jaromir Jagr, Pittsburgh 67
Peter Forsberg, Colorado 66
Ron Francis, Pittsburgh 62
Adam Oates, Washington 58
Jozef Stumpel, Los Angeles 58

Points

Jaromir Jagr, Pittsburgh 102
Peter Forsberg, Colorado 91
Pavel Bure, Vancouver 90
Wayne Gretzky, N.Y. Rangers 90
John LeClair, Philadelphia 87
Zigmund Palffy, N.Y. Islanders 87
Ron Francis, Pittsburgh 87

Penalty minutes

Donald Brashear, Vancouver 372
Tie Domi, Toronto 365
Krzysztof Oliwa, New Jersey 295
Paul Laus, Florida..................................293
Richard Pilon, N.Y. Islanders..............291

**Lowest goals-against average
(Min. 25 games)**

Ed Belfour, Dallas 1.88
Martin Brodeur, New Jersey 1.89
Tom Barrasso, Pittsburgh 2.07
Dominik Hasek, Buffalo 2.09
Ron Hextall, Philadelphia 2.165
Trevor Kidd, Carolina..........................2.168
Jamie McLennan, St. Louis 2.171

Shutouts

Dominik Hasek, Buffalo 13
Martin Brodeur, New Jersey 10
Ed Belfour, Dallas 9
Jeff Hackett, Chicago 8
Curtis Joseph, Edmonton........................8

Wins by goaltenders

Martin Brodeur, New Jersey 41
Ed Belfour, Dallas 37
Dominik Hasek, Buffalo 33
Olaf Kolzig, Washington 33
Chris Osgood, Detroit..............................33

1998-99

Goals
Teemu Selanne, Anaheim 47
Tony Amonte, Chicago 44
Jaromir Jagr, Pittsburgh 44
Alexei Yashin, Ottawa 44
John LeClair, Philadelphia 43

Assists
Jaromir Jagr, Pittsburgh 83
Peter Forsberg, Colorado 67
Paul Kariya, Anaheim 62
Teemu Selanne, Anaheim 60
Joe Sakic, Colorado 55

Points
Jaromir Jagr, Pittsburgh 127
Teemu Selanne, Anaheim 107
Paul Kariya, Anaheim 101
Peter Forsberg, Colorado 97
Joe Sakic, Colorado 96

Penalty minutes
Rob Ray, Buffalo 261
Jeff Odgers, Colorado 259
Peter Worrell, Florida 258
Patrick Cote, Nashville 242
Krzysztof Oliwa, New Jersey 240

Lowest goals-against average
(Min. 25 games)
Ron Tugnutt, Ottawa 1.79
Dominik Hasek, Buffalo 1.87
Byron Dafoe, Boston 1.9845
Ed Belfour, Dallas 1.9953
Roman Turek, Dallas 2.08

Shutouts
Byron Dafoe, Boston 10
Dominik Hasek, Buffalo 9
Nikolai Khabibulin, Phoenix....................8
Guy Hebert, Anaheim 6
Arturs Irbe, Carolina 6
Garth Snow, Vancouver..........................6
John Vanbiesbrouck, Philadelphia.........6

Wins by goaltenders
Martin Brodeur, New Jersey 39
Ed Belfour, Dallas 35
Curtis Joseph, Toronto..........................35
Chris Osgood, Detroit............................34
Byron Dafoe, Boston 32
Nikolai Khabibulin, Phoenix.................32
Patrick Roy, Colorado...........................32

1999-2000

Goals
Pavel Bure, Florida 58
Owen Nolan, San Jose 44
Tony Amonte, Chicago 43
Jaromir Jagr, Pittsburgh 42
Paul Kariya, Anaheim 42

Assists
Mark Recchi, Philadelphia....................63
Adam Oates, Washington......................56
Jaromir Jagr, Pittsburgh 54
Viktor Kozlov, Florida 53
Nicklas Lidstrom, Detroit 53

Points
Jaromir Jagr, Pittsburgh 96
Pavel Bure, Florida 94

Mark Recchi, Philadelphia....................91
Paul Kariya, Anaheim 86
Teemu Selanne, Anaheim 85

Penalty minutes
Denny Lambert, Atlanta.......................219
Todd Simpson, Florida 202
Tie Domi, Toronto 198
Matthew Barnaby, Pittsburgh 197
Eric Cairns, N.Y. Islanders.................196

Lowest goals-against average
(Min. 25 games)
Damian Rhodes, Atlanta.....................3.88
Dan Cloutier, Tampa Bay 3.491
Norm Maracle, Atlanta 3.486
Kevin Weekes, Van.-NYI.....................3.23
Robbie Tallas, Boston....................3.169
Tom Barrasso, Pit.-Ott. 3.168

Shutouts
Roman Turek, St. Louis..........................7
Martin Brodeur, New Jersey...................6
Chris Osgood, Detroit.............................6
Martin Biron, Buffalo 5
Fred Brathwaite, Calgary 5
Arturs Irbe, Carolina...............................5
Olaf Kolzig, Washington 5
Jose Theodore, Montreal 5

Wins by goaltenders
Martin Brodeur, New Jersey.................43
Roman Turek, St. Louis........................42
Olaf Kolzig, Washington 41
Curtis Joseph, Toronto..........................36
Arturs Irbe, Carolina.............................34

AWARD WINNERS

LEAGUE AWARDS

ART ROSS TROPHY

(Leading scorer)

Season	Player, Team	Pts.
1917-18	Joe Malone, Montreal	44
1918-19	Newsy Lalonde, Montreal	32
1919-20	Joe Malone, Quebec Bulldogs	45
1920-21	Newsy Lalonde, Montreal	41
1921-22	Punch Broadbelt, Ottawa	46
1922-23	Babe Dye, Toronto	37
1923-24	Cy Denneny, Ottawa	23
1924-25	Babe Dye, Toronto	44
1925-26	Nels Stewart, Montreal Maroons	42
1926-27	Bill Cook, N.Y. Rangers	37
1927-28	Howie Morenz, Montreal	51
1928-29	Ace Bailey, Toronto	32
1929-30	Cooney Weiland, Boston	73
1930-31	Howie Morenz, Montreal	51
1931-32	Harvey Jackson, Toronto	53
1932-33	Bill Cook, N.Y. Rangers	50
1933-34	Charlie Conacher, Toronto	52
1934-35	Charlie Conacher, Toronto	57
1935-36	Dave Schriner, N.Y. Americans	45
1936-37	Dave Schriner, N.Y. Americans	46
1937-38	Gordie Drillion, Toronto	52
1938-39	Toe Blake, Montreal	47
1939-40	Milt Schmidt, Boston	52
1940-41	Bill Cowley, Boston	62
1941-42	Bryan Hextall, N.Y. Rangers	56
1942-43	Doug Bentley, Chicago	73
1943-44	Herbie Cain, Boston	82
1944-45	Elmer Lach, Montreal	80
1945-46	Max Bentley, Chicago	61
1946-47	Max Bentley, Chicago	72
1947-48	Elmer Lach, Montreal	61
1948-49	Roy Conacher, Chicago	68
1949-50	Ted Lindsay, Detroit	78
1950-51	Gordie Howe, Detroit	86
1951-52	Gordie Howe, Detroit	86
1952-53	Gordie Howe, Detroit	95
1953-54	Gordie Howe, Detroit	81
1954-55	Bernie Geoffrion, Montreal	75
1955-56	Jean Beliveau, Montreal	88
1956-57	Gordie Howe, Detroit	89
1957-58	Dickie Moore, Montreal	84
1958-59	Dickie Moore, Montreal	96
1959-60	Bobby Hull, Chicago	81
1960-61	Bernie Geoffrion, Montreal	95
1961-62	Bobby Hull, Chicago	84
1962-63	Gordie Howe, Detroit	86
1963-64	Stan Mikita, Chicago	89
1964-65	Stan Mikita, Chicago	87
1965-66	Bobby Hull, Chicago	97
1966-67	Stan Mikita, Chicago	97
1967-68	Stan Mikita, Chicago	87
1968-69	Phil Esposito, Boston	126
1969-70	Bobby Orr, Boston	120
1970-71	Phil Esposito, Boston	152
1971-72	Phil Esposito, Boston	133
1972-73	Phil Esposito, Boston	130
1973-74	Phil Esposito, Boston	145
1974-75	Bobby Orr, Boston	135
1975-76	Guy Lafleur, Montreal	125
1976-77	Guy Lafleur, Montreal	136
1977-78	Guy Lafleur, Montreal	132
1978-79	Bryan Trottier, N.Y. Islanders	134

Season	Player, Team	Pts.
1979-80	Marcel Dionne, Los Angeles	137
1980-81	Wayne Gretzky, Edmonton	164
1981-82	Wayne Gretzky, Edmonton	212
1982-83	Wayne Gretzky, Edmonton	196
1983-84	Wayne Gretzky, Edmonton	205
1984-85	Wayne Gretzky, Edmonton	208
1985-86	Wayne Gretzky, Edmonton	215
1986-87	Wayne Gretzky, Edmonton	183
1987-88	Mario Lemieux, Pittsburgh	168
1988-89	Mario Lemieux, Pittsburgh	199
1989-90	Wayne Gretzky, Los Angeles	142
1990-91	Wayne Gretzky, Los Angeles	163
1991-92	Mario Lemieux, Pittsburgh	131
1992-93	Mario Lemieux, Pittsburgh	160
1993-94	Wayne Gretzky, Los Angeles	130
1994-95	Jaromir Jagr, Pittsburgh	70
1995-96	Mario Lemieux, Pittsburgh	161
1996-97	Mario Lemieux, Pittsburgh	122
1997-98	Jaromir Jagr, Pittsburgh	102
1998-99	Jaromir Jagr, Pittsburgh	127
1999-00	Jaromir Jagr, Pittsburgh	96
2000-01	Jaromir Jagr, Pittsburgh	121

The award was originally known as the Leading Scorer Trophy. The present trophy, first given in 1947, was presented to the NHL by Art Ross, former manager-coach of the Boston Bruins. In event of a tie, the player with the most goals receives the award.

MAURICE RICHARD TROPHY

(Leading goal scorer)

Season	Player, Team	Goals
1998-99	Teemu Selanne, Anaheim	47
1999-00	Pavel Bure, Florida	58
2000-01	Pavel Bure, Florida	59

HART MEMORIAL TROPHY

(Most Valuable Player)

Season	Player, Team
1923-24	Frank Nighbor, Ottawa
1924-25	Billy Burch, Hamilton
1925-26	Nels Stewart, Montreal Maroons
1926-27	Herb Gardiner, Montreal
1927-28	Howie Morenz, Montreal
1928-29	Roy Worters, N.Y. Americans
1929-30	Nels Stewart, Montreal Maroons
1930-31	Howie Morenz, Montreal
1931-32	Howie Morenz, Montreal
1932-33	Eddie Shore, Boston
1933-34	Aurel Joliat, Montreal
1934-35	Eddie Shore, Boston
1935-36	Eddie Shore, Boston
1936-37	Babe Siebert, Montreal
1937-38	Eddie Shore, Boston
1938-39	Toe Blake, Montreal
1939-40	Ebbie Goodfellow, Detroit
1940-41	Bill Cowley, Boston
1941-42	Tom Anderson, N.Y. Americans
1942-43	Bill Cowley, Boston
1943-44	Babe Pratt, Toronto
1944-45	Elmer Lach, Montreal
1945-46	Max Bentley, Chicago
1946-47	Maurice Richard, Montreal
1947-48	Buddy O'Connor, N.Y. Rangers
1948-49	Sid Abel, Detroit
1949-50	Chuck Rayner, N.Y. Rangers

Season	Player, Team
1950-51	Milt Schmidt, Boston
1951-52	Gordie Howe, Detroit
1952-53	Gordie Howe, Detroit
1953-54	Al Rollins, Chicago
1954-55	Ted Kennedy, Toronto
1955-56	Jean Beliveau, Montreal
1956-57	Gordie Howe, Detroit
1957-58	Gordie Howe, Detroit
1958-59	Andy Bathgate, N.Y. Rangers
1959-60	Gordie Howe, Detroit
1960-61	Bernie Geoffrion, Montreal
1961-62	Jacques Plante, Montreal
1962-63	Gordie Howe, Detroit
1963-64	Jean Beliveau, Montreal
1964-65	Bobby Hull, Chicago
1965-66	Bobby Hull, Chicago
1966-67	Stan Mikita, Chicago
1967-68	Stan Mikita, Chicago
1968-69	Phil Esposito, Boston
1969-70	Bobby Orr, Boston
1970-71	Bobby Orr, Boston
1971-72	Bobby Orr, Boston
1972-73	Bobby Clarke, Philadelphia
1973-74	Phil Esposito, Boston
1974-75	Bobby Clarke, Philadelphia
1975-76	Bobby Clarke, Philadelphia
1976-77	Guy Lafleur, Montreal
1977-78	Guy Lafleur, Montreal
1978-79	Bryan Trottier, N.Y. Islanders
1979-80	Wayne Gretzky, Edmonton
1980-81	Wayne Gretzky, Edmonton
1981-82	Wayne Gretzky, Edmonton
1982-83	Wayne Gretzky, Edmonton
1983-84	Wayne Gretzky, Edmonton
1984-85	Wayne Gretzky, Edmonton
1985-86	Wayne Gretzky, Edmonton
1986-87	Wayne Gretzky, Edmonton
1987-88	Mario Lemieux, Pittsburgh
1988-89	Wayne Gretzky, Los Angeles
1989-90	Mark Messier, Edmonton
1990-91	Brett Hull, St. Louis
1991-92	Mark Messier, N.Y. Rangers
1992-93	Mario Lemieux, Pittsburgh
1993-94	Sergei Fedorov, Detroit
1994-95	Eric Lindros, Philadelphia
1995-96	Mario Lemieux, Pittsburgh
1996-97	Dominik Hasek, Buffalo
1997-98	Dominik Hasek, Buffalo
1998-99	Jaromir Jagr, Pittsburgh
1999-00	Chris Pronger, St. Louis
2000-01	Joe Sakic, Colorado

JAMES NORRIS MEMORIAL TROPHY

(Outstanding defenseman)

Season	Player, Team
1953-54	Red Kelly, Detroit
1954-55	Doug Harvey, Montreal
1955-56	Doug Harvey, Montreal
1956-57	Doug Harvey, Montreal
1957-58	Doug Harvey, Montreal
1958-59	Tom Johnson, Montreal
1959-60	Doug Harvey, Montreal
1960-61	Doug Harvey, Montreal
1961-62	Doug Harvey, N.Y. Rangers
1962-63	Pierre Pilote, Chicago
1963-64	Pierre Pilote, Chicago
1964-65	Pierre Pilote, Chicago
1965-66	Jacques Laperriere, Montreal
1966-67	Harry Howell, N.Y. Rangers
1967-68	Bobby Orr, Boston
1968-69	Bobby Orr, Boston

Season	Player, Team
1969-70	Bobby Orr, Boston
1970-71	Bobby Orr, Boston
1971-72	Bobby Orr, Boston
1972-73	Bobby Orr, Boston
1973-74	Bobby Orr, Boston
1974-75	Bobby Orr, Boston
1975-76	Denis Potvin, N.Y. Islanders
1976-77	Larry Robinson, Montreal
1977-78	Denis Potvin, N.Y. Islanders
1978-79	Denis Potvin, N.Y. Islanders
1979-80	Larry Robinson, Montreal
1980-81	Randy Carlyle, Pittsburgh
1981-82	Doug Wilson, Chicago
1982-83	Rod Langway, Washington
1983-84	Rod Langway, Washington
1984-85	Paul Coffey, Edmonton
1985-86	Paul Coffey, Edmonton
1986-87	Ray Bourque, Boston
1987-88	Ray Bourque, Boston
1988-89	Chris Chelios, Montreal
1989-90	Ray Bourque, Boston
1990-91	Ray Bourque, Boston
1991-92	Brian Leetch, N.Y. Rangers
1992-93	Chris Chelios, Chicago
1993-94	Ray Bourque, Boston
1994-95	Paul Coffey, Detroit
1995-96	Chris Chelios, Chicago
1996-97	Brian Leetch, N.Y. Rangers
1997-98	Rob Blake, Los Angeles
1998-99	Al MacInnis, St. Louis
1999-00	Chris Pronger, St. Louis
2000-01	Nicklas Lidstrom, Detroit

VEZINA TROPHY

(Outstanding goaltender)

Season	Player, Team	GAA
1926-27	George Hainsworth, Montreal	1.52
1927-28	George Hainsworth, Montreal	1.09
1928-29	George Hainsworth, Montreal	0.98
1929-30	Tiny Thompson, Boston	2.23
1930-31	Roy Worters, N.Y. Americans	1.68
1931-32	Charlie Gardiner, Chicago	2.10
1932-33	Tiny Thompson, Boston	1.83
1933-34	Charlie Gardiner, Chicago	1.73
1934-35	Lorne Chabot, Chicago	1.83
1935-36	Tiny Thompson, Boston	1.71
1936-37	Normie Smith, Detroit	2.13
1937-38	Tiny Thompson, Boston	1.85
1938-39	Frank Brimsek, Boston	1.60
1939-40	Dave Kerr, N.Y. Rangers	1.60
1940-41	Turk Broda, Toronto	2.60
1941-42	Frank Brimsek, Boston	2.38
1942-43	Johnny Mowers, Detroit	2.48
1943-44	Bill Durnan, Montreal	2.18
1944-45	Bill Durnan, Montreal	2.42
1945-46	Bill Durnan, Montreal	2.60
1946-47	Bill Durnan, Montreal	2.30
1947-48	Turk Broda, Toronto	2.38
1948-49	Bill Durnan, Montreal	2.10
1949-50	Bill Durnan, Montreal	2.20
1950-51	Al Rollins, Toronto	1.75
1951-52	Terry Sawchuk, Detroit	1.98
1952-53	Terry Sawchuk, Detroit	1.94
1953-54	Harry Lumley, Toronto	1.85
1954-55	Terry Sawchuk, Detroit	1.94
1955-56	Jacques Plante, Montreal	1.86
1956-57	Jacques Plante, Montreal	2.02
1957-58	Jacques Plante, Montreal	2.09
1958-59	Jacques Plante, Montreal	2.15
1959-60	Jacques Plante, Montreal	2.54
1960-61	Johnny Bower, Toronto	2.50

Season	Player, Team	GAA
1961-62	Jacques Plante, Montreal	2.37
1962-63	Glenn Hall, Chicago	2.51
1963-64	Charlie Hodge, Montreal	2.26
1964-65	Terry Sawchuk, Toronto	2.56
	Johnny Bower, Toronto	2.38
1965-66	Lorne Worsley, Montreal	2.36
	Charlie Hodge, Montreal	2.58
1966-67	Glenn Hall, Chicago	2.38
	Denis DeJordy, Chicago	2.46
1967-68	Lorne Worsley, Montreal	1.98
	Rogatien Vachon, Montreal	2.48
1968-69	Glenn Hall, St. Louis	2.17
	Jacques Plante, St. Louis	1.96
1969-70	Tony Esposito, Chicago	2.17
1970-71	Ed Giacomin, N.Y. Rangers	2.15
	Gilles Villemure, N.Y. Rangers	2.29
1971-72	Tony Esposito, Chicago	1.76
	Gary Smith, Chicago	2.41
1972-73	Ken Dryden, Montreal	2.26
1973-74	Bernie Parent, Philadelphia	1.89
	Tony Esposito, Chicago	2.04
1974-75	Bernie Parent, Philadelphia	2.03
1975-76	Ken Dryden, Montreal	2.03
1976-77	Ken Dryden, Montreal	2.14
	Michel Larocque, Montreal	2.09
1977-78	Ken Dryden, Montreal	2.05
	Michel Larocque, Montreal	2.67
1978-79	Ken Dryden, Montreal	2.30
	Michel Larocque, Montreal	2.84
1979-80	Bob Sauve, Buffalo	2.36
	Don Edwards, Buffalo	2.57
1980-81	Richard Sevigny, Montreal	2.40
	Michel Larocque, Montreal	3.03
	Denis Herron, Montreal	3.50
1981-82	Billy Smith, N.Y. Islanders	2.97
1982-83	Pete Peeters, Boston	2.36
1983-84	Tom Barrasso, Buffalo	2.84
1984-85	Pelle Lindbergh, Philadelphia	3.02
1985-86	John Vanbiesbrouck, N.Y. Rangers	3.32
1986-87	Ron Hextall, Philadelphia	3.00
1987-88	Grant Fuhr, Edmonton	3.43
1988-89	Patrick Roy, Montreal	2.47
1989-90	Patrick Roy, Montreal	2.53
1990-91	Ed Belfour, Chicago	2.47
1991-92	Patrick Roy, Montreal	2.36
1992-93	Ed Belfour, Chicago	2.59
1993-94	Dominik Hasek, Buffalo	1.95
1994-95	Dominik Hasek, Buffalo	2.11
1995-96	Jim Carey, Washington	2.26
1996-97	Dominik Hasek, Buffalo	2.27
1997-98	Dominik Hasek, Buffalo	2.09
1998-99	Dominik Hasek, Buffalo	1.87
1999-00	Olaf Kolzig, Washington	2.24
2000-01	Dominik Hasek, Buffalo	2.11

The award was formerly presented to the goaltender(s) having played a minimum of 25 games for the team with the fewest goals scored against. Beginning with the 1981-82 season, it was awarded to the outstanding goaltender.

BILL JENNINGS TROPHY

(Leading goaltender)

Season	Player, Team	GAA
1981-82	Denis Herron, Montreal	2.64
	Rick Wamsley, Montreal	2.75
1982-83	Roland Melanson, N.Y. Islanders	2.66
	Billy Smith, N.Y. Islanders	2.87
1983-84	Pat Riggin, Washington	2.66
	Al Jensen, Washington	2.91
1984-85	Tom Barrasso, Buffalo	2.66
	Bob Sauve, Buffalo	3.22

Season	Player, Team	GAA
1985-86	Bob Froese, Philadelphia	2.55
	Darren Jensen, Philadelphia	3.68
1986-87	Brian Hayward, Montreal	2.81
	Patrick Roy, Montreal	2.93
1987-88	Brian Hayward, Montreal	2.86
	Patrick Roy, Montreal	2.90
1988-89	Patrick Roy, Montreal	2.47
	Brian Hayward, Montreal	2.90
1989-90	Rejean Lemelin, Boston	2.81
	Andy Moog, Boston	2.89
1990-91	Ed Belfour, Chicago	2.47
1991-92	Patrick Roy, Montreal	2.36
1992-93	Ed Belfour, Chicago	2.59
1993-94	Dominik Hasek, Buffalo	1.95
	Grant Fuhr, Buffalo	3.68
1994-95	Ed Belfour, Chicago	2.28
1995-96	Chris Osgood, Detroit	2.17
	Mike Vernon, Detroit	2.26
1996-97	Martin Brodeur, New Jersey	1.88
	Mike Dunham, New Jersey	2.55
1997-98	Martin Brodeur, New Jersey	1.89
1998-99	Ed Belfour, Dallas	1.99
	Roman Turek, Dallas	2.08
1999-00	Roman Turek, St. Louis	1.95
2000-01	Dominik Hasek, Buffalo	2.11

The award is presented to the goaltender(s) having played a minimum of 25 games for the team with the fewest goals scored against.

CALDER MEMORIAL TROPHY

(Rookie of the year)

Season	Player, Team
1932-33	Carl Voss, Detroit
1933-34	Russ Blinco, Montreal Maroons
1934-35	Dave Schriner, N.Y. Americans
1935-36	Mike Karakas, Chicago
1936-37	Syl Apps, Toronto
1937-38	Cully Dahlstrom, Chicago
1938-39	Frank Brimsek, Boston
1939-40	Kilby Macdonald, N.Y. Rangers
1940-41	John Quilty, Montreal
1941-42	Grant Warwick, N.Y. Rangers
1942-43	Gaye Stewart, Toronto
1943-44	Gus Bodnar, Toronto
1944-45	Frank McCool, Toronto
1945-46	Edgar Laprade, N.Y. Rangers
1946-47	Howie Meeker, Toronto
1947-48	Jim McFadden, Detroit
1948-49	Pentti Lund, N.Y. Rangers
1949-50	Jack Gelineau, Boston
1950-51	Terry Sawchuk, Detroit
1951-52	Bernie Geoffrion, Montreal
1952-53	Lorne Worsley, N.Y. Rangers
1953-54	Camille Henry, N.Y. Rangers
1954-55	Ed Litzenberger, Chicago
1955-56	Glenn Hall, Detroit
1956-57	Larry Regan, Boston
1957-58	Frank Mahovlich, Toronto
1958-59	Ralph Backstrom, Montreal
1959-60	Bill Hay, Chicago
1960-61	Dave Keon, Toronto
1961-62	Bobby Rousseau, Montreal
1962-63	Kent Douglas, Toronto
1963-64	Jacques Laperriere, Montreal
1964-65	Roger Crozier, Detroit
1965-66	Brit Selby, Toronto
1966-67	Bobby Orr, Boston
1967-68	Derek Sanderson, Boston
1968-69	Danny Grant, Minnesota
1969-70	Tony Esposito, Chicago
1970-71	Gilbert Perreault, Buffalo
1971-72	Ken Dryden, Montreal

Season   Player, Team
1972-73—Steve Vickers, N.Y. Rangers
1973-74—Denis Potvin, N.Y. Islanders
1974-75—Eric Vail, Atlanta
1975-76—Bryan Trottier, N.Y. Islanders
1976-77—Willi Plett, Atlanta
1977-78—Mike Bossy, N.Y. Islanders
1978-79—Bobby Smith, Minnesota
1979-80—Ray Bourque, Boston
1980-81—Peter Stastny, Quebec
1981-82—Dale Hawerchuk, Winnipeg
1982-83—Steve Larmer, Chicago
1983-84—Tom Barrasso, Buffalo
1984-85—Mario Lemieux, Pittsburgh
1985-86—Gary Suter, Calgary
1986-87—Luc Robitaille, Los Angeles
1987-88—Joe Nieuwendyk, Calgary
1988-89—Brian Leetch, N.Y. Rangers
1989-90—Sergei Makarov, Calgary
1990-91—Ed Belfour, Chicago
1991-92—Pavel Bure, Vancouver
1992-93—Teemu Selanne, Winnipeg
1993-94—Martin Brodeur, New Jersey
1994-95—Peter Forsberg, Quebec
1995-96—Daniel Alfredsson, Ottawa
1996-97—Bryan Berard, N.Y. Islanders
1997-98—Sergei Samsonov, Boston
1998-99—Chris Drury, Colorado
1999-00—Scott Gomez, New Jersey
2000-01—Evgeni Nabokov, San Jose

The award was originally known as the Leading Rookie Award. It was renamed the Calder Trophy in 1936-37 and became the Calder Memorial Trophy in 1942-43, following the death of NHL President Frank Calder.

LADY BYNG MEMORIAL TROPHY

(Most gentlemanly player)

Season   Player, Team
1924-25—Frank Nighbor, Ottawa
1925-26—Frank Nighbor, Ottawa
1926-27—Billy Burch, N.Y. Americans
1927-28—Frank Boucher, N.Y. Rangers
1928-29—Frank Boucher, N.Y. Rangers
1929-30—Frank Boucher, N.Y. Rangers
1930-31—Frank Boucher, N.Y. Rangers
1931-32—Joe Primeau, Toronto
1932-33—Frank Boucher, N.Y. Rangers
1933-34—Frank Boucher, N.Y. Rangers
1934-35—Frank Boucher, N.Y. Rangers
1935-36—Doc Romnes, Chicago
1936-37—Marty Barry, Detroit
1937-38—Gordie Drillon, Toronto
1938-39—Clint Smith, N.Y. Rangers
1939-40—Bobby Bauer, Boston
1940-41—Bobby Bauer, Boston
1941-42—Syl Apps, Toronto
1942-43—Max Bentley, Chicago
1943-44—Clint Smith, Chicago
1944-45—Bill Mosienko, Chicago
1945-46—Toe Blake, Montreal
1946-47—Bobby Bauer, Boston
1947-48—Buddy O'Connor, N.Y. Rangers
1948-49—Bill Quackenbush, Detroit
1949-50—Edgar Laprade, N.Y. Rangers
1950-51—Red Kelly, Detroit
1951-52—Sid Smith, Toronto
1952-53—Red Kelly, Detroit
1953-54—Red Kelly, Detroit
1954-55—Sid Smith, Toronto
1955-56—Earl Reibel, Detroit
1956-57—Andy Hebenton, N.Y. Rangers
1957-58—Camille Henry, N.Y. Rangers

Season   Player, Team
1958-59—Alex Delvecchio, Detroit
1959-60—Don McKenney, Boston
1960-61—Red Kelly, Toronto
1961-62—Dave Keon, Toronto
1962-63—Dave Keon, Toronto
1963-64—Ken Wharram, Chicago
1964-65—Bobby Hull, Chicago
1965-66—Alex Delvecchio, Detroit
1966-67—Stan Mikita, Chicago
1967-68—Stan Mikita, Chicago
1968-69—Alex Delvecchio, Detroit
1969-70—Phil Goyette, St. Louis
1970-71—John Bucyk, Boston
1971-72—Jean Ratelle, N.Y. Rangers
1972-73—Gilbert Perreault, Buffalo
1973-74—John Bucyk, Boston
1974-75—Marcel Dionne, Detroit
1975-76—Jean Ratelle, N.Y. R.-Boston
1976-77—Marcel Dionne, Los Angeles
1977-78—Butch Goring, Los Angeles
1978-79—Bob MacMillan, Atlanta
1979-80—Wayne Gretzky, Edmonton
1980-81—Rick Kehoe, Pittsburgh
1981-82—Rick Middleton, Boston
1982-83—Mike Bossy, N.Y. Islanders
1983-84—Mike Bossy, N.Y. Islanders
1984-85—Jari Kurri, Edmonton
1985-86—Mike Bossy, N.Y. Islanders
1986-87—Joe Mullen, Calgary
1987-88—Mats Naslund, Montreal
1988-89—Joe Mullen, Calgary
1989-90—Brett Hull, St. Louis
1990-91—Wayne Gretzky, Los Angeles
1991-92—Wayne Gretzky, Los Angeles
1992-93—Pierre Turgeon, N.Y. Islanders
1993-94—Wayne Gretzky, Los Angeles
1994-95—Ron Francis, Pittsburgh
1995-96—Paul Kariya, Anaheim
1996-97—Paul Kariya, Anaheim
1997-98—Ron Francis, Pittsburgh
1998-99—Wayne Gretzky, N.Y. Rangers
1999-00—Pavol Demitra, St. Louis
2000-01—Joe Sakic, Colorado

The award was originally known as the Lady Byng Trophy. After winning the award seven times, Frank Boucher received permanent possession and a new trophy was donated to the NHL in 1936. After Lady Byng's death in 1949, the NHL changed the name to Lady Byng Memorial Trophy.

CONN SMYTHE TROPHY

(Playoff MVP)

Season   Player, Team
1964-65—Jean Beliveau, Montreal
1965-66—Roger Crozier, Detroit
1966-67—Dave Keon, Toronto
1967-68—Glenn Hall, St. Louis
1968-69—Serge Savard, Montreal
1969-70—Bobby Orr, Boston
1970-71—Ken Dryden, Montreal
1971-72—Bobby Orr, Boston
1972-73—Yvan Cournoyer, Montreal
1973-74—Bernie Parent, Philadelphia
1974-75—Bernie Parent, Philadelphia
1975-76—Reggie Leach, Philadelphia
1976-77—Guy Lafleur, Montreal
1977-78—Larry Robinson, Montreal
1978-79—Bob Gainey, Montreal
1979-80—Bryan Trottier, N.Y. Islanders
1980-81—Butch Goring, N.Y. Islanders
1981-82—Mike Bossy, N.Y. Islanders
1982-83—Billy Smith, N.Y. Islanders

Season Player, Team	Season Player, Team
1983-84—Mark Messier, Edmonton	1983-84—Doug Jarvis, Washington
1984-85—Wayne Gretzky, Edmonton	1984-85—Craig Ramsay, Buffalo
1985-86—Patrick Roy, Montreal	1985-86—Troy Murray, Chicago
1986-87—Ron Hextall, Philadelphia	1986-87—Dave Poulin, Philadelphia
1987-88—Wayne Gretzky, Edmonton	1987-88—Guy Carbonneau, Montreal
1988-89—Al MacInnis, Calgary	1988-89—Guy Carbonneau, Montreal
1989-90—Bill Ranford, Edmonton	1989-90—Rick Meagher, St. Louis
1990-91—Mario Lemieux, Pittsburgh	1990-91—Dirk Graham, Chicago
1991-92—Mario Lemieux, Pittsburgh	1991-92—Guy Carbonneau, Montreal
1992-93—Patrick Roy, Montreal	1992-93—Doug Gilmour, Toronto
1993-94—Brian Leetch, N.Y. Rangers	1993-94—Sergei Fedorov, Detroit
1994-95—Claude Lemieux, New Jersey	1994-95—Ron Francis, Pittsburgh
1995-96—Joe Sakic, Colorado	1995-96—Sergei Fedorov, Detroit
1996-97—Mike Vernon, Detroit	1996-97—Michael Peca, Buffalo
1997-98—Steve Yzerman, Detroit	1997-98—Jere Lehtinen, Dallas
1998-99—Joe Nieuwendyk, Dallas	1998-99—Jere Lehtinen, Dallas
1999-00—Scott Stevens, New Jersey	1999-00—Steve Yzerman, Detroit
2000-01—Patrick Roy, Colorado	2000-01—John Madden, New Jersey

BILL MASTERTON MEMORIAL TROPHY

(Sportsmanship—dedication to hockey)

Season Player, Team
1967-68—Claude Provost, Montreal
1968-69—Ted Hampson, Oakland
1969-70—Pit Martin, Chicago
1970-71—Jean Ratelle, N.Y. Rangers
1971-72—Bobby Clarke, Philadelphia
1972-73—Lowell MacDonald, Pittsburgh
1973-74—Henri Richard, Montreal
1974-75—Don Luce, Buffalo
1975-76—Rod Gilbert, N.Y. Rangers
1976-77—Ed Westfall, N.Y. Islanders
1977-78—Butch Goring, Los Angeles
1978-79—Serge Savard, Montreal
1979-80—Al MacAdam, Minnesota
1980-81—Blake Dunlop, St. Louis
1981-82—Glenn Resch, Colorado
1982-83—Lanny McDonald, Calgary
1983-84—Brad Park, Detroit
1984-85—Anders Hedberg, N.Y. Rangers
1985-86—Charlie Simmer, Boston
1986-87—Doug Jarvis, Hartford
1987-88—Bob Bourne, Los Angeles
1988-89—Tim Kerr, Philadelphia
1989-90—Gord Kluzak, Boston
1990-91—Dave Taylor, Los Angeles
1991-92—Mark Fitzpatrick, N.Y. Islanders
1992-93—Mario Lemieux, Pittsburgh
1993-94—Cam Neely, Boston
1994-95—Pat LaFontaine, Buffalo
1995-96—Gary Roberts, Calgary
1996-97—Tony Granato, San Jose
1997-98—Jamie McLennan, St. Louis
1998-99—John Cullen, Tampa Bay
1999-00—Ken Daneyko, New Jersey
2000-01—Adam Graves, N.Y. Rangers

Presented by the Professional Hockey Writers' Association to the player who best exemplifies the qualities of perseverance, sportsmanship and dedication to hockey.

FRANK J. SELKE TROPHY

(Best defensive forward)

Season Player, Team
1977-78—Bob Gainey, Montreal
1978-79—Bob Gainey, Montreal
1979-80—Bob Gainey, Montreal
1980-81—Bob Gainey, Montreal
1981-82—Steve Kasper, Boston
1982-83—Bobby Clarke, Philadelphia

JACK ADAMS TROPHY

(Coach of the year)

Season Coach, Team
1973-74—Fred Shero, Philadelphia
1974-75—Bob Pulford, Los Angeles
1975-76—Don Cherry, Boston
1976-77—Scotty Bowman, Montreal
1977-78—Bobby Kromm, Detroit
1978-79—Al Arbour, N.Y. Islanders
1979-80—Pat Quinn, Philadelphia
1980-81—Red Berenson, St. Louis
1981-82—Tom Watt, Winnipeg
1982-83—Orval Tessier, Chicago
1983-84—Bryan Murray, Washington
1984-85—Mike Keenan, Philadelphia
1985-86—Glen Sather, Edmonton
1986-87—Jacques Demers, Detroit
1987-88—Jacques Demers, Detroit
1988-89—Pat Burns, Montreal
1989-90—Bob Murdoch, Winnipeg
1990-91—Brian Sutter, St. Louis
1991-92—Pat Quinn, Vancouver
1992-93—Pat Burns, Toronto
1993-94—Jacques Lemaire, New Jersey
1994-95—Marc Crawford, Quebec
1995-96—Scotty Bowman, Detroit
1996-97—Ted Nolan, Buffalo
1997-98—Pat Burns, Boston
1998-99—Jacques Martin, Ottawa
1999-00—Joel Quenneville, St. Louis
2000-01—Bill Barber, Philadelphia

KING CLANCY TROPHY

(Humanitarian contributions)

Season Player, Team
1987-88—Lanny McDonald, Calgary
1988-89—Bryan Trottier, N.Y. Islanders
1989-90—Kevin Lowe, Edmonton
1990-91—Dave Taylor, Los Angeles
1991-92—Ray Bourque, Boston
1992-93—Dave Poulin, Boston
1993-94—Adam Graves, N.Y. Rangers
1994-95—Joe Nieuwendyk, Calgary
1995-96—Kris King, Winnipeg
1996-97—Trevor Linden, Vancouver
1997-98—Kelly Chase, St. Louis
1998-99—Rob Ray, Buffalo
1999-00—Curtis Joseph, Toronto
2000-01—Shjon Podein, Colorado

ALL-STAR TEAMS

(As selected by members of the Professional
Hockey Writers' Association at the end of each season)

1930-31

First team		Second team
Aurel Joliet, Mon. C.	LW	Bun Cook, N.Y.R.
Howie Morenz, Mon. C.	C	Frank Boucher, N.Y.R.
Bill Cook, N.Y.R.	RW	Dit Clapper, Bos.
Eddie Shore, Bos.	D	Sylvio Mantha, Mon.
King Clancy, Tor.	D	Ching Johnson, N.Y.R.
Charlie Gardiner, Chi.	G	Tiny Thompson, Bos.

1931-32

First team		Second team
Harvey Jackson, Tor.	LW	Aurel Joliat, Mon. C.
Howie Morenz, Mon. C.	C	Hooley Smith, Mon. M.
Bill Cook, N.Y.R.	RW	Charlie Conacher, Tor.
Eddie Shore, Bos.	D	Sylvio Mantha, Mon. C.
Ching Johnson, N.Y.R.	D	King Clancy, Tor.
Charlie Gardiner, Chi.	G	Roy Worters, N.Y.A.

1932-33

First team		Second team
Baldy Northcott, Mon. M.	LW	Harvey Jackson, Tor.
Frank Boucher, N.Y.R.	C	Howie Morenz, Mon.
Bill Cook, N.Y.R.	RW	Charlie Conacher, Tor.
Eddie Shore, Bos.	D	King Clancy, Tor.
Ching Johnson, N.Y.R.	D	Lionel Conacher, Mon. M.
John Ross Roach, Det.	G	Charlie Gardiner, Chi.

1933-34

First team		Second team
Harvey Jackson, Tor.	LW	Aurel Joliat, Mon. C.
Frank Boucher, N.Y.R.	C	Joe Primeau, Tor.
Charlie Conacher, Tor.	RW	Bill Cook, N.Y.R.
King Clancy, Tor.	D	Eddie Shore, Bos.
Lionel Conacher, Chi.	D	Ching Johnson, N.Y.R.
Charlie Gardiner, Chi.	G	Roy Worters, N.Y.A.

1934-35

First team		Second team
Harvey Jackson, Tor.	LW	Aurel Joliat, Mon. C.
Frank Boucher, N.Y.R.	C	Cooney Welland, Det.
Charlie Conacher, Tor.	RW	Dit Clapper, Bos.
Eddie Shore, Bos.	D	Cy Wentworth, Mon. M.
Earl Seibert, N.Y.R.	D	Art Coulter, Chi.
Lorne Chabot, Chi.	G	Tiny Thompson, Bos.

1935-36

First team		Second team
Dave Schriner, N.Y.A.	LW	Paul Thompson, Chi.
Hooley Smith, Mon. M.	C	Bill Thoms, Tor.
Charlie Conacher, Tor.	RW	Cecil Dillon, N.Y.R.
Eddie Shore, Bos.	D	Earl Seibert, Chi.
Babe Siebert, Bos.	D	Ebbie Goodfellow, Det.
Tiny Thompson, Bos.	G	Wilf Cude, Mon. C.

1936-37

First team		Second team
Harvey Jackson, Tor.	LW	Dave Schriner, N.Y.A.
Marty Barry, Det.	C	Art Chapman, N.Y.A.
Larry Aurie, Det.	RW	Cecil Dillon, N.Y.R.
Babe Siebert, Mon. C.	D	Earl Seibert, Chi.
Ebbie Goodfellow, Det.	D	Lionel Conacher, Mon. M.
Norm Smith, Det.	G	Wilf Cude, Mon. C.

1937-38

First team		Second team
Paul Thompson, Chi.	LW	Toe Blake, Mon. C.
Bill Cowley, Bos.	C	Syl Apps, Tor.
Cecil Dillon, N.Y.R.	RW	Cecil Dillon, N.Y.R.
Gord Drillon, Tor.	(tied)	Gord Drillon, Tor.
Eddie Shore, Bos.	D	Art Coulter, N.Y.R.
Babe Siebert, Mon. C.	D	Earl Seibert, Chi.
Tiny Thompson, Bos.	G	Dave Kerr, N.Y.R.

1938-39

First team		Second team
Toe Blake, Mon.	LW	Johnny Gottselig, Chi.
Syl Apps, Tor.	C	Neil Colville, N.Y.R.
Gord Drillon, Tor.	RW	Bobby Bauer, Bos.
Eddie Shore, Bos.	D	Earl Seibert, Chi.
Dit Clapper, Bos.	D	Art Coulter, N.Y.R.
Frank Brimsek, Bos.	G	Earl Robertson, N.Y.A.

1939-40

First team		Second team
Toe Blake, Mon.	LW	Woody Dumart, Bos.
Milt Schmidt, Bos.	C	Neil Colville, N.Y.R.
Bryan Hextall, N.Y.R.	RW	Bobby Bauer, Bos.
Dit Clapper, Bos.	D	Art Coulter, N.Y.R.
Ebbie Goodfellow, Det.	D	Earl Seibert, Chi.
Dave Kerr, N.Y.R.	G	Frank Brimsek, Bos.

1940-41

First team		Second team
Dave Schriner, Tor.	LW	Woody Dumart, Bos.
Bill Cowley, Bos.	C	Syl Apps, Tor.
Bryan Hextall, N.Y.R.	RW	Bobby Bauer, Bos.
Dit Clapper, Bos.	D	Earl Seibert, Chi.
Wally Stanowski, Tor.	D	Ott Heller, N.Y.R.
Turk Broda, Tor.	G	Frank Brimsek, Bos.

1941-42

First team		Second team
Lynn Patrick, N.Y.R.	LW	Sid Abel, Det.
Syl Apps, Tor.	C	Phil Watson, N.Y.R.
Bryan Hextall, N.Y.R.	RW	Gord Drillon, Tor.
Earl Seibert, Chi.	D	Pat Egan, Bkl.
Tommy Anderson, Bkl.	D	Bucko McDonald, Tor.
Frank Brimsek, Bos.	G	Turk Broda, Tor.

1942-43

First team		Second team
Doug Bentley, Chi.	LW	Lynn Patrick, N.Y.R.
Bill Cowley, Bos.	C	Syl Apps, Tor.
Lorne Carr, Tor.	RW	Bryan Hextall, N.Y.R.
Earl Seibert, Chi.	D	Jack Crawford, Bos.
Jack Stewart, Det.	D	Bill Hollett, Bos.
Johnny Mowers, Det.	G	Frank Brimsek, Bos.

1943-44

First team		Second team
Doug Bentley, Chi.	LW	Herb Cain, Bos.
Bill Cowley, Bos.	C	Elmer Lach, Mon.
Lorne Carr, Tor.	RW	Maurice Richard, Mon.
Earl Seibert, Chi.	D	Emile Bouchard, Mon.
Babe Pratt, Tor.	D	Dit Clapper, Bos.
Bill Durnan, Mon.	G	Paul Bibeault, Tor.

1944-45

First team		Second team
Toe Blake, Mon.	LW	Syd Howe, Det.
Elmer Lach, Mon.	C	Bill Cowley, Bos.
Maurice Richard, Mon.	RW	Bill Mosienko, Chi.
Emile Bouchard, Mon.	D	Glen Harmon, Mon.
Bill Hollett, Det.	D	Babe Pratt, Tor.
Bill Durnan, Mon.	G	Mike Karakas, Chi.

1945-46

First team		Second team
Gaye Stewart, Tor.	LW	Toe Blake, Mon.
Max Bentley, Chi.	C	Elmer Lach, Mon.
Maurice Richard, Mon.	RW	Bill Mosienko, Chi.
Jack Crawford, Bos.	D	Kenny Reardon, Mon.
Emile Bouchard, Mon.	D	Jack Stewart, Det.
Bill Durnan, Mon.	G	Frank Brimsek, Bos.

1946-47

First team		Second team
Doug Bentley, Chi.	LW	Woody Dumart, Bos.
Milt Schmidt, Bos.	C	Max Bentley, Chi.
Maurice Richard, Mon.	RW	Bobby Bauer, Bos.
Kenny Reardon, Mon.	D	Jack Stewart, Det.
Emile Bouchard, Mon.	D	Bill Quackenbush, Det.
Bill Durnan, Mon.	G	Frank Brimsek, Bos.

1947-48

First team		Second team
Ted Lindsay, Det.	LW	Gaye Stewart, Chi.
Elmer Lach, Mon.	C	Buddy O'Connor, N.Y.R.
Maurice Richard, Mon.	RW	Bud Poile, Chi.
Bill Quackenbush, Det.	D	Kenny Reardon, Mon.
Jack Stewart, Det.	D	Neil Colville, N.Y.R.
Turk Broda, Tor.	G	Frank Brimsek, Bos.

1948-49

First team		Second team
Roy Conacher, Chi.	LW	Ted Lindsay, Det.
Sid Abel, Det.	C	Doug Bentley, Chi.
Maurice Richard, Mon.	RW	Gordie Howe, Det.
Bill Quackenbush, Det.	D	Glen Harmon, Mon.
Jack Stewart, Det.	D	Kenny Reardon, Mon.
Bill Durnan, Mon.	G	Chuck Rayner, N.Y.R.

1949-50

First team		Second team
Ted Lindsay, Det.	LW	Tony Leswick, N.Y.R.
Sid Abel, Det.	C	Ted Kennedy, Tor.
Maurice Richard, Mon.	RW	Gordie Howe, Det.
Gus Mortson, Tor.	D	Leo Reise, Det.
Kenny Reardon, Mon.	D	Red Kelly, Det.
Bill Durnan, Mon.	G	Chuck Rayner, N.Y.R.

1950-51

First team		Second team
Ted Lindsay, Det.	LW	Sid Smith, Tor.
Milt Schmidt, Bos.	C	Sid Abel, Det.
	(tied)	Ted Kennedy, Tor.
Gordie Howe, Det.	RW	Maurice Richard, Mon.
Red Kelly, Det.	D	Jim Thomson, Tor.
Bill Quackenbush, Bos.	D	Leo Reise, Det.
Terry Sawchuk, Det.	G	Chuck Rayner, N.Y.R.

1951-52

First team		Second team
Ted Lindsay, Det.	LW	Sid Smith, Tor.
Elmer Lach, Mon.	C	Milt Schmidt, Bos.
Gordie Howe, Det.	RW	Maurice Richard, Mon.
Red Kelly, Det.	D	Hy Buller, N.Y.R.
Doug Harvey, Mon.	D	Jim Thomson, Tor.
Terry Sawchuk, Det.	G	Jim Henry, Bos.

1952-53

First team		Second team
Ted Lindsay, Det.	LW	Bert Olmstead, Mon.
Fleming Mackell, Bos.	C	Alex Delvecchio, Det.
Gordie Howe, Det.	RW	Maurice Richard, Mon.
Red Kelly, Det.	D	Bill Quackenbush, Bos.
Doug Harvey, Mon.	D	Bill Gadsby, Chi.
Terry Sawchuk, Det.	G	Gerry McNeil, Mon.

1953-54

First team		Second team
Ted Lindsay, Det.	LW	Ed Sandford, Bos.
Ken Mosdell, Mon.	C	Ted Kennedy, Tor.
Gordie Howe, Det.	RW	Maurice Richard, Mon.
Red Kelly, Det.	D	Bill Gadsby, Chi.
Doug Harvey, Mon.	D	Tim Horton, Tor.
Harry Lumley, Tor.	G	Terry Sawchuk, Det.

1954-55

First team		Second team
Sid Smith, Tor.	LW	Danny Lewicki, N.Y.R.
Jean Beliveau, Mon.	C	Ken Mosdell, Mon.
Maurice Richard, Mon.	RW	Bernie Geoffrion, Mon.
Doug Harvey, Mon.	D	Bob Goldham, Det.
Red Kelly, Det.	D	Fern Flaman, Bos.
Harry Lumley, Tor.	G	Terry Sawchuk, Det.

1955-56

First team		Second team
Ted Lindsay, Det.	LW	Bert Olmstead, Mon.
Jean Beliveau, Mon.	C	Tod Sloan, Tor.
Maurice Richard, Mon.	RW	Gordie Howe, Det.
Doug Harvey, Mon.	D	Red Kelly, Det.
Bill Gadsby, N.Y.R.	D	Tom Johnson, Mon.
Jacques Plante, Mon.	G	Glenn Hall, Det.

1956-57

First team		Second team
Ted Lindsay, Det.	LW	Real Chevrefils, Bos.
Jean Beliveau, Mon.	C	Eddie Litzenberger, Chi.
Gordie Howe, Det.	RW	Maurice Richard, Mon.
Doug Harvey, Mon.	D	Fern Flaman, Bos.
Red Kelly, Det.	D	Bill Gadsby, N.Y.R.
Glenn Hall, Det.	G	Jacques Plante, Mon.

1957-58

First team		Second team
Dickie Moore, Mon.	LW	Camille Henry, N.Y.R.
Henri Richard, Mon.	C	Jean Beliveau, Mon.
Gordie Howe, Det.	RW	Andy Bathgate, N.Y.R.
Doug Harvey, Mon.	D	Fern Flaman, Bos.
Bill Gadsby, N.Y.R.	D	Marcel Pronovost, Det.
Glenn Hall, Chi.	G	Jacques Plante, Mon.

1958-59

First team		Second team
Dickie Moore, Mon.	LW	Alex Delvecchio, Det.
Jean Beliveau, Mon.	C	Henri Richard, Mon.
Andy Bathgate, N.Y.R.	RW	Gordie Howe, Det.
Tom Johnson, Mon.	D	Marcel Pronovost, Det.
Bill Gadsby, N.Y.R.	D	Doug Harvey, Mon.
Jacques Plante, Mon.	G	Terry Sawchuk, Det.

1959-60

First team		Second team
Bobby Hull, Chi.	LW	Dean Prentice, N.Y.R.
Jean Beliveau, Mon.	C	Bronco Horvath, Bos.
Gordie Howe, Det.	RW	Bernie Geoffrion, Mon.
Doug Harvey, Mon.	D	Allan Stanley, Tor.
Marcel Pronovost, Det.	D	Pierre Pilote, Chi.
Glenn Hall, Chi.	G	Jacques Plante, Mon.

1960-61

First team		Second team
Frank Mahovlich, Mon.	LW	Dickie Moore, Mon.
Jean Beliveau, Mon.	C	Henri Richard, Mon.
Bernie Geoffrion, Mon.	RW	Gordie Howe, Det.
Doug Harvey, Mon.	D	Allan Stanley, Tor.
Marcel Pronovost, Det.	D	Pierre Pilote, Chi.
Johnny Bower, Tor.	G	Glenn Hall, Chi.

1961-62

First team		Second team
Bobby Hull, Chi.	LW	Frank Mahovlich, Tor.
Stan Mikita, Chi.	C	Dave Keon, Tor.
Andy Bathgate, N.Y.R.	RW	Gordie Howe, Det.
Doug Harvey, N.Y.R.	D	Carl Brewer, Tor.
Jean-Guy Talbot, Mon.	D	Pierre Pilote, Chi.
Jacques Plante, Mon.	G	Glenn Hall, Chi.

1962-63

First team		Second team
Frank Mahovlich, Tor.	LW	Bobby Hull, Chi.
Stan Mikita, Chi.	C	Henri Richard, Mon.
Gordie Howe, Det.	RW	Andy Bathgate, N.Y.R.
Pierre Pilote, Chi.	D	Tim Horton, Tor.
Carl Brewer, Tor.	D	Elmer Vasko, Chi.
Glenn Hall, Chi.	G	Terry Sawchuk, Det.

1963-64

First team		Second team
Bobby Hull, Chi.	LW	Frank Mahovlich, Tor.
Stan Mikita, Chi.	C	Jean Beliveau, Mon.
Ken Wharram, Chi.	RW	Gordie Howe, Det.
Pierre Pilote, Chi.	D	Elmer Vasko, Chi.
Tim Horton, Tor.	D	Jacques Laperriere, Mon.
Glenn Hall, Chi.	G	Charlie Hodge, Mon.

1964-65

First team		Second team
Bobby Hull, Chi.	LW	Frank Mahovlich, Tor.
Norm Ullman, Det.	C	Stan Mikita, Chi.
Claude Provost, Mon.	RW	Gordie Howe, Det.
Pierre Pilote, Chi.	D	Bill Gadsby, Det.
Jacques Laperriere, Mon.	D	Carl Brewer, Tor.
Roger Crozier, Det.	G	Charlie Hodge, Mon.

1965-66

First team		Second team
Bobby Hull, Chi.	LW	Frank Mahovlich, Tor.
Stan Mikita, Chi.	C	Jean Beliveau, Mon.
Gordie Howe, Det.	RW	Bobby Rousseau, Mon.
Jacques Laperriere, Mon.	D	Allan Stanley, Tor.
Pierre Pilote, Chi.	D	Pat Stapleton, Chi.
Glenn Hall, Chi.	G	Gump Worsley, Mon.

1966-67

First team		Second team
Bobby Hull, Chi.	LW	Don Marshall, N.Y.R.
Stan Mikita, Chi.	C	Norm Ullman, Det.
Ken Wharram, Chi.	RW	Gordie Howe, Det.
Pierre Pilote, Chi.	D	Tim Horton, Tor.
Harry Howell, N.Y.R.	D	Bobby Orr, Bos.
Ed Giacomin, N.Y.R.	G	Glenn Hall, Chi.

1967-68

First team		Second team
Bobby Hull, Chi.	LW	Johnny Bucyk, Bos.
Stan Mikita, Chi.	C	Phil Esposito, Bos.
Gordie Howe, Det.	RW	Rod Gilbert, N.Y.R.
Bobby Orr, Bos.	D	J.C. Tremblay, Mon.
Tim Horton, Tor.	D	Jim Neilson, N.Y.R.
Gump Worsley, Mon.	G	Ed Giacomin, N.Y.R.

1968-69

First team		Second team
Bobby Hull, Chi.	LW	Frank Mahovlich, Det.
Phil Esposito, Bos.	C	Jean Beliveau, Mon.
Gordie Howe, Det.	RW	Yvan Cournoyer, Mon.
Bobby Orr, Bos.	D	Ted Green, Bos.
Tim Horton, Tor.	D	Ted Harris, Mon.
Glenn Hall, St.L.	G	Ed Giacomin, N.Y.R.

1969-70

First team		Second team
Bobby Hull, Chi.	LW	Frank Mahovlich, Det.
Phil Esposito, Bos.	C	Stan Mikita, Chi.
Gordie Howe, Det.	RW	John McKenzie, Bos.
Bobby Orr, Bos.	D	Carl Brewer, Det.
Brad Park, N.Y.R.	D	Jacques Laperriere, Mon.
Tony Esposito, Chi.	G	Ed Giacomin, N.Y.R.

1970-71

First team		Second team
Johnny Bucyk, Bos.	LW	Bobby Hull, Chi.
Phil Esposito, Bos.	C	Dave Keon, Tor.
Ken Hodge, Bos.	RW	Yvan Cournoyer, Mon.
Bobby Orr, Bos.	D	Brad Park, N.Y.R.
J.C. Tremblay, Mon.	D	Pat Stapleton, Chi.
Ed Giacomin, N.Y.R.	G	Jacques Plante, Tor.

1971-72

First team		Second team
Bobby Hull, Chi.	LW	Vic Hadfield, N.Y.R.
Phil Esposito, Bos.	C	Jean Ratelle, N.Y.R.
Rod Gilbert, N.Y.R.	RW	Yvan Cournoyer, Mon.
Bobby Orr, Bos.	D	Bill White, Chi.
Brad Park, N.Y.R.	D	Pat Stapleton, Chi.
Tony Esposito, Chi.	G	Ken Dryden, Mon.

1972-73

First team		Second team
Frank Mahovlich, Mon.	LW	Dennis Hull, Chi.
Phil Esposito, Bos.	C	Bobby Clarke, Phi.
Mickey Redmond, Det.	RW	Yvan Cournoyer, Mon.
Bobby Orr, Bos.	D	Brad Park, N.Y.R.
Guy Lapointe, Mon.	D	Bill White, Chi.
Ken Dryden, Mon.	G	Tony Esposito, Chi.

1973-74

First team		Second team
Richard Martin, Buf.	LW	Wayne Cashman, Bos.
Phil Esposito, Bos.	C	Bobby Clarke, Phi.
Ken Hodge, Bos.	RW	Mickey Redmond, Det.
Bobby Orr, Bos.	D	Bill White, Chi.
Brad Park, N.Y.R.	D	Barry Ashbee, Phi.
Bernie Parent, Phi.	G	Tony Esposito, Chi.

1974-75

First team		Second team
Richard Martin, Buf.	LW	Steve Vickers, N.Y.R.
Bobby Clarke, Phi.	C	Phil Esposito, Bos.
Guy Lafleur, Mon.	RW	Rene Robert, Buf.
Bobby Orr, Bos.	D	Guy Lapointe, Mon.
Denis Potvin, N.Y.I.	D	Borje Salming, Tor.
Bernie Parent, Phi.	G	Rogie Vachon, L.A.

1975-76

First team		Second team
Bill Barber, Phi.	LW	Richard Martin, Buf.
Bobby Clarke, Phi.	C	Gilbert Perreault, Buf.
Guy Lafleur, Mon.	RW	Reggie Leach, Phi.
Denis Potvin, N.Y.I.	D	Borje Salming, Tor.
Brad Park, Bos.	D	Guy Lapointe, Mon.
Ken Dryden, Mon.	G	Glenn Resch, N.Y.I.

1976-77

First team		Second team
Steve Shutt, Mon.	LW	Richard Martin, Buf.
Marcel Dionne, L.A.	C	Gilbert Perreault, Buf.
Guy Lafleur, Mon.	RW	Lanny McDonald, Tor.
Larry Robinson, Mon.	D	Denis Potvin, N.Y.I.
Borje Salming, Tor.	D	Guy Lapointe, Mon.
Ken Dryden, Mon.	G	Rogie Vachon, L.A.

1977-78

First team		Second team
Clark Gillies, N.Y.I.	LW	Steve Shutt, Mon.
Bryan Trottier, N.Y.I.	C	Darryl Sittler, Tor.
Guy Lafleur, Mon.	RW	Mike Bossy, N.Y.I.
Denis Potvin, N.Y.I.	D	Larry Robinson, Mon.
Brad Park, Bos.	D	Borje Salming, Tor.
Ken Dryden, Mon.	G	Don Edwards, Buf.

1978-79

First team		Second team
Clark Gillies, N.Y.I.	LW	Bill Barber, Phi.
Bryan Trottier, N.Y.I.	C	Marcel Dionne, L.A.
Guy Lafleur, Mon.	RW	Mike Bossy, N.Y.I.
Denis Potvin, N.Y.I.	D	Borje Salming, Tor.
Larry Robinson, Mon.	D	Serge Savard, Mon.
Ken Dryden, Mon.	G	Glenn Resch, N.Y.I.

1979-80

First team		Second team
Charlie Simmer, L.A.	LW	Steve Shutt, Mon.
Marcel Dionne, L.A.	C	Wayne Gretzky, Edm.
Guy Lafleur, Mon.	RW	Danny Gare, Buf.
Larry Robinson, Mon.	D	Borje Salming, Tor.
Ray Bourque, Bos.	D	Jim Schoenfeld, Buf.
Tony Esposito, Chi.	G	Don Edwards, Buf.

1980-81

First team		Second team
Charlie Simmer, L.A.	LW	Bill Barber, Phi.
Wayne Gretzky, Edm.	C	Marcel Dionne, L.A.
Mike Bossy, N.Y.I.	RW	Dave Taylor, L.A.
Denis Potvin, N.Y.I.	D	Larry Robinson, Mon.
Randy Carlyle, Pit.	D	Ray Bourque, Bos.
Mike Liut, St.L.	G	Mario Lessard, L.A.

1981-82

First team		Second team
Mark Messier, Edm.	LW	John Tonelli, N.Y.I.
Wayne Gretzky, Edm.	C	Bryan Trottier, N.Y.I.
Mike Bossy, N.Y.I.	RW	Rick Middleton, Bos.
Doug Wilson, Chi.	D	Paul Coffey, Edm.
Ray Bourque, Bos.	D	Brian Engblom, Mon.
Bill Smith, N.Y.I.	G	Grant Fuhr, Edm.

1982-83

First team		Second team
Mark Messier, Edm.	LW	Michel Goulet, Que.
Wayne Gretzky, Edm.	C	Denis Savard, Chi.
Mike Bossy, N.Y.I.	RW	Lanny McDonald, Cal.
Mark Howe, Phi.	D	Ray Bourque, Bos.
Rod Langway, Was.	D	Paul Coffey, Edm.
Pete Peeters, Bos.	G	Roland Melanson, N.Y.I.

1983-84

First team		Second team
Michel Goulet, Que.	LW	Mark Messier, Edm.
Wayne Gretzky, Edm.	C	Bryan Trottier, N.Y.I.
Mike Bossy, N.Y.I.	RW	Jari Kurri, Edm.
Rod Langway, Was.	D	Paul Coffey, Edm.
Ray Bourque, Bos.	D	Denis Potvin, N.Y.I.
Tom Barrasso, Buf.	G	Pat Riggin, Was.

1984-85

First team		Second team
John Ogrodnick, Det.	LW	John Tonelli, N.Y.I.
Wayne Gretzky, Edm.	C	Dale Hawerchuk, Win.
Jari Kurri, Edm.	RW	Mike Bossy, N.Y.I.
Paul Coffey, Edm.	D	Rod Langway, Was.
Ray Bourque, Bos.	D	Doug Wilson, Chi.
Pelle Lindbergh, Phi.	G	Tom Barrasso, Buf.

1985-86

First team		Second team
Michel Goulet, Que.	LW	Mats Naslund, Mon.
Wayne Gretzky, Edm.	C	Mario Lemieux, Pit.
Mike Bossy, N.Y.I.	RW	Jari Kurri, Edm.
Paul Coffey, Edm.	D	Larry Robinson, Mon.
Mark Howe, Phi.	D	Ray Bourque, Bos.
John Vanbiesbrouck, N.Y.R.	G	Bob Froese, Phi.

1986-87

First team		Second team
Michel Goulet, Que.	LW	Luc Robitaille, L.A.
Wayne Gretzky, Edm.	C	Mario Lemieux, Pit.
Jari Kurri, Edm.	RW	Tim Kerr, Phi.
Ray Bourque, Bos.	D	Larry Murphy, Was.
Mark Howe, Phi.	D	Al MacInnis, Cal.
Ron Hextall, Phi.	G	Mike Liut, Har.

1987-88

First team		Second team
Luc Robitaille, L.A.	LW	Michel Goulet, Que.
Mario Lemieux, Pit.	C	Wayne Gretzky, Edm.
Hakan Loob, Cal.	RW	Cam Neely, Bos.
Ray Bourque, Bos.	D	Gary Suter, Cal.
Scott Stevens, Was.	D	Brad McCrimmon, Cal.
Grant Fuhr, Edm.	G	Patrick Roy, Mon.

1988-89

First team		Second team
Luc Robitaille, L.A.	LW	Gerard Gallant, Det.
Mario Lemieux, Pit.	C	Wayne Gretzky, L.A.
Joe Mullen, Cal.	RW	Jari Kurri, Edm.
Chris Chelios, Mon.	D	Al MacInnis, Cal.
Paul Coffey, Pit.	D	Ray Bourque, Bos.
Patrick Roy, Mon.	G	Mike Vernon, Cal.

1989-90

First team		Second team
Luc Robitaille, L.A.	LW	Brian Bellows, Min.
Mark Messier, Edm.	C	Wayne Gretzky, L.A.
Brett Hull, St.L.	RW	Cam Neely, Bos.
Ray Bourque, Bos.	D	Paul Coffey, Pit.
Al MacInnis, Cal.	D	Doug Wilson, Chi.
Patrick Roy, Mon.	G	Daren Puppa, Buf.

1990-91

First team		Second team
Luc Robitaille, L.A.	LW	Kevin Stevens, Pit.
Wayne Gretzky, L.A.	C	Adam Oates, St.L.
Brett Hull, St.L.	RW	Cam Neely, Bos.
Ray Bourque, Bos.	D	Chris Chelios, Chi.
Al MacInnis, Cal.	D	Brian Leetch, N.Y.R.
Ed Belfour, Chi.	G	Patrick Roy, Mon.

1991-92

First team		Second team
Kevin Stevens, Pit.	LW	Luc Robitaille, L.A.
Mark Messier, N.Y.R.	C	Mario Lemieux, Pit.
Brett Hull, St.L.	RW	Mark Recchi, Pit., Phi.
Brian Leetch, N.Y.R.	D	Phil Housley, Win.
Ray Bourque, Bos.	D	Scott Stevens, N.J.
Patrick Roy, Mon.	G	Kirk McLean, Van.

1992-93

First team		Second team
Luc Robitaille, L.A.	LW	Kevin Stevens, Pit.
Mario Lemieux, Pit.	C	Pat LaFontaine, Buf.
Teemu Selanne, Win.	RW	Alexander Mogilny, Buf.
Chris Chelios, Chi.	D	Larry Murphy, Pit.
Ray Bourque, Bos.	D	Al Iafrate, Was.
Ed Belfour, Chi.	G	Tom Barrasso, Pit.

1993-94

First team		Second team
Brendan Shanahan, St.L.	LW	Adam Graves, N.Y.R.
Sergei Fedorov, Det.	C	Wayne Gretzky, L.A.
Pavel Bure, Van.	RW	Cam Neely, Bos.
Ray Bourque, Bos.	D	Al MacInnis, Cal.
Scott Stevens, N.J.	D	Brian Leetch, N.Y.R.
Dominik Hasek, Buf.	G	John Vanbiesbrouck, Fla.

1994-95

First team		Second team
John LeClair, Mon., Phi.	LW	Keith Tkachuk, Win.
Eric Lindros, Phi.	C	Alexei Zhamnov, Win.
Jaromir Jagr, Pit.	RW	Theoren Fleury, Cal.
Paul Coffey, Det.	D	Ray Bourque, Bos.
Chris Chelios, Chi.	D	Larry Murphy, Pit.
Dominik Hasek, Buf.	G	Ed Belfour, Chi.

1995-96

First team		Second team
Paul Kariya, Ana.	LW	John LeClair, Phi.
Mario Lemieux, Pit.	C	Eric Lindros, Phi.
Jaromir Jagr, Pit.	RW	Alexander Mogilny, Van.
Chris Chelios, Chi.	D	Vladimir Konstantinov, Det.
Ray Bourque, Bos.	D	Brian Leetch, N.Y.R.
Jim Carey, Was.	G	Chris Osgood, Det.

1996-97

First team		Second team
Paul Kariya, Ana.	LW	John LeClair, Phi.
Mario Lemieux, Pit.	C	Wayne Gretzky, N.Y.R.
Teemu Selanne, Ana.	RW	Jaromir Jagr, Pit.
Brian Leetch, N.Y.R.	D	Chris Chelios, Chi.
Sandis Ozolinsh, Col.	D	Scott Stevens, N.J.
Dominik Hasek, Buf.	G	Martin Brodeur, N.J.

1997-98

First team		Second team
John LeClair, Phi.	LW	Keith Tkachuk, Pho.
Peter Forsberg, Col.	C	Wayne Gretzky, N.Y.R.
Jaromir Jagr, Pit.	RW	Teemu Selanne, Ana.
Nicklas Lidstrom, Det.	D	Chris Pronger, St.L.
Rob Blake, L.A.	D	Scott Niedermayer, N.J.
Dominik Hasek, Buf.	G	Martin Brodeur, N.J.

1998-99

First team		Second team
Paul Kariya, Ana.	LW	John LeClair, Phi.
Peter Forsberg, Col.	C	Alexei Yashin, Ott.
Jaromir Jagr, Pit.	RW	Teemu Selanne, Ana.
Nicklas Lidstrom, Det.	D	Ray Bourque, Bos.
Al MacInnis, St.L.	D	Eric Desjardins, Phi.
Dominik Hasek, Buf.	G	Byron Dafoe, Bos.

1999-2000

First team		Second team
Brendan Shanahan, Det.	LW	Paul Kariya, Ana.
Steve Yzerman, Det.	C	Mike Modano, Dal.
Jaromir Jagr, Pit.	RW	Pavel Bure, Florida
Nicklas Lidstrom, Det.	D	Rob Blake, L.A.-Colo.
Chris Pronger, St.L.	D	Eric Desjardins, Phi.
Olaf Kolzig, Was.	G	Roman Turek, St.L.

2000-01

First team		Second team
Patrik Elias, N.J.	LW	Luc Robitaille, L.A.
Joe Sakic, Col.	C	Mario Lemieux, Pit.
Jaromir Jagr, Pit.	RW	Pavel Bure, Fla.
Ray Bourque, Colorado	D	Rob Blake, L.A.
Nicklas Lidstrom, Det.	D	Scott Stevens, N.J.
Dominik Hasek, Buf.	G	Roman Cechmanek, Phi.

THE SPORTING NEWS AWARDS

PLAYER OF THE YEAR

1967-68—E. Div.: Stan Mikita, Chicago
　　　　　 W. Div.: Red Berenson, St. Louis
1968-69—E. Div.: Phil Esposito, Boston
　　　　　 W. Div.: Red Berenson, St. Louis
1969-70—E. Div.: Bobby Orr, Boston
　　　　　 W. Div.: Red Berenson, St. Louis
1970-71—E. Div.: Phil Esposito, Boston
　　　　　 W. Div.: Bobby Hull, Chicago
1971-72—E. Div.: Jean Ratelle, N.Y. Rangers
　　　　　 W. Div.: Bobby Hull, Chicago
1972-73—E. Div.: Phil Esposito, Boston
　　　　　 W. Div.: Bobby Clarke, Philadelphia
1973-74—E. Div.: Phil Esposito, Boston
　　　　　 W. Div.: Bernie Parent, Philadelphia
1974-75—Camp. Conf.: Bobby Clarke, Philadelphia
　　　　　 Wales Conf.: Guy Lafleur, Montreal
1975-76—Bobby Clarke, Philadelphia
1976-77—Guy Lafleur, Montreal
1977-78—Guy Lafleur, Montreal
1978-79—Bryan Trottier, N.Y. Islanders
1979-80—Marcel Dionne, Los Angeles
1980-81—Wayne Gretzky, Edmonton
1981-82—Wayne Gretzky, Edmonton
1982-83—Wayne Gretzky, Edmonton
1983-84—Wayne Gretzky, Edmonton
1984-85—Wayne Gretzky, Edmonton
1985-86—Wayne Gretzky, Edmonton
1986-87—Wayne Gretzky, Edmonton
1987-88—Mario Lemieux, Pittsburgh
1988-89—Mario Lemieux, Pittsburgh
1989-90—Mark Messier, Edmonton
1990-91—Brett Hull, St. Louis
1991-92—Mark Messier, N.Y. Rangers

1992-93—Mario Lemieux, Pittsburgh
1993-94—Sergei Fedorov, Detroit
1994-95—Eric Lindros, Philadelphia
1995-96—Mario Lemieux, Pittsburgh
1996-97—Dominik Hasek, Buffalo
1997-98—Dominik Hasek, Buffalo
1998-99—Jaromir Jagr, Pittsburgh
1999-00—Jaromir Jagr, Pittsburgh
2000-01—Joe Sakic, Colorado

ROOKIE OF THE YEAR

1967-68—E. Div.: Derek Sanderson, Boston
　　　　　 W. Div.: Bill Flett, Los Angeles
1968-69—E. Div.: Brad Park, N.Y. Rangers
　　　　　 W. Div.: Norm Ferguson, Oakland
1969-70—E. Div.: Tony Esposito, Chicago
　　　　　 W. Div.: Bobby Clarke, Philadelphia
1970-71—E. Div.: Gil Perreault, Buffalo
　　　　　 W. Div.: Jude Drouin, Minnesota
1971-72—E. Div.: Richard Martin, Buffalo
　　　　　 W. Div.: Gilles Meloche, California
1972-73—E. Div.: Steve Vickers, N.Y. Rangers
　　　　　 W. Div.: Bill Barber, Philadelphia
1973-74—E. Div.: Denis Potvin, N.Y. Islanders
　　　　　 W. Div.: Tom Lysiak, Atlanta
1974-75—Camp. Conf.: Eric Vail, Atlanta
　　　　　 Wales Conf.: Pierre Larouche, Pittsburgh
1975-76—Bryan Trottier, N.Y. Islanders
1976-77—Willi Plett, Atlanta
1977-78—Mike Bossy, N.Y. Islanders
1978-79—Bobby Smith, Minnesota
1979-80—Ray Bourque, Boston
1980-81—Peter Stastny, Quebec
1981-82—Dale Hawerchuk, Winnipeg

1982-83—Steve Larmer, Chicago
1983-84—Steve Yzerman, Detroit
1984-85—Mario Lemieux, Pittsburgh
1985-86—Wendel Clark, Toronto
1986-87—Ron Hextall, Philadelphia
1987-88—Joe Nieuwendyk, Calgary
1988-89—Brian Leetch, N.Y. Rangers
1989-90—Jeremy Roenick, Chicago
1990-91—Ed Belfour, Chicago
1991-92—Tony Amonte, N.Y. Rangers
1992-93—Teemu Selanne, Winnipeg
1993-94—Jason Arnott, Edmonton
1994-95—Peter Forsberg, Quebec
1995-96—Eric Daze, Chicago
1996-97—Bryan Berard, N.Y. Islanders
1997-98—Sergei Samsonov, Boston
1998-99—Chris Drury, Colorado
1999-00—Scott Gomez, New Jersey
2000-01—Evgeni Nabokov, San Jose

NHL COACH OF THE YEAR

1944-45—Dick Irvin, Montreal
1945-46—Johnny Gottselig, Chicago
1979-80—Pat Quinn, Philadelphia
1980-81—Red Berenson, St. Louis
1981-82—Herb Brooks, N.Y. Rangers
1982-83—Gerry Cheevers, Boston
1983-84—Bryan Murray, Washington
1984-85—Mike Keenan, Philadelphia
1985-86—Jacques Demers, St. Louis
1986-87—Jacques Demers, Detroit
1987-88—Terry Crisp, Calgary
1988-89—Pat Burns, Montreal
1989-90—Mike Milbury, Boston
1990-91—Tom Webster, Los Angeles
1991-92—Pat Quinn, Vancouver
1992-93—Pat Burns, Toronto
1993-94—Jacques Lemaire, New Jersey
1994-95—Marc Crawford, Quebec
1995-96—Scotty Bowman, Detroit
1996-97—Ken Hitchcock, Dallas
1997-98—Pat Burns, Boston
1998-99—Jacques Martin, Ottawa
1999-00—Joel Quenneville, St. Louis
2000-01—Scotty Bowman, Detroit
NOTE: The Coach of the Year Award was not given from 1946-47 through 1978-79 seasons.

NHL EXECUTIVE OF THE YEAR

1972-73—Sam Pollock, Montreal
1973-74—Keith Allen, Philadelphia
1974-75—Bill Torrey, N.Y. Islanders
1975-76—Sam Pollock, Montreal
1976-77—Harry Sinden, Boston
1977-78—Ted Lindsay, Detroit
1978-79—Bill Torrey, N.Y. Islanders
1979-80—Scotty Bowman, Buffalo
1980-81—Emile Francis, St. Louis
1981-82—John Ferguson, Winnipeg
1982-83—David Poile, Washington
1983-84—David Poile, Washington
1984-85—John Ferguson, Winnipeg
1985-86—Emile Francis, Hartford
1986-87—John Ferguson, Winnipeg
1987-88—Cliff Fletcher, Calgary
1988-89—Bruce McNall, Los Angeles
1989-90—Harry Sinden, Boston
1990-91—Craig Patrick, Pittsburgh
1991-92—Neil Smith, N.Y. Rangers
1992-93—Cliff Fletcher, Toronto
1993-94—Bobby Clarke, Florida
1994-95—Bobby Clarke, Philadelphia
1995-96—Bryan Murray, Florida

1996-97—John Muckler, Buffalo
1997-98—Craig Patrick, Pittsburgh
1998-99—Craig Patrick, Pittsburgh
1999-00—Larry Pleau, St. Louis
2000-01—Brian Burke, Vancouver

THE SPORTING NEWS ALL-STAR TEAMS

(As selected by six hockey writers in 1944-45 and 1945-46
and by a vote of league players since 1967-68;
no teams selected from 1946-47 through 1966-67)

1944-45

First team		Second team
Maurice Richard, Mon.	W	Bill Mosienko, Chi.
Toe Blake, Mon.	W	Sweeney Schriner, Tor.
Elmer Lach, Mon.	C	Bill Cowley, Bos.
Emile Bouchard, Mon.	D	Earl Seibert, Det.
Bill Hollett, Det.	D	Babe Pratt, Tor.
Bill Durnan, Mon.	G	Frank McCool, Tor.

1945-46

First team		Second team
Gaye Stewart, Tor.	LW	Doug Bentley, Chi.
Max Bentley, Chi.	C	Elmer Lach, Mon.
Bill Mosienko, Chi.	RW	Maurice Richard, Mon.
Emile Bouchard, Mon.	D	Jack Crawford, Bos.
Jack Stewart, Det.	D	Babe Pratt, Tor.
Bill Durnan, Mon.	G	Harry Lumley, Det.

1967-68

EAST DIVISION First team		WEST DIVISION First team
Bobby Hull, Chi.	LW	Ab McDonald, Pit.
Stan Mikita, Chi.	C	Red Berenson, St.L.
Gordie Howe, Det.	RW	Wayne Connelly, Min.
Bobby Orr, Bos.	D	Bill White, L.A.
Tim Horton, Tor.	D	Mike McMahon, Min.
Ed Giacomin, N.Y.R.	G	Glenn Hall, St.L.

Second team		Second team
Johnny Bucyk, Bos.	LW	Bill Sutherland, Phi.
Phil Esposito, Bos.	C	Ray Cullen, Min.
Rod Gilbert, N.Y.R.	RW	Bill Flett, L.A.
J.C. Tremblay, Mon.	D	Ar Arbour, St.L.
Gary Bergman, Det.	D	Ed Van Impe, Phi.
Gump Worsley, Mon.	G	Doug Favell, Phi.

1968-69

EAST DIVISION First team		WEST DIVISION First team
Bobby Hull, Chi.	LW	Danny Grant, Min.
Phil Esposito, Bos.	C	Red Berenson, St.L.
Gordie Howe, Det.	RW	Norm Ferguson, Oak.
Bobby Orr, Bos.	D	Bill White, L.A.
Tim Horton, Tor.	D	Ar Arbour, St.L.
Ed Giacomin, N.Y.R.	G	Glenn Hall, St.L.

Second team		Second team
Frank Mahovlich, Det.	LW	Ab McDonald, St.L.
Stan Mikita, Chi.	C	Ted Hampson, Oak.
Yvan Cournoyer, Mon.	RW	Claude LaRose, Min.
J.C. Tremblay, Mon.	D	Carol Vadnais, Oak.
Jim Neilson, N.Y.R.	D	Ed Van Impe, Phi.
Bruce Gamble, Tor.	G	Bernie Parent, Phi.

1969-70

EAST DIVISION		WEST DIVISION
Bobby Hull, Chi.	LW	Dean Prentice, Pit.
Stan Mikita, Chi.	C	Red Berenson, St.L.
Ron Ellis, Tor.	RW	Bill Goldsworthy, Min.
Bobby Orr, Bos.	D	Al Arbour, St.L.
Brad Park, N.Y.R.	D	Bob Woytowich, Pit.
Tony Esposito, Chi.	G	Bernie Parent, Phi.

1970-71

EAST DIVISION		WEST DIVISION
Johnny Bucyk, Bos.	LW	Bobby Hull, Chi.
Phil Esposito, Bos.	C	Stan Mikita, Chi.
Ken Hodge, Bos.	RW	Bill Goldsworthy, Min.
Bobby Orr, Bos.	D	Pat Stapleton, Chi.
J.C. Tremblay, Mon.	D	Bill White, Chi.
Ed Giacomin, N.Y.R.	G	Tony Esposito, Chi.

1971-72

EAST DIVISION		WEST DIVISION
Vic Hadfield, N.Y.R.	LW	Bobby Hull, Chi.
Phil Esposito, Bos.	C	Bobby Clarke, Phi.
Rod Gilbert, N.Y.R.	RW	Bill Goldsworthy, Min.
Bobby Orr, Bos.	D	Pat Stapleton, Chi.
Brad Park, N.Y.R.	D	Bill White, Chi.
Ken Dryden, Mon.	G	Tony Esposito, Chi.

1972-73

EAST DIVISION		WEST DIVISION
Frank Mahovlich, Mon.	LW	Dennis Hull, Chi.
Phil Esposito, Bos.	C	Bobby Clarke, Phi.
Mickey Redmond, Det.	RW	Bill Flett, Phi.
Bobby Orr, Bos.	D	Bill White, Chi.
Guy Lapointe, Mon.	D	Barry Gibbs, Min.
Ken Dryden, Mon.	G	Tony Esposito, Chi.

1973-74

EAST DIVISION		WEST DIVISION
First team		First team
Richard Martin, Buf.	LW	Lowell MacDonald, Pit.
Phil Esposito, Bos.	C	Bobby Clarke, Phi.
Ken Hodge, Bos.	RW	Bill Goldsworthy, Min.
Bobby Orr, Bos.	D	Bill White, Chi.
Brad Park, N.Y.R.	D	Barry Ashbee, Phi.
Gilles Gilbert, Bos.	G	Bernie Parent, Phi.
Second team		Second team
Frank Mahovlich, Mon.	LW	Dennis Hull, Chi.
Darryl Sittler, Tor.	C	Stan Mikita, Chi.
Mickey Redmond, Det.	RW	Jean Pronovost, Pit.
Guy Lapointe, Mon.	D	Don Awrey, St.L.
Borje Salming, Tor.	D	Dave Burrows, Pit.
Ed Giacomin, N.Y.R.	D	Tony Esposito, Chi.

1974-75

CAMPBELL CONFERENCE		WALES CONFERENCE
First team		First team
Steve Vickers, N.Y.R.	LW	Richard Martin, Buf.
Bobby Clarke, Phi.	C	Phil Esposito, Bos.
Rod Gilbert, N.Y.R.	RW	Guy Lafleur, Mon.
Denis Potvin, N.Y.I.	D	Bobby Orr, Bos.
Brad Park, N.Y.R.	D	Guy Lapointe, Mon.
Bernie Parent, Phi.	G	Rogie Vachon, L.A.
Second team		Second team
Eric Vail, Atl.	LW	Danny Grant, Det.
Stan Mikita, Chi.	C	Gilbert Perreault, Buf.
Reggie Leach, Phi.	RW	Rene Robert, Buf.
Jim Watson, Phi.	D	Borje Salming, Tor.
Phil Russell, Chi.	D	Terry Harper, L.A.
Gary Smith, Van.	D	Ken Dryden, Mon.

1975-76

First team		Second team
Bill Barber, Phi.	LW	Richard Martin, Buf.
Bobby Clarke, Phi.	C	Pete Mahovlich, Mon.
Guy Lafleur, Mon.	RW	Reggie Leach, Phi.
Denis Potvin, N.Y.I.	D	Guy Lapointe, Mon.
Brad Park, Bos.	D	Borje Salming, Tor.
Ken Dryden, Mon.	G	Glenn Resch, N.Y.I.

1976-77

First team		Second team
Steve Shutt, Mon.	LW	Clark Gillies, N.Y.I.
Marcel Dionne, L.A.	C	Gilbert Perreault, Buf.
Guy Lafleur, Mon.	RW	Lanny McDonald, Tor.
Larry Robinson, Mon.	D	Guy Lapointe, Mon.
Borje Salming, Tor.	D	Serge Savard, Mon.
	(tied)	Denis Potvin, N.Y.I.
Rogie Vachon, L.A.	G	Ken Dryden, Mon.

1977-78

First team		Second team
Clark Gillies, N.Y.I.	LW	Steve Shutt, Mon.
Bryan Trottier, N.Y.I.	C	Darryl Sittler, Tor.
Guy Lafleur, Mon.	RW	Terry O'Reilly, Bos.
Borje Salming, Tor.	D	Denis Potvin, N.Y.I.
Larry Robinson, Mon.	D	Serge Savard, Mon.
Ken Dryden, Mon.	G	Don Edwards, Buf.

1978-79

First team		Second team
Clark Gillies, N.Y.I.	LW	Bob Gainey, Mon.
Bryan Trottier, N.Y.I.	C	Marcel Dionne, L.A.
Guy Lafleur, Mon.	RW	Mike Bossy, N.Y.I.
Denis Potvin, N.Y.I.	D	Borje Salming, Tor.
Larry Robinson, Mon.	D	Serge Savard, Mon.
Ken Dryden, Mon.	G	Glenn Resch, N.Y.I.

1979-80

First team		Second team
Charlie Simmer, L.A.	LW	Steve Shutt, Mon.
Marcel Dionne, L.A.	C	Wayne Gretzky, Edm.
Guy Lafleur, Mon.	RW	Danny Gare, Buf.
Larry Robinson, Mon.	D	Barry Beck, Col., N.Y.R.
Borje Salming, Tor.	D	Mark Howe, Har.
Tony Esposito, Chi.	G	Don Edwards, Buf.

1980-81

First team		Second team
Charlie Simmer, L.A.	LW	Bill Barber, Phi.
Wayne Gretzky, Edm.	C	Marcel Dionne, L.A.
Mike Bossy, N.Y.I.	RW	Dave Taylor, L.A.
Randy Carlyle, Pit.	D	Larry Robinson, Mon.
Denis Potvin, N.Y.I.	D	Ray Bourque, Bos.
Mike Liut, St.L.	G	Don Beaupre, Min.

1981-82

First team		Second team
Mark Messier, Edm.	LW	John Tonelli, N.Y.I.
Wayne Gretzky, Edm.	C	Bryan Trottier, N.Y.I.
Mike Bossy, N.Y.I.	RW	Rick Middleton, Bos.
Doug Wilson, Chi.	D	Paul Coffey, Edm.
Ray Bourque, Bos.	D	Larry Robinson, Mon.
Bill Smith, N.Y.I.	G	Grant Fuhr, Edm.

1982-83

First team		Second team
Mark Messier, Edm.	LW	Michel Goulet, Que.
Wayne Gretzky, Edm.	C	Denis Savard, Chi.
Lanny McDonald, Cal.	RW	Mike Bossy, N.Y.I.
Mark Howe, Phi.	D	Ray Bourque, Bos.
Rod Langway, Was.	D	Paul Coffey, Edm.
Pete Peeters, Bos.	G	Andy Moog, Edm.

1983-84

First team		Second team
Michel Goulet, Que.	LW	John Ogrodnick, Det.
Wayne Gretzky, Edm.	C	Bryan Trottier, N.Y.I.
Rick Middleton, Bos.	RW	Mike Bossy, N.Y.I.
Ray Bourque, Bos.	D	Paul Coffey, Edm.
Rod Langway, Was.	D	Denis Potvin, N.Y.I.
Pat Riggin, Was.	G	Tom Barrasso, Buf.

1984-85

First team		Second team
Michel Goulet, Que.	LW	John Ogrodnick, Det.
Wayne Gretzky, Edm.	C	Dale Hawerchuk, Win.
Jari Kurri, Edm.	RW	Mike Bossy, N.Y.I.
Ray Bourque, Bos.	D	Rod Langway, Was.
Paul Coffey, Edm.	D	Doug Wilson, Chi.
Pelle Lindbergh, Phi.	G	Tom Barrasso, Buf.

1985-86

First team		Second team
Michel Goulet, Que.	LW	Mats Naslund, Mon.
Wayne Gretzky, Edm.	C	Mario Lemieux, Pit.
Mike Bossy, N.Y.I.	RW	Jari Kurri, Edm.
Paul Coffey, Edm.	D	Ray Bourque, Bos.
Mark Howe, Phi.	D	Larry Robinson, Mon.
John Vanbiesbrouck, N.Y.R.	G	Grant Fuhr, Edm.

1986-87

First team		Second team
Michel Goulet, Que.	LW	Luc Robitaille, L.A.
Wayne Gretzky, Edm.	C	Mark Messier, Edm.
Tim Kerr, Phi.	RW	Kevin Dineen, Har.
Ray Bourque, Bos.	D	Larry Murphy, Was.
Mark Howe, Phi.	D	Paul Coffey, Edm.
Mike Liut, Har.	G	Ron Hextall, Phi.

1987-88

First team		Second team
Luc Robitaille, L.A.	LW	Michel Goulet, Que.
Mario Lemieux, Pit.	C	Wayne Gretzky, Edm.
Cam Neely, Bos.	RW	Hakan Loob, Cal.
Ray Bourque, Bos.	D	Scott Stevens, Was.
Gary Suter, Cal.	D	Brad McCrimmon, Cal.
Grant Fuhr, Edm.	G	Tom Barrasso, Buf.

1988-89

First team		Second team
Luc Robitaille, L.A.	LW	Mats Naslund, Mon.
Mario Lemieux, Pit.	C	Wayne Gretzky, L.A.
Joe Mullen, Cal.	RW	Jari Kurri, Edm.
Paul Coffey, Pit.	D	Ray Bourque, Bos.
Chris Chelios, Mon.	D	Gary Suter, Cal.
Patrick Roy, Mon.	G	Mike Vernon, Cal.

1989-90

First team		Second team
Luc Robitaille, L.A.	LW	Brian Bellows, Min.
Mark Messier, Edm.	C	Pat LaFontaine, N.Y.I.
Brett Hull, St.L.	RW	Cam Neely, Bos.
Ray Bourque, Bos.	D	Doug Wilson, Chi.
Al MacInnis, Cal.	D	Paul Coffey, Pit.
Patrick Roy, Mon.	G	Daren Puppa, Buf.

1990-91

First team		Second team
Luc Robitaille, L.A.	LW	Kevin Stevens, Pit.
Wayne Gretzky, L.A.	C	Adam Oates, St.L.
Brett Hull, St.L.	RW	Cam Neely, Bos.
Ray Bourque, Bos.	D	Brian Leetch, N.Y.R.
Al MacInnis, Cal.	D	Chris Chelios, Chi.
Ed Belfour, Chi.	G	Patrick Roy, Mon.

1991-92

First team		Second team
Kevin Stevens, Pit.	LW	Luc Robitaille, L.A.
Mark Messier, N.Y.R.	C	Wayne Gretzky, L.A.
Brett Hull, St.L.	RW	Joe Mullen, Pit.
Brian Leetch, N.Y.R.	D	Phil Housley, Win.
Ray Bourque, Bos.	D	Chris Chelios, Chi.
Patrick Roy, Mon.	G	Kirk McLean, Van.

1992-93

First team		Second team
Luc Robitaille, L.A.	LW	Kevin Stevens, Pit.
Mario Lemieux, Pit.	C	Doug Gilmour, Tor.
Teemu Selanne, Win.	RW	Alexander Mogilny, Buf.
Chris Chelios, Chi.	D	Larry Murphy, Pit.
Ray Bourque, Bos.	D	Al Iafrate, Was.
Tom Barrasso, Pit.	G	Ed Belfour, Chi.

1993-94

First team		Second team
Adam Graves, N.Y.R.	LW	Dave Andreychuk, Tor.
Sergei Fedorov, Det.	C	Wayne Gretzky, L.A.
Cam Neely, Bos.	RW	Pavel Bure, Van.
Ray Bourque, Bos.	D	Brian Leetch, N.Y.R.
Scott Stevens, N.J.	D	Al MacInnis, Cal.
John Vanbiesbrouck, Fla.	G	Dominik Hasek, Buf.

1994-95

	LW	John LeClair, Mon.-Phi.
	C	Eric Lindros, Philadelphia
	RW	Jaromir Jagr, Pittsburgh
	D	Paul Coffey, Detroit
	D	Ray Bourque, Boston
	G	Dominik Hasek, Buffalo

1995-96

	LW	Keith Tkachuk, Winnipeg
	C	Mario Lemieux, Pittsburgh
	RW	Jaromir Jagr, Pittsburgh
	D	Chris Chelios, Chicago
	D	Ray Bourque, Boston
	G	Chris Osgood, Detroit

1996-97

	LW	John LeClair, Philadelphia
	C	Mario Lemieux, Pittsburgh
	RW	Teemu Selanne, Anaheim
	D	Chris Chelios, Chicago
	D	Brian Leetch, N.Y. Rangers
	G	Dominik Hasek, Buffalo

1997-98

	LW	John LeClair, Philadelphia
	C	Peter Forsberg, Colorado
	RW	Teemu Selanne, Anaheim
	D	Rob Blake, Los Angeles
	D	Nicklas Lidstrom, Detroit
	G	Dominik Hasek, Buffalo

1998-99

	LW	Paul Kariya, Anaheim
	C	Alexei Yashin, Ottawa
	RW	Jaromir Jagr, Pittsburgh
	D	Al MacInnis, St. Louis
	D	Nicklas Lidstrom, Detroit
	G	Dominik Hasek, Buffalo

1999-2000

	LW	Paul Kariya, Anaheim
	C	Steve Yzerman, Detroit
	RW	Jaromir Jagr, Pittsburgh
	D	Nicklas Lidstrom, Detroit
	D	Chris Pronger, St. Louis
	G	Roman Turek, St. Louis

2000-01

First team		Second team
Alexei Kovalev, Pit.	LW	Patrik Elias, N.J.
Joe Sakic, Col.	C	Mario Lemieux, Pit.
Jaromir Jagr, Pit.	RW	Pavel Bure, Fla.
Rob Blake, L.A.-Col.	D	Brian Leetch, N.Y.R.
Nicklas Lidstrom, Det.	D	Chris Pronger, St.L.
Martin Brodeur, N.J.	G	Sean Burke, Pho.

HALL OF FAME

ROSTER OF MEMBERS

NOTE: Leagues other than the NHL with which Hall of Fame members are associated are denoted in parentheses. Abbreviations: **AAHA:** Alberta Amateur Hockey Association. **AHA:** Amateur Hockey Association of Canada. **CAHL:** Canadian Amateur Hockey League. **EAA:** Eaton Athletic Association. **ECAHA:** Eastern Canada Amateur Hockey Association. **ECHA:** Eastern Canada Hockey Association. **FAHL:** Federal Amateur Hockey League. **IHL:** International Professional Hockey League. **MHL:** Manitoba Hockey League. **MNSHL:** Manitoba and Northwestern Senior Hockey League. **MPHL:** Maritime Pro Hockey League. **MSHL:** Manitoba Senior Hockey League. **NHA:** National Hockey Association. **NOHA:** Northern Ontario Hockey Association. **OHA:** Ontario Hockey Association. **OPHL:** Ontario Professional Hockey League. **PCHA:** Pacific Coast Hockey Association. **WCHL:** Western Canada Hockey League. **WHA:** World Hockey Association. **WHL:** Western Hockey League. **WinHL:** Winnipeg Hockey League. **WOHA:** Western Ontario Hockey Association.

PLAYERS

Player	Elec. year/ how elected*	Pos.†	First season	Last season	Stanley Cup wins‡	Teams as player
Abel, Sid	1969/P	C	1938-39	1953-54	3	Detroit Red Wings, Chicago Blackhawks
Adams, Jack	1959/P	C	1917-18	1926-27	2	Toronto Arenas, Vancouver Millionaires (PCHA), Toronto St. Pats, Ottawa Senators
Apps, Syl	1961/P	C	1936-37	1947-48	3	Toronto Maple Leafs
Armstrong, George	1975/P	RW	1949-50	1970-71	4	Toronto Maple Leafs
Bailey, Ace	1975/P	RW	1926-27	1933-34	1	Toronto Maple Leafs
Bain, Dan	1945/P	C	1895-96	1901-02	3	Winnipeg Victorias (MHL)
Baker, Hobey	1945/P	Ro.	1910	1915	0	Princeton University, St. Nicholas
Barber, Bill	1990/P	LW	1972-73	1983-84	2	Philadelphia Flyers
Barry, Marty	1965/P	C	1927-28	1939-40	2	New York Americans, Boston Bruins, Detroit Red Wings, Montreal Canadiens
Bathgate, Andy	1978/P	RW	1952-53	1974-75	1	New York Rangers, Toronto Maple Leafs, Detroit Red Wings, Pittsburgh Penguins, Vancouver Blazers (WHA)
Bauer, Bobby	1996/V	LW	1935-36	1951-52	2	Boston Bruins
Beliveau, Jean	1972/P	C	1950-51	1970-71	10	Montreal Canadiens
Benedict, Clint	1965/P	G	1917-18	1929-30	4	Ottawa Senators, Montreal Maroons
Bentley, Doug	1964/P	LW	1939-40	1953-54	0	Chicago Blackhawks, New York Rangers
Bentley, Max	1966/P	C	1940-41	1953-54	3	Toronto Maple Leafs, New York Rangers
Blake, Toe	1966/P	LW	1932-33	1947-48	3	Montreal Maroons, Montreal Canadiens
Boivin, Leo	1986/P	D	1951-52	1969-70	0	Toronto Maple Leafs, Boston Bruins, Detroit Red Wings, Pittsburgh Penguins, Minnesota North Stars
Boon, Dickie	1952/P	D	1897	1905	2	Montreal Monarchs, Montreal AAA (CAHL), Montreal Wanderers (FAHL)
Bossy, Mike	1991/P	RW	1977-78	1986-87	4	New York Islanders
Bouchard, Butch	1966/P	D	1941-42	1955-56	4	Montreal Canadiens
Boucher, Frank	1958/P	C	1921-22	1943-44	2	Ottawa Senators, Vancouver Maroons, New York Rangers
Boucher, George	1960/P	F/D	1915-16	1931-32	4	Ottawa Senators, Montreal Maroons, Chicago Blackhawks
Bower, Johnny	1976/P	G	1953-54	1969-70	0	New York Rangers, Toronto Maple Leafs
Bowie, Russell	1945/P	C	1898-99	1907-08	1	Montreal Victorias
Brimsek, Frank	1966/P	G	1938-39	1951-52	0	Boston Bruins, Chicago Blackhawks
Broadbent, Punch	1962/P	RW	1912-13	1928-29	4	Ottawa Senators, Montreal Maroons, New York Americans
Broda, Turk	1967/P	G	1936-37	1928-29	0	Toronto Maple Leafs
Bucyk, John	1981/P	LW	1955-56	1977-78	2	Detroit Red Wings, Boston Bruins
Burch, Billy	1974/P	C	1922-23	1932-33	0	Hamilton Tigers, New York Americans, Chicago Blackhawks
Cameron, Harry	1962/P	D	1912-13	1925-26	3	Toronto Blueshirts, Toronto Arenas, Montreal Wanderers, Ottawa Senators, Toronto St. Pats, Montreal Canadiens, Saskatoon (WCHL)
Cheevers, Gary	1985/P	G	1961-62	1979-80	2	Toronto Maple Leafs, Boston Bruins, Cleveland Crusaders (WHA)
Clancy, King	1958/P	D	1921-22	1936-37	3	Ottawa Senators, Toronto Maple Leafs
Clapper, Dit	1947/P	RW	1927-28	1946-47	3	Boston Bruins
Clarke, Bobby	1987/P	C	1969-70	1983-84	2	Philadelphia Flyers
Cleghorn, Sprague	1958/P	D	1909-10	1927-28	3	New York Crescents, Renfrew Creamery Kings (NHA), Montreal Wanderers, Ottawa Senators, Toronto St. Pats, Toronto St. Pats, Montreal Canadiens, Boston Bruins
Colville, Neil	1967/P	C/D	1935-36	1948-49	1	New York Rangers
Conacher, Charlie	1961/P	RW	1929-30	1940-41	1	Toronto Maple Leafs, Detroit Red Wings, New York Americans
Conacher, Lionel	1994/V	D	1925-26	1936-37	2	Pittsburgh Pirates, New York Americans, Montreal Maroons, Chicago Blackhawks
Conacher, Roy	1998/V	LW	1938-39	1951-52	2	Boston Bruins, Detroit Red Wings, Chicago Blackhawks
Connell, Alex	1958/P	G	1924-25	1936-37	2	Ottawa Senators, Detroit Red Wings, New York Americans, Montreal Maroons
Cook, Bill	1952/P	RW	1921-22	1936-37	2	Saskatoon, New York Rangers

Player	Elec. year/ how elected*	Pos.†	First season	Last season	Stanley Cup wins‡	Teams as player
Cook, Bun	1995/V	LW	1926-27	1936-37	2	New York Rangers, Boston Bruins
Coulter, Art	1974/P	D	1931-32	1941-42	2	Chicago Blackhawks, New York Rangers
Cournoyer, Yvan	1982/P	RW	1963-64	1978-79	10	Montreal Canadiens
Cowley, Bill	1968/P	C	1934-35	1946-47	2	St. Louis Eagles, Boston Bruins
Crawford, Rusty	1962/P	LW	1912-13	1925-26	1	Quebec Bulldogs, Ottawa Senators, Toronto Arenas, Saskatoon (WCHL), Calgary (WCHL), Vancouver (WHL)
Darragh, Jack	1962/P	RW	1910-11	1923-24	4	Ottawa Senators
Davidson, Scotty	1950/P	RW	1912-13	1913-14	0	Toronto (NHA)
Day, Hap	1961/P	LW	1924-25	1937-38	1	Toronto St. Pats, Toronto Maple Leafs, New York Americans
Delvecchio, Alex	1977/P	C	1950-51	1973-74	3	Detroit Red Wings
Denneny, Cy	1959/P	LW	1914-15	1928-29	5	Toronto Shamrocks (NHA), Toronto Arenas (NHA), Ottawa Senators, Boston Bruins
Dionne, Marcel	1992/P	C	1971-72	1988-89	0	Detroit Red Wings, Los Angeles Kings, New York Rangers
Drillon, Gord	1975/P	LW	1936-37	1942-43	1	Toronto Maple Leafs, Montreal Canadiens
Drinkwater, Graham	1950/P	F/D	1892-93	1898-99	5	Montreal Victorias
Dryden, Ken	1983/P	G	1970-71	1978-79	6	Montreal Canadiens
Dumart, Woody	1992/V	LW	1935-36	1953-54	2	Boston Bruins
Dunderdale, Tommy	1974/P	C	1906-07	1923-24	0	Winnipeg Maple Leafs (MHL), Montreal Shamrocks (NHA), Quebec Bulldogs (NHA), Victoria (PCHA), Portland (PCHA), Saskatoon (WCHL), Edmonton (WCHL)
Durnan, Bill	1964/P	G	1943-44	1949-50	2	Montreal Canadiens
Dutton, Red	1958/P	D	1921-22	1935-36	0	Calgary Tigers (WCHL), Montreal Maroons, New York Americans
Dye, Babe	1970/P	RW	1919-20	1930-31	1	Toronto St. Pats, Hamilton Tigers, Chicago Blackhawks, New York Americans, Toronto Maple Leafs
Esposito, Phil	1984/P	C	1963-64	1980-81	2	Chicago Blackhawks, Boston Bruins, New York Rangers
Esposito, Tony	1988/P	G	1968-69	1983-84	1	Montreal Canadiens, Chicago Blackhawks
Farrell, Arthur	1965/P	F	1896-97	1900-01	2	Montreal Shamrocks (AHA/CAHL)
Fetisov, Viacheslav	2001/P	D	1974-75	1997-98	2	CSKA Moscow, New Jersey Devils, Detroit Red Wings
Flaman, Fern	1990/V	D	1944-45	1960-61	1	Boston Bruins, Toronto Maple Leafs
Foyston, Frank	1958/P	C	1912-13	1927-28	3	Toronto Blueshirts (NHA), Seattle Metropolitans (PCHA), Victoria Cougars (WCHL/WHL), Detroit Cougars
Fredrickson, Frank	1958/P	C	1920-21	1930-31	1	Victoria Aristocrats (PCHA), Victoria Cougars (PCHA/WCHL/WHL), Detroit Cougars, Boston Bruins, Pittsburgh Pirates, Detroit Falcons
Gadsby, Bill	1970/P	D	1946-47	1965-66	0	Chicago Blackhawks, New York Rangers, Detroit Red Wings
Gainey, Bob	1992/P	LW	1973-74	1988-89	5	Montreal Canadiens
Gardiner, Chuck	1945/P	G	1927-28	1933-34	1	Chicago Blackhawks
Gardiner, Herb	1958/P	D	1921-22	1928-29	0	Calgary Tigers (WCHL), Montreal Canadiens, Chicago Blackhawks
Gardner, Jimmy	1962/P	LW	1900-01	1914-15	3	Montreal Hockey Club (CAHL), Montreal Wanderers (FAHL/ECAHA/NHA), Calumet (IHL), Pittsburgh (IHL), Montreal Shamrocks (ECAHA),New Westminster Royals (PCHA), Montreal Canadiens (NHA)
Gartner, Mike	2001/P	RW	1978-79	1997-98	0	Cincinnati Stingers (WHA), Washington Capitals, Minnesota North Stars, New York Rangers, Toronto Maple Leafs, Phoenix Coyotes
Geoffrion, Boom Boom	1972/P	RW	1950-51	1967-68	6	Montreal Canadiens, New York Rangers
Gerard, Eddie	1945/P	F/D	1913-14	1922-23	4	Ottawa Senators (NHA/NHL), Toronto St. Pats
Giacomin, Eddie	1987/P	G	1965-66	1977-78	0	New York Rangers, Detroit Red Wings
Gilbert, Rod	1982/P	RW	1960-61	1977-78	0	New York Rangers
Gilmour, Billy	1962/P	RW	1902-03	1915-16	5	Ottawa Silver Seven (CAHL/FAHL/ECAHA), Montreal Victorias (ECAHA), Ottawa Senators (ECHA/NHA)
Goheen, Moose	1952/P	D	1914	1918	0	St. Paul Athletic Club, 1920 U.S. Olympic Team
Goodfellow, Ebbie	1963/P	C	1929-30	1942-43	3	Detroit Cougars, Detroit Falcons, Detroit Red Wings
Goulet, Michel	1998/P	LW	1978-79	1993-94	0	Birmingham Bulls (WHA), Quebec Nordiques, Chicago Blackhawks
Grant, Mike	1950/P	D	1893-94	1901-02	5	Montreal Victorias (AHA/CAHL), Montreal Shamrocks (CAHL)
Green, Shorty	1962/P	RW	1923-24	1926-27	0	Hamilton Tigers, New York Americans
Gretzky, Wayne	1999/P	C	1978-79	1998-99	4	Indianapolis Racers (WHA), Edmonton (WHA/NHL), Los Angeles Kings, St. Louis Blues, New York Rangers
Griffis, Si	1950/P	Ro./D	1902-03	1918-19	2	Rat Portage Thistles (MNSHL), Kenora Thistles (MSHL), Vancouver Millionaires (PCHA)
Hainsworth, George	1961/P	G	1923-24	1936-37	2	Saskatoon Crescents (WCHL/WHL), Montreal Canadiens
Hall, Glenn	1975/P	G	1952-53	1970-71	1	Detriot Red Wings, Chicago Blackhawks, St. Louis Blues
Hall, Joe	1961/P	F/D	1903-04	1918-19	2	Winnipeg (MSHL), Quebec Bulldogs (ECAHA/NHA), Brandon (MHL), Montreal (ECAHA), Montreal Shamrocks (ECAHA/NHA), Montreal Wanderers (ECHA), Montreal Canadiens

Player	Elec. year/ how elected*	Pos.†	First season	Last season	Stanley Cup wins‡	Teams as player
Harvey, Doug	1973/P	D	1947-48	1968-69	6	Montreal Canadiens, New York Rangers, Detroit Red Wings, St. Louis Blues
Hawerchuk, Dale	2001/P	C	1981-82	1996-97	0	Winnipeg Jets, Buffalo Sabres, St. Louis Blues, Philadelphia Flyers
Hay, George	1958/P	LW	1921-22	1933-34	0	Regina Capitals (WCHL), Portland Rosebuds (WHL), Chicago Blackhawks, Detroit Cougars, Detroit Falcons, Detroit Red Wings
Hern, Riley	1962/P	G	1906-07	1910-11	3	Montreal Wanderers (ECAHA/ECHA/NHA)
Hextall, Bryan	1969/P	RW	1936-37	1947-48	1	New York Rangers
Holmes, Hap	1972/P	G	1912-13	1927-28	0	Toronto Blueshirts (NHA), Seattle Metropolitans (PCHA), Toronto Arenas, Victoria Cougars, Detroit Cougars
Hooper, Tom	1962/P	F	1904-05	1907-08	2	Rat Portage Thistles (MNSHL), Kenora Thistles (SHL), Montreal Wanderers (ECAHA), Montreal (ECAHA)
Horner, Red	1965/P	D	1928-29	1939-40	1	Toronto Maple Leafs
Horton, Tim	1977/P	D	1949-50	1973-74	4	Toronto Maple Leafs, New York Rangers, Pittsburgh Penguins, Buffalo Sabres
Howe, Gordie	1972/P	RW	1946-47	1979-80	4	Detroit Red Wings, Houston Aeros (WHA), New England Whalers (WHA), Hartford Whalers
Howe, Syd	1965/P	F/D	1929-30	1945-46	3	Ottawa Senators, Philadelphia Quakers, Toronto Maple Leafs, St. Louis Eagles, Detroit Red Wings
Howell, Harry	1979/P	D	1952-53	1975-76	0	New York Rangers, Oakland Seals, California Golden Seals, New York Golden Blades/Jersey Knights (WHA), San Diego Mariners (WHA), Calgary Cowboys (WHA)
Hull, Bobby	1983/P	LW	1957-58	1979-80	1	Chicago Blackhawks, Winnipeg Jets (WHA/NHL), Hartford Whalers
Hutton, Bouse	1962/P	G	1898-99	1903-04	1	Ottawa Silver Seven (CAHL)
Hyland, Harry	1962/P	RW	1908-09	1917-18	1	Montreal Shamrocks (ECHA), Montreal Wanderers (NHA), New Westminster Royals (PCHA), Ottawa Senators
Irvin, Dick	1958/P	C	1916-17	1928-29	0	Portland Rosebuds (PCHA), Regina Capitals (WCHL), Chicago Blackhawks
Jackson, Busher	1971/P	LW	1929-30	1943-44	1	Toronto Maple Leafs, New York Americans, Boston Bruins
Johnson, Ching	1958/P	D	1926-27	1937-38	2	New York Rangers, New York Americans
Johnson, Moose	1952/P	LW/D	1903-04	1921-22	4	Montreal AAA (CAHL), Montreal Wanderers (ECAHA/ECHA/NHA), New Westminster Royals (PCHA), Portland Rosebuds (PCHA), Victoria Aristocrats (PCHA)
Johnson, Tom	1970/P	D	1947-48	1964-65	6	Montreal Canadiens, Boston Bruins
Joliat, Aurel	1947/P	LW	1922-23	1937-38	3	Montreal Canadiens
Keats, Duke	1958/P	C	1915-16	1928-29	0	Toronto Arenas (NHA), Edmonton Eskimos (WCHL/WHL), Detroit Cougars, Chicago Blackhawks
Kelly, Red	1969/P	C	1947-48	1966-67	8	Detroit Red Wings, Toronto Maple Leafs
Kennedy, Ted	1966/P	C	1942-43	1956-57	5	Toronto Maple Leafs
Keon, Dave	1986/P	C	1960-61	1981-82	4	Toronto Maple Leafs, Minnesota Fighting Saints (WHA), Indianapolis Racers (WHA), New England Whalers (WHA), Hartford Whalers
Kurri, Jari	2001/P	C/RW	1980-81	1997-98	5	Edmonton Oilers, Los Angeles Kings, New York Rangers, Mighty Ducks of Anaheim, Colorado Avalanche
Lach, Elmer	1966/P	C	1940-41	1953-54	3	Montreal Canadiens
Lafleur, Guy	1988/P	RW	1971-72	1990-91	5	Montreal Canadiens, New York Rangers, Quebec Nordiques
Lalonde, Newsy	1950/P	C/Ro.	1904-05	1926-27	1	Cornwall (FAHL), Portage La Prairie (MHL), Toronto (OPHL), Montreal Canadiens (NHA/NHL), Renfrew Creamery Kings (NHA), Vancouver Millionaires (PCHA), Saskatoon Sheiks (WCHL), Saskatoon Crescents (WCHL/WHL), New York Americans
Laperriere, Jacques	1987/P	D	1962-63	1973-74	6	Montreal Canadiens
Lapointe, Guy	1993/P	D	1968-69	1983-84	6	Montreal Canadiens, St. Louis Blues, Boston Bruins
Laprade, Edgar	1993/V	C	1945-46	1954-55	0	New York Rangers
Laviolette, Jack	1962/P	D/LW	1903-04	1917-18	1	Montreal Nationals (FAHL), Montreal Shamrocks (ECAHA/ECHA), Montreal Canadiens (NHA/NHL)
Lehman, Hughie	1958/P	G	1908-09	1927-28	1	Berlin Dutchmen (OPHL), Galt (OPHL), New Westminster Royals (PCHA), Vancouver Millionaires, Vancouver Maroons, Chicago Blackhawks
Lemaire, Jacques	1984/P	C	1967-68	1978-79	8	Montreal Canadiens
Lemieux, Mario	1997/P	C	1984-85	1996-97	2	Pittsburgh Penguins
LeSueur, Percy	1961/P	G	1905-06	1915-16	3	Smith Falls (FAHL), Ottawa Senators (ECAHA/ECHA/NHA), Toronto Shamrocks (NHA), Toronto Blueshirts (NHA)
Lewis, Herbie	1989/V	LW	1928-29	1938-39	2	Detroit Cougars, Detroit Falcons, Detroit Red Wings
Lindsay, Ted	1966/P	LW	1944-45	1964-65	4	Detroit Red Wings, Chicago Blackhawks

Player	Elec. year/ how elected*	Pos.†	First season	Last season	Stanley Cup wins‡	Teams as player
Lumley, Harry	1980/P	G	1943-44	1959-60	1	Detroit Red Wings, New York Rangers, Chicago Blackhawks, Toronto Maple Leafs, Boston Bruins
MacKay, Mickey	1952/P	C/Ro.	1914-15	1929-30	1	Vancouver Millionaires (PCHA), Vancouver Maroons (PCHA/WCHL/WHL), Chicago Blackhawks, Pittsburgh Pirates, Boston Bruins
Mahovlich, Frank	1981/P	LW	1956-57	1977-78	6	Toronto Maple Leafs, Detroit Red Wings, Montreal Canadiens, Toronto Toros (WHA), Birmingham Bulls (WHA)
Malone, Joe	1950/P	C/LW	1908-09	1923-24	3	Quebec (ECHA), Waterloo (OPHL), Quebec Bulldogs (NHA/NHL), Montreal Canadiens, Hamilton Tigers
Mantha, Sylvio	1960/P	D	1923-24	1936-37	3	Montreal Canadiens, Boston Bruins
Marshall, Jack	1965/P	C/D	1900-01	1916-17	6	Winnipeg Victorias, Montreal AAA (CAHL), Montreal Wanderers (FAHL/ECAHA/NHA), Montreal Montagnards (FAHL), Montreal Shamrocks (ECAHA/ECHA), Toronto Blueshirts (NHA)
Maxwell, Fred	1962/P	Ro.	1914	1925	0	Winnipeg Monarchs (MSHL), Winnipeg Falcons (MSHL)
McDonald, Lanny	1992/P	RW	1973-74	1988-89	1	Toronto Maple Leafs, Colorado Rockies, Calgary Flames
McGee, Frank	1945/P	C/Ro.	1902-03	1905-06	4	Ottawa Silver Seven
McGimsie, Billy	1962/P	F	1902-03	1906-07	1	Rat Portage Thistles (MNSHL/MSHL), Kenora Thistles (MSHL)
McNamara, George	1958/P	D	1907-08	1916-17	1	Montreal Shamrocks (ECAHA/ECHA), Waterloo (OPHL), Toronto Tecumsehs (NHA), Toronto Ontarios (NHA), Toronto Blueshirts (NHA), Toronto Shamrocks (NHA), 228th Battalion (NHA)
Mikita, Stan	1983/P	C	1958-59	1979-80	1	Chicago Blackhawks
Moore, Dickie	1974/P	RW	1951-52	1967-68	6	Montreal Canadiens, Toronto Maple Leafs, St. Louis Blues
Moran, Paddy	1958/P	G	1901-02	1916-17	2	Quebec Bulldogs (CAHL/ECAHA/ECHA/NHA), Haileybury (NHA)
Morenz, Howie	1945/P	C	1923-24	1936-37	3	Montreal Canadiens, Chicago Blackhawks, New York Rangers
Mosienko, Bill	1965/P	RW	1941-42	1954-55	0	Chicago Blackhawks
Mullen, Joe	2000/P	RW	1979-80	1996-97	3	St. Louis Blues, Calgary Flames, Pittsburgh Penguins, Boston Bruins
Nighbor, Frank	1947/P	LW/C	1912-13	1929-30	5	Toronto Blueshirts (NHA), Vancouver Millionaires, (PCHA), Ottawa Senators, Toronto Maple Leafs
Noble, Reg	1962/P	LW/C/D	1916-17	1932-33	3	Toronto Blueshirts (NHA), Montreal Canadiens (NHA), Toronto Arenas, Toronto St. Pats, Montreal Maroons, Detroit Cougars, Detroit Falcons, Detroit Red Wings
O'Connor, Buddy	1988/V	C	1941-42	1950-51	2	Montreal Canadiens, New York Rangers
Oliver, Harry	1967/P	F	1921-22	1936-37	1	Calgary Tigers (WCHL/WHL), Boston Bruins, New York Americans
Olmstead, Bert	1985/P	LW	1948-49	1961-62	5	Chicago Blackhawks, Montreal Canadiens, Toronto Maple Leafs
Orr, Bobby	1979/P	D	1966-67	1978-79	2	Boston Bruins, Chicago Blackhawks
Parent, Bernie	1984/P	G	1965-66	1978-79	2	Boston Bruins, Philadelphia Flyers, Toronto Maple Leafs, Philadelphia Blazers (WHA)
Park, Brad	1988/P	D	1968-69	1984-85	0	New York Rangers, Boston Bruins, Detroit Red Wings
Patrick, Lester	1947/P	D/Ro./G	1903-04	1926-27	3	Brandon, Westmount (CAHL), Montreal Wanderers (ECAHA), Edmonton Eskimos (AAHA), Renfrew Millionaires (NHA), Victoria Aristocrats (PCHA), Spokane Canaries (PCHA), Seattle Metropolitans (PCHA), Seattle Metropolitans(PCHA), Victoria Cougars (WHA), New York Rangers
Patrick, Lynn	1980/P	LW	1934-35	1945-46	1	New York Rangers
Perreault, Gilbert	1990/P	C	1970-71	1986-87	0	Buffalo Sabres
Phillips, Tommy	1945/P	LW	1902-03	1911-12	1	Montreal AAA (CAHL), Toronto Marlboros (OHA), Rat Portage Thistles, Kenora Thistles (MHL), Ottawa Ottawa Senators (ECAHA), Edmonton Eskimos (AAHA), Vancouver Millionaires (PCHA)
Pilote, Pierre	1975/P	D	1955-56	1968-69	1	Chicago Blackhawks, Toronto Maple Leafs
Pitre, Didier	1962/P	D/Ro.	1903-04	1922-23	0	Montreal Nationals (FAHL/CAHL), Montreal Shamrocks (ECAHA), Edmonton Eskimos (AAHA), Montreal Canadiens (NHA/NHL), Vancouver Millionaires (PCHA)
Plante, Jacques	1978/P	G	1952-53	1974-75	6	Montreal Canadiens, New York Rangers, St. Louis Blues, Toronto Maple Leafs, Boston Bruins, Edmonton Oilers
Potvin, Denis	1991/P	D	1973-74	1987-88	4	New York Islanders
Pratt, Babe	1966/P	D	1935-36	1946-47	2	New York Rangers, Toronto Maple Leafs, Boston Bruins
Primeau, Joe	1963/P	C	1927-28	1935-36	1	Toronto Maple Leafs
Pronovost, Marcel	1978/P	D	1950-51	1966-67	5	Detroit Red Wings, Toronto Maple Leafs
Pulford, Bob	1991/P	LW	1956-57	1971-72	4	Toronto Maple Leafs, Los Angeles Kings
Pulford, Harvey	1945/P	D	1893-94	1907-08	4	Ottawa Silver Seven/Senators (AHA/CAHL/FAHL/ECAHA)

Player	Elec. year/ how elected*	Pos.†	First season	Last season	Stanley Cup wins‡	Teams as player
Quackenbush, Bill	1976/P	D	1942-43	1955-56	0	Detroit Red Wings, Boston Bruins
Rankin, Frank	1961/P	Ro.	1906	1914	0	Stratford (OHA), Eatons (EAA), Toronto St. Michaels (OHA)
Ratelle, Jean	1985/P	C	1960-61	1980-81	0	New York Rangers, Boston Bruins
Rayner, Chuck	1973/P	G	1940-41	1952-53	0	New York Americans, New York Rangers
Reardon, Ken	1966/P	D	1940-41	1949-50	1	Montreal Canadiens
Richard, Henri	1979/P	C	1955-56	1974-75	11	Montreal Canadiens
Richard, Rocket	1961/P	RW	1942-43	1959-60	8	Montreal Canadiens
Richardson, George	1950/P		1906	1912	0	14th Regiment, Queen's University
Roberts, Gordon	1971/P	LW	1909-10	1919-20	0	Ottawa Senators (NHA), Montreal Wanderers (NHA), Vancouver Millionaires (PCHA), Seattle Metropolitans (PCHA)
Robinson, Larry	1995/P	D	1972-73	1991-92	6	Montreal Canadiens, Los Angeles Kings
Ross, Art	1945/P	D	1904-05	1917-18	2	Westmount (CAHL), Brandon (MHL), Kenora Thistles (MHL), Montreal Wanderers (ECAHA/ECHA/NHA/NHL), Haileybury (NHA), Ottawa Senators (NHA)
Russell, Blair	1965/P	RW/C	1899-00	1907-08	0	Montreal Victorias (CAHL/ECAHA)
Russell, Ernie	1965/P	Ro./C	1904-05	1913-14	4	Montreal Winged Wheelers (CAHL), Montreal Wanderers (ECAHA/NHA)
Ruttan, Jack	1962/P		1905	1913	0	Armstrong's Point, Rustler, St. John's College, Manitoba Varsity (WSHL), Winnipeg (WinHL)
Salming, Borje	1996/P	D	1973-74	1989-90	0	Toronto Maple Leafs, Detroit Red Wings
Savard, Dennis	2000/P	C	1980-81	1996-97	1	Chicago Blackhawks, Montreal Canadiens, Tampa Bay Lightning
Savard, Serge	1986/P	D	1966-67	1982-83	7	Montreal Canadiens, Winnipeg Jets
Sawchuk, Terry	1971/P	G	1949-50	1969-70	4	Detroit Red Wings, Boston Bruins, Toronto Maple Leafs, Los Angeles Kings, New York Rangers
Scanlan, Fred	1965/P	F	1897-98	1902-03	3	Montreal Shamrocks (AHA/CAHL), Winnipeg Victorias (MSHL)
Schmidt, Milt	1961/P	C	1936-37	1954-55	2	Boston Bruins
Schriner, Sweeney	1962/P	LW	1934-35	1945-46	2	New York Americans, Toronto Maple Leafs
Seibert, Earl	1963/P	D	1931-32	1945-46	2	New York Rangers, Chicago Blackhawks, Detroit Red Wings
Seibert, Oliver	1961/P	D	1900	1906	0	Berlin Rangers (WOHA), Houghton (IHL), Guelph (OPHL), London (OPHL)
Shore, Eddie	1947/P	D	1924-25	1939-40	2	Regina Capitals (WCHL), Edmonton Eskimos (WHL), Boston Bruins, New York Americans
Shutt, Steve	1993/P	LW	1972-73	1984-85	5	Montreal Canadiens, Los Angeles Kings
Siebert, Babe	1964/P	LW/D	1925-26	1938-39	2	Montreal Maroons, New York Rangers, Boston Bruins, Montreal Canadiens
Simpson, Joe	1962/P	D	1921-22	1930-31	0	Edmonton Eskimos (WCHL), New York Americans
Sittler, Darryl	1989/P	C	1970-71	1984-85	0	Toronto Maple Leafs, Philadelphia Flyers, Detroit Red Wings
Smith, Alf	1962/P	RW	1894-95	1907-08	4	Ottawa Silver Seven/Senators (AHA/CAHL/FAHL/ECAHA), Kenora Thistles (MHL)
Smith, Billy	1993/P	G	1971-72	1988-89	4	Los Angeles Kings, New York Islanders
Smith, Clint	1991/V	C	1936-37	1946-47	1	New York Rangers, Chicago Blackhawks
Smith, Hooley	1972/P	RW	1924-25	1940-41	2	1924 Canadian Olympic Team, Ottawa Senators, Montreal Maroons, Boston Bruins, New York Americans
Smith, Tommy	1973/P	LW/C	1905-06	1919-20	1	Ottawa Vics (FAHL), Ottawa Senators (ECAHA), Brantford (OPHL), Moncton (MPHL), Quebec Bulldogs (NHA/NHL), Toronto Ontarios (NHA), Montreal Canadiens (NHA)
Stanley, Allan	1981/P	D	1948-49	1968-69	4	New York Rangers, Chicago Blackhawks, Boston Bruins, Toronto Maple Leafs, Philadelphia Flyers
Stanley, Barney	1962/P	RW/D	1914-15	1925-26	1	Vancouver Millionaires (PCHA), Calgary Tigers (WCHL), Regina Capitals (WCHL), Edmonton Eskimos (WCHL/WHL)
Stastny, Peter	1998/P	C	1980-81	1994-95	0	Quebec Nordiques, New Jersey Devils, St. Louis Blues
Stewart, Black Jack	1964/P	D	1938-39	1951-52	2	Detroit Red Wings, Chicago Blackhawks
Stewart, Nels	1962/P	C	1925-26	1939-40	1	Montreal Maroons, Boston Bruins, New York Americans, Boston Bruins
Stuart, Bruce	1961/P	F	1989-99	1910-11	3	Ottawa Senators (CAHL/ECHA/NHA), Quebec Bulldogs (CAHL), Pittsburgh (IHL), Houghton (IHL), Portage Lake (IHL), Montreal Wanderers (ECAHA)
Stuart, Hod	1945/P	D	1898-99	1906-07	1	Ottawa Senators, Quebec Bulldogs, Calumet (IHL), Pittsburgh (IHL), Montreal Wanderers
Taylor, Cyclone	1947/P	D/Ro./C	1907-08	1922-23	2	Ottawa Senators (ECAHA/ECHA), Renfrew Creamery Kings (NHA), Vancouver Maroons (PCHA)
Thompson, Tiny	1959/P	G	1928-29	1939-40	1	Boston Bruins, Detroit Red Wings
Tretiak, Vladislav	1989/P	G	1969	1984	0	Central Red Army
Trihey, Harry	1950/P	C	1896-97	1900-01	2	Montreal Shamrocks (AHA/CAHL)
Trottier, Bryan	1997/P	C	1975-76	1993-94	6	New York Islanders, Pittsburgh Penguins

Player	Elec. year/ how elected*	Pos.†	First season	Last season	Stanley Cup wins‡	Teams as player
Ullman, Norm	1982/P	C	1955-56	1976-77	0	Detroit Red Wings, Toronto Maple Leafs, Edmonton Oilers (WHA)
Vezina, Georges	1945/P	G	1910-11	1925-26	2	Montreal Canadiens (NHA/NHL)
Walker, Jack	1960/P	LW/Ro.	1910-11	1927-28	3	Port Arthur, Toronto Blueshirts (NHA), Seattle Metropolitans (PCHA), Victoria Cougars (WCHL/WHL), Detroit Cougars
Walsh, Marty	1962/P	C	1905-06	1911-12	2	Queens University (OHA), Ottawa Senators (ECAHA/ECHA/NHA)
Watson, Harry E.	1962/P	C	1915	1931	0	St. Andrews (OHA), Aura Lee Juniors (OHA), Toronto Dentals (OHA), Toronto Granites (OHA), 1924 Canadian Olympic Team, Toronto National Sea Fleas (OHA)
Watson, Harry P.	1994/V	LW	1941-42	1956-57	5	Brooklyn Americans, Detroit Red Wings, Toronto Maple Leafs, Chicago Blackhawks
Weiland, Cooney	1971/P	C	1928-29	1938-39	0	Boston Bruins, Ottawa Senators, Detroit Red Wings
Westwick, Harry	1962/P	Ro.	1894-95	1907-08	4	Ottawa Senators/Silver Seven (AHA/CAHL/FAHL/ECAHA/), Kenora Thistles
Whitcroft, Frederick	1962/P	Ro.	1906-07	1909-10	0	Kenora Thistles (MSHL), Edmonton Eskimos (AAHA), Renfrew Millionaires (NHA)
Wilson, Gord	1962/P	D	1918	1933	0	Port Arthur War Veterans (OHA), Iroquois Falls (NOHA), Port Arthur Bearcats (OHA)
Worsley, Gump	1980/P	G	1952-53	1973-74	4	New York Rangers, Montreal Canadiens, Minnesota North Stars
Worters, Roy	1969/P	G	1925-26	1936-37	0	Pittsburgh Pirates, New York Americans, Montreal Canadiens

*Denotes whether enshrinee was elected by regular election (P) or veterans committee (V).
†Primary positions played during career: C—center; D—defense; G—goaltender; LW—left wing; Ro.—rover; RW—right wing.
‡Stanley Cup wins column refers to wins as a player in the players section and as a coach in the coaches section.

BUILDERS

Builder	Election year	Stanley Cup wins‡	Designation for induction
Adams, Charles F.	1960		Founder, Boston Bruins (1924)
Adams, Weston W.	1972		President and chairman, Boston Bruins(1936-69)
Aheam, Frank	1962		Owner, Ottawa Senators (1924-34)
Ahearne, Bunny	1977		President, International Hockey Federation (1957-75)
Allan, Sir Montagu	1945		Donator of Allan Cup, awarded anually to senior amateur champion of Canada (1908)
Allen, Keith	1992	0	Coach, Philadelphia Flyers (1967-68 and 1968-69); general manager and executive, Philadelphia Flyers (1966-present)
Arbour, Al	1996	4	Coach, St. Louis Blues, New York Islanders, 1970-71, 1971-72 to 1972-73, 1973-74 through 1985-86 and 1988-89 to 1993-94; vice president of hockey operations and consultant, New York Islanders (1994 to 1998)
Ballard, Harold	1977		Owner and chief executive, Toronto Maple Leafs (1961-90)
Bauer, Father David	1989		Developer and coach of first Canadian National Hockey Team
Bickell, J.P.	1978		First president and chairman of the board, Toronto Maple Leafs (1927-51)
Bowman, Scotty	1991	8	Coach, St. Louis Blues, Montreal Canadiens, Buffalo Sabres, Pittsburgh Penguins, Detroit Red Wings (1967-68 through 1979-80, 1981-82 through 1986-87 and 1991-92 through present); general manager, St. Louis Blues, Buffalo Sabres (1969-70, 1970-71 and 1979-80 through 1986-87)
Brown, George V.	1961		U.S. hockey pioneer; organizer, Boston Athletic Association hockey team (1910); general manager, Boston Arena and Boston Garden (1934-37)
Brown, Walter A.	1962		Co-owner and president, Boston Bruins (1951-64); general manager, Boston Gardens
Buckland, Frank	1975		Amateur hockey coach and manager; president and treasurer, Ontario Hockey Association
Bush, Walter L.	2000		President, Minnesota North Stars (1967-1978); president, USA Hockey; vice president, International Ice Hockey Federation
Butterfield, Jack	1980		President, American Hockey League
Calder, Frank	1947		First president, National Hockey League (1917-43)
Campbell, Angus	1964		First president, Northern Ontario Hockey Association (1919); executive, Ontario Hockey Association
Campbell, Clarence	1966		Referee (1929-40); president, National Hockey League (1946-77)
Cattarinich, Joseph	1977		General manager, Montreal Canadiens (1909-10); co-owner, Montreal Canadiens (1921-35)
Dandurand, Leo	1963	1	Co-owner, Montreal Canadiens (1921-35); coach, Montreal Canadiens (1920-21 through 1924-25 and 1934-35); general manager, Montreal Canadiens (1920-21 through 1934-35)
Dilio, Frank	1964		Secretary and president, Junior Amateur Hockey Association; registrar and secretary, Quebec Amateur Hockey League (1943-62)
Dudley, George	1958		President, Canadian Amateur Hockey Association (1940-42); treasurer, Ontario Hockey Association; president, International Ice Hockey Federation

Builder	Election year	Stanley Cup wins‡	Designation for induction
Dunn, Jimmy	1968		President, Manitoba Amateur Hockey Association (1945-51); president, Canadian Amateur Hockey Association
Francis, Emile	1982	0	General manager, New York Rangers,St. Louis Blues, Hartford Whalers (1964-65 through 1988-89); coach, New York Rangers, St. Louis Blues (1965-66 through 1974-75, 1976-77, 1981-82 and 1982-83); president, Hartford Whalers (1983-1993)
Gibson, Jack	1976		Organizer, International League (1903-07), world's first professional hockey league
Gorman, Tommy	1963	2	Co-founder, National Hockey League (1917); coach, Ottawa Senators, New York Americans, Chicago Blackhawks, Montreal Maroons (1917-1938); general manager, Montreal Canadiens (1941-42 through 1945-46)
Griffiths, Frank	1993		Chairman, Vancouver Canucks (1974 through 1994)
Hanley, Bill	1986		Secretary-manager, Ontario Hockey Association
Hay, Charles	1974		Coordinator, 1972 series between Canada and Soviet Union; president, Hockey Canada
Hendy, Jim	1968		President, United States Hockey League; general manager, Cleveland Barons (AHL); publisher, Hockey Guide (1933-51)
Hewitt, Foster	1965		Hockey broadcaster
Hewitt, William	1947		Sports editor, Toronto Star; secretary, Ontario Hockey Association (1903-61); registrar and treasurer, Canadian Amateur Hockey Association
Hume, Fred	1962		Co-developer, Western Hockey League, New Westminster Royals
Imlach, Punch	1984	4	Coach, Toronto Maple Leafs, Buffalo Sabres (1958-59 through 1968-69, 1970-71, 1971-72 and 1979-80); general manager, Toronto Maple Leafs, Buffalo Sabres (1958-59 through 1968-69, 1970-71 through 1977-78 and 1979-80 through 1981-82)
Ivan, Tommy	1974	3	Coach, Detroit Red Wings, Chicago Blackhawks (1947-48 through 1953-54, 1956-57 and 1957-58); general manager, Chicago Blackhawks (1954-55 through 1976-77)
Jennings, Bill	1975		President, New York Rangers
Johnson, Bob	1992	1	Coach, Calgary Flames, Pittsburgh Penguins (1982-83 through 1986-87, 1990-91 and 1991-92)
Juckes, Gordon	1979		President, Saskatchewan Amateur Hockey Association; director, Canadian Amateur Hockey Association (1960-78)
Kilpatrick,General J.R.	1960		President, New York Rangers, Madison Square Garden; director, NHL Players' Pension Society; NHL Governor
Knox III, Seymour	1993		Chairman and president, Buffalo Sabres (1970-71 through 1995-96)
Leader, Al	1969		President, Western Hockey League (1944-69)
LeBel, Bob	1970		Founder and president, Interprovincial Senior League (1944-47); president, Quebec Amateur Hockey League, Canadian Amateur Hockey Association, International Ice Hockey Federation (1955-63)
Lockhart, Tommy	1965		Organizer and president, Eastern Amateur Hockey League, Amateur Hockey Association of the United States; business manager, New York Rangers
Loicq, Paul	1961		President and referee, International Ice Hockey Federation (1922-47)
Mariucci, John	1985		Minnesota hockey pioneer; coach, 1956 U.S. Olympic Team
Mathers, Frank	1992		Coach, president and general manager, Hershey Bears (AHL)
McLaughlin, Major Frederic	1963		Owner and first president, Chicago Blackhawks; general manager, Chicago Blackhawks (1926-27 through 1941-42)
Milford, Jake	1984		Coach, New York Rangers organization; general manager, Los Angeles Kings, Vancouver Canucks (1973-74 through 1981-82)
Molson, Senator Hartland De Montarville	1973		President and chairman, Montreal Canadiens (1957-68)
Morrison, Scotty	1999		Referee-in-chief; chairman, Hall of Fame
Murray, Monsignor Athol	1998		Founded hockey programs in Saskatchewan; founded Notre Dame College in Wilcox
Nelson, Francis	1947		Sports editor, Toronto Globe; vice president, Ontario Hockey Association (1903-05); Governor, Amateur Athletic Union of Canada
Norris, Bruce	1969		Owner, Detroit Red Wings, Olympic Stadium (1955-82)
Norris, James Sr.	1958		Co-owner, Detroit Red Wings (1933-43)
Norris, James Dougan	1962		Co-owner, Detroit Red Wings (1933-43), Chicago Blackhawks (1946-66)
Northey, William	1947		President, Montreal Amateur Athletic Association; managing director, Montreal Forum; first trustee, Allan Cup (1908)
O'Brien, J. Ambrose	1962		Organizer, National Hockey Association (1909); co-founder, Montreal Canadiens
O'Neil, Brian	1994		Director of administration, NHL (1966); executive director, NHL (1971); executive vice-president, NHL (1977)
Page, Fred	1993		President, Canadian Amateur Hockey Association (1966-68); chairman of the board, British Columbia Junior Hockey League (1983 through present)
Patrick, Craig	2001		Builder of U.S. National & Olympic programs; general manager, New York Rangers (1981 through 1986), general manager, Pittsburgh Penguins (1989 to present), coach, Pittsburgh Penguins (1989-90 and1996-97)
Patrick, Frank	1958		Co-organizer and president, Pacific Coast Hockey Association (1911); owner, manager, player/coach, Vancouver Millionaires (PCHA); managing director, National Hockey League; coach, Boston Bruins (1934-35 and 1935-36); manager, Montreal Canadiens
Pickard, Allan	1958		President, Saskatchewan Amateur Hockey Association, Saskatchewan Senior League, Western Canada Senior League;governor, Saskatchewan Junior League, Western Canada Junior League; president, Canadian Amateur Hockey Association (1947-50)

Builder	Election year	Stanley Cup wins‡	Designation for induction
Pilous, Rudy	1985	1	Coach, Chicago Blackhawks, Winnipeg Jets (1957-58 through 1962-63 and 1974-75); manager, Winnipeg Jets (WHA); scout, Detroit Red Wings, Los Angeles Kings
Poile, Bud	1990		General manager, Philadelphia Flyers, Vancouver Canucks (1967-68 through 1972-73); vice president, World Hockey Association; commissioner, Central Hockey League, International Hockey League
Pollock, Sam	1978		Director of personnel, Montreal Canadiens (1950-64); general manager, Montreal Canadiens (1964-65 through 1977-78)
Raymond, Sen. Donat	1958		President, Canadian Arena Company (Montreal Maroons, Montreal Canadiens) (1924-25 through 1955); chairman, Canadian Arena Company (1955-63)
Robertson, John Ross	1947		President, Ontario Hockey Association (1901-05)
Robinson, Claude	1947		First secretary, Canadian Amateur Hockey Association (1914); manager, 1932 Canadian Olympic Team
Ross, Philip	1976		Trustee, Stanley Cup (1893-1949)
Sabetzki, Gunther	1995		President, International Ice Hockey Federation (1975-1994)
Sather, Glen	1997	4	Coach, Edmonton Oilers (1976-89 and 1993-94); general manager, Edmonton Oilers (1979 to present)
Selke, Frank	1960		Assistant general manager, Toronto Maple Leafs; general manager, Montreal Canadiens (1946-47 through 1963-64)
Sinden, Harry	1983	1	Coach, Boston Bruins (1966-67 through 1969-70, 1979-80 and 1984-85); coach, 1972 Team Canada; general manager, Boston Bruins (1972-73 through present)
Smith, Frank	1962		Co-founder and secretary, Beaches Hockey League (later Metropolitan Toronto Hockey League) (1911-62)
Smythe, Conn	1958	0	President, Toronto Maple Leafs, Maple Leaf Gardens, general manager, Toronto Maple Leafs (1927-28 through 1956-57); coach, Toronto Maple Leafs (1926-27 through 1930-31)
Snider, Ed	1988		Owner, Philadelphia Flyers (1967-68 through present)
Stanley of Preston, Lord	1945		Donator, Stanley Cup (1893)
Sutherland, Capt. James	1947		President, Ontario Hockey Association (1915-17); president, Canadian Amateur Hockey Association (1919-21)
Tarasov, Anatoli	1974		Coach, Soviet National Team
Torrey, Bill	1995		Executive vice president, California Seals; general manager, New York Islanders; president, Florida Panthers (1967-present)
Turner, Lloyd	1958		Co-organizer, Western Canadian Hockey League (1918); organizer, Calgary Tigers
Tutt, Thayer	1978		President, International Ice Hockey Federation (1966-69), Amateur Hockey Association of the United States
Voss, Carl	1974		President, U.S. Hockey League; first NHL referee-in-chief
Waghorne, Fred	1961		Pioneer and hockey official, Toronto Hockey League
Wirtz, Arthur	1971		Co-owner, Detroit Red Wings, Olympia Stadium, Chicago Stadium, St. Louis Arena, Madison Square Garden, Chicago Blackhawks
Wirtz, Bill	1976		President, Chicago Blackhawks (1966 through present); chairman, NHL Board of Governors
Ziegler, John	1987		President, National Hockey League (1977-92)

‡Stanley Cup wins column refers to wins as a player in the players section and as a coach in the builders section.

REFEREES/LINESMEN

Referee/linesman	Election year	First season	Last season	Position
Armstrong, Neil	1991	1957	1977	Linesman and referee
Ashley, John	1981	1959	1972	Referee
Chadwick, Bill	1964	1940	1955	Linesman and referee
D'Amico, John	1993	1964-65	1987-88	Linesman
Elliott, Chaucer	1961	1903	1913	Referee (OHA)
Hayes, George	1988	1946-47	1964-65	Linesman
Hewitson, Bobby	1963	1924	1934	Referee
Ion, Mickey	1961	1913	1943	Referee (PCHL/NHL)
Pavelich, Marty	1987	1956-57	1978-79	Linesman
Rodden, Mike	1962			Referee
Smeaton, Cooper	1961			Referee (NHA/NHL); referee-in-chief (NHL) (1931-37); trustee, Stanley Cup (1946-78)
Storey, Red	1967	1951	1959	Referee
Udvari, Frank	1973	1951-52	1965-66	Referee; supervisor of NHL officials
Van Hellemond, Andy	1999	1972-73	1995-96	Referee

MILESTONES

(Players and coaches active in the NHL in the 2000-01 season are in boldface)

CAREER

FORWARDS/DEFENSEMEN

20 SEASONS

Rk.	Player	No.
1.	Gordie Howe	26
2.	Alex Delvecchio	24
	Tim Horton	24
4.	John Bucyk	23
5.	**Ray Bourque**	**22**
	Mark Messier	**22**
	Stan Mikita	22
	Doug Mohns	22
	Dean Prentice	22
10.	George Armstrong	21
	Paul Coffey	**21**
	Harry Howell	21
	Larry Murphy	**21**
	Eric Nesterenko	21
	Marcel Pronovost	21
	Jean Ratelle	21
	Allan Stanley	21
	Ron Stewart	21
19.	Jean Beliveau	20
	Ron Francis	**20**
	Bill Gadsby	20
	Wayne Gretzky	20
	Red Kelly	20
	Al MacInnis	**20**
	Henri Richard	20
	Larry Robinson	20
	Norm Ullman	20

Total number of players: (27)

1,200 GAMES

Rk.	Player	No.
1.	Gordie Howe	1,767
2.	**Larry Murphy**	**1,615**
3.	**Ray Bourque**	**1,612**
4.	**Mark Messier**	**1,561**
5.	Alex Delvecchio	1,549
6.	John Bucyk	1,540
7.	**Ron Francis**	**1,489**
8.	Wayne Gretzky	1,487
9.	Tim Horton	1,446
10.	**Scott Stevens**	**1,434**
11.	Mike Gartner	1,432
12.	Harry Howell	1,411
13.	Norm Ullman	1,410
14.	**Paul Coffey**	**1,409**
15.	Dale Hunter	1,407
16.	Stan Mikita	1,394
17.	Doug Mohns	1,390
18.	Larry Robinson	1,384
19.	Dean Prentice	1,378
20.	**Dave Andreychuk**	**1,361**
21.	**Pat Verbeek**	**1,360**
22.	**Phil Housley**	**1,357**
23.	Ron Stewart	1,353
24.	Marcel Dionne	1,348
25.	**Doug Gilmour**	**1,342**
26.	Guy Carbonneau	1,318
27.	Red Kelly	1,316
28.	**Steve Yzerman**	**1,310**
29.	Dave Keon	1,296
30.	Phil Esposito	1,282

Rk.	Player	No.
31.	Jean Ratelle	1,281
32.	Bryan Trottier	1,279
33.	**Al MacInnis**	**1,262**
34.	Craig Ludwig	1,256
35.	Henri Richard	1,256
36.	Kevin Lowe	1,254
37.	Jari Kurri	1,251
38.	Bill Gadsby	1,248
39.	Allan Stanley	1,244
40.	Dino Ciccarelli	1,232
41.	Eddie Westfall	1,227
42.	Brad McCrimmon	1,222
43.	Eric Nesterenko	1,219
44.	**Kirk Muller**	**1,216**
45.	Marcel Pronovost	1,206

Total number of players: (45)

500 GOALS

Rk.	Player	No.
1.	Wayne Gretzky	894
2.	Gordie Howe	801
3.	Marcel Dionne	731
4.	Phil Esposito	717
5.	Mike Gartner	708
6.	**Mark Messier**	**651**
7.	**Brett Hull**	**649**
8.	**Mario Lemieux**	**648**
9.	**Steve Yzerman**	**645**
10.	Bobby Hull	610
11.	Dino Ciccarelli	608
12.	Jari Kurri	601
13.	**Luc Robitaille**	**590**
14.	Mike Bossy	573
15.	**Dave Andreychuk**	**572**
16.	Guy Lafleur	560
17.	John Bucyk	556
18.	Michel Goulet	548
19.	Maurice Richard	544
20.	Stan Mikita	541
21.	Frank Mahovlich	533
22.	Bryan Trottier	524
23.	Dale Hawerchuk	518
24.	**Pat Verbeek**	**515**
25.	Gilbert Perreault	512
26.	Jean Beliveau	507
27.	Joe Mullen	502
28.	Lanny McDonald	500

Total number of players: (28)

700 ASSISTS

Rk.	Player	No.
1.	Wayne Gretzky	1,963
2.	**Ray Bourque**	**1,169**
3.	**Ron Francis**	**1,137**
4.	**Paul Coffey**	**1,135**
5.	**Mark Messier**	**1,130**
6.	Gordie Howe	1,049
7.	Marcel Dionne	1,040
8.	**Steve Yzerman**	**969**
9.	**Adam Oates**	**963**
10.	**Larry Murphy**	**929**
11.	Stan Mikita	926
12.	**Mario Lemieux**	**922**
13.	**Doug Gilmour**	**914**
14.	Bryan Trottier	901

Rk.	Player	No.
15.	Dale Hawerchuk	891
16.	Phil Esposito	873
17.	Denis Savard	865
18.	Bobby Clarke	852
19.	**Phil Housley**	**847**
20.	**Al MacInnis**	**845**
21.	Alex Delvecchio	825
22.	Gilbert Perreault	814
23.	John Bucyk	813
24.	Jari Kurri	797
25.	Guy Lafleur	793
26.	Peter Stastny	789
27.	Jean Ratelle	776
28.	Bernie Federko	761
29.	Larry Robinson	750
30.	Denis Potvin	742
31.	Norm Ullman	739
32.	Bernie Nicholls	734
33.	**Joe Sakic**	**721**
34.	Jean Beliveau	712

Total number of players: (34)

1,000 POINTS

Rk.	Player	No.
1.	Wayne Gretzky	2,857
2.	Gordie Howe	1,850
3.	**Mark Messier**	**1,781**
4.	Marcel Dionne	1,771
5.	**Ron Francis**	**1,624**
6.	**Steve Yzerman**	**1,614**
7.	Phil Esposito	1,590
8.	**Ray Bourque**	**1,579**
9.	**Mario Lemieux**	**1,570**
10.	**Paul Coffey**	**1,531**
11.	Stan Mikita	1,467
12.	Bryan Trottier	1,425
13.	Dale Hawerchuk	1,409
14.	Jari Kurri	1,398
15.	John Bucyk	1,369
16.	Guy Lafleur	1,353
17.	**Doug Gilmour**	**1,343**
18.	Denis Savard	1,338
19.	Mike Gartner	1,335
20.	Gilbert Perreault	1,326
21.	Alex Delvecchio	1,281
22.	**Adam Oates**	**1,279**
23.	Jean Ratelle	1,267
24.	Peter Stastny	1,239
25.	**Luc Robitaille**	**1,238**
26.	Norm Ullman	1,229
27.	Jean Beliveau	1,219
28.	**Larry Murphy**	**1,216**
29.	Bobby Clarke	1,210
30.	**Dave Andreychuk**	**1,209**
	Bernie Nicholls	1,209
32.	Dino Ciccarelli	1,200
33.	**Brett Hull**	**1,183**
34.	**Joe Sakic**	**1,178**
35.	Bobby Hull	1,170
36.	**Phil Housley**	**1,164**
37.	**Al MacInnis**	**1,158**
38.	Michel Goulet	1,152
39.	**Pierre Turgeon**	**1,145**
40.	Bernie Federko	1,130
41.	Mike Bossy	1,126

Rk.	Player	No.
42.	Darryl Sittler	1,121
43.	Frank Mahovlich	1,103
44.	Glenn Anderson	1,099
45.	**Jaromir Jagr**	**1,079**
46.	Dave Taylor	1,069
47.	Joe Mullen	1,063
48.	Denis Potvin	1,052
49.	Henri Richard	1,046
50.	**Vincent Damphousse**	**1,045**
51.	**Pat Verbeek**	**1,040**
52.	Bobby Smith	1,036
53.	Brian Bellows	1,022
54.	Rod Gilbert	1,021
55.	Dale Hunter	1,020
56.	Pat LaFontaine	1,013
57.	Steve Larmer	1,012
58.	**Mark Recchi**	**1,010**
59.	Lanny McDonald	1,006
60.	Brian Propp	1,004

Total number of players: (60)

2,000 PENALTY MINUTES

Rk.	Player	No.
1.	Dave Williams	3,966
2.	Dale Hunter	3,565
3.	Marty McSorley	3,381
4.	Tim Hunter	3,146
5.	**Bob Probert**	**3,124**
6.	Chris Nilan	3,043
7.	**Rick Tocchet**	**2,946**
8.	**Rob Ray**	**2,897**
9.	**Craig Berube**	**2,885**
10.	**Tie Domi**	**2,870**
11.	**Pat Verbeek**	**2,833**
12.	**Dave Manson**	**2,759**
13.	**Scott Stevens**	**2,678**
14.	Willi Plett	2,572
15.	Joey Kocur	2,519
16.	**Gino Odjick**	**2,463**
17.	Basil McRae	2,457
18.	Ulf Samuelsson	2,453
19.	**Chris Chelios**	**2,430**
20.	**Ken Daneyko**	**2,426**
21.	Jay Wells	2,359
22.	Garth Butcher	2,302
23.	Shane Churla	2,301
24.	Dave Schultz	2,294
25.	Laurie Boschman	2,265
26.	Ken Baumgartner	2,244
27.	Rob Ramage	2,226
28.	Bryan Watson	2,212
29.	**Gary Roberts**	**2,188**
30.	**Shayne Corson**	**2,159**
31.	**Kevin Dineen**	**2,155**
32.	**Steve Smith**	**2,139**
33.	Terry O'Reilly	2,095
34.	Al Secord	2,093
35.	Ronnie Stern	2,077
36.	Mick Vukota	2,071
37.	Gord Donnelly	2,069
38.	**Jeff Odgers**	**2,058**
39.	Mike Foligno	2,049
40.	Phil Russell	2,038
41.	**Stu Grimson**	**2,037**
42.	**Kris King**	**2,030**
43.	Kelly Chase	2,017
44.	**Scott Mellanby**	**2,016**
45.	Harold Snepsts	2,009
46.	**Lyle Odelein**	**2,003**

Total number of players: (46)

GOALTENDERS

15 SEASONS

Rk.	Goaltender	No.
1.	Terry Sawchuk	21
	Gump Worsley	21
3.	Grant Fuhr	19
	John Vanbiesbrouck	**19**
5.	Glenn Hall	18
	Gilles Meloche	18
	Andy Moog	18
	Jacques Plante	18
	Billy Smith	18
	Mike Vernon	**18**
11.	Tom Barrasso	17
	Don Beaupre	17
	Patrick Roy	**17**
	Ken Wregget	17
15.	Tony Esposito	16
	Eddie Johnston	16
	Harry Lumley	16
	Kirk McLean	**16**
	Rogie Vachon	16
20.	Johnny Bower	15
	Kelly Hrudey	15
	Reggie Lemelin	15
	Cesare Maniago	15
	Darren Puppa	15
	Bill Ranford	15

Total number of goaltenders: (25)

600 GAMES

Rk.	Goaltender	No.
1.	Terry Sawchuk	971
2.	Glenn Hall	906
3.	**Patrick Roy**	**903**
4.	Tony Esposito	886
5.	**John Vanbiesbrouck**	**877**
6.	Grant Fuhr	868
7.	Gump Worsley	862
8.	Jacques Plante	837
9.	Harry Lumley	804
10.	Rogie Vachon	795
11.	Gilles Meloche	788
12.	**Mike Vernon**	**763**
13.	Tom Barrasso	733
14.	Andy Moog	713
15.	Billy Smith	680
16.	Kelly Hrudey	677
17.	**Ed Belfour**	**675**
18.	Don Beaupre	667
19.	Mike Liut	663
20.	Dan Bouchard	655
	Curtis Joseph	**655**
22.	Bill Ranford	647
23.	Turk Broda	629
	Sean Burke	**629**
25.	**Kirk McLean**	**612**
26.	Ed Giacomin	610
27.	Ron Hextall	608
	Bernie Parent	608
29.	Greg Millen	604

Total number of goaltenders: (29)

30,000 MINUTES

Rk.	Goaltender	No.
1.	Terry Sawchuk	57,205
2.	Glenn Hall	53,484
3.	**Patrick Roy**	**52,693**
4.	Tony Esposito	52,585
5.	Gump Worsley	50,232

Rk.	Goaltender	No.
6.	**John Vanbiesbrouck**	**50,175**
7.	Jacques Plante	49,553
8.	Grant Fuhr	48,945
9.	Harry Lumley	48,107
10.	Rogie Vachon	46,298
11.	Gilles Meloche	45,401
12.	**Mike Vernon**	**43,624**
13.	Tom Barrasso	41,760
14.	Andy Moog	40,151
15.	**Ed Belfour**	**38,860**
16.	Billy Smith	38,431
17.	Turk Broda	38,173
18.	Mike Liut	38,155
19.	Kelly Hrudey	38,084
20.	**Curtis Joseph**	**38,057**
21.	Dan Bouchard	37,919
22.	Don Beaupre	37,396
23.	**Sean Burke**	**35,964**
24.	Bill Ranford	35,937
25.	Ed Giacomin	35,693
26.	Greg Millen	35,377
27.	Bernie Parent	35,136
28.	**Kirk McLean**	**35,090**
29.	Ron Hextall	34,750
30.	**Mike Richter**	**34,294**
31.	Eddie Johnston	34,209
32.	Tiny Thompson	34,174
33.	Cesare Maniago	32,570
34.	Glenn Resch	32,279
35.	Johnny Bower	32,077
36.	Ken Wregget	31,663
37.	Frank Brimsek	31,210
38.	John Roach	30,423
39.	**Martin Brodeur**	**30,235**
40.	Roy Worters	30,175

Total number of goaltenders: (40)

2.50 OR UNDER GOALS-AGAINST AVERAGE

(Goaltenders with 10,000 or more minutes)

Rk.	Goaltender	Min.	GAA
1.	Alex Connell	26,030	1.91
	George Hainsworth	29,415	1.91
3.	Chuck Gardiner	19,687	2.02
4.	Lorne Chabot	25,309	2.04
5.	Tiny Thompson	34,174	2.08
6.	Dave Kerr	26,519	2.17
7.	**Martin Brodeur**	**30,235**	**2.21**
8.	Ken Dryden	23,352	2.24
	Dominik Hasek	**29,873**	**2.24**
10.	Roy Worters	30,175	2.27
11.	Clint Benedict	22,321	2.32
	Norman Smith	12,297	2.32
13.	Bill Durnan	22,945	2.36
	Gerry McNeil	16,535	2.36
15.	Jacques Plante	49,553	2.38
16.	**Chris Osgood**	**22,475**	**2.40**
17.	**Ed Belfour**	**38,860**	**2.45**
18.	John Roach	30,423	2.46
19.	**Olaf Kolzig**	**19,653**	**2.49**

Total number of goaltenders: (19)

200 GAMES WON

Rk.	Goaltender	No.
1.	**Patrick Roy**	**484**
2.	Terry Sawchuk	447
3.	Jacques Plante	434
4.	Tony Esposito	423
5.	Glenn Hall	407
6.	Grant Fuhr	403
7.	**Mike Vernon**	**383**
8.	Andy Moog	372

Rk.	Goaltender	No.
	John Vanbiesbrouck	372
10.	Rogie Vachon	355
11.	Tom Barrasso	353
12.	**Ed Belfour**	**343**
13.	Gump Worsley	335
14.	Harry Lumley	332
15.	**Curtis Joseph**	**317**
16.	Billy Smith	305
17.	Turk Broda	302
18.	Ron Hextall	296
19.	Mike Liut	293
20.	Ed Giacomin	289
21.	Dan Bouchard	286
	Martin Brodeur	**286**
23.	Tiny Thompson	284
24.	**Mike Richter**	**272**
25.	Kelly Hrudey	271
26.	Gilles Meloche	270
	Bernie Parent	270
28.	Don Beaupre	268
29.	Ken Dryden	258
30.	Frank Brimsek	252
31.	Johnny Bower	251
32.	George Hainsworth	247
	Dominik Hasek	**247**
34.	Pete Peeters	246
35.	**Kirk McLean**	**245**
36.	**Sean Burke**	**243**
37.	Bill Ranford	240
38.	Eddie Johnston	236
	Reggie Lemelin	236
40.	Glenn Resch	231
41.	Gerry Cheevers	230
42.	Ken Wregget	225
43.	**Chris Osgood**	**221**
44.	John Roach	218
45.	Greg Millen	215
46.	Bill Durnan	208
	Don Edwards	208
48.	Lorne Chabot	206
	Roger Crozier	206
	Felix Potvin	**206**
51.	Rick Wamsley	204
52.	Dave Kerr	203

Total number of goaltenders: (52)

200 GAMES LOST

Rk.	Goaltender	No.
1.	Gump Worsley	353
2.	Gilles Meloche	351
3.	**John Vanbiesbrouck**	**343**
4.	Terry Sawchuk	337
5.	Glenn Hall	327
6.	Harry Lumley	324
7.	Tony Esposito	307
8.	Grant Fuhr	295
9.	Rogie Vachon	291
10.	Greg Millen	284
11.	Bill Ranford	279
12.	Don Beaupre	277
	Patrick Roy	**277**
14.	**Sean Burke**	**274**
15.	Mike Liut	271
16.	Kelly Hrudey	265
17.	**Mike Vernon**	**264**
18.	**Kirk McLean**	**262**
19.	Cesare Maniago	261
20.	Tom Barrasso	259
21.	Eddie Johnston	256
22.	Ken Wregget	248
23.	Jacques Plante	246
24.	**Curtis Joseph**	**243**
25.	Gary Smith	237

Rk.	Goaltender	No.
26.	Billy Smith	233
	Roy Worters	233
28.	Dan Bouchard	232
29.	Jim Rutherford	227
30.	**Mike Richter**	**226**
31.	Turk Broda	224
	Glenn Resch	224
33.	**Guy Hebert**	**222**
34.	**Ed Belfour**	**215**
35.	Ron Hextall	214
36.	**Jeff Hackett**	**212**
37.	Andy Moog	209
	Chuck Rayner	209
39.	Ed Giacomin	206
40.	**Felix Potvin**	**205**
	Al Rollins	205
42.	John Roach	204
43.	Denis Herron	203
	Ron Low	203
45.	Glen Hanlon	202

Total number of goaltenders: (45)

75 GAMES TIED

Rk.	Goaltender	No.
1.	Terry Sawchuk	188
2.	Glenn Hall	165
3.	Tony Esposito	151
4.	Gump Worsley	150
5.	Harry Lumley	143
6.	Jacques Plante	137
7.	Gilles Meloche	131
8.	Bernie Parent	121
9.	**John Vanbiesbrouck**	**119**
10.	Rogie Vachon	115
11.	Grant Fuhr	114
12.	Dan Bouchard	113
13.	**Patrick Roy**	**110**
14.	Billy Smith	105
15.	Turk Broda	101
16.	Ed Giacomin	97
17.	Cesare Maniago	96
18.	**Mike Vernon**	**91**
19.	Johnny Bower	90
20.	**Ed Belfour**	**89**
	Greg Millen	89
22.	Kelly Hrudey	88
	Andy Moog	88
24.	Eddie Johnston	87
25.	**Sean Burke**	**86**
26.	Al Rollins	84
27.	Glenn Resch	82
28.	Tom Barrasso	81
29.	Frank Brimsek	80
30.	Don Edwards	77
	Chuck Rayner	77
32.	**Martin Brodeur**	**76**
	Denis Herron	76
	Curtis Joseph	**76**
	Phil Myre	76
	Bill Ranford	76
37.	**Don Beaupre**	**75**
	Dave Kerr	75
	Tiny Thompson	75

Total number of goaltenders: (39)

25 SHUTOUTS

Rk.	Goaltender	No.
1.	Terry Sawchuk	103
2.	George Hainsworth	94
3.	Glenn Hall	84
4.	Jacques Plante	82
5.	Tiny Thompson	81
	Alex Connell	81

Rk.	Goaltender	No.
7.	Tony Esposito	76
8.	Lorne Chabot	73
9.	Harry Lumley	71
10.	Roy Worters	67
11.	Turk Broda	62
12.	John Roach	58
13.	**Ed Belfour**	**57**
	Clint Benedict	57
15.	**Dominik Hasek**	**56**
16.	Ed Giacomin	54
	Bernie Parent	54
18.	**Patrick Roy**	**52**
19.	**Martin Brodeur**	**51**
	Dave Kerr	51
	Rogie Vachon	51
22.	Ken Dryden	46
23.	Gump Worsley	43
24.	Charlie Gardiner	42
25.	Frank Brimsek	40
	John Vanbiesbrouck	**40**
27.	Johnny Bower	37
28.	Tom Barrasso	35
29.	Bill Durnan	34
30.	Eddie Johnston	32
	Curtis Joseph	**32**
32.	Roger Crozier	30
	Arturs Irbe	**30**
	Cesare Maniago	30
	Chris Osgood	**30**
36.	**Guy Hebert**	**28**
	Jim Henry	28
	Mike Karakas	28
	Gerry McNeil	28
	Andy Moog	28
	Al Rollins	28
42.	Dan Bouchard	27
43.	**Sean Burke**	**26**
	Gerry Cheevers	26
	Glenn Resch	26
	Gary Smith	26
	Mike Vernon	**26**
48.	Grant Fuhr	25
	Mike Liut	25
	Chuck Rayner	25

Total number of goaltenders: (50)

COACHES

500 GAMES

Rk.	Coach	No.
1.	**Scotty Bowman**	**2,059**
2.	Al Arbour	1,606
3.	Dick Irvin	1,449
4.	Billy Reay	1,102
5.	**Mike Keenan**	**1,069**
6.	Jacques Demers	1,006
7.	Roger Neilson	998
8.	**Pat Quinn**	**990**
9.	Bryan Murray	975
10.	Sid Abel	964
	Jack Adams	964
12.	Toe Blake	914
13.	Punch Imlach	879
14.	Bob Berry	860
15.	**Pat Burns**	**855**
16.	Glen Sather	842
17.	Bob Pulford	829
18.	Michel Bergeron	792
19.	Brian Sutter	782
20.	Emile Francis	778
21.	Milt Schmidt	770
22.	Art Ross	758

Rk. Coach	No.
23. Terry Murray	743
24. Red Kelly	742
25. Fred Shero	734
26. John Muckler	648
27. Pierre Page	636
28. Terry Crisp	631
29. Ron Wilson	624
30. Jack Evans	614
31. Jacques Martin	608
32. Lester Patrick	604
33. Eddie Johnston	596
34. Jim Schoenfeld	580
35. Tommy Ivan	573
36. Jacques Lemaire	557
37. Hap Day	546
38. Darryl Sutter	544
39. Frank Boucher	527
40. Johnny Wilson	517
41. Bob McCammon	512
42. Herb Brooks	507
Total number of coaches: (42)	

250 GAMES WON

Rk. Coach	No.
1. Scotty Bowman	1,193
2. Al Arbour	781
3. Dick Irvin	692
4. Billy Reay	542
Mike Keenan	542
6. Toe Blake	500
7. Bryan Murray	484
Pat Quinn	484
9. Glen Sather	464
10. Roger Neilson	459
11. Jack Adams	413
12. Pat Burns	412
13. Jacques Demers	409
14. Punch Imlach	402
15. Fred Shero	390
16. Emile Francis	388
17. Bob Berry	384
18. Sid Abel	382
19. Art Ross	368
20. Bob Pulford	363
21. Terry Murray	360
Brian Sutter	360
23. Michel Bergeron	338
24. Tommy Ivan	288
25. Ron Wilson	287
26. Terry Crisp	286
27. Lester Patrick	281
28. Red Kelly	278
29. John Muckler	276
30. Jacques Martin	274
31. Jacques Lemaire	272
32. Eddie Johnston	266
33. Hap Day	259
34. Jim Schoenfeld	256
35. Ken Hitchcock	254
36. Pierre Page	253

Rk. Coach	No.
37. Don Cherry	250
Milt Schmidt	250
Darryl Sutter	250
Total number of coaches: (39)	

250 GAMES LOST

Rk. Coach	No.
1. Al Arbour	577
2. Scotty Bowman	559
3. Dick Irvin	527
4. Jacques Demers	467
5. Sid Abel	427
6. Mike Keenan	398
7. Milt Schmidt	394
8. Jack Adams	390
9. Billy Reay	385
10. Roger Neilson	380
11. Pat Quinn	374
12. Bryan Murray	368
13. Bob Berry	355
14. Michel Bergeron	350
15. Punch Imlach	337
16. Red Kelly	330
Bob Pulford	330
18. Brian Sutter	319
19. Pat Burns	314
20. Jack Evans	303
21. Pierre Page	301
22. Art Ross	300
23. Terry Murray	283
24. Rick Bowness	277
25. John Muckler	276
26. Emile Francis	273
Ron Wilson	273
28. Glen Sather	268
29. Terry Crisp	267
30. Frank Boucher	263
Tom McVie	263
32. Toe Blake	255
33. Tom Watt	252
34. Eddie Johnston	251
Total number of coaches: (34)	

100 GAMES TIED

Rk. Coach	No.
1. Scotty Bowman	303
2. Al Arbour	248
3. Dick Irvin	230
4. Billy Reay	175
5. Jack Adams	161
6. Toe Blake	159
Roger Neilson	159
8. Sid Abel	155
9. Punch Imlach	150
10. Bob Pulford	136
11. Red Kelly	134
12. Jacques Demers	130
13. Pat Burns	129
14. Pat Quinn	127
15. Milt Schmidt	126
16. Mike Keenan	124

Rk. Coach	No.
17. Bryan Murray	123
18. Bob Berry	121
19. Fred Shero	119
20. Emile Francis	117
21. Tommy Ivan	111
22. Glen Sather	110
23. Lester Patrick	107
24. Michel Bergeron	104
25. Brian Sutter	103
Total number of coaches: (25)	

.550 WINNING PERCENTAGE

(Coaches with 300 or more games)

Rk. Coach	Games	Pct.
1. Scotty Bowman	2,059	.654
2. Claude Ruel	305	.648
3. Toe Blake	914	.634
4. Floyd Smith	309	.626
5. Ken Hitchcock	453	.623
6. Glen Sather	842	.616
7. Fred Shero	734	.612
8. Gerry Cheevers	376	.604
9. Joel Quenneville	368	.603
10. Don Cherry	480	.601
11. Tommy Ivan	573	.599
12. Cecil Hart	394	.590
13. Emile Francis	778	.574
14. Marc Crawford	495	.572
15. Billy Reay	1,102	.571
16. Mike Keenan	1,069	.566
Jacques Lemaire	557	.566
18. Al Arbour	1,606	.564
19. Bryan Murray	975	.559
20. Dick Irvin	1,449	.557
Pat Quinn	990	.557
Pat Burns	855	.557
Harry Sinden	327	.557
24. Lester Patrick	604	.554
Terry Murray	743	.552
Total number of coaches: (25)		

STANLEY CUP CHAMPIONSHIPS

(Includes Stanley Cup championships as NHL coach only)

Rk. Coach	No.
1. Toe Blake	8
Scotty Bowman	8
3. Hap Day	5
4. Al Arbour	4
Dick Irvin	4
Punch Imlach	4
Glen Sather	4
8. Jack Adams	3
Pete Green	3
Tommy Ivan	3
11. Tommy Gorman	2
Cecil Hart	2
Lester Patrick	2
Fred Shero	2
Total number of coaches: (14)	

SEASON

FORWARDS/DEFENSEMEN

60 GOALS

Season	Player, Team	No.
1981-82	Wayne Gretzky, Edm.	92
1983-84	Wayne Gretzky, Edm.	87
1990-91	Brett Hull, St.L.	86
1988-89	Mario Lemieux, Pit.	85

Season	Player, Team	No.
1971-72	Phil Esposito, Bos.	76
1992-93	Alexander Mogilny, Buf.	76
1992-93	Teemu Selanne, Win.	76
1984-85	Wayne Gretzky, Edm.	73
1989-90	Brett Hull, St.L.	72
1982-83	Wayne Gretzky, Edm.	71
1984-85	Jari Kurri, Edm.	71
1991-92	Brett Hull, St.L.	70

Season	Player, Team	No.
1987-88	Mario Lemieux, Pit.	70
1988-89	Bernie Nicholls, L.A.	70
1978-79	Mike Bossy, NYI	69
1992-93	Mario Lemieux, Pit.	69
1995-96	Mario Lemieux, Pit.	69
1980-81	Mike Bossy, NYI	68
1973-74	Phil Esposito, Bos.	68
1985-86	Jari Kurri, Edm.	68

Season	Player, Team	No.
1972-73	Phil Esposito, Bos.	66
1982-83	Lanny McDonald, Cal.	66
1988-89	**Steve Yzerman, Det.**	**65**
1981-82	Mike Bossy, NYI	64
1992-93	**Luc Robitaille, L.A.**	**63**
1986-87	Wayne Gretzky, Edm.	62
1995-96	**Jaromir Jagr, Pit.**	**62**
1989-90	**Steve Yzerman, Det.**	**62**
1985-86	Mike Bossy, NYI	61
1974-75	Phil Esposito, Bos.	61
1975-76	Reggie Leach, Phi.	61
1982-83	Mike Bossy, NYI	60
1992-93	**Pavel Bure, Van.**	**60**
1993-94	**Pavel Bure, Van.**	**60**
1977-78	Guy Lafleur, Mon.	60
1981-82	Dennis Maruk, Was.	60
1976-77	Steve Shutt, Mon.	60

Total number of occurrences: (37)

50-GOAL SEASONS

Rk.	Player	No.	Cons.
1.	Mike Bossy	9	9
	Wayne Gretzky	9	8
3.	Guy Lafleur	6	6
	Marcel Dionne	6	5
	Mario Lemieux	**6**	**3**
6.	Phil Esposito	5	5
	Brett Hull	**5**	**5**
	Steve Yzerman	**5**	**4**
	Bobby Hull	5	2
	Pavel Bure	**5**	**2**
11.	Michel Goulet	4	4
	Tim Kerr	4	4
	Jari Kurri	4	4
14.	**John LeClair**	**3**	**3**
	Rick Vaive	3	3
	Cam Neely	3	2
	Teemu Selanne	**3**	**2**
	Luc Robitaille	**3**	**1**
19.	**Dave Andreychuk**	**2**	**2**
	Rick Martin	2	2
	Dennis Maruk	2	2
	Joe Nieuwendyk	**2**	**2**
	Mickey Redmond	2	2
	Jeremy Roenick	**2**	**2**
	Brendan Shanahan	**2**	**2**
	Charlie Simmer	2	2
	Kevin Stevens	**2**	**2**
	Keith Tkachuk	**2**	**2**
	Glenn Anderson	2	1
	Peter Bondra	**2**	**1**
	Dino Ciccarelli	2	1
	Danny Gare	2	1
	Jaromir Jagr	**2**	**1**
	Pat LaFontaine	2	1
	Pierre Larouche	2	1
	Reggie Leach	2	1
	Alexander Mogilny	**2**	**1**
	Stephane Richer	2	1
	Joe Sakic	**2**	**1**
	Blaine Stoughton	2	1
41.	Wayne Babych	1	1
	Bill Barber	1	1
	Brian Bellows	1	1
	John Bucyk	1	1
	Mike Bullard	1	1
	Bob Carpenter	1	1
	Jimmy Carson	1	1
	Guy Chouinard	1	1
	Sergei Fedorov	**1**	**1**
	Theoren Fleury	**1**	**1**
	Mike Gartner	1	1

Rk.	Player	No.	Cons.
	Bernie Geoffrion	1	1
	Danny Grant	1	1
	Adam Graves	**1**	**1**
	Vic Hadfield	1	1
	Dale Hawerchuk	1	1
	Ken Hodge	1	1
	Paul Kariya	**1**	**1**
	Rick Kehoe	1	1
	Gary Leeman	1	1
	Hakan Loob	1	1
	Rick MacLeish	1	1
	Lanny McDonald	1	1
	Mark Messier	**1**	**1**
	Rick Middleton	1	1
	Mike Modano	**1**	**1**
	Joe Mullen	1	1
	Bernie Nicholls	1	1
	John Ogrodnick	1	1
	Jean Pronovost	1	1
	Mark Recchi	**1**	**1**
	Jacques Richard	1	1
	Maurice Richard	1	1
	Gary Roberts	**1**	**1**
	Al Secord	1	1
	Ray Sheppard	1	1
	Steve Shutt	1	1
	Craig Simpson	1	1
	Bryan Trottier	1	1
	Pierre Turgeon	**1**	**1**

Total number of players: (80)

40 GOALS BY ROOKIES

Season	Player, Team	No.
1992-93	**Teemu Selanne, Win.**	**76**
1977-78	Mike Bossy, NYI	53
1987-88	**Joe Nieuwendyk, Cal.**	**51**
1981-82	Dale Hawerchuk, Win.	45
1986-87	**Luc Robitaille, L.A.**	**45**
1971-72	Rick Martin, Buf.	44
1981-82	Barry Pederson, Bos.	44
1982-83	Steve Larmer, Chi.	43
1984-85	**Mario Lemieux, Pit.**	**43**
1992-93	Eric Lindros, Phi.	41
1980-81	Darryl Sutter, Chi.	40
1983-84	Sylvain Turgeon, Har.	40
1984-85	Warren Young, Pit.	40

Total number of players: (13)

125 POINTS

Season	Player	No.
1985-86	Wayne Gretzky, Edm.	215
1981-82	Wayne Gretzky, Edm.	212
1984-85	Wayne Gretzky, Edm.	208
1983-84	Wayne Gretzky, Edm.	205
1988-89	**Mario Lemieux, Pit.**	**199**
1982-83	Wayne Gretzky, Edm.	196
1986-87	Wayne Gretzky, Edm.	183
1988-89	Wayne Gretzky, L.A.	168
1987-88	**Mario Lemieux, Pit.**	**168**
1980-81	Wayne Gretzky, Edm.	164
1990-91	Wayne Gretzky, L.A.	163
1995-96	**Mario Lemieux, Pit.**	**161**
1992-93	**Mario Lemieux, Pit.**	**160**
1988-89	**Steve Yzerman, Det.**	**155**
1970-71	Phil Esposito, Bos.	152
1988-89	Bernie Nicholls, L.A.	150
1987-88	Wayne Gretzky, Edm.	149
1995-96	**Jaromir Jagr, Pit.**	**149**
1992-93	Pat LaFontaine, Buf.	148
1981-82	Mike Bossy, NYI	147
1973-74	Phil Esposito, Bos.	145
1989-90	Wayne Gretzky, L.A.	142

Season	Player	No.
1992-93	**Adam Oates, Bos.**	**142**
1985-86	**Mario Lemieux, Pit.**	**141**
1970-71	Bobby Orr, Bos.	139
1981-82	Peter Stastny, Que.	139
1985-86	**Paul Coffey, Edm.**	**138**
1979-80	Wayne Gretzky, Edm.	137
1979-80	Marcel Dionne, L.A.	137
1992-93	**Steve Yzerman, Det.**	**137**
1976-77	Guy Lafleur, Mon.	136
1981-82	Dennis Maruk, Was.	136
1980-81	Marcel Dionne, L.A.	135
1984-85	Jari Kurri, Edm.	135
1974-75	Bobby Orr, Bos.	135
1978-79	Bryan Trottier, NYI	134
1971-72	Phil Esposito, Bos.	133
1977-78	Guy Lafleur, Mon.	132
1992-93	**Pierre Turgeon, NYI**	**132**
1992-93	**Teemu Selanne, Win.**	**132**
1990-91	**Brett Hull, St.L.**	**131**
1991-92	**Mario Lemieux, Pit.**	**131**
1985-86	Jari Kurri, Edm.	131
1980-81	Kent Nilsson, Cal.	131
1987-88	Denis Savard, Chi.	131
1972-73	Phil Esposito, Bos.	130
1978-79	Marcel Dionne, L.A.	130
1984-85	Dale Hawerchuk, Win.	130
1993-94	Wayne Gretzky, L.A.	130
1989-90	**Mark Messier, Edm.**	**129**
1978-79	Guy Lafleur, Mon.	129
1981-82	Bryan Trottier, NYI	129
1974-75	Phil Esposito, Bos.	127
1992-93	**Doug Gilmour, Tor.**	**127**
1992-93	**Alexander Mogilny, Buf.**	**127**
1989-90	**Steve Yzerman, Det.**	**127**
1998-99	**Jaromir Jagr, Pit.**	**127**
1968-69	Phil Esposito, Bos.	126
1978-79	Mike Bossy, NYI	126
1983-84	**Paul Coffey, Edm.**	**126**
1984-85	Marcel Dionne, L.A.	126
1975-76	Guy Lafleur, Mon.	125
1979-80	Guy Lafleur, Mon.	125

Total number of occurrences: (63)

100-POINT SEASONS

Rk.	Player	No.	Cons.
1.	Wayne Gretzky	15	13
2.	**Mario Lemieux**	**10**	**6**
3.	Marcel Dionne	8	5
4.	Mike Bossy	7	6
	Peter Stastny	7	6
6.	Guy Lafleur	6	6
	Bobby Orr	6	6
	Steve Yzerman	**6**	**6**
	Phil Esposito	6	5
	Dale Hawerchuk	6	5
	Jari Kurri	6	5
	Bryan Trottier	6	5
	Mark Messier	**6**	**2**
14.	**Joe Sakic**	**5**	**2**
	Denis Savard	5	2
16.	**Brett Hull**	**4**	**4**
	Paul Coffey	**4**	**3**
	Bernie Federko	4	3
	Michel Goulet	4	2
	Adam Oates	**4**	**2**
	Luc Robitaille	**4**	**2**
	Jaromir Jagr	**4**	**1**
23.	Mike Rogers	3	3
	Glenn Anderson	3	2
	Bobby Clarke	3	2
	Doug Gilmour	**3**	**2**
	Bernie Nicholls	3	2

Rk.	Player	No.	Cons.
	Mark Recchi	3	2
29.	Pavel Bure	2	2
	Jimmy Carson	2	2
	Pete Mahovlich	2	2
	Barry Pederson	2	2
	Jeremy Roenick	2	2
	Charlie Simmer	2	2
	Kevin Stevens	2	2
	Dave Taylor	2	2
	Dino Ciccarelli	2	1
	Sergei Fedorov	2	1
	Theoren Fleury	2	1
	Ron Francis	3	1
	Pat LaFontaine	2	1
	Rick Middleton	2	1
	Alexander Mogilny	2	1
	Kent Nilsson	2	1
	Gilbert Perreault	2	1
	Jean Ratelle	2	1
	Darryl Sittler	2	1
	Teemu Selanne	2	1
	Pierre Turgeon	2	1

Total number of players: (49)

75 POINTS BY ROOKIES

Season	Player, Team	No.
1992-93	Teemu Selanne, Win.	132
1980-81	Peter Stastny, Que.	109
1981-82	Dale Hawerchuk, Win.	103
1992-93	Joe Juneau, Bos.	102
1984-85	Mario Lemieux, Pit.	100
1981-82	Neal Broten, Min.	98
1975-76	Bryan Trottier, NYI	95
1987-88	Joe Nieuwendyk, Cal.	92
1981-82	Barry Pederson, Bos.	92
1977-78	Mike Bossy, NYI	91
1982-83	Steve Larmer, Chi.	90
1981-82	Marian Stastny, Que.	89
1983-84	Steve Yzerman, Det.	87
1989-90	Sergei Makarov, Cal.	86
1980-81	Anton Stastny, Que.	85
1986-87	Luc Robitaille, L.A.	84
1993-94	Mikael Renberg, Phi.	82
1986-87	Jimmy Carson, L.A.	79
1990-91	Sergei Fedorov, Det.	79
1993-94	Alexei Yashin, Ott.	79
1971-72	Marcel Dionne, L.A.	77

Season	Player, Team	No.
1980-81	Larry Murphy, L.A.	76
1981-82	Mark Pavelich, NYR	76
1983-84	Dave Poulin, Phi.	76
1992-93	Eric Lindros, Phi.	75
1980-81	Jari Kurri, Edm.	75
1989-90	Mike Modano, Min.	75
1979-80	Brian Propp, Phi.	75
1980-81	Denis Savard, Chi.	75

Total number of players: (29)

350 PENALTY MINUTES

Season	Player, Team	No.
1974-75	Dave Schultz, Phi.	472
1981-82	Paul Baxter, Pit.	409
1991-92	Mike Peluso, Chi.	408
1977-78	Dave Schultz, L.A.-Pit.	405
1992-93	Marty McSorley, L.A.	399
1987-88	Bob Probert, Det.	398
1987-88	Basil McRae, Min.	378
1985-86	Joey Kocur, Det.	377
1988-89	Tim Hunter, Cal.	375
1997-98	Donald Brashear, Van.	372
1996-97	Gino Odjick, Van.	371
1975-76	Steve Durbano, Pit.-K.C.	370
1992-93	Gino Odjick, Van.	370
1988-89	Basil McRae, Min.	365
1997-98	Tie Domi, Tor.	365
1986-87	Tim Hunter, Cal.	361
1984-85	Chris Nilan, Mon.	358
1985-86	Torrie Robertson, Har.	358
1986-87	Tiger Williams, L.A.	358
1986-87	Brian Curran, NYI	356
1991-92	Rob Ray, Buf.	354
1988-89	Dave Manson, Chi.	352
1977-78	Tiger Williams, Tor.	351
1989-90	Basil McRae, Min.	351
1988-89	Marty McSorley, L.A.	350
1990-91	Rob Ray, Buf.	350

Total number of occurrences: (26)

GOALTENDERS

10 SHUTOUTS

Season	Goaltender, Team	No.
1928-29	George Hainsworth, Mon. C.	22
1925-26	Alex Connell, Ott.	15

Season	Goaltender, Team	No.
1927-28	Alex Connell, Ott.	15
1927-28	Hal Winkler, Bos.	15
1969-70	Tony Esposito, Chi.	15
1926-27	George Hainsworth, Mon. C.	14
1926-27	Clint Benedict, Mon. M.	13
1926-27	Alex Connell, Ott.	13
1927-28	George Hainsworth, Mon. C.	13
1928-29	John Roach, NYR	13
1928-29	Roy Worters, NYA	13
1953-54	Harry Lumley, Tor.	13
1997-98	Dominik Hasek, Buf.	13
1928-29	Lorne Chabot, Tor.	12
1928-29	Tiny Thompson, Bos.	12
1930-31	Chuck Gardiner, Chi.	12
1951-52	Terry Sawchuk, Det.	12
1953-54	Terry Sawchuk, Det.	12
1954-55	Terry Sawchuk, Det.	12
1955-56	Glenn Hall, Det.	12
1973-74	Bernie Parent, Phi.	12
1974-75	Bernie Parent, Phi.	12
1927-28	Lorne Chabot, NYR	11
1927-28	Harry Holmes, Det.	11
1928-29	Clint Benedict, Mon. M.	11
1928-29	Joe Miller, Pit.	11
1932-33	Tiny Thompson, Bos.	11
1950-51	Terry Sawchuk, Det.	11
2000-01	Dominik Hasek, Buf.	11
1926-27	Lorne Chabot, NYR	10
1927-28	Roy Worters, Pit.	10
1928-29	Clarence Dolson, Det.	10
1932-33	John Roach, Det.	10
1933-34	Chuck Gardiner, Chi.	10
1935-36	Tiny Thompson, Bos.	10
1938-39	Frank Brimsek, Bos.	10
1948-49	Bill Durnan, Mon.	10
1952-53	Harry Lumley, Tor.	10
1952-53	Gerry McNeil, Mon.	10
1973-74	Tony Esposito, Chi.	10
1976-77	Ken Dryden, Mon.	10
1996-97	Martin Brodeur, N.J.	10
1997-98	Martin Brodeur, N.J.	10
1998-99	Byron Dafoe, Bos.	10
2000-01	Roman Cechmanek, Phi.	10

Total number of occurrences: (45)

GAME

FORWARDS/DEFENSEMEN

FIVE GOALS

Date	Player	Team	Opponents	Goals
December 19, 1917	Joe Malone	Montreal	at Ottawa	5
December 19, 1917	Harry Hyland	Montreal Wanderers	vs. Toronto	5
January 12, 1918	Joe Malone	Montreal	vs. Ottawa	5
February 2, 1918	Joe Malone	Montreal	vs. Toronto	5
January 10, 1920	Newsy Lalonde	Montreal	vs Toronto	6
January 31, 1920	Joe Malone	Quebec Bulldogs	vs. Toronto	7
March 6, 1920	Mickey Roach	Toronto St. Pats	vs. Quebec	5
March 10, 1920	Joe Malone	Quebec Bulldogs	vs. Ottawa	6
January 26, 1921	Corb Denneny	Toronto St. Pats	vs. Hamilton	6
February 16, 1921	Newsy Lalonde	Montreal	vs. Hamilton	5
March 7, 1921	Cy Denneny	Ottawa Senators	vs. Hamilton	6
December 16, 1922	Babe Dye	Toronto St. Pats	vs. Montreal	5
December 5, 1924	Redvers Green	Hamilton Tigers	at Toronto	5
December 22, 1924	Babe Dye	Toronto St. Pats	at Boston	5
January 7, 1925	Harry Broadbent	Montreal Maroons	at Hamilton	5
December 14, 1929	Pit Lepine	Montreal	vs. Ottawa	5
March 18, 1930	Howie Morenz	Montreal	vs. New York Americans	5
January 19, 1932	Charlie Conacher	Toronto	vs. New York Americans	5

Date	Player	Team	Opponents	Goals
February 6, 1943	Ray Getliffe	Montreal	vs. Boston	5
December 28, 1944	Maurice Richard	Montreal	vs. Detroit	5
February 3, 1944	Syd Howe	Detroit	vs. New York Rangers	6
January 8, 1947	Howie Meeker	Toronto	vs. Chicago	5
February 19, 1955	Bernie Geoffrion	Montreal	vs. New York Rangers	5
February 1, 1964	Bobby Rousseau	Montreal	vs. Detroit	5
November 7, 1968	Red Berenson	St. Louis	at Philadelphia	6
February 15, 1975	Yvan Cournoyer	Montreal	vs. Chicago	5
October 12, 1976	Don Murdoch	New York Rangers	at Minnesota	5
November 7, 1976	Darryl Sittler	Toronto	vs. Boston	6
February 2, 1977	Ian Turnbull	Toronto	vs. Detroit	5
December 23, 1978	Bryan Trottier	New York Islanders	vs. New York Rangers	5
January 15, 1979	Tim Young	Minnesota	at New York Rangers	5
January 6, 1981	John Tonelli	New York Islanders	vs. Toronto	5
February 18, 1981	Wayne Gretzky	Edmonton	vs. St. Louis	5
December 30, 1981	Wayne Gretzky	Edmonton	vs. Philadelphia	5
February 3, 1982	Grant Mulvey	Chicago	vs. St. Louis	5
February 13, 1982	Bryan Trottier	New York Islanders	vs. Philadelphia	5
March 2, 1982	Willie Lindstrom	Winnipeg	at Philadelphia	5
February 23, 1983	Mark Pavelich	New York Rangers	vs. Hartford	5
November 19, 1983	Jari Kurri	Edmonton	vs. New Jersey	5
January 8, 1984	Bengt Gustafsson	Washington	at Philadelphia	5
February 3, 1984	Pat Hughes	Edmonton	vs. Calgary	5
December 15, 1984	Wayne Gretzky	Edmonton	at St. Louis	5
February 6, 1986	**Dave Andreychuk**	**Buffalo**	**at Boston**	**5**
December 6, 1987	Wayne Gretzky	Edmonton	vs. Minnesota	5
December 31, 1988	**Mario Lemieux**	**Pittsburgh**	**vs. New Jersey**	**5**
January 11, 1989	**Joe Nieuwendyk**	**Calgary**	**vs. Winnipeg**	**5**
March 5, 1992	**Mats Sundin**	**Quebec**	**at Hartford**	**5**
April 9, 1993	**Mario Lemieux**	**Pittsburgh**	**at New York Rangers**	**5**
February 5, 1994	**Peter Bondra**	**Washington**	**vs. Tampa Bay**	**5**
February 17, 1994	**Mike Ricci**	**Quebec**	**vs. San Jose**	**5**
April 1, 1995	**Alexei Zhamnov**	**Winnipeg**	**at Los Angeles**	**5**
March 26, 1996	**Mario Lemieux**	**Pittsburgh**	**vs. St. Louis**	**5**
December 26, 1996	**Sergei Fedorov**	**Detroit**	**vs. Washington**	**5**

Total number of occurrences: (53)

TEAM BY TEAM

MIGHTY DUCKS OF ANAHEIM
YEAR-BY-YEAR RECORDS

Season	W	L	T	RT	Pts.	Finish	W	L	Highest round	Coach
									PLAYOFFS	
1993-94	33	46	5	—	71	4th/Pacific	—	—		Ron Wilson
1994-95	16	27	5	—	37	6th/Pacific	—	—		Ron Wilson
1995-96	35	39	8	—	78	4th/Pacific	—	—		Ron Wilson
1996-97	36	33	13	—	85	2nd/Pacific	4	7	Conference semifinals	Ron Wilson
1997-98	26	43	13	—	65	6th/Pacific	—	—		Pierre Page
1998-99	35	34	13	—	83	3rd/Pacific	0	4	Conference quarterfinals	Craig Hartsburg
1999-00	34	36	12	3	83	5th/Pacific	—	—		Craig Hartsburg
2000-01	25	41	11	5	66	5th/Pacific	—	—		Craig Hartsburg, Guy Charron

FIRST-ROUND ENTRY DRAFT CHOICES

Year   Player, Overall, Last amateur team (league)
1993—Paul Kariya, 4, University of Maine
1994—Oleg Tverdovsky, 2, Krylja Sovetov, CIS
1995—Chad Kilger, 4, Kingston (OHL)
1996—Ruslan Salei, 9, Las Vegas (IHL)
1997—Mikael Holmqvist, 18, Djurgarden Stockholm (Sweden)

Year   Player, Overall, Last amateur team (league)
1998—Vitali Vishnevsky, 5, Torpedo Yaroslavl (Russia)
1999—No first-round selection
2000—Alexei Smirnov, 12, Dynamo (Russia)
2001—Stanislav Chistov, 5, OMDK (Russia)

SINGLE-SEASON INDIVIDUAL RECORDS

FORWARDS/DEFENSEMEN

Most goals
52—Teemu Selanne, 1997-98

Most assists
62—Paul Kariya, 1998-99

Most points
109—Teemu Selanne, 1996-97

Most penalty minutes
285—Todd Ewen, 1995-96

Most power play goals
25—Teemu Selanne, 1998-99

Most shorthanded goals
3—Bob Corkum, 1993-94
  Paul Kariya, 1995-96

Paul Kariya, 1996-97
Paul Kariya, 1999-00
Paul Kariya, 2000-01

Most games with three or more goals
3—Teemu Selanne, 1997-98

Most shots
429—Paul Kariya, 1998-99

GOALTENDERS

Most games
69—Guy Hebert, 1998-99

Most minutes
4,083—Guy Hebert, 1998-99

Most shots against
2,133—Guy Hebert, 1996-97

Most goals allowed
172—Guy Hebert, 1996-97

Lowest goals-against average
2.42—Guy Hebert, 1998-99

Most shutouts
6—Guy Hebert, 1998-99

Most wins
31—Guy Hebert, 1998-99

Most losses
29—Guy Hebert, 1998-99

Most ties
12—Guy Hebert, 1996-97

FRANCHISE LEADERS

Players in boldface played for club in 2000-01

FORWARDS/DEFENSEMEN

Games
Paul Kariya 442
Steve Rucchin 414
Teemu Selanne 394
Jason Marshall 347
Joe Sacco 333

Goals
Paul Kariya 243
Teemu Selanne 225
Steve Rucchin 106
Joe Sacco 62
Marty McInnis 48

Assists
Paul Kariya 288
Teemu Selanne 257
Steve Rucchin 202
Oleg Tverdovsky 99
Matt Cullen 91

Points
Paul Kariya 531
Teemu Selanne 482
Steve Rucchin 308
Matt Cullen 141
Oleg Tverdovsky 138

Penalty minutes
David Karpa 788
Jason Marshall 706
Todd Ewen 650
Stu Grimson 583
Warren Rychel 416

GOALTENDERS

Games
Guy Hebert 441
Mikhail Shtalenkov 122
Dominic Roussel 51
Jean-Sebastien Giguere 34
Ron Tugnutt 28

Shutouts
Guy Hebert 27
Jean-Sebastien Giguere 4
Mikhail Shtalenkov 3
Dominic Roussel 2
Ron Tugnutt 1

Goals-against average
(2400 minutes minimum)
Guy Hebert 2.75
Dominic Roussel 2.85
Mikhail Shtalenkov 3.14

Wins
Guy Hebert 173
Mikhail Shtalenkov 34
Dominic Roussel 12
Jean-Sebastien Giguere 11
Ron Tugnutt 10

ATLANTA FLAMES (DEFUNCT)

YEAR-BY-YEAR RECORDS

	REGULAR SEASON						PLAYOFFS			
Season	W	L	T	Pts.	Finish	W	L	Highest round		Coach
1972-73	25	38	15	65	7th/West	—	—			Bernie Geoffrion
1973-74	30	34	14	74	4th/West	0	4	Division semifinals		Bernie Geoffrion
1974-75	34	31	15	83	4th/Patrick	—	—			Bernie Geoffrion, Fred Creighton
1975-76	35	33	12	82	3rd/Patrick	0	2	Preliminaries		Fred Creighton
1976-77	34	34	12	80	3rd/Patrick	1	2	Preliminaries		Fred Creighton
1977-78	34	27	19	87	3rd/Patrick	0	2	Preliminaries		Fred Creighton
1978-79	41	31	8	90	4th/Patrick	0	2	Preliminaries		Fred Creighton
1979-80	35	32	13	83	4th/Patrick	1	3	Preliminaries		Al MacNeil

Franchise relocated to Calgary following 1979-80 season.

FIRST-ROUND ENTRY DRAFT CHOICES

Year   Player, Overall, Last amateur team (league)
1972—Jacques Richard, 2, Quebec (QMJHL)
1973—Tom Lysiak, 2, Medicine Hat (WCHL)
        Vic Mercredi, 16, New Westminster (WCHL)
1974—No first-round selection
1975—Richard Mulhern, 8, Sherbrooke (QMJHL)

Year   Player, Overall, Last amateur team (league)
1976—Dave Shand, 8, Peterborough (OHL)
        Harold Phillipoff, 10, New Westminster (WCHL)
1977—No first-round selection
1978—Brad Marsh, 11, London (OHL)
1979—Paul Reinhart, 12, Kitchener (OHL)

SINGLE-SEASON INDIVIDUAL RECORDS

FORWARDS/DEFENSEMEN

Most goals
50—Guy Chouinard, 1978-79

Most assists
71—Bob MacMillan, 1978-79

Most points
108—Bob MacMillan, 1978-79

Most penalty minutes
231—Willi Plett, 1979-80

Most power play goals
14—Kent Nilsson, 1979-80

Most shorthanded goals
3—Bill Clement, 1976-77

Most games with three or more goals
3—Eric Vail, 1974-75

Most shots
277—Tom Lysiak, 1976-77

GOALTENDERS

Most games
64—Dan Bouchard, 1978-79

Most minutes
3,624—Dan Bouchard, 1978-79

Most goals allowed
201—Dan Bouchard, 1978-79

Lowest goals-against average
2.54—Dan Bouchard, 1975-76

Most shutouts
5—Dan Bouchard, 1973-74
    Phil Myre, 1974-75

Most wins
32—Dan Bouchard, 1978-79

Most losses
23—Phil Myre, 1972-73

Most ties
19—Dan Bouchard, 1977-78

FRANCHISE LEADERS

FORWARDS/DEFENSEMEN

Games
Eric Vail	469
Rey Comeau	468
Tom Lysiak	445
Curt Bennett	405
Randy Manery	377

Goals
Eric Vail	174
Tom Lysiak	155
Curt Bennett	126
Guy Chouinard	126
Ken Houston	91
Willi Plett	91

Assists
Tom Lysiak	276
Eric Vail	209
Guy Chouinard	168
Randy Manery	142
Curt Bennett	140

Points
Tom Lysiak	431
Eric Vail	383
Guy Chouinard	294
Curt Bennett	266
Bob MacMillan	221

Penalty minutes
Willi Plett	740
Ken Houston	332
Tom Lysiak	329
Ed Kea	283
Randy Manery	242

GOALTENDERS

Games
Dan Bouchard	384
Phil Myre	211
Pat Riggin	25
Yves Belanger	22
Reggie Lemelin	21

Shutouts
Dan Bouchard	20
Phil Myre	11
Pat Riggin	2
Yves Belanger	1

Goals-against average (2400 minutes minimum)
Dan Bouchard	3.00
Phil Myre	3.21

Wins
Dan Bouchard	166
Phil Myre	76
Pat Riggin	11
Yves Belanger	8
Reggie Lemelin	8

NHL HISTORY Team by team

ATLANTA THRASHERS
YEAR-BY-YEAR RECORDS

		REGULAR SEASON					PLAYOFFS			
Season	W	L	T	RT	Pts.	Finish	W	L	Highest round	Coach
1999-00	14	61	7	4	39	5th/Southeast	—	—		Curt Fraser
2000-01	23	45	12	2	60	4th/Southeast	—	—		Curt Fraser

FIRST-ROUND ENTRY DRAFT CHOICES

Year   Player, Overall, Last amateur team (league)
1999—Patrik Stefan, 1, Long Beach (IHL)
2000—Dany Heatley, 2, Wisconsin (WCHA)

Year   Player, Overall, Last amateur team (league)
2001—Ilja Kovalchuk, 1, Spartak Jr. (Russia)*
*Designates first player chosen in draft.

SINGLE-SEASON INDIVIDUAL RECORDS

FORWARDS/DEFENSEMEN

Most goals
32—Donald Audette, 2000-01

Most assists
47—Ray Ferraro, 2000-01

Most points
76—Ray Ferraro, 2000-01

Most penalty minutes
226—Jeff Odgers, 2000-01

Most power play goals
13—Donald Audette, 2000-01

Most shorthanded goals
3—Shean Donovan, 2000-01

Most games with three or more goals
2—Donald Audette, 2000-01
Ray Ferraro, 2000-01

Most shots
187—Donald Audette, 2000-01

GOALTENDERS

Most games
38—Damian Rhodes, 2000-01

Most minutes
2,072—Damian Rhodes, 2000-01

Most shots against
1,129—Damian Rhodes, 2000-01

Most goals allowed
116—Damian Rhodes, 2000-01

Lowest goals-against average
3.35—Milan Hnilicka, 2000-01

Most shutouts
2—Milan Hnilicka, 2000-01

Most wins
12—Milan Hnilicka, 2000-01

Most losses
19—Norm Maracle, 1999-2000
Damian Rhodes, 1999-2000
Milan Hnilicka, 2000-01
Damian Rhodes, 2000-01

Most ties
7—Damian Rhodes, 2000-01

FRANCHISE LEADERS

Players in boldface played for club in 2000-01

FORWARDS/DEFENSEMEN

Games
Ray Ferraro 162
Andrew Brunette 158
Chris Tamer 151
Denny Lambert 140
Patrik Stefan 138

Goals
Ray Ferraro 48
Donald Audette 39
Andrew Brunette 38
Hnat Domenichelli 21
Dean Sylvester 21

Assists
Ray Ferraro 72
Andrew Brunette 71
Donald Audette 43
Patrik Stefan 41
Stephen Guolla 25

Points
Ray Ferraro 120
Andrew Brunette 109
Donald Audette 82
Patrik Stefan 56
Yannick Tremblay 43

Penalty minutes
Denny Lambert 434
Jeff Odgers 226
Steve Staios 203
Chris Tamer 219
Ray Ferraro 179

GOALTENDERS

Games
Damian Rhodes 66
Norm Maracle 45
Milan Hnilicka 36
Scott Fankhouser 23
Scott Langkow 15

Shutouts
Milan Hnilicka 2
Norm Maracle 1
Damian Rhodes 1

Goals-against average
(1200 minutes minimum)
Milan Hnilicka 3.35
Norm Maracle 3.47
Damian Rhodes 3.58

Wins
Milan Hnilicka 12
Damian Rhodes 12
Norm Maracle 6
Scott Fankhouser 4
Scott Langkow 3

BOSTON BRUINS
YEAR-BY-YEAR RECORDS

		REGULAR SEASON					PLAYOFFS			
Season	W	L	T	RT	Pts.	Finish	W	L	Highest round	Coach
1924-25	6	24	0	—	12	6th	—	—		Art Ross
1925-26	17	15	4	—	38	4th	—	—		Art Ross
1926-27	21	20	3	—	45	2nd/American	*2	2	Stanley Cup finals	Art Ross
1927-28	20	13	11	—	51	1st/American	*0	1	Semifinals	Art Ross
1928-29	26	13	5	—	57	1st/American	5	0	Stanley Cup champ	Cy Denneny
1929-30	38	5	1	—	77	1st/American	3	3	Stanley Cup finals	Art Ross

		REGULAR SEASON						PLAYOFFS		
Season	W	L	T	RT	Pts.	Finish	W	L	Highest round	Coach
1930-31	28	10	6	—	62	1st/American	2	3	Semifinals	Art Ross
1931-32	15	21	12	—	42	4th/American	—	—		Art Ross
1932-33	25	15	8	—	58	1st/American	2	3	Semifinals	Art Ross
1933-34	18	25	5	—	41	4th/American	—	—		Art Ross
1934-35	26	16	6	—	58	1st/American	1	3	Semifinals	Frank Patrick
1935-36	22	20	6	—	50	2nd/American	1	1	Quarterfinals	Frank Patrick
1936-37	23	18	7	—	53	2nd/American	1	2	Quarterfinals	Art Ross
1937-38	30	11	7	—	67	1st/American	0	3	Semifinals	Art Ross
1938-39	36	10	2	—	74	1st	8	4	Stanley Cup champ	Art Ross
1939-40	31	12	5	—	67	1st	2	4	Semifinals	Ralph (Cooney) Weiland
1940-41	27	8	13	—	67	1st	8	3	Stanley Cup champ	Ralph (Cooney) Weiland
1941-42	25	17	6	—	56	3rd	2	3	Semifinals	Art Ross
1942-43	24	17	9	—	57	2nd	4	5	Stanley Cup finals	Art Ross
1943-44	19	26	5	—	43	5th	—	—		Art Ross
1944-45	16	30	4	—	36	4th	3	4	League semifinals	Art Ross
1945-46	24	18	8	—	56	2nd	5	5	Stanley Cup finals	Dit Clapper
1946-47	26	23	11	—	63	3rd	1	4	League semifinals	Dit Clapper
1947-48	23	24	13	—	59	3rd	1	4	League semifinals	Dit Clapper
1948-49	29	23	8	—	66	2nd	1	4	League semifinals	Dit Clapper
1949-50	22	32	16	—	60	5th	—	—		George Boucher
1950-51	22	30	18	—	62	4th	†1	4	League semifinals	Lynn Patrick
1951-52	25	29	16	—	66	4th	3	4	League semifinals	Lynn Patrick
1952-53	28	29	13	—	69	3rd	5	6	League semifinals	Lynn Patrick
1953-54	32	28	10	—	74	4th	0	4	League semifinals	Lynn Patrick
1954-55	23	26	21	—	67	4th	1	4	League semifinals	Lynn Patrick, Milt Schmidt
1955-56	23	34	13	—	59	5th	—	—		Milt Schmidt
1956-57	34	24	12	—	80	3rd	5	5	Stanley Cup finals	Milt Schmidt
1957-58	27	28	15	—	69	4th	6	6	Stanley Cup finals	Milt Schmidt
1958-59	32	29	9	—	73	2nd	3	4	League semifinals	Milt Schmidt
1959-60	28	34	8	—	64	5th	—	—		Milt Schmidt
1960-61	15	42	13	—	43	6th	—	—		Milt Schmidt
1961-62	15	47	8	—	38	6th	—	—		Phil Watson
1962-63	14	39	17	—	45	6th	—	—		Phil Watson, Milt Schmidt
1963-64	18	40	12	—	48	6th	—	—		Milt Schmidt
1964-65	21	43	6	—	48	6th	—	—		Milt Schmidt
1965-66	21	43	6	—	48	5th	—	—		Milt Schmidt
1966-67	17	43	10	—	44	6th	—	—		Harry Sinden
1967-68	37	27	10	—	84	3rd/East	0	4	Division semifinals	Harry Sinden
1968-69	42	18	16	—	100	2nd/East	6	4	Division finals	Harry Sinden
1969-70	40	17	19	—	99	2nd/East	12	2	Stanley Cup champ	Harry Sinden
1970-71	57	14	7	—	121	1st/East	3	4	Division semifinals	Tom Johnson
1971-72	54	13	11	—	119	1st/East	12	3	Stanley Cup champ	Tom Johnson
1972-73	51	22	5	—	107	2nd/East	1	4	Division semifinals	Tom Johnson, Bep Guidolin
1973-74	52	17	9	—	113	1st/East	10	6	Stanley Cup finals	Bep Guidolin
1974-75	40	26	14	—	94	2nd/Adams	1	2	Preliminaries	Don Cherry
1975-76	48	15	17	—	113	1st/Adams	5	7	Semifinals	Don Cherry
1976-77	49	23	8	—	106	1st/Adams	8	6	Stanley Cup finals	Don Cherry
1977-78	51	18	11	—	113	1st/Adams	10	5	Stanley Cup finals	Don Cherry
1978-79	43	23	14	—	100	1st/Adams	7	4	Semifinals	Don Cherry
1979-80	46	21	13	—	105	2nd/Adams	4	6	Quarterfinals	Fred Creighton, Harry Sinden
1980-81	37	30	13	—	87	2nd/Adams	0	3	Preliminaries	Gerry Cheevers
1981-82	43	27	10	—	96	2nd/Adams	6	5	Division finals	Gerry Cheevers
1982-83	50	20	10	—	110	1st/Adams	9	8	Conference finals	Gerry Cheevers
1983-84	49	25	6	—	104	1st/Adams	0	3	Division semifinals	Gerry Cheevers
1984-85	36	34	10	—	82	4th/Adams	2	3	Division semifinals	Gerry Cheevers, Harry Sinden
1985-86	37	31	12	—	86	3rd/Adams	0	3	Division semifinals	Butch Goring
1986-87	39	34	7	—	85	3rd/Adams	0	4	Division semifinals	Butch Goring, Terry O'Reilly
1987-88	44	30	6	—	94	2nd/Adams	12	6	Stanley Cup finals	Terry O'Reilly
1988-89	37	29	14	—	88	2nd/Adams	5	5	Division finals	Terry O'Reilly
1989-90	46	25	9	—	101	1st/Adams	13	8	Stanley Cup finals	Mike Milbury
1990-91	44	24	12	—	100	1st/Adams	10	9	Conference finals	Mike Milbury
1991-92	36	32	12	—	84	2nd/Adams	8	7	Conference finals	Rick Bowness
1992-93	51	26	7	—	109	1st/Adams	0	4	Division semifinals	Brian Sutter
1993-94	42	29	13	—	97	2nd/Northeast	6	7	Conference semifinals	Brian Sutter
1994-95	27	18	3	—	57	3rd/Northeast	1	4	Conference quarterfinals	Brian Sutter
1995-96	40	31	11	—	91	2nd/Northeast	1	4	Conference quarterfinals	Steve Kasper
1996-97	26	47	9	—	61	6th/Northeast	—	—		Steve Kasper
1997-98	39	30	13	—	91	2nd/Northeast	2	4	Conference quarterfinals	Pat Burns
1998-99	39	30	13	—	91	3th/Northeast	6	6	Conference semifinals	Pat Burns
1999-00	24	39	19	6	73	5th/Northeast	—	—		Pat Burns
2000-01	36	30	8	8	88	4th/Northeast	—	—		Pat Burns, Mike Keenan

*Won-lost record does not indicate tie(s) resulting from two-game, total-goals series that year (two-game, total-goals series were played from 1917-18 through 1935-36).

†Tied after one overtime (curfew law).

FIRST-ROUND ENTRY DRAFT CHOICES

Year	Player, Overall, Last amateur team (league)
1969	Don Tannahill, 3, Niagara Falls (OHL)
	Frank Spring, 4, Edmonton (WCHL)
	Ivan Boldirev, 11, Oshawa (OHL)
1970	Reggie Leach, 3, Flin Flon (WCHL)
	Rick MacLeish, 4, Peterborough (OHL)
	Ron Plumb, 9, Peterborough (OHL)
	Bob Stewart, 13, Oshawa (OHL)
1971	Ron Jones, 6, Edmonton (WCHL)
	Terry O'Reilly, 14, Oshawa (OHL)
1972	Mike Bloom, 16, St. Catharines (OHL)
1973	Andre Savard, 6, Quebec (QMJHL)
1974	Don Laraway, 18, Swift Current (WCHL)
1975	Doug Halward, 14, Peterborough (OHL)
1976	Clayton Pachal, 16, New Westminster (WCHL)
1977	Dwight Foster, 16, Kitchener (OHL)
1978	Al Secord, 16, Hamilton (OHL)
1979	Ray Bourque, 8, Verdun (QMJHL)
	Brad McCrimmon, 15, Brandon (WHL)
1980	Barry Pederson, 18, Victoria (WHL)
1981	Norm Leveille, 14, Chicoutimi (QMJHL)
1982	Gord Kluzak, 1, Billings (WHL)*
1983	Nevin Markwart, 21, Regina (WHL)
1984	Dave Pasin, 19, Prince Albert (WHL)

Year	Player, Overall, Last amateur team (league)
1985	No first-round selection
1986	Craig Janney, 13, Boston College
1987	Glen Wesley, 3, Portland (WHL)
	Stephane Quintal, 14, Granby (QMJHL)
1988	Robert Cimetta, 18, Toronto (OHL)
1989	Shayne Stevenson, 17, Kitchener (OHL)
1990	Bryan Smolinski, 21, Michigan State University
1991	Glen Murray, 18, Sudbury (OHL)
1992	Dmitri Kvartalnov, 16, San Diego (IHL)
1993	Kevyn Adams, 25, Miami of Ohio
1994	Evgeni Riabchikov, 21, Molot-Perm (Russia)
1995	Kyle McLaren, 9, Tacoma (WHL)
	Sean Brown, 21, Belleville (OHL)
1996	Johnathan Aitken, 8, Medicine Hat (WHL)
1997	Joe Thornton, 1, Sault Ste. Marie (OHL)*
	Sergei Samsonov, 8, Detroit (IHL)
1998	No first-round selection
1999	Nicholas Boynton, 21, Ottawa (OHL)
2000	Lars Jonsson, 7, Leksand, Sweden
	Martin Samuelsson, 27, MoDo, Sweden
2001	Shaone Morrisonn, 19, Kamloops (WHL)

*Designates first player chosen in draft.

SINGLE-SEASON INDIVIDUAL RECORDS

FORWARDS/DEFENSEMEN

Most goals
76—Phil Esposito, 1970-71

Most assists
102—Bobby Orr, 1970-71

Most points
152—Phil Esposito, 1970-71

Most penalty minutes
302—Jay Miller, 1987-88

Most power play goals
28—Phil Esposito, 1971-72

Most shorthanded goals
7—Jerry Toppazzini, 1957-58
Ed Westfall, 1970-71
Derek Sanderson, 1971-72

Most games with three or more goals
7—Phil Esposito, 1970-71

Most shots
550—Phil Esposito, 1970-71

GOALTENDERS

Most games
70—Frank Brimsek, 1949-50
Jack Gelineau, 1950-51
Eddie Johnston, 1964-64

Most minutes
4,200—Frank Brimsek, 1949-50
Jack Gelineau, 1950-51
Eddie Johnston, 1964-64

Most goals allowed
244—Frank Brimsek, 1949-50

Lowest goals-against average
1.18—Tiny Thompson, 1928-29

Most shutouts
15—Hal Winkler, 1927-28

Most wins
40—Pete Peeters, 1982-83

FRANCHISE LEADERS

Players in boldface played for club in 2000-01

FORWARDS/DEFENSEMEN

Games

Ray Bourque	1518
John Bucyk	1436
Wayne Cashman	1027
Terry O'Reilly	891
Rick Middleton	881

Goals

John Bucyk	545
Phil Esposito	459
Rick Middleton	402
Ray Bourque	395
Cam Neely	344

Assists

Ray Bourque	1111
John Bucyk	794
Bobby Orr	624
Phil Esposito	553
Wayne Cashman	516

Points

Ray Bourque	1506
John Bucyk	1339
Phil Esposito	1012
Rick Middleton	898
Bobby Orr	888

Penalty minutes

Terry O'Reilly	2095
Mike Milbury	1552
Keith Crowder	1261
Wayne Cashman	1041
Ray Bourque	1087

GOALTENDERS

Games

Cecil Thompson	468
Frankie Brimsek	444
Eddie Johnston	443
Gerry Cheevers	416
Gilles Gilbert	277

Shutouts

Cecil Thompson	74
Frankie Brimsek	35
Eddie Johnston	27
Gerry Cheevers	26
Jim Henry	24

Goals-against average
(2400 minutes minimum)

Hal Winkler	1.56
Cecil Thompson	1.99
Byron Dafoe	**2.33**
Charles Stewart	2.46
John Henderson	2.52

Wins

Tiny Thompson	252
Frankie Brimsek	230
Gerry Cheevers	229
Eddie Johnston	182
Gilles Gilbert	155

BUFFALO SABRES
YEAR-BY-YEAR RECORDS

Season	W	L	T	RT	Pts.	Finish	W	L	Highest round	Coach
		REGULAR SEASON					PLAYOFFS			
1970-71	24	39	15	—	63	5th/East	—	—		Punch Imlach
1971-72	16	43	19	—	51	6th/East	—	—		Punch Imlach, Joe Crozier
1972-73	37	27	14	—	88	4th/East	2	4	Division semifinals	Joe Crozier
1973-74	32	34	12	—	76	5th/East	—	—		Joe Crozier
1974-75	49	16	15	—	113	1st/Adams	10	7	Stanley Cup finals	Floyd Smith
1975-76	46	21	13	—	105	2nd/Adams	4	5	Quarterfinals	Floyd Smith
1976-77	48	24	8	—	104	2nd/Adams	2	4	Quarterfinals	Floyd Smith
1977-78	44	19	17	—	105	2nd/Adams	3	5	Quarterfinals	Marcel Pronovost
1978-79	36	28	16	—	88	2nd/Adams	1	2	Preliminaries	Marcel Pronovost, Bill Inglis
1979-80	47	17	16	—	110	1st/Adams	9	5	Semifinals	Scotty Bowman
1980-81	39	20	21	—	99	1st/Adams	4	4	Quarterfinals	Roger Neilson
1981-82	39	26	15	—	93	3rd/Adams	1	3	Division semifinals	Jim Roberts, Scotty Bowman
1982-83	38	29	13	—	89	3rd/Adams	6	4	Division finals	Scotty Bowman
1983-84	48	25	7	—	103	2nd/Adams	0	3	Division semifinals	Scotty Bowman
1984-85	38	28	14	—	90	3rd/Adams	2	3	Divison semifinals	Scotty Bowman
1985-86	37	37	6	—	80	5th/Adams	—	—		Jim Schoenfeld, Scotty Bowman
1986-87	28	44	8	—	64	5th/Adams	—	—		Scotty Bowman, Craig Ramsay
1987-88	37	32	11	—	85	3rd/Adams	2	4	Division semifinals	Ted Sator
1988-89	38	35	7	—	83	3rd/Adams	1	4	Division semifinals	Ted Sator
1989-90	45	27	8	—	98	2nd/Adams	2	4	Division semifinals	Rick Dudley
1990-91	31	30	19	—	81	3rd/Adams	2	4	Division semifinals	Rick Dudley, Ted Sator
1991-92	31	37	12	—	74	3rd/Adams	3	4	Division semifinals	Rick Dudley, John Muckler
1992-93	38	36	10	—	86	4th/Adams	4	4	Division finals	John Muckler
1993-94	43	32	9	—	95	4th/Northeast	3	4	Conference quarterfinals	John Muckler
1994-95	22	19	7	—	51	4th/Northeast	1	4	Conference quarterfinals	John Muckler
1995-96	33	42	7	—	73	5th/Northeast	—	—		Ted Nolan
1996-97	40	30	12	—	92	1st/Northeast	5	7	Conference semifinals	Ted Nolan
1997-98	36	29	17	—	89	3rd/Northeast	10	5	Conference finals	Lindy Ruff
1998-99	37	28	17	—	91	4rd/Northeast	14	7	Stanley Cup finals	Lindy Ruff
1999-00	35	36	11	4	85	3rd/Northeast	1	4	Conference quarterfinals	Lindy Ruff
2000-01	46	30	5	1	98	2nd/Northeast	7	6	Conference semifinals	Lindy Ruff

FIRST-ROUND ENTRY DRAFT CHOICES

Year   Player, Overall, Last amateur team (league)

1970—Gilbert Perreault, 1, Montreal (OHL)*
1971—Rick Martin, 5, Montreal (OHL)
1972—Jim Schoenfeld, 5, Niagara Falls (OHL)
1973—Morris Titanic, 12, Sudbury (OHL)
1974—Lee Fogolin, 11, Oshawa (OHL)
1975—Robert Sauve, 17, Laval (QMJHL)
1976—No first-round selection
1977—Ric Seiling, 14, St. Catharines (OHL)
1978—Larry Playfair, 13, Portland (WHL)
1979—Mike Ramsey, 11, University of Minnesota
1980—Steve Patrick, 20, Brandon (WHL)
1981—Jiri Dudacek, 17, Kladno (Czechoslovakia)
1982—Phil Housley, 6, South St. Paul H.S. (Minn.)
    Paul Cyr, 9, Victoria (WHL)
    Dave Andreychuk, 16, Oshawa (OHL)
1983—Tom Barrasso, 5, Acton Boxboro H.S. (Mass.)
    Norm Lacombe, 10, Univ. of New Hampshire
    Adam Creighton, 11, Ottawa (OHL)
1984—Bo Andersson, 18, Vastra Frolunda (Sweden)

Year   Player, Overall, Last amateur team (league)

1985—Carl Johansson, 14, Vastra Frolunda (Sweden)
1986—Shawn Anderson, 5, Team Canada
1987—Pierre Turgeon, 1, Granby (QMJHL)*
1988—Joel Savage, 13, Victoria (WHL)
1989—Kevin Haller, 14, Regina (WHL)
1990—Brad May, 14, Niagara Falls (OHL)
1991—Philippe Boucher, 13, Granby (QMJHL)
1992—David Cooper, 11, Medicine Hat (WHL)
1993—No first-round selection
1994—Wayne Primeau, 17, Owen Sound (OHL)
1995—Jay McKee, 14, Niagara Falls (OHL)
    Martin Biron, 16, Beauport (QMJHL)
1996—Erik Rasmussen, 7, University of Minnesota
1997—Mika Noronen, 21, Tappara Tampere (Finland)
1998—Dimitri Kalinin, 18, Traktor Chelyabinsk (Russia)
1999—Barrett Heisten, 20, Maine (H. East)
2000—Artem Kriukov, 15, Yaroslavl (Russia)
2001—Jiri Novotny, 22, Budejovice (Czech. Rep.)
*Designates first player chosen in draft.

SINGLE-SEASON INDIVIDUAL RECORDS

FORWARDS/DEFENSEMEN

Most goals
76—Alexander Mogilny, 1992-93

Most assists
95—Pat LaFontaine, 1992-93

Most points
148—Pat LaFontaine, 1992-93

Most penalty minutes
354—Rob Ray, 1991-92

Most power play goals
28—Dave Andreychuk, 1991-92

Most shorthanded goals
8—Don Luce, 1994-95

Most games with three or more goals
7—Rick Martin, 1995-96
    Alexander Mogilny, 1992-93

Most shots
360—Alexander Mogilny, 1992-93

GOALTENDERS

Most games
72—Don Edwards, 1997-78
Dominik Hasek, 1997-98

Most minutes
4,220—Dominik Hasek, 1997-98

Most shots against
2,190—Roger Crozier, 1971-72

Most goals allowed
214—Roger Crozier, 1971-72
Tom Barrasso, 1985-86

Lowest goals-against average
1.87—Dominik Hasek, 1998-99

Most shutouts
13—Dominik Hasek, 1997-98

Most wins
38—Don Edwards, 1977-78

Most losses
34—Roger Crozier, 1971-72

Most ties
17—Don Edwards, 1977-78

FRANCHISE LEADERS

Players in boldface played for club in 2000-01

FORWARDS/DEFENSEMEN

Games
Gilbert Perreault 1191
Craig Ramsay...................................1070
Mike Ramsey.....................................911
Bill Hajt...854
Rob Ray...777

Goals
Gilbert Perreault 512
Rick Martin..382
Dave Andreychuk 348
Danny Gare 267
Craig Ramsay 252

Assists
Gilbert Perreault 814
Dave Andreychuk 423
Craig Ramsay.....................................420
Phil Housley 380
Rene Robert 330

Points

Gilbert Perreault 1326
Dave Andreychuk 771
Rick Martin..695
Craig Ramsay 672
Phil Housley 558

Penalty minutes
Rob Ray 2897
Mike Foligno......................................1450
Larry Playfair.....................................1390
Brad May 1323
Matthew Barnaby 1248

GOALTENDERS

Games
Dominik Hasek..........................491
Don Edwards.............................307
Tom Barrasso............................266
Bob Sauve................................246
Daren Puppa.............................215

Shutouts

Dominik Hasek 55
Don Edwards..................................14
Tom Barrasso.................................13
Roger Crozier.................................10
Martin Biron....................................7
Bob Sauve.......................................7

Goals-against average
(2400 minutes minimum)
Dominik Hasek.........................2.23
Martin Biron.............................2.52
Gerry Desjardins 2.81
Don Edwards.............................2.90
Dave Dryden.............................3.06

Wins
Dominik Hasek.........................234
Don Edwards.............................156
Tom Barrasso............................124
Bob Sauve................................119
Daren Puppa..............................96

CALGARY FLAMES
YEAR-BY-YEAR RECORDS

			REGULAR SEASON				PLAYOFFS			
Season	W	L	T	RT	Pts.	Finish	W	L	Highest round	Coach
1980-81	39	27	14	—	92	3rd/Patrick	9	7	Semifinals	Al MacNeil
1981-82	29	34	17	—	75	3rd/Smythe	0	3	Division semifinals	Al MacNeil
1982-83	32	34	14	—	78	2nd/Smythe	4	5	Division finals	Bob Johnson
1983-84	34	32	14	—	82	2nd/Smythe	6	5	Division finals	Bob Johnson
1984-85	41	27	12	—	94	3rd/Smythe	1	3	Division semifinals	Bob Johnson
1985-86	40	31	9	—	89	2nd/Smythe	12	10	Stanley Cup finals	Bob Johnson
1986-87	46	31	3	—	95	2nd/Smythe	2	4	Division semifinals	Bob Johnson
1987-88	48	23	9	—	105	1st/Smythe	4	5	Division finals	Terry Crisp
1988-89	54	17	9	—	117	1st/Smythe	16	6	Stanley Cup champ	Terry Crisp
1989-90	42	23	15	—	99	1st/Smythe	2	4	Division semifinals	Terry Crisp
1990-91	46	26	8	—	100	2nd/Smythe	3	4	Division semifinals	Doug Risebrough
1991-92	31	37	12	—	74	5th/Smythe	—	—		Doug Risebrough, Guy Charron
1992-93	43	30	11	—	97	2nd/Smythe	2	4	Division semifinals	Dave King
1993-94	42	29	13	—	97	1st/Pacific	3	4	Conference quarterfinals	Dave King
1994-95	24	17	7	—	55	1st/Pacific	3	4	Conference quarterfinals	Dave King
1995-96	34	37	11	—	79	T2nd/Pacific	0	4	Conference quarterfinals	Pierre Page
1996-97	32	41	9	—	73	5th/Pacific	—	—		Pierre Page
1997-98	26	41	15	—	67	5th/Pacific	—	—		Brian Sutter
1998-99	30	40	12	—	72	3rd/Pacific	—	—		Brian Sutter
1999-00	31	41	10	5	77	4th/Pacific	—	—		Brian Sutter
2000-01	27	36	15	4	73	4th/Pacific	—	—		Don Hay, Greg Gilbert

Franchise was formerly in Atlanta from 1972-73 through 1979-80 seasons.

FIRST-ROUND ENTRY DRAFT CHOICES

Year   Player, Overall, Last amateur team (league)
1980—Denis Cyr, 13, Montreal (OHL)
1981—Al MacInnis, 15, Kitchener (OHL)
1982—No first-round selection
1983—Dan Quinn, 13, Belleville (OHL)
1984—Gary Roberts, 12, Ottawa (OHL)
1985—Chris Biotti, 17, Belmont Hill H.S. (Mass.)

Year   Player, Overall, Last amateur team (league)
1986—George Pelawa, 16, Bemidji H.S. (Minn.)
1987—Bryan Deasley, 19, University of Michigan
1988—Jason Muzzatti, 21, Michigan State University
1989—No first-round selection
1990—Trevor Kidd, 11, Brandon (WHL)
1991—Niklas Sundblad, 19, AIK (Sweden)

Year	Player, Overall, Last amateur team (league)
1992—Cory Stillman, 6, Windsor (OHL)
1993—Jesper Mattsson, 18, Malmo (Sweden)
1994—Chris Dingman, 19, Brandon (WHL)
1995—Denis Gauthier, 20, Drummondville (QMJHL)
1996—Derek Morris, 13, Regina (WHL)

Year	Player, Overall, Last amateur team (league)
1997—Daniel Tkaczuk, 6, Barrie (OHL)
1998—Rico Fata, 6, London (OHL)
1999—Oleg Saprykin, 11, Seattle (WHL)
2000—Brent Krahn, 9, Calgary (WHL)
2001—Chuck Kobasew, 14, Boston College

SINGLE-SEASON INDIVIDUAL RECORDS

FORWARDS/DEFENSEMEN

Most goals
66—Lanny McDonald, 1982-83

Most assists
82—Kent Nilsson, 1980-81

Most points
131—Kent Nilsson, 1980-81

Most penalty minutes
375—Tim Hunter, 1988-89

Most power play goals
31—Joe Nieuwendyk, 1987-88

Most shorthanded goals
9—Kent Nilsson, 1984-85

Most games with three or more goals
5—Hakan Loob, 1987-88
　Theo Fleury, 1990-91

Most shots
353—Theo Fleury, 1995-96

GOALTENDERS

Most games
64—Mike Vernon, 1987-88
　Mike Vernon, 1992-93

Most minutes
3,732—Mike Vernon, 1992-93

Most goals allowed
229—Rejean Lemelin, 1985-86

Lowest goals-against average
2.32—Fred Brathwaite, 2000-01

Most shutouts
5—Fred Brathwaite, 1999-2000
　Fred Brathwaite, 2000-01

Most wins
39—Mike Vernon, 1987-88

Most losses
30—Mike Vernon, 1991-92

Most ties
11—Pat Riggin, 1981-82

FRANCHISE LEADERS

Players in boldface played for club in 2000-01

FORWARDS/DEFENSEMEN

Games

Al MacInnis	803
Theo Fleury	791
Joel Otto	730
Jim Peplinski	711
Gary Suter	617

Goals

Theo Fleury	364
Joe Nieuwendyk	314
Gary Roberts	257
Kent Nilsson	229
Lanny McDonald	215

Assists

Al MacInnis	609
Theo Fleury	466
Gary Suter	437
Joe Nieuwendyk	302
Paul Reinhart	297

Points

Theo Fleury	830
Al MacInnis	822
Joe Nieuwendyk	616
Gary Suter	565
Gary Roberts	505

Penalty minutes

Tim Hunter	2405
Gary Roberts	1736
Joel Otto	1642
Jim Peplinski	1467
Ronnie Stern	1288

GOALTENDERS

Games

Mike Vernon	**508**
Reggie Lemelin	303
Trevor Kidd	178
Fred Brathwaite	**138**
Don Edwards	114

Shutouts

Mike Vernon	**12**
Fred Brathwaite	**11**
Trevor Kidd	10
Reggie Lemelin	6
Rick Tabaracci	4
Rick Wamsley	4

Goals-against average
(2400 minutes minimum)

Fred Brathwaite	**2.54**
Rick Tabaracci	2.81
Trevor Kidd	2.83
Dwayne Roloson	2.95
Mike Vernon	**3.28**

Wins

Mike Vernon	**257**
Reggie Lemelin	136
Trevor Kidd	72
Rick Wamsley	53
Fred Brathwaite	**51**

CALIFORNIA GOLDEN SEALS (DEFUNCT)
YEAR-BY-YEAR RECORDS

	REGULAR SEASON					PLAYOFFS			
Season	W	L	T	Pts.	Finish	W	L	Highest round	Coach
1967-68*	15	42	17	42	6th/West	—	—		Bert Olmstead, Gordie Fashoway
1968-69*	29	36	11	69	2nd/West	3	4	Division semifinals	Fred Glover
1969-70*	22	40	14	58	4th/West	0	4	Division semifinals	Fred Glover
1970-71	20	53	5	45	7th/West	—	—		Fred Glover
1971-72	21	39	18	60	6th/West	—	—		Fred Glover, Vic Stasiuk
1972-73	16	46	16	48	8th/West	—	—		Garry Young, Fred Glover
1973-74	13	55	10	36	8th/West	—	—		Fred Glover, Marsh Johnston
1974-75	19	48	13	51	4th/Adams	—	—		Marsh Johnston
1975-76	27	42	11	65	4th/Adams	—	—		Jack Evans

*Oakland Seals.
Franchise relocated and became Cleveland Barons following 1975-76 season.

FIRST-ROUND ENTRY DRAFT CHOICES

Year   Player, Overall, Last amateur team (league)
1969—Tony Featherstone, 7, Peterborough (OHA)
1970—Chris Oddleifson, 10 Winnipeg (WCHL)
1971—No first-round selection
1972—No first-round selection

Year   Player, Overall, Last amateur team (league)
1973—No first-round selection
1974—Rick Hampton, 3, St. Catharines (OHA)
        Ron Chipperfield, 17, Brandon (WCHL)
1975—Ralph Klassen, 3, Saskatoon (WCHL)

INDIVIDUAL SINGLE-SEASON RECORDS

FORWARDS/DEFENSEMEN

Most goals
34—Norm Ferguson, 1968-69

Most assists
49—Ted Hampson, 1968-69

Most points
75—Ted Hampson, 1968-69

Most penalty minutes
217—Dennis Hextall, 1970-71

Most power play goals
12—Bill Hicke, 1967-68

Most shorthanded goals
5—Dennis Maruk, 1975-76

Most games with three or more goals
2—Earl Ingarfield, 1969-70
    Reggie Leach, 1973-74
    Al MacAdam, 1975-76
    Wayne Merrick, 1975-76

Most shots
274—Carol Vadnais, 1968-69

GOALTENDERS

Most games
71—Gary Smith, 1970-71

Most minutes
3,975—Gary Smith, 1970-71

Most goals allowed
256—Gary Smith, 1970-71

Lowest goals-against average
2.86—Charlie Hodge, 1967-68

Most shutouts
4—Gary Smith, 1968-69
    Gilles Meloche, 1971-72

Most wins
19—Gary Smith, 1969-70
    Gary Smith, 1970-71

Most losses
48—Gary Smith, 1970-71

Most ties
14—Gilles Meloche, 1972-73

FRANCHISE LEADERS

FORWARDS/DEFENSEMEN

Games
Bert Marshall 313
Gary Ehman 297
Joey Johnston 288
Norm Ferguson 279
Gary Croteau 270

Goals
Joey Johnston 84
Bill Hicke 79
Norm Ferguson 73
Gary Ehman 69
Carol Vadnais 63

Assists
Ted Hampson 123
Bill Hicke 101
Joey Johnston 101
Gary Ehman 86
Carol Vadnais 83

Points
Joey Johnston 185
Ted Hampson 184
Bill Hicke 180
Gary Ehman 155
Carol Vadnais 146

Penalty minutes
Carol Vadnais 560
Bob Stewart 499
Bert Marshall 395
Joey Johnston 308
Doug Roberts 280

GOALTENDERS

Games
Gilles Meloche 250
Gary Smith 211
Charlie Hodge 86
Gary Simmons 74
Marv Edwards 35

Shutouts
Gary Smith 9
Gilles Meloche 8
Gary Simmons 4
Charlie Hodge 3
Marv Edwards 1

Goals-against average
(2400 minutes minimum)
Charlie Hodge 3.09
Gary Smith 3.33
Gary Simmons 3.49
Gilles Meloche 3.83

Wins
Charlie Hodge 3.09
Gary Smith 3.33
Gary Simmons 3.49
Gilles Meloche 3.83

CAROLINA HURRICANES
YEAR-BY-YEAR RECORDS

	REGULAR SEASON						PLAYOFFS			
Season	W	L	T	RT	Pts.	Finish	W	L	Highest round	Coach
1997-98	33	41	8	—	74	6th/Northeast	—	—		Paul Maurice
1998-99	34	30	18	—	86	1st/Southeast	2	4	Conference quarterfinals	Paul Maurice
1999-00	37	35	10	0	84	3rd/Southeast	—	—		Paul Maurice
2000-01	38	32	9	3	88	2nd/Southeast	2	4	Conference quarterfinals	Paul Maurice

Franchise was formerly known as Hartford Whalers and relocated to Carolina following 1996-97 season.

FIRST-ROUND ENTRY DRAFT CHOICES

Year   Player, Overall, Last amateur team (league)
1998—Jeff Heerema, 11, Sarnia (OHL)
1999—David Tanabe, 16, Wisconsin (WCHA)

Year   Player, Overall, Last amateur team (league)
2000—No first-round selection
2001—Igor Knyazev, 15, Spartak Jr. (Russia)

FORWARDS/DEFENSEMEN

Most goals
41—Jeff O'Neill, 2000-01

Most assists
50—Ron Francis, 1999-2000
　　Ron Francis, 2000-01

Most points
73—Ron Francis, 1999-2000

Most penalty minutes
204—Stu Grimson, 1997-98

Most power play goals
17—Jeff O'Neill, 2000-01

Most shorthanded goals
3—Keith Primeau, 1997-98

Most games with three or more goals
2—Sami Kapanen, 1997-98

Most shots
254—Sami Kapanen, 1998-99

GOALTENDERS

Most games
77—Arturs Irbe, 2000-01

Most minutes
4,406—Arturs Irbe, 2000-01

Most shots against
1,947—Arturs Irbe, 2000-01

Most goals allowed
180—Arturs Irbe, 2000-01

Lowest goals-against average
2.17—Trevor Kidd, 1997-98

Most shutouts
6—Arturs Irbe, 1998-99
　　Arturs Irbe, 2000-01

Most wins
37—Arturs Irbe, 2000-01

Most losses
29—Arturs Irbe, 2000-01

Most ties
12—Arturs Irbe, 1998-99

FRANCHISE LEADERS

Players in boldface played for club in 2000-01

FORWARDS/DEFENSEMEN

Games

Sami Kapanen	320
Jeff O'Neill	311
Glen Wesley	305
Martin Gelinas	276
Bates Battaglia	250

Goals

Jeff O'Neill	101
Sami Kapanen	94
Martin Gelinas	62
Ron Francis	59
Gary Roberts	57

Assists

Sami Kapanen	133
Ron Francis	131
Jeff O'Neill	99
Gary Roberts	87
Martin Gelinas	74

Points

Sami Kapanen	227
Jeff O'Neill	200
Ron Francis	190
Gary Roberts	144
Martin Gelinas	136

Penalty minutes

Gary Roberts	343
Jeff O'Neill	311
Dave Karpa	266
Nolan Pratt	229
Stu Grimson	204

GOALTENDERS

Games

Arturs Irbe	214
Trevor Kidd	72
Sean Burke	25
Tyler Moss	12
Eric Fichaud	9

Shutouts

Arturs Irbe	17
Trevor Kidd	5
Sean Burke	1
Eric Fichaud	1

Goals-against average
(2400 minutes minimum)

Trevor Kidd	2.34
Arturs Irbe	2.37

Wins

Arturs Irbe	98
Trevor Kidd	28
Sean Burke	7
Kirk McLean	4
Eric Fichaud	3

CHICAGO BLACKHAWKS
YEAR-BY-YEAR RECORDS

	REGULAR SEASON						PLAYOFFS			
Season	W	L	T	RT	Pts.	Finish	W	L	Highest round	Coach
1926-27	19	22	3	—	41	3rd/American	*0	1	Quarterfinals	Pete Muldoon
1927-28	7	34	3	—	17	5th/American	—	—		Barney Stanley, Hugh Lehman
1928-29	7	29	8	—	22	5th/American	—	—		Herb Gardiner
1929-30	21	18	5	—	47	2nd/American	*0	1	Quarterfinals	Tom Schaughnessy, Bill Tobin
1930-31	24	17	3	—	51	2nd/American	*5	3	Stanley Cup finals	Dick Irvin
1931-32	18	19	11	—	47	2nd/American	1	1	Quarterfinals	Dick Irvin, Bill Tobin
1932-33	16	20	12	—	44	4th/American	—	—		Godfrey Matheson, Emil Iverson
1933-34	20	17	11	—	51	2nd/American	6	2	Stanley Cup champ	Tom Gorman
1934-35	26	17	5	—	57	2nd/American	*0	1	Quarterfinals	Clem Loughlin
1935-36	21	19	8	—	50	3rd/American	1	1	Quarterfinals	Clem Loughlin
1936-37	14	27	7	—	35	4th/American	—	—		Clem Loughlin
1937-38	14	25	9	—	37	3rd/American	7	3	Stanley Cup champ	Bill Stewart
1938-39	12	28	8	—	32	7th	—	—		Bill Stewart, Paul Thompson
1939-40	23	19	6	—	52	4th	0	2	Quarterfinals	Paul Thompson
1940-41	16	25	7	—	39	5th	2	3	Semifinals	Paul Thompson
1941-42	22	23	3	—	47	4th	1	2	Quarterfinals	Paul Thompson
1942-43	17	18	15	—	49	5th	—	—		Paul Thompson
1943-44	22	23	5	—	49	4th	4	5	Stanley Cup finals	Paul Thompson
1944-45	13	30	7	—	33	5th	—	—		Paul Thompson, John Gottselig
1945-46	23	20	7	—	53	3rd	0	4	League semifinals	John Gottselig

NHL HISTORY Team by team

| | REGULAR SEASON | | | | | | PLAYOFFS | | | |
Season	W	L	T	RT	Pts.	Finish	W	L	Highest round	Coach
1946-47	19	37	4	—	42	6th	—	—		John Gottselig
1947-48	20	34	6	—	46	6th	—	—		John Gottselig, Charlie Conacher
1948-49	21	31	8	—	50	5th	—	—		Charlie Conacher
1949-50	22	38	10	—	54	6th	—	—		Charlie Conacher
1950-51	13	47	10	—	36	6th	—	—		Ebbie Goodfellow
1951-52	17	44	9	—	43	6th	—	—		Ebbie Goodfellow
1952-53	27	28	15	—	69	4th	3	4	League semifinals	Sid Abel
1953-54	12	51	7	—	31	6th	—	—		Sid Abel
1954-55	13	40	17	—	43	6th	—	—		Frank Eddolls
1955-56	19	39	12	—	50	6th	—	—		Dick Irvin
1956-57	16	39	15	—	47	6th	—	—		Tommy Ivan
1957-58	24	39	7	—	55	5th	—	—		Tommy Ivan, Rudy Pilous
1958-59	28	29	13	—	69	3rd	2	4	League semifinals	Rudy Pilous
1959-60	28	29	13	—	69	3rd	0	4	League semifinals	Rudy Pilous
1960-61	29	24	17	—	75	3rd	8	4	Stanley Cup champ	Rudy Pilous
1961-62	31	26	13	—	75	3rd	6	6	Stanley Cup finals	Rudy Pilous
1962-63	32	21	17	—	81	2nd	2	4	League semifinals	Rudy Pilous
1963-64	36	22	12	—	84	2nd	3	4	League semifinals	Billy Reay
1964-65	34	28	8	—	76	3rd	7	7	Stanley Cup finals	Billy Reay
1965-66	37	25	8	—	82	2nd	2	4	League semifinals	Billy Reay
1966-67	41	17	12	—	94	1st	2	4	League semifinals	Billy Reay
1967-68	32	26	16	—	80	4th/East	5	6	Division finals	Billy Reay
1968-69	34	33	9	—	77	6th/East	—	—		Billy Reay
1969-70	45	22	9	—	99	1st/East	4	4	Division finals	Billy Reay
1970-71	49	20	9	—	107	1st/West	11	7	Stanley Cup finals	Billy Reay
1971-72	46	17	15	—	107	1st/West	4	4	Division finals	Billy Reay
1972-73	42	27	9	—	93	1st/West	10	6	Stanley Cup finals	Billy Reay
1973-74	41	14	23	—	105	2nd/West	6	5	Division finals	Billy Reay
1974-75	37	35	8	—	82	3rd/Smythe	3	5	Quarterfinals	Billy Reay
1975-76	32	30	18	—	82	1st/Smythe	0	4	Quarterfinals	Billy Reay
1976-77	26	43	11	—	63	3rd/Smythe	0	2	Preliminaries	Billy Reay, Bill White
1977-78	32	29	19	—	83	1st/Smythe	0	4	Quarterfinals	Bob Pulford
1978-79	29	36	15	—	73	1st/Smythe	0	4	Quarterfinals	Bob Pulford
1979-80	34	27	19	—	87	1st/Smythe	3	4	Quarterfinals	Eddie Johnston
1980-81	31	33	16	—	78	2nd/Smythe	0	3	Preliminaries	Keith Magnuson
1981-82	30	38	12	—	72	4th/Norris	8	7	Conference finals	Keith Magnuson, Bob Pulford
1982-83	47	23	10	—	104	1st/Norris	7	6	Conference finals	Orval Tessier
1983-84	30	42	8	—	68	4th/Norris	2	3	Division semifinals	Orval Tessier
1984-85	38	35	7	—	83	2nd/Norris	9	6	Conference finals	Orval Tessier, Bob Pulford
1985-86	39	33	8	—	86	1st/Norris	0	3	Division semifinals	Bob Pulford
1986-87	29	37	14	—	72	3rd/Norris	0	4	Division semifinals	Bob Pulford
1987-88	30	41	9	—	69	3rd/Norris	1	4	Division semifinals	Bob Murdoch
1988-89	27	41	12	—	66	4th/Norris	9	7	Conference finals	Mike Keenan
1989-90	41	33	6	—	88	1st/Norris	10	10	Conference finals	Mike Keenan
1990-91	49	23	8	—	106	1st/Norris	2	4	Division semifinals	Mike Keenan
1991-92	36	29	15	—	87	2nd/Norris	12	6	Stanley Cup finals	Mike Keenan
1992-93	47	25	12	—	106	1st/Norris	0	4	Division semifinals	Darryl Sutter
1993-94	39	36	9	—	87	5th/Central	2	4	Conference quarterfinals	Darryl Sutter
1994-95	24	19	5	—	53	3rd/Central	9	7	Conference finals	Darryl Sutter
1995-96	40	28	14	—	94	2nd/Central	6	4	Conference semifinals	Craig Hartsburg
1996-97	34	35	13	—	81	5th/Central	2	4	Conference quarterfinals	Craig Hartsburg
1997-98	30	39	13	—	73	5th/Central	—	—		Craig Hartsburg
1998-99	29	41	12	—	70	3rd/Central	—	—		Dirk Graham, Lorne Molleken
1999-00	33	39	10	2	78	3rd/Central	—	—		Lorne Molleken, Bob Pulford
2000-01	29	40	8	5	71	T4th/Central	—	—		Alpo Suhonen, Denis Savard, Al MacAdam

*Won-lost record does not indicate tie(s) resulting from two-game, total-goals series that year (two-game, total-goals series were played from 1917-18 through 1935-36).

FIRST-ROUND ENTRY DRAFT CHOICES

Year   Player, Overall, Last amateur team (league)

1969—J.P. Bordeleau, 13, Montreal (OHL)
1970—Dan Maloney, 14, London (OHL)
1971—Dan Spring, 12, Edmonton (WCHL)
1972—Phil Russell, 13, Edmonton (WCHL)
1973—Darcy Rota, 13, Edmonton (WCHL)
1974—Grant Mulvey, 16, Calgary (WCHL)
1975—Greg Vaydik, 7, Medicine Hat (WCHL)
1976—Real Cloutier, 9, Quebec (WHA)
1977—Doug Wilson, 6, Ottawa (OHL)

Year   Player, Overall, Last amateur team (league)

1978—Tim Higgins, 10, Ottawa (OHL)
1979—Keith Brown, 7, Portland (WHL)
1980—Denis Savard, 3, Montreal (QMJHL)
      Jerome Dupont, 15, Toronto (OHL)
1981—Tony Tanti, 12, Oshawa (OHL)
1982—Ken Yaremchuk, 7, Portland (WHL)
1983—Bruce Cassidy, 18, Ottawa (OHL)
1984—Ed Olczyk, 3, U.S. Olympic Team
1985—Dave Manson, 11, Prince Albert (WHL)

Year	Player, Overall, Last amateur team (league)
1986	Everett Sanipass, 14, Verdun (QMJHL)
1987	Jimmy Waite, 8, Chicoutimi (QMJHL)
1988	Jeremy Roenick, 8, Thayer Academy (Mass.)
1989	Adam Bennett, 6, Sudbury (OHL)
1990	Karl Dykhuis, 16, Hull (QMJHL)
1991	Dean McAmmond, 22, Prince Albert (WHL)
1992	Sergei Krivokrasov, 12, Central Red Army, CIS
1993	Eric Lecompte, 24, Hull (QMJHL)
1994	Ethan Moreau, 14, Niagara Falls (OHL)
1995	Dimitri Nabokov, 19, Krylja Sovetov, CIS

Year	Player, Overall, Last amateur team (league)
1996	No first-round selection
1997	Daniel Cleary, 13, Belleville (OHL)
	Ty Jones, 16, Spokane (WHL)
1998	Mark Bell, 8, Ottawa (OHL)
1999	Steve McCarthy, 23, Kootenay (WHL)
2000	Mikhail Yakubov, 10, Togliatta (Russia)
	Pavel Vorobiev, 11, Yaroslavl (Russia)
2001	Tuomo Ruutu, 9, Jokerit (Finland)
	Adam Munro, 29, Erie (OHL)

SINGLE-SEASON INDIVIDUAL RECORDS

FORWARDS/DEFENSEMEN

Most goals
58—Bobby Hull, 1968-69

Most assists
87—Denis Savard, 1981-82
Denis Savard, 1987-88

Most points
131—Denis Savard, 1987-88

Most penalty minutes
408—Mike Peluso, 1991-92

Most power play goals
24—Jeremy Roenick, 1993-94

Most shorthanded goals
10—Dirk Graham, 1988-89

Most games with three or more goals
4—Bobby Hull, 1959-60
Bobby Hull, 1965-66

Most shots
414—Bobby Hull, 1968-69

GOALTENDERS

Most games
74—Ed Belfour, 1990-91

Most minutes
4,219—Tony Esposito, 1974-75

Most goals allowed
246—Harry Lumley, 1950-51
Tony Esposito, 1980-81

Lowest goals-against average
1.73—Charles Gardiner, 1933-34

Most shutouts
15—Tony Esposito, 1969-70

Most wins
43—Ed Belfour, 1990-91

Most losses
47—Al Rollins, 1953-54

Most ties
21—Tony Esposito, 1973-74

FRANCHISE LEADERS

Players in boldface played for club in 2000-01

FORWARDS/DEFENSEMEN

Games

Stan Mikita	1394
Bobby Hull	1036
Eric Nesterenko	1013
Bob Murray	1008
Doug Wilson	938

Goals

Bobby Hull	604
Stan Mikita	541
Steve Larmer	406
Denis Savard	377
Dennis Hull	298

Assists

Stan Mikita	926
Denis Savard	719
Doug Wilson	554
Bobby Hull	549
Steve Larmer	517

Points

Stan Mikita	1467
Bobby Hull	1153
Denis Savard	1096
Steve Larmer	923
Doug Wilson	779

GOALTENDERS

Games

Tony Esposito	873
Glenn Hall	618
Ed Belfour	415
Mike Karakas	331
Charlie Gardiner	316

Shutouts

Tony Esposito	74
Glenn Hall	51
Chuck Gardiner	42
Ed Belfour	30
Mike Karakas	28

Goals-against average
(2400 minutes minimum)

Lorne Chabot	1.83
Charlie Gardiner	2.02
Paul Goodman	2.17
Jeff Hackett	2.45
Dominik Hasek	2.58

Wins

Tony Esposito	418
Glenn Hall	275
Ed Belfour	201
Murray Bannerman	116
Mike Karakas	114

CLEVELAND BARONS (DEFUNCT)
YEAR-BY-YEAR RECORDS

	REGULAR SEASON					PLAYOFFS			
Season	W	L	T	Pts.	Finish	W	L	Highest round	Coach
1976-77	25	42	13	63	4th/Adams	—	—		Jack Evans
1977-78	22	45	13	57	4th/Adams	—	—		Jack Evans

Franchise was formerly known as California Golden Seals and relocated to Cleveland following 1995-96 season. Barons disbanded after 1977-78 season. Owners bought Minnesota franchise and a number of Cleveland players were awarded to North Stars; remaining players were dispersed to other clubs in draft.

Year   Player, Overall, Last amateur team (league)
1976—Bjorn Johansson, 5, Orebro IK (Sweden)

Year   Player, Overall, Last amateur team (league)
1977—Mike Crombeen, 5, Kingston (OHA)

SINGLE-SEASON INDIVIDUAL RECORDS

FORWARDS/DEFENSEMEN

Most goals
36—Dennis Maruk, 1977-78

Most assists
50—Dennis Maruk, 1976-77

Most points
78—Dennis Maruk, 1976-77

Most penalty minutes
229—Randy Holt, 1977-78

Most power play goals
7—Mike Fidler, 1976-77
   Kris Manery, 1977-78

Most shorthanded goals
2—Dennis Maruk, 1977-78

Most games with three or more goals
1—Bob Murdoch, 1976-77
   Dennis Maruk, 1977-78
   Chuck Arnason, 1977-78

Most shots
268—Dennis Maruk, 1976-77

GOALTENDERS

Most games
54—Gilles Meloche, 1977-78

Most minutes
3,100—Gilles Meloche, 1977-78

Most goals allowed
195—Gilles Meloche, 1977-78

Lowest goals-against average
3.47—Gilles Meloche, 1976-77

Most shutouts
2—Gary Edwards, 1976-77
   Gilles Meloche, 1976-77

Most wins
19—Gilles Meloche, 1976-77

Most losses
27—Gilles Meloche, 1977-78

Most ties
8—Gilles Meloche, 1977-78

FRANCHISE LEADERS

FORWARDS/DEFENSEMEN

Games

Al MacAdam	160
Dennis Maruk	156
Greg Smith	154
Dave Gardner	151
Bob Stewart	145

Goals

Dennis Maruk	64
Mike Fidler	40
Al MacAdam	38
Bob Murdoch	37
Dave Gardner	35

Assists

Dennis Maruk	85
Al MacAdam	73
Dave Gardner	47
Greg Smith	47
Bob Murdoch	45

Points

Dennis Maruk	149
Al MacAdam	111
Mike Fidler	84
Dave Gardner	82
Bob Murdoch	82

Penalty minutes

Randy Holt	229
Len Frig	213
Bob Stewart	192
Greg Smith	157
Mike Christie	128

GOALTENDERS

Games

Gilles Meloche	105
Gary Edwards	47
Gary Simmons	15

Shutouts

Gilles Meloche	3
Gary Edwards	2
Gary Simmons	1

**Goals-against average
(2400 minutes minimum)**

Gary Edwards	4.36
Gilles Meloche	3.62

Wins

Gilles Meloche	35
Gary Edwards	10
Gary Simmons	2

COLORADO AVALANCHE
YEAR-BY-YEAR RECORDS

	REGULAR SEASON						PLAYOFFS			
Season	W	L	T	RT	Pts.	Finish	W	L	Highest round	Coach
1995-96	47	25	10	—	104	1st/Pacific	16	6	Stanley Cup champ	Marc Crawford
1996-97	49	24	9	—	107	1st/Pacific	10	7	Conference finals	Marc Crawford
1997-98	39	26	17	—	95	1st/Pacific	3	4	Conference quarterfinals	Marc Crawford
1998-99	44	28	10	—	98	1st/Northwest	11	8	Conference finals	Bob Hartley
1999-00	42	29	11	1	96	1st/Northwest	11	6	Conference finals	Bob Hartley
2000-01	52	16	10	4	118	1st/Northwest	16	7	Stanley Cup champ	Bob Hartley

Franchise was formerly known as Quebec Nordiques and relocated to Colorado following 1994-95 season.

FIRST-ROUND ENTRY DRAFT CHOICES

Year   Player, Overall, Last amateur team (league)
1996—Peter Ratchuk, 25, Shattuck-St. Mary's H.S. (Min.)
1997—Kevin Grimes, 26, Kingston (OHL)
1998—Alex Tanguay, 12, Halifax (QMJHL)
   Martin Skoula, 17, Barrie (OHL)
   Robyn Regehr, 19, Kamloops (WHL)

Year   Player, Overall, Last amateur team (league)
   Scott Parker, 20, Kelowna (WHL)
1999—Mihail Kuleshov, 25, Cherepovec, Russia
2000—Vaclav Nedorost, 14, Budejovice, Czech Republic
2001—No first-round selection

SINGLE-SEASON INDIVIDUAL RECORDS

FORWARDS/DEFENSEMEN

Most goals
54—Joe Sakic, 2000-01

Most assists
86—Peter Forsberg, 1995-96

Most points
120—Joe Sakic, 1995-96

Most penalty minutes
259—Jeff Odgers, 1998-99

Most power play goals
19—Joe Sakic, 2000-01

Most shorthanded goals
6—Joe Sakic, 1995-96

Most games with three or more goals
2—Peter Forsberg, 1995-96
   Valeri Kamensky, 1995-96
   Claude Lemieux, 1995-96
   Joe Sakic, 1999-2000
   Joe Sakic, 2000-01

Most shots
332—Joe Sakic, 2000-01

GOALTENDERS

Most games
65—Patrick Roy, 1997-98

Most minutes
3,835—Patrick Roy, 1997-98

Most shots against
1,861—Patrick Roy, 1996-97

Most goals allowed
153—Patrick Roy, 1997-98

Lowest goals-against average
2.21—Patrick Roy, 2000-01

Most shutouts
7—Patrick Roy, 1996-97

Most wins
40—Patrick Roy, 2000-01

Most losses
21—Patrick Roy, 1999-2000

Most ties
13—Patrick Roy, 1997-98

FRANCHISE LEADERS

Players in boldface played for club in 2000-01

FORWARDS/DEFENSEMEN

Games
Stephane Yelle............................432
Joe Sakic 426
Peter Forsberg 419
Adam Deadmarsh 405
Jon Klemm 393

Goals
Joe Sakic 223
Peter Forsberg 154
Adam Deadmarsh 129
Valeri Kamensky................................106
Claude Lemieux.................................106

Assists
Peter Forsberg 376
Joe Sakic 329
Sandis Ozolinsh.................................181
Valeri Kamensky................................155
Adam Deadmarsh 142

Points
Joe Sakic 552
Peter Forsberg 530
Adam Deadmarsh 271
Valeri Kamensky................................261
Sandis Ozolinsh.................................253

Penalty minutes
Adam Deadmarsh 667
Adam Foote 579
Jeff Odgers..472
Peter Forsberg 428
Claude Lemieux.................................381

GOALTENDERS

Games
Patrick Roy 352
Craig Billington....................................67
Stephane Fiset.....................................37
Marc Denis...28
David Aebischer 26

Shutouts
Patrick Roy..................................23
David Aebischer 3
Marc Denis...3
Craig Billington......................................2
Stephane Fiset.......................................1

Goals-against average
(2400 minutes minimum)
Patrick Roy 2.34
Craig Billington.................................2.61

Wins
Patrick Roy 195
Craig Billington....................................30
Stephane Fiset.....................................22
David Aebischer..........................12
Marc Denis...10

COLORADO ROCKIES (DEFUNCT)
YEAR-BY-YEAR RECORDS

| | REGULAR SEASON | | | | | PLAYOFFS | | | |
Season	W	L	T	Pts.	Finish	W	L	Highest round	Coach
1976-77	20	46	14	54	5th/Smythe	—	—		John Wilson
1977-78	19	40	21	59	2nd/Smythe	0	2	Preliminaries	Pat Kelly
1978-79	15	53	12	42	4th/Smythe	—	—		Pat Kelly, Bep Guidolin
1979-80	19	48	13	51	6th/Smythe	—	—		Don Cherry
1980-81	22	45	13	57	5th/Smythe	—	—		Billy MacMillan
1981-82	18	49	13	49	5th/Smythe	—	—		Bert Marshall, Marshall Johnston

Franchise was formerly known as Kansas City Scouts and relocated to Colorado following 1975-76 season; franchise relocated and became New Jersey Devils following 1981-82 season.

FIRST-ROUND ENTRY DRAFT CHOICES

Year   Player, Overall, Last amateur team (league)
1976—Paul Gardner, 11, Oshawa (OHL)
1977—Barry Beck, 2, New Westminster (WCHL)
1978—Mike Gillis, 5, Kingston (OHL)
1979—Rob Ramage, 1, Birmingham (WHA)*

Year   Player, Overall, Last amateur team (league)
1980—Paul Gagne, 19, Windsor (OHL)
1981—Joe Cirella, 5, Oshawa (OHL)
*Designates first player chosen in draft.

SINGLE-SEASON INDIVIDUAL RECORDS

FORWARDS/DEFENSEMEN

Most goals
41—Wilf Paiement, 1976-77

Most assists
56—Wilf Paiement, 1977-78

Most points
87—Wilf Paiement, 1977-78

Most penalty minutes
201—Rob Ramage, 1981-82

Most power play goals
14—Paul Gardner, 1978-79

Most shorthanded goals
5—Wilf Paiement, 1976-77

Most games with three or more goals
1—Held by many players

Most shots
298—Lanny McDonald, 1980-81

GOALTENDERS

Most games
61—Chico Resch, 1981-82

Most minutes
3,424—Chico Resch, 1981-82

Most goals allowed
230—Chico Resch, 1981-82

Lowest goals-against average
3.49—Bill McKechnie, 1979-80

Most shutouts
1—Held by many goaltenders

Most wins
16—Chico Resch, 1981-82

Most losses
31—Chico Resch, 1981-82

Most ties
11—Chico Resch, 1981-82
Doug Favell, 1977-78

FRANCHISE LEADERS

FORWARDS/DEFENSEMEN

Games

Mike Kitchen	354
Ron Delorme	314
Wilf Paiement	257
Randy Pierce	240
Gary Croteau	234
Rob Ramage	234

Goals

Wilf Paiement	106
Paul Gardner	83
Ron Delorme	66
Lanny McDonald	66
Gary Croteau	65

Assists

Wilf Paiement	148
Rob Ramage	91
Merlin Malinowski	86
Paul Gardner	77
Lanny McDonald	75

Points

Wilf Paiement	254
Paul Gardner	160
Lanny McDonald	141
Gary Croteau	136
Merlin Malinowski	132
Rob Ramage	132

Penalty minutes

Rob Ramage	529
Wilf Paiement	336
Mike Kitchen	294
Ron Delorme	284
Randy Pierce	206

GOALTENDERS

Games

Michel Plasse	126
Doug Favell	84
Hardy Astrom	79
Chico Resch	69
Bill Oleschuk	54

Shutouts

Doug Favell	1
Bill McKenzie	1
Bill Oleschuk	1

**Goals-against average
(2400 minutes minimum)**

Hardy Astrom	3.77
Doug Favell	3.82
Michel Plasse	3.91
Chico Resch	3.97
Bill Oleschuk	4.00

Wins

Michel Plasse	24
Doug Favell	21
Chico Resch	18
Hardy Astrom	15
Bill McKenzie	12

COLUMBUS BLUE JACKETS
YEAR-BY-YEAR RECORDS

		REGULAR SEASON					PLAYOFFS			
Season	W	L	T	RT	Pts.	Finish	W	L	Highest round	Coach
2000-01	28	39	9	6	71	T4th/Central	—	—		Dave King

FIRST-ROUND ENTRY DRAFT CHOICES

Year Player, Overall, Last amateur team (league)
2000—Rostislav Klesla, 4, Brampton (OHL)

Year Player, Overall, Last amateur team (league)
2001—Pascal LeClaire, 8, Halifax (QMJHL)

SINGLE-SEASON INDIVIDUAL RECORDS

FORWARDS/DEFENSEMEN

Most goals
30—Geoff Sanderson, 2000-01

Most assists
42—Espen Knutsen, 2000-01

Most points
56—Geoff Sanderson, 2000-01

Most penalty minutes
140—Tyler Wright, 2000-01

Most power play goals
14—Steve Heinze, 2000-01

Most shorthanded goals
1—Robert Kron, 2000-01
Jamie Pushor, 2000-01
Tyler Wright, 2000-01

Most games with three or more goals
1—Deron Quint, 2000-01
Geoff Sanderson, 2000-01
Tyler Wright, 2000-01

Most shots
199—Geoff Sanderson, 2000-01

GOALTENDERS

Most games
53—Ron Tugnutt, 2000-01

Most minutes
3,129—Ron Tugnutt, 2000-01

Most goals allowed
127—Ron Tugnutt, 2000-01

Lowest goals-against average
2.44—Ron Tugnutt, 2000-01

Most shutouts
4—Ron Tugnutt, 2000-01

Most wins
22—Ron Tugnutt, 2000-01

Most losses
25—Ron Tugnutt, 2000-01

Most ties
5—Ron Tugnutt, 2000-01

FRANCHISE LEADERS

Players in boldface played for club in 2000-01

FORWARDS/DEFENSEMEN

Games
Serge Aubin...............................81
Lyle Odelein 81
David Vyborny 79
Mattias Timander 76
Tyler Wright..............................76

Goals
Geoff Sanderson 30
Steve Heinze.............................22
Tyler Wright...............................16
Serge Aubin...............................13
David Vyborny 13

Assists
Espen Knutsen...........................42
Geoff Sanderson 26

Steve Heinze..............................20
David Vyborny 19
Serge Aubin...............................17

Points
Geoff Sanderson 56
Espen Knutsen...........................53
Steve Heinze.............................42
David Vyborny 32
Tyler Wright...............................32

Penalty minutes
Tyler Wright 140
Kevin Dineen 126
Lyle Odelein............................118
Serge Aubin 107
Jamie Pushor...........................94

GOALTENDERS

Games
Ron Tugnutt 53
Marc Denis................................32

Shutouts
Ron Tugnutt 4

Goals-against average
(1200 minutes minimum)
Ron Tugnutt 2.44
Marc Denis 3.25

Wins
Ron Tugnutt 22
Marc Denis 6

DALLAS STARS
YEAR-BY-YEAR RECORDS

	REGULAR SEASON						PLAYOFFS			
Season	W	L	T	RT	Pts.	Finish	W	L	Highest round	Coach
1993-94	42	29	13	—	97	3rd/Central	5	4	Conference semifinals	Bob Gainey
1994-95	17	23	8	—	42	5th/Central	1	4	Conference quartertinals	Bob Gainey
1995-96	26	42	14	—	66	6th/Central	—	—		Bob Gainey, Ken Hitchcock
1996-97	48	26	8	—	104	1st/Central	3	4	Conference quarterfinals	Ken Hitchcock
1997-98	49	22	11	—	109	1st/Central	10	7	Conference finals	Ken Hitchcock
1998-99	51	19	12	—	114	1st/Pacific	16	7	Stanley Cup champ	Ken Hitchcock
1999-00	43	29	10	6	102	1st/Pacific	14	9	Stanley Cup finals	Ken Hitchcock
2000-01	48	24	8	2	106	1st/Pacific	4	6	Conference semifinals	Ken Hitchcock

Franchise was formerly known as Minnesota North Stars and relocated to Dallas following 1992-93 season.

FIRST-ROUND ENTRY DRAFT CHOICES

Year   Player, Overall, Last amateur team (league)
1993—Todd Harvey, 9, Detroit (OHL)
1994—Jason Botterill, 20, Michigan (CCHA)
1995—Jarome Iginla, 11, Kamloops (WHL)
1996—Richard Jackman, 5, Sault Ste. Marie (OHL)
1997—Brenden Morrow, 25, Portland (WHL)

Year   Player, Overall, Last amateur team (league)
1998—No first-round selection
1999—No first-round selection
2000—Steve Ott, 25, Windsor (OHL)
2001—Jason Bacashihua, 26, Chicago (NAHL)

SINGLE-SEASON INDIVIDUAL RECORDS

FORWARDS/DEFENSEMEN

Most goals
50—Mike Modano, 1993-94

Most assists
57—Russ Courtnall, 1993-94

Most points
93—Mike Modano, 1993-94

Most penalty minutes
333—Shane Churla, 1993-94

Most power play goals
18—Mike Modano, 1993-94

Most shorthanded goals
5—Mike Modano, 1996-97
   Mike Modano, 1997-98

Most games with three or more goals
3—Mike Modano, 1998-99

Most shots
320—Mike Modano, 1995-96

GOALTENDERS

Most games
63—Ed Belfour, 2000-01

Most minutes
3,687—Ed Belfour, 2000-01

Most shots against
1,604—Andy Moog, 1993-94

Most goals allowed
170—Andy Moog, 1993-94

Lowest goals-against average
1.88—Ed Belfour, 1997-98

Most shutouts
9—Ed Belfour, 1997-98

Most wins
37—Ed Belfour, 1997-98

Most losses
21—Ed Belfour, 1999-2000

Most ties
10—Ed Belfour, 1997-98

FRANCHISE LEADERS

Players in boldface played for club in 2000-01

FORWARDS/DEFENSEMEN

Games
Derian Hatcher..........................555
Mike Modano 551
Richard Matvichuk 455
Craig Ludwig............................433
Darryl Sydor............................416

Goals
Mike Modano 259
Joe Nieuwendyk 155
Brett Hull...............................95
Jere Lehtinen...........................88
Jamie Langenbrunner...................80

Assists
Mike Modano 332
Darryl Sydor...........................178
Derian Hatcher........................161
Sergei Zubov 151
Joe Nieuwendyk 138

Points
Mike Modano 591
Joe Nieuwendyk 293
Sergei Zubov...........................244
Darryl Sydor............................231
Jere Lehtinen 218

Penalty minutes
Derian Hatcher........................921
Shane Churla...........................687
Craig Ludwig 534
Grant Marshall 492
Todd Harvey 449

GOALTENDERS

Games
Ed Belfour 247
Andy Moog..............................175
Darcy Wakaluk 88
Roman Turek.............................55
Arturs Irbe...............................35

Shutouts
Ed Belfour.................................26
Andy Moog.................................8
Darcy Wakaluk 6
Arturs Irbe.................................3
Marty Turco................................3

Goals-against average
(2400 minutes minimum)
Ed Belfour 2.08
Roman Turek...........................2.14
Andy Moog.............................2.75
Darcy Wakaluk 3.21

Wins
Ed Belfour 139
Andy Moog...............................75
Darcy Wakaluk 31
Roman Turek.............................30
Arturs Irbe................................17

DETROIT RED WINGS
YEAR-BY-YEAR RECORDS

	REGULAR SEASON					PLAYOFFS			
Season	W	L	T	RT	Pts.	Finish	W	L	Highest round	Coach
1926-27†	12	28	4	—	28	5th/American	—	—		Art Duncan, Duke Keats
1927-28†	19	19	6	—	44	4th/American	—	—		Jack Adams
1928-29†	19	16	9	—	47	3rd/American	0	2	Quarterfinals	Jack Adams
1929-30†	14	24	6	—	34	4th/American	—	—		Jack Adams
1930-31†	16	21	7	—	39	4th/American	—	—		Jack Adams
1931-32‡	18	20	10	—	46	3rd/American	*0	1	Quarterfinals	Jack Adams
1932-33	25	15	8	—	58	2nd/American	2	2	Semifinals	Jack Adams
1933-34	24	14	10	—	58	1st/American	4	5	Stanley Cup finals	Jack Adams
1934-35	19	22	7	—	45	4th/American	—	—		Jack Adams
1935-36	24	16	8	—	56	1st/American	6	1	Stanley Cup champ	Jack Adams
1936-37	25	14	9	—	59	1st/American	6	4	Stanley Cup champ	Jack Adams
1937-38	12	25	11	—	35	4th/American	—	—		Jack Adams
1938-39	18	24	6	—	42	5th	3	3	Semifinals	Jack Adams
1939-40	16	26	6	—	38	5th	2	3	Semifinals	Jack Adams
1940-41	21	16	11	—	53	3rd	4	5	Stanley Cup finals	Jack Adams
1941-42	19	25	4	—	42	5th	7	5	Stanley Cup finals	Jack Adams
1942-43	25	14	11	—	61	1st	8	2	Stanley Cup champ	Jack Adams
1943-44	26	18	6	—	58	2nd	1	4	League semifinals	Jack Adams
1944-45	31	14	5	—	67	2nd	7	7	Stanley Cup finals	Jack Adams
1945-46	20	20	10	—	50	4th	1	4	League semifinals	Jack Adams
1946-47	22	27	11	—	55	4th	1	4	League semifinals	Jack Adams
1947-48	30	18	12	—	72	2nd	4	6	Stanley Cup finals	Tommy Ivan
1948-49	34	19	7	—	75	1st	4	7	Stanley Cup finals	Tommy Ivan
1949-50	37	19	14	—	88	1st	8	6	Stanley Cup champ	Tommy Ivan
1950-51	44	13	13	—	101	1st	2	4	League semifinals	Tommy Ivan
1951-52	44	14	12	—	100	1st	8	0	Stanley Cup champ	Tommy Ivan
1952-53	36	16	18	—	90	1st	2	4	League semifinals	Tommy Ivan
1953-54	37	19	14	—	88	1st	8	4	Stanley Cup champ	Tommy Ivan
1954-55	42	17	11	—	95	1st	8	3	Stanley Cup champ	Jimmy Skinner
1955-56	30	24	16	—	76	2nd	5	5	Stanley Cup finals	Jimmy Skinner
1956-57	38	20	12	—	88	1st	1	4	League semifinals	Jimmy Skinner
1957-58	29	29	12	—	70	3rd	0	4	League semifinals	Jimmy Skinner, Sid Abel
1958-59	25	37	8	—	58	6th	—	—		Sid Abel
1959-60	26	29	15	—	67	4th	2	4	League semifinals	Sid Abel
1960-61	25	29	16	—	66	4th	6	5	Stanley Cup finals	Sid Abel
1961-62	23	33	14	—	60	5th	—	—		Sid Abel
1962-63	32	25	13	—	77	4th	5	6	Stanley Cup finals	Sid Abel
1963-64	30	29	11	—	71	4th	7	7	Stanley Cup finals	Sid Abel
1964-65	40	23	7	—	87	1st	3	4	League semifinals	Sid Abel
1965-66	31	27	12	—	74	4th	6	6	Stanley Cup finals	Sid Abel

							PLAYOFFS			
	REGULAR SEASON									
Season	W	L	T	RT	Pts.	Finish	W	L	Highest round	Coach
1966-67	27	39	4	—	58	5th	—	—		Sid Abel
1967-68	27	35	12	—	66	6th/East	—	—		Sid Abel
1968-69	33	31	12	—	78	5th/East	—	—		Bill Gadsby
1969-70	40	21	15	—	95	3rd/East	0	4	Division semifinals	Bill Gadsby, Sid Abel
1970-71	22	45	11	—	55	7th/East	—	—		Ned Harkness, Doug Barkley
1971-72	33	35	10	—	76	5th/East	—	—		Doug Barkley, Johnny Wilson
1972-73	37	29	12	—	86	5th/East	—	—		Johnny Wilson
1973-74	29	39	10	—	68	6th/East	—	—		Ted Garvin, Alex Delvecchio
1974-75	23	45	12	—	58	4th/Norris	—	—		Alex Delvecchio
1975-76	26	44	10	—	62	4th/Norris	—	—		Ted Garvin, Alex Delvecchio
1976-77	16	55	9	—	41	5th/Norris	—	—		Alex Delvecchio, Larry Wilson
1977-78	32	34	14	—	78	2nd/Norris	3	4	Quarterfinals	Bobby Kromm
1978-79	23	41	16	—	62	5th/Norris	—	—		Bobby Kromm
1979-80	26	43	11	—	63	5th/Norris	—	—		Bobby Kromm, Ted Lindsay
1980-81	19	43	18	—	56	5th/Norris	—	—		Ted Lindsay, Wayne Maxner
1981-82	21	47	12	—	54	6th/Norris	—	—		Wayne Maxner, Billy Dea
1982-83	21	44	15	—	57	5th/Norris	—	—		Nick Polano
1983-84	31	42	7	—	69	3rd/Norris	1	3	Division semifinals	Nick Polano
1984-85	27	41	12	—	66	3rd/Norris	0	3	Division semifinals	Nick Polano
1985-86	17	57	6	—	40	5th/Norris	—	—		Harry Neale, Brad Park, Dan Belisle
1986-87	34	36	10	—	78	2nd/Norris	9	7	Conference finals	Jacques Demers
1987-88	41	28	11	—	93	1st/Norris	9	7	Conference finals	Jacques Demers
1988-89	34	34	12	—	80	1st/Norris	2	4	Division semifinals	Jacques Demers
1989-90	28	38	14	—	70	5th/Norris	—	—		Jacques Demers
1990-91	34	38	8	—	76	3rd/Norris	3	4	Division semifinals	Bryan Murray
1991-92	43	25	12	—	98	1st/Norris	4	7	Division finals	Bryan Murray
1992-93	47	28	9	—	103	2nd/Norris	3	4	Division semifinals	Bryan Murray
1993-94	46	30	8	—	100	1st/Central	3	4	Division semifinals	Scotty Bowman
1994-95	33	11	4	—	70	1st/Central	12	6	Stanley Cup finals	Scotty Bowman
1995-96	62	13	7	—	131	1st/Central	10	9	Conference finals	Scotty Bowman
1996-97	38	26	18	—	94	2nd/Central	16	4	Stanley Cup champ	Scotty Bowman
1997-98	44	23	15	—	103	2nd/Central	16	6	Stanley Cup champ	Scotty Bowman
1998-99	43	32	7	—	93	1st/Central	6	4	Conference semifinals	Scotty Bowman
1999-00	48	24	10	2	108	2nd/Central	5	4	Conference semifinals	Scotty Bowman
2000-01	49	20	9	4	111	1st/Central	2	4	Conference quarterfinals	Scotty Bowman

*Won-lost record does not indicate tie(s) resulting from two-game, total goals series that year (two-game, total-goals series were played from 1917-18 through 1935-36).

†Detroit Cougars.

‡Detroit Falcons.

FIRST-ROUND ENTRY DRAFT CHOICES

Year   Player, Overall, Last amateur team (league)

1969—Jim Rutherford, 10, Hamilton (OHL)
1970—Serge Lajeunesse, 12, Montreal (OHL)
1971—Marcel Dionne, 2, St. Catharines (OHL)
1972—No first-round selection
1973—Terry Richardson, 11, New Westminster (WCHL)
1974—Bill Lochead, 9, Oshawa (OHL)
1975—Rick Lapointe, 5, Victoria (WCHL)
1976—Fred Williams, 4, Saskatoon (WCHL)
1977—Dale McCourt, 1, St. Catharines (OHL)*
1978—Willie Huber, 9, Hamilton (OHL)
          Brent Peterson, 12, Portland (WCHL)
1979—Mike Foligno, 3, Sudbury (OHL)
1980—Mike Blaisdell, 11, Regina (WHL)
1981—No first-round selection
1982—Murray Craven, 17, Medicine Hat (WHL)
1983—Steve Yzerman, 4, Peterborough (OHL)
1984—Shawn Burr, 7, Kitchener (OHL)
1985—Brent Fedyk, 8, Regina (WHL)

Year   Player, Overall, Last amateur team (league)

1986—Joe Murphy, 1, Michigan State University*
1987—Yves Racine, 11, Longueuil (QMJHL)
1988—Kory Kocur, 17, Saskatoon (WHL)
1989—Mike Sillinger, 11, Regina (WHL)
1990—Keith Primeau, 3, Niagara Falls (OHL)
1991—Martin Lapointe, 10, Laval (QMJHL)
1992—Curtis Bowen, 22, Ottawa (OHL)
1993—Anders Eriksson, 22, MoDo, Sweden
1994—Yan Golvbovsky, 23, Dynamo Moscow, CIS
1995—Maxim Kuznetsov, 26, Dynamo Moscow, CIS
1996—Jesse Wallin, 26, Red Deer (WHL)
1997—No first-round selection
1998—Jiri Fischer, 25, Hull (QMJHL)
1999—No first-round selection
2000—Niklas Kronvall, 29, Djurgarden, Sweden
2001—No first-round selection
*Designates first player chosen in draft.

SINGLE-SEASON INDIVIDUAL RECORDS

FORWARDS/DEFENSEMEN

Most goals
65—Steve Yzerman, 1988-89

Most assists
90—Steve Yzerman, 1988-89

Most points
155—Steve Yzerman, 1988-89

Most penalty minutes
398—Bob Probert, 1987-88

Most power play goals
21—Mickey Redmond, 1973-74
      Dino Ciccarelli, 1992-93

Most shorthanded goals
10—Marcel Dionne, 1974-75

Most games with three or more goals
4—Frank Mahovlich, 1968-69
  Steve Yzerman, 1990-91

Most shots
388—Steve Yzerman, 1988-89

GOALTENDERS

Most games
72—Tim Cheveldae, 1991-92

Most minutes
4,236—Tim Cheveldae, 1991-92

Most goals allowed
226—Tim Cheveldae, 1991-92

Lowest goals-against average
1.43—Dolly Dodson, 1928-29

Most shutouts
12—Terry Sawchuk, 1951-52
  Terry Sawchuk, 1953-54
  Terry Sawchuk, 1954-55
  Glenn Hall, 1955-56

Most wins
44—Terry Sawchuk, 1950-51
  Terry Sawchuk, 1951-52

FRANCHISE LEADERS

Players in boldface played for club in 2000-01

FORWARDS/DEFENSEMEN

Games

Gordie Howe	1687
Alex Delvecchio	1549
Steve Yzerman	**1310**
Marcel Pronovost	983
Norm Ullman	875

Goals

Gordie Howe	786
Steve Yzerman	**645**
Alex Delvecchio	456
Ted Lindsay	335
Sergei Fedorov	**333**

Assists

Gordie Howe	1023
Steve Yzerman	**969**
Alex Delvecchio	825
Sergei Fedorov	**470**
Norm Ullman	434

Points

Gordie Howe	1809
Steve Yzerman	**1614**
Alex Delvecchio	1281
Sergei Fedorov	**803**
Norm Ullman	758

GOALTENDERS

Games

Terry Sawchuk	734
Chris Osgood	**389**
Harry Lumley	324
Jim Rutherford	314
Roger Crozier	310

Shutouts

Terry Sawchuk	85
Chris Osgood	**30**
Harry Lumley	26
Roger Crozier	20
Clarence Dolson	17
Glenn Hall	17

Harry Holmes	17
Norm Smith	17

Goals-against average
(2400 minutes minimum)

Clarence Dolson	2.06
Harry Holmes	2.11
Glenn Hall	2.14
Alex Connell	2.25
John Ross Roach	2.26

Wins

Terry Sawchuk	352
Chris Osgood	**221**
Harry Lumley	163
Roger Crozier	130
Tim Cheveldae	128

EDMONTON OILERS
YEAR-BY-YEAR RECORDS

			REGULAR SEASON				PLAYOFFS			
Season	W	L	T	RT	Pts.	Finish	W	L	Highest round	Coach
1972-73*	38	37	3	—	79	5th	—	—		Ray Kinasewich
1973-74†	38	37	3	—	79	3rd	1	4	League quarterfinals	Brian Shaw
1974-75†	36	38	4	—	76	5th	—	—		Brian Shaw, Bill Hunter
1975-76†	27	49	5	—	59	4th	0	4	League quarterfinals	Clare Drake, Bill Hunter
1976-77†	34	43	4	—	72	4th	1	4	League quarterfinals	Bep Guidolin, Glen Sather
1977-78†	38	39	3	—	79	5th	1	4	League quarterfinals	Glen Sather
1978-79†	48	30	2	—	98	1st	6	7	Avco World Cup finals	Glen Sather
1979-80	28	39	13	—	69	4th/Smythe	0	3	Preliminaries	Glen Sather
1980-81	29	35	16	—	74	4th/Smythe	5	4	Quarterfinals	Glen Sather
1981-82	48	17	15	—	111	1st/Smythe	2	3	Division semifinals	Glen Sather
1982-83	47	21	12	—	106	1st/Smythe	11	5	Stanley Cup finals	Glen Sather
1983-84	57	18	5	—	119	1st/Smythe	15	4	Stanley Cup champ	Glen Sather
1984-85	49	20	11	—	109	1st/Smythe	15	3	Stanley Cup champ	Glen Sather
1985-86	56	17	7	—	119	1st/Smythe	6	4	Division finals	Glen Sather
1986-87	50	24	6	—	106	1st/Smythe	16	5	Stanley Cup champ	Glen Sather
1987-88	44	25	11	—	99	2nd/Smythe	16	2	Stanley Cup champ	Glen Sather
1988-89	38	34	8	—	84	3rd/Smythe	3	4	Division semifinals	Glen Sather
1989-90	38	28	14	—	90	2nd/Smythe	16	6	Stanley Cup champ	John Muckler
1990-91	37	37	6	—	80	3rd/Smythe	9	9	Conference finals	John Muckler
1991-92	36	34	10	—	82	3rd/Smythe	8	8	Conference finals	Ted Green
1992-93	26	50	8	—	60	5th/Smythe	—	—		Ted Green
1993-94	25	45	14	—	64	6th/Pacific	—	—		Ted Green, Glen Sather
1994-95	17	27	4	—	38	5th/Pacific	—	—		George Burnett, Ron Low
1995-96	30	44	8	—	68	5th/Pacific	—	—		Ron Low
1996-97	36	37	9	—	81	3rd/Pacific	5	7	Conference semifinals	Ron Low
1997-98	35	37	10	—	80	3rd/Pacific	5	7	Conference semifinals	Ron Low
1998-99	33	37	12	—	78	2nd/Northwest	0	4	Conference quarterfinals	Ron Low
1999-00	32	34	16	8	88	2nd/Northwest	1	4	Conference quarterfinals	Kevin Lowe
2000-01	39	28	12	3	93	2nd/Northwest	2	4	Conference quarterfinals	Craig MacTavish

*Alberta Oilers, members of World Hockey Association.
†Members of World Hockey Association.

FIRST-ROUND ENTRY DRAFT CHOICES

Year   Player, Overall, Last amateur team (league)
1979—Kevin Lowe, 21, Quebec (QMJHL)
1980—Paul Coffey, 6, Kitchener (OHL)
1981—Grant Fuhr, 8, Victoria (WHL)
1982—Jim Playfair, 20, Portland (WHL)
1983—Jeff Beukeboom, 19, Sault Ste. Marie (OHL)
1984—Selmar Odelein, 21, Regina (WHL)
1985—Scott Metcalfe, 20, Kingston (OHL)
1986—Kim Issel, 21, Prince Albert (WHL)
1987—Peter Soberlak, 21, Swift Current (WHL)
1988—Francois Leroux, 19, St. Jean (QMJHL)
1989—Jason Soules, 15, Niagara Falls (OHL)
1990—Scott Allison, 17, Prince Albert (WHL)
1991—Tyler Wright, 12, Swift Current (WHL)
      Martin Rucinsky, 20, Litvinov, Czechoslovakia
1992—Joe Hulbig, 13, St. Sebastian H.S. (Mass.)

Year   Player, Overall, Last amateur team (league)
1993—Jason Arnott, 7, Oshawa (OHL)
      Nick Stajduhar, 16, London (OHL)
1994—Jason Bonsignore, 4, Niagara Falls (OHL)
      Ryan Smyth, 6, Moose Jaw (WHL)
1995—Steve Kelly, 6, Prince Albert (WHL)
1996—Boyd Devereaux, 6, Kitchener (OHL)
      Matthieu Descoteaux, 19, Shawinigan (QMJHL)
1997—Michel Riessen, 14, HC Biel, Switzerland
1998—Michael Henrich, 13, Barrie (OHL)
1999—Jani Rita, 13, Jokerit Helsinki, Finland
2000—Alexei Mikhnov, 17, Yaroslavl, Russia
2001—Ales Hemsky, 13, Hull (QMJHL)
NOTE: Edmonton chose Dave Dryden, Bengt Gustafsson and Ed Mio as priority selections before the 1979 expansion draft.

SINGLE-SEASON INDIVIDUAL RECORDS

FORWARDS/DEFENSEMEN

Most goals
92—Wayne Gretzky, 1981-82

Most assists
163—Wayne Gretzky, 1985-86

Most points
215—Wayne Gretzky, 1985-86

Most penalty minutes
286—Steve Smith, 1987-88

Most power play goals
20—Wayne Gretzky, 1983-84
    Ryan Smyth, 1996-97

Most shorthanded goals
12—Wayne Gretzky, 1983-84

Most games with three or more goals
10—Wayne Gretzky, 1981-82
    Wayne Gretzky, 1983-84

Most shots
369—Wayne Gretzky, 1981-82

GOALTENDERS

Most games
75—Grant Fuhr, 1987-88

Most minutes
4,364—Tommy Salo, 2000-01

Most goals allowed
246—Grant Fuhr, 1987-88

Lowest goals-against average
2.33—Tommy Salo, 1999-2000

Most shutouts
8—Curtis Joseph, 1997-98
   Tommy Salo, 2000-01

Most wins
40—Grant Fuhr, 1987-88

Most losses
38—Bill Ranford, 1992-93

Most ties
14—Grant Fuhr, 1981-82

FRANCHISE LEADERS

Players in boldface played for club in 2000-01

FORWARDS/DEFENSEMEN

Games
Kevin Lowe	1037
Mark Messier	851
Glenn Anderson	828
Kelly Buchberger	795
Jari Kurri	754

Goals
Wayne Gretzky	583
Jari Kurri	474
Glenn Anderson	413
Mark Messier	392
Paul Coffey	209

Assists
Wayne Gretzky	1086
Mark Messier	642
Jari Kurri	569
Glenn Anderson	483
Paul Coffey	460

Points
Wayne Gretzky	1669
Jari Kurri	1043
Mark Messier	1034
Glenn Anderson	896
Paul Coffey	669

Penalty minutes
Kelly Buchberger	1747
Kevin McClelland	1298
Kevin Lowe	1236
Mark Messier	1122
Steve Smith	1080

GOALTENDERS

Games
Bill Ranford	433
Grant Fuhr	423
Andy Moog	235
Curtis Joseph	177
Tommy Salo	**156**

Shutouts
Curtis Joseph	14
Tommy Salo	**10**
Grant Fuhr	9
Bill Ranford	8
Andy Moog	4

Goals-against average
(2400 minutes minimum)
Tommy Salo	**2.42**
Bob Essensa	2.73
Curtis Joseph	2.90
Bill Ranford	3.51
Andy Moog	3.61

Wins
Grant Fuhr	226
Bill Ranford	163
Andy Moog	143
Curtis Joseph	76
Tommy Salo	**71**

NHL HISTORY *Team by team*

FLORIDA PANTHERS
YEAR-BY-YEAR RECORDS

	REGULAR SEASON						PLAYOFFS			
Season	W	L	T	RT	Pts.	Finish	W	L	Highest round	Coach
1993-94	33	34	17	—	83	5th/Atlantic	—	—		Roger Neilson
1994-95	20	22	6	—	46	5th/Atlantic	—	—		Roger Neilson
1995-96	41	31	10	—	92	3rd/Atlantic	12	10	Stanley Cup finals	Doug MacLean
1996-97	35	28	19	—	89	3rd/Atlantic	1	4	Conference quarterfinals	Doug MacLean
1997-98	24	43	15	—	63	6th/Atlantic	—	—		Doug MacLean, Bryan Murray
1998-99	30	34	18	—	78	2nd/Southeast	—	—		Terry Murray
1999-00	43	33	6	6	98	2nd/Southeast	0	4	Conference quarterfinals	Terry Murray
2000-01	22	38	13	9	66	3rd/Southeast	—	—		Terry Murray

FIRST-ROUND ENTRY DRAFT CHOICES

Year   Player, Overall, Last amateur team (league)
1993—Rob Niedermayer, 5, Medicine Hat (WHL)
1994—Ed Jovanovski, 1, Windsor (OHL)*
1995—Radek Dvorak, 10, Budejovice, Czech Republic
1996—Marcus Nilson, 20, Djurgarden-Stockholm, Sweden
1997—Mike Brown, 20, Red Deer (WHL)
1998—No first-round selection

Year   Player, Overall, Last amateur team (league)
1999—Denis Shvidki, 12, Barrie (OHL)
2000—No first-round selection
2001—Stephen Weiss, 4, Plymouth (OHL)
       Lukas Krajicek, 24, Peterborough (OHL)
*Designates first player chosen in draft.

SINGLE-SEASON INDIVIDUAL RECORDS

FORWARDS/DEFENSEMEN

Most goals
59—Pavel Bure, 2000-01

Most assists
53—Viktor Kozlov, 1999-2000

Most points
94—Pavel Bure, 1999-2000

Most penalty minutes
313—Paul Laus, 1996-97

Most power play goals
19—Scott Mellanby, 1995-96
Pavel Bure, 2000-01

Most shorthanded goals
6—Tom Fitzgerald, 1995-96

Most games with three or more goals
4—Pavel Bure, 1999-2000
Pavel Bure, 2000-01

Most shots
384—Pavel Bure, 2000-01

GOALTENDERS

Most games
60—John Vanbiesbrouck, 1996-97

Most minutes
3,451—John Vanbiesbrouck, 1997-98

Most shots against
1,912—John Vanbiesbrouck, 1993-94

Most goals allowed
165—John Vanbiesbrouck, 1997-98

Lowest goals-against average
2.29—John Vanbiesbrouck, 1996-97

Most shutouts
5—Robert Luongo, 2000-01

Most wins
27—John Vanbiesbrouck, 1996-97

Most losses
29—John Vanbiesbrouck, 1997-98

Most ties
11—Sean Burke, 1998-99

FRANCHISE LEADERS

Players in boldface played for club in 2000-01

FORWARDS/DEFENSEMEN

Games
Scott Mellanby...........................542
Rob Niedermayer......................518
Robert Svehla.........................491
Paul Laus.............................485
Bill Lindsay..............................443

Goals
Scott Mellanby...........................157
Pavel Bure.............................130
Rob Niedermayer......................101
Ray Whitney 97
Radek Dvorak..............................69

Assists
Robert Svehla...........................207
Scott Mellanby.........................197
Rob Niedermayer......................165
Ray Whitney............................130
Viktor Kozlov 122

Points
Scott Mellanby...........................354
Rob Niedermayer......................266
Robert Svehla.........................261
Ray Whitney............................227
Pavel Bure.............................202

Penalty minutes
Paul Laus 1545
Scott Mellanby..........................953
Peter Worrell...........................828
Ed Jovanovski...........................549
Robert Svehla.........................516

GOALTENDERS

Games
John Vanbiesbrouck.........................268
Mark Fitzpatrick......................119
Trevor Kidd................................70
Sean Burke................................66
Robert Luongo..............................47

Shutouts
John Vanbiesbrouck.............................13
Robert Luongo.........................5
Mark Fitzpatrick.............................4
Sean Burke.................................3
Kirk McLean 2
Trevor Kidd 2

Goals-against average
(2400 minutes minimum)
Robert Luongo 2.44
John Vanbiesbrouck......................2.58
Sean Burke................................2.65
Mark Fitzpatrick.............................2.71
Trevor Kidd 3.04

Wins
John Vanbiesbrouck............................106
Mark Fitzpatrick......................43
Sean Burke................................23
Trevor Kidd..............................24
Mike Vernon...............................18

HAMILTON TIGERS (DEFUNCT)
YEAR-BY-YEAR RECORDS

		REGULAR SEASON					PLAYOFFS		
Season	W	L	T	Pts.	Finish	W	L	Highest round	Coach
1920-21	6	18	0	12	4th	—	—		Percy Thompson
1921-22	7	17	0	14	4th	—	—		Percy Thompson
1922-23	6	18	0	12	4th	—	—		Art Ross
1923-24	9	15	0	18	4th	—	—		Percy Lesueur
1924-25	19	10	1	39	1st	*—	—		Jimmy Gardner

*Refused to participate in playoffs—held out for more compensation.
Franchise was formerly known as Quebec Bulldogs and relocated to Hamilton following 1919-20 season; franchise relocated and became New York Americans following 1924-1925 season.

HARTFORD WHALERS (DEFUNCT)
YEAR-BY-YEAR RECORDS

		REGULAR SEASON					PLAYOFFS		
Season	W	L	T	Pts.	Finish	W	L	Highest round	Coach
1972-73*	46	30	2	94	1st	12	3	Avco World Cup champ	Jack Kelley
1973-74*	43	31	4	90	1st	3	4	League quarterfinals	Ron Ryan
1974-75*	43	30	5	91	1st	2	4	League quarterfinals	Ron Ryan, Jack Kelley
1975-76*	33	40	7	73	3rd	6	4	League semifinals	Jack Kelley, Don Blackburn, Harry Neale
1976-77*	35	40	6	76	4th	1	4	League quarterfinals	Harry Neale
1977-78*	44	31	5	93	2nd	8	6	Avco World Cup finals	Harry Neale
1978-79*	37	34	9	83	4th	5	5	League semifinals	Bill Dineen, Don Blackburn
1979-80	27	34	19	73	4th/Norris	0	3	Preliminaries	Don Blackburn
1980-81	21	41	18	60	4th/Norris	—	—		Don Blackburn, Larry Pleau
1981-82	21	41	18	60	5th/Adams	—	—		Larry Pleau
1982-83	19	54	7	45	5th/Adams	—	—		Larry Kish, Larry Pleau, John Cunniff
1983-84	28	42	10	66	5th/Adams	—	—		Jack Evans
1984-85	30	41	9	69	5th/Adams	—	—		Jack Evans
1985-86	40	36	4	84	4th/Adams	6	4	Division finals	Jack Evans
1986-87	43	30	7	93	1st/Adams	2	4	Division semifinals	Jack Evans
1987-88	35	38	7	77	4th/Adams	2	4	Division semifinals	Jack Evans, Larry Pleau
1988-89	37	38	5	79	4th/Adams	0	4	Division semifinals	Larry Pleau
1989-90	38	33	9	85	4th/Adams	3	4	Division semifinals	Rick Ley
1990-91	31	38	11	73	4th/Adams	2	4	Division semifinals	Rick Ley
1991-92	26	41	13	65	4th/Adams	3	4	Division semifinals	Jim Roberts
1992-93	26	52	6	58	5th/Adams	—	—		Paul Holmgren
1993-94	27	48	9	63	6th/Northeast	—	—		Paul Holmgren, Pierre McGuire
1994-95	19	24	5	43	5th/Northeast	—	—		Paul Holmgren
1995-96	34	39	9	77	4th/Northeast	—	—		Paul Holmgren, Paul Maurice
1996-97	32	39	11	75	5th/Northeast	—	—		Paul Maurice

*New England Whalers, members of World Hockey Association.
Franchise relocated and became Carolina Hurricanes following 1996-97 season.

FIRST-ROUND ENTRY DRAFT CHOICES

Year   Player, Overall, Last amateur team (league)
1979—Ray Allison, 18, Brandon (WHL)
1980—Fred Arthur, 8, Cornwall (QMJHL)
1981—Ron Francis, 4, Sault Ste. Marie (OHL)
1982—Paul Lawless, 14, Windsor (OHL)
1983—Sylvain Turgeon, 2, Hull (QMJHL)
     David A. Jensen, 20, Lawrence Academy (Mass.)
1984—Sylvain Cote, 11, Quebec (QMJHL)
1985—Dana Murzyn, 5, Calgary (WHL)
1986—Scott Young, 11, Boston University
1987—Jody Hull, 18, Peterborough (OHL)
1988—Chris Govedaris, 11, Toronto (OHL)

Year   Player, Overall, Last amateur team (league)
1989—Robert Holik, 10, Jihlava (Czechoslovakia)
1990—Mark Greig, 15, Lethbridge (WHL)
1991—Patrick Poulin, 9, St. Hyacinthe (QMJHL)
1992—Robert Petrovicky, 9, Dukla Trencin (Czech.)
1993—Chris Pronger, 2, Peterborough (OHL)
1994—Jeff O'Neill, 5, Guelph (OHL)
1995—Jean-Sebastien Giguere, 13, Halifax (QMJHL)
1996—No first-round selection
1997—Nikos Tselios, 22, Belleville (OHL)
NOTE: Hartford chose Jordy Douglas, John Garrett and Mark Howe as priority selections before the 1979 expansion draft.

SINGLE-SEASON INDIVIDUAL RECORDS

FORWARDS/DEFENSEMEN

Most goals
56—Blaine Stoughton, 1979-80

Most assists
69—Ron Francis, 1989-90

Most points
105—Mike Rogers, 1979-80
     Mike Rogers, 1980-81

Most penalty minutes
358—Torrie Robertson, 1985-86

Most power play goals
21—Geoff Sanderson, 1992-93

Most shorthanded goals
4—Mike Rogers, 1980-81
   Kevin Dineen, 1984-85

Most games with three or more goals
3—Mike Rogers, 1980-81
   Blaine Stoughton, 1981-82

GOALTENDERS

Most games
66—Sean Burke, 1995-96

Most minutes
3,669—Sean Burke, 1995-96

Most goals allowed
282—Greg Millen, 1982-83

Lowest goals-against average
2.64—Mike Liut, 1989-90

Most shutouts
4—Mike Liut, 1986-87
   Peter Sidorkiewicz, 1988-89
   Sean Burke, 1995-96
   Sean Burke, 1996-97

Most wins
31—Mike Liut, 1986-87

Most losses
38—Greg Millen, 1982-83

Most ties
12—John Garrett, 1980-81
   Greg Millen, 1982-83

FRANCHISE LEADERS

FORWARDS/DEFENSEMEN

Games
Ron Francis 714
Kevin Dineen 587
Adam Burt...499
Dave Tippett......................................483
Ulf Samuelsson 463

Goals
Ron Francis 264
Kevin Dineen 235
Blaine Stoughton..............................219
Pat Verbeek.......................................192
Geoff Sanderson 189

Assists
Ron Francis 557
Kevin Dineen 268
Andrew Cassels.................................253
Pat Verbeek.......................................211
Dave Babych 196

Points
Ron Francis 821
Kevin Dineen 503
Pat Verbeek.......................................403
Blaine Stoughton..............................377
Geoff Sanderson 352

Penalty minutes
Torrie Robertson 1368
Kevin Dineen 1239
Pat Verbeek......................................1144
Ulf Samuelsson 1108
Adam Burt..723

GOALTENDERS

Games
Sean Burke..256
Mike Liut 252
Greg Millen 219
Peter Sidorkiewicz............................178
John Garrett 122

Shutouts
Mike Liut 13
Sean Burke..10
Peter Sidorkiewicz...............................8
Greg Millen...4
Steve Weeks...4

**Goals-against average
(2400 minutes minimum)**
Sean Burke..3.12
Jason Muzzatti 3.23
Peter Sidorkiewicz............................3.33
Mike Liut 3.36
Kay Whitmore 3.61

Wins
Mike Liut 115
Sean Burke..101
Peter Sidorkiewicz..............................71
Greg Millen..62
Steve Weeks..42

KANSAS CITY SCOUTS (DEFUNCT)
YEAR-BY-YEAR RECORDS

		REGULAR SEASON				PLAYOFFS			
Season	W	L	T	Pts.	Finish	W	L	Highest round	Coach
1974-75	15	54	11	41	5th/Smythe	—	—		Bep Guidolin
1975-76	12	56	12	36	5th/Smythe	—	—		Bep Guidolin, Sid Abel, Eddie Bush

Franchise relocated and became Colorado Rockies following 1975-76 season; franchise later relocated and became New Jersey Devils after 1981-82 season.

FIRST-ROUND ENTRY DRAFT CHOICES

Year   Player, Overall, Last amateur team (league)
1974—Wilf Paiement, 2, St. Catharines (OHL)

Year   Player, Overall, Last amateur team (league)
1975—Barry Dean, 2, Medicine Hat (WCHL)

SINGLE-SEASON INDIVIDUAL RECORDS

FORWARDS/DEFENSEMEN

Most goals
27—Guy Charron, 1975-76

Most assists
44—Guy Charron, 1975-76

Most points
71—Guy Charron, 1975-76

Most penalty minutes
209—Steve Durbano, 1975-76

Most power play goals
11—Simon Nolet, 1974-75

Most shorthanded goals
2—Ed Gilbert, 1974-75
   Simon Nolet, 1974-75

Most games with three or more goals
1—Wilf Paiement, 1975-76

Most shots
226—Guy Charron, 1975-76

GOALTENDERS

Most games
64—Denis Herron, 1975-76

Most minutes
3,620—Denis Herron, 1975-76

Most goals allowed
243—Denis Herron, 1975-76

Lowest goals-against average
4.03—Denis Herron, 1975-76

Most shutouts
Never accomplished

Most wins
11—Denis Herron, 1975-76

Most losses
39—Denis Herron, 1975-76

Most ties
11—Denis Herron, 1975-76

FORWARDS/DEFENSEMEN

Games

Gary Croteau	156
Randy Rota	151
Robin Burns	149
Dave Hudson	144
Wilf Paiement	135

Goals

Wilf Paiement	47
Guy Charron	40
Simon Nolet	36
Robin Burns	31
Gary Croteau	27
Randy Rota	27

Assists

Guy Charron	73
Dave Hudson	52
Simon Nolet	47
Wilf Paiement	35

Gary Bergman	33
Robin Burns	33

Points

Guy Charron	113
Simon Nolet	83
Wilf Paiement	82
Dave Hudson	72
Robin Burns	64

Penalty minutes

Wilf Paiement	222
Steve Durbano	209
Jean-Guy Lagace	130
Larry Johnston	122
Robin Burns	107

GOALTENDERS

Games

Denis Herron	86
Peter McDuffe	36
Michel Plasse	24
Bill McKenzie	22
Bill Oleschuk	1

Shutouts
Never occurred

Goals-against average
(2400 minutes minimum)

Denis Herron	3.96

Wins

Denis Herron	15
Peter McDuffe	7
Michel Plasse	4
Bill McKenzie	1

LOS ANGELES KINGS
YEAR-BY-YEAR RECORDS

	REGULAR SEASON						PLAYOFFS			
Season	W	L	T	RT	Pts.	Finish	W	L	Highest round	Coach
1967-68	31	33	10	—	72	2nd/West	3	4	Division semifinals	Red Kelly
1968-69	24	42	10	—	58	4th/West	4	7	Division finals	Red Kelly
1969-70	14	52	10	—	38	6th/West	—	—		Hal Laycoe, Johnny Wilson
1970-71	25	40	13	—	63	5th/West	—	—		Larry Regan
1971-72	20	49	9	—	49	7th/West	—	—		Larry Regan, Fred Glover
1972-73	31	36	11	—	73	6th/West	—	—		Bob Pulford
1973-74	33	33	12	—	78	3rd/West	1	4	Division semifinals	Bob Pulford
1974-75	42	17	21	—	105	2nd/Norris	1	2	Preliminaries	Bob Pulford
1975-76	38	33	9	—	85	2nd/Norris	5	4	Quarterfinals	Bob Pulford
1976-77	34	31	15	—	83	2nd/Norris	4	5	Quarterfinals	Bob Pulford
1977-78	31	34	15	—	77	3rd/Norris	0	2	Preliminaries	Ron Stewart
1978-79	34	34	12	—	80	3rd/Norris	0	2	Preliminaries	Bob Berry
1979-80	30	36	14	—	74	2nd/Norris	1	3	Preliminaries	Bob Berry
1980-81	43	24	13	—	99	2nd/Norris	1	3	Preliminaries	Bob Berry
1981-82	24	41	15	—	63	4th/Smythe	4	6	Division finals	Parker MacDonald, Don Perry,
1982-83	27	41	12	—	66	5th/Smythe	—	—		Don Perry
1983-84	23	44	13	—	59	5th/Smythe	—	—		Don Perry, Rogie Vachon, Roger Neilson
1984-85	34	32	14	—	82	4th/Smythe	0	3	Division semifinals	Pat Quinn
1985-86	23	49	8	—	54	5th/Smythe	—	—		Pat Quinn
1986-87	31	41	8	—	70	4th/Smythe	1	4	Division semifinals	Pat Quinn, Mike Murphy
1987-88	30	42	8	—	68	4th/Smythe	1	4	Division semifinals	Mike Murphy, Rogie Vachon, Robbie Ftorek
1988-89	42	31	7	—	91	2nd/Smythe	4	7	Division finals	Robbie Ftorek
1989-90	34	39	7	—	75	4th/Smythe	4	6	Division finals	Tom Webster
1990-91	46	24	10	—	102	1st/Smythe	6	6	Division finals	Tom Webster
1991-92	35	31	14	—	84	2nd/Smythe	2	4	Division semifinals	Tom Webster
1992-93	39	35	10	—	88	3rd/Smythe	13	11	Stanley Cup finals	Barry Melrose
1993-94	27	45	12	—	66	5th/Pacific	—	—		Barry Melrose
1994-95	16	23	9	—	41	4th/Pacific	—	—		Barry Melrose, Rogie Vachon
1995-96	24	40	18	—	66	6th/Pacific	—	—		Larry Robinson
1996-97	28	43	11	—	67	6th/Pacific	—	—		Larry Robinson
1997-98	38	33	11	—	87	2nd/Pacific	0	4	Conference quarterfinals	Larry Robinson
1998-99	32	45	5	—	69	5th/Pacific	—	—		Larry Robinson
1999-00	39	31	12	4	94	2nd/Pacific	0	4	Conference quarterfinals	Andy Murray
2000-01	38	28	13	3	92	3rd/Pacific	7	6	Conference semifinals	Andy Murray

FIRST-ROUND ENTRY DRAFT CHOICES

Year   Player, Overall, Last amateur team (league)
1969—No first-round selection
1970—No first-round selection

Year   Player, Overall, Last amateur team (league)
1971—No first-round selection
1972—No first-round selection

NHL HISTORY *Team by team*

Year	Player, Overall, Last amateur team (league)
1973—No first-round selection
1974—No first-round selection
1975—Tim Young, 16, Ottawa (OHL)
1976—No first-round selection
1977—No first-round selection
1978—No first-round selection
1979—Jay Wells, 16, Kingston (OHL)
1980—Larry Murphy, 4, Peterborough (OHL)
Jim Fox, 10, Ottawa (OHL)
1981—Doug Smith, 2, Ottawa (OHL)
1982—No first-round selection
1983—No first-round selection
1984—Craig Redmond, 6, Canadian Olympic Team
1985—Craig Duncanson, 9, Sudbury (OHL)
Dan Gratton, 10, Oshawa (OHL)
1986—Jimmy Carson, 2, Verdun (QMJHL)
1987—Wayne McBean, 4, Medicine Hat (WHL)

Year	Player, Overall, Last amateur team (league)
1988—Martin Gelinas, 7, Hull (QMJHL)
1989—No first-round selection
1990—Darryl Sydor, 7, Kamloops (WHL)
1991—No first-round selection
1992—No first-round selection
1993—No first-round selection
1994—Jamie Storr, 7, Owen Sound (OHL)
1995—Aki-Petteri Berg, 3, TPS Jrs., Finland
1996—No first-round selection
1997—Olli Jokinen, 3, IFK Helsinki, Finland
Matt Zultek, 15, Ottawa (OHL)
1998—Mathieu Biron, 21, Shawinigan (QMJHL)
1999—No first-round selection
2000—Alexander Frolov, 20, Yaroslavl, Russia
2001—Jens Karlsson, 18, Frolunda, Sweden
David Steckel, 30, Ohio State

SINGLE-SEASON INDIVIDUAL RECORDS

FORWARDS/DEFENSEMEN

Most goals
70—Bernie Nicholls, 1988-89

Most assists
122—Wayne Gretzky, 1990-91

Most points
168—Wayne Gretzky, 1988-89

Most penalty minutes
399—Marty McSorley, 1992-93

Most power play goals
26—Luc Robitaille, 1991-92

Most shorthanded goals
8—Bernie Nicholls, 1988-89

Most games with three or more goals
5—Jimmy Carson, 1987-88

Most shots
385—Bernie Nicholls, 1988-89

GOALTENDERS

Most games
70—Rogie Vachon, 1977-78

Most minutes
4,107—Rogie Vachon, 1977-78

Most shots against
2,219—Kelly Hrudey, 1993-94

Most goals allowed
228—Kelly Hrudey, 1993-94

Lowest goals-against average
2.24—Rogie Vachon, 1974-75

Most shutouts
8—Rogie Vachon, 1977-78

Most wins
35—Mario Lessard, 1980-81

Most losses
31—Kelly Hrudey, 1993-94

Most ties
13—Rogie Vachon, 1974-75
    Rogie Vachon, 1977-78
    Kelly Hrudey, 1991-92

FRANCHISE LEADERS

Players in boldface played for club in 2000-01

FORWARDS/DEFENSEMEN

Games
Dave Taylor	1111
Luc Robitaille	**932**
Marcel Dionne	921
Butch Goring	736
Mike Murphy	673

Goals
Marcel Dionne	550
Luc Robitaille	**520**
Dave Taylor	431
Bernie Nicholls	327
Butch Goring	275

Assists
Marcel Dionne	757
Wayne Gretzky	672
Dave Taylor	638
Luc Robitaille	**559**
Bernie Nicholls	431

Points
Marcel Dionne	1307
Luc Robitaille	**1079**
Dave Taylor	1069
Wayne Gretzky	918
Bernie Nicholls	758

Penalty minutes
Marty McSorley	1846
Dave Taylor	1589
Jay Wells	1446
Rob Blake	**1051**
Mark Hardy	858

GOALTENDERS

Games
Rogie Vachon	389
Kelly Hrudey	360
Mario Lessard	240
Stephane Fiset	**200**
Gary Edwards	155

Shutouts
Rogie Vachon	32
Jamie Storr	**11**
Stephane Fiset	**10**
Kelly Hrudey	10
Mario Lessard	9

Goals-against average
(2400 minutes minimum)
Jamie Storr	**2.52**
Stephane Fiset	**2.80**
Rogie Vachon	2.86
Wayne Rutledge	3.34
Gary Edwards	3.39

Wins
Rogie Vachon	171
Kelly Hrudey	145
Mario Lessard	92
Stephane Fiset	**80**
Jamie Storr	**64**

Season	W	L	T	RT	Pts.	Finish	W	L	Highest round	Coach
				REGULAR SEASON					**PLAYOFFS**	
1967-68	27	32	15	—	69	4th/West	7	7	Division finals	Wren Blair
1968-69	18	43	15	—	51	6th/West	—	—		Wren Blair, John Muckler
1969-70	19	35	22	—	60	3rd/West	2	4	Division semifinals	Wren Blair, Charlie Burns
1970-71	28	34	16	—	72	4th/West	6	6	Division finals	Jack Gordon
1971-72	37	29	12	—	86	2nd/West	3	4	Division semifinals	Jack Gordon
1972-73	37	30	11	—	85	3rd/West	2	4	Division semifinals	Jack Gordon
1973-74	23	38	17	—	63	7th/West	—	—		Jack Gordon, Parker MacDonald
1974-75	23	50	7	—	53	4th/Smythe	—	—		Jack Gordon, Charlie Burns
1975-76	20	53	7	—	47	4th/Smythe	—	—		Ted Harris
1976-77	23	39	18	—	64	2nd/Smythe	0	2	Preliminaries	Ted Harris
1977-78	18	53	9	—	45	5th/Smythe	—	—		Ted Harris, Andre Beaulieu, Lou Nanne
1978-79	28	40	12	—	68	4th/Adams	—	—		Harry Howell, Glen Sonmor
1979-80	36	28	16	—	88	3rd/Adams	8	7	Semifinals	Glen Sonmor
1980-81	35	28	17	—	87	3rd/Adams	12	7	Stanley Cup finals	Glen Sonmor
1981-82	37	23	20	—	94	1st/Norris	1	3	Division semifinals	Glen Sonmor, Murray Oliver
1982-83	40	24	16	—	96	2nd/Norris	4	5	Division finals	Glen Sonmor, Murray Oliver
1983-84	39	31	10	—	88	1st/Norris	7	9	Conference finals	Bill Maloney
1984-85	25	43	12	—	62	4th/Norris	5	4	Division finals	Bill Maloney, Glen Sonmor
1985-86	38	33	9	—	85	2nd/Norris	2	3	Division semifinals	Lorne Henning
1986-87	30	40	10	—	70	5th/Norris	—	—		Lorne Henning, Glen Sonmor
1987-88	19	48	13	—	51	5th/Norris	—	—		Herb Brooks
1988-89	27	37	16	—	70	3rd/Norris	1	4	Division semifinals	Pierre Page
1989-90	36	40	4	—	76	4th/Norris	3	4	Division semifinals	Pierre Page
1990-91	27	39	14	—	68	4th/Norris	14	9	Stanley Cup finals	Bob Gainey
1991-92	32	42	6	—	70	4th/Norris	3	4	Division semifinals	Bob Gainey
1992-93	36	38	10	—	82	5th/Norris	—	—		Bob Gainey

Franchise relocated and became Dallas Stars following 1992-93 season.

FIRST-ROUND ENTRY DRAFT CHOICES

Year   Player, Overall, Last amateur team (league)

1969—Dick Redmond, 5, St. Catharines (OHL)
　　　Dennis O'Brien, 14, St. Catharines (OHL)
1970—No first-round selection
1971—No first-round selection
1972—Jerry Byers, 12, Kitchener (OHL)
1973—No first-round selection
1974—Doug Hicks, 6, Flin Flon (WCHL)
1975—Brian Maxwell, 4, Medicine Hat (WCHL)
1976—Glen Sharpley, 3, Hull (QMJHL)
1977—Brad Maxwell, 7, New Westminster (WCHL)
1978—Bobby Smith, 1, Ottawa (OHL)*
1979—Craig Hartsburg, 6, Birmingham (WHA)
　　　Tom McCarthy, 10, Oshawa (OHL)
1980—Brad Palmer, 16, Victoria (WHL)

Year   Player, Overall, Last amateur team (league)

1981—Ron Meighan, 13, Niagara Falls (OHL)
1982—Brian Bellows, 2, Kitchener (OHL)
1983—Brian Lawton, 1, Mount St. Charles H.S. (R.I.)*
1984—David Quinn, 13, Kent H.S. (Ct.)
1985—No first-round selection
1986—Warren Babe, 12, Lethbridge (WHL)
1987—Dave Archibald, 6, Portland (WHL)
1988—Mike Modano, 1, Prince Albert (WHL)*
1989—Doug Zmolek, 7, John Marshall H.S. (Minn.)
1990—Derian Hatcher, 8, North Bay (OHL)
1991—Richard Matvichuk, 8, Saskatoon (WHL)
1992—No first-round selection
*Designates first player chosen in draft.

SINGLE-SEASON INDIVIDUAL RECORDS

FORWARDS/DEFENSEMEN

Most goals
55—Dino Ciccarelli, 1981-82
　　Brian Bellows, 1989-90

Most assists
76—Neal Broten, 1985-86

Most points
114—Bobby Smith, 1981-82

Most penalty minutes
382—Basil McRae, 1987-88

Most power play goals
22—Dino Ciccarelli, 1986-87

Most shorthanded goals
6—Bill Collins, 1969-70

Most games with three or more goals
3—Bill Goldsworthy, 1973-74
　　Dino Ciccarelli, 1981-82
　　Dino Ciccarelli, 1983-84
　　Tom McCarthy, 1984-85
　　Scott Bjugstad, 1985-86
　　Dino Ciccarelli, 1985-86

Most shots
321—Bill Goldsworthy, 1973-74

GOALTENDERS

Most games
64—Cesare Maniago, 1968-69

Most minutes
3,599—Cesare Maniago, 1968-69

Most goals allowed
216—Pete LoPresti, 1977-78

Lowest goals-against average
2.12—Gump Worsley, 1971-72

Most shutouts
6—Cesare Maniago, 1967-68

Most wins
31—Jon Casey, 1989-90

Most losses
35—Pete LoPresti, 1977-78

Most ties
16—Cesare Maniago, 1969-70

NHL HISTORY *Team by team*

FRANCHISE LEADERS

FORWARDS/DEFENSEMEN

Games
Neal Broten	876
Curt Giles	760
Brian Bellows	753
Fred Barrett	730
Bill Goldsworthy	670

Goals
Brian Bellows	342
Dino Ciccarelli	332
Bill Goldsworthy	267
Neal Broten	249
Steve Payne	228

Assists
Neal Broten	547
Brian Bellows	380
Bobby Smith	369
Dino Ciccarelli	319
Tim Young	316

Points
Neal Broten	796
Brian Bellows	722
Dino Ciccarelli	651
Bobby Smith	554
Bill Goldsworthy	506

Penalty minutes
Basil McRae	1567
Shane Churla	1194
Willi Plett	1137
Brad Maxwell	1031
Mark Tinordi	872

GOALTENDERS

Games
Cesare Maniago	420
Gilles Meloche	328
Jon Casey	325
Don Beaupre	316
Pete LoPresti	173

Shutouts
Cesare Maniago	29
Jon Casey	12
Gilles Meloche	9
Pete LoPresti	5
Don Beaupre	4
Brian Hayward	4

Goals-against average (2400 minutes minimum)
Gump Worsley	2.62
Cesare Maniago	3.17
Jon Casey	3.28
Gilles Gilbert	3.39
Gary Edwards	3.44
Darcy Wakaluk	3.44

Wins
Cesare Maniago	143
Gilles Meloche	141
Jon Casey	128
Don Beaupre	126
Pete LoPresti	43

MINNESOTA WILD

YEAR-BY-YEAR RECORDS

		REGULAR SEASON					PLAYOFFS			
Season	W	L	T	RT	Pts.	Finish	W	L	Highest round	Coach
2000-01	25	39	13	5	68	5th/Northwest	—	—		Jacques Lemaire

FIRST-ROUND ENTRY DRAFT CHOICES

Year   Player, Overall, Last amateur team (league)
2000—Marian Gaborik, 3, Trencin, Slovakia

Year   Player, Overall, Last amateur team (league)
2001—Mikko Koivu, 6, TPS, Finland

SINGLE-SEASON INDIVIDUAL RECORDS

FORWARDS/DEFENSEMEN

Most goals
18—Marian Gaborik, 2000-01
Darby Hendrickson, 2000-01
Wes Walz, 2000-01

Most assists
28—Scott Pellerin, 2000-01

Most points
39—Scott Pellerin, 2000-01

Most penalty minutes
137—Matt Johnson, 2000-01

Most power play goals
4—Filip Kuba, 2000-01

Most shorthanded goals
7—Wes Walz, 2000-01

Most games with three or more goals
1—Antti Laaksonen, 2000-01

Most shots
179—Marian Gaborik, 2000-01

GOALTENDERS

Most games
42—Manny Fernandez, 2000-01

Most minutes
2,461—Manny Fernandez, 2000-01

Most goals allowed
98—Jamie McLennan, 2000-01

Lowest goals-against average
2.24—Manny Fernandez, 2000-01

Most shutouts
4—Manny Fernandez, 2000-01

Most wins
19—Manny Fernandez, 2000-01

Most losses
23—Jamie McLennan, 2000-01

Most ties
9—Jamie McLennan, 2000-01

FRANCHISE LEADERS

Players in boldface played for club in 2000-01

FORWARDS/DEFENSEMEN

Games
Antti Laaksonen	82
Wes Walz	82
Lubomir Sekeras	80
Stacy Roest	76
Aaron Gavey	75
Filip Kuba	75

Goals
Marian Gaborik	18
Darby Hendrickson	18
Wes Walz	18
Antti Laaksonen	12
Scott Pellerin	11
Lubomir Sekeras	11

Assists
Scott Pellerin	28
Lubomir Sekeras	23

Jim Dowd	22
Filip Kuba	21
Stacy Roest	20

Points
Scott Pellerin	39
Marian Gaborik	36
Lubomir Sekeras	34
Filip Kuba	30
Wes Walz	30

MONTREAL CANADIENS
YEAR-BY-YEAR RECORDS

		REGULAR SEASON					PLAYOFFS			
Season	W	L	T	RT	Pts.	Finish	W	L	Highest round	Coach
1917-18	13	9	0	—	26	1st/3rd	1	1	Semifinals	George Kennedy
1918-19	10	8	0	—	20	1st/2nd	†*6	3	Stanley Cup finals	George Kennedy
1919-20	13	11	0	—	26	2nd/3rd	—	—		George Kennedy
1920-21	13	11	0	—	26	3rd/2nd	—	—		George Kennedy
1921-22	12	11	1	—	25	3rd	—	—		Leo Dandurand
1922-23	13	9	2	—	28	2nd	1	1	Quarterfinals	Leo Dandurand
1923-24	13	11	0	—	26	2nd	6	0	Stanley Cup champ	Leo Dandurand
1924-25	17	11	2	—	36	3rd	3	3	Stanley Cup finals	Leo Dandurand
1925-26	11	24	1	—	23	7th	—	—		Cecil Hart
1926-27	28	14	2	—	58	2nd/Canadian	*1	1	Semifinals	Cecil Hart
1927-28	26	11	7	—	59	1st/Canadian	*0	1	Semifinals	Cecil Hart
1928-29	22	7	15	—	59	1st/Canadian	0	3	Semifinals	Cecil Hart
1929-30	21	14	9	—	51	2nd/Canadian	*5	0	Stanley Cup champ	Cecil Hart
1930-31	26	10	8	—	60	1st/Canadian	6	4	Stanley Cup champ	Cecil Hart
1931-32	25	16	7	—	57	1st/Canadian	1	3	Semifinals	Cecil Hart
1932-33	18	25	5	—	41	3rd/Canadian	*0	1	Quarterfinals	Newsy Lalonde
1933-34	22	20	6	—	50	2nd/Canadian	*0	1	Quarterfinals	Newsy Lalonde
1934-35	19	23	6	—	44	3rd/Canadian	*0	1	Quarterfinals	Newsy Lalonde, Leo Dandurand
1935-36	11	26	11	—	33	4th/Canadian	—	—		Sylvio Mantha
1936-37	24	18	6	—	54	1st/Canadian	2	3	Semifinals	Cecil Hart
1937-38	18	17	13	—	49	3rd/Canadian	1	2	Quarterfinals	Cecil Hart
1938-39	15	24	9	—	39	6th	1	2	Quarterfinals	Cecil Hart, Jules Dugal
1939-40	10	33	5	—	25	7th	—	—		Pit Lepine
1940-41	16	26	6	—	38	6th	1	2	Quarterfinals	Dick Irvin
1941-42	18	27	3	—	39	6th	1	2	Quarterfinals	Dick Irvin
1942-43	19	19	12	—	50	4th	1	4	League semifinals	Dick Irvin
1943-44	38	5	7	—	83	1st	8	1	Stanley Cup champ	Dick Irvin
1944-45	38	8	4	—	80	1st	2	4	League semifinals	Dick Irvin
1945-46	28	17	5	—	61	1st	8	1	Stanley Cup champ	Dick Irvin
1946-47	34	16	10	—	78	1st	6	5	Stanley Cup finals	Dick Irvin
1947-48	20	29	11	—	51	5th	—	—		Dick Irvin
1948-49	28	23	9	—	65	3rd	3	4	League semifinals	Dick Irvin
1949-50	29	22	19	—	77	2nd	1	4	League semifinals	Dick Irvin
1950-51	25	30	15	—	65	3rd	5	6	Stanley Cup finals	Dick Irvin
1951-52	34	26	10	—	78	2nd	4	7	Stanley Cup finals	Dick Irvin
1952-53	28	23	19	—	75	2nd	8	4	Stanley Cup champ	Dick Irvin
1953-54	35	24	11	—	81	2nd	7	4	Stanley Cup finals	Dick Irvin
1954-55	41	18	11	—	93	2nd	7	5	Stanley Cup finals	Dick Irvin
1955-56	45	15	10	—	100	1st	8	2	Stanley Cup champ	Toe Blake
1956-57	35	23	12	—	82	2nd	8	2	Stanley Cup champ	Toe Blake
1957-58	43	17	10	—	96	1st	8	2	Stanley Cup champ	Toe Blake
1958-59	39	18	13	—	91	1st	8	3	Stanley Cup champ	Toe Blake
1959-60	40	18	12	—	92	1st	8	0	Stanley Cup champ	Toe Blake
1960-61	41	19	10	—	92	1st	2	4	League semifinals	Toe Blake
1961-62	42	14	14	—	98	1st	2	4	League semifinals	Toe Blake
1962-63	28	19	23	—	79	3rd	1	4	League semifinals	Toe Blake
1963-64	36	21	13	—	85	1st	3	4	League semifinals	Toe Blake
1964-65	36	23	11	—	83	2nd	8	5	Stanley Cup champ	Toe Blake
1965-66	41	21	8	—	90	1st	8	2	Stanley Cup champ	Toe Blake
1966-67	32	25	13	—	77	2nd	6	4	Stanley Cup finals	Toe Blake
1967-68	42	22	10	—	94	1st/East	12	1	Stanley Cup champ	Toe Blake
1968-69	46	19	11	—	103	1st/East	12	2	Stanley Cup champ	Claude Ruel
1969-70	38	22	16	—	92	5th/East	—	—		Claude Ruel
1970-71	42	23	13	—	97	3rd/East	12	8	Stanley Cup champ	Claude Ruel, Al MacNeil
1971-72	46	16	16	—	108	3rd/East	2	4	Division semifinals	Scotty Bowman
1972-73	52	10	16	—	120	1st/East	12	5	Stanley Cup champ	Scotty Bowman

Season	W	L	T	RT	Pts.	Finish	W	L	Highest round	Coach
REGULAR SEASON							PLAYOFFS			
1973-74	45	42	9	—	99	2nd/East	2	4	Division semifinals	Scotty Bowman
1974-75	47	14	19	—	113	1st/Norris	6	5	Semifinals	Scotty Bowman
1975-76	58	11	11	—	127	1st/Norris	12	1	Stanley Cup champ	Scotty Bowman
1976-77	60	8	12	—	132	1st/Norris	12	2	Stanley Cup champ	Scotty Bowman
1977-78	59	10	11	—	129	1st/Norris	12	3	Stanley Cup champ	Scotty Bowman
1978-79	52	17	11	—	115	1st/Norris	12	4	Stanley Cup champ	Scotty Bowman
1979-80	47	20	13	—	107	1st/Norris	6	4	Quarterfinals	Bernie Geoffrion, Claude Ruel
1980-81	45	22	13	—	103	1st/Norris	0	3	Preliminaries	Claude Ruel
1981-82	46	17	17	—	109	1st/Adams	2	3	Division semifinals	Bob Berry
1982-83	42	24	14	—	98	2nd/Adams	0	3	Division semifinals	Bob Berry
1983-84	35	40	5	—	75	4th/Adams	9	6	Conference finals	Bob Berry, Jacques Lemaire
1984-85	41	27	12	—	94	1st/Adams	6	6	Division finals	Jacques Lemaire
1985-86	40	33	7	—	87	2nd/Adams	15	5	Stanley Cup champ	Jean Perron
1986-87	41	29	10	—	92	2nd/Adams	10	7	Conference finals	Jean Perron
1987-88	45	22	13	—	103	1st/Adams	5	6	Division finals	Jean Perron
1988-89	53	18	9	—	115	1st/Adams	14	7	Stanley Cup finals	Pat Burns
1989-90	41	28	11	—	93	3rd/Adams	5	6	Division finals	Pat Burns
1990-91	39	30	11	—	89	2nd/Adams	7	6	Division finals	Pat Burns
1991-92	41	28	11	—	93	1st/Adams	4	7	Division finals	Pat Burns
1992-93	48	30	6	—	102	3rd/Adams	16	4	Stanley Cup champ	Jacques Demers
1993-94	41	29	14	—	96	3rd/Northeast	3	4	Conference quarterfinals	Jacques Demers
1994-95	18	23	7	—	43	6th/Northeast	—	—		Jacques Demers
1995-96	40	32	10	—	90	3rd/Northeast	2	4	Conference quarterfinals	Jacques Demers, Mario Tremblay
1996-97	31	36	15	—	77	T3rd/Northeast	1	4	Conference quarterfinals	Mario Tremblay
1997-98	37	32	13	—	87	4th/Northeast	4	6	Conference semifinals	Alain Vigneault
1998-99	32	39	11	—	75	5th/Northeast	—	—		Alain Vigneault
1999-00	35	38	9	4	83	4th/Northeast	—	—		Alain Vigneault
2000-01	28	40	8	6	70	5th/Northeast	—	—		Alain Vigneault, Michel Therrien

*Won-lost record does not indicate tie(s) resulting from two-game, total-goals series that year (two-game, total-goals series were played from 1917-18 through 1935-36).

†1918-19 series abandoned with no Cup holder due to influenza epidemic.

FIRST-ROUND ENTRY DRAFT CHOICES

Year   Player, Overall, Last amateur team (league)
1969—Rejean Houle, 1, Montreal (OHL)*
　　　Marc Tardif, 2, Montreal (OHL)
1970—Ray Martiniuk, 5, Flin Flon (WCHL)
　　　Chuck Lefley, 6, Canadian Nationals
1971—Guy Lafleur, 1, Quebec (QMJHL)*
　　　Chuck Arnason, 7, Flin Flon (WCHL)
　　　Murray Wilson, 11, Ottawa (OHL)
1972—Steve Shutt, 4, Toronto (OHL)
　　　Michel Larocque, 6, Ottawa (OHL)
　　　Dave Gardner, 8, Toronto (OHL)
　　　John Van Boxmeer, 14, Guelph (SOJHL)
1973—Bob Gainey, 8, Peterborough (OHL)
1974—Cam Connor, 5, Flin Flon (WCHL)
　　　Doug Risebrough, 7, Kitchener (OHL)
　　　Rick Chartraw, 10, Kitchener (OHL)
　　　Mario Tremblay, 12, Montreal (OHL)
　　　Gord McTavish, 15, Sudbury (OHL)
1975—Robin Sadler, 9, Edmonton (WCHL)
　　　Pierre Mondou, 15, Montreal (QMJHL)
1976—Peter Lee, 12, Ottawa (OHL)
　　　Rod Schutt, 13, Sudbury (OHL)
　　　Bruce Baker, 18, Ottawa (OHL)
1977—Mark Napier, 10, Birmingham (WHA)
　　　Normand Dupont, 18, Montreal (QMJHL)
1978—Danny Geoffrion, 8, Cornwall (QMJHL)
　　　Dave Hunter, 17, Sudbury (OHL)
1979—No first-round selection
1980—Doug Wickenheiser, 1, Regina (WHL)*

Year   Player, Overall, Last amateur team (league)
1981—Mark Hunter, 7, Brantford (OHL)
　　　Gilbert Delorme, 18, Chicoutimi (QMJHL)
　　　Jan Ingman, 19, Farjestads (Sweden)
1982—Alain Heroux, 19, Chicoutimi (QMJHL)
1983—Alfie Turcotte, 17, Portland (WHL)
1984—Petr Svoboda, 5, Czechoslovakia
　　　Shayne Corson, 8, Brantford (OHL)
1985—Jose Charbonneau, 12, Drummondville (QMJHL)
　　　Tom Chorske, 16, Minneapolis SW H.S. (Minn.)
1986—Mark Pederson, 15, Medicine Hat (WHL)
1987—Andrew Cassels, 17, Ottawa (OHL)
1988—Eric Charron, 20, Trois-Rivieres (QMJHL)
1989—Lindsay Vallis, 13, Seattle (WHL)
1990—Turner Stevenson, 12, Seattle (WHL)
1991—Brent Bilodeau, 17, Seattle (WHL)
1992—David Wilkie, 20, Kamloops (WHL)
1993—Saku Koivu, 21, TPS Turku (Finland)
1994—Brad Brown, 18, North Bay (OHL)
1995—Terry Ryan, 8, Tri-City (WHL)
1996—Matt Higgins, 18, Moose Jaw (WHL)
1997—Jason Ward, 11, Erie (OHL)
1998—Eric Chouinard, 16, Quebec (QMJHL)
1999—No first-round selection
2000—Ron Hainsey, 13, Univ. of Mass.-Lowell
　　　Marcel Hossa, 16, Portland (WHL)
2001—Michael Komisarek, 7, Univ. of Michigan
　　　Alexander Perezhogin, 25, OMSK, Russia
*Designates first player chosen in draft.

SINGLE-SEASON INDIVIDUAL RECORDS

FORWARDS/DEFENSEMEN

Most goals
60—Steve Shutt, 1976-77
　　Guy Lafleur, 1977-78

Most assists
82—Pete Mahovlich, 1974-75

Most points
136—Guy Lafleur, 1976-77

Most penalty minutes
358—Chris Nilan, 1984-85

Most power play goals
20—Yvan Cournoyer, 1966-67

Most shorthanded goals
8—Guy Carbonneau, 1983-84

Most games with three or more goals
7—Joe Malone, 1917-18

GOALTENDERS

Most games
70—Gerry McNeil, 1950-51
    Gerry McNeil, 1951-52
    Jacques Plante, 1961-62

Most minutes
4,200—Gerry McNeil, 1950-51
       Gerry McNeil, 1951-52
       Jacques Plante, 1961-62

Lowest goals-against average
0.92—George Hainsworth, 1928-29

Most shutouts
22—George Hainsworth, 1928-29

Most wins
42—Jacques Plante, 1955-56
    Jacques Plante, 1961-62
    Ken Dryden, 1975-76

FRANCHISE LEADERS

Players in boldface played for club in 2000-01

FORWARDS/DEFENSEMEN

Games

Henri Richard	1256
Larry Robinson	1202
Bob Gainey	1160
Jean Beliveau	1125
Claude Provost	1005

Goals

Maurice Richard	544
Guy Lafleur	518
Jean Beliveau	507
Yvan Cournoyer	428
Steve Shutt	408

Assists

Guy Lafleur	728
Jean Beliveau	712
Henri Richard	688
Larry Robinson	686
Jacques Lemaire	469

Points

Guy Lafleur	1246
Jean Beliveau	1219
Henri Richard	1046
Maurice Richard	965
Larry Robinson	883

Penalty minutes

Chris Nilan	2248
Lyle Odelein	1367
Shayne Corson	1341
Maurice Richard	1285
John Ferguson	1214

GOALTENDERS

Games

Jacques Plante	556
Patrick Roy	551
Ken Dryden	397
Bill Durnan	383
George Hainsworth	318

Shutouts

George Hainsworth	75
Jacques Plante	58
Ken Dryden	46
Bill Durnan	34
Patrick Roy	29

Wins

Jacques Plante	314
Patrick Roy	289
Ken Dryden	258
Bill Durnan	208
George Hainsworth	167

MONTREAL MAROONS (DEFUNCT)
YEAR-BY-YEAR RECORDS

	REGULAR SEASON					PLAYOFFS			
Season	W	L	T	Pts.	Finish	W	L	Highest round	Coach
1924-25	9	19	2	20	5th	—	—		Eddie Gerard
1925-26	20	11	5	45	2nd	3	1	Stanley Cup champ	Eddie Gerard
1926-27	20	20	4	44	3rd/Canadian	*0	1	Quarterfinals	Eddie Gerard
1927-28	24	14	6	54	2nd/Canadian	*5	3	Stanley Cup finals	Eddie Gerard
1928-29	15	20	9	39	5th/Canadian	—	—		Eddie Gerard
1929-30	23	16	5	51	1st/Canadian	1	3	Semifinals	Dunc Munro
1930-31	20	18	6	46	3rd/Canadian	*0	2	Quarterfinals	Dunc Munro, George Boucher
1931-32	19	22	7	45	3rd/Canadian	*1	1	Semifinals	Sprague Cleghorn
1932-33	22	20	6	50	2nd/Canadian	0	2	Quarterfinals	Eddie Gerard
1933-34	19	18	11	49	3rd/Canadian	*1	2	Semifinals	Eddie Gerard
1934-35	24	19	5	53	2nd/Canadian	*5	0	Stanley Cup champ	Tommy Gorman
1935-36	22	16	10	54	1st/Canadian	0	3	Semifinals	Tommy Gorman
1936-37	22	17	9	53	2nd/Canadian	2	3	Semifinals	Tommy Gorman
1937-38	12	30	6	30	4th/Canadian	—	—		King Clancy, Tommy Gorman

*Won-lost record does not indicate tie(s) resulting from two-game, total goals series that year (two-game, total-goals series were played from 1917-18 through 1935-36).

MONTREAL WANDERERS (DEFUNCT)
YEAR-BY-YEAR RECORDS

	REGULAR SEASON					PLAYOFFS			
Season	W	L	T	Pts.	Finish	W	L	Highest round	Coach
1917-18*	1	5	0	2	4th	—	—		Art Ross

*Franchise disbanded after Montreal Arena burned down. Montreal Canadiens and Toronto each counted one win for defaulted games with Wanderers.

NHL HISTORY *Team by team*

NASHVILLE PREDATORS
YEAR-BY-YEAR RECORDS

	REGULAR SEASON						PLAYOFFS			
Season	W	L	T	RT	Pts.	Finish	W	L	Highest round	Coach
1998-99	28	47	7	—	63	4th/Central	—	—		Barry Trotz
1999-00	28	47	7	7	70	4th/Central	—	—		Barry Trotz
2000-01	34	36	9	3	80	3rd/Central	—	—		Barry Trotz

FIRST-ROUND ENTRY DRAFT CHOICES

Year   Player, Overall, Last amateur team (league)
1998—David Legwand, 2, Plymouth (OHL)
1999—Brian Finley, 6, Barrie (OHL)

Year   Player, Overall, Last amateur team (league)
2000—Scott Hartnell, 6, Prince Albert (WHL)
2001—Dan Hamhuis, 12, Prince George (WHL)

SINGLE-SEASON INDIVIDUAL RECORDS

FORWARDS/DEFENSEMEN

Most goals
26—Cliff Ronning, 1999-2000

Most assists
43—Cliff Ronning, 2000-01

Most points
62—Cliff Ronning, 1999-2000
Cliff Ronning, 2000-01

Most penalty minutes
242—Patrick Cote, 1998-99

Most power play goals
10—Sergei Krivokrasov, 1998-99

Most shorthanded goals
3—Greg Johnson, 1998-99
Tom Fitzgerald, 1999-2000
Scott Walker, 2000-01

Most games with three or more goals
1—Robert Valicevic, 1999-2000
Scott Walker, 2000-01

Most shots
248—Cliff Ronning, 1999-2000

GOALTENDERS

Most games
52—Mike Dunham, 1999-2000

Most minutes
3,077—Mike Dunham, 1999-2000

Most goals allowed
146—Mike Dunham, 1999-2000

Lowest goals-against average
2.28—Mike Dunham, 2000-01

Most shutouts
1—Mike Dunham, 2000-01

Most wins
21—Mike Dunham, 2000-01

Most losses
27—Mike Dunham, 1999-2000

Most ties
6—Mike Dunham, 1999-2000

FRANCHISE LEADERS

Players in boldface played for club in 2000-01

FORWARDS/DEFENSEMEN

Games
Tom Fitzgerald 244
Patric Kjellberg 234
Cliff Ronning 234
Greg Johnson 232
Drake Berehowsky 219

Goals
Cliff Ronning..............................63
Patric Kjellberg 48
Scott Walker 47
Greg Johnson 42
Vitali Yachmenev 38

Assists
Cliff Ronning 114
Greg Johnson.............................84
Scott Walker 75

Patric Kjellberg 74
Drake Berehowsky 53

Points
Cliff Ronning 177
Greg Johnson 126
Patric Kjellberg 122
Scott Walker 122
Sergei Krivokrasov 74

Penalty minutes
Drake Berehowsky 327
Patrick Cote...............................312
Scott Walker 259
Bob Boughner............................234
Denny Lambert...........................218

GOALTENDERS

Games
Mike Dunham 144
Tomas Vokoun 107
Eric Fichaud...................................9
Chris Mason.................................4

Shutouts
Mike Dunham................................5
Tomas Vokoun 4

Goals-against average
(2400 minutes minimum)
Tomas Vokoun 2.72
Mike Dunham 2.73

Wins
Mike Dunham..............................56
Tomas Vokoun............................34

NEW JERSEY DEVILS
YEAR-BY-YEAR RECORDS

	REGULAR SEASON						PLAYOFFS			
Season	W	L	T	RT	Pts.	Finish	W	L	Highest round	Coach
1982-83	17	49	14	—	48	5th/Patrick	—	—		Billy MacMillan
1983-84	17	56	7	—	41	5th/Patrick	—	—		Billy MacMillan, Tom McVie
1984-85	22	48	10	—	54	5th/Patrick	—	—		Doug Carpenter
1985-86	28	49	3	—	59	5th/Patrick	—	—		Doug Carpenter
1986-87	29	45	6	—	64	6th/Patrick	—	—		Doug Carpenter
1987-88	38	36	6	—	82	4th/Patrick	11	9	Conference finals	Doug Carpenter, Jim Schoenfeld

Season	W	L	T	RT	Pts.	Finish	W	L	Highest round	Coach
						REGULAR SEASON			**PLAYOFFS**	
1988-89	27	41	12	—	66	5th/Patrick	—	—		Jim Schoenfeld
1989-90	37	34	9	—	83	2nd/Patrick	2	4	Division semifinals	Jim Schoenfeld, John Cunniff
1990-91	32	33	15	—	79	4th/Patrick	3	4	Division semifinals	John Cunniff, Tom McVie
1991-92	38	31	11	—	87	4th/Patrick	3	4	Division semifinals	Tom McVie
1992-93	40	37	7	—	87	4th/Patrick	1	4	Division semifinals	Herb Brooks
1993-94	47	25	12	—	106	2nd/Atlantic	11	9	Conference finals	Jacques Lemaire
1994-95	22	18	8	—	52	2nd/Atlantic	16	4	Stanley Cup champ	Jacques Lemaire
1995-96	37	33	12	—	86	6th/Atlantic	—	—		Jacques Lemaire
1996-97	45	23	14	—	104	1st/Atlantic	5	5	Conference semifinals	Jacques Lemaire
1997-98	48	23	11	—	107	1st/Atlantic	2	4	Conference quarterfinals	Jacques Lemaire
1998-99	47	24	11	—	105	1st/Atlantic	3	4	Conference quarterfinals	Robbie Ftorek
1999-00	45	29	8	5	103	2nd/Atlantic	16	7	Stanley Cup champ	Robbie Ftorek, Larry Robinson
2000-01	48	19	12	3	111	1st/Atlantic	15	10	Stanley Cup finals	Larry Robinson

Franchise was originally known as Kansas City Scouts and relocated to become Colorado Rockies following 1975-76 season; franchise relocated and became New Jersey Devils following 1981-82 season.

FIRST-ROUND ENTRY DRAFT CHOICES

Year   Player, Overall, Last amateur team (league)
1982—Rocky Trottier, 8, Billings (WHL)
      Ken Daneyko, 18, Seattle (WHL)
1983—John MacLean, 6, Oshawa (OHL)
1984—Kirk Muller, 2, Guelph (OHL)
1985—Craig Wolanin, 3, Kitchener (OHL)
1986—Neil Brady, 3, Medicine Hat (WHL)
1987—Brendan Shanahan, 2, London (OHL)
1988—Corey Foster, 12, Peterborough (OHL)
1989—Bill Guerin, 5, Springfield (Mass.) Jr.
      Jason Miller, 18, Medicine Hat (WHL)
1990—Martin Brodeur, 20, St. Hyacinthe (QMJHL)
1991—Scott Niedermayer, 3, Kamloops (WHL)
      Brian Rolston, 11, Detroit Compuware Jr.

Year   Player, Overall, Last amateur team (league)
1992—Jason Smith, 18, Regina (WHL)
1993—Denis Pederson, 13, Prince Albert (WHL)
1994—Vadim Sharifjanov, 25, Salavat (Russia)
1995—Petr Sykora, 18, Detroit (IHL)
1996—Lance Ward, 10, Red Deer (WHL)
1997—Jean-Francois Damphousse, 24, Moncton (QMJHL)
1998—Mike Van Ryn, 26, Michigan
      Scott Gomez, 27, Tri-City (WHL)
1999—Ari Ahonen, 27, Jyvaskyla, Finland
2000—David Hale, 22, Sioux City (USHL)
2001—Adrian Foster, 28, Saskatoon (WHL)

SINGLE-SEASON INDIVIDUAL RECORDS

FORWARDS/DEFENSEMEN

Most goals
46—Pat Verbeek, 1987-88

Most assists
60—Scott Stevens, 1993-94

Most points
96—Patrik Elias, 2000-01

Most penalty minutes
295—Krzysztof Oliwa, 1997-98

Most power play goals
19—John MacLean, 1990-91

Most shorthanded goals
6—John Madden, 1999-2000

Most games with three or more goals
3—Kirk Muller, 1987-88
    John MacLean, 1988-89
    Patrik Elias, 2000-01

Most shots
322—John MacLean, 1989-90

GOALTENDERS

Most games
77—Martin Brodeur, 1995-96

Most minutes
4,433—Martin Brodeur, 1995-96

Most goals allowed
242—Chico Resch, 1982-83

Lowest goals-against average
1.88—Martin Brodeur, 1996-97

Most shutouts
10—Martin Brodeur, 1996-97
    Martin Brodeur, 1997-98

Most wins
43—Martin Brodeur, 1997-98
    Martin Brodeur, 1999-2000

Most losses
35—Chico Resch, 1982-83

Most ties
13—Martin Brodeur, 1996-97

FRANCHISE LEADERS

Players in boldface played for club in 2000-01

FORWARDS/DEFENSEMEN

Games
Ken Daneyko..........................**1147**
John MacLean............................934
Scott Stevens **755**
Randy McKay **705**
Bruce Driver...............................702

Goals
John MacLean............................347
Kirk Muller.................................185
Bobby Holik **173**
Pat Verbeek...............................170
Aaron Broten.............................147

Assists
John MacLean............................354
Kirk Muller.................................335
Bruce Driver...............................316
Scott Stevens **296**
Aaron Broten.............................283

Points
John MacLean............................701
Kirk Muller.................................520
Aaron Broten.............................430
Bobby Holik **409**
Bruce Driver...............................399

Penalty minutes
Ken Daneyko..........................**2426**
Randy McKay **1353**
John MacLean............................1168
Pat Verbeek...............................943
Scott Stevens **900**

GOALTENDERS

Games
Martin Brodeur........................**519**
Chris Terreri **302**
Chico Resch...............................198
Sean Burke................................162
Alain Chevrier............................140

Shutouts		Goals-against average		Wins	
Martin Brodeur	51	(2400 minutes minimum)		Martin Brodeur	286
Chris Terreri	7	Martin Brodeur	2.21	Chris Terreri	118
Craig Billington	4	Chris Terreri	3.07	Sean Burke	62
Sean Burke	4	Sean Burke	3.66	Alain Chevrier	53
Mike Dunham	3	Bob Sauve	3.87	Chico Resch	49
		Craig Billington	3.98		

NEW YORK AMERICANS (DEFUNCT)
YEAR-BY-YEAR RECORDS

	REGULAR SEASON					PLAYOFFS			
Season	W	L	T	Pts.	Finish	W	L	Highest round	Coach
1925-26	12	20	4	28	5th	—	—		Tommy Gorman
1926-27	17	25	2	36	4th/Canadian	—	—		Newsy Lalonde
1927-28	11	27	6	28	5th/Canadian	—	—		Wilf Green
1928-29	19	13	12	50	2nd/Canadian	*0	1	Semifinals	Tommy Gorman
1929-30	14	25	5	33	4th/Canadian	—	—		Lionel Conacher
1930-31	18	16	10	46	4th/Canadian	—	—		Eddie Gerard
1931-32	16	24	8	40	4th/Canadian	—	—		Eddie Gerard
1932-33	15	22	11	41	4th/Canadian	—	—		Joe Simpson
1933-34	15	23	10	40	4th/Canadian	—	—		Joe Simpson
1934-35	12	27	9	33	4th/Canadian	—	—		Joe Simpson
1935-36	16	25	7	39	3rd/Canadian	2	3	Semifinals	Red Dutton
1936-37	15	29	4	34	4th/Canadian	—	—		Red Dutton
1937-38	19	18	11	49	2nd/Canadian	3	3	Semifinals	Red Dutton
1938-39	17	21	10	44	4th	0	2	Quarterfinals	Red Dutton
1939-40	15	29	4	34	6th	1	2	Quarterfinals	Red Dutton
1940-41	8	29	11	27	7th	—	—		Red Dutton
1941-42†	16	29	3	35	7th	—	—		Red Dutton

Franchise was originally known as Quebec Bulldogs and relocated to become Hamilton Tigers following 1919-20 season; franchise relocated and became New York Americans following 1924-25 season.

*Won-lost record does not indicate tie(s) resulting from two-game, total goals series that year (two-game, total-goals series were played from 1917-18 through 1935-36).

†Brooklyn Americans.

NEW YORK ISLANDERS
YEAR-BY-YEAR RECORDS

	REGULAR SEASON						PLAYOFFS			
Season	W	L	T	RT	Pts.	Finish	W	L	Highest round	Coach
1972-73	12	60	6	—	30	8th/East	—	—		Phil Goyette, Earl Ingarfield
1973-74	19	41	18	—	56	8th/East	—	—		Al Arbour
1974-75	33	25	22	—	88	3rd/Patrick	9	8	Semifinals	Al Arbour
1975-76	42	21	17	—	101	2nd/Patrick	7	6	Semifinals	Al Arbour
1976-77	47	21	12	—	106	2nd/Patrick	8	4	Semifinals	Al Arbour
1977-78	48	17	15	—	111	1st/Patrick	3	4	Quarterfinals	Al Arbour
1978-79	51	15	14	—	116	1st/Patrick	6	4	Semifinals	Al Arbour
1979-80	39	28	13	—	91	2nd/Patrick	15	6	Stanley Cup champ	Al Arbour
1980-81	48	18	14	—	110	1st/Patrick	15	3	Stanley Cup champ	Al Arbour
1981-82	54	16	10	—	118	1st/Patrick	15	4	Stanley Cup champ	Al Arbour
1982-83	42	26	12	—	96	2nd/Patrick	15	5	Stanley Cup champ	Al Arbour
1983-84	50	26	4	—	104	1st/Patrick	12	9	Stanley Cup finals	Al Arbour
1984-85	40	34	6	—	86	3rd/Patrick	4	6	Division finals	Al Arbour
1985-86	39	29	12	—	90	3rd/Patrick	0	3	Division semifinals	Al Arbour
1986-87	35	33	12	—	82	3rd/Patrick	7	7	Division finals	Terry Simpson
1987-88	39	31	10	—	88	1st/Patrick	2	4	Division semifinals	Terry Simpson
1988-89	28	47	5	—	61	6th/Patrick	—	—		Terry Simpson, Al Arbour
1989-90	31	38	11	—	73	4th/Patrick	1	4	Division semifinals	Al Arbour
1990-91	25	45	10	—	60	6th/Patrick	—	—		Al Arbour
1991-92	34	35	11	—	79	5th/Patrick	—	—		Al Arbour
1992-93	40	37	7	—	87	3rd/Patrick	9	9	Conference finals	Al Arbour
1993-94	36	36	12	—	84	4th/Atlantic	0	4	Conference quarterfinals	Al Arbour, Lorne Henning
1994-95	15	28	5	—	35	7th/Atlantic	—	—		Lorne Henning
1995-96	22	50	10	—	54	7th/Atlantic	—	—		Mike Milbury
1996-97	29	41	12	—	70	7th/Atlantic	—	—		Mike Milbury, Rick Bowness
1997-98	30	41	11	—	71	4th/Atlantic	—	—		Rick Bowness, Mike Milbury
1998-99	24	48	10	—	58	5th/Atlantic	—	—		Mike Milbury, Bill Stewart
1999-00	24	49	9	1	58	5th/Atlantic	—	—		Butch Goring
2000-01	21	51	7	3	52	5th/Atlantic	—	—		Butch Goring, Lorne Henning

FIRST-ROUND ENTRY DRAFT CHOICES

Year	Player, Overall, Last amateur team (league)
1972	Billy Harris, 1, Toronto (OHL)*
1973	Denis Potvin, 1, Ottawa (OHL)*
1974	Clark Gillies, 4, Regina (WCHL)
1975	Pat Price, 11, Vancouver (WHA)
1976	Alex McKendry, 14, Sudbury (OHL)
1977	Mike Bossy, 15, Laval (QMJHL)
1978	Steve Tambellini, 15, Lethbridge (WCHL)
1979	Duane Sutter, 17, Lethbridge (WHL)
1980	Brent Sutter, 17, Red Deer (AJHL)
1981	Paul Boutilier, 21, Sherbrooke (QMJHL)
1982	Pat Flatley, 21, University of Wisconsin
1983	Pat LaFontaine, 3, Verdun (QMJHL)
	Gerald Diduck, 16, Lethbridge (WHL)
1984	Duncan MacPherson, 20, Saskatoon (WHL)
1985	Brad Dalgarno, 6, Hamilton (OHL)
	Derek King, 13, Sault Ste. Marie (OHL)
1986	Tom Fitzgerald, 17, Austin Prep (Mass.)
1987	Dean Chynoweth, 13, Medicine Hat (WHL)
1988	Kevin Cheveldayoff, 16, Brandon (WHL)

Year	Player, Overall, Last amateur team (league)
1989	Dave Chyzowski, 2, Kamloops (WHL)
1990	Scott Scissons, 6, Saskatoon (WHL)
1991	Scott Lachance, 4, Boston University
1992	Darius Kasparaitis, 5, Dynamo Moscow (CIS)
1993	Todd Bertuzzi, 23, Guelph (OHL)
1994	Brett Lindros, 9, Kingston (OHL)
1995	Wade Redden, 2, Brandon (WHL)
1996	Jean-Pierre Dumont, 3, Val-d'Or (QMJHL)
1997	Roberto Luongo, 4, Val d'Or (QMJHL)
	Eric Brewer, 5, Prince George (WHL)
1998	Michael Rupp, 9, Erie (OHL)
1999	Tim Connolly, 5, Erie (OHL)
	Taylor Pyatt, 8, Sudbury (OHL)
	Branislav Mezei, 10, Belleville (OHL)
	Kristian Kudroc, 28, Michalovce, Slovakia
2000	Rick DiPietro, 1, Boston University*
	Raffi Torres, 5, Brampton (OHL)
2001	No first-round selection

*Designates first player chosen in draft.

SINGLE-SEASON INDIVIDUAL RECORDS

FORWARDS/DEFENSEMEN

Most goals
69—Mike Bossy, 1978-79

Most assists
87—Bryan Trottier, 1978-79

Most points
147—Mike Bossy, 1981-82

Most penalty minutes
356—Brian Curran, 1986-87

Most power play goals
28—Mike Bossy, 1980-81

Most shorthanded goals
7—Bob Bourne, 1980-81

Most games with three or more goals
9—Mike Bossy, 1980-81

GOALTENDERS

Most games
65—Ron Hextall, 1993-94

Most minutes
3,581—Ron Hextall, 1993-94

Most goals allowed
195—Gerry Desjardins, 1972-73

Lowest goals-against average
2.07—Chico Resch, 1975-76

Most shutouts
7—Chico Resch, 1975-76

Most wins
32—Billy Smith, 1981-82

Most losses
35—Gerry Desjardins, 1972-73

Most ties
17—Billy Smith, 1974-75

FRANCHISE LEADERS

Players in boldface played for club in 2000-01

FORWARDS/DEFENSEMEN

Games
Bryan Trottier	1123
Denis Potvin	1060
Bob Nystrom	900
Clark Gillies	872
Bob Bourne	814

Goals
Mike Bossy	573
Bryan Trottier	500
Denis Potvin	310
Clark Gillies	304
Pat LaFontaine	287
Brent Sutter	287

Assists
Bryan Trottier	853
Denis Potvin	742
Mike Bossy	553
Clark Gillies	359
John Tonelli	338

Points
Bryan Trottier	1353
Mike Bossy	1126
Denis Potvin	1052
Clark Gillies	663
Brent Sutter	610

Penalty minutes
Mick Vukota	1879
Rich Pilon	1525
Garry Howatt	1466
Denis Potvin	1354
Bob Nystrom	1248

GOALTENDERS

Games
Billy Smith	675
Chico Resch	282
Kelly Hrudey	241
Tommy Salo	187
Glenn Healy	176

Shutouts
Chico Resch	25
Billy Smith	22
Tommy Salo	14
Kelly Hrudey	6
Wade Flaherty	**4**

Goals-against average
(2400 minutes minimum)
Chico Resch	2.56
Tommy Salo	2.77
Wade Flaherty	**2.84**
Ron Hextall	3.08
Eric Fichaud	3.14
Roland Melanson	3.14

Wins
Billy Smith	304
Chico Resch	157
Kelly Hrudey	106
Roland Melanson	77
Glenn Healy	66

NEW YORK RANGERS
YEAR-BY-YEAR RECORDS

Season	W	L	T	RT	Pts.	Finish	W	L	Highest round	Coach
						REGULAR SEASON			**PLAYOFFS**	
1926-27	25	13	6	—	56	1st/American	*0	1	Semifinals	Lester Patrick
1927-28	19	16	9	—	47	2nd/American	*5	3	Stanley Cup champ	Lester Patrick
1928-29	21	13	10	—	52	2nd/American	*3	2	Stanley Cup finals	Lester Patrick
1929-30	17	17	10	—	44	3rd/American	*1	2	Semifinals	Lester Patrick
1930-31	19	16	9	—	47	3rd/American	2	2	Semifinals	Lester Patrick
1931-32	23	17	8	—	54	1st/American	3	4	Stanley Cup finals	Lester Patrick
1932-33	23	17	8	—	54	3rd/American	*6	1	Stanley Cup champ	Lester Patrick
1933-34	21	19	8	—	50	3rd/American	*0	1	Quarterfinals	Lester Patrick
1934-35	22	20	6	—	50	3rd/American	*1	1	Semifinals	Lester Patrick
1935-36	19	17	12	—	50	4th/American	—	—		Lester Patrick
1936-37	19	20	9	—	47	3rd/American	6	3	Stanley Cup finals	Lester Patrick
1937-38	27	15	6	—	60	2nd/American	1	2	Quarterfinals	Lester Patrick
1938-39	26	16	6	—	58	2nd	3	4	Semifinals	Lester Patrick
1939-40	27	11	10	—	64	2nd	8	4	Stanley Cup champ	Frank Boucher
1940-41	21	19	8	—	50	4th	1	2	Quarterfinals	Frank Boucher
1941-42	29	17	2	—	60	1st	2	4	Semifinals	Frank Boucher
1942-43	11	31	8	—	30	6th	—	—		Frank Boucher
1943-44	6	39	5	—	17	6th	—	—		Frank Boucher
1944-45	11	29	10	—	32	6th	—	—		Frank Boucher
1945-46	13	28	9	—	35	6th	—	—		Frank Boucher
1946-47	22	32	6	—	50	5th	—	—		Frank Boucher
1947-48	21	26	13	—	55	4th	2	4	League semifinals	Frank Boucher
1948-49	18	31	11	—	47	6th	—	—		Frank Boucher, Lynn Patrick
1949-50	28	31	11	—	67	4th	7	5	Stanley Cup finals	Lynn Patrick
1950-51	20	29	21	—	61	5th	—	—		Neil Colville
1951-52	23	34	13	—	59	5th	—	—		Neil Colville, Bill Cook
1952-53	17	37	16	—	50	6th	—	—		Bill Cook
1953-54	29	31	10	—	68	5th	—	—		Frank Boucher, Muzz Patrick
1954-55	17	35	18	—	52	5th	—	—		Muzz Patrick
1955-56	32	28	10	—	74	3rd	1	4	League semifinals	Phil Watson
1956-57	26	30	14	—	66	4th	1	4	League semifinals	Phil Watson
1957-58	32	25	13	—	77	2nd	2	4	League semifinals	Phil Watson
1958-59	26	32	12	—	64	5th	—	—		Phil Watson
1959-60	17	38	15	—	49	6th	—	—		Phil Watson, Alf Pike
1960-61	22	38	10	—	54	5th	—	—		Alf Pike
1961-62	26	32	12	—	64	4th	2	4	League semifinals	Doug Harvey
1962-63	22	36	12	—	56	5th	—	—		Muzz Patrick, Red Sullivan
1963-64	22	38	10	—	54	5th	—	—		Red Sullivan
1964-65	20	38	12	—	52	5th	—	—		Red Sullivan
1965-66	18	41	11	—	47	6th	—	—		Red Sullivan, Emile Francis
1966-67	30	28	12	—	72	4th	0	4	League semifinals	Emile Francis
1967-68	39	23	12	—	90	2nd/East	2	4	Division semifinals	Emile Francis
1968-69	41	26	9	—	91	3rd/East	0	4	Division semifinals	Bernie Geoffrion, Emile Francis
1969-70	38	22	16	—	92	4th/East	2	4	Division semifinals	Emile Francis
1970-71	49	18	11	—	109	2nd/East	7	6	Division finals	Emile Francis
1971-72	48	17	13	—	109	2nd/East	10	6	Stanley Cup finals	Emile Francis
1972-73	47	23	8	—	102	3rd/East	5	5	Division finals	Emile Francis
1973-74	40	24	14	—	94	3rd/East	7	6	Division finals	Larry Popein, Emile Francis
1974-75	37	29	14	—	88	2nd/Patrick	1	2	Preliminaries	Emile Francis
1975-76	29	42	9	—	67	4th/Patrick	—	—		Ron Stewart, John Ferguson
1976-77	29	37	14	—	72	4th/Patrick	—	—		John Ferguson
1977-78	30	37	13	—	73	4th/Patrick	1	2	Preliminaries	Jean-Guy Talbot
1978-79	40	29	11	—	91	3rd/Patrick	11	7	Stanley Cup finals	Fred Shero
1979-80	38	32	10	—	86	3rd/Patrick	4	5	Quarterfinals	Fred Shero
1980-81	30	36	14	—	74	4th/Patrick	7	7	Semifinals	Fred Shero, Craig Patrick
1981-82	39	27	14	—	92	2nd/Patrick	5	5	Division finals	Herb Brooks
1982-83	35	35	10	—	80	4th/Patrick	5	4	Division finals	Herb Brooks
1983-84	42	29	9	—	93	4th/Patrick	2	3	Division semifinals	Herb Brooks
1984-85	26	44	10	—	62	4th/Patrick	0	3	Division semifinals	Herb Brooks, Craig Patrick
1985-86	36	38	6	—	78	4th/Patrick	8	8	Conference finals	Ted Sator
1986-87	34	38	8	—	76	4th/Patrick	2	4	Division semifinals	Ted Sator, Tom Webster, Phil Esposito
1987-88	36	34	10	—	82	4th/Patrick	—	—		Michel Bergeron
1988-89	37	35	8	—	82	3rd/Patrick	0	4	Division semifinals	Michel Bergeron, Phil Esposito
1989-90	36	31	13	—	85	1st/Patrick	5	5	Division finals	Roger Neilson
1990-91	36	31	13	—	85	2nd/Patrick	2	4	Division semifinals	Roger Neilson

			REGULAR SEASON				PLAYOFFS			
Season	W	L	T	RT	Pts.	Finish	W	L	Highest round	Coach
1991-92	50	25	5	—	105	1st/Patrick	6	7	Division finals	Roger Neilson
1992-93	34	39	11	—	79	6th/Patrick	—	—		Roger Neilson, Ron Smith
1993-94	52	24	8	—	112	1st/Atlantic	16	7	Stanley Cup champ	Mike Keenan
1994-95	22	23	3	—	47	4th/Atlantic	4	6	Conference semifinals	Colin Campbell
1995-96	41	27	14	—	96	2nd/Atlantic	5	6	Conference semifinals	Colin Campbell
1996-97	38	34	10	—	86	4th/Atlantic	9	6	Conference finals	Colin Campbell
1997-98	25	39	18	—	68	5th/Atlantic	—	—		Colin Campbell, John Muckler
1998-99	33	38	11	—	77	4th/Atlantic	—	—		John Muckler
1999-00	29	41	12	3	73	4th/Atlantic	—	—		John Muckler, John Tortorella
2000-01	33	43	5	1	72	4th/Atlantic	—	—		Ron Low

*Won-lost record does not indicate tie(s) resulting from two-game, total goals series that year (two-game, total-goals series were played from 1917-18 through 1935-36).

FIRST-ROUND ENTRY DRAFT CHOICES

Year   Player, Overall, Last amateur team (league)

1969—Andre Dupont, 8, Montreal (OHL)
　　　Pierre Jarry, 12, Ottawa (OHL)
1970—Normand Gratton, 11, Montreal (OHL)
1971—Steve Vickers, 10, Toronto (OHL)
　　　Steve Durbano, 13, Toronto (OHL)
1972—Albert Blanchard, 10, Kitchener (OHL)
　　　Bobby MacMillan, 15, St. Catharines (OHL)
1973—Rick Middleton, 14, Oshawa (OHL)
1974—Dave Maloney, 14, Kitchener (OHL)
1975—Wayne Dillon, 12, Toronto (WHA)
1976—Don Murdoch, 6, Medicine Hat (WCHL)
1977—Lucien DeBlois, 8, Sorel (QMJHL)
　　　Ron Duguay, 13, Sudbury (OHL)
1978—No first-round selection
1979—Doug Sulliman, 13, Kitchener (OHL)
1980—Jim Malone, 14, Toronto (OHL)
1981—James Patrick, 9, Prince Albert (AJHL)
1982—Chris Kontos, 15, Toronto (OHL)
1983—Dave Gagner, 12, Brantford (OHL)

Year   Player, Overall, Last amateur team (league)

1984—Terry Carkner, 14, Peterborough (OHL)
1985—Ulf Dahlen, 7, Ostersund (Sweden)
1986—Brian Leetch, 9, Avon Old Farms Prep (Ct.)
1987—Jayson More, 10, New Westminster (WCHL)
1988—No first-round selection
1989—Steven Rice, 20, Kitchener (OHL)
1990—Michael Stewart, 13, Michigan State University
1991—Alexei Kovalev, 15, Dynamo Moscow (USSR)
1992—Peter Ferraro, 24, Waterloo (USHL)
1993—Niklas Sundstrom, 8, Ornskoldsvik (Sweden)
1994—Dan Cloutier, 26, Sault Ste. Marie (OHL)
1995—No first-round selection
1996—Jeff Brown, 22, Sarnia (OHL)
1997—Stefan Cherneski, 19, Brandon (WHL)
1998—Manny Malhotra, 7, Guelph (OHL)
1999—Pavel Brendl, 4, Calgary (WHL)
　　　Jamie Lundmark, 9, Moose Jaw (WHL)
2000—No first-round selection
2001—Daniel Blackburn, 10, Kootenay (WHL)

SINGLE-SEASON INDIVIDUAL RECORDS

FORWARDS/DEFENSEMEN

Most goals
52—Adam Graves, 1993-94

Most assists
88—Brian Leetch, 1991-92

Most points
109—Jean Ratelle, 1971-72

Most penalty minutes
305—Troy Mallette, 1989-90

Most power play goals
23—Vic Hadfield, 1971-72

Most shorthanded goals
7—Theoren Fleury, 2000-01

Most games with three or more goals
4—Tomas Sandstrom, 1986-87

Most shots
344—Phil Esposito, 1976-77

GOALTENDERS

Most games
72—Mike Richter, 1997-98

Most minutes
4,143—Mike Richter, 1997-98

Lowest goals-against average
1.48—John Ross Roach, 1928-29

Most shutouts
13—John Ross Roach, 1928-29

Most wins
42—Mike Richter, 1993-94

FRANCHISE LEADERS

Players in boldface played for club in 2000-01

FORWARDS/DEFENSEMEN

Games
Harry Howell 1160
Rod Gilbert 1065
Ron Greschner 982
Walt Tkaczuk 945
Brian Leetch **939**

Goals
Rod Gilbert 406
Jean Ratelle 336
Andy Bathgate 272

Adam Graves 270
Vic Hadfield 262

Assists
Brian Leetch **655**
Rod Gilbert 615
Jean Ratelle 481
Andy Bathgate 457
Walt Tkaczuk 451

Points
Rod Gilbert 1021
Brian Leetch **860**

Jean Ratelle 817
Andy Bathgate 729
Walt Tkaczuk 678

Penalty minutes
Ron Greschner 1226
Jeff Beukeboom 1157
Harry Howell 1147
Don Maloney 1113
Vic Hadfield 1036

GOALTENDERS

Games

Mike Richter 598
Gump Worsley 583
Ed Giacomin....................................539
John Vanbiesbrouck.......................449
Chuck Rayner.................................377

Shutouts

Ed Giacomin..49
Dave Kerr 40

John Ross Roach...............................30
Chuck Rayner...................................24
Gump Worsley 24

Goals-against average
(2400 minutes minimum)

Lorne Chabot.................................1.61
Dave Kerr 2.07
John Ross Roach............................2.16
Andy Aitkenhead 2.42
Johnny Bower.................................2.62
Gilles Villemure 2.62

Wins

Mike Richter 272
Ed Giacomin....................................266
Gump Worsley 204
John Vanbiesbrouck.......................200
Dave Kerr 157

OTTAWA SENATORS (FIRST CLUB—DEFUNCT)
YEAR-BY-YEAR RECORDS

	REGULAR SEASON					PLAYOFFS			
Season	W	L	T	Pts.	Finish	W	L	Highest round	Coach
1917-18	9	13	0	18	3rd	—	—		Eddie Gerard
1918-19	12	6	0	24	1st	1	4	Semifinals	Alf Smith
1919-20	19	5	0	38	1st	3	2	Stanley Cup champ	Pete Green
1920-21	14	10	0	28	2nd	*4	2	Stanley Cup champ	Pete Green
1921-22	14	8	2	30	1st	*0	1	Semifinals	Pete Green
1922-23	14	9	1	29	1st	6	2	Stanley Cup champ	Pete Green
1923-24	16	8	0	32	1st	0	2	Semifinals	Pete Green
1924-25	17	12	1	35	4th	—	—		Pete Green
1925-26	24	8	4	52	1st	*0	1	Semifinals	Pete Green
1926-27	30	10	4	64	1st/Canadian	*3	0	Stanley Cup champ	Dave Gill
1927-28	20	14	10	50	3rd/Canadian	0	2	Quarterfinals	Dave Gill
1928-29	14	17	13	41	4th/Canadian	—	—		Dave Gill
1929-30	21	15	8	50	3rd/Canadian	*0	1	Semifinals	Newsy Lalonde
1930-31	10	30	4	24	5th/Canadian	—	—		Newsy Lalonde
1931-32					Club suspended operations for one season.				
1932-33	11	27	10	32	5th/Canadian	—	—		Cy Denneny
1933-34	13	29	6	32	5th/Canadian	—	—		George Boucher

*Won-lost record does not indicate tie(s) resulting from two-game, total goals series that year (two-game, total-goals series were played from 1917-18 through 1935-36).

Franchise relocated and became St. Louis Eagles following 1933-34 season.

OTTAWA SENATORS (SECOND CLUB)
YEAR-BY-YEAR RECORDS

	REGULAR SEASON						PLAYOFFS			
Season	W	L	T	RT	Pts.	Finish	W	L	Highest round	Coach
1992-93	10	70	4	—	24	6th/Adams	—	—		Rick Bowness
1993-94	14	61	9	—	37	7th/Northeast	—	—		Rick Bowness
1994-95	9	34	5	—	23	7th/Northeast	—	—		Rick Bowness
1995-96	18	59	5	—	41	6th/Northeast	—	—		Rick Bowness, Dave Allison, Jacques Martin
1996-97	31	36	15	—	77	T3rd/Northeast	3	4	Conference quarterfinals	Jacques Martin
1997-98	34	33	15	—	83	5th/Northeast	5	6	Conference semifinals	Jacques Martin
1998-99	44	23	15	—	103	1st/Northeast	0	4	Conference quarterfinals	Jacques Martin
1999-00	41	30	11	2	95	2nd/Northeast	2	4	Conference quarterfinals	Jacques Martin
2000-01	48	21	9	4	109	1st/Northeast	0	4	Conference quarterfinals	Jacques Martin

FIRST-ROUND ENTRY DRAFT CHOICES

Year   Player, Overall, Last amateur team (league)
1992—Alexei Yashin, 2, Dynamo Moscow (CIS)
1993—Alexandre Daigle, 1, Victoriaville (QMJHL)*
1994—Radek Bonk, 3, Las Vegas (IHL)
1995—Bryan Berard, 1, Detroit (OHL)*
1996—Chris Phillips, 1, Prince Albert (WHL)*
1997—Marian Hossa, 12, Dukla Trencin, Czechoslovakia

Year   Player, Overall, Last amateur team (league)
1998—Mathieu Chouinard, 15, Shawinigan (QMJHL)
1999—Martin Havlat, 26, Trinec, Czech Republic
2000—Anton Volchenkov, 21, CSKA, Russia
2001—Jason Spezza, 2, Windsor (OHL)
      Tim Gleason, 23, Windsor (OHL)
*Designates first player chosen in draft.

FORWARDS/DEFENSEMEN

Most goals
44—Alexei Yashin, 1998-99

Most assists
50—Alexei Yashin, 1998-99

Most points
94—Alexei Yashin, 1998-99

Most penalty minutes
318—Mike Peluso, 1992-93

Most power play goals
19—Alexei Yashin, 1998-99

Most shorthanded goals
4—Magnus Arvedson, 1998-99

Most games with three or more goals
1—Held by many players

Most shots
337—Alexei Yashin, 1998-99

GOALTENDERS

Most games
64—Peter Sidorkiewicz, 1992-93

Most minutes
3,607—Patrick Lalime, 2000-01

Most shots against
1,801—Craig Billington, 1993-94

Most goals allowed
254—Craig Billington, 1993-94

Lowest goals-against average
1.79—Ron Tugnutt, 1998-99

Most shutouts
7—Patrick Lalime, 2000-01

Most wins
36—Patrick Lalime, 2000-01

Most losses
46—Peter Sidorkiewicz, 1992-93

Most ties
14—Damian Rhodes, 1996-97

FRANCHISE LEADERS

Players in boldface played for club in 2000-01

FORWARDS/DEFENSEMEN

Games

Alexei Yashin 504
Radek Bonk...............................471
Andreas Dackell 401
Daniel Alfredsson 396
Wade Redden 393

Goals

Alexei Yashin 218
Daniel Alfredsson 123
Shawn McEachern.....................127
Radek Bonk 93
Marian Hossa............................76

Assists

Alexei Yashin 225
Daniel Alfredsson 216
Radek Bonk...............................138
Shawn McEachern.....................131
Wade Redden 122

Points

Alexei Yashin 491
Daniel Alfredsson 339
Shawn McEachern.....................258
Radek Bonk...............................231
Alexandre Daigle 172

Penalty minutes

Dennis Vial 625
Denny Lambert..........................467
Troy Mallette 372
Randy Cunneyworth...................360
Mike Peluso..............................318

GOALTENDERS

Games

Damian Rhodes..........................181
Ron Tugnutt...............................166
Patrick Lalime............................98
Craig Billington..........................72
Don Beaupre 71

Shutouts

Ron Tugnutt 13
Damian Rhodes..........................11
Patrick Lalime............................10
Don Beaupre 2
Jani Hurme 2

Goals-against average
(2400 minutes minimum)

Ron Tugnutt 2.32
Patrick Lalime 2.34
Damian Rhodes..........................2.56
Don Beaupre 3.53
Peter Sidorkiewicz......................4.43

Wins

Ron Tugnutt 72
Damian Rhodes..........................65
Patrick Lalime............................55
Don Beaupre 14
Jani Hurme 13

PHILADELPHIA FLYERS
YEAR-BY-YEAR RECORDS

| | REGULAR SEASON | | | | | PLAYOFFS | | | |
Season	W	L	T	RT	Pts.	Finish	W	L	Highest round	Coach
1967-68	31	32	11	—	73	1st/West	3	4	Division semifinals	Keith Allen
1968-69	20	35	21	—	61	3rd/West	0	4	Division semifinals	Keith Allen
1969-70	17	35	24	—	58	5th/West	—	—		Vic Stasiuk
1970-71	28	33	17	—	73	3rd/West	0	4	Division semifinals	Vic Stasiuk
1971-72	26	38	14	—	66	5th/West	—	—		Fred Shero
1972-73	37	30	11	—	85	2nd/West	5	6	Division finals	Fred Shero
1973-74	50	16	12	—	112	1st/West	12	5	Stanley Cup champ	Fred Shero
1974-75	51	18	11	—	113	1st/Patrick	12	5	Stanley Cup champ	Fred Shero
1975-76	51	13	16	—	118	1st/Patrick	8	8	Stanley Cup finals	Fred Shero
1976-77	48	16	16	—	112	1st/Patrick	4	6	Semifinals	Fred Shero
1977-78	45	20	15	—	105	2nd/Patrick	7	5	Semifinals	Fred Shero
1978-79	40	25	15	—	95	2nd/Patrick	3	5	Quarterfinals	Bob McCammon, Pat Quinn
1979-80	48	12	20	—	116	1st/Patrick	13	6	Stanley Cup finals	Pat Quinn
1980-81	41	24	15	—	97	2nd/Patrick	6	6	Quarterfinals	Pat Quinn
1981-82	38	31	11	—	87	3rd/Patrick	1	3	Division semifinals	Pat Quinn, Bob McCammon
1982-83	49	23	8	—	106	1st/Patrick	0	3	Division semifinals	Bob McCammon
1983-84	44	26	10	—	98	3rd/Patrick	0	3	Division semifinals	Bob McCammon
1984-85	53	20	7	—	113	1st/Patrick	12	7	Stanley Cup finals	Mike Keenan
1985-86	53	23	4	—	110	1st/Patrick	2	3	Division semifinals	Mike Keenan

NHL HISTORY *Team by team*

| Season | REGULAR SEASON | | | | | | PLAYOFFS | | | |
	W	L	T	RT	Pts.	Finish	W	L	Highest round	Coach
1986-87	46	26	8	—	100	1st/Patrick	15	11	Stanley Cup finals	Mike Keenan
1987-88	38	33	9	—	85	2nd/Patrick	3	4	Division semifinals	Mike Keenan
1988-89	36	36	8	—	80	4th/Patrick	10	9	Conference finals	Paul Holmgren
1989-90	30	39	11	—	71	6th/Patrick	—	—		Paul Holmgren
1990-91	33	37	10	—	76	5th/Patrick	—	—		Paul Holmgren
1991-92	32	37	11	—	75	6th/Patrick	—	—		Paul Holmgren, Bill Dineen
1992-93	36	37	11	—	83	5th/Patrick	—	—		Bill Dineen
1993-94	35	39	10	—	80	6th/Atlantic	—	—		Terry Simpson
1994-95	28	16	4	—	60	1st/Atlantic	10	5	Conference finals	Terry Murray
1995-96	45	24	13	—	103	1st/Atlantic	6	6	Conference semifinals	Terry Murray
1996-97	45	24	13	—	103	2nd/Atlantic	12	7	Stanley Cup finals	Terry Murray
1997-98	42	29	11	—	95	2nd/Atlantic	1	4	Conference quarterfinals	Wayne Cashman, Roger Neilson
1998-99	37	26	19	—	93	2nd/Atlantic	2	4	Conference quarterfinals	Roger Neilson
1999-00	45	25	12	3	105	1st/Atlantic	11	7	Conference finals	Roger Neilson, Craig Ramsay
2000-01	43	25	11	3	100	2nd/Atlantic	2	4	Conference quarterfinals	Craig Ramsay, Bill Barber

FIRST-ROUND ENTRY DRAFT CHOICES

Year Player, Overall, Last amateur team (league)
1969—Bob Currier, 6, Cornwall (QMJHL)
1970—No first-round selection
1971—Larry Wright, 8, Regina (WCHL)
      Pierre Plante, 9, Drummondville (QMJHL)
1972—Bill Barber, 7, Kitchener (OHL)
1973—No first-round selection
1974—No first-round selection
1975—Mel Bridgeman, 1, Victoria (WCHL)*
1976—Mark Suzor, 17, Kingston (OHL)
1977—Kevin McCarthy, 17, Winnipeg (WCHL)
1978—Behn Wilson, 6, Kingston (OHL)
      Ken Linseman, 7, Birmingham (WHA)
      Dan Lucas, 14, Sault Ste. Marie (OHL)
1979—Brian Propp, 14, Brandon (WHL)
1980—Mike Stothers, 21, Kingston (OHL)
1981—Steve Smith, 16, Sault Ste. Marie (OHL)
1982—Ron Sutter, 4, Lethbridge (WHL)
1983—No first-round selection
1984—No first-round selection

Year Player, Overall, Last amateur team (league)
1985—Glen Seabrooke, 21, Peterborough (OHL)
1986—Kerry Huffman, 20, Guelph (OHL)
1987—Darren Rumble, 20, Kitchener (OHL)
1988—Claude Boivin, 14, Drummondville (QMJHL)
1989—No first-round selection
1990—Mike Ricci, 4, Peterborough (OHL)
1991—Peter Forsberg, 6, Modo, Sweden
1992—Ryan Sittler, 7, Nichols H.S. (N.Y.)
      Jason Bowen, 15, Tri-City (WHL)
1993—No first-round selection
1994—No first-round selection
1995—Brian Boucher, 22, Tri-City (WHL)
1996—Dainius Zubrus, 15, Pembroke, Tier II
1997—No first-round selection
1998—Simon Gagne, 22, Quebec (QMJHL)
1999—Maxime Ouellet, 22, Quebec (QMJHL)
2000—Justin Williams, 28, Plymouth (OHL)
2001—Jeff Woywitka, 27, Red Deer (WHL)
*Designates first player chosen in draft.

SINGLE-SEASON INDIVIDUAL RECORDS

FORWARDS/DEFENSEMEN

Most goals
61—Reggie Leach, 1975-76

Most assists
89—Bobby Clarke, 1974-75
    Bobby Clarke, 1975-76

Most points
123—Mark Recchi, 1992-93

Most penalty minutes
472—Dave Schultz, 1974-75

Most power play goals
34—Tim Kerr, 1985-86

Most shorthanded goals
7—Brian Propp, 1984-85
   Mark Howe, 1985-86

Most games with three or more goals
5—Tim Kerr, 1984-85

Most shots
380—Bill Barber, 1975-76

GOALTENDERS

Most games
73—Bernie Parent, 1973-74

Most minutes
4,314—Bernie Parent, 1973-74

Most goals allowed
208—Ron Hextall, 1987-88

Lowest goals-against average
1.89—Bernie Parent, 1973-74

Most shutouts
12—Bernie Parent, 1973-74
    Bernie Parent, 1974-75

Most wins
47—Bernie Parent, 1973-74

Most losses
29—Bernie Parent, 1969-70

Most ties
20—Bernie Parent, 1969-70

FRANCHISE LEADERS

Players in boldface played for club in 2000-01

FORWARDS/DEFENSEMEN

Games
Bobby Clarke 1144
Bill Barber 903
Brian Propp 790
Joe Watson 746

Bob Kelly 741
Rick MacLeish 741

Goals
Bill Barber 420
Brian Propp 369
Tim Kerr 363

Bobby Clarke 358
Rick MacLeish 328

Assists
Bobby Clarke 852
Brian Propp 480
Bill Barber 463

Rick MacLeish.....................................369
Eric Lindros..369

Points
Bobby Clarke......................................1210
Bill Barber 883
Brian Propp..849
Rick MacLeish.....................................697
Eric Lindros...659

Penalty minutes
Rick Tocchet 1789
Paul Holmgren 1600
Andre Dupont......................................1505
Bobby Clarke.......................................1453
Dave Schultz..1386

GOALTENDERS
Games
Ron Hextall...489
Bernie Parent......................................486
Doug Favell...215
Pete Peeters 179
Wayne Stephenson 165

Shutouts
Bernie Parent......................................50
Ron Hextall..18
Doug Favell 16
Bob Froese...12
Roman Cechmanek.....................10
Wayne Stephenson 10

Goals-against average
(2400 minutes minimum)
Roman Cechmanek 2.01
John Vanbiesbrouck.........................2.19
Bernie Parent.....................................2.42
Garth Snow 2.59
Bob Froese...2.74

Wins
Ron Hextall...240
Bernie Parent......................................232
Wayne Stephenson 93
Bob Froese...92
Pelle Lindbergh 87

PHOENIX COYOTES
YEAR-BY-YEAR RECORDS

| | REGULAR SEASON | | | | | | PLAYOFFS | | | |
Season	W	L	T	RT	Pts.	Finish	W	L	Highest round	Coach
1996-97	38	37	7	—	83	T3rd/Central	3	4	Conference quarterfinals	Don Hay
1997-98	35	35	12	—	82	4th/Central	2	4	Conference quarterfinals	Jim Schoenfeld
1998-99	39	31	12	—	90	2nd/Pacific	3	4	Conference quarterfinals	Jim Schoenfeld
1999-00	39	35	8	4	90	3rd/Pacific	1	4	Conference quarterfinals	Bob Francis
2000-01	35	27	17	3	90	4th/Pacific	—	—		Bob Francis

Franchise was formerly known as Winnipeg Jets and relocated to Phoenix following 1995-96 season.

FIRST-ROUND ENTRY DRAFT CHOICES

Year   Player, Overall, Last amateur team (league)
1997—No first-round selection
1998—Patrick DesRochers, 14, Sarnia (OHL)
1999—Scott Kelman, 15, Seattle (WHL)
        Kirill Safronov, 19, SKA St. Petersburg, Russia

Year   Player, Overall, Last amateur team (league)
2000—Krystofer Kolanos, 19, Boston College
2001—Fredrik Sjostrom, 11, Frolunda, Sweden

SINGLE-SEASON INDIVIDUAL RECORDS

FORWARDS/DEFENSEMEN

Most goals
52—Keith Tkachuk, 1996-97

Most assists
48—Jeremy Roenick, 1998-99

Most points
86—Keith Tkachuk, 1996-97

Most penalty minutes
228—Keith Tkachuk, 1996-97

Most power play goals
15—Keith Tkachuk, 2000-01

Most shorthanded goals
5—Bob Corkum, 1997-98

Most games with three or more goals
3—Keith Tkachuk, 1996-97
      Keith Tkachuk, 1997-98

Most shots
296—Keith Tkachuk, 1996-97

GOALTENDERS

Most games
72—Nikolai Khabibulin, 1996-97

Most minutes
4,091—Nikolai Khabibulin, 1996-97

Most shots against
2,094—Nikolai Khabibulin, 1996-97

Most goals allowed
193—Nikolai Khabibulin, 1996-97

Lowest goals-against average
2.27—Sean Burke, 2000-01

Most shutouts
8—Nikolai Khabibulin, 1998-99

Most wins
32—Nikolai Khabibulin, 1998-99

Most losses
33—Nikolai Khabibulin, 1996-97

Most ties
13—Sean Burke, 2000-01

FRANCHISE LEADERS

Players in boldface played for club in 2000-1

FORWARDS/DEFENSEMEN

Games
Teppo Numminen.......................397
Jeremy Roenick 384
Shane Doan 332
Keith Tkachuk 332
Keith Carney 266

Goals
Keith Tkachuk 179
Jeremy Roenick 141
Shane Doan...............................67
Rick Tocchet.................................64
Dallas Drake.................................52

Assists
Jeremy Roenick 210
Teppo Numminen......................155

Keith Tkachuk 155
Dallas Drake...............................100
Shane Doan...............................92

Points
Jeremy Roenick 351
Keith Tkachuk 334
Teppo Numminen.......................191
Shane Doan 159
Dallas Drake...............................152

Penalty minutes

Keith Tkachuk 716
Jeremy Roenick 564
Rick Tocchet...............................371
Jim McKenzie..............................346
Shane Doan 293

GOALTENDERS

Games

Nikolai Khabibulin 205
Sean Burke................................97

Jim Waite 33
Bob Essensa...................................30
Robert Esche 25

Shutouts

Nikolai Khabibulin 19
Sean Burke 7
Mikhail Shtalenkov 2
Robert Esche 2
Jim Waite 2

Goals-against average
(2400 minutes minimum)

Sean Burke 2.37
Nikolai Khabibulin 2.58

Wins

Nikolai Khabibulin 92
Sean Burke................................42
Bob Essensa.............................13
Jim Waite 11
Robert Esche 10

PITTSBURGH PENGUINS
YEAR-BY-YEAR RECORDS

Season	W	L	T	RT	Pts.	Finish	W	L	Highest round	Coach
			REGULAR SEASON				PLAYOFFS			
1967-68	27	34	13	—	67	5th/West	—	—		Red Sullivan
1968-69	20	45	11	—	51	5th/West	—	—		Red Sullivan
1969-70	26	38	12	—	64	2nd/West	6	4	Division finals	Red Kelly
1970-71	21	37	20	—	62	6th/West	—	—		Red Kelly
1971-72	26	38	14	—	66	4th/West	0	4	Division semifinals	Red Kelly
1972-73	32	37	9	—	73	5th/West	—	—		Red Kelly, Ken Schinkel
1973-74	28	41	9	—	65	5th/West	—	—		Ken Schinkel, Marc Boileau
1974-75	37	28	15	—	89	3rd/Norris	5	4	Quarterfinals	Marc Boileau
1975-76	35	33	12	—	82	3rd/Norris	1	2	Preliminaries	Marc Boileau, Ken Schinkel
1976-77	34	33	13	—	81	3rd/Norris	1	2	Preliminaries	Ken Schinkel
1977-78	25	37	18	—	68	4th/Norris	—	—		Johnny Wilson
1978-79	36	31	13	—	85	2nd/Norris	2	5	Quarterfinals	Johnny Wilson
1979-80	30	37	13	—	73	3rd/Norris	2	3	Preliminaries	Johnny Wilson
1980-81	30	37	13	—	73	3rd/Norris	2	3	Preliminaries	Eddie Johnston
1981-82	31	36	13	—	75	4th/Patrick	2	3	Division semifinals	Eddie Johnston
1982-83	18	53	9	—	45	6th/Patrick	—	—		Eddie Johnston
1983-84	16	58	6	—	38	6th/Patrick	—	—		Lou Angotti
1984-85	24	51	5	—	53	5th/Patrick	—	—		Bob Berry
1985-86	34	38	8	—	76	5th/Patrick	—	—		Bob Berry
1986-87	30	38	12	—	72	5th/Patrick	—	—		Bob Berry
1987-88	36	35	9	—	81	6th/Patrick	—	—		Pierre Creamer
1988-89	40	33	7	—	87	2nd/Patrick	7	4	Division finals	Gene Ubriaco
1989-90	32	40	8	—	72	5th/Patrick	—	—		Gene Ubriaco, Craig Patrick
1990-91	41	33	6	—	88	1st/Patrick	16	8	Stanley Cup champ	Bob Johnson
1991-92	39	32	9	—	87	3rd/Patrick	16	5	Stanley Cup champ	Scotty Bowman
1992-93	56	21	7	—	119	1st/Patrick	7	5	Division finals	Scotty Bowman
1993-94	44	27	13	—	101	1st/Northeast	2	4	Conference quarterfinals	Eddie Johnston
1994-95	29	16	3	—	61	2nd/Northeast	5	7	Conference semifinals	Eddie Johnston
1995-96	49	29	4	—	102	1st/Northeast	11	7	Conference finals	Eddie Johnston
1996-97	38	36	8	—	84	2nd/Northeast	1	4	Conference quarterfinals	Eddie Johnston, Craig Patrick
1997-98	40	24	18	—	98	1st/Northeast	2	4	Conference quarterfinals	Kevin Constantine
1998-99	38	30	14	—	90	3rd/Atlantic	6	7	Conference semifinals	Kevin Constantine
1999-00	37	37	8	6	88	3rd/Atlantic	6	5	Conference semifinals	Kevin Constantine, Herb Brooks
2000-01	42	28	9	3	96	3rd/Atlantic	9	9	Conference finals	Ivan Hlinka

FIRST-ROUND ENTRY DRAFT CHOICES

Year Player, Overall, Last amateur team (league)
1969—No first-round selection
1970—Greg Polis, 7, Estevan (WCHL)
1971—No first-round selection
1972—No first-round selection
1973—Blaine Stoughton, 7, Flin Flon (WCHL)
1974—Pierre Larouche, 8, Sorel (QMJHL)
1975—Gord Laxton, 13, New Westminster (WCHL)
1976—Blair Chapman, 2, Saskatoon (WCHL)
1977—No first-round selection
1978—No first-round selection
1979—No first-round selection
1980—MIke Bullard, 9, Brantford (OHL)
1981—No first-round selection
1982—Rich Sutter, 10, Lethbridge (WHL)

Year Player, Overall, Last amateur team (league)
1983—Bob Errey, 15, Peterborough (OHL)
1984—Mario Lemieux, 1, Laval (QMJHL)*
         Doug Bodger, 9, Kamloops (WHL)
         Roger Belanger, 16, Kingston (OHL)
1985—Craig Simpson, 2, Michigan State University
1986—Zarley Zalapski, 4, Team Canada
1987—Chris Joseph, 5, Seattle (WHL)
1988—Darrin Shannon, 4, Windsor (OHL)
1989—Jamie Heward, 16, Regina (WHL)
1990—Jaromir Jagr, 5, Poldi Kladno, Czech. Republic
1991—Markus Naslund, 16, MoDo, Sweden
1992—Martin Straka, 19, Skoda Plzen, Czech. Republic
1993—Stefan Bergqvist, 26, Leksand, Sweden
1994—Chris Wells, 24, Seattle (WHL)

NHL HISTORY Team by team

Year	Player, Overall, Last amateur team (league)
1995	Alexei Morozov, 24, Krylja Sovetov, CIS
1996	Craig Hillier, 23, Ottawa (OHL)
1997	Robert Dome, 17, Las Vegas (IHL)
1998	Milan Kraft, 23, Plzen (Czech.)

Year	Player, Overall, Last amateur team (league)
1999	Konstantin Koltsov, 18, Cherepovec, Russia
2000	Brooks Orpik, 18, Boston College
2001	Colby Armstrong, 21, Red Deer (WHL)

*Designates first player chosen in draft.

SINGLE-SEASON INDIVIDUAL RECORDS

FORWARDS/DEFENSEMEN

Most goals
85—Mario Lemieux, 1988-89

Most assists
114—Mario Lemieux, 1988-89

Most points
199—Mario Lemieux, 1988-89

Most penalty minutes
409—Paul Baxter, 1981-82

Most power play goals
31—Mario Lemieux, 1988-89
Mario Lemieux, 1995-96

Most shorthanded goals
13—Mario Lemieux, 1988-89

Most games with three or more goals
9—Mario Lemieux, 1988-89

Most shots
403—Jaromir Jagr, 1995-96

GOALTENDERS

Most games
63—Greg Millen, 1980-81
Tom Barrasso, 1992-93
Tom Barrasso, 1997-98

Most minutes
3,721—Greg Millen, 1980-81

Most goals allowed
258—Greg Millen, 1980-81

Lowest goals-against average
2.07—Tom Barrasso, 1997-98

Most shutouts
7—Tom Barrasso, 1997-98

Most wins
43—Tom Barrasso, 1992-93

Most losses
31—Les Binkley, 1968-69

Most ties
15—Denis Herron, 1977-78

FRANCHISE LEADERS

Players in boldface played for club in 2000-01

FORWARDS/DEFENSEMEN

Games

Jaromir Jagr	**806**
Mario Lemieux	**788**
Jean Pronovost	753
Rick Kehoe	722
Ron Stackhouse	621

Goals

Mario Lemieux	**648**
Jaromir Jagr	**439**
Jean Pronovost	316
Rick Kehoe	312
Kevin Stevens	251

Assists

Mario Lemieux	**922**
Jaromir Jagr	**640**
Ron Francis	449
Syl Apps	349
Paul Coffey	332

Points

Mario Lemieux	**1570**
Jaromir Jagr	**1079**
Rick Kehoe	636
Ron Francis	613
Jean Pronovost	603

Penalty minutes

Troy Loney	980
Kevin Stevens	968
Rod Buskas	959
Bryan Watson	871
Paul Baxter	851

GOALTENDERS

Games

Tom Barrasso	458
Denis Herron	290
Ken Wregget	212
Les Binkley	196
Michel Dion	151

Shutouts

Tom Barrasso	22
Les Binkley	11
Denis Herron	6
Ken Wregget	6
Dunc Wilson	5

Goals-against average
(2400 minutes minimum)

Peter Skudra	2.65
Jean-Sebastien Aubin	**2.73**
Al Smith	3.07
Les Binkley	3.12
Jim Rutherford	3.14

Wins

Tom Barrasso	226
Ken Wregget	104
Denis Herron	88
Les Binkley	58
Greg Millen	57

PITTSBURGH PIRATES (DEFUNCT)
YEAR-BY-YEAR RECORDS

	REGULAR SEASON					PLAYOFFS			
Season	W	L	T	Pts.	Finish	W	L	Highest round	Coach
1925-26	19	16	1	39	3rd	—	—		Odie Cleghorn
1926-27	15	26	3	33	4th/American	—	—		Odie Cleghorn
1927-28	19	17	8	46	3rd/American	1	1	Quarterfinals	Odie Cleghorn
1928-29	9	27	8	26	4th/American	—	—		Odie Cleghorn
1929-30	5	36	3	13	5th/American	—	—		Frank Frederickson
1930-31*	4	36	4	12	5th/American	—	—		Cooper Smeaton

*Philadelphia Quakers.

NHL HISTORY *Team by team*

QUEBEC BULLDOGS (DEFUNCT)
YEAR-BY-YEAR RECORDS

		REGULAR SEASON					PLAYOFFS		
Season	W	L	T	Pts.	Finish	W	L	Highest round	Coach
1919-20	4	20	0	8	4th	—	—		Mike Quinn

Franchise relocated and became Hamilton Tigers following 1919-20 season; franchise later relocated and became New York Americans after 1924-25 season.

QUEBEC NORDIQUES (DEFUNCT)
YEAR-BY-YEAR RECORDS

		REGULAR SEASON					PLAYOFFS		
Season	W	L	T	Pts.	Finish	W	L	Highest round	Coach
1972-73*	33	40	5	71	5th	—	—		Maurice Richard, Maurice Filion
1973-74*	38	36	4	80	5th	—	—		Jacques Plante
1974-75*	46	32	0	92	1st	8	7	Avco World Cup finals	Jean-Guy Gendron
1975-76*	50	27	4	104	2nd	1	4	League quarterfinals	Jean-Guy Gendron
1976-77*	47	31	3	97	1st	12	5	Avco World Cup champ	Marc Boileau
1977-78*	40	37	3	83	4th	5	6	League semifinals	Marc Boileau
1978-79*	41	34	5	87	2nd	0	4	League semifinals	Jacques Demers
1979-80	25	44	11	61	5th/Adams	—	—		Jacques Demers
1980-81	30	32	18	78	4th/Adams	2	3	Preliminaries	Maurice Filion, Michel Bergeron
1981-82	33	31	16	82	4th/Adams	7	9	Conference finals	Michel Bergeron
1982-83	34	34	12	80	4th/Adams	1	3	Division semifinals	Michel Bergeron
1983-84	42	28	10	94	3rd/Adams	5	4	Division finals	Michel Bergeron
1984-85	41	30	9	91	2nd/Adams	9	9	Conference finals	Michel Bergeron
1985-86	43	31	6	92	1st/Adams	0	3	Division semifinals	Michel Bergeron
1986-87	31	39	10	72	4th/Adams	7	6	Division finals	Michel Bergeron
1987-88	32	43	5	69	5th/Adams	—	—		Andre Savard, Ron Lapointe
1988-89	27	46	7	61	5th/Adams	—	—		Ron Lapointe, Jean Perron
1989-90	12	61	7	31	5th/Adams	—	—		Michel Bergeron
1990-91	16	50	14	46	5th/Adams	—	—		Dave Chambers
1991-92	20	48	12	52	5th/Adams	—	—		Dave Chambers, Pierre Page
1992-93	47	27	10	104	2nd/Adams	2	4	Division semifinals	Pierre Page
1993-94	34	42	8	76	5th/Northeast	—	—		Pierre Page
1994-95	30	13	5	65	1st/Northeast	2	4	Conference quarterfinals	Marc Crawford

*Members of World Hockey Association.
Franchise relocated and became Colorado Avalanche following 1994-95 season.

FIRST-ROUND ENTRY DRAFT CHOICES

Year   Player, Overall, Last amateur team (league)
1979—Michel Goulet, 20, Birmingham (WHA)
1980—No first-round selection
1981—Randy Moller, 11, Lethbridge (WHL)
1982—David Shaw, 13, Kitchener (OHL)
1983—No first-round selection
1984—Trevor Steinburg, 15, Guelph (OHL)
1985—Dave Latta, 15, Kitchener (OHL)
1986—Ken McRae, 18, Sudbury (OHL)
1987—Bryan Fogarty, 9, Kingston (OHL)
      Joe Sakic, 15, Swift Current (WHL)
1988—Curtis Leschyshyn, 3, Saskatoon (WHL)
      Daniel Dore, 5, Drummondville (QMJHL)

Year   Player, Overall, Last amateur team (league)
1989—Mats Sundin, 1, Nacka (Sweden)*
1990—Owen Nolan, 1, Cornwall (OHL)*
1991—Eric Lindros, 1, Oshawa (OHL)*
1992—Todd Warriner, 4, Windsor (OHL)
1993—Jocelyn Thibault, 10, Sherbrooke (QMJHL)
      Adam Deadmarsh, 14, Portland (WHL)
1994—Wade Belak, 12, Saskatoon (WHL)
      Jeffrey Kealty, 22, Catholic Memorial H.S.
1995—Marc Denis, 25, Chicoutimi (QMJHL)
*Designates first player chosen in draft.
NOTE: Quebec chose Paul Baxter, Richard Brodeur and Garry Larivierre as priority selections before the 1979 expansion draft.

SINGLE-SEASON INDIVIDUAL RECORDS

FORWARDS/DEFENSEMEN

Most goals
57—Michel Goulet, 1982-83

Most assists
93—Peter Stastny, 1981-82

Most points
139—Peter Stastny, 1981-82

Most penalty minutes
301—Gord Donnelly, 1987-88

Most power play goals
29—Michel Goulet, 1987-88

Most shorthanded goals
6—Michel Goulet, 1981-82
   Scott Young, 1992-93

Most games with three or more goals
4—Miroslav Frycer, 1981-82
   Peter Stastny, 1982-83

GOALTENDERS

Most games
60—Dan Bouchard, 1981-82

Most minutes
3,572—Dan Bouchard, 1981-82

Most goals allowed
230—Dan Bouchard, 1981-82

Lowest goals-against average
2.78—Stephane Fiset, 1994-95

Most shutouts
4—Clint Malarchuk, 1985-86

Most losses
29—Ron Tugnutt, 1990-91

Most ties
11—Dan Bouchard, 1981-82

Most wins
29—Dan Bouchard, 1983-84
   Ron Hextall, 1992-93

FRANCHISE LEADERS

FORWARDS/DEFENSEMEN

Games
Michel Goulet	813
Peter Stastny	737
Alain Cote	696
Anton Stastny	650
Steven Finn	606

Goals
Michel Goulet	456
Peter Stastny	380
Anton Stastny	252
Joe Sakic	235
Dale Hunter	140

Assists
Peter Stastny	668
Michel Goulet	489
Joe Sakic	391
Anton Stastny	384
Dale Hunter	318

Points
Peter Stastny	1048
Michel Goulet	945
Anton Stastny	636
Joe Sakic	626
Dale Hunter	458

Penalty minutes
Dale Hunter	1545
Steven Finn	1511
Paul Gillis	1351
Randy Moller	1002
Mario Marois	778

GOALTENDERS

Games
Dan Bouchard	225
Marlo Gosselin	192
Ron Tugnutt	153
Stephane Fiset	152
Clint Malarchuk	140

Shutouts
Mario Gosselin	6
Dan Bouchard	5
Stephane Fiset	5
Clint Malarchuk	5
Michel Dion	2

Goals-against average
(2400 minutes minimum)
Jocelyn Thibault	2.95
Ron Hextall	3.45
Dan Bouchard	3.59
Clint Malarchuk	3.63
Maril Gosselin	3.67

Wins
Dan Bouchard	107
Mario Gosselin	79
Stephane Fiset	62
Clint Malarchuk	62
Ron Tugnutt	35

ST. LOUIS BLUES
YEAR-BY-YEAR RECORDS

		REGULAR SEASON						PLAYOFFS			
Season	W	L	T	RT	Pts.	Finish	W	L	Highest round	Coach
1967-68	27	31	16	—	70	3rd/West	8	10	Stanley Cup finals	Lynn Patrick, Scotty Bowman
1968-69	37	25	14	—	88	1st/West	8	4	Stanley Cup finals	Scotty Bowman
1969-70	37	27	12	—	86	1st/West	8	8	Stanley Cup finals	Scotty Bowman
1970-71	34	25	19	—	87	2nd/West	2	4	Division semifinals	Al Arbour, Scotty Bowman
1971-72	28	39	11	—	67	3rd/West	4	7	Division finals	Sid Abel, Bill McCreary, Al Arbour
1972-73	32	34	12	—	76	4th/West	1	4	Division semifinals	Al Arbour, Jean-Guy Talbot
1973-74	26	40	12	—	64	6th/West	—	—		Jean-Guy Talbot, Lou Angotti
1974-75	35	31	14	—	84	2nd/Smythe	0	2	Preliminaries	Lou Angotti, Lynn Patrick, Garry Young
1975-76	29	37	14	—	72	3rd/Smythe	1	2	Preliminaries	Garry Young, Lynn Patrick, Leo Boivin
1976-77	32	39	9	—	73	1st/Smythe	0	4	Quarterfinals	Emile Francis
1977-78	20	47	13	—	53	4th/Smythe	—	—		Leo Boivin, Barclay Plager
1978-79	18	50	12	—	48	3rd/Smythe	—	—		Barclay Plager
1979-80	34	34	12	—	80	2nd/Smythe	0	3	Preliminaries	Barclay Plager, Red Berenson
1980-81	45	18	17	—	107	1st/Smythe	5	6	Quarterfinals	Red Berenson
1981-82	32	40	8	—	72	3rd/Norris	5	5	Division finals	Red Berenson, Emile Francis
1982-83	25	40	15	—	65	4th/Norris	1	3	Division semifinals	Emile Francis, Barclay Plager
1983-84	32	41	7	—	71	2nd/Norris	6	5	Division finals	Jacques Demers
1984-85	37	31	12	—	86	1st/Norris	0	3	Division semifinals	Jacques Demers
1985-86	37	34	9	—	83	3rd/Norris	10	9	Conference finals	Jacques Demers
1986-87	32	33	15	—	79	1st/Norris	2	4	Division semifinals	Jacques Martin
1987-88	34	38	8	—	76	2nd/Norris	5	5	Division finals	Jacques Martin
1988-89	33	35	12	—	78	2nd/Norris	5	5	Division finals	Brian Sutter
1989-90	37	34	9	—	83	2nd/Norris	7	5	Division finals	Brian Sutter
1990-91	47	22	11	—	105	2nd/Norris	6	7	Division finals	Brian Sutter
1991-92	36	33	11	—	83	3rd/Norris	2	4	Division semifinals	Brian Sutter
1992-93	37	36	11	—	85	4th/Norris	7	4	Division finals	Bob Plager, Bob Berry
1993-94	40	33	11	—	91	4th/Central	0	4	Conference quarterfinals	Bob Berry
1994-95	28	15	5	—	61	2nd/Central	3	4	Conference quarterfinals	Mike Keenan
1995-96	32	34	16	—	80	T3rd/Central	7	6	Conference semifinals	Mike Keenan
1996-97	36	35	11	—	83	T3rd/Central	2	4	Conference quarterfinals	Mike Keenan, Jimmy Roberts, Joel Quenneville
1997-98	45	29	8	—	98	3rd/Central	6	4	Conference semifinals	Joel Quenneville

	REGULAR SEASON						PLAYOFFS			
Season	W	L	T	RT	Pts.	Finish	W	L	Highest round	Coach
1998-99	37	32	13	—	87	2nd/Central	6	7	Conference semifinals	Joel Quenneville
1999-00	51	20	11	1	114	1st/Central	3	4	Conference quarterfinals	Joel Quenneville
2000-01	43	22	12	5	103	2nd/Central	9	6	Conference finals	Joel Quenneville

FIRST-ROUND ENTRY DRAFT CHOICES

Year   Player, Overall, Last amateur team (league)
1969—No first-round selection
1970—No first-round selection
1971—Gene Carr, 4, Flin Flon (WCHL)
1972—Wayne Merrick, 9, Ottawa (OHL)
1973—John Davidson, 5, Calgary (WCHL)
1974—No first-round selection
1975—No first-round selection
1976—Bernie Federko, 7, Saskatoon (WCHL)
1977—Scott Campbell, 9, London (OHL)
1978—Wayne Babych, 3, Portland (WCHL)
1979—Perry Turnbull, 2, Portland (WHL)
1980—Rik Wilson, 12, Kingston (OHL)
1981—Marty Ruff, 20, Lethbridge (WHL)
1982—No first-round selection
1983—No first-round selection
1984—No first-round selection
1985—No first-round selection

Year   Player, Overall, Last amateur team (league)
1986—Jocelyn Lemieux, 10, Laval (QMJHL)
1987—Keith Osborne, 12, North Bay (OHL)
1988—Rod Brind'Amour, 9, Notre Dame Academy (Sask.)
1989—Jason Marshall, 9, Vernon (B.C.) Tier II
1990—No first-round selection
1991—No first-round selection
1992—No first-round selection
1993—No first-round selection
1994—No first-round selection
1995—No first-round selection
1996—Marty Reasoner, 14, Boston College
1997—No first-round selection
1998—Christian Backman, 24, Frolunda HC Goteborg (Sweden)
1999—Barret Jackman, 17, Regina (WHL)
2000—Jeff Taffe, 30, University of Minnesota
2001—No first-round selection

SINGLE-SEASON INDIVIDUAL RECORDS

FORWARDS/DEFENSEMEN

Most goals
86—Brett Hull, 1990-91

Most assists
90—Adam Oates, 1990-91

Most points
131—Brett Hull, 1990-91

Most penalty minutes
306—Bob Gassoff, 1975-76

Most power play goals
29—Brett Hull, 1990-91
   Brett Hull, 1992-93

Most shorthanded goals
8—Chuck Lefley, 1975-76
   Larry Patey, 1980-81

Most games with three or more goals
8—Brett Hull, 1991-92

Most shots
408—Brett Hull, 1991-92

GOALTENDERS

Most games
79—Grant Fuhr, 1995-96

Most minutes
4,365—Grant Fuhr, 1995-96

Most shots against
2,382—Curtis Joseph, 1993-94

Most goals allowed
250—Mike Liut, 1991-92

Lowest goals-against average
1.95—Roman Turek, 1999-2000

Most shutouts
8—Glenn Hall, 1968-69

Most wins
42—Roman Turek, 1999-2000

Most losses
29—Mike Liut, 1983-84

Most ties
16—Grant Fuhr, 1995-96

FRANCHISE LEADERS

Players in boldface played for club in 2000-01

FORWARDS/DEFENSEMEN

Games
Bernie Federko 927
Brian Sutter.......................................779
Brett Hull 744
Garry Unger 662
Bob Plager..615

Goals
Brett Hull...527
Bernie Federko 352
Brian Sutter.......................................303
Garry Unger 292
Red Berenson....................................172

Assists
Bernie Federko 721
Brett Hull...409
Brian Sutter.......................................334

Garry Unger 283
Red Berenson....................................240

Points
Bernie Federko 1073
Brett Hull...936
Brian Sutter.......................................636
Garry Unger 575
Red Berenson....................................412

Penalty minutes
Brian Sutter......................................1786
Kelly Chase......................................1497
Barclay Plager..................................1115
Rob Ramage 998
Bob Gassoff.......................................866

GOALTENDERS

Games
Mike Liut...347
Curtis Joseph 280
Grant Fuhr...249
Greg Millen..209
Rick Wamsley 154

Shutouts
Glenn Hall...16
Grant Fuhr...11
Mike Liut...10
Jacques Plante....................................10
Greg Millen...9

Goals-against average
(2400 minutes minimum)
Jacques Plante................................2.07
Roman Turek.........................2.10

Glenn Hall	2.43
Grant Fuhr	2.68
Ernie Wakely	2.77

Wins

| Mike Liut | 151 |
| Curtis Joseph | 137 |

Grant Fuhr	108
Greg Millen	85
Rick Wamsley	75

ST. LOUIS EAGLES (DEFUNCT)
YEAR-BY-YEAR RECORDS

	REGULAR SEASON					PLAYOFFS			
Season	W	L	T	Pts.	Finish	W	L	Highest round	Coach
1934-35	11	31	6	28	5th/Canadian	—	—		Eddie Gerard, George Boucher

Franchise was formerly known as Ottawa Senators and relocated to St. Louis following 1933-34 season.

SAN JOSE SHARKS
YEAR-BY-YEAR RECORDS

	REGULAR SEASON						PLAYOFFS			
Season	W	L	T	RT	Pts.	Finish	W	L	Highest round	Coach
1991-92	17	58	5	—	39	6th/Smythe	—	—		George Kingston
1992-93	11	71	2	—	24	6th/Smythe	—	—		George Kingston
1993-94	33	35	16	—	82	3rd/Pacific	7	7	Conference semifinals	Kevin Constantine
1994-95	19	25	4	—	42	3rd/Pacific	4	7	Conference semifinals	Kevin Constantine
1995-96	20	55	7	—	47	7th/Pacific	—	—		Kevin Constantine, Jim Wiley
1996-97	27	47	8	—	62	7th/Pacific	—	—		Al Sims
1997-98	34	38	10	—	78	4th/Pacific	2	4	Conference quarterfinals	Darryl Sutter
1998-89	31	33	18	—	80	4th/Pacific	2	4	Conference quarterfinals	Darryl Sutter
1999-00	35	37	10	7	87	4th/Pacific	5	7	Conference semifinals	Darryl Sutter
2000-01	40	27	12	3	95	2nd/Pacific	2	4	Conference quarterfinals	Darryl Sutter

OFIRST-ROUND ENTRY DRAFT CHOICES

Year   Player, Overall, Last amateur team (league)

1991—Pat Falloon, 2, Spokane (WHL)
1992—Mike Rathje, 3, Medicine Hat (WHL)
    Andrei Nazarov, 10, Dynamo Moscow, CIS
1993—Viktor Kozlov, 6, Moscow, CIS
1994—Jeff Friesen, 11, Regina (WHL)
1995—Teemu Riihijarvi, 12, Espoo Jrs., Finland
1996—Andrei Zyuzin, 2, Salavat Yulayev UFA, CIS
    Marco Sturm, 21, Landshut, Germany

Year   Player, Overall, Last amateur team (league)

1997—Patrick Marleau, 2, Seattle (WHL)
    Scott Hannan, 23, Kelowna (WHL)
1998—Brad Stuart, 3, Regina (WHL)
1999—Jeff Jillson, 14, University of Michigan
2000—No first-round selection
2001—Marcel Goc, 20, Schwennigen, Germany

SINGLE-SEASON INDIVIDUAL RECORDS

FORWARDS/DEFENSEMEN

Most goals
44—Owen Nolan, 1999-2000

Most assists
52—Kelly Kisio, 1992-93

Most points
84—Owen Nolan, 1999-2000

Most penalty minutes
326—Link Gaetz, 1991-92

Most power play goals
18—Owen Nolan, 1999-2000

Most shorthanded goals
6—Jamie Baker, 1995-96

Most games with three or more goals
2—Rob Gaudreau, 1992-93
    Igor Larionov, 1993-94
    Tony Granato, 1996-97

Most shots
261—Tony Granato, 1996-97

GOALTENDERS

Most games
74—Arturs Irbe, 1993-94

Most minutes
4,412—Arturs Irbe, 1993-94

Most shots against
2,064—Arturs Irbe, 1993-94

Most goals allowed
209—Arturs Irbe, 1993-94

Lowest goals-against average
2.19—Evgeni Nabokov, 2000-01

Most shutouts
6—Evgeni Nabokov, 2000-01

Most wins
32—Evgeni Nabokov, 2000-01

Most losses
30—Jeff Hackett, 1992-93

Most ties
16—Arturs Irbe, 1993-94

FRANCHISE LEADERS

Players in boldface played for club in 2000-01

FORWARDS/DEFENSEMEN

Games

Jeff Friesen	514
Mike Rathje	457
Owen Nolan	432
Marcus Ragnarsson	424
Jeff Odgers	334

Goals

Owen Nolan	161
Jeff Friesen	149
Pat Falloon	76
Patrick Marleau	76
Mike Ricci	64

Assists

Jeff Friesen	201
Owen Nolan	182
Marcus Ragnarsson	103
Patrick Marleau	93
Vincent Damphousse	92

Points

Jeff Friesen	**350**
Owen Nolan	**343**
Patrick Marleau	**169**
Pat Falloon	162
Mike Ricci	**150**

Penalty minutes

Jeff Odgers	1001
Owen Nolan	**750**
Jay More	545
Andrei Nazarov	490
Dody Wood	471

GOALTENDERS

Games

Arturs Irbe	183
Mike Vernon	126
Steve Shields	**125**
Jeff Hackett	78
Evgeni Nabokov	**77**

Shutouts

Steve Shields	**10**
Mike Vernon	9
Arturs Irbe	8
Evgeni Nabokov	**7**
Ed Belfour	1
Wade Flaherty	1
Kelly Hrudey	1

Goals-against average
(2400 minutes minimum)

Evgeni Nabokov	**2.19**
Mike Vernon	2.39
Steve Shields	**2.44**
Kelly Hrudey	3.04
Chris Terreri	3.39

Wins

Arturs Irbe	57
Mike Vernon	52
Steve Shields	**48**
Evgeni Nabokov	**34**
Kelly Hrudey	20

TAMPA BAY LIGHTNING
YEAR-BY-YEAR RECORDS

	REGULAR SEASON						PLAYOFFS			
Season	W	L	T	RT	Pts.	Finish	W	L	Highest round	Coach
1992-93	23	54	7	—	53	6th/Norris	—	—		Terry Crisp
1993-94	30	43	11	—	71	7th/Atlantic	—	—		Terry Crisp
1994-95	17	28	3	—	37	6th/Atlantic	—	—		Terry Crisp
1995-96	38	32	12	—	88	5th/Atlantic	2	4	Conference quarterfinals	Terry Crisp
1996-97	32	40	10	—	74	6th/Atlantic	—	—		Terry Crisp
1997-98	17	55	10	—	44	7th/Atlantic	—	—		Terry Crisp, Rick Paterson, Jacques Demers
1998-99	19	54	9	—	47	4th/Southeast	—	—		Jacques Demers
1999-00	19	54	9	7	54	4th/Southeast	—	—		Steve Ludzik
2000-01	24	47	6	5	59	5th/Southeast	—	—		Steve Ludzik, John Tortorella

FIRST-ROUND ENTRY DRAFT CHOICES

Year   Player, Overall, Last amateur team (league)
1992—Roman Hamrlik, 1, Zlin, Czechoslovakia*
1993—Chris Gratton, 3, Kingston (OHL)
1994—Jason Weimer, 8, Portland (WHL)
1995—Daymond Langkow, 5, Tri-City (WHL)
1996—Mario Larocque, 16, Hull (QMJHL)
1997—Paul Mara, 7, Sudbury (OHL)

Year   Player, Overall, Last amateur team (league)
1998—Vincent Lecavalier, 1, Rimouski (QMJHL)*
1999—No first-round selection
2000—Nikita Alexeev, 8, Erie (OHL)
2001—Alexander Svitov, 3, OMSK, Russia
*Designates first player chosen in draft.

SINGLE-SEASON INDIVIDUAL RECORDS

FORWARDS/DEFENSEMEN

Most goals
42—Brian Bradley, 1992-93

Most assists
56—Brian Bradley, 1995-96

Most points
86—Brian Bradley, 1992-93

Most penalty minutes
258—Enrico Ciccone, 1995-96

Most power play goals
16—Brian Bradley, 1992-93

Most shorthanded goals
4—Rob Zamuner, 1994-95
   Rob Zamuner, 1995-96

Most games with three or more goals
3—Wendel Clark, 1998-99

Most shots
281—Roman Hamrlik, 1995-96

GOALTENDERS

Most games
63—Daren Puppa, 1993-94

Most minutes
3,653—Daren Puppa, 1993-94

Most shots against
1,742—Kevin Weekes, 2000-01

Most goals allowed
177—Kevin Weekes, 2000-01

Lowest goals-against average
2.46—Daren Puppa, 1995-96

Most shutouts
5—Daren Puppa, 1995-96

Most wins
29—Daren Puppa, 1995-96

Most losses
33—Daren Puppa, 1993-94
   Kevin Weekes, 2000-01

Most ties
9—Daren Puppa, 1995-96

FRANCHISE LEADERS

Players in boldface played for club in 2000-01

FORWARDS/DEFENSEMEN

Games

Rob Zamuner	475
Mikael Andersson	435
Chris Gratton	404
Roman Hamrlik	377
Cory Cross	336

Goals

Brian Bradley	111
Chris Gratton	88
Rob Zamuner	84
Alexander Selivanov	78
Petr Klima	63

Assists

Brian Bradley	189
Chris Gratton	148
Roman Hamrlik	133
Rob Zamuner	116
Vincent Lecavalier	**85**

Points

Brian Bradley	300
Chris Gratton	236
Rob Zamuner	200
Roman Hamrlik	185
Vincent Lecavalier	**161**

Penalty minutes

Chris Gratton	741
Enrico Ciccone	604
Roman Hamrlik	472
Rudy Poeschek	418
Jason Wiemer	391

GOALTENDERS

Games

Daren Puppa	206
Corey Schwab	87
Dan Cloutier	**76**
Kevin Weekes	**61**
Pat Jablonski	58

Shutouts

Daren Puppa	12
Rick Tabaracci	4
Kevin Weekes	**4**
Corey Schwab	3
Six players tied with	1

Goals-against average (2400 minutes minimum)

Daren Puppa	2.68
Rick Tabaracci	2.75
Kevin Weekes	**3.14**
Corey Schwab	3.25
Dan Cloutier	**3.50**

Wins

Daren Puppa	77
Corey Schwab	21
Rick Tabaracci	20
Kevin Weekes	**20**
J.C. Bergeron	14

TORONTO MAPLE LEAFS
YEAR-BY-YEAR RECORDS

Season	W	L	T	RT	Pts.	Finish	W	L	Highest round	Coach
1917-18‡	13	9	0	—	26	2nd	4	3	Stanley Cup champ	Dick Carroll
1918-19‡	5	13	0	—	10	3rd	—	—		Dick Carroll
1919-20§	12	12	0	—	24	3rd	—	—		Frank Heffernan, Harry Sproule
1920-21§	15	9	0	—	30	1st	0	2	Semifinals	Dick Carroll
1921-22§	13	10	1	—	27	2nd	*4	2	Stanley Cup champ	Eddie Powers
1922-23§	13	10	1	—	27	3rd	—	—		Charlie Querrie, Jack Adams
1923-24§	10	14	0	—	20	3rd	—	—		Eddie Powers
1924-25§	19	11	0	—	38	2nd	0	2	Semifinals	Eddie Powers
1925-26§	12	21	3	—	27	6th	—	—		Eddie Powers
1926-27§	15	24	5	—	35	5th/Canadian	—	—		Conn Smythe
1927-28	18	18	8	—	44	4th/Canadian	—	—		Alex Roveril, Conn Smythe
1928-29	21	18	5	—	47	3rd/Canadian	2	2	Semifinals	Alex Roveril, Conn Smythe
1929-30	17	21	6	—	40	4th/Canadian	—	—		Alex Roveril, Conn Smythe
1930-31	22	13	9	—	53	2nd/Canadian	*0	1	Quarterfinals	Conn Smythe, Art Duncan
1931-32	23	18	7	—	53	2nd/Canadian	5	2	Stanley Cup champ	Art Duncan, Dick Irvin
1932-33	24	18	6	—	54	1st/Canadian	4	5	Stanley Cup finals	Dick Irvin
1933-34	26	13	9	—	61	1st/Canadian	2	3	Semifinals	Dick Irvin
1934-35	30	14	4	—	64	1st/Canadian	3	4	Stanley Cup finals	Dick Irvin
1935-36	23	19	6	—	52	2nd/Canadian	4	5	Stanley Cup finals	Dick Irvin
1936-37	22	21	5	—	49	3rd/Canadian	0	2	Quarterfinals	Dick Irvin
1937-38	24	15	9	—	57	1st/Canadian			Stanley Cup finals	Dick Irvin
1938-39	19	20	9	—	47	3rd	5	5	Stanley Cup finals	Dick Irvin
1939-40	25	17	6	—	56	3rd	6	4	Stanley Cup finals	Dick Irvin
1940-41	28	14	6	—	62	2nd	3	4	Semifinals	Hap Day
1941-42	27	18	3	—	57	2nd	8	5	Stanley Cup champ	Hap Day
1942-43	22	19	9	—	53	3rd	2	4	League semifinals	Hap Day
1943-44	23	23	4	—	50	3rd	1	4	League semifinals	Hap Day
1944-45	24	22	4	—	52	3rd	8	5	Stanley Cup champ	Hap Day
1945-46	19	24	7	—	45	5th	—	—		Hap Day
1946-47	31	19	10	—	72	2nd	8	3	Stanley Cup champ	Hap Day
1947-48	32	15	13	—	77	1st	8	1	Stanley Cup champ	Hap Day
1948-49	22	25	13	—	57	4th	8	1	Stanley Cup champ	Hap Day
1949-50	31	27	12	—	74	3rd	3	4	League semifinals	Hap Day
1950-51	41	16	13	—	95	2nd	†8	2	Stanley Cup champ	Joe Primeau
1951-52	29	25	16	—	74	3rd	0	4	League semifinals	Joe Primeau
1952-53	27	30	13	—	67	5th	—	—		Joe Primeau
1953-54	32	24	14	—	78	3rd	1	4	League semifinals	King Clancy
1954-55	24	24	22	—	70	3rd	0	4	League semifinals	King Clancy
1955-56	24	33	13	—	61	4th	1	4	League semifinals	King Clancy

			REGULAR SEASON				PLAYOFFS			
Season	W	L	T	RT	Pts.	Finish	W	L	Highest round	Coach
1956-57	21	34	15	—	57	5th	—	—		Howie Meeker
1957-58	21	38	11	—	53	6th	—	—		Billy Reay
1958-59	27	32	11	—	65	4th	5	7	Stanley Cup finals	Billy Reay, Punch Imlach
1959-60	35	26	9	—	79	2nd	4	6	Stanley Cup finals	Punch Imlach
1960-61	39	19	12	—	90	2nd	1	4	League semifinals	Punch Imlach
1961-62	37	22	11	—	85	2nd	8	4	Stanley Cup champ	Punch Imlach
1962-63	35	23	12	—	82	1st	8	2	Stanley Cup champ	Punch Imlach
1963-64	33	25	12	—	78	3rd	8	6	Stanley Cup champ	Punch Imlach
1964-65	30	26	14	—	74	4th	2	4	League semifinals	Punch Imlach
1965-66	34	25	11	—	79	3rd	0	4	League semifinals	Punch Imlach
1966-67	32	27	11	—	75	3rd	8	4	Stanley Cup champ	Punch Imlach
1967-68	33	31	10	—	76	5th/East	—	—		Punch Imlach
1968-69	35	26	15	—	85	4th/East	0	4	Division semifinals	Punch Imlach
1969-70	29	34	13	—	71	6th/East	—	—		John McLellan
1970-71	37	33	8	—	82	4th/East	2	4	Division semifinals	John McLellan
1971-72	33	31	14	—	80	4th/East	1	4	Division semifinals	John McLellan
1972-73	27	41	10	—	64	6th/East	—	—		John McLellan
1973-74	35	27	16	—	86	4th/East	0	4	Division semifinals	Red Kelly
1974-75	31	33	16	—	78	3rd/Adams	2	5	Quarterfinals	Red Kelly
1975-76	34	31	15	—	83	3rd/Adams	5	5	Quarterfinals	Red Kelly
1976-77	33	32	15	—	81	3rd/Adams	4	5	Quarterfinals	Red Kelly
1977-78	41	29	10	—	92	3rd/Adams	4	2	Quarterfinals	Roger Neilson
1978-79	34	33	13	—	81	3rd/Adams	4	7	Quarterfinals	Roger Neilson
1979-80	35	40	5	—	75	4th/Adams	0	3	Preliminaries	Floyd Smith
1980-81	28	37	15	—	71	5th/Adams	0	3	Preliminaries	Punch Imlach, Joe Crozier
1981-82	20	44	16	—	56	5th/Norris	—	—		Mike Nykoluk
1982-83	28	40	12	—	68	3rd/Norris	1	3	Division semifinals	Mike Nykoluk
1983-84	26	45	9	—	61	5th/Norris	—	—		Mike Nykoluk
1984-85	20	52	8	—	48	5th/Norris	—	—		Dan Maloney
1985-86	25	48	7	—	57	4th/Norris	6	4	Division finals	Dan Maloney
1986-87	32	42	6	—	70	4th/Norris	7	6	Division finals	John Brophy
1987-88	21	49	10	—	52	4th/Norris	2	4	Division semifinals	John Brophy
1988-89	28	46	6	—	62	5th/Norris	—	—		John Brophy, George Armstrong
1989-90	38	38	4	—	80	3rd/Norris	1	4	Division semifinals	Doug Carpenter
1990-91	23	46	11	—	57	5th/Norris	—	—		Doug Carpenter, Tom Watt
1991-92	30	43	7	—	67	5th/Norris	—	—		Tom Watt
1992-93	44	29	11	—	99	3rd/Norris	11	10	Conference finals	Pat Burns
1993-94	43	29	12	—	98	2nd/Central	9	9	Conference finals	Pat Burns
1994-95	21	19	8	—	50	4th/Central	3	4	Conference quarterfinals	Pat Burns
1995-96	34	36	12	—	80	T3rd/Central	2	4	Conference quarterfinals	Pat Burns, Nick Beverley
1996-97	30	44	8	—	68	6th/Central	—	—		Mike Murphy
1997-98	30	43	9	—	69	6th/Central	—	—		Mike Murphy
1998-99	45	30	7	—	97	2nd/Northeast	9	8	Conference finals	Pat Quinn
1999-00	45	30	7	3	100	1st/Northeast	6	6	Conference semifinals	Pat Quinn
2000-01	37	29	11	5	90	3rd/Northeast	7	4	Conference semifinals	Pat Quinn

*Won-lost record does not indicate tie(s) resulting from two-game, total-goals series that year (two-game, total-goals series were played from 1917-18 through 1935-36).
†Tied after one overtime (curfew law).
‡Toronto Arenas.
§Toronto St. Patricks (until April 14, 1927).

FIRST-ROUND ENTRY DRAFT CHOICES

Year	Player, Overall, Last amateur team (league)
1969	Ernie Moser, 9, Esteven (WCHL)
1970	Darryl Sittler, 8, London (OHL)
1971	No first-round selection
1972	George Ferguson, 11, Toronto (OHL)
1973	Lanny McDonald, 4, Medicine Hat (WCHL)
	Bob Neely, 10, Peterborough (OHL)
	Ian Turnbull, 15, Ottawa (OHL)
1974	Jack Valiquette, 13, Sault Ste. Marie (OHL)
1975	Don Ashby, 6, Calgary (WCHL)
1976	No first-round selection
1977	John Anderson, 11, Toronto (OHA)
	Trevor Johansen, 12, Toronto (OHA)
1978	No first-round selection
1979	Laurie Boschman, 9, Brandon (WHL)
1980	No first-round selection
1981	Jim Benning, 6, Portland (WHL)

Year	Player, Overall, Last amateur team (league)
1982	Gary Nylund, 3, Portland (WHL)
1983	Russ Courtnall, 7, Victoria (WHL)
1984	Al Iafrate, 4, U.S. Olympics/Belleville (OHL)
1985	*Wendel Clark, 1, Saskatoon (WHL)
1986	Vincent Damphousse, 6, Laval (QMJHL)
1987	Luke Richardson, 7, Peterborough (OHL)
1988	Scott Pearson, 6, Kingston (OHL)
1989	Scott Thornton, 3, Belleville (OHL)
	Rob Pearson, 12, Belleville (OHL)
	Steve Bancroft, 21, Belleville (OHL)
1990	Drake Berehowsky, 10, Kingston (OHL)
1991	No first-round selection
1992	Brandon Convery, 8, Sudbury (OHL)
	Grant Marshall, 23, Ottawa (OHL)
1993	Kenny Jonsson, 12, Rogle, Sweden
	Landon Wilson, 19, Dubuque (USHL)

Year	Player, Overall, Last amateur team (league)
1994—Eric Fichaud, 16, Chicoutimi (QMJHL)
1995—Jeff Ware, 15, Oshawa (OHL)
1996—No first-round selection
1997—No first-round selection
1998—Nikolai Antropov, 10, Torpedo, Russia

Year	Player, Overall, Last amateur team (league)
1999—Luca Cereda, 24, Ambri, Switzerland
2000—Brad Boyes, 24, Erie (OHL)
2001—Carlo Colaiacovo, 17, Erie (OHL)
*Designates first player chosen in draft.

SINGLE-SEASON INDIVIDUAL RECORDS

FORWARDS/DEFENSEMEN

Most goals
54—Rick Vaive, 1981-82

Most assists
95—Doug Gilmour, 1992-93

Most points
127—Doug Gilmour, 1992-93

Most penalty minutes
351—Tiger Williams, 1977-78

Most shorthanded goals
8—Dave Keon, 1970-71
  Dave Reid, 1990-91

Most games with three or more goals
5—Darryl Sittler, 1980-81

GOALTENDERS

Most games
74—Felix Potvin, 1996-97

Most minutes
4,271—Felix Potvin, 1996-97

Lowest goals-against average
1.56—Lorne Chabot, 1928-29

Most shutouts
13—Harry Lumley, 1953-54

Most wins
36—Curtis Joseph, 1999-2000

Most losses
38—Ed Chadwick, 1957-58

Most ties
22—Harry Lumley, 1954-55

FRANCHISE LEADERS

Players in boldface played for club in 2000-01

FORWARDS/DEFENSEMEN

Games

George Armstrong	1187
Tim Horton	1185
Borje Salming	1099
Dave Keon	1062
Ron Ellis	1034

Goals

Darryl Sittler	389
Dave Keon	365
Ron Ellis	332
Rick Vaive	299
Frank Mahovlich	296
George Armstrong	296

Assists

Borje Salming	620
Darryl Sittler	527
Dave Keon	493
George Armstrong	417
Tim Horton	349

Points

Darryl Sittler	916
Dave Keon	858
Borje Salming	768
George Armstrong	713
Ron Ellis	640

Penalty minutes

Dave Williams	1670
Tie Domi	**1620**
Wendel Clark	1535
Tim Horton	1389
Borje Salming	1292

GOALTENDERS

Games

Turk Broda	629
Johnny Bower	472
Felix Potvin	369
Mike Palmateer	296
Harry Lumley	267

Shutouts

Turk Broda	62
Harry Lumley	34
Lorne Chabot	33
Johnny Bower	32
George Hainsworth	19

Goals-against average (2400 minutes minimum)

John Ross Roach	2.00
Al Rollins	2.05
Lorne Chabot	2.20
Harry Lumley	2.21
George Hainsworth	2.26

Wins

Turk Broda	302
Johnny Bower	220
Felix Potvin	160
Mike Palmateer	129
Lorne Chabot	108

VANCOUVER CANUCKS
YEAR-BY-YEAR RECORDS

	REGULAR SEASON						PLAYOFFS			
Season	W	L	T	RT	Pts.	Finish	W	L	Highest round	Coach
1970-71	24	46	8	—	56	6th/East	—	—		Hal Laycoe
1971-72	20	50	8	—	48	7th/East	—	—		Hal Laycoe
1972-73	22	47	9	—	53	7th/East	—	—		Vic Stasiuk
1973-74	24	43	11	—	59	7th/East	—	—		Bill McCreary, Phil Maloney
1974-75	38	32	10	—	86	1st/Smythe	1	4	Quarterfinals	Phil Maloney
1975-76	33	32	15	—	81	2nd/Smythe	0	2	Preliminaries	Phil Maloney
1976-77	25	42	13	—	63	4th/Smythe	—	—		Phil Maloney, Orland Kurtenbach
1977-78	20	43	17	—	57	3rd/Smythe	—	—		Orland Kurtenbach
1978-79	25	42	13	—	63	2nd/Smythe	1	2	Preliminaries	Harry Neale
1979-80	27	37	16	—	70	3rd/Smythe	1	3	Preliminaries	Harry Neale
1980-81	28	32	20	—	76	3rd/Smythe	0	3	Preliminaries	Harry Neale
1981-82	30	33	17	—	77	2nd/Smythe	11	6	Stanley Cup finals	Harry Neale, Roger Neilson
1982-83	30	35	15	—	75	3rd/Smythe	1	3	Division semifinals	Roger Neilson
1983-84	32	39	9	—	73	3rd/Smythe	1	3	Division semifinals	Roger Neilson, Harry Neale
1984-85	25	46	9	—	59	5th/Smythe	—	—		Bill Laforge, Harry Neale

NHL HISTORY *Team by team*

	REGULAR SEASON					PLAYOFFS			
Season	W	L	T	RT	Pts.	Finish	W	L	Highest round	Coach
1985-86	23	44	13	—	59	4th/Smythe	0	3	Division semifinals	Tom Watt
1986-87	29	43	8	—	66	5th/Smythe	—	—		Tom Watt
1987-88	25	46	9	—	59	5th/Smythe	—	—		Bob McCammon
1988-89	33	39	8	—	74	4th/Smythe	3	4	Division semifinals	Bob McCammon
1989-90	25	41	14	—	64	5th/Smythe	—	—		Bob McCammon
1990-91	28	43	9	—	65	4th/Smythe	2	4	Division semifinals	Bob McCammon, Pat Quinn
1991-92	42	26	12	—	96	1st/Smythe	6	7	Division finals	Pat Quinn
1992-93	46	29	9	—	101	1st/Smythe	6	6	Division finals	Pat Quinn
1993-94	41	40	3	—	85	2nd/Pacific	15	9	Stanley Cup finals	Pat Quinn
1994-95	18	18	12	—	48	2nd/Pacific	4	7	Conference semifinals	Rick Ley
1995-96	32	35	15	—	79	T2nd/Pacific	2	4	Conference quarterfinals	Rick Ley, Pat Quinn
1996-97	35	40	7	—	77	4th/Pacific	—	—		Tom Renney
1997-98	25	43	14	—	64	7th/Pacific	—	—		Tom Renney, Mike Keenan
1998-99	23	47	12	—	58	4th/Northwest	—	—		Mike Keenan, Marc Crawford
1999-00	30	37	15	8	83	3rd/Northwest	—	—		Marc Crawford
2000-01	36	28	11	7	90	3rd/Northwest	0	4	Conference quarterfinals	Marc Crawford

FIRST-ROUND ENTRY DRAFT CHOICES

Year   Player, Overall, Last amateur team (league)
1970—Dale Tallon, 2, Toronto (OHL)
1971—Jocelyn Guevremont, 3, Montreal (OHL)
1972—Don Lever, 3, Niagara Falls (OHL)
1973—Dennis Ververgaert, 3, London (OHL)
      Bob Dailey, 9, Toronto (OHL)
1974—No first-round selection
1975—Rick Blight, 10, Brandon (WCHL)
1976—No first-round selection
1977—Jere Gillis, 4, Sherbrooke (QMJHL)
1978—Bill Derlago, 4, Brandon (WCHL)
1979—Rick Vaive, 5, Birmingham (WHA)
1980—Rick Lanz, 7, Oshawa (OHL)
1981—Garth Butcher, 10, Regina (WHL)
1982—Michel Petit, 11, Sherbrooke (QMJHL)
1983—Cam Neely, 9, Portland (WHL)
1984—J.J. Daigneault, 10, Can. Ol./Longueuil (QMJHL)
1985—Jim Sandlak, 4, London (OHL)
1986—Dan Woodley, 7, Portland (WHL)

Year   Player, Overall, Last amateur team (league)
1987—No first-round selection
1988—Trevor Linden, 2, Medicine Hat (WHL)
1989—Jason Herter, 8, University of North Dakota
1990—Petr Nedved, 2, Seattle (WHL)
      Shawn Antoski, 18, North Bay (OHL)
1991—Alex Stojanov, 7, Hamilton (OHL)
1992—Libor Polasek, 21, TJ Vikovice (Czech.)
1993—Mike Wilson, 20, Sudbury (OHL)
1994—Mattias Ohlund, 13, Pitea Div. I (Sweden)
1995—No first-round selection
1996—Josh Holden, 12, Regina (WHL)
1997—Brad Ference, 10, Spokane (WHL)
1998—Bryan Allen, 4, Oshawa (OHL)
1999—Daniel Sedin, 2, Modo Ornskoldsvik, Sweden
      Henrik Sedin, 3, Modo Ornskoldsvik, Sweden
2000—Nathan Smith, 23, Swift Current (WHL)
2001—R.J. Umberger, 16, Ohio State

SINGLE-SEASON INDIVIDUAL RECORDS

FORWARDS/DEFENSEMEN

Most goals
60—Pavel Bure, 1992-93
    Pavel Bure, 1993-94

Most assists
62—Andre Boudrias, 1974-75

Most points
110—Pavel Bure, 1992-93

Most penalty minutes
372—Donald Brashear, 1997-98

Most power play goals
25—Pavel Bure, 1993-94

Most shorthanded goals
7—Pavel Bure, 1992-93

Most games with three or more goals
4—Petri Skriko, 1986-87

Most shots
407—Pavel Bure, 1992-93

GOALTENDERS

Most games
72—Gary Smith, 1974-75

Most minutes
3,852—Kirk McLean, 1991-92

Most goals allowed
240—Richard Brodeur, 1985-86

Lowest goals-against average
2.59—Felix Potvin, 1999-2000

Most shutouts
6—Gary Smith, 1974-75
   Garth Snow, 1998-99

Most wins
38—Kirk McLean, 1991-92

Most losses
33—Gary Smith, 1973-74

Most ties
16—Richard Brodeur, 1980-81

FRANCHISE LEADERS

Players in boldface played for club in 2000-01

FORWARDS/DEFENSEMEN

Games
Stan Smyl.............................896
Harold Snepsts.....................781
Trevor Linden 702
Dennis Kearns 677
Doug Lidster 666

Goals
Stan Smyl...........................262
Pavel Bure..........................254
Tony Tanti..........................250
Trevor Linden 247
Thomas Gradin 197

Assists
Stan Smyl...........................411
Thomas Gradin....................353
Trevor Linden 322
Dennis Kearns 290
Andre Boudrias 267

Points

Stan Smyl	673
Trevor Linden	569
Thomas Gradin	550
Pavel Bure	478
Tony Tanti	470

Penalty minutes

Gino Odjick	2127
Garth Butcher	1668
Stan Smyl	1556
Harold Snepsts	1446
Tiger Williams	1324

GOALTENDERS

Games

Kirk McLean	516
Richard Brodeur	377
Gary Smith	208
Dunc Wilson	148
Glen Hanlon	137

Shutouts

Kirk McLean	20
Gary Smith	11
Richard Brodeur	6
Garth Snow	6
Glen Hanlon	5

Goals-against average
(2400 minutes minimum)

Felix Potvin	**2.84**
Garth Snow	2.87
Corey Hirsch	3.12
Kirk McLean	3.28
Gary Smith	3.33

Wins

Kirk McLean	211
Richard Brodeur	126
Gary Smith	72
Glen Hanlon	43
Kay Whitmore	36

WASHINGTON CAPITALS
YEAR-BY-YEAR RECORDS

	REGULAR SEASON						PLAYOFFS			
Season	W	L	T	RT	Pts.	Finish	W	L	Highest round	Coach
1974-75	8	67	5	—	21	5th/Norris	—	—		Jim Anderson, Red Sullivan, Milt Schmidt
1975-76	11	59	10	—	32	5th/Norris	—	—		Milt Schmidt, Tom McVie
1976-77	24	42	14	—	62	4th/Norris	—	—		Tom McVie
1977-78	17	49	14	—	48	5th/Norris	—	—		Tom McVie
1978-79	24	41	15	—	63	4th/Norris	—	—		Dan Belisle
1979 80	27	40	13	—	67	5th/Patrick	—	—		Dan Belisle, Gary Green
1980-81	26	36	18	—	70	5th/Patrick	—	—		Gary Green
1981-82	26	41	13	—	65	5th/Patrick	—	—		Gary Green, Roger Crozier, Bryan Murray
1982-83	39	25	16	—	94	3rd/Patrick	1	3	Division semifinals	Bryan Murray
1983-84	48	27	5	—	101	2nd/Patrick	4	4	Division finals	Bryan Murray
1984-85	46	25	9	—	101	2nd/Patrick	2	3	Division semifinals	Bryan Murray
1985-86	50	23	7	—	107	2nd/Patrick	5	4	Division finals	Bryan Murray
1986-87	38	32	10	—	86	2nd/Patrick	3	4	Division semifinals	Bryan Murray
1987-88	38	33	9	—	85	2nd/Patrick	7	7	Division finals	Bryan Murray
1988-89	41	29	10	—	92	1st/Patrick	2	4	Division semifinals	Bryan Murray
1989-90	36	38	6	—	78	3rd/Patrick	8	7	Conference finals	Bryan Murray, Terry Murray
1990-91	37	36	7	—	81	3rd/Patrick	5	6	Division finals	Terry Murray
1991-92	45	27	8	—	98	2nd/Patrick	3	4	Division semifinals	Terry Murray
1992-93	43	34	7	—	93	2nd/Patrick	2	4	Division semifinals	Terry Murray
1993-94	39	35	10	—	88	3rd/Atlantic	5	6	Conference semifinals	Terry Murray, Jim Schoenfeld
1994-95	22	18	8	—	52	3rd/Atlantic	4	3	Conference quarterfinals	Jim Schoenfeld
1995-96	39	32	11	—	89	4th/Atlantic	2	4	Conference quarterfinals	Jim Schoenfeld
1996-97	33	40	9	—	75	5th/Atlantic	—	—		Jim Schoenfeld
1997-98	40	30	12	—	92	3rd/Atlantic	12	9	Stanley Cup finals	Ron Wilson
1998-99	31	45	6	—	68	3rd/Southeast	—	—		Ron Wilson
1999-00	44	26	12	2	102	1st/Southeast	1	4	Conference quarterfinals	Ron Wilson
2000-01	41	27	10	4	96	1st/Southeast	2	4	Conference quarterfinals	Ron Wilson

FIRST-ROUND ENTRY DRAFT CHOICES

Year   Player, Overall, Last amateur team (league)

1974—Greg Joly, 1, Regina (WCHL)*
1975—Alex Forsyth, 18, Kingston (OHA)
1976—Rick Green, 1, London (OHL)*
      Greg Carroll, 15, Medicine Hat (WCHL)
1977—Robert Picard, 3, Montreal (QMJHL)
1978—Ryan Walter, 2, Seattle (WCHL)
      Tim Coulis, 18, Hamilton (OHL)
1979—Mike Gartner, 4, Cincinnati (WHA)
1980—Darren Veitch, 5, Regina (WHL)
1981—Bobby Carpenter, 3, St. John's H.S. (Mass.)
1982—Scott Stevens, 5, Kitchener (OHL)
1983—No first-round selection
1984—Kevin Hatcher, 17, North Bay (OHL)
1985—Yvon Corriveau, 19, Toronto (OHL)
1986—Jeff Greenlaw, 19, Team Canada
1987—No first-round selection
1988—Reggie Savage, 15, Victoriaville (QMJHL)
1989—Olaf Kolzig, 19, Tri-City (WHL)

Year   Player, Overall, Last amateur team (league)

1990—John Slaney, 9, Cornwall (OHL)
1991—Pat Peake, 14, Detroit (OHL)
      Trevor Halverson, 21, North Bay (OHL)
1992—Sergei Gonchar, 14, Dynamo Moscow, CIS
1993—Brendan Witt, 11, Seattle (WHL)
      Jason Allison, 17, London (OHL)
1994—Nolan Baumgartner, 10, Kamloops (WHL)
      Alexander Kharlamov, 15, CSKA Moscow, CIS
1995—Brad Church, 17, Prince Albert (WHL)
      Miikka Elomo, 23, Kiekko-67, Finland
1996—Alexander Volchkov, 4, Barrie (OHL)
1997—Nick Boynton, 9, Ottawa (OHL)
      Jaroslav Svejkovsky, 17, Tri-City (WHL)
1998—No first-round selection
1999—Kris Breech, 7, Calgary (WHL)
2000—Brian Sutherby, 26, Moose Jaw (WHL)
2001—No first-round selection
*Designates first player chosen in draft.

SINGLE-SEASON INDIVIDUAL RECORDS

FORWARDS/DEFENSEMEN

Most goals
60—Dennis Maruk, 1981-82

Most assists
76—Dennis Maruk, 1981-82

Most points
136—Dennis Maruk, 1981-82

Most penalty minutes
339—Alan May, 1989-90

Most power play goals
22—Peter Bondra, 2000-01

Most shorthanded goals
6—Mike Gartner, 1986-87
  Peter Bondra, 1994-95

Most games with three or more goals
4—Dennis Maruk, 1980-81
  Dennis Maruk, 1981-82
  Peter Bondra, 1995-96

Most shots
330—Mike Gartner, 1984-85

GOALTENDERS

Most games
73—Olaf Kolzig, 1999-2000

Most minutes
4,371—Olaf Kolzig, 1999-2000

Most shots against
1,957—Olaf Kolzig, 1999-2000

Most goals allowed
235—Ron Low, 1974-75

Lowest goals-against average
2.13—Jim Carey, 1994-95

Most shutouts
9—Jim Carey, 1995-96

Most wins
41—Olaf Kolzig, 1999-2000

Most losses
36—Ron Low, 1974-75

Most ties
11—Olaf Kolzig, 1999-2000

FRANCHISE LEADERS

Players in boldface played for club in 2000-01

FORWARDS/DEFENSEMEN

Games
Kelly Miller	940
Calle Johansson	**890**
Dale Hunter	872
Michal Pivonka	825
Mike Gartner	758

Goals
Mike Gartner	397
Peter Bondra	**382**
Mike Ridley	218
Bengt Gustafsson	196
Dave Christian	193

Assists
Michal Pivonka	418
Mike Gartner	392
Dale Hunter	375
Bengt Gustafsson	359
Calle Johansson	**349**

Points
Mike Gartner	789
Peter Bondra	**664**
Michal Pivonka	599
Dale Hunter	556
Bengt Gustafsson	555

Penalty minutes
Dale Hunter	2003
Scott Stevens	1630
Craig Berube	**1220**
Alan May	1189
Kevin Hatcher	998

GOALTENDERS

Games
Olaf Kolzig	**344**
Don Beaupre	269
Al Jensen	173
Ron Low	145
Pat Riggin	143

Goals-against average
(2400 minutes minimum)
Jim Carey	2.37
Olaf Kolzig	**2.49**
Rick Tabaracci	2.71
Pat Riggin	3.02
Don Beaupre	3.05

Wins
Olaf Kolzig	**151**
Don Beaupre	128
Al Jensen	94
Jim Carey	70
Pete Peeters	70

Shutouts
Olaf Kolzig	**21**
Jim Carey	14
Don Beaupre	12
Al Jensen	8
Pete Peeters	7

WINNIPEG JETS (DEFUNCT)
YEAR-BY-YEAR RECORDS

	REGULAR SEASON					PLAYOFFS			
Season	W	L	T	Pts.	Finish	W	L	Highest round	Coach
1972-73*	43	31	4	90	1st	9	5	Avco World Cup finals	Nick Mickoski, Bobby Hull
1973-74*	34	39	5	73	4th	0	4	League quarterfinals	Nick Mickoski, Bobby Hull
1974-75*	38	35	5	81	3rd	—	—		Rudy Pilous
1975-76*	52	27	2	106	1st	12	1	Avco World Cup champ	Bobby Kromm
1976-77*	46	32	2	94	2nd	11	9	Avco World Cup finals	Bobby Kromm
1977-78*	50	28	2	102	1st	8	1	Avco World Cup champ	Larry Hillman
1978-79*	39	35	6	84	3rd	8	2	Avco World Cup champ	Larry Hillman, Tom McVie
1979-80	20	49	11	51	5th/Smythe	—	—		Tom McVie
1980-81	9	57	14	32	6th/Smythe	—	—		Tom McVie, Bill Sutherland, Mike Smith
1981-82	33	33	14	80	2nd/Norris	1	3	Division semifinals	Tom Watt
1982-83	33	39	8	74	4th/Smythe	0	3	Division semifinals	Tom Watt
1983-84	31	38	11	73	3rd/Smythe	0	3	Division semifinals	Tom Watt, Barry Long
1984-85	43	27	10	96	2nd/Smythe	3	5	Division finals	Barry Long
1985-86	26	47	7	59	3rd/Smythe	0	3	Division semifinals	Barry Long, John Ferguson
1986-87	40	32	8	88	3rd/Smythe	4	6	Division finals	Dan Maloney
1987-88	33	36	11	77	3rd/Smythe	1	4	Division semifinals	Dan Maloney
1988-89	26	42	12	64	5th/Smythe	—	—		Dan Maloney, Rick Bowness
1989-90	37	32	11	85	3rd/Smythe	3	4	Division semifinals	Bob Murdoch

Season	W	L	T	Pts.	Finish	W	L	Highest round	Coach
			REGULAR SEASON					PLAYOFFS	
1990-91	26	43	11	63	5th/Smythe	—	—		Bob Murdoch
1991-92	33	32	15	81	4th/Smythe	3	4	Division semifinals	John Paddock
1992-93	40	37	7	87	4th/Smythe	2	4	Division semifinals	John Paddock
1993-94	24	51	9	57	6th/Central	—	—		John Paddock
1994-95	16	25	7	39	6th/Central	—	—		John Paddock, Terry Simpson
1995-96	36	40	6	78	5th/Central	—	—		Terry Simpson

*Members of World Hockey Association.
Franchise relocated and became Phoenix Coyotes following 1995-96 season.

FIRST-ROUND ENTRY DRAFT CHOICES

Year   Player, Overall, Last amateur team (league)
1979—Jimmy Mann, 19, Sherbrooke (QMJHL)
1980—David Babych, 2, Portland (WHL)
1981—Dale Hawerchuk, 1, Cornwall (QMJHL)*
1982—Jim Kyte, 12, Cornwall (OHL)
1983—Andrew McBain, 8, North Bay (OHL)
        Bobby Dollas, 14, Laval (QMJHL)
1984—No first-round selection
1985—Ryan Stewart, 18, Kamloops (WHL)
1986—Pat Elynuik, 8, Prince Albert (WHL)
1987—Bryan Marchment, 16, Belleville (OHL)
1988—Teemu Selanne, 10, Jokerit (Finland)
1989—Stu Barnes, 4, Tri-City (WHL)

Year   Player, Overall, Last amateur team (league)
1990—Keith Tkachuk, 19, Malden Cath. H.S. (Mass.)
1991—Aaron Ward, 5, University of Michigan
1992—Sergei Bautin, 17, Dynamo Moscow (CIS)
1993—Mats Lindgren, 15, Skelleftea (Sweden)
1994—No first-round selection
1995—Shane Doan, 7, Kamloops (WHL)
1996—Dan Focht, 11, Tri-City (WHL)
        Daniel Briere, 24, Drummondville (QMJHL)
*Designates first player chosen in draft.
NOTE: Winnipeg chose Scott Campbell, Morris Lukowich and Markus Mattsson as priority selections before the 1979 expansion draft.

SINGLE-SEASON INDIVIDUAL RECORDS

FORWARDS/DEFENSEMEN

Most goals
76—Teemu Selanne, 1992-93

Most assists
79—Phil Housley, 1992-93

Most points
132—Teemu Selanne, 1992-93

Most penalty minutes
347—Tie Domi, 1993-94

Most power play goals
24—Teemu Selanne, 1992-93

Most shorthanded goals
7—Dave McLlwain, 1989-90

Most games with three or more goals
5—Teemu Selanne, 1992-93

Most shots
387—Teemu Selanne, 1992-93

GOALTENDERS

Most games
67—Bob Essensa, 1992-93

Most minutes
3,855—Bob Essensa, 1992-93

Most goals allowed
227—Bob Essensa, 1992-93

Lowest goals-against average
2.88—Bob Essensa, 1991-92

Most shutouts
5—Bob Essensa, 1991-92

Most wins
33—Brian Hayward, 1984-85
        Bob Essensa, 1992-93

Most losses
30—Bob Essensa, 1993-94

Most ties
8—Doug Soetaert, 1981-82

FRANCHISE LEADERS

FORWARDS/DEFENSEMEN

Games
Thomas Steen 950
Dale Hawerchuk 713
Doug Smail 691
Randy Carlyle 564
Teppo Numminen 547

Goals
Dale Hawerchuk 379
Thomas Steen 264
Paul MacLean 248
Doug Smail 189
Morris Lukowich 168

Assists
Thomas Steen 553
Dale Hawerchuk 550
Paul MacLean 270
Fredrik Olausson 249
Dave Babych 248

Points
Dale Hawerchuk 929
Thomas Steen 817
Paul MacLean 518
Doug Smail 397
Laurie Boschman 379

Penalty minutes
Laurie Boschman 1338
Keith Tkachuk 792
Jim Kyte 772
Tim Watters 760
Thomas Steen 753

GOALTENDERS

Games
Bob Essensa 281
Brian Hayward 165
Doug Soetaert 130
Daniel Berthiaume 120
Pokey Reddick 117

Shutouts
Bob Essensa 14
Daniel Berthiaume 4
Markus Mattsson 3
Stephane Beauregard 2
Dan Bouchard 2
Doug Soetaert 2
Ed Staniowski 2

**Goals-against average
(2400 minutes minimum)**
Nikolai Khabibulin 3.22
Bob Essensa 3.38
Stephane Beauregard 3.48
Daniel Berthiaume 3.63
Pokey Reddick 3.73

Wins
Bob Essensa 116
Brian Hayward 63
Daniel Berthiaume 50
Doug Soetaert 50
Pokey Reddick 41

MINOR LEAGUES

American Hockey League

International Hockey League

East Coast Hockey League

Central Hockey League

United Hockey League

AMERICAN HOCKEY LEAGUE

LEAGUE OFFICE

Chairman of the board
Jack A. Butterfield
President/CEO and treasurer
David A. Andrews
General counsel
Joe Rodio
Director, finance and administration
Drew Griffin
Director of hockey operations
Jim Mill

Dir. of corporate sales & bus. dev.
Ross Yanco
Exec. assistant to the president
Liz Sylvia
Coordinator of event mgmt. & licensing
Sean Lavoine
Coordinator of marketing services
Megan Rowe
Dir. of communications & media rel.
Bret Stothart

Address
1 Monarch Place
Springfield, MA 01144
Phone
413-781-2030
Fax
413-733-4767

TEAMS

ALBANY RIVER RATS

Chief executive officer
Garen Szableski
Head coach
John Cunniff
Home ice
Pepsi Arena
Address
51 South Pearl St.
Albany, NY 12207
Seating capacity
6,500
Phone
518-487-2244
FAX
518-487-2248

BRIDGEPORT SOUND TIGERS

General manager
Gordie Clark
Head coach
Steve Stirling
Home ice
Bridgeport Arena
Address
855 Main Street
Bridgeport, CT 06604
Seating capacity
8,800
Phone
203-334-4625
FAX
203-333-1719

CHICAGO WOLVES

General manager
Kevin Cheveldayoff
Head coach
John Anderson
Home ice
Allstate Arena
Address
2301 Ravine Way
Glenview, IL 60025
Seating capacity
16,682
Phone
847-724-4625
FAX
847-724-1652

CINCINNATI MIGHTY DUCKS

General manager
David McNab
Head coach
Mike Babcock
Home ice
Cincinnati Gardens
Address
2250 Seymour Ave.
Cincinnati, OH 45212
Seating capacity
10,326
Phone
513-351-3999
FAX
513-351-5898

CLEVELAND BARONS

General manager
Wayne Thomas
Head coach
Roy Sommer
Home ice
Gund Arena
Address
One Center Ice
200 Huron Road
Cleveland, OH 44115
Seating capacity
19,941
Phone
216-420-0000
FAX
216-420-2500

GRAND RAPIDS GRIFFINS

General manager
Bob McNamara
Head coach
Bruce Cassidy
Home ice
Van Andel Arena
Address
130 W. Fulton
Grand Rapids, MI 49503
Seating capacity
10,834
Phone
616-774-4585
FAX
616-336-5464

HAMILTON BULLDOGS

President
Cary Kaplan
Head coach
Claude Julien
Home ice
Copps Coliseum
Address
85 York Blvd.
Hamilton, Ont. L8R 3L4
Seating capacity
8,919
Phone
905-529-8500
FAX
905-529-1188

HARTFORD WOLFPACK

Senior vice president
Don Maloney
Head coach
John Paddock
Home ice
Hartford Civic Center
Address
196 Trumbull Street
Hartford, CT 06103
Seating capacity
15,635
Phone
860-246-7825
FAX
860-240-7618

HERSHEY BEARS

General manager
Doug Yingst
Head coach
Mike Foligno
Home ice
Hersheypark Arena
Address
P.O. Box 866
Hershey, PA 17033
Seating capacity
7,225
Phone
717-534-3380
FAX
717-534-3383

– 256 –

HOUSTON AEROS

General manager
Dave Barr
Head coach
Todd McLellan
Home ice
Compaq Center
Address
3100 Wilcrest Drive
Houston, TX 77042
Seating capacity
11,207
Phone
713-974-7825
FAX
713-361-7900

LOWELL LOCK MONSTERS

Executive v.p./general manager
Tom Rowe
Head coach
Ron Smith
Home ice
Tsongas Arena
Address
300 Arcand Dr.
Lowell, MA 01852
Seating capacity
6,400
Phone
978-458-7825
FAX
978-453-8452

MANCHESTER MONARCHS

President
Jeff Eisenberg
Head coach
Bruce Boudreau
Home Ice
Manchester Civic Center
Address
832 Elm Street
Manchester, NH 03101
Seating capacity
10,000
Phone
603-626-7825
FAX
603 626 7022

MANITOBA MOOSE

President
Mark Chipman
Head coach
Stan Smyl
Home ice
Winnipeg Arena
Address
1430 Maroons Road
Winnipeg, Manitoba, Canada R3G 0L5
Seating capacity
10,842
Phone
204-987-7825
FAX
204-896-6673

MILWAUKEE ADMIRALS

General manager and executive v.p.
Phil Wittliff

Head coach
Al Sims
Home ice
Bradley Center
Address
1001 North Fourth St.
Milwaukee, WI 53203
Seating capacity
18,394
Phone
414-227-0550
FAX
414-227-0568

NORFOLK ADMIRALS

General manager
Al MacIsaac
Head coach
Trent Yawney
Home ice
Norfolk Scope
Address
2181 Landstown Road
Virginia Beach, VA 23456
Seating capacity
8,974
Phone
757-430-8873
FAX
757-430-8803

PHILADELPHIA PHANTOMS

Chief operating officer
Frank Miceli
Head coach
John Stevens
Home ice
First Union Spectrum
Address
3601 S. Broad Street
Philadelphia, PA 19148
Seating capacity
17,380
Phone
215-465-4522
FAX
215-952-5245

PORTLAND PIRATES

President
Brian Petrovek
Head coach
Glen Hanlon
Home ice
Cumberland County Civic Center
Address
85 Free St.
Portland, ME 04101
Seating capacity
6,746
Phone
207-828-4665
FAX
207-773-3278

PROVIDENCE BRUINS

Chief executive officer
Ed Anderson
Head coach
Bill Armstrong
Home ice
Providence Civic Center

Address
1 LaSalle Square
Providence, RI 02903
Seating capacity
11,605
Phone
401-273-5000
FAX
401-273-5004

QUEBEC CITADELLES

General manager
Raymond Bolduc
Head coach
Eric Lavigne
Home ice
Colisee de Quebec
Address
250 Hamel Blvd.
Quebec City, Que. G1L 5A7
Seating capacity
15,399
Phone
418-525-5333
FAX
418-525-5057

ROCHESTER AMERICANS

General manager
Jody Gage
Head coach
Randy Cunneyworth
Home ice
Blue Cross Arena
Address
One War Memorial Square
Rochester, NY 14614
Seating capacity
11,200
Phone
716-454-5335
FAX
716-454-3954

SAINT JOHN FLAMES

General manager
Stew MacDonald
Head coach
Jim Playfair
Home ice
Harbour Station
Address
P.O. Box 4040, Station B
Saint John, NB E2M 5E6
Seating capacity
6,153
Phone
506-635-2637
FAX
506-633-4625

ST. JOHN'S MAPLE LEAFS

Director of operations
Glenn Stanford
Head coach
Lou Crawford
Home ice
St. John's Memorial Stadium
Address
49 Elizabeth Ave., Suite 302
St. John's, Newfoundland A1A 1W9

Seating capacity
3,765
Phone
709-726-1010
FAX
709-726-1511

SPRINGFIELD FALCONS
President
Bruce Landon
Head coach
Marc Potvin
Home ice
Springfield Civic Center
Address
P.O. Box 3190
Springfield, MA 01101
Seating capacity
7,452
Phone
413-739-3344
FAX
413-739-3389

SYRACUSE CRUNCH
General manager/chief financial officer
Vance Lederman
Head coach
Gary Agnew
Home ice
Onondaga County War Memorial

Address
800 South State St.
Syracuse, NY 13202
Seating capacity
6,230
Phone
315-473-4444
FAX
315-473-4449

UTAH GRIZZLIES
President
Tim Mouser
Head coach
Don Hay
Home ice
The "E" Center
Address
3200 S. Decker Lake Dr.
West Valley City, UT 84119
Seating capacity
10,207
Phone
801-988-8000
FAX
801-988-8001

WILKES-BARRE/SCRANTON PENGUINS
President
Jeff Barrett

Head coach
Glenn Patrick
Home ice
First Union Arena at Casey Plaza
Address
60 Public Square, Suite 150
Wilkes-Barre, PA 18701
Seating capacity
8,457
Phone
570-208-7367
FAX
570-208-5432

WORCESTER ICECATS
Executive vice president
Peter Ricciardi
Head coach
Don Granato
Home ice
Worcester's Centrum Centre
Address
303 Main St.
Worcester, MA 01608
Seating capacity
12,316
Phone
508-798-5400
FAX
508-799-5267

2000-01 REGULAR SEASON
FINAL STANDINGS

EASTERN CONFERENCE

CANADIAN DIVISION

Team	G	W	L	T	OTL	Pts.	GF	GA
Saint John	80	44	24	7	5	100	269	210
Quebec	80	41	32	3	4	89	264	252
St. John's	80	35	35	8	2	80	247	244
Hamilton	80	28	41	6	5	67	227	281

NEW ENGLAND DIVISION

Team	G	W	L	T	OTL	Pts.	GF	GA
Worcester	80	48	20	9	3	108	264	205
Hartford	80	40	26	8	6	94	263	247
Providence	80	35	31	10	4	84	245	242
Lowell	80	35	35	5	5	80	225	244
Portland	80	34	40	4	2	74	250	280
Springfield	80	29	37	8	6	72	253	280

WESTERN CONFERENCE

SOUTHERN DIVISION

Team	G	W	L	T	OTL	Pts.	GF	GA
Kentucky	80	42	25	12	1	97	273	212
Cincinnati	80	41	26	9	4	95	254	240
Norfolk	80	36	26	13	5	90	241	208
Louisville	80	21	51	5	3	50	200	285

MID-ATLANTIC DIVISION

Team	G	W	L	T	OTL	Pts.	GF	GA
Rochester	80	46	22	9	3	104	224	192
Wilkes-Barre	80	36	33	9	2	83	252	248
Syracuse	80	33	30	12	5	83	235	254
Philadelphia	80	36	34	5	5	82	246	244
Hershey	80	34	39	4	3	75	216	234
Albany	80	30	40	6	4	70	216	262

INDIVIDUAL LEADERS

Goals: Brad Smyth, Hartford (50)
Assists: Derek Armstrong, Hartford (69)
Points: Derek Armstrong, Hartford (101)
Penalty minutes: Jody Shelley, Syracuse (357)
Goaltending average: Dwayne Roloson, Worcester (2.17)
Shutouts: Dwayne Roloson, Worcester (6)

TOP SCORERS

	Games	G	A	Pts.
Derek Armstrong, Hartford	75	32	69	101
Jean-Guy Trudel, Springfield	80	34	65	99
Ryan Kraft, Kentucky	77	38	50	88
Mark Greig, Philadelphia	74	31	57	88
Brad Smyth, Hartford	77	50	29	79
Bill Bowler, Syracuse	72	21	58	79
Mikael Samuelsson, Kentucky	66	32	46	78
Marty Murray, Saint John	56	24	52	76
Jim Montgomery, Kentucky	55	22	52	74
Steve Bancroft, Kentucky	80	23	50	73
Mark Freer, Philadelphia	76	31	41	72
Paul Healey, Hamilton	79	39	32	71
Peter Ferraro, Providence	78	26	45	71
Michel Picard, Philadelphia	72	31	39	70
Eric Boguniecki, Lou.-Wor.	73	30	40	70
Mark Murphy, Portland	76	29	41	70
Bobby House, St. John's	65	36	33	69
Jason Williams, Cincinnati	76	24	45	69
Paul Brousseau, Louisville	73	29	39	68
Jeff Farkas, St. John's	77	28	40	68

ALBANY RIVER RATS

SCORING

	Games	G	A	Pts.	PIM
Chris Ferraro	74	24	42	66	111
Pierre Dagenais	69	34	28	62	52
Sylvain Cloutier	79	16	35	51	115
Jiri Bicek	73	12	29	41	73
Richard Rochefort	75	16	24	40	18
Sasha Goc	55	10	29	39	49
Josef Boumedienne	79	8	29	37	117
Mike Jefferson	69	19	15	34	195
Ed Ward	65	14	19	33	71
Alexander Zinevich	61	10	17	27	20
Stanislav Gron	61	16	9	25	19
Andre Lakos	51	1	20	21	29
Mike Rupp	71	10	10	20	63
Willie Mitchell	41	3	13	16	94
Jason Lehoux	52	8	7	15	101
Maxim Birbraer	50	7	6	13	24
Daryl Andrews	80	2	8	10	49
Henrik Rehnberg	80	1	8	9	78
Carlyle Lewis	68	1	7	8	175
Mike Commodore	41	2	5	7	59
Geordie Kinnear	14	1	1	2	48
Lucas Nehrling	33	1	1	2	92
Bryan Duce	11	0	1	1	4
Jean-Francois Damphousse (g)	55	0	1	1	10
Pascal Gasse (goalie)	1	0	0	0	0
Corey Hirsch (goalie)	4	0	0	0	2
Frederic Henry (goalie)	32	0	0	0	19
Rob Skrlac	38	0	0	0	105

GOALTENDING

	Gms.	Min.	W	L	T	G	SO	Avg.
Pascal Gasse	1	25	0	0	0	0	0	0.00
J.-F. Damphousse	55	2963	24	23	3	141	1	2.86
Frederic Henry	32	1651	6	17	3	99	1	3.60
Corey Hirsch	4	199	0	4	0	19	0	5.72

CINCINNATI MIGHTY DUCKS

SCORING

	Games	G	A	Pts.	PIM
Jason Williams	76	24	45	69	48
Bob Wren	70	20	47	67	103
Chris O'Sullivan	60	9	40	49	31
Yuri Butsayev	54	29	17	46	26
Andy McDonald	46	15	25	40	21
Antti Aalto	40	14	26	40	39
Jay Legault	57	18	19	37	44
B.J. Young	42	14	22	36	111
Toivo Suursoo	51	14	12	26	37
Torrey DiRoberto	67	11	13	24	86
Sean Avery	58	8	15	23	304
Marc Chouinard	32	10	9	19	4
Petr Tenkrat	25	9	9	18	24
Jesse Wallin	76	2	15	17	50
Maxim Balmochnykh	65	6	9	15	45
Dwayne Zinger	68	6	9	15	120
Jarrett Smith	46	5	9	14	28
Kevin Sawyer	41	2	12	14	211
Marc Rodgers	32	7	5	12	53
Cam Severson	20	4	7	11	60
Antti-Jussi Niemi	36	3	8	11	26
Peter Podhradsky	59	4	5	9	27
Yan Golubovsky	28	4	4	8	16
Alexei Tezikov	13	2	6	8	8
Jiri Fischer	18	2	6	8	22
Jonas Ronnqvist	13	3	2	5	6
Sergei Vyshedkevich	17	3	2	5	2
Dean Malkoc	65	1	4	5	232
John Wikstrom	43	3	1	4	35
Doug Nolan	13	0	4	4	6
Jason Lawmaster	12	2	1	3	19
Todd Gill	2	0	1	1	2

	Games	G	A	Pts.	PIM
Justin Harney	5	0	1	1	0
Jean-Sebastien Giguere (goalie)	23	0	1	1	21
Gregg Naumenko (goalie)	39	0	1	1	6
Ryan Barnes	1	0	0	0	7
Martin Engren (goalie)	1	0	0	0	0
Alexandre Jacques	1	0	0	0	0
Tomas Kopecky	1	0	0	0	0
Tom Lawson (goalie)	1	0	0	0	0
Brian Leitza (goalie)	1	0	0	0	0
Paxton Schafer (goalie)	1	0	0	0	0
Shawn Timm (goalie)	1	0	0	0	0
Brad Guzda (goalie)	2	0	0	0	0
Hugh Hamilton	2	0	0	0	0
Judd Lambert (goalie)	2	0	0	0	0
Aren Miller (goalie)	2	0	0	0	0
Tim Verbeek	2	0	0	0	4
Ryan Hoople (goalie)	3	0	0	0	0
Scott Langkow (goalie)	15	0	0	0	0

GOALTENDING

	Gms.	Min.	W	L	T	G	SO	Avg.
Paxton Schafer	1	16	0	0	0	0	0	0.00
Brian Leitza	1	8	0	0	0	0	0	0.00
Shawn Timm	1	1	0	0	0	0	0	0.00
J.-S. Giguere	23	1306	12	7	2	53	0	2.43
Tom Lawson	1	23	0	0	0	1	0	2.58
Gregg Naumenko	39	2079	20	12	3	101	2	2.91
Brad Guzda	2	120	1	1	0	6	0	3.00
Scott Langkow	15	838	6	4	4	44	1	3.15
Ryan Hoople	3	182	2	1	0	10	0	3.29
Judd Lambert	2	102	0	2	0	7	0	4.11
Martin Engren	1	58	0	1	0	4	0	4.12
Aren Miller	2	110	0	2	0	9	0	4.92

HAMILTON BULLDOGS

SCORING

	Games	G	A	Pts.	PIM
Paul Healey	79	39	32	71	34
Peter Sarno	79	19	46	65	64
Jason Chimera	78	29	25	54	93
Michel Riesen	69	26	28	54	14
Brian Swanson	40	18	29	47	20
Chad Hinz	78	13	22	35	30
Shawn Horcoff	24	10	18	28	19
Fernando Pisani	52	12	13	25	28
Scott Ferguson	42	3	18	21	79
Rory Fitzpatrick	34	3	17	20	29
Brian Urick	50	11	8	19	22
Alain Nasreddine	74	4	14	18	164
Brad Norton	46	3	15	18	114
Maxim Spiridonov	62	15	2	17	62
Michael Henrich	73	5	10	15	36
Ryan Risidore	48	2	12	14	51
Terran Sandwith	59	1	12	13	154
Chris Hajt	70	0	10	10	48
Mark Deyell	17	4	5	9	10
Todd Robinson	15	2	7	9	0
Lloyd Shaw	50	1	7	8	192
Andrew Long	17	0	6	6	8
Alex Henry	56	2	3	5	87
Chris Albert	32	0	5	5	109
Martin Laitre	44	1	3	4	152
Kurtis Drummond	20	0	4	4	16
Kevin Mitchell	8	0	3	3	2
Josh Green	2	2	0	2	2
Jason Morgan (goalie)	11	2	0	2	10
Patrick Cote	16	0	1	1	61
Chris Madden	26	0	1	1	2
Jared Smyth	2	0	0	0	10
Joel Theriault	2	0	0	0	0
Alex Fomitchev (goalie)	6	0	0	0	0
Devin Hartnell	6	0	0	0	14
Eric Heffler (goalie)	19	0	0	0	0
Joaquin Gage (goalie)	37	0	0	0	2

GOALTENDING

	Gms.	Min.	W	L	T	G	SO	Avg.
Alex Fomitchev.......	6	316	2	2	1	14	0	2.66
Chris Madden.......	26	1345	9	11	3	70	0	3.12
Joaquin Gage.........	37	2129	12	22	2	118	0	3.33
Eric Heffler.............	19	1037	5	11	0	68	0	3.93

HARTFORD WOLFPACK

SCORING

	Games	G	A	Pts.	PIM
Derek Armstrong	75	32	69	101	73
Brad Smyth............................	77	50	29	79	110
Ken Gernander........................	80	22	27	49	39
Mike Mottau...........................	61	10	33	43	45
Drew Bannister.......................	73	9	30	39	143
Burke Henry............................	80	8	30	38	133
Tony Tuzzolino	47	12	23	35	136
Mike Harder...........................	36	10	19	29	27
Terry Virtue...........................	71	5	24	29	166
Boyd Kane.............................	56	11	17	28	81
David Duerden	43	16	9	25	10
Jeff Ulmer.............................	48	11	14	25	34
Jason Doig.............................	52	4	20	24	178
Johan Witehall.......................	19	10	8	18	19
Chris Kenady..........................	42	5	12	17	58
Todd Hall..............................	79	5	12	17	13
Michal Grosek.........................	12	8	7	15	12
Jeff Toms..............................	12	4	9	13	2
Bert Robertsson......................	27	7	5	12	27
Manny Malhotra.......................	28	5	6	11	69
Brad Mehalko..........................	27	4	7	11	60
Brandon Dietrich......................	44	3	8	11	11
Francois Fortier.......................	28	2	6	8	8
Stefan Cherneski.....................	28	1	7	8	43
Richard Scott..........................	64	2	5	7	320
Ryan Tobler...........................	13	1	5	6	71
Wes Jarvis.............................	20	1	2	3	24
Jason Dawe	4	2	0	2	2
Ryan Bast..............................	50	1	1	2	146
Tomas Kloucek	21	0	2	2	44
Vitali Yeremeyev (goalie)	36	0	2	2	4
Garett Bembridge.....................	7	1	0	1	0
Mathieu Benoit........................	9	1	0	1	0
Dale Purinton..........................	11	0	1	1	75
Johan Holmqvist (goalie)	43	0	1	1	4
Martin Richter.........................	1	0	0	0	0
Bryce Wandler (goalie)..............	1	0	0	0	0
Stefan Rivard	2	0	0	0	12
Jeff Brown	3	0	0	0	2
Jason LaBarbera (goalie)...........	4	0	0	0	0
Jean-Francois Labbe (goalie)	8	0	0	0	0
Benjamin Carpentier	25	0	0	0	63

GOALTENDING

	Gms.	Min.	W	L	T	G	SO	Avg.
Bryce Wandler	1	29	0	0	0	1	0	2.04
Johan Holmqvist.....	43	2305	19	14	4	111	2	2.89
Vitali Yeremeyev.....	36	1977	16	15	3	98	2	2.97
J.-Francois Labbe ...	8	394	4	2	1	20	0	3.04
Jason LaBarbera ...	4	156	1	1	0	12	0	4.61

HERSHEY BEARS

SCORING

	Games	G	A	Pts.	PIM
Kelly Fairchild........................	70	23	40	63	68
Rob Shearer...........................	73	18	34	52	64
Brad Larsen...........................	67	21	25	46	93
Mike Craig.............................	57	21	22	43	73
Brian Willsie..........................	48	18	23	41	20
Joel Prpic.............................	74	16	23	39	128
Yevgeny Lazarev	80	17	21	38	50
Yuri Babenko..........................	71	17	18	35	80
Steffon Walby.........................	69	12	21	33	48
Rick Berry.............................	48	6	17	23	87
Alex Riazantsev.......................	66	5	18	23	26
Ville Nieminen........................	28	10	11	21	48

	Games	G	A	Pts.	PIM
Nick Bootland	71	6	8	14	110
Dan Smith..............................	58	2	12	14	34
Ben Storey.............................	58	2	12	14	71
Bryan Muir.............................	26	5	8	13	50
K.C. Timmons.........................	39	3	9	12	69
Matt Scorsune.........................	57	3	9	12	25
Brian White............................	75	2	9	11	44
Olaf Kjenstad..........................	9	3	1	4	4
Duane Harmer.........................	15	2	2	4	14
Kelly Perrault..........................	7	1	2	3	12
Vlad Serov	7	1	2	3	2
Garry Gulash	14	1	2	3	92
Stewart Malgunas.....................	25	0	2	2	39
Steve Parsons.........................	30	1	0	1	98
Bruce Richardson	4	0	1	1	4
John Tripp.............................	5	0	1	1	0
Terry Ryan............................	8	0	1	1	36
Brent Thompson	15	0	1	1	44
Philippe Sauve (goalie).............	42	0	1	1	17
Frederic Cassivi (goalie)............	49	0	1	1	2
Frederic Bouchard	1	0	0	0	2
Kiley Hill..............................	1	0	0	0	0
Dominic Maltais	1	0	0	0	0
Argris Saviels.........................	1	0	0	0	0
Dana Stover	1	0	0	0	0
Martin Villeneuve (goalie)..........	1	0	0	0	0
Hugues Gervais	2	0	0	0	2
Raitis Ivanans	2	0	0	0	0
Mark Major	2	0	0	0	10
Brent Bilodeau	2	0	0	0	0
Mikhail Kuleshov......................	3	0	0	0	4
Jason Ulmer...........................	3	0	0	0	2
Sanny Lindstrom	24	0	0	0	61

GOALTENDING

	Gms.	Min.	W	L	T	G	SO	Avg.
Martin Villeneuve	1	1	0	0	0	0	0	0.00
Philippe Sauve	42	2182	17	18	1	100	3	2.75
Frederic Cassivi....	49	2620	17	24	3	124	2	2.84

KENTUCKY THOROUGHBLADES

SCORING

	Games	G	A	Pts.	PIM
Ryan Kraft............................	77	38	50	88	36
Mikael Samuelsson	66	32	46	78	58
Jim Montgomery	55	22	52	74	44
Steve Bancroft........................	80	23	50	73	162
Jonathan Cheechoo	75	32	34	66	63
Chris Lipsett..........................	71	21	34	55	45
Jarrett Deuling	54	10	29	39	61
Larry Courville	71	20	16	36	112
Dave MacIsaac........................	73	9	24	33	178
Zoltan Batovsky.......................	79	9	19	28	36
Miroslav Zalesak	60	14	11	25	26
Andy Lundbohm	63	7	15	22	41
Adam Colagiacomo....................	67	10	11	21	48
Robert Jindrich........................	62	4	16	20	36
Greg Andrusak........................	58	5	14	19	63
Matt Bradley..........................	22	5	8	13	16
Eric LaPlante..........................	62	5	8	13	181
Mark Smith............................	6	2	6	8	23
Robert Mulick	71	0	6	6	55
Christian Gosselin	42	2	3	5	145
Rob Davison	72	0	4	4	230
Adam Nittel............................	40	2	0	2	203
Chad Dameworth	17	1	1	2	8
Tim Lovell.............................	8	0	2	2	19
Mikka Kiprusoff (goalie)	36	0	2	2	2
Vesa Toskala (goalie)................	44	0	1	1	6
Chris Aldous	1	0	0	0	0
Jeff Sullivan	1	0	0	0	4
Dan Vandermeer	1	0	0	0	0
Kam White	3	0	0	0	6
Chad Ackerman	4	0	0	0	0
Jan Vodrazka	6	0	0	0	31
Terry Friesen (goalie)	7	0	0	0	4

GOALTENDING

	Gms.	Min.	W	L	T	G	SO	Avg.
Miikka Kiprusoff	36	2038	19	9	6	76	2	2.24
Vesa Toskala	44	2466	22	13	5	114	2	2.77
Terry Friesen	7	356	1	4	1	17	1	2.87

LOUISVILLE PANTHERS
SCORING

	Games	G	A	Pts.	PIM
Paul Brousseau	73	29	39	68	21
David Emma	55	22	28	50	63
Mike Harder	38	13	24	37	8
Travis Brigley	49	14	21	35	34
Denis Shvidki	34	15	11	26	20
Ryan Jardine	77	12	14	26	38
Eric Beaudoin	71	15	10	25	78
Eric Boguniecki	28	13	12	25	56
Brad Ference	52	3	21	24	200
David Duerden	34	9	14	23	8
Peter Ratchuk	64	5	13	18	85
Andrej Podkonicky	41	6	10	16	31
Evgeny Korolev	36	2	14	16	68
Tim Findlay	27	3	11	14	9
Yan Golubovsky	30	1	12	13	36
Serge Payer	32	6	6	12	15
Mike Cirillo	61	4	8	12	146
Ivan Novoseltsev	34	2	10	12	8
Brent Thompson	59	1	9	10	170
Maxim Galanov	9	4	5	9	11
Rocky Thompson	55	3	5	8	193
Paul Harvey	34	2	5	7	37
Kyle Rossiter	78	2	5	7	110
Lance Ward	35	3	2	5	78
Doug Schueller	11	1	4	5	11
Joey Tetarenko	29	1	4	5	74
Dan Boyle	6	0	5	5	12
Chris Kenady	20	2	1	3	36
Roger Trudeau	23	2	1	3	6
Mike Green	24	2	1	3	4
Nick Smith	23	1	2	3	25
Remi Royer	18	1	1	2	50
Mike Wilson	4	0	2	2	5
Simon Olivier	3	1	0	1	2
Steve Leach	2	0	1	1	0
Chris Allen	7	0	1	1	4
Michel Periard	7	0	1	1	0
John Jakopin	8	0	1	1	21
Ryan Bach (goalie)	30	0	1	1	0
Richard Shulmistra (goalie)	1	0	0	0	0
Christian Soucy (goalie)	1	0	0	0	2
Alex Dumas	2	0	0	0	0
Roberto Luongo (goalie)	3	0	0	0	0
Kevin St. Pierre (goalie)	3	0	0	0	0
Chris Eade	4	0	0	0	0
Tyler Prosofsky	6	0	0	0	2
Maxime Gingras (goalie)	9	0	0	0	2
Eric Godard	45	0	0	0	132
Sean Gauthier (goalie)	54	0	0	0	17

GOALTENDING

	Gms.	Min.	W	L	T	G	SO	Avg.
Ryan Bach	30	1297	6	13	1	66	1	3.05
Roberto Luongo	3	178	1	2	0	10	0	3.38
Maxime Gingras	9	372	2	3	0	22	0	3.55
Sean Gauthier	54	2725	11	33	4	165	2	3.63
Kevin St. Pierre	3	128	1	1	0	8	0	3.75
Richard Shulmistra	1	60	0	1	0	4	0	4.00
Christian Soucy	1	60	0	1	0	5	0	5.00

LOWELL LOCK MONSTERS
SCORING

	Games	G	A	Pts.	PIM
Marko Tuomainen	59	28	39	67	73
Jeff Daw	65	28	28	56	33
Chris Schmidt	79	21	32	53	84
Brad Chartrand	72	17	34	51	44

	Games	G	A	Pts.	PIM
Rich Brennan	69	10	31	41	146
Andreas Lilja	61	7	29	36	149
Joe Corvo	77	10	23	33	31
David Hymovitz	60	14	15	29	52
Jason Krog	26	11	16	27	6
Nate Miller	80	15	10	25	61
Mike Pudlick	57	7	13	20	39
Stewart Bodtker	33	6	14	20	26
Peter LeBoutillier	70	6	13	19	175
Eric Belanger	13	8	10	18	4
Reggie Berg	30	6	7	13	22
Kevin Baker	26	6	5	11	18
Greg Phillips	33	5	5	10	33
Richard Seeley	55	2	8	10	102
Juraj Kolnik	25	2	6	8	18
Mike Omicioli	10	1	5	6	2
Stefan Rivard	14	2	3	5	15
Kip Brennan	23	2	3	5	117
Harold Hersh	22	3	1	4	20
Glenn Stewart	10	2	2	4	2
Mathieu Biron	22	1	3	4	17
Branislav Mezei	20	0	3	3	28
Chad Power	6	1	1	2	0
Duane Harmer	14	1	1	2	10
Jerred Smithson	24	1	1	2	10
Joe Rullier	63	1	1	2	162
Paul Spadafora	2	1	0	1	0
Jason Blake	2	0	1	1	2
Kam White	2	0	1	1	0
Brendan Brooks	5	0	1	1	17
Tomas Vlasak	5	0	1	1	5
Quinn Fair	8	0	1	1	8
Petr Mika	13	0	1	1	7
Ray Schultz	13	0	1	1	33
Eric Veilleux	15	0	1	1	22
Andre Payette	23	0	1	1	94
Tom Ashe	1	0	0	0	2
Francois Drainville	1	0	0	0	0
Robert Ferraris	1	0	0	0	0
Sean Molina	1	0	0	0	0
Andrew Dale	2	0	0	0	0
Benoit Morin	2	0	0	0	0
Greg Callahan	3	0	0	0	4
Steve Cheredaryk	3	0	0	0	2
Louis Dumont	3	0	0	0	0
Stephane Fiset (goalie)	3	0	0	0	0
Mike Hall	3	0	0	0	2
Martin Lapointe	3	0	0	0	0
Terry Lindgren	3	0	0	0	7
James Patterson	3	0	0	0	2
Cody Bowtell	5	0	0	0	2
Mitch Fritz	5	0	0	0	20
Mike Nicholishen	5	0	0	0	4
Alexei Volkov (goalie)	5	0	0	0	0
Brad Essex	6	0	0	0	12
Steve Passmore (goalie)	6	0	0	0	2
Steve O'Brien	7	0	0	0	0
Travis Scott (goalie)	34	0	0	0	17
Marcel Cousineau (goalie)	37	0	0	0	29

GOALTENDING

	Gms.	Min.	W	L	T	G	SO	Avg.
Travis Scott	34	1977	16	15	1	83	2	2.52
Marcel Cousineau	37	2135	15	20	2	101	1	2.84
Stephane Fiset	3	190	1	0	2	9	0	2.84
Steve Passmore	6	334	2	4	0	24	0	4.32
Alexei Volkov	5	202	1	1	0	16	0	4.75

NORFOLK ADMIRALS
SCORING

	Games	G	A	Pts.	PIM
Casey Hankinson	69	30	21	51	74
Marty Wilford	80	7	41	48	102
Josef Marha	60	18	28	46	44
Reto Von Arx	49	16	26	42	28
Mark Bell	61	15	27	42	126

	Games	G	A	Pts.	PIM
Matt Henderson	78	14	24	38	80
Ajay Baines	73	18	18	36	92
Nolan Baumgartner	63	5	28	33	75
Mike Souza	75	14	17	31	44
Ty Jones	64	11	17	28	114
Nathan Perrott	73	11	17	28	268
Kyle Calder	37	12	15	27	21
Dmitri Tolkunov	78	5	18	23	93
Geoff Peters	73	11	10	21	48
Aaron Downey	67	6	15	21	234
Blair Atcheynum	37	12	8	20	16
Valeri Zelepukin	29	10	9	19	28
Mark Janssens	28	3	9	12	41
Steve Dubinsky	14	6	5	11	4
Jeff Paul	59	5	6	11	171
Chris McAlpine	13	4	7	11	6
Arne Ramholt	62	3	8	11	25
Steve Poapst	37	1	8	9	14
Jeff Helperl	45	1	8	9	82
Chris Herperger	9	1	4	5	9
Steve McCarthy	7	0	4	4	2
Rumun Ndur	21	1	2	3	93
Jeff Maund (goalie)	42	0	3	3	19
Jeff Sproat	6	1	0	1	2
Quintin Laing	10	0	1	1	10
Jason Ialongo	1	0	0	0	0
Erasmo Saltarelli (goalie)	1	0	0	0	0
Travis Smith	1	0	0	0	0
Bobby Russell	2	0	0	0	0
Adam Calder	3	0	0	0	2
Robbie Tallas (goalie)	6	0	0	0	0
Jean-Paul Tessier	9	0	0	0	6
Michel LaRocque (goalie)	35	0	0	0	10

GOALTENDING

	Gms.	Min.	W	L	T	G	SO	Avg.
Erasmo Saltarelli	1	60	1	0	1	0	1	1.00
Robbie Tallas	6	333	2	2	2	12	0	2.16
Jeff Maund	42	2385	20	12	7	94	3	2.36
Michel Larocque	35	2087	13	17	4	96	2	2.76

PHILADELPHIA PHANTOMS

SCORING

	Games	G	A	Pts.	PIM
Mark Greig	74	31	57	88	98
Mark Freer	76	31	41	72	42
Michel Picard	72	31	39	70	22
Kirby Law	78	27	34	61	150
Derek Plante	57	18	35	53	19
Vaclav Pletka	71	20	21	41	51
Tomas Divisek	45	10	22	32	33
Brad Tiley	56	11	19	30	10
Steve Washburn	46	12	16	28	52
Mikhail Chernov	50	8	12	20	32
John Slaney	25	6	11	17	10
Bruno St. Jacques	45	1	16	17	83
Chris Heron	57	8	8	16	12
Dan Peters	73	2	14	16	71
Petr Hubacek	62	3	9	12	29
Jason Beckett	56	2	10	12	107
Francis Lessard	64	3	7	10	330
Rob Murray	46	3	6	9	65
Joe Dipenta	71	3	5	8	65
Jesse Boulerice	60	3	4	7	256
Chris Bogas	15	1	6	7	8
Matt Herr	11	2	4	6	18
Dean Melanson	15	1	4	5	48
Matt Zultek	16	1	4	5	6
Steve McLaren	48	3	1	4	177
Francis Belanger	13	1	3	4	32
P.J. Stock	9	1	2	3	37
Sean Ritchlin	11	2	0	2	6
Neil Little (goalie)	58	0	2	2	60
Ruslan Fedotenko	8	1	0	1	8
Sergei Skrobot	5	0	1	1	0
Cail MacLean	9	0	1	1	4

	Games	G	A	Pts.	PIM
Todd Fedoruk	14	0	1	1	49
Arpad Mihaly	2	0	0	0	0
Dan Murphy (goalie)	2	0	0	0	0
Maxime Ouellet (goalie)	2	0	0	0	0
Roman Cechmanek (goalie)	3	0	0	0	17
Russ Hewson	5	0	0	0	0
Brian Regan (goalie)	30	0	0	0	2

GOALTENDING

	Gms.	Min.	W	L	T	G	SO	Avg.
Roman Cechmanek	3	160	1	1	0	3	0	1.12
Maxime Ouellet	2	86	1	0	0	4	0	2.78
Neil Little	58	3117	22	27	4	148	2	2.85
Brian Regan	30	1386	12	9	1	73	2	3.16
Dan Murphy	2	80	0	2	0	9	0	6.75

PORTLAND PIRATES

SCORING

	Games	G	A	Pts.	PIM
Mark Murphy	76	29	41	70	92
Glen Metropolit	51	25	42	67	59
Jeff Nelson	80	18	37	55	63
Terry Yake	55	11	38	49	47
Matt Pettinger	64	19	17	36	92
Derek Bekar	58	19	16	35	49
Matt Herr	40	21	13	34	58
Brad Church	61	14	18	32	90
Martin Hlinka	60	13	19	32	50
Alexei Tezikov	58	7	24	31	58
Jakub Ficenec	62	10	16	26	41
Krys Barch	76	10	15	25	91
Michael Farrell	79	6	18	24	61
Mike Peluso	19	12	10	22	17
Trent Whitfield	19	9	11	20	27
Patrick Boileau	77	6	14	20	50
Kent Hulst	47	6	13	19	36
Todd Rohloff	58	3	8	11	59
David Emma	16	2	8	10	6
Rob Zettler	36	1	9	10	84
Jean-Francois Fortin	32	1	7	8	22
Remi Royer	40	1	7	8	140
James Black	5	2	3	5	0
Dean Melanson	13	1	4	5	14
Jason Ulmer	5	1	2	3	0
Derek Schutz	20	1	2	3	14
Marty Standish	6	1	1	2	31
Jan Bulis	4	0	2	2	0
Nathan Forster	27	0	2	2	25
Corey Hirsch (goalie)	36	0	2	2	0
Brantt Myhres	9	1	0	1	53
Chris Corrinet	6	0	1	1	4
Jamie Huscroft	6	0	1	1	12
Harold Hersh	1	0	0	0	0
Stephen Moon	1	0	0	0	0
Kyle Clark	2	0	0	0	2
Harold Hersh	2	0	0	0	2
Kiley Hill	2	0	0	0	0
Brian Sotherby	2	0	0	0	2
David Bell	3	0	0	0	7
Mike Siklenka	3	0	0	0	0
Rastislav Stana (goalie)	3	0	0	0	0
Gerad Adams	4	0	0	0	2
Stephen Peat	6	0	0	0	16
Cam Severson	8	0	0	0	11
Curtis Cruickshank (goalie)	10	0	0	0	0
Ryan Van Buskirk	18	0	0	0	16
Jason Shmyr	32	0	0	0	141
Sebastien Charpentier (goalie)	34	0	0	0	19

GOALTENDING

	Gms.	Min.	W	L	T	G	SO	Avg.
Corey Hirsch	36	2142	17	17	2	104	1	2.91
S. Charpentier	34	1978	16	16	1	113	1	3.43
Rastislav Stana	3	161	0	2	1	11	0	4.09
Curtis Cruickshank	10	533	1	7	0	44	0	4.95

PROVIDENCE BRUINS
SCORING

	Games	G	A	Pts.	PIM
Peter Ferraro	78	26	45	71	109
Eric Manlow	60	16	51	67	18
Cameron Mann	39	24	23	47	59
Eric Nickulas	62	20	23	43	100
Brandon Smith	63	11	28	39	30
Peter Vandermeer	62	19	18	37	240
Lee Goren	54	15	18	33	72
Nick Boynton	78	6	27	33	105
Andre Savage	35	13	15	28	47
Jeremy Brown	60	11	17	28	57
Jonathan Girard	39	3	21	24	6
Terry Hollinger	70	8	14	22	73
Ivan Huml	79	13	6	19	28
Jon Coleman	49	4	15	19	14
Marquis Mathieu	57	10	7	17	205
Jay Henderson	41	9	7	16	121
Kent Hulst	23	4	12	16	16
Joe Hulbig	36	4	11	15	19
Mattias Karlin	68	3	12	15	28
Shawn Bates	11	5	8	13	12
Pavel Kolarik	51	5	6	11	14
Zdenek Kutlak	62	4	5	9	16
Mike Hall	18	3	5	8	6
Mike Omicioli	16	2	4	6	14
Keith McCambridge	63	1	5	6	215
Duane Harmer	6	1	4	5	2
Ken Belanger	10	1	4	5	47
Elias Abrahamsson	39	2	2	4	54
Danny Bousquet	7	1	2	3	0
Aniket Dhadphale	3	1	0	1	2
Ben Schust	8	0	1	1	2
Jason Renard	11	0	1	1	35
Chad Cabana	14	0	1	1	43
John Grahame (goalie)	16	0	1	1	12
Kay Whitmore (goalie)	26	0	1	1	8
Andy Bezeau	1	0	0	0	8
Steve Briere (goalie)	2	0	0	0	0
Sean Matile (goalie)	3	0	0	0	0
Stefan Rivard	3	0	0	0	4
Peter Skudra (goalie)	3	0	0	0	0
Vratislav Cech	4	0	0	0	2
Judd Lambert (goalie)	10	0	0	0	0
Andrew Raycroft (goalie)	26	0	0	0	11

GOALTENDING

	Gms.	Min.	W	L	T	G	SO	Avg.
Peter Skudra	3	180	3	0	0	5	0	1.67
Sean Matile	3	164	1	2	0	6	1	2.20
Steve Briere	2	118	0	2	0	5	0	2.54
Kay Whitmore	26	1460	13	8	2	65	2	2.67
Judd Lambert	10	569	6	2	1	26	0	2.74
John Grahame	16	893	4	7	3	47	0	3.16
Andrew Raycroft	26	1459	8	14	4	82	1	3.37

QUEBEC CITADELLES
SCORING

	Games	G	A	Pts.	PIM
Pierre Sevigny	74	29	37	66	138
Mike Ribeiro	74	26	40	66	44
Miloslav Guren	75	11	40	51	24
Barry Richter	68	4	47	51	45
Xavier Delisle	62	18	29	47	34
Mathieu Descoteaux	73	16	27	43	38
Eric Bertrand	66	21	21	42	113
Andrei Bashkirov	53	17	25	42	6
Eric Chouinard	48	12	21	33	6
Marc Beaucage	65	18	14	32	44
Eric Landry	27	14	18	32	90
Matt Higgins	66	10	18	28	18
Jonathan Delisle	71	6	18	24	201
Gennady Razin	69	3	19	22	25
Francis Belanger	22	15	4	19	101
Jason Ward	23	7	12	19	69

	Games	G	A	Pts.	PIM
Arron Asham	15	7	9	16	51
Michael Ryder	61	6	9	15	14
Josh DeWolf	58	3	8	11	65
Francois Fortier	28	5	5	10	17
Francois Beauchemin	56	3	6	9	44
Mathieu Raby	76	3	3	6	193
Jim Campbell	3	5	0	5	6
Andrei Markov	14	0	5	5	4
Matt O'Dette	38	1	3	4	124
Patrick Gingras	7	1	2	3	23
Juha Lind	3	1	1	2	0
Daniel Payette	19	1	1	2	6
Eric Fichaud (goalie)	42	0	2	2	6
Michael McBain	50	0	2	2	31
Ron Hainsey	4	1	0	1	0
Darryl Shannon	4	0	1	1	4
Evan Lindsay (goalie)	1	0	0	0	0
Johan Witehall	1	0	0	0	0
Enrico Ciccone	2	0	0	0	22
Darcy Harris	3	0	0	0	4
Jose Theodore (goalie)	3	0	0	0	0
Francis Bouillon	4	0	0	0	0
Christian Bronsard (goalie)	10	0	0	0	0
Mathieu Garon (goalie)	31	0	0	0	14

GOALTENDING

	Gms.	Min.	W	L	T	G	SO	Avg.
Evan Lindsay	1	2	0	0	0	0	0	0.00
Mathieu Garon	31	1768	16	13	1	86	1	2.92
Jose Theodore	3	180	3	0	0	9	0	3.00
Eric Fichaud	42	2441	19	19	2	127	1	3.12
Christian Bronsard	10	416	3	4	0	22	0	3.17

ROCHESTER AMERICANS
SCORING

	Games	G	A	Pts.	PIM
Francois Methot	79	22	33	55	35
Joromy Adduono	76	24	30	54	53
Craig Charron	73	18	32	50	53
Norm Milley	77	20	27	47	56
Chris Taylor	45	20	24	44	25
Jason Cipolla	72	12	25	37	61
Joe Murphy	74	20	15	35	43
Brian Campbell	65	7	25	32	24
Mike Hurlbut	53	6	26	32	36
Dane Jackson	69	16	12	28	104
Quinn Hancock	57	9	19	28	29
Doug Houda	43	6	20	26	106
Todd Nelson	74	6	20	26	32
Jason Holland	63	4	19	23	45
Darren VanOene	64	10	12	22	147
Mike Mader	60	7	7	14	103
Sasha Lakovic	51	3	9	12	161
Paul Traynor	67	1	8	9	36
Jaroslav Kristek	35	5	3	8	20
Kevin Bolibruck	76	2	5	7	52
Craig Brunel	37	3	2	5	96
Ryan Brindley	22	2	3	5	26
Andrew Peters	49	0	4	4	118
Milan Bartovic	2	1	1	2	0
Mika Noronen (goalie)	47	0	2	2	28
Marc Busenburg	12	0	1	1	2
Tom Askey (goalie)	29	0	1	1	4
Kirk Daubenspeck (goalie)	1	0	0	0	0
Joel Irving	1	0	0	0	10
Peter Skudra (goalie)	2	0	0	0	0
David Kudelka	3	0	0	0	10
Martin Biron (goalie)	4	0	0	0	2

GOALTENDING

	Gms.	Min.	W	L	T	G	SO	Avg.
Martin Biron	4	239	3	1	0	4	1	1.00
Mika Noronen	47	2753	26	15	5	100	4	2.18
Peter Skudra	2	120	2	0	0	5	0	2.50
Tom Askey	29	1671	15	8	4	71	1	2.55
Kirk Daubenspeck	1	60	0	1	0	6	0	6.00

SAINT JOHN FLAMES

SCORING

	Games	G	A	Pts.	PIM
Marty Murray	56	24	52	76	36
Dave Roche	79	32	26	58	179
Derrick Walser	76	19	36	55	36
Rico Fata	70	23	29	52	129
Sergei Varlamov	55	21	30	51	56
Darrel Scoville	76	15	32	47	125
Benoit Gratton	53	10	36	46	153
Daniel Tkaczuk	50	15	21	36	48
Chris Clark	48	18	17	35	131
Jason Botterill	60	13	20	33	101
Miika Elomo	72	10	21	31	109
Micki Dupont	67	8	21	29	28
Steve Begin	58	14	14	28	109
Blair Betts	75	13	15	28	28
Mike Martin	60	7	16	23	69
Rick Mrozik	76	5	11	16	26
Doug Doull	49	3	10	13	167
Gaetan Royer	58	8	4	12	134
Marc Bureau	17	4	7	11	13
Kenny Corupe	44	3	4	7	26
Steve Montador	58	1	6	7	95
Ryan Chaytors	11	1	4	5	0
Chris St. Croix	69	0	4	4	66
Derek Morris	3	1	2	3	2
Jeff Dewar	3	1	0	1	5
Levente Szuper (goalie)	34	0	1	1	0
Martin Brochu (goalie)	55	0	1	1	8
Quade Lightbody	1	0	0	0	0
John McNabb	1	0	0	0	0
Dany Sabourin (goalie)	1	0	0	0	0
Shaun Sutter	1	0	0	0	0
Mike Vellinga	1	0	0	0	0
Dustin Virag	1	0	0	0	0
Jeff Walker	1	0	0	0	0
Jeff Sullivan	2	0	0	0	0

GOALTENDING

	Gms.	Min.	W	L	T	G	SO	Avg.
Dany Sabourin	1	40	1	0	0	0	0	0.00
Levente Szuper	34	1750	16	10	2	73	2	2.50
Martin Brochu	55	3049	27	19	5	132	2	2.60

ST. JOHN'S MAPLE LEAFS

SCORING

	Games	G	A	Pts.	PIM
Bobby House	65	36	33	69	49
Jeff Farkas	77	28	40	68	62
Donald MacLean	61	26	34	60	48
Mikael Hakanson	64	10	40	50	46
Adam Mair	47	18	27	45	69
Alyn McCauley	47	16	28	44	12
David Cooper	71	16	26	42	117
Nathan Dempsey	55	11	28	39	60
Alexei Ponikarovsky	49	12	24	36	44
Allan Rourke	64	9	19	28	36
Michal Travnicek	80	3	21	24	70
Tyler Harlton	80	5	18	23	68
D.J. Smith	59	7	12	19	106
Konstantin Kalmikov	47	7	10	17	8
Shawn Thornton	79	5	12	17	320
Petr Svoboda	38	7	7	14	48
Syl Apps	69	6	8	14	73
Frantisek Mrazek	51	4	9	13	24
Morgan Warren	57	2	10	12	16
Chad Allan	73	4	5	9	50
Maxim Glalanov	17	2	7	9	10
Jason Sessa	9	4	4	8	4
Jonathan Roy	7	2	3	5	4
Jacques Lariviere	37	3	0	3	95
David Nemirovsky	9	1	2	3	10
Mike Minard (goalie)	43	0	3	3	4

SPRINGFIELD FALCONS (continued header column)

	Games	G	A	Pts.	PIM
Dimitri Yakushin	45	2	0	2	61
Vladimir Antipov	9	1	1	2	2
Jimmy Waite (goalie)	43	0	2	2	12
Peter Reynolds	2	0	0	0	0
Jamie Hodson (goalie)	4	0	0	0	0
Hugo Marchand	5	0	0	0	4

GOALTENDING

	Gms.	Min.	W	L	T	G	SO	Avg.
Mike Minard	43	2252	23	10	4	91	1	2.42
Jimmy Waite	43	2447	12	25	4	132	1	3.24
Jamie Hodson	4	137	0	2	0	13	0	5.71

SPRINGFIELD FALCONS

SCORING

	Games	G	A	Pts.	PIM
Jean-Guy Trudel	80	34	65	99	89
Philippe Audet	80	26	31	57	113
Daniel Briere	30	21	25	46	30
David Cullen	69	13	29	42	40
Trent Hunter	57	18	17	35	14
Juraj Kolnik	29	15	20	35	20
Eric Healey	66	16	17	33	53
Jason Krog	24	7	23	30	4
Anders Myrvold	69	5	25	30	129
Chris Winnes	62	13	14	27	6
James Desmarais	37	8	16	24	6
Brad Ralph	50	5	13	18	23
Kirill Safronov	66	5	13	18	77
Tavis Hansen	24	6	10	16	81
Ryan Lauzon	37	5	10	15	6
David MacIntyre	20	2	12	14	14
Craig Mills	64	8	5	13	131
Wyatt Smith	18	5	7	12	11
Stewart Bodtker	14	4	8	12	2
Jeff Toms	5	6	5	11	0
Scott Swanson	22	1	10	11	10
Ramzi Abid	17	6	4	10	38
Frederic Bouchard	12	5	5	10	24
Francois Leroux	65	4	6	10	180
John Spoltore	10	3	4	7	6
Justin Hocking	60	0	7	7	114
Mathieu Biron	34	0	6	6	18
Dan Focht	69	0	6	6	156
Rob Murray	30	3	2	5	43
Jason Morgan	16	1	4	5	19
Rob Bonneau	10	2	2	4	14
Sergei Kuznetsov	22	0	4	4	10
Robert Francz	24	2	1	3	26
Robert Schnabel	22	1	2	3	38
Chris Aldous	6	1	1	2	0
Petr Mika	27	0	2	2	8
Simon Olivier	2	1	0	1	4
David Bell	5	1	0	1	14
Blair Allison (goalie)	1	0	0	0	0
Brent Gauvreau	1	0	0	0	0
Jeff Kozakowski	1	0	0	0	2
Mike Pomichter	1	0	0	0	2
Cody Bowtell	3	0	0	0	0
Steven Low	3	0	0	0	12
Denis Chalifoux	4	0	0	0	0
Mike Martone	4	0	0	0	0
Pierre-Luc Therrien (goalie)	4	0	0	0	0
Dan Murphy (goalie)	16	0	0	0	0
Steve Valiquette (goalie)	20	0	0	0	0
Patrick DesRochers (goalie)	50	0	0	0	21

GOALTENDING

	Gms.	Min.	W	L	T	G	SO	Avg.
Steve Valiquette	20	1066	7	10	1	54	0	3.04
Patrick DesRochers	50	2807	17	24	5	156	0	3.33
Dan Murphy	16	824	4	7	2	51	0	3.71
Pierre-Luc Therrien	4	116	1	1	0	9	0	4.64
Blair Allison	1	33	0	1	0	3	0	5.39

SYRACUSE CRUNCH
SCORING

	Games	G	A	Pts.	PIM
Bill Bowler	72	21	58	79	50
Radim Bicanek	68	22	43	65	124
Reggie Savage	78	37	24	61	90
Mike Gaul	70	16	45	61	80
Jeff Williams	76	22	27	49	36
Mathieu Darche	66	16	24	40	21
Brad Moran	71	11	19	30	30
Sean Selmser	75	11	15	26	151
Matt Davidson	72	14	11	25	24
Martin Spanhel	67	11	13	24	75
Chris Nielsen	47	10	11	21	24
Scott Hollis	38	10	10	20	92
Deron Quint	21	5	15	20	30
Jonas Junkka	58	5	14	19	49
Jeremy Reich	56	6	9	15	108
Blake Bellefeuille	50	5	5	10	18
Jody Shelley	69	1	7	8	357
Dan Watson	59	3	4	7	12
Adam Borzecki	29	1	6	7	39
Andrei Sryubko	70	1	6	7	169
Kent McDonell	32	3	3	6	36
Marc Lamothe (goalie)	42	0	6	6	2
Jeff Ware	71	0	4	4	174
Jean-Francois Labbe (goalie)	37	0	3	3	27
Mike Garrow	4	0	2	2	2
Greg Labenski	1	1	0	1	0
Ben Keup	4	1	0	1	0
Brian Cummings	5	1	0	1	0
Robert Ek	28	1	0	1	28
Jonathan Schill	4	0	1	1	8
Greg Gardner (goalie)	9	0	1	1	0
Robb Palahnuk	1	0	0	0	0
Jeff Ambrosio	4	0	0	0	0
Shawn Legault	5	0	0	0	41
Tim O'Connell	11	0	0	0	2

GOALTENDING

	Gms.	Min.	W	L	T	G	SO	Avg.
J.-Francois Labbe	37	2201	15	15	5	105	2	2.86
Marc Lamothe	42	2323	17	15	7	112	2	2.89
Greg Gardner	9	351	1	5	0	28	0	4.78

WILKES-BARRE/SCRANTON PENGUINS
SCORING

	Games	G	A	Pts.	PIM
Toby Petersen	73	26	41	67	22
Greg Crozier	77	24	36	60	81
Tom Kostopoulos	80	16	36	52	120
John Slaney	40	12	38	50	4
Milan Kraft	40	21	23	44	27
Eric Meloche	79	20	20	40	72
William Tibbetts	38	14	24	38	185
Sven Butenschon	55	7	28	35	85
Jason MacDonald	74	17	16	33	290
Martin Sonnenberg	73	14	18	32	89
Alexandre Mathieu	77	11	17	28	32
Trent Cull	71	11	15	26	166
Alexander Zevakhin	77	14	11	25	16
Darcy Verot	78	10	15	25	347
Andrew Ference	43	6	18	24	95
Dennis Bonvie	65	5	18	23	221
Dylan Gyori	70	5	15	20	86
Chris Kelleher	66	6	13	19	37
Michal Rozsival	29	8	8	16	32
Brendan Buckley	63	2	8	10	62
Josef Melichar	46	2	5	7	69
Jean-Philippe Soucy	13	0	2	2	33
Sebastien Caron (goalie)	30	0	2	2	21
Shaun Peet	8	1	0	1	7
Brian Gaffaney	2	0	1	1	0
Chris Bogas	5	0	1	1	0

	Games	G	A	Pts.	PIM
Chris Slater	7	0	1	1	20
Justin Harney	14	0	1	1	12
Joel Laing (goalie)	16	0	1	1	0
Rich Parent (goalie)	35	0	1	1	26
Mark Scally (goalie)	1	0	0	0	0
Garth Snow (goalie)	3	0	0	0	2
Steve Parsons	4	0	0	0	12
Mark Moore	11	0	0	0	2
Jim Leger	18	0	0	0	4

GOALTENDING

	Gms.	Min.	W	L	T	G	SO	Avg.
Rich Parent	35	2043	17	12	5	80	2	2.35
Garth Snow	3	178	2	1	0	7	0	2.36
Joel Laing	16	864	5	8	1	47	0	3.26
Sebastien Caron	30	1746	12	14	3	103	4	3.54
Mark Scally	1	6	0	0	0	3	0	29.43

WORCESTER ICECATS
SCORING

	Games	G	A	Pts.	PIM
Pascal Rheaume	56	23	36	59	63
Daniel Corso	52	19	37	56	47
Mark Rycroft	71	24	26	50	68
Eric Boguniecki	45	17	28	45	100
Andrei Troschinsky	78	17	28	45	32
Mike Peluso	44	17	23	40	22
Marty Reasoner	34	17	18	35	25
Dale Clarke	67	7	25	32	26
Ed Campbell	78	5	27	32	207
Darren Rumble	53	6	24	30	65
Justin Papineau	43	7	22	29	33
Jame Pollock	55	15	8	23	36
Jaroslav Obsut	47	9	12	21	20
Ladislav Nagy	20	6	14	20	36
Marc Brown	34	9	10	19	27
Doug Friedman	41	9	10	19	78
Chris Murray	21	9	8	17	60
Darren Clark	34	6	10	16	12
Jamie Thompson	37	8	6	14	35
Mike Van Ryn	37	3	10	13	12
Matt Walker	61	4	8	12	131
Tyler Rennette	29	3	8	11	24
Shawn Mamane	51	4	6	10	68
Dan Trebil	14	2	7	9	0
Peter Smrek	50	2	7	9	71
Todd Reirden	7	2	6	8	20
Derek Bekar	18	5	2	7	10
Jason Lawmaster	15	3	4	7	55
Vladimir Chebaturkin	33	0	7	7	73
Andrej Podkonicky	16	2	3	5	15
J.F. Boutin	13	0	5	5	14
Tyler Willis	16	2	1	3	50
Jessie Rezansoff	17	1	2	3	67
Didier Tremblay	7	1	1	2	2
Sebastien Bordeleau	2	0	2	2	9
Cody Rudkowsky (goalie)	25	0	2	2	2
Dustin Kuk	7	0	1	1	13
Jan Horacek	11	0	1	1	20
Dwayne Roloson (goalie)	52	0	1	1	24
Tom Ashe	1	0	0	0	2
Alex Westlund (goalie)	1	0	0	0	0
Lars Pettersen	5	0	0	0	0
Curtis Sanford (goalie)	5	0	0	0	0
Lauri Kinos	11	0	0	0	8
Jason Payne	11	0	0	0	46
Brandon Sugden	11	0	0	0	56

GOALTENDING

	Gms.	Min.	W	L	T	G	SO	Avg.
Dwayne Roloson	52	3127	32	15	5	113	6	2.17
Cody Rudkowsky	25	1477	13	8	3	66	3	2.68
Curtis Sanford	5	236	3	0	1	16	0	4.06
Alex Westlund	1	8	0	0	0	1	0	7.86

PLAYERS WITH TWO OR MORE TEAMS

SCORING

	Games	G	A	Pts.	PIM
Chris Aldous, Kentucky	1	0	0	0	0
Chris Aldous, Springfield	6	1	1	2	0
Totals	7	1	1	2	0
Tom Ashe, Worcester	1	0	0	0	2
Tom Ashe, Lowell	1	0	0	0	2
Totals	2	0	0	0	4
Derek Bekar, Worcester	18	5	2	7	10
Derek Bekar, Portland	58	19	16	35	49
Totals	76	24	18	42	59
Francis Belanger, Philadelphia	13	1	3	4	32
Francis Belanger, Quebec	22	15	4	19	101
Totals	35	16	7	23	133
David Bell, Springfield	5	1	0	1	14
David Bell, Portland	3	0	0	0	7
Totals	8	1	0	1	21
Mathieu Biron, Lowell	22	1	3	4	17
Mathieu Biron, Springfield	34	0	6	6	18
Totals	56	1	9	10	35
Stewart Bodtker, Springfield	14	4	8	12	2
Stewart Bodtker, Lowell	33	6	14	20	26
Totals	47	10	22	32	28
Chris Bogas, Philadelphia	15	1	6	7	8
Chris Bogas, W.-B./Scran.	5	0	1	1	0
Totals	20	1	7	8	8
Eric Boguniecki, Louisville	28	13	12	25	56
Eric Boguniecki, Worcester	45	17	28	45	100
Totals	73	30	40	70	156
Frederic Bouchard, Hershey	1	0	0	0	2
Frederic Bouchard, Springfield	12	5	5	10	24
Totals	13	5	5	10	26
Cody Bowtell, Lowell	5	0	0	0	2
Cody Bowtell, Springfield	3	0	0	0	0
Totals	8	0	0	0	2
David Duerden, Louisville	34	9	14	23	8
David Duerden, Hartford	43	16	9	25	10
Totals	77	25	23	48	18
David Emma, Louisville	55	22	28	50	63
David Emma, Portland	16	2	8	10	6
Totals	71	24	36	60	69
Francois Fortier, Hartford	28	2	6	8	8
Francois Fortier, Quebec	28	5	5	10	17
Totals	56	7	11	18	25
Yan Golubovsky, Cincinnati	28	4	4	8	16
Yan Golubovsky, Louisville	30	1	12	13	36
Totals	58	5	16	21	52
Mike Hall, Lowell	3	0	0	0	2
Mike Hall, Providence	18	3	5	8	6
Totals	21	3	5	8	8
Mike Harder, Hartford	36	10	19	29	27
Mike Harder, Louisville	38	13	24	37	8
Totals	74	23	43	66	35
Duane Harmer, Lowell	14	1	1	2	10
Duane Harmer, Providence	6	1	4	5	2
Duane Harmer, Hershey	15	2	2	4	14
Totals	35	4	7	11	26
Justin Harney, Cincinnati	5	0	1	1	0
Justin Harney, W.-B./Scran.	14	0	1	1	12
Totals	19	0	2	2	12
Matt Herr, Portland	40	21	13	34	58
Matt Herr, Philadelphia	11	2	4	6	18
Totals	51	23	17	40	76
Harold Hersh, Lowell	22	3	1	4	20
Harold Hersh, Portland	1	0	0	0	0
Harold Hersh, Portland	2	0	0	0	2
Totals	25	3	1	4	22
Kiley Hill, Hershey	1	0	0	0	0
Kiley Hill, Portland	2	0	0	0	0
Totals	3	0	0	0	0
Corey Hirsch, Albany (g)	4	0	0	0	2
Corey Hirsch, Portland (g)	36	0	2	2	0
Totals	40	0	2	2	2
Kent Hulst, Portland	47	6	13	19	36
Kent Hulst, Providence	23	4	12	16	16
Totals	70	10	25	35	52
Chris Kenady, Louisville	20	2	1	3	36
Chris Kenady, Hartford	42	5	12	17	58
Totals	62	7	13	20	94
Juraj Kolnik, Lowell	25	2	6	8	18
Juraj Kolnik, Springfield	29	15	20	35	20
Totals	54	17	26	43	38
Jason Krog, Lowell	26	11	16	27	6
Jason Krog, Springfield	24	7	23	30	4
Totals	50	18	39	57	10
Jean-Francois Labbe, Hart. (g)	8	0	0	0	0
Jean-Francois Labbe, Syr. (g)	37	0	3	3	27
Totals	45	0	3	3	27
Judd Lambert, Providence (g)	10	0	0	0	0
Judd Lambert, Cincinnati (g)	2	0	0	0	0
Totals	12	0	0	0	0
Jason Lawmaster, Worcester	15	3	4	7	55
Jason Lawmaster, Cincinnati	12	2	1	3	19
Totals	27	5	5	10	74
Dean Melanson, Philadelphia	15	1	4	5	48
Dean Melanson, Portland	13	1	4	5	14
Totals	28	2	8	10	62
Petr Mika, Lowell	13	0	1	1	7
Petr Mika, Springfield	27	0	2	2	8
Totals	40	0	3	3	15
Jason Morgan, Hamilton	11	2	0	2	10
Jason Morgan, Springfield	16	1	4	5	19
Totals	27	3	4	7	29
Dan Murphy, Philadelphia (g)	2	0	0	0	0
Dan Murphy, Springfield (g)	16	0	0	0	0
Totals	18	0	0	0	0
Rob Murray, Philadelphia	46	3	6	9	65
Rob Murray, Springfield	30	3	2	5	43
Totals	76	6	8	14	108
Simon Olivier, Louisville	3	1	0	1	2
Simon Olivier, Springfield	2	1	0	1	4
Totals	5	2	0	2	6
Mike Omicioli, Providence	16	2	4	6	14
Mike Omicioli, Lowell	10	1	5	6	2
Totals	26	3	9	12	16
Steve Parsons, W.-B./Scran.	4	0	0	0	12
Steve Parsons, Hershey	30	1	0	1	98
Totals	34	1	0	1	110
Mike Peluso, Portland	19	12	10	22	17
Mike Peluso, Worcester	44	17	23	40	22
Totals	63	29	33	62	39
Andrej Podkonicky, Worcester	16	2	3	5	15
Andrej Podkonicky, Louisville	41	6	10	16	31
Totals	57	8	13	21	46
Stefan Rivard, Providence	3	0	0	0	4
Stefan Rivard, Hartford	2	0	0	0	12
Stefan Rivard, Lowell	14	2	3	5	15
Totals	19	2	3	5	31
Remi Royer, Portland	40	1	7	8	140
Remi Royer, Louisville	18	1	1	2	50
Totals	58	2	8	10	190
Cam Severson, Portland	8	0	0	0	11
Cam Severson, Cincinnati	20	4	7	11	60
Totals	28	4	7	11	71
Peter Skudra, Rochester (g)	2	0	0	0	0
Peter Skudra, Providence (g)	3	0	0	0	0
Totals	5	0	0	0	0
John Slaney, W.-B./Scran.	40	12	38	50	4
John Slaney, Philadelphia	25	6	11	17	10
Totals	65	18	49	67	14
Jeff Sullivan, Kentucky	1	0	0	0	4
Jeff Sullivan, Saint John	2	0	0	0	0
Totals	3	0	0	0	4
Alexei Tezikov, Portland	58	7	24	31	58
Alexei Tezikov, Cincinnati	13	2	6	8	8
Totals	71	9	30	39	66
Brent Thompson, Louisville	59	1	9	10	170
Brent Thompson, Hershey	15	0	1	1	44
Totals	74	1	10	11	214
Jeff Toms, Springfield	5	6	5	11	0

	Games	G	A	Pts.	PIM
Jeff Toms, Hartford..................	12	4	9	13	2
Totals	17	10	14	24	2
Jason Ulmer, Hershey..............	3	0	0	0	2
Jason Ulmer, Portland	5	1	2	3	0
Totals	8	1	2	3	2
Kam White, Kentucky	3	0	0	0	6
Kam White, Lowell....................	2	0	1	1	0
Totals	5	0	1	1	6
Johan Witehall, Hartford...........	19	10	8	18	19
Johan Witehall, Quebec............	1	0	0	0	0
Totals	20	10	8	18	19

GOALTENDING

	Gms.	Min.	W	L	T	G	SO	Avg.
Corey Hirsch, Alb. ..	4	199	0	4	0	19	0	5.72
Corey Hirsch, Por. ..	36	2142	17	17	2	104	1	2.91
Totals	40	2341	17	21	2	123	1	3.15
J.-F. Labbe, Har.	8	394	4	2	1	20	0	3.04
J.-F. Labbe, Syr.	37	2201	15	15	5	105	2	2.86
Totals	45	2595	19	17	6	125	2	2.89
Judd Lambert, Pro....	10	569	6	2	1	26	0	2.74
Judd Lambert, Cin. ..	2	102	0	2	0	7	0	4.11
Totals	12	671	6	4	1	33	0	2.95
Dan Murphy, Phi.	2	80	0	2	0	9	0	6.75
Dan Murphy, Spr.	16	824	4	7	2	51	0	3.71
Totals	18	904	4	9	2	60	0	3.98
Peter Skudra, Roc. .	2	120	2	0	0	5	0	2.50
Peter Skudra, Pro. .	3	180	3	0	0	5	0	1.67
Totals	5	300	5	0	0	10	0	2.14

2001 CALDER CUP PLAYOFFS
RESULTS

CONFERENCE QUARTERFINALS

	W	L	Pts.	GF	GA
Saint John	3	0	6	10	5
Portland...................................	0	3	0	5	10

(Saint John won series, 3-0)

	W	L	Pts.	GF	GA
Quebec	3	1	6	15	7
St. John's	1	3	2	7	15

(Quebec won series, 3-1)

	W	L	Pts.	GF	GA
Worcester................................	3	1	6	11	12
Lowell......................................	1	3	2	12	11

(Worcester won series, 3-1)

	W	L	Pts.	GF	GA
Providence	3	2	6	13	13
Hartford...................................	2	3	4	13	13

(Providence won series, 3-2)

	W	L	Pts.	GF	GA
Philadelphia............................	3	1	6	11	7
Rochester................................	1	3	2	7	11

(Philadelphia won series, 3-1)

	W	L	Pts.	GF	GA
Wilkes-Barre............................	3	2	6	19	13
Syracuse..................................	2	3	4	13	19

(Wilkes-Barre won series, 3-2)

	W	L	Pts.	GF	GA
Hershey	3	0	6	8	5
Kentucky..................................	0	3	0	5	8

(Hershey won series, 3-0)

	W	L	Pts.	GF	GA
Norfolk	3	1	6	18	14
Cincinnati	1	3	2	14	18

(Norfolk won series, 3-1)

CONFERENCE SEMIFINALS

	W	L	Pts.	GF	GA
Saint John	4	1	8	19	10
Quebec	1	4	2	10	19

(Saint John won series, 4-1)

	W	L	Pts.	GF	GA
Providence	4	3	8	13	17
Worcester................................	3	4	6	17	13

(Providence won series, 4-3)

	W	L	Pts.	GF	GA
Wilkes-Barre............................	4	2	8	18	18
Philadelphia............................	2	4	4	18	18

(Wilkes-Barre won series, 4-2)

	W	L	Pts.	GF	GA
Hershey	4	1	8	12	7
Norfolk	1	4	2	7	12

(Hershey won series, 4-1)

CONFERENCE FINALS

	W	L	Pts.	GF	GA
Saint John	4	1	8	16	9
Providence	1	4	2	9	16

(Saint John won series, 4-1)

	W	L	Pts.	GF	GA
Wilkes-Barre............................	4	0	8	12	7
Hershey	0	4	0	7	12

(Wilkes-Barre won series, 4-0)

CALDER CUP FINALS

	W	L	Pts.	GF	GA
Saint John	4	2	8	20	17
Wilkes-Barre............................	2	4	4	17	20

(Saint John won series, 4-2)

INDIVIDUAL LEADERS

Goals: Sergei Varlamov, Saint John (15)
Assists: Michal Rozsival, W.-B./Scran. (19)
Points: Chris Kelleher, W.-B./Scran. (25)
Penalty minutes: Jason McDonald, W.-B./Scran. (66)
Goaltending average: Frederic Cassivi, Hershey (1.49)
Shutouts: Martin Brochu, Saint John (4)

TOP SCORERS

	Games	G	A	Pts.
Chris Kelleher, W.-B./Scran.	21	7	18	25
Sergei Varlamov, Saint John	19	15	8	23
Michal Rozsival, W.-B./Scran.	21	3	19	22
Marty Murray, Saint John.................	19	4	16	20
Milan Kraft, W.-B./Scran.	14	12	7	19
Daniel Tkaczuk, Saint John..............	14	10	9	19
Steve Begin, Saint John	19	10	7	17
Derrick Walser, Saint John	19	7	9	16
Eric Meloche, W.-B./Scran.	21	6	10	16
Chris Clark, Saint John.....................	18	4	10	14

CINCINNATI MIGHTY DUCKS
(Lost conference quarterfinals to Norfolk, 3-1)

SCORING

	Games	G	A	Pts.	PIM
Bob Wren	4	4	2	6	2
Petr Tenkrat	4	3	2	5	0
Antti Aalto	3	2	1	3	2
Todd Robinson	3	1	2	3	4
Jay Legault	4	0	3	3	0
Chris O'Sullivan	4	0	3	3	0
Cam Severson	3	1	1	2	0
Marc Rodgers	4	1	1	2	8
Dwayne Zinger	4	1	1	2	2
Yuri Butsayev	4	0	2	2	2
Sean Avery	4	1	0	1	19
Torrey DiRoberto	3	0	1	1	2
Andy McDonald	3	0	1	1	2
Doug Nolan	3	0	1	1	2
Alexei Tezikov	4	0	1	1	0
Jesse Wallin	4	0	1	1	4
Jason Williams	1	0	0	0	2
Gregg Naumenko (goalie)	2	0	0	0	0
Peter Podhradsky	2	0	0	0	0
John Wikstrom	2	0	0	0	2
Scott Langkow (goalie)	3	0	0	0	0
Jason Lawmaster	3	0	0	0	4
Dean Malkoc	4	0	0	0	6

GOALTENDING

	Gms.	Min.	W	L	T	G	SO	Avg.
Scott Langkow	3	142	1	1	0	7	0	2.95
Gregg Naumenko	2	123	0	2	0	10	0	4.90

HARTFORD WOLFPACK
(Lost conference quarterfinals to Providence, 3-2)

SCORING

	Games	G	A	Pts.	PIM
Jeff Toms	5	6	0	6	2
Derek Armstrong	5	0	6	6	6
Brad Smyth	5	2	3	5	8
Boyd Kane	5	2	0	2	2
Chris Kenady	5	2	0	2	7
Drew Bannister	5	0	2	2	6
David Duerden	5	0	2	2	0
Peter Smrek	5	0	2	2	2
Tony Tuzzolino	5	0	2	2	6
Terry Virtue	5	1	0	1	2
Jason Doig	5	0	1	1	4
Mike Mottau	5	0	1	1	19
Richard Scott	1	0	0	0	0
Ken Gernander	2	0	0	0	0
Brad Mehalko	3	0	0	0	10
Todd Hall	5	0	0	0	2
Burke Henry	5	0	0	0	2
Johan Holmqvist (goalie)	5	0	0	0	0
Manny Malhotra	5	0	0	0	0
Ryan Tobler	5	0	0	0	2

GOALTENDING

	Gms.	Min.	W	L	T	G	SO	Avg.
Johan Holmqvist	5	314	2	3	0	13	0	2.48

HERSHEY BEARS
(Lost conference finals to Wilkes-Barre, 4-0)

SCORING

	Games	G	A	Pts.	PIM
Yevgeny Lazarev	12	3	8	11	10
Kelly Fairchild	12	2	9	11	10
Brian Willsie	12	7	2	9	14
Steffon Walby	12	2	6	8	12
Mike Craig	12	3	2	5	20
Rick Berry	12	2	2	4	18

	Games	G	A	Pts.	PIM
Ben Storey	4	1	3	4	2
Brad Larsen	10	1	3	4	6
Nick Bootland	12	1	3	4	2
Rob Shearer	12	1	3	4	0
Yuri Babenko	12	2	1	3	6
Joel Prpic	12	1	1	2	26
Mikhail Kuleshov	11	1	0	1	0
Radim Vrbata	1	0	1	1	2
Brian White	9	0	1	1	12
Stewart Malgunas	11	0	1	1	14
Dan Smith	12	0	1	1	4
Duane Harmer	1	0	0	0	0
Steve Parsons	1	0	0	0	0
Jordan Krestanovich	2	0	0	0	0
Philippe Sauve (goalie)	3	0	0	0	2
Frederic Cassivi (goalie)	9	0	0	0	0
Alex Riazantsev	11	0	0	0	2
Brent Thompson	12	0	0	0	10

GOALTENDING

	Gms.	Min.	W	L	T	G	SO	Avg.
Frederic Cassivi	9	564	7	2	0	14	1	1.49
Philippe Sauve	3	218	0	3	0	10	0	2.75

KENTUCKY THOROUGHBLADES
(Lost conference quarterfinals to Hershey, 3-0)

SCORING

	Games	G	A	Pts.	PIM
Jim Montgomery	3	1	2	3	5
Ryan Kraft	3	2	0	2	0
Steve Bancroft	3	0	2	2	8
Zoltan Batovsky	3	0	2	2	0
Matt Bradley	1	1	0	1	5
Mikael Samuelsson	3	1	0	1	0
Christian Gosselin	3	0	1	1	6
Miroslav Zalesak	3	0	1	1	4
Terry Friesen (goalie)	1	0	0	0	0
Greg Andrusak	2	0	0	0	0
Adam Colagiacomo	2	0	0	0	0
Robert Jindrich	2	0	0	0	0
Robert Mulick	2	0	0	0	0
Jonathan Cheechoo	3	0	0	0	0
Larry Courville	3	0	0	0	6
Rob Davison	3	0	0	0	0
Jarrett Deuling	3	0	0	0	0
Eric LaPlante	3	0	0	0	6
Chris Lipsett	3	0	0	0	0
Dave MacIsaac	3	0	0	0	6
Vesa Toskala (goalie)	3	0	0	0	2

GOALTENDING

	Gms.	Min.	W	L	T	G	SO	Avg.
Terry Friesen	1	0	0	0	0	0	0	0.00
Vesa Toskala	3	197	0	3	0	8	0	2.43

LOWELL LOCK MONSTERS
(Lost conference quarterfinals to Worcester, 3-1)

SCORING

	Games	G	A	Pts.	PIM
Marko Tuomainen	4	3	3	6	10
Andreas Lilja	4	0	6	6	6
Joe Corvo	4	3	1	4	0
Chris Schmidt	4	2	2	4	2
David Hymovitz	4	2	1	3	17
Cody Bowtell	4	1	1	2	0
Stewart Bodtker	4	0	1	1	2
Jeff Daw	3	0	1	1	2
Brad Chartrand	4	0	1	1	8
Quinn Fair	4	0	1	1	6
Peter LeBoutillier	4	0	1	1	2
Andre Payette	4	0	1	1	6
Mike Pudlick	4	0	1	1	2

	Games	G	A	Pts.	PIM
Joe Rullier	4	0	1	1	2
Marcel Cousineau (goalie)	1	0	0	0	0
Chris Aldous	4	0	0	0	2
Nate Miller	4	0	0	0	2
Stefan Rivard	4	0	0	0	10
Travis Scott (goalie)	4	0	0	0	0
Jerred Smithson	4	0	0	0	2

GOALTENDING

	Gms.	Min.	W	L	T	G	SO	Avg.
Travis Scott	4	209	1	2	0	7	1	2.01
Marcel Cousineau	1	58	0	1	0	4	0	4.10

NORFOLK ADMIRALS
(Lost conference semifinals to Hershey, 4-1)

SCORING

	Games	G	A	Pts.	PIM
Casey Hankinson	9	5	4	9	2
Josef Marha	9	1	8	9	6
Valeri Zelepukin	9	5	3	8	6
Kyle Calder	9	2	6	8	2
Mark Bell	9	4	3	7	10
Marty Wilford	9	1	5	6	8
Nolan Baumgartner	9	2	3	5	11
Reto Von Arx	9	1	2	3	8
Nathan Perrott	9	2	0	2	18
Matt Henderson	9	1	1	2	16
Jeff Paul	9	0	2	2	12
Rumun Ndur	9	1	0	1	26
Geoff Peters	6	0	1	1	6
Ajay Baines	9	0	1	1	2
Dmitri Tolkunov	9	0	1	1	4
Mike Souza	3	0	0	0	2
Blair Atcheynum	4	0	0	0	6
Jeff Maund (goalie)	4	0	0	0	0
Michel LaRocque (goalie)	5	0	0	0	0
Jeff Helperl	8	0	0	0	16
Aaron Downey	9	0	0	0	4

GOALTENDING

	Gms.	Min.	W	L	T	G	SO	Avg.
Michel Larocque	5	304	2	3	0	13	0	2.57
Jeff Maund	4	259	2	2	0	13	0	3.01

PHILADELPHIA PHANTOMS
(Lost conference semifinals to Wilkes-Barre, 4-2)

SCORING

	Games	G	A	Pts.	PIM
Tomas Divisek	10	4	9	13	4
Mark Greig	10	6	5	11	4
Michel Picard	10	4	5	9	4
John Slaney	10	2	6	8	6
Kirby Law	10	1	6	7	16
Dan Peters	6	1	4	5	8
Mark Freer	10	3	1	4	10
Vaclav Pletka	10	1	3	4	4
Matt Herr	9	2	1	3	8
Mikhail Chernov	6	1	2	3	4
Joe Dipenta	10	1	2	3	15
Brad Tiley	10	1	2	3	2
Jesse Boulerice	10	1	1	2	28
Bruno St. Jacques	10	1	0	1	16
Petr Hubacek	9	0	1	1	6
Guillaume Lefebvre	9	0	1	1	2
Matt Zultek	9	0	1	1	8
Russ Hewson	2	0	0	0	0
Steve Washburn	2	0	0	0	2
Steve McLaren	8	0	0	0	38
Francis Lessard	10	0	0	0	33
Neil Little (goalie)	10	0	0	0	0

GOALTENDING

	Gms.	Min.	W	L	T	G	SO	Avg.
Neil Little	10	631	5	5	0	23	1	2.19

PORTLAND PIRATES
(Lost conference quarterfinals to Saint John, 3-0)

SCORING

	Games	G	A	Pts.	PIM
Martin Hlinka	3	1	2	3	2
Mark Murphy	3	2	0	2	2
Brad Church	3	1	1	2	18
Michael Farrell	3	0	2	2	2
Jeff Nelson	3	0	2	2	6
Chris Corrinet	2	1	0	1	0
Jakub Ficenec	3	0	1	1	2
Terry Yake	3	0	1	1	12
Sebastien Charpentier (goalie)	1	0	0	0	0
Jean-Francois Fortin	1	0	0	0	0
Krys Barch	2	0	0	0	0
David Emma	2	0	0	0	0
Corey Hirsch (goalie)	2	0	0	0	0
Dean Melanson	2	0	0	0	10
Matt Pettinger	2	0	0	0	4
Steve Sherriffs	2	0	0	0	2
Brian Sotherby	2	0	0	0	0
Derek Bekar	3	0	0	0	0
David Bell	3	0	0	0	0
Patrick Boileau	3	0	0	0	8
Nathan Forster	3	0	0	0	0
Todd Rohloff	3	0	0	0	2

GOALTENDING

	Gms.	Min.	W	L	T	G	SO	Avg.
S. Charpentier	1	102	0	1	0	3	0	1.76
Corey Hirsch	2	118	0	2	0	7	0	3.55

PROVIDENCE BRUINS
(Lost conference finals to Saint John, 4-1)

SCORING

	Games	G	A	Pts.	PIM
Eric Manlow	17	6	7	13	6
Peter Ferraro	17	4	5	9	34
Eric Nickulas	12	4	4	8	24
Shawn Bates	8	2	6	8	8
Jeremy Brown	17	2	6	8	12
Lee Goren	17	5	2	7	11
Andre Savage	17	3	4	7	18
Terry Hollinger	17	2	5	7	24
Marquis Mathieu	17	3	2	5	64
Jonathan Girard	17	0	5	5	4
Brandon Smith	17	0	5	5	6
Joe Hulbig	15	2	2	4	20
Pavel Kolarik	17	0	4	4	4
Mattias Karlin	16	1	2	3	2
Kent Hulst	10	1	1	2	4
Nick Boynton	17	0	2	2	35
Jay Henderson	1	0	0	0	2
Ken Belanger	2	0	0	0	4
Peter Vandermeer	4	0	0	0	16
Keith McCambridge	10	0	0	0	18
Elias Abrahamsson	14	0	0	0	20
John Grahame (goalie)	17	0	0	0	6
Ivan Huml	17	0	0	0	2

GOALTENDING

	Gms.	Min.	W	L	T	G	SO	Avg.
John Grahame	17	1043	8	9	0	46	2	2.65

QUEBEC CITADELLES
(Lost conference semifinals to Saint John, 4-1)

SCORING

	Games	G	A	Pts.	PIM
Eric Landry	9	4	4	8	35
Johan Witehall	9	3	5	8	6
Francis Belanger	9	2	5	7	20
Miloslav Guren	8	4	2	6	6
Eric Bertrand	9	4	2	6	12
Xavier Delisle	9	1	5	6	2
Mike Ribeiro	9	1	5	6	23

	Games	G	A	Pts.	PIM
Arron Asham	7	1	2	3	2
Barry Richter	6	0	3	3	2
Mathieu Descoteaux	7	0	3	3	4
Eric Chouinard	9	2	0	2	2
Andrei Bashkirov	6	1	1	2	0
Andrei Markov	7	1	1	2	2
Jonathan Delisle	6	1	0	1	53
Josh DeWolf	7	0	1	1	16
Mathieu Garon (goalie)	8	0	1	1	4
Matt Higgins	8	0	1	1	4
Pierre Sevigny	8	0	1	1	17
Ron Hainsey	1	0	0	0	0
Eric Fichaud (goalie)	2	0	0	0	0
Mathieu Raby	5	0	0	0	2
Matt O'Dette	7	0	0	0	16
Gennady Razin	9	0	0	0	4

GOALTENDING

	Gms.	Min.	W	L	T	G	SO	Avg.
Eric Fichaud	2	98	0	1	0	3	0	1.84
Mathieu Garon	8	459	4	4	0	22	1	2.88

ROCHESTER AMERICANS
(Lost conference quarterfinals to Philadelphia, 3-1)

SCORING

	Games	G	A	Pts.	PIM
Francois Methot	4	1	3	4	0
Dane Jackson	4	1	1	2	4
Sasha Lakovic	4	1	1	2	32
Todd Nelson	4	0	2	2	2
Jeremy Adduono	4	1	0	1	4
Jason Holland	4	1	0	1	6
Mike Hurlbut	4	1	0	1	6
Darren VanOene	4	1	0	1	4
Milan Bartovic	4	0	1	1	2
Brian Campbell	4	0	1	1	0
Craig Charron	4	0	1	1	2
Joe Murphy	4	0	1	1	4
Paul Traynor	1	0	0	0	0
Kevin Bolibruck	3	0	0	0	0
Jason Cipolla	4	0	0	0	2
Quinn Hancock	4	0	0	0	0
Doug Houda	4	0	0	0	4
Mike Mader	4	0	0	0	4
Norm Milley	4	0	0	0	2
Mika Noronen (goalie)	4	0	0	0	0

GOALTENDING

	Gms.	Min.	W	L	T	G	SO	Avg.
Mika Noronen	4	250	1	3	0	11	0	2.64

SAINT JOHN FLAMES
(Winner of 2001 Calder Cup playoffs)

SCORING

	Games	G	A	Pts.	PIM
Sergei Varlamov	19	15	8	23	10
Marty Murray	19	4	16	20	18
Daniel Tkaczuk	14	10	9	19	4
Steve Begin	19	10	7	17	18
Derrick Walser	19	7	9	16	14
Chris Clark	18	4	10	14	49
Darrel Scoville	19	3	7	10	12
Micki Dupont	19	1	9	10	14
Dave Roche	19	3	6	9	43
Jason Botterill	19	2	7	9	30
Steve Montador	19	0	8	8	13
Blair Betts	19	2	3	5	4
Rico Fata	19	2	3	5	22
Mike Martin	16	1	2	3	14
Rick Mrozik	19	1	1	2	6
Miika Elomo	6	0	2	2	12
Martin Brochu (goalie)	19	0	2	2	4
Chris St. Croix	5	0	1	1	4

	Games	G	A	Pts.	PIM
Jason Morgan	6	0	1	1	2
Doug Doull	16	0	1	1	32
Bobby Russell	1	0	0	0	0
Levente Szuper (goalie)	1	0	0	0	0
Jeff Dewar	3	0	0	0	0
Gaetan Royer	14	0	0	0	16

GOALTENDING

	Gms.	Min.	W	L	T	G	SO	Avg.
Levente Szuper	1	36	1	0	0	0	0	0.00
Martin Brochu	19	1148	14	4	0	39	4	2.04

ST. JOHN'S MAPLE LEAFS
(Lost conference quarterfinals to Quebec, 3-1)

SCORING

	Games	G	A	Pts.	PIM
Nathan Dempsey	4	0	4	4	8
Donald MacLean	4	2	1	3	2
Shawn Thornton	3	1	2	3	2
Jeff Farkas	4	1	2	3	4
Chad Allan	4	1	1	2	9
David Cooper	4	1	1	2	10
Jason Sessa	3	1	0	1	6
Michal Travnicek	4	0	1	1	4
Jacques Lariviere	1	0	0	0	0
Peter Reynolds	1	0	0	0	0
Dimitri Yakushin	1	0	0	0	0
Syl Apps	4	0	0	0	0
Maxim Glalanov	4	0	0	0	2
Mikael Hakanson	4	0	0	0	0
Tyler Harlton	4	0	0	0	0
Mike Minard (goalie)	4	0	0	0	2
Alexei Ponikarovsky	4	0	0	0	4
Jonathan Roy	4	0	0	0	2
D.J. Smith	4	0	0	0	11
Petr Svoboda	4	0	0	0	4
Morgan Warren	4	0	0	0	0

GOALTENDING

	Gms.	Min.	W	L	T	G	SO	Avg.
Mike Minard	4	252	1	3	0	15	0	3.57

SYRACUSE CRUNCH
(Lost conference quarterfinals to Wilkes-Barre, 3-2)

SCORING

	Games	G	A	Pts.	PIM
Brad Moran	5	3	4	7	2
Radim Bicanek	5	4	2	6	2
Chris Nielsen	5	2	2	4	4
Bill Bowler	4	1	3	4	2
Matt Davidson	5	1	2	3	2
Mike Gaul	5	1	2	3	8
Reggie Savage	5	0	2	2	16
Kent McDonell	3	1	0	1	0
Adam Borzecki	5	0	1	1	8
Mathieu Darche	5	0	1	1	4
Jean-Francois Labbe (goalie)	5	0	1	1	2
Jeff Williams	5	0	1	1	0
Jonas Junkka	2	0	0	0	0
Martin Spanhel	2	0	0	0	8
Dan Watson	4	0	0	0	6
Blake Bellefeuille	5	0	0	0	0
Jeremy Reich	5	0	0	0	6
Sean Selmser	5	0	0	0	14
Jody Shelley	5	0	0	0	21
Andrei Sryubko	5	0	0	0	0
Jeff Ware	5	0	0	0	16

GOALTENDING

	Gms.	Min.	W	L	T	G	SO	Avg.
J.-Francois Labbe	5	323	2	3	0	18	0	3.34

WILKES-BARRE/SCRANTON PENGUINS
(Lost league finals to Saint John, 4-2)

SCORING

	Games	G	A	Pts.	PIM
Chris Kelleher	21	7	18	25	4
Michal Rozsival	21	3	19	22	23
Milan Kraft	14	12	7	19	6
Eric Meloche	21	6	10	16	17
Toby Petersen	21	7	6	13	4
Tom Kostopoulos	21	3	9	12	6
Greg Crozier	21	6	5	11	16
William Tibbetts	12	4	6	10	55
Martin Sonnenberg	21	4	3	7	6
Alexandre Mathieu	16	4	2	6	14
Alexander Zevakhin	21	2	4	6	0
Trent Cull	21	3	2	5	28
Darcy Verot	21	2	3	5	40
Josef Melichar	21	0	5	5	6
Jason MacDonald	17	1	3	4	66
Dylan Gyori	18	1	3	4	24
Dennis Bonvie	21	0	4	4	35
Brendan Buckley	21	0	2	2	33
Andrew Ference	3	1	0	1	12
Brian Gaffaney	1	0	0	0	0
Jim Leger	1	0	0	0	0
Mark Moore	3	0	0	0	0
Shaun Peet	7	0	0	0	2
Rich Parent (goalie)	21	0	0	0	4

GOALTENDING

	Gms.	Min.	W	L	T	G	SO	Avg.
Rich Parent	21	1347	13	8	0	58	1	2.58

WORCESTER ICECATS
(Lost conference semifinals to Providence, 4-3)

SCORING

	Games	G	A	Pts.	PIM
Justin Papineau	11	7	3	10	8
Sebastien Bordeleau	11	1	7	8	23
Jame Pollock	11	1	7	8	10
Mark Rycroft	11	2	5	7	4
Mike Peluso	11	3	3	6	4
Pascal Rheaume	11	2	4	6	2
Eric Boguniecki	9	3	2	5	10
Dan Trebil	9	0	5	5	2
Andrei Troschinsky	11	2	2	4	2
Jeff Panzer	5	1	2	3	0
Jamie Thompson	6	1	2	3	2
Doug Friedman	8	2	0	2	22
Mike Van Ryn	7	1	1	2	2
Ed Campbell	10	1	0	1	10
Vladimir Chebaturkin	10	1	0	1	10
Jaroslav Obsut	7	0	1	1	4
Darren Rumble	8	0	1	1	10
Marc Brown	10	0	1	1	6
Dale Clarke	1	0	0	0	0
Didier Tremblay	1	0	0	0	0
Jan Horacek	2	0	0	0	2
Darren Clark	4	0	0	0	0
Shawn Mamane	4	0	0	0	2
Trevor Gillies	6	0	0	0	24
Dwayne Roloson (goalie)	11	0	0	0	2
Matt Walker	11	0	0	0	6

GOALTENDING

	Gms.	Min.	W	L	T	G	SO	Avg.
Dwayne Roloson	11	697	6	5	0	23	1	1.98

2000-01 AWARD WINNERS

ALL-STAR TEAMS

First team	Pos.	Second team
Dwayne Roloson, Worcester	G	Mika Noronen, Rochester
Stevo Bancroft, Kentucky	D	Mike Gaul, Syracuse
John Slaney, Philadelphia	D	Radim Bicanek, Syracuse
Jean-Guy Trudel, Springfield	LW	Pierre Dagenais, Albany
Derek Armstrong, Hartford	C	Ryan Kraft, Kentucky
Mark Greig, Philadelphia	RW	Bobby House, St. John's
Brad Smyth, Hartford		

TROPHY WINNERS

John B. Sollenberger Trophy: Derek Armstrong, Hartford
Les Cunningham Award: Derek Armstrong, Hartford
Harry (Hap) Holmes Memorial Trophy: Mika Noronen, Rochester
Dudley (Red) Garrett Memorial Trophy: Ryan Kraft, Kentucky
Eddie Shore Award: John Slaney, Philadelphia
Fred Hunt Memorial Award: Kent Hulst, Providence
Louis A.R. Pieri Memorial Award: Don Granato, Worcester
Baz Bastien Trophy: Dwayne Roloson, Worcester
Jack Butterfield Trophy: Steve Begin, Saint John

ALL-TIME AWARD WINNERS

JOHN B. SOLLENBERGER TROPHY
(Leading scorer)

Season	Player, Team
1936-37	Jack Markle, Syracuse
1937-38	Jack Markle, Syracuse
1938-39	Don Deacon, Pittsburgh
1939-40	Norm Locking, Syracuse
1940-41	Les Cunningham, Cleveland
1941-42	Pete Kelly, Springfield
1942-43	Wally Kilrea, Hershy
1943-44	Tommy Burlington, Cleveland
1944-45	Bob Gracie, Pittsburgh
	Bob Walton, Pittsburgh
1945-46	Les Douglas, Indianapolis
1946-47	Phil Hergesheimer, Philadelphia
1947-48	Carl Liscombe, Providence
1948-49	Sid Smith, Pittsburgh
1949-50	Les Douglas, Cleveland
1950-51	Ab DeMarco, Buffalo
1951-52	Ray Powell, Providence
1952-53	Eddie Olson, Cleveland
1953-54	George Sullivan, Hershey
1954-55	Eddie Olson, Cleveland

Season	Player, Team
1955-56	Zellio Toppazzini, Providence
1956-57	Fred Glover, Cleveland
1957-58	Willie Marshall, Hershey
1958-59	Bill Hicke, Rochester
1959-60	Fred Glover, Cleveland
1960-61	Bill Sweeney, Springfield
1961-62	Bill Sweeney, Springfield
1962-63	Bill Sweeney, Springfield
1963-64	Gerry Ehman, Rochester
1964-65	Art Stratton, Buffalo
1965-66	Dick Gamble, Rochester
1966-67	Gordon Labossiere, Quebec
1967-68	Simon Nolet, Quebec
1968-69	Jeannot Gilbert, Hershey
1969-70	Jude Drouin, Montreal
1970-71	Fred Speck, Baltimore
1971-72	Don Blackburn, Providence
1972-73	Yvon Lambert, Nova Scotia
1973-74	Steve West, New Haven
1974-75	Doug Gibson, Rochester
1975-76	Jean-Guy Gratton, Hershey
1976-77	Andre Peloffy, Springfield

Season	Player, Team
1977-78	Gord Brooks, Philadelphia
	Rick Adduono, Rochester
1978-79	Bernie Johnston, Maine
1979-80	Norm Dube, Nova Scotia
1980-81	Mark Lofthouse, Hershey
1981-82	Mike Kasczyki, New Brunswick
1982-83	Ross Yates, Binghamton
1983-84	Claude Larose, Sherbrooke
1984-85	Paul Gardner, Binghamton
1985-86	Paul Gardner, Rochester
1986-87	Tim Tookey, Hershey
1987-88	Bruce Boudreau, Springfield
1988-89	Stephan Lebeau, Sherbrooke
1989-90	Paul Ysebaert, Utica
1990-91	Kevin Todd, Utica
1991-92	Shaun Van Allen, Cape Breton
1992-93	Don Biggs, Binghamton
1993-94	Tim Taylor, Adirondack
1994-95	Peter White, Cape Breton
1995-96	Brad Smyth, Carolina
1996-97	Peter White, Philadelphia
1997-98	Peter White, Philadelphia
1998-99	Domenic Pittis, Rochester
1999-00	Christian Matte, Hershey
2000-01	Derek Armstrong, Hartford

LES CUNNINGHAM AWARD
(Most Valuable Player)

Season	Player, Team
1947-48	Carl Liscombe, Providence
1948-49	Carl Liscombe, Providence
1949-50	Les Douglas, Cleveland
1950-51	Ab DeMarco, Buffalo
1951-52	Ray Powell, Providence
1952-53	Eddie Olson, Cleveland
1953-54	George "Red" Sullivan, Hershey
1954-55	Ross Lowe, Springfield
1955-56	Johnny Bower, Providence
1956-57	Johnny Bower, Providence
1957-58	Johnny Bower, Cleveland
1958-59	Bill Hicke, Rochester
	Rudy Migay, Rochester
1959-60	Fred Glover, Cleveland
1960-61	Phil Maloney, Buffalo
1961-62	Fred Glover, Cleveland
1962-63	Denis DeJordy, Buffalo
1963-64	Fred Glover, Cleveland
1964-65	Art Stratton, Buffalo
1965-66	Dick Gamble, Rochester
1966-67	Mike Nykoluk, Hershey
1967-68	Dave Creighton, Providence
1968-69	Gilles Villemure, Buffalo
1969-70	Gilles Villemure, Buffalo
1970-71	Fred Speck, Baltimore
1971-72	Garry Peters, Boston
1972-73	Billy Inglis, Cincinnati
1973-74	Art Stratton, Rochester
1974-75	Doug Gibson, Rochester
1975-76	Ron Andruff, Nova Scotia
1976-77	Doug Gibson, Rochester
1977-78	Blake Dunlop, Maine
1978-79	Rocky Saganiuk, New Brunswick
1979-80	Norm Dube, Nova Scotia
1980-81	Pelle Lindbergh, Maine
1981-82	Mike Kasczyki, New Brunswick
1982-83	Ross Yates, Binghamton
1983-84	Mal Davis, Rochester
	Garry Lariviere, St. Catharines
1984-85	Paul Gardner, Binghamton
1985-86	Paul Gardner, Rochester
1986-87	Tim Tookey, Hershey
1987-88	Jody Gage, Rochester
1988-89	Stephan Lebeau, Sherbrooke
1989-90	Paul Ysebaert, Utica
1990-91	Kevin Todd, Utica
1991-92	John Anderson, Hew Haven

Season	Player, Team
1992-93	Don Biggs, Binghamton
1993-94	Rich Chernomaz, St. John's
1994-95	Steve Larouche, Prince Edward Island
1995-96	Brad Smyth, Carolina
1996-97	Jean-Francois Labbe, Hershey
1997-98	Steve Guolla, Kentucky
1998-99	Randy Robitaille, Providence
1999-00	Martin Brochu, Portland
2000-01	Derek Armstrong, Hartford

HARRY (HAP) HOLMES MEMORIAL TROPHY
(Outstanding goaltender)

Season	Player, Team
1936-37	Bert Gardiner, Philadelphia
1937-38	Frank Brimsek, Providence
1938-39	Alfie Moore, Hershey
1939-40	Moe Roberts, Cleveland
1940-41	Chuck Rayner, Springfield
1941-42	Bill Beveridge, Cleveland
1942-43	Gordie Bell, Buffalo
1943-44	Nick Damore, Hershey
1944-45	Yves Nadon, Buffalo
1945-46	Connie Dion, St. Louis-Buffalo
1946-47	Baz Bastien, Pittsburgh
1947-48	Baz Bastien, Pittsburgh
1948-49	Baz Bastien, Pittsburgh
1949-50	Gil Mayer, Pittsburgh
1950-51	Gil Mayer, Pittsburgh
1951-52	Johnny Bower, Cleveland
1952-53	Gil Mayer, Pittsburgh
1953-54	Jacques Plante, Buffalo
1954-55	Gil Mayer, Pittsburgh
1955-56	Gil Mayer, Pittsburgh
1956-57	Johnny Bower, Providence
1957-58	Johnny Bower, Cleveland
1958-59	Bob Perreault, Hershey
1959-60	Ed Chadwick, Rochester
1960-61	Marcel Paille, Springfield
1961-62	Marcel Paille, Springfield
1962-63	Denis DeJordy, Buffalo
1963-64	Roger Crozier, Pittsburgh
1964-65	Gerry Cheevers, Rochester
1965-66	Les Binkley, Cleveland
1966-67	Andre Gill, Hershey
1967-68	Bob Perreault, Rochester
1968-69	Gilles Villemure, Buffalo
1969-70	Gilles Villemure, Buffalo
1970-71	Gary Kurt, Cleveland
1971-72	Dan Bouchard, Boston
	Ross Brooks, Boston
1972-73	Michel Larocque, Nova Scotia
1973-74	Jim Shaw, Nova Scotia
	Dave Elenbaas, Nova Scotia
1974-75	Ed Walsh, Nova Scotia
	Dave Elenbaas, Nova Scotia
1975-76	Dave Elenbaas, Nova Scotia
	Ed Walsh, Nova Scotia
1976-77	Ed Walsh, Nova Scotia
	Dave Elenbaas, Nova Scotia
1977-78	Bob Holland, Nova Scotia
	Maurice Barrette, Nova Scotia
1978-79	Pete Peeters, Maine
	Robbie Moore, Maine
1979-80	Rick St. Croix, Maine
	Robbie Moore, Maine
1980-81	Pelle Lindbergh, Maine
	Robbie Moore, Maine
1981-82	Bob Janecyk, New Brunswick
	Warren Skorodenski, New Brunswick
1982-83	Brian Ford, Fredericton
	Clint Malarchuk, Fredericton
1983-84	Brian Ford, Fredericton
1984-85	Jon Casey, Baltimore
1985-86	Sam St. Laurent, Maine
	Karl Friesen, Maine
1986-87	Vincent Riendeau, Sherbrooke

Season	Player, Team
1987-88	Vincent Riendeau, Sherbrooke
	Jocelyn Perreault, Sherbrooke
1988-89	Randy Exelby, Sherbrooke
	Francois Gravel, Sherbrooke
1989-90	Jean Claude Bergeron, Sherbrooke
	Andre Racicot, Sherbrooke
1990-91	David Littman, Rochester
	Darcy Wakaluk, Rochester
1991-92	David Littman, Rochester
1992-93	Corey Hirsch, Binghamton
	Boris Rousson, Binghamton
1993-94	Byron Dafoe, Portland
	Olaf Kolzig, Portland
1994-95	Mike Dunham, Albany
	Corey Schwab, Albany
1995-96	Scott Langkow, Springfield
	Manny Legace, Springfield
1996-97	Jean-Francois Labbe, Hershey
1997-98	Jean-Sebastien Giguere, Saint John
	Tyler Moss, Saint John
1998-99	Martin Biron, Rochester
	Tom Draper, Rochester
1999-00	Milan Hnilicka, Hartford
	Jean-Francois Labbe, Hartford
2000-01	Mika Noronen, Rochester

Beginning with the 1983-84 season, the award goes to the top goaltending team with each goaltender having played a minimum of 25 games for the team with the fewest goals against.

DUDLEY (RED) GARRETT MEMORIAL TROPHY
(Top rookie)

Season	Player, Team
1947-48	Bob Solinger, Cleveland
1948-49	Terry Sawchuk, Indianapolis
1949-50	Paul Meger, Buffalo
1950-51	Wally Hergesheimer, Cleveland
1951-52	Earl "Dutch" Reibel, Indianapolis
1952-53	Guyle Fielder, St. Louis
1953-54	Don Marshall, Buffalo
1954-55	Jimmy Anderson, Springfield
1955-56	Bruce Cline, Providence
1956-57	Boris "Bo" Elik, Cleveland
1957-58	Bill Sweeney, Providence
1958-59	Bill Hicke, Rochester
1959-60	Stan Baluik, Providence
1960-61	Ronald "Chico" Maki, Buffalo
1961-62	Les Binkley, Cleveland
1962-63	Doug Robinson, Buffalo
1963-64	Roger Crozier, Pittsburgh
1964-65	Ray Cullen, Buffalo
1965-66	Mike Walton, Rochester
1966-67	Bob Rivard, Quebec
1967-68	Gerry Desjardins, Cleveland
1968-69	Ron Ward, Rochester
1969-70	Jude Drouin, Montreal
1970-71	Fred Speck, Baltimore
1971-72	Terry Caffery, Cleveland
1972-73	Ron Anderson, Boston
1973-74	Rick Middleton, Providence
1974-75	Jerry Holland, Providence
1975-76	Greg Holst, Providence
	Pierre Mondou, Nova Scotia
1976-77	Rod Schutt, Nova Scotia
1977-78	Norm Dupont, Nova Scotia
1978-79	Mike Meeker, Binghamton
1979-80	Darryl Sutter, New Brunswick
1980-81	Pelle Lindbergh, Maine
1981-82	Bob Sullivan, Binghamton
1982-83	Mitch Lamoureux, Baltimore
1983-84	Claude Verret, Rochester
1984-85	Steve Thomas, St. Catharines
1985-86	Ron Hextall, Hershey
1986-87	Brett Hull, Moncton
1987-88	Mike Richard, Binghamton
1988-89	Stephan Lebeau, Sherbrooke
1989-90	Donald Audette, Rochester

Season	Player, Team
1990-91	Patrick Lebeau, Fredericton
1991-92	Felix Potvin, St. John's
1992-93	Corey Hirsch, Binghamton
1993-94	Rene Corbet, Cornwall
1994-95	Jim Carey, Portland
1995-96	Darcy Tucker, Fredericton
1996-97	Jaroslav Svejkovsky, Portland
1997-98	Daniel Briere, Springfield
1998-99	Shane Willis, New Haven
1999-00	Mika Noronen, Rochester
2000-01	Ryan Kraft, Kentucky

EDDIE SHORE PLAQUE
(Outstanding defenseman)

Season	Player, Team
1958-59	Steve Kraftcheck, Rochester
1959-60	Larry Hillman, Providence
1960-61	Bob McCord, Springfield
1961-62	Kent Douglas, Springfield
1962-63	Marc Reaume, Hershey
1963-64	Ted Harris, Cleveland
1964-65	Al Arbour, Rochester
1965-66	Jim Morrison, Quebec
1966-67	Bob McCord, Pittsburgh
1967-68	Bill Needham, Cleveland
1968-69	Bob Blackburn, Buffalo
1969-70	Noel Price, Springfield
1970-71	Marshall Johnston, Cleveland
1971-72	Noel Price, Nova Scotia
1972-73	Ray McKay, Cincinnati
1973-74	Gordon Smith, Springfield
1974-75	Joe Zanussi, Providence
1975-76	Noel Price, Nova Scotia
1976-77	Brian Engblom, Nova Scotia
1977-78	Terry Murray, Maine
1978-79	Terry Murray, Maine
1979-80	Rick Vasko, Adirondack
1980-81	Craig Levie, Nova Scotia
1981-82	Dave Farrish, New Brunswick
1982-83	Greg Tebbutt, Baltimore
1983-84	Garry Lariviere, St. Catharines
1984-85	Richie Dunn, Binghamton
1985-86	Jim Wiemer, New Haven
1986-87	Brad Shaw, Binghamton
1987-88	Dave Fenyves, Hershey
1988-89	Dave Fenyves, Hershey
1989-90	Eric Weinrich, Utica
1990-91	Norm Maciver, Cape Breton
1991-92	Greg Hawgood, Cape Breton
1992-93	Bobby Dollas, Adirondack
1993-94	Chris Snell, St. John's
1994-95	Jeff Serowik, Providence
1995-96	Barry Richter, Binghamton
1996-97	Darren Rumble, Philadelphia
1997-98	Jamie Heward, Philadelphia
1998-99	Ken Sutton, Albany
1999-00	Brad Tiley, Springfield
2000-01	John Slaney, Philadelphia

FRED HUNT MEMORIAL AWARD
(Sportsmanship, determination and dedication)

Season	Player, Team
1977-78	Blake Dunlop, Maine
1978-79	Bernie Johnston, Maine
1979-80	Norm Dube, Nova Scotia
1980-81	Tony Cassolato, Hershey
1981-82	Mike Kasczyki, New Brunswick
1982-83	Ross Yates, Binghamton
1983-84	Claude Larose, Sherbrooke
1984-85	Paul Gardner, Binghamton
1985-86	Steve Tsujiura, Maine
1986-87	Glenn Merkosky, Adirondack
1987-88	Bruce Boudreau, Springfield
1988-89	Murray Eaves, Adirondack
1989-90	Murray Eaves, Adirondack
1990-91	Glenn Merkosky, Adirondack

Season	Player, Team
1991-92	John Anderson, New Haven
1992-93	Tim Tookey, Hershey
1993-94	Jim Nesich, Cape Breton
1994-95	Steve Larouche, Prince Edward Island
1995-96	Ken Gernander, Binghamton
1996-97	Steve Passmore, Hamilton
1997-98	Craig Charron, Rochester
1998-99	Mitch Lamoureux, Hershey
1999-00	Randy Cunneyworth, Rochester\
2000-01	Kent Hulst, Providence

LOUIS A.R. PIERI MEMORIAL AWARD
(Top coach)

Season	Coach, Team
1967-68	Vic Stasiuk, Quebec
1968-69	Frank Mathers, Hershey
1969-70	Fred Shero, Buffalo
1970-71	Terry Reardon, Baltimore
1971-72	Al MacNeil, Nova Scotia
1972-73	Floyd Smith, Cincinnati
1973-74	Don Cherry, Rochester
1974-75	John Muckler, Providence
1975-76	Chuck Hamilton, Hershey
1976-77	Al MacNeil, Nova Scotia
1977-78	Bob McCammon, Maine
1978-79	Parker MacDonald, New Haven
1979-80	Doug Gibson, Hershey
1980-81	Bob McCammon, Maine
1981-82	Orval Tessier, New Brunswick
1982-83	Jacques Demers, Fredericton
1983-84	Gene Ubriaco, Baltimore
1984-85	Bill Dineen, Adirondack
1985-86	Bill Dineen, Adirondack
1986-87	Larry Pleau, Binghamton
1987-88	John Paddock, Hershey
	Mike Milbury, Maine
1988-89	Tom McVie, Utica
1989-90	Jimmy Roberts, Springfield
1990-91	Don Lever, Rochester
1991-92	Doug Carpenter, New Haven
1992-93	Marc Crawford, St. John's
1993-94	Barry Trotz, Portland
1994-95	Robbie Ftorek, Albany
1995-96	Robbie Ftorek, Albany
1996-97	Greg Gilbert, Worcester
1997-98	Bill Stewart, Saint John
1998-99	Peter Laviolette, Providence
1999-00	Glen Hanlon, Portland
2000-01	Don Granato, Worcester

BAZ BASTIEN TROPHY
(Coaches pick as top goaltender)

Season	Player, Team
1983-84	Brian Ford, Fredericton
1984-85	Jon Casey, Baltimore
1985-86	Sam St. Laurent, Maine
1986-87	Mark Laforest, Adirondack
1987-88	Wendell Young, Hershey
1988-89	Randy Exelby, Sherbrooke
1989-90	Jean Claude Bergeron, Sherbrooke
1990-91	Mark Laforest, Binghamton
1991-92	Felix Potvin, St. John's
1992-93	Corey Hirsch, Binghamton
1993-94	Frederic Chabot, Hershey
1994-95	Jim Carey, Portland
1995-96	Manny Legace, Springfield
1996-97	Jean-Francois Labbe, Hershey
1997-98	Scott Langkow, Springfield
1998-99	Martin Biron, Rochester
1999-00	Martin Brochu, Portland
2000-01	Dwayne Roloson, Worcester

JACK BUTTERFIELD TROPHY
(Calder Cup playoff MVP)

Season	Player, Team
1983-84	Bud Stefanski, Maine
1984-85	Brian Skrudland, Sherbrooke
1985-86	Tim Tookey, Hershey
1986-87	Dave Fenyves, Rochester
1987-88	Wendell Young, Hershey
1988-89	Sam St. Laurent, Adirondack
1989-90	Jeff Hackett, Springfield
1990-91	Kay Whitmore, Springfield
1991-92	Allan Bester, Adirondack
1992-93	Bill McDougall, Cape Breton
1993-94	Olaf Kolzig, Portland
1994-95	Mike Dunham, Albany
	Corey Schwab, Albany
1995-96	Dixon Ward, Rochester
1996-97	Mike McHugh, Hershey
1997-98	Mike Maneluk, Philadelphia
1998-99	Peter Ferraro, Providence
1999-00	Derek Armstrong, Hartford
2000-01	Steve Begin, Saint John

ALL-TIME LEAGUE CHAMPIONS

	REGULAR-SEASON CHAMPION		PLAYOFF CHAMPION	
Season	Team	Coach	Team	Coach
1936-37	Philadelphia (E)	Herb Gardiner	Syracuse	Eddie Powers
	Syracuse (W)	Eddie Powers		
1937-38	Providence (E)	Bun Cook	Providence	Bun Cook
	Cleveland (W)	Bill Cook		
1938-39	Philadelphia (E)	Herb Gardiner	Cleveland	Bill Cook
	Hershey (W)	Herb Mitchell		
1939-40	Providence (E)	Bun Cook	Providence	Bun Cook
	Indianapolis (W)	Herb Lewis		
1940-41	Providence (E)	Bun Cook	Cleveland	Bill Cook
	Cleveland (W)	Bill Cook		
1941-42	Springfield (E)	Johnny Mitchell	Indianapolis	Herb Lewis
	Indianapolis (W)	Herb Lewis		
1942-43	Hershey	Cooney Weiland	Buffalo	Art Chapman
1943-44	Hershey (E)	Cooney Weiland	Buffalo	Art Chapman
	Cleveland (W)	Bun Cook		
1944-45	Buffalo (E)	Art Chapman	Cleveland	Bun Cook
	Cleveland (W)	Bun Cook		
1945-46	Buffalo (E)	Frank Beisler	Buffalo	Frank Beisler
	Indianapolis (W)	Earl Seibert		

REGULAR-SEASON CHAMPION   PLAYOFF CHAMPION

Season	Team	Coach	Team	Coach
1946-47—	Hershey (E)	Don Penniston	Hershey	Don Penniston
	Cleveland (W)	Bun Cook		
1947-48—	Providence (E)	Terry Reardon	Cleveland	Bun Cook
	Cleveland (W)	Bun Cook		
1948-49—	Providence (E)	Terry Reardon	Providence	Terry Reardon
	St. Louis (W)	Ebbie Goodfellow		
1949-50—	Buffalo (E)	Roy Goldsworthy	Indianapolis	Ott Heller
	Cleveland (W)	Bun Cook		
1950-51—	Buffalo (E)	Roy Goldsworthy	Cleveland	Bun Cook
	Cleveland (W)	Bun Cook		
1951-52—	Hershey (E)	John Crawford	Pittsburgh	King Clancy
	Pittsburgh (W)	King Clancy		
1952-53—	Cleveland	Bun Cook	Cleveland	Bun Cook
1953-54—	Buffalo	Frank Eddolls	Cleveland	Bun Cook
1954-55—	Pittsburgh	Howie Meeker	Pittsburgh	Howie Meeker
1955-56—	Providence	John Crawford	Providence	John Crawford
1956-57—	Providence	John Crawford	Cleveland	Jack Gordon
1957-58—	Hershey	Frank Mathers	Hershey	Frank Mathers
1958-59—	Buffalo	Bobby Kirk	Hershey	Frank Mathers
1959-60—	Springfield	Pat Egan	Springfield	Pat Egan
1960-61—	Springfield	Pat Egan	Springfield	Pat Egan
1961-62—	Springfield (E)	Pat Egan	Springfield	Pat Egan
	Cleveland (W)	Jack Gordon		
1962-63—	Providence (E)	Fern Flaman	Buffalo	Billy Reay
	Buffalo (W)	Billy Reay		
1963-64—	Quebec (E)	Floyd Curry	Cleveland	Fred Glover
	Pittsburgh (W)	Vic Stasiuk		
1964-65—	Quebec (E)	Bernie Geoffrion	Rochester	Joe Crozier
	Rochester (W)	Joe Crozier		
1965-66—	Quebec (E)	Bernie Geoffrion	Rochester	Joe Crozier
	Rochester (W)	Joe Crozier		
1966-67—	Hershey (E)	Frank Mathers	Pittsburgh	Baz Bastien
	Pittsburgh (W)	Baz Bastien		
1967-68—	Hershey (E)	Frank Mathers	Rochester	Joe Crozier
	Rochester (W)	Joe Crozier		
1968-69—	Hershey (E)	Frank Mathers	Hershey	Frank Mathers
	Buffalo (W)	Fred Shero		
1969-70—	Montreal (E)	Al MacNeil	Buffalo	Fred Shero
	Buffalo (W)	Fred Shero		
1970-71—	Providence (E)	Larry Wilson	Springfield	John Wilson
	Baltimore (W)	Terry Reardon		
1971-72—	Boston (E)	Bep Guidolin	Nova Scotia	Al MacNeil
	Baltimore (W)	Terry Reardon		
1972-73—	Nova Scotia (E)	Al MacNeil	Cincinnati	Floyd Smith
	Cincinnati (W)	Floyd Smith		
1973-74—	Rochester (N)	Don Cherry	Hershey	Chuck Hamilton
	Baltimore (S)	Terry Reardon		
1974-75—	Providence (N)	John Muckler	Springfield	Ron Stewart
	Virginia (S)	Doug Barkley		
1975-76—	Nova Scotia (N)	Al MacNeil	Nova Scotia	Al MacNeil
	Hershey (S)	Chuck Hamilton		
1976-77—	Nova Scotia	Al MacNeil	Nova Scotia	Al MacNeil
1977-78—	Maine (N)	Bob McCammon	Maine	Bob McCammon
	Rochester (S)	Duane Rupp		
1978-79—	Maine (N)	Bob McCammon	Maine	Bob McCammon
	New Haven (S)	Parker MacDonald		
1979-80—	New Brunswick (N)	Joe Crozier-Lou Angotti	Hershey	Doug Gibson
	New Haven (S)	Parker MacDonald		
1980-81—	Maine (N)	Bob McCammon	Adirondack	Tom Webster-J.P. LeBlanc
	Hershey (S)	Bryan Murray		
1981-82—	New Brunswick (N)	Orval Tessier	New Brunswick	Orval Tessier
	Binghamton (S)	Larry Kish		
1982-83—	Fredericton (N)	Jacques Demers	Rochester	Mike Keenan
	Rochester (S)	Mike Keenan		
1983-84—	Fredericton (N)	Earl Jessiman	Maine	John Paddock
	Baltimore (S)	Gene Ubriaco		
1984-85—	Maine (N)	Tom McVie-John Paddock	Sherbrooke	Pierre Creamer
	Binghamton (S)	Larry Pleau		
1985-86—	Adirondack (N)	Bill Dineen	Adirondack	Bill Dineen
	Hershey (S)	John Paddock		
1986-87—	Sherbrooke (N)	Pierre Creamer	Rochester	John Van Boxmeer
	Rochester (S)	John Van Boxmeer*		

REGULAR-SEASON CHAMPION   PLAYOFF CHAMPION

Season	Team	Coach	Team	Coach
1987-88—	Maine (N)	Mike Milbury	Hershey	John Paddock
	Hershey (S)	John Paddock		
1988-89—	Sherbrooke (N)	Jean Hamel	Adirondack	Bill Dineen
	Adirondack (S)	Bill Dineen		
1989-90—	Sherbrooke (N)	Jean Hamel	Springfield	Jimmy Roberts
	Rochester (S)	John Van Boxmeer		
1990-91—	Springfield (N)	Jimmy Roberts	Springfield	Jimmy Roberts
	Rochester (S)	Don Lever		
1991-92—	Springfield (N)	Jay Leach	Adirondack	Barry Melrose
	Binghamton (S)	Ron Smith		
	Fredericton (A)	Paulin Bordeleau		
1992-93—	Providence (N)	Mike O'Connell	Cape Breton	George Burnett
	Binghamton (S)	Ron Smith-Colin Campbell		
	St. John's (A)	Marc Crawford		
1993-94—	Adirondack (N)	Newell Brown	Portland	Barry Trotz
	Hershey (S)	Jay Leach		
	St. John's (A)	Marc Crawford		
1994-95—	Albany (N)	Robbie Ftorek	Albany	Robbie Ftorek
	Binghamton (S)	Al Hill		
	Prince Edward Island (A)	Dave Allison		
1995-96—	Albany (N)	Robbie Ftorek	Rochester	John Tortorella
1996-97—	Philadelphia (MA)	Bill Barber	Hershey	Bob Hartley
1997-98—	Philadelphia (MA)	Bill Barber	Philadelphia	Bill Barber
1998-99—	Providence (NE)	Peter Laviolette	Providence	Peter Laviolette
1999-00—	Hartford (NE)	John Paddock	Hartford	John Paddock
2000-01—	Worcester (NE)	Don Granato	Saint John	Jim Playfair

*Rochester awarded division championship based on season-series record.

INTERNATIONAL HOCKEY LEAGUE

(NOTE: The International League folded following the 2000-01 season, and some of its teams joined the American Hockey League for the 2001-02 season.)

2000-01 REGULAR SEASON
FINAL STANDINGS

EAST DIVISION

Team	G	W	L	OTP	Pts.	GF	GA
Grand Rapids	82	53	22	7	113	279	196
Orlando	82	47	28	7	101	241	193
Cincinnati	82	44	29	9	97	267	258
Cleveland	82	43	32	7	93	270	258
Milwaukee	82	42	33	7	91	244	217
Detroit	82	23	53	6	52	184	311

WEST DIVISION

Team	G	W	L	OTP	Pts.	GF	GA
Chicago	82	43	32	7	93	267	249
Houston	82	42	32	8	92	229	245
Manitoba	82	39	31	12	90	222	230
Utah	82	38	36	8	84	208	220
Kansas City	82	37	42	3	77	239	273

Note: OTP denotes overtime point. Teams earn one point when game is tied at the end of regulation and enters overtime. The team that wins the overtime earns an additional point and is credited with a win in the standings.

INDIVIDUAL LEADERS

Goals: Christian Matte, Cleveland (38)
Assists: Brett Harkins, Houston (64)
Points: Derek King, Grand Rapids (83)
        Steve Larouche, Chicago (83)
Penalty minutes: Darcy Hordichuk, Orlando (369)
Goaltending average: Norm Maracle, Orlando (2.02)
Shutouts: Norm Maracle, Orlando (8)

	Games	G	A	Pts.
Kai Nurminen, Cleveland	74	28	46	74
Niklas Andersson, Chicago	66	33	39	72
Greg Koehler, Cincinnati	80	35	36	71
Steve Brule, Manitoba	78	21	48	69
Viacheslav Butsayev, Grand Rapids	75	33	35	68
Christian Matte, Cleveland	58	38	29	67
Byron Ritchie, Cincinnati	77	31	35	66
Gilbert Dionne, Cincinnati	80	23	43	66
Brian Felsner, Cincinnati	73	27	38	65
Ivan Ciernik, Grand Rapids	66	27	38	65
Greg Leeb, Utah	78	25	40	65
Mark Beaufait, Orlando	54	23	42	65
Dave Roberts, Grand Rapids	72	27	36	63
Vadim Sharifijanov, Kansas City	70	20	43	63
Ville Peltonen, Milwaukee	53	27	33	60

TOP SCORERS

	Games	G	A	Pts.
Derek King, Grand Rapids	76	32	51	83
Steve Larouche, Chicago	75	31	52	83
Brett Harkins, Houston	81	16	64	80
Brian Bonin, Cleveland	72	35	42	77
Rob Brown, Chicago	75	24	53	77

INDIVIDUAL STATISTICS

CHICAGO WOLVES
SCORING

	Games	G	A	Pts.	PIM
Steve Larouche	75	31	52	83	78
Rob Brown	75	24	53	77	99
Niklas Andersson	66	33	39	72	81
Brian Noonan	82	21	32	53	103
Steve Maltais	50	25	26	51	57
Bob Nardella	78	9	40	49	58
Ted Drury	68	21	21	42	53
Jesse Belanger	58	17	22	39	28
Guy Larose	81	13	22	35	32
Dan Plante	76	15	11	26	58
Robert Petrovicky	23	13	10	23	22
Glen Featherstone	71	6	16	22	152
Paul Kruse	71	8	12	20	180
Dallas Eakins	64	3	16	19	49
Mark Lawrence	32	8	6	14	26
David Shaw	30	0	10	10	23
Kevin Dahl	72	2	6	8	63
Dean Melanson	42	1	7	8	80
Chris LiPuma	64	2	5	7	184
Eric Houde	30	2	4	6	10
Michel Petit	23	2	3	5	26
Mike Maneluk	10	2	2	4	11
Aris Brimanis	20	2	2	4	14
Tom Tilley	10	1	3	4	10

	Games	G	A	Pts.	PIM
Steve Martins	5	1	2	3	0
Wendell Young (goalie)	38	0	3	3	24
Neil Brady	24	1	1	2	12
Darren Clark	1	0	2	2	0
Glenn Crawford	5	0	2	2	0
Dan Trebil	6	0	2	2	4
Glenn Stewart	3	1	0	1	0
Blair Atcheynum	7	1	0	1	0
Todd Robinson	2	0	1	1	0
Evgeny Korolev	4	0	1	1	0
Vlad Serov	4	0	1	1	2
Michael McBain	13	0	1	1	2
Rick DiPietro (goalie)	14	0	1	1	2
Trevor Baker	1	0	0	0	0
Chad Ford (goalie)	1	0	0	0	0
J.F. Tremblay	1	0	0	0	0
Frederick Jobin	2	0	0	0	0
Doug Zmolek	2	0	0	0	2
Robbie Tallas (goalie)	3	0	0	0	0
Steve Passmore (goalie)	6	0	0	0	0
Adam Borzecki	9	0	0	0	10
Richard Shulmistra (goalie)	29	0	0	0	0

GOALTENDING

	Gms.	Min.	W	L	OTP	G	SO	Avg.
Chad Ford	1	44	0	0	0	1	0	1.38
Richard Shulmistra	29	1616	20	8	0	51	4	1.89

	Gms.	Min.	W	L	OTP	G	SO	Avg.
Wendell Young	38	2074	17	16	3	109	3	3.15
Rick DiPietro	14	778	4	5	2	44	0	3.39
Steve Passmore	6	340	2	2	2	22	0	3.88
Robbie Tallas	3	87	0	1	0	6	0	4.13

CINCINNATI CYCLONES

SCORING

	Games	G	A	Pts.	PIM
Greg Koehler	80	35	36	71	122
Byron Ritchie	77	31	35	66	166
Gilbert Dionne	80	23	43	66	46
Brian Felsner	73	27	38	65	62
Stefan Ustorf	71	19	38	57	43
Brad Defauw	82	20	31	51	39
Craig MacDonald	82	20	28	48	104
Erik Cole	69	23	20	43	28
Ian MacNeil	82	17	22	39	139
Jeff Heerema	73	17	16	33	42
Harlan Pratt	73	6	23	29	45
Nikos Tselios	79	7	18	25	98
Mike Rucinski	79	1	22	23	46
Len Esau	68	3	16	19	61
Jon Rohloff	66	2	17	19	62
Jeremiah McCarthy	69	6	12	18	34
Jaroslav Svoboda	52	4	10	14	25
Greg Kuznik	73	0	7	7	72
Niclas Wallin	8	1	2	3	4
Aaron Brand	1	1	0	1	2
Mark McMahon	2	0	1	1	4
Craig Adams	4	0	1	1	9
Randy Petruk (goalie)	8	0	1	1	4
Tyler Moss (goalie)	9	0	1	1	0
Corey Hirsch (goalie)	13	0	1	1	2
Jean-Marc Pelletier (goalie)	39	0	1	1	0
Brendan Brooks	1	0	0	0	0
Mike McKay	1	0	0	0	0
Bujar Amidovski (goalie)	3	0	0	0	0
Reggie Berg	3	0	0	0	2
Marc Magliarditi (goalie)	17	0	0	0	0

GOALTENDING

	Gms.	Min.	W	L	OTP	G	SO	Avg.
Corey Hirsch	13	783	11	2	0	28	1	2.15
Tyler Moss	9	506	5	3	1	24	2	2.85
Jean-Marc Pelletier	39	2261	18	14	5	119	2	3.16
Marc Magliarditi	17	893	6	6	3	48	0	3.22
Randy Petruk	8	420	4	3	0	23	1	3.29
Bujar Amidovski	3	94	0	1	0	6	0	3.83

CLEVELAND LUMBERJACKS

SCORING

	Games	G	A	Pts.	PIM
Brian Bonin	72	35	42	77	45
Kai Nurminen	74	28	46	74	34
Christian Matte	58	38	29	67	59
Pavel Patera	54	8	44	52	22
Nick Naumenko	77	5	45	50	60
Richard Park	75	27	21	48	29
Peter Bartos	60	18	28	46	18
Brett McLean	74	20	24	44	54
Pascal Dupuis	70	19	24	43	37
Chris Armstrong	77	9	32	41	42
Steve Aronson	64	9	17	26	23
Darryl Laplante	67	6	19	25	43
Chris Longo	63	8	12	20	68
Eric Charron	60	9	10	19	99
J.J. Daigneault	44	8	9	17	18
Lawrence Nycholat	42	3	7	10	69
Ian Herbers	78	3	7	10	179
Ray Schultz	44	3	5	8	127
Mike Matteucci	69	0	7	7	189
Garrett Burnett	54	2	4	6	250

	Games	G	A	Pts.	PIM
Jeff Daw	8	2	3	5	2
Eduard Pershin	10	3	1	4	11
Allan Egeland	10	0	3	3	19
Jonathan Shockey	24	0	3	3	23
Zac Bierk (goalie)	49	0	3	3	14
Cory Larose	4	1	1	2	6
Nick Schultz	4	1	1	2	2
Brendan Walsh	10	1	1	2	45
Derek Holland	2	0	1	1	0
David Brumby (goalie)	17	0	1	1	2
Jeff Johnstone	1	0	0	0	0
James Patterson	1	0	0	0	2
Doug Schmidt	1	0	0	0	0
Jamie O'Leary	2	0	0	0	2
Justin Cardwell	3	0	0	0	0
Derek Gustafson (goalie)	24	0	0	0	0

GOALTENDING

	Gms.	Min.	W	L	OTP	G	SO	Avg.
Derek Gustafson	24	1293	14	7	1	59	2	2.74
Zac Bierk	49	2785	24	18	5	134	6	2.89
David Brumby	17	893	5	7	1	53	1	3.56

DETROIT VIPERS

SCORING

	Games	G	A	Pts.	PIM
Martin Cibak	79	10	28	38	88
Dmitri Afanasenkov	65	15	22	37	26
Nils Ekman	33	22	14	36	63
Jason Podollan	63	15	16	31	98
Scott Nichol	67	7	24	31	198
Matt Elich	60	12	16	28	12
Thomas Ziegler	67	8	19	27	40
Michael Jones	71	9	17	26	41
Marek Posmyk	49	7	14	21	58
Kaspars Astashenko	51	6	10	16	58
Samuel St. Pierre	69	7	7	14	25
Ben Clymer	53	5	8	13	88
Sheldon Keefe	13	7	5	12	23
Dale Rominski	65	6	6	12	52
Bryan Muir	21	5	7	12	36
Daniel Goneau	15	6	4	10	8
Steve Martins	8	5	4	9	4
Kyle Kos	46	0	9	9	165
Kristian Kudroc	44	4	3	7	80
Paul Mara	10	3	3	6	22
Kyle Freadrich	29	3	3	6	120
Mikko Kuparinen	43	1	5	6	73
Gordie Dwyer	24	2	3	5	169
Sergey Gusev	13	1	4	5	10
Dieter Kochan (goalie)	49	0	5	5	6
Jaroslav Svejkovsky	2	2	2	4	2
Kenton Smith	59	1	3	4	24
Jan Sulc	16	2	1	3	4
Konstantin Kalmikov	18	2	1	3	2
Michael Kiesman	37	2	1	3	59
Mario Larocque	71	2	1	3	233
Eric Schneider	6	0	3	3	2
Darren Meek	8	0	3	3	4
Maxim Galanov	16	0	3	3	6
Edo Turglav	1	2	0	2	0
Mark Thompson	16	1	1	2	8
Cory Sarich	3	0	2	2	2
Craig Millar	11	0	2	2	32
Travis Clayton	1	0	1	1	0
Maxim Potapov	1	0	1	1	0
Andrei Zyuzin	2	0	1	1	0
Phil Crowe	4	0	1	1	0
Paul Lawson	6	0	1	1	2
Kahill Thomas	6	0	1	1	0
Mark Fitzpatrick (goalie)	9	0	1	1	4
Evgeny Konstantinov (goalie)	27	0	1	1	0
Dan Cloutier (goalie)	1	0	0	0	0

	Games	G	A	Pts.	PIM
David Mitchell (goalie)	1	0	0	0	0
Rhett Trombley	1	0	0	0	5
Likit Andersson	2	0	0	0	0
Chris Bogas	2	0	0	0	0
Chris Cummings	3	0	0	0	0
Markus Helanen (goalie)	4	0	0	0	0
Ryan Hoople (goalie)	12	0	0	0	0

GOALTENDING

	Gms.	Min.	W	L	OTP	G	SO	Avg.
Mark Fitzpatrick	9	485	4	4	0	21	0	2.60
Dan Cloutier	1	59	0	1	0	3	0	3.05
Ryan Hoople	12	512	2	5	1	27	0	3.16
Dieter Kochan	49	2606	13	28	3	154	0	3.55
Evgeny Konstantinov	27	1197	4	15	2	85	0	4.26
Markus Helanen	4	83	0	0	0	6	0	4.33
David Mitchell	1	3	0	0	0	2	0	43.11

GRAND RAPIDS GRIFFINS

SCORING

	Games	G	A	Pts.	PIM
Derek King	76	32	51	83	19
Viacheslav Butsayev	75	33	35	68	65
Ivan Ciernik	66	27	38	65	53
Dave Roberts	72	27	36	63	47
Todd White	64	22	32	54	20
Ed Patterson	70	19	23	42	90
Chris Neil	78	15	21	36	354
Kip Miller	34	16	19	35	12
Travis Richards	75	5	30	35	42
David Oliver	51	14	17	31	35
Chris Szysky	70	15	13	28	108
Konstantin Gorovikov	68	7	19	26	48
Petr Schastlivy	43	10	14	24	10
Joel Kwiatkowski	77	4	17	21	58
Sean Gagnon	70	4	16	20	226
Mike Crowley	22	4	12	16	10
Joel Bouchard	19	3	9	12	8
Keith Aldridge	36	3	8	11	99
Sean Berens	37	3	8	11	26
John Gruden	34	2	6	8	18
Dave Van Drunen	36	2	5	7	24
Ilya Demidov	54	1	4	5	65
Craig Millar	12	1	2	3	2
Mike Fountain (goalie)	52	0	3	3	4
Cail MacLean	16	2	0	2	0
Derek Wood	6	1	1	2	2
Bobby Stewart	7	0	2	2	2
Josh Harrold	14	0	2	2	4
Marty McSorley	14	0	2	2	36
Mike Hall	7	1	0	1	0
John Emmons	9	1	0	1	4
Mike Maurice	6	0	1	1	0
Jeff DaCosta	1	0	0	0	2
Sylvain Daigle (goalie)	1	0	0	0	0
Rastislav Pavlikovsky	1	0	0	0	0
Eric Brule	2	0	0	0	0
Shane Hnidy	2	0	0	0	2
Jamie Rivers	2	0	0	0	2
J.F Tremblay	2	0	0	0	0
Chad Alban (goalie)	3	0	0	0	2
Judd Lambert (goalie)	3	0	0	0	0
Philippe Plante	3	0	0	0	0
Kevin Grimes	5	0	0	0	4
Justin Hocking	6	0	0	0	12
Sean Blanchard	10	0	0	0	7
Mathieu Chouinard (goalie)	28	0	0	0	2

GOALTENDING

	Gms.	Min.	W	L	OTP	G	SO	Avg.
Chad Alban	3	180	2	1	0	4	1	1.33
Mike Fountain	52	3005	34	10	6	104	6	2.08
Mathieu Chouinard	28	1567	17	7	1	69	1	2.64
Judd Lambert	3	148	0	3	0	9	0	3.65
Sylvain Daigle	1	60	0	1	0	5	0	5.00

HOUSTON AEROS

SCORING

	Games	G	A	Pts.	PIM
Brett Harkins	81	16	64	80	51
Shawn Carter	82	23	36	59	54
Tom Chorske	78	27	25	52	36
Greg Pankewicz	74	22	24	46	231
Bobby Reynolds	80	15	31	46	61
Sandy Moger	63	18	24	42	58
Jeff Tory	70	12	23	35	24
Sean McCann	82	12	18	30	50
Barry Dreger	80	7	20	27	235
Bobby Brown	58	7	18	25	28
Lane Lambert	66	10	12	22	70
David Wilkie	49	8	11	19	29
Rudy Poeschek	67	3	13	16	66
Scott Hollis	22	7	6	13	22
Greg Walters	66	4	9	13	186
Russ Romaniuk	35	5	7	12	29
Blake Sloan	20	7	4	11	18
Brad Williamson	54	3	8	11	24
Paul Dyck	65	4	5	9	34
John Tripp	15	0	6	6	14
Mark Janssens	4	2	1	3	2
Troy Stonier	16	2	1	3	6
Dmitri Mironov	3	2	0	2	2
Kelly Smart	7	2	0	2	0
Philippe Plante	13	1	1	2	17
Mike Gaffney	9	0	2	2	0
Zarley Zalapski	9	0	2	2	12
Frederic Chabot (goalie)	47	0	2	2	4
Terry Marchant	6	1	0	1	4
Chris Lipsett	1	0	0	0	0
James Patterson	1	0	0	0	0
Jeff Kungle	2	0	0	0	0
Bryan McMullen (goalie)	2	0	0	0	2
Andre Signoretti	2	0	0	0	0
Trevor Roenick	3	0	0	0	2
Sergei Klimentiev	7	0	0	0	6
Grant Richison	8	0	0	0	8
Bert Robertsson	14	0	0	0	26
Terran Sandwith	14	0	0	0	17
Nick Stajduhar	22	0	0	0	16
Jason Elliott (goalie)	41	0	0	0	4

GOALTENDING

	Gms.	Min.	W	L	OTP	G	SO	Avg.
Frederic Chabot	47	2705	23	16	5	119	3	2.64
Jason Elliott	41	2235	19	16	3	113	0	3.03
Bryan McMullen	2	33	0	0	0	4	0	7.24

KANSAS CITY BLADES

SCORING

	Games	G	A	Pts.	PIM
Vadim Sharifijanov	70	20	43	63	48
Josh Holden	60	27	26	53	136
Sean Tallaire	80	23	28	51	44
Steve Kariya	43	15	29	44	51
Pat Kavanagh	78	26	15	41	86
Brad Leeb	53	18	16	34	53
Jarkko Ruutu	46	11	18	29	111
Zenith Komarniski	70	7	22	29	191
Mike Brown	78	14	13	27	214
Ryan Ready	67	10	15	25	75
Bryan Allen	75	5	20	25	99
Jeff Scissons	68	5	19	24	24
Dody Wood	45	9	14	23	211

	Games	G	A	Pts.	PIM
Greg Hawgood	46	6	16	22	21
Steve Lingren	66	5	14	19	50
Bryan Helmer	42	4	15	19	76
Colin Chaulk	37	5	13	18	31
Harold Druken	15	5	9	14	20
Jan Vodrazka	65	3	11	14	227
Artem Chubarov	10	7	4	11	12
Ryan Bonni	80	2	9	11	127
Rob Bonneau	8	1	6	7	4
Regan Darby	55	1	5	6	164
Corey Schwab (goalie)	50	0	4	4	12
Patrick Yetman	3	2	1	3	0
Greg Eisler	4	1	1	2	0
Travis Clayton	11	0	2	2	4
Alfie Michaud (goalie)	32	0	2	2	19
David Vallieres	9	1	0	1	0
Glen Crawford	3	0	1	1	0
Brent Sopel	4	0	1	1	0
Trevor Sherban	6	0	1	1	19
Rene Vydareny	39	0	1	1	25
Blair Manning	1	0	0	0	0
Jonas Soling	1	0	0	0	0
Benoit Thibert (goalie)	1	0	0	0	2
Richard Shulmistra (goalie)	4	0	0	0	0
Darrell Hay	9	0	0	0	19

GOALTENDING

	Gms.	Min.	W	L	OTP	G	SO	Avg.
Corey Schwab	50	2866	22	24	1	150	2	3.14
Alfie Michaud	32	1778	14	14	2	93	1	3.14
Richard Shulmistra	4	239	1	3	0	13	0	3.26
Benoit Thibert	1	53	0	1	0	6	0	6.82

MANITOBA MOOSE
SCORING

	Games	G	A	Pts.	PIM
Steve Brule	78	21	48	69	22
Brett Hauer	82	17	42	59	52
Dan Kesa	79	16	31	47	48
Rusty Fitzgerald	77	30	15	45	35
Sean Pronger	82	18	21	39	85
Doug Ast	82	15	23	38	77
Philippe Boucher	45	10	22	32	39
Jimmy Roy	77	18	13	31	150
Justin Kurtz	69	8	22	30	62
Brian Chapman	82	5	21	26	126
Daniel Goneau	58	10	14	24	26
Scott Thomas	22	9	14	23	21
John MacLean	32	6	12	18	28
Bruce Richardson	51	8	9	17	131
B.J. Young	33	8	7	15	47
Dmitri Leonov	57	6	8	14	67
Mike Ruark	81	0	8	8	194
Jason Podollan	16	5	2	7	10
Cory Cyrenne	15	2	5	7	8
Dion Darling	72	0	7	7	188
Mel Angelstad	67	1	5	6	232
Simon Olivier	17	1	3	4	18
Bobby Dollas	8	1	2	3	2
Scott Morrow	8	1	2	3	6
Cal Benazic	22	0	2	2	40
Randy Copley	3	0	1	1	2
Nathan Rempel	12	0	1	1	19
Johan Hedberg (goalie)	46	0	1	1	10
Steve Briere (goalie)	1	0	0	0	0
Aren Miller (goalie)	1	0	0	0	0
Marc Tropper	1	0	0	0	0
Barrie Moore	2	0	0	0	0
Trevor Demmans	4	0	0	0	0
Sean Blanchard	7	0	0	0	4
Jeff Salajko (goalie)	11	0	0	0	2
Ken Wregget (goalie)	30	0	0	0	6

GOALTENDING

	Gms.	Min.	W	L	OTP	G	SO	Avg.
Steve Briere	1	10	0	0	0	0	0	0.00
Aren Miller	1	60	1	0	0	1	0	1.00
Jeff Salajko	11	621	4	5	1	26	0	2.51
Johan Hedberg	46	2697	23	13	7	115	1	2.56
Ken Wregget	30	1601	11	13	4	72	2	2.70

MILWAUKEE ADMIRALS
SCORING

	Games	G	A	Pts.	PIM
Ville Peltonen	53	27	33	60	26
Sean Haggerty	76	27	23	50	59
Mark Mowers	63	25	25	50	54
Mike Watt	60	20	20	40	48
Jason Goulet	54	19	21	40	22
Bubba Berenzweig	72	10	26	36	38
Randy Robitaille	19	10	23	33	4
Jeremy Stevenson	60	16	13	29	262
Petr Sachl	76	12	17	29	33
John Namestnikov	56	7	22	29	36
Pavel Skrbek	54	2	22	24	55
Dan Riva	75	12	9	21	23
Alexei Vasiliev	69	6	12	18	20
Denis Arkhipov	40	9	8	17	11
Ryan Tobler	49	7	9	16	196
Greg Classen	23	5	10	15	31
Mark Eaton	34	3	12	15	27
David Gosselin	32	5	9	14	56
Jonas Andersson	52	6	7	13	44
Alexandre Boikov	56	2	11	13	147
Jayme Filipowicz	68	0	13	13	101
Marian Cisar	15	4	7	11	4
Marc Moro	68	2	9	11	190
Matt Eldred	45	0	5	5	63
Rory Fitzpatrick	22	0	2	2	32
Chris Mason (goalie)	37	0	2	2	21
Jason Ulmer	6	1	0	1	4
Martin Bartek	14	1	0	1	2
Richard Keyes	1	0	1	1	0
Matt Loen	1	0	1	1	0
Brantt Myhres	6	0	1	1	10
John Tripp	12	0	1	1	31
Alexandre Krevsun	1	0	0	0	0
Jim Logan	1	0	0	0	0
Kent Sauer	1	0	0	0	0
Frederic Bouchard	5	0	0	0	8
Alex Westlund (goalie)	7	0	0	0	0
Bert Robertson	10	0	0	0	0
Jan Lasak (goalie)	43	0	0	0	4

GOALTENDING

	Gms.	Min.	W	L	OTP	G	SO	Avg.
Chris Mason	37	2226	17	14	5	87	5	2.35
Alex Westlund	7	304	2	2	0	13	0	2.57
Jan Lasak	43	2439	23	17	2	106	1	2.61

ORLANDO SOLAR BEARS
SCORING

	Games	G	A	Pts.	PIM
Mark Beaufait	54	23	42	65	34
Jarrod Skalde	60	14	40	54	56
Curtis Murphy	51	19	30	49	55
Herbert Vasiljevs	58	22	26	48	32
Bryan Adams	61	18	28	46	43
Dan Snyder	78	13	30	43	127
Brian Pothier	76	12	29	41	69
J.P. Vigier	78	23	17	40	66
Todd Richards	75	9	28	37	60
Yves Sarault	35	17	17	34	42
Wes Mason	45	13	14	27	52
Ben Simon	77	8	12	20	47
Dean Sylvester	27	9	9	18	20

	Games	G	A	Pts.	PIM
Hugo Boisvert	68	6	12	18	41
Brad Tapper	45	7	9	16	39
Scott Ricci	51	3	11	14	27
Dmitri Vlasenkov	49	5	8	13	10
Brett Clark	43	2	9	11	32
Darcy Hordichuk	69	7	3	10	369
Jon Coleman	19	1	7	8	6
Mike Weaver	68	0	8	8	34
Andrei Skopintsev	25	0	6	6	22
Sergei Vyshedkevich	10	2	3	5	2
Vladimir Sicak	33	1	3	4	15
Scott Fankhouser (goalie)	28	0	3	3	10
Brian Wesenberg	12	2	0	2	19
Jason Norrie	7	1	1	2	22
David Gove	9	1	1	2	2
Norm Maracle (goalie)	51	0	2	2	0
Vince Williams	4	0	1	1	4
Wade Brookbank	29	0	1	1	122
Sean Gillam	1	0	0	0	0
Shep Harder (goalie)	1	0	0	0	0
Sean Ritchlin	1	0	0	0	0
Kirk Daubenspeck (goalie)	2	0	0	0	0
Scott LaGrand (goalie)	2	0	0	0	0
Scott Langkow (goalie)	4	0	0	0	2
Briane Thompson	7	0	0	0	0
Geordie Kinnear	11	0	0	0	41
Rumun Ndur	16	0	0	0	50

GOALTENDING

	Gms.	Min.	W	L	OTP	G	SO	Avg.
Norm Maracle	51	2963	33	13	3	100	8	2.02
Scott LaGrand	2	88	0	1	0	3	0	2.05
Kirk Daubenspeck	2	77	0	1	0	3	0	2.34
Scott Fankhouser	28	1603	13	12	3	69	1	2.58
Scott Langkow	4	187	1	1	1	9	0	2.88
Shep Harder	1	32	0	0	0	3	0	5.64

UTAH GRIZZLIES

SCORING

	Games	G	A	Pts.	PIM
Greg Leeb	78	25	40	65	36
John Purves	78	22	36	58	32
Jamie Wright	74	25	27	52	126
David Ling	79	15	28	43	202
Ryan Christie	69	22	16	38	88
Brad Lauer	73	15	23	38	70
Alan Letang	79	6	24	30	26
Jon Sim	39	16	13	29	44
Richard Jackman	57	9	19	28	24
Gavin Morgan	79	7	14	21	187
Jeff MacMillan	81	5	15	20	105
Patrick Neaton	75	4	16	20	78
Geno Tsybouk	61	4	12	16	157
Eric Houde	34	2	13	15	18
Steve Gainey	61	7	7	14	167
Chris Wells	43	6	6	12	33
Mike Barrie	20	2	7	9	15
John Erskine	77	1	8	9	284
Jeff Shevalier	8	5	3	8	2
Tyler Bouck	24	2	6	8	39
Gregor Baumgartner	31	3	2	5	4
Mike Bales (goalie)	50	0	5	5	10
Mark Wotton	63	2	2	4	64
Jeff Tory	10	1	3	4	7
Neil Brady	26	0	4	4	34
Adam Borzecki	9	0	2	2	9
Mike Legg	6	0	1	1	0
Roman Lyashenko	6	0	1	1	2
Jason Shmyr	25	0	1	1	167
Rick Tabaracci (goalie)	30	0	1	1	31
Chad Alban (goalie)	11	0	0	0	0

GOALTENDING

	Gms.	Min.	W	L	OTP	G	SO	Avg.
Chad Alban	11	597	2	4	4	23	0	2.31
Rick Tabaracci	30	1648	14	13	1	67	1	2.44
Mike Bales	50	2697	22	19	3	111	5	2.47

PLAYERS WITH TWO OR MORE TEAMS

SCORING

	Games	G	A	Pts.	PIM
Chad Alban, Grand Rapids (g)	3	0	0	0	2
Chad Alban, Utah (goalie)	11	0	0	0	0
Totals	14	0	0	0	2
Sean Blanchard, Grand Rapids	10	0	0	0	7
Sean Blanchard, Manitoba	7	0	0	0	4
Totals	17	0	0	0	11
Adam Borzecki, Chicago	9	0	0	0	10
Adam Borzecki, Utah	9	0	2	2	9
Totals	18	0	2	2	19
Neil Brady, Chicago	24	1	1	2	12
Neil Brady, Utah	26	0	4	4	34
Totals	50	1	5	6	46
Travis Clayton, Detroit	1	0	1	1	0
Travis Clayton, Kansas City	11	0	2	2	4
Totals	12	0	3	3	4
Daniel Goneau, Manitoba	58	10	14	24	26
Daniel Goneau, Detroit	15	6	4	10	8
Totals	73	16	18	34	34
Eric Houde, Utah	34	2	13	15	18
Eric Houde, Chicago	30	2	4	6	10
Totals	64	4	17	21	28
Steve Martins, Detroit	8	5	4	9	4
Steve Martins, Chicago	5	1	2	3	0
Totals	13	6	6	12	4
Craig Millar, Detroit	11	0	2	2	32
Craig Millar, Grand Rapids	12	1	2	3	2
Totals	23	1	4	5	34
James Patterson, Houston	1	0	0	0	0
James Patterson, Cleveland	1	0	0	0	2
Totals	2	0	0	0	2
Philippe Plante, Houston	13	1	1	2	17
Philippe Plante, Grand Rapids	3	0	0	0	0
Totals	16	1	1	2	17
Jason Podollan, Detroit	63	15	16	31	98
Jason Podollan, Manitoba	16	5	2	7	10
Totals	79	20	18	38	108
Richard Shulmistra, K.C. (g)	4	0	0	0	0
Richard Shulmistra, Chi. (g)	29	0	0	0	0
Totals	33	0	0	0	0
Jeff Tory, Utah	10	1	3	4	7
Jeff Tory, Houston	70	12	23	35	24
Totals	80	13	26	39	31
J.F Tremblay, Grand Rapids	2	0	0	0	0
J.F Tremblay, Chicago	1	0	0	0	0
Totals	3	0	0	0	0
John Tripp, Houston	15	0	6	6	14
John Tripp, Milwaukee	12	0	1	1	31
Totals	27	0	7	7	45

GOALTENDING

	Gms.	Min.	W	L	OTP	G	SO	Avg.
Chad Alban	3	180	2	1	0	4	1	1.33
Chad Alban	11	597	2	4	4	23	0	2.31
Totals	14	777	4	5	4	27	1	2.09
Richard Shulmistra	4	239	1	3	0	13	0	3.26
Richard Shulmistra	29	1616	20	8	0	51	4	1.89
Totals	33	1855	21	11	0	64	4	2.07

RESULTS

CONFERENCE SEMIFINALS

	W	L	Pts.	GF	GA
Grand Rapids	4	0	8	17	6
Cleveland	0	4	0	6	17

(Grand Rapids won series, 4-0)

	W	L	Pts.	GF	GA
Orlando	4	1	8	16	12
Cincinnati	1	4	2	12	16

(Orlando won series, 4-1)

	W	L	Pts.	GF	GA
Chicago	4	1	8	19	10
Milwaukee	1	4	2	10	19

(Chicago won series, 4-1)

	W	L	Pts.	GF	GA
Manitoba	4	3	8	15	16
Houston	3	4	6	16	15

(Manitoba won series, 4-3)

CONFERENCE FINALS

	W	L	Pts.	GF	GA
Orlando	4	2	8	20	21
Grand Rapids	2	4	4	21	20

(Orlando won series, 4-2)

	W	L	Pts.	GF	GA
Chicago	4	2	8	20	13
Manitoba	2	4	4	13	20

(Chicago won series, 4-2)

TURNER CUP FINALS

	W	L	Pts.	GF	GA
Orlando	4	1	8	20	8
Chicago	1	4	2	8	20

(Orlando won series, 4-1)

INDIVIDUAL LEADERS

Goals: Steve Larouche, Chicago (12)
Assists: Niklas Andersson, Chicago (14)
Points: Steve Larouche, Chicago (18)
Penalty minutes: Darcy Hordichuk, Orlando (41)
Goaltending average: Mathieu Chouinard, Grand Rapids (1.78)
Shutouts: Richard Shulmistra, Chicago (2)

TOP SCORERS

	Games	G	A	Pts.
Steve Larouche, Chicago	15	12	6	18
Steve Maltais, Chicago	16	7	10	17
Rob Brown, Chicago	16	4	13	17
Niklas Andersson, Chicago	16	1	14	15
Curtis Murphy, Orlando	16	3	11	14
Wes Mason, Orlando	16	6	7	13
Kip Miller, Grand Rapids	10	5	8	13
Steve Brule, Manitoba	13	3	10	13
Todd Richards, Orlando	16	2	11	13
J.P. Vigier, Orlando	16	6	6	12

INDIVIDUAL STATISTICS

CHICAGO WOLVES

(Lost league finals to Orlando, 4-1)

SCORING

	Games	G	A	Pts.	PIM
Steve Larouche	15	12	6	18	6
Steve Maltais	16	7	10	17	2
Rob Brown	16	4	13	17	26
Niklas Andersson	16	1	14	15	14
Ted Drury	14	5	4	9	4
Jesse Belanger	14	3	4	7	10
Bob Nardella	16	3	4	7	34
Steve Martins	16	1	6	7	22
Brian Noonan	16	1	6	7	38
Paul Kruse	16	2	3	5	22
Guy Larose	16	2	3	5	10
Aris Brimanis	16	3	1	4	8
Kevin Dahl	16	2	2	4	16
David Shaw	16	0	3	3	18
Glen Featherstone	13	0	2	2	37
Dan Plante	16	1	0	1	27
Eric Houde	1	0	0	0	0
Mark Lawrence	2	0	0	0	0
Chris LiPuma	2	0	0	0	8
Lonnie Loach	2	0	0	0	0
Mike McBain	3	0	0	0	0
Wendell Young (goalie)	7	0	0	0	0
Richard Shulmistra (goalie)	10	0	0	0	0
Dallas Eakins	14	0	0	0	24

GOALTENDING

	Gms.	Min.	W	L	SP	G	SO	Avg.
Richard Shulmistra	10	591	7	2	1	20	2	2.03
Wendell Young	7	373	2	3	1	21	0	3.38

CINCINNATI CYCLONES

(Lost conference semifinals to Orlando, 4-1)

SCORING

	Games	G	A	Pts.	PIM
Stefan Ustorf	5	0	6	6	4
Brian Felsner	5	3	2	5	6
Byron Ritchie	5	3	2	5	10
Greg Koehler	5	2	2	4	6
Nikos Tselios	5	0	3	3	0
Brad Defauw	4	2	0	2	8
Len Esau	5	1	1	2	8
Gilbert Dionne	5	0	2	2	0
Erik Cole	5	1	0	1	2
Harlan Pratt	2	0	1	1	2
Greg Kuznik	5	0	1	1	4
Craig MacDonald	5	0	1	1	6
Ian MacNeil	5	0	1	1	4
Craig Adams	1	0	0	0	2
Jeremiah McCarthy	3	0	0	0	0
Josef Vasicek	3	0	0	0	0
Niclas Wallin	3	0	0	0	2
Jeff Heerema	4	0	0	0	0
Jon Rohloff	4	0	0	0	6
Jean-Marc Pelletier (goalie)	5	0	0	0	0
Mike Rucinski	5	0	0	0	2

GOALTENDING

	Gms.	Min.	W	L	SP	G	SO	Avg.
Jean-Marc Pelletier	5	318	1	3	1	15	0	2.83

CLEVELAND LUMBERJACKS

(Lost conference semifinals to Grand Rapids, 4-0)

SCORING

	Games	G	A	Pts.	PIM
Brian Bonin	4	2	0	2	0
Christian Matte	4	1	1	2	0
Chris Armstrong	4	0	2	2	2
Richard Park	4	0	2	2	4
Ray Schultz	3	1	0	1	16
Steve Aronson	4	1	0	1	0
Chris Longo	4	1	0	1	4
Nick Schultz	3	0	1	1	0
Peter Bartos	4	0	1	1	2
Ian Herbers	4	0	1	1	10
Darryl Laplante	4	0	1	1	6
Kai Nurminen	1	0	0	0	0
Derek Gustafson (goalie)	2	0	0	0	0
Zac Bierk (goalie)	4	0	0	0	0
Pascal Dupuis	4	0	0	0	0
Mike Matteucci	4	0	0	0	15
Brett McLean	4	0	0	0	18
Nick Naumenko	4	0	0	0	4
Lawrence Nycholat	4	0	0	0	2
Brendan Walsh	4	0	0	0	11

GOALTENDING

	Gms.	Min.	W	L	SP	G	SO	Avg.
Zac Bierk	4	182	0	3	0	10	0	3.29
Derek Gustafson	2	53	0	1	0	5	0	5.64

GRAND RAPIDS GRIFFINS

(Lost conference finals to Orlando, 4-2)

SCORING

	Games	G	A	Pts.	PIM
Kip Miller	10	5	8	13	2
Ivan Ciernik	10	5	6	11	26
Derek King	10	5	5	10	4
David Oliver	10	6	2	8	8
Petr Schastlivy	7	4	4	8	0
Todd White	10	4	4	8	10
Viacheslav Butsayev	10	1	5	6	18
Sean Gagnon	10	2	3	5	30
John Gruden	10	1	4	5	8
Ed Patterson	10	1	4	5	17
Travis Richards	10	0	5	5	8
Chris Neil	10	2	2	4	22
Dave Roberts	10	1	2	3	8
Chris Szysky	7	0	2	2	13
Mike Fountain (goalie)	8	0	2	2	0
Keith Aldridge	10	0	2	2	8
Joel Kwiatkowski	10	1	0	1	4
Ilya Demidov	2	0	1	1	21
Dave Van Drunen	10	0	1	1	22
Mathieu Chouinard (goalie)	3	0	0	0	0
Sean Berens	4	0	0	0	0

GOALTENDING

	Gms.	Min.	W	L	SP	G	SO	Avg.
Mathieu Chouinard	3	135	1	1	0	4	0	1.78
Mike Fountain	8	522	5	1	2	21	1	2.41

HOUSTON AEROS

(Lost conference semifinals to Manitoba, 4-3)

SCORING

	Games	G	A	Pts.	PIM
Shawn Carter	7	2	5	7	2
Sandy Moger	7	5	0	5	2
Tom Chorske	7	3	2	5	4
Jeff Tory	7	1	4	5	2
Sean McCann	7	1	2	3	0
Bobby Reynolds	7	1	2	3	6
Brett Harkins	7	0	3	3	8
Greg Pankewicz	7	1	1	2	10

	Games	G	A	Pts.	PIM
David Wilkie	7	1	1	2	4
Scott Hollis	7	1	0	1	10
Bobby Brown	7	0	1	1	7
Barry Dreger	7	0	1	1	8
Lane Lambert	7	0	1	1	11
Brad Williamson	7	0	1	1	8
Greg Walters	3	0	0	0	5
Terran Sandwith	5	0	0	0	6
Paul Dyck	6	0	0	0	2
Frederic Chabot (goalie)	7	0	0	0	0
Rudy Poeschek	7	0	0	0	8

GOALTENDING

	Gms.	Min.	W	L	SP	G	SO	Avg.
Frederic Chabot	7	482	3	2	2	15	0	1.87

MANITOBA MOOSE

(Lost conference finals to Chicago, 4-2)

SCORING

	Games	G	A	Pts.	PIM
Steve Brule	13	3	10	13	12
Brett Hauer	13	1	9	10	12
Sean Pronger	13	3	6	9	2
Rusty Fitzgerald	12	6	2	8	10
B.J. Young	13	4	2	6	14
Dan Kesa	13	2	3	5	12
Justin Kurtz	13	2	3	5	12
Cory Cyrenne	11	1	3	4	6
Scott Thomas	3	1	2	3	0
Brian Chapman	13	1	2	3	12
Dmitri Leonov	13	0	3	3	6
Doug Ast	13	2	0	2	14
Jimmy Roy	12	1	1	2	22
Dion Darling	12	0	2	2	21
Bruce Richardson	12	0	2	2	26
Mike Ruark	13	1	0	1	23
Scott Morrow	2	0	0	0	0
Jeff Salajko (goalie)	2	0	0	0	0
Jason Podollan	4	0	0	0	2
Simon Olivier	5	0	0	0	0
Mel Angelstad	8	0	0	0	26
Cal Benazic	10	0	0	0	8
Ken Wregget (goalie)	12	0	0	0	2

GOALTENDING

	Gms.	Min.	W	L	SP	G	SO	Avg.
Ken Wregget	12	774	6	5	0	30	0	2.33
Jeff Salajko	2	71	0	1	1	6	0	5.05

MILWAUKEE ADMIRALS

(Lost conference semifinals to Chicago, 4-1)

SCORING

	Games	G	A	Pts.	PIM
Bubba Berenzweig	5	0	4	4	4
Alexandre Boikov	5	2	1	3	0
Ville Peltonen	5	2	1	3	6
Mark Mowers	5	1	2	3	2
Mike Watt	5	1	2	3	6
Jeremy Stevenson	5	2	0	2	12
Jason Goulet	5	1	1	2	4
Marc Moro	5	1	0	1	10
John Namestnikov	3	0	1	1	0
Sean Haggerty	5	0	1	1	8
Dan Riva	5	0	1	1	2
Bert Robertson	5	0	1	1	2
Timo Helbling	1	0	0	0	0
Jayme Filipowicz	2	0	0	0	2
Jan Lasak (goalie)	3	0	0	0	0
Chris Mason (goalie)	4	0	0	0	0
Alexei Vasiliev	4	0	0	0	2
Jonas Andersson	5	0	0	0	2
Greg Classen	5	0	0	0	0

	Games	G	A	Pts.	PIM
Petr Sachl	5	0	0	0	4
Pavel Skrbek	5	0	0	0	2

GOALTENDING

	Gms.	Min.	W	L	SP	G	SO	Avg.
Chris Mason	4	239	1	3	0	12	0	3.02
Jan Lasak	3	60	0	1	0	5	0	4.97

ORLANDO SOLAR BEARS
(Winner of 2001 Turner Cup playoffs)

SCORING

	Games	G	A	Pts.	PIM
Curtis Murphy	16	3	11	14	18
Wes Mason	16	6	7	13	24
Todd Richards	16	2	11	13	8
J.P. Vigier	16	6	6	12	14
Herbert Vasiljevs	12	8	3	11	14
Ben Simon	16	6	5	11	20
Dan Snyder	16	7	3	10	20
Mark Beaufait	9	1	9	10	2

	Games	G	A	Pts.	PIM
Hugo Boisvert	16	4	5	9	23
Jarrod Skalde	15	3	6	9	20
Brian Pothier	16	3	5	8	11
Bryan Adams	16	3	4	7	20
Brett Clark	15	1	6	7	2
Darcy Hordichuk	16	3	3	6	41
Mike Weaver	16	0	2	2	8
Dean Sylvester	9	0	1	1	6
Jon Coleman	12	0	1	1	2
Scott Ricci	16	0	1	1	6
Scott Fankhouser (goalie)	1	0	0	0	0
David Gove	1	0	0	0	0
Dmitri Vlasenkov	1	0	0	0	0
Brad Tapper	2	0	0	0	2
Wade Brookbank	4	0	0	0	6
Norm Maracle (goalie)	16	0	0	0	0

GOALTENDING

	Gms.	Min.	W	L	SP	G	SO	Avg.
Norm Maracle	16	1003	12	4	0	37	1	2.21
Scott Fankhouser	1	37	0	0	0	3	0	4.83

2000-01 AWARD WINNERS

ALL-STAR TEAMS

First team	Pos.	Second team
Norm Maracle, Orlando	G	Mike Fountain, Grand Rapids
Brett Hauer, Manitoba	D	Bubba Berenzweig, Mil.
Curtis Murphy, Orlando	D	Travis Richards, G. Rapids
Derek King, Grand Rapids	LW	Ville Peltonen, Milwaukee
Steve Larouche, Chicago	C	Brian Bonin, Cleveland
Niklas Anderson, Chicago	RW	Greg Koehler, Cincinnati

TROPHY WINNERS

James Gatschene Memorial Trophy: Norm Maracle, Orlando
Leo P. Lamoureux Memorial Trophy: Derek King, Grand Rapids
Steve Larouche, Chicago
James Norris Memorial Trophy: Norm Maracle, Orlando
Scott Fankhouser, Orlando
Larry D. Gordon Trophy: Brett Hauer, Manitoba
Garry F. Longman Memorial Trophy: Brian Pothier, Orlando
Ken McKenzie Trophy: Brian Pothier, Orlando
Commissioner's Trophy: Peter Horachek, Orlando
N.R. (Bud) Poile Trophy: Norm Maracle, Orlando

ALL-TIME AWARD WINNERS

JAMES GATSCHENE MEMORIAL TROPHY
(Most Valuable Player)

Season   Player, Team
1946-47—Herb Jones, Detroit Auto Club
1947-48—Lyle Dowell, Det. Bright's Goodyears
1948-49—Bob McFadden, Det. Jerry Lynch
1949-50—Dick Kowcinak, Sarnia
1950-51—John McGrath, Toledo
1951-52—Ernie Dick, Chatham
1952-53—Donnie Marshall, Cincinnati
1953-54—No award given
1954-55—Phil Goyette, Cincinnati
1955-56—George Hayes, Grand Rapids
1956-57—Pierre Brillant, Indianapolis
1957-58—Pierre Brillant, Indianapolis
1958-59—Len Thornson, Fort Wayne
1959-60—Billy Reichart, Minneapolis
1960-61—Len Thornson, Fort Wayne
1961-62—Len Thornson, Fort Wayne
1962-63—Len Thornson, Fort Wayne
Eddie Lang, Fort Wayne
1963-64—Len Thornson, Fort Wayne
1964-65—Chick Chalmers, Toledo
1965-66—Gary Schall, Muskegon
1966-67—Len Thornson, Fort Wayne
1967-68—Len Thornson, Fort Wayne
Don Westbrooke, Dayton
1968-69—Don Westbrooke, Dayton
1969-70—Cliff Pennington, Des Moines
1970-71—Lyle Carter, Muskegon
1971-72—Len Fontaine, Port Huron
1972-73—Gary Ford, Muskegon

Season   Player, Team
1973-74—Pete Mara, Des Moines
1974-75—Gary Ford, Muskegon
1975-76—Len Fontaine, Port Huron
1976-77—Tom Mellor, Toledo
1977-78—Dan Bonar, Fort Wayne
1978-79—Terry McDougall, Fort Wayne
1979-80—Al Dumba, Fort Wayne
1980-81—Marcel Comeau, Saginaw
1981-82—Brent Jarrett, Kalamazoo
1982-83—Claude Noel, Toledo
1983-84—Darren Jensen, Fort Wayne
1984-85—Scott Gruhl, Muskegon
1985-86—Darrell May, Peoria
1986-87—Jeff Pyle, Saginaw
Jock Callander, Muskegon
1987-88—John Cullen, Flint
1988-89—Dave Michayluk, Muskegon
1989-90—Michel Mongeau, Peoria
1990-91—David Bruce, Peoria
1991-92—Dmitri Kvartalnov, San Diego
1992-93—Tony Hrkac, Indianapolis
1993-94—Rob Brown, Kalamazoo
1994-95—Tommy Salo, Denver
1995-96—Stephane Beauregard, San Francisco
1996-97—Frederic Chabot, Houston
1997-98—Patrice Lefebvre, Las Vegas
1998-99—Brian Wiseman, Houston
1999-00—Frederic Chabot, Houston
Nikolai Khabibulin, Long Beach
2000-01—Norm Maracle, Orlando

LEO P. LAMOUREUX MEMORIAL TROPHY
(Leading scorer)

Season   Player, Team
1946-47—Harry Marchand, Windsor
1947-48—Dick Kowcinak, Det. Auto Club
1948-49—Leo Richard, Toledo
1949-50—Dick Kowcinak, Sarnia
1950-51—Herve Parent, Grand Rapids
1951-52—George Parker, Grand Rapids
1952-53—Alex Irving, Milwaukee
1953-54—Don Hall, Johnstown
1954-55—Phil Goyette, Cincinnati
1955-56—Max Mekilok, Cincinnati
1956-57—Pierre Brillant, Indianapolis
1957-58—Warren Hynes, Cincinnati
1958-59—George Ranieri, Louisville
1959-60—Chick Chalmers, Louisville
1960-61—Ken Yackel, Minneapolis
1961-62—Len Thornson, Fort Wayne
1962-63—Moe Bartoli, Minneapolis
1963-64—Len Thornson, Fort Wayne
1964-65—Lloyd Maxfield, Port Huron
1965-66—Bob Rivard, Fort Wayne
1966-67—Len Thornson, Fort Wayne
1967-68—Gary Ford, Muskegon
1968-69—Don Westbrooke, Dayton
1969-70—Don Westbrooke, Dayton
1970-71—Darrel Knibbs, Muskegon
1971-72—Gary Ford, Muskegon
1972-73—Gary Ford, Muskegon
1973-74—Pete Mara, Des Moines
1974-75—Rick Bragnalo, Dayton
1975-76—Len Fontaine, Port Huron
1976-77—Jim Koleff, Flint
1977-78—Jim Johnston, Flint
1978-79—Terry McDougall, Fort Wayne
1979-80—Al Dumba, Fort Wayne
1980-81—Marcel Comeau, Saginaw
1981-82—Brent Jarrett, Kalamazoo
1982-83—Dale Yakiwchuk, Milwaukee
1983-84—Wally Schreiber, Fort Wayne
1984-85—Scott MacLeod, Salt Lake
1985-86—Scott MacLeod, Salt Lake
1986-87—Jock Callander, Muskegon
        Jeff Pyle, Saginaw
1987-88—John Cullen, Flint
1988-89—Dave Michayluk, Muskegon
1989-90—Michel Mongeau, Peoria
1990-91—Lonnie Loach, Fort Wayne
1991-92—Dmitri Kvartalnov, San Diego
1992-93—Tony Hrkac, Indianapolis
1993-94—Rob Brown, Kalamazoo
1994-95—Stephane Morin, Minnesota
1995-96—Rob Brown, Chicago
1996-97—Rob Brown, Chicago
1997-98—Patrice Lefebvre, Las Vegas
1998-99—Brian Wiseman, Houston
1999-00—Steve Maltais, Chicago
2000-01—Derek King, Grand Rapids
        Steve Larouche, Chicago

The award was originally known as the George H. Wilkinson Trophy from 1946-47 through 1959-60.

JAMES NORRIS MEMORIAL TROPHY
(Outstanding goaltenders)

Season   Player, Team
1955-56—Bill Tibbs,Troy
1956-57—Glenn Ramsey, Cincinnati
1957-58—Glenn Ramsey, Cincinnati
1958-59—Don Rigazio, Louisville
1959-60—Rene Zanier, Fort Wayne
1960-61—Ray Mikulan, Minneapolis
1961-62—Glenn Ramsey, Omaha
1962-63—Glenn Ramsey, Omaha
1963-64—Glenn Ramsey, Toledo

Season   Player, Team
1964-65—Chuck Adamson, Fort Wayne
1965-66—Bob Sneddon, Port Huron
1966-67—Glenn Ramsey, Toledo
1967-68—Tim Tabor, Muskegon
        Bob Perani, Muskegon
1968-69—Pat Rupp, Dayton
        John Adams, Dayton
1969-70—Gaye Cooley, Des Moines
        Bob Perreault, Des Moines
1970-71—Lyle Carter, Muskegon
1971-72—Glenn Resch, Muskegon
1972-73—Robbie Irons, Fort Wayne
        Don Atchison, Fort Wayne
1973-74—Bill Hughes, Muskegon
1974-75—Bob Volpe, Flint
        Merlin Jenner, Flint
1975-76—Don Cutts, Muskegon
1976-77—Terry Richardson, Kalamazoo
1977-78—Lorne Molleken, Saginaw
        Pierre Chagnon, Saginaw
1978-79—Gord Laxton, Grand Rapids
1979-80—Larry Lozinski, Kalamazoo
1980-81—Claude Legris, Kalamazoo
        Georges Gagnon, Kalamazoo
1981-82—Lorne Molleken, Toledo
        Dave Tardich, Toledo
1982-83—Lorne Molleken, Toledo
1983-84—Darren Jensen, Fort Wayne
1984-85—Rick Heinz, Peoria
1985-86—Rick St. Croix, Fort Wayne
        Pokey Reddick, Fort Wayne
1986-87—Alain Raymond, Fort Wayne
        Michel Dufour, Fort Wayne
1987-88—Steve Guenette, Muskegon
1988-89—Rick Knickle, Fort Wayne
1989-90—Jimmy Waite, Indianapolis
1990-91—Guy Hebert, Peoria
        Pat Jablonski, Peoria
1991-92—Arturs Irbe, Kansas City
        Wade Flaherty, Kansas City
1992-93—Rick Knickle, San Diego
        Clint Malarchuk, San Diego
1993-94—J.C. Bergeron, Atlanta
        Mike Greenlay, Atlanta
1994-95—Tommy Salo, Denver
1995-96—Mark McArthur, Utah
        Tommy Salo, Utah
1996-97—Rich Parent, Detroit
        Jeff Reese, Detroit
1997-98—Mike Buzak, Long Beach
        Kay Whitmore, Long Beach
1998-99—Andrei Trefilov, Detroit
        Steve Weekes, Detroit
1999-00—Frederic Chabot, Houston
2000-01—Norm Maracle, Orlando
        Scott Fankhouser, Orlando

LARRY D. GORDON TROPHY
(Outstanding defenseman)

Season   Player, Team
1964-65—Lionel Repka, Fort Wayne
1965-66—Bob Lemieux, Muskegon
1966-67—Larry Mavety, Port Huron
1967-68—Carl Brewer, Muskegon
1968-69—Al Breaule, Dayton
        Moe Benoit, Dayton
1969-70—John Gravel, Toledo
1970-71—Bob LaPage, Des Moines
1971-72—Rick Pagnutti, Fort Wayne
1972-73—Bob McCammon, Port Huron
1973-74—Dave Simpson, Dayton
1974-75—Murry Flegel, Muskegon
1975-76—Murry Flegel, Muskegon
1976-77—Tom Mellor, Toledo

Season	Player, Team
1977-78	Michel LaChance, Milwaukee
1978-79	Guido Tenesi, Grand Rapids
1979-80	John Gibson, Saginaw
1980-81	Larry Goodenough, Saginaw
1981-82	Don Waddell, Saginaw
1982-83	Jim Burton, Fort Wayne
	Kevin Willison, Milwaukee
1983-84	Kevin Willison, Milwaukee
1984-85	Lee Norwood, Peoria
1985-86	Jim Burton, Fort Wayne
1986-87	Jim Burton, Fort Wayne
1987-88	Phil Bourque, Muskegon
1988-89	Randy Boyd, Milwaukee
1989-90	Brian Glynn, Salt Lake
1990-91	Brian McKee, Fort Wayne
1991-92	Jean-Marc Richard, Fort Wayne
1992-93	Bill Houlder, San Diego
1993-94	Darren Veitch, Peoria
1994-95	Todd Richards, Las Vegas
1995-96	Greg Hawgood, Las Vegas
1996-97	Brad Werenka, Indianapolis
1997-98	Dan Lambert, Long Beach
1998-99	Greg Hawgood, Houston
1999-00	Brett Hauer, Manitoba
2000-01	Brett Hauer, Manitoba

The award was originally known as the Governors Trophy from 1964-65 through 1998-99.

GARRY F. LONGMAN MEMORIAL TROPHY
(Outstanding rookie)

Season	Player, Team
1961-62	Dave Richardson, Fort Wayne
1962-63	John Gravel, Omaha
1963-64	Don Westbrooke, Toledo
1964-65	Bob Thomas, Toledo
1965-66	Frank Golembrowsky, Port Huron
1966-67	Kerry Bond, Columbus
1967-68	Gary Ford, Muskegon
1968-69	Doug Volmar, Columbus
1969-70	Wayne Zuk, Toledo
1970-71	Corky Agar, Flint
	Herb Howdle, Dayton
1971-72	Glenn Resch, Muskegon
1972-73	Danny Gloor, Des Moines
1973-74	Frank DeMarco, Des Moines
1974-75	Rick Bragnalo, Dayton
1975-76	Sid Veysey, Fort Wayne
1976-77	Ron Zanussi, Fort Wayne
	Garth MacGuigan, Muskegon
1977-78	Dan Bonar, Fort Wayne
1978-79	Wes Jarvis, Port Huron
1979-80	Doug Robb, Milwaukee
1980-81	Scott Vanderburgh, Kalamazoo
1981-82	Scott Howson, Toledo
1982-83	Tony Fiore, Flint
1983-84	Darren Jensen, Fort Wayne
1984-85	Gilles Thibaudeau, Flint
1965-66	Guy Benoit, Muskegon
1986-87	Michel Mongeau, Saginaw
1987-88	Ed Belfour, Saginaw
	John Cullen, Flint
1988-89	Paul Ranheim, Salt Lake
1989-90	Rob Murphy, Milwaukee
1990-91	Nelson Emerson, Peoria
1991-92	Dmitri Kvartalnov, Kansas City
1992-93	Mikhail Shtalenkov, Milwaukee
1993-94	Radek Bonk, Las Vegas
1994-95	Tommy Salo, Denver
1995-96	Konstantin Shafranov, Fort Wayne
1996-97	Sergei Samsonov, Detroit
1997-98	Todd White, Indianapolis
1998-99	Marty Turco, Michigan
1999-00	Nils Ekman, Long Beach
2000-01	Brian Pothier, Orlando

KEN MC KENZIE TROPHY
(Outstanding American-born rookie)

Season	Player, Team
1977-78	Mike Eruzione, Toledo
1978-79	Jon Fontas, Saginaw
1979-80	Bob Janecyk, Fort Wayne
1980-81	Mike Labianca, Toledo
	Steve Janaszak, Fort Wayne
1981-82	Steve Salvucci, Saginaw
1982-83	Paul Fenton, Peoria
1983-84	Mike Krensing, Muskegon
1984-85	Bill Schafhauser, Kalamazoo
1985-86	Brian Noonan, Saginaw
1986-87	Ray LeBlanc, Flint
1987-88	Dan Woodley, Flint
1988-89	Paul Ranheim, Salt Lake
1989-90	Tim Sweeney, Salt Lake
1990-91	C.J. Young, Salt Lake
1991-92	Kevin Wortman, Salt Lake
1992-93	Mark Beaufait, Kansas City
1993-94	Chris Rogles, Indianapolis
1994-95	Chris Marinucci, Denver
1995-96	Brett Lievers, Utah
1996-97	Brian Felsner, Orlando
1997-98	Eric Nickulas, Orlando
1998-99	Mark Mowers, Milwaukee
1999-00	Andrew Berenzweig, Milwaukee
2000-01	Brian Pothier, Orlando

COMMISSIONER'S TROPHY
(Coach of the year)

Season	Coach, Team
1984-85	Rick Ley, Muskegon
	Pat Kelly, Peoria
1985-86	Rob Laird, Fort Wayne
1986-87	Wayne Thomas, Salt Lake
1987-88	Rick Dudley, Flint
1988-89	B. J. MacDonald, Muskegon
	Phil Russell, Muskegon
1989-90	Darryl Sutter, Indianapolis
1990-91	Bob Plager, Peoria
1991-92	Kevin Constantine, Kansas City
1992-93	Al Sims, Fort Wayne
1993-94	Bruce Boudreau, Fort Wayne
1994-95	Butch Goring, Denver
1995-96	Butch Goring, Utah
1996-97	John Van Boxmeer, Long Beach
1997-98	John Torchetti, Fort Wayne
1998-99	Dave Tippett, Houston
1999-00	Guy Charron, Grand Rapids
2000-01	Peter Horachek, Orlando

N.R. (BUD) POILE TROPHY
(Playoff MVP)

Season	Player, Team
1984-85	Denis Cyr, Peoria
1985-86	Jock Callander, Muskegon
1986-87	Rick Heinz, Salt Lake
1987-88	Peter Lappin, Salt Lake
1988-89	Dave Michayluk, Muskegon
1989-90	Mike McNeill, Indianapolis
1990-91	Michel Mongeau, Peoria
1991-92	Ron Handy, Kansas City
1992-93	Pokey Reddick, Fort Wayne
1993-94	Stan Drulia, Atlanta
1994-95	Kip Miller, Denver
1995-96	Tommy Salo, Utah
1996-97	Peter Ciavaglia, Detroit
1997-98	Alexander Semak, Chicago
1998-99	Mark Freer, Houston
1999-00	Andre Trefilov, Chicago
2000-01	Norm Maracle, Orlando

The award was originally known as the Turner Cup Playoff MVP from 1984-85 through 1988-89.

	REGULAR-SEASON CHAMPION		PLAYOFF CHAMPION	
Season	**Team**	**Coach**	**Team**	**Coach**
1945-46—	No trophy awarded		Detroit Auto Club	Jack Ward
1946-47—	Windsor Staffords	Jack Ward	Windsor Spitfires	Ebbie Goodfellow
1947-48—	Windsor Hettche Spitfires	Dent-Goodfellow	Toledo Mercurys	Andy Mulligan
1948-49—	Toledo Mercurys	Andy Mulligan	Windsor Hettche Spitfires	Jimmy Skinner
1949-50—	Sarnia Sailors	Dick Kowcinak	Catham Maroons	Bob Stoddart
1950-51—	Grand Rapids Rockets	Lou Trudell	Toledo Mercurys	Alex Wood
1951-52—	Grand Rapids Rockets	Lou Trudell	Toledo Mercurys	Alex Wood
1952-53—	Cincinnati Mohawks	Buddy O'Conner	Cincinnati Mohawks	Buddy O'Conner
1953-54—	Cincinnati Mohawks	Roly McLenahan	Cincinnati Mohawks	Roly McLenahan
1954-55—	Cincinnati Mohawks	Roly McLenahan	Cincinnati Mohawks	Roly McLenahan
1955-56—	Cincinnati Mohawks	Roly McLenahan	Cincinnati Mohawks	Roly McLenahan
1956-57—	Cincinnati Mohawks	Roly McLenahan	Cincinnati Mohawks	Roly McLenahan
1957-58—	Cincinnati Mohawks	Bill Gould	Indiana. Chiefs	Leo Lamoureux
1958-59—	Louisville Rebels	Leo Gasparini	Louisville Rebels	Leo Gasparini
1959-60—	Fort Wayne Komets	Ken Ullyot	St. Paul Saints	Fred Shero
1960-61—	Minneapolis Millers	Ken Yachel	St. Paul Saints	Fred Shero
1961-62—	Muskegon Zephrys	Moose Lallo	Muskegon Zephrys	Moose Lallo
1962-63—	Fort Wayne Komets	Ken Ullyot	Fort Wayne Komets	Ken Ullyot
1963-64—	Toledo Blades	Moe Benoit	Toledo Blades	Moe Benoit
1964-65—	Port Huron Flags	Lloyd Maxfield	Fort Wayne Komets	Eddie Long
1965-66—	Muskegon Mohawks	Moose Lallo	Port Huron Flags	Lloyd Maxfield
1966-67—	Dayton Gems	Warren Back	Toledo Blades	Terry Slater
1967-68—	Muskegon Mohawks	Moose Lallo	Muskegon Mohawks	Moose Lallo
1968-69—	Dayton Gems	Larry Wilson	Dayton Gems	Larry Wilson
1969-70—	Muskegon Mohawks	Moose Lallo	Dayton Gems	Larry Wilson
1970-71—	Muskegon Mohawks	Moose Lallo	Port Huron Flags	Ted Garvin
1971-72—	Muskegon Mohawks	Moose Lallo	Port Huron Flags	Ted Garvin
1972-73—	Fort Wayne Komets	Marc Boileau	Fort Wayne Komets	Marc Boileau
1973-74—	Des Moines Capitals	Dan Belisle	Des Moines Capitals	Dan Belisle
1974-75—	Muskegon Mohawks	Moose Lallo	Toledo Goaldiggers	Ted Garvin
1975-76—	Dayton Gems	Ivan Prediger	Dayton Gems	Ivan Prediger
1976-77—	Saginaw Gears	Don Perry	Saginaw Gears	Don Perry
1977-78—	Fort Wayne Komets	Gregg Pilling	Toledo Goaldiggers	Ted Garvin
1978-79—	Grand Rapids Owls	Moe Bartoli	Kalamazoo Wings	Bill Purcell
1979-80—	Kalamazoo Wings	Doug McKay	Kalamazoo Wings	Doug McKay
1980-81—	Kalamazoo Wings	Doug McKay	Saginaw Gears	Don Perry
1981-82—	Toledo Goaldiggers	Bill Inglis	Toledo Goaldiggers	Bill Inglis
1982-83—	Toledo Goaldiggers	Bill Inglis	Toledo Goaldiggers	Bill Inglis
1983-84—	Fort Wayne Komets	Ron Ullyot	Flint Generals	Dennis Desrosiers
1984-85—	Peoria Rivermen	Pat Kelly	Peoria Rivermen	Pat Kelly
1985-86—	Fort Wayne Komets	Rob Laird	Muskegon Lumberjacks	Rick Ley
1986-87—	Fort Wayne Komets	Rob Laird	Salt Lake Golden Eagles	Wayne Thomas
1987-88—	Muskegon Lumberjacks	Rick Ley	Salt Lake Golden Eagles	Paul Baxter
1988-89—	Muskegon Lumberjacks	B.J. MacDonald	Muskegon Lumberjacks	B.J. MacDonald
1989-90—	Muskegon Lumberjacks	B.J. MacDonald	Indianapolis Ice	Darryl Sutter
1990-91—	Peoria Rivermen	Bob Plager	Peoria Rivermen	Bob Plager
1991-92—	Kansas City Blades	Kevin Constantine	Kansas City Blades	Kevin Constantine
1992-93—	San Diego Gulls	Rick Dudley	Fort Wayne Komets	Al Sims
1993-94—	Las Vegas Thunder	Butch Goring	Atlanta Knights	Gene Ubriaco
1994-95—	Denver Grizzlies	Butch Goring	Denver Grizzlies	Butch Goring
1995-96—	Las Vegas Thunder	Chris McSorley	Utah Grizzlies	Butch Goring
1996-97—	Detroit Vipers	Steve Ludzik	Detroit Vipers	Steve Ludzik
1997-98—	Long Beach Ice Dogs	John Van Boxmeer	Chicago Wolves	John Anderson
1998-99—	Houston Aeros	Dave Tippett	Houston Aeros	Dave Tippett
1999-00—	Chicago Wolves	John Anderson	Chicago Wolves	John Anderson
2000-01—	Grand Rapids	Guy Charron	Orlando Solar Bears	Peter Horachek

The IHL regular-season champion is awarded the Fred A. Huber Trophy and the playoff champion is awarded the Joseph Turner Memorial Cup.

The regular-season championship award was originally called the J.P. McGuire Trophy from 1946-47 through 1953-54.

EAST COAST HOCKEY LEAGUE

LEAGUE OFFICE

President/chief executive officer
Richard W. Adams
Commissioner emeritus
Patrick J. Kelly
Sr. v.p. of business operations
Scott Sabatino
Vice president of hockey administration
Doug Price
V.p of marketing/sales
Glen Thornborough

Director of communications
Jack Carnefix
Assistant director of communications
Diana Danforth
Director of special projects
Melissa Adams
Director of marketing/licensing
Kelly Jutras
Director of officiating
Bryan Graham

Address
103 Main Street, Suite 300
Princeton, NJ 08540
Phone
609-452-0770
FAX
609-452-7147

TEAMS

ARKANSAS RIVERBLADES
President and chief executive officer
Dave Berryman
Head coach
Chris Cichocki
Home ice
Alltel Arena
Address
425 W. Broadway, Suite A
North Little Rock, AR 72114
Seating capacity
16,377
Phone
501-975-2327
FAX
501-907-2327

ATLANTIC CITY HOCKEY CLUB
General manager
Matt Loughran
Head coach
To be announced
Home ice
Boardwalk Hall
Address
2301 Boardwalk
Atlantic City, NJ 08401
Seating capacity
10,500
Phone
609-348-7825
FAX
609-348-7828

AUGUSTA LYNX
General manager
Mike Pierson
Head coach
Jim Burton
Home ice
Richmond County Civic Center
Address
712 Telfair St.
Augusta, GA 30901
Seating capacity
6,604
Phone
706-724-4423
FAX
706-724-2423

BATON ROUGE KINGFISH
General manager
Ron Hansis

Head coach
Dave Lohrei
Home ice
Centroplex
Address
P.O. Box 2142
Baton Rouge, LA 70821
Seating capacity
8,600
Phone
225-336-4625
FAX
225-336-4011

CHARLOTTE CHECKERS
General manager
Sam Russo
Head coach
Don MacAdam
Home ice
Independence Arena
Address
2700 E. Independence Blvd.
Charlotte, NC 28205
Seating capacity
9,570
Phone
704-342-4423
FAX
704-377-4595

CINCINNATI CYCLONES
General manager
To be announced
Head coach
Ray Edwards
Home ice
Firstar Center
Address
100 Broadway
Cincinnati, OH 45202
Seating capacity
12,056
Phone
513-521-7825
FAX
513-421-1210

COLUMBIA INFERNO
General manager
Rick Woodard
Head coach
Scott White
Home ice
Carolina Coliseum

Address
701 Assembly Street
Columbia, S.C. 29201
Seating capacity
6,300
Phone
803-256-7825
FAX
803-256-7866

COLUMBUS COTTONMOUTHS
General manager
Phil Roberto
Head coach
Bruce Garber
Home ice
Columbus Civic Center
Address
400 Fourth Street
Columbus, GA 31901
Seating capacity
7,509
Phone
706-571-0086
FAX
706-571-0080

DAYTON BOMBERS
General manager
Ed Gingher
Head coach
Greg Ireland
Home ice
Nutter Center
Address
3640 Colonel Glenn Hwy, Suite 417
Dayton, OH 45435
Seating capacity
9,950
Phone
937-775-4747
FAX
937-775-4749

FLORIDA EVERBLADES
President
Craig Brush
Head coach
Gerry Fleming
Home ice
TECO Arena
Address
11000 Everblades Parkway
Estero, FL 33928

Seating capacity
7,181
Phone
941-948-7825
FAX
941-948-2248

GREENSBORO GENERALS

President
Art Donaldson
Head coach
Graeme Townshend
Home ice
Greensboro Coliseum
Address
P.O. Box 3387
Greensboro, NC 27402
Seating capacity
20,800
Phone
336-218-5428
FAX
336-218-5498

GREENVILLE GRRROWL

President
Carl Scheer
Head coach
John Marks
Home ice
BI-LO Center
Address
P.O. Box 10348
Greenville, SC 29603
Seating capacity
14,108
Phone
864-467-4777
FAX
864-241-3872

JOHNSTOWN CHIEFS

General manager
Toby O'Brien
Head coach
Scott Allen
Home ice
Cambria County War Memorial
Address
326 Napoleon Street
Johnstown, PA 15901
Seating capacity
4,050
Phone
814-539-1799
FAX
814-536-1316

LOUISIANA ICEGATORS

General manager
Rudy Bourg
Head coach
Dave Farrish
Home ice
Cajundome
Address
444 Cajundome Blvd.
Lafayette, LA 70506
Seating capacity
11,700
Phone
337-234-4423
FAX
337-232-1254

MACON WHOOPEE

President
Keith Burdette
Head coach
To be announced
Home ice
Macon Centreplex
Address
200 Coliseum Dr.
Macon, GA 31217
Seating capacity
7,100
Phone
478-741-1000
FAX
478-464-0655

MISSISSIPPI SEA WOLVES

General manager
Jean Gagnon
Head coach
Bob Woods
Home ice
Mississippi Coast Coliseum
Address
2350 Beach Blvd.
Biloxi, MS 39531
Seating capacity
9,150
Phone
228-388-6151
FAX
228-388-5848

MOBILE MYSTICKS

General manager
Brian Genard
Head coach
Jeff Pyle
Home ice
Mobile Civic Center
Address
P.O. Box 263
Mobile, AL 36601-0263
Seating capacity
8,033
Phone
334-208-7825
FAX
334-434-7931

NEW ORLEANS BRASS

Vice president/general manager
Dan Belisle
Head coach
Ted Sator
Home ice
New Orleans Arena
Address
1660 Girod Street
New Orleans, LA 70113
Seating capacity
17,000
Phone
504-522-7825
FAX
504-523-7295

PEE DEE PRIDE

Senior vice president
Jack Capuano
Head coach
Davis Payne
Home ice
Florence City-County Civic Center

Address
One Civic Center Plaza
3300 West Radio Drive
Florence, SC 29501
Seating capacity
7,426
Phone
843-669-7825
FAX
843-669-7149

PENSACOLA ICE PILOTS

Director of business operations
Neil Hoyt
Head coach
Todd Gordon
Home ice
Pensacola Civic Center
Address
201 East Gregory St.-Rear
Pensacola, FL 32501-4956
Seating capacity
8,150
Phone
850-432-7825
FAX
850-432-1929

PEORIA RIVERMEN

President
John Butler
Head coach
Jason Christie
Home ice
Peoria Civic Center
Address
201 SW Jefferson
Peoria, IL 61602
Seating capacity
9,470
Phone
309-676-1040
FAX
309-676-2488

READING ROYALS

General manager
Ray Delia
Head coach
Al Sims
Home ice
Sovereign Center
Address
35 N. 6th Street, 1st Floor
Reading, PA 19601
Seating capacity
7,200
Phone
610-898-7825
FAX
610-898-4625

RICHMOND RENEGADES

President/hockey operations
Paul Gamsby
Head coach
Mark Kaufman
Home ice
Richmond Coliseum
Address
601 East Leigh St.
Richmond, VA 23219
Seating capacity
11,088

Phone
804-643-7865
FAX
804-649-0651

ROANOKE EXPRESS
General manager
Tony Benizio
Head coach
Perry Florie
Home ice
Roanoke Civic Center
Address
101 SW Campbell Ave.
Roanoke, VA 24011
Seating capacity
8,706
Phone
540-343-4500
FAX
540-343-4523

SOUTH CAROLINA STRINGRAYS
President
Matt Klidjian
Head coach
Rick Adduono
Home ice
North Charleston Coliseum
Address
3107 Firestone Road
N. Charleston, SC 29418

Seating capacity
10,529
Phone
843-744-2248
FAX
843-744-2898

TOLEDO STORM
General manager
Pat Pylypuik
Head coach
Dennis Holland
Home ice
Toledo Sports Arena
Address
One Main Street
Toledo, OH 43605
Seating capacity
5,160
Phone
419-691-0200
FAX
419-698-8998

TRENTON TITANS
President and general manager
Brian McKenna
Head coach
Troy Ward
Home ice
Sovereign Bank Arena

Address
650 S. Broad Street
Trenton, NJ 08611
Seating capacity
7,850
Phone
609-599-9500
FAX
609-599-3600

WHEELING NAILERS
Vice president/general manager
Eddie Johnston
Head coach
John Brophy
Home ice
Wheeling Civic Center
Address
1144 Market Street, Suite 202
Wheeling, WV 26003
Seating capacity
5,406
Phone
304-234-4625
FAX
304-233-4846

2000-01 REGULAR SEASON
FINAL STANDINGS

NORTHERN CONFERENCE

NORTHEAST DIVISION

Team	G	W	L	T	Pts.	GF	GA
Trenton	72	50	18	4	104	236	164
Roanoke	72	38	30	4	80	231	195
Charlotte	72	34	26	12	80	247	252
Richmond	72	35	31	6	76	223	228
Greensboro	72	26	39	7	59	215	277

NORTHWEST DIVISION

Team	G	W	L	T	Pts.	GF	GA
Peoria	72	45	17	10	100	238	182
Dayton	72	45	21	6	96	247	194
Toledo	72	37	27	8	82	262	259
Johnstown	72	28	36	8	64	207	238
Wheeling	72	24	40	8	56	192	277

SOUTHERN CONFERENCE

SOUTHEAST DIVISION

Team	G	W	L	T	Pts.	GF	GA
South Carolina	72	42	23	7	91	240	210
Florida	72	38	26	8	84	236	242
Tallahassee	72	38	27	7	83	248	219
Pee Dee	72	38	28	6	82	242	231
Augusta	72	36	29	7	79	259	253
Greenville	72	34	33	5	73	219	239

SOUTHWEST DIVISION

Team	G	W	L	T	Pts.	GF	GA
Louisiana	72	42	24	6	90	237	209
Jackson	72	39	24	9	87	206	209
Mobile	72	38	28	6	82	240	233
New Orleans	72	35	25	12	82	247	239
Arkansas	72	34	24	14	82	237	232
Baton Rouge	72	35	26	11	81	216	225
Mississippi	72	34	33	5	73	221	218
Birmingham	72	28	40	4	60	224	296
Pensacola	72	27	40	5	59	201	250

INDIVIDUAL LEADERS

Goals: Andrew Williamson, Toledo (52)
Assists: John Spoltore, Louisiana (71)
Points: Scott King, Charlotte (101)
Penalty minutes: Jason Hamilton, B.R.-Whe. (412)
Goaltending average: Curtis Sanford, Peoria (1.91)
Shutouts: Brian Leitza, Baton Rouge (5)
Scott Stirling, Trenton (5)

TOP SCORERS

	Games	G	A	Pts.
King, Scott, Charlotte	72	40	61	101
Bes, Jeff, Pen.-Jack.	68	35	65	100
Williamson, Andrew, Toledo	66	52	45	97
Patterson, James, Toledo	65	40	56	96
Ling, Jamie, Dayton	72	26	67	93
Morrow, Scott, Augusta	70	33	53	86
Spoltore, John, Louisiana	59	14	71	85
Bousquet, Dany, Pee Dee	56	39	45	84
Hicks, Jamey, Birmingham	68	34	50	84

	Games	G	A	Pts.			Games	G	A	Pts.
Vincent, Paul, Ark.-Aug.	61	34	49	83		Edinger, Adam, New Orleans	58	31	45	76
Cadotte, Mark, Arkansas	72	37	44	81		Cullaton, Brent, Tallahassee	54	27	47	74
McNeil, Shawn, Louisiana	72	36	45	81		Benoit, Mathieu, Charlotte	62	43	30	73
Buckley, Tom, Florida	71	27	53	80		Soling, Jonas, Augusta	71	41	31	72
Hilton, Kevin, Charlotte	71	19	61	80		Tropper, Marc, Charlotte	63	29	43	72
Elders, Jason, Mobile	71	36	41	77		Calder, Adam, South Carolina	67	28	44	72
Turner, Mark, Mobile	69	30	47	77		Dumont, Louis, Augusta	60	25	47	72

INDIVIDUAL STATISTICS

ARKANSAS RIVERBLADES

SCORING

	Games	G	A	Pts.	PIM
Mark Cadotte	72	37	44	81	76
Aaron Brand	71	29	39	68	66
Jason Bermingham	71	21	34	55	67
Eric Long	72	8	41	49	76
Trevor Roenick	37	16	29	45	64
Paul Vincent	35	16	24	40	57
Lee Jinman	34	11	26	37	26
Dan Heilman	65	13	23	36	42
Eric Brule	53	6	30	36	48
Shane Kenny	63	10	18	28	116
Mike Bodnarchuk	24	12	11	23	28
Dan Harrison	63	5	14	19	105
Russ Guzior	25	10	8	18	24
Nic Beaudoin	17	9	7	16	6
Travis Dillabough	47	5	10	15	50
Neal Rech	22	7	7	14	42
Jason Payne	45	6	5	11	178
Matt Masterson	31	4	7	11	20
Dean Stork	70	3	7	10	87
Brent Ozarowski	41	1	7	8	17
Mark McMahon	59	2	5	7	147
Rob Smillie	16	2	3	5	0
Paul Giblin	26	1	3	4	4
Hugo Belanger	1	2	0	2	0
Jeff Potter	7	1	1	2	4
Bob Janosz (goalie)	28	0	2	2	2
Vern Fiddler	3	0	1	1	2
Peter MacKellar	1	0	0	0	0
Mark Spence	1	0	0	0	0
Kevin Tucker	3	0	0	0	4
Luc Roy	4	0	0	0	4
Troy Khaler	7	0	0	0	4
Ryan Lee	8	0	0	0	43
Keith Cassidy	11	0	0	0	27
Jeff Salajko (goalie)	47	0	0	0	34

GOALTENDING

	Gms.	Min.	W	L	T	G	SO	Avg.
Jeff Salajko	47	2779	24	13	8	129	3	2.79
Bob Janosz	28	1611	10	11	6	93	0	3.46

AUGUSTA LYNX

SCORING

	Games	G	A	Pts.	PIM
Scott Morrow	70	33	53	86	143
Jonas Soling	71	41	31	72	63
Louis Dumont	60	25	47	72	108
Dean Tiltgen	72	30	38	68	51
Lars Pettersen	51	24	37	61	28
Wes Swinson	60	10	37	47	186
Likit Andersson	71	8	36	44	65
Paul Vincent	26	18	25	43	19
Martin Lapointe	72	9	30	39	52
Sandy Lamarre	63	20	14	34	143
Russ Guzior	41	6	17	23	66
John Whitwell	71	5	18	23	91
Rob Bonneau	21	5	17	22	16
Tomas Groschl	59	5	11	16	52
Tom O'Connor	68	1	11	12	52

	Games	G	A	Pts.	PIM
Cal Benazic	22	5	6	11	68
Chris Thompson	17	3	6	9	76
Andrei Chouroupov	33	2	5	7	29
Peter Nylander	26	3	3	6	4
Ken Tasker	45	2	4	6	123
Denis Chervyakov	52	0	6	6	51
Dorian Anneck	15	3	2	5	4
Andrew Rodgers	10	1	0	1	53
Patrick Yetman	1	0	1	1	0
Jeff McKercher	2	0	1	1	0
Reg Bourcier (goalie)	22	0	1	1	6
Danny Bigras	1	0	0	0	0
Jeff Blanchard	3	0	0	0	6
Bob Thorton	3	0	0	0	6
J.R. Prestifilippo (goalie)	9	0	0	0	0
Troy Stevens	10	0	0	0	0
Judd Lambert (goalie)	17	0	0	0	0
Erasmo Saltarelli (goalie)	30	0	0	0	2

GOALTENDING

	Gms.	Min.	W	L	T	G	SO	Avg.
Judd Lambert	17	1033	10	6	1	48	2	2.79
Erasmo Saltarelli	30	1764	17	10	3	98	1	3.33
Reg Bourcier	22	1217	9	7	3	74	0	3.65
J.R. Prestifilippo	9	348	0	6	0	25	0	4.31

BATON ROUGE KINGFISH

SCORING

	Games	G	A	Pts.	PIM
Mike Rucinski	64	31	33	64	81
Jon Sturgis	71	23	36	59	40
Cam Brown	71	18	28	46	131
Shane Calder	67	22	21	43	95
Dane Litke	69	10	33	43	24
Andy Doktorchik	56	19	20	39	89
Matt Erredge	53	18	20	38	16
C.J. Buzzell	58	12	23	35	28
Josh Mizerek	69	11	18	29	54
Sylvain Dufresne	72	5	22	27	45
Chris Chelios	53	5	20	25	91
Sean Berens	18	12	9	21	26
Forrest Gore	16	8	11	19	17
Per Ledin	27	4	8	12	37
Keith Bland	69	3	9	12	177
Jarrett Smith	18	4	7	11	16
Jay McKee	20	2	9	11	24
Ronalds Ozolinsh	62	2	9	11	86
Jay Legault	8	3	5	8	6
Jesse Rooney	6	3	2	5	2
Kris Mallette	45	1	4	5	114
Torrey DiRoberto	3	0	3	3	2
John Peterman	10	0	3	3	8
Paxton Schafer (goalie)	45	0	3	3	10
Chris Cerrella	6	0	2	2	4
Kevin Magnuson	66	0	2	2	98
Rob Sinclair	4	0	1	1	0
D.J. Mando	5	0	1	1	6
Samy Nasreddine	5	0	1	1	18
Chris Ford	7	0	1	1	2
Jason Hamilton	12	0	1	1	79
Brian Leitza (goalie)	32	0	1	1	2
Mike Barrie	1	0	0	0	17

GOALTENDING

	Gms.	Min.	W	L	T	G	SO	Avg.
Brian Leitza	32	1806	14	16	2	82	5	2.72
Paxton Schafer	44	2564	21	10	9	130	0	3.04

BIRMINGHAM BULLS

SCORING

	Games	G	A	Pts.	PIM
Jamey Hicks	68	34	50	84	64
Eduard Pershin	61	24	36	60	127
John Campbell	72	20	34	54	57
Dennis Maxwell	53	22	31	53	231
Stefan Rivard	51	20	30	50	243
Tyler Johnston	48	8	23	31	78
Hugo Belanger	29	11	16	27	21
Ian Walterson	42	8	18	26	22
Matt Turek	37	16	9	25	30
Ted Laviolette	34	1	20	21	44
Mark Biesenthal	39	11	8	19	87
Dion Hagan	72	4	14	18	64
Brandon Merli	53	7	10	17	53
Denis Smakovsky	22	8	4	12	26
Ryan Pepperall	21	7	2	9	37
Mike Barrie	10	5	4	9	41
Ryan Moynihan	15	4	5	9	2
Neal Rech	27	4	5	9	70
Mark Loeding	68	2	7	9	75
Rob Stanfield	65	2	5	7	140
Ian Hebert	9	1	6	7	8
Branoslav Kvetan	35	0	6	6	76
Peter Constantine	46	1	4	5	216
Ryan Hoople (goalie)	34	0	5	5	8
Louie Colsant	31	2	2	4	26
Jay McKee	13	0	3	3	8
Craig Lutes	14	2	0	2	14
Duncan Dalmao	10	0	2	2	6
Josh MacNevin	16	0	2	2	32
Randy Davidson	6	0	1	1	4
Shane Stewart	8	0	1	1	8
Leorr Shtrom (goalie)	22	0	1	1	12
Shawn Timm (goalie)	1	0	0	0	0
Greg Dreveny (goalie)	2	0	0	0	0
Corey Batten (goalie)	4	0	0	0	0
Jeff Blair (goalie)	5	0	0	0	2
Piero Greco (goalie)	7	0	0	0	0
Everett Caldwell	11	0	0	0	12

GOALTENDING

	Gms.	Min.	W	L	T	G	SO	Avg.
Cory Batten	4	238	1	3	0	11	0	2.77
Leorr Shtrom	22	1286	13	9	0	71	0	3.31
Ryan Hoople	34	2003	12	17	3	129	0	3.86
Piero Greco	7	428	2	4	1	33	0	4.63
Greg Dreveny	2	105	0	1	0	10	0	5.69
Jeff Blair	5	298	0	5	0	29	0	5.84
Shawn Timm	1	15	0	1	0	3	0	12.39

CHARLOTTE CHECKERS

SCORING

	Games	G	A	Pts.	PIM
Scott King	72	40	61	101	34
Kevin Hilton	71	19	61	80	38
Mathieu Benoit	62	43	30	73	16
Marc Tropper	63	29	43	72	97
David Oliver	66	15	29	44	226
Paul Giblin	45	19	19	38	14
Mike Hurley	33	13	13	26	24
Tyler Deis	58	9	16	25	105
Kurt Seher	62	5	19	24	54
Josh MacNevin	52	2	19	21	47
Brad Mehalko	26	8	11	19	47
Kevin Pozzo	44	3	16	19	33
Boyd Kane	12	9	8	17	6
Mark Spence	59	6	9	15	40

	Games	G	A	Pts.	PIM
Justin Harney	23	3	10	13	18
Wes Jarvis	39	4	8	12	185
Dennis Maxwell	9	6	5	11	13
Lee Hamilton	53	3	8	11	77
Brandon Dietrich	20	2	9	11	19
Andre Signoretti	27	0	9	9	8
Martin Cerven	30	1	7	8	26
Bob MacIsaac	67	2	4	6	106
Francois Fortier	7	1	5	6	15
Steve Wilson	14	1	4	5	23
Steve Duke	23	1	3	4	22
Eric Silverman	8	0	4	4	2
Scott Wray	8	1	2	3	2
Mike Hartman	16	1	2	3	21
Richard Scott	4	1	1	2	22
Oak Hewer	12	0	2	2	2
Scott Bailey (goalie)	29	0	2	2	14
Jason Labarbera (goalie)	35	0	2	2	2
Vitali Yeremeyev (goalie)	5	0	1	1	0
Chris Manchakowski	7	0	1	1	14
Shep Harder (goalie)	1	0	0	0	0
Benjamin Carpentier	2	0	0	0	10
Shawn Mansoff	2	0	0	0	0
Matt Mulhern	2	0	0	0	0
Bryce Wandler (goalie)	4	0	0	0	0
Mark Moore	7	0	0	0	4

GOALTENDING

	Gms.	Min.	W	L	T	G	SO	Avg.
Shep Harder	1	60	1	0	0	2	0	2.00
Scott Bailey	29	1682	10	12	5	89	1	3.17
Jason LaBarbera	35	2100	18	10	7	112	1	3.20
Vitali Yeremeyev	5	298	3	2	0	21	0	4.23
Bryce Wandler	4	240	2	2	0	18	0	4.50

DAYTON BOMBERS

SCORING

	Games	G	A	Pts.	PIM
Jamie Ling	72	26	67	93	40
Tom Nemeth	72	20	48	68	87
Brad Holzinger	66	20	39	59	77
Bill McCauley	65	13	46	59	48
Jeff Mitchell	56	21	35	56	236
Brendan Brooks	65	29	18	47	95
Ben Keup	66	23	21	44	154
Dan Preston	68	12	24	36	66
Mike Isherwood	58	11	16	27	51
Greg Labenski	71	8	18	26	116
Kent McDonell	28	16	9	25	94
Jonathan Schill	58	18	6	24	153
Dave Flanagan	21	8	8	16	4
Chris Thompson	15	7	6	13	71
Doug Nolan	42	1	12	13	137
Blaine McCauley	62	0	12	12	255
Dan Price	17	6	5	11	46
Rick Gorman	31	4	5	9	24
Mike Mulligan	31	3	3	6	98
Robert Ek	18	0	4	4	2
Derek Ernest	65	0	4	4	321
Alex Westlund (goalie)	29	0	3	3	8
Sean Seyferth	2	0	2	2	2
Ernie Hartlieb	5	0	2	2	2
Trevor Prior (goalie)	14	0	2	2	2
Cody Leibel	18	0	2	2	21
Greg Gardner (goalie)	28	0	2	2	44
Mark Shalawylo	7	1	0	1	4
Andrei Kuznetsov	5	0	1	1	0
Chad Ford (goalie)	2	0	0	0	0
Mike Garrow	2	0	0	0	2
Shane Kuss	2	0	0	0	0
Dan Powell	2	0	0	0	0
Andrew Allen (goalie)	4	0	0	0	0
Jeremy Cornish	4	0	0	0	10
Bryan McKinney	5	0	0	0	8

	Games	G	A	Pts.	PIM
Troy Kahler	7	0	0	0	10
Adam Nittel	9	0	0	0	30

GOALTENDING

	Gms.	Min.	W	L	T	G	SO	Avg.
Andrew Allen	4	240	4	0	0	5	2	1.25
Alex Westlund	29	1731	19	5	4	64	3	2.22
Greg Gardner	28	1600	14	9	2	70	2	2.62
Trevor Prior	14	743	8	6	0	45	0	3.64
Chad Ford	2	71	0	1	0	7	0	5.94

FLORIDA EVERBLADES

SCORING

	Games	G	A	Pts.	PIM
Tom Buckley	71	27	53	80	88
Matt Demarski	63	30	33	63	55
Andy MacIntyre	71	28	30	58	34
Reggie Berg	33	19	29	48	39
Randy Copley	69	22	18	40	55
Jason Morgan	37	15	22	37	41
David Vallieres	45	10	24	34	66
Peter Hogan	70	7	23	30	80
Sean Blanchard	51	5	25	30	60
Devin Hartnell	60	14	14	28	103
Mike Jickling	40	7	19	26	34
Brent McDonald	67	11	11	22	55
Terry Lindgren	68	4	18	22	149
Hugh Hamilton	60	7	13	20	68
Shane Belter	35	3	16	19	34
Anthony Terzo	21	3	8	11	14
Jonathan Sorg	19	3	7	10	24
Darrell Hay	40	5	4	9	26
Ryan Pepperall	29	3	6	9	51
Joel Trottier	24	5	2	7	25
Tim Wolfe	12	2	5	7	6
Nathan Rocheleau	23	2	3	5	16
Sandy Cohen	19	1	4	5	0
Brent Pope	31	0	5	5	51
Kevin McDonald	13	1	2	3	67
Jason Metcalfe	31	0	2	2	56
Colin Anderson	2	1	0	1	0
Jean-Francois Dufour	3	1	0	1	0
Josh Mizerek	2	0	1	1	2
Kevin Bertram	5	0	1	1	4
Nathan Rempel	8	0	1	1	9
Bryce Macken	13	0	1	1	6
Marc Magliarditi (goalie)	26	0	1	1	0
Bujar Amidovski (goalie)	31	0	1	1	17
Leorr Shtrom (goalie)	1	0	0	0	0
Richard Shulmistra (goalie)	2	0	0	0	0
Greg Callahan	7	0	0	0	18
Oleg Timchenko	9	0	0	0	0
Brant Nicklin (goalie)	11	0	0	0	0
Randy Petruk (goalie)	13	0	0	0	10

GOALTENDING

	Gms.	Min.	W	L	T	G	SO	Avg.
Marc Magliarditi	26	1445	16	6	2	65	1	2.70
Richard Shulmistra	2	130	2	0	0	7	0	3.23
Randy Petruk	13	742	5	7	1	41	0	3.31
Brant Nicklin	11	544	4	4	2	31	0	3.42
Bujar Amidovski	30	1456	11	8	3	88	0	3.63
Leorr Shtrom	1	60	0	1	0	4	0	4.00

GREENSBORO GENERALS

SCORING

	Games	G	A	Pts.	PIM
Sal Manganaro	67	33	34	67	127
Joel Irwin	68	23	40	63	64
Lukas Smital	68	26	32	58	58
Jamie Sokolsky	72	19	29	48	66
Mike Sylvia	56	15	28	43	50
Curtis Huppe	47	18	23	41	23
Jason Ialongo	46	8	24	32	16

	Games	G	A	Pts.	PIM
Oleg Timchenko	48	12	18	30	14
Joe Ritson	71	13	11	24	51
Duane Harmer	39	3	21	24	64
Kevin Paden	30	9	12	21	31
Mike Perna	61	2	17	19	221
Curtis Wilgosh	38	4	10	14	34
Martin Masa	13	5	6	11	12
Andrew Taylor	19	4	7	11	37
Juraj Slovak	65	5	5	10	52
Martin Galik	21	3	6	9	8
Jason Robinson	51	1	8	9	132
Mike Sgroi	9	3	4	7	44
Bob Halkidis	33	1	6	7	50
Trevor Gillies	63	1	6	7	303
Kris Waltze	32	3	3	6	170
Nathan Rempel	22	2	2	4	31
Roger Larche	5	1	1	2	7
David Whitworth	5	0	2	2	4
Chris Thompson	8	0	2	2	19
Jason Windle	17	0	2	2	14
Darryl Campbell	4	1	0	1	2
Troy Stevens	7	0	1	1	2
Martin Cerven	11	0	1	1	4
Bob Thornton	11	0	1	1	6
Erasmo Saltarelli (goalie)	8	0	0	0	0
J.R. Prestifilippo (goalie)	9	0	0	0	4
Eric Heffler (goalie)	15	0	0	0	0
Trevor Prior (goalie)	18	0	0	0	2
Sergei Naumov (goalie)	31	0	0	0	2

GOALTENDING

	Gms.	Min.	W	L	T	G	SO	Avg.
Erasmo Saltarelli	8	396	4	2	0	20	0	3.03
Sergei Naumov	31	1767	11	14	5	95	1	3.23
Trevor Prior	18	992	6	9	1	66	1	3.99
Eric Heffler	15	821	4	10	0	55	0	4.02
J.R. Prestifilippo	9	402	1	4	1	32	0	4.77

GREENVILLE GRRROWL

SCORING

	Games	G	A	Pts.	PIM
Scott Kirton	70	20	42	62	148
Brad Federenko	65	21	31	52	34
Colln Pepperall	62	25	20	45	106
Neil Fewster	72	10	34	44	57
Martin Masa	56	15	26	41	128
Ryan Stewart	70	19	21	40	179
Sean Venedam	51	15	22	37	42
Vratisla Cech	64	10	19	29	96
Jason Kelly	63	6	23	29	85
Andrew Taylor	50	12	16	28	61
Jason Windle	44	10	9	19	29
Doug Kirton	45	6	12	18	42
Sean Ritchlin	25	9	8	17	20
Kelly Harper	16	6	11	17	6
Jason Ialongo	21	6	11	17	6
David Bell	67	4	13	17	190
Cam Kryway	54	5	10	15	61
Vladimir Sicak	34	4	6	10	16
Mike Sylvia	14	5	4	9	6
Curtis Huppe	20	4	5	9	2
Dwayne Blais	9	1	6	7	2
Matt Masterson	12	1	3	4	2
Jeff Zehr	23	2	1	3	76
Eric Van Acker	59	1	2	3	149
Dan Heilman	5	2	0	2	0
Scott Ricci	15	0	2	2	8
Tyrone Garner (goalie)	36	0	1	1	2
Todd Bisson	3	0	0	0	2
Blaz Emersic	3	0	0	0	0
Charles Paquette	3	0	0	0	4
Denis Timofeev	3	0	0	0	8
Kirby Tokarski	3	0	0	0	2
Derek Gosselin	4	0	0	0	4

	Games	G	A	Pts.	PIM
Brian Wesenberg	4	0	0	0	7
Craig Minard	5	0	0	0	0
Antti Kohvakka	6	0	0	0	2
Shep Harder (goalie)	9	0	0	0	0
Nick Vitucci (goalie)	29	0	0	0	0

GOALTENDING

	Gms.	Min.	W	L	T	G	SO	Avg.
Tyrone Garner	35	2114	17	15	3	99	3	2.81
Nick Vitucci	29	1719	14	12	2	91	1	3.18
Shep Harder	9	538	3	6	0	35	0	3.91

JACKSON BANDITS
SCORING

	Games	G	A	Pts.	PIM
Denny Felsner	70	25	45	70	30
Bobby Russell	69	38	30	68	44
Cory Larose	63	21	32	53	73
Quintin Laing	60	13	24	37	39
Brian Callahan	72	23	13	36	151
Ryan Mougenel	57	15	19	34	80
Jeff Bes	20	11	21	32	34
Jim Bermingham	45	11	17	28	50
Chris Peyton	65	5	17	22	58
Ryan Gillis	26	2	20	22	37
Bobby Stewart	26	9	12	21	16
Dave Stewart	69	6	9	15	283
J.P. O'Connor	44	2	11	13	77
Chris Wismer	47	2	11	13	77
Brad Peddle	43	3	8	11	61
Jonathan Shockey	43	0	10	10	95
Brendan Walsh	25	3	6	9	179
Jean-Paul Tessier	38	3	6	9	40
Milt Mastad	70	0	9	9	172
Steve Wilson	17	3	4	7	33
Jeff Helperl	34	1	6	7	75
Lee Jinman	10	2	4	6	6
Mike Jozefowicz	10	2	4	6	2
Dan Carney	49	2	3	5	30
Lawrence Nycholat	5	1	2	3	5
Bryan McKinney	6	1	1	2	8
Mike Tamburro (goalie)	49	0	2	2	16
Sam Katsuras	2	1	0	1	0
Randy Fitzgerald	21	1	0	1	23
Steve Aronson	3	0	1	1	2
Marco Emond (goalie)	4	0	0	0	0
Pete Gardiner	5	0	0	0	0
Derek Gustafson (goalie)	7	0	0	0	0
Denis Berthelot	8	0	0	0	2
David Brumby (goalie)	15	0	0	0	6

GOALTENDING

	Gms.	Min.	W	L	T	G	SO	Avg.
Derek Gustafson	7	404	4	3	0	15	1	2.23
Mike Tamburro	49	2927	26	15	6	130	2	2.66
David Brumby	15	877	6	6	3	47	0	3.21
Marco Emond	4	182	3	0	0	10	0	3.29

JOHNSTOWN CHIEFS
SCORING

	Games	G	A	Pts.	PIM
Eric Schneider	66	33	37	70	32
Andrew Dale	71	23	38	61	72
Ryan Chaytors	50	20	30	50	28
Jim Shepherd	44	14	26	40	135
Dorian Anneck	47	15	20	35	32
Mike Vellinga	66	5	25	30	85
Brent Bilodeau	64	7	22	29	123
Dmitri Tarabrin	61	14	11	25	61
Andrew Clark	42	12	13	25	35
Jan Sulc	54	6	17	23	41
Ryan Tocher	70	2	19	21	75
Chris Brassard	25	11	8	19	83
Mike Rodrigues	61	4	13	17	78

	Games	G	A	Pts.	PIM
Jim Leger	40	9	7	16	48
John McNabb	25	9	6	15	20
Jeff Sullivan	69	2	9	11	302
Maxim Potapov	15	4	4	8	2
Kenny Corupe	12	2	6	8	20
Samuel St. Pierre	6	3	2	5	2
Benoit Dusablon	11	2	3	5	4
Mark Thompson	41	2	3	5	82
Mikko Kuparinen	13	1	4	5	10
Mike Kiesman	30	1	3	4	56
Blair Stayzer	37	1	3	4	104
Jason Spence	47	1	3	4	217
Jeff Lukasak	12	1	2	3	17
Kenton Smith	13	0	3	3	12
Ted Laviolette	7	1	1	2	6
Edo Terglav	6	1	0	1	0
Brent Ozarowski	11	1	0	1	4
Karl Infanger	2	0	1	1	0
Tyrone Garner (goalie)	5	0	1	1	0
Roman Marakhovski	9	0	1	1	6
Dany Sabourin (goalie)	19	0	1	1	17
Ryan Moynihan	1	0	0	0	0
Rick Boyd	2	0	0	0	6
Pat Glenday	3	0	0	0	4
D.J. Maracle	3	0	0	0	2
Frederic Deschenes (goalie)	54	0	0	0	8

GOALTENDING

	Gms.	Min.	W	L	T	G	SO	Avg.
Tyrone Garner	5	306	3	1	1	15	0	2.94
Frederic Deschenes	54	3158	21	26	6	157	2	2.98
Dany Sabourin	19	903	4	9	1	56	0	3.72

LOUISIANA ICEGATORS
SCORING

	Games	G	A	Pts.	PIM
John Spoltore	59	14	71	85	58
Shawn McNeil	72	36	45	81	70
Jay Murphy	54	32	32	64	200
Chris Valicevic	72	13	41	54	56
Mike Murray	51	15	31	46	68
Ryan Shanahan	51	20	22	42	136
Corey Neilson	64	15	25	40	128
Dan Tessier	60	20	15	35	116
Bruce Richardson	22	10	21	31	83
Magnus Nilsson	68	13	11	24	66
Matthew Pagnutti	72	6	18	24	99
Kevin Karlander	56	7	12	19	54
Jason McQuat	47	9	6	15	130
John McNabb	18	4	10	14	22
Roger Maxwell	62	4	9	13	257
Mike Kucsulain	34	8	4	12	123
Dalen Hrooshkin	42	4	4	8	14
Briane Thompson	9	2	5	7	9
Roman Marakhovski	51	2	4	6	32
Stan Melanson	72	2	4	6	138
Nathan Borega	57	0	5	5	35
Murray Kuntz	7	1	1	2	2
Jason Saal (goalie)	40	0	1	1	6
David Belitski (goalie)	1	0	0	0	0
Matt Ouellette	2	0	0	0	0
Shep Harder (goalie)	3	0	0	0	0
Ryan Marsh	3	0	0	0	2
Kris Mallette	5	0	0	0	25
Evgeny Konstantinov (goalie)	8	0	0	0	2
Greg Callahan	20	0	0	0	34
Mike Valley (goalie)	25	0	0	0	4

GOALTENDING

	Gms.	Min.	W	L	T	G	SO	Avg.
David Belitski	1	65	0	0	1	2	0	1.85
Jason Saal	40	2270	27	11	0	102	2	2.70
E. Konstantinov	8	458	4	4	0	21	0	2.75
Mike Valley	25	1481	11	7	5	71	0	2.88
Shep Harder	3	115	0	2	0	6	0	3.13

MISSISSIPPI SEA WOLVES
SCORING

	Games	G	A	Pts.	PIM
Bob Woods	69	17	43	60	23
J.F. Aube	62	26	33	59	25
Cody Bowtell	67	28	28	56	50
Dave Paradise	71	24	30	54	78
Joel Dezainde	58	10	38	48	77
Dustin Whitecotton	72	17	24	41	10
John Evangelista	67	17	22	39	97
Brent Gauvreau	67	11	21	32	63
Mike Oliveira	58	12	17	29	29
Sergei Kuznetsov	55	11	17	28	34
Patrick Rochon	72	4	21	25	123
Robert Francz	32	9	15	24	56
Brad Essex	57	8	12	20	165
Mike Martone	66	3	12	15	135
Chris Brassard	11	6	6	12	50
Anthony Terzo	34	4	7	11	30
Greg Willers	31	4	5	9	19
Wes Blevins	63	1	8	9	55
Sean Gillam	58	0	8	8	91
Wesley Scanzano	7	2	5	7	0
Chris Baxter	10	1	6	7	15
Keith Cassidy	29	2	4	6	32
Jeff McKercher	16	2	3	5	14
Jan Melichercik	2	1	1	2	0
Chris Lipsett	3	0	2	2	0
Brad Goulet	2	1	0	1	2
Chuck Thuss (goalie)	35	0	1	1	16
Jon Gaskins	1	0	0	0	0
Steve Briere (goalie)	41	0	0	0	13

GOALTENDING

	Gms.	Min.	W	L	T	G	SO	Avg.
Steve Briere	41	2413	19	17	3	116	1	2.88
Chuck Thuss	34	1942	15	16	2	95	3	2.93

MOBILE MYSTICKS
SCORING

	Games	G	A	Pts.	PIM
Jason Elders	71	36	41	77	26
Mark Turner	69	30	47	77	67
Chad Onufrechuk	71	19	42	61	51
Hugues Gervais	61	32	19	51	196
B.J. Kilbourne	71	15	35	50	76
Jason Clarke	69	16	31	47	354
Brent Wishart	71	18	26	44	27
Bobby Stewart	35	18	20	38	36
Sam Ftorek	72	15	18	33	89
Jim Nagle	57	9	15	24	10
David Van Drunnen	33	2	18	20	52
Josh Harrold	37	2	16	18	34
Paul Fioroni	38	7	10	17	110
Jonathan Sorg	30	6	11	17	37
Brad Peddle	26	1	12	13	21
J.P. O'Connor	21	6	6	12	40
Jason Reid	65	2	7	9	92
Benoit Cotnoir	20	3	5	8	43
Jason Metcalfe	41	1	5	6	89
Dennis Mullen	33	2	1	3	126
Ian Walterson	13	0	3	3	6
Maxime Gingras (goalie)	18	0	3	3	0
Kevin Grimes	52	0	2	2	255
Chris Bell	6	0	1	1	0
Scott Langkow (goalie)	6	0	0	0	2
Reg Bourcier (goalie)	9	0	0	0	2
Dave Haimson (goalie)	13	0	0	0	6
Tyler Palmer	28	0	0	0	10
Chris Wickenheiser (goalie)	28	0	0	0	2

GOALTENDING

	Gms.	Min.	W	L	T	G	SO	Avg.
Maxime Gingras	18	1059	12	4	1	41	2	2.32
Chris Wickenheiser	28	1659	13	13	2	88	1	3.18
Dave Haimson	13	771	6	5	1	41	0	3.19
Reg Bourcier	9	526	5	2	2	31	0	3.53
Scott Langkow	6	358	2	4	0	23	0	3.86

NEW ORLEANS BRASS
SCORING

	Games	G	A	Pts.	PIM
Adam Edinger	58	31	45	76	63
Martin Bartek	51	30	33	63	16
Sylvai Deschatelets	70	25	33	58	106
Bryan Forslund	72	20	37	57	126
Ryan Fultz	43	21	29	50	16
Jeff Lazaro	58	21	27	48	103
Lee Ruff	72	6	23	29	103
Steve Cheredaryk	57	5	24	29	219
Rick Smith	68	16	12	28	67
David Whitworth	45	5	17	22	77
Alexandre Krevsun	48	8	13	21	24
Kevin Colley	23	11	8	19	27
Tyson Holly	42	8	11	19	58
Kent Sauer	46	4	11	15	84
Mark Polak	27	2	13	15	38
Mike Sgroi	39	7	7	14	104
Chris Aldous	37	2	8	10	38
Chad Dameworth	53	1	9	10	64
Jed Whitchurch	22	5	4	9	2
Denis Timofeev	38	2	6	8	49
Brad Hodgins	15	1	7	8	31
Craig Foddrill	7	3	4	7	0
Mike Sandbeck	6	3	2	5	2
Andrew Taylor	4	3	1	4	14
Corey Waring	7	3	1	4	2
Chris Bell	8	1	2	3	0
Doug Bonner (goalie)	20	0	3	3	2
Omar Ennaffati	2	1	1	2	0
Ville Liukko	4	1	0	1	0
Antti Ahokas	37	1	0	1	96
Jomi Santala	1	0	1	1	0
Oleg Timchenko	7	0	1	1	2
Sean Peach	18	0	1	1	17
Antti Kohvakka	20	0	1	1	17
Craig Desjarlais	1	0	0	0	0
Pascal Gasse (goalie)	2	0	0	0	4
Klage Kaebel	2	0	0	0	0
Francis Larivee (goalie)	5	0	0	0	10
Matti Wallenius	10	0	0	0	11
Ron Vogel (goalie)	27	0	0	0	4
Alexei Volkov (goalie)	29	0	0	0	2

GOALTENDING

	Gms.	Min.	W	L	T	G	SO	Avg.
Ron Vogel	27	1557	17	7	3	63	2	2.43
Alexei Volkov	29	1577	12	9	5	81	1	3.08
Doug Bonner	20	1007	6	6	4	58	1	3.46
Pascal Gasse	2	110	0	1	0	9	0	4.93
Francis Larivee	4	133	0	2	0	14	0	6.30

PEE DEE PRIDE
SCORING

	Games	G	A	Pts.	PIM
Dany Bousquet	56	39	45	84	74
Casey Kesselring	71	19	47	66	39
Allan Sirois	71	26	37	63	118
Peter Geronazzo	72	31	28	59	92
Wes Goldie	71	33	22	55	60
Trevor Demmans	69	11	41	52	50
Matt Reid	70	16	34	50	15
Ryan Petz	72	21	21	42	81
Eric Naud	67	13	21	34	204
Kevin Haupt	68	8	19	27	16
Jeff Burgoyne	56	4	16	20	45
Vince Malts	52	5	13	18	214
Ryan Jestadt	62	2	10	12	93
Kyle Knopp	29	3	8	11	12
Bryan Tapper	67	4	6	10	58

	Games	G	A	Pts.	PIM
Curtis Wilgosh	20	2	5	7	16
Aaron Gates	44	0	6	6	72
Leigh Dean	54	0	6	6	46
Ryan Moynihan	11	2	2	4	0
Ted Laviolette	8	1	3	4	18
Duncan Dalmao	5	0	4	4	6
Martin Galik	28	0	3	3	12
Matt Ulewlling	6	2	0	2	16
Jeff Potter	13	0	1	1	11
Jeff Blanchard	3	0	0	0	0
Trent Walford	5	0	0	0	2
J.R. Prestifilippo (goalie)	11	0	0	0	0
Cory Cadden (goalie)	22	0	0	0	4
Sandy Allan (goalie)	44	0	0	0	10

GOALTENDING

	Gms.	Min.	W	L	T	G	SO	Avg.
J.R. Prestifilippo	11	601	8	1	1	27	0	2.69
Cory Cadden	22	1292	11	9	0	64	0	2.97
Sandy Allan	44	2476	19	18	5	130	2	3.15

PENSACOLA ICE PILOTS

SCORING

	Games	G	A	Pts.	PIM
Jeff Bes	48	24	44	68	69
Allan Egeland	59	18	42	60	186
Jonathan Gagnon	70	24	15	39	52
Pat Staerker	61	14	25	39	22
Briane Thompson	53	11	28	39	121
Rob Sinclair	68	19	16	35	12
John Tripp	36	19	14	33	110
Chris Brassard	17	6	16	22	35
John McNabb	26	5	14	19	18
Matt Cusson	45	4	14	18	21
Kevin Colley	23	6	11	17	44
Brent Dodginghorse	38	7	9	16	60
Jim Bermingham	23	6	8	14	22
Jay McGee	60	4	10	14	47
Oak Hewer	30	2	12	14	18
Scott McCallum	40	3	10	13	64
Tyson Holly	24	6	6	12	31
Sean Peach	32	2	10	12	36
Todd Barclay	42	5	3	8	6
Chris Wismer	24	3	4	7	19
Chris Newans	9	2	5	7	34
John Poapst	23	2	5	7	14
Jesse Black	28	0	5	5	16
Keith Cassidy	23	2	2	4	20
Chris Aldous	12	1	3	4	8
Denis Timofeev	20	0	4	4	28
Rob Smillie	7	1	2	3	2
Greg Willers	24	1	2	3	26
Dalen Hrooshkin	14	1	1	2	4
Leon Delorme	30	1	1	2	147
Curtis Valentine	3	1	0	1	0
Shane Calder	4	1	0	1	10
Nick Jones	3	0	1	1	11
Kevin Karlander	3	0	1	1	7
Louis Mass	3	0	1	1	2
John Day	6	0	1	1	4
Scott Easton (goalie)	1	0	0	0	0
David Bilik	2	0	0	0	16
Darren Cameron	2	0	0	0	0
Josh LeRoy	2	0	0	0	0
Nick Reiser (goalie)	2	0	0	0	0
Paul Bailley	3	0	0	0	0
Jeff Blair (goalie)	3	0	0	0	0
Matt Interbartolo	3	0	0	0	0
Craig Stahl	3	0	0	0	15
Mark Scott	4	0	0	0	16
Pavel Smirnov	4	0	0	0	2
Randy Best	5	0	0	0	4
Anthony Belza	9	0	0	0	17

	Games	G	A	Pts.	PIM
David Belitski (goalie)	16	0	0	0	0
Nathan Borega	16	0	0	0	10
Scott LaGrand (goalie)	24	0	0	0	4
Shawn Degagne (goalie)	34	0	0	0	11

GOALTENDING

	Gms.	Min.	W	L	T	G	SO	Avg.
Jeff Blair	3	179	1	2	0	8	0	2.68
David Belitski	16	946	4	11	1	46	0	2.92
Shawn Degagne	34	1799	14	12	4	99	1	3.30
Scott LaGrand	24	1341	8	14	0	81	0	3.62
Scott Easton	1	60	0	1	0	5	0	5.00
Nick Reiser	2	23	0	0	0	3	0	7.98

PEORIA RIVERMEN

SCORING

	Games	G	A	Pts.	PIM
Joe Rybar	72	17	44	61	42
J.F. Boutin	59	24	30	54	97
Bret Meyers	53	27	26	53	46
Dustin Kuk	63	22	26	48	119
Darren Clark	40	14	24	38	14
Blaine Fitzpatrick	53	19	15	34	169
Arvid Rekis	64	12	21	33	99
Tyler Willis	58	14	18	32	251
Didier Tremblay	51	5	23	28	63
Aaron Fox	34	10	16	26	14
Matt Golden	52	5	19	24	70
Trevor Wasyluk	21	8	15	23	36
Jason Lawmaster	40	9	11	20	211
Trevor Baker	60	9	11	20	228
Tomaz Razingar	52	10	9	19	28
Shawn Mamane	19	9	8	17	47
Lauri Kinos	55	4	12	16	56
Darren Maloney	68	1	12	13	128
John Varga	13	3	7	10	6
Daniel Hodge	46	2	8	10	26
Tyler Rennette	7	5	1	6	6
Luke Gruden	28	2	4	6	35
Andrei Petrakov	12	2	2	4	0
Chad Stauffacher	29	2	2	4	69
Jaroslav Obsut	3	0	4	4	2
Jason Polera	9	1	2	3	2
Jan Horacek	6	0	3	3	8
Dale Clarke	2	1	0	1	0
Matt Walker	8	1	0	1	70
Grant McCune (goalie)	3	0	1	1	0
Curtis Sanford (goalie)	27	0	1	1	2
Kenric Exner (goalie)	47	0	1	1	4
Anthony Belza	1	0	0	0	8
Daniel Jacques (goalie)	1	0	0	0	0
Brandon Sugden	1	0	0	0	0
Josh Bennett	2	0	0	0	7
Kevin Tucker	8	0	0	0	4
Blaz Emersic	12	0	0	0	0
Jessie Rezansoff	19	0	0	0	175

GOALTENDING

	Gms.	Min.	W	L	T	G	SO	Avg.
Daniel Jacques	1	20	0	0	0	0	0	0.00
Curtis Sanford	27	1511	15	7	4	48	3	1.91
Grant McCune	3	161	2	1	0	6	0	2.24
Kenric Exner	47	2708	28	9	6	118	1	2.61

RICHMOND RENEGADES

SCORING

	Games	G	A	Pts.	PIM
Brian McCullough	67	31	27	58	56
Richard Pitirri	66	18	40	58	46
Rod Taylor	61	34	22	56	67
Brian Goudie	70	8	35	43	204
George Awada	72	18	23	41	49
Mike Siklenka	65	19	18	37	117

	Games	G	A	Pts.	PIM
Matt Noga	52	11	25	36	76
Frank Novock	62	12	23	35	28
Joe Blaznek	29	13	12	25	14
Dan Vandermeer	72	9	15	24	268
Forrest Gore	38	12	10	22	70
Derek Schutz	35	9	13	22	79
Andrew Shier	24	6	14	20	38
Gerad Adams	48	4	16	20	120
Joe Vandermeer	72	1	17	18	73
Neal Rech	24	6	8	14	48
Kevin Knopp	31	3	11	14	22
Chad Ackerman	32	1	13	14	26
Nate Forster	30	2	7	9	55
Jim Shepherd	11	3	4	7	19
Bob Thornton	23	0	6	6	37
Jean-Francois Fortin	15	0	4	4	2
Ryan Skaleski	47	0	4	4	14
Jay McKee	17	1	2	3	19
Kyle Clark	18	1	2	3	110
Ryan Van Buskirk	15	0	2	2	16
Doug Altschul	16	1	0	1	6
Rastislav Stana (goalie)	38	0	1	1	0
Jason Jarrelle	1	0	0	0	0
Ben Lesshaftt (goalie)	1	0	0	0	0
John Lovell	4	0	0	0	0
Sean Matile (goalie)	20	0	0	0	0
Maxime Gingras (goalie)	22	0	0	0	2

GOALTENDING

	Gms.	Min.	W	L	T	G	SO	Avg.
Rastislav Stana	38	2111	15	16	2	90	1	2.56
Maxime Gingras	22	1147	11	5	3	62	1	3.24
Sean Matile	20	1089	9	10	1	65	0	3.58

ROANOKE EXPRESS

SCORING

	Games	G	A	Pts.	PIM
Doug Sheppard	69	30	39	69	34
Adam Dewan	53	32	36	68	205
Mike Peron	71	21	35	56	174
Calvin Elfring	70	16	37	53	79
Jeff Sproat	64	12	37	49	14
Ben Schust	64	18	30	48	14
John Sadowski	62	14	25	39	96
Troy Lake	47	15	21	36	92
Pete Gardiner	58	15	19	34	130
Travis Smith	66	7	25	32	96
Mike Omicioli	28	11	19	30	28
Joe Dusbabek	55	9	14	23	52
Kevin McDonald	57	8	12	20	296
Nate Handrahan	60	5	12	17	25
Todd Compeau	50	3	10	13	49
Duncan Dalmao	55	2	10	12	75
Anthony Terzo	14	3	5	8	13
Jeff Burgoyne	16	0	6	6	12
Jason Shipulski	11	4	0	4	4
John Poapst	9	1	2	3	0
Colin Anderson	12	1	2	3	4
Aaron Gates	19	1	2	3	46
Anthony Belza	56	1	2	3	246
Tim Wolfe	6	0	3	3	6
Sean Peach	13	1	1	2	20
Rob Smillie	16	1	1	2	6
Brent Ozarowski	2	0	0	0	0
Nick Jones	3	0	0	0	9
Jeff Potter	17	0	0	0	2
Dave Gagnon (goalie)	32	0	0	0	0
Daniel Berthiaume (goalie)	45	0	0	0	2

GOALTENDING

	Gms.	Min.	W	L	T	G	SO	Avg.
Daniel Berthiaume	45	2604	26	17	1	104	4	2.40
Dave Gagnon	32	1732	12	13	3	84	3	2.91

SOUTH CAROLINA STINGRAYS

SCORING

	Games	G	A	Pts.	PIM
Adam Calder	67	28	44	72	103
Jason Sessa	58	34	30	64	113
Brett Marietti	61	22	40	62	120
Dave Seitz	58	14	43	57	55
Greg Schmidt	56	25	26	51	75
Brad Dexter	72	7	40	47	46
Joel Irving	68	20	24	44	203
Ryan Brindley	48	10	27	37	65
Damian Prescott	71	15	19	34	93
Buddy Wallace	39	10	22	32	56
Marty Clapton	69	8	14	22	62
Zach Ham	69	8	14	22	53
Scott Swanson	28	4	14	18	8
Jared Bednar	57	6	9	15	155
Trevor Johnson	64	6	9	15	158
Mike Nicholishen	48	5	10	15	74
Chris Wheaton	55	9	3	12	180
Luc Theoret	19	4	2	6	19
Chad Remackel	5	2	4	6	6
Hugo Marchand	50	1	5	6	122
Andrei Chouroupov	12	2	3	5	6
Jody Lehman (goalie)	32	0	4	4	13
Craig Brunel	8	0	3	3	34
Martin Cerven	8	0	3	3	2
Kirk Daubenspeck (goalie)	46	0	3	3	37
Jacques Lariviere	6	0	2	2	7

GOALTENDING

	Gms.	Min.	W	L	T	G	SO	Avg.
Kirk Daubenspeck	45	2624	26	13	3	119	3	2.72
Jody Lehman	32	1746	16	10	4	81	4	2.78

TALLAHASSEE TIGER SHARKS

SCORING

	Games	G	A	Pts.	PIM
Brent Cullaton	54	27	47	74	56
Andrew Long	51	28	33	61	20
Olivier Morin	69	23	36	59	102
David Thibeault	70	25	27	52	93
Benoit Dusablon	49	21	29	50	33
Adam Copeland	58	26	21	47	69
Jim Baxter	72	15	32	47	30
J.F. Houle	56	12	34	46	92
Patrick Gingras	47	18	23	41	184
Ben Guite	68	11	18	29	34
Simon Tremblay	56	7	20	27	72
Jared Smyth	67	6	17	23	56
Kurtis Drummond	41	4	18	22	53
Darren McAusland	31	1	13	14	18
John Varga	13	6	6	12	4
Todd Kidd	69	1	11	12	153
Michael Ryder	5	4	5	9	6
Mitch Fritz	42	5	3	8	79
Martin Menard	11	3	5	8	30
Marc Gaudet	66	1	7	8	60
Daniel Payette	20	1	6	7	13
Brent Pope	39	0	6	6	81
Rick Hayward	16	0	4	4	74
Ryan Risidore	2	1	1	2	5
Michael Henrich	6	1	1	2	0
Brandon Sugden	12	1	0	1	75
Evan Lindsay (goalie)	17	0	1	1	0
Christian Bronsard (goalie)	22	0	1	1	8
Kent Paterson	1	0	0	0	2
Aren Miller (goalie)	2	0	0	0	0
Joel Theriault	2	0	0	0	25
Chad Mehlenbacher (goalie)	3	0	0	0	0
Stan Reddick (goalie)	3	0	0	0	0
Alex Fomitchev (goalie)	28	0	0	0	0

GOALTENDING

	Gms.	Min.	W	L	T	G	SO	Avg.
Alex Fomitchev	28	1628	16	8	2	72	2	2.65
Christian Bronsard	22	1291	12	8	2	59	1	2.74
Evan Lindsay	17	1017	8	7	2	50	0	2.95
Stan Reddick	3	180	1	2	0	12	0	4.00
Aren Miller	2	99	1	1	0	8	0	4.86
Chad Mehlenbacher	3	131	0	1	1	11	0	5.04

TOLEDO STORM

SCORING

	Games	G	A	Pts.	PIM
Andrew Williamson	66	52	45	97	53
James Patterson	65	40	56	96	59
Jeff Johnstone	56	26	40	66	48
Ryan Gaucher	53	10	46	56	81
Tim Verbeek	70	23	32	55	220
Rob Thorpe	63	24	24	48	91
Shawn Maltby	64	12	29	41	133
Derek Booth	67	12	22	34	126
Sam Katsuras	63	10	21	31	63
Jason Norrie	57	9	17	26	251
B.J. Adams	69	2	14	16	110
Kelly Miller	56	7	8	15	82
Alexandre Jacques	25	5	10	15	16
Chris Bogas	43	9	5	14	56
Mike Christian	15	4	6	10	70
Ryan Pepperall	17	3	3	6	11
Phillippe Lakos	66	3	3	6	193
Ryan Barnes	16	2	4	6	31
Bryan McKinney	16	1	5	6	56
Todd Gillingham	18	1	4	5	107
Mark Bernard (goalie)	56	1	4	5	47
Ted Laviolette	14	2	2	4	48
J.J Hunter	6	1	1	2	2
Nick Edinger	7	1	1	2	6
Shawn Skolney	11	1	1	2	40
Jeff Petrie	3	0	2	2	0
Curtis Rich	64	0	2	2	143
Chris Cava	4	1	0	1	0
Jon Barkman	3	0	1	1	2
Dave Cameron	3	0	1	1	0
Klage Kaebel	3	0	1	1	0
Jeff Schmidt	8	0	1	1	6
Valeri Ermolov	1	0	0	0	0
Ron Vogel (goalie)	1	0	0	0	0
Craig Desjarlais	2	0	0	0	0
Chris George	3	0	0	0	4
Andrei Sharkevich	3	0	0	0	0
Todd Steinmetz	3	0	0	0	2
Rusty McKie	4	0	0	0	14
Avi Karunakar (goalie)	9	0	0	0	2
Aren Miller (goalie)	10	0	0	0	10
Mike Sgroi	10	0	0	0	62

GOALTENDING

	Gms.	Min.	W	L	T	G	SO	Avg.
Avi Karunakar	9	513	3	2	3	28	0	3.28
Mark Bernard	56	3275	30	21	5	180	2	3.30
Aren Miller	10	548	4	4	0	38	0	4.16
Ron Vogel	1	40	0	0	0	4	0	6.00

TRENTON TITANS

SCORING

	Games	G	A	Pts.	PIM
Aniket Dhadphale	68	30	35	65	79
Scott Bertoli	72	18	38	56	79
Alain St. Hilaire	56	16	34	50	33
Paul Spadafora	66	14	33	47	60
Mike Hall	49	15	31	46	39
Cail MacLean	49	28	17	45	26
Steve O'Brien	65	11	34	45	40
Butch Kaebel	49	13	21	34	20
Jed Whitchurch	49	12	16	28	7

	Games	G	A	Pts.	PIM
Sasha Cucuz	55	12	13	25	34
Sergei Skrobot	65	7	18	25	48
Shane Belter	23	6	15	21	22
Sandy Cohen	45	8	12	20	23
Rick Kowalsky	12	7	10	17	22
Benoit Morin	23	9	5	14	107
Stewart Bodtker	13	7	5	12	42
Vince Williams	59	3	8	11	50
Lee Jinman	15	2	8	10	18
Chris Heron	9	3	5	8	2
David Whitworth	13	3	5	8	21
Sean Molina	62	2	5	7	41
Kam White	59	3	3	6	224
Jason Beckett	17	2	2	4	24
Eric Brule	4	1	2	3	0
Chad Ackerman	4	0	3	3	4
Todd Barclay	4	0	3	3	2
Jeff Schmidt	12	2	0	2	2
Ryan Moynihan	14	1	1	2	8
Richard Seeley	9	0	2	2	18
Ian Forbes	33	0	2	2	133
Eric Silverman	17	1	0	1	6
Jarred Smithson	3	0	1	1	2
Francois Bourbeau (goalie)	1	0	0	0	0
Kirk Lamb	1	0	0	0	0
Mike Pietrangelo	3	0	0	0	2
Randy Best	4	0	0	0	4
Dennis Bassett (goalie)	5	0	0	0	2
Greg Callahan	5	0	0	0	0
Brian Regan (goalie)	8	0	0	0	0
Scott Kelsey	9	0	0	0	6
Dan Murphy (goalie)	15	0	0	0	0
Jeff Potter	22	0	0	0	6
Scott Stirling (goalie)	48	0	0	0	10

GOALTENDING

	Gms.	Min.	W	L	T	G	SO	Avg.
Brian Regan	8	485	8	0	0	15	1	1.86
Scott Stirling	48	2722	32	10	3	97	5	2.14
Dan Murphy	15	862	7	7	1	33	2	2.30
Dennis Bassett	5	264	3	1	0	12	1	2.73
Francois Bourbeau	1	24	0	0	0	2	0	5.03

WHEELING NAILERS

SCORING

	Games	G	A	Pts.	PIM
Jamie O'Leary	61	16	40	56	103
Buddy Smith	52	13	30	43	20
Chris Slater	57	12	25	37	116
Derek Smith	63	8	29	37	62
Alexei Podalinski	68	20	16	36	90
Mike Hurley	38	18	15	33	40
Boris Protsenko	48	15	11	26	42
Kevin Caulfield	56	13	12	25	62
Doug Schmidt	54	7	18	25	166
Chris Newans	40	7	17	24	124
Vitali Kozel	41	11	12	23	24
Justin Harney	34	7	13	20	43
Stefan Brannare	67	8	10	18	224
Scott McCallum	32	4	10	14	24
Butch Kaebel	20	5	6	11	4
Valeri Ermolov	26	2	9	11	8
Steve Parsons	19	5	4	9	178
Karson Kaebel	13	1	8	9	10
Rob Smillie	17	3	5	8	4
Brandon Bagnell	48	3	5	8	22
Eric Normandin	15	3	3	6	30
Antti Kohvakka	27	3	2	5	22
Arped Mihaly	9	0	5	5	0
Kevin Paden	12	2	2	4	8
Scott Wray	17	2	2	4	23
Jason Hamilton	41	2	2	4	333
Jean-Philippe Soucy	5	0	4	4	4
Alexei Kolkunov	8	1	2	3	4

	Games	G	A	Pts.	PIM
Mark Moore	20	0	2	2	19
Sean Seyferth	17	1	0	1	7
Michal Stastny	3	0	1	1	2
Jeff Schmidt	8	0	1	1	4
Craig Hillier (goalie)	19	0	1	1	4
Joel Laing (goalie)	47	0	1	1	15
Martin Duval	1	0	0	0	0
Shep Harder (goalie)	1	0	0	0	0
Samuel Polomsky	2	0	0	0	0
Rob Millar	3	0	0	0	0
Jason Ricci	3	0	0	0	0
Andrei Sharkevich	3	0	0	0	0
Brandon Christian	4	0	0	0	17
Mila Cermak	7	0	0	0	0
Mark Scally (goalie)	17	0	0	0	4

GOALTENDING

	Gms.	Min.	W	L	T	G	SO	Avg.
Joel Laing	47	2615	17	18	7	125	1	2.87
Craig Hillier	19	889	4	10	1	62	0	4.19
Mark Scally	17	825	3	11	0	71	0	5.16
Shep Harder	1	44	0	1	0	4	0	5.48

PLAYERS WITH TWO OR MORE TEAMS

SCORING

	Games	G	A	Pts.	PIM
Chad Ackerman, Richmond	32	1	13	14	26
Chad Ackerman, Trenton	4	0	3	3	4
Totals	36	1	16	17	30
Chris Aldous, New Orleans	37	2	8	10	38
Chris Aldous, Pensacola	12	1	3	4	8
Totals	49	3	11	14	46
Colin Anderson, Roanoke	12	1	2	3	4
Colin Anderson, Florida	2	1	0	1	0
Totals	14	2	2	4	4
Dorian Anneck, Johnstown	47	15	20	35	32
Dorian Anneck, Augusta	15	3	2	5	4
Totals	62	18	22	40	36
Todd Barclay, Trenton	4	0	3	3	2
Todd Barclay, Pensacola	42	5	3	8	6
Totals	46	5	6	11	8
Mike Barrie, Birmingham	10	5	4	9	41
Mike Barrie, Baton Rouge	1	0	0	0	17
Totals	11	5	4	9	58
David Belitski, Louisiana (g)	1	0	0	0	0
David Belitski, Pensacola (g)	16	0	0	0	0
Totals	17	0	0	0	0
Chris Bell, Mobile	6	0	1	1	0
Chris Bell, New Orleans	8	1	2	3	0
Totals	14	1	3	4	0
Shane Belter, Florida	35	3	16	19	34
Shane Belter, Trenton	23	6	15	21	22
Totals	58	9	31	40	56
Anthony Belza, Peoria	1	0	0	0	8
Anthony Belza, Pensacola	9	0	0	0	17
Anthony Belza, Roanoke	56	1	2	3	246
Totals	66	1	2	3	271
Jim Bermingham, Jackson	45	11	17	28	50
Jim Bermingham, Pensacola	23	6	8	14	22
Totals	68	17	25	42	72
Jeff Bes, Pensacola	48	24	44	68	69
Jeff Bes, Jackson	20	11	21	32	34
Totals	68	35	65	100	103
Randy Best, Pensacola	5	0	0	0	4
Randy Best, Trenton	4	0	0	0	4
Totals	9	0	0	0	8
Jeff Blanchard, Augusta	3	0	0	0	6
Jeff Blanchard, Pee Dee	3	0	0	0	0
Totals	6	0	0	0	6
Nathan Borega, Louisiana	57	0	5	5	35
Nathan Borega, Pensacola	16	0	0	0	10
Totals	73	0	5	5	45
Reg Bourcier, Augusta (goalie)	22	0	1	1	6
Reg Bourcier, Mobile (goalie)	9	0	0	0	2
Totals	31	0	1	1	8
Chris Brassard, Johnstown	25	11	8	19	83
Chris Brassard, Pensacola	17	6	16	22	35
Chris Brassard, Mississippi	11	6	6	12	50
Totals	53	23	30	53	168
Eric Brule, Trenton	4	1	2	3	0
Eric Brule, Arkansas	53	6	30	36	48
Totals	57	7	32	39	48
Jeff Burgoyne, Roanoke	16	0	6	6	12
Jeff Burgoyne, Pee Dee	56	4	16	20	45
Totals	72	4	22	26	57
Shane Calder, Pensacola	4	1	0	1	10
Shane Calder, Baton Rouge	67	22	21	43	95
Totals	71	23	21	44	105
Greg Callahan, Florida	7	0	0	0	18
Greg Callahan, Trenton	5	0	0	0	0
Greg Callahan, Louisiana	20	0	0	0	34
Totals	32	0	0	0	52
Keith Cassidy, Arkansas	11	0	0	0	27
Keith Cassidy, Mississippi	29	2	4	6	32
Keith Cassidy, Pensacola	23	2	2	4	20
Totals	63	4	6	10	79
Martin Cerven, Charlotte	30	1	7	8	26
Martin Cerven, South Carolina	8	0	3	3	2
Martin Cerven, Greensboro	11	0	1	1	4
Totals	49	1	11	12	32
Andrei Chouroupov, Augusta	33	2	5	7	29
Andrei Chouroupov, S.C.	12	2	3	5	6
Totals	45	4	8	12	35
Sandy Cohen, Trenton	45	8	12	20	23
Sandy Cohen, Florida	19	1	4	5	0
Totals	64	9	16	25	23
Kevin Colley, Pensacola	23	6	11	17	44
Kevin Colley, New Orleans	23	11	8	19	27
Totals	46	17	19	36	71
Duncan Dalmao, Birmingham	10	0	2	2	6
Duncan Dalmao, Pee Dee	5	0	4	4	6
Duncan Dalmao, Roanoke	55	2	10	12	75
Totals	70	2	16	18	87
Craig Desjarlais, New Orleans	1	0	0	0	0
Craig Desjarlais, Toledo	2	0	0	0	0
Totals	3	0	0	0	0
Benoit Dusablon, Johnstown	11	2	3	5	4
Benoit Dusablon, Tallahassee	49	21	29	50	33
Totals	60	23	32	55	37
Blaz Emersic, Greenville	3	0	0	0	0
Blaz Emersic, Peoria	12	0	0	0	0
Totals	15	0	0	0	0
Valeri Ermolov, Wheeling	26	2	9	11	8
Valeri Ermolov, Toledo	1	0	0	0	0
Totals	27	2	9	11	8
Martin Galik, Greensboro	21	3	6	9	8
Martin Galik, Pee Dee	28	0	3	3	12
Totals	49	3	9	12	20
Pete Gardiner, Jackson	5	0	0	0	2
Pete Gardiner, Roanoke	58	15	19	34	130
Totals	63	15	19	34	132
Tyrone Garner, Johnstown (g)	5	0	1	1	0
Tyrone Garner, Greenville (g)	36	0	1	1	2
Totals	41	0	2	2	2
Aaron Gates, Roanoke	19	1	2	3	46
Aaron Gates, Pee Dee	44	0	6	6	72
Totals	63	1	8	9	118
Paul Giblin, Arkansas	26	1	3	4	4
Paul Giblin, Charlotte	45	19	19	38	14
Totals	71	20	22	42	18
Maxime Gingras, Richmond (g)	22	0	0	0	2
Maxime Gingras, Mobile (g)	18	0	3	3	0
Totals	40	0	3	3	2
Forrest Gore, Richmond	38	12	10	22	70
Forrest Gore, Baton Rouge	16	8	11	19	17
Totals	54	20	21	41	87
Russ Guzior, Augusta	41	6	17	23	66
Russ Guzior, Arkansas	25	10	8	18	24

	Games	G	A	Pts.	PIM
Totals	66	16	25	41	90
Jason Hamilton, Baton Rouge	12	0	1	1	79
Jason Hamilton, Wheeling	41	2	2	4	333
Totals	53	2	3	5	412
Shep Harder, Greenville (g)	9	0	0	0	0
Shep Harder, Charlotte (g)	1	0	0	0	0
Shep Harder, Louisiana (g)	3	0	0	0	0
Shep Harder, Wheeling (g)	1	0	0	0	0
Totals	14	0	0	0	0
Justin Harney, Wheeling	34	7	13	20	43
Justin Harney, Charlotte	23	3	10	13	18
Totals	57	10	23	33	61
Dan Heilman, Greenville	5	2	0	2	0
Dan Heilman, Arkansas	65	13	23	36	42
Totals	70	15	23	38	42
Oak Hewer, Charlotte	12	0	2	2	2
Oak Hewer, Pensacola	30	2	12	14	18
Totals	42	2	14	16	20
Tyson Holly, New Orleans	42	8	11	19	58
Tyson Holly, Pensacola	24	6	6	12	31
Totals	66	14	17	31	89
Dalen Hrooshkin, Louisiana	42	4	4	8	14
Dalen Hrooshkin, Pensacola	14	1	1	2	4
Totals	56	5	5	10	18
Curtis Huppe, Greenville	20	4	5	9	2
Curtis Huppe, Greensboro	47	18	23	41	23
Totals	67	22	28	50	25
Mike Hurley, Charlotte	33	13	13	26	24
Mike Hurley, Wheeling	38	18	15	33	40
Totals	71	31	28	59	64
Jason Ialongo, Greenville	21	6	11	17	6
Jason Ialongo, Greensboro	46	8	24	32	16
Totals	67	14	35	49	22
Lee Jinman, Jackson	10	2	4	6	6
Lee Jinman, Trenton	15	2	8	10	18
Lee Jinman, Arkansas	34	11	26	37	26
Totals	59	15	38	53	50
Nick Jones, Roanoke	3	0	0	0	9
Nick Jones, Pensacola	3	0	1	1	11
Totals	6	0	1	1	20
Butch Kaebel, Wheeling	20	5	6	11	4
Butch Kaebel, Trenton	49	13	21	34	20
Totals	69	18	27	45	24
Klage Kaebel, Toledo	3	0	1	1	0
Klage Kaebel, New Orleans	2	0	0	0	0
Totals	5	0	1	1	0
Kevin Karlander, Louisiana	56	7	12	19	54
Kevin Karlander, Pensacola	3	0	1	1	7
Totals	59	7	13	20	61
Sam Katsuras, Toledo	63	10	21	31	63
Sam Katsuras, Jackson	2	1	0	1	0
Totals	65	11	21	32	63
Antti Kohvakka, New Orleans	20	0	1	1	17
Antti Kohvakka, Greenville	6	0	0	0	2
Antti Kohvakka, Wheeling	27	3	2	5	22
Totals	53	3	3	6	41
Ted Laviolette, Pee Dee	8	1	3	4	18
Ted Laviolette, Birmingham	34	1	20	21	44
Ted Laviolette, Toledo	14	2	2	4	48
Ted Laviolette, Johnstown	7	1	1	2	6
Totals	63	5	26	31	116
Josh MacNevin, Charlotte	52	2	19	21	47
Josh MacNevin, Birmingham	16	0	2	2	32
Totals	68	2	21	23	79
Kris Mallette, Louisiana	5	0	0	0	25
Kris Mallette, Baton Rouge	45	1	4	5	114
Totals	50	1	4	5	139
Roman Marakhovski, Lou.	51	2	4	6	32
Roman Marakhovski, Johns.	9	0	1	1	6
Totals	60	2	5	7	38
Martin Masa, Greenville	56	15	26	41	128
Martin Masa, Greensboro	13	5	6	11	12
Totals	69	20	32	52	140
Matt Masterson, Arkansas	31	4	7	11	20
Matt Masterson, Greenville	12	1	3	4	2
Totals	43	5	10	15	22

	Games	G	A	Pts.	PIM
Dennis Maxwell, Birmingham	53	22	31	53	231
Dennis Maxwell, Charlotte	9	6	5	11	13
Totals	62	28	36	64	244
Scott McCallum, Pensacola	40	3	10	13	64
Scott McCallum, Wheeling	32	4	10	14	24
Totals	72	7	20	27	88
Kevin McDonald, Florida	13	1	2	3	67
Kevin McDonald, Roanoke	57	8	12	20	296
Totals	70	9	14	23	363
Jay McGee, Pensacola	60	4	10	14	47
Jay McKee, Richmond	17	1	2	3	19
Jay McKee, Baton Rouge	20	2	9	11	24
Jay McKee, Birmingham	13	0	3	3	8
Totals	50	3	14	17	51
Jeff McKercher, Mississippi	16	2	3	5	14
Jeff McKercher, Augusta	2	0	1	1	0
Totals	18	2	4	6	14
Bryan McKinney, Jackson	6	1	1	2	8
Bryan McKinney, Toledo	16	1	5	6	56
Bryan McKinney, Dayton	5	0	0	0	8
Totals	27	2	6	8	72
John McNabb, Pensacola	26	5	14	19	18
John McNabb, Johnstown	25	9	6	15	20
John McNabb, Louisiana	18	4	10	14	22
Totals	69	18	30	48	60
Jason Metcalfe, Mobile	41	1	5	6	89
Jason Metcalfe, Florida	31	0	2	2	56
Totals	72	1	7	8	145
Aren Miller, Toledo (goalie)	10	0	0	0	10
Aren Miller, Tallahassee (g)	2	0	0	0	0
Totals	12	0	0	0	10
Josh Mizerek, Florida	2	0	1	1	2
Josh Mizerek, Baton Rouge	69	11	18	29	54
Totals	71	11	19	30	56
Mark Moore, Wheeling	20	0	2	2	19
Mark Moore, Charlotte	7	0	0	0	4
Totals	27	0	2	2	23
Ryan Moynihan, Johnstown	1	0	0	0	0
Ryan Moynihan, Pee Dee	11	2	2	4	0
Ryan Moynihan, Trenton	14	1	1	2	8
Ryan Moynihan, Birmingham	15	4	5	9	2
Totals	41	7	8	15	10
Chris Newans, Wheeling	40	7	17	24	124
Chris Newans, Pensacola	9	2	5	7	34
Totals	49	9	22	31	158
J.P. O'Connor, Jackson	44	2	11	13	77
J.P. O'Connor, Mobile	21	6	6	12	40
Totals	65	8	17	25	117
Brent Ozarowski, Roanoke	2	0	0	0	0
Brent Ozarowski, Johnstown	11	1	0	1	4
Brent Ozarowski, Arkansas	41	1	7	8	17
Totals	54	2	7	9	21
Kevin Paden, Wheeling	12	2	2	4	8
Kevin Paden, Greensboro	30	9	12	21	31
Totals	42	11	14	25	39
Sean Peach, Roanoke	13	1	1	2	20
Sean Peach, Pensacola	32	2	10	12	36
Sean Peach, New Orleans	18	0	1	1	17
Totals	63	3	12	15	73
Brad Peddle, Jackson	43	3	8	11	61
Brad Peddle, Mobile	26	1	12	13	21
Totals	69	4	20	24	82
Ryan Pepperall, Florida	29	3	6	9	51
Ryan Pepperall, Toledo	17	3	3	6	11
Ryan Pepperall, Birmingham	21	7	2	9	37
Totals	67	13	11	24	99
John Poapst, Roanoke	9	1	2	3	0
John Poapst, Pensacola	23	2	5	7	14
Totals	32	3	7	10	14
Brent Pope, Tallahassee	39	0	6	6	81
Brent Pope, Florida	31	0	5	5	51
Totals	70	0	11	11	132
Jeff Potter, Pee Dee	13	0	1	1	11
Jeff Potter, Roanoke	17	0	0	0	2
Jeff Potter, Arkansas	7	1	1	2	4
Jeff Potter, Trenton	22	0	0	0	6

	Games	G	A	Pts.	PIM
Totals	59	1	2	3	23
J.R. Prestifilippo, Augusta (g) ..	9	0	0	0	0
J.R. Prestifilippo, G'boro (g)	9	0	0	0	4
J.R. Prestifilippo, Pee Dee (g) ..	11	0	0	0	0
Totals	29	0	0	0	4
Trevor Prior, Dayton (goalie)	14	0	2	2	2
Trevor Prior, Greensboro (g)	18	0	0	0	2
Totals	32	0	2	2	4
Neal Rech, Richmond	24	6	8	14	48
Neal Rech, Birmingham	27	4	5	9	70
Neal Rech, Arkansas	22	7	7	14	42
Totals	73	17	20	37	160
Nathan Rempel, Florida	8	0	1	1	9
Nathan Rempel, Greensboro	22	2	2	4	31
Totals	30	2	3	5	40
Erasmo Saltarelli, G'boro (g)	8	0	0	0	0
Erasmo Saltarelli, Augusta (g)...	30	0	0	0	2
Totals	38	0	0	0	2
Jeff Schmidt, Trenton	12	2	0	2	2
Jeff Schmidt, Wheeling	8	0	1	1	4
Jeff Schmidt, Toledo	8	0	1	1	6
Totals	28	2	2	4	12
Sean Seyferth, Dayton	2	0	2	2	2
Sean Seyferth, Wheeling	17	1	0	1	7
Totals	19	1	2	3	9
Mike Sgroi, Toledo	10	0	0	0	62
Mike Sgroi, New Orleans	39	7	7	14	104
Mike Sgroi, Greensboro	9	3	4	7	44
Totals	58	10	11	21	210
Andrei Sharkevich, Wheeling	3	0	0	0	0
Andrei Sharkevich, Toledo	3	0	0	0	0
Totals	6	0	0	0	0
Jim Shepherd, Richmond	11	3	4	7	19
Jim Shepherd, Johnstown	44	14	26	40	135
Totals	55	17	30	47	154
Leorr Shtrom, Florida (g)	1	0	0	0	0
Leorr Shtrom, Birmingham (g) .	22	0	1	1	12
Totals	23	0	1	1	12
Eric Silverman, Charlotte	8	0	4	4	2
Eric Silverman, Trenton	17	1	0	1	6
Totals	25	1	4	5	8
Rob Sinclair, Baton Rouge	4	0	1	1	0
Rob Sinclair, Pensacola	68	19	16	35	12
Totals	72	19	17	36	12
Rob Smillie, Pensacola	7	1	2	3	2
Rob Smillie, Roanoke	16	1	1	2	6
Rob Smillie, Arkansas	16	2	3	5	0
Rob Smillie, Wheeling	17	3	5	8	4
Totals	56	7	11	18	12
Jonathan Sorg, Florida	19	3	7	10	24
Jonathan Sorg, Mobile	30	6	11	17	37
Totals	49	9	18	27	61
Mark Spence, Arkansas	1	0	0	0	0
Mark Spence, Charlotte	59	6	9	15	40
Totals	60	6	9	15	40
Troy Stevens, Augusta	10	0	0	0	0
Troy Stevens, Greensboro	7	0	1	1	2
Totals	17	0	1	1	2
Bobby Stewart, Mobile	35	18	20	38	36
Bobby Stewart, Jackson	26	9	12	21	16
Totals	61	27	32	59	52
Brandon Sugden, Tallahassee....	12	1	0	1	75
Brandon Sugden, Peoria	1	0	0	0	0
Totals	13	1	0	1	75
Mike Sylvia, Greensboro	56	15	28	43	50
Mike Sylvia, Greenville	14	5	4	9	6
Totals	70	20	32	52	56
Andrew Taylor, New Orleans	4	3	1	4	14
Andrew Taylor, Greensboro	19	4	7	11	37
Andrew Taylor, Greenville	50	12	16	28	61
Totals	73	19	24	43	112
Anthony Terzo, Roanoke	14	3	5	8	13
Anthony Terzo, Florida	21	3	8	11	14
Anthony Terzo, Mississippi	34	4	7	11	30
Totals	69	10	20	30	57
Briane Thompson, Pensacola....	53	11	28	39	121

	Games	G	A	Pts.	PIM
Briane Thompson, Louisiana.....	9	2	5	7	9
Totals	62	13	33	46	130
Chris Thompson, Augusta	17	3	6	9	76
Chris Thompson, Greensboro ...	8	0	2	2	19
Chris Thompson, Dayton	15	7	6	13	71
Totals	40	10	14	24	166
Bob Thornton, Richmond	23	0	6	6	37
Bob Thornton, Greensboro	11	0	1	1	6
Totals	34	0	7	7	43
Oleg Timchenko, Greensboro	48	12	18	30	14
Oleg Timchenko, Florida	9	0	0	0	0
Oleg Timchenko, New Orleans ..	7	0	1	1	2
Totals	64	12	19	31	16
Denis Timofeev, Greenville	3	0	0	0	8
Denis Timofeev, Pensacola	20	0	4	4	28
Denis Timofeev, New Orleans....	38	2	6	8	49
Totals	61	2	10	12	85
Kevin Tucker, Arkansas	3	0	0	0	4
Kevin Tucker, Peoria	8	0	0	0	4
Totals	11	0	0	0	8
John Varga, Tallahassee	13	6	6	12	4
John Varga, Peoria	13	3	7	10	6
Totals	26	9	13	22	10
Paul Vincent, Arkansas	35	16	24	40	57
Paul Vincent, Augusta	26	18	25	43	19
Totals	61	34	49	83	76
Ron Vogel, Toledo (goalie)	1	0	0	0	0
Ron Vogel, New Orleans (g)	27	0	0	0	4
Totals	28	0	0	0	4
Ian Walterson, Mobile	13	0	3	3	6
Ian Walterson, Birmingham	42	8	18	26	22
Totals	55	8	21	29	28
Jed Whitchurch, Trenton	49	12	16	28	7
Jed Whitchurch, New Orleans	22	5	4	9	2
Totals	71	17	20	37	9
David Whitworth, Greensboro ...	5	0	2	2	4
David Whitworth, New Orleans .	45	5	17	22	77
David Whitworth, Trenton	13	3	5	8	21
Totals	63	8	24	32	102
Curtis Wilgosh, Pee Dee	20	2	5	7	16
Curtis Wilgosh, Greensboro	38	4	10	14	34
Totals	58	6	15	21	50
Greg Willers, Mississippi	31	4	5	9	19
Greg Willers, Pensacola	24	1	2	3	26
Totals	55	5	7	12	45
Steve Wilson, Jackson	17	3	4	7	33
Steve Wilson, Charlotte	14	1	4	5	23
Totals	31	4	8	12	56
Jason Windle, Greensboro	17	0	2	2	14
Jason Windle, Greenville	44	10	9	19	29
Totals	61	10	11	21	43
Chris Wismer, Jackson	47	2	11	13	77
Chris Wismer, Pensacola	24	3	4	7	19
Totals	71	5	15	20	96
Tim Wolfe, Florida	12	2	5	7	6
Tim Wolfe, Roanoke	6	0	3	3	6
Totals	18	2	8	10	12
Scott Wray, Charlotte	8	1	2	3	2
Scott Wray, Wheeling	17	2	2	4	23
Totals	25	3	4	7	25

GOALTENDING

	Gms.	Min.	W	L	T	G	SO	Avg.
David Belitski, Lou. .	1	65	0	0	1	2	0	1.85
David Belitski, Pen. .	16	946	4	11	1	46	0	2.92
Totals	17	1011	4	11	2	48	0	2.85
Reg Bourcier, Aug. .	22	1217	9	7	3	74	0	3.65
Reg Bourcier, Mob. .	9	526	5	2	2	31	0	3.53
Totals	31	1744	14	9	5	105	0	3.61
T. Garner, John. .	5	306	3	1	1	15	0	2.94
T. Garner, G'ville	35	2114	17	15	3	99	3	2.81
Totals	40	2420	20	16	4	114	3	2.83
M. Gingras, Rich. ...	22	1147	11	5	3	62	1	3.24
M. Gingras, Mob. ...	18	1059	12	4	1	41	2	2.32
Totals	40	2206	23	9	4	103	3	2.80
S. Harder, G'ville ...	9	538	3	6	0	35	0	3.91

	Gms.	Min.	W	L	T	G	SO	Avg.
Shep Harder, Char. .	1	60	1	0	0	2	0	2.00
Shep Harder, Lou. . .	3	115	0	2	0	6	0	3.13
Shep Harder, Whe. .	1	44	0	1	0	4	0	5.48
Totals	14	756	4	9	0	47	0	3.88
Aren Miller, Toledo..	10	548	4	4	0	38	0	4.16
Aren Miller, Tal.	2	99	1	1	0	8	0	4.86
Totals	12	647	5	5	0	46	0	4.27
Prestifilippo, Aug. ...	9	348	0	6	0	25	0	4.31
Prestifilippo, G'boro.	9	402	1	4	1	32	0	4.77
J. Prestifilippo, P.D.	11	601	8	1	1	27	0	2.69
Totals	29	1352	9	11	2	84	0	3.73
Trevor Prior, Dayton	14	743	8	6	0	45	0	3.64

	Gms.	Min.	W	L	T	G	SO	Avg.
T. Prior, G'boro........	18	992	6	9	1	66	1	3.99
Totals	32	1735	14	15	1	111	1	3.84
E. Saltarelli, G'boro .	8	396	4	2	0	20	0	3.03
E. Saltarelli, Aug. ...	30	1764	17	10	3	98	1	3.33
Totals	38	2160	21	12	3	118	1	3.28
Leorr Shtrom, Fla. ...	1	60	0	1	0	4	0	4.00
L. Shtrom, Birm.	22	1286	13	9	0	71	0	3.31
Totals	23	1346	13	10	0	75	0	3.34
Ron Vogel, Toledo...	1	40	0	0	0	4	0	6.00
Ron Vogel, N.O.	27	1557	17	7	3	63	2	2.43
Totals	28	1597	17	7	3	67	2	2.52

2001 KELLY CUP PLAYOFFS

RESULTS

WILD-CARD ROUND

	W	L	Pts.	GF	GA
New Orleans	2	1	4	8	11
Augusta	1	2	2	11	8

(New Orleans won series, 2-1)

	W	L	Pts.	GF	GA
Arkansas......................................	2	0	4	8	6
Baton Rouge................................	0	2	0	6	8

(Arkansas won series, 2-0)

CONFERENCE QUARTERFINALS

	W	L	Pts.	GF	GA
Trenton	3	1	6	12	7
Johnstown....................................	1	3	2	7	12

(Trenton won series, 3-1)

	W	L	Pts.	GF	GA
Peoria	3	1	6	11	6
Richmond.....................................	1	3	2	6	11

(Peoria won series, 3-1)

	W	L	Pts.	GF	GA
Dayton..	3	2	6	16	15
Charlotte.......................................	2	3	4	15	16

(Dayton won series, 3-2)

	W	L	Pts.	GF	GA
Toledo...	3	2	6	15	13
Roanoke	2	3	4	13	15

(Toledo won series, 3-2)

	W	L	Pts.	GF	GA
Mobile	3	2	6	16	14
Jackson	2	3	4	14	16

(Mobile won series, 3-2)

	W	L	Pts.	GF	GA
Pee Dee	3	2	6	16	14
Florida	2	3	4	14	16

(Pee Dee won series, 3-2)

	W	L	Pts.	GF	GA
South Carolina.............................	3	1	6	20	12
Arkansas......................................	1	3	2	12	20

(South Carolina won series, 3-1)

	W	L	Pts.	GF	GA
Louisiana......................................	3	2	6	20	17
New Orleans	2	3	4	17	20

(Louisiana won series, 3-2)

CONFERENCE SEMIFINALS

	W	L	Pts.	GF	GA
Trenton	3	0	6	13	4
Toledo...	0	3	0	4	13

(Trenton won series, 3-0)

	W	L	Pts.	GF	GA
Peoria	3	0	6	10	6
Dayton..	0	3	0	6	10

(Peoria won series, 3-0)

	W	L	Pts.	GF	GA
South Carolina.............................	3	2	6	22	19
Mobile	2	3	4	19	22

(South Carolina won series, 3-2)

	W	L	Pts.	GF	GA
Louisiana......................................	3	2	6	20	17
Pee Dee	2	3	4	17	20

(Louisiana won series, 3-2)

CONFERENCE FINALS

	W	L	Pts.	GF	GA
Trenton	4	3	8	19	19
Peoria	3	4	6	19	19

(Trenton won series, 4-3)

	W	L	Pts.	GF	GA
South Carolina.............................	4	0	8	14	9
Louisiana......................................	0	4	0	9	14

(South Carolina won series, 4-0)

LEAGUE FINALS

	W	L	Pts.	GF	GA
South Carolina.............................	4	1	8	20	16
Trenton	1	4	2	16	20

(South Carolina won series, 4-1)

INDIVIDUAL LEADERS

Goals: Cail MacLean, Trenton (13)
Dave Seitz, South Carolina (13)
Assists: Dave Seitz, South Carolina (15)
Points: Dave Seitz, South Carolina (28)
Penalty minutes: Jay Murphy, Louisiana (62)
Goaltending average: Jody Lehman, South Carolina (2.00)
Shutouts: Curtis Sanford, Peoria (2)
Scott Stirling, Trenton (2)

TOP SCORERS

	Games	G	A	Pts.
Dave Seitz, South Carolina	18	13	15	28
Chad Remackel, South Carolina........	18	8	13	21
Scott Bertoli, Trenton.......................	19	7	14	21
Buddy Wallace, South Carolina	18	7	13	20
Shawn McNeil, Louisiana	14	7	12	19
Adam Calder, South Carolina............	17	7	12	19
Greg Schmidt, South Carolina..........	18	9	9	18
Cail MacLean, Trenton	19	13	4	17
Mike Hall, Trenton...........................	19	3	12	15
Ryan Brindley, South Carolina...........	18	3	11	14
Shane Belter, Trenton	17	0	14	14

MINOR LEAGUES *ECHL*

ARKANSAS RIVERBLADES
(Lost conference quarterfinals to South Carolina, 3-1)

SCORING

	Games	G	A	Pts.	PIM
Aaron Brand	6	2	6	8	6
Lee Jinman	6	2	5	7	4
Trevor Roenick	6	4	2	6	10
Mark Cadotte	6	3	3	6	4
Nic Beaudoin	5	2	3	5	2
Dan Harrison	6	0	4	4	26
Vern Fiddler	5	3	0	3	5
Brent Ozarowski	3	1	1	2	0
Shane Kenny	6	1	1	2	12
Eric Long	6	1	1	2	4
Jason Bermingham	6	0	2	2	6
Eric Brule	6	0	2	2	12
Mark McMahon	6	1	0	1	14
Russ Guzior	5	0	1	1	0
Dan Heilman	6	0	1	1	4
Dean Stork	6	0	1	1	16
Derek Dolson (goalie)	1	0	0	0	0
Bob Janosz (goalie)	6	0	0	0	0
Neal Rech	6	0	0	0	6

GOALTENDING

	Gms.	Min.	W	L	T	G	SO	Avg.
Derek Dolson	1	20	0	0	0	1	0	3.00
Bob Janosz	6	340	3	3	0	25	0	4.41

AUGUSTA LYNX
(Lost wild-card round to New Orleans, 2-1)

SCORING

	Games	G	A	Pts.	PIM
Paul Vincent	3	3	4	7	0
Louis Dumont	3	1	4	5	0
Lars Pettersen	3	3	1	4	2
Scott Morrow	3	1	3	4	2
Likit Andersson	3	1	2	3	2
Wes Swinson	3	1	1	2	2
Jonas Soling	3	0	2	2	2
Dean Tiltgen	3	1	0	1	2
Dorian Anneck	3	0	1	1	0
Cal Benazic	3	0	1	1	4
Sandy Lamarre	3	0	1	1	4
John Whitwell	3	0	1	1	0
Tamas Groschl	3	0	0	0	0
Judd Lambert (goalie)	3	0	0	0	0
Martin Lapointe	3	0	0	0	0
Tom O'Connor	3	0	0	0	0
Ken Tasker	3	0	0	0	0

GOALTENDING

	Gms.	Min.	W	L	T	G	SO	Avg.
Judd Lambert	3	145	1	2	0	8	0	3.32

BATON ROUGE KINGFISH
(Lost wild-card round to Arkansas, 2-0)

SCORING

	Games	G	A	Pts.	PIM
Jon Sturgis	2	2	1	3	0
Mike Rucinski	2	1	2	3	0
Josh Mizerek	2	0	3	3	2
Dane Litke	2	1	1	2	2
C.J. Buzzell	2	1	0	1	2
Shane Calder	2	1	0	1	0
Matt Erredge	2	0	1	1	0
Jesse Rooney	2	0	1	1	2
Keith Bland	2	0	0	0	0
Cam Brown	2	0	0	0	2
Chris Cerrella	2	0	0	0	0

	Games	G	A	Pts.	PIM
Sylvain Dufresne	2	0	0	0	0
Forrest Gore	2	0	0	0	0
Kris Mallette	2	0	0	0	0
Ronalds Ozolinsh	2	0	0	0	6
John Peterman	2	0	0	0	2
Paxton Schafer (goalie)	2	0	0	0	0

GOALTENDING

	Gms.	Min.	W	L	T	G	SO	Avg.
Paxton Schafer	2	120	0	1	1	8	0	4.00

CHARLOTTE CHECKERS
(Lost conference finals to Dayton, 3-2)

SCORING

	Games	G	A	Pts.	PIM
Brandon Dietrich	5	5	1	6	6
Mathieu Benoit	5	3	3	6	10
David Oliver	5	2	2	4	43
Andre Signoretti	5	2	2	4	2
Kevin Hilton	4	0	4	4	4
Marc Tropper	5	2	1	3	4
Scott King	5	1	1	2	12
Paul Giblin	5	0	2	2	2
Steve Wilson	5	0	2	2	6
Wes Jarvis	3	0	1	1	10
Dennis Maxwell	4	0	1	1	29
Kurt Seher	4	0	1	1	23
Steve Duke	5	0	1	1	14
Justin Harney	5	0	1	1	2
Mark Spence	5	0	1	1	4
Tyler Deis	1	0	0	0	0
Jason Labarbera (goalie)	2	0	0	0	0
Scott Bailey (goalie)	3	0	0	0	0
Bob MacIsaac	4	0	0	0	12
Chris Manchakowski	5	0	0	0	8

GOALTENDING

	Gms.	Min.	W	L	T	G	SO	Avg.
Jason LaBarbera	2	143	1	0	1	5	0	2.09
Scott Bailey	3	199	1	1	1	10	0	3.02

DAYTON BOMBERS
(Lost conference semifinals to Peoria, 3-0)

SCORING

	Games	G	A	Pts.	PIM
Jeff Mitchell	8	4	4	8	18
Jamie Ling	8	3	5	8	0
Ben Keup	8	3	2	5	10
Jonathan Schill	6	2	3	5	22
Brendan Brooks	8	2	3	5	20
Tom Nemeth	8	2	3	5	6
Dan Preston	8	0	5	5	4
Mike Isherwood	7	1	3	4	16
Bill McCauley	8	1	3	4	24
Brad Holzinger	8	2	1	3	14
Chris Thompson	7	1	2	3	36
Mike Garrow	6	0	3	3	2
Greg Labenski	8	0	2	2	20
Jeff Ambrosio	7	1	0	1	0
Greg Gardner (goalie)	3	0	1	1	2
Ernie Hartlieb	3	0	0	0	0
Kent McDonell	3	0	0	0	4
Alex Westlund (goalie)	5	0	0	0	0
Blaine McCauley	8	0	0	0	33
Mike Mulligan	8	0	0	0	14

GOALTENDING

	Gms.	Min.	W	L	T	G	SO	Avg.
Alex Westlund	5	350	2	1	2	15	0	2.57
Greg Gardner	3	183	1	2	0	9	0	2.96

FLORIDA EVERBLADES
(Lost conference quarterfinals to Pee Dee, 3-2)

SCORING

	Games	G	A	Pts.	PIM
Tom Buckley	5	2	4	6	8
Jason Morgan	5	2	3	5	17
Reggie Berg	5	1	3	4	6
Hugh Hamilton	5	1	3	4	4
Andy MacIntyre	5	1	3	4	0
Matt Demarski	5	2	1	3	6
Darrell Hay	5	2	1	3	0
Peter Hogan	5	1	1	2	4
Sean Blanchard	5	0	2	2	2
Sandy Cohen	5	1	0	1	2
Brent McDonald	5	1	0	1	4
Mike Jickling	4	0	1	1	2
Randy Copley	5	0	1	1	2
Brent Pope	5	0	1	1	8
Devin Hartnell	1	0	0	0	0
Terry Lindgren	5	0	0	0	11
Marc Magliarditi (goalie)	5	0	0	0	0
Jason Metcalfe	5	0	0	0	14

GOALTENDING

	Gms.	Min.	W	L	T	G	SO	Avg.
Marc Magliarditi	5	311	2	2	1	15	0	2.89

JACKSON BANDITS
(Lost conference quarterfinals to Mobile, 3-2)

SCORING

	Games	G	A	Pts.	PIM
Ryan Mougenel	5	3	4	7	15
Chris Peyton	5	2	3	5	6
Mike Jozefowicz	5	1	4	5	8
Denny Felsner	5	2	2	4	4
Cory Larose	5	2	2	4	12
Jeff Bes	5	1	3	4	10
Jonathan Shockey	5	1	1	2	15
Bobby Stewart	5	1	1	2	17
Bobby Russell	5	0	2	2	4
Brian Callahan	5	1	0	1	6
Jean-Paul Tessier	5	0	1	1	4
David Brumby (goalie)	1	0	0	0	0
Ryan Gillis	2	0	0	0	2
Dan Carney	4	0	0	0	0
Sam Katsuras	4	0	0	0	0
Milt Mastad	4	0	0	0	4
Mike Tamburro (goalie)	4	0	0	0	0
Quintin Laing	5	0	0	0	0
Dave Stewart	5	0	0	0	16

GOALTENDING

	Gms.	Min.	W	L	T	G	SO	Avg.
Mike Tamburro	4	239	2	2	0	11	0	2.76
David Brumby	1	60	0	1	0	5	0	5.00

JOHNSTOWN CHIEFS
(Lost conference quarterfinals to Trenton, 3-1)

SCORING

	Games	G	A	Pts.	PIM
Samuel St. Pierre	4	2	1	3	2
Jim Shepherd	4	1	2	3	10
Brent Bilodeau	4	1	1	2	7
Andrew Clark	4	1	1	2	2
Mike Vellinga	4	0	2	2	0
Ryan Chaytors	4	1	0	1	4
Andrew Dale	4	1	0	1	0
Eric Schneider	4	0	1	1	6
Kenton Smith	4	0	1	1	2
Jason Spence	4	0	1	1	2
Dany Sabourin (goalie)	1	0	0	0	0
Edo Terglav	1	0	0	0	0
Mike Kiesman	3	0	0	0	17
Frederic Deschenes (goalie)	4	0	0	0	0

	Games	G	A	Pts.	PIM
Ted Laviolette	4	0	0	0	18
Jim Leger	4	0	0	0	2
Jeff Sullivan	4	0	0	0	9
Dmitri Tarabrin	4	0	0	0	0
Ryan Tocher	4	0	0	0	4

GOALTENDING

	Gms.	Min.	W	L	T	G	SO	Avg.
Frederic Deschenes	4	207	1	2	1	9	0	2.61
Dany Sabourin	1	40	0	0	0	2	0	3.00

LOUISIANA ICEGATORS
(Lost conference finals to South Carolina, 4-0)

SCORING

	Games	G	A	Pts.	PIM
Shawn McNeil	14	7	12	19	11
Jay Murphy	14	9	4	13	62
John Spoltore	14	4	8	12	12
Corey Neilson	14	2	10	12	24
Mike Kucsulain	14	5	4	9	34
Dan Tessier	14	3	6	9	10
Ryan Shanahan	14	6	2	8	46
Chris Valicevic	13	3	5	8	8
Mike Murray	14	2	6	8	16
Briane Thompson	14	0	8	8	6
Magnus Nilsson	11	3	2	5	8
John McNabb	12	1	4	5	0
Jason McQuat	12	1	3	4	0
Matthew Pagnutti	13	0	4	4	6
Ryan Marsh	14	1	1	2	12
Stan Melanson	13	0	2	2	12
Jason Saal (goalie)	4	0	0	0	0
Murray Kuntz	5	0	0	0	6
Evgeny Konstantinov (goalie)	12	0	0	0	4

GOALTENDING

	Gms.	Min.	W	L	T	G	SO	Avg.
E. Konstantinov	12	637	5	6	0	32	0	3.01
Jason Saal	4	229	1	2	0	17	0	4.45

MOBILE MYSTICS
(Lost conference semifinals to South Carolina, 3-2)

SCORING

	Games	G	A	Pts.	PIM
Mark Turner	10	5	6	11	8
Jason Elders	8	4	7	11	6
Hugues Gervais	9	7	3	10	33
Brad Peddle	10	1	8	9	21
B.J. Kilbourne	10	5	3	8	10
Jason Clarke	10	3	5	8	61
J.P. O'Connor	10	2	3	5	14
Chad Onufrechuk	10	0	5	5	12
Brent Wishart	10	3	1	4	10
Jonathan Sorg	10	2	2	4	6
Sam Ftorek	10	2	1	3	29
Josh Harrold	10	0	3	3	4
Jason Reid	10	1	1	2	28
Kevin Grimes	8	0	1	1	32
Jim Nagle	10	0	1	1	16
Reg Bourcier (goalie)	5	0	0	0	0
Greg Hewitt (goalie)	5	0	0	0	0
Tyler Palmer	9	0	0	0	4

GOALTENDING

	Gms.	Min.	W	L	T	G	SO	Avg.
Reg Bourcier	5	332	2	2	1	18	1	3.26
Greg Hewitt	5	300	3	2	0	18	0	3.60

NEW ORLEANS BRASS
(Lost conference quarterfinals to Louisiana, 3-2)

SCORING

	Games	G	A	Pts.	PIM
Adam Edinger	8	8	5	13	8
Martin Bartek	8	5	4	9	4

	Games	G	A	Pts.	PIM
Ryan Fultz	8	1	8	9	6
Steve Cheredaryk	8	1	5	6	14
Bryan Forslund	8	3	1	4	8
Lee Ruff	8	0	4	4	4
Jeff Lazaro	4	2	1	3	2
Sylvai Deschatelets	8	2	1	3	6
Craig Foddrill	8	1	2	3	2
Mike Sandbeck	8	0	3	3	12
Kevin Colley	8	1	1	2	12
Sean Peach	8	1	1	2	13
Chad Dameworth	6	0	1	1	4
Omar Ennaffati	8	0	1	1	8
Ron Vogel (goalie)	8	0	1	1	4
Jed Whitchurch	8	0	1	1	0
Rob Garrick (goalie)	1	0	0	0	0
Denis Timofeev	3	0	0	0	0
Alexandre Krevsun	4	0	0	0	0
Antti Ahokas	7	0	0	0	8

GOALTENDING

	Gms.	Min.	W	L	T	G	SO	Avg.
Ron Vogel	8	445	4	3	1	26	1	3.51
Rob Garrick	1	32	0	0	0	5	0	9.49

PEE DEE PRIDE
(Lost conference semifinals to Louisiana, 3-2)

SCORING

	Games	G	A	Pts.	PIM
Ryan Petz	10	4	8	12	4
Peter Geronazzo	10	6	4	10	8
Casey Kesselring	10	6	4	10	4
Wes Goldie	10	7	1	8	8
Matt Reid	10	2	5	7	4
Eric Naud	10	2	4	6	12
Allan Sirois	10	2	4	6	10
Trevor Demmans	8	1	3	4	25
Kyle Knopp	10	0	4	4	9
Kevin Haupt	9	1	2	3	2
Ryan Jestadt	10	1	2	3	14
Vince Malts	9	0	3	3	27
Jeff Burgoyne	10	0	3	3	10
Matt Ulewlling	10	1	1	2	8
Aaron Gates	10	0	2	2	10
Martin Galik	1	0	0	0	0
J.R. Prestifilippo (goalie)	1	0	0	0	0
Bryan Tapper	3	0	0	0	0
Leigh Dean	8	0	0	0	8
Sandy Allan (goalie)	10	0	0	0	4

GOALTENDING

	Gms.	Min.	W	L	T	G	SO	Avg.
J.R. Prestifilippo	1	20	0	0	0	0	0	0.00
Sandy Allan	10	585	5	5	0	33	0	3.38

PEORIA RIVERMEN
(Lost conference finals to Trenton, 4-3)

SCORING

	Games	G	A	Pts.	PIM
J.F. Boutin	14	6	7	13	28
Tyler Rennette	14	9	2	11	14
Arvid Rekis	14	6	3	9	22
Joe Rybar	14	3	6	9	4
Jason Lawmaster	10	0	8	8	15
Bret Meyers	14	3	4	7	16
Darren Maloney	14	2	5	7	24
Blaine Fitzpatrick	14	3	3	6	14
Matt Golden	13	0	6	6	12
Didier Tremblay	14	2	3	5	8
Dustin Kuk	14	3	1	4	20
Trevor Baker	13	1	3	4	54
Tomaz Razingar	11	1	2	3	4
Tyler Willis	14	1	2	3	45
Darren Clark	6	0	3	3	25

	Games	G	A	Pts.	PIM
Lauri Kinos	9	0	1	1	6
Kenric Exner (goalie)	1	0	0	0	0
Jessie Rezansoff	5	0	0	0	15
Curtis Sanford (goalie)	14	0	0	0	0
Kevin Tucker	14	0	0	0	10

GOALTENDING

	Gms.	Min.	W	L	T	G	SO	Avg.
Curtis Sanford	14	813	9	4	0	28	2	2.07
Kenric Exner	1	40	0	1	0	3	0	4.50

RICHMOND RENEGADES
(Lost conference quarterfinals to Peoria, 3-1)

SCORING

	Games	G	A	Pts.	PIM
Brian McCullough	4	1	2	3	0
Derek Schutz	4	0	3	3	12
Frank Novock	4	2	0	2	2
Rod Taylor	4	2	0	2	18
Ryan Van Buskirk	3	0	2	2	6
Andrew Shier	4	0	2	2	0
George Awada	4	1	0	1	8
Brian Goudie	4	0	1	1	45
Richard Pitirri	4	0	1	1	4
Dan Vandermeer	4	0	1	1	11
Gerad Adams	1	0	1	1	4
Sean Matile (goalie)	1	0	0	0	0
Kyle Clark	3	0	0	0	5
Rastislav Stana (goalie)	3	0	0	0	0
Kevin Knopp	4	0	0	0	6
Matt Noga	4	0	0	0	6
Mike Siklenka	4	0	0	0	34
Ryan Skaleski	4	0	0	0	4
Joe Vandermeer	4	0	0	0	8

GOALTENDING

	Gms.	Min.	W	L	T	G	SO	Avg.
Rastislav Stana	3	180	1	2	0	7	1	2.34
Sean Matile	1	60	0	1	0	3	0	3.03

ROANOKE EXPRESS
(Lost conference quarterfinals to Toledo, 3-2)

SCORING

	Games	G	A	Pts.	PIM
Mike Omicioli	5	2	4	6	21
Doug Sheppard	5	1	4	5	5
Mike Peron	5	2	2	4	18
Adam Dewan	5	2	1	3	18
Nate Handrahan	5	1	1	2	4
Troy Lake	5	1	1	2	16
Travis Smith	5	1	1	2	4
Jeff Sproat	5	1	1	2	4
Calvin Elfring	5	0	2	2	0
Duncan Dalmao	5	1	0	1	8
John Sadowski	5	1	0	1	16
Anthony Belza	5	0	1	1	4
Joe Dusbabek	5	0	1	1	10
Dave Gagnon (goalie)	1	0	0	0	0
Daniel Berthiaume (goalie)	5	0	0	0	2
Todd Compeau	5	0	0	0	4
Kevin McDonald	5	0	0	0	4
Ben Schust	5	0	0	0	4

GOALTENDING

	Gms.	Min.	W	L	T	G	SO	Avg.
Dave Gagnon	1	2	0	0	0	0	0	0.00
Daniel Berthiaume	5	339	2	2	1	15	0	2.65

SOUTH CAROLINA STINGRAYS
(Winner of 2001 Kelly Cup playoffs)

SCORING

	Games	G	A	Pts.	PIM
Dave Seitz	18	13	15	28	16
Chad Remackel	18	8	13	21	12

	Games	G	A	Pts.	PIM
Buddy Wallace	18	7	13	20	34
Adam Calder	17	7	12	19	22
Greg Schmidt	18	9	9	18	36
Ryan Brindley	18	3	11	14	30
Damian Prescott	17	7	5	12	28
Brett Marietti	11	5	7	12	8
Joel Irving	18	5	7	12	36
Marty Clapton	17	3	9	12	30
Brad Dexter	18	3	8	11	10
Scott Swanson	17	2	9	11	12
Zach Ham	17	4	5	9	20
Jared Bednar	15	0	5	5	24
Mike Nicholishen	18	1	3	4	24
Trevor Johnson	18	1	2	3	24
Hugo Marchand	3	0	1	1	2
Kirk Daubenspeck (goalie)	13	0	1	1	4
Jody Lehman (goalie)	7	0	0	0	2
Chris Wheaton	7	0	0	0	8

GOALTENDING

	Gms.	Min.	W	L	T	G	SO	Avg.
Jody Lehman	7	389	5	1	0	13	1	2.00
Kirk Daubenspeck	13	754	9	1	2	39	0	3.10

TOLEDO STORM

(Lost conference semifinals to Trenton, 3-0)

SCORING

	Games	G	A	Pts.	PIM
Jason Norrie	8	4	2	6	7
Chris Bogas	8	1	5	6	19
Andrew Williamson	8	3	2	5	2
J.J Hunter	7	1	4	5	2
James Patterson	8	2	2	4	14
Chris Cava	8	0	4	4	23
Jeff Petrie	6	2	1	3	4
Derek Booth	8	2	1	3	12
Alexandre Jacques	8	1	2	3	10
Ryan Gaucher	8	1	1	2	10
Rob Thorpe	8	1	1	2	4
Tim Verbeek	8	1	1	2	8
Jeff Johnstone	7	0	2	2	6

	Games	G	A	Pts.	PIM
Chris George	4	0	1	1	14
Shawn Maltby	6	0	1	1	4
Phillippe Lakos	7	0	1	1	4
Kelly Miller	3	0	0	0	0
B.J. Adams	8	0	0	0	10
Mark Bernard (goalie)	8	0	0	0	8

GOALTENDING

	Gms.	Min.	W	L	T	G	SO	Avg.
Mark Bernard	8	525	3	3	2	25	0	2.86

TRENTON TITANS

(Lost finals to South Carolina, 4-1)

SCORING

	Games	G	A	Pts.	PIM
Scott Bertoli	19	7	14	21	24
Cail MacLean	19	13	4	17	10
Mike Hall	19	3	12	15	6
Shane Belter	17	0	14	14	17
Rick Kowalsky	13	8	4	12	12
Alain St. Hilaire	19	7	4	11	8
Chris Heron	19	6	5	11	10
Paul Spadafora	19	4	7	11	21
Aniket Dhadphale	19	3	6	9	6
Steve O'Brien	19	3	6	9	4
Chad Ackerman	19	2	5	7	2
Sasha Cucuz	16	1	5	6	11
Sergei Skrobot	13	2	3	5	5
Butch Kaebel	15	1	4	5	2
Sean Molina	19	0	5	5	12
Kam White	19	0	2	2	52
Benoit Morin	3	0	1	1	23
Jason Beckett	15	0	1	1	26
Scott Stirling (goalie)	18	0	1	1	6
Dan Murphy (goalie)	3	0	0	0	0

GOALTENDING

	Gms.	Min.	W	L	T	G	SO	Avg.
Scott Stirling	18	1026	10	6	2	40	2	2.34
Dan Murphy	3	156	1	0	0	8	0	3.08

2000-01 AWARD WINNERS

ALL-STAR TEAMS

First team	Pos.	Second team
Scott Stirling, Trenton	G	Curtis Sanford, Peoria
Tom Nemeth, Dayton	D	Bob Woods, Mississippi
Trevor Demmans, Pee Dee	D	Eric Long, Arkansas
James Patterson, Toledo	LW	Jason Elders, Mobile
Dany Bousquet, Pee Dee	C	Scott King, Charlotte
Andrew Williamson, Toledo	RW	Brent Cullaton, Tallahassee

TROPHY WINNERS

Most Valuable Player: Scott King, Charlotte
Scoring leader: Scott King, Charlotte
Outstanding defenseman: Tom Nemeth, Dayton
Outstanding goaltender: Scott Stirling, Trenton
Rookie of the Year: Scott Stirling, Trenton
Playoff MVP: Dave Seitz, South Carolina
Coach of the Year: Troy Ward, Trenton

ALL-TIME AWARD WINNERS

MOST VALUABLE PLAYER

Season   Player, Team
1988-89—Daryl Harpe, Erie
1989-90—Bill McDougall, Erie
1990-91—Stan Drulia, Knoxville
1991-92—Phil Berger, Greensboro
1992-93—Trevor Jobe, Nashville
1993-94—Joe Flanagan, Birmingham
1994-95—Vadim Slivchenko, Wheeling
1995-96—Hugo Belanger, Nashville
1996-97—Mike Ross, South Carolina
1997-98—Jamey Hicks, Birmingham
1998-99—Chris Valicevic, Louisiana
1999-00—Andrew Williamson, Toledo
2000-01—Scott King, Charlotte

TOP SCORER

Season   Player, Team
1988-89—Daryl Harpe, Erie
1989-90—Bill McDougall, Erie
1990-91—Stan Drulia, Knoxville
1991-92—Phil Berger, Greensboro
1992-93—Trevor Jobe, Nashville
1993-94—Phil Berger, Greensboro
1994-95—Scott Burfoot, Erie
1995-96—Hugo Belanger, Nashville
1996-97—Ed Courtenay, South Carolina
            Mike Ross, South Carolina
1997-98—Jamey Hicks, Birmingham
1998-99—John Spoltore, Louisiana
1999-00—John Spoltore, Louisiana
2000-01—Scott King, Charlotte

ROOKIE OF THE YEAR

Season	Player, Team
1988-89	Tom Sasso, Johnstown
1989-90	Bill McDougall, Erie
1990-91	Dan Gauthier, Knoxville
1991-92	Darren Colbourne, Dayton
1992-93	Joe Flanagan, Birmingham
1993-94	Dan Gravelle, Greensboro
1994-95	Kevin McKinnon, Erie
1995-96	Keli Corpse, Wheeling
1996-97	Dany Bousquet, Birmingham
1997-98	Sean Venedam, Toledo
1998-99	Maxime Gingras, Richmond
1999-00	Jan Lasak, Hampton Roads
2000-01	Scott Stirling, Trenton

TOP GOALTENDER

Season	Player, Team
1988-89	Scott Gordon, Johnstown
1989-90	Alain Raymond, Hampton Roads
1990-91	Dean Anderson, Knoxville
1991-92	Frederic Chabot, Winston-Salem
1992-93	Nick Vitucci, Hampton Roads
1993-94	Cory Cadden, Knoxville
1994-95	Chris Gordon, Huntington
1995-96	Alain Morissette, Louisville
1996-97	Marc Delorme, Louisiana
1997-98	Nick Vitucci, Toledo
1998-99	Maxime Gingras, Richmond
1999-00	Jan Lasak, Hampton Roads
2000-01	Scott Stirling, Trenton

PLAYOFF MVP

Season	Player, Team
1988-89	Nick Vitucci, Carolina
1989-90	Wade Flaherty, Greensboro
1990-91	Dave Gagnon, Hampton Rds.
	Flanagan, Hampton Roads
1991-92	Mark Bernard, Hampton Roads
1992-93	Rick Judson, Toledo
1993-94	Dave Gagnon, Toledo

Season	Player, Team
1994-95	Blaine Moore, Richmond
1995-96	Nick Vitucci, Charlotte
1996-97	Jason Fitzsimmons, South Carolina
1997-98	Sebastian Charpentier, Hampton Roads
1998-99	Travis Scott, Mississippi
1999-00	J.F. Boutin, Peoria
	Jason Christie, Peoria
2000-01	Dave Seitz, South Carolina

COACH OF THE YEAR

Season	Coach, Team
1988-89	Ron Hansis, Erie
1989-90	Dave Allison, Virginia
1990-91	Don Jackson, Knoxville
1991-92	Doug Sauter, Winston-Salem
1992-93	Kurt Kleinendorst, Raleigh
1993-94	Barry Smith, Knoxville
1994-95	Jim Playfair, Dayton
1995-96	Roy Sommer, Richmond
1996-97	Brian McCutcheon, Columbus
1997-98	Chris Nilan, Chesapeake
1998-99	Bob Ferguson, Florida
1999-00	Bob Ferguson, Florida
2000-01	Troy Ward, Trenton

TOP DEFENSEMAN

Season	Player, Team
1988-89	Kelly Szautner, Erie
1989-90	Bill Whitfield, Virginia
1990-91	Brett McDonald, Nashville
1991-92	Scott White, Greensboro
1992-93	Derek Booth, Toledo
1993-94	Tom Nemeth, Dayton
1994-95	Brandon Smith, Dayton
1995-96	Chris Valicevic, Louisiana
1996-97	Chris Valicevic, Louisiana
1997-98	Chris Valicevic, Louisiana
1998-99	Chris Valicevic, Louisiana
1999-00	Tom Nemeth, Dayton
2000-01	Tom Nemeth, Dayton

ALL-TIME LEAGUE CHAMPIONS

	REGULAR-SEASON CHAMPION		PLAYOFF CHAMPION	
Season	Team	Coach	Team	Coach
1988-89	Erie Panthers	Ron Hansis	Carolina Thunderbirds	Brendon Watson
1989-90	Winston-Salem Thunderbirds	C. McSorley, J. Fraser	Greensboro Monarchs	Jeff Brubaker
1990-91	Knoxville Cherokees	Don Jackson	Hampton Roads Admirals	John Brophy
1991-92	Toledo Storm	Chris McSorley	Hampton Roads Admirals	John Brophy
1992-93	Wheeling Thunderbirds	Doug Sauter	Toledo Storm	Chris McSorley
1993-94	Knoxville Cherokees	Barry Smith	Toledo Storm	Chris McSorley
1994-95	Wheeling Thunderbirds	Doug Sauter	Richmond Renegades	Roy Sommer
1995-96	Richmond Renegades	Roy Sommer	Charlotte Checkers	John Marks
1996-97	South Carolina Stingrays	Rick Vaive	South Carolina Stingrays	Rick Vaive
1997-98	Louisiana Icegators	Doug Shedden	Hampton Roads Admirals	John Brophy
1998-99	Pee Dee Pride	Jack Capuano	Mississippi Sea Wolves	Bruce Boudreau
1999-00	Florida Everblades	Bob Ferguson	Peoria Rivermen	Don Granato
2000-01	Trenton Titans	Troy Ward	South Carolina Stingrays	Rick Adduono

The ECHL regular season champion is awarded the Brabham Cup. The playoff champion was awarded the Riley Cup through the 1995-96 season. Playoff champions are now awarded the Patrick J. Kelly Cup.

MINOR LEAGUES ECHL

CENTRAL HOCKEY LEAGUE

LEAGUE OFFICE

Commissioner
N. Thomas Berry Jr.
President
Brad Treliving
Sr. vice president/CFO
Dan Ciarametaro
Dir. of communications
Steve Cherwonak
Director of hockey operations
Dwane Lewis

Manager of hockey operations
Rod Pasma
Director of officiating
Leon Stickle
Marketing manager
Aaron Jackson
Controller
Phil Lajoie

Address
14040 North Cave Creek Rd., Ste. 100
Phoenix, AZ 85022
Phone
602-485-9399
FAX
602-485-9449

TEAMS

AMARILLO RATTLERS

General manager
Grant Buckborough
Head coach
Joe Ferras
Home ice
Amarillo Civic Center
Address
P.O. Box 9087
Amarillo, TX 79105
Seating capacity
4,900
Phone
806-374-7825
FAX
806-374-7835

AUSTIN ICE BATS

General manager
Craig Jenkins
Head coach
Brent Hughes
Home ice
Travis County Expo Center
Address
7311 Decker Lane
Austin, TX 78724
Seating Capacity
7,741
Phone
512-927-7825
FAX
512-927-7828

BOSSIER-SHREVEPORT MUDBUGS

General manager
Jason Rent
Head coach
Scott Muscutt
Home ice
CenturyTel Center
Address
2000 CenturyTel Center Drive
Bossier City, LA 71112
Seating Capacity
12,307
Phone
318-752-2847
FAX
318-752-2878

CORPUS CHRISTI ICERAYS

General manager
Taylor Hall

Head coach
Dale Henry
Home ice
Memorial Coliseum
Address
500 North Water Street, Suite 412
Corpus Christi, TX 78471
Seating Capacity
3,500
Phone
361-814-7825
FAX
361-980-0003

EL PASO BUZZARDS

General manager
Tommy Benizio
Head coach
Trent Eigner
Home ice
El Paso County Coliseum
Address
1 TX Tower
109 N. Oregon, Suite 1402
El Paso, TX 79901
Seating Capacity
5,200
Phone
915-533-7825
FAX
915-533-7826

FORT WORTH BRAHMAS

General manager
Mike Barack
Head coach
Todd Lalonde
Home ice
Fort Worth Convention Center
Address
1314 Lake Street, Suite 200
Fort Worth, TX 76102
Seating Capacity
11,200
Phone
817-336-4423
FAX
817-336-3334

INDIANAPOLIS ICE

General manager and head coach
Rod Davidson
Home ice
Pepsi Coliseum

Address
1202 East 38th Street
Indianapolis, IN 46205
Seating capacity
8,200
Phone
317-925-4423
FAX
317-931-4511

LUBBOCK COTTON KINGS

General manager
Mark Adams
Coach
Bill McDonald
Home ice
Lubbock Municipal Coliseum
Address
1309 University
Lubbock, TX 79401
Seating capacity
7,050
Phone
806-747-7825
FAX
806-792-8396

MEMPHIS RIVERKINGS

General manager
Jim Riggs
Head coach
Doug Shedden
Home ice
DeSoto Civic Center
Address
P.O. Box 808
Southhaven, MS 38671
Seating capacity
8,444
Phone
662-342-1755
FAX
662-342-1156

NEW MEXICO SCORPIONS

General manager
Pat Dunn
Head coach
Tony Martino
Home ice
Tingley Coliseum
Address
5111 San Mateo N.E.
Albuquerque, NM 87109

Seating capacity
9,738
Phone
505-881-7825
FAX
505-883-7829

ODESSA JACKALOPES

General manager
Monty Hoppel
Head coach
Don McKee
Home ice
Ector County Coliseum
Address
P.O. Box 51187
Midland, TX 79710
Seating Capacity
5,200
Phone
915-683-4251
FAX
915-683-0994

OKLAHOMA CITY BLAZERS

General manager
Chris Presson
Head coach
Doug Sauter
Home ice
Myriad Convention Center
Address
119 North Robinson
Oklahoma City, OK 73102
Seating capacity
13,479

Phone
405-235-7825
FAX
405-272-9875

SAN ANGELO OUTLAWS

General manager
George Posejpal
Head coach
Ed Johnstone
Home ice
San Angelo Coliseum
Address
3260 Sherwood Way
San Angelo, TX 76901
Seating Capacity
5,260
Phone
915-949-7825
FAX
915-223-0999

SAN ANTONIO IGUANAS

General manager
Rick Carden
Head coach
Chris Stewart
Home ice
Freeman Coliseum
Address
8546 Broadway, Suite 165
San Antonio, TX 78217
Seating Capacity
8,500
Phone
210-227-4449

FAX
210-821-4592

TULSA OILERS

General manager
Tommy Thompson
Head coach
Garry Unger
Home ice
Tulsa Convention Center
Address
9128 46th Street
Tulsa, OK 74145
Seating Capacity
7,111
Phone
918-632-7825
FAX
918-632-0006

WICHITA THUNDER

General manager
Bill Shuck
Head coach
Jim Latos
Home ice
Kansas Coliseum
Address
505 West Maple Street
Wichita, KS 67213
Seating Capacity
9,686
Phone
316-264-4625
FAX
316-264-3037

2000-01 REGULAR SEASON
FINAL STANDINGS

EASTERN DIVISION

Team	G	W	L	SOL	Pts.	GF	GA
Memphis	70	43	21	6	92	296	236
Columbus	70	41	21	8	90	248	199
Fayetteville	70	31	30	9	71	216	243
Indianapolis	70	31	32	7	69	239	260
Huntsville	70	31	36	3	65	217	275
Macon	70	23	36	11	57	218	262

WESTERN DIVISION

Team	G	W	L	SOL	Pts.	GF	GA
Oklahoma City	70	48	19	3	99	273	185
San Antonio	70	42	21	7	91	288	229
Topeka	69	38	23	8	84	256	245
Tulsa	70	36	26	8	80	259	250
Wichita	70	30	32	8	68	251	251
Border City	51	11	36	4	26	132	283

Note. League suspended operation of Border City and Topeka clubs on Feb. 20. Topeka club was reinstated by a temporary restraining order and completed its season.

INDIVIDUAL LEADERS

Goals: Yvan Corbin, Indianapolis (75)
Assists: Chris MacKenzie, Indianapolis (93)
Points: Yvan Corbin, Indianapolis (129)
Penalty minutes: Marty Melnychuk, San Antonio (437)
Goaltending average: Brant Nicklin, Oklahoma City (2.37)
Shutouts: Francis Ouellette, Columbus (4)

TOP SCORERS

	Games	G	A	Pts.
Yvan Corbin, Indianapolis	69	75	54	129
Chris MacKenzie, Indianapolis	66	30	93	123
Don Parsons, Memphis	69	56	57	113
Joe Burton, Oklahoma City	70	51	59	110
Michael Martens, Columbus	70	53	52	105

	Games	G	A	Pts.
Doug Lawrence, Tulsa	63	15	80	95
Jason Duda, Wichita	70	38	52	90
Bob Berg, Topeka	69	25	63	88
Marty Standish, Oklahoma City	63	43	44	87
Blair Manning, Topeka	61	35	50	85
Johnny Brdarovic, San Antonio	70	29	56	85
Bernie John, Indianapolis	67	23	62	85
Darryl Noren, Fayetteville	70	48	36	84
Jamie Steer, Fayetteville	70	32	51	83
Pete Brearley, Topeka	66	44	38	82
Jean-Francois Gregoire, Tulsa	70	37	44	81
Scott Green, San Antonio	70	38	42	80
Jonathan DuBois, San Antonio	65	22	58	80
Cory Cyrenne, Memphis	52	33	46	79
Tom Gomes, B.C.-Tul.	69	35	41	76

MINOR LEAGUES *Central*

BORDER CITY BANDITS

SCORING

	Games	G	A	Pts.	PIM
Jason Sangiuliano	33	11	14	25	18
Trevor Jobe	21	12	11	23	46
Shawn Yakimishyn	43	10	11	21	144
Rusty McKie	35	7	13	20	204
Keli Corpse	16	5	14	19	10
Tom Gomes	16	7	9	16	85
Blaz Emersic	28	6	8	14	6
Jason Desloover	44	4	10	14	67
Aaron Porter	29	3	10	13	13
Jeff Parrott	31	1	12	13	13
Nolan Weir	38	1	12	13	41
Jim Gattolliat	42	5	7	12	124
Chris Ross	28	8	3	11	8
Bobby Hanson	22	3	8	11	4
Garth Gartner	40	4	5	9	126
Eric Pinoul	13	3	6	9	23
Daniel Shank	9	2	7	9	14
Darcy Anderson	9	4	4	8	4
Sean Freeman	18	4	3	7	26
Thomas Migdal	13	4	2	6	6
Marek Babic	35	4	2	6	32
Sam Fields	28	3	3	6	113
Cam Werfelman	26	2	4	6	77
Sandis Girvitch	15	3	2	5	16
Don Sauter	7	2	3	5	0
Rostyslav Saglo	8	1	4	5	6
Cam Law	8	0	5	5	10
Randy Hankinson	17	3	1	4	15
Stefan Simoes	4	1	3	4	0
Marian Csorich	15	0	4	4	14
Matt Miller	14	2	1	3	14
Francis Boulay	4	1	1	2	2
Kyle Gizowski	6	1	1	2	0
Scott Ross	30	1	1	2	79
Mike L'Heureux	8	1	0	1	22
Dan McGuire (goalie)	1	0	0	0	0
Brad Mueller	1	0	0	0	0
Per Fernhall	2	0	0	0	0
Kristoffer Eriksson	4	0	0	0	8
Greg MacInnis	4	0	0	0	14
Ron Vogal (goalie)	4	0	0	0	17
Alan Hitchen (goalie)	5	0	0	0	2
Jean-Ian Filiatrault (goalie)	6	0	0	0	10
Cameron MacDonald (goalie)	7	0	0	0	24
Trevor Bremner	9	0	0	0	36
Jason Wright (goalie)	14	0	0	0	23
Trevor Matter (goalie)	23	0	0	0	14

GOALTENDING

	Games	Min.	W	L	SOL	G	SO	Avg.
Trevor Matter	23	1141	6	11	3	88	0	4.63
Jean-Ian Filliatrault	6	320	2	4	0	26	0	4.88
Ron Vogal	4	207	1	2	0	19	0	5.52
Alan Hitchen	5	268	0	4	0	26	0	5.81
Jason Wright	14	800	2	11	0	81	0	6.08
Cameron MacDonald	7	299	0	4	1	32	0	6.43
Dan McGuire	1	23	0	0	0	4	0	10.26

COLUMBUS COTTONMOUTHS

SCORING

	Games	G	A	Pts.	PIM
Michael Martens	70	53	52	105	48
Martin Menard	48	35	29	64	112
Bobby Marshall	68	6	46	52	95
Riley Nelson	70	20	27	47	37
Kris Cantu	37	20	24	44	59
Mick Kempffer	70	4	40	44	30
Rob Schweyer	57	14	25	39	109

	Games	G	A	Pts.	PIM
Andy Powers	60	9	24	33	40
Jerome Bechard	65	10	18	28	421
Kris Schultz	49	10	15	25	163
Craig Stahl	67	7	12	19	160
Daniel Payette	14	9	9	18	28
Drew Schoneck	70	9	9	18	51
Ryan Brown	41	4	10	14	77
Jaroslav Kerestes	68	5	6	11	144
Denis Lamoureux	19	7	3	10	15
Doug Mann	37	5	4	9	148
Jeremy Stasiuk	8	4	5	9	17
Greg Quebec	20	3	4	7	6
Scott Schoneck	34	2	5	7	29
Rich Metro	24	3	3	6	6
Kamil Kuriplach	15	1	3	4	30
Per Fernhall	2	0	3	3	0
Mark Scott	9	1	1	2	38
Jayme Adduono	5	1	0	1	12
Blake Sheane	3	0	1	1	5
Bobby Hanson	6	0	1	1	0
Todd Miller	6	0	1	1	10
Brad Mueller	7	0	1	1	15
Francis Ouellette (goalie)	41	0	1	1	16
Jeff Cheeseman	1	0	0	0	0
Richard Kazada	1	0	0	0	0
Anthony DiPalma	5	0	0	0	2
Darren McLean	11	0	0	0	38
Blaine Russell (goalie)	34	0	0	0	6

GOALTENDING

	Games	Min.	W	L	SOL	G	SO	Avg.
Blaine Russell	34	1910	17	11	4	82	3	2.58
Francis Ouellette	41	2292	24	10	4	105	4	2.75

FAYETTEVILLE FORCE

SCORING

	Games	G	A	Pts.	PIM
Darryl Noren	70	48	36	84	76
Jamie Steer	70	32	51	83	39
David Hoogsteen	70	23	43	66	46
Alex Chunchukov	57	19	46	65	24
Mike Torkoff	49	11	25	36	65
Jason Tatarnic	42	11	14	25	70
Jasen Rintala	70	11	13	24	121
Mark Shalawylo	25	11	9	20	8
Eric Linkowski	31	9	11	20	20
Tyler McMillan	28	2	18	20	8
Jason Rushton	21	8	9	17	64
Rob Concannon	13	5	7	12	25
Sandis Girvitch	38	5	6	11	33
Brad Cruikshank	68	4	7	11	302
John Gibson	25	1	7	8	33
Mike Jaros	70	1	7	8	163
Colin Muldoon	44	0	7	7	38
Ales Dvorak	13	4	2	6	10
Kris Currie	63	1	5	6	186
Normand Fay	14	0	5	5	6
Lenny Bonanno	12	1	3	4	15
Jeff Corbett	46	1	2	3	227
Chris Bonvie	12	0	2	2	2
Erik Olsen	13	0	2	2	32
Marty Melnychuk	40	1	0	1	380
Darcy Anderson	9	0	1	1	13
Jake Harney	1	0	0	0	2
Alex Lachance	1	0	0	0	0
Joe Wassilyn	1	0	0	0	0
Dave Wilejto	1	0	0	0	0
Derek Beuselinck	5	0	0	0	8
Mike Moran	5	0	0	0	41
Ross Dufresne	7	0	0	0	4
Darren McLean	21	0	0	0	115

	Games	G	A	Pts.	PIM
Ian Olsen (goalie)	35	0	0	0	14
Ken Shepard (goalie)	40	0	0	0	46
Jim McLean	41	0	0	0	10

GOALTENDING

	Games	Min.	W	L	SOL	G	SO	Avg.
Ken Shepard	40	2239	17	16	5	112	3	3.00
Ian Olsen	35	1960	14	14	4	119	0	3.64

HUNTSVILLE CHANNEL CATS
SCORING

	Games	G	A	Pts.	PIM
Chris George	69	46	19	65	16
Igor Bondarev	67	13	41	54	53
Derek Reynolds	68	22	31	53	253
Marek Jass	69	20	19	39	52
Blake Sheane	43	16	18	34	121
Josh Boni	23	6	27	33	46
Mike Dick	48	10	20	30	39
Josh Tymchak	59	11	18	29	177
Shane Stewart	58	11	17	28	66
Doug Pirnak	70	9	18	27	180
Doug Merrell	49	7	15	22	14
Erik Olsen	57	2	17	19	124
Alex Chunchukov	10	3	7	10	4
Chad Nelson	17	4	5	9	64
Jason Sangiuliano	16	3	6	9	10
Brian Tutt	30	3	6	9	34
Greg Wilkinson	18	5	3	8	13
Curtis Voth	28	4	4	8	233
Trevor Folk	30	1	7	8	65
Sheldon Szmata	21	3	4	7	8
B.J. Stephens	17	1	6	7	6
Kevin Carr	38	0	6	6	18
Phil Daigle	15	4	1	5	74
Bryan Fogarty	11	1	4	5	16
Shaun Byrne	53	1	4	5	168
Marek Babic	16	1	2	3	23
Kelly Selix	8	1	1	2	8
Nathan Bowen	4	1	0	1	0
Brad Gratton	5	0	1	1	2
Matt Carmichael (goalie)	48	0	1	1	37
Mark Macera	2	0	0	0	0
Al Rooney (goalie)	2	0	0	0	0
Mike Brusseau (goalie)	5	0	0	0	2
Jason Genik (goalie)	22	0	0	0	22

GOALTENDING

	Games	Min.	W	L	SOL	G	SO	Avg.
Mike Brusseau	5	269	3	2	0	14	1	3.12
Matt Carmichael	48	2686	20	21	1	158	1	3.53
Jason Genik	22	1112	7	12	2	80	1	4.32
Al Rooney	2	120	1	1	0	14	0	7.00

INDIANAPOLIS ICE
SCORING

	Games	G	A	Pts.	PIM
Yvan Corbin	69	75	54	129	130
Chris MacKenzie	66	30	93	123	126
Bernie John	67	23	62	85	12
Chris Richards	56	14	44	58	24
Jason Selleke	70	16	21	37	116
Dan Cousineau	69	3	22	25	95
Ken Boone	42	13	8	21	315
Jan Jas	45	12	7	19	22
Peter Jas	54	8	10	18	14
Casey Harris	59	8	7	15	182
Derek Grant	10	4	11	15	23
Dave Jesiolowski	38	4	11	15	189
Todd Norman	33	2	6	8	12
Kevin Schmidt	70	1	7	8	26
Sebastian Pajerski	18	3	4	7	7
Jamie Morris (goalie)	37	0	7	7	2
Corey Payment	40	5	1	6	32

	Games	G	A	Pts.	PIM
Aigars Mironovics	34	3	3	6	42
Marc Laforge	49	1	5	6	175
Chad Spurr	7	1	4	5	0
Dan Passero	7	1	1	2	2
Brandon Christian	10	1	1	2	116
Ryan Reid	10	1	1	2	49
Duncan Paterson	14	1	1	2	30
Robert Davidson	35	1	1	2	51
Dan Back	32	0	2	2	17
Charlie Elezi	3	1	0	1	17
Brandon Lafrance	3	1	0	1	0
Lubos Krajcovic	17	1	0	1	2
Ray Aho (goalie)	38	0	1	1	10
Chris Bonvie	1	0	0	0	0
Steven Kirkpatrick (goalie)	1	0	0	0	0
Tom Viola	12	0	0	0	14

GOALTENDING

	Games	Min.	W	L	SOL	G	SO	Avg.
Steven Kirkpatrick	1	0	0	0	0	0	0	0.00
Ray Aho	38	2123	19	13	5	108	1	3.05
Jamie Morris	37	2060	12	19	2	142	0	4.14

MACON WHOOPEE
SCORING

	Games	G	A	Pts.	PIM
Rob Sandrock	70	17	53	70	95
Bobby Davis	56	25	31	56	15
Todd MacIsaac	69	21	31	52	167
Ryan Campbell	57	26	18	44	43
Joe Suk	39	13	17	30	48
Ryan Kummu	51	9	13	22	132
Jamie Pegg	36	6	13	19	58
Jason Gudmundson	31	8	10	18	24
Chris Richards	16	7	10	17	46
Bobby Hanson	15	5	11	16	18
Shaun Peet	47	5	11	16	145
Mark Green	10	8	7	15	8
Mike Payne	59	3	12	15	290
Bill Monkman	26	7	6	13	41
Derek Grant	14	5	8	13	62
Greg Quebec	31	10	2	12	6
Kevin Pucovsky	27	5	7	12	39
Eric Linkowski	27	2	10	12	19
A.J. Aitken	30	4	7	11	25
Vitali Andreev	21	3	8	11	31
Lenny Bonanno	15	0	10	10	63
Keith Osborne	16	3	6	9	24
Francis Boulay	11	3	5	8	11
Phil Valk	33	0	8	8	139
Aigars Mironovics	15	3	4	7	6
Per Fernhall	20	3	4	7	41
Oleg Tsirkounov	18	4	2	6	5
Klage Kaebel	9	1	4	5	4
Bryan Kennedy	14	1	3	4	23
Don Sauter	16	1	3	4	14
Jason Tatarnic	10	0	4	4	29
Ales Dvorak	22	1	2	3	12
Duane Hergenhein	2	0	3	3	0
Joe Pavone	8	2	0	2	32
Chris Ross	3	1	1	2	2
Eric Peterson	6	0	2	2	4
Hiro Murakami	13	0	2	2	8
Andrei Sharkevich	6	1	0	1	2
Ryan Naismith	7	1	0	1	0
Eric Pinoul	4	0	1	1	0
David Mills	5	0	1	1	0
Sam Fields	8	0	1	1	43
Sebastian Pajerski	16	0	1	1	11
Brian Elder (goalie)	44	0	1	1	2
Drew Norman	1	0	0	0	0
Trevor Anderson (goalie)	2	0	0	0	0
Nathan Bowen	2	0	0	0	0
Matt Hill	2	0	0	0	0

	Games	G	A	Pts.	PIM
Denis Lamoureux	2	0	0	0	2
Fred Slukynsky	2	0	0	0	0
Derek Sylvester	2	0	0	0	0
Mattias Wraak	2	0	0	0	0
Kris Currie	4	0	0	0	19
Jeff Washbrook	4	0	0	0	7
Andrei Kuznetsov	7	0	0	0	0
Colin Muldoon	11	0	0	0	12
Steve Vezina (goalie)	14	0	0	0	2
Aaron Vickar (goalie)	16	0	0	0	0

GOALTENDING

	Games	Min.	W	L	SOL	G	SO	Avg.
Aaron Vickar	16	957	6	7	3	46	2	2.88
Brian Elder	44	2510	14	21	5	156	2	3.73
Trevor Anderson	2	64	0	1	0	4	0	3.73
Steve Vezina	14	660	3	7	3	42	0	3.82

MEMPHIS RIVERKINGS

SCORING

	Games	G	A	Pts.	PIM
Don Parsons	69	56	57	113	131
Cory Cyrenne	52	33	46	79	24
Nick Stajduhar	36	9	45	54	104
Derek Landmesser	59	7	41	48	121
Brian Tucker	68	17	28	45	286
Jason Simon	61	24	19	43	301
Matt Johnson	70	18	25	43	30
Derek Grant	23	21	20	41	14
Brad Mueller	53	20	15	35	47
A.J. Aitken	35	11	18	29	35
Travis Riggin	62	15	13	28	31
Greg Lakovic	49	12	11	23	165
Jason Gudmundson	26	9	14	23	6
Lenny Bonanno	26	4	12	16	81
Don Martin	19	4	11	15	64
Jamie Pegg	35	1	14	15	24
Jeremy Kyte	22	5	6	11	27
Ales Dvorak	27	4	6	10	17
Kevin Fricke	64	4	6	10	38
Kevin Holliday	46	0	9	9	393
Mike Marostega	10	2	5	7	15
Kevin Ryan	32	0	5	5	70
Dan Lupo	9	2	2	4	8
Curtis Voth	15	1	3	4	160
Sloawomir Krzak	8	3	0	3	0
Francis Boulay	7	2	1	3	4
Matt Interbartolo	9	2	0	2	4
Aaron Vickar (goalie)	18	0	2	2	0
Mark Richards (goalie)	47	0	2	2	45
Domininc Gagnon	4	1	0	1	2
Stas Tkatch	2	0	1	1	0
Jeremy Goetzinger	4	0	1	1	0
Marek Babic	10	0	1	1	0
Martin Fillion (goalie)	2	0	0	0	0
Alan Hitchen (goalie)	2	0	0	0	0
Tom Field	3	0	0	0	4
David Garofalo	3	0	0	0	0
Jeremy Griffis	3	0	0	0	2
Mike Brusseau (goalie)	4	0	0	0	0
Hardy Gensel	4	0	0	0	0
Vlad Kulikov (goalie)	8	0	0	0	17
Ryan Lee	8	0	0	0	19

GOALTENDING

	Games	Min.	W	L	SOL	G	SO	Avg.
Martin Fillion	2	67	2	0	0	3	0	2.67
Aaron Vickar	18	972	10	5	1	46	0	2.84
Mark Richards	47	2581	27	11	4	134	2	3.12
Mike Brusseau	4	195	1	3	0	13	0	4.01
Vlad Kulikov	8	335	2	2	1	25	0	4.48
Alan Hitchen	2	50	1	0	0	4	0	4.83

OKLAHOMA CITY BLAZERS

SCORING

	Games	G	A	Pts.	PIM
Joe Burton	70	51	59	110	32
Marty Standish	63	43	44	87	161
Jared Dumba	70	36	39	75	54
Hardy Sauter	70	16	47	63	50
Peter Arvanitis	69	19	29	48	163
Peter Robertson	67	7	30	37	45
Dave Shields	61	20	12	32	191
Sheldon Szmata	45	12	17	29	39
Guy Girouard	62	2	20	22	74
Marco Cefalo	52	12	9	21	149
Joakim Andersson	35	11	9	20	58
Chris Dashney	68	2	18	20	89
Wade Brookbank	46	1	13	14	267
Don Sauter	26	6	6	12	18
Tyler Fleck	55	3	9	12	166
Frank DeFrenza	13	5	4	9	11
Oleg Tsirkounov	35	4	5	9	57
Thomas Migdal	14	3	3	6	4
Mark Scott	20	3	3	6	49
Paul Johnson	58	2	4	6	86
Gregor Baumgartner	6	2	3	5	8
Josh Dobbyn	16	2	2	4	45
Garth Gartner	15	1	2	3	65
Barkley Sauter	5	2	0	2	11
Aaron Porter	3	0	2	2	2
Chris Low	13	0	2	2	4
Rod Branch (goalie)	41	0	2	2	10
Mike Markell	4	1	0	1	0
David Kontzie	5	1	0	1	15
Luke Murphy	5	0	1	1	2
Brant Nicklin (goalie)	19	0	1	1	0
Jeff Allen	2	0	0	0	0
Willy Mason	6	0	0	0	19
Bjorn Leonhardt (goalie)	12	0	0	0	4

GOALTENDING

	Games	Min.	W	L	SOL	G	SO	Avg.
Brant Nicklin	19	1115	15	3	0	44	2	2.37
Rod Branch	41	2357	26	12	2	98	3	2.50
Bjorn Leonhardt	12	718	7	4	1	36	0	3.01

SAN ANTONIO IGUANAS

SCORING

	Games	G	A	Pts.	PIM
Johnny Brdarovic	70	29	56	85	40
Scott Green	70	38	42	80	45
Jonathan DuBois	65	22	58	80	212
Henry Kuster	65	28	39	67	34
Tyler Quiring	69	22	45	67	79
Paul Buczkowski	70	21	33	54	57
Ken Richardson	66	25	23	48	266
Jeff Trembecky	68	18	30	48	56
Greg Gatto	63	21	22	43	222
Andrei Lupandin	70	10	30	40	93
Brian Shantz	23	11	22	33	18
Darcy Dallas	62	7	23	30	130
Chris Smith	31	10	7	17	37
Garnet Jacobson	65	6	6	12	238
Mike Moran	43	4	6	10	86
Ryan Edwards	37	3	7	10	78
Jeff Parrott	16	0	9	9	2
Marty Melnychuk	15	4	3	7	57
Aaron Boh	12	3	4	7	61
Nathan Grobins (goalie)	31	0	6	6	22
Peter Zurba	3	1	1	2	24
Debb Carpenter	5	1	1	2	2
Nathan Rocheleau	8	1	1	2	2
Marian Csorich	11	1	1	2	0
Mike Marostega	10	0	2	2	0
Rob Galatiuk (goalie)	8	0	1	1	31
Mark Falkowski	13	0	1	1	19

	Games	G	A	Pts.	PIM
Ian Perkins (goalie)	26	0	1	1	14
Joe Gray	3	0	0	0	0
Craig Hayden	3	0	0	0	0
Derek Watson	3	0	0	0	0
Dale Masson (goalie)	10	0	0	0	0

GOALTENDING

	Games	Min.	W	L	SOL	G	SO	Avg.
Rob Galatiuk	8	407	4	2	1	18	0	2.66
Nathan Grobins	31	1776	17	10	3	89	1	3.01
Dale Masson	10	551	7	1	0	30	0	3.27
Ian Perkins	26	1454	14	8	3	82	1	3.38

TOPEKA SCARECROWS

SCORING

	Games	G	A	Pts.	PIM
Bob Berg	69	25	63	88	98
Blair Manning	61	35	50	85	45
Pete Brearley	66	44	38	82	40
John Vary	69	12	59	71	65
Paul Strand	64	25	24	49	170
Mark Edmundson	67	21	24	45	65
Chris Felix	68	7	38	45	100
Jeff Goldie	58	16	25	41	43
Shawn Gervais	67	10	19	29	103
Ryan Hartung	56	11	13	24	40
John McCabe	67	10	11	21	148
Jay Hern	58	11	8	19	151
Duke Bouskill	56	8	9	17	39
Chris Maillet	46	3	5	8	89
Blake Sheane	11	3	4	7	8
Lannie McCabe	64	0	4	4	118
Sergei Deshevyy	68	0	4	4	141
Scott Hay (goalie)	31	0	3	3	33
Ryan McCormack	10	2	0	2	2
Anthony Zurfluh	13	0	2	2	14
Luciano Caravaggio (goalie)	40	0	1	1	17
Chris Burke	4	0	0	0	0

GOALTENDING

	Games	Min.	W	L	SOL	G	SO	Avg.
Luciano Caravaggio	40	2345	22	11	5	123	0	3.15
Scott Hay	31	1790	16	12	3	111	0	3.72

TULSA OILERS

SCORING

	Games	G	A	Pts.	PIM
Doug Lawrence	63	15	80	95	170
Jean-Francois Gregoire	70	37	44	81	44
Tom Gomes	53	28	32	60	78
Craig Hamelin	56	24	32	56	80
Jon Cameron	70	21	30	51	81
Jorin Welsh	70	20	30	50	90
David Rattray	70	14	23	37	202
Craig Bilick	62	17	16	33	132
Brad Englehart	29	14	9	23	29
Mike Mohr	70	8	15	23	134
Chris Fawcett	38	11	7	18	4
Peter Campbell	19	6	12	18	4
Carlos Soke	46	8	9	17	172
Dan Hopfner	57	2	12	14	24
Chris Smith	27	1	9	10	28
Derek Stone	70	4	4	8	94
Ryan Reid	42	3	5	8	135
Dallas Anderson	44	2	6	8	309
Brian Secord	11	3	4	7	14
Richard Uniacke	15	2	4	6	8
Sylvain Naud	15	1	5	6	22
Aldo Iaquinta	27	1	5	6	77
Trevor Shoaf	7	2	2	4	4
Joe Eagan	11	2	2	4	14
Aaron Parenteau	11	1	2	3	2
Chris Jamieson	11	1	1	2	9
Matt Barnes (goalie)	21	0	2	2	2

	Games	G	A	Pts.	PIM
James Ronayne (goalie)	39	0	2	2	0
Curtis Voth	1	0	0	0	5
Richard Peacock	9	0	0	0	51
Chad Erickson (goalie)	17	0	0	0	2

GOALTENDING

	Games	Min.	W	L	SOL	G	SO	Avg.
Matt Barnes	21	1234	10	6	3	64	1	3.11
James Ronayne	39	2101	16	13	5	116	2	3.31
Chad Erickson	17	853	10	7	0	55	0	3.87

WICHITA THUNDER

SCORING

	Games	G	A	Pts.	PIM
Jason Duda	70	38	52	90	68
Travis Clayton	63	34	39	73	130
John Gurskis	69	28	36	64	22
Stephane Larocque	49	25	23	48	175
Sean O'Reilly	70	4	42	46	217
Terry Menard	44	14	21	35	74
Bruce Ramsay	60	11	24	35	364
Jay Banach	68	18	16	34	255
Jeff Leiter	69	10	21	31	236
Andrew Dickson	66	6	22	28	105
Jon Austin	32	11	14	25	4
Jerod Bina	44	9	15	24	60
Trevor Jobe	14	9	11	20	20
Mark Strohack	25	4	13	17	20
Kamil Kuriplach	53	2	12	14	93
Kris Schultz	17	3	7	10	65
Todd Newton	22	3	7	10	26
Allan Roulette	20	2	6	8	34
Thomas Migdal	19	4	3	7	8
Ken Fels	63	2	5	7	215
Joey Bastien	8	3	3	6	4
Corey Payment	13	1	3	4	2
Jason Desloover	19	1	3	4	14
Ryan Dencurik	5	1	1	2	2
Cam Werfelman	11	1	1	2	35
Kevin Lewis	13	1	1	2	20
Chris Dearden	10	0	2	2	6
Dale Masson (goalie)	13	0	2	2	0
Pat Glenday	18	0	2	2	18
Stephen Wagner (goalie)	23	0	2	2	2
Troy Yarosh	2	0	0	0	4
Marek Babic	3	0	0	0	0
Darren Cameron	3	0	0	0	0
Scott Simpson (goalie)	5	0	0	0	0
Derek Warren	8	0	0	0	15
Jason Neath	11	0	0	0	53
Stan Reddick (goalie)	37	0	0	0	2

GOALTENDING

	Games	Min.	W	L	SOL	G	SO	Avg.
Stan Reddick	37	2056	14	15	5	103	3	3.01
Scott Simpson	5	264	1	3	1	15	0	3.41
Dale Masson	13	614	3	6	2	37	0	3.61
Stephen Wagner	23	1250	12	8	0	80	0	3.84

PLAYERS WITH TWO OR MORE TEAMS

SCORING

	Games	G	A	Pts.	PIM
A.J. Aitken, Macon	30	4	7	11	25
A.J. Aitken, Memphis	35	11	18	29	35
Totals	65	15	25	40	60
Darcy Anderson, Fayetteville	9	0	1	1	13
Darcy Anderson, Border City	9	4	4	8	4
Totals	18	4	5	9	17
Marek Babic, Border City	35	4	2	6	32
Marek Babic, Memphis	10	0	1	1	0
Marek Babic, Wichita	3	0	0	0	0
Marek Babic, Huntsville	16	1	2	3	23
Totals	64	5	5	10	55

	Games	G	A	Pts.	PIM
Lenny Bonanno, Memphis	26	4	12	16	81
Lenny Bonanno, Macon	15	0	10	10	63
Lenny Bonanno, Fayetteville	12	1	3	4	15
Totals	53	5	25	30	159
Chris Bonvie, Indianapolis	1	0	0	0	0
Chris Bonvie, Fayetteville	12	0	2	2	2
Totals	13	0	2	2	2
Francis Boulay, Border City	4	1	1	2	2
Francis Boulay, Memphis	7	2	1	3	4
Francis Boulay, Macon	11	3	5	8	11
Totals	22	6	7	13	17
Nathan Bowen, Macon	2	0	0	0	0
Nathan Bowen, Huntsville	4	1	0	1	0
Totals	6	1	0	1	0
Mike Brusseau, Memphis (g)	4	0	0	0	0
Mike Brusseau, Huntsville (g)	5	0	0	0	2
Totals	9	0	0	0	2
Alex Chunchukov, Fayetteville	57	19	46	65	24
Alex Chunchukov, Huntsville	10	3	7	10	4
Totals	67	22	53	75	28
Marian Csorich, San Antonio	11	1	1	2	16
Marian Csorich, Border City	15	0	4	4	14
Totals	26	1	5	6	30
Kris Currie, Macon	4	0	0	0	19
Kris Currie, Fayetteville	63	1	5	6	186
Totals	67	1	5	6	205
Jason Desloover, Border City	44	4	10	14	67
Jason Desloover, Wichita	19	1	3	4	14
Totals	63	5	13	18	81
Ales Dvorak, Memphis	27	4	6	10	17
Ales Dvorak, Macon	22	1	2	3	12
Ales Dvorak, Fayetteville	13	4	2	6	10
Totals	62	9	10	19	39
Per Fernhall, Columbus	2	0	3	3	0
Per Fernhall, Macon	20	3	4	7	41
Per Fernhall, Border City	2	0	0	0	0
Totals	24	3	7	10	41
Sam Fields, Border City	28	3	3	6	113
Sam Fields, Macon	8	0	1	1	43
Totals	36	3	4	7	156
Garth Gartner, Border City	40	4	5	9	126
Garth Gartner, Oklahoma City	15	1	2	3	65
Totals	55	5	7	12	191
Sandis Girvitch, Fayetteville	38	5	6	11	33
Sandis Girvitch, Border City	15	3	2	5	16
Totals	53	8	8	16	49
Tom Gomes, Border City	16	7	9	16	85
Tom Gomes, Tulsa	53	28	32	60	78
Totals	69	35	41	76	163
Derek Grant, Memphis	23	21	20	41	14
Derek Grant, Macon	14	5	8	13	62
Derek Grant, Indianapolis	10	4	11	15	23
Totals	47	30	39	66	99
Jason Gudmundson, Macon	31	8	10	18	24
Jason Gudmundson, Memphis	26	9	14	23	6
Totals	57	17	24	41	30
Bobby Hanson, Columbus	6	0	1	1	0
Bobby Hanson, Border City	22	3	8	11	4
Bobby Hanson, Macon	15	5	11	16	18
Totals	43	8	20	28	22
Alan Hitchen, Memphis (goalie)	2	0	0	0	0
Alan Hitchen, Border City (g)	5	0	0	0	2
Totals	7	0	0	0	2
Trevor Jobe, Border City	21	12	11	23	46
Trevor Jobe, Wichita	14	9	11	20	20
Totals	35	21	22	43	66
Kamil Kuriplach, Columbus	15	1	3	4	30
Kamil Kuriplach, Wichita	53	2	12	14	93
Totals	68	3	15	18	123
Denis Lamoureux, Macon	2	0	0	0	2
Denis Lamoureux, Columbus	19	7	3	10	15
Totals	21	7	3	10	17
Eric Linkowski, Macon	27	2	10	12	19
Eric Linkowski, Fayetteville	31	9	11	20	20
Totals	58	11	21	32	39
Mike Marostega, Memphis	10	2	5	7	15
Mike Marostega, San Antonio	10	0	2	2	0
Totals	20	2	7	9	15
Dale Masson, Wichita (goalie)	13	0	2	2	0
Dale Masson, San Antonio (g)	10	0	0	0	0
Totals	23	0	2	2	0
Darren McLean, Columbus	11	0	0	0	38
Darren McLean, Fayetteville	21	0	0	0	115
Totals	32	0	0	0	153
Marty Melnychuk, Fayetteville	40	1	0	1	380
Marty Melnychuk, San Antonio	15	4	3	7	57
Totals	55	5	3	8	437
Thomas Migdal, Border City	13	4	2	6	6
Thomas Migdal, Wichita	19	4	3	7	8
Thomas Migdal, Oklahoma City	14	3	3	6	4
Totals	46	11	8	19	18
Aigars Mironovics, Indianapolis	34	3	3	6	42
Aigars Mironovics, Macon	15	3	4	7	6
Totals	49	6	7	13	48
Mike Moran, San Antonio	43	4	6	10	86
Mike Moran, Fayetteville	5	0	0	0	41
Totals	48	4	6	10	127
Brad Mueller, Columbus	7	0	1	1	15
Brad Mueller, Border City	1	0	0	0	0
Brad Mueller, Memphis	53	20	15	35	47
Totals	61	20	16	36	62
Colin Muldoon, Fayetteville	44	0	7	7	38
Colin Muldoon, Macon	11	0	0	0	12
Totals	55	0	7	7	50
Erik Olsen, Huntsville	57	2	17	19	124
Erik Olsen, Fayetteville	13	0	2	2	32
Totals	70	2	19	21	156
Sebastian Pajerski, Indianapolis	18	3	4	7	7
Sebastian Pajerski, Macon	16	0	1	1	11
Totals	34	3	5	8	18
Jeff Parrott, Border City	31	1	12	13	13
Jeff Parrott, San Antonio	16	0	9	9	2
Totals	47	1	21	22	15
Corey Payment, Wichita	13	1	3	4	2
Corey Payment, Indianapolis	40	5	1	6	32
Totals	53	6	4	10	34
Jamie Pegg, Macon	36	6	13	19	58
Jamie Pegg, Memphis	35	1	14	15	24
Totals	71	7	27	34	82
Eric Pinoul, Border City	13	3	6	9	23
Eric Pinoul, Macon	4	0	1	1	0
Totals	17	3	7	10	23
Aaron Porter, Oklahoma City	3	0	2	2	2
Aaron Porter, Border City	29	3	10	13	13
Totals	32	3	12	15	15
Greg Quebec, Macon	31	10	2	12	6
Greg Quebec, Columbus	20	3	4	7	6
Totals	51	13	6	19	12
Ryan Reid, Tulsa	42	3	5	8	135
Ryan Reid, Indianapolis	10	1	1	2	49
Totals	52	4	6	10	184
Chris Richards, Indianapolis	56	14	44	58	24
Chris Richards, Macon	16	7	10	17	46
Totals	72	21	54	75	70
Chris Ross, Macon	3	1	1	2	2
Chris Ross, Border City	28	8	3	11	8
Totals	31	9	4	13	10
Jason Sangiuliano, Border City	33	11	14	25	18
Jason Sangiuliano, Huntsville	16	3	6	9	10
Totals	49	14	20	34	28
Don Sauter, Oklahoma City	26	6	6	12	18
Don Sauter, Border City	7	2	3	5	0
Don Sauter, Macon	16	1	3	4	14
Totals	49	9	12	21	32
Kris Schultz, Wichita	17	3	7	10	65
Kris Schultz, Columbus	49	10	15	25	163

	Games	G	A	Pts.	PIM
Totals	66	13	22	35	228
Mark Scott, Columbus	9	1	1	2	38
Mark Scott, Oklahoma City	20	3	3	6	49
Totals	29	4	4	8	87
Blake Sheane, Huntsville	43	16	18	34	121
Blake Sheane, Columbus	3	0	1	1	5
Blake Sheane, Topeka	11	3	4	7	8
Totals	57	19	23	42	134
Chris Smith, Tulsa	27	1	9	10	28
Chris Smith, San Antonio	31	10	7	17	37
Totals	58	11	16	27	65
Sheldon Szmata, Huntsville	21	3	4	7	8
Sheldon Szmata, Oklahoma City	45	12	17	29	39
Totals	66	15	21	36	47
Jason Tatarnic, Fayetteville	42	11	14	25	70
Jason Tatarnic, Macon	10	0	4	4	29
Totals	52	11	18	29	99
Oleg Tsirkounov, Oklahoma City	35	4	5	9	57
Oleg Tsirkounov, Macon	18	4	2	6	5
Totals	53	8	7	15	62
Aaron Vickar, Macon (goalie)	16	0	0	0	0
Aaron Vickar, Memphis (goalie)	18	0	2	2	0
Totals	34	0	2	2	0

	Games	G	A	Pts.	PIM
Curtis Voth, Tulsa	1	0	0	0	5
Curtis Voth, Huntsville	28	4	4	8	233
Curtis Voth, Memphis	15	1	3	4	160
Totals	44	5	7	12	398
Cam Werfelman, Wichita	11	1	1	2	35
Cam Werfelman, Border City	26	2	4	6	77
Totals	37	3	5	8	112

GOALTENDING

	Gms.	Min.	W	L	SOL	G	SO	Avg.
M. Brusseau, Mem.	4	195	1	3	0	13	0	4.01
M. Brusseau, Hun.	5	269	3	2	0	14	1	3.12
Totals	9	464	4	5	0	27	1	3.49
A. Hitchen, Mem.	2	50	1	0	0	4	0	4.83
A. Hitchen, B.C.	5	268	0	4	0	26	0	5.81
Totals	7	318	1	4	0	30	0	5.66
D. Masson, Wich.	13	614	3	6	2	37	0	3.61
D. Masson, S.A.	10	551	7	1	0	30	0	3.27
Totals	23	1165	10	7	2	67	0	3.45
A. Vickar, Macon	16	957	6	7	3	46	2	2.88
A. Vickar, Memphis	18	972	10	5	1	46	0	2.84
Totals	34	1929	16	12	4	92	2	2.86

2001 PLAYOFFS
RESULTS

CONFERENCE SEMIFINALS

	W	L	Pts.	GF	GA
Memphis	3	0	6	11	7
Indianapolis	0	3	0	7	11

(Memphis won series, 3-0)

	W	L	Pts.	GF	GA
Columbus	3	2	6	16	14
Fayetteville	2	3	4	14	16

(Columbus won series, 3-2)

	W	L	Pts.	GF	GA
Oklahoma City	3	0	6	11	6
Tulsa	0	3	0	6	11

(Oklahoma City won series, 3-0)

	W	L	Pts.	GF	GA
San Antonio	3	1	6	15	13
Topeka	1	3	2	13	15

(San Antonio won series, 3-1)

CONFERENCE FINALS

	W	L	Pts.	GF	GA
Columbus	3	1	6	10	7
Memphis	1	3	2	7	10

(Columbus won series, 3-1)

	W	L	Pts.	GF	GA
Oklahoma City	3	2	6	14	13
San Antonio	2	3	4	13	14

(Oklahoma City won series, 3-2)

FINALS

	W	L	Pts.	GF	GA
Oklahoma City	4	1	8	13	5
Columbus	1	4	2	5	13

(Oklahoma City won series, 4-1)

INDIVIDUAL LEADERS

Goals: Michael Martens, Columbus (8)
Assists: Guy Girouard, Oklahoma City (9)
Points: Marty Standish, Oklahoma City (13)
Penalty minutes: Jerome Bechard, Columbus (106)
Goaltending average: Aaron Vickar, Memphis (1.51)
Shutouts: Rod Branch, Oklahoma City (2)

TOP SCORERS

	Games	G	A	Pts.
Marty Standish, Oklahoma City	12	6	7	13
Michael Martens, Columbus	14	8	4	12
Don Parsons, Memphis	7	5	6	11
Joe Burton, Oklahoma City	13	5	6	11
Hardy Sauter, Oklahoma City	13	3	8	11
Ken Richardson, San Antonio	9	7	3	10
Jared Dumba, Oklahoma City	11	5	5	10
Jonathan DuBois, San Antonio	9	4	5	9
Daniel Payette, Columbus	14	3	6	9
Guy Girouard, Oklahoma City	13	0	9	9

INDIVIDUAL STATISTICS

COLUMBUS COTTONMOUTHS
(Lost finals to Oklahoma City, 4-1)

SCORING

	Games	G	A	Pts.	PIM
Michael Martens	14	8	4	12	6
Daniel Payette	14	3	6	9	35
Jeremy Stasiuk	13	5	3	8	20
Mick Kempffer	14	0	8	8	8
Martin Menard	13	3	4	7	36
Bobby Marshall	14	0	6	6	16
Kris Cantu	14	2	3	5	12
Craig Stahl	13	2	2	4	15
Jerome Bechard	14	2	2	4	106
Rob Schweyer	13	1	3	4	15

	Games	G	A	Pts.	PIM
Riley Nelson	14	1	3	4	4
Drew Schoneck	13	2	1	3	2
Ryan Brown	13	2	0	2	18
Kris Schultz	12	0	1	1	6
Jaroslav Kerestes	14	0	1	1	26
Blaine Russell (goalie)	3	0	0	0	0
Anthony DiPalma	8	0	0	0	12
Francis Ouellette (goalie)	13	0	0	0	0
Doug Mann	14	0	0	0	28

GOALTENDING

	Games	Min.	W	L	T	G	SO	Avg.
Blaine Russell	3	170	1	1	0	5	0	1.77
Francis Ouellette	13	742	6	4	2	27	1	2.18

FAYETTEVILLE FORCE
(Lost conference semifinals to Columbus, 3-2)

SCORING

	Games	G	A	Pts.	PIM
Darryl Noren	5	2	3	5	4
David Hoogsteen	5	2	2	4	2
Jamie Steer	5	2	2	4	0
Rob Concannon	5	0	4	4	12
Ales Dvorak	5	1	2	3	0
Brad Cruikshank	5	2	0	2	2
Jasen Rintala	5	2	0	2	17
Darren McLean	4	1	1	2	12
Mark Shalawylo	5	1	1	2	0
John Gibson	5	1	0	1	25
Eric Linkowski	5	0	1	1	2
Tyler McMillan	5	0	1	1	4
Ken Shepard (goalie)	5	0	1	1	0
Lenny Bonanno	5	0	0	0	8
Kris Currie	5	0	0	0	4
Mike Jaros	5	0	0	0	9
Erik Olsen	5	0	0	0	16

GOALTENDING

	Games	Min.	W	L	T	G	SO	Avg.
Ken Shepard	5	365	2	2	1	16	0	2.63

INDIANAPOLIS ICE
(Lost conference semifinals to Memphis, 3-0)

SCORING

	Games	G	A	Pts.	PIM
Chris MacKenzie	3	1	5	6	2
Jason Selleke	3	2	0	2	0
Yvan Corbin	2	1	1	2	0
Bernie John	3	1	1	2	2
Dan Passero	3	1	1	2	0
Casey Harris	2	1	0	1	6
Dan Cousineau	3	0	1	1	4
Peter Jas	3	0	1	1	0
Chad Spurr	3	0	1	1	2
Jamie Morris (goalie)	1	0	0	0	0
Ray Aho (goalie)	2	0	0	0	0
Ken Boone	3	0	0	0	35
Robert Davidson	3	0	0	0	0
Dave Jesiolowski	3	0	0	0	34
Duncan Paterson	3	0	0	0	2
Ryan Reid	3	0	0	0	8
Kevin Schmidt	3	0	0	0	4
Jarrett Thompson	3	0	0	0	0

GOALTENDING

	Games	Min.	W	L	T	G	SO	Avg.
Jamie Morris	1	59	1	0	3	0	3.06
Ray Aho	2	118	0	2	0	8	0	4.06

MEMPHIS RIVERKINGS
(Lost conference finals to Columbus, 3-1)

SCORING

	Games	G	A	Pts.	PIM
Don Parsons	7	5	6	11	6
Derek Landmesser	7	2	5	7	24

	Games	G	A	Pts.	PIM
Brian Tucker	7	3	3	6	16
Don Martin	7	0	6	6	22
Jason Simon	5	3	1	4	19
Greg Lakovic	6	1	1	2	28
Kevin Fricke	7	1	1	2	0
Matt Johnson	7	1	1	2	2
Curtis Voth	6	0	2	2	50
Kevin Ryan	7	0	2	2	8
A.J. Aitken	7	1	0	1	4
Travis Riggin	7	1	0	1	6
Mark Richards (goalie)	5	0	1	1	6
Brad Mueller	7	0	1	1	8
Aaron Vickar (goalie)	2	0	0	0	0
Matt Interbartolo	3	0	0	0	0
Jeremy Goetzinger	6	0	0	0	0
Kevin Holliday	7	0	0	0	0
Jamie Pegg	7	0	0	0	6

GOALTENDING

	Games	Min.	W	L	T	G	SO	Avg.
Aaron Vickar	2	119	1	1	0	3	0	1.51
Mark Richards	5	299	3	2	0	14	0	2.81

OKLAHOMA CITY BLAZERS
(Winner of 2001 playoffs)

SCORING

	Games	G	A	Pts.	PIM
Marty Standish	12	6	7	13	46
Joe Burton	13	5	6	11	0
Hardy Sauter	13	3	8	11	6
Jared Dumba	11	5	5	10	10
Guy Girouard	13	0	9	9	10
Peter Robertson	13	5	2	7	22
Dave Shields	13	5	2	7	48
Peter Arvanitis	13	3	3	6	4
Thomas Migdal	13	1	5	6	0
Garth Gartner	11	2	0	2	29
Marco Cefalo	13	1	1	2	8
Tyler Fleck	13	1	1	2	19
Sheldon Szmata	13	1	1	2	10
Chris Dashney	13	0	2	2	4
Mike Markell	1	0	0	0	0
Brant Nicklin (goalie)	1	0	0	0	0
Wade Brookbank	5	0	0	0	24
Jason Weitzel	5	0	0	0	18
Barkley Sauter	8	0	0	0	39
Rod Branch (goalie)	12	0	0	0	4
Paul Johnson	12	0	0	0	6

GOALTENDING

	Games	Min.	W	L	T	G	SO	Avg.
Rod Branch	12	740	10	2	0	20	2	1.62
Brant Nicklin	1	78	0	0	1	4	0	3.08

SAN ANTONIO IGUANAS
(Lost conference finals to Oklahoma City, 3-2)

SCORING

	Games	G	A	Pts.	PIM
Ken Richardson	9	7	3	10	16
Jonathan DuBois	9	4	5	9	41
Chris Smith	9	1	7	8	32
Scott Green	9	2	5	7	8
Andrei Lupandin	9	2	5	7	8
Johnny Brdarovic	9	4	2	6	6
Tyler Quiring	8	2	4	6	30
Greg Gatto	9	2	4	6	20
Henry Kuster	9	3	1	4	6
Jeff Parrott	9	0	3	3	18
Joe Gray	5	0	2	2	2
Marty Melnychuk	9	0	2	2	59
Jeff Trembecky	9	1	0	1	24
Paul Buczkowski	3	0	1	1	2
Darcy Dallas	9	0	1	1	34
Mike Marostega	9	0	1	1	4

	Games	G	A	Pts.	PIM
Dale Masson (goalie)	4	0	0	0	0
Nathan Grobins (goalie)	5	0	0	0	0
Garnet Jacobson	7	0	0	0	27

GOALTENDING

	Games	Min.	W	L	T	G	SO	Avg.
Nathan Grobins	5	318	2	2	1	14	0	2.64
Dale Masson	4	239	3	1	0	13	0	3.26

TOPEKA SCARECROWS
(Lost conference semifinals to San Antonio, 3-1)

SCORING

	Games	G	A	Pts.	PIM
Blair Manning	4	1	5	6	8
Pete Brearley	4	3	2	5	0
Jeff Goldie	4	3	2	5	0
Bob Berg	4	2	3	5	7
Ryan Hartung	4	1	2	3	4
John Vary	4	0	3	3	6
Shawn Gervais	4	2	0	2	6
Sergei Deshevyy	4	0	2	2	2
Lannie McCabe	4	0	2	2	5
John McCabe	4	1	0	1	5
Paul Strand	2	0	1	1	12
Luciano Caravaggio (goalie)	4	0	1	1	2
Mark Edmundson	4	0	1	1	2
Blake Sheane	4	0	1	1	4
Lannie McCabe	2	0	0	0	0
Chris Felix	4	0	0	0	12
Jay Hern	4	0	0	0	7
Anthony Zurfluh	4	0	0	0	12

GOALTENDING

	Games	Min.	W	L	T	G	SO	Avg.
Luciano Caravaggio	4	239	1	3	0	15	0	3.77

TULSA OILERS
(Lost conference semifinals to Oklahoma City, 3-0)

SCORING

	Games	G	A	Pts.	PIM
Brad Englehart	3	2	0	2	4
Jon Cameron	3	1	1	2	2
Peter Campbell	3	1	1	2	7
Mike Mohr	3	1	1	2	10
Jean-Francois Gregoire	3	0	2	2	2
Doug Lawrence	3	0	2	2	10
Tom Gomes	3	1	0	1	4
Craig Bilick	3	0	1	1	0
Craig Hamelin	3	0	1	1	2
David Rattray	3	0	1	1	14
Trevor Shoaf	3	0	1	1	0
Dallas Anderson	1	0	0	0	2
Dan Hopfner	2	0	0	0	0
Carlos Soke	2	0	0	0	0
Matt Barnes (goalie)	3	0	0	0	0
Aldo Iaquinta	3	0	0	0	12
Derek Stone	3	0	0	0	0
Jorin Welsh	3	0	0	0	6

GOALTENDING

	Games	Min.	W	L	T	G	SO	Avg.
Matt Barnes	3	185	0	2	1	11	0	3.56

2000-01 AWARD WINNERS

ALL-STAR TEAMS

The Central Hockey League did not name an
All-Star team for the 2000-01 season.

TROPHY WINNERS

Most Valuable Player: Joe Burton, Oklahoma City
Ken McKenzie Trophy: Yvan Corbin, Indianapolis
Goaltender of the Year: Brant Niklin, Oklahoma City
Defenseman of the Year: Derek Landmesser, Memphis
Rookie of the Year: Derek Reynolds, Huntsville
President's Trophy: Rod Branch, Oklahoma City
Commissioner's Trophy: Paul Kelly, Topeka

ALL-TIME AWARD WINNERS

MOST VALUABLE PLAYER

Season	Player, Team
1992-93	Sylvain Fleury, Oklahoma City
1993-94	Robert Desjardins, Wichita
1994-95	Paul Jackson, San Antonio
1995-96	Brian Shantz, San Antonio
1996-97	Trevor Jobe, Columbus-Wichita
1997-98	Joe Burton, Oklahoma City
1998-99	Derek Puppa, Huntsville
1999-00	Yvan Corbin, Indianapolis
	Chris MacKenzie, Indianapolis
2000-01	Joe Burton, Oklahoma City

KEN MCKENZIE TROPHY
(Leading Scorer)

Season	Player, Team
1992-93	Sylvain Fleury, Oklahoma City
1993-94	Paul Jackson, Wichita
1994-95	Brian Shantz, San Antonio
1995-96	Brian Shantz, San Antonio
1996-97	Trevor Jobe, Columbus-Wichita
1997-98	Luc Beausoleil, Tulsa
1998-99	Derek Grant, Memphis
1999-00	Yvan Corbin, Indianapolis
	Chris MacKenzie, Indianapolis
2000-01	Yvan Corbin, Indianapolis

GOALTENDER OF THE YEAR

Season	Player, Team
1992-93	Tony Martino, Tulsa
1993-94	Alan Perry, Oklahoma City
1994-95	Alan Perry, Oklahoma City
1995-96	Jean-Ian Filiatrault, Oklahoma City
1996-97	Jean-Ian Filiatrault, Oklahoma City
1997-98	Brian Elder, Oklahoma City
1998-99	Jean-Ian Filiatrault, Oklahoma City
1999-00	Frankie Ouellette, Columbus
2000-01	Brant Nicklin, Oklahoma City

DEFENSEMAN OF THE YEAR

Season	Player, Team
1992-93	Dave Doucette, Dallas
1993-94	Guy Girouard, Oklahoma City
1994-95	Eric Ricard, Fort Worth
1995-96	Dan Brown, Memphis
1996-97	Hardy Sauter, Oklahoma City
1997-98	Hardy Sauter, Oklahoma City
1998-99	Igor Bondarev, Huntsville
1999-00	Brett Colborne, Fayetteville
2000-01	Derek Landmesser, Memphis

ROOKIE OF THE YEAR

Season	Player, Team
1992-93	Robert Desjardins, Wichita
1993-94	Chad Seibel, Memphis
1994-95	Michel St. Jacques, Oklahoma City
1995-96	Derek Grant, Memphis
1996-97	Cory Dosdall, Wichita
1997-98	David Beauregard, Wichita
1998-99	Johnny Brdarovic, San Antonio
1999-00	James Patterson, Huntsville
2000-01	Derek Reynolds, Huntsville

PRESIDENT'S TROPHY
(Playoff MVP)

Season	Player, Team
1992-93	Tony Fiore, Tulsa
1993-94	Ron Handy, Wichita
1994-95	Ron Handy, Wichita
1995-96	Jean-Ian Filiatrault, Oklahoma City

Season	Player, Team
1996-97	Steve Plouffe, Fort Worth
1997-98	Mike Martens, Columbus
1998-99	Derek Puppa, Huntsville
1999-00	Jamie Morris, Indianapolis
2000-01	Rod Branch, Oklahoma City

COMMISSIONER'S TROPHY
(Coach of the year)

Season	Coach, Team
1992-93	Garry Unger, Tulsa
1993-94	Doug Shedden, Wichita
1994-95	John Torchetti, San Antonio
1995-96	Doug Sauter, Oklahoma City
1996-97	Bill McDonald, Fort Worth
1997-98	David Lohrei, Nashville
1998-99	Chris Stewart, Huntsville
1999-00	David Lohrie, Fayetteville
2000-01	Paul Kelly, Topeka

ALL-TIME LEAGUE CHAMPIONS

	REGULAR-SEASON CHAMPION		PLAYOFF CHAMPION	
Season	Team	Coach	Team	Coach
1992-93—	Oklahoma City Blazers	Michael McEwen	Tulsa Oilers	Garry Unger
1993-94—	Wichita Thunder	Doug Shedden	Wichita Thunder	Doug Shedden
1994-95—	Wichita Thunder	Doug Shedden	Wichita Thunder	Doug Shedden
1995-96—	Oklahoma City Blazers	Doug Sauter	Oklahoma City Blazers	Doug Sauter
1996-97—	Oklahoma City Blazers	Doug Sauter	Fort Worth Fire	Bill McDonald
1997-98—	Columbus Cottonmouths	Bruce Garber	Columbus Cottonmouths	Bruce Garber
1998-99—	Oklahoma City Blazers	Doug Sauter	Huntsville Channel Cats	Chris Stewart
1999-00—	Fayetteville Force	David Lohrie	Indianapolis Ice	Rod Davidson
2000-01—	Oklahoma City Blazers	Doug Sauter	Oklahoma City Blazers	Doug Sauter

The Central League regular season champion is awarded the Adams Cup. The playoff champion is awarded the Ray Miron Cup. Prior to the 1999-2000 season, the playoff champion was awarded the William "Bill" Levins Cup.

UNITED HOCKEY LEAGUE

(NOTE: The United Hockey League operated under the name Colonial Hockey League through the 1996-97 season.)

LEAGUE OFFICE

Commissioner/chief executive officer
Richard Brosal
Vice president of hockey operations
Mitch Lamoureux
Director of business operations
Ron Caron
Director of hockey administration
Lori Kessel

Director of media relations
Lisa Peppin
Supervisors of officials
Gary Como, Mike Hobert, Matt
Pavelich
Assistant to the president
Sharlynn Roberts

Address
1831 Lake St. Louis Blvd.
Lake St. Louis, MO 63367
Phone
636-625-6011
FAX
636-625-2009

TEAMS

ADIRONDACK ICEHAWKS
President
Art Shaver
Head coach
Gates Orlando
Home ice
Glens Falls Civic Center
Address
1 Civic Center Plaza
Glens Falls, NY 12801
Seating capacity
4,806
Phone
518-926-7825
FAX
518-761-9112

ASHEVILLE SMOKE
President
Dan Wilhelm
General manager/head coach
Pat Bingham
Home ice
Asheville Civic Center
Address
87 Haywood Street
Asheville, NC 28801
Seating capacity
5,522
Phone
828-252-7825
FAX
828-252-8756

B.C. ICEMEN
General manager
Patrick Snyder
Head coach
Brad Jones
Home ice
Broome County Veterans Mem. Arena
Address
One Stuart Street
Binghamton, NY 13901
Seating capacity
4,680
Phone
607-772-9300
FAX
607-772-0707

ELMIRA JACKALS
President
Tamer Afr
Head coach
Todd Brost
Home ice
Coach USA Center
Address
P.O. Box 669
Elmira, NY 14902
Seating capacity
4,700
Phone
607-734-7825
FAX
607-733-2237

FLINT GENERALS
General manager
Dan Heisserer
Head coach
Bill Thurlow
Home ice
IMA Sports Arena
Address
3501 Lapeer Road
Flint, MI 48503
Seating capacity
4,021
Phone
810-742-9422
FAX
810-742-5892

FORT WAYNE KOMETS
General manager
David Franke
Head coach
Greg Puhalski
Home ice
Allen County War Mem. Coliseum
Address
1010 Memorial Way, Suite 100
Fort Wayne, IN 46805
Seating capacity
8,003
Phone
219-483-0011
FAX
219-483-3899

KALAMAZOO WINGS
Vice president/general manager
Steve Doherty
Head coach
Dennis Desrosiers
Home ice
Wings Stadium
Address
3620 Van Rick Drive
Kalamazoo, MI 49001
Seating capacity
5,113
Phone
616-349-9772
FAX
616-345-6584

KNOXVILLE SPEED
President
Andrew Wilhelm
General manager/head coach
Terry Ruskowski
Home ice
Knoxville Civic Coliseum
Address
500 East Church Street
Knoxville, TN 37915
Seating capacity
4,900
Phone
865-521-9991
FAX
865-524-2639

MISSOURI RIVER OTTERS
General manager
Matt McSparin
Head coach
Mark Reeds
Home ice
Family Arena
Address
324 Main Street
St. Charles, MO 63301
Seating capacity
10,000
Phone
636-946-0003
FAX
636-946-3844

MUSKEGON FURY

General manager
Tony Lisman
Head coach
Rich Kromm
Home ice
L.C. Walker Arena
Address
470 West Western Avenue
Muskegon, MI 49440
Seating capacity
5,000
Phone
231-726-3879
FAX
231-728-0428

NEW HAVEN KNIGHTS

General manager
Angelo Mazzella
Head coach
Paul Gillis
Home ice
New Haven Veterans Mem. Coliseum
Address
275 South Orange St.
New Haven, CT 06510
Seating capacity
8,829

Phone
203-498-7825
FAX
203-503-6049

PORT HURON BORDER CATS

President
Tamer Afr
Head coach
Jean Laforest
Home ice
Kimball Entertainment and Sports
Center
Address
1661 Range Road, Ste. B-130
Kimball, MI 48074
Seating capacity
7,000
Phone
810-388-2287
FAX
810-388-4625

QUAD CITY MALLARDS

Vice President
Howard Cornfield
Head coach
Paul MacLean
Home ice
The MARK of the Quad Cities

Address
1509 Third Avenue A
Moline, IL 61265
Seating capacity
9,175
Phone
309-764-7825
FAX
309-764-7858

ROCKFORD ICEHOGS

General manager
Kevin Cummings
Head coach
Dale DeGray
Home ice
Rockford MetroCentre
Address
P.O. Box 5984
Rockford, IL 61125-0984
Seating capacity
7,000
Phone
815-986-6465
FAX
815-963-0974

2000-01 REGULAR SEASON
FINAL STANDINGS

EASTERN CONFERENCE

NORTHEAST DIVISION

Team	G	W	L	SOL	Pts.	GF	GA
Adirondack	74	40	28	6	86	259	235
Elmira	74	32	33	9	73	260	289
B.C. (Binghamtom)	74	31	34	9	71	263	290

SOUTHEAST DIVISION

Team	G	W	L	SOL	Pts.	GF	GA
Asheville	74	45	22	7	97	297	240
New Haven	74	41	26	7	89	268	217
Knoxville	74	39	31	4	82	238	233

WESTERN CONFERENCE

NORTHWEST DIVISION

Team	G	W	L	SOL	Pts.	GF	GA
Fort Wayne	74	42	26	6	90	261	253
Muskegon	74	37	28	9	83	242	240
Flint	74	30	34	10	70	253	303
Port Huron	74	30	34	10	70	234	260

SOUTHWEST DIVISION

Team	G	W	L	SOL	Pts.	GF	GA
Quad City	74	55	12	7	117	341	216
Missouri	74	41	24	9	91	268	259
Kalamazoo	74	37	31	6	80	220	220
Rockford	74	30	38	6	66	207	256

INDIVIDUAL LEADERS

Goals: Chris Grenville, B.C. (52)
Assists: Hugo Belanger, Adirondack (78)
Points: Hugo Belanger, Adirondack (125)
Penalty minutes: Shawn Legault, Elmira (413)
     Kerry Toporowski, Quincy (413)
Goaltending average: Brad Guzda, Knoxville (2.52)
Shutouts: Blair Allison, New Haven (3)
     Kevin St. Pierre, Port Huron (3)
     Bryan Schoen, B.C. (3)
     Sergei Zvyagin, Adirondack (3)

TOP SCORERS

	Games	G	A	Pts.
Hugo Belanger, Adirondack	73	47	78	125
Chris Grenville, B.C.	74	52	57	109
Kevin St. Jacques, Adirondack	70	30	76	106

	Games	G	A	Pts.
Eric Murano, Missouri	66	33	69	102
Dominic Maltais, Asheville	72	40	61	101
Todd Robinson, Muskegon	61	36	64	100
Jason Ulmer, Quad City	60	26	71	97
Steve Gibson, Quad City	71	37	55	92
Jeremy Rebek, Missouri	68	26	63	89
Derek Wood, B.C.	70	27	58	85
Robin Bouchard, Muskegon	73	44	40	84
Derek Crimin, Asheville	72	28	56	84
Jay Mazur, M.V.-N.H.	64	23	60	83
Brent Gretzky, P.H.-F.W.	70	16	66	82
Andrew Tortorella, Knoxville	71	29	51	80
Jim Brown, New Haven	70	35	44	79
Hugo Proulx, Quad City	69	26	53	79
Brett Colborne, Asheville	66	15	62	77
J.C. Ruid, Asheville	74	34	41	75
Andrew Luciuk, Muskegon	72	29	44	73

ADIRONDACK ICEHAWKS

SCORING

	Games	G	A	Pts.	PIM
Hugo Belanger	73	47	78	125	59
Kevin St. Jacques	70	30	76	106	130
Trent Schachle	71	17	38	55	84
John Batten	61	13	40	53	131
Frank Littlejohn	57	29	20	49	193
Eric Seidel	64	27	22	49	60
Rob Millar	68	18	25	43	8
Doug Stienstra	73	19	13	32	67
Bryan Duce	52	17	13	30	18
Brad Shaver	52	6	23	29	70
David Dartsch	55	4	9	13	204
David Insalaco	64	3	10	13	44
Trevor Senn	38	4	8	12	364
Marc Busenburg	64	2	10	12	36
James Duval	15	2	8	10	9
Alex Johnstone	72	2	8	10	240
Mike Varhaug	68	3	5	8	364
Eric Boyte	67	1	7	8	51
Lucas Nehrling	23	1	4	5	99
Darcy Anderson	12	2	2	4	12
Guillaume Rodrigue	7	1	1	2	4
Frank Esposito	2	0	2	2	7
Joe Bianchi	6	0	1	1	4
Derek Young	8	0	1	1	6
Sergei Zvyagin (goalie)	59	0	1	1	10
Niklas Henrikkson	1	0	0	0	0
Avi Karunakar (goalie)	1	0	0	0	0
Dan McGuire (goalie)	1	0	0	0	0
Steve Sangermano	1	0	0	0	4
Kroamann	1	0	0	0	0
Greg Heffernan	2	0	0	0	7
Chad Ford (goalie)	3	0	0	0	2
Peter DeSantis	6	0	0	0	2
Pascal Gasse (goalie)	14	0	0	0	4

GOALTENDING

	Gms.	Min.	W	L	SOL	G	SO	Avg.
Dan McGuire	1	59	0	1	0	2	0	2.05
Pascal Gasse	14	765	5	5	2	36	1	2.82
Sergei Zvyagin	59	3373	35	19	3	163	3	2.90
Chad Ford	3	172	0	2	1	13	0	4.55
Avi Karunakar	1	60	0	1	0	5	0	5.04

ASHEVILLE SMOKE

SCORING

	Games	G	A	Pts.	PIM
Dominic Maltais	72	40	61	101	111
Derek Crimin	72	28	56	84	43
Brett Colborne	66	15	62	77	143
J.C. Ruid	74	34	41	75	101
Shawn Ulrich	73	24	37	61	89
Olaf Kjenstad	50	23	34	57	115
Tyler Prosofsky	70	21	28	49	187
Bogdan Rudenko	43	28	18	46	122
Blue Bennefield	70	19	16	35	178
Alex Dumas	70	12	20	32	74
Bruce Watson	61	16	15	31	401
Ryan Aikia	74	2	27	29	161
Vitali Andreev	30	9	15	24	16
Rob Marshall	60	8	14	22	24
Bob Rapoza	74	6	11	17	48
Lee Svangstu	37	4	9	13	179
Tom Wilson	71	3	6	9	210
Rich Metro	22	1	7	8	23
John Hewitt	43	1	2	3	232
Colin Muldoon	9	0	3	3	13
Terence Craven (goalie)	1	0	0	0	0
Bogdan Rudenko	1	0	0	0	2

	Games	G	A	Pts.	PIM
Trevor Ross	2	0	0	0	0
Andreas Sjolund	2	0	0	0	0
Evan Lindsay (goalie)	5	0	0	0	0
Alex Fomitchev (goalie)	14	0	0	0	0
Brent Belecki (goalie)	56	0	0	0	5

GOALTENDING

	Gms.	Min.	W	L	SOL	G	SO	Avg.
Terence Craven	1	1	0	0	0	0	0	0.00
Alex Fomitchev	14	838	9	3	2	37	0	2.65
Brent Belecki	56	3308	34	17	4	168	1	3.05
Evan Lindsay	5	279	2	1	20	0	4.30

B.C. ICEMEN

SCORING

	Games	G	A	Pts.	PIM
Chris Grenville	74	52	57	109	81
Derek Wood	70	27	58	85	56
Rob Voltera	69	25	24	49	277
Mark Dutiaume	45	22	25	47	40
Justin Plamondon	74	12	33	45	52
James Desmarais	33	17	23	40	18
Derek Knorr	43	14	23	37	105
Matt Ruchty	68	15	20	35	322
Jeff Kozakowski	60	6	25	31	50
Glendon Cominetti	60	11	17	28	29
Jason Polera	29	14	9	23	37
Pat Stachniak	74	3	20	23	144
Chris Palmer	18	11	10	21	4
Tim Ferguson	24	4	12	16	10
Josh Boni	16	4	9	13	31
Martin Belanger	62	2	9	11	8
Alex Andreyev	66	0	9	9	146
Chris Torkoff	53	1	7	8	53
Ben Murray	64	4	3	7	12
Steve Moore	19	3	4	7	34
Eddie Kowalski	18	4	2	6	8
M. Torkoff	8	1	2	3	2
Jason MacIntyre	28	0	3	3	76
Kyle Adams	19	1	1	2	4
Vaclav Pazourek	29	1	1	2	46
Bryan Schoen (goalie)	57	0	2	2	8
Mark Kotary	2	1	0	1	0
Sean Honeysett	3	1	0	1	6
Brad Erbsland (goalie)	1	0	0	0	0
Greg Tsouklas	1	0	0	0	5
Pierre-Luc Therrien (goalie)	30	0	0	0	4

GOALTENDING

	Gms.	Min.	W	L	SOL	G	SO	Avg.
Bryan Schoen	57	3157	24	21	9	191	3	3.63
Pierre-Luc Thierrien	30	1262	7	13	0	78	2	3.71
Brad Erbsland	1	3	0	0	0	1	0	18.46

ELMIRA JACKALS

SCORING

	Games	G	A	Pts.	PIM
David Bernier	68	23	44	67	70
Jeff Antonovich	61	23	36	59	38
Ed Lowe	74	25	28	53	60
Greg Olsen	73	32	19	51	133
Jeremy Vanin	72	15	27	42	104
Mike Thompson	35	17	20	37	40
Kelly Hultgren	60	11	23	34	51
Carl Drakensjo	61	7	22	29	54
David Lessard	20	16	12	28	46
James Sheehan	73	6	20	26	107
Tim O'Connell	64	7	17	24	131
Valentin Oletskky	46	6	18	24	14
Bob Cunningham	22	13	10	23	2
Brad Domonsky	39	12	10	22	228

MINOR LEAGUES UHL

	Games	G	A	Pts.	PIM
Nic Bilotto	53	5	16	21	142
Rick Gorman	31	5	15	20	41
Michal Stastny	45	7	12	19	35
Trevor Jobe	15	6	8	14	10
Rob Guinn	37	4	10	14	38
Shawn Legault	65	2	11	13	413
Bryan Fogarty	18	1	8	9	16
Scott Chartier	11	3	4	7	26
John Murphy	15	2	2	4	64
Darren Wright	9	1	3	4	45
Eric Peterson	14	1	2	3	19
Peter MacKellar	9	2	0	2	2
Tom O'Grady	3	0	2	2	0
Matt Saper	17	0	2	2	29
Robert Ek	6	0	1	1	2
Danny Lavoie (goalie)	27	0	1	1	2
Mike Cirillo	1	0	0	0	4
Dan Watson	1	0	0	0	0
Troy Mann	3	0	0	0	0
Andy Stephenson	4	0	0	0	0
Ken Goetz	6	0	0	0	27
Jason Rose	7	0	0	0	4
Christian Soucy (goalie)	54	0	0	0	6

GOALTENDING

	Gms.	Min.	W	L	SOL	G	SO	Avg.
Christian Soucy	54	3030	27	19	6	186	1	3.68
Danny Lavoie	27	1397	5	14	3	87	1	3.74

FLINT GENERALS
SCORING

	Games	G	A	Pts.	PIM
Kahlil Thomas	72	23	49	72	52
Jim Duhart	58	32	34	66	132
Troy Mann	39	17	33	50	12
Mark Major	53	16	30	46	163
Lorne Knauft	57	14	32	46	155
Kevin Kerr	30	18	23	41	97
Gary Roach	46	7	28	35	23
Luch Nasato	62	13	20	33	304
Dale Greenwood	57	12	18	30	164
Slav Krzak	51	17	11	28	30
Chad Grills	55	8	19	27	211
Paul Lawson	72	12	14	26	138
Peter Cermak	32	13	12	25	23
John Maksymiu	62	9	11	20	28
Dariusz Zabawa	42	6	14	20	8
Ken Ruddick	37	8	11	19	49
Mike Maurice	23	6	13	19	8
Chris Libett	46	4	10	14	45
Darren Meek	65	3	11	14	54
Ross Wilson	17	7	6	13	12
Stephen Brochu	17	0	8	8	14
Jason Modopoulos	18	2	4	6	117
John Guirestante	24	1	4	5	60
Dean Roach	11	0	5	5	12
Stephane Dugal	27	1	3	4	26
Ryan Townsend	4	0	1	1	6
Francois Hardy	13	0	1	1	60
Steve Vezina (goalie)	21	0	1	1	2
Lou Mastromarino (goalie)	35	0	1	1	8
Nick Ross	1	0	0	0	0
Jason Rapcewicz	7	0	0	0	9
Bobby Dacosta (goalie)	8	0	0	0	0
Patrick Charbonneau (goalie)	23	0	0	0	12

GOALTENDING

	Gms.	Min.	W	L	SOL	G	SO	Avg.
P. Charbonneau	23	1207	8	9	3	72	1	3.58
Bobby Dacosta	8	414	2	4	2	25	0	3.62
Steve Vezina	21	1062	9	10	1	69	1	3.90
Lou Mastromarino	35	1738	11	11	4	124	0	4.28

FORT WAYNE KOMETS
SCORING

	Games	G	A	Pts.	PIM
Brent Gretzky	61	16	58	74	22
Mike McKay	70	38	25	63	50
Frederic Bouchard	56	26	33	59	88
Jim Logan	60	25	31	56	113
Keli Corpse	54	16	39	55	35
Kelly Hurd	56	23	29	52	57
Rick Judson	53	16	28	44	8
Brad Twordik	72	16	25	41	50
Dave Lemay	71	13	28	41	176
Derek Gauthier	57	14	25	39	161
Fred Slukynsky	59	9	19	28	69
Igor Malykhin	63	7	11	18	66
Sergei Radchenko	62	3	11	14	116
Darren Martens	43	7	6	13	6
Jason Goulet	13	7	5	12	12
Daniel Ronan	72	0	12	12	74
Gary Ricciardi	71	4	5	9	161
Jeff Loder	10	3	4	7	9
Greg Pajor	16	1	6	7	6
Christian Bragnalo	23	1	4	5	16
Krikor Arman	14	1	3	4	17
Geno Parrish	19	1	3	4	14
Dave Butler	27	0	3	3	8
Kevin Popp	12	2	0	2	47
Rhett Trombley	18	1	1	2	74
Steve Lowe	4	0	2	2	18
Joe Coombs	3	1	0	1	4
Joe Sewell	9	1	0	1	24
Nathan Grobins (goalie)	2	0	1	1	0
Ian Lampshire	7	0	1	1	0
Stephen Wagner (goalie)	8	0	1	1	0
Konstantin Simchuk (goalie)	26	0	1	1	0
Mike Correia (goalie)	1	0	0	0	0
Chris Dearden	4	0	0	0	2
Nick Jones	6	0	0	0	33
Doug Teskey (goalie)	47	0	0	0	8

GOALTENDING

	Gms.	Min.	W	L	SOL	G	SO	Avg.
K. Simchuk	26	1404	14	5	3	73	0	3.12
Mike Correia	1	19	0	1	0	1	0	3.16
Doug Teskey	47	2517	26	15	3	137	2	3.27
Steve Wagner	8	366	1	4	0	21	0	3.45
Nathan Grobins	2	120	1	1	0	12	0	6.00

KALAMAZOO WINGS
SCORING

	Games	G	A	Pts.	PIM
Randy Holmes	71	30	31	61	90
Jeff Scharf	74	22	37	59	59
Matt Loen	72	21	36	57	68
Richard Keyes	56	29	27	56	79
Mike Ford	71	23	17	40	60
Mike Maurice	33	14	19	33	18
Steve Moore	48	15	17	32	64
Jeff Winter	71	3	27	30	56
Aaron Plumb	62	4	17	21	146
Brian Wilson	70	4	15	19	16
Jason Hughes	74	6	11	17	119
Jeff Foster	47	3	14	17	32
Josh Boni	23	7	9	16	19
Erich Dumpis	51	4	11	15	32
Andrew Huggett	72	3	11	14	29
Craig Paterson	74	2	10	12	103
Jeff Lukasak	59	3	7	10	86
Derek Toninato	26	1	7	8	9
Jeff Turner	11	2	5	7	15
Alain O'Driscoll	29	4	2	6	22
Janis Tomans	9	2	4	6	19
Benoit Beausoleil	36	3	1	4	105
Kory Cooper (goalie)	54	0	4	4	2

	Games	G	A	Pts.	PIM
Vitali Andreev	13	2	1	3	6
Chad Ford (goalie)	3	0	0	0	2
Tyler Palmer	17	0	0	0	11
Tim Knudsen (goalie)	22	0	0	0	18

GOALTENDING

	Gms.	Min.	W	L	SOL	G	SO	Avg.
Kory Cooper	54	3108	25	24	3	146	2	2.82
Chad Ford	3	145	2	1	0	7	0	2.89
Tim Knudsen	22	1174	10	6	3	59	0	3.02

KNOXVILLE SPEED

SCORING

	Games	G	A	Pts.	PIM
Andrew Tortorella	71	29	51	80	125
Dan Myre	61	26	29	55	30
Sergei Petrov	54	25	28	53	161
Alain Savage	43	20	31	51	95
Mike Green	48	18	24	42	35
Dmitry Ustyuzhanin	74	9	33	42	61
Mikko Sivonen	73	25	16	41	16
Mike Schultz	72	12	18	30	40
Alexandre Alepin	68	8	15	23	283
David Lessard	25	11	10	21	57
Mike Vandenberghe	74	4	17	21	91
Michael Henderson	28	9	11	20	195
Brad Domonsky	28	6	11	17	183
Yannick Latour	59	6	11	17	55
Francis Boulay	23	4	9	13	4
Geno Parrish	19	1	12	13	22
Darren Banks	20	4	7	11	50
Bradley Denis	63	0	10	10	114
David Mayes	21	2	7	9	26
John Kachur	7	4	4	8	4
Craig Desjarlais	35	2	6	8	23
Travis Brigley	4	2	4	6	4
Oleg Kouzmin	20	1	4	5	14
Michael Murray	18	1	3	4	4
Wade Simpson	18	0	3	3	22
Ianniuc Renaud	27	1	1	2	224
Robert Fail	14	0	2	2	14
Mike Gamble	3	1	0	1	0
Pat Noiseulx	3	1	0	1	2
Todd Steinmetz	12	0	1	1	15
Mark Karpen	20	0	1	1	0
Trevor Ross	1	0	0	0	0
Adam Weber	1	0	0	0	2
Anatchy Buliga	2	0	0	0	2
Jon Gaskins	2	0	0	0	2
Jeff Lindsay	2	0	0	0	6
Cam Werfelman	2	0	0	0	2
Chad Thompson	3	0	0	0	4
Ernie Thorp	7	0	0	0	66
Dean Shmyr	21	0	0	0	148
Tom Lawson (goalie)	35	0	0	0	21
Brad Guzda (goalie)	45	0	0	0	15

GOALTENDING

	Gms.	Min.	W	L	SOL	G	SO	Avg.
Brad Guzda	45	2424	23	15	2	102	1	2.52
Tom Lawson	35	2002	16	16	2	116	0	3.48

MISSOURI RIVER OTTERS

SCORING

	Games	G	A	Pts.	PIM
Eric Murano	66	33	69	102	73
Jeremy Rebek	68	26	63	89	115
Lonnie Loach	56	27	37	64	29
Colin Chaulk	39	14	39	53	144
Darin Kimble	62	29	22	51	114
Kiley Hill	58	30	19	49	108
Jay Hebert	56	15	28	43	66
Kevin Plager	52	10	25	35	69
Trevor Sherban	50	6	26	32	73
Glenn Crawford	20	10	19	29	26

	Games	G	A	Pts.	PIM
Mike Bayrack	43	10	15	25	16
Jay Woodcroft	56	7	12	19	64
Randy Gallatin	74	9	9	18	51
Lee Cole	71	3	14	17	232
Anthony Cappelletti	65	1	16	17	93
Ryan Johnston	42	8	7	15	80
Troy Michalski	66	2	12	14	98
Chris Tok	38	1	13	14	50
Jared Reigstad	46	3	10	13	41
Robert Starke	52	7	5	12	122
Per Fernhall	24	4	5	9	12
Andrew Merrick	20	1	4	5	33
George Cantrall	23	2	2	4	56
Nick Lamia	3	1	0	1	2
John Glavota	3	0	1	1	6
Krikor Arman	5	0	1	1	6
Mike Correia (goalie)	2	0	0	0	0
Richard Spence	6	0	0	0	6
Vaclav Pazourek	9	0	0	0	4
Dave Arsenault (goalie)	12	0	0	0	2
Doug Bonner (goalie)	18	0	0	0	2
Benoit Thibert (goalie)	46	0	0	0	16

GOALTENDING

	Gms.	Min.	W	L	SOL	G	SO	Avg.
Benoit Thibert	46	2662	24	13	6	139	1	3.13
Doug Bonner	18	991	8	7	2	54	0	3.27
Dave Arsenault	12	699	8	3	1	46	0	3.95
Mike Correia	2	80	1	1	0	7	0	5.25

MOHAWK VALLEY PROWLERS

SCORING

	Games	G	A	Pts.	PIM
Jay Mazur	43	15	45	60	12
Nic Beaudoin	46	16	24	40	24
Harold Hersh	28	12	23	35	66
Steven Low	47	9	22	31	81
Andre Payette	45	9	18	27	244
James Duval	48	9	18	27	18
Bob Cunningham	18	12	11	23	4
J.J Wrobel	48	12	11	23	17
Justin Martin	25	7	10	17	64
Jeremy Vokes	23	8	8	16	6
Mark Kotary	24	5	8	13	24
Tim Harris	26	5	4	9	73
Don Martin	20	2	7	9	47
Bob Ferraris	25	0	9	9	31
Kevin Tucker	48	1	6	7	72
Tim Ferguson	12	4	2	6	6
Adam Lewis	14	2	4	6	9
Mike Marostega	42	1	5	6	51
Kirk LLano	28	1	4	5	51
B.J. Stephens	10	3	1	4	4
Trevor Jobe	2	2	1	3	2
Chris Palmer	4	1	2	3	0
Dana Guilbert	5	1	2	3	0
Marc Lauzon	5	1	2	3	2
Doug Altschul	4	2	0	2	2
Serge Roberge	26	2	0	2	124
Greg Wilkinson	14	1	1	2	4
Andy Stephenson	24	1	1	2	33
Greg Murray	4	0	2	2	2
Koona Briggs	5	1	0	1	8
Andrew Plumb	5	1	0	1	2
Jake Ream	9	1	0	1	6
Christian Bragnalo	10	1	0	1	4
Francois Hardy	15	1	0	1	11
John Dowd	3	0	1	1	0
Ryan Simpson	3	0	1	1	2
Rocky Florio	4	0	1	1	12
Jason Rapcewicz	5	0	1	1	21
Arpad Mihaly	7	0	1	1	0
Vaclav Pazourek	13	0	1	1	17

	Games	G	A	Pts.	PIM
Marc Champagne (goalie)	1	0	0	0	0
Terence Craven (goalie)	1	0	0	0	0
Jake Harney	1	0	0	0	0
Sean Kelly	1	0	0	0	0
Francois Landreville	1	0	0	0	0
John Turner (goalie)	1	0	0	0	0
Sean Honeysett	2	0	0	0	0
Alexander Vasko	2	0	0	0	0
Burke	2	0	0	0	2
Al Rooney (goalie)	4	0	0	0	0
Peter Ward	4	0	0	0	2
Pat Leahy	5	0	0	0	2
David Desrosiers	6	0	0	0	6
Olie Sundstrom (goalie)	16	0	0	0	26
Patrick Charbonneau (goalie)	18	0	0	0	6
Mike Brusseau (goalie)	21	0	0	0	6

GOALTENDING

	Gms.	Min.	W	L	SOL	G	SO	Avg.
Mike Brusseau	21	1045	5	10	1	69	0	3.96
P. Charbonneau	18	901	4	8	4	61	0	4.06
Olie Sundstrom	16	924	6	9	1	63	1	4.09
Al Rooney	4	220	0	3	0	26	0	7.09
Marc Champagne	1	54	0	0	0	13	0	14.56
John Turner	1	20	0	1	0	6	0	18.00
Terence Craven	1	6	0	1	0	5	0	46.75

MUSKEGON FURY
SCORING

	Games	G	A	Pts.	PIM
Todd Robinson	61	36	64	100	82
Robin Bouchard	73	44	40	84	179
Andrew Luciuk	72	29	44	73	96
Philippe Roy	73	14	31	45	72
Glenn Crawford	46	10	33	43	86
Scott Feasby	72	10	28	38	138
Sergei Kharin	66	8	30	38	46
Frankie Nault	74	10	14	24	38
Alexei Krovopuskov	38	7	13	20	44
Bob Cunningham	20	9	8	17	13
Quinn Hancock	13	7	10	17	2
Mike Bayrack	19	7	10	17	34
Eddie Kowalski	34	7	8	15	28
Andrew Merrick	49	7	7	14	69
Mark Vilneff	69	5	9	14	62
Rob Melanson	73	1	11	12	164
Justin Martin	39	2	7	9	63
Rick Emmett	19	1	7	8	20
Krikor Arman	43	5	2	7	66
J.F Tremblay	39	4	3	7	54
Maxim Linnik	41	3	4	7	43
Scott Hlady	19	1	5	6	4
Rob Hutson	12	4	1	5	29
Jared Reigstad	16	3	1	4	18
Alain O'Driscoll	20	1	3	4	10
Dean Mayrand	42	2	1	3	190
Scott Myers (goalie)	7	0	1	1	2
James Duval	11	0	1	1	2
Sylvain Daigle (goalie)	48	0	1	1	28
Jason Rapcewicz	2	0	0	0	0
Kiril Ladygin	7	0	0	0	0
Joe Dimaline (goalie)	24	0	0	0	6

GOALTENDING

	Gms.	Min.	W	L	SOL	G	SO	Avg.
Sylvain Daigle	48	2742	23	20	5	135	2	2.95
Joe Dimaline	24	1330	10	7	4	67	0	3.02
Scott Myers	7	354	4	1	0	23	0	3.90

NEW HAVEN KNIGHTS
SCORING

	Games	G	A	Pts.	PIM
Jim Brown	70	35	44	79	90
Brian Bolf	72	23	39	62	32
Mike Pomichter........................	71	31	25	56	47
Glenn Stewart	37	21	35	56	16
John Vecchiarelli......................	45	18	36	54	69
Simon Olivier	59	19	33	52	163
Jason Stewart..........................	59	25	21	46	68
Mike Melas..............................	43	18	24	42	81
Greg Pajor..............................	49	6	24	30	24
Keith Dupee	41	8	19	27	32
Jay Mazur	21	8	15	23	10
Jeff Brown	67	7	16	23	116
Daniel Lyons	48	9	11	20	19
Chad Cabana	51	9	11	20	207
Kenzie Homer	69	4	13	17	161
Raitis Ivanans	66	4	10	14	270
Keith Fitzpatrick	57	1	12	13	43
Tomas Baluch	17	5	5	10	6
Nick Lent................................	26	3	5	8	48
Chris Winnes	6	2	6	8	4
John Poapst..............................	14	1	6	7	8
Bob Ferraris	31	0	5	5	41
Christian Bragnalo	38	0	5	5	33
Arpad Mihaly	20	2	1	3	10
Kevin Popp..............................	16	0	3	3	58
Robert Curtis	6	2	0	2	10
Jussi Eloranta	3	1	1	2	0
Steve Lowe	7	0	2	2	10
Andy Disch..............................	13	0	2	2	20
Clint Cabana............................	15	0	2	2	49
Blair Allison (goalie)	50	0	2	2	21
Eric Germain	7	0	1	1	23
Bryce Wandler (goalie)	26	0	1	1	0
Jeff Brow	2	0	0	0	0
David Desrosiers......................	2	0	0	0	0
John Dowd	2	0	0	0	0
Brent Ozarowski	2	0	0	0	0
Eric Carmody (goalie)	3	0	0	0	0
Phil Esposito	5	0	0	0	56
Ales Dvorak............................	7	0	0	0	4

GOALTENDING

	Gms.	Min.	W	L	SOL	G	SO	Avg.
Blair Allison............	50	2831	29	13	6	124	3	2.63
Bryce Wandler	26	1429	10	13	1	71	0	2.98
Eric Carmody	3	95	1	0	0	7	0	4.41

PORT HURON BORDER CATS
SCORING

	Games	G	A	Pts.	PIM
David-Al Beauregard..................	56	33	30	63	31
Ryan Pawluk............................	64	21	39	60	61
Jason Glover............................	56	21	25	46	102
Yannick Carpentier....................	71	14	24	38	41
Mike Bondy..............................	63	13	25	38	80
Jeff Loder..............................	40	19	18	37	34
Bob McKillop	64	13	24	37	38
Tim Findlay	36	19	13	32	24
Stephane Madore	57	4	25	29	167
Ian Jacobs..............................	68	9	18	27	34
Michel Massie..........................	42	8	12	20	98
Kraig Nienhuis	16	9	10	19	28
Curtis Sayler	62	7	10	17	276
Kevin Bertram	65	7	8	15	173
Shayne Tomlinson	70	2	12	14	100
Paul Harvey............................	11	9	3	12	2
David Mayes............................	23	2	8	10	38
Michel Periard..........................	23	1	8	9	30
Brent Gretzky	9	0	8	8	18
Mike Cirillo............................	5	2	5	7	22
Mike Green..............................	11	1	5	6	6
Mikhail Nemirovsky	10	2	3	5	12
Adam Lewis	17	1	4	5	6
Wade Simpson	42	2	2	4	54
John Glavota............................	17	1	3	4	38
John Varga..............................	7	0	4	4	0

	Games	G	A	Pts.	PIM
Samuel Paquet	10	3	0	3	10
Peter Campbell	12	2	1	3	2
David Dartsch	14	1	2	3	44
Jason Tartarnic	15	0	3	3	7
Paul Polillo	2	0	2	2	0
Chris Allen	4	0	1	1	4
Darryl Campbell	7	0	1	1	4
Hugo Hamelin (goalie)	42	0	1	1	6
Darren Banks	4	0	0	0	4
David Desrosiers	5	0	0	0	4
Jeremy Cornish	13	0	0	0	69
Kevin St. Pierre (goalie)	39	0	0	0	23

GOALTENDING

	Gms.	Min.	W	L	SOL	G	SO	Avg.
Kevin St. Pierre	39	2107	16	13	5	106	3	3.02
Hugo Hamelin	42	2323	14	21	5	139	1	3.59

QUAD CITY MALLARDS

SCORING

	Games	G	A	Pts.	PIM
Jason Ulmer	60	26	71	97	40
Steve Gibson	71	37	55	92	91
Hugo Proulx	69	26	53	79	107
Chad Power	67	34	31	65	38
Kelly Perrault	61	14	46	60	106
Ryan Lindsay	61	20	35	55	107
Garry Gulash	61	14	38	52	311
Cam Severson	46	22	26	48	129
Vlad Serov	29	33	13	46	26
Patrick Nadeau	53	19	24	43	22
Mark McFarlane	73	11	24	35	249
Peter Armbrust	53	14	15	29	12
Frederick Jobin	67	13	16	29	197
Rick Emmett	44	7	22	29	20
Etienne Drapeau	61	13	13	26	205
Dan Bjornlie	38	6	14	20	27
Paul Johnson	63	4	16	20	79
Andy Fermoyle	55	3	15	18	60
Kerry Toporowski	63	2	15	17	413
Harold Hersh	19	6	10	16	32
Martin Hlinka	11	4	10	14	0
Mike Sim	28	3	5	8	22
Joe Dimaline (goalie)	17	0	3	3	0
Martin Villeneuve (goalie)	40	0	3	3	19
Sanny Lindstrom	5	1	1	2	10
Andy Disch	10	1	1	2	21
Yan Turgeon	4	1	0	1	2
Matt Eldred	3	0	1	1	8
Andy Faulkner	1	0	0	0	0
Ryan McIntosh (goalie)	2	0	0	0	0
Mike Coveny	5	0	0	0	2
Scott Myers (goalie)	22	0	0	0	2

GOALTENDING

	Gms.	Min.	W	L	SOL	G	SO	Avg.
Ryan McIntosh	2	120	2	0	0	2	1	1.00
Joe Dimaline	17	929	13	0	2	35	1	2.26
Martin Villeneuve	40	2198	28	6	4	98	2	2.68
Scott Myers	22	1191	12	6	1	67	1	3.38

ROCKFORD ICEHOGS

SCORING

	Games	G	A	Pts.	PIM
Mike Figliomeni	72	23	39	62	97
Nick Checco	63	23	36	59	33
Justin Kearns	66	27	20	47	85
Jocelyn Langlois	66	16	30	46	44
Steve Dumonski	69	23	20	43	215
Jeff DaCosta	59	6	30	36	62
Evgeny Krivomaz	71	11	23	34	76
Francois Sasseville	63	17	14	31	70
Dan Davies	69	13	10	23	138
Curtis Bois	68	9	13	22	112

	Games	G	A	Pts.	PIM
Mike Tobin	58	4	16	20	125
Chris Fattey	69	5	14	19	52
Yan Turgeon	25	5	13	18	18
Michel Periard	31	3	14	17	20
Eduard Zankovets	27	7	5	12	4
Patrice Charbonneau	70	0	10	10	74
Jeremy Vokes	10	2	6	8	4
Shawn Smith	67	0	5	5	73
Randy Hankinson	9	0	2	2	8
Matt Miller	18	0	2	2	9
J.F. Rivard (goalie)	60	0	2	2	12
David Runge	65	0	2	2	185
Sean Flynn	3	1	0	1	0
Andy Faulkner	9	1	0	1	6
Dave Butler	4	0	1	1	2
Vitali Kozel	6	0	1	1	8
Shane Fukushima	1	0	0	0	0
Tomasz Rysz	1	0	0	0	0
Patrick Brownlee	2	0	0	0	0
Mike Correia (goalie)	3	0	0	0	0
Mike Coveny	3	0	0	0	6
Kelly Von Hiltgen	3	0	0	0	16
Zoran Bennbicak	4	0	0	0	2
Maxim Linnik	5	0	0	0	10
Chad Ford (goalie)	6	0	0	0	0
B.J. Stephens	6	0	0	0	8
John Varga	8	0	0	0	2
Curtis Cruickshank (goalie)	9	0	0	0	0

GOALTENDING

	Gms.	Min.	W	L	SOL	G	SO	Avg.
J.F. Rivard	60	3466	26	27	4	180	1	3.12
Curtis Cruickshank	9	489	3	5	1	29	0	3.56
Chad Ford	6	310	1	3	1	22	0	4.26
Mike Correia	3	159	0	3	0	13	0	4.91

PLAYERS WITH TWO OR MORE TEAMS

SCORING

	Games	G	A	Pts.	PIM
Vitali Andreev, Kalamazoo	13	2	1	3	6
Vitali Andreev, Asheville	30	9	15	24	16
Totals	43	11	16	27	22
Krikor Arman, Fort Wayne	14	1	3	4	17
Krikor Arman, Muskegon	43	5	2	7	66
Krikor Arman, Missouri	5	0	1	1	6
Totals	62	6	6	12	89
Darren Banks, Knoxville	20	4	7	11	50
Darren Banks, Port Huron	4	0	0	0	4
Totals	24	4	7	11	54
John Batten, Adirondack	61	13	40	53	131
Mike Bayrack, Missouri	43	10	15	25	16
Mike Bayrack, Muskegon	19	7	10	17	34
Totals	62	17	25	42	50
Josh Boni, Kalamazoo	23	7	9	16	19
Josh Boni, B.C.	16	4	9	13	31
Totals	39	11	18	29	50
Christian Bragnalo, New Haven	38	0	5	5	33
Christian Bragnalo, M.V.	10	1	0	1	4
Christian Bragnalo, Fort Wayne	23	1	4	5	16
Totals	71	2	9	11	53
Dave Butler, Fort Wayne	27	0	3	3	8
Dave Butler, Rockford	4	0	1	1	2
Totals	31	0	4	4	10
Patrick Charbonneau, M.V. (g	18	0	0	0	6
Patrick Charbonneau, Flint (g)	23	0	0	0	12
Totals	41	0	0	0	18
Mike Cirillo, Elmira	1	0	0	0	4
Mike Cirillo, Port Huron	5	2	5	7	22
Totals	6	2	5	7	26
Mike Correia, Rockford (g)	3	0	0	0	0
Mike Correia, Missouri (g)	2	0	0	0	0
Mike Correia, Fort Wayne (g)	1	0	0	0	0
Totals	6	0	0	0	0

	Games	G	A	Pts.	PIM
Mike Coveny, Rockford	3	0	0	0	6
Mike Coveny, Quad City	5	0	0	0	2
Totals	8	0	0	0	8
Terence Craven, Asheville (g)	1	0	0	0	0
Terence Craven, M.V. (goalie)	1	0	0	0	0
Totals	2	0	0	0	0
Glenn Crawford, Muskegon	46	10	33	43	86
Glenn Crawford, Missouri	20	10	19	29	26
Totals	66	20	52	72	112
Bob Cunningham, Muskegon	20	9	8	17	13
Bob Cunningham, M.V.	18	12	11	23	4
Bob Cunningham, Elmira	22	13	10	23	2
Totals	60	34	29	63	19
David Dartsch, Adirondack	55	4	9	13	204
David Dartsch, Port Huron	14	1	2	3	44
Totals	69	5	11	16	248
David Desrosiers, Port Huron	5	0	0	0	4
David Desrosiers, New Haven	2	0	0	0	0
David Desrosiers, M.V.	6	0	0	0	6
Totals	13	0	0	0	10
Joe Dimaline, Muskegon (g)	24	0	0	0	6
Joe Dimaline, Quad City (g)	17	0	3	3	0
Totals	41	0	3	3	6
Andy Disch, New Haven	13	0	2	2	20
Andy Disch, Quad City	10	1	1	2	21
Totals	23	1	3	4	41
Brad Domonsky, Elmira	39	12	10	22	228
Brad Domonsky, Knoxville	28	6	11	17	183
Totals	67	18	21	39	411
John Dowd, New Haven	2	0	0	0	0
John Dowd, Mohawk Valley	3	0	1	1	0
Totals	5	0	1	1	0
James Duval, Mohawk Valley	48	9	18	27	18
James Duval, Adirondack	15	2	8	10	9
James Duval, Muskegon	11	0	1	1	2
Totals	74	11	27	38	29
Rick Emmett, Quad City	44	7	22	29	20
Rick Emmett, Muskegon	19	1	7	8	20
Totals	63	8	29	37	40
Andy Faulkner, Rockford	9	1	0	1	6
Andy Faulkner, Quad City	1	0	0	0	0
Totals	10	1	0	1	6
Tim Ferguson, Mohawk Valley	12	4	2	6	6
Tim Ferguson, B.C.	24	4	12	16	10
Totals	36	8	14	22	16
Bob Ferraris, Mohawk Valley	25	0	9	9	31
Bob Ferraris, New Haven	31	0	5	5	41
Totals	56	0	14	14	72
Chad Ford, Adirondack (goalie)	3	0	0	0	2
Chad Ford, Rockford (goalie)	6	0	0	0	0
Chad Ford, Kalamazoo (goalie)	3	0	0	0	2
Totals	12	0	0	0	4
John Glavota, Missouri	3	0	1	1	6
John Glavota, Port Huron	17	1	3	4	38
Totals	20	1	4	5	44
Mike Green, Port Huron	11	1	5	6	6
Mike Green, Knoxville	48	18	24	42	35
Totals	59	19	29	48	41
Brent Gretzky, Port Huron	9	0	8	8	18
Brent Gretzky, Fort Wayne	61	16	58	74	22
Totals	70	16	66	82	40
Francois Hardy, Mohawk Valley	15	1	0	1	11
Francois Hardy, Flint	13	0	1	1	60
Totals	28	1	1	2	71
Harold Hersh, Mohawk Valley	28	12	23	35	66
Harold Hersh, Quad City	19	6	10	16	32
Totals	47	18	33	51	98
Sean Honeysett, B.C.	3	1	0	1	6
Sean Honeysett, M.V.	2	0	0	0	0
Totals	5	1	0	1	6
Trevor Jobe, Elmira	15	6	8	14	10
Trevor Jobe, Mohawk Valley	2	2	1	3	2
Totals	17	8	9	17	12

	Games	G	A	Pts.	PIM
Mark Kotary, Mohawk Valley	24	5	8	13	24
Mark Kotary, B.C.	2	1	0	1	0
Totals	26	6	8	14	24
Eddie Kowalski, Muskegon	34	7	8	15	28
Eddie Kowalski, B.C.	18	4	2	6	8
Totals	52	11	10	21	36
David Lessard, Knoxville	25	11	10	21	57
David Lessard, Elmira	20	16	12	28	46
Totals	45	27	22	49	103
Adam Lewis, Mohawk Valley	14	2	4	6	9
Adam Lewis, Port Huron	17	1	4	5	6
Totals	31	3	8	11	15
Maxim Linnik, Rockford	5	0	0	0	10
Maxim Linnik, Muskegon	41	3	4	7	43
Totals	46	3	4	7	53
Jeff Loder, Fort Wayne	10	3	4	7	9
Jeff Loder, Port Huron	40	19	18	37	34
Totals	50	22	22	44	43
Steve Lowe, Fort Wayne	4	0	2	2	18
Steve Lowe, New Haven	7	0	2	2	10
Totals	11	0	4	4	28
Troy Mann, Elmira	3	0	0	0	0
Troy Mann, Flint	39	17	33	50	12
Totals	42	17	33	50	12
Justin Martin, Mohawk Valley	25	7	10	17	64
Justin Martin, Muskegon	39	2	7	9	63
Totals	64	9	17	26	127
Mike Maurice, Flint	23	6	13	19	8
Mike Maurice, Kalamazoo	33	14	19	33	18
Totals	56	20	32	52	26
David Mayes, Port Huron	23	2	8	10	38
David Mayes, Knoxville	21	2	7	9	26
Totals	44	4	15	19	64
Jay Mazur, Mohawk Valley	43	15	45	60	12
Jay Mazur, New Haven	21	8	15	23	10
Totals	64	23	60	83	22
Andrew Merrick, Muskegon	49	7	7	14	69
Andrew Merrick, Missouri	20	1	4	5	33
Totals	69	8	11	19	102
Arpad Mihaly, New Haven	20	2	1	3	10
Arpad Mihaly, Mohawk Valley	7	0	1	1	0
Totals	27	2	2	4	10
Steve Moore, B.C.	19	3	4	7	34
Steve Moore, Kalamazoo	48	15	17	32	68
Totals	67	18	21	39	102
Scott Myers, Quad City (g)	22	0	0	0	2
Scott Myers, Muskegon (g)	7	0	1	1	2
Totals	29	0	1	1	4
Alain O'Driscoll, Muskegon	20	1	3	4	10
Alain O'Driscoll, Kalamazoo	29	4	2	6	22
Totals	49	5	5	10	32
Greg Pajor, Fort Wayne	16	1	6	7	6
Greg Pajor, New Haven	49	6	24	30	24
Totals	65	7	30	37	30
Chris Palmer, Mohawk Valley	4	1	2	3	0
Chris Palmer, B.C.	18	11	10	21	4
Totals	22	12	12	24	4
Geno Parrish, Fort Wayne	19	1	3	4	14
Geno Parrish, Knoxville	19	1	12	13	22
Totals	38	2	15	17	36
Vaclav Pazourek, M.V.	13	0	1	1	17
Vaclav Pazourek, B.C.	29	1	1	2	46
Vaclav Pazourek, Missouri	9	0	0	0	4
Totals	51	1	2	3	67
Michel Periard, Port Huron	23	1	8	9	30
Michel Periard, Rockford	31	3	14	17	20
Totals	54	4	22	26	50
Kevin Popp, New Haven	16	0	3	3	58
Kevin Popp, Fort Wayne	12	2	0	2	47
Totals	28	2	3	5	105
Jason Rapcewicz, Muskegon	2	0	0	0	0
Jason Rapcewicz, Flint	7	0	0	0	9
Jason Rapcewicz, M.V.	5	0	1	1	21
Totals	14	0	1	1	30

	Games	G	A	Pts.	PIM
Jared Reigstad, Missouri..........	46	3	10	13	41
Jared Reigstad, Muskegon........	16	3	1	4	18
Totals	62	6	11	17	59
Wade Simpson, Knoxville.........	18	0	3	3	22
Wade Simpson, Port Huron	42	2	2	4	54
Totals	60	2	5	7	76
Andy Stephenson, Elmira	4	0	0	0	0
Andy Stephenson, M.V.	24	1	1	2	33
Totals	28	1	1	2	33
Yan Turgeon, Quad City	4	1	0	1	2
Yan Turgeon, Rockford..............	25	5	13	18	18
Totals	29	6	13	19	20
John Varga, Rockford................	8	0	0	0	2
John Varga, Port Huron............	7	0	4	4	0
Totals	15	0	4	4	2
Jeremy Vokes, Rockford	10	2	6	8	4
Jeremy Vokes, Mohawk Valley ..	23	8	8	16	6
Totals	33	10	14	24	10

GOALTENDING

	Gms.	Min.	W	L	SOL	G	SO	Avg.
P. Charbonneau, M.V.	18	901	4	8	4	61	0	4.06
P. Charbonneau, Fli.	23	1207	8	9	3	72	1	3.58
Totals	41	2108	12	17	7	133	1	3.79
M. Correia, Rock. ...	3	159	0	3	0	13	0	4.91
M. Correia, Mo.	2	80	1	1	0	7	0	5.25
M. Correia, F.W.	1	19	0	1	0	1	0	3.16
Totals	6	258	1	5	0	21	0	4.88
T. Craven, Ash.	1	1	0	0	0	0	0	0.00
T. Craven, M.V.	1	6	0	1	0	5	0	46.75
Totals	2	7	0	1	0	5	0	42.45
J. Dimaline, Musk. .	24	1330	10	7	4	67	0	3.02
Joe Dimaline, Quin. .	17	929	13	0	2	35	1	2.26
Totals	41	2258	23	7	6	102	1	2.71
Chad Ford, Adi.	3	172	0	2	1	13	0	4.55
Chad Ford, Rock. ...	6	310	1	3	1	22	0	4.26
Chad Ford, Kal.	3	145	2	1	0	7	0	2.89
Totals	12	627	3	6	2	42	0	4.02
Scott Myers, Quin...	22	1191	12	6	1	67	1	3.38
Scott Myers, Musk. .	7	354	4	1	0	23	0	3.90
Totals	29	1544	16	7	1	90	1	3.50

2001 COLONIAL CUP PLAYOFFS

RESULTS

WILD-CARD ROUND

	W	L	Pts.	GF	GA
Knoxville..	1	0	2	1	0
Elmira..	0	1	0	0	1

(Knoxville won series, 1-0)

	W	L	Pts.	GF	GA
Muskegon..	1	0	2	6	3
Kalamazoo..	0	1	0	3	6

(Muskegon won series, 1-0)

CONFERENCE SEMIFINALS

	W	L	Pts.	GF	GA
Asheville...	3	0	6	14	4
Knoxville..	0	3	0	4	14

(Asheville won series, 3-0)

	W	L	Pts.	GF	GA
New Haven	3	2	6	19	20
Adirondack	2	3	4	20	19

(New Haven won series, 3-2)

	W	L	Pts.	GF	GA
Quad City...	3	1	6	16	10
Muskegon..	1	3	2	10	16

(Quad City won series, 3-1)

	W	L	Pts.	GF	GA
Fort Wayne	3	1	6	17	11
Missouri	1	3	2	11	17

(Fort Wayne won series, 3-1)

CONFERENCE FINALS

	W	L	Pts.	GF	GA
Asheville...	3	0	6	12	6
New Haven	0	3	0	6	12

(Asheville won series, 3-0)

	W	L	Pts.	GF	GA
Quad City...	3	0	6	17	5
Fort Wayne	0	3	0	5	17

(Quad City won series, 3-0)

FINALS

	W	L	Pts.	GF	GA
Quad City...	4	1	8	22	10
Asheville...	1	4	2	10	22

(Quad City won series, 4-1)

INDIVIDUAL LEADERS

Goals: Vlad Serov, Quad City (12)
Assists: Steve Gibson, Quad City (15)
Points: Jason Ulmer, Quad City (21)
Penalty minutes: Kerry Toporowski, Quad City (65)
Goaltending average: Martin Villeneuve, Quad City (1.81)
Shutouts: Brent Belecki, Asheville (2)

TOP SCORERS

	Games	G	A	Pts.
Jason Ulmer, Quad City	12	8	13	21
Vlad Serov, Quad City	12	12	7	19
Steve Gibson, Quad City...................	12	4	15	19
J.C. Ruid, Asheville...........................	11	1	5	16
Hugo Proulx, Quad City	12	9	5	14
Bogdan Rudenko, Asheville..............	11	5	8	13
Dominic Maltais, Asheville	8	3	9	12
Olaf Kjenstad, Asheville	10	5	5	10
Mike McKay, Fort Wayne	7	4	6	10
Kelly Perrault, Quad City...................	12	2	8	10

MINOR LEAGUES *UHL*

ADIRONDACK ICEHAWKS
(Lost conference semifinals to New Haven, 3-2)
SCORING

	Games	G	A	Pts.	PIM
Kevin St. Jacques	5	2	6	8	4
John Batten	5	1	6	7	8
Rob Millar	5	2	4	6	0
Hugo Belanger	5	4	1	5	0
Frank Littlejohn	5	3	1	4	25
Bryan Duce	5	3	0	3	0
Joe Bianchi	5	1	2	3	6
Marc Busenburg	5	0	3	3	8
Eric Boyte	5	1	1	2	2
Trent Schachle	5	1	1	2	8
Eric Seidel	5	1	1	2	2
Brad Shaver	3	0	2	2	4
Doug Stienstra	5	0	2	2	2
David Dartsch	5	1	0	1	20
Lucas Nehrling	5	0	1	1	19
Darcy Anderson	1	0	0	0	2
Alex Johnstone	1	0	0	0	0
David Insalaco	2	0	0	0	0
Mike Varhaug	2	0	0	0	0
Sergei Zvyagin (goalie)	5	0	0	0	0

GOALTENDING

	Gms.	Min.	W	L	T	G	SO	Avg.
Sergei Zvyagin	5	316	2	2	1	19	0	3.61

ASHEVILLE SMOKE
(Lost finals to Quad City, 4-1)
SCORING

	Games	G	A	Pts.	PIM
J.C. Ruid	11	11	5	16	13
Bogdan Rudenko	11	5	8	13	24
Dominic Maltais	8	3	9	12	30
Olaf Kjenstad	10	5	5	10	40
Derek Crimin	10	3	4	7	14
Brett Colborne	9	0	7	7	33
Blue Bennefield	11	0	6	6	28
Shawn Ulrich	8	1	4	5	22
Ryan Aikia	11	0	5	5	43
Vitali Andreev	11	2	2	4	12
Bob Rapoza	11	2	1	3	0
Bruce Watson	8	1	1	2	43
Tyler Prosofsky	9	1	1	2	39
Alex Dumas	11	1	1	2	12
Tom Wilson	11	1	1	2	34
Rob Marshall	11	0	1	1	0
Rich Metro	2	0	0	0	0
Colin Muldoon	2	0	0	0	0
Lee Svangstu	9	0	0	0	34
Brent Belecki (goalie)	11	0	0	0	0

GOALTENDING

	Gms.	Min.	W	L	T	G	SO	Avg.
Brent Belecki	11	659	7	4	0	32	2	2.91

ELMIRA JACKALS
(Lost wild-card round to Knoxville, 1-0)
SCORING

	Games	G	A	Pts.	PIM
Jeff Antonovich	1	0	0	0	0
David Bernier	1	0	0	0	2
Nic Bilotto	1	0	0	0	2
Bob Cunningham	1	0	0	0	0
Rick Gorman	1	0	0	0	4
Rob Guinn	1	0	0	0	0
Shawn Legault	1	0	0	0	0
David Lessard	1	0	0	0	0

	Games	G	A	Pts.	PIM
Ed Lowe	1	0	0	0	0
John Murphy	1	0	0	0	0
Tim O'Connell	1	0	0	0	0
Greg Olsen	1	0	0	0	0
James Sheehan	1	0	0	0	0
Christian Soucy (goalie)	1	0	0	0	0
Michal Stastny	1	0	0	0	0
Mike Thompson	1	0	0	0	0
Jeremy Vanin	1	0	0	0	0

GOALTENDING

	Gms.	Min.	W	L	T	G	SO	Avg.
Christian Soucy	1	59	0	1	0	1	0	1.02

FORT WAYNE KOMETS
(Lost conference finals to Quad City, 3-0)
SCORING

	Games	G	A	Pts.	PIM
Mike McKay	7	4	6	10	10
Brent Gretzky	7	5	3	8	2
Keli Corpse	7	6	0	6	0
Christian Bragnalo	7	1	5	6	18
Dave Lemay	7	0	6	6	18
Derek Gauthier	7	2	3	5	6
Jim Logan	7	2	3	5	13
Frederic Bouchard	7	1	3	4	6
Rick Judson	6	0	4	4	2
Brad Twordik	6	1	2	3	12
Igor Malykhin	5	0	2	2	6
Fred Slukynsky	7	0	2	2	8
Doug Teskey (goalie)	7	0	1	1	0
Konstantin Simchuk (goalie)	2	0	0	0	0
Ian Lampshire	3	0	0	0	0
Joe Sewell	3	0	0	0	4
Nick Jones	4	0	0	0	30
Darren Martens	4	0	0	0	0
Sergei Radchenko	4	0	0	0	2
Gary Ricciardi	7	0	0	0	10
Daniel Ronan	7	0	0	0	6

GOALTENDING

	Gms.	Min.	W	L	T	G	SO	Avg.
Doug Teskey	7	369	3	3	0	23	0	3.74
Konstantin Simchuk	2	50	0	1	0	4	0	4.79

KALAMAZOO WINGS
(Lost wild-card round to Muskegon, 1-0)
SCORING

	Games	G	A	Pts.	PIM
Steve Moore	1	2	0	2	0
Matt Loen	1	1	0	1	2
Mike Ford	1	0	1	1	0
Andrew Huggett	1	0	1	1	0
Jeff Lukasak	1	0	1	1	2
Mike Maurice	1	0	1	1	0
Jeff Scharf	1	0	1	1	0
Kory Cooper (goalie)	1	0	0	0	0
Jeff Foster	1	0	0	0	0
Randy Holmes	1	0	0	0	0
Jason Hughes	1	0	0	0	2
Alain O'Driscoll	1	0	0	0	0
Craig Paterson	1	0	0	0	0
Aaron Plumb	1	0	0	0	0
Jeff Turner	1	0	0	0	2
Brian Wilson	1	0	0	0	0
Jeff Winter	1	0	0	0	0

GOALTENDING

	Gms.	Min.	W	L	T	G	SO	Avg.
Kory Cooper	1	59	0	1	0	5	0	5.10

KNOXVILLE SPEED
(Lost conference semifinals to Asheville, 3-0)

SCORING

	Games	G	A	Pts.	PIM
Sergei Petrov	4	1	2	3	11
Dan Myre	4	1	1	2	0
Geno Parrish	4	1	1	2	4
Adam Rivet	2	0	2	2	0
Mike Schultz	4	1	0	1	6
Andrew Tortorella	4	1	0	1	6
Michael Henderson	3	0	1	1	32
Brad Domonsky	4	0	1	1	33
Mikko Sivonen	4	0	1	1	2
Mike Green	1	0	0	0	0
Oleg Kouzmin	1	0	0	0	0
Tom Lawson (goalie)	1	0	0	0	0
Dean Shmyr	2	0	0	0	0
Yannick Latour	3	0	0	0	0
Alexandre Alepin	4	0	0	0	13
David Cameron	4	0	0	0	0
Bradley Denis	4	0	0	0	6
Brad Guzda (goalie)	4	0	0	0	0
Iannique Renaud	4	0	0	0	24
Dmitry Ustyuzhanin	4	0	0	0	2
Mike Vandenberghe	4	0	0	0	2

GOALTENDING

	Gms.	Min.	W	L	T	G	SO	Avg.
Tom Lawson	1	20	0	0	0	0	0	0.00
Brad Guzda	4	219	1	3	0	13	1	3.57

MISSOURI RIVER OTTERS
(Lost conference semifinals to Fort Wayne, 3-1)

SCORING

	Games	G	A	Pts.	PIM
Lonnie Loach	4	2	6	8	2
Colin Chaulk	4	4	2	6	4
Jeremy Rebek	4	3	3	6	2
Eric Murano	4	0	4	4	0
Darin Kimble	4	0	3	3	4
Anthony Cappelletti	1	1	0	1	0
Kiley Hill	4	1	0	1	20
Glenn Crawford	4	0	1	1	6
Randy Gallatin	4	0	1	1	6
Jay Hebert	4	0	1	1	8
Ryan Johnston	1	0	0	0	0
Andrew Merrick	1	0	0	0	0
Robert Starke	1	0	0	0	0
Doug Bonner (goalie)	2	0	0	0	0
Andy Burnham	2	0	0	0	2
Benoit Thibert (goalie)	2	0	0	0	0
Lee Cole	3	0	0	0	8
Trevor Sherban	3	0	0	0	14
Richard Spence	3	0	0	0	4
Troy Michalski	4	0	0	0	6
Kevin Plager	4	0	0	0	2
Chris Tok	4	0	0	0	16

GOALTENDING

	Gms.	Min.	W	L	T	G	SO	Avg.
Doug Bonner	2	120	1	1	0	8	0	4.00
Benoit Thibert	2	118	0	2	0	9	0	4.56

MUSKEGON FURY
(Lost conference semifinals to Quad City, 3-1)

SCORING

	Games	G	A	Pts.	PIM
Andrew Luciuk	5	3	5	8	4
Todd Robinson	5	3	4	7	16
Robin Bouchard	5	2	4	6	18
Rick Emmett	5	2	3	5	4
Scott Feasby	5	1	3	4	14
Scott Hlady	3	0	3	3	2
Alexei Krovopuskov	5	1	1	2	18
Sergei Kharin	4	1	0	1	0
Mike Bayrack	5	1	0	1	4

	Games	G	A	Pts	PIM
Rob Hutson	5	1	0	1	38
Philippe Roy	5	1	0	1	12
Igor Valeev	3	0	1	1	2
Sylvain Daigle (goalie)	5	0	1	1	4
James Duval	3	0	0	0	2
Rob Melanson	5	0	0	0	2
Frankie Nault	5	0	0	0	4
Jared Reigstad	5	0	0	0	4
Mark Vilneff	5	0	0	0	6

GOALTENDING

	Gms.	Min.	W	L	T	G	SO	Avg.
Sylvain Daigle	5	298	2	3	0	17	0	3.42

NEW HAVEN KNIGHTS
(Lost conference finals to Asheville, 3-0)

SCORING

	Games	G	A	Pts.	PIM
Glenn Stewart	8	5	4	9	17
Mike Melas	7	2	4	6	10
Mike Pomichter	8	0	6	6	0
Jason Stewart	8	2	3	5	6
Nick Lent	8	3	1	4	7
Keith Dupee	6	2	2	4	6
Brian Bolf	7	2	2	4	2
Clint Cabana	8	2	2	4	25
John Poapst	8	1	3	4	4
Chris Winnes	5	1	2	3	2
Jeff Brown	8	1	2	3	8
Greg Pajor	6	0	3	3	0
Bob Ferraris	8	0	3	3	8
Jim Brown	6	1	1	2	6
Kenzie Homer	6	1	1	2	8
Daniel Lyons	7	1	1	2	8
Raitis Ivanans	8	1	0	1	4
Chad Cabana	1	0	0	0	22
Brycc Wandler (goalie)	2	0	0	0	0
Keith Fitzpatrick	5	0	0	0	4
Blair Allison (goalie)	7	0	0	0	0

GOALTENDING

	Gms.	Min.	W	L	T	G	SO	Avg.
Blair Allison	7	422	3	4	0	24	1	3.41
Bryce Wandler	2	71	0	1	0	6	0	5.04

QUAD CITY MALLARDS
(Winner of 2001 playoffs)

SCORING

	Games	G	A	Pts.	PIM
Jason Ulmer	12	8	13	21	2
Vlad Serov	12	12	7	19	6
Steve Gibson	12	4	15	19	6
Hugo Proulx	12	9	5	14	18
Kelly Perrault	12	2	8	10	14
Chad Power	12	6	3	9	6
Garry Gulash	12	0	9	9	24
Dan Bjornlie	12	1	6	7	4
Mark McFarlane	9	3	3	6	48
Harold Hersh	11	3	3	6	24
Patrick Nadeau	10	2	4	6	4
Ryan Lindsay	8	2	3	5	28
Frederick Jobin	12	1	4	5	49
Kerry Toporowski	11	0	3	3	65
Etienne Drapeau	4	1	1	2	14
Martin Hlinka	5	1	1	2	11
Andy Fermoyle	5	0	2	2	6
Peter Armbrust	12	0	2	2	6
Joe Dimaline (goalie)	7	0	1	1	2
Martin Villeneuve (goalie)	5	0	0	0	0
Paul Johnson	9	0	0	0	16

GOALTENDING

	Gms.	Min.	W	L	T	G	SO	Avg.
Martin Villeneuve	5	299	4	1	0	9	0	1.81
Joe Dimaline	7	419	6	1	0	14	0	2.00

2000-01 AWARD WINNERS

ALL-STAR TEAMS

First team	Pos.	Second team
Blair Allison, New Haven	G	Brad Guzda, Knoxville
Frederic Bouchard, Ft. Wayne	D	Brett Colborne, Asheville
Jeremy Rebek, Missouri	D	Simon Olivier, New Haven
Jason Ulmer, Quad City	C	Dominic Maltais, Asheville
Hugo Belanger, Adirondack	LW	Andrew Tortorella, Knoxville
Chris Grenville, B.C.	RW	Steve Gibson, Quad City

TROPHY WINNERS

Most Valuable Player: Hugo Belanger, Adirondack
Scoring leader: Hugo Belanger, Adirondack
Outstanding defenseman: Jeremy Rebek, Missouri
Outstanding defensive forward: Jason Ulmer, Quad City
Outstanding goaltender: Blair Allison, New Haven
Rookie of the Year: Jason Ulmer, Quad City
Most sportsmanlike player: Brent Gretzky, Fort Wayne
Playoff MVP: Jason Ulmer, Quad City
Coach of the Year: Terry Ruskowski, Knoxville

ALL-TIME AWARD WINNERS

MOST VALUABLE PLAYER

Season	Player, Team
1991-92	Terry McCutcheon, Brantford
1992-93	Jason Firth, Thunder Bay
1993-94	Kevin Kerr, Flint
1994-95	Mark Green, Utica
	Paul Polillo, Brantford
1995-96	Paul Polillo, Brantford
1996-97	Paul Polillo, Brantford
1997-98	Jason Firth, Thunder Bay
1998-99	Jason Firth, Thunder Bay
1999-00	Brian Regan, Missouri
2000-01	Hugo Belanger, Adirondack
1995-96	Brian Downey, Madison
1996-97	Brian Downey, Madison
1997-98	Brad Jones, B.C.
1998-99	Paul Willett, Muskegon
1999-00	Jay Neal, Port Huron
2000-01	Jason Ulmer, Quad City

SCORING LEADER

Season	Player, Team
1991-92	Tom Sasso, Flint
1992-93	Len Soccio, St. Thomas
1993-94	Paul Polillo, Brantford
1994-95	Paul Polillo, Brantford
1995-96	Paul Polillo, Brantford
1996-97	Paul Polillo, Brantford
1997-98	Paul Polillo, Brantford
1998-99	Jason Firth, Thunder Bay
1999-00	Brent Gretzky, Asheville
2000-01	Hugo Belanger, Adirondack

BEST GOALTENDER

Season	Player, Team
1991-92	Jamie Stewart, Detroit
1992-93	Jamie Stewart, Detroit
1993-94	J.F. Labbe, Thunder Bay
1994-95	Maxim Machialovsky, Detroit
1995-96	Rich Parent, Muskegon
1996-97	Sergei Zvyagin, Quad City
1997-98	Darryl Gilmour, Madison
1998-99	Joe Dimaline, Muskegon
1999-00	Brian Regan, Missouri
2000-01	Blair Allison, Quad City

ROOKIE OF THE YEAR

Season	Player, Team
1991-92	Kevin Butt, St. Thomas
1992-93	Jason Firth, Thunder Bay
1993-94	Jean-Francois Labbe, Thunder Bay
1994-95	Lance Leslie, Thunder Bay
1995-96	Matt Loen, Madison
1996-97	Forbes MacPherson, Thunder Bay
1997-98	Jason Weaver, Muskegon
1998-99	Mike Melas, Quad City
1999-00	Jason Goulet, Fort Wayne
2000-01	Jason Ulmer, Quad City

MOST SPORTSMANLIKE PLAYER

Season	Player, Team
1991-92	Tom Sasso, Flint
1992-93	Paul Polillo, Brantford
1993-94	Paul Polillo, Brantford
1994-95	Paul Polillo, Brantford
1995-96	Scott Burfoot, Flint
1996-97	Kent Hawley, Madison
1997-98	Brian Sakic, Flint
1998-99	Brian Sakic, Flint
1999-00	Keli Corpse, Fort Wayne
2000-01	Brent Gretzky, Fort Wayne

DEFENSEMAN OF THE YEAR

Season	Player, Team
1991-92	Tom Searle, Brantford
1992-93	Tom Searle, Brantford
1993-94	Barry McKinlay, Thunder Bay
1994-95	Barry McKinlay, Thunder Bay
1995-96	Chris Hynnes, Thunder Bay
1996-97	Barry McKinlay, Thunder Bay
1997-98	John Vary, Muskegon
1998-99	Stephan Brochu, Flint
1999-00	Gary Roach, Flint
2000-01	Jeremy Rebek, Missouri

PLAYOFF MVP

Season	Player, Team
1991-92	Gary Callaghan, Thunder Bay
1992-93	Roland Melanson, Brantford
1993-94	Jean-Francois Labbe, Thunder Bay
1994-95	Lance Leslie, Thunder Bay
1995-96	Scott Burfoot, Flint
1996-97	Sergei Zvyagin, Quad City
1997-98	Jim Brown, Quad City
1998-99	Sergei Kharin, Muskegon
1999-00	Nick Stajduhar, Flint
2000-01	Jason Ulmer, Quad City

BEST DEFENSIVE FORWARD

Season	Player, Team
1991-92	Tim Bean, St. Thomas
1992-93	Todd Howarth, Thunder Bay
1993-94	Jamie Hicks, Brantford
1994-95	Terry Menard, Thunder Bay

COACH OF THE YEAR

Season	Coach, Team
1991-92	Peter Horachek, St. Thomas
1992-93	Bill McDonald, Thunder Bay
1993-94	Tom Barrett, Chatham
1994-95	Steve Ludzik, Muskegon
1995-96	Mark Johnson, Madison
1996-97	Robbie Nichols, Flint
1997-98	Robert Dirk, Winston-Salem
1998-99	Rich Kromm, Muskegon
1999-00	Brad Jones, B.C.
2000-01	Terry Ruskowski, Knoxville

REGULAR-SEASON CHAMPION

Season	Team	Coach
1991-92—	Michigan Falcons	Terry Christensen
1992-93—	Brantford Smoke	Ken Mann & Ken Gratton
1993-94—	Thunder Bay Senators	Bill MacDonald
1994-95—	Thunder Bay Senators	Bill MacDonald
1995-96—	Flint Generals	Robbie Nichols
1996-97—	Flint Generals	Robbie Nichols
1997-98—	Quad City Mallards	Paul Gillis
1998-99—	Muskegon Fury	Rich Kromm
1999-00—	Flint Generals	Doug Shedden
2000-01—	Quad City Mallards	Paul MacLean

PLAYOFF CHAMPION

Team	Coach
Thunder Bay Thunder Hawks	Bill MacDonald
Brantford Smoke	Ken Gratton
Thunder Bay Senators	Bill MacDonald
Thunder Bay Senators	Bill MacDonald
Flint Generals	Robbie Nichols
Quad City Mallards	John Anderson
Quad City Mallards	Paul Gillis
Muskegon Fury	Rich Kromm
Flint Generals	Doug Shedden
Quad City Mallards	Paul MacLean

MINOR LEAGUES *UHL*

MAJOR JUNIOR LEAGUES

Canadian Hockey League

Ontario Hockey League

Quebec Major Junior Hockey League

Western Hockey League

CANADIAN HOCKEY LEAGUE

GENERAL INFORMATION

The Canadian Hockey League is an alliance of the three Major Junior leagues—Ontario Hockey League, Quebec Major Junior Hockey League and Western Hockey League. After the regular season, the three leagues compete in a round-robin tournament to decide the Memorial Cup championship. Originally awarded to the national Junior champion, the Memorial Cup later signified Junior A supremacy (after Junior hockey in Canada was divided into ``A'' and ``B'' classes). Beginning in 1971, when Junior A hockey was split into Major Junior and Tier II Junior A, the Memorial Cup was awarded to the Major Junior champion.

LEAGUE OFFICE

Member leagues
Ontario Hockey League
Quebec Major Junior Hockey League
Western Hockey League
President
David E. Branch
Vice president
Gilles Courteau
V.p., marketing and corp. development
John Hudson

Directors
Bruce Hamilton
Charles Henry
Jim Rooney
Secretary treasurer
John Horman
Director of marketing
Norm Webb
Director of special events
Dave Lord

Director of information
Roger Lajoie
Director of officiating
Richard Doerksen
Address
305 Milner Ave., Suite 201
Scarborough, Ont. M1B 3V4
Phone
416-332-9711
FAX
416-332-1477

2001 MEMORIAL CUP

FINAL STANDINGS

Team (League)	W	L	Pts.	GF	GA
Red Deer (WHL)	3	1	6	17	16
Val-d'Or (QMJHL)	3	2	6	25	18
Regina (WHL)	2	3	4	17	17
Ottawa (OHL)	1	3	2	8	16

RESULTS

SATURDAY, MAY 19
Ottawa 5, Regina 2

SUNDAY, MAY 20
Red Deer 5, Val-d'Or 4 (OT)

MONDAY, MAY 21
Val-d'Or 5, Regina 2

TUESDAY, MAY 22
Red Deer 4, Ottawa 2

WEDNESDAY, MAY 23
Val-d'Or 6, Ottawa 1

THURSDAY, MAY 24
Regina 5, Red Deer 2

FRIDAY, MAY 25
Regina 4, Ottawa 0

SATURDAY, MAY 26
Val-d'Or 5, Regina 4 (OT)

SUNDAY, MAY 27
Red Deer 6, Val-d'Or 5 (OT)

TOP TOURNAMENT SCORERS

	Games	G	A	Pts.
Simon Gamache, Val-d'Or	5	*4	3	*7
Brett Lysak, Regina	5	3	4	*7
Ross Lupaschuk, Red Deer	4	2	5	*7
Chris Lyness, Val-d'Or	5	1	*6	*7
Stephane Veilleux, Val-d'Or	5	3	3	6
Brandon Reid, Val-d'Or	5	3	3	6
Karel Mosovsky, Regina	5	3	3	6
Kevin Korol, Regina	5	3	3	6
Kyle Wanvig, Red Deer	4	2	4	6
Paul Elliott, Regina	5	2	4	6
Martin Erat, Red Deer	4	1	5	6
Eric Fortier, Val-d'Or	5	1	5	6

*Indicates tournament leader.

2000-01 AWARD WINNERS

ALL-STAR TEAMS

First team	Pos.	Second team
Dan Blackburn, Kootenay	G	Frederic Cloutier, Shaw.
M.-Andre Bergeron, Shaw.	D	Ross Lupaschuck, Red Deer
Matt Kinch, Calgary	D	Jonathan Zion, Ottawa
Simon Gamache, Val-d'Or	LW	Steve Ott, Kitchener
Justin Mapletoft, Red Deer	C	Brandon Reid, Val-d'Or
Jarrett Stoll, Kootenay	RW	Kyle Wanvig, Red Deer

TROPHY WINNERS

Player of the year: Simon Gamache, Val-d'Or
Top scorer award: Simon Gamache, Val-d'Or
Plus/minus award: Simon Gamache, Val-d'Or
Face-off award: Derek MacKenzie, Sudbury
Rookie of the year: Scottie Upshall, Kamloops
Defenseman of the year: Marc-Andre Bergeron, Shawinigan
Goaltender of the year: Dan Blackburn, Kootenay
Scholastic player of the year: Dan Hulak, Portland
Coach of the year: Brent Sutter, Red Deer
Executive of the year: Mario Boucher, Shawinigan
Most sportsmanlike player of the year: Brandon Reid, Val-d'Or
Top draft prospect award: Jason Spezza, Windsor
Humanitarian award: Jim Vandermeer, Red Deer

HISTORY

ALL-TIME MEMORIAL CUP WINNERS

Season	Team	Season	Team	Season	Team
1918-19	Univ. of Toronto Schools	1946-47	Toronto St. Michael's	1974-75	Toronto Marlboros
1919-20	Toronto Canoe Club	1947-48	Port Arthur W. End Bruins	1975-76	Hamilton Fincups
1920-21	Winnipeg Falcons	1948-49	Montreal Royals	1976-77	New Westminster Bruins
1921-22	Fort William War Veterans	1949-50	Montreal Jr. Canadiens	1977-78	New Westminster Bruins
1922-23	Univ. of Manitoba-Winnipeg	1950-51	Barrie Flyers	1978-79	Peterborough Petes
1923-24	Owen Sound Greys	1951-52	Guelph Biltmores	1979-80	Cornwall Royals
1924-25	Regina Pats	1952-53	Barrie Flyers	1980-81	Cornwall Royals
1925-26	Calgary Canadians	1953-54	St. Catharines Tee Pees	1981-82	Kitchener Rangers
1926-27	Owen Sound Greys	1954-55	Toronto Marlboros	1982-83	Portland Winter Hawks
1927-28	Regina Monarchs	1955-56	Toronto Marlboros	1983-84	Ottawa 67's
1928-29	Toronto Marlboros	1956-57	Flin Flon Bombers	1984-85	Prince Albert Raiders
1929-30	Regina Pats	1957-58	Ottawa-Hull Jr. Canadiens	1985-86	Guelph Platers
1930-31	Winnipeg Elmwoods	1958-59	Winnipeg Braves	1986-87	Medicine Hat Tigers
1931-32	Sudbury Wolves	1959-60	St. Catharines Tee Pees	1987-88	Medicine Hat Tigers
1932-33	Newmarket	1960-61	Tor. St. Michael's Majors	1988-89	Swift Current Broncos
1933-34	Toronto St. Michael's	1961-62	Hamilton Red Wings	1989-90	Oshawa Generals
1934-35	Winnipeg Monarchs	1962-63	Edmonton Oil Kings	1990-91	Spokane Chiefs
1935-36	West Toronto Redmen	1963-64	Toronto Marlboros	1991-92	Kamloops Blazers
1936-37	Winnipeg Monarchs	1964-65	Niagara Falls Flyers	1992-93	Sault Ste. Marie Greyhounds
1937-38	St. Boniface Seals	1965-66	Edmonton Oil Kings	1993-94	Kamloops Blazers
1938-39	Oshawa Generals	1966-67	Toronto Marlboros	1994-95	Kamloops Blazers
1939-40	Oshawa Generals	1967-68	Niagara Falls Flyers	1995-96	Granby Predateurs
1940-41	Winnipeg Rangers	1968-69	Montreal Jr. Canadiens	1996-97	Hull Olympics
1941-42	Portage la Prairie	1969-70	Montreal Jr. Canadiens	1997-98	Portland Winter Hawks
1942-43	Winnipeg Rangers	1970-71	Quebec Remparts	1998-99	Ottawa 67's
1943-44	Oshawa Generals	1971-72	Cornwall Royals	1999-00	Rimouski Oceanic
1944-45	Toronto St. Michael's	1972-73	Toronto Marlboros	2000-01	Red Deer Rebels
1945-46	Winnipeg Monarchs	1973-74	Regina Pats		

ALL-TIME AWARD WINNERS

PLAYER OF THE YEAR AWARD

Season	Player, Team
1974-75	Ed Staniowski, Regina
1975-76	Peter Lee, Ottawa
1976-77	Dale McCourt, Ste. Catharines
1977-78	Bobby Smith, Ottawa
1978-79	Pierre LaCroix, Trois-Rivieres
1979-80	Doug Wickenheiser, Regina
1980-81	Dale Hawerchuk, Cornwall
1981-82	Dave Simpson, London
1982-83	Pat LaFontaine, Verdun
1983-84	Mario Lemieux, Laval
1984-85	Dan Hodgson, Prince Albert
1985-86	Luc Robitaille, Hull
1986-87	Rob Brown, Kamloops
1987-88	Joe Sakic, Swift Current
1988-89	Bryan Fogarty, Niagara Falls
1989-90	Mike Ricci, Peterborough
1990-91	Eric Lindros, Oshawa
1991-92	Charles Poulin, St. Hyacinthe
1992-93	Pat Peake, Detroit
1993-94	Jason Allison, London
1994-95	David Ling, Kingston
1995-96	Christian Dube, Sherbrooke
1996-97	Alyn McCauley, Ottawa
1997-98	Sergei Varlamov, Swift Current
1998-99	Brian Campbell, Ottawa
1999-00	Brad Richards, Rimouski
2000-01	Simon Gamache, Val-d'Or

TOP SCORER AWARD

Season	Player, Team
1993-94	Jason Allison, London
1994-95	Marc Savard, Oshawa
1995-96	Daniel Briere, Drummondville
1996-97	Pavel Rosa, Hull
1997-98	Ramzi Abid, Chicoutimi
1998-99	Mike Ribeiro, Rouyn-Noranda

Season	Player, Team
1999-00	Brad Richards, Rimouski
2000-01	Simon Gamache, Val-d'Or

PLUS/MINUS AWARD

Season	Player, Team
1986-87	Rob Brown, Kamloops
1987-88	Marc Saumier, Hull
1988-89	Bryan Fogarty, Niagara Falls
1989-90	Len Barrie, Kamloops
1990-91	Eric Lindros, Oshawa
1991-92	Dean McAmmond, Prince Albert
1992-93	Chris Pronger, Peterborough
1993-94	Mark Wotton, Saskatoon
1994-95	Darren Ritchie, Brandon
1995-96	Daniel Goneau, Granby
1996-97	Nick Boynton, Ottawa
1997-98	Andrew Ference, Portland
1998-99	Simon Tremblay, Quebec
1999-00	Brad Richards, Rimouski
2000-01	Simon Gamache, Val-d'Or

FACE-OFF AWARD

Season	Player, Team
1997-98	Mark Smith, Lethbridge
1998-99	Dan Tessier, Ottawa
1999-00	Dan Tessier, Ottawa
2000-01	Derek MacKenzie, Sudbury

ROOKIE AWARD

Season	Player, Team
1987-88	Martin Gelinas, Hull
1988-89	Yanic Perreault, Trois-Rivieres
1989-90	Petr Nedved, Seattle
1990-91	Philippe Boucher, Granby
1991-92	Alexandre Daigle, Victoriaville
1992-93	Jeff Freisen, Regina
1993-94	Vitali Yachmenev, North Bay

Season	Player, Team
1994-95	Bryan Berard, Detroit
1995-96	Joe Thornton, Sault Ste. Marie
1996-97	Vincent Lecavalier, Rimouski
1997-98	David Legwand, Plymouth
1998-99	Pavel Brendl, Calgary
1999-00	Dan Blackburn, Kootenay
2000-01	Scottie Upshall, Kamloops

DEFENSEMAN OF THE YEAR AWARD

Season	Player, Team
1987-88	Greg Hawgood, Kamloops
1988-89	Bryan Fogarty, Niagara Falls
1989-90	John Slaney, Cornwall
1990-91	Patrice Brisebois, Drummondville
1991-92	Drake Berehowsky, North Bay
1992-93	Chris Pronger, Peterborough
1993-94	Steve Gosselin, Chicoutimi
1994-95	Nolan Baumgartner, Kamloops
1995-96	Bryan Berard, Detroit
1996-97	Sean Blanchard, Ottawa
1997-98	Derrick Walser, Rimouski
1998-99	Brad Stuart, Calgary
1999-00	Micki Dupont, Kootenay
2000-01	Marc-Andre Bergeron, Shawinigan

GOALTENDER OF THE YEAR AWARD

Season	Player, Team
1987-88	Stephane Beauregard, St. Jean
1988-89	Stephane Fiset, Victoriaville
1989-90	Trevor Kidd, Brandon
1990-91	Felix Potvin, Chicoutimi
1991-92	Corey Hirsch, Kamloops
1992-93	Jocelyn Thibault, Sherbrooke
1993-94	Norm Maracle, Saskatoon
1994-95	Martin Biron, Beauport
1995-96	Frederic Deschenes, Granby
1996-97	Marc Denis, Chicoutimi
1997-98	Mathieu Garon, Victoriaville
1998-99	Cody Rudkowsky, Seattle
1999-00	Andrew Raycroft, Kingston
2000-01	Dan Blackburn, Kootenay

SCHOLASTIC PLAYER OF THE YEAR AWARD

Season	Player, Team
1987-88	Darrin Shannon, Windsor
1988-89	Jeff Nelson, Prince Albert
1989-90	Jeff Nelson, Prince Albert
1990-91	Scott Niedermayer, Kamloops
1991-92	Nathan LaFayette, Cornwall
1992-93	David Trofimenkoff, Lethbridge
1993-94	Patrick Boileau, Laval
1994-95	Perry Johnson, Regina
1995-96	Boyd Devereaux, Kitchener
1996-97	Stefan Cherneski, Brandon
1997-98	Kyle Rossiter, Spokane
1998-99	Rob Zepp, Plymouth
1999-00	Brad Boyes, Erie
2000-01	Dan Hulak, Portland

COACH OF THE YEAR AWARD

Season	Coach, Team
1987-88	Alain Vigneault, Hull
1988-89	Joe McDonnell, Kitchener
1989-90	Ken Hitchcock, Kamloops
1990-91	Joe Canale, Chicoutimi
1991-92	Bryan Maxwell, Spokane
1992-93	Marcel Comeau, Tacoma
1993-94	Bert Templeton, North Bay
1994-95	Craig Hartsburg, Guelph
1995-96	Bob Lowes, Brandon
1996-97	Brian Kilrea, Ottawa
1997-98	Dean Clark, Calgary
1998-99	Guy Chouinard, Quebec
1999-00	Peter DeBoer, Plymouth
2000-01	Brent Sutter, Red Deer

EXECUTIVE OF THE YEAR AWARD

Season	Executive, Team or League
1988-89	John Horman, QMJHL
1989-90	Russ Farwell, Seattle
1990-91	Sherwood Bassin, Sault Ste. Marie
1991-92	Bert Templeton, North Bay
1992-93	Jim Rutherford, Detroit
1993-94	Bob Brown, Kamloops
1994-95	Kelly McCrimmon, Brandon
1995-96	Tim Speltz, Spokane
1996-97	Harold MacKay, Halifax
1997-98	Paul McIntosh, London
1998-99	Jeff Hunt, Ottawa
1999-00	Maurice Tanguay, Rimouski
2000-01	Mario Boucher, Shawinigan

MOST SPORTSMANLIKE PLAYER OF THE YEAR AWARD

Season	Player, Team
1989-90	Andrew McKim, Hull
1990-91	Pat Falloon, Spokane
1991-92	Martin Gendron, St. Hyacinthe
1992-93	Rick Girard, Swift Current
1993-94	Yanick Dube, Laval
1994-95	Eric Daze, Beauport
1995-96	Hnat Domenichelli, Kamloops
1996-97	Kelly Smart, Brandon
1997-98	Cory Cyrenne, Brandon
1998-99	Matt Kinch, Calgary
1999-00	Jonathan Roy, Moncton
2000-01	Brandon Reid, Val-d'Or

TOP DRAFT PROSPECT AWARD

Season	Player, Team
1990-91	Eric Lindros, Oshawa
1991-92	Todd Warriner, Windsor
1992-93	Alexandre Daigle, Victoriaville
1993-94	Jeff O'Neill, Guelph
1994-95	Bryan Berard, Detroit
1995-96	Chris Phillips, Prince Albert
1996-97	Joe Thornton, Sault Ste. Marie
1997-98	Vincent Lecavalier, Rimouski
1998-99	Pavel Brendl, Calgary
1999-00	Rostislav Klesla, Brampton
2000-01	Jason Spezza, Windsor

HUMANITARIAN AWARD

Season	Player, Team
1992-93	Keli Corpse, Kingston
1993-94	Stephane Roy, Val d'Or
1994-95	David-Alexandre Beauregard, St. Hyacinthe
1995-96	Craig Mills, Belleville
1996-97	Jesse Wallin, Red Deer
1997-98	Jason Metcalfe, London
1998-99	Philippe Sauve, Rimouski
1999-00	Simon Gamache, Val-d'Or
2000-01	Jim Vandermeer, Red Deer

ONTARIO HOCKEY LEAGUE

LEAGUE OFFICE

Commissioner
David E. Branch
Chairman of the board
Jim Rooney
Director of administration
Herb Morell
Dir. of hockey op./referee in chief
Ted Baker

Director of information & special events
Aaron Bell
Director of central scouting
Bill Neeham
Address
305 Milner Avenue
Suite 200
Scarborough, Ontario M1B 3V4

Phone
416-299-8700
FAX
416-299-8787

2000-01 REGULAR SEASON
FINAL STANDINGS

EAST DIVISION

Team	G	W	L	T	RT	Pts.	GF	GA
Belleville	68	37	23	5	3	82	275	224
Ottawa	68	33	21	10	4	80	249	201
Peterborough	68	30	28	8	2	70	221	213
Kingston	68	28	28	11	1	68	232	218
Oshawa	68	20	36	7	5	52	184	254

CENTRAL DIVISION

Team	G	W	L	T	RT	Pts.	GF	GA
Sudbury	68	35	22	8	3	81	237	196
Toronto	68	35	23	8	2	80	213	188
North Bay	68	32	28	6	2	72	232	220
Barrie	68	29	28	7	4	69	214	230
Mississauga	68	3	56	7	2	15	157	380

MIDWEST DIVISION

Team	G	W	L	T	RT	Pts.	GF	GA
Erie	68	45	11	10	2	102	264	171
Guelph	68	34	23	9	2	79	227	205
Brampton	68	33	22	9	4	79	231	210
Owen Sound	68	31	27	7	3	72	256	236
Kitchener	68	26	36	6	0	58	183	247

WEST DIVISION

Team	G	W	L	T	RT	Pts.	GF	GA
Plymouth	68	43	15	5	5	96	253	162
Windsor	68	34	22	8	4	80	257	221
Sarnia	68	28	31	7	2	65	235	244
London	68	26	34	5	3	60	222	263
Sault Ste. Marie	68	23	38	4	3	53	188	256

INDIVIDUAL LEADERS

Goals: Randy Rowe, Belleville (64)
Assists: Kyle Wellwood, Belleville (83)
Points: Kyle Wellwood, Belleville (118)
Penalty minutes: Mike Amodeo, Kitchener (244)
Goaltending average: Rob Zepp, Plymouth (2.26)
Shutouts: Andy Chiodo, Toronto (4)
Peter Hamerlik, Kingston (4)
Adam Munro, Erie (4)
J.F. Perras, Erie (4)
Rob Zepp, Plymouth (4)

	Games	G	A	Pts.
Brad Boyes, Erie	59	45	45	90
Derek MacKenzie, Sudbury	62	40	49	89
Jason Baird, Erie	68	30	58	88
Steve Ott, Windsor	55	50	37	87
Stephen Weiss, Plymouth	62	40	47	87
Jason Jaspers, Sudbury	63	42	42	84
Derek Roy, Kitchener	65	42	39	81
Scott Cameron, North Bay	68	37	43	80
Cory Pecker, SSM-Erie	61	41	38	79
Joe Talbot, Ottawa	68	39	40	79
Fedor Fedorov, Sudbury	67	33	45	78
Igor Valeev, North Bay	62	17	61	78
Michael Zigomanis, Kingston	52	40	37	77
Kevin Dallman, Guelph	66	25	52	77
Charlie Stephens, Guelph	67	38	38	76
Shawn Snider, Owen Sound	61	27	49	76
Chris Kelly, Lon.-Sud.	50	26	50	76

TOP SCORERS

	Games	G	A	Pts.
Kyle Wellwood, Belleville	68	35	83	118
Jason Spezza, Miss.-Wind.	56	43	73	116
Branko Radivojevic, Belleville	61	34	70	104
Randy Rowe, Belleville	63	64	38	102

INDIVIDUAL STATISTICS

BARRIE COLTS
SCORING

	Games	G	A	Pts.	PIM
Blaine Down	62	35	38	73	80
Mike Henderson	64	31	37	68	56
Matthew Dzieduszycki	45	33	30	63	49
Tim Branham	68	7	25	32	77
Joey Tenute	61	13	18	31	38
Fraser Clair	43	16	14	30	41
Eric Reitz	68	5	21	26	178
Shayne Fryia	43	16	9	25	66
Jan Platil	60	6	18	24	114
Dean Byvelds	46	4	19	23	21
Aaron Power	66	3	20	23	103
Ed Hill	60	3	19	22	104
Frantisek Bakrlik	54	11	10	21	70
Matt Passfield	27	5	9	14	30
Neill Posillico	55	6	5	11	69
Brent Sullivan	33	2	9	11	35
Steven Morris	39	5	5	10	16
Tyler Hanchuck	31	1	6	7	71
Matt Grennier	30	4	2	6	6
Jordan Brenner	55	3	3	6	18
William Wellman	34	1	5	6	42

MAJOR JUNIOR LEAGUES OHL

MAJOR JUNIOR LEAGUES OHL

	Games	G	A	Pts.	PIM
Greg Mizzi	34	2	3	5	63
Ryan O'Keefe	8	1	4	5	32
Kyle Wailes	21	1	2	3	10
Jason Davies	5	0	2	2	2
Brian Finley (goalie)	16	0	1	1	0
Mike D'Alessandro (goalie)	37	0	1	1	8
Bryan Hayes	43	0	1	1	4
Steve Lajeunesse	1	0	0	0	0
Joe Bowcock	5	0	0	0	0
Daniel Girardi	6	0	0	0	0
Rick Hwodeky	6	0	0	0	13
Alex Butkus	20	0	0	0	19
David Chant (goalie)	23	0	0	0	2

GOALTENDING

	Gms.	Min.	W	L	T	G	SO	Avg.
David Chant	23	1255	10	10	2	64	1	3.06
Brian Finley	16	818	5	8	0	42	0	3.08
Mike D'Alessandro	37	1850	12	13	5	108	1	3.50

BELLEVILLE BULLS

SCORING

	Games	G	A	Pts.	PIM
Kyle Wellwood	68	35	83	118	24
Branko Radivojevic	61	34	70	104	77
Randy Rowe	63	64	38	102	30
Nathan Robinson	66	32	37	69	57
Mike Renzi	67	28	28	56	98
Michael Jacobsen	63	16	34	50	24
David Cornacchia	68	9	37	46	104
Malcolm Hutt	68	8	20	28	48
Matthew Stajan	57	9	18	27	27
Cody McCormick	66	7	16	23	135
Adam Paiement	58	9	10	19	50
Nick Policelli	62	4	14	18	176
Alex White	52	6	8	14	19
Dan Growden	48	4	10	14	18
David Silverstone	65	4	7	11	202
Matt Coughlin	61	1	10	11	145
Andre Deveaux	58	3	6	9	65
Brad Efthimiou	48	1	7	8	0
Rob Dmytruk	41	1	1	2	27
Andrew Brown	25	0	2	2	31
Jan Chovan (goalie)	39	0	2	2	0
Blake Orr	11	0	1	1	12
Paulo Colaiacovo (goalie)	32	0	1	1	0
Jesse Olden	1	0	0	0	2
Cory Campbell (goalie)	8	0	0	0	2

GOALTENDING

	Gms.	Min.	W	L	T	G	SO	Avg.
Jan Chovan	39	2074	19	15	2	98	2	2.84
Paulo Colaiacovo	32	1627	15	7	3	88	1	3.25
Cory Campbell	8	415	3	4	0	34	0	4.92

BRAMPTON BATTALION

SCORING

	Games	G	A	Pts.	PIM
Raffi Torres	55	33	37	70	76
Aaron Van Leusen	68	25	40	65	33
Jeff Bateman	53	15	44	59	81
Rostislav Klesla	45	18	36	54	59
Lukas Havel	58	20	33	53	91
Jay McClement	66	30	19	49	61
Kurt MacSweyn	66	17	24	41	37
Jason Maleyko	63	11	30	41	78
Chris Rowan	67	18	18	36	88
Scott Thompson	64	8	18	26	27
Paul Flache	68	8	16	24	100
Jay Harrison	53	4	15	19	112
Ryan Bowness	52	5	10	15	51
Jonah Leroux	48	4	7	11	24
Matt Grennier	32	4	6	10	13
Adam Henrich	48	5	4	9	27

	Games	G	A	Pts.	PIM
Chris Clayton	52	1	7	8	14
Tyler Hanchuck	34	1	5	6	55
Mike Rice	15	1	4	5	18
Brad Woods	14	0	5	5	14
Alex MacDonell	36	0	3	3	47
Travis Parent	40	0	3	3	30
David Chant (goalie)	29	0	2	2	0
Brad Topping (goalie)	31	0	1	1	0
Corey LeClair	56	0	1	1	18
Brian Finley (goalie)	11	0	0	0	0

GOALTENDING

	Gms.	Min.	W	L	T	G	SO	Avg.
Brad Topping	31	1800	14	10	4	86	1	2.87
Brian Finley	11	631	7	3	1	31	0	2.95
David Chant	29	1706	12	13	4	88	1	3.09

ERIE OTTERS

SCORING

	Games	G	A	Pts.	PIM
Brad Boyes	59	45	45	90	42
Jason Baird	68	30	58	88	237
Nikita Alexeev	64	31	41	72	45
Brad Yeo	66	28	41	69	186
Joe Guenther	68	34	32	66	27
Mike Nelson	61	25	38	63	62
Cory Pecker	30	17	22	39	32
Carlo Colaiacovo	62	12	27	39	59
Darren McMillan	60	2	26	28	42
Scott Rozendal	38	8	12	20	115
Sean Dixon	63	3	17	20	31
Brandon Cullen	30	7	11	18	71
Scott Dobben	57	8	9	17	18
Troy Ilijow	37	3	7	10	71
Chris Campoli	52	1	9	10	47
Pavel Shtefan	18	4	5	9	6
Patrick Lamesse	30	1	6	7	10
Chris Berti	19	0	6	6	42
Riley Moher	39	2	3	5	72
Derrick Byfuglien	31	1	4	5	37
Brian Lee	50	0	3	3	35
Mike McKeown	49	1	1	2	70
Kenny Jung	28	0	2	2	8
Bobby John Byfuglien	37	0	2	2	31
Joey Sullivan	47	1	0	1	104
Adam Munro (goalie)	41	0	1	1	2
J.F. Perras (goalie)	33	0	0	0	4

GOALTENDING

	Gms.	Min.	W	L	T	G	SO	Avg.
Adam Munro	41	2283	26	6	6	88	4	2.31
J.F. Perras	33	1856	19	7	4	82	4	2.65

GUELPH STORM

SCORING

	Games	G	A	Pts.	PIM
Kevin Dallman	66	25	52	77	88
Charlie Stephens	67	38	38	76	53
Martin St. Pierre	68	20	49	69	40
Daniel Paille	64	22	31	53	57
Brent Kelly	67	17	36	53	35
Colt King	65	25	27	52	129
Brian Passmore	57	16	32	48	105
Dustin Brown D.	53	23	22	45	45
Derek Hennessey	56	17	14	31	38
Steve Chabbert	66	3	18	21	84
Morgan McCormick	45	5	6	11	75
Nick Lees	65	5	4	9	26
Niko Tuomi	40	0	8	8	51
Peter Flache	55	3	3	6	32
Andrew Brown	35	2	4	6	20
Frank Burgio	63	1	5	6	56
Adam Campbell	28	0	6	6	52
Ben Pilon	27	0	4	4	2

	Games	G	A	Pts.	PIM
Barry Graham	48	0	4	4	76
Ryan Thompson	36	1	2	3	39
Andrew Archer	50	0	2	2	59
Craig Andersson (goalie)	59	0	2	2	22
Jon Hedberg	2	1	0	1	4
Cory Campbell (goalie)	4	0	0	0	0
Andrew Sim (goalie)	5	0	0	0	0
Dan McNeill	29	0	0	0	8

GOALTENDING

	Gms.	Min.	W	L	T	G	SO	Avg.
Craig Andersson	59	3555	30	19	9	156	3	2.63
Cory Campbell	4	240	2	2	0	14	0	3.50
Andrew Sim	5	220	2	2	0	13	0	3.55

KINGSTON FRONTENACS

SCORING

	Games	G	A	Pts.	PIM
Michael Zigomanis	52	40	37	77	44
Derek Campbell	57	25	44	69	130
Andrew Ianiero	66	25	39	64	42
Brett Clouthier	68	28	29	57	165
Cory Stillman	68	29	27	56	39
Travis Lisabeth	62	22	25	47	69
Nathan Tennant	67	7	23	30	130
Tomas Skvaridlo	58	10	19	29	33
Eric Braff	68	3	21	24	47
Jean-Francois Seguin	49	6	17	23	16
Chris Cook	68	10	10	20	25
Corey Sabourin	51	1	18	19	35
Doug MacIver	54	3	13	16	171
Justin McCutcheon	67	6	9	15	75
Shane O'Brien	61	2	12	14	89
Lou Dickenson	25	4	6	10	10
Brody Todd	63	4	5	9	31
Brad Horan	61	3	5	8	7
Darryl Thomson	39	2	5	7	28
Sean Langdon	20	2	4	6	6
Peter Hamerlik (goalie)	56	0	2	2	8
Sean McMorrow	7	0	1	1	22
Sean Burke	12	0	1	1	0
Glen Ridler (goalie)	22	0	1	1	2
Mike Smith (goalie)	3	0	0	0	0
Aaron Wilson	7	0	0	0	0
Matt Timmins	22	0	0	0	17

GOALTENDING

	Gms.	Min.	W	L	T	G	SO	Avg.
Peter Hamerlik	56	3026	21	21	8	153	4	3.03
Glen Ridler	22	964	7	8	1	52	0	3.24
Mike Smith	3	136	0	0	2	8	0	3.53

KITCHENER RANGERS

SCORING

	Games	G	A	Pts.	PIM
Derek Roy	65	42	39	81	114
Andre Benoit	65	16	19	35	37
Steve Eminger	54	6	26	32	66
Chris Brannen	65	5	27	32	48
Josh Bennett	62	15	15	30	191
Matt Passfield	39	15	12	27	33
Scott Sheppard	67	11	16	27	35
Vasily Bizyayev	53	10	14	24	10
Ryan Ramsay	22	5	18	23	39
Jimmy Gagnon	41	10	11	21	118
Chris Cava	56	6	15	21	153
Matt Armstrong	41	9	11	20	58
John Dunphy	26	7	12	19	14
Marcus Smith	59	4	13	17	43
Mike Amodeo	60	5	11	16	244
Travis Chapman	59	4	10	14	22
Matt Rock	65	2	10	12	65
Sam Skwarchuk	58	5	5	10	10
Jamie Minchella	30	4	2	6	6

	Games	G	A	Pts.	PIM
Scott Dickie (goalie)	60	0	4	4	14
Mike Gresdal	20	1	1	2	29
Brad Larter	52	1	1	2	74
T.J. Eason	27	0	2	2	30
Steve Richards	11	0	0	0	20
Jeff Johnston (goalie)	17	0	0	0	0
Brock Yates	55	0	0	0	64

GOALTENDING

	Gms.	Min.	W	L	T	G	SO	Avg.
Scott Dickie	60	3381	24	26	5	179	0	3.18
Jeff Johnston	17	746	2	10	1	60	0	4.83

LONDON KNIGHTS

SCORING

	Games	G	A	Pts.	PIM
Mike Stathopulos	68	17	54	71	16
Rick Nash	58	31	35	66	56
Joel Scherban	65	24	31	55	22
Chris Kelly	31	21	34	55	46
Aaron Lobb	67	23	25	48	93
Daniel Bois	66	21	16	37	218
Ian Turner	64	8	22	30	87
Dan Jancevski	39	4	23	27	95
Lou Dickenson	35	12	13	25	23
Jason Davies	54	13	11	24	56
Ryan Held	28	6	17	23	30
Logan Hunter	64	8	11	19	128
Petr Hemsky	54	7	11	18	4
Dennis Wideman	24	8	8	16	38
John Eminger	59	4	12	16	110
Andy Burnham	33	7	4	11	140
Matt Junkins	65	2	9	11	60
Bobby Turner	49	0	8	8	108
Kyle Neufeld	27	2	3	5	39
Bovan Seljan	15	2	2	4	6
Mike Clarke	59	0	4	4	89
Josh Chambers	43	1	2	3	26
Sean McMorrow	29	0	3	3	75
Matthew Albiani	17	0	2	2	12
Brent Varty	41	1	0	1	30
Mike Anning	5	0	1	1	7
Aaron Molnar (goalie)	68	0	1	1	4
Chris Lawrence (goalie)	3	0	0	0	0
Matt Cooper (goalie)	8	0	0	0	0

GOALTENDING

	Gms.	Min.	W	L	T	G	SO	Avg.
Chris Lawrence	3	49	0	0	0	0	0	0.00
Aaron Molnar	68	3925	26	37	5	245	1	3.75
Matt Cooper	8	151	0	0	0	13	0	5.17

MISSISSAUGA ICEDOGS

SCORING

	Games	G	A	Pts.	PIM
Patrick Jarrett	60	15	38	53	22
Chad Wiseman	30	15	29	44	22
Omar Ennaffati	65	11	29	40	104
Jason Spezza	15	7	23	30	11
Brian McGrattan	31	20	9	29	83
Mike Wehrstedt	37	12	16	28	12
Ryan Courtney	49	6	16	22	23
Andrew Davis	65	4	16	20	89
Nathan O'Nabigon	35	8	8	16	33
Brandon Robinson	60	12	3	15	20
Chris Osborne	59	8	6	14	44
David Dalliday	60	5	8	13	52
Chris Thaler	64	4	9	13	36
Grant Buckley	61	2	10	12	67
Tyler Eady	27	4	6	10	19
John Jarram	60	3	7	10	63
Steven Rawski	43	3	6	9	20
Jeff Paisley	47	4	3	7	18
Adam Midgely	22	2	4	6	32

	Games	G	A	Pts.	PIM
Mike Oliveira	10	1	5	6	6
Brent Labre	48	0	6	6	102
Mark Cranley	43	3	1	4	42
Mike James	17	2	2	4	24
Fraser Clair	14	3	0	3	14
Mark Ridout	6	1	2	3	13
Jason Francis	11	0	3	3	4
Brett Angel	19	0	2	2	51
Michael Mole (goalie)	45	0	2	2	0
Dan Sullivan	9	1	0	1	4
Matt Timmins	16	0	1	1	15
Matt Coughlin	2	0	0	0	6
Andrew Sim (goalie)	6	0	0	0	0
Chris Curran	11	0	0	0	12
Sean McMorrow	13	0	0	0	34
Rob Garrick (goalie)	22	0	0	0	0

GOALTENDING

	Gms.	Min.	W	L	T	G	SO	Avg.
Rob Garrick	22	1232	1	17	2	107	1	5.21
Michael Mole	45	2435	2	35	4	219	0	5.40
Andrew Sim	6	209	0	3	1	19	0	5.45

NORTH BAY CENTENNIALS

SCORING

	Games	G	A	Pts.	PIM
Scott Cameron	68	37	43	80	45
Igor Valeev	62	17	61	78	175
Ryan Armstrong	63	36	20	56	52
Chris Thorburn	66	22	32	54	64
Jeffrey Doyle	41	16	20	36	76
Kyle Werner	65	16	20	36	112
Chris Eade	64	3	26	29	117
Peter Reynolds	58	2	27	29	85
Josh Tataryn	40	19	9	28	12
Adam Gibson	56	13	14	27	24
Kevin Werner	53	8	12	20	59
George Halkidis	58	3	15	18	31
Craig Foster	59	10	6	16	51
Nick Vernelli	59	5	10	15	21
Brad Pierce	67	2	11	13	133
Ryan McGregor	51	4	8	12	40
Kevin Hurley	49	3	9	12	27
Peter Veltman	39	5	5	10	47
Matt Bacon	23	1	5	6	33
Vladimir Sapozhnikov	53	0	6	6	70
Brad Walford	8	3	2	5	2
Josh Legge	16	0	4	4	52
Ryan Morgan	33	0	1	1	30
Alex Auld (goalie)	40	0	1	1	6
Andrew Penner (goalie)	32	0	0	0	4

GOALTENDING

	Gms.	Min.	W	L	T	G	SO	Avg.
Alex Auld	40	2319	22	11	5	98	1	2.54
Andrew Penner	32	1787	10	19	1	117	1	3.93

OSHAWA GENERALS

SCORING

	Games	G	A	Pts.	PIM
Jamie Johnson	56	8	38	46	14
John Kozoriz	59	16	23	39	26
Kevin Mitchell	54	10	29	39	139
Brandon Nolan	52	15	23	38	21
Brandon Cullen	34	16	14	30	85
Ryan Healy	49	15	14	29	75
Mike Rice	43	12	17	29	32
Jon Hedberg	63	7	22	29	68
Chris Minard	28	12	12	24	18
Ladislav Kolda	65	7	17	24	20
Lindsay Plunkett	31	11	9	20	67
Scott Rozendal	20	12	4	16	53
Sean Stefanski	59	7	8	15	86

	Games	G	A	Pts.	PIM
Pat Montgomery	53	6	8	14	137
Pavel Shtefan	23	4	9	13	9
Brad Walford	52	1	12	13	25
Eric Larochelle	58	3	9	12	35
Ben Eager	61	4	6	10	120
Tobias Whelan	56	5	3	8	14
Richard Spence	66	0	8	8	94
Brad Woods	38	0	5	5	26
Ryan Fraser	10	2	0	2	24
Nick Lees	2	1	1	2	0
Jonah Leroux	15	1	1	2	6
Derek McEvoy	16	1	1	2	2
Mike Rusenstrom	8	0	2	2	6
T.J. Reynolds	2	0	1	1	5
Steve Thomas	5	0	1	1	4
Paul Ranger	32	0	1	1	2
Mitch Hugli	1	0	0	0	0
Chris Whitley (goalie)	1	0	0	0	0
Andrew Archer	2	0	0	0	4
Neill Posillico	2	0	0	0	0
Jarrett Winn	7	0	0	0	0
T.J. Aceti (goalie)	26	0	0	0	6
Derek Dolson (goalie)	45	0	0	0	9

GOALTENDING

	Gms.	Min.	W	L	T	G	SO	Avg.
Chris Whitley	1	60	0	1	0	3	0	3.00
Derek Dolson	45	2635	14	26	4	147	0	3.35
T.J. Aceti	26	1436	6	14	3	94	0	3.93

OTTAWA 67'S

SCORING

	Games	G	A	Pts.	PIM
Joe Talbot	68	39	40	79	28
Jonathan Zion	59	22	51	73	38
Miguel Delisle	61	34	38	72	89
Zenon Konopka	66	20	45	65	120
Lance Galbraith	58	16	40	56	190
Vadim Sozinov	57	21	18	39	57
Brendan Bell	68	7	32	39	59
Adam Chapman	60	14	18	32	41
Sean Scully	67	12	18	30	22
Luke Sellars	59	9	21	30	136
Matthew Albiani	36	6	16	22	20
Sebastien Savage	42	10	10	20	73
Carter Trevisani	35	9	10	19	22
Rodney Bauman	47	9	9	18	82
Brett McGrath	60	4	13	17	10
Jeremy Van Hoof	65	1	14	15	49
Bryan Rodney	65	0	15	15	26
Russ Moyer	51	4	10	14	48
Josh Tataryn	24	3	5	8	6
Pierre Mitsou	51	2	5	7	33
Marc Lefebvre	28	3	2	5	21
Adam Smyth	24	2	2	4	63
Derek McDonald	11	1	2	3	14
Seamus Kotyk (goalie)	55	0	1	1	4
Corey Sabourin	4	0	0	0	2
John Ceci (goalie)	22	0	0	0	0

GOALTENDING

	Gms.	Min.	W	L	T	G	SO	Avg.
Seamus Kotyk	55	3087	24	20	7	141	2	2.74
John Ceci	22	1054	9	5	3	56	0	3.19

OWEN SOUND ATTACK

SCORING

	Games	G	A	Pts.	PIM
Shawn Snider	61	27	49	76	96
Kyle McAllister	68	28	44	72	40
Joel Ward	67	26	36	62	45
Daniel Sisca	67	25	35	60	69
Greg Jacina	57	25	26	51	101

	Games	G	A	Pts.	PIM
Agris Saviels	68	14	37	51	46
Bryan Kazarian	68	16	28	44	73
Brandon Verner	66	8	28	36	78
Trevor Blanchard	65	15	18	33	153
Luc Chaisson	52	13	16	29	18
Bill Zalba	26	10	13	23	37
Dan Sullivan	43	10	13	23	50
Mike Barrett	58	9	14	23	77
Nick Vukovic	65	6	17	23	67
Brent Sullivan	22	8	9	17	29
Ryan Sharp	54	5	6	11	47
Richard Power	54	3	5	8	25
Richard Colwill	40	3	3	6	8
Josh Legge	41	1	5	6	70
John Osborne	18	3	2	5	26
Dene Poulin	56	1	3	4	49
Justin Hodgins	33	0	4	4	14
Corey Roberts (goalie)	56	0	3	3	4
Kris Fraser	17	0	2	2	6
Michael Lymer	1	0	0	0	0
Justin Day (goalie)	20	0	0	0	0

GOALTENDING

	Gms.	Min.	W	L	T	G	SO	Avg.
Corey Roberts	56	3130	22	25	6	168	1	3.22
Justin Day	20	977	8	5	1	60	0	3.68

PETERBOROUGH PETES

SCORING

	Games	G	A	Pts.	PIM
Marcel Rodman	61	36	35	71	14
Brad Self	68	19	47	66	28
Eric Staal	63	19	30	49	23
Jamie Chamberlain	66	14	28	42	75
John Brioux	68	14	28	42	34
Kurtis Foster	62	17	24	41	78
Lukas Krajicek	61	8	27	35	53
Greg Chambers	60	9	18	27	10
Ryan Ramsay	36	16	10	26	67
Dustin Wood	64	5	20	25	41
Jon Howse	58	11	11	22	34
Matt Herrielsen	60	9	13	22	59
Stephen Hoar	56	9	10	19	58
Matt Carkner	53	8	8	16	128
Bill Zalba	24	7	8	15	20
Matt Armstrong	25	5	6	11	22
Adam Elzinga	66	1	10	11	76
Dan Buccella	39	5	4	9	128
Jimmy Gagnon	25	3	6	9	65
Ryan Card	55	3	2	5	16
Josh Patterson	8	1	2	3	9
T.J. Eason	39	0	3	3	64
Kerry Gillis	27	1	1	2	30
Brian Croswell	9	1	0	1	4
Mike Self	13	0	1	1	8
Bryan Faulkner	2	0	0	0	0
Kyle Aitken	8	0	0	0	0
Brent Hughes	8	0	0	0	4
David Currie (goalie)	17	0	0	0	0
Joey MacDonald (goalie)	57	0	0	0	15

GOALTENDING

	Gms.	Min.	W	L	T	G	SO	Avg.
Joey MacDonald	57	3284	25	21	7	161	1	2.94
David Currie	17	852	5	9	1	44	2	3.10

PLYMOUTH WHALERS

SCORING

	Games	G	A	Pts.	PIM
Stephen Weiss	62	40	47	87	45
Damian Surma	55	26	34	60	62
Stacey Britstone	59	24	27	51	90
Cole Jarrett	60	12	36	48	98
Tomas Kurka	47	15	29	44	20

	Games	G	A	Pts.	PIM
George Nistas	46	10	26	36	14
Kristopher Vernarsky	60	14	21	35	35
Rob McBride	54	15	17	32	19
Preston Mizzi	29	15	16	31	49
Bryan Thompson	59	11	20	31	55
James Wisniewski	53	6	23	29	72
Chad Wiseman	32	11	16	27	12
Chad Larose	32	18	7	25	24
Karl Stewart	68	9	14	23	87
Ryan O'Keefe	55	5	16	21	138
Libor Ustrnul	35	3	13	16	66
Gregory Campbell	65	2	12	14	40
Andre Robichaud	68	1	12	13	25
James Ramsay	43	4	5	9	88
Nate Kiser	62	1	8	9	105
Nathan O'Nabigon	29	5	3	8	21
Steven Morris	10	3	3	6	4
Tony Williams	8	2	2	4	21
Jared Newman	34	0	4	4	114
Stephane Gervais	6	1	0	1	0
Rob Zepp (goalie)	55	0	1	1	2
Larry Sterling (goalie)	2	0	0	0	0
Paul Drew (goalie)	14	0	0	0	0
Mike Gresdal	30	0	0	0	22

GOALTENDING

	Gms.	Min.	W	L	T	G	SO	Avg.
Larry Sterling	2	27	0	0	0	0	0	0.00
Rob Zepp	55	3246	34	18	3	122	4	2.26
Paul Drew	14	718	9	1	1	29	1	2.42

SARNIA STING

SCORING

	Games	G	A	Pts.	PIM
Eric Himelfarb	49	31	44	75	48
Maxim Rybin	67	34	36	70	60
Alexander Buturlin	57	28	37	65	27
Kris Newbury	64	28	30	58	126
Dusty Jamieson	66	14	35	49	22
Robb Palahnuk	66	25	19	44	93
Julius Halfkenny	66	12	22	34	75
Adam Campbell	39	9	16	25	109
Scott Heffernan	51	2	20	22	30
Preston Mizzi	25	10	11	21	10
Tyler Coleman	67	9	12	21	11
Ryan Hare	44	7	13	20	24
John Hecimovic	62	6	11	17	27
Chris Berti	25	5	10	15	38
Corey Brekelmans	28	2	9	11	32
Reg Thomas	63	1	9	10	122
Jason Penner	52	4	5	9	49
Jeff Luckovitch	51	0	8	8	108
Mike Craigen	30	5	2	7	65
Riley Moher	29	1	5	6	59
Kenny Jung	30	1	4	5	24
Jamie Johnson	9	0	5	5	7
Ryan Chapman	20	1	1	2	6
Cory Campbell (goalie)	23	0	2	2	8
Andrew Oke	16	0	1	1	8
Ryan Fraser	17	0	1	1	40
Brad Beloungea	29	0	1	1	7
Robert Gherson (goalie)	41	0	1	1	2
Chandon Hill	4	0	0	0	0
Tom Rogerson (goalie)	6	0	0	0	0
Andrew Sim (goalie)	8	0	0	0	0
Billy Rochefort	15	0	0	0	12

GOALTENDING

	Gms.	Min.	W	L	T	G	SO	Avg.
Cory Campbell	23	1304	14	6	2	62	0	2.85
Andrew Sim	8	327	2	2	0	18	1	3.30
Robert Gherson	41	2230	11	22	5	136	1	3.66
Tom Rogerson	6	260	1	3	0	21	0	4.85

SAULT STE. MARIE GREYHOUNDS

SCORING

	Games	G	A	Pts.	PIM
Jeff Richards	52	20	23	43	102
Trevor Daley	58	14	27	41	105
Cory Pecker	31	24	16	40	37
Paul Ballantyne	63	12	28	40	60
Ryan Held	31	12	16	28	26
Rob Chapman	51	12	15	27	83
John Osborne	32	12	14	26	37
Brent Theobald	45	9	15	24	50
Ryan Weistche	66	9	14	23	28
Martin Bonda	53	8	13	21	29
Brett Trudell	56	12	6	18	36
Mike Melinko	58	6	10	16	24
Nick Jones	25	5	10	15	111
Kyle Wailes	39	4	10	14	18
Vaclav Zavoral	55	4	6	10	116
Chris Martin	41	1	9	10	19
Derek Fox	50	1	9	10	72
Patrick Lamesse	30	6	2	8	12
Kyle Neufeld	25	4	4	8	27
Malcolm MacMillan	21	3	5	8	90
Preston Mizzi	12	2	6	8	15
Alan Nolan	57	2	5	7	109
Shayne Fryia	22	1	6	7	19
Jeremy Swanson	54	1	6	7	60
Dustin VanBallegooie	59	1	5	6	85
Troy Ilijow	30	2	3	5	31
Ray Emery (goalie)	52	0	2	2	42
Jeremy Day (goalie)	23	0	1	1	0
Tyler Mercier (goalie)	1	0	0	0	0
Jordan Kennedy	6	0	0	0	9

GOALTENDING

	Gms.	Min.	W	L	T	G	SO	Avg.
Ray Emery	52	2938	18	29	2	174	1	3.55
Tyler Mercier	1	33	0	0	0	2	0	3.64
Jeremy Day	23	1144	5	12	2	76	0	3.99

SUDBURY WOLVES

SCORING

	Games	G	A	Pts.	PIM
Derek MacKenzie	62	40	49	89	89
Jason Jaspers	63	42	42	84	77
Fedor Fedorov	67	33	45	78	88
Alexei Semenov	65	21	42	63	106
T.J. Warkus	63	19	28	47	69
Mike Vaillaincourt	61	7	22	29	49
Jerry Connell	67	15	11	26	168
Tom Kotsopoulos	58	11	15	26	105
Kip Brennan	27	7	14	21	94
Chris Kelly	19	5	16	21	17
Dennis Wideman	25	7	11	18	37
Josh Gratton	44	5	13	18	110
Dan Jancevski	31	3	14	17	42
Steven Ellis	60	5	11	16	27
Chad Starling	51	3	12	15	118
Adam Keefe	50	4	10	14	62
Ladislav Reznicek	59	1	11	12	14
Corey Brekelmans	29	0	7	7	15
Walter Prawdzik	50	3	1	4	40
Drew Kivell	67	0	4	4	75
Mike Smith (goalie)	43	0	3	3	8
Jason Hicks	48	0	2	2	35
Sebastien Savage	8	1	0	1	11
Miguel Beaudry (goalie)	25	0	1	1	0
Mark McArthur	1	0	0	0	0

GOALTENDING

	Gms.	Min.	W	L	T	G	SO	Avg.
Mike Smith	43	2571	22	13	7	108	3	2.52
Miguel Beaudry	25	1393	12	10	1	74	1	3.19

TORONTO ST. MICHAEL'S MAJORS

SCORING

	Games	G	A	Pts.	PIM
Ryan Walsh	65	26	45	71	81
Darryl Bootland	56	32	33	65	136
Frank Lukes	61	23	33	56	37
Matt Bannan	56	19	28	47	52
Matt Ellis	68	21	24	45	19
Mark Popovic	61	7	35	42	54
Lorne Misita	52	16	23	39	52
Tim Brent	64	9	19	28	31
Adam DeLeeuw	54	11	14	25	122
Drew Fata	58	5	15	20	134
Chris Minard	40	11	8	19	28
Kevin Klein	58	3	16	19	21
Lindsay Plunkett	20	8	6	14	27
Michael Gough	55	6	8	14	84
Jeffrey Doyle	23	2	10	12	40
Chris Boucher	68	0	12	12	100
Steve Farquharson	58	7	4	11	133
Tyler Cook	54	2	8	10	48
Matt Bacon	35	3	6	9	44
T.J. Reynolds	50	1	3	4	163
Ryan Robert	27	1	1	2	4
Mike Sellan	58	0	2	2	129
Greg Mizzi	8	0	1	1	10
Scott Talbot (goalie)	2	0	0	0	0
Peter Budaj (goalie)	37	0	0	0	0
Andy Chiodo (goalie)	38	0	0	0	9

GOALTENDING

	Gms.	Min.	W	L	T	G	SO	Avg.
Andy Chiodo	38	2069	18	12	5	86	4	2.49
Scott Talbot	2	70	0	1	0	3	0	2.57
Peter Budaj	37	1996	17	12	3	95	3	2.86

WINDSOR SPITFIRES

SCORING

	Games	G	A	Pts.	PIM
Steve Ott	55	50	37	87	164
Jason Spezza	41	36	50	86	32
Shawn Mather	68	29	45	74	41
Steve Hildenbrand	68	23	41	64	90
Robin Boucher	65	19	29	48	37
Craig Kennedy	67	16	28	44	55
Tim Gleason	47	8	28	36	124
Joey Sewell	42	14	18	32	142
Craig Mahon	65	5	20	25	174
Timo Helbling	54	7	14	21	90
Rob Hennigar	43	7	13	20	27
David Bowman	67	7	13	20	42
Kyle Chapman	45	11	7	18	96
Ahren Nittel	46	6	4	10	56
Ryan Courtney	14	3	7	10	7
Brett Angel	40	2	8	10	165
Matt Maccarone	59	2	7	9	21
Steven Rawski	17	1	8	9	5
Frank Sinacori	44	2	6	8	43
Mike James	14	3	3	6	14
Sal Peralta	28	3	3	6	6
Tyler Eady	15	0	5	5	12
John Scott Dickson	44	3	1	4	24
Dan Growden	10	0	3	3	12
Mark Ridout	27	0	2	2	56
Matt Livingston	38	0	1	1	13
Ryan Aschaber (goalie)	19	0	0	0	4
Mike Leighton (goalie)	54	0	0	0	12

GOALTENDING

	Gms.	Min.	W	L	T	G	SO	Avg.
Mike Leighton	54	3035	32	13	5	138	2	2.73
Ryan Aschaber	19	1043	2	12	3	69	0	3.97

PLAYERS WITH TWO OR MORE TEAMS

SCORING

	Games	G	A	Pts.	PIM
Matthew Albiani, London	17	0	2	2	12
Matthew Albiani, Ottawa	36	6	16	22	20
Totals	53	6	18	24	32
Brett Angel, Mississauga	19	0	2	2	51
Brett Angel, Windsor	40	2	8	10	165
Totals	59	2	10	12	216
Andrew Archer, Oshawa	2	0	0	0	4
Andrew Archer, Guelph	50	0	2	2	59
Totals	52	0	2	2	63
Matt Armstrong, Kitchener	41	9	11	20	58
Matt Armstrong, Peterborough	25	5	6	11	22
Totals	66	14	17	31	80
Matt Bacon, North Bay	23	1	5	6	33
Matt Bacon, Toronto	35	3	6	9	44
Totals	58	4	11	15	77
Chris Berti, Sarnia	25	5	10	15	38
Chris Berti, Erie	19	0	6	6	42
Totals	44	5	16	21	80
Corey Brekelmans, Sarnia	28	2	9	11	32
Corey Brekelmans, Sudbury	29	0	7	7	15
Totals	57	2	16	18	47
Andrew Brown, Guelph	35	2	4	6	20
Andrew Brown, Belleville	25	0	2	2	31
Totals	60	2	6	8	51
Adam Campbell, Sarnia	39	9	16	25	109
Adam Campbell, Guelph	28	0	6	6	52
Totals	67	9	22	31	161
Cory Campbell, Belleville (g)	8	0	0	0	2
Cory Campbell, Guelph (g)	4	0	0	0	0
Cory Campbell, Sarnia (g)	23	0	2	2	8
Totals	35	0	2	2	10
David Chant, Brampton (g)	29	0	2	2	0
David Chant, Barrie (g)	23	0	0	0	2
Totals	52	0	2	2	2
Fraser Clair, Mississauga	14	3	0	3	14
Fraser Clair, Barrie	43	16	14	30	41
Totals	57	19	14	33	55
Matt Coughlin, Mississauga	2	0	0	0	6
Matt Coughlin, Belleville	61	1	10	11	145
Totals	63	1	10	11	151
Ryan Courtney, Windsor	14	3	7	10	7
Ryan Courtney, Mississauga	49	6	16	22	23
Totals	63	9	23	32	30
Brandon Cullen, Oshawa	34	16	14	30	85
Brandon Cullen, Erie	30	7	11	18	71
Totals	64	23	25	48	156
Jason Davies, Barrie	5	0	2	2	2
Jason Davies, London	54	13	11	24	56
Totals	59	13	13	26	58
Lou Dickenson, London	35	12	13	25	23
Lou Dickenson, Kingston	25	4	6	10	10
Totals	60	16	19	35	33
Jeffrey Doyle, Toronto	23	2	10	12	40
Jeffrey Doyle, North Bay	41	16	20	36	76
Totals	64	18	30	48	116
Tyler Eady, Windsor	15	0	5	5	12
Tyler Eady, Mississauga	27	4	6	10	19
Totals	42	4	11	15	31
T.J. Eason, Peterborough	39	0	3	3	64
T.J. Eason, Kitchener	27	0	2	2	30
Totals	66	0	5	5	94
Brian Finley, Barrie (g)	16	0	1	1	0
Brian Finley, Brampton (g)	11	0	0	0	0
Totals	27	0	1	1	0
Ryan Fraser, Oshawa	10	2	0	2	24
Ryan Fraser, Sarnia	17	0	1	1	40
Totals	27	2	1	3	64
Shayne Fryia, Sault Ste. Marie	22	1	6	7	19
Shayne Fryia, Barrie	43	16	9	25	66
Totals	65	17	15	32	85

	Games	G	A	Pts.	PIM
Jimmy Gagnon, Kitchener	41	10	11	21	118
Jimmy Gagnon, Peterborough	25	3	6	9	65
Totals	66	13	17	30	183
Matt Grennier, Brampton	32	4	6	10	13
Matt Grennier, Barrie	30	4	2	6	6
Totals	62	8	8	16	19
Mike Gresdal, Plymouth	30	0	0	0	22
Mike Gresdal, Kitchener	20	1	1	2	29
Totals	50	1	1	2	51
Dan Growden, Windsor	10	0	3	3	12
Dan Growden, Belleville	48	4	10	14	18
Totals	58	4	13	17	30
Tyler Hanchuck, Brampton	34	1	5	6	55
Tyler Hanchuck, Barrie	31	1	6	7	71
Totals	65	2	11	13	126
Jon Hedberg, Guelph	2	1	0	1	4
Jon Hedberg, Oshawa	63	7	22	29	68
Totals	65	8	22	30	72
Ryan Held, Sault Ste. Marie	31	12	16	28	26
Ryan Held, London	28	6	17	23	30
Totals	59	18	33	51	56
Troy Ilijow, Erie	37	3	7	10	71
Troy Ilijow, Sault Ste. Marie	30	2	3	5	31
Totals	67	5	10	15	102
Mike James, Windsor	14	3	3	6	14
Mike James, Mississauga	17	2	2	4	24
Totals	31	5	5	10	38
Dan Jancevski, London	39	4	23	27	95
Dan Jancevski, Sudbury	31	3	14	17	42
Totals	70	7	37	44	137
Jamie Johnson, Sarnia	9	0	5	5	7
Jamie Johnson, Oshawa	56	8	38	46	14
Totals	65	8	43	51	21
Kenny Jung, Erie	28	0	2	2	8
Kenny Jung, Sarnia	30	1	4	5	24
Totals	58	1	6	7	32
Chris Kelly, London	31	21	34	55	46
Chris Kelly, Sudbury	19	5	16	21	17
Totals	50	26	50	76	63
Patrick Lamesse, Erie	30	1	6	7	10
Patrick Lamesse, S. Ste. Marie	30	6	2	8	12
Totals	60	7	8	15	22
Nick Lees, Oshawa	2	1	1	2	0
Nick Lees, Guelph	65	5	4	9	26
Totals	67	6	5	11	26
Josh Legge, North Bay	16	0	4	4	52
Josh Legge, Owen Sound	41	1	5	6	70
Totals	57	1	9	10	122
Jonah Leroux, Oshawa	15	1	1	2	6
Jonah Leroux, Brampton	48	4	7	11	24
Totals	63	5	8	13	30
Sean McMorrow, Mississauga	13	0	0	0	34
Sean McMorrow, Kingston	7	0	1	1	22
Sean McMorrow, London	29	0	3	3	75
Totals	49	0	4	4	131
Chris Minard, Toronto	40	11	8	19	28
Chris Minard, Oshawa	28	12	12	24	18
Totals	68	23	20	43	46
Greg Mizzi, Toronto	8	0	1	1	10
Greg Mizzi, Barrie	34	2	3	5	63
Totals	42	2	4	6	73
Preston Mizzi, Sault Ste. Marie	12	2	6	8	15
Preston Mizzi, Sarnia	25	10	11	21	10
Preston Mizzi, Plymouth	29	15	16	31	49
Totals	66	27	33	60	74
Riley Moher, Erie	39	2	3	5	72
Riley Moher, Sarnia	29	1	5	6	59
Totals	68	3	8	11	131
Steven Morris, Plymouth	10	3	3	6	4
Steven Morris, Barrie	39	5	5	10	16
Totals	49	8	8	16	20

	Games	G	A	Pts.	PIM
Kyle Neufeld, London	27	2	3	5	39
Kyle Neufeld, Sault Ste. Marie	25	4	4	8	27
Totals	52	6	7	13	66
Ryan O'Keefe, Barrie	8	1	4	5	32
Ryan O'Keefe, Plymouth	55	5	16	21	138
Totals	63	6	20	26	170
Nathan O'Nabigon, Plymouth	29	5	3	8	21
Nathan O'Nabigon, Miss.	35	8	8	16	33
Totals	64	13	11	24	54
John Osborne, Sault Ste. Marie	32	12	14	26	37
John Osborne, Owen Sound	18	3	2	5	26
Totals	50	15	16	31	63
Matt Passfield, Barrie	27	5	9	14	30
Matt Passfield, Kitchener	39	15	12	27	33
Totals	66	20	21	41	63
Cory Pecker, Sault Ste. Marie	31	24	16	40	37
Cory Pecker, Erie	30	17	22	39	32
Totals	61	41	38	79	69
Lindsay Plunkett, Oshawa	31	11	9	20	67
Lindsay Plunkett, Toronto	20	8	6	14	27
Totals	51	19	15	34	94
Neill Posillico, Oshawa	2	0	0	0	0
Neill Posillico, Barrie	55	6	5	11	69
Totals	57	6	5	11	69
Ryan Ramsay, Peterborough	36	16	10	26	67
Ryan Ramsay, Kitchener	22	5	18	23	39
Totals	58	21	28	49	106
Steven Rawski, Windsor	17	1	8	9	5
Steven Rawski, Mississauga	43	3	6	9	20
Totals	60	4	14	18	25
T.J. Reynolds, Oshawa	2	0	1	1	5
T.J. Reynolds, Toronto	50	1	3	4	163
Totals	52	1	4	5	168
Mike Rice, Brampton	15	1	4	5	18
Mike Rice, Oshawa	43	12	17	29	32
Totals	58	13	21	34	50
Mark Ridout, Mississauga	6	1	2	3	13
Mark Ridout, Windsor	27	0	2	2	56
Totals	33	1	4	5	69
Scott Rozendal, Erie	38	8	12	20	115
Scott Rozendal, Oshawa	20	12	4	16	53
Totals	58	20	16	36	168
Corey Sabourin, Ottawa	4	0	0	0	2
Corey Sabourin, Kingston	51	1	18	19	35
Totals	55	1	18	19	37
Sebastien Savage, Sudbury	8	1	0	1	11
Sebastien Savage, Ottawa	42	10	10	20	73
Totals	50	11	10	21	84
Pavel Shtefan, Erie	18	4	5	9	6
Pavel Shtefan, Oshawa	23	4	9	13	9
Totals	41	8	14	22	15
Andrew Sim, Sarnia (g)	8	0	0	0	0
Andrew Sim, Mississauga (g)	6	0	0	0	0
Andrew Sim, Guelph (g)	5	0	0	0	0
Totals	19	0	0	0	0
Mike Smith, Kingston (g)	3	0	0	0	0

	Games	G	A	Pts.	PIM
Mike Smith, Sudbury (g)	43	0	3	3	8
Totals	46	0	3	3	8
Jason Spezza, Mississauga	15	7	23	30	11
Jason Spezza, Windsor	41	36	50	86	32
Totals	56	43	73	116	43
Brent Sullivan, Owen Sound	22	8	9	17	29
Brent Sullivan, Barrie	33	2	9	11	35
Totals	55	10	18	28	64
Dan Sullivan, Mississauga	9	1	0	1	4
Dan Sullivan, Owen Sound	43	10	13	23	50
Totals	52	11	13	24	54
Josh Tataryn, Ottawa	24	3	5	8	6
Josh Tataryn, North Bay	40	19	9	28	12
Totals	64	22	14	36	18
Matt Timmins, Kingston	22	0	0	0	17
Matt Timmins, Mississauga	16	0	1	1	15
Totals	38	0	1	1	32
Kyle Wailes, Barrie	21	1	2	3	10
Kyle Wailes, Sault Ste. Marie	39	4	10	14	18
Totals	60	5	12	17	28
Brad Walford, North Bay	8	3	2	5	2
Brad Walford, Oshawa	52	1	12	13	25
Totals	60	4	14	18	27
Dennis Wideman, Sudbury	25	7	11	18	37
Dennis Wideman, London	24	8	8	16	38
Totals	49	15	19	34	75
Chad Wiseman, Mississauga	30	15	29	44	22
Chad Wiseman, Plymouth	32	11	16	27	12
Totals	62	26	45	71	34
Brad Woods, Brampton	14	0	5	5	14
Brad Woods, Oshawa	38	0	5	5	26
Totals	52	0	10	10	40
Bill Zalba, Owen Sound	26	10	13	23	37
Bill Zalba, Peterborough	24	7	8	15	20
Totals	50	17	21	38	57

GOALTENDING

	Games	Min.	W	L	T	G	SO	Avg.
C. Campbell, Bell.	8	415	3	4	0	34	0	4.92
C. Campbell, Gue.	4	240	2	2	0	14	0	3.50
C. Campbell, Sar.	23	1304	14	6	2	62	0	2.85
Totals	45	1959	19	12	2	110	0	3.37
David Chant, Bram.	29	1706	12	13	4	88	1	3.09
David Chant, Bar.	23	1255	10	10	2	64	1	3.06
Totals	52	2961	22	23	6	152	2	3.08
Brian Finley, Bar.	16	818	5	8	0	42	0	3.08
Brian Finley, Bram.	11	631	7	3	1	31	0	2.95
Totals	27	1449	12	11	1	73	0	3.02
Andrew Sim, Sar.	8	327	2	2	0	18	1	3.30
Andrew Sim, Miss.	6	209	0	3	1	19	0	5.45
Andrew Sim, Gue.	5	220	2	2	0	13	0	3.55
Totals	19	756	4	7	1	50	1	3.97
Mike Smith, King.	3	136	0	0	2	8	0	3.53
Mike Smith, Sud.	43	2571	22	13	7	108	3	2.52
Totals	46	2707	22	13	9	116	3	2.57

2001 J. ROSS ROBERTSON CUP PLAYOFFS
RESULTS

CONFERENCE QUARTERFINALS

	W	L	Pts.	GF	GA
Belleville	4	0	8	24	12
Kingston	0	4	0	12	24
(Belleville won series, 4-0)					
Sudbury	4	1	8	15	8
Barrie	1	4	2	8	15
(Subury won series, 4-1)					
Toronto	4	3	8	18	20
Peterborough	3	4	6	20	18
(Toronto won series, 4-3)					

	W	L	Pts.	GF	GA
Ottawa	4	0	8	15	6
North Bay	0	4	0	6	15
(Ottawa won series, 4-0)					
Erie	4	1	8	22	14
London	1	4	2	14	22
(Erie won series, 4-1)					
Plymouth	4	0	8	22	11
Sarnia	0	4	0	11	22
(Plymouth won series, 4-0)					

	W	L	Pts.	GF	GA
Windsor	4	1	8	23	13
Owen Sound	1	4	2	13	23

(Windsor won series, 4-1)

	W	L	Pts.	GF	GA
Brampton	4	0	8	17	5
Guelph	0	4	0	5	17

(Brampton won series, 4-0)

CONFERENCE SEMIFINALS

	W	L	Pts.	GF	GA
Ottawa	4	2	8	30	22
Belleville	2	4	4	22	30

(Ottawa won series, 4-2)

	W	L	Pts.	GF	GA
Toronto	4	3	8	19	25
Sudbury	3	4	6	25	19

(Toronto won series, 4-3)

	W	L	Pts.	GF	GA
Erie	4	1	8	23	12
Brampton	1	4	2	12	23

(Erie won series, 4-1)

	W	L	Pts.	GF	GA
Plymouth	4	0	8	16	10
Windsor	0	4	0	16	10

(Plymouth won series, 4-0)

CONFERENCE FINALS

	W	L	Pts.	GF	GA
Ottawa	4	0	8	15	5
Toronto	0	4	0	5	15

(Ottawa won series, 4-0)

	W	L	Pts.	GF	GA
Plymouth	4	1	8	21	13
Erie	1	4	2	13	21

(Plymouth won series, 4-1)

J. ROSS ROBERTSON CUP FINALS

	W	L	Pts.	GF	GA
Ottawa	4	2	8	19	15
Plymouth	2	4	4	15	19

(Ottawa won series, 4-2)

INDIVIDUAL LEADERS

Goals: Cory Pecker, Erie (14)
Assists: Jonathan Zion, Ottawa (19)
Points: Lance Galbraith, Ottawa (28)
Joe Talbot, Ottawa (28)
Penalty minutes: Kip Brennan, Sudbury (92)
Goaltending average: Mike Smith, Sudbury (2.12)
Shutouts: Seamus Kotyk, Ottawa (3)

TOP SCORERS

	Games	G	A	Pts.
Lance Galbraith, Ottawa	20	13	15	28
Joe Talbot, Ottawa	20	13	15	28
Miguel Delisle, Ottawa	20	8	17	25
Cory Pecker, Erie	15	14	9	23
Brad Boyes, Erie	15	10	13	23
Stephen Weiss, Plymouth	18	7	16	23
Jonathan Zion, Ottawa	20	3	19	22
Tomas Kurka, Plymouth	16	8	13	21
Chad Wiseman, Plymouth	19	12	8	20
Chad Larose, Plymouth	19	10	10	20
Zenon Konopka, Ottawa	20	7	13	20

INDIVIDUAL STATISTICS

BARRIE COLTS

(Lost conference quarterfinals to Sudbury, 4-1)

SCORING

	Games	G	A	Pts.	PIM
Fraser Clair	5	1	2	3	8
Mike Henderson	5	1	2	3	2
Blaine Down	5	2	0	2	10
Matthew Dzieduszycki	5	2	0	2	4
Joey Tenute	5	1	1	2	10
Shayne Fryia	5	0	2	2	8
Eric Reitz	5	1	0	1	21
Tim Branham	3	0	1	1	6
William Wellman	4	0	1	1	7
Ed Hill	5	0	1	1	2
Aaron Power	5	0	1	1	8
Jordan Brenner	1	0	0	0	0
Mike D'Alessandro (goalie)	1	0	0	0	2
Neill Posillico	1	0	0	0	0
Bryan Hayes	2	0	0	0	0
Greg Mizzi	4	0	0	0	4
Frantisek Bakrlik	5	0	0	0	10
Alex Butkus	5	0	0	0	0
David Chant (goalie)	5	0	0	0	0
Matt Grennier	5	0	0	0	6
Tyler Hanchuck	5	0	0	0	26
Rick Hwodeky	5	0	0	0	4
Jan Platil	5	0	0	0	12

GOALTENDING

	Gms.	Min.	W	L	T	G	SO	Avg.
David Chant	5	272	1	4	0	12	0	2.65
Mike D'Alessandro	1	27	0	0	0	3	0	6.67

BELLEVILLE BULLS

(Lost conference semifinals to Ottawa, 4-2)

SCORING

	Games	G	A	Pts.	PIM
Kyle Wellwood	10	3	16	19	4
Mike Renzi	10	8	8	16	12
Branko Radivojevic	10	6	10	16	18
Nathan Robinson	10	6	10	16	7
Randy Rowe	10	9	6	15	6
Andre Deveaux	10	3	6	9	6
Nick Policelli	10	2	5	7	28
Matthew Stajan	7	1	6	7	5
Michael Jacobsen	10	2	4	6	4
Malcolm Hutt	10	2	3	5	10
David Cornacchia	10	1	3	4	26
Matt Coughlin	8	1	1	2	17
Adam Paiement	9	1	1	2	8
Cody McCormick	10	1	1	2	23
David Silverstone	10	0	2	2	21
Dan Growden	10	0	1	1	2
Alex White	10	0	1	1	2
Paulo Colaiacovo (goalie)	2	0	0	0	0
Rob Dmytruk	2	0	0	0	2
Brad Efthimiou	5	0	0	0	0
Andrew Brown	9	0	0	0	2
Jan Chovan (goalie)	10	0	0	0	0

GOALTENDING

	Gms.	Min.	W	L	T	G	SO	Avg.
Jan Chovan	10	618	6	4	0	38	0	3.69
Paulo Colaiacovo	2	22	0	0	0	4	0	10.91

BRAMPTON BATTALION
(Lost conference semifinals to Erie, 4-1)

SCORING

	Games	G	A	Pts.	PIM
Jeff Bateman	9	5	7	12	18
Raffi Torres	8	7	4	11	19
Rostislav Klesla	9	2	9	11	26
Aaron Van Leusen	9	3	4	7	4
Lukas Havel	9	1	6	7	15
Jay McClement	9	4	2	6	10
Jason Maleyko	9	2	3	5	10
Kurt MacSweyn	9	1	4	5	20
Scott Thompson	9	0	4	4	6
Paul Flache	9	1	1	2	18
Jay Harrison	9	1	1	2	17
Ryan Bowness	9	0	2	2	9
Corey LeClair	9	1	0	1	2
Chris Rowan	9	1	0	1	11
Jonah Leroux	9	0	1	1	6
Brad Topping (goalie)	2	0	0	0	0
Travis Parent	4	0	0	0	0
Alex MacDonell	6	0	0	0	4
Chris Clayton	9	0	0	0	0
Brian Finley (goalie)	9	0	0	0	0
Adam Henrich	9	0	0	0	6

GOALTENDING

	Gms.	Min.	W	L	T	G	SO	Avg.
Brian Finley	9	503	5	4	0	26	1	3.10
Brad Topping	2	36	0	0	0	2	0	3.33

ERIE OTTERS
(Lost conference finals to Plymouth, 4-1)

SCORING

	Games	G	A	Pts.	PIM
Cory Pecker	15	14	9	23	16
Brad Boyes	15	10	13	23	8
Nikita Alexeev	12	7	7	14	12
Jason Baird	14	4	8	12	47
Carlo Colaiacovo	14	4	7	11	16
Joe Guenther	15	2	9	11	12
Brad Yeo	15	4	4	8	59
Chris Berti	15	3	5	8	33
Darren McMillan	15	0	8	8	10
Sean Dixon	15	1	6	7	4
Mike Nelson	15	4	2	6	18
Brandon Cullen	13	1	4	5	30
Derrick Byfuglien	15	3	1	4	29
J.F. Perras (goalie)	9	0	2	2	0
Mike McKeown	15	1	0	1	8
Scott Dobben	15	0	1	1	10
Brian Lee	9	0	0	0	4
Adam Munro (goalie)	10	0	0	0	0
Bobby John Byfuglien	13	0	0	0	2
Chris Campoli	15	0	0	0	4
Joey Sullivan	15	0	0	0	6

GOALTENDING

	Gms.	Min.	W	L	T	G	SO	Avg.
J.F. Perras	9	390	3	4	0	19	0	2.92
Adam Munro	10	509	6	2	0	27	1	3.18

GUELPH STORM
(Lost conference quarterfinals to Brampton, 4-0)

SCORING

	Games	G	A	Pts.	PIM
Daniel Paille	4	2	0	2	2
Brian Passmore	4	1	1	2	9
Charlie Stephens	4	0	2	2	2
Frank Burgio	4	1	0	1	6
Peter Flache	4	1	0	1	0
Adam Campbell	4	0	1	1	4
Steve Chabbert	4	0	1	1	2
Derek Hennessey	4	0	1	1	2

	Games	G	A	Pts.	PIM
Colt King	4	0	1	1	8
Morgan McCormick	4	0	1	1	6
Kevin Dallman	1	0	0	0	0
Ben Pilon	1	0	0	0	0
Dan McNeill	2	0	0	0	0
Craig Andersson (goalie)	4	0	0	0	0
Andrew Archer	4	0	0	0	4
Dustin Brown	4	0	0	0	10
Brent Kelly	4	0	0	0	0
Nick Lees	4	0	0	0	0
Martin St. Pierre	4	0	0	0	4
Ryan Thompson	4	0	0	0	4
Niko Tuomi	4	0	0	0	2

GOALTENDING

	Gms.	Min.	W	L	T	G	SO	Avg.
Craig Andersson	4	240	0	4	0	17	0	4.25

KINGSTON FRONTENACS
(Lost conference quarterfinals to Belleville, 4-0)

SCORING

	Games	G	A	Pts.	PIM
Andrew Ianiero	4	3	3	6	4
Travis Lisabeth	4	2	4	6	6
Derek Campbell	4	1	2	3	8
Eric Braff	4	0	3	3	0
Tomas Skvaridlo	4	2	0	2	6
Cory Stillman	4	2	0	2	0
Doug MacIver	4	0	2	2	4
Brett Clouthier	4	1	0	1	10
Lou Dickenson	4	1	0	1	4
Peter Hamerlik (goalie)	3	0	1	1	0
Shane O'Brien	4	0	1	1	6
Corey Sabourin	4	0	1	1	2
Nathan Tennant	4	0	1	1	2
Chris Cook	3	0	0	0	0
Glen Ridler (goalie)	3	0	0	0	0
Brad Horan	4	0	0	0	0
Sean Langdon	4	0	0	0	2
Justin McCutcheon	4	0	0	0	5
Darryl Thomson	4	0	0	0	11
Brody Todd	4	0	0	0	0

GOALTENDING

	Gms.	Min.	W	L	T	G	SO	Avg.
Glen Ridler	3	146	0	2	0	10	0	4.11
Peter Hamerlik	3	131	0	2	0	13	0	5.95

LONDON KNIGHTS
(Lost conference quarterfinals to Erie, 4-1)

SCORING

	Games	G	A	Pts.	PIM
Ryan Held	5	4	5	9	2
Rick Nash	4	3	3	6	8
Dennis Wideman	5	0	4	4	6
Jason Davies	5	3	0	3	0
Daniel Bois	5	2	1	3	19
Andy Burnham	4	1	1	2	17
Mike Stathopulos	5	1	1	2	0
John Eminger	5	0	2	2	10
Aaron Lobb	5	0	2	2	12
Ian Turner	5	0	2	2	10
Logan Hunter	5	0	1	1	12
Joel Scherban	5	0	1	1	0
Chris Lawrence (goalie)	1	0	0	0	0
Petr Hemsky	2	0	0	0	0
Josh Chambers	3	0	0	0	0
Brent Varty	3	0	0	0	0
Mike Clarke	4	0	0	0	2
Matt Junkins	5	0	0	0	4
Sean McMorrow	5	0	0	0	0
Aaron Molnar (goalie)	5	0	0	0	0
Bovan Seljan	5	0	0	0	4
Bobby Turner	5	0	0	0	15

GOALTENDING

	Gms.	Min.	W	L	T	G	SO	Avg.
Aaron Molnar	5	285	1	4	0	19	0	4.00
Chris Lawrence	1	14	0	0	0	3	0	12.86

NORTH BAY CENTENNIALS
(Lost conference quarterfinals to Ottawa, 4-0)

SCORING

	Games	G	A	Pts.	PIM
Chris Eade	4	1	2	3	4
Ryan Armstrong	4	2	0	2	10
Jeffrey Doyle	4	1	1	2	8
Josh Tataryn	4	1	1	2	2
George Halkidis	4	1	0	1	4
Scott Cameron	4	0	1	1	2
Peter Reynolds	4	0	1	1	7
Chris Thorburn	4	0	1	1	9
Igor Valeev	4	0	1	1	22
Nick Vernelli	4	0	1	1	2
Ryan McGregor	2	0	0	0	4
Adam Gibson	3	0	0	0	0
Kevin Hurley	3	0	0	0	0
Alex Auld (goalie)	4	0	0	0	0
Craig Foster	4	0	0	0	2
Brad Pierce	4	0	0	0	2
Vladimir Sapozhnikov	4	0	0	0	2
Peter Veltman	4	0	0	0	7
Kyle Werner	4	0	0	0	2
Kevin Werner	4	0	0	0	4

GOALTENDING

	Gms.	Min.	W	L	T	G	SO	Avg.
Alex Auld	4	240	0	4	0	15	0	3.75

OTTAWA 67'S
(Winner of 2001 J. Ross Robertson Cup)

SCORING

	Games	G	A	Pts.	PIM
Lance Galbraith	20	13	15	28	74
Joe Talbot	20	13	15	28	6
Miguel Delisle	20	8	17	25	30
Jonathan Zion	20	3	19	22	18
Zenon Konopka	20	7	13	20	47
Vadim Sozinov	20	7	8	15	4
Luke Sellars	18	4	10	14	47
Brendan Bell	20	1	11	12	22
Rodney Bauman	17	4	6	10	4
Matthew Albiani	20	3	5	8	8
Adam Chapman	20	3	4	7	10
Jeremy Van Hoof	20	3	4	7	27
Russ Moyer	19	3	3	6	6
Sebastien Savage	20	3	3	6	41
Bryan Rodney	20	1	4	5	20
Carter Trevisani	20	1	4	5	26
Sean Scully	20	2	1	3	0
Pierre Mitsou	6	0	2	2	4
Brett McGrath	20	0	2	2	2
John Ceci (goalie)	3	0	0	0	0
Seamus Kotyk (goalie)	20	0	0	0	8

GOALTENDING

	Gms.	Min.	W	L	T	G	SO	Avg.
Seamus Kotyk	20	1157	16	4	0	46	3	2.39
John Ceci	3	44	0	0	0	2	0	2.73

OWEN SOUND ATTACK
(Lost conference quarterfinals to Windsor, 4-1)

SCORING

	Games	G	A	Pts.	PIM
Joel Ward	5	2	4	6	4
Bryan Kazarian	5	3	1	4	26
Shawn Snider	5	2	2	4	8
Kyle McAllister	5	1	3	4	4
Trevor Blanchard	5	1	2	3	14

	Games	G	A	Pts.	PIM
Ryan Sharp	3	1	1	2	2
Dan Sullivan	4	1	1	2	11
Mike Barrett	5	1	1	2	4
John Osborne	4	1	0	1	4
Daniel Sisca	2	0	1	1	2
Luc Chaisson	4	0	1	1	2
Greg Jacina	4	0	1	1	15
Agris Saviels	5	0	1	1	2
Brandon Verner	5	0	1	1	6
Nick Vukovic	5	0	1	1	8
Justin Day (goalie)	2	0	0	0	0
Richard Colwill	3	0	0	0	6
Justin Hodgins	4	0	0	0	0
Josh Legge	4	0	0	0	16
Dene Poulin	5	0	0	0	2
Richard Power	5	0	0	0	0
Corey Roberts (goalie)	5	0	0	0	6

GOALTENDING

	Gms.	Min.	W	L	T	G	SO	Avg.
Corey Roberts	5	253	1	3	0	19	0	4.51
Justin Day	2	46	0	1	0	4	0	5.22

PETERBOROUGH PETES
(Lost conference quarterfinals to Toronto, 4-3)

SCORING

	Games	G	A	Pts.	PIM
Brad Self	7	6	3	9	8
Eric Staal	7	2	5	7	4
Marcel Rodman	7	4	2	6	2
Lukas Krajicek	7	0	5	5	0
Matt Armstrong	7	3	1	4	15
Jamie Chamberlain	7	1	2	3	8
Matt Carkner	7	0	3	3	25
Dustin Wood	7	0	3	3	11
John Brioux	7	1	1	2	13
Kurtis Foster	7	1	1	2	10
Matt Herneisen	7	1	1	2	20
Stephen Hoar	7	0	2	2	0
Greg Chambers	5	1	0	1	0
Bill Zalba	5	0	1	1	4
Jimmy Gagnon	7	0	1	1	15
Jon Howse	7	0	1	1	0
Joey MacDonald (goalie)	7	0	1	1	2
Dan Buccella	2	0	0	0	9
Josh Patterson	2	0	0	0	0
Ryan Card	7	0	0	0	0
Adam Elzinga	7	0	0	0	2

GOALTENDING

	Gms.	Min.	W	L	T	G	SO	Avg.
Joey MacDonald	7	425	3	4	0	18	0	2.54

PLYMOUTH WHALERS
(Lost finals to Ottawa, 4-2)

SCORING

	Games	G	A	Pts.	PIM
Stephen Weiss	18	7	16	23	10
Tomas Kurka	16	8	13	21	13
Chad Wiseman	19	12	8	20	22
Chad Larose	19	10	10	20	22
Cole Jarrett	19	6	12	18	29
Damian Surma	19	8	9	17	25
Kristopher Vernarsky	19	7	10	17	19
James Wisniewski	19	3	10	13	34
Karl Stewart	19	3	4	7	14
Stacey Britstone	15	1	6	7	18
Preston Mizzi	19	4	2	6	22
George Nistas	16	3	3	6	6
Libor Ustrnul	19	1	4	5	19
Jared Newman	6	0	3	3	26
Rob McBride	16	1	1	2	11
Bryan Thompson	14	1	0	1	11
Nate Kiser	13	0	1	1	26

	Games	G	A	Pts.	PIM
Ryan O'Keefe	19	0	1	1	26
Andre Robichaud	19	0	1	1	6
Paul Drew (goalie)	1	0	0	0	0
James Ramsay	9	0	0	0	0
Gregory Campbell	10	0	0	0	7
Rob Zepp (goalie)	19	0	0	0	4

GOALTENDING

	Gms.	Min.	W	L	T	G	SO	Avg.
Paul Drew	1	0	0	0	0	0	0	0.00
Rob Zepp	19	1139	14	5	0	51	2	2.69

SARNIA STING
(Lost conference quarterfinals to Plymouth, 4-0)

SCORING

	Games	G	A	Pts.	PIM
Dusty Jamieson	4	4	4	8	0
Eric Himelfarb	4	1	7	8	4
Alexander Buturlin	4	3	1	4	0
Kris Newbury	4	1	3	4	20
Maxim Rybin	4	0	3	3	2
Robb Palahnuk	4	2	0	2	9
Ryan Fraser	4	0	1	1	2
Scott Heffernan	4	0	1	1	0
Ryan Chapman	1	0	0	0	0
Chandon Hill	1	0	0	0	0
Brad Beloungea	2	0	0	0	2
Cory Campbell (goalie)	2	0	0	0	0
Tyler Coleman	4	0	0	0	0
Mike Craigen	4	0	0	0	11
Robert Gherson (goalie)	4	0	0	0	0
Julius Halfkenny	4	0	0	0	9
Ryan Hare	4	0	0	0	6
John Hecimovic	4	0	0	0	5
Kenny Jung	4	0	0	0	2
Jeff Luckovitch	4	0	0	0	12
Riley Moher	4	0	0	0	4
Reg Thomas	4	0	0	0	13

GOALTENDING

	Gms.	Min.	W	L	T	G	SO	Avg.
Roberg Gherson	4	158	0	2	0	9	0	3.42
Cory Campbell	2	81	0	2	0	10	0	7.41

SUDBURY WOLVES
(Lost conference semifinals to Toronto, 4-3)

SCORING

	Games	G	A	Pts.	PIM
Jason Jaspers	12	3	16	19	18
Alexei Semenov	12	4	13	17	17
Chris Kelly	12	11	5	16	14
Derek MacKenzie	12	6	8	14	16
Kip Brennan	12	5	6	11	92
Fedor Fedorov	12	4	6	10	36
Dan Jancevski	12	0	9	9	17
T.J. Warkus	12	2	4	6	4
Mike Vaillaincourt	12	2	0	2	6
Josh Gratton	9	1	1	2	25
Steven Ellis	12	1	1	2	2
Chad Starling	12	1	1	2	29
Corey Brekelmans	12	0	2	2	14
Jerry Connell	12	0	1	1	27
Drew Kivell	12	0	1	1	6
Tom Kotsopoulos	12	0	1	1	31
Jason Hicks	3	0	0	0	4
Walter Prawdzik	7	0	0	0	7
Adam Keefe	8	0	0	0	2
Ladislav Reznicek	9	0	0	0	0
Mike Smith (goalie)	12	0	0	0	2

GOALTENDING

	Gms.	Min.	W	L	T	G	SO	Avg.
Mike Smith	12	735	7	5	0	26	2	2.12

TORONTO ST. MICHAEL'S MAJORS
(Lost conference finals to Ottawa, 4-0)

SCORING

	Games	G	A	Pts.	PIM
Frank Lukes	18	4	9	13	12
Matt Ellis	18	4	8	12	6
Lindsay Plunkett	13	7	4	11	27
Michael Gough	18	4	7	11	45
Matt Bannan	18	5	5	10	14
Ryan Walsh	18	5	5	10	14
Tim Brent	18	2	8	10	6
Mark Popovic	18	3	5	8	22
Lorne Misita	18	2	5	7	25
Kevin Klein	18	0	5	5	17
Darryl Bootland	11	3	1	4	20
Drew Fata	18	1	3	4	26
Tyler Cook	18	0	3	3	16
T.J. Reynolds	18	0	3	3	70
Adam DeLeeuw	18	1	1	2	21
Steve Farquharson	18	1	0	1	48
Matt Bacon	15	0	1	1	15
Chris Boucher	18	0	1	1	25
Andy Chiodo (goalie)	9	0	0	0	0
Ryan Robert	10	0	0	0	0
Peter Budaj (goalie)	11	0	0	0	0

GOALTENDING

	Gms.	Min.	W	L	T	G	SO	Avg.
Peter Budaj	11	621	6	4	0	26	1	2.51
Andy Chiodo	9	479	2	6	0	30	0	3.76

WINDSOR SPITFIRES
(Lost conference semifinals to Plymouth, 4-0)

SCORING

	Games	G	A	Pts.	PIM
Steve Ott	9	3	8	11	27
Jason Spezza	9	4	5	9	10
Steve Hildenbrand	9	3	6	9	21
Craig Kennedy	9	1	8	9	11
Shawn Mather	9	7	1	8	4
Kyle Chapman	9	5	3	8	15
John Scott Dickson	9	3	4	7	2
Ahren Nittel	7	3	1	4	16
David Bowman	9	1	2	3	10
Tim Gleason	9	1	2	3	23
Robin Boucher	8	0	3	3	0
Timo Helbling	7	0	2	2	11
Craig Mahon	7	0	2	2	9
Frank Sinacori	7	1	0	1	2
Matt Maccarone	8	1	0	1	2
Rob Hennigar	5	0	1	1	4
Matt Livingston	6	0	1	1	6
Ryan Aschaber (goalie)	2	0	0	0	0
Brett Angel	4	0	0	0	2
Sal Peralta	8	0	0	0	0
Mike Leighton (goalie)	9	0	0	0	4
Mark Ridout	9	0	0	0	17

GOALTENDING

	Gms.	Min.	W	L	T	G	SO	Avg.
Ryan Aschaber	2	20	0	0	0	1	0	3.00
Mike Leighton	9	519	4	5	0	27	1	3.12

ALL-STAR TEAMS

First team	Pos.	Second team
Craig Andersson, Guelph	G	Rob Zepp, Plymouth
Rostislav Klesla, Brandon	D	Kevin Dallman, Guelph
Alexei Semenov, Sudbury	D	Jon Zion, Ottawa
Randy Rowe, Belleville	LW	Raffi Torres, Brampton
Kyle Wellwood, Belleville	C	Brad Boyes, Erie
Branko Radivojevic, Bel.	RW	Cory Pecker, Erie

TROPHY WINNERS

Red Tilson Trophy: Brad Boyes, Erie
Eddie Powers Memorial Trophy: Kyle Wellwood, Belleville
Dave Pinkney Trophy: Rob Zepp, Plymouth
                            Paul Drew, Plymouth
Max Kaminsky Trophy: Alexei Semenov, Sudbury
William Hanley Trophy: Brad Boyes, Erie
Emms Family Award: Rick Nash, London
Matt Leyden Trophy: Dave MacQueen, Erie
Jim Mahon Memorial Trophy: Branko Radivojevic, Belleville
F.W. Dinty Moore Trophy: Andy Chiodo, Toronto
Leo Lalonde Memorial Trophy: Randy Rowe, Belleville
Hamilton Spectator Trophy: Erie Otters
J. Ross Robertson Cup: Ottawa 67's

ALL-TIME AWARD WINNERS

RED TILSON TROPHY
(Outstanding player)

Season	Player, Team
1944-45	Doug McMurdy, St. Catharines
1945-46	Tod Sloan, St. Michael's
1946-47	Ed Sanford, St. Michael's
1947-48	George Armstrong, Stratford
1948-49	Gil Mayer, Barrie
1949-50	George Armstrong, Marlboros
1950-51	Glenn Hall, Windsor
1951-52	Bill Harrington, Kitchener
1952-53	Bob Attersley, Oshawa
1953-54	Brian Cullen, St. Catharines
1954-55	Hank Ciesla, St. Catharines
1955-56	Ron Howell, Guelph
1956-57	Frank Mahovlich, St. Michael's
1957-58	Murray Oliver, Hamilton
1958-59	Stan Mikita, St. Catharines
1959-60	Wayne Connelly, Peterborough
1960-61	Rod Gilbert, Guelph
1961-62	Pit Martin, Hamilton
1962-63	Wayne Maxner, Niagara Falls
1963-64	Yvan Cournoyer, Montreal
1964-65	Andre Lacroix, Peterborough
1965-66	Andre Lacroix, Peterborough
1966-67	Mickey Redmond, Peterborough
1967-68	Walt Tkaczuk, Kitchener
1968-69	Rejean Houle, Montreal
1969-70	Gilbert Perreault, Montreal
1970-71	Dave Gardner, Marlboros
1971-72	Don Lever, Niagara Falls
1972-73	Rick Middleton, Oshawa
1973-74	Jack Valiquette, Sault Ste. Marie
1974-75	Dennis Maruk, London
1975-76	Peter Lee, Ottawa
1976-77	Dale McCourt, St. Catharines
1977-78	Bobby Smith, Ottawa
1978-79	Mike Foligno, Sudbury
1979-80	Jim Fox, Ottawa
1980-81	Ernie Godden, Windsor
1981-82	Dave Simpson, London
1982-83	Doug Gilmour, Cornwall
1983-84	John Tucker, Kitchener
1984-85	Wayne Groulx, Sault Ste. Marie
1985-86	Ray Sheppard, Cornwall
1986-87	Scott McCrory, Oshawa
1987-88	Andrew Cassels, Ottawa
1988-89	Bryan Fogarty, Niagara Falls
1989-90	Mike Ricci, Peterborough
1990-91	Eric Lindros, Oshawa
1991-92	Todd Simon, Niagara Falls

Season	Player, Team
1992-93	Pat Peake, Detroit
1993-94	Jason Allison, London
1994-95	David Ling, Kingston
1995-96	Alyn McCauley, Ottawa
1996-97	Alyn McCauley, Ottawa
1997-98	David Legwand, Plymouth
1998-99	Brian Campbell, Ottawa
1999-00	Andrew Raycroft, Kingston
2000-01	Brad Boyes, Erie

EDDIE POWERS MEMORIAL TROPHY
(Scoring champion)

Season	Player, Team
1933-34	J. Groboski, Oshawa
1934-35	J. Good, Toronto Lions
1935-36	John O'Flaherty, West Toronto
1936-37	Billy Taylor, Oshawa
1937-38	Hank Goldup, Tor. Marlboros
1938-39	Billy Taylor, Oshawa
1939-40	Jud McAtee, Oshawa
1940-41	Gaye Stewart, Tor. Marlboros
1941-42	Bob Wiest, Brantford
1942-43	Norman ``Red'' Tilson, Oshawa
1943-44	Ken Smith, Oshawa
1944-45	Leo Gravelle, St. Michael's
1945-46	Tod Sloan, St. Michael's
1946-47	Fleming Mackell, St. Michael's
1947-48	George Armstrong, Stratford
1940-49	Bert Giesebrecht, Windsor
1949-50	Earl Reibel, Windsor
1950-51	Lou Jankowski, Oshawa
1951-52	Ken Laufman, Guelph
1952-53	Jim McBurney, Galt
1953-54	Brian Cullen, St. Catharines
1954-55	Hank Ciesla, St. Catharines
1955-56	Stan Baliuk, Kitchener
1956-57	Bill Sweeney, Guelph
1957-58	John McKenzie, St. Catharines
1958-59	Stan Mikita, St. Catharines
1959-60	Chico Maki, St. Catharines
1960-61	Rod Gilbert, Guelph
1961-62	Andre Boudrias, Montreal
1962-63	Wayne Maxner, Niagara Falls
1963-64	Andre Boudrias, Montreal
1964-65	Ken Hodge, St. Catharines
1965-66	Andre Lacroix, Peterborough
1966-67	Derek Sanderson, Niagara Falls
1967-68	Tom Webster, Niagara Falls
1968-69	Rejean Houle, Montreal
1969-70	Marcel Dionne, St. Catharines
1970-71	Marcel Dionne, St. Catharines

Season	Player, Team
1971-72	Bill Harris, Toronto
1972-73	Blake Dunlop, Ottawa
1973-74	Jack Valiquette, Sault Ste. Marie
	Rick Adduono, St. Catharines
1974-75	Bruce Boudreau, Toronto
1975-76	Mike Kaszycki, Sault Ste. Marie
1976-77	Dwight Foster, Kitchener
1977-78	Bobby Smith, Ottawa
1978-79	Mike Foligno, Sudbury
1979-80	Jim Fox, Ottawa
1980-81	John Goodwin, Sault Ste. Marie
1981-82	Dave Simpson, London
1982-83	Doug Gilmour, Cornwall
1983-84	Tim Salmon, Kingston
1984-85	Dave MacLean, Belleville
1985-86	Ray Sheppard, Cornwall
1986-87	Scott McCrory, Oshawa
1987-88	Andrew Cassels, Ottawa
1988-89	Bryan Fogarty, Niagara Falls
1989-90	Keith Primeau, Niagara Falls
1990-91	Eric Lindros, Oshawa
1991-92	Todd Simon, Niagara Falls
1992-93	Andrew Brunette, Owen Sound
1993-94	Jason Allison, London
1994-95	Marc Savard, Oshawa
1995-96	Aaron Brand, Sarnia
1996-97	Marc Savard, Oshawa
1997-98	Peter Sarno, Windsor
1998-99	Peter Sarno, Sarnia
1999-00	Sheldon Keefe, Barrie
2000-01	Kyle Wellwood, Belleville

DAVE PINKNEY TROPHY
(Top team goaltending)

Season	Player, Team
1948-49	Gil Mayer, Barrie
1949-50	Don Lockhart, Marlboros
1950-51	Don Lockhart, Marlboros
	Lorne Howes, Barrie
1951-52	Don Head, Marlboros
1952-53	John Henderson, Marlboros
1953-54	Dennis Riggin, Hamilton
1954-55	John Albani, Marlboros
1955-56	Jim Crockett, Marlboros
1956-57	Len Broderick, Marlboros
1957-58	Len Broderick, Marlboros
1958-59	Jacques Caron, Peterborough
1959-60	Gerry Cheevers, St. Michael's
1960-61	Bud Blom, Hamilton
1961-62	George Holmes, Montreal
1962-63	Chuck Goddard, Peterborough
1963-64	Bernie Parent, Niagara Falls
1964-65	Bernie Parent, Niagara Falls
1965-66	Ted Quimet, Montreal
1966-67	Peter MacDuffe, St. Catharines
1967-68	Bruce Mullet, Montreal
1968-69	Wayne Wood, Montreal
1969-70	John Garrett, Peterborough
1970-71	John Garrett, Peterborough
1971-72	Michel Larocque, Ottawa
1972-73	Mike Palmateer, Toronto
1973-74	Don Edwards, Kitchener
1974-75	Greg Millen, Peterborough
1975-76	Jim Bedard, Sudbury
1976-77	Pat Riggin, London
1977-78	Al Jensen, Hamilton
1978-79	Nick Ricci, Niagara Falls
1979-80	Rick LaFerriere, Peterborough
1980-81	Jim Ralph, Ottawa
1981-82	Marc D'Amour, Sault Ste. Marie
1982-83	Peter Sidorkiewicz, Oshawa
	Jeff Hogg, Oshawa

Season	Player, Team
1983-84	Darren Pang, Ottawa
	Greg Coram, Ottawa
1984-85	Scott Mosey, Sault Ste. Marie
	Marty Abrams, Sault Ste. Marie
1985-86	Kay Whitmore, Peterborough
	Ron Tugnutt, Peterborough
1986-87	Sean Evoy, Oshawa
	Jeff Hackett, Oshawa
1987-88	Todd Bojcun, Peterborough
	John Tanner, Peterborough
1988-89	Todd Bojcun, Peterborough
	John Tanner, Peterborough
1989-90	Jeff Wilson, Peterborough
	Sean Gauthier, Kingston
1990-91	Kevin Hodson, Sault Ste. Marie
	Mike Lenarduzzi, Sault Ste. Marie
1991-92	Kevin Hodson, Sault Ste. Marie
1992-93	Chad Lang, Peterborough
	Ryan Douglas, Peterborough
1993-94	Sandy Allan, North Bay
	Scott Roche, North Bay
1994-95	Andy Adams, Guelph
	Mark McArthur, Guelph
1995-96	Dan Cloutier, Guelph
	Brett Thompson, Guelph
1996-97	Craig Hillier, Ottawa
	Tim Keyes, Ottawa
1997-98	Craig Hillier, Ottawa
	Seamus Kotyk, Ottawa
1998-99	Robert Holsinger, Plymouth
	Rob Zepp, Plymouth
1999-00	Bill Ruggiero, Plymouth
	Rob Zepp, Plymouth
2000-01	Rob Zepp, Plymouth
	Paul Drew, Plymouth

MAX KAMINSKY TROPHY
(Outstanding defenseman)

Season	Player, Team
1969-70	Ron Plumb, Peterborough
1970-71	Jocelyn Guevremont, Montreal
1971-72	Denis Potvin, Ottawa
1972-73	Denis Potvin, Ottawa
1973-74	Jim Turkiewicz, Peterborough
1974-75	Mike O'Connell, Kingston
1975-76	Rick Green, London
1976-77	Craig Hartsburg, S. Ste. Marie
1977-78	Brad Marsh, London
	Rob Ramage, London
1978-79	Greg Theberge, Peterborough
1979-80	Larry Murphy, Peterborough
1980-81	Steve Smith, Sault Ste. Marie
1981-82	Ron Meighan, Niagara Falls
1982-83	Allan MacInnis, Kitchener
1983-84	Brad Shaw, Ottawa
1984-85	Bob Halkidis, London
1985-86	Terry Carkner, Peterborough
	Jeff Brown, Sudbury
1986-87	Kerry Huffman, Guelph
1987-88	Darryl Shannon, Windsor
1988-89	Bryan Fogarty, Niagara Falls
1989-90	John Slaney, Cornwall
1990-91	Chris Snell, Ottawa
1991-92	Drake Berehowsky, North Bay
1992-93	Chris Pronger, Peterborough
1993-94	Jamie Rivers, Sudbury
1994-95	Bryan Berard, Detroit
1995-96	Bryan Berard, Detroit
1996-97	Sean Blanchard, Ottawa
1997-98	Chris Allen, Kingston
1998-99	Brian Campbell, Ottawa
1999-00	John Erskine, London
2000-01	Alexei Semenov, Sudbury

WILLIAM HANLEY TROPHY
(Most gentlemanly)

Season	Player, Team
1960-61	Bruce Draper, St. Michael's
1961-62	Lowell MacDonald, Hamilton
1962-63	Paul Henderson, Hamilton
1963-64	Fred Stanfield, St. Catharines
1964-65	Jimmy Peters, Hamilton
1965-66	Andre Lacroix, Peterborough
1966-67	Mickey Redmond, Peterborough
1967-68	Tom Webster, Niagara Falls
1968-69	Rejean Houle, Montreal
1969-74	No award presented
1974-75	Doug Jarvis, Peterborough
1975-76	Dale McCourt, Hamilton
1976-77	Dale McCourt, St. Catharines
1977-78	Wayne Gretzky, S.S. Marie
1978-79	Sean Simpson, Ottawa
1979-80	Sean Simpson, Ottawa
1980-81	John Goodwin, Sault Ste. Marie
1981-82	Dave Simpson, London
1982-83	Kirk Muller, Guelph
1983-84	Kevin Conway, Kingston
1984-85	Scott Tottle, Peterborough
1985-86	Jason Lafreniere, Belleville
1986-87	Scott McCrory, Oshawa
	Keith Gretzky, Hamilton
1987-88	Andrew Cassels, Ottawa
1988-89	Kevin Miehm, Oshawa
1989-90	Mike Ricci, Peterborough
1990-91	Dale Craigwell, Oshawa
1991-92	John Spoltore, North Bay
1992-93	Pat Peake, Detroit
1993-94	Jason Allison, London
1994-95	Vitali Yachmenev, North Bay
1995-96	Jeff Williams, Guelph
1996-97	Alyn McCauley, Ottawa
1997-98	Matt Bradley, Kingston
1998-99	Brian Campbell, Ottawa
1999-00	Mike Zigomanis, Kingston
2000-01	Brad Boyes, Erie

EMMS FAMILY AWARD
(Rookie of the year)

Season	Player, Team
1972-73	Dennis Maruk, London
1973-74	Jack Valiquette, Sault Ste. Marie
1974-75	Danny Shearer, Hamilton
1975-76	John Travella, Sault Ste. Marie
1976-77	Yvan Joly, Ottawa
1977-78	Wayne Gretzky, S.S. Marie
1978-79	John Goodwin, Sault Ste. Marie
1979-80	Bruce Dowie, Toronto
1980-81	Tony Tanti, Oshawa
1981-82	Pat Verbeek, Sudbury
1982-83	Bruce Cassidy, Ottawa
1983-84	Shawn Burr, Kitchener
1984-85	Derek King, Sault Ste. Marie
1985-86	Lonnie Loach, Guelph
1986-87	Andrew Cassels, Ottawa
1987-88	Rick Corriveau, London
1988-89	Owen Nolan, Cornwall
1989-90	Chris Longo, Peterborough
1990-91	Cory Stillman, Windsor
1991-92	Chris Gratton, Kingston
1992-93	Jeff O'Neill, Guelph
1993-94	Vitali Yachmenev, North Bay
1994-95	Bryan Berard, Detroit
1995-96	Joe Thornton, Sault Ste. Marie
1996-97	Peter Sarno, Windsor
1997-98	David Legwand, Plymouth
1998-99	Sheldon Keefe, Barrie
1999-00	Derek Roy, Kitchener
2000-01	Rick Nash, London

MATT LEYDEN TROPHY
(Coach of the year)

Season	Coach, Team
1971-72	Gus Bodnar, Oshawa
1972-73	George Armstrong, Toronto
1973-74	Jack Bownass, Kingston
1974-75	Bert Templeton, Hamilton
1975-76	Jerry Toppazzini, Sudbury
1976-77	Bill Long, London
1977-78	Bill White, Oshawa
1978-79	Gary Green, Peterborough
1979-80	Dave Chambers, Toronto
1980-81	Brian Kilrea, Ottawa
1981-82	Brian Kilrea, Ottawa
1982-83	Terry Crisp, Sault Ste. Marie
1983-84	Tom Barrett, Kitchener
1984-85	Terry Crisp, Sault Ste. Marie
1985-86	Jacques Martin, Guelph
1986-87	Paul Theriault, Oshawa
1987-88	Dick Todd, Peterborough
1988-89	Joe McDonnell, Kitchener
1989-90	Larry Mavety, Kingston
1990-91	George Burnett, Niagara Falls
1991-92	George Burnett, Niagara Falls
1992-93	Gary Agnew, London
1993-94	Bert Templeton, North Bay
1994-95	Craig Hartsburg, Guelph
1995-96	Brian Kilrea, Ottawa
1996-97	Brian Kilrea, Ottawa
1997-98	Gary Agnew, London
1998-99	Peter DeBoer, Plymouth
1999-00	Peter DeBoer, Plymouth
2000-01	Dave MacQueen, Erie

JIM MAHON MEMORIAL TROPHY
(Top scoring right wing)

Season	Player, Team
1971-72	Bill Harris, Toronto
1972-73	Dennis Ververgaert, London
1973-74	Dave Gorman, St. Catharines
1974-75	Mark Napier, Toronto
1975-76	Peter Lee, Ottawa
1976-77	John Anderson, Toronto
1977-78	Dino Ciccarelli, London
1978-79	Mike Foligno, Sudbury
1979-80	Jim Fox, Ottawa
1980-81	Tony Tanti, Oshawa
1981-82	Tony Tanti, Oshawa
1982-83	Ian MacInnis, Cornwall
1983-84	Wayne Presley, Kitchener
1984-85	Dave MacLean, Belleville
1985-86	Ray Sheppard, Cornwall
1986-87	Ron Goodall, Kitchener
1987-88	Sean Williams, Oshawa
1988-89	Stan Drulia, Niagara Falls
1989-90	Owen Nolan, Cornwall
1990-91	Rob Pearson, Oshawa
1991-92	Darren McCarty, Belleville
1992-93	Kevin J. Brown, Detroit
1993-94	Kevin J. Brown, Detroit
1994-95	David Ling, Kingston
1995-96	Cameron Mann, Peterborough
1996-97	Joe Seroski, Sault Ste. Marie
1997-98	Maxim Spiridonov, London
1998-99	Norm Milley, Sudbury
1999-00	Sheldon Keefe, Barrie
2000-01	Branko Radivojevic, Belleville

F.W. DINTY MOORE TROPHY
(Lowest average by a rookie goalie)

Season	Player, Team
1975-76	Mark Locken, Hamilton
1976-77	Barry Heard, London
1977-78	Ken Ellacott, Peterborough

Season	Player, Team
1978-79	Nick Ricci, Niagara Falls
1979-80	Mike Vezina, Ottawa
1980-81	John Vanbiesbrouck, Sault Ste. Marie
1981-82	Shawn Kilroy, Peterborough
1982-83	Dan Burrows, Belleville
1983-84	Jerry Iuliano, Sault Ste. Marie
1984-85	Ron Tugnutt, Peterborough
1985-86	Paul Henriques, Belleville
1986-87	Jeff Hackett, Oshawa
1987-88	Todd Bojcun, Peterborough
1988-89	Jeff Wilson, Kingston
1989-90	Sean Basilio, London
1990-91	Kevin Hodson, Sault Ste. Marie
1991-92	Sandy Allan, North Bay
1992-93	Ken Shepard, Oshawa
1993-94	Scott Roche, North Bay
1994-95	David MacDonald, Sudbury
1995-96	Brett Thompson, Guelph
1996-97	Shawn Degane, Kitchener
1997-98	Seamus Kotyk, Ottawa
1998-99	Lavente Szuper, Ottawa
1999-00	Andrew Sim, Sarnia
2000-01	Andy Chiodo, Toronto

LEO LALONDE MEMORIAL TROPHY
(Overage player of the year)

Season	Player, Team
1983-84	Don McLaren, Ottawa
1984-85	Dunc MacIntyre, Belleville
1985-86	Steve Guenette, Guelph
1986-87	Mike Richard, Toronto
1987-88	Len Soccio, North Bay
1988-89	Stan Drulia, Niagara Falls
1989-90	Iain Fraser, Oshawa
1990-91	Joey St. Aubin, Kitchener
1991-92	John Spoltore, North Bay
1992-93	Scott Hollis, Oshawa
1993-94	B.J. MacPherson, North Bay
1994-95	Bill Bowler, Windsor
1995-96	Aaron Brand, Sarnia
1996-97	Zac Bierk, Peterborough
1997-98	Bujar Amidovski, Toronto
1998-99	Ryan Ready, Belleville
1999-00	Dan Tessier, Ottawa
2000-01	Randy Rowe, Belleville

ALL-TIME LEAGUE CHAMPIONS

REGULAR-SEASON CHAMPION

PLAYOFF CHAMPION

Season	Team (Regular-Season)	Team (Playoff)
1933-34	No trophy awarded	St. Michael's College
1934-35	No trophy awarded	Kitchener
1935-36	No trophy awarded	West Toronto Redmen
1936-37	No trophy awarded	St. Michael's College
1937-38	No trophy awarded	Oshawa Generals
1938-39	No trophy awarded	Oshawa Generals
1939-40	No trophy awarded	Oshawa Generals
1940-41	No trophy awarded	Oshawa Generals
1941-42	No trophy awarded	Oshawa Generals
1942-43	No trophy awarded	Oshawa Generals
1943-44	No trophy awarded	Oshawa Generals
1944-45	No trophy awarded	St. Michael's College
1945-46	No trophy awarded	St. Michael's College
1946-47	No trophy awarded	St. Michael's College
1947-48	No trophy awarded	Barrie Flyers
1948-49	No trophy awarded	Barrie Flyers
1949-50	No trophy awarded	Guelph Biltmores
1950-51	No trophy awarded	Barrie Flyers
1951-52	No trophy awarded	Guelph Biltmores
1952-53	No trophy awarded	Barrie Flyers
1953-54	No trophy awarded	St. Catharines Tee Pees
1954-55	No trophy awarded	Toronto Marlboros
1955-56	No trophy awarded	Toronto Marlboros
1956-57	No trophy awarded	Guelph Biltmores
1957-58	St. Catharines Tee Pees	Toronto Marlboros
1958-59	St. Catharines Tee Pees	Peterborough TPTs
1959-60	Toronto Marlboros	St. Catharines Tee Pees
1960-61	Guelph Royals	St. Michael's College
1961-62	Montreal Jr. Canadiens	Hamilton Red Wings
1962-63	Niagara Falls Flyers	Niagara Falls Flyers
1963-64	Toronto Marlboros	Toronto Marlboros
1964-65	Niagara Falls Flyers	Niagara Falls Flyers
1965-66	Peterborough Petes	Oshawa Generals
1966-67	Kitchener Rangers	Toronto Marlboros
1967-68	Kitchener Rangers	Niagara Falls Flyers
1968-69	Montreal Jr. Canadiens	Montreal Jr. Canadiens
1969-70	Montreal Jr. Canadiens	Montreal Jr. Canadiens
1970-71	Peterborough Petes	St. Catharines Black Hawks
1971-72	Toronto Marlboros	Peterborough Petes
1972-73	Toronto Marlboros	Toronto Marlboros
1973-74	Kitchener Rangers	St. Catharines Black Hawks
1974-75	Toronto Marlboros	Toronto Marlboros
1975-76	Sudbury Wolves	Hamilton Steelhawks

	REGULAR-SEASON CHAMPION	PLAYOFF CHAMPION
Season	Team	Team
1976-77—	St. Catharines Fincups	Ottawa 67's
1977-78—	Ottawa 67's	Peterborough Petes
1978-79—	Peterborough Petes	Peterborough Petes
1979-80—	Peterborough Petes	Peterborough Petes
1980-81—	Sault St. Marie Greyhounds	Kitchener Rangers
1981-82—	Ottawa 67's	Kitchener Rangers
1982-83—	Sault Ste. Marie Greyhounds	Oshawa Generals
1983-84—	Kitchener Rangers	Ottawa 67's
1984-85—	Sault Ste. Marie Greyhounds	Sault Ste. Marie Greyhounds
1985-86—	Peterborough Petes	Guelph Platers
1986-87—	Oshawa Generals	Oshawa Generals
1987-88—	Windsor Compuware Spitfires	Windsor Compuware Spitfires
1988-89—	Kitchener Rangers	Peterborough Petes
1989-90—	Oshawa Generals	Oshawa Generals
1990-91—	Oshawa Generals	Sault Ste. Marie Greyhounds
1991-92—	Peterborough Petes	Sault Ste. Marie Greyhounds
1992-93—	Peterborough Petes	Peterborough Petes
1993-94—	North Bay Centennials	North Bay Centennials
1994-95—	Guelph Storm	Detroit Jr. Red Wings
1995-96—	Guelph Storm	Peterborough Petes
1996-97—	Ottawa 67's	Oshawa Generals
1997-98—	Guelph Storm	Guelph Storm
1998-99—	Plymouth Whalers	Belleville Bulls
1999-00—	Plymouth Whalers	Barrie Colts
2000-01—	Erie Otters	Ottawa 67's

The OHL regular-season champion is awarded the Hamilton Spectator Trophy and the playoff champion is awarded the J. Ross Robertson Cup.

MAJOR JUNIOR LEAGUES OHL

QUEBEC MAJOR JUNIOR HOCKEY LEAGUE

LEAGUE OFFICE

President
Gilles Courteau
Prefect of discipline
Maurice Filion
Statistician
Denis Demers
Director of public relations
Manon Gagnon-Leroux
Referee in chief
Doug Hayward

Director of hockey operations
Marcel Patenaude
Director of marketing
Paul Girard
Controller
Pierre Daoust

Address
255 Roland-Therien Blvd.
Suite 101
Longueuil, Quebec J4H 4A6
Phone
450-442-3590
FAX
450-442-3593

2000-01 REGULAR SEASON
FINAL STANDINGS

ROBERT LE BEL CONFERENCE

West Division

Team	G	W	L	T	RT	Pts.	GF	GA
Val-d'Or	72	46	19	7	2	101	369	235
Rouyn-Noranda	72	43	24	5	2	93	318	251
Hull	72	34	31	7	3	78	288	284
Montreal	72	24	41	7	6	61	249	310

Central Division

Team	G	W	L	T	RT	Pts.	GF	GA
Shawinigan	72	54	12	6	2	116	375	192
Victoriaville	72	45	24	3	3	96	341	269
Drummondville	72	31	36	5	6	73	246	267
Sherbrooke	72	28	40	4	3	63	245	274

FRANK DILIO CONFERENCE

East Division

Team	G	W	L	T	RT	Pts.	GF	GA
Baie-Comeau	72	41	23	8	0	90	283	255
Quebec	72	22	41	9	5	58	225	303
Chicoutimi	72	22	40	10	1	55	242	313
Rimouski	72	25	45	2	2	54	268	328

Maritime Division

Team	G	W	L	T	RT	Pts.	GF	GA
Halifax	72	32	30	10	6	80	235	253
Cape Breton	72	30	38	4	1	65	270	292
Acadie-Bathurst	72	29	39	4	1	63	239	281
Moncton	72	23	43	6	2	54	246	323

INDIVIDUAL LEADERS

Goals: Simon Gamache, Val-d'Or (74)
Assists: Simon Gamache, Val-d'Or (110)
Points: Simon Gamache, Val-d'Or (184)
Penalty minutes: Tommy Bolduc, Que.-Vic. (468)
Goaltending average: Frederic Cloutier, Shawinigan (2.50)
Shutouts: Frederic Cloutier, Shawinigan (6)

	Games	G	A	Pts.
Radim Vrbata, Shawinigan	55	56	64	120
Antoine Vermette, Victoriaville	71	57	62	119
Sebastien Thinel, Victoriaville	72	45	73	118
Stephane Veilleux, Val-d'Or	68	48	67	115
Jason Pominville, Shawinigan	71	46	67	113
Marco Charpentier, Baie-Comeau	71	57	55	112
Wesley Scanzano, Rouyn-Noranda	50	40	70	110
Eric Fortier, Val-d'Or	71	39	68	107
Marc-Andre Bergeron, Shawinigan	69	42	59	101
Patrick Yetman, Moncton	71	33	68	101
Joseph Yann, Mont.-A.B.	69	27	74	101
Ales Hemsky, Hull	68	36	64	100
Chris Lyness, Mont.-V.d.	66	28	72	100
Pierre-Marc Bouchard, Chicoutimi	67	38	57	95
Jonathan Bellemarre, Shawinigan	71	34	61	95

TOP SCORERS

	Games	G	A	Pts.
Simon Gamache, Val-d'Or	72	74	110	184
Marc-Andre Thinel, Victoriaville	70	62	88	150
Dominic Forget, Shawinigan	71	47	94	141
Yanick Lehoux, Baie-Comeau	70	67	68	135
Brandon Reid, Val-d'Or	57	45	81	126

INDIVIDUAL STATISTICS

ACADIE-BATHURST TITANS
SCORING

	Games	G	A	Pts.	PIM
Simon Laliberte	68	33	48	81	69
Alexandre Vigneault	71	13	65	78	127
Samuel Seguin	68	34	31	65	58
Alex Matieroukhine	59	25	34	59	127
Mirko Murovic	54	20	39	59	50
Olivier Fillion	62	21	33	54	45
Yann Joseph	35	11	30	41	66
Jonathan Ferland	70	17	11	28	135

	Games	G	A	Pts.	PIM
Karl Fournier	60	11	16	27	44
Antoine Bergeron	26	8	19	27	72
Miroslav Durak	27	5	13	18	95
Tyler Reid	72	5	13	18	122
Darrell Jerrett	72	6	8	14	198
Patrick Mbaraga	71	5	7	12	167
Michael Tessier	55	4	8	12	110
Michael Lambert	23	2	5	7	15
Eric Labelle	29	3	2	5	77
Eric Cloutier	25	2	3	5	20

	Games	G	A	Pts.	PIM
Garip Saliji	13	3	1	4	4
Luc Ratelle	11	1	3	4	46
Michael Lanthier	19	1	3	4	162
Colin Keith	19	1	3	4	94
Remi Doucet	22	2	1	3	14
Carl McLean	57	2	1	3	78
Sergei Kaltygen	11	1	2	3	14
Tim Sinasac	23	1	2	3	126
Kevin Lavallee	22	1	1	2	33
Matthew Doherty	26	1	1	2	14
Jean-Francois Laniel (goalie)	11	0	2	2	2
Louis Alfred	40	0	2	2	45
George Cantrall	9	0	1	1	67
Jonathan Lomax	32	0	1	1	35
Adam Russo (goalie)	35	0	1	1	17
Robert Purdy	1	0	0	0	0
Matthew Baker	1	0	0	0	0
Louis Deault	2	0	0	0	2
Charline Labonte (goalie)	2	0	0	0	0
Daniel Robert	2	0	0	0	0
Yannick Guay	4	0	0	0	0
Simon Lajeunesse (goalie)	36	0	0	0	0
Joey Francois Blacksmith	37	0	0	0	160

GOALTENDING

	Games	Min.	W	L	T	G	SO	Avg.
Adam Russo	35	1807	15	13	2	98	1	3.25
Simon Lajeunesse	36	1879	10	19	2	121	1	3.86
Jean-Francois Laniel	11	590	4	7	0	44	0	4.48
Charline Labonte	2	60	0	0	0	6	0	6.00

BAIE-COMEAU DRAKKAR
SCORING

	Games	G	A	Pts.	PIM
Yanick Lehoux	70	67	68	135	62
Marco Charpentier	71	57	55	112	88
Jonathan Gautier	59	22	43	65	45
Robin Leblanc	61	24	38	62	33
Pascal Pelletier	70	15	44	59	176
Charles Linglet	70	21	34	55	61
Duilio Grande	68	15	27	42	201
Maxime Fortunus	71	10	31	41	106
Evgeny Gusakov	32	11	20	31	68
Jean Morin	27	9	21	30	75
Joel Perreault	68	10	14	24	46
Dominic Periard	69	4	18	22	207
Kevin Deslauriers	64	5	14	19	57
Jonathan Walsh	67	4	8	12	47
Daniel Bergoron	67	3	5	8	380
Premysl Duben	32	0	8	8	36
Martin Mandeville	53	2	4	6	23
Matthew Hyde	67	3	1	4	157
Luis Tremblay	52	1	3	4	51
David St. Germain (goalie)	53	0	4	4	8
Thierry Douville	65	0	4	4	408
Jonathan Jolette	40	0	2	2	67
Pierre-Andre Leblanc	7	0	1	1	6
Ghyslain Rousseau (goalie)	29	0	1	1	19
Jerome Petit	1	0	0	0	0
Jessy-Luc Richard	1	0	0	0	10
Yanick Sabourin	1	0	0	0	0
Jean-Philippe Chartier	2	0	0	0	0
Jonathan Lachance	3	0	0	0	0
Guy Turmel	4	0	0	0	39
Marc-Andre Roy	5	0	0	0	5
Alexandre Desormeaux	24	0	0	0	46

GOALTENDING

	Games	Min.	W	L	T	G	SO	Avg.
David St. Germain	53	2913	32	13	4	169	3	3.48
Ghyslain Rousseau	29	1445	9	10	4	86	1	3.57

CAPE BRETON SCREAMING EAGLES
SCORING

	Games	G	A	Pts.	PIM
Olivier Proulx	71	37	56	93	172
Kevin Cloutier	67	32	60	92	92
Dominic Noel	72	38	46	84	38
Dustin Russell	72	38	38	76	42
Andre Martineau	71	24	37	61	41
Pierre-Luc Laprise	71	20	31	51	85
Stuart MacRae	58	17	28	45	53
Mathieu Dumas	71	5	33	38	79
Jean-Philippe Cote	71	6	29	35	90
Ryan Flinn	57	16	17	33	280
Maxime Lessard	65	8	17	25	40
Robert Horak	65	7	15	22	93
Charles Gauthier	52	12	9	21	23
Hunter Lahache	60	3	9	12	466
Vladimir Artushin	25	2	7	9	23
Pascal Morency	32	3	5	8	79
Rodrigue Boucher	61	1	7	8	59
Matthew French	39	1	3	4	17
Jason Melo	11	0	3	3	2
Jason Harshaw	25	0	3	3	43
Tyler Noye	22	0	2	2	4
Marc-Andre Fleury (goalie)	35	0	2	2	0
Gaby Beaudet	42	0	2	2	34
Jean-Francois Beaudet	59	0	2	2	58
George Davis	44	0	1	1	196
Joel Isenor	1	0	0	0	0
Neil Logan (goalie)	1	0	0	0	0
P.J. Lynch	1	0	0	0	0
Marc-Olivier Vary	2	0	0	0	2
Scott Gouthro (goalie)	3	0	0	0	0
Rob Dunphy	4	0	0	0	0
Daniel Boisclair (goalie)	47	0	0	0	0

GOALTENDING

	Games	Min.	W	L	T	G	SO	Avg.
Scott Gouthro	3	184	2	1	0	9	0	2.94
Neil Logan	1	19	0	1	0	1	0	3.16
Daniel Boisclair	47	2426	16	23	2	161	0	3.98
Marc-Andre Fleury	35	1705	12	13	2	115	0	4.05

CHICOUTIMI SAGUEENEENS
SCORING

	Games	G	A	Pts.	PIM
Pierre-Marc Bouchard	67	38	57	95	20
Christian Larrivee	72	32	48	80	46
Eric Betournay	72	18	43	61	101
Mathieu Betournay	70	24	26	50	14
Jonathan Francoeur	38	24	23	47	20
Sylvain Watt	70	9	38	47	25
Sebastien Lucier	38	13	13	26	47
Guillaume Karrer	58	10	16	26	119
Karl St. Pierre	69	5	21	26	162
P.-Alexandre Parenteau	28	10	13	23	14
Sebastien Laprise	33	12	10	22	18
Stanislav Hudec	68	4	16	20	72
Alex Turcotte	29	7	12	19	22
Sylvain Plamondon	39	5	13	18	120
Jean-Francois Demers	59	4	12	16	308
Eric Beaudin	68	4	12	16	121
David Beaudry-Ouellet	60	5	8	13	46
Eric Dufour	28	5	7	12	10
Bruno Champagne	31	2	9	11	6
Jean-Michel Martin	41	3	6	9	68
Jonathan St. Louis	6	2	5	7	28
Martin Beauchesne	51	1	6	7	137
Alexandre Blackburn	27	1	5	6	36
Francois Caron	24	1	3	4	6
Yannick Dallaire	42	2	1	3	154
Michael Parent	22	0	3	3	33
Dominic Deblois	3	1	1	2	0
Michel Finn	4	0	2	2	0
Simon Lagace-Daigle	2	0	1	1	2

	Games	G	A	Pts.	PIM
Alain Chenard	49	0	1	1	24
Dave Verville (goalie)	56	0	1	1	16
Eric Bourbeau (goalie)	1	0	0	0	0
Martin Fecteau	1	0	0	0	0
Hughes Verpaelst	1	0	0	0	0
Francois Miville	2	0	0	0	5
Dave Belanger	3	0	0	0	22
Guillaume Bouchard (goalie)	5	0	0	0	0
Luc St. Pierre	5	0	0	0	2
Sebastien Hains	6	0	0	0	0
Olivier Dannel (goalie)	20	0	0	0	0

GOALTENDING

	Games	Min.	W	L	T	G	SO	Avg.
Dave Verville	56	3128	19	27	7	193	1	3.70
Olivier Dannel	20	1039	3	11	3	86	0	4.97
Guillaume Bouchard	5	175	0	2	0	24	0	8.26
Eric Bourbeau	1	19	0	0	0	3	0	9.69

DRUMMONDVILLE VOLTIGEURS
SCORING

	Games	G	A	Pts.	PIM
Julien Desrosiers	57	32	45	77	90
Frederic Faucher	58	33	35	68	82
Vincent Tougas	57	30	28	58	136
Eric Dubois	48	22	26	48	68
Pierre-Luc Emond	62	10	36	46	110
Martin Frolik	65	13	27	40	10
Francis Deslauriers	62	11	27	38	58
Louis-Philippe Lessard	71	14	22	36	116
Jean-Philippe Morin	58	2	32	34	204
Simon Nadeau	66	14	19	33	99
J.-Francois Cyr	54	19	10	29	20
Jean-Philippe Glaude	46	2	27	29	129
Joey D'Amico	71	10	14	24	311
Daniel Clermont	31	5	10	15	43
Eric Jean	57	5	7	12	286
Simon Duplessis	61	4	7	11	297
Thierry Kaszap	54	5	5	10	67
Martin Chabot	51	5	3	8	13
Steve Villeneuve	68	4	4	8	62
Evgueni Nourislamov	35	1	7	8	35
Sebastien Lapierre	59	2	5	7	46
Didier Bochatay	29	1	3	4	50
Jerome Briere	10	2	0	2	2
Jean-Francois Racine (goalie)	61	0	2	2	19
Bernard Lahaie	12	0	1	1	4
Patrick Turbide	2	0	0	0	4
Benoit Paris	3	0	0	0	0
Michael McIntyre	4	0	0	0	9
Dominic Fiset	5	0	0	0	7
David Lessard	5	0	0	0	15
Mathieu Audet (goalie)	7	0	0	0	0
Frederick Malette (goalie)	17	0	0	0	0

GOALTENDING

	Games	Min.	W	L	T	G	SO	Avg.
Jean-Francois Racine	61	3362	27	26	3	189	4	3.37
Frederick Malette	17	820	4	8	2	57	0	4.17
Mathieu Audet	7	169	0	2	0	18	0	6.38

HALIFAX MOOSEHEADS
SCORING

	Games	G	A	Pts.	PIM
Jason King	72	48	41	89	78
Brandon Benedict	67	23	44	67	57
Sergei Klyazmin	65	33	28	61	76
Robbie Sutherland	60	24	27	51	68
Jules-Edy Laraque	48	16	30	46	48
Ali MacEachern	62	12	29	41	129
Sebastien Laprise	30	18	18	36	12
Derrick Kent	68	11	20	31	58
Giulio Scandella	69	7	23	30	59
Louis Mandeville	28	2	20	22	36
Bruce Gillis	72	7	10	17	71
Conor McGuire	49	7	8	15	27

	Games	G	A	Pts.	PIM
Jonathan Boone	58	7	8	15	124
Gary Zinck	59	2	11	13	218
Hugo Lehoux	71	5	6	11	412
Nick Greenough	22	2	9	11	214
A.J. MacLean	59	2	5	7	30
Jean-Francois Laplante	11	2	4	6	11
Jules Saulnier	23	2	4	6	10
Ryan MacPherson	66	2	3	5	87
Milan Jurcina	68	0	5	5	56
Ryan White	55	0	4	4	113
Dany Dallaire (goalie)	22	0	3	3	4
Randy Upshall	36	0	3	3	64
Michael Couch	31	2	0	2	18
Joe Groleau	11	1	0	1	21
Shawn Lewis	6	0	1	1	2
Yannick McNamara	15	0	1	1	6
Pascal Leclaire (goalie)	35	0	1	1	0
Mitchell Hardy	4	0	0	0	0
Carlos Sayde (goalie)	4	0	0	0	0
Matt Nichol	5	0	0	0	10
Benoit-Luc Gauthier	6	0	0	0	4
Stephane Lavoie	7	0	0	0	0
Todd Veary (goalie)	7	0	0	0	2
Yann Collin (goalie)	9	0	0	0	2

GOALTENDING

	Games	Min.	W	L	T	G	SO	Avg.
Dany Dallaire	22	1340	15	4	3	54	0	2.42
Yann Collin	9	493	1	5	2	29	0	3.53
Pascal Leclaire	35	2111	14	16	5	126	1	3.58
Todd Veary	7	300	2	4	0	26	0	5.20
Carlos Sayde	4	142	0	1	0	16	0	6.79

HULL OLYMPIQUES
SCORING

	Games	G	A	Pts.	PIM
Ales Hemsky	68	36	64	100	67
Bruno Lemire	70	41	51	92	68
Philippe Lacasse	65	29	56	85	55
Alexandre Giroux	38	31	32	63	62
Roberto Bissonnette	71	31	31	62	381
Philippe Choiniere	71	25	30	55	117
Jean-Michel Daoust	68	23	27	50	84
Adam Rivet	71	9	38	47	117
Mario Joly	60	7	23	30	310
Andrew Carver	69	5	22	27	132
Brent Roach	72	11	14	25	12
Derick Martin	64	2	22	24	102
Dale Sullivan	72	8	14	22	31
Jonathan Labelle	54	7	15	22	85
Maxime Talbot	24	6	7	13	60
Bobby Clarke	58	3	7	10	84
Ian Courville	40	2	8	10	33
Jason Kostadine	53	1	9	10	103
Doug O'Brien	47	1	6	7	16
John Cilladi	46	3	3	6	158
Chris Moher	25	1	5	6	39
Vladimir Artushin	14	3	1	4	67
Carle Rochon	15	1	3	4	42
Ivan Curic	7	0	2	2	34
Olivier Dannel (goalie)	10	0	2	2	10
Eric Lafrance (goalie)	40	0	2	2	0
Jens Dubreuil	21	1	0	1	84
Nick Watroba	22	1	0	1	38
Jeff Thomson (goalie)	12	0	1	1	0
Joel Pajuelo	1	0	0	0	0
Pascal Lapensee	1	0	0	0	0
Benoit Beaudoin	1	0	0	0	0
Paul Davison	2	0	0	0	4
Kevin Beaumont	2	0	0	0	5
Jean-Francois Kingsley (goalie)	6	0	0	0	0

GOALTENDING

	Games	Min.	W	L	T	G	SO	Avg.
Eric Lafrance	40	2024	21	11	3	114	0	3.38
Olivier Dannel	10	538	3	5	0	38	0	4.24

MAJOR JUNIOR LEAGUES

	Games	Min.	W	L	T	G	SO	Avg.
Jeff Thomson	12	496	2	4	1	37	0	4.48
Jean-Francois Kingsley	6	271	2	1	0	23	0	5.10

MONCTON WILDCATS
SCORING

	Games	G	A	Pts.	PIM
Patrick Yetman	71	33	68	101	32
Jonathan Roy	45	29	29	58	31
Collin Circelli	67	21	36	57	41
Johnny Oduya	44	11	38	49	147
Mikhail Deev	67	24	20	44	70
Scott O'Connor	64	9	33	42	109
Olivier Dubuc	49	16	20	36	63
Daniel Hudgin	71	16	20	36	121
P.-Alexandre Parenteau	45	10	19	29	38
Michael Smith	50	10	14	24	49
P.J. Lynch	34	10	10	20	28
Bobby Naylor	41	8	12	20	165
Matthew Seymour	56	3	8	11	76
Michel Dube	46	7	3	10	34
Teddy Kyres	26	1	9	10	35
A.J. Howe	33	6	3	9	24
James Sanford	26	4	5	9	40
Dion Hyman	60	3	6	9	304
Francois Caron	24	0	9	9	24
Stephen Knowles	33	5	3	8	32
Trevor Ettinger	44	3	5	8	206
Julien Lavoie	37	2	6	8	32
David Philpott	30	4	2	6	10
Marc Higginbotham	41	2	4	6	75
Ian Seguin	63	1	5	6	182
Greg Mizzi	8	3	1	4	12
Kory Baker	5	2	2	4	10
Simon St. Pierre	18	1	3	4	9
Dallas Beaton	50	1	3	4	49
Jonathan Billy	11	0	3	3	4
Tyler Durham	2	1	0	1	0
Leon Martin	2	0	0	0	4
Steve Richards	3	0	0	0	2
Scott Della Vedova (goalie)	3	0	0	0	0
Danny Corriveau	6	0	0	0	0
Todd Meehan	8	0	0	0	14
Mike Fournier	10	0	0	0	6
Justin Roy	12	0	0	0	9
Patrice Cadieux	13	0	0	0	0
Matthew Davis (goalie)	18	0	0	0	6
Bill Ruggiero (goalie)	62	0	0	0	37

GOALTENDING

	Games	Min.	W	L	T	G	SO	Avg.
Bill Ruggiero	62	3452	23	32	4	231	1	4.02
Matthew Davis	18	777	0	9	2	75	0	5.80
Scott Della Vedova	3	114	0	2	0	11	0	5.82

MONTREAL ROCKETS
SCORING

	Games	G	A	Pts.	PIM
Edo Terglav	71	32	39	71	83
Chris Montgomery	69	23	46	69	30
Jean-Michel Boisvert	67	29	38	67	34
Brett Lutes	72	29	37	66	90
Yann Joseph	34	16	44	60	26
Chris Lyness	35	18	40	58	46
Marc Villeneuve	72	22	20	42	64
Francis Emery	69	7	22	29	131
Jonathan St. Louis	29	14	9	23	80
Pierre-Andre Bureau	65	8	11	19	24
Michael Lambert	33	6	12	18	14
Maxime Pelletier	49	6	11	17	147
Mathieu Paul	62	2	13	15	72
Tyler Noye	33	4	10	14	29
Louis Robitaille	69	2	10	12	269
Nicolas Pelletier	26	6	5	11	22

	Games	G	A	Pts.	PIM
Jean-Francois Soucy	27	3	8	11	37
Pierre-Olivier Beaulieu	61	3	8	11	31
Michael Riendeau	26	4	5	9	6
Jordan Trew	34	6	2	8	113
Marc-Andre Beaulieu	53	2	5	7	8
Sebastien Beaudin	31	0	7	7	56
Kevin Lavallee	36	0	7	7	48
Guillaume Lajeunesse	53	2	4	6	16
Gregory Dupre	4	1	3	4	4
Tuukka Makela	9	2	1	3	14
Michael Lanthier	32	1	2	3	148
Guillaume Lamoureux	7	0	2	2	2
Sylvain Angers	35	1	0	1	103
Patrice Poissant (goalie)	36	0	1	1	6
Jonathan Cayer (goalie)	43	0	1	1	4
Jean-Olivier Deling	1	0	0	0	0
Travis Clock	3	0	0	0	4
Jean-Philippe Paradis	3	0	0	0	0
Alexandre Charest	4	0	0	0	0
Alexandre Simoneau	5	0	0	0	2
Olivier Maltais	6	0	0	0	2
Rosario Ruggeri	9	0	0	0	8
Dany Dallaire (goalie)	10	0	0	0	0

GOALTENDING

	Games	Min.	W	L	T	G	SO	Avg.
Patrice Poissant	36	1687	12	15	1	108	0	3.84
Jonathan Cayer	43	2193	10	21	4	157	1	4.30
Dany Dallaire	10	485	2	5	2	38	0	4.71

QUEBEC REMPARTS
SCORING

	Games	G	A	Pts.	PIM
Shawn Collymore	71	24	43	67	32
Yannick Searles	70	28	36	64	30
Cory Urquhart	60	25	24	49	32
Petr Preucil	70	12	35	47	121
Philippe Paris	52	19	27	46	61
Guillaume Berube	70	12	22	34	23
Guillaume Fournier	69	14	16	30	20
Remi Bergeron	64	7	20	27	140
Jean Mallette	59	9	16	25	108
David Masse	28	14	8	22	20
Martin Grenier	26	5	16	21	82
Mike Bray	41	10	10	20	317
Didier Bochatay	34	7	9	16	73
Steven Levac	32	3	13	16	35
Robert Pearce	54	7	8	15	61
Tommy Bolduc	37	5	9	14	342
Eric Cloutier	28	6	6	12	27
David Boilard	64	3	8	11	108
Sylvain Plamondon	14	5	4	9	48
Jeff Hadley	55	1	7	8	283
Sebastien Bourgon	53	1	6	7	57
Justin Stewart	59	1	6	7	51
Philippe Parent	32	2	4	6	46
Sebastien Morissette	23	3	2	5	14
Ivan Curic	10	0	5	5	32
Karl Morin	34	2	2	4	34
Martin Pare (goalie)	5	0	1	1	0
Andre Hart	8	0	1	1	42
Richard Paul	20	0	1	1	141
Alexandre Reuben	47	0	1	1	16
Daniel Gervais-Houle	2	0	0	0	2
Mariano D'Agostino	4	0	0	0	4
Mike McGuigan	5	0	0	0	7
Scott Della Vedova (goalie)	31	0	0	0	38
Kevin Lachance (goalie)	56	0	0	0	8

GOALTENDING

	Games	Min.	W	L	T	G	SO	Avg.
Kevin Lachance	56	2756	17	20	8	168	1	3.66
Scott Della Vedova	31	1416	5	19	1	107	0	4.54
Martin Pare	5	202	0	2	0	22	0	6.55

RIMOUSKI OCEANIC

SCORING

	Games	G	A	Pts.	PIM
Michel Ouellet	63	42	50	92	50
Nicolas Poirier	70	39	53	92	119
Benoit Martin	70	20	49	69	53
Tomas Malec	64	13	50	63	198
Thatcher Bell	46	27	32	59	77
Jean-Philippe Briere	70	26	33	59	52
Jonathan Beaulieu	41	14	41	55	178
Aaron Johnson	64	12	41	53	128
Jean-Francois Plourde	67	17	20	37	82
Brent MacLellan	62	7	19	26	155
Mathieu Simard	72	16	9	25	58
Ryan Clowe	32	15	10	25	43
Gabriel Balasescu	67	8	7	15	124
Alexis Castonguay	39	3	10	13	194
Samuel Gibbons	55	0	10	10	92
Jean-Francois Babin	47	3	4	7	205
Tim Sinasac	19	2	3	5	84
Philippe Lauze	68	1	4	5	208
Charles-Erick Gagnon	24	0	3	3	6
Martin Senechal	7	1	1	2	21
Daniel Petiquay	57	1	1	2	331
Sebastien Bolduc	63	1	1	2	332
Mathieu Fournier	27	0	2	2	92
Jonathan Pelletier (goalie)	31	0	2	2	0
Nicolas Pilote	34	0	2	2	33
Eric Salvail (goalie)	38	0	2	2	23
David Young	1	0	0	0	0
David Bouchard	2	0	0	0	0
Dany Dufour	8	0	0	0	24
Denis Berube (goalie)	15	0	0	0	0
Ronnie Decontie	20	0	0	0	82
Carle Rochon	24	0	0	0	47

GOALTENDING

	Games	Min.	W	L	T	G	SO	Avg.
Jonathan Pelletier	31	1749	12	17	0	107	1	3.67
Denis Berube	15	710	5	7	0	54	0	4.57
Eric Salvail	38	1876	8	21	2	165	0	5.28

ROUYN-NORANDA HUSKIES

SCORING

	Games	G	A	Pts.	PIM
Wesley Scanzano	50	40	70	110	57
Maxime Bouchard	67	33	51	84	290
Jerome Marois	68	36	47	83	119
Jonathan Gauthier	69	30	45	75	176
Guillaume Lefebvre	61	24	43	67	160
Michal Pinc	64	16	46	62	220
Marc-Andre Binette	36	22	33	55	61
Sebastian Strozynski	70	16	36	52	169
Patrice Theriault	72	9	38	47	48
Alexandre Morel	60	6	25	31	224
Alexandre Giroux	25	13	14	27	56
Maxime Talbot	40	9	15	24	78
Jonathan St. Louis	37	9	14	23	97
Matthew Quinn	69	11	9	20	51
Jonathan Gagnon	69	10	8	18	45
Shawn Scanzano	18	7	11	18	55
Patrick Gilbert	71	5	13	18	155
Louis Mandeville	42	2	15	17	59
Steve Waters	16	5	10	15	18
Jonathan Francoeur	10	2	6	8	10
Bruno Cadieux	49	1	7	8	33
Philippe Parent	19	3	4	7	22
Bertrand-Pierre Plouffe	34	3	4	7	54
Mathieu Leclerc	36	2	5	7	42
Sebastien Laprise	7	3	3	6	6
Jonathan Jolette	27	1	5	6	36
Kirill Alexeev	15	0	2	2	27
Sebastien Centomo (goalie)	46	0	2	2	48
Eric L'Italien	15	0	1	1	4

	Games	G	A	Pts.	PIM
Jean-Philippe Hamel	29	0	1	1	10
Jean Morin	1	0	0	0	2
Benoit Bibeau	2	0	0	0	0
Mathieu Poitras (goalie)	2	0	0	0	0
Michel Bergevin-Robinson	4	0	0	0	0
Pierre-Olivier Girouard (goalie)	8	0	0	0	0
Dominic D'Amour	18	0	0	0	10
Dominic Soucy	20	0	0	0	13
Maxime Ouellet (goalie)	25	0	0	0	2

GOALTENDING

	Games	Min.	W	L	T	G	SO	Avg.
Maxime Ouellet	25	1471	18	6	1	65	3	2.65
Sebastien Centomo	46	2599	25	14	4	158	3	3.65
Pierre-Olivier Girouard	8	234	0	4	0	16	0	4.11
Mathieu Poitras	2	47	0	0	0	8	0	10.19

SHAWINIGAN CATARACTES

SCORING

	Games	G	A	Pts.	PIM
Dominic Forget	71	47	94	141	78
Radim Vrbata	55	56	64	120	67
Jason Pominville	71	46	67	113	24
Marc-Andre Bergeron	69	42	59	101	185
Jonathan Bellemarre	71	34	61	95	91
Jean-Francois Dufort	46	21	32	53	194
Jean-Francois David	65	14	38	52	160
Anthony Quessy	65	20	30	50	267
David Chicoine	72	14	35	49	168
Yannick Noiseux	62	18	21	39	86
Zbynek Michalek	69	10	29	39	52
Gilbert Lefrancois	72	11	24	35	103
Alexandre Menard-Burrows	63	16	14	30	105
Kevin Bergin	56	5	17	22	168
Denis Desmarais	68	4	13	17	160
Jimmy Cuddihy	61	5	11	16	46
Mathieu Payette	57	3	8	11	86
Francois Gagnon	44	5	3	8	24
Jonathan Lessard	65	2	5	7	208
Trevor Ettinger	28	1	5	6	122
Alexandre Blackburn	44	1	1	2	179
Frederic Cloutier (goalie)	58	0	2	2	16
Paul-Andre Bourgoin	4	0	1	1	0
Patrick Bolduc	6	0	1	1	6
Olivier Michaud (goalie)	21	0	1	1	0
Conor McGuire	2	0	0	0	0
Patrick Desaulniers	2	0	0	0	0
Justin Roy	10	0	0	0	19

GOALTENDING

	Games	Min.	W	L	T	G	SO	Avg.
Frederic Cloutier	58	3270	42	8	2	136	6	2.50
Olivier Michaud	21	1096	12	4	4	54	1	2.96

SHERBROOKE FAUCONS

SCORING

	Games	G	A	Pts.	PIM
Nicolas Corbeil	68	33	51	84	159
Steve Morency	72	38	32	70	40
Benoit Genesse	67	24	44	68	87
Francois Belanger	72	28	37	65	134
Pierre-Luc Courchesne	71	15	44	59	86
Simon Tremblay	72	25	33	58	131
Eric Lavigne	71	13	39	52	75
Francis Trudel	72	3	29	32	78
Jonathan Robert	58	10	18	28	79
Jean Morin	33	11	11	22	88
Patrick Vincent	21	9	9	18	112
Sebastien Courcelles	67	4	14	18	76
Artem Ternavski	65	3	15	18	143
Miroslav Durak	34	0	17	17	24
Sandro Sbrocca	26	7	8	15	108
Joey Neale	41	5	10	15	22
Mathieu Thibodeau	67	3	9	12	52

	Games	G	A	Pts.	PIM
Jeremy Knight	33	4	2	6	59
Mike Ouellet	12	3	1	4	11
Bertrand-Pierre Plouffe	29	2	2	4	44
Mathieu Wathier	32	2	2	4	6
Patrick Gosselin	45	1	3	4	98
Patrick Levesque	19	1	2	3	12
Eric Dagenais	33	0	3	3	81
Jean Gravel	8	1	0	1	23
Jonathan Leclerc (goalie)	6	0	1	1	0
Guy Turmel	23	0	1	1	174
Drew MacIntyre (goalie)	48	0	1	1	2
Patrice Tassy	1	0	0	0	0
Michel Beausoleil	1	0	0	0	0
Yan Gaudette	2	0	0	0	2
Stephane Valois	4	0	0	0	0
Jimmy Arsenault	4	0	0	0	0
Maxime-Charles	4	0	0	0	7
Mathieu Landry	24	0	0	0	22
Louis-Philippe Lemay (goalie)	35	0	0	0	4

GOALTENDING

	Games	Min.	W	L	T	G	SO	Avg.
Drew MacIntyre	48	2552	17	22	3	139	4	3.27
Louis-Philippe Lemay	35	1655	10	16	1	115	2	4.17
Jonathan Leclerc	6	128	1	2	0	12	0	5.62

VAL D'OR FOREURS

SCORING

	Games	G	A	Pts.	PIM
Simon Gamache	72	74	110	184	70
Brandon Reid	57	45	81	126	18
Stephane Veilleux	68	48	67	115	90
Eric Fortier	71	39	68	107	58
Seneque Hyacinthe	66	32	54	86	68
Jerome Bergeron	69	33	33	66	145
Antoine Bergeron	36	16	26	42	95
Chris Lyness	31	10	32	42	46
Kory Baker	44	12	24	36	80
David Cloutier	72	14	20	34	200
Alexandre Rouleau	70	8	17	25	124
Hugo Levesque	72	3	19	22	59
Luc Girard	72	3	18	21	88
Pierre Morvan	65	8	6	14	77
Alex Turcotte	26	4	9	13	41
Mathieu Bastien	47	4	6	10	230
Samuel Duplain	68	1	9	10	297
Steve Pelletier	51	5	4	9	56
Jean-Francois Soucy	38	3	4	7	57
Eric Labelle	36	1	6	7	127
Mathieu Roy	30	0	7	7	60
Nicolas Pelletier	15	2	4	6	4
Tomas Psenka	56	1	4	5	145
Mathieu Lendick	9	0	3	3	15
Frederic Bedard	20	2	0	2	2
Yan Hallee	21	1	0	1	63
Patrick Perrier (goalie)	1	0	0	0	0
Jean-Francois Payant	2	0	0	0	0
Adam Morneau	2	0	0	0	0
Steve Vallee (goalie)	2	0	0	0	0
Jean-Philippe Paradis	3	0	0	0	0
Jonathan Charette	3	0	0	0	0
Jan Choteborsky	3	0	0	0	6
Simon Lajeunesse (goalie)	21	0	0	0	2
Maxime Daigneault (goalie)	28	0	0	0	0
Jean-Francois Laniel (goalie)	31	0	0	0	0

GOALTENDING

	Games	Min.	W	L	T	G	SO	Avg.
Patrick Perrier	1	2	0	0	0	0	0	0.00
Simon Lajeunesse	21	1159	16	3	1	54	1	2.80
Jean-Francois Laniel	31	1755	15	8	5	90	2	3.08
Maxime Daigneault	28	1386	14	8	1	82	0	3.55
Steve Vallee	2	64	1	0	0	4	0	3.74

VICTORIAVILLE TIGRES

SCORING

	Games	G	A	Pts.	PIM
Marc-Andre Thinel	70	62	88	150	101
Antoine Vermette	71	57	62	119	102
Sebastien Thinel	72	45	73	118	84
Danny Groulx	72	16	71	87	164
Carl Mallette	61	28	55	83	99
Matthew Lombardi	72	28	39	67	66
Pierre-Luc Sleigher	70	16	20	36	240
Martin Autotte	68	13	23	36	178
Kristian Kovac	51	10	20	30	38
Martin Grenier	28	9	19	28	108
Jonathan Fauteux	55	9	18	27	133
Sandro Sbrocca	39	11	15	26	238
Johnny Oduya	24	3	16	19	112
Mathieu Brunelle	65	7	11	18	39
Teddy Kyres	40	5	9	14	42
Patrick Vincent	24	5	8	13	130
Sergei Kaltygen	14	5	6	11	23
Carl Gagnon	28	4	5	9	4
Ivan Curic	21	0	8	8	78
Simon St. Pierre	31	2	5	7	6
Steve Richards	23	2	4	6	33
Pierre-Luc Daneau	67	1	5	6	27
James Sanford	41	0	6	6	60
Tommy Bolduc	25	1	2	3	126
Mathieu Wathier	37	0	3	3	57
Jean-Francois Nogues (goalie)	41	0	3	3	31
Karl Morin	21	0	2	2	8
Adam Wojcik	8	1	0	1	12
David Masse	14	1	0	1	6
Hugo Beaudet	4	0	1	1	0
Mike Fournier	1	0	0	0	0
Daniel Gervais-Houle	2	0	0	0	2
Simon Ebacher	2	0	0	0	0
Francis Debilly (goalie)	3	0	0	0	0
Alexandre Turgeon-Cote (g)	3	0	0	0	0
Patrice Cadieux (goalie)	4	0	0	0	0
Philippe Ozga (goalie)	9	0	0	0	0
Nicolas Joyal (goalie)	13	0	0	0	0
Frederick Malette (goalie)	13	0	0	0	27
Sebastien Morissette	19	0	0	0	5
Luc Levesque	22	0	0	0	48
Richard Paul	34	0	0	0	155

GOALTENDING

	Games	Min.	W	L	T	G	SO	Avg.
Francis Debilly	3	36	0	1	0	1	0	1.69
Philippe Ozga	9	522	6	2	0	28	0	3.22
Jean-Francois Nogues	41	2240	25	11	2	129	2	3.46
Frederick Malette	13	676	9	3	0	41	0	3.64
Patrice Cadieux	4	134	1	0	0	9	0	4.05
Nicolas Joyal	13	645	4	6	1	52	0	4.84
Alexandre Turgeon-Cote	3	96	0	1	0	8	0	4.99

PLAYERS WITH TWO OR MORE TEAMS

SCORING

	Games	G	A	Pts.	PIM
Vladimir Artushin, Hull	14	3	1	4	67
Vladimir Artushin, Cape Breton	25	2	7	9	23
Totals	39	5	8	13	90
Kory Baker, Moncton	5	2	2	4	10
Kory Baker, Val-d'Or	44	12	24	36	80
Totals	49	14	26	40	90
Antoine Bergeron, Val-d'Or	36	16	26	42	95
Antoine Bergeron, A.-Bathurst	26	8	19	27	72
Totals	62	24	45	69	167
Alexandre Blackburn, Shaw.	44	1	1	2	179
Alexandre Blackburn, Chi.	27	1	5	6	36
Totals	71	2	6	8	215
Didier Bochatay, Drum.	29	1	3	4	50

	Games	G	A	Pts.	PIM
Didier Bochatay, Quebec	34	7	9	16	73
Totals	63	8	12	20	123
Tommy Bolduc, Quebec	37	5	9	14	342
Tommy Bolduc, Victoriaville	25	1	2	3	126
Totals	62	6	11	17	468
Francois Caron, Chicoutimi	24	1	3	4	6
Francois Caron, Moncton	24	0	9	9	24
Totals	48	1	12	13	30
Eric Cloutier, Quebec	28	6	6	12	27
Eric Cloutier, Acadie-Bathurst	25	2	3	5	20
Totals	53	8	9	17	47
Ivan Curic, Hull	7	0	2	2	34
Ivan Curic, Quebec	10	0	5	5	32
Ivan Curic, Victoriaville	21	0	8	8	78
Totals	38	0	15	15	144
Dany Dallaire, Montreal	10	0	0	0	0
Dany Dallaire, Halifax	22	0	3	3	4
Totals	32	0	3	3	4
Olivier Dannel, Chicoutimi	20	0	0	0	0
Olivier Dannel, Hull	10	0	2	2	10
Totals	30	0	2	2	10
Miroslav Durak, Sherbrooke	34	0	17	17	24
Miroslav Durak, A.-Bathurst	27	5	13	18	95
Totals	61	5	30	35	119
Trevor Ettinger, Moncton	44	3	5	8	206
Trevor Ettinger, Shawinigan	28	1	5	6	122
Totals	72	4	10	14	328
Mike Fournier, Moncton	10	0	0	0	6
Mike Fournier, Victoriaville	1	0	0	0	0
Totals	11	0	0	0	6
Jonathan Francoeur, Chi.	38	24	23	47	20
Jonathan Francoeur, R.-N.	10	2	6	8	10
Totals	48	26	29	55	30
Daniel Gervais-Houle, Vic.	2	0	0	0	2
Daniel Gervais-Houle, Quebec	2	0	0	0	2
Totals	4	0	0	0	4
Alexandre Giroux, Hull	38	31	32	63	62
Alexandre Giroux, R.-Noranda	25	13	14	27	56
Totals	63	44	46	90	118
Martin Grenier, Quebec	26	5	16	21	82
Martin Grenier, Victoriaville	28	9	19	28	108
Totals	54	14	35	49	190
Jonathan Jolette, Baie-Comeau	40	0	2	2	67
Jonathan Jolette, R.-Noranda	27	1	5	6	36
Totals	67	1	7	8	103
Yann Joseph, Montreal	34	16	44	60	26
Yann Joseph, Acadie-Bathurst	35	11	30	41	66
Totals	69	27	74	101	92
Sergei Kaltygen, A.-Bathurst	11	1	2	3	14
Sergei Kaltygen, Victoriaville	14	5	6	11	23
Totals	25	6	8	14	37
Teddy Kyres, Victoriaville	40	5	9	14	42
Teddy Kyres, Moncton	26	1	9	10	35
Totals	66	6	18	24	77
Eric Labelle, Val-d'Or	36	1	6	7	127
Eric Labelle, Acadie-Bathurst	29	3	2	5	77
Totals	65	4	8	12	204
Simon Lajeunesse, A.-Bathurst	36	0	0	0	0
Simon Lajeunesse, Val-d'Or	21	0	0	0	2
Totals	57	0	0	0	2
Michael Lambert, A.-Bathurst	23	2	5	7	15
Michael Lambert, Montreal	33	6	12	18	14
Totals	56	8	17	25	29
Jean-Francois Laniel, Val-d'Or	31	0	0	0	0
Jean-Francois Laniel, A.-B.	11	0	2	2	2
Totals	42	0	2	2	2
Michael Lanthier, Montreal	32	1	2	3	148
Michael Lanthier, A.-Bathurst	19	1	3	4	162
Totals	51	2	5	7	310
Sebastien Laprise, Chicoutimi	33	12	10	22	18
Sebastien Laprise, R.-Noranda	7	3	3	6	6
Sebastien Laprise, Halifax	30	18	18	36	12
Totals	70	33	31	64	36
Kevin Lavallee, A.-Bathurst	22	1	1	2	33

	Games	G	A	Pts.	PIM
Kevin Lavallee, Montreal	36	0	7	7	48
Totals	58	1	8	9	81
P.J. Lynch, Cape Breton	1	0	0	0	0
P.J. Lynch, Moncton	34	10	10	20	28
Totals	35	10	10	20	28
Chris Lyness, Montreal	35	18	40	58	46
Chris Lyness, Val-d'Or	31	10	32	42	46
Totals	66	28	72	100	92
Frederick Malette, Drum.	17	0	0	0	0
Frederick Malette, Victoriaville	13	0	0	0	27
Totals	30	0	0	0	27
Louis Mandeville, R.-Noranda	42	2	15	17	59
Louis Mandeville, Halifax	28	2	20	22	36
Totals	70	4	35	39	95
David Masse, Victoriaville	14	1	0	1	6
David Masse, Quebec	28	14	8	22	20
Totals	42	15	8	23	26
Conor McGuire, Shawinigan	2	0	0	0	0
Conor McGuire, Halifax	49	7	8	15	27
Totals	51	7	8	15	27
Jean Morin, Sherbrooke	33	11	11	22	88
Jean Morin, Rouyn-Noranda	1	0	0	0	2
Jean Morin, Baie-Comeau	27	9	21	30	75
Totals	61	20	32	52	165
Karl Morin, Quebec	34	2	2	4	34
Karl Morin, Victoriaville	21	0	2	2	8
Totals	55	2	4	6	42
Sebastien Morissette, Vic.	19	0	0	0	5
Sebastien Morissette, Quebec	23	3	2	5	14
Totals	42	3	2	5	19
Tyler Noye, Cape Breton	22	0	2	2	4
Tyler Noye, Montreal	33	4	10	14	29
Totals	55	4	12	16	33
Johnny Oduya, Moncton	44	11	38	49	147
Johnny Oduya, Victoriaville	24	3	16	19	112
Totals	68	14	54	68	259
Jean-Philippe Paradis, Val-d'Or	3	0	0	0	0
Jean-Philippe Paradis, Mont.	3	0	0	0	0
Totals	6	0	0	0	0
Philippe Parent, R.-Noranda	19	3	4	7	22
Philippe Parent, Quebec	32	2	4	6	46
Totals	51	5	8	13	68
P.-Alexandre Parenteau, Monc.	45	10	19	29	38
P.-Alexandre Parenteau, Chi.	28	10	13	23	14
Totals	73	20	32	52	52
Richard Paul, Victoriaville	34	0	0	0	155
Richard Paul, Quebec	20	0	1	1	141
Totals	54	0	1	1	296
Nicolas Pelletier, Montreal	26	6	5	11	22
Nicolas Pelletier, Val-d'Or	15	2	4	6	4
Totals	41	8	9	17	26
Sylvain Plamondon, Quebec	14	5	4	9	48
Sylvain Plamondon, Chicoutimi	39	5	13	18	120
Totals	53	10	17	27	168
Bertrand-Pierre Plouffe, R.-N.	34	3	4	7	54
Bertrand-Pierre Plouffe, Sher.	29	2	2	4	44
Totals	63	5	6	11	98
Steve Richards, Moncton	3	0	0	0	2
Steve Richards, Victoriaville	23	2	4	6	33
Totals	26	2	4	6	35
Carle Rochon, Rimouski	24	0	0	0	47
Carle Rochon, Hull	15	1	3	4	42
Totals	39	1	3	4	89
Justin Roy, Shawinigan	10	0	0	0	19
Justin Roy, Moncton	12	0	0	0	9
Totals	22	0	0	0	28
James Sanford, Victoriaville	41	0	6	6	60
James Sanford, Moncton	26	4	5	9	40
Totals	67	4	11	15	100
Jonathan St. Louis, R.-N.	37	9	14	23	97
Jonathan St. Louis, Chicoutimi	6	2	5	7	28
Jonathan St. Louis, Montreal	29	14	9	23	80
Totals	72	25	28	53	205
Simon St. Pierre, Victoriaville	31	2	5	7	6

	Games	G	A	Pts.	PIM
Simon St. Pierre, Moncton	18	1	3	4	9
Totals	49	3	8	11	15
Sandro Sbrocca, Victoriaville	39	11	15	26	238
Sandro Sbrocca, Sherbrooke	26	7	8	15	108
Totals	65	18	23	41	346
Tim Sinasac, Acadie-Bathurst	23	1	2	3	126
Tim Sinasac, Rimouski	19	2	3	5	84
Totals	42	3	5	8	210
Jean-Francois Soucy, Val-d'Or	38	3	4	7	57
Jean-Francois Soucy, Montreal	27	3	8	11	37
Totals	65	6	12	18	94
Maxime Talbot, R.-Noranda	40	9	15	24	78
Maxime Talbot, Hull	24	6	7	13	60
Totals	64	15	22	37	138
Alex Turcotte, Chicoutimi	29	7	12	19	22
Alex Turcotte, Val-d'Or	26	4	9	13	41
Totals	55	11	21	32	63
Guy Turmel, Baie-Comeau	4	0	0	0	39
Guy Turmel, Sherbrooke	23	0	1	1	174
Totals	27	0	1	1	213
Scott Della Vedova, Moncton	3	0	0	0	0
Scott Della Vedova, Quebec	31	0	0	0	38
Totals	34	0	0	0	38
Patrick Vincent, Sherbrooke	21	9	9	18	112
Patrick Vincent, Victoriaville	24	5	8	13	130

	Games	G	A	Pts.	PIM
Totals	45	14	17	31	242
Mathieu Wathier, Victoriaville	37	0	3	3	57
Mathieu Wathier, Sherbrooke	32	2	2	4	6
Totals	69	2	5	7	63

GOALTENDING

	Games	Min.	W	L	T	G	SO	Avg.
Dany Dallaire, Mont.	10	485	2	5	2	38	0	4.71
Dany Dallaire, Halifax	22	1340	15	4	3	54	0	2.42
Totals	32	1825	17	9	5	92	0	3.02
Olivier Dannel, Chi.	20	1039	3	11	3	86	0	4.97
Olivier Dannel, Hull	10	538	3	5	0	38	0	4.24
Totals	30	1577	6	16	3	124	0	4.72
S. Della Vedova, Monc.	3	114	0	2	0	11	0	5.82
S. Della Vedova, Que.	31	1416	5	19	1	107	0	4.54
Totals	34	1530	5	21	1	118	0	4.63
S. Lajeunesse, A.-B.	36	1879	10	19	2	121	1	3.86
S. Lajeunesse, V.-d'Or	21	1159	16	3	1	54	1	2.80
Totals	57	3038	26	22	3	175	2	3.46
J.-F. Laniel, V.-d'Or	31	1755	15	8	5	90	2	3.08
J.-F. Laniel, A.-B.	11	590	4	7	0	44	0	4.48
Totals	42	2345	19	15	5	134	2	3.43
Frederick Malette, Drum.	17	820	4	8	2	57	0	4.17
Frederick Malette, Vic.	13	676	9	3	0	41	0	3.64
Totals	30	1496	13	11	2	98	0	3.93

2001 PRESIDENT CUP PLAYOFFS

RESULTS

DIVISION QUARTERFINALS

	W	L	Pts.	GF	GA
Rouyn-Noranda	4	1	8	22	13
Hull	1	4	2	13	22

(Rouyn-Noranda won series, 4-1)

	W	L	Pts.	GF	GA
Val-d'Or	4	0	8	21	13
Sherbrooke	0	4	0	13	21

(Val-d'Or won series, 4-0)

	W	L	Pts.	GF	GA
Victoriaville	4	3	8	34	29
Drummondville	3	4	6	29	34

(Victoriaville won series, 4-3)

	W	L	Pts.	GF	GA
Rimouski	4	2	8	26	18
Halifax	2	4	4	18	26

(Rimouski won series, 4-2)

	W	L	Pts.	GF	GA
Acadie-Bathurst	4	0	8	16	4
Quebec	0	4	0	4	16

(Acadie-Bathurst won series, 4-0)

	W	L	Pts.	GF	GA
Cape Breton	4	3	8	24	21
Chicoutimi	3	4	6	21	24

(Cape Breton won series, 4-3)

DIVISION SEMIFINALS

	W	L	Pts.	GF	GA
Shawinigan	4	0	8	16	6
Rouyn-Noranda	0	4	0	6	16

(Shawinigan won series, 4-0)

	W	L	Pts.	GF	GA
Val-d'Or	4	3	8	36	32
Victoriaville	3	4	6	32	36

(Val-d'Or won series, 4-3)

	W	L	Pts.	GF	GA
Baie-Comeau	4	1	8	27	11
Rimouski	1	4	2	11	27

(Baie-Comeau won series, 4-1)

	W	L	Pts.	GF	GA
Acadie-Bathurst	4	1	8	20	12
Cape Breton	1	4	2	12	20

(Acadie-Bathurst won series, 4-1)

DIVISION FINALS

	W	L	Pts.	GF	GA
Acadie-Bathurst	4	2	8	21	18
Baie-Comeau	2	4	4	18	21

(Acadie-Bathurst won series, 4-2)

	W	L	Pts.	GF	GA
Val-d'Or	4	2	8	25	20
Shawinigan	2	4	4	20	25

(Val-d'Or won series, 4-2)

LEAGUE FINALS

	W	L	Pts.	GF	GA
Val-d'Or	4	0	8	21	10
Acadie-Bathurst	0	4	0	10	21

(Val-d'Or won series, 4-0)

INDIVIDUAL LEADERS

Goals: Simon Gamache, Val-d'Or (22)
Assists: Simon Gamache, Val-d'Or (35)
Points: Simon Gamache, Val-d'Or (57)
Penalty minutes: Patrick Vincent, Victoriaville (59)
Goaltending average: Adam Russo, Acadie-Bathurst (2.50)
Maxime Daigneault, Val-d'Or (2.50)
Shutouts: Adam Russo, Acadie-Bathurst (3)

TOP SCORERS

	Games	G	A	Pts.
Simon Gamache, Val-d'Or	21	22	35	57
Brandon Reid, Val-d'Or	21	13	29	42
Stephane Veilleux, Val-d'Or	21	15	18	33
Seneque Hyacinthe, Val-d'Or	21	10	17	27
Marc-Andre Thinel, Victoriaville	13	12	13	25
Eric Fortier, Val-d'Or	21	7	18	25
Yanick Lehoux, Baie-Comeau	11	8	16	24
Chris Lyness, Val-d'Or	21	7	14	21
Danny Groulx, Victoriaville	13	2	19	21
Mirko Murovic, Acadie-Bathurst	19	9	11	20

INDIVIDUAL STATISTICS

ACADIE-BATHURST TITANS
(Lost league finals to Val-d'Or, 4-0)

SCORING

	Games	G	A	Pts.	PIM
Mirko Murovic	19	9	11	20	8
Alex Matieroukhine	19	11	6	17	46
Simon Laliberte	19	5	12	17	16
Antoine Bergeron	19	6	10	16	46
Yann Joseph	19	5	11	16	22
Alexandre Vigneault	19	1	13	14	20
Eric Cloutier	17	6	7	13	19
Samuel Seguin	19	5	7	12	12
Olivier Fillion	19	3	8	11	12
Karl Fournier	19	6	4	10	20
Darrell Jerrett	19	2	7	9	42
Miroslav Durak	18	4	3	7	45
Patrick Mbaraga	19	1	4	5	39
Jonathan Ferland	13	0	4	4	47
Tyler Reid	19	1	2	3	20
Michael Tessier	13	1	0	1	2
Michael Lanthier	16	1	0	1	47
Jean-Francois Laniel (goalie)	4	0	0	0	0
Carl McLean	9	0	0	0	10
Joey Francois Blacksmith	11	0	0	0	2
Eric Labelle	17	0	0	0	37
Adam Russo (goalie)	19	0	0	0	0

GOALTENDING

	Games	Min.	W	L	T	G	SO	Avg.
Adam Russo	19	1082	11	5	0	45	3	2.50
Jean-Francois Laniel	4	133	1	2	0	10	0	4.51

BAIE-COMEAU DRAKKAR
(Lost division finals to Acadie-Bathurst, 4-2)

SCORING

	Games	G	A	Pts.	PIM
Yanick Lehoux	11	8	16	24	0
Marco Charpentier	11	9	10	19	10
Robin Leblanc	11	7	8	15	8
Pascal Pelletier	11	2	11	13	6
Jonathan Gautier	11	3	6	9	4
Dominic Periard	10	2	6	8	58
Jean Morin	11	4	3	7	16
Maxime Fortunus	11	2	4	6	6
Duilio Grande	11	2	3	5	24
Charles Linglet	11	2	2	4	10
Martin Mandeville	10	1	2	3	4
Kevin Deslauriers	11	1	2	3	4
Joel Perreault	11	1	1	2	10
Daniel Bergeron	11	0	2	2	34
Premysl Duben	9	1	0	1	12
Jonathan Walsh	8	0	1	1	0
Luis Tremblay	9	0	1	1	6
Ghyslain Rousseau (goalie)	1	0	0	0	0
Matthew Hyde	9	0	0	0	2

	Games	G	A	Pts.	PIM
Thierry Douville	11	0	0	0	16
David St. Germain (goalie)	11	0	0	0	0

GOALTENDING

	Games	Min.	W	L	T	G	SO	Avg.
David St. Germain	11	683	6	4	0	29	1	2.55
Ghyslain Rousseau	1	47	0	1	0	3	0	3.88

CAPE BRETON SCREAMING EAGLES
(Lost division semifinals to Acadie-Bathurst, 4-1)

SCORING

	Games	G	A	Pts.	PIM
Dominic Noel	12	9	6	15	22
Stuart MacRae	12	6	7	13	2
Dustin Russell	12	2	8	10	4
Pierre-Luc Laprise	12	3	6	9	6
Olivier Proulx	12	4	3	7	18
Mathieu Dumas	12	1	6	7	4
Hunter Lahache	12	0	7	7	35
Andre Martineau	9	3	3	6	10
Pascal Morency	12	1	5	6	29
Charles Gauthier	9	2	3	5	4
Maxime Lessard	12	2	2	4	8
Robert Horak	12	1	3	4	18
Ryan Flinn	9	1	1	2	43
Vladimir Artushin	6	1	0	1	2
Matthew French	4	0	1	1	25
Jason Harshaw	12	0	1	1	26
Kevin Cloutier	2	0	0	0	0
Marc-Andre Fleury (goalie)	2	0	0	0	0
Rob Dunphy	3	0	0	0	0
George Davis	5	0	0	0	14
Gaby Beaudet	6	0	0	0	0
Jean-Francois Beaudet	7	0	0	0	0
Jean-Philippe Cote	12	0	0	0	18
Rodrigue Boucher	12	0	0	0	4
Daniel Boisclair (goalie)	12	0	0	0	0

GOALTENDING

	Games	Min.	W	L	T	G	SO	Avg.
Daniel Boisclair	12	685	5	6	0	36	0	3.16
Marc-Andre Fleury	2	32	0	1	0	4	0	7.50

CHICOUTIMI SAGUENEENS
(Lost division quarterfinals to Cape Breton, 4-3)

SCORING

	Games	G	A	Pts.	PIM
Pierre-Marc Bouchard	6	5	8	13	0
P.-Alexandre Parenteau	7	4	7	11	2
Eric Betournay	7	3	6	9	6
Christian Larrivee	7	3	1	4	4
Sylvain Plamondon	7	1	3	4	2
Eric Beaudin	7	0	4	4	12
David Beaudry-Ouellet	7	2	1	3	4
Stanislav Hudec	7	1	2	3	6

MAJOR JUNIOR LEAGUES

	Games	G	A	Pts.	PIM
Eric Dufour	7	1	2	3	0
Bruno Champagne	7	1	0	1	0
Alain Chenard	6	0	1	1	0
Mathieu Betournay	7	0	1	1	0
Karl St. Pierre	7	0	1	1	10
Sylvain Watt	7	0	1	1	2
Dave Verville (goalie)	7	0	1	1	0
Martin Beauchesne	2	0	0	0	0
Sebastien Hains	4	0	0	0	0
Alexandre Blackburn	7	0	0	0	9
Jean-Francois Demers	7	0	0	0	4
Yannick Dallaire	7	0	0	0	0
Guillaume Bouchard	7	0	0	0	0

GOALTENDING

	Games	Min.	W	L	T	G	SO	Avg.
Dave Verville	7	418	3	4	0	22	0	3.16

DRUMMONDVILLE VOLTIGEURS
(Lost division quarterfinals to Victoriaville, 4-3)

SCORING

	Games	G	A	Pts.	PIM
Julien Desrosiers	6	6	4	10	4
Francis Deslauriers	6	3	3	6	10
Eric Dubois	6	2	4	6	4
Vincent Tougas	6	2	3	5	6
Simon Duplessis	6	2	1	3	17
Jean-Francois Cyr	6	1	2	3	4
Evgueni Nourislamov	3	0	3	3	2
Pierre-Luc Emond	6	2	0	2	10
Thierry Kaszap	6	0	2	2	25
Martin Chabot	4	1	0	1	0
Eric Jean	5	1	0	1	17
David Bergeron	1	0	1	1	0
Simon Nadeau	5	0	1	1	0
Martin Frolik	5	0	1	1	2
Jean-Philippe Morin	5	0	1	1	6
Jean-Francois Racine (goalie)	5	0	1	1	0
Louis-Philippe Lessard	6	0	1	1	6
Joey D'Amico	6	0	1	1	44
David Bergeron (goalie)	1	0	0	0	0
Mathieu Audet (goalie)	2	0	0	0	0
Jean-Philippe Glaude	2	0	0	0	2
Sebastien Lapierre	2	0	0	0	0
Bernard Lahaie	3	0	0	0	2
Frederic Faucher	3	0	0	0	2
Jerome Briere	4	0	0	0	0
Steve Villeneuve	6	0	0	0	2

GOALTENDING

	Games	Min.	W	L	T	G	SO	Avg.
Jean-Francois Racine	5	303	2	3	0	20	0	3.97
David Bergeron	1	30	0	1	0	3	0	5.99
Mathieu Audet	2	42	0	0	0	5	0	7.22

HALIFAX MOOSEHEADS
(Lost division quarterfinals to Rimouski, 4-2)

SCORING

	Games	G	A	Pts.	PIM
Robbie Sutherland	6	5	2	7	20
Jason King	6	3	2	5	16
Brandon Benedict	6	0	5	5	12
Derrick Kent	6	1	3	4	10
Louis Mandeville	6	0	4	4	6
Sebastien Laprise	6	2	1	3	16
Gary Zinck	5	1	2	3	29
Sergei Klyazmin	6	1	2	3	8
A.J. MacLean	6	2	0	2	4
Bruce Gillis	6	1	1	2	12
Jonathan Boone	6	1	1	2	9
Jules-Edy Laraque	6	1	1	2	6
Ali MacEachern	4	0	2	2	13
Milan Jurcina	6	0	2	2	12

	Games	G	A	Pts.	PIM
Conor McGuire	6	0	1	1	4
Dany Dallaire (goalie)	5	0	1	1	0
Jules Saulnier	1	0	0	0	0
Michael Couch	2	0	0	0	0
Pascal Leclaire (goalie)	2	0	0	0	0
Ryan MacPherson	2	0	0	0	0
Randy Upshall	2	0	0	0	0
Ryan White	4	0	0	0	14
Giulio Scandella	5	0	0	0	0
Hugo Lehoux	5	0	0	0	17

GOALTENDING

	Games	Min.	W	L	T	G	SO	Avg.
Dany Dallaire	5	250	2	2	0	15	0	3.61
Pascal Leclaire	2	109	0	2	0	10	0	5.49

HULL OLYMPIQUES
(Lost division quarterfinals to Rouyn-Noranda, 4-1)

SCORING

	Games	G	A	Pts.	PIM
Ales Hemsky	5	2	3	5	2
Bruno Lemire	5	2	3	5	6
Philippe Lacasse	5	2	2	4	2
Dale Sullivan	5	2	1	3	0
Brent Roach	5	2	1	3	0
Mario Joly	5	0	3	3	18
Roberto Bissonnette	3	1	1	2	4
Philippe Choiniere	5	1	1	2	8
Maxime Talbot	5	1	0	1	2
Jason Kostadine	4	0	1	1	0
Doug O'Brien	5	0	1	1	0
John Cilladi	1	0	0	0	0
Olivier Dannel (goalie)	1	0	0	0	0
Chris Moher	2	0	0	0	4
Ian Courville	4	0	0	0	0
Jean-Michel Daoust	5	0	0	0	8
Carle Rochon	5	0	0	0	0
Bobby Clarke	5	0	0	0	4
Derick Martin	5	0	0	0	8
Andrew Carver	5	0	0	0	10
Adam Rivet	5	0	0	0	14
Eric Lafrance (goalie)	5	0	0	0	2

GOALTENDING

	Games	Min.	W	L	T	G	SO	Avg.
Eric Lafrance	5	293	1	4	0	19	0	3.89
Olivier Dannel	1	5	0	0	0	1	0	13.67

QUEBEC REMPARTS
(Lost division quarterfinals to Acadie-Bathurst, 4-0)

SCORING

	Games	G	A	Pts.	PIM
Shawn Collymore	4	0	3	3	0
Mike Bray	4	1	1	2	35
Guillaume Berube	4	1	0	1	2
Petr Preucil	4	1	0	1	11
David Masse	4	1	0	1	22
Remi Bergeron	4	0	1	1	16
Guillaume Fournier	4	0	1	1	2
Kevin Lachance (goalie)	4	0	1	1	6
Scott Della Vedova (goalie)	1	0	0	0	0
Alexandre Reuben	1	0	0	0	0
Cory Urquhart	2	0	0	0	2
Robert Pearce	2	0	0	0	0
Sebastien Morissette	3	0	0	0	17
Jeff Hadley	4	0	0	0	19
Didier Bochatay	4	0	0	0	24
Justin Stewart	4	0	0	0	6
Yannick Searles	4	0	0	0	2
Richard Paul	4	0	0	0	24
David Boilard	4	0	0	0	26
Philippe Paris	4	0	0	0	16
Philippe Parent	4	0	0	0	24
Jean Mallette	4	0	0	0	4

MAJOR JUNIOR LEAGUES QMJHL

GOALTENDING

	Games	Min.	W	L	T	G	SO	Avg.
Kevin Lachance	4	265	0	4	0	15	0	3.40
Scott Della Vedova	1	5	0	0	0	1	0	11.83

RIMOUSKI OCEANIC
(Lost division semifinals to Baie-Comeau, 4-1)

SCORING

	Games	G	A	Pts.	PIM
Michel Ouellet	11	6	7	13	8
Thatcher Bell	11	6	7	13	14
Jonathan Beaulieu	11	4	7	11	18
Jean-Philippe Briere	11	3	8	11	2
Tomas Malec	11	0	11	11	26
Ryan Clowe	11	8	1	9	12
Aaron Johnson	11	2	4	6	35
Benoit Martin	11	2	4	6	4
Jean-Francois Plourde	11	3	2	5	28
Mathieu Simard	11	2	2	4	10
Nicolas Poirier	11	0	4	4	31
Gabriel Balasescu	11	0	3	3	36
Philippe Lauze	11	1	0	1	22
Samuel Gibbons	11	0	1	1	10
Eric Salvail (goalie)	1	0	0	0	2
Tim Sinasac	3	0	0	0	29
Jean-Francois Babin	8	0	0	0	0
Sebastien Bolduc	11	0	0	0	14
Daniel Petiquay	11	0	0	0	4
Brent MacLellan	11	0	0	0	41
Jonathan Pelletier (goalie)	11	0	0	0	2

GOALTENDING

	Games	Min.	W	L	T	G	SO	Avg.
Jonathan Pelletier	11	677	5	6	0	44	0	3.90
Eric Salvail	1	7	0	0	0	1	0	8.49

ROUYN-NORANDA HUSKIES
(Lost division semifinals to Shawinigan, 4-0)

SCORING

	Games	G	A	Pts.	PIM
Wesley Scanzano	9	3	8	11	0
Maxime Bouchard	9	5	5	10	22
Shawn Scanzano	9	2	7	9	20
Marc-Andre Binette	9	6	2	8	8
Alexandre Giroux	9	2	6	8	22
Jonathan Gauthier	9	1	5	6	22
Sebastian Strozynski	9	3	2	5	17
Guillaume Lefebvre	9	3	1	4	22
Alexandre Morel	9	1	3	4	10
Jonathan Gagnon	9	1	2	3	8
Patrick Gilbert	9	0	3	3	6
Michal Pinc	9	0	3	3	12
Matthew Quinn	9	0	2	2	2
Jerome Marois	6	1	0	1	17
Sebastien Centomo (goalie)	1	0	0	0	0
Eric L'Italien	3	0	0	0	0
Bruno Cadieux	3	0	0	0	0
Dominic Soucy	8	0	0	0	0
Jonathan Jolette	8	0	0	0	4
Maxime Ouellet (goalie)	8	0	0	0	0
Patrice Theriault	8	0	0	0	8
Mathieu Leclerc	9	0	0	0	17

GOALTENDING

	Games	Min.	W	L	T	G	SO	Avg.
Maxime Ouellet	8	490	4	4	0	25	0	3.06
Sebastien Centomo	1	60	0	1	0	4	0	4.00

SHAWINIGAN CATARACTES
(Lost division finals to Val-d'Or, 4-2)

SCORING

	Games	G	A	Pts.	PIM
Marc-Andre Bergeron	10	4	11	15	24
Jonathan Bellemarre	8	3	11	14	18

	Games	G	A	Pts.	PIM
Jason Pominville	10	6	6	12	0
Radim Vrbata	10	4	7	11	4
Anthony Quessy	10	4	6	10	36
Dominic Forget	10	4	5	9	8
Jean-Francois Dufort	10	3	3	6	18
Jean-Francois David	10	2	4	6	14
Alexandre Menard-Burrows	10	2	1	3	8
David Chicoine	10	2	1	3	14
Jonathan Lessard	10	0	3	3	16
Yannick Noiseux	10	2	0	2	4
Denis Desmarais	10	0	2	2	18
Gilbert Lefrancois	10	0	2	2	14
Trevor Ettinger	10	0	1	1	14
Zbynek Michalek	3	0	0	0	0
Olivier Michaud (goalie)	3	0	0	0	0
Francois Gagnon	4	0	0	0	2
Mathieu Payette	5	0	0	0	0
Frederic Cloutier (goalie)	9	0	0	0	0
Kevin Bergin	10	0	0	0	0
Jimmy Cuddihy	10	0	0	0	0

GOALTENDING

	Games	Min.	W	L	T	G	SO	Avg.
Olivier Michaud	3	150	1	2	0	6	0	2.41
Frederic Cloutier	9	467	5	2	0	24	1	3.08

SHERBROOKE FAUCONS
(Lost division quarterfinals to Val-d'Or, 4-0)

SCORING

	Games	G	A	Pts.	PIM
Sandro Sbrocca	4	2	3	5	24
Francois Belanger	4	1	4	5	16
Benoit Genesse	4	2	2	4	4
Nicolas Corbeil	3	1	3	4	4
Simon Tremblay	4	2	1	3	2
Francis Trudel	4	1	2	3	12
Jeremy Knight	4	1	2	3	2
Bertrand-Pierre Plouffe	4	1	2	3	24
Pierre-Luc Courchesne	4	0	3	3	2
Sebastien Courcelles	4	1	1	2	2
Steve Morency	4	1	1	2	4
Yan Gaudette	1	0	0	0	0
Mathieu Duquette	1	0	0	0	0
Guy Turmel	1	0	0	0	15
Stephane Valois	2	0	0	0	0
Mathieu Thibodeau	4	0	0	0	0
Mathieu Wathier	4	0	0	0	0
Jonathan Robert	4	0	0	0	14
Eric Dagenais	4	0	0	0	2
Joey Neale	4	0	0	0	0
Eric Lavigne	4	0	0	0	0
Louis-Philippe Lemay	4	0	0	0	0
Drew MacIntyre (goalie)	4	0	0	0	0

GOALTENDING

	Games	Min.	W	L	T	G	SO	Avg.
Drew MacIntyre	4	238	0	4	0	19	0	4.78

VAL-D'OR FOREURS
(Winner of 2001 President Cup playoffs)

SCORING

	Games	G	A	Pts.	PIM
Simon Gamache	21	22	35	57	18
Brandon Reid	21	13	29	42	14
Stephane Veilleux	21	15	18	33	42
Seneque Hyacinthe	21	10	17	27	22
Eric Fortier	21	7	18	25	22
Chris Lyness	21	7	14	21	50
Nicolas Pelletier	21	7	5	12	6
David Cloutier	21	3	9	12	36
Kory Baker	17	3	8	11	30
Jerome Bergeron	21	7	3	10	56
Hugo Levesque	21	2	8	10	28

	Games	G	A	Pts.	PIM
Alex Turcotte	21	3	2	5	8
Mathieu Bastien	21	2	3	5	22
Pierre Morvan	21	0	3	3	26
Luc Girard	18	0	2	2	10
Tomas Psenka	7	1	0	1	4
Alexandre Rouleau	21	1	0	1	46
Steve Pelletier	2	0	0	0	2
Frederic Bedard	2	0	0	0	0
Maxime Daigneault (goalie)	10	0	0	0	0
Simon Lajeunesse (goalie)	14	0	0	0	0
Mathieu Roy	17	0	0	0	4
Samuel Duplain	20	0	0	0	17

GOALTENDING

	Games	Min.	W	L	T	G	SO	Avg.
Maxime Daigneault	10	504	8	1	0	21	0	2.50
Simon Lajeunesse	14	760	8	4	0	52	0	4.10

VICTORIAVILLE TIGRES
(Lost division semifinals to Val-d'Or, 4-3)

SCORING

	Games	G	A	Pts.	PIM
Marc-Andre Thinel	13	12	13	25	18
Danny Groulx	13	2	19	21	46
Matthew Lombardi	13	12	6	18	10

	Games	G	A	Pts.	PIM
Carl Mallette	13	10	8	18	42
Johnny Oduya	13	4	9	13	10
Sebastien Thinel	13	4	8	12	6
Martin Autotte	13	4	7	11	30
Antoine Vermette	9	4	6	10	14
Martin Grenier	13	2	8	10	51
Jonathan Fauteux	13	0	6	6	10
Patrick Vincent	11	2	3	5	59
Kristian Kovac	13	2	3	5	4
Pierre-Luc Sleigher	10	1	1	2	27
Mathieu Brunelle	13	1	1	2	0
Carl Gagnon	13	0	2	2	12
Frederick Malette (goalie)	4	0	1	1	0
Steve Richards	8	0	1	1	12
Jean-Francois Nogues (goalie)	11	0	1	1	0
Pierre-Luc Daneau	13	0	1	1	4
Hugo Beaudet	2	0	0	0	0
Tommy Bolduc	12	0	0	0	28
Karl Morin	13	0	0	0	0

GOALTENDING

	Games	Min.	W	L	T	G	SO	Avg.
Jean-Francois Nogues	11	575	6	3	0	38	0	3.96
Frederick Malette	4	219	1	3	0	18	0	4.93

2000-01 AWARD WINNERS

ALL-STAR TEAMS

First team	Pos.	Second team
Frederic Cloutier, Shawinigan	G	Maxime Ouellet, R.-Noranda
Marc-Andre Bergeron, Shaw.	D	Chris Lyness, Val-d'Or
Danny Groulx, Victoriaville	D	Alexandre Vigneault, A.-Bath.
Simon Gamache, Val-d'Or	LW	Jason King, Halifax
Brandon Reid, Val-d'Or	C	Dominic Forget, Shawinigan
Radim Vrbata, Shawinigan	RW	Marc-Andre Thinel, Vic.

TROPHY WINNERS

Frank Selke Trophy: Brandon Reid, Val-d'Or
Michel Bergeron Trophy: Pierre-Marc Bouchard, Chicoutimi
Raymond Lagace Trophy: Tomas Malec, Rimouski
Jean Beliveau Trophy: Simon Gamache, Val-d'Or
Michel Briere Trophy: Simon Gamache, Val-d'Or
Marcel Robert Trophy: Jean-Philippe Briere, Rimouski
Mike Bossy Trophy: Ales Hemsky, Hull
Emile "Butch" Bouchard Trophy: Marc-Andre Bergeron, Shaw.
Jacques Plante Trophy: Frederic Cloutier, Shawinigan
Guy Lafleur Trophy: Simon Gamache, Val-d'Or
Robert LeBel Trophy: Shawinigan Cataractes
John Rougeau Trophy: Shawinigan Cataractes
President Cup: Val-d'Or Foreurs

ALL-TIME AWARD WINNERS

FRANK SELKE TROPHY
(Most gentlemanly player)

Season	Player, Team
1970-71	Norm Dube, Sherbrooke
1971-72	Gerry Teeple, Cornwall
1972-73	Claude Larose, Drummondville
1973-74	Gary MacGregor, Cornwall
1974-75	Jean-Luc Phaneuf, Montreal
1975-76	Norm Dupont, Montreal
1976-77	Mike Bossy, Laval
1977-78	Kevin Reeves, Montreal
1978-79	Ray Bourque, Verdun
	Jean-Francois Sauve, Trois-Rivieres
1979-80	Jean-Francois Sauve, Trois-Rivieres
1980-81	Claude Verret, Trois-Rivieres
1981-82	Claude Verret, Trois-Rivieres
1982-83	Pat LaFontaine, Verdun
1983-84	Jerome Carrier, Verdun
1984-85	Patrick Emond, Chicoutimi
1985-86	Jimmy Carson, Verdun
1986-87	Luc Beausoleil, Laval
1987-88	Stephan Lebeau, Shawinigan
1988-89	Steve Cadieux, Shawinigan
1989-90	Andrew McKim, Hull
1990-91	Yanic Perreault, Trois-Rivieres
1991-92	Martin Gendron, St. Hyacinthe

Season	Player, Team
1992-93	Martin Gendron, St. Hyacinthe
1993-94	Yanick Dube, Laval
1994-95	Eric Daze, Beauport
1995-96	Christian Dube, Sherbrooke
1996-97	Daniel Briere, Drummondville
1997-98	Simon Laliberte, Moncton
1998-99	Eric Chouinard, Quebec
1999-00	Jonathan Roy, Moncton
2000-01	Brandon Reid, Val-d'Or

MICHEL BERGERON TROPHY
(Top rookie forward)

Season	Player, Team
1969-70	Serge Martel, Verdun
1970-71	Bob Murphy, Cornwall
1971-72	Bob Murray, Cornwall
1972-73	Pierre Larouche, Sorel
1973-74	Mike Bossy, Laval
1974-75	Dennis Pomerleau, Hull
1975-76	Jean-Marc Bonamie, Shawinigan
1976-77	Rick Vaive, Sherbrooke
1977-78	Norm Rochefort, Trois-Rivieres
	Denis Savard, Montreal
1978-79	Alan Grenier, Laval
1979-80	Dale Hawerchuk, Cornwall

Season	Player, Team
1980-81	Claude Verret, Trois-Rivieres
1981-82	Sylvain Turgeon, Hull
1982-83	Pat LaFontaine, Verdun
1983-84	Stephane Richer, Granby
1984-85	Jimmy Carson, Verdun
1985-86	Pierre Turgeon, Granby
1986-87	Rob Murphy, Laval
1987-88	Martin Gelinas, Hull
1988-89	Yanic Perreault, Trois-Rivieres
1989-90	Martin Lapointe, Laval
1990-91	Rene Corbet, Drummondville
1991-92	Alexandre Daigle, Victoriaville
1992-93	Steve Brule, St. Jean
1993-94	Christian Dube, Sherbrooke
1994-95	Daniel Briere, Drummondville
1995-96	Pavel Rosa, Hull
1996-97	Vincent Lecavalier, Rimouski
1997-98	Mike Ribeiro, Rouyn-Noranda
1998-99	Ladislav Nagy, Halifax
1999-00	Chris Montgomery, Montreal
2000-01	Pierre-Marc Bouchard, Chicoutimi

Prior to 1980-81 season, award was given to QMJHL rookie of the year.

RAYMOND LAGACE TROPHY
(Top rookie defenseman or goaltender)

Season	Player, Team
1980-81	Billy Campbell, Montreal
1981-82	Michel Petit, Sherbrooke
1982-83	Bobby Dollas, Laval
1983-84	James Gasseau, Drummondville
1984-85	Robert Desjardins, Shawinigan
1985-86	Stephane Guerard, Shawinigan
1986-87	Jimmy Waite, Chicoutimi
1987-88	Stephane Beauregard, St. Jean
1988-89	Karl Dykhuis, Hull
1989-90	Francois Groleau, Shawinigan
1990-91	Philippe Boucher, Granby
1991-92	Philippe DeRouville, Longueuil
1992-93	Stephane Routhier, Drummondville
1993-94	Jimmy Drolet, St. Hyacinthe
1994-95	Martin Biron, Beauport
1995-96	Mathieu Garon, Victoriaville
1996-97	Christian Bronsard, Hull
1997-98	Alexei Tezikov, Moncton
1998-99	Alexei Volkov, Halifax
1999-00	Kirill Safronov, Quebec
2000-01	Tomas Malec, Rimouski

JEAN BELIVEAU TROPHY
(Scoring leader)

Season	Player, Team
1969-70	Luc Simard, Trois-Rivieres
1970-71	Guy Lafleur, Quebec
1971-72	Jacques Richard, Quebec
1972-73	Andre Savard, Quebec
1973-74	Pierre Larouche, Sorel
1974-75	Norm Dupont, Montreal
1975-76	Richard Dalpe, Trois-Rivieres
	Sylvain Locas, Chicoutimi
1976-77	Jean Savard, Quebec
1977-78	Ron Carter, Sherbooke
1978-79	Jean-Francois Sauve, Trois-Rivieres
1979-80	Jean-Francois Sauve, Trois-Rivieres
1980-81	Dale Hawerchuk, Cornwall
1981-82	Claude Verret, Trois-Rivieres
1982-83	Pat LaFontaine, Verdun
1983-84	Mario Lemieux, Laval
1984-85	Guy Rouleau, Longueuil
1985-86	Guy Rouleau, Hull
1986-87	Marc Fortier, Chicoutimi
1987-88	Patrice Lefebvre, Shawinigan
1988-89	Stephane Morin, Chicoutimi
1989-90	Patrick Lebeau, Victoriaville

Season	Player, Team
1990-91	Yanic Perreault, Trois-Rivieres
1991-92	Patrick Poulin, St. Hyacinthe
1992-93	Rene Corbet, Drummondville
1993-94	Yanick Dube, Laval
1994-95	Patrick Carignan, Shawinigan
1995-96	Daniel Briere, Drummondville
1996-97	Pavel Rosa, Hull
1997-98	Ramzi Abid, Chicoutimi
1998-99	Mike Ribeiro, Rouyn-Noranda
1999-00	Brad Richards, Rimouski
2000-01	Simon Gamache, Val-d'Or

MICHEL BRIERE TROPHY
(Most Valuable Player)

Season	Player, Team
1972-73	Andre Savard, Quebec
1973-74	Gary MacGregor, Cornwall
1974-75	Mario Viens, Cornwall
1975-76	Peter Marsh, Sherbrooke
1976-77	Lucien DeBlois, Sorel
1977-78	Kevin Reeves, Montreal
1978-79	Pierre Lacroix, Trois-Rivieres
1979-80	Denis Savard, Montreal
1980-81	Dale Hawerchuk, Cornwall
1981-82	John Chabot, Sherbrooke
1982-83	Pat LaFontaine, Verdun
1983-84	Mario Lemieux, Laval
1984-85	Daniel Berthiaume, Chicoutimi
1985-86	Guy Rouleau, Hull
1986-87	Robert Desjardins, Longueuil
1987-88	Marc Saumier, Hull
1988-89	Stephane Morin, Chicoutimi
1989-90	Andrew McKim, Hull
1990-91	Yanic Perreault, Trois-Rivieres
1991-92	Charles Poulin, St. Hyacinthe
1992-93	Jocelyn Thibault, Sherbrooke
1993-94	Emmanuel Fernandez, Laval
1994-95	Frederic Chartier, Laval
1995-96	Christian Dube, Sherbrooke
1996-97	Daniel Corso, Victoriaville
1997-98	Ramzi Abid, Chicoutimi
1998-99	Mathieu Chouinard, Shawinigan
1999-00	Brad Richards, Rimouski
2000-01	Simon Gamache, Val-d'Or

MARCEL ROBERT TROPHY
(Top scholastic/athletic performer)

Season	Player, Team
1981-82	Jacques Sylvestre, Granby
1982-83	Claude Gosselin, Quebec
1983-84	Gilbert Paiement, Chicoutimi
1984-85	Claude Gosselin, Longueuil
1985-86	Bernard Morin, Laval
1986-87	Patrice Tremblay, Chicoutimi
1987-88	Stephane Beauregard, St. Jean
1988-89	Daniel Lacroix, Granby
1989-90	Yanic Perreault, Trois-Rivieres
1990-91	Benoit Larose, Laval
1991-92	Simon Toupin, Beauport
1992-93	Jocelyn Thibault, Sherbrooke
1993-94	Patrick Boileau, Laval
1994-95	Daniel Briere, Drummondville
1995-96	Marc Denis, Chicoutimi
1996-97	Luc Vaillancourt, Beauport
1997-98	Michel Tremblay, Shawinigan
1998-99	Christian Robichaud, Victoriaville
1999-00	Yanick Lehoux, Baie-Comeau
2000-01	Jean-Philippe Briere, Rimouski

MIKE BOSSY TROPHY
(Top pro prospect)

Season	Player, Team
1980-81	Dale Hawerchuk, Cornwall
1981-82	Michel Petit, Sherbrooke

Season	Player, Team
1982-83	Pat LaFontaine, Verdun
	Sylvain Turgeon, Hull
1983-84	Mario Lemieux, Laval
1984-85	Jose Charbonneau, Drummondville
1985-86	Jimmy Carson, Verdun
1986-87	Pierre Turgeon, Granby
1987-88	Daniel Dore, Drummondville
1988-89	Patrice Brisebois, Laval
1989-90	Karl Dykhuis, Hull
1990-91	Philippe Boucher, Granby
1991-92	Paul Brousseau, Hull
1992-93	Alexandre Daigle, Victoriaville
1993-94	Eric Fichaud, Chicoutimi
1994-95	Martin Biron, Beauport
1995-96	Jean-Pierre Dumont, Val d'Or
1996-97	Roberto Luongo, Val d'Or
1997-98	Vincent Lecavalier, Rimouski
1998-99	Maxime Ouellet, Quebec
1999-00	Antoine Vermette, Victoriaville
2000-01	Ales Hemsky, Hull

Originally known as Association of Journalism of Hockey Trophy from 1980-81 through 1982-83.

EMILE "BUTCH" BOUCHARD TROPHY
(Top defenseman)

Season	Player, Team
1975-76	Jean Gagnon, Quebec
1976-77	Robert Picard, Montreal
1977-78	Mark Hardy, Montreal
1978-79	Ray Bourque, Verdun
1979-80	Gaston Therrien, Quebec
1980-81	Fred Boimistruck, Cornwall
1981-82	Paul Andre Boutilier, Sherbrooke
1982-83	J.J. Daigneault, Longueuil
1983-84	Billy Campbell, Verdun
1984-85	Yves Beaudoin, Shawinigan
1985-86	Sylvain Cote, Hull
1986-87	Jean Marc Richard, Chicoutimi
1987-88	Eric Desjardins, Granby
1988-89	Yves Racine, Victoriaville
1989-90	Claude Barthe, Victoriaville
1990-91	Patrice Brisebois, Drummondville
1991-92	Francois Groleau, Shawinigan
1992-93	Benoit Larose, Laval
1993-94	Steve Gosselin, Chicoutimi
1994-95	Stephane Julien, Sherbrooke
1995-96	Denis Gauthier, Drummondville
1996-97	Stephane Robidas, Shawinigan
1997-98	Derrick Walser, Rimouski
1998-99	Jiri Fischer, Hull
1999-00	Michel Periard, Rimouski
2000-01	Marc-Andre Bergeron, Shawiningan

JACQUES PLANTE TROPHY
(Top goaltender)

Season	Player, Team
1969-70	Michael Deguise, Sorel
1970-71	Reynald Fortier, Quebec
1971-72	Richard Brodeur, Cornwall
1972-73	Pierre Perusee, Quebec
1973-74	Claude Legris, Sorel
1974-75	Nick Sanza, Sherbrooke
1975-76	Tim Bernhardt, Cornwall
1976-77	Tim Bernhardt, Cornwall
1977-78	Tim Bernhardt, Cornwall
1978-79	Jacques Cloutier, Trois-Rivieres
1979-80	Corrado Micalef, Sherbrooke
1980-81	Michel Dufour,Sorel
1981-82	Jeff Barratt, Montreal
1982-83	Tony Haladuick, Laval
1983-84	Tony Haladuick, Laval
1984-85	Daniel Berthiaume, Chicoutimi

Season	Player, Team
1985-86	Robert Desjardins, Hull
1986-87	Robert Desjardins, Longueuil
1987-88	Stephane Beauregard, St. Jean
1988-89	Stephane Fiset, Victoriaville
1989-90	Pierre Gagnon, Victoriaville
1990-91	Felix Potvin, Chicoutimi
1991-92	Jean-Francois Labbe, Trois-Rivieres
1992-93	Jocelyn Thibault, Sherbrooke
1993-94	Philippe DeRouville, Verdun
1994-95	Martin Biron, Beauport
1995-96	Frederic Deschenes, Granby
1996-97	Marc Denis, Chicoutimi
1997-98	Mathieu Garon, Victoriaville
1998-99	Maxime Ouellet, Quebec
1999-00	Simon Lajeunesse, Moncton
2000-01	Frederic Cloutier, Shawinigan

GUY LAFLEUR TROPHY
(Playoff MVP)

Season	Player, Team
1977-78	Richard David, Trois-Rivieres
1978-79	Jean-Francois Sauve, Trois-Rivieres
1979-80	Dale Hawerchuk, Cornwall
1980-81	Alain Lemieux, Trois-Rivieres
1981-82	Michel Morissette, Sherbrooke
1982-83	Pat LaFontaine, Verdun
1983-84	Mario Lemieux, Laval
1984-85	Claude Lemieux, Verdun
1985-86	Sylvain Cote, Hull
	Luc Robitaille, Hull
1986-87	Marc Saumier, Longueuil
1987-88	Marc Saumier, Hull
1988-89	Donald Audette, Laval
1989-90	Denis Chalifoux, Laval
1990-91	Felix Potvin, Chicoutimi
1991-92	Robert Guillet, Longueuil
1992-93	Emmanuel Fernandez, Laval
1993-94	Eric Fichaud, Chicoutimi
1994-95	Jose Theodore, Hull
1995-96	Jason Doig, Granby
1996-97	Christian Bronsard, Hull
1997-98	Jean-Pierre Dumont, Val d'Or
1998-99	Mathieu Benoit, Acadie-Bathurst
1999-00	Brad Richards, Rimouski
2000-01	Simon Gamache, Val-d'Or

ROBERT LEBEL TROPHY
(Best team defensive average)

Season	Team
1977-78	Trois-Rivieres Draveurs
1978-79	Trois-Rivieres Draveurs
1979-80	Sherbrooke Beavers
1980-81	Sorel Black Hawks
1981-82	Montreal Juniors
1982-83	Shawinigan Cataracts
1983-84	Shawinigan Cataracts
1984-85	Shawinigan Cataracts
1985-86	Hull Olympiques
1986-78	Longueuil Chevaliers
1987-88	St. Jean Castors
1988-89	Hull Olympiques
1989-90	Victoriaville Tigres
1990-91	Chicoutimi Sagueneens
1991-92	Trois-Rivieres Draveurs
1992-93	Sherbrooke Faucons
1993-94	College Francais de Verdun
1994-95	Beauport Harfangs
1995-96	Granby Predateurs
1996-97	Hull Olympics
1997-98	Quebec Remparts
1998-99	Halifax Mooseheads
1999-00	Moncton Wildcats
2000-01	Shawinigan Cataractes

	REGULAR-SEASON CHAMPION	PLAYOFF CHAMPION
Season	**Team**	**Team**
1969-70—	Quebec Remparts	Quebec Remparts
1970-71—	Quebec Remparts	Quebec Remparts
1971-72—	Cornwall Royals	Cornwall Royals
1972-73—	Quebec Remparts	Quebec Remparts
1973-74—	Sorel Black Hawks	Quebec Remparts
1974-75—	Sherbrooke Beavers	Sherbrooke Beavers
1975-76—	Sherbrooke Beavers	Quebec Remparts
1976-77—	Quebec Remparts	Sherbrooke Beavers
1977-78—	Trois-Rivieres Draveurs	Trois-Rivieres Draveurs
1978-79—	Trois-Rivieres Draveurs	Trois-Rivieres Draveurs
1979-80—	Sherbrooke Beavers	Cornwall Royals
1980-81—	Cornwall Royals	Cornwall Royals
1981-82—	Sherbrooke Beavers	Sherbrooke Beavers
1982-83—	Laval Voisins	Verdun Juniors
1983-84—	Laval Voisins	Laval Voisins
1984-85—	Shawinigan Cataracts	Verdun Junior Canadiens
1985-86—	Hull Olympiques	Hull Olympiques
1986-87—	Granby Bisons	Longueuil Chevaliers
1987-88—	Hull Olympiques	Hull Olympiques
1988-89—	Trois-Rivieres Draveurs	Laval Titans
1989-90—	Victoriaville Tigres	Laval Titans
1990-91—	Chicoutimi Sagueneens	Chicoutimi Sagueneens
1991-92—	Longueuil College Francais	Longueuil College Francais
1992-93—	Sherbrooke Faucons	Laval Titans
1993-94—	Laval Titans	Chicoutimi Sagueneens
1994-95—	Laval Titans	Hull Olympiques
1995-96—	Granby Predateurs	Granby Predateurs
1996-97—	Hull Olympics	Hull Olympics
1997-98—	Quebec Remparts	Val d'Or Foreurs
1998-99—	Quebec Remparts	Acadie-Bathurst Titans
1999-00—	Rimouski Oceanic	Rimouski Oceanic
2000-01—	Shawinigan Cataractes	Val-d'Or Foreurs

The QMJHL regular-season champion is awarded the John Rougeau Trophy and the playoff champion is awarded the Presidents Cup. The John Rougeau Trophy was originally called the Governors Trophy from 1969-70 through 1982-83.

MAJOR JUNIOR LEAGUES *QMJHL*

WESTERN HOCKEY LEAGUE

LEAGUE OFFICE

Note: League was known as Canadian Major Junior Hockey League in 1966-67 and Western Canadian Hockey League from 1967-68 through 1977-78.

Commissioner
Ron Robison
Chairman of the board
Bruce Hamilton
Vice president
Richard Doerksen
Director of communications/events
Leroy McKinnon

Education consultant
Jim Donlevy
Secretary
Connie Watson
Bookkeeping
Dianne Hayes

Address
Suite 308, 8989 Macleod Trail S.
Calgary, Alberta T2H 0M2
Phone
403-253-8113
FAX
403-258-1455

2000-01 REGULAR SEASON

FINAL STANDINGS

EAST DIVISION

Team	G	W	L	T	RT	Pts.	GF	GA
Swift Current	72	43	20	7	2	95	275	215
Regina	72	40	27	3	2	85	285	242
Moose Jaw	72	34	29	4	5	77	287	291
Brandon	72	32	32	5	3	72	244	242
Saskatoon	72	19	43	5	5	48	193	265
Prince Albert	72	18	47	3	4	43	204	348

CENTRAL DIVISION

Team	G	W	L	T	RT	Pts.	GF	GA
Red Deer	72	54	12	3	3	114	304	168
Kootenay	72	45	17	4	6	100	286	213
Calgary	72	37	27	5	3	82	284	250
Lethbridge	72	29	35	4	4	66	200	229
Medicine Hat	72	24	40	5	3	56	271	316

WEST DIVISION

Team	G	W	L	T	RT	Pts.	GF	GA
Kelowna	72	37	23	7	5	86	259	240
Portland	72	37	27	5	3	82	254	237
Kamloops	72	35	28	7	2	79	289	274
Spokane	72	35	28	7	2	79	242	219
Prince George	72	31	33	4	4	70	242	266
Seattle	72	30	33	8	1	69	262	299
Tri-City	72	21	36	8	7	57	217	284

INDIVIDUAL LEADERS

Goals: Layne Ulmer, Swift Current (63)
Assists: Jared Aulin, Kamloops (77)
  Justin Mapletoft, Red Deer (77)
Points: Justin Mapletoft, Red Deer (120)
Penalty minutes: David Kaczowka, Regina (414)
Goaltending average: Shane Bendera, Red Deer (2.49)
Shutouts: Shane Bendera, Red Deer (5)
  Lanny Ramage, Portland (5)

	Games	G	A	Pts.
Blake Evans, T.C.-Reg.	67	52	50	102
Kyle Wanvig, Red Deer	69	55	46	101
Konstantin Panov, Kamloops	69	44	56	100
Jordan Krestanovich, Calgary	70	40	60	100
Nathan Barrett, Lethbridge	70	46	53	99
Rory McDade, Kelowna	72	28	70	98
Duncan Milroy, Swift Current	68	38	54	92
Marcel Hossa, Portland	58	34	56	90
Tim Smith, Spo.-S.C.	68	31	59	90
Nathan Smith, Swift Current	67	28	62	90
Scott Upshall, Kamloops	70	42	45	87
Carsen Germyn, Kelowna	71	35	52	87
Zdenek Blatny, Kootenay	58	37	48	85
Garrett Prosofsky, P.A.-Port.	68	37	48	85
Matt Kinch, Calgary	70	18	66	84
Brett Lysak, Regina	64	35	48	83

TOP SCORERS

	Games	G	A	Pts.
Justin Mapletoft, Red Deer	70	43	77	120
Layne Ulmer, Swift Current	68	63	56	119
Jared Aulin, Kamloops	70	31	77	108
Jarret Stoll, Kootenay	62	40	66	106

INDIVIDUAL STATISTICS

BRANDON WHEAT KINGS

SCORING

	Games	G	A	Pts.	PIM
Ryan Craig	70	38	33	71	49
Colin McRae	71	25	40	65	36
Aaron Goldade	65	22	34	56	84
Jordin Tootoo	60	20	28	48	172
Kevin Harris	72	11	34	45	47
Milan Bartovic	34	15	25	40	40
Brett Girard	42	17	22	39	12
Jiri Jakes	64	22	16	38	73
Brett Thurston	72	4	21	25	88
Tim Konsorada	67	9	14	23	33
Lance Monych	53	14	8	22	34
Justin Hansen	18	7	12	19	22
Randy Ponte	68	8	9	17	283
Nolan Yonkman	51	6	10	16	94
Mark Ardelan	66	2	14	16	65

	Games	G	A	Pts.	PIM
Richard Mueller	33	5	10	15	16
Reagan Leslie	61	4	11	15	69
Wade Skolney	28	2	9	11	37
Travis Young	54	4	6	10	21
Travis Eagles	25	4	5	9	32
Brett Dickie	66	1	8	9	24
Bart Rushmer	6	0	8	8	24
Caine Pearpoint	42	2	3	5	26
James Marquis	34	1	4	5	16
J.D. Kehler	27	0	5	5	26
Jan Fadrny	2	1	1	2	6
Houston Hair	6	0	1	1	6
Shaun Fleming (goalie)	1	0	0	0	0
Richard Mueller	1	0	0	0	0
Mike Wirll	2	0	0	0	4
Eric Fehr	4	0	0	0	0
Krister Toews (goalie)	4	0	0	0	0
Geoff McIntosh (goalie)	17	0	0	0	0
Robert McVicar (goalie)	27	0	0	0	2
Jamie Hodson (goalie)	29	0	0	0	6

GOALTENDING

	Games	Min.	W	L	T	G	SO	Avg.
Robert McVicar	27	1537	12	10	2	76	0	2.97
Geoff McIntosh	17	947	8	7	1	50	1	3.17
Jamie Hodson	29	1587	9	17	1	92	0	3.48
Krister Toews	4	205	2	1	0	13	0	3.80
Shaun Fleming	1	60	1	0	0	5	0	5.00

CALGARY HITMEN
SCORING

	Games	G	A	Pts.	PIM
Jordan Krestanovich	70	40	60	100	32
Matt Kinch	70	18	66	84	52
Pavel Brendl	49	40	35	75	66
Kris Beech	40	22	44	66	103
Shaun Sutter	63	29	35	64	102
Sean McAslan	51	21	32	53	137
Shaun Norrie	72	24	24	48	106
Wade Davis	67	11	21	32	77
Chad Wolkowski	60	8	24	32	34
Rod Sarich	62	5	27	32	84
Michael Bubnick	68	8	22	30	50
Brandon Segal	72	16	11	27	103
Owen Fussey	48	15	10	25	33
Robin Gomez	65	5	15	20	253
Toni Bader	65	7	8	15	138
Jared Carli	68	2	13	15	149
Johnny Boychuk	66	4	8	12	61
David Vrbata	37	3	9	12	39
Adam Breitkreuz	48	3	3	6	37
Taggart Desmet	7	0	2	2	4
Brady Block (goalie)	37	0	2	2	18
Chris Beston	6	1	0	1	6
Mike Egener	52	1	0	1	91
Danny Ehrmen	41	0	1	1	35
Mark Shefchyk	1	0	0	0	0
Marcus Wright (goalie)	1	0	0	0	0
Richard McPherson	4	0	0	0	0
Ryan Martin (goalie)	5	0	0	0	0
Brent Krahn (goalie)	37	0	0	0	0

GOALTENDING

	Games	Min.	W	L	T	G	SO	Avg.
Brent Krahn	37	2087	22	10	3	104	1	2.99
Brady Block	37	1997	15	17	1	120	0	3.61
Ryan Martin	5	238	0	2	1	20	0	5.04
Marcus Wright	1	27	0	1	0	4	0	8.89

KAMLOOPS BLAZERS
SCORING

	Games	G	A	Pts.	PIM
Jared Aulin	70	31	77	108	62
Konstantin Panov	69	44	56	100	54
Scott Upshall	70	42	45	87	111

	Games	G	A	Pts.	PIM
Jonathan Hobson	71	31	33	64	77
Erik Christensen	72	21	23	44	36
Paul Elliott	40	10	33	43	37
Shaonne Morrison	61	13	25	38	132
Gable Gross	40	20	14	34	41
Tyler Sloan	70	5	28	33	146
Ryan Annesley	30	9	19	28	35
Jarret Lukin	61	11	7	18	43
Mark Rooneem	62	8	9	17	77
Paul Brown	30	6	11	17	118
Derek Krestanovich	67	4	13	17	72
Conlan Seder	50	1	13	14	29
Josh Bonar	40	3	8	11	28
Pat Brandreth	49	3	8	11	163
Kyle Ladobruk	39	2	8	10	18
Colton Orr	41	8	1	9	179
Paul Deniset	20	3	6	9	16
Tyler Boldt	58	3	6	9	58
Shon Jones-Parry	24	2	6	8	99
Aaron Gionet	68	5	2	7	231
Nikita Korovkin	46	3	1	4	58
Jack Redlick	17	0	2	2	50
Steve Belanger (goalie)	27	0	1	1	9
Davis Parley (goalie)	52	0	1	1	0
Josh Pokol	2	0	0	0	2

GOALTENDING

	Games	Min.	W	L	T	G	SO	Avg.
Davis Parley	52	2948	27	16	3	170	1	3.46
Steve Belanger	27	1407	8	14	4	97	1	4.14

KELOWNA ROCKETS
SCORING

	Games	G	A	Pts.	PIM
Rory McDade	72	28	70	98	50
Carsen Germyn	71	35	52	87	102
Jan Fadrny	56	32	45	77	58
Kiel McLeod	65	38	28	66	94
Tomas Oravec	65	21	44	65	28
Ryan Cuthbert	66	12	25	37	54
Richie Regehr	71	10	27	37	68
Chris Di Ubaldo	47	13	15	28	47
Cam Paddock	72	14	10	24	110
David Selthun	55	5	18	23	45
Paul Hurd	59	9	12	21	116
Gavin McLeod	71	4	15	19	127
Travis Moen	40	8	8	16	106
Tyler Mosienko	60	5	10	15	24
Seth Leonard	46	6	8	14	21
Bart Rushmer	65	6	6	12	134
Joe Suderman	64	4	7	11	114
Josh Gorges	57	4	6	10	24
Randall Gelech	51	1	9	10	19
J.J. Hunter	12	1	5	6	4
Blaine Depper	55	2	0	2	87
Vernon Fiddler	3	0	2	2	0
Nolan Yonkman	7	0	1	1	19
Vaughn Watson (goalie)	3	0	0	0	0
Kyle Stanton (goalie)	13	0	0	0	0
Jason Stone (goalie)	16	0	0	0	0
Brett Palin	39	0	0	0	25
Kevin Swanson (goalie)	49	0	0	0	0

GOALTENDING

	Games	Min.	W	L	T	G	SO	Avg.
Jason Stone	16	772	7	6	0	39	1	3.03
Kevin Swanson	49	2854	27	16	5	148	0	3.11
Kyle Stanton	13	717	3	6	2	45	0	3.77
Vaughn Watson	3	18	0	0	0	2	0	6.67

KOOTENAY ICE
SCORING

	Games	G	A	Pts.	PIM
Jarret Stoll	62	40	66	106	105
Zdenek Blatny	58	37	48	85	120
Mike Comrie	37	39	40	79	79

	Games	G	A	Pts.	PIM
Jason Jaffray	70	31	42	73	108
Tyler Beechey	70	32	40	72	72
Bret DeCecco	51	32	28	60	61
Trevor Johnson	68	11	42	53	98
Marek Svatos	39	23	18	41	47
Colin Sinclair	72	10	17	27	70
Cole Fischer	55	3	16	19	73
Richard Hamula	71	4	12	16	20
Andy Thompson	56	2	12	14	142
Pat Iannone	68	4	8	12	139
Dean Arsene	68	1	10	11	178
Aaron Rome	53	2	8	10	43
Lance Morrison	44	4	5	9	16
Brennan Evans	55	2	7	9	105
Tyler Dyck	42	4	2	6	92
Craig Weller	30	1	5	6	40
Eric Bowen	22	1	3	4	71
Kyle Sheen	35	1	3	4	48
Adam Taylor	36	1	2	3	17
Dion Lassu	14	0	3	3	50
Steven Makway	44	0	3	3	62
Mike Lee	22	1	1	2	45
Dan Blackburn (goalie)	50	0	2	2	8
Michael Salekin	1	0	0	0	2
Dale Mahovsky	2	0	0	0	0
Jordy Dudka	3	0	0	0	2
B.J. Boxma (goalie)	4	0	0	0	2
Jeff Harvey (goalie)	23	0	0	0	2

GOALTENDING

	Games	Min.	W	L	T	G	SO	Avg.
B.J. Boxma	4	210	2	1	0	9	0	2.57
Dan Blackburn	50	2922	33	14	2	135	1	2.77
Jeff Harvey	23	1221	10	8	2	68	0	3.34

LETHBRIDGE HURRICANES
SCORING

	Games	G	A	Pts.	PIM
Nathan Barrett	70	46	53	99	66
Tomas Kopecky	49	22	28	50	52
Warren McCutcheon	69	17	29	46	69
Brian Ballman	69	21	19	40	135
Scott Borders	62	17	22	39	93
Tim Green	51	13	23	36	33
Thomas Scantlebury	71	6	23	29	162
Derek Atkinson	45	8	16	24	41
Simon Ferguson	63	5	18	23	169
Derek Ruck	72	4	19	23	40
Phil Cole	63	6	15	21	129
Ryley Layden	19	6	11	17	22
Martin Podlesak	21	8	6	14	23
Adam Johnson	44	5	6	11	88
Darren Lynch	27	4	4	8	9
Brett O'Malley	45	1	7	8	19
Mark Forth	58	0	8	8	51
Brian Patterson	65	1	5	6	52
Andrew Jungwirth	45	1	3	4	108
Jerry Eckel	32	2	1	3	2
Tristan Grant	23	2	0	2	75
Matt Jacques	53	2	0	2	20
Dustin Kazak	1	0	1	1	0
Matt Fetzner	49	0	1	1	62
Charles Allen	1	0	0	0	0
Justin Ossachuk	1	0	0	0	5
Brent Seabrooke	4	0	0	0	0
Colin Johnson	9	0	0	0	0
Shaun Lee (goalie)	9	0	0	0	0
Ryan Jorde	11	0	0	0	49
Derek Parker	23	0	0	0	125
Blake Ward (goalie)	30	0	0	0	22
Joel Martin (goalie)	42	0	0	0	2

GOALTENDING

	Games	Min.	W	L	T	G	SO	Avg.
Blake Ward	30	1676	10	15	3	79	2	2.83
Joel Martin	42	2225	17	18	1	107	2	2.89
Shaun Lee	9	444	2	6	0	34	0	4.59

MEDICINE HAT TIGERS
SCORING

	Games	G	A	Pts.	PIM
Chris St. Jacques	70	37	36	73	84
Ben Thomson	71	31	42	73	27
Vernon Fiddler	67	33	38	71	100
Ryan Hollweg	65	19	39	58	125
Joffrey Lupul	69	30	26	56	39
Jay Bouwmeester	61	14	39	53	44
Brett Draney	57	20	28	48	84
Ken Davis	69	19	15	34	75
Tyson Mulock	63	13	21	34	16
Ryan Kinasewich	66	12	20	32	36
Jeremy Goetzinger	63	4	26	30	115
Denny Johnston	56	11	18	29	75
Petr Chvojka	59	3	18	21	102
Brad Voth	45	9	9	18	215
B. J. Fehr	71	1	15	16	105
Brett Scheffelmaier	62	3	10	13	279
Ryan Chieduch	54	1	10	11	75
David Ullmann	44	5	4	9	52
Josh Morrow	46	0	7	7	111
Ryan Olynyk	51	2	3	5	220
Stefan Meyer	4	1	1	2	0
Ben McMullin (goalie)	23	0	1	1	12
Riley Day	1	0	0	0	0
Steven Regier	1	0	0	0	0
Tomas Netik	3	0	0	0	2
Brett Jaeger (goalie)	11	0	0	0	0
Kyle Kettles (goalie)	47	0	0	0	20

GOALTENDING

	Games	Min.	W	L	T	G	SO	Avg.
Brett Jaeger	11	638	4	6	1	41	0	3.86
Kyle Kettles	47	2586	15	24	2	183	0	4.25
Ben McMullin	23	1136	5	12	2	83	0	4.38

MOOSE JAW WARRIORS
SCORING

	Games	G	A	Pts.	PIM
Brian Sutherby	59	34	43	77	138
Shawn Limpright	69	31	43	74	160
Jason Weitzel	70	24	42	66	117
Nathan Paetsch	70	8	54	62	118
Steven Crampton	72	26	33	59	153
Ben Knopp	58	22	34	56	105
Jarrett Thompson	63	23	32	55	163
Harlan Anderson	72	11	42	53	50
Sean O'Connor	71	34	15	49	192
Tomas Mojzis	72	11	25	36	115
Scott Kelman	60	15	18	33	130
Brooks Laich	71	9	21	30	28
Bobby Chad Mitchell	45	9	12	21	175
Renat Mamachev	72	5	12	17	63
David Bararuk	53	6	9	15	9
Deryk Engelland	65	4	11	15	157
Kyle Brodziak	57	2	8	10	49
Mitch Love	51	5	4	9	97
Shaun Landolt	49	4	4	8	40
Dustin Bru	26	3	4	7	9
Sean Connors (goalie)	43	0	4	4	20
Tim Barlow (goalie)	35	0	3	3	0
Cole Byers	42	0	3	3	31
Tyler Dietrich	5	1	0	1	2
Nathan Deobald (goalie)	2	0	0	0	0

GOALTENDING

	Games	Min.	W	L	T	G	SO	Avg.
Nathan Deobald	2	64	1	0	0	3	0	2.81
Tim Barlow	35	1914	17	14	0	121	2	3.79
Sean Connors	43	2377	16	20	4	163	1	4.11

PORTLAND WINTER HAWKS
SCORING

	Games	G	A	Pts.	PIM
Marcel Hossa	58	34	56	90	58
Josh Olson	72	22	38	60	86

	Games	G	A	Pts.	PIM
Josef Balej	46	32	21	53	18
Jesse Ferguson	67	12	41	53	108
Shawn Roed	53	20	29	49	94
Paul Gaustad	70	11	30	41	168
Dean Beuker	72	14	23	37	46
Garrett Prosofsky	27	21	15	36	18
Dan Hulak	72	6	26	32	50
Joey Hope	56	6	24	30	103
Nick Marach	45	13	15	28	74
Matthew Girling	61	11	13	24	27
Kevin Young	57	4	20	24	108
Kris Callaway	60	6	11	17	144
Craig Valette	39	8	6	14	39
Daniel McIvor	52	6	8	14	15
Willy Glover	55	5	9	14	34
Eric Bowen	34	5	5	10	107
John Togiai	58	5	5	10	43
Patrick Wellar	57	2	7	9	65
Blake Robson	9	5	2	7	8
Brad Priestlay	35	2	4	6	32
Ryan Kehrig	8	1	4	5	0
Luke Molotowsky	32	1	4	5	2
James DeMone	18	2	2	4	52
Dustin Bauer	47	0	2	2	97
Lanny Ramage (goalie)	55	0	2	2	19
Braydon Coburn	2	0	1	1	0
Travis Mitchell (goalie)	1	0	0	0	0
Tyler Grover	2	0	0	0	2
Chad Grisdale	8	0	0	0	20
Jomar Cruz (goalie)	22	0	0	0	4

GOALTENDING

	Games	Min.	W	L	T	G	SO	Avg.
Lanny Ramage	55	3167	30	21	3	166	5	3.14
Jomar Cruz	22	1116	7	8	2	59	1	3.17
Travis Mitchell	1	60	0	1	0	6	0	6.00

PRINCE ALBERT RAIDERS

SCORING

	Games	G	A	Pts.	PIM
Riley Cote	64	17	35	52	114
Greg Watson	71	22	28	50	72
Garrett Prosofsky	41	16	33	49	32
Igor Pohanka	70	16	33	49	24
Nick Schultz	59	17	30	47	120
J.J. Hunter	58	28	17	45	40
Blaine Stowards	65	14	23	37	43
Jesse Schultz	35	14	18	32	14
Anton Borodkin	52	9	20	29	52
Chris Harper	60	17	4	21	85
Dustin Kazak	33	4	15	19	14
Kyle Bruce	68	8	8	16	193
Jon Kress	69	3	10	13	164
Mike Wirll	29	5	6	11	6
Scott C. McQueen	42	3	7	10	35
Grant McNeill	61	2	6	8	280
Ryan Haggerty	56	2	4	6	78
James DeMone	29	0	6	6	89
Jeff Schmidt	54	2	2	4	39
Connor Lowe	60	1	3	4	62
Landon Lillejord	36	1	1	2	40
Jordan Clarke	37	1	1	2	97
Jay Batchelor	53	1	1	2	55
Jon Mirasty	30	0	2	2	109
Rob MacGregor	5	1	0	1	0
Clayton Chartrand	3	0	1	1	4
Aaron Sorochan (goalie)	25	0	1	1	8
Brett Novak	2	0	0	0	0
Grant McCune (goalie)	60	0	0	0	7

GOALTENDING

	Games	Min.	W	L	T	G	SO	Avg.
Grant McCune	60	3203	14	38	3	239	0	4.48
Aaron Sorochan	25	1141	4	12	0	100	0	5.26

PRINCE GEORGE COUGARS

SCORING

	Games	G	A	Pts.	PIM
Berkeley Buchko	72	39	30	69	47
Justin Cox	71	30	38	68	91
Christian Chartier	63	12	56	68	99
Dan Hamhuis	62	13	47	60	125
Blake Robson	58	24	35	59	98
Brett Allan	65	26	22	48	68
Chris Falloon	72	19	22	41	27
Tim Wedderburn	68	9	25	34	54
John Filewich	61	9	16	25	32
Aaron Foster	47	11	12	23	100
Dan Baum	59	9	14	23	169
Adam Stefishen	70	11	9	20	195
Tomas Tesarek	61	6	13	19	18
Travis Eagles	23	3	11	14	13
Willy Glover	14	6	5	11	18
David Koci	70	2	7	9	155
Derek Boogaard	61	1	8	9	245
Nathan Brice	58	4	4	8	96
Devin Wilson	63	3	5	8	63
Gary Gladue	48	2	6	8	18
Scott Lynch	53	1	4	5	56
Joey Hope	13	1	3	4	6
Mark Kitts	24	1	2	3	21
Chad Grisdale	15	0	2	2	43
Kyle Stanton (goalie)	16	0	1	1	4
Marty Maurice (goalie)	3	0	0	0	2
Duane Perillat (goalie)	5	0	0	0	2
Billy Thompson (goalie)	57	0	0	0	6

GOALTENDING

	Games	Min.	W	L	T	G	SO	Avg.
Billy Thompson	57	3185	24	24	3	178	1	3.35
Kyle Stanton	16	779	6	8	0	46	1	3.54
Marty Maurice	3	180	1	2	0	15	0	5.00
Duane Perillat	5	188	0	3	0	19	0	6.06

RED DEER REBELS

SCORING

	Games	G	A	Pts.	PIM
Justin Mapletoft	70	43	77	120	111
Kyle Wanvig	69	55	46	101	202
Colby Armstrong	72	36	42	78	156
Ross Lupaschuk	65	28	37	65	135
Jim Vandermeer	72	21	44	65	180
Doug Lynch	72	12	37	49	181
Andrew Bergen	71	16	28	44	74
Boyd Gordon	72	12	27	39	89
Joel Stepp	70	24	13	37	89
Jeff Woywitka	72	7	28	35	113
Jeff Smith	72	22	11	33	187
Martin Erat	17	4	24	28	24
Justin Wallin	39	6	14	20	58
Ladislav Kouba	62	5	7	12	29
Devin Francon	72	4	7	11	188
Diarmuid Kelly	44	2	7	9	50
Derek Meech	60	2	7	9	40
Bryce Thoma	69	2	4	6	34
Darcy Robinson	30	1	5	6	70
Shay Stephenson	44	1	4	5	30
Martin Vymazal	24	0	2	2	6
Shane Grypuik	25	0	2	2	22
Donovan Rattray	11	1	0	1	13
Cam Ondrik (goalie)	10	0	1	1	2
Michael Garnett (goalie)	21	0	1	1	2
Jason Ertl	1	0	0	0	2
Colin Johnson	1	0	0	0	0
Cam Ward (goalie)	1	0	0	0	0
Adam Dombrowski	4	0	0	0	8
Shane Bendera (goalie)	45	0	0	0	9

GOALTENDING

	Games	Min.	W	L	T	G	SO	Avg.
Cam Ward	1	60	1	0	0	0	1	0.00
Michael Garnett	21	1133	14	5	1	39	3	2.07

	Games	Min.	W	L	T	G	SO	Avg.
Cam Ondrik	10	551	7	2	0	20	2	2.18
Shane Bendera	45	2603	32	8	2	108	5	2.49

REGINA PATS

SCORING

	Games	G	A	Pts.	PIM
Brett Lysak	64	35	48	83	44
Filip Novak	64	17	50	67	75
Kevin Korol	69	19	46	65	66
Karel Mosovsky	61	25	26	51	59
Joey Bastien	37	17	28	45	36
Garth Murray	72	28	16	44	183
Blake Evans	27	24	19	43	50
Barret Jackman	43	9	27	36	138
Grant Jacobsen	64	10	25	35	40
Matt Hubbauer	61	20	14	34	131
Gable Gross	27	11	18	29	44
Paul Elliott	27	8	17	25	51
Ryan Thomas	55	3	19	22	191
Curtis Austring	59	12	5	17	54
Ryan Annesley	41	9	8	17	43
David McDonald	51	7	7	14	32
Chad Bassen	50	9	4	13	47
Jeff Feniak	28	2	10	12	63
David Kaczowka	63	4	6	10	414
Garnet Exelby	22	2	8	10	51
Shon Jones-Parry	26	2	7	9	97
Kyle Ladobruk	24	4	3	7	10
Scott Balan	42	2	5	7	69
Tyler Findlay	44	1	5	6	14
Paul Brown	33	3	1	4	83
Shawn Belle	4	0	3	3	0
Landon Boyko	15	0	3	3	30
Brett Bartel	18	0	3	3	8
Chad Grisdale	32	0	3	3	47
Justin Lucyshyn	37	1	1	2	80
Donald Choukalos (goalie)	60	0	1	1	14
Dustin Molleken	1	0	0	0	4
Chris Schlenker	1	0	0	0	0
Derek Sunderland	1	0	0	0	0
Zack Roe	2	0	0	0	0
Daniel Waschuk	2	0	0	0	0
Jonathan Parker	4	0	0	0	0
Chad Davidson (goalie)	20	0	0	0	0

GOALTENDING

	Games	Min.	W	L	T	G	SO	Avg.
Chad Davidson	20	949	7	6	1	48	1	3.03
Donald Choukalos	60	3376	33	23	2	187	3	3.32

SASKATOON BLADES

SCORING

	Games	G	A	Pts.	PIM
Garrett Bembridge	72	38	40	78	40
Justin Kelly	60	16	40	56	38
Martin Erat	31	19	35	54	48
David Cameron	67	19	35	54	30
Warren Peters	63	27	14	41	111
Justin Wallin	30	6	25	31	25
Derek Halldorson	52	13	6	19	97
Ryan Stempfle	61	5	11	16	84
Garnet Exelby	43	5	10	15	110
Ryan Kehrig	52	5	8	13	20
Davin Heintz	67	5	8	13	6
Kane Ludwar	35	5	7	12	79
Jade Galbraith	24	5	5	10	10
Trent Adamus	62	3	7	10	52
Matt Suderman	70	1	8	9	116
Justin Kanigan	66	4	4	8	111
Darcy Robinson	41	2	6	8	80
Petr Prochazka	33	3	4	7	17
Chris Manchakowski	39	1	6	7	77
Jeff Coulter	66	4	1	5	191
Adrian Foster	5	0	5	5	4

	Games	G	A	Pts.	PIM
Martin Vymazal	22	0	5	5	4
Scott Balan	28	0	5	5	49
Rob Woods	42	1	3	4	26
Derek Couture	7	2	1	3	6
Craig Valette	24	2	0	2	19
Aaron Starr	40	1	1	2	10
Mike Green	7	0	2	2	2
Paul Gentile	2	0	0	0	0
Curtis Yausie	2	0	0	0	2
Kyle Harris	3	0	0	0	2
Aaron Rome	3	0	0	0	2
Mark Forth	5	0	0	0	4
Jason Goulet	22	0	0	0	12
Michael Garnett (goalie)	28	0	0	0	0
Tony Kolewaski (goalie)	28	0	0	0	9
Cam Ondrik (goalie)	30	0	0	0	2

GOALTENDING

	Games	Min.	W	L	T	G	SO	Avg.
Michael Garnett	28	1501	7	17	2	83	1	3.32
Cam Ondrik	30	1763	7	20	2	104	0	3.54
Tony Kolewaski	28	1073	5	11	1	67	0	3.75

SEATTLE THUNDERBIRDS

SCORING

	Games	G	A	Pts.	PIM
Shane Endicott	72	36	43	79	86
Jamie Lundmark	52	35	42	77	49
Barrett Heisten	58	20	57	77	61
David Morisset	61	32	36	68	95
Dustin Johner	72	25	31	56	45
Gerard DiCaire	69	15	36	51	33
Tim Preston	67	13	22	35	74
Jake Riddle	67	13	20	33	109
Brad Tutschek	59	11	15	26	79
Craig Olynick	62	5	20	25	105
Keegan McAvoy	72	7	17	24	197
Dion Lassu	54	3	18	21	165
Greg Black	59	9	11	20	178
Darren McLachlan	42	10	9	19	161
Tyler Metcalfe	50	6	7	13	23
Scott Kelman	10	5	6	11	10
Matthew Spiller	71	4	7	11	174
Jeffrey Beatch	71	2	9	11	67
Scott C. McQueen	29	0	7	7	23
Bret DeCecco	6	2	3	5	8
Matthew Chacho	43	2	3	5	41
Igor Agarunov	38	3	1	4	20
Shon Jones-Parry	11	0	4	4	34
Eric Benke	48	0	3	3	16
Paul Hurd	10	0	2	2	17
Mark Lindsay	3	1	0	1	0
Brennan Evans	11	1	0	1	25
David Ullmann	5	0	1	1	2
Nick Pannoni (goalie)	41	0	1	1	9
Thomas Vicars (goalie)	41	0	1	1	4
Matthew Hansen	2	0	0	0	0
Craig Perry	2	0	0	0	2
Ryan Cyr (goalie)	3	0	0	0	0
Alex Lentowich	3	0	0	0	7

GOALTENDING

	Games	Min.	W	L	T	G	SO	Avg.
Thomas Vicars	41	2025	13	15	2	129	2	3.82
Nick Pannoni	41	2165	17	17	5	150	0	4.16
Ryan Cyr	3	177	0	2	1	16	0	5.42

SPOKANE CHIEFS

SCORING

	Games	G	A	Pts.	PIM
Lynn Loyns	66	31	43	74	81
Brandin Cote	69	27	43	70	117
Roman Tvrdon	62	28	34	62	55
Tim Smith	38	19	37	56	65
Jeff Lucky	53	20	21	41	26

	Games	G	A	Pts.	PIM
Mason Wallin	72	14	25	39	48
Tim Krymusa	72	12	23	35	34
Shawn Thompson	66	7	24	31	99
Steven Mann	47	7	21	28	20
Chris Ovington	63	4	24	28	90
Scott Henkelman	30	15	12	27	49
Matthew Keith	33	13	14	27	63
Ryan Thorpe	51	8	17	25	89
Chris Heid	51	2	15	17	76
Kurt Sauer	48	5	10	15	85
Brad Schell	60	7	6	13	10
Joff Kehler	61	6	6	12	56
David Boychuk	69	5	7	12	224
Chris Barr	71	3	7	10	140
Justin Keller	27	4	3	7	4
Jordan Clarke	32	0	5	5	98
Ratislav Lipka	35	1	3	4	12
Barry Horman	33	3	0	3	23
Jevon Desautels	49	1	2	3	83
Tyler MacKay (goalie)	62	0	3	3	30
Barry Brust (goalie)	16	0	2	2	4
Darrell Stoddard	5	0	1	1	5
Drew Lamontagne	1	0	0	0	0
Craig Perry	26	0	0	0	42

GOALTENDING

	Games	Min.	W	L	T	G	SO	Avg.
Tyler MacKay	62	3567	31	24	6	174	3	2.93
Barry Brust	16	777	4	6	1	42	0	3.24

SWIFT CURRENT BRONCOS

SCORING

	Games	G	A	Pts.	PIM
Layne Ulmer	68	63	56	119	75
Duncan Milroy	68	38	54	92	51
Nathan Smith	67	28	62	90	78
Jay Langager	64	12	40	52	79
Brent Twordik	71	18	32	50	75
Ian White	69	12	31	43	24
Tim Smith T.	30	12	22	34	38
Scott Henkelman	39	13	18	31	22
Ben Ondrus	69	13	17	30	151
Paul Deniset	46	11	14	25	31
James Hiebert	58	12	12	24	123
Dean Serdachny	69	4	10	14	203
Clay Thoring	69	8	5	13	38
Craig Priestlay	70	8	5	13	53
Jakub Cutta	47	5	8	13	102
Dustin Friesen	61	3	8	11	33
Matt Sommerfeld	62	5	5	10	258
John Dahl	45	3	6	9	4
Adam Dombrowski	55	1	8	9	78
Ales Cerny	60	2	5	7	38
Kevin Seibel	58	3	3	6	51
Colton Orr	19	0	4	4	67
Jay Batchelor	9	0	2	2	6
Houston Hair	5	1	0	1	5
Tyson Motz (goalie)	14	0	1	1	9
B.J. Boxma (goalie)	44	0	1	1	6
Jarad Bourassa	1	0	0	0	0
Jeremy Williams	2	0	0	0	2
Todd Ford (goalie)	20	0	0	0	0

GOALTENDING

	Games	Min.	W	L	T	G	SO	Avg.
B.J. Boxma	44	2576	26	14	2	114	0	2.66
Todd Ford	20	1066	12	4	2	53	0	2.98
Tyson Motz	14	716	5	4	3	43	1	3.60

TRI-CITY AMERICANS

SCORING

	Games	G	A	Pts.	PIM
Eric Johannson	72	36	44	80	72
Ben Kilgour	70	23	41	64	90
Blake Evans	40	28	31	59	70

	Games	G	A	Pts.	PIM
Eric Clark	65	16	25	41	57
Jordan Cameron	52	10	20	30	90
Martin Podlesak	39	13	13	26	36
Joey Bastien	19	8	13	21	27
Mike Lee	40	6	14	20	140
Brad Zanon	70	5	15	20	147
Andrew Davidson	71	10	9	19	104
Dustin Barker	63	7	12	19	35
Justin Hansen	39	13	4	17	55
Sean Curry	72	5	12	17	113
Dylan Stanley	60	6	7	13	22
Jesse Schultz	30	5	8	13	16
Tyler Dyck	27	7	3	10	57
Martin Liba	41	4	5	9	8
Derek Atkinson	19	5	3	8	19
Andrew DeSousa	60	0	8	8	118
Darrell May	49	3	4	7	57
Tim Green	13	2	5	7	4
Ryan Jorde	56	1	6	7	170
Colin Johnson	44	0	7	7	24
Ryley Layden	13	1	4	5	20
Jeff Feniak	40	1	4	5	105
Adam Johnson	13	1	3	4	32
Aaron Winterholt	14	0	4	4	13
Tyson Motz (goalie)	18	0	2	2	8
Tyler Weiman (goalie)	44	0	2	2	8
Jon Mirasty	37	1	0	1	122
Shawn Belle	2	0	1	1	0
Ian McDonald	3	0	1	1	0
Justin Lucyshyn	31	0	1	1	55
Bob Graham	1	0	0	0	2
Chris Marchand	1	0	0	0	4
Chris Stubel	8	0	0	0	0
Blake Ward (goalie)	8	0	0	0	10
Chris Houle (goalie)	9	0	0	0	0

GOALTENDING

	Games	Min.	W	L	T	G	SO	Avg.
Tyler Weiman	44	2464	10	25	4	155	0	3.77
Blake Ward	8	470	2	3	3	30	0	3.83
Tyson Motz	18	1007	7	10	0	65	0	3.87
Chris Houle	9	427	2	5	1	28	0	3.93

PLAYERS WITH TWO OR MORE TEAMS

SCORING

	Games	G	A	Pts.	PIM
Ryan Annesley, Regina	41	9	8	17	43
Ryan Annesley, Kamloops	30	9	19	28	35
Totals	71	18	27	45	78
Derek Atkinson, Lethbridge	45	8	16	24	41
Derek Atkinson, Tri-City	19	5	3	8	19
Totals	64	13	19	32	60
Scott Balan, Regina	42	2	5	7	69
Scott Balan, Saskatoon	28	0	5	5	49
Totals	70	2	10	12	118
Joey Bastien, Regina	37	17	28	45	36
Joey Bastien, Tri-City	19	8	13	21	27
Totals	56	25	41	66	63
Jay Batchelor, Swift Current	9	0	2	2	6
Jay Batchelor, Prince Albert	53	1	1	2	55
Totals	62	1	3	4	61
Shawn Belle, Regina	4	0	3	3	0
Shawn Belle, Tri-City	2	0	1	1	0
Totals	6	0	4	4	0
Eric Bowen, Portland	34	5	5	10	107
Eric Bowen, Kootenay	22	1	3	4	71
Totals	56	6	8	14	178
B.J. Boxma, Kootenay	4	0	0	0	2
B.J. Boxma, Swift Current	44	0	1	1	6
Totals	48	0	1	1	8
Paul Brown, Regina	33	3	1	4	83
Paul Brown, Kamloops	30	6	11	17	118
Totals	63	9	12	21	201

	Games	G	A	Pts.	PIM
Jordan Clarke, Prince Albert.....	37	1	1	2	97
Jordan Clarke, Spokane.............	32	0	5	5	98
Totals...............................	69	1	6	7	195
Bret DeCecco, Seattle..............	6	2	3	5	8
Bret DeCecco, Kootenay............	51	32	28	60	61
Totals...............................	57	34	31	65	69
James DeMone, Portland...........	18	2	2	4	52
James DeMone, Prince Albert...	29	0	6	6	89
Totals...............................	47	2	8	10	141
Paul Deniset, Kamloops...........	20	3	6	9	16
Paul Deniset, Swift Current.......	46	11	14	25	31
Totals...............................	66	14	20	34	47
Adam Dombrowski, Red Deer...	4	0	0	0	8
Adam Dombrowski, S. Current..	55	1	8	9	78
Totals...............................	59	1	8	9	86
Tyler Dyck, Kootenay..............	42	4	2	6	92
Tyler Dyck, Tri-City...............	27	7	3	10	57
Totals...............................	69	11	5	16	149
Travis Eagles, Prince George.....	23	3	11	14	13
Travis Eagles, Brandon............	25	4	5	9	32
Totals...............................	48	7	16	23	45
Paul Elliott, Kamloops.............	40	10	33	43	37
Paul Elliott, Regina................	27	8	17	25	51
Totals...............................	67	18	50	68	88
Martin Erat, Saskatoon............	31	19	35	54	48
Martin Erat, Red Deer..............	17	4	24	28	24
Totals...............................	48	23	59	82	72
Blake Evans, Tri-City..............	40	28	31	59	70
Blake Evans, Regina...............	27	24	19	43	50
Totals...............................	67	52	50	102	120
Brennan Evans, Seattle............	11	1	0	1	25
Brennan Evans, Kootenay.........	55	2	7	9	105
Totals...............................	66	3	7	10	130
Garnet Exelby, Saskatoon	43	5	10	15	110
Garnet Exelby, Regina.............	22	2	8	10	51
Totals...............................	65	7	18	25	161
Jan Fadrny, Brandon................	2	1	1	2	6
Jan Fadrny, Kelowna...............	56	32	45	77	58
Totals...............................	58	33	46	79	64
Jeff Feniak, Tri-City	40	1	4	5	105
Jeff Feniak, Regina	28	2	10	12	63
Totals...............................	68	3	14	17	168
Vernon Fiddler, Kelowna	3	0	2	2	0
Vernon Fiddler, Medicine Hat.....	67	33	38	71	100
Totals...............................	70	33	40	73	100
Mark Forth, Saskatoon	5	0	0	0	4
Mark Forth, Lethbridge............	58	0	8	8	51
Totals...............................	63	0	8	8	55
Michael Garnett, Red Deer........	21	0	1	1	2
Michael Garnett, Saskatoon.......	28	0	0	0	0
Totals...............................	49	0	1	1	2
Willy Glover, Prince George......	14	6	5	11	18
Willy Glover, Portland	55	5	9	14	34
Totals...............................	69	11	14	25	52
Tim Green, Tri-City................	13	2	5	7	4
Tim Green, Lethbridge.............	51	13	23	36	33
Totals...............................	64	15	28	43	37
Chad Grisdale, Portland...........	8	0	0	0	20
Chad Grisdale, Prince George....	15	0	2	2	43
Chad Grisdale, Regina.............	32	0	3	3	47
Totals...............................	55	0	5	5	110
Gable Gross, Kamloops............	40	20	14	34	41
Gable Gross, Regina................	27	11	18	29	44
Totals...............................	67	31	32	63	85
Houston Hair, Swift Current.......	5	1	0	1	5
Houston Hair, Brandon	6	0	1	1	6
Totals...............................	11	1	1	2	11
Justin Hansen, Brandon	18	7	12	19	22
Justin Hansen, Tri-City.............	39	13	4	17	55
Totals...............................	57	20	16	36	77
Scott Henkelman, Swift Current	39	13	18	31	22
Scott Henkelman, Spokane........	30	15	12	27	49
Totals...............................	69	28	30	58	71
Joey Hope, Prince George........	13	1	3	4	6

	Games	G	A	Pts.	PIM
Joey Hope, Portland	56	6	24	30	103
Totals...............................	69	7	27	34	109
J.J. Hunter, Kelowna................	12	1	5	6	4
J.J. Hunter, Prince Albert...........	58	28	17	45	40
Totals...............................	70	29	22	51	44
Paul Hurd, Seattle....................	10	0	2	2	17
Paul Hurd, Kelowna.................	59	9	12	21	116
Totals...............................	69	9	14	23	133
Adam Johnson, Tri-City............	13	1	3	4	32
Adam Johnson, Lethbridge	44	5	6	11	88
Totals...............................	57	6	9	15	120
Colin Johnson, Red Deer..........	1	0	0	0	0
Colin Johnson, Lethbridge.........	9	0	0	0	0
Colin Johnson, Tri-City	44	0	7	7	24
Totals...............................	54	0	7	7	24
Shon Jones-Parry, Seattle.........	11	0	4	4	34
Shon Jones-Parry, Regina.........	26	2	7	9	97
Shon Jones-Parry, Kamloops....	24	2	6	8	99
Totals...............................	61	4	17	21	230
Ryan Jorde, Lethbridge	11	0	0	0	49
Ryan Jorde, Tri-City	56	1	6	7	170
Totals...............................	67	1	6	7	219
Dustin Kazak, Lethbridge..........	1	0	1	1	0
Dustin Kazak, Prince Albert	33	4	15	19	14
Totals...............................	34	4	16	20	14
Ryan Kehrig, Portland..............	8	1	4	5	0
Ryan Kehrig, Saskatoon...........	52	5	8	13	20
Totals...............................	60	6	12	18	20
Scott Kelman, Seattle...............	10	5	6	11	10
Scott Kelman, Moose Jaw........	60	15	18	33	130
Totals...............................	70	20	24	44	140
Kyle Ladobruk, Kamloops.........	39	2	8	10	18
Kyle Ladobruk, Regina.............	24	4	3	7	10
Totals...............................	63	6	11	17	28
Dion Lassu, Kootenay..............	14	0	3	3	50
Dion Lassu, Seattle..................	54	3	18	21	165
Totals...............................	68	3	21	24	215
Ryley Layden, Tri-City.............	13	1	4	5	20
Ryley Layden, Lethbridge	19	6	11	17	22
Totals...............................	32	7	15	22	42
Mike Lee, Tri-City...................	40	6	14	20	140
Mike Lee, Kootenay	22	1	1	2	45
Totals...............................	62	7	15	22	185
Justin Lucyshyn, Regina...........	37	1	1	2	80
Justin Lucyshyn, Tri-City	31	0	1	1	55
Totals...............................	68	1	2	3	135
Scott McQueen, Prince Albert ...	42	3	7	10	35
Scott McQueen, Seattle	29	0	7	7	23
Totals...............................	71	3	14	17	58
Jon Mirasty, Prince Albert	30	0	2	2	109
Jon Mirasty, Tri-City................	37	1	0	1	122
Totals...............................	67	1	2	3	231
Tyson Motz, Swift Current........	14	0	1	1	9
Tyson Motz, Tri-City................	18	0	2	2	8
Totals...............................	32	0	3	3	17
Richard Mueller, Brandon.........	1	0	0	0	0
Richard Mueller, Brandon.........	33	5	10	15	16
Totals...............................	34	5	10	15	16
Cam Ondrik, Saskatoon	30	0	0	0	2
Cam Ondrik, Red Deer.............	10	0	1	1	0
Totals...............................	40	0	1	1	2
Colton Orr, Swift Current..........	19	0	4	4	67
Colton Orr, Kamloops..............	41	8	1	9	179
Totals...............................	60	8	5	13	246
Craig Perry, Seattle	2	0	0	0	2
Craig Perry, Spokane...............	26	0	0	0	42
Totals...............................	28	0	0	0	44
Martin Podlesak, Tri-City..........	39	13	13	26	36
Martin Podlesak, Lethbridge......	21	8	6	14	23
Totals...............................	60	21	19	40	59
Garrett Prosofsky, Prince Albert	41	16	33	49	32
Garrett Prosofsky, Portland	27	21	15	36	18
Totals...............................	68	37	48	85	50
Darcy Robinson, Saskatoon	41	2	6	8	80

	Games	G	A	Pts.	PIM
Darcy Robinson, Red Deer	30	1	5	6	70
Totals	71	3	11	14	150
Blake Robson, Portland	9	5	2	7	8
Blake Robson, Prince George....	58	24	35	59	98
Totals	67	29	37	66	106
Aaron Rome, Saskatoon............	3	0	0	0	2
Aaron Rome, Kootenay..............	53	2	8	10	43
Totals	56	2	8	10	45
Bart Rushmer, Brandon	6	0	8	8	24
Bart Rushmer, Kelowna.............	65	6	6	12	134
Totals	71	6	14	20	158
Kyle Stanton, Kelowna..............	13	0	0	0	0
Kyle Stanton, Prince George......	16	0	1	1	4
Totals	29	0	1	1	4
Jesse Schultz, Tri-City	30	5	8	13	16
Jesse Schultz, Prince Albert	35	14	18	32	14
Totals	65	19	26	45	30
Tim Smith T., Spokane	38	19	37	56	65
Tim Smith T., Swift Current	30	12	22	34	38
Totals	68	31	59	90	103
David Ullmann, Seattle	5	0	1	1	2
David Ullmann, Medicine Hat	44	5	4	9	52
Totals	49	5	5	10	54
Martin Vymazal, Red Deer	24	0	2	2	6
Martin Vymazal, Saskatoon	22	0	5	5	4
Totals	46	0	7	7	10
Craig Valette, Saskatoon............	24	2	0	2	19
Craig Valette, Portland	39	8	6	14	39
Totals	63	10	6	16	58
Justin Wallin, Red Deer	39	6	14	20	58
Justin Wallin, Saskatoon	30	6	25	31	25

	Games	G	A	Pts.	PIM
Totals	69	12	39	51	83
Blake Ward, Tri-City	8	0	0	0	10
Blake Ward, Lethbridge	30	0	0	0	22
Totals	38	0	0	0	32
Mike Wirll, Brandon..................	2	0	0	0	4
Mike Wirll, Prince Albert............	29	5	6	11	6
Totals	31	5	6	11	10
Nolan Yonkman, Kelowna..........	7	0	1	1	19
Nolan Yonkman, Brandon..........	51	6	10	16	94
Totals	58	6	11	17	113

GOALTENDING

	Games	Min.	W	L	T	G	SO	Avg.
B.J. Boxma, Koo. ...	4	210	2	1	0	9	0	2.57
B.J. Boxma, S.C. ...	44	2576	26	14	2	114	0	2.66
Totals	48	2786	28	15	2	123	0	2.65
M. Garnett, R.D.	21	1133	14	5	1	39	3	2.07
M. Garnett, Sask. ...	28	1501	7	17	2	83	1	3.32
Totals	49	2634	21	22	3	122	4	2.78
Tyson Motz, S.C. ...	14	716	5	4	3	43	0	3.60
Tyson Motz, T.-C. ...	18	1007	7	10	0	65	0	3.87
Totals	32	1723	12	14	3	108	1	3.76
Cam Ondrik, Sask. .	30	1763	7	20	2	104	0	3.54
Cam Ondrik, R.D. ...	10	551	7	2	0	20	2	2.18
Totals	40	2314	14	22	2	124	2	3.22
Kyle Stanton, Kel. ...	13	717	3	6	2	45	0	3.77
Kyle Stanton, P.G. ..	16	779	6	8	0	46	1	3.54
Totals	29	1496	9	14	2	91	1	3.65
Blake Ward, T.-C. ...	8	470	2	3	3	30	0	3.83
Blake Ward, Leth. ...	30	1676	10	15	3	79	2	2.83
Totals	38	2146	12	18	6	109	2	3.05

2001 PLAYOFFS
RESULTS

FIRST ROUND

	W	L	Pts.	GF	GA
Red Deer	4	1	8	26	6
Lethbridge.....................................	1	4	2	6	26

(Red Deer won series, 4-1)

	W	L	Pts.	GF	GA
Swift Current	4	2	8	16	17
Brandon..	2	4	4	17	16

(Swift Current won series, 4-2)

	W	L	Pts.	GF	GA
Kootenay	4	0	8	23	6
Moose Jaw....................................	0	4	0	6	23

(Kootenay won series, 4-0)

	W	L	Pts.	GF	GA
Calgary	4	2	8	22	18
Regina	2	4	4	18	22

(Calgary won series, 4-2)

	W	L	Pts.	GF	GA
Seattle	4	2	8	18	16
Kelowna..	2	4	4	16	18

(Seattle won series, 4-2)

	W	L	Pts.	GF	GA
Portland...	4	2	8	25	17
Prince George...............................	2	4	4	17	25

(Portland won series, 4-2)

	W	L	Pts.	GF	GA
Spokane	4	0	8	20	5
Kamloops	0	4	0	5	20

(Spokane won series, 4-0)

SECOND ROUND

	W	L	Pts.	GF	GA
Red Deer	4	2	8	19	14
Calgary	2	4	4	14	19

(Red Deer won series, 4-2)

	W	L	Pts.	GF	GA
Swift Current	4	3	8	18	21
Kootenay	3	4	6	21	18

(Swift Current won series, 4-3)

	W	L	Pts.	GF	GA
Spokane	3	0	6	12	6
Seattle	0	3	0	6	12

(Spokane won series, 3-0)

SEMIFINALS

	W	L	Pts.	GF	GA
Portland...	4	1	8	11	6
Spokane	1	4	2	6	11

(Portland won series, 4-1)

	W	L	Pts.	GF	GA
Red Deer	4	2	8	17	11
Swift Current	2	4	4	11	17

(Red Deer won series, 4-2)

WHL FINALS

	W	L	Pts.	GF	GA
Red Deer	4	1	8	18	13
Portland...	1	4	2	13	18

(Red Deer won series, 4-1)

INDIVIDUAL LEADERS

Goals: Martin Erat, Red Deer (15)
Assists: Martin Erat, Red Deer (21)
        Justin Mapletoft, Red Deer (21)
Points: Martin Erat, Red Deer (36)
Penalty minutes: Dean Serdachny, Swift Current (60)
Goaltending average: Tyler MacKay, Spokane (1.71)
Shutouts: Shane Bendera, Red Deer (4)

TOP SCORERS

	Games	G	A	Pts.
Martin Erat, Red Deer	22	15	21	36
Justin Mapletoft, Red Deer	22	13	21	34
Tim Smith, Swift Current	19	10	14	24
Kyle Wanvig, Red Deer	22	10	12	22
Duncan Milroy, Swift Current	19	9	12	21
Zdenek Blatny, Kootenay	11	8	10	18
Lynn Loyns, Spokane	12	6	12	18
Bret DeCecco, Kootenay	11	6	11	17
Paul Gaustad, Portland	16	10	6	16
Roman Tvrdon, Spokane	12	5	11	16
Jim Vandermeer, Red Deer	22	3	13	16

INDIVIDUAL STATISTICS

BRANDON WHEAT KINGS
(Lost first round to Swift Current, 4-2)
SCORING

	Games	G	A	Pts.	PIM
Jordin Tootoo	6	2	4	6	18
Tim Konsorada	6	2	3	5	11
Aaron Goldade	6	2	2	4	16
Colin McRae	6	0	4	4	7
Ryan Craig	6	3	0	3	7
Milan Bartovic	6	1	2	3	8
Travis Young	3	0	3	3	6
Travis Eagles	6	1	1	2	8
Brett Girard	6	1	1	2	6
Jiri Jakes	6	1	1	2	4
Reagan Leslie	6	0	2	2	8
Richard Mueller	6	0	2	2	4
Brett Dickie	6	1	0	1	6
Kevin Harris	6	1	0	1	8
Lance Monych	6	1	0	1	0
Randy Ponte	6	1	0	1	29
Mark Ardelan	6	0	1	1	9
Nolan Yonkman	6	0	1	1	12
Jamie Hodson (goalie)	1	0	0	0	0
Brett Thurston	3	0	0	0	7
Robert McVicar (goalie)	5	0	0	0	0

GOALTENDING

	Games	Min.	W	L	T	G	SO	Avg.
Robert McVicar	5	324	2	3	0	13	1	2.41
Jamie Hodson	1	59	0	1	0	3	0	3.05

CALGARY HITMEN
(Lost second round to Red Deer, 4-2)
SCORING

	Games	G	A	Pts.	PIM
Pavel Brendl	10	7	6	13	6
Jordan Krestanovich	12	8	4	12	8
Kris Beech	10	2	8	10	26
Matt Kinch	12	3	6	9	6
Sean McAslan	12	3	5	8	29
Michael Bubnick	11	0	7	7	2
Robin Gomez	12	5	0	5	9
Owen Fussey	12	2	1	3	6
Shaun Norrie	12	1	2	3	18
Shaun Sutter	12	1	2	3	12
Jared Carli	11	0	3	3	10
Rod Sarich	7	1	1	2	10
Johnny Boychuk	12	1	1	2	17
Brandon Segal	12	1	1	2	17
Wade Davis	12	0	2	2	16
Chad Wolkowski	12	0	2	2	6
Toni Bader	12	1	0	1	12
Adam Breitkreuz	6	0	0	0	2
Mike Egener	6	0	0	0	5
Danny Ehrmen	8	0	0	0	0
Brady Block (goalie)	12	0	0	0	7

GOALTENDING

	Games	Min.	W	L	T	G	SO	Avg.
Brady Block	12	759	6	6	0	35	0	2.77

KAMLOOPS BLAZERS
(Lost first round to Spokane, 4-0)
SCORING

	Games	G	A	Pts.	PIM
Ryan Annesley	4	2	0	2	4
Erik Christensen	4	1	1	2	0
Jared Aulin	4	0	2	2	0
Jonathan Hobson	4	0	2	2	8
Scott Upshall	4	0	2	2	10
Konstantin Panov	4	1	0	1	2
Mark Rooneem	4	1	0	1	0
Jack Redlick	2	0	1	1	4
Tyler Boldt	4	0	1	1	6
Nikita Korovkin	1	0	0	0	0
Steve Belanger (goalie)	2	0	0	0	0
Paul Brown	2	0	0	0	4
Josh Bonar	3	0	0	0	0
Pat Brandreth	3	0	0	0	0
Shon Jones-Parry	3	0	0	0	15
Derek Krestanovich	3	0	0	0	6
Colton Orr	3	0	0	0	20
Davis Parley (goalie)	3	0	0	0	0
Aaron Gionet	4	0	0	0	6
Jarret Lukin	4	0	0	0	4
Shaonne Morrison	4	0	0	0	6
Conlan Seder	4	0	0	0	0
Tyler Sloan	4	0	0	0	4

GOALTENDING

	Games	Min.	W	L	T	G	SO	Avg.
Steve Belanger	2	84	0	1	0	7	0	5.00
Davis Parley	3	154	0	3	0	13	0	5.06

KELOWNA ROCKETS
(Lost first round to Seattle, 4-2)
SCORING

	Games	G	A	Pts.	PIM
Carsen Germyn	6	2	6	8	10
Jan Fadrny	6	3	4	7	8
Kiel McLeod	4	4	1	5	8
Rory McDade	6	1	4	5	6
Chris Di Ubaldo	6	3	1	4	8
Tomas Oravec	6	0	3	3	0
Josh Gorges	6	1	1	2	4
David Selthun	6	0	2	2	4
Seth Leonard	3	1	0	1	2
Paul Hurd	6	1	0	1	4
Ryan Cuthbert	6	0	1	1	6
Gavin McLeod	6	0	1	1	9
Tyler Mosienko	6	0	1	1	2
Richie Regehr	6	0	1	1	4
Jason Stone (goalie)	1	0	0	0	0

	Games	G	A	Pts.	PIM
Blaine Depper	5	0	0	0	2
Randall Gelech	6	0	0	0	4
Cam Paddock	6	0	0	0	4
Bart Rushmer	6	0	0	0	19
Joe Suderman	6	0	0	0	10
Kevin Swanson (goalie)	6	0	0	0	0

GOALTENDING

	Games	Min.	W	L	T	G	SO	Avg.
Jason Stone	1	8	0	0	0	0	0	0.00
Kevin Swanson	6	361	2	4	0	17	1	2.83

KOOTENAY ICE
(Lost second round to Swift Current, 4-3)
SCORING

	Games	G	A	Pts.	PIM
Zdenek Blatny	11	8	10	18	24
Bret DeCecco	11	6	11	17	12
Jarret Stoll	11	5	9	14	22
Jason Jaffray	11	5	7	12	10
Marek Svatos	11	7	2	9	26
Cole Fischer	11	3	4	7	8
Colin Sinclair	11	0	7	7	23
Mike Lee	11	3	3	6	25
Richard Hamula	11	3	2	5	4
Trevor Johnson	10	1	4	5	12
Tyler Beechey	11	1	3	4	6
Aaron Rome	11	1	3	4	6
Pat Iannone	11	1	1	2	2
Craig Weller	11	0	2	2	26
Dean Arsene	11	0	1	1	34
Andy Thompson	11	0	1	1	14
Jeff Harvey (goalie)	1	0	0	0	0
Adam Taylor	1	0	0	0	0
Lance Morrison	3	0	0	0	0
Steven Makway	8	0	0	0	11
Dan Blackburn (goalie)	11	0	0	0	4
Brennan Evans	11	0	0	0	25

GOALTENDING

	Games	Min.	W	L	T	G	SO	Avg.
Jeff Harvey	1	4	0	0	0	0	0	0.00
Dan Blackburn	11	706	7	4	0	23	1	1.95

LETHBRIDGE HURRICANES
(Lost first round to Red Deer, 4-1)
SCORING

	Games	G	A	Pts.	PIM
Martin Podlesak	3	1	1	2	2
Nathan Barrett	5	1	1	2	6
Tomas Kopecky	5	1	1	2	6
Adam Johnson	5	0	2	2	17
Warren McCutcheon	4	1	0	1	11
Brett O'Malley	5	1	0	1	15
Brian Patterson	5	1	0	1	6
Tim Green	3	0	1	1	2
Brian Ballman	5	0	1	1	18
Mark Forth	5	0	1	1	4
Andrew Jungwirth	5	0	1	1	8
Darren Lynch	5	0	1	1	14
Phil Cole	1	0	0	0	2
Thomas Scantlebury	1	0	0	0	0
Scott Borders	2	0	0	0	8
Joel Martin (goalie)	2	0	0	0	0
Matt Fetzner	4	0	0	0	2
Blake Ward (goalie)	4	0	0	0	4
Simon Ferguson	5	0	0	0	36
Tristan Grant	5	0	0	0	11
Matt Jacques	5	0	0	0	0
Derek Ruck	5	0	0	0	4

GOALTENDING

	Games	Min.	W	L	T	G	SO	Avg.
Blake Ward	4	238	1	3	0	20	0	5.04
Joel Martin	2	69	0	1	0	6	0	5.22

MOOSE JAW WARRIORS
(Lost first round to Kootenay, 4-0)
SCORING

	Games	G	A	Pts.	PIM
Brian Sutherby	4	2	1	3	10
Steven Crampton	4	1	2	3	10
Nathan Paetsch	4	1	2	3	6
Shawn Limpright	4	1	0	1	12
Jarrett Thompson	4	1	0	1	15
Harlan Anderson	4	0	1	1	4
Scott Kelman	4	0	1	1	12
Tomas Mojzis	4	0	1	1	8
Sean O'Connor	4	0	1	1	15
Jason Weitzel	4	0	1	1	4
Bobby Chad Mitchell	2	0	0	0	17
David Bararuk	3	0	0	0	0
Kyle Brodziak	3	0	0	0	0
Tim Barlow	4	0	0	0	2
Deryk Engelland	4	0	0	0	10
Ben Knopp	4	0	0	0	11
Brooks Laich	4	0	0	0	5
Shaun Landolt	4	0	0	0	0
Mitch Love	4	0	0	0	2
Renat Mamachev	4	0	0	0	0

GOALTENDING

	Games	Min.	W	L	T	G	SO	Avg.
Tim Barlow	4	237	0	4	0	22	0	5.57

PORTLAND WINTER HAWKS
(Lost finals to Red Deer, 4-1)
SCORING

	Games	G	A	Pts.	PIM
Paul Gaustad	16	10	6	16	59
Josef Balej	16	6	9	15	6
Marcel Hossa	16	5	7	12	14
Shawn Roed	16	3	9	12	42
Josh Olson	16	5	4	9	17
Joey Hope	13	1	7	8	10
Jesse Ferguson	16	1	7	8	48
Dan Hulak	16	1	6	7	4
Garrett Prosofsky	12	5	1	6	22
Dean Beuker	16	3	3	6	15
Nick Marach	16	3	3	6	32
Willy Glover	15	2	4	6	10
Kevin Young	14	1	4	5	24
Braydon Coburn	14	0	4	4	2
Matthew Girling	15	2	0	2	4
Brad Priestlay	16	1	1	2	11
Kris Callaway	16	0	2	2	26
Craig Valette	16	0	2	2	27
Patrick Wellar	10	0	1	1	13
Jomar Cruz (goalie)	2	0	0	0	0
John Togiai	3	0	0	0	0
Lanny Ramage (goalie)	16	0	0	0	2

GOALTENDING

	Games	Min.	W	L	T	G	SO	Avg.
Jomar Cruz	2	44	0	1	0	1	0	1.36
Lanny Ramage	16	952	9	6	0	40	2	2.52

PRINCE GEORGE COUGARS
(Lost first round to Portland, 4-2)
SCORING

	Games	G	A	Pts.	PIM
Justin Cox	6	3	4	7	20
Blake Robson	6	1	5	6	2
Berkeley Buchko	6	3	2	5	2
Dan Hamhuis	6	2	3	5	15
Christian Chartier	6	1	4	5	6
Aaron Foster	6	3	1	4	14
Dan Baum	6	1	2	3	27
Brett Allan	6	0	3	3	6
Chris Falloon	6	0	3	3	0
Tim Wedderburn	6	1	1	2	6

	Games	G	A	Pts.	PIM
Mark Kitts	5	1	0	1	0
Derek Boogaard	6	1	0	1	31
Gary Gladue	6	0	1	1	0
Devin Wilson	6	0	1	1	8
Kyle Stanton (goalie)	1	0	0	0	0
Nathan Brice	6	0	0	0	9
David Koci	6	0	0	0	20
Scott Lynch	6	0	0	0	2
Adam Stefishen	6	0	0	0	16
Billy Thompson (goalie)	6	0	0	0	0

GOALTENDING

	Games	Min.	W	L	T	G	SO	Avg.
Kyle Stanton	1	37	0	0	0	2	0	3.24
Billy Thompson	6	324	2	4	0	22	0	4.07

RED DEER REBELS
(Winner of 2001 WHL playoffs)

SCORING

	Games	G	A	Pts.	PIM
Martin Erat	22	15	21	36	32
Justin Mapletoft	22	13	21	34	59
Kyle Wanvig	22	10	12	22	47
Jim Vandermeer	22	3	13	16	43
Ross Lupaschuk	22	5	10	15	54
Andrew Bergen	22	7	6	13	14
Colby Armstrong	21	6	6	12	39
Jeff Woywitka	22	2	8	10	25
Doug Lynch	21	1	9	10	30
Joel Stepp	22	6	3	9	24
Boyd Gordon	22	3	6	9	2
Jeff Smith	22	4	4	8	40
Bryce Thoma	22	2	3	5	8
Diarmuid Kelly	22	1	3	4	8
Darcy Robinson	20	1	1	2	20
Devin Francon	22	1	0	1	26
Shane Bendera (goalie)	22	0	1	1	2
Ladislav Kouba	3	0	0	0	2
Derek Meech	22	0	0	0	9
Shay Stephenson	22	0	0	0	15

GOALTENDING

	Games	Min.	W	L	T	G	SO	Avg.
Shane Bendera	22	1404	16	6	0	43	4	1.84

REGINA PATS
(Lost first round to Calgary, 4-2)

SCORING

	Games	G	A	Pts.	PIM
Blake Evans	6	6	2	8	8
Brett Lysak	6	5	1	6	4
Filip Novak	6	1	4	5	6
Karel Mosovsky	6	1	3	4	8
Paul Elliott	6	0	4	4	2
Curtis Austring	6	3	0	3	2
Barret Jackman	6	0	3	3	8
Garth Murray	6	1	1	2	10
Garnet Exelby	6	0	2	2	2
Gable Gross	6	0	2	2	12
Kevin Korol	6	1	0	1	6
Chad Grisdale	4	0	1	1	5
Chad Bassen	6	0	1	1	2
Jeff Feniak	6	0	1	1	13
Grant Jacobsen	6	0	1	1	4
Ryan Thomas	6	0	1	1	15
Chad Davidson (goalie)	2	0	0	0	2
Kyle Ladobruk	2	0	0	0	0
David McDonald	2	0	0	0	0
Matt Hubbauer	4	0	0	0	5
Donald Choukalos (goalie)	6	0	0	0	4
David Kaczowka	6	0	0	0	6

GOALTENDING

	Games	Min.	W	L	T	G	SO	Avg.
Donald Choukalos	6	315	1	4	0	18	0	3.43
Chad Davidson	2	53	1	0	0	4	0	4.53

SEATTLE THUNDERBIRDS
(Lost second round to Spokane, 3-0)

SCORING

	Games	G	A	Pts.	PIM
Shane Endicott	9	4	5	9	12
Jamie Lundmark	9	4	4	8	16
Barrett Heisten	9	2	6	8	20
Tim Preston	9	4	3	7	6
David Morisset	9	4	2	6	12
Dustin Johner	9	1	5	6	6
Darren McLachlan	9	1	3	4	18
Brad Tutschek	9	2	1	3	4
Greg Black	9	1	1	2	26
Jake Riddle	6	0	2	2	2
Gerard DiCaire	9	0	2	2	2
Dion Lassu	9	0	2	2	23
Keegan McAvoy	9	0	2	2	17
Craig Olynick	9	0	2	2	14
Matthew Spiller	9	1	0	1	22
Scott McQueen	9	0	1	1	0
Jeffrey Beatch	1	0	0	0	2
Thomas Vicars (goalie)	2	0	0	0	0
Matthew Chacho	3	0	0	0	0
Nick Pannoni (goalie)	7	0	0	0	0
Eric Benke	8	0	0	0	0
Tyler Metcalfe	9	0	0	0	0

GOALTENDING

	Games	Min.	W	L	T	G	SO	Avg.
Nick Pannoni	7	426	3	4	0	18	0	2.54
Thomas Vicars	2	122	1	1	0	9	0	4.43

SPOKANE CHIEFS
(Lost semifinals to Portland, 4-1)

SCORING

	Games	G	A	Pts.	PIM
Lynn Loyns	12	6	12	18	18
Roman Tvrdon	12	5	11	16	0
Scott Henkelman	12	5	9	14	14
Tim Krymusa	12	4	3	7	4
Mason Wallin	12	4	3	7	6
David Boychuk	12	2	3	5	54
Ryan Thorpe	10	3	1	4	6
Matthew Keith	12	1	3	4	14
Chris Heid	12	0	4	4	12
Joff Kehler	11	2	1	3	10
Steven Mann	10	0	3	3	0
Shawn Thompson	12	2	0	2	33
Brandin Cote	8	1	1	2	12
Chris Ovington	12	1	1	2	10
Brad Schell	12	0	2	2	2
Kurt Sauer	3	1	0	1	2
Justin Keller	12	1	0	1	0
Chris Barr	10	0	1	1	22
Tyler MacKay (goalie)	12	0	1	1	10
Barry Brust (goalie)	1	0	0	0	0
Barry Horman	2	0	0	0	0
Jevon Desautels	4	0	0	0	0
Jordan Clarke	12	0	0	0	24

GOALTENDING

	Games	Min.	W	L	T	G	SO	Avg.
Barry Brust	1	0	0	0	0	0	0	0.00
Tyler MacKay	12	736	8	4	0	21	2	1.71

SWIFT CURRENT BRONCOS
(Lost semifinals to Red Deer, 4-2)

SCORING

	Games	G	A	Pts.	PIM
Tim Smith	19	10	14	24	38
Duncan Milroy	19	9	12	21	6
Brent Twordik	19	4	7	11	30
Layne Ulmer	19	7	3	10	20
Nathan Smith	19	4	3	7	20
Paul Deniset	19	4	2	6	10

	Games	G	A	Pts.	PIM
Dean Serdachny	19	0	6	6	60
Ben Ondrus	19	2	3	5	46
James Hiebert	16	1	4	5	39
Ian White	19	1	4	5	6
Jakub Cutta	16	1	3	4	32
Jay Langager	19	1	3	4	18
Clay Thoring	19	1	3	4	10
Matt Sommerfeld	15	0	2	2	42
John Dahl	8	0	1	1	2
Jarad Bourassa	1	0	0	0	0
Todd Ford (goalie)	1	0	0	0	0

	Games	G	A	Pts.	PIM
Craig Priestlay	9	0	0	0	21
Kevin Seibel	14	0	0	0	2
Dustin Friesen	17	0	0	0	0
Ales Cerny	18	0	0	0	19
B.J. Boxma (goalie)	19	0	0	0	2
Adam Dombrowski	19	0	0	0	8

GOALTENDING

	Games	Min.	W	L	T	G	SO	Avg.
B.J. Boxma	19	1217	10	9	0	52	0	2.56
Todd Ford	1	26	0	0	0	2	0	4.62

2000-01 AWARD WINNERS

ALL-STAR TEAMS

EASTERN CONFERENCE

First team	Pos.	Second team
Dan Blackburn, Kootenay	G	Shane Bendera, Red Deer
Matt Kinch, Calgary	D	Ross Lupaschuk, Red Deer
Jim Vandermeer, Red Deer	D	Filip Novak, Regina
Justin Mapletoft, Red Deer	F	Nathan Barrett, Lethbridge
Jarret Stoll, Kootenay	F	Blake Evans, Regina
Layne Ulmer, Swift Current	F	Kyle Wanvig, Red Deer

WESTERN CONFERENCE

First team	Pos.	Second team
Tyler McKay, Spokane	G	Kevin Swanson, Kelowna
Christian Chartier, P. George	D	Dan Hulak, Portland
Dan Hamhuis, P. George	D	Gerard Dicaire, Seattle
		Kurt Sauer, Spokane
Jared Aulin, Kamloops	F	Brandin Cote, Spokane
Jamie Lundmark, Seattle	F	Marcel Hossa, Portland
Konstantin Panov, Kamloops	F	Rory McDade, Kelowna

TROPHY WINNERS

Four Broncos Memorial Trophy: Justin Mapletoft, Red Deer
Bob Clarke Trophy: Justin Mapletoft, Red Deer
Jim Piggott Memorial Trophy: Scottie Upshall, Kamloops
Brad Hornung Trophy: Matt Kinch, Calgary
Bill Hunter Trophy: Christian Chartier, Prince George
Del Wilson Trophy: Dan Blackburn, Kootenay
Dunc McCallum Memorial Trophy: Brent Sutter, Red Deer
Scott Munro Memorial Trophy: Red Deer Rebels
President's Cup: Red Deer Rebels
Playoff MVP: Shane Bendera, Red Deer

ALL-TIME AWARD WINNERS

FOUR BRONCOS MEMORIAL TROPHY
(Player of the year—selected by coaches)

Season	Player, Team
1966-67	Gerry Pinder, Saskatoon
1967-68	Jim Harrison, Estevan
1968-69	Bobby Clarke, Flin Flon
1969-70	Reggie Leach, Flin Flon
1970-71	Ed Dyck, Calgary
1971-72	John Davidson, Calgary
1972-73	Dennis Sobchuk, Regina
1973-74	Ron Chipperfield, Brandon
1974-75	Bryan Trottier, Lethbridge
1975-76	Bernie Federko, Saskatoon
1976-77	Barry Beck, New Westminster
1977-78	Ryan Walter, Seattle
1978-79	Perry Turnbull, Portland
1979-80	Doug Wickenheiser, Regina
1980-81	Steve Tsujiura, Medicine Hat
1981-82	Mike Vernon, Calgary
1982-83	Mike Vernon, Calgary
1983-84	Ray Ferraro, Brandon
1984-85	Cliff Ronning, New Westminster
1985-86	Emanuel Viveiros, Prince Albert (East Div.)
	Rob Brown, Kamloops (West Div.)
1986-87	Joe Sakic, Swift Current (East Div.)
	Rob Brown, Kamloops (West Div.)
1987-88	Joe Sakic, Swift Current
1988-89	Stu Barnes, Tri-City
1989-90	Glen Goodall, Seattle
1990-91	Ray Whitney, Spokane
1991-92	Steve Konowalchuk, Portland
1992-93	Jason Krywulak, Swift Current
1993-94	Sonny Mignacca, Medicine Hat

Season	Player, Team
1994-95	Marty Murray, Brandon
1995-96	Jarome Iginla, Kamloops
1996-97	Peter Schaefer, Brandon
1997-98	Sergei Varlamov, Swift Current
1998-99	Cody Rudkowsky, Seattle
1999-00	Brad Moran, Calgary
2000-01	Justin Mapletoft, Red Deer

The trophy was awarded to the most valuable player prior to the 1994-95 season.

BOB CLARKE TROPHY
(Top scorer)

Season	Player, Team
1966-67	Gerry Pinder, Saskatoon
1967-68	Bobby Clarke, Flin Flon
1968-69	Bobby Clarke, Flin Flon
1969-70	Reggie Leach, Flin Flon
1970-71	Chuck Arnason, Flin Flon
1971-72	Tom Lysiak, Medicine Hat
1972-73	Tom Lysiak, Medicine Hat
1973-74	Ron Chipperfield, Brandon
1974-75	Mel Bridgman, Victoria
1975-76	Bernie Federko, Saskatoon
1976-77	Bill Derlago, Brandon
1977-78	Brian Propp, Brandon
1978-79	Brian Propp, Brandon
1979-80	Doug Wickenheiser, Regina
1980-81	Brian Varga, Regina
1981-82	Jack Callander, Regina
1982-83	Dale Derkatch, Regina
1983-84	Ray Ferraro, Brandon
1984-85	Cliff Ronning, New Westminster

Season	Player, Team
1985-86	Rob Brown, Kamloops
1986-87	Rob Brown, Kamloops
1987-88	Joe Sakic, Swift Current
	Theo Fleury, Moose Jaw
1988-89	Dennis Holland, Portland
1989-90	Len Barrie, Kamloops
1990-91	Ray Whitney, Spokane
1991-92	Kevin St. Jacques, Lethbridge
1992-93	Jason Krywulak, Swift Current
1993-94	Lonny Bohonos, Portland
1994-95	Daymond Langkow, Tri-City
1995-96	Mark Deyell, Saskatoon
1996-97	Todd Robinson, Portland
1997-98	Sergei Varlamov, Swift Current
1998-99	Pavel Brendl, Calgary
1999-00	Brad Moran, Calgary
2000-01	Justin Mapletoft, Red Deer

The award was originally known as the Bob Brownridge Memorial Trophy.

JIM PIGGOTT MEMORIAL TROPHY
(Rookie of the year)

Season	Player, Team
1966-67	Ron Garwasiuk, Regina
1967-68	Ron Fairbrother, Saskatoon
1968-69	Ron Williams, Edmonton
1969-70	Gene Carr, Flin Flon
1970-71	Stan Weir, Medicine Hat
1971-72	Dennis Sobchuk, Regina
1972-73	Rick Blight, Brandon
1973-74	Cam Connor, Flin Flon
1974-75	Don Murdoch, Medicine Hat
1975-76	Steve Tambellini, Lethbridge
1976-77	Brian Propp, Brandon
1977-78	John Orgrodnick, New Westminster
	Keith Brown, Portland
1978-79	Kelly Kisio, Calgary
1979-80	Grant Fuhr, Victoria
1980-81	Dave Michayluk, Regina
1981-82	Dale Derkatch, Regina
1982-83	Dan Hodgson, Prince Albert
1983-84	Cliff Ronning, New Westminster
1984-85	Mark Mackay, Moose Jaw
1985-86	Neil Brady, Medicine Hat (East Div.)
	Ron Shudra, Kamloops, (West Div.)
	Dave Waldie, Portland (West Div.)
1986-87	Joe Sakic, Swift Current (East Div.)
	Dennis Holland, Portland (West Div.)
1987-88	Stu Barnes, New Westminster
1988-89	Wes Walz, Lethbridge
1989-90	Petr Nedved, Seattle
1990-91	Donevan Hextall, Prince Albert
1991-92	Ashley Buckberger, Swift Current
1992-93	Jeff Friesen, Regina
1993-94	Wade Redden, Brandon
1994-95	Todd Robinson, Portland
1995-96	Chris Phillips, Prince Albert
1996-97	Donovan Nunweiler, Moose Jaw
1997-98	Marian Hossa, Portland
1998-99	Pavel Brendl, Calgary
1999-00	Dan Blackburn, Kootenay
2000-01	Scottie Upshall, Kamloops

The award was originally known as the Stewart "Butch" Paul Memorial Trophy.

BRAD HORNUNG TROPHY
(Most sportsmanlike player)

Season	Player, Team
1966-67	Morris Stefaniw, Estevan
1967-68	Bernie Blanchette, Saskatoon
1968-69	Bob Liddington, Calgary
1969-70	Randy Rota, Calgary
1970-71	Lorne Henning, Estevan

Season	Player, Team
1971-72	Ron Chipperfield, Brandon
1972-73	Ron Chipperfield, Brandon
1973-74	Mike Rogers, Calgary
1974-75	Danny Arndt, Saskatoon
1975-76	Blair Chapman, Saskatoon
1976-77	Steve Tambellini, Lethbridge
1977-78	Steve Tambellini, Lethbridge
1978-79	Errol Rausse, Seattle
1979-80	Steve Tsujiura, Medicine Hat
1980-81	Steve Tsujiura, Medicine Hat
1981-82	Mike Moller, Lethbridge
1982-83	Darren Boyko, Winnipeg
1983-84	Mark Lamb, Medicine Hat
1984-85	Cliff Ronning, New Westminster
1985-86	Randy Smith, Saskatoon (East Division)
	Ken Morrison, Kamloops (West Division)
1986-87	Len Nielsen, Regina (East Division)
	Dave Archibald, Portland (West Division)
1987-88	Craig Endean, Regina
1988-89	Blair Atcheynum, Moose Jaw
1989-90	Bryan Bosch, Lethbridge
1990-91	Pat Falloon, Spokane
1991-92	Steve Junker, Spokane
1992-93	Rick Girard, Swift Current
1993-94	Lonny Bohonos, Portland
1994-95	Darren Ritchie, Brandon
1995-96	Hnat Domenichelli, Kamloops
1996-97	Kelly Smart, Brandon
1997-98	Cory Cyrenne, Brandon
1998-99	Matt Kinch, Calgary
1999-00	Trent Hunter, Prince George
2000-01	Matt Kinch, Calgary

The award was originally known as the Frank Boucher Memorial Trophy for most gentlemanly player.

BILL HUNTER TROPHY
(Top defenseman)

Season	Player, Team
1966-67	Barry Gibbs, Estevan
1967-68	Gerry Hart, Flin Flon
1968-69	Dale Hoganson, Estevan
1969-70	Jim Hargreaves, Winnipeg
1970-71	Ron Jones, Edmonton
1971-72	Jim Watson, Calgary
1972-73	George Pesut, Saskatoon
1973-74	Pat Price, Saskatoon
1974-75	Rick LaPointe, Victoria
1975-76	Kevin McCarthy, Winnipeg
1976-77	Barry Beck, New Westminster
1977-78	Brad McCrimmon, Brandon
1978-79	Keith Brown, Portland
1979-80	David Babych, Portland
1980-81	Jim Benning, Portland
1981-82	Gary Nylund, Portland
1982-83	Gary Leeman, Regina
1983-84	Bob Rouse, Lethbridge
1984-85	Wendel Clark, Saskatoon
1985-86	Emanuel Viveiros, Prince Albert (East Division)
	Glen Wesley, Portland (West Division)
1986-87	Wayne McBean, Medicine Hat (East Division)
	Glen Wesley, Portland (West Division)
1987-88	Greg Hawgood, Kamloops
1988-89	Dan Lambert, Swift Current
1989-90	Kevin Haller, Regina
1990-91	Darryl Sydor, Kamloops
1991-92	Richard Matvichuk, Saskatoon
1992-93	Jason Smith, Regina
1993-94	Brendan Witt, Seattle
1994-95	Nolan Baumgartner, Kamloops
1995-96	Nolan Baumgartner, Kamloops
1996-97	Chris Phillips, Lethbridge
1997-98	Michal Rozsival, Swift Current
1998-99	Brad Stuart, Calgary

Season	Player, Team
1999-00	Micki Dupont, Kamloops
2000-01	Christian Chartier, Prince George

DEL WILSON TROPHY
(Top goaltender)

Season	Player, Team
1966-67	Ken Brown, Moose Jaw
1967-68	Chris Worthy, Flin Flon
1968-69	Ray Martyniuk, Flin Flon
1969-70	Ray Martyniuk, Flin Flon
1970-71	Ed Dyck, Calgary
1971-72	John Davidson, Calgary
1972-73	Ed Humphreys, Saskatoon
1973-74	Garth Malarchuk, Calgary
1974-75	Bill Oleschuk, Saskatoon
1975-76	Carey Walker, New Westminster
1976-77	Glen Hanlon, Brandon
1977-78	Bart Hunter, Portland
1978-79	Rick Knickle, Brandon
1979-80	Kevin Eastman, Victoria
1980-81	Grant Fuhr, Victoria
1981-82	Mike Vernon, Calgary
1982-83	Mike Vernon, Calgary
1983-84	Ken Wregget, Lethbridge
1984-85	Troy Gamble, Medicine Hat
1985-86	Mark Fitzpatrick, Medicine Hat
1986-87	Kenton Rein, Prince Albert (East Division)
	Dean Cook, Kamloops (West Division)
1987-88	Troy Gamble, Spokane
1988-89	Danny Lorenz, Seattle
1989-90	Trevor Kidd, Brandon
1990-91	Jamie McLennan, Lethbridge
1991-92	Corey Hirsch, Kamloops
1992-93	Trevor Wilson, Brandon
1993-94	Norm Maracle, Saskatoon
1994-95	Paxton Schafer, Medicine Hat
1995-96	David Lemanowicz, Spokane
1996-97	Brian Boucher, Tri-City
1997-98	Brent Belecki, Portland
1998-99	Cody Rudkowsky, Seattle
1999-00	Bryce Wandler, Swift Current
2000-01	Dan Blackburn, Kootenay

PLAYER OF THE YEAR
(Selected by fans and media)

Season	Player, Team
1974-75	Ed Staniowski, Regina
1975-76	Bernie Federko, Saskatoon
1976-77	Kevin McCarthy, Winnipeg
1977-78	Ryan Walter, Seattle
1978-79	Brian Propp, Brandon
1979-80	Doug Wickenheiser, Regina
1980-81	Barry Pederson, Victoria
1981-82	Mike Vernon, Calgary
1982-83	Dean Evason, Kamloops
1983-84	Ray Ferraro, Brandon
1984-85	Dan Hodgson, Prince Albert
1985-86	Emanuel Viveiros, Prince Albert
1986-87	Rob Brown, Kamloops
1987-88	Joe Sakic, Swift Current

Season	Player, Team
1988-89	Dennis Holland, Portland
1989-90	Wes Walz, Lethbridge
1990-91	Ray Whitney, Spokane
1991-92	Corey Hirsch, Kamloops
1992-93	Jason Krywulak, Swift Current
1993-94	Sonny Mignacca, Medicine Hat

The award merged with the Four Broncos Memorial Trophy after the 1993-94 season.

DUNC MC CALLUM MEMORIAL TROPHY
(Coach of the year)

Season	Coach, Team
1968-69	Scotty Munro, Calgary
1969-70	Pat Ginnell, Flin Flon
1970-71	Pat Ginnell, Flin Flon
1971-72	Earl Ingarfield, Regina
1972-73	Pat Ginnell, Flin Flon
1973-74	Stan Dunn, Swift Current
1974-75	Pat Ginnell, Victoria
1975-76	Ernie McLean, New Westminster
1976-77	Dunc McCallum, Brandon
1977-78	Jack Shupe, Victoria
	Dave King, Billings
1978-79	Dunc McCallum, Brandon
1979-80	Doug Sauter, Calgary
1980-81	Ken Hodge, Portland
1981-82	Jack Sangster, Seattle
1982-83	Darryl Lubiniecki, Saskatoon
1983-84	Terry Simpson, Prince Albert
1984-85	Doug Sauter, Medicine Hat
1985-86	Terry Simpson, Prince Albert
1986-87	Ken Hitchcock, Kamloops (West Division)
	Graham James, Swift Current (East Division)
1987-88	Marcel Comeau, Saskatoon
1988-89	Ron Kennedy, Medicine Hat
1989-90	Ken Hitchcock, Kamloops
1990-91	Tom Renney, Kamloops
1991-92	Bryan Maxwell, Spokane
1992-93	Marcel Comeau, Tacoma
1993-94	Lorne Molleken, Saskatoon
1994-95	Don Nachbaur, Seattle
1995-96	Bob Lowes, Brandon
1996-97	Brent Peterson, Portland
1997-98	Dean Clark, Brandon
1998-99	Don Hay, Tri-City
1999-00	Todd McLellan, Swift Current
2000-01	Brent Sutter, Red Deer

PLAYOFF MVP

Season	Player, Team
1991-92	Jarrett Deuling, Kamloops
1992-93	Andy Schneider, Swift Current
1993-94	Steve Passmore, Kamloops
1994-95	Nolan Baumgartner, Kamloops
1995-96	Bob Brown, Brandon
1996-97	Blaine Russell, Lethbridge
1997-98	Brent Belecki, Portland
1998-99	Brad Moran, Calgary
1999-00	Dan Blackburn, Kootenay
2000-01	Shane Bendera, Red Deer

ALL-TIME LEAGUE CHAMPIONS

	REGULAR-SEASON CHAMPION	PLAYOFF CHAMPION
Season	**Team**	**Team**
1966-67—	Edmonton Oil Kings	Moose Jaw Canucks
1967-68—	Flin Flon Bombers	Estevan Bruins
1968-69—	Flin Flon Bombers	Flin Flon Bombers
1969-70—	Flin Flon Bombers	Flin Flon Bombers
1970-71—	Edmonton Oil Kings	Edmonton Oil Kings
1971-72—	Calgary Centennials	Edmonton Oil Kings
1972-73—	Saskatoon Blades	Medicine Hat Tigers
1973-74—	Regina Pats	Regina Pats
1974-75—	Victoria Cougars	New Westminster Bruins
1975-76—	New Westminster Bruins	New Westminster Bruins
1976-77—	New Westminster Bruins	New Westminster Bruins
1977-78—	Brandon Wheat Kings	New Westminster Bruins
1978-79—	Brandon Wheat Kings	Brandon Wheat Kings
1979-80—	Portland Winter Hawks	Regina Pats
1980-81—	Victoria Cougars	Victoria Cougars
1981-82—	Lethbridge Broncos	Portland Winter Hawks
1982-83—	Saskatoon Blades	Lethbridge Broncos
1983-84—	Kamloops Junior Oilers	Kamloops Junior Oilers
1984-85—	Prince Albert Raiders	Prince Albert Raiders
1985-86—	Medicine Hat Tigers	Kamloops Blazers
1986-87—	Kamloops Blazers	Medicine Hat Tigers
1987-88—	Saskatoon Blades	Medicine Hat Tigers
1988-89—	Swift Current Broncos	Swift Current Broncos
1989-90—	Kamloops Blazers	Kamloops Blazers
1990-91—	Kamloops Blazers	Spokane Chiefs
1991-92—	Kamloops Blazers	Kamloops Blazers
1992-93—	Swift Current Broncos	Swift Current Broncos
1993-94—	Kamloops Blazers	Kamloops Blazers
1994-95—	Kamloops Blazers	Kamloops Blazers
1995-96—	Brandon Wheat Kings	Brandon Wheat Kings
1996-97—	Lethbridge Hurricanes	Lethbridge Hurricanes
1997-98—	Portland Winter Hawks	Portland Winter Hawks
1998-99—	Calgary Hitmen	Calgary Hitmen
1999-00—	Calgary Hitmen	Kootenay Ice
2000-01—	Red Deer Rebels	Red Deer Rebels

The WHL regular-season champion is awarded the Scott Munro Memorial Trophy and the playoff champion Is awarded the President's Cup.

MAJOR JUNIOR LEAGUES *WHL*

COLLEGE HOCKEY

NCAA Division I

Central Collegiate Hockey Association

Eastern College Athletic Conference

Hockey East

Western Collegiate Hockey Association

Independents

Canadian Interuniversity Athletic Union

Canadian colleges

NCAA DIVISION I

NCAA TOURNAMENT

EAST REGIONAL
(Worcester, Mass.)
FIRST ROUND
Colorado College 3, St. Lawrence 2 (2OT)
Maine 5, Minnesota 4 (OT)
QUARTERFINALS
North Dakota 4, Colorado College 1
Boston College 3, Maine 1

WEST REGIONAL
(Grand Rapids, Mich.)
FIRST ROUND
Wisconsin 4, Providence 1
Michigan 4, Mercyhurst 3
QUARTERFINALS
Michigan State 5, Wisconsin 1
Michigan 4, St. Cloud State 3

NCAA FINALS
(Albany, N.Y.)
North Dakota 2, Michigan State 0
Boston College 4, Michigan 2

CHAMPIONSHIP GAME
(Providence, R.I.)
Boston College 3, North Dakota 2 (OT)

ALL-TOURNAMENT TEAM

Player	Pos.	College
Scott Clemmensen	G	Boston College
Travis Roche	D	North Dakota
Rob Scuderi	D	Boston College
Chuck Kobasew	F	Boston College
Krys Kolanos	F	Boston College
Bryan Lundbohm	F	North Dakota

ALL-AMERICA TEAMS

EAST

First team	Pos.	Second team
Ty Conklin, New Hampshire	G	Nolan Schaefer, Providence
Bobby Allen, Boston College	D	Matt Desrosiers, St. Law.
Kent Huskins, Clarkson	D	Ron Hainsey, Lowell
Erik Anderson, St. Lawrence	F	Carl Corazzini, Boston Univ.
Brian Gionta, Boston College	F	Krys Kolanos, Boston College
Jeff Hamilton, Yale	F	Devin Rask, Providence

WEST

First team	Pos.	Second team
Ryan Miller, Michigan State	G	Scott Meyer, St. Cloud State
Jordan Leopold, Minnesota	D	Jeff Jillson, Michigan
Travis Roche, North Dakota	D	Greg Zanon, Neb.-Omaha
Dany Heatley, Wisconsin	F	Mike Bishai, W. Michigan
Andy Hilbert, Michigan	F	Mike Cammalleri, Michigan
Jeff Panzer, North Dakota	F	Mark Cullen, Colo. College
	F	Bryan Lundbohm, N. Dakota

HISTORY

TOURNAMENT CHAMPIONS

Year	Champion	Coach	Score	Runner-up	Most outstanding player
1948	Michigan	Vic Heyliger	8-4	Dartmouth	Joe Riley, F, Dartmouth
1949	Boston College	John Kelley	4-3	Dartmouth	Dick Desmond, G, Dartmouth
1950	Colorado College	Cheddy Thompson	13-4	Boston University	Ralph Bevins, G, Boston University
1951	Michigan	Vic Heyliger	7-1	Brown	Ed Whiston, G, Brown
1952	Michigan	Vic Heyliger	4-1	Colorado College	Kenneth Kinsley, G, Colorado College
1953	Michigan	Vic Heyliger	7-3	Minnesota	John Matchefts, F, Michigan
1954	Rensselaer	Ned Harkness	*5-4	Minnesota	Abbie Moore, F, Rensselaer
1955	Michigan	Vic Heyliger	5-3	Colorado College	Philip Hilton, D, Colorado College
1956	Michigan	Vic Heyliger	7-5	Michigan Tech	Lorne Howes, G, Michigan
1957	Colorado College	Thomas Bedecki	13-6	Michigan	Bob McCusker, F, Colorado College
1958	Denver	Murray Armstrong	6-2	North Dakota	Murray Massier, F, Denver
1959	North Dakota	Bob May	*4-3	Michigan State	Reg Morelli, F, North Dakota
1960	Denver	Murray Armstrong	5-3	Michigan Tech	Bob Marquis, F, Boston University
					Barry Urbanski, G, Boston University
					Louis Angotti, F, Michigan Tech
1961	Denver	Murray Armstrong	12-2	St. Lawrence	Bill Masterton, F, Denver
1962	Michigan Tech	John MacInnes	7-1	Clarkson	Louis Angotti, F, Michigan Tech
1963	North Dakota	Barney Thorndycraft	6-5	Denver	Al McLean, F, North Dakota
1964	Michigan	Allen Renfrew	6-3	Denver	Bob Gray, G, Michigan
1965	Michigan Tech	John MacInnes	8-2	Boston College	Gary Milroy, F, Michigan Tech
1966	Michigan State	Amo Bessone	6-1	Clarkson	Gaye Cooley, G, Michigan State
1967	Cornell	Ned Harkness	4-1	Boston University	Walt Stanowski, D, Cornell
1968	Denver	Murray Armstrong	4-0	North Dakota	Gerry Powers, G, Denver
1969	Denver	Murray Armstrong	4-3	Cornell	Keith Magnuson, D, Denver
1970	Cornell	Ned Harkness	6-4	Clarkson	Daniel Lodboa, D, Cornell
1971	Boston University	Jack Kelley	4-2	Minnesota	Dan Brady, G, Boston University
1972	Boston University	Jack Kelley	4-0	Cornell	Tim Regan, G, Boston University
1973	Wisconsin	Bob Johnson	4-2	Vacated	Dean Talafous, F, Wisconsin
1974	Minnesota	Herb Brooks	4-2	Michigan Tech	Brad Shelstad, G, Minnesota
1975	Michigan Tech	John MacInnes	6-1	Minnesota	Jim Warden, G, Michigan Tech

Year	Champion	Coach	Score	Runner-up	Most outstanding player
1976	Minnesota	Herb Brooks	6-4	Michigan Tech	Tom Vanelli, F, Minnesota
1977	Wisconsin	Bob Johnson	*6-5	Michigan	Julian Baretta, G, Wisconsin
1978	Boston University	Jack Parker	5-3	Boston College	Jack O'Callahan, D, Boston University
1979	Minnesota	Herb Brooks	4-3	North Dakota	Steve Janaszak, G, Minnesota
1980	North Dakota	John Gasparini	5-2	Northern Michigan	Doug Smail, F, North Dakota
1981	Wisconsin	Bob Johnson	6-3	Minnesota	Marc Behrend, G, Wisconsin
1982	North Dakota	John Gasparini	5-2	Wisconsin	Phil Sykes, F, North Dakota
1983	Wisconsin	Jeff Sauer	6-2	Harvard	Marc Behrend, G, Wisconsin
1984	Bowling Green State	Jerry York	*5-4	Minnesota-Duluth	Gary Kruzich, G, Bowling Green State
1985	Rensselaer	Mike Addesa	2-1	Providence	Chris Terreri, G, Providence
1986	Michigan State	Ron Mason	6-5	Harvard	Mike Donnelly, F, Michigan State
1987	North Dakota	John Gasparini	5-3	Michigan State	Tony Hrkac, F, North Dakota
1988	Lake Superior State	Frank Anzalone	*4-3	St. Lawrence	Bruce Hoffort, G, Lake Superior State
1989	Harvard	Bill Cleary	*4-3	Minnesota	Ted Donato, F, Harvard
1990	Wisconsin	Jeff Sauer	7-3	Colgate	Chris Tancill, F, Wisconsin
1991	Northern Michigan	Rick Comley	*8-7	Boston University	Scott Beattie, F, Northern Michigan
1992	Lake Superior State	Jeff Jackson	5-3	Wisconsin	Paul Constantin, F, Lake Superior State
1993	Maine	Shawn Walsh	5-4	Lake Superior State	Jim Montgomery, F, Maine
1994	Lake Superior State	Jeff Jackson	9-1	Boston University	Sean Tallaire, F, Lake Superior State
1995	Boston University	Jack Parker	6-2	Maine	Chris O'Sullivan, F, Boston University
1996	Michigan	Red Berenson	*3-2	Colorado College	Brendan Morrison, F, Michigan
1997	North Dakota	Dean Blais	6-4	Boston University	Matt Henderson, F, North Dakota
1998	Michigan	Red Berenson	*3-2	Boston College	Marty Turco, G, Michigan
1999	Maine	Shawn Walsh	*3-2	New Hampshire	Alfie Michaud, G, Maine
2000	North Dakota	Dean Blais	4-2	Boston College	Lee Goren, F, North Dakota
2001	Boston College	Jerry York	*3-2	North Dakota	Chuck Kobasew, F, Boston College

*Overtime.

ALL-TIME TOURNAMENT RECORDS

	Visits	W	L	GF	GA	Pct.	Finished 1st	2nd
Michigan	24	38	17	276	185	.691	9	2
North Dakota	18	30	14	172	124	.682	7	4
‡Lake Superior State	10	20	11	143	105	.645	3	1
§Wisconsin	19	30	17	189	148	.638	5	2
Maine	10	20	12	126	115	.625	2	1
Denver	14	19	12	144	91	.613	5	2
Colgate	2	3	2	13	15	.600	0	1
Michigan Tech	10	13	9	118	85	.591	3	4
Boston University	25	33	29	252	250	.532	4	5
Minnesota	23	28	25	263	239	.528	3	6
†Michigan State	20	24	24	193	182	.500	2	2
Northern Michigan	7	8	8	66	67	.500	1	1
‡Rensselaer Polytechnic Institute	8	8	8	52	55	.500	2	0
Northeastern	3	3	3	30	30	.500	0	0
Merrimack	1	2	2	14	16	.500	0	0
Niagara	1	1	1	5	5	.500	0	0
Ohio State	2	2	2	12	12	.500	0	0
Cornell	11	10	12	76	84	.455	2	2
Minnesota-Duluth	4	5	6	43	41	.455	0	1
Colorado College	15	13	16	115	129	.448	2	3
Dartmouth	5	4	5	38	37	.444	0	2
Boston College	22	23	30	186	132	.434	2	4
Providence	8	9	13	73	82	.409	0	1
*Bowling Green State	9	8	12	66	88	.400	1	0
§Lowell	3	2	3	19	23	.400	0	0
Clarkson	17	12	20	103	135	.375	0	3
†Harvard	16	14	24	143	166	.368	1	2
Yale	2	1	2	7	9	.333	0	0
New Hampshire	11	7	15	65	101	.318	0	1
Alaska-Anchorage	3	2	5	22	39	.286	0	0
Brown	4	2	5	31	45	.286	0	1
St. Lawrence	15	6	24	85	137	.200	0	2
Vermont	3	1	4	10	21	.200	0	0
Princeton	1	0	1	1	2	.000	0	0
Mercyhurst	1	0	1	3	4	.000	0	0
Miami of Ohio	2	0	2	3	7	.000	0	0
St. Cloud State	3	0	4	11	19	.000	0	0
Western Michigan	3	0	4	8	23	.000	0	0

(Denver also participated in 1973 tournament but its record was voided by the NCAA in 1977 upon discovery of violations by the University. The team had finished second in '73.)

COLLEGE HOCKEY *NCAA Division I*

*Bowling Green State and Northeastern played to a 2-2 tie in 1981-82.
†Harvard and Michigan State played to a 3-3 tie in 1982-83.
‡Lake Superior State and RPI played to a 3-3 tie in 1984-85.
§Wisconsin and Lowell played to a 4-4 tie in 1987-88.

HOBEY BAKER AWARD WINNERS

(Top college hockey player in United States)

Year—Player, College
1981—Neal Broten, Minnesota
1982—George McPhee, Bowling Green St.
1983—Mark Fusco, Harvard
1984—Tom Kurvers, Minnesota-Duluth
1985—Bill Watson, Minnesota-Duluth
1986—Scott Fusco, Harvard
1987—Tony Hrkac, North Dakota

Year—Player, College
1988—Robb Stauber, Minnesota
1989—Lane MacDonald, Harvard
1990—Kip Miller, Michigan State
1991—David Emma, Boston College
1992—Scott Pellerin, Maine
1993—Paul Kariya, Maine
1994—Chris Marinucci, Min.-Duluth

Year—Player, College
1995—Brian Holzinger, Bowling Green St.
1996—Brian Bonin, Minnesota
1997—Brendan Morrison, Michigan
1998—Chris Drury, Boston University
1999—Jason Krog, New Hampshire
2000—Mike Mottau, Boston College
2001—Ryan Miller, Michigan State

COLLEGE HOCKEY *NCAA Division I*

CENTRAL COLLEGIATE
HOCKEY ASSOCIATION

2000-01 SEASON

FINAL STANDINGS

Team	G	W	L	T	Pts.	GF	GA
Michigan St. (33-5-4) ..	28	21	4	3	45	86	37
Mia. of Ohio (20-16-2).	28	17	10	1	35	95	71
Michigan (27-13-5)......	28	16	9	3	35	102	60
Neb.-Omaha (24-15-3)	28	15	10	3	33	86	80
N. Michigan (18-13-7).	28	12	10	6	30	76	71
W. Michigan (20-13-6).	28	12	10	6	30	97	96
Ohio State (17-18-2)....	28	13	13	2	28	81	89
Ferris St. (13-20-5)......	28	9	15	4	22	64	81
Bowl. Green (16-19-5).	28	8	15	5	21	72	82
A. Fairbanks (9-19-8)...	28	7	14	7	21	67	91
Notre Dame (10-22-7).	28	7	15	6	20	72	98
Lake Sup. St. (13-23-0).	28	8	20	0	16	53	95

Overall record in parentheses.

PLAYOFF RESULTS

FIRST ROUND

Michigan 8, Ferris State 3
Michigan 3, Ferris State 0
(Michigan won series, 2-0)

Michigan State 5, Alaska-Fairbanks 2
Michigan State 3, Alaska-Fairbanks 2 (OT)
(Michigan State won series, 2-0)

Bowling Green State 4, Miami of Ohio 3
Bowling Green State 4, Miami of Ohio 3 (OT)
(Bowling Green State won series, 2-0)

Ohio State 5, Nebraska-Omaha 4 (OT)
Nebraska-Omaha 2, Ohio State 1
Nebraska-Omaha 4, Ohio State 3 (2OT)
(Nebraska-Omaha won series, 2-1)

Northern Michigan 3, Western Michigan 2 (OT)
Western Michigan 9, Northern Michigan 7
Northern Michigan 5, Western Michigan 4 (OT)
(Northern Michigan won series, 2-1)

PLAY-IN GAME

Bowling Green State 2, Northern Michigan 1 (OT)

SEMIFINALS

Michigan 3, Nebraska-Omaha 2
Michigan State 2, Bowling Green State 1

FINALS

Michigan State 2, Michigan 0

ALL-STAR TEAMS

First team	Pos.	Second team
Ryan Miller, Michigan State	G	Josh Blackburn, Michigan
		Phil Osaer, Ferris State
Jeff Jillson, Michigan	D	Andrew Hutchinson, Mich. St.
Greg Zanon, Neb.-Omaha	D	John-Michael Liles, Mich. St.
David Brisson, Neb.-Omaha	F	Mike Bishai, Western Mich.
Mike Cammalleri, Michigan	F	Jason Deskins, Mia. of Ohio
Andy Hilbert, Michigan	F	David Gove, Western Mich.

AWARD WINNERS

Player of the year: Ryan Miller, Michigan State
Rookie of the year: R.J. Umberger, Ohio State
Coach of the year: Enrico Blasi, Miami of Ohio
Leading scorer: Mike Bishai, Western Michigan
Playoff MVP: Ryan Miller, Michigan State

INDIVIDUAL LEADERS

Goals: Mike Cammalleri, Michigan (29)
Assists: Mike Bishai, Western Michigan (45)
Points: Mike Bishai, Western Michigan (68)
Penalty minutes: Brian Pasko, Western Michigan (195)
Goaltending average: Ryan Miller, Michigan State (1.32)

TOP SCORERS

	Games	G	A	Pts.
Mike Bishai, Western Michigan	37	23	45	68
Andy Hilbert, Michigan	42	26	38	64
Mike Cammalleri, Michigan	42	29	32	61
David Gove, Western Michigan	39	22	37	59
Steve Rymsha, Western Michigan	38	25	29	54
Jeff Campbell, Western Michigan......	37	26	27	53
David Brisson, Nebraska-Omaha......	41	22	25	47
Greg Day, Bowling Green State	40	20	27	47
Dan Carlson, Notre Dame.................	39	17	25	42
Jason Deskins, Miami of Ohio..........	38	19	20	39
Rustyn Dolyny, Michigan State	42	13	26	39

INDIVIDUAL STATISTICS

ALASKA-FAIRBANKS NANOOKS

SCORING

	Pos.	Class	Games	G	A	Pts.	PIM
Jim Lawrence...........	F	Sr.	35	15	15	30	26
Bobby Andrews........	F	Jr.	36	9	16	25	46
Blaine Bablitz	F	So.	33	7	17	24	10
Cam Keith	F	Fr.	35	9	11	20	18
Daniel Carriere	D	Jr.	36	7	12	19	38
Ryan Reinheller........	F	Sr.	34	9	8	17	79
Tom Herman	F	Fr.	36	6	9	15	34
Felipe Larranaga.......	D	Fr.	36	4	10	14	10
Pat Hallett	F	Sr.	30	7	5	12	67
Cory Rask	F	Fr.	36	5	6	11	16
Ryan Lang................	F	Fr.	32	3	7	10	24
Scott McIlroy	F	Sr.	33	5	1	6	45
Chad Hamilton	D	Sr.	35	1	5	6	42
Aaron Grosul............	D	Jr.	36	0	6	6	16
Ryan Campbell.........	F	Fr.	30	3	2	5	16
Efren Larranaga	F	Sr.	26	0	4	4	14
Scott Farrell	D	So.	35	0	4	4	24
Darren Tiemstra	D	Sr.	26	0	3	3	26
Paul Austin	F	Fr.	22	0	2	2	6
Gabe Palmer	G	Fr.	1	0	0	0	0
Pat Glenday.............	D	Fr.	4	0	0	0	0
Jake Flora................	F	Jr.	8	0	0	0	4
John Duggan	D	Fr.	14	0	0	0	12
Lance Mayes............	G	So.	19	0	0	0	0
Preston McKay........	G	Fr.	23	0	0	0	2

GOALTENDING

	Games	Min.	W	L	T	Goals	SO	Avg.
Gabe Palmer	1	20	0	0	0	0	0	0.00
Preston McKay	23	1197	6	10	4	54	0	2.71
Lance Mayes	19	987	3	9	4	52	0	3.16

BOWLING GREEN STATE FALCONS
SCORING

	Pos.	Class	Games	G	A	Pts.	PIM
Greg Day	F	Jr.	40	20	27	47	26
Ryan Murphy	F	Sr.	38	23	15	38	22
Scott Hewson	F	Jr.	40	9	20	29	88
D'Arcy McConvey	F	Fr.	39	4	15	19	34
Marc Barlow	D	Jr.	36	5	12	17	18
Curtis Valentine	F	Sr.	40	9	7	16	8
Ryan Fultz	F	So.	16	5	9	14	4
Kevin Bieksa	D	Fr.	35	4	9	13	90
Roger Leonard	F	Fr.	34	5	7	12	53
Grady Moore	D	Jr.	36	3	8	11	40
Austin de Luis	F	Jr.	29	5	5	10	54
Brian Escobedo	D	Fr.	37	1	9	10	30
Tyler Knight	F	So.	39	4	4	8	24
Doug Schueller	D	Sr.	33	2	6	8	50
Ryan Wetterberg	F	Jr.	40	2	6	8	10
Mark Wires	F	Fr.	40	4	1	5	34
Dennis Williams	F	Sr.	37	2	3	5	64
Phil Barski	F	Fr.	17	1	3	4	10
Joe Statkus	D	Jr.	33	0	3	3	34
Louis Mass	D	Sr.	38	0	3	3	42
Erik Eaton	D	Fr.	8	1	0	1	10
Shawn Timm	G	Sr.	4	0	0	0	0
Sean Kotary	F	Fr.	5	0	0	0	4
Paul Weismann	D	Fr.	8	0	0	0	20
Tyler Masters	G	So.	38	0	0	0	2

GOALTENDING

	Games	Min.	W	L	T	Goals	SO	Avg.
Tyler Masters	38	2237	16	17	4	92	3	2.47
Shawn Timm	4	204	0	2	1	15	0	4.41

FERRIS STATE BULLDOGS
SCORING

	Pos.	Class	Games	G	A	Pts.	PIM
Kevin Swider	F	Sr.	38	17	17	34	2
Rob Collins	F	Jr.	35	15	17	32	23
Chris Kunitz	F	So.	37	16	13	29	81
Jim Dube	D	Sr.	36	3	13	16	37
Scott Lewis	D	Sr.	37	5	7	12	42
Phil Lewandowski	F	So.	29	3	9	12	79
Troy Milam	D	So.	38	4	7	11	58
Josh Bowers	F	So.	37	5	4	9	55
Derrick McIver	F	Fr.	28	4	5	9	39
Rob Lightfoot	F	Sr.	37	4	2	6	28
Phil Meyer	D	So.	36	2	4	6	60
Brett Smith	F	Fr.	37	2	4	6	30
Jason Basile	F	Jr.	38	2	4	6	34
Chad McIver	D	Jr.	34	0	6	6	59
Jon Rogger	F	Sr.	33	3	1	4	23
Simon Mangos	D	Fr.	37	2	2	4	24
Trevor Large	F	Fr.	28	2	1	3	4
Christian Schroder	D	Jr.	21	1	2	3	40
Kevin Caudill	F	So.	12	0	2	2	14
Scott Markowsky	F	So.	13	0	2	2	0
Nick Field	F	So.	9	1	0	1	6
Matt Gossett	D	Fr.	8	0	1	1	8
Vince Owen	G	Sr.	17	0	1	1	15
Phil Osaer	G	Jr.	25	0	1	1	2
Martin Sellgren	D	Fr.	13	0	0	0	14
Don Patrick	F	Fr.	15	0	0	0	0

GOALTENDING

	Games	Min.	W	L	T	Goals	SO	Avg.
Phil Osaer	25	1449	9	12	3	57	3	2.36
Vince Owen	17	848	4	8	2	53	0	3.75

LAKE SUPERIOR STATE LAKERS
SCORING

	Pos.	Class	Games	G	A	Pts.	PIM
Aaron Davis	F	So.	34	10	15	25	53
Jason Nightingale	F	So.	34	14	8	22	48
Ryan Vince	F	Sr.	36	5	16	21	66
Mike Vigilante	F	Sr.	35	5	13	18	31
Ryan Knox	D	Sr.	25	6	8	14	26
Chris McNamara	F	Jr.	35	6	7	13	63
Aaron Phillips	F	So.	35	6	7	13	26
Yevgeniy Dubravin	F	Jr.	35	8	1	9	12
Bart Redden	F	Sr.	36	2	6	8	68
Jeremy Bachusz	F	Jr.	12	2	5	7	6
Kyle Anderson	F	Fr.	28	3	2	5	40
Justin Micek	F	Fr.	29	3	2	5	28
Matt Frick	D	Sr.	36	2	3	5	30
Chris Peterson	F	So.	30	1	4	5	6
Trevor Weisgerber	F	So.	18	2	2	4	8
Kevin Wilson	D	So.	31	1	3	4	51
Chad Dahlen	D	Fr.	17	1	2	3	4
Tyson Turgeon	D	Jr.	35	1	2	3	16
Will Magnuson	D	Jr.	33	0	3	3	54
Chris Thompson	D	Jr.	35	1	1	2	134
Matt Kuharski	F	Fr.	11	0	1	1	18
Klemen Kelgar	D	Sr.	1	0	0	0	0
Scott Murray	G	So.	7	0	0	0	0
Ryan Branham	D	Fr.	12	0	0	0	10
Adam Nightingale	F	Fr.	18	0	0	0	32
Jayme Platt	G	Sr.	34	0	0	0	6

GOALTENDING

	Games	Min.	W	L	T	Goals	SO	Avg.
Jayme Platt	34	1884	12	21	0	96	0	3.06
Scott Murray	7	275	1	2	0	17	0	3.72

MIAMI OF OHIO REDSKINS
SCORING

	Pos.	Class	Games	G	A	Pts.	PIM
Jason Deskins	F	Jr.	38	19	20	39	60
Gregor Krajnc	F	Sr.	38	15	17	32	14
Pat Leahy	F	Sr.	37	13	19	32	52
Derek Edwardson	F	Fr.	37	6	20	26	18
Mike Kompon	F	Fr.	35	10	12	22	24
Ernie Hartlieb	F	Sr.	37	10	12	22	22
Evan Cheverie	F	Jr.	38	13	7	20	30
Mike Glumac	F	Jr.	37	9	10	19	46
Nick Jardine	F	So.	37	9	8	17	34
Ken Marsch	D	Jr.	20	0	16	16	18
Greg Hogeboom	F	Fr.	38	8	5	13	20
Bart Stevens	D	Jr.	38	0	10	10	12
Matt Chandler	F	Jr.	23	1	5	6	12
Matt Medvecz	D	So.	38	1	5	6	30
Pavel Nejezchleb	D	Jr.	30	0	6	6	26
Chris Knupp	F	So.	35	3	2	5	26
Anthony Donskov	F	Sr.	4	1	2	3	4
AJ Kratofil	D	Fr.	24	1	2	3	10
Danny Stewart	F	So.	31	0	3	3	64
Jake Ortmeyer	D	So.	36	1	1	2	48
Brian Sipotz	D	Fr.	32	0	1	1	48
David Burleigh	G	So.	35	0	1	1	2
Clarke Walford	D	Sr.	1	0	0	0	0
Nick Petraglia	D	Fr.	2	0	0	0	0
David Bowen	G	Fr.	9	0	0	0	0

GOALTENDING

	Games	Min.	W	L	T	Goals	SO	Avg.
David Bowen......	9	295	2	1	0	11	0	2.24
David Burleigh ...	35	2000	18	15	2	92	2	2.76

MICHIGAN WOLVERINES
SCORING

	Pos.	Class	Games	G	A	Pts.	PIM
Andy Hilbert	F	So.	42	26	38	64	72
Mike Cammalleri	F	So.	42	29	32	61	24
John Shouneyia	F	So.	45	10	25	35	28
Mark Kosick	F	Sr.	41	14	17	31	14
Jeff Jillson	D	Jr.	43	10	20	30	74
Josh Langfeld	F	Sr.	42	16	12	28	44
Scott Matzka	F	Sr.	45	9	18	27	100
Geoff Koch	F	Sr.	40	10	16	26	34
Mark Mink	F	So.	45	8	14	22	32
Jed Ortmeyer	F	So.	27	10	11	21	52
Craig Murray	F	Jr.	42	10	7	17	32
Mike Komisarek	D	Fr.	41	4	12	16	77
Bill Trainor	F	Sr.	43	3	9	12	4
Mike Roemensky	D	So.	45	2	8	10	26
Joe Kautz	F	Fr.	35	4	5	9	30
Jay Vancik...............	D	Jr.	39	1	8	9	64
Dave Huntzicker	D	Sr.	30	0	5	5	45
Josh Blackburn	G	Jr.	45	0	5	5	6
Andy Burnes	D	Fr.	41	0	4	4	44
Dave Wyzgowski	F	Fr.	14	1	2	3	41
Bob Gassoff	D	Sr.	24	0	1	1	56
J.J. Swistak.............	F	So.	31	0	1	1	20
Rob Kohen	F	Fr.	1	0	0	0	0
Kevin O'Malley	G	Jr.	2	0	0	0	15
L.J. Scarpace	G	Sr.	3	0	0	0	0
Brad Fraser	D	So.	13	0	0	0	12

GOALTENDING

	Games	Min.	W	L	T	Goals	SO	Avg.
Kevin O'Malley ...	2	32	0	0	0	0	0	0.00
Josh Blackburn..	45	2647	26	13	5	101	5	2.29
L.J. Scarpace	3	36	1	0	0	2	0	3.31

MICHIGAN STATE SPARTANS
SCORING

	Pos.	Class	Games	G	A	Pts.	PIM
Rustyn Dolyny	F	Sr.	42	13	26	39	30
Brian Maloney..........	F	So.	41	15	22	37	86
Adam Hall	F	Jr.	42	18	12	30	42
John Nail.................	F	Sr.	42	20	8	28	32
Brad Fast................	D	So.	42	4	24	28	16
Sean Patchell	F	Sr.	42	8	19	27	58
John-Michael Liles...	D	So.	42	7	18	25	28
Damon Whitten	F	Sr.	42	12	12	24	42
Andrew Hutchinson .	D	Jr.	42	5	19	24	46
Andrew Bogle	F	Sr.	39	9	13	22	26
Jeremy Jackson	F	Fr.	23	7	12	19	40
Troy Ferguson	F	So.	41	4	10	14	12
Joe Goodenow	F	Jr.	29	4	6	10	18
Joe Markusen	D	Fr.	41	1	4	5	39
Jon Insana	D	Jr.	42	3	1	4	61
Steve Jackson	F	So.	40	1	3	4	4
Tim Hearon	F	Fr.	38	0	4	4	8
Steve Clark.............	F	So.	41	2	1	3	14
Ryan Miller..............	G	So.	40	0	3	3	0
Aaron Hundt	D	Fr.	10	1	0	1	0
Pat Brush	F	Fr.	1	0	0	0	0
Mike Porter	D	Fr.	1	0	0	0	0
Steve Swistak..........	F	Fr.	1	0	0	0	0
Joe Blackburn	G	Sr.	3	0	0	0	0
Kris Koski	F	So.	31	0	0	0	12

GOALTENDING

	Games	Min.	W	L	T	Goals	SO	Avg.
Joe Blackburn....	3	123	2	0	0	2	1	0.97
Ryan Miller	40	2447	31	5	4	54	10	1.32

NEBRASKA-OMAHA MAVERICKS
SCORING

	Pos.	Class	Games	G	A	Pts.	PIM
David Brisson..........	F	So.	41	22	25	47	26
Jeff Hoggan	F	Jr.	42	12	17	29	78
Greg Zanon	D	So.	39	12	16	28	64
Andrew Wong	F	Fr.	35	12	12	24	16
James Chalmers	F	Sr.	37	6	15	21	96
Scott Turner	F	Fr.	32	3	15	18	26
Billy Pugliese	F	Sr.	36	10	6	16	22
Allan Carr	F	Sr.	18	9	7	16	10
Dave Noel-Bernier....	F	Sr.	40	5	11	16	32
Mike Gabinet...........	D	Fr.	30	2	13	15	14
Aaron Smith............	F	Fr.	32	8	6	14	38
Jason White	F	Sr.	28	5	7	12	20
Jason Jaworski	F	So.	37	3	9	12	72
Jason Cupp	F	Sr.	40	3	9	12	26
Zach Scribner..........	D	Jr.	34	2	7	9	34
Joe Pereira	F	So.	25	4	2	6	18
Shane Glover	F	Jr.	31	2	4	6	41
Ed Cassin	D	Sr.	27	1	4	5	28
Nick Fohr	F	Jr.	41	2	2	4	14
Daniel Samuelsson ..	D	Jr.	40	2	1	3	18
Kyle O'Keefe	F	So.	22	1	2	3	31
Dan Ellis.................	G	Fr.	40	0	2	2	2
Joe Yurecko	F	Sr.	28	1	0	1	24
Josh Lampman	D	Sr.	4	0	1	1	6
John Rosso	D	Sr.	13	0	1	1	8
Dan Zaluski	D	Sr.	1	0	0	0	0
Brian Haaland..........	G	Fr.	1	0	0	0	0
Rodney McLeod........	G	Jr.	7	0	0	0	0

GOALTENDING

	Games	Min.	W	L	T	Goals	SO	Avg.
Brian Haaland ...	1	24	0	0	0	0	0	0.00
Rodney McLeod.	7	246	3	1	0	7	1	1.70
Dan Ellis.............	40	2285	21	14	3	95	1	2.49

NORTHERN MICHIGAN WILDCATS
SCORING

	Pos.	Class	Games	G	A	Pts.	PIM
Chad Theuer	F	Jr.	38	10	27	37	42
Bryce Cockburn	F	So.	37	21	11	32	30
Terry Harrison.........	F	So.	34	15	16	31	22
Fred Mattersdorfer...	F	Sr.	38	12	19	31	16
Jimmy Jackson........	D	So.	38	7	24	31	36
Chris Gobert	F	So.	31	10	20	30	14
Sean Connolly	D	Jr.	38	5	14	19	80
Mike Sandbeck........	D	Sr.	38	3	15	18	34
Ryan Riipi	F	Sr.	38	10	7	17	26
Sean Owens	D	Jr.	31	2	9	11	22
Mike Stutzel	F	So.	16	3	5	8	6
Brent Robertson.......	F	Fr.	36	3	5	8	84
Dan Donnette	F	So.	38	2	6	8	4
Peter Michelutti.......	F	So.	35	4	3	7	4
Colin Young	D	Sr.	36	2	4	6	40
Alex Sawruk............	F	Fr.	24	3	2	5	14
Matt Hunter	F	Fr.	30	3	2	5	20
Justin Kinnunen.......	F	Fr.	35	1	4	5	35
Tim Lindberg	D	So.	16	2	2	4	22
Ryan Carrigan	D	Fr.	33	2	2	4	46
Ambrose Tappe........	F	Fr.	15	1	2	3	8
Dan Ragusett...........	G	Sr.	21	0	3	3	0
Dave Bonk...............	F	Fr.	5	0	1	1	4
Kevin Gardner	F	Fr.	1	0	0	0	0
Joe Borro	F	Fr.	2	0	0	0	0
Craig Kowalski	G	Fr.	19	0	0	0	2

GOALTENDING

	Games	Min.	W	L	T	Goals	SO	Avg.
Dan Ragusett.....	21	1272	11	5	3	52	1	2.45
Craig Kowalski...	19	1078	7	8	4	49	1	2.73

NOTRE DAME FIGHTING IRISH

SCORING

	Pos.	Class	Games	G	A	Pts.	PIM
Dan Carlson	F	Sr.	39	17	25	42	20
Ryan Dolder............	F	Sr.	39	15	19	34	26
Rob Globke	F	Fr.	33	17	9	26	74
Aaron Gill................	F	Fr.	38	11	15	26	37
Brett Lebda	D	Fr.	39	7	19	26	109
Connor Dunlop	F	So.	30	7	12	19	38
David Inman	F	Jr.	37	11	6	17	10
Evan Nielsen	D	So.	37	2	10	12	54
Matt Van Arkel	F	Sr.	39	3	5	8	69
Chad Chipchase	F	Sr.	33	3	4	7	20
Neil Komadoski........	D	Fr.	30	2	5	7	106
John Wroblewski	F	So.	36	2	4	6	22
Jon Maruk...............	F	Jr.	37	0	5	5	24
Jay Kopischke..........	F	Sr.	19	2	2	4	26
Paul Harris	D	So.	19	1	3	4	10
Jake Wiegand...........	F	So.	37	1	3	4	32
Tom Galvin...............	D	Fr.	26	0	4	4	18
Brett Henning..........	F	Jr.	15	1	2	3	14
Michael Chin	F	So.	36	1	2	3	10
Ryan Clark	D	Sr.	33	0	2	2	79
Sam Cornelius	D	Jr.	25	1	0	1	12
Jeremiah Kimento....	G	Jr.	19	0	1	1	0
Kyle Kolquist	G	Sr.	7	0	0	0	0
Kyle Dolder	F	Fr.	10	0	0	0	0
T.J. Mathieson........	D	Fr.	17	0	0	0	14
Tony Zasowski	G	So.	22	0	0	0	2

GOALTENDING

	Games	Min.	W	L	T	Goals	SO	Avg.
Kyle Kolquist......	7	296	0	4	2	16	0	3.24
J. Kimento	19	949	5	7	2	57	0	3.60
Tony Zasowski ...	22	1122	5	11	3	75	0	4.01

OHIO STATE BUCKEYES

SCORING

	Pos.	Class	Games	G	A	Pts.	PIM
R.J. Umberger	F	Fr.	32	14	23	37	18
J.-Francois Dufour ...	F	Sr.	37	15	21	36	28
Dave Steckel	F	Fr.	33	17	18	35	80
Paul Caponigri	F	Fr.	35	13	18	31	56
Doug Andress	D	Fr.	36	5	16	21	22
Nick Ganga..............	F	Jr.	31	9	10	19	54
Scott May	F	Fr.	37	9	9	18	26
Mike McCormick......	F	Jr.	33	4	14	18	18
Andre Signoretti.......	D	Sr.	16	3	10	13	48
Miguel Lafleche........	F	So.	37	8	4	12	26
Luke Pavlas.............	F	So.	34	3	9	12	34

	Pos.	Class	Games	G	A	Pts.	PIM
Eric Skaug................	D	Fr.	30	3	6	9	34
Jaisen Freeman........	D	Sr.	37	2	6	8	32
Daymen Bencharski .	F	Fr.	26	3	4	7	12
Pete Broccoli............	D	So.	37	2	5	7	38
Chris Olsgard...........	F	Fr.	31	2	4	6	58
Jason Crain..............	D	Jr.	36	2	4	6	36
Yan Des Gagne........	F	Jr.	29	2	3	5	6
T.J. Latorre.............	F	So.	29	1	4	5	40
Ryan Smith..............	F	So.	22	1	2	3	25
Reed Whiting	D	Fr.	16	0	2	2	14
Mike Betz	G	Fr.	36	0	2	2	0
Carter Trevisani	D	Fr.	10	0	1	1	2
Scott Titus	D	Jr.	1	0	0	0	0
Kelly Holowaty	G	Fr.	4	0	0	0	0
Peter Wishloff..........	G	So.	4	0	0	0	0

GOALTENDING

	Games	Min.	W	L	T	Goals	SO	Avg.
Kelly Holowaty ...	4	12	0	0	0	0	0	0.00
Peter Wishloff....	4	79	1	1	0	3	0	2.27
Mike Betz..........	36	2178	16	17	2	109	1	3.00

WESTERN MICHIGAN BRONCOS

SCORING

	Pos.	Class	Games	G	A	Pts.	PIM
Mike Bishai	F	Jr.	37	23	45	68	37
David Gove..............	F	Sr.	39	22	37	59	16
Steve Rymsha..........	F	Sr.	38	25	29	54	107
Jeff Campbell	F	Fr.	37	26	27	53	10
Mike Jarmuth...........	D	Fr.	34	3	18	21	30
David Cousineau	D	So.	34	4	15	19	66
Anthony Battaglia.....	F	Jr.	35	3	12	15	8
Dana Lattery	F	Fr.	34	11	3	14	58
Brent Rumble..........	F	So.	34	7	6	13	32
Lucas Drake	F	Fr.	36	4	8	12	20
Ryan Crane	D	Jr.	17	3	8	11	28
Andy Townsend	D	So.	34	0	11	11	14
Brett Mills	F	Sr.	36	5	5	10	50
Austin Miller	D	Jr.	39	2	8	10	31
Paul Davies	F	Fr.	38	2	6	8	30
Chad Kline..............	F	Jr.	29	2	4	6	30
Ben Gagnon	F	So.	36	2	4	6	20
Mark Wilkinson........	F	Sr.	12	2	2	4	6
Shaun Rose	F	So.	16	1	3	4	2
Brian Pasko.............	D	Fr.	35	1	3	4	195
Rob Yamashita........	D	So.	10	0	2	2	20
Josh Akright	D	So.	36	0	2	2	86
Bryan Farquhar	F	Jr.	9	1	0	1	14
Jeff Reynaert...........	G	Jr.	38	0	1	1	0
J.J. Weaks	G	So.	6	0	0	0	0

GOALTENDING

	Games	Min.	W	L	T	Goals	SO	Avg.
Jeff Reynaert	38	2269	19	12	6	118	2	3.12
J.J. Weaks	6	123	1	1	0	8	0	3.92

EASTERN COLLEGE ATHLETIC CONFERENCE

FINAL STANDINGS

Team	G	W	L	T	Pts.	GF	GA
Clarkson (21-11-3)	22	15	5	2	32	81	45
St. Lawrence (20-13-4)	22	13	6	3	29	83	70
Harvard (16-15-2)........	22	12	8	2	26	68	60
Cornell (16-12-5).........	22	11	8	3	25	44	44
Dartmouth (16-14-4) ...	22	10	8	4	24	67	62
Rensselaer (17-15-2)...	22	11	9	2	24	62	54
Princeton (10-16-5).....	22	9	9	4	22	70	66
Yale (14-16-1)..............	22	10	11	1	21	72	80
Union (12-18-4)..........	22	8	12	2	18	54	75
Vermont (14-18-2).......	22	8	12	2	18	68	69
Colgate (10-20-4)	22	8	13	1	17	60	67
Brown (4-21-4).............	22	2	16	4	8	43	80

Overall record in parentheses.

PLAYOFF RESULTS

FIRST ROUND

St. Lawrence 6, Union 3
St. Lawrence 4, Union 2
    (St. Lawrence won series, 2-0)

Harvard 5, Yale 4
Harvard 7, Yale 4
    (Harvard won series, 2-0)

Vermont 5, Clarkson 3
Clarkson 3, Vermont 2 (2OT)
Vermont 3, Clarkson 2 (OT)
    (Vermont won series, 2-1)

Cornell 3, Princeton 2
Cornell 2, Princeton 1
    (Cornell won series, 2-0)

Dartmouth 4, Rensselaer 2
Dartmouth 5, Rensselaer 1
    (Dartmouth won series, 2-0)

PLAY-IN GAME

Dartmouth 3, Vermont 2 (OT)

SEMIFINALS

Cornell 5, Harvard 2
St. Lawrence 2, Dartmouth 0

CONSOLATION GAME

Harvard 3, Dartmouth 2 (OT)

CHAMPIONSHIP GAME

St. Lawrence 3, Cornell 1

ALL-STAR TEAMS

First team	Pos.	Second team
Oliver Jonas, Harvard	G	Mike Walsh, Clarkson
Matt Desrosiers, St. Law.	D	Trevor Byrne, Dartmouth
Kent Huskins, Clarkson	D	Cory Murphy, Colgate
Erik Anderson, St. Lawrence	F	Dominic Moore, Harvard
Mike Gellard, St. Lawrence	F	Sean Nolan, Colgate
Jeff Hamilton, Yale	F	Matt Poapst, Clarkson

AWARD WINNERS

Player of the year: Erik Anderson, St. Lawrence
Rookie of the year: Rob McFeeters, Clarkson
Coach of the year: Mark Morris, Clarkson
Leading scorer: Mike Gellard, St. Lawrence
Playoff MVP: Jeremy Symington, St. Lawrence

INDIVIDUAL LEADERS

Goals: Matt Murley, Rensselaer (24)
Assists: Mike Gellard, St. Lawrence (38)
Points: Mike Gellard, St. Lawrence (57)
Penalty minutes: David McCulloch, Harvard (102)
Goaltending average: Mike Walsh, Clarkson (1.86)

TOP SCORERS

	Games	G	A	Pts.
Mike Gellard, St. Lawrence...............	37	19	38	57
Jeff Hamilton, Yale............................	31	23	32	55
Erik Anderson, St. Lawrence	32	17	34	51
Ben Stafford, Yale	31	14	32	46
Russ Bartlett, St. Lawrence...............	37	18	25	43
Dominic Moore, Harvard....................	32	15	28	43
Matt Murley, Rensselaer....................	34	24	18	42
Alan Fyfe, St. Lawrence	36	16	23	39
Nick Deschenes, Yale........................	31	17	20	37
J.F. Caudron, Vermont	34	16	21	37

INDIVIDUAL STATISTICS

BROWN BEARS

SCORING

	Pos.	Class	Games	G	A	Pts.	PIM
Matt Kohansky.........	F	Sr.	27	10	13	23	24
Doug Janjevich	F	Sr.	28	7	7	14	12
Jon Zielinski.............	F	Sr.	29	7	7	14	36
Paul Esdale	D	So.	26	6	8	14	30
Keith Kirley	F	So.	22	4	6	10	29
John Petricig............	F	Sr.	26	5	3	8	33
Chris Legg	F	So.	26	3	5	8	6
Scott Ford	D	Fr.	23	2	6	8	18
Brent Robinson........	F	Fr.	23	1	7	8	2
Josh Barker.............	D	Jr.	29	3	4	7	30

	Pos.	Class	Games	G	A	Pts.	PIM
Shane Mudryk..........	F	Fr.	23	2	5	7	12
Tye Korbl.................	F	So.	28	3	3	6	10
Adam Saunders	F	Fr.	26	2	4	6	2
Christian Warrington.	D	Sr.	25	1	3	4	22
Chris Busby	D	Fr.	25	1	3	4	10
Pascal Denis	F	Fr.	28	0	4	4	10
J.-Francois Labarre..	F	Jr.	12	2	1	3	20
Owen Walter	D	So.	14	1	2	3	10
Gianni Cantini	F	Jr.	15	1	2	3	2
Vincent Macri...........	D	Fr.	16	1	1	2	16
Jason Wilson	F	So.	16	0	2	2	14
Nick Ringstad..........	F	Fr.	16	1	0	1	4

	Pos.	Class	Games	G	A	Pts.	PIM
Chris Dirkes	D	Jr.	7	0	1	1	6
Scott Pratt	F	Fr.	3	0	0	0	2
Mike Pratt	D	Sr.	9	0	0	0	12
Yann Danis	G	Fr.	12	0	0	0	0
Brian Eklund	G	Jr.	19	0	0	0	0

GOALTENDING

	Games	Min.	W	L	T	Goals	SO	Avg.
Brian Eklund	19	1084	2	13	3	62	0	3.43
Yann Danis	12	667	2	8	1	40	0	3.60

CLARKSON GOLDEN KNIGHTS
SCORING

	Pos.	Class	Games	G	A	Pts.	PIM
Matt Poapst	F	Jr.	35	17	18	35	56
Kent Huskins	D	Sr.	35	6	28	34	22
David Evans	F	Jr.	33	12	19	31	8
Rob McFeeters	F	Fr.	32	15	15	30	10
Kevin O'Flaherty	F	So.	35	8	20	28	28
Don Smith	F	Sr.	31	12	13	25	18
Dave Reid	D	So.	35	5	20	25	24
K. Ellis-Toddington	D	Jr.	34	4	18	22	24
Murray Kuntz	F	Sr.	35	10	11	21	32
Jean Desrochers	F	Fr.	32	4	13	17	16
Tristan Lush	F	Fr.	35	3	10	13	10
Chris Line	F	Jr.	27	5	7	12	4
Trevor Edwards	F	Fr.	33	5	5	10	18
Chris Bahen	D	So.	34	3	7	10	45
Mike Nagai	D	Fr.	32	5	4	9	28
Gasper Sekelj	D	Sr.	19	4	4	8	10
Marc Garceau	F	Jr.	13	2	4	6	2
Joe Carosa	D	So.	32	1	4	5	8
Adam Campana	F	So.	19	2	1	3	14
Ian Manzano	D	Jr.	34	0	2	2	41
Craig Foddrill	F	Jr.	12	0	1	1	8
Zach Schwan	F	Fr.	3	0	0	0	4
Karl Mattson	G	So.	7	0	0	0	0
Shawn Grant	G	Jr.	12	0	0	0	4
Mike Walsh	G	So.	21	0	0	0	4

GOALTENDING

	Games	Min.	W	L	T	Goals	SO	Avg.
Mike Walsh	21	1291	15	4	1	40	4	1.86
Shawn Grant	12	591	6	3	1	32	0	3.25
Karl Mattson	7	276	0	4	1	16	0	3.48

COLGATE RED RAIDERS
SCORING

	Pos.	Class	Games	G	A	Pts.	PIM
Sean Nolan	F	Sr.	34	21	14	35	24
Cory Murphy	D	Sr.	34	7	22	29	34
Scooter Smith	F	So.	30	10	14	24	36
Mike O'Malley	F	Sr.	30	8	10	18	10
Etienne Morin	F	Jr.	34	9	7	16	24
Chad MacDonald	F	Sr.	32	7	7	14	100
P.J. Yedon	F	So.	31	6	8	14	12
Kyle Doyle	F	Fr.	29	6	7	13	34
Bryan Long	D	Sr.	31	5	8	13	24
Rob Brown	D	Fr.	33	1	10	11	18
Kevin Johns	F	Sr.	25	3	7	10	18
Ben Bryce	D	Jr.	32	1	7	8	50
Dan Stay	F	Sr.	32	2	5	7	48
Pat Varecka	F	Sr.	32	1	5	6	14
Sam Sturgis	F	Sr.	27	1	4	5	6
Paul Kelley	F	Fr.	24	3	1	4	24
Bob Vandersluis	F	Jr.	28	3	1	4	12
Steve Silversides	D	So.	32	0	3	3	14
Matt Nicholson	D	Fr.	25	1	1	2	50
Brad D'Arco	F	So.	23	0	2	2	6
Tucker Veenis	D	Fr.	14	0	0	0	4
David Cann	G	Fr.	21	0	0	0	2
Jason Lefevre	G	Jr.	21	0	0	0	2

GOALTENDING

	Games	Min.	W	L	T	Goals	SO	Avg.
David Cann	21	941	5	9	0	43	0	2.74
Jason Lefevre	21	1107	5	11	4	64	0	3.47

CORNELL BIG RED
SCORING

	Pos.	Class	Games	G	A	Pts.	PIM
Stephen Baby	F	So.	32	8	20	28	47
Ryan Vesce	F	Fr.	33	7	20	27	10
Sam Paolini	F	So.	33	8	13	21	16
Mark McRae	D	So.	33	8	11	19	14
Doug Murray	D	So.	25	5	13	18	39
David Kozier	F	Jr.	33	7	5	12	22
K. Wieckowski	F	Jr.	32	4	6	10	24
Denis Ladouceur	F	Jr.	23	6	3	9	14
Matt McRae	F	So.	27	3	6	9	10
David Francis	F	Jr.	33	5	1	6	16
Andrew McNiven	F	Sr.	27	2	4	6	10
Larry Pierce	D	Sr.	24	1	5	6	14
Shane Palahicky	F	So.	27	1	4	5	14
Dan Svoboda	F	Sr.	30	1	4	5	27
Danny Powell	D	Sr.	31	0	5	5	30
Brian McMeekin	D	Jr.	31	2	1	3	24
Ben Wallace	D	Fr.	32	2	0	2	8
Scott Krahn	F	Fr.	14	1	1	2	4
Kelly Hughes	F	Fr.	11	1	0	1	4
Jason Kuczmanski	F	Fr.	11	1	0	1	6
Ian Burt	G	Sr.	8	0	1	1	0
Greg Hornby	F	Fr.	10	0	1	1	40
Alex Gregory	D	Jr.	18	0	1	1	12
Chris Gartman	G	So.	2	0	0	0	8
Travis Bell	D	So.	23	0	0	0	6
Matt Underhill	G	Jr.	25	0	0	0	0

GOALTENDING

	Games	Min.	W	L	T	Goals	SO	Avg.
Matt Underhill	25	1504	13	8	3	47	1	1.88
Ian Burt	8	420	2	4	2	16	1	2.29
Chris Gartman	2	86	1	0	0	4	0	2.79

DARTMOUTH BIG GREEN
SCORING

	Pos.	Class	Games	G	A	Pts.	PIM
Mike Maturo	F	Jr.	34	18	15	33	20
Kent Gillings	F	So.	34	11	18	29	20
Trevor Byrne	D	So.	34	5	21	26	52
Chris Baldwin	F	Jr.	34	14	10	24	16
Jamie Herrington	F	Jr.	33	7	16	23	10
Frank Nardella	F	Jr.	34	4	18	22	16
Mike Murray	F	So.	34	7	14	21	24
Chris Taliercio	F	Jr.	32	10	7	17	22
Pete Summerfelt	D	So.	34	2	15	17	42
Michael Byrne	F	Sr.	34	5	5	10	26
P.J. Martin	D	So.	34	2	8	10	30
Peter Mahler	F	Sr.	34	3	6	9	32
Dory Tisdale	D	Sr.	25	3	5	8	8
Dan Casella	F	Jr.	34	2	6	8	36
Mike Turner	D	Fr.	34	2	4	6	14
Gary Hunter	F	Jr.	18	2	2	4	8
Jason Costa	F	Fr.	24	2	2	4	16
Brian Van Abel	D	Fr.	33	1	1	2	12
Halsey Coughlin	F	So.	7	1	0	1	10
Craig Lund	F	Jr.	1	0	1	1	0
Ryan Sinclair	F	Jr.	5	0	1	1	0
Pascal Lalonde	D	Jr.	6	0	1	1	6
Chris Hontvet	F	So.	15	0	1	1	20
Mike Wheelihan	F	Fr.	1	0	0	0	0
Darren Gastrock	G	Fr.	3	0	0	0	0
Carl Desjardins	D	Jr.	4	0	0	0	0
Nick Boucher	G	So.	33	0	0	0	0

GOALTENDING

	Games	Min.	W	L	T	Goals	SO	Avg.
Nick Boucher	33	1966	16	12	4	84	1	2.56
Darren Gastrock.	3	97	0	2	0	8	0	4.96

HARVARD CRIMSON

SCORING

	Pos.	Class	Games	G	A	Pts.	PIM
Dominic Moore	F	So.	32	15	28	43	40
Steve Moore	F	Sr.	32	7	26	33	43
Tim Pettit	F	Fr.	31	14	17	31	22
Chris Bala	F	Sr.	32	14	16	30	24
Tyler Kolarik	F	Fr.	32	13	15	28	36
Peter Capouch	D	Jr.	33	7	14	21	8
Brett Nowak	F	So.	24	7	9	16	26
Kenny Turano..........	F	Fr.	31	8	5	13	14
Harry Schwefel	F	Sr.	33	5	5	10	8
Dennis Packard........	F	Fr.	33	4	4	8	28
David McCulloch......	D	Fr.	30	1	7	8	102
Jared Cantanucci	F	Jr.	32	1	7	8	16
Rob Fried	F	Fr.	30	4	1	5	22
Aaron Kim...............	F	So.	30	0	5	5	80
Blair Barlow	D	Fr.	33	1	3	4	24
Jeff Stonehouse.......	F	Jr.	24	1	2	3	12
Abe Kinkopf	F	Fr.	5	1	1	2	2
Graham Morrell........	D	Jr.	10	0	2	2	12
Kyle Clark	F	Jr.	18	0	2	2	20
Kenny Smith	D	Fr.	21	0	2	2	37
Tim Stay.................	D	Sr.	26	0	2	2	2
Derek Nowak...........	F	Jr.	3	0	1	1	2
Kevin McCafferty......	D	Jr.	2	0	0	0	0
Will Crothers...........	G	Fr.	2	0	0	0	0
Leif Ericson............	D	Jr.	14	0	0	0	2
Oliver Jonas............	G	Sr.	32	0	0	0	0

GOALTENDING

	Games	Min.	W	L	T	Goals	SO	Avg.
Oliver Jonas.......	32	1903	15	15	2	95	2	2.99
Will Crothers......	2	80	1	0	0	6	0	4.50

PRINCETON TIGERS

SCORING

	Pos.	Class	Games	G	A	Pts.	PIM
Kirk Lamb	F	Sr.	27	6	25	31	60
Chris Corrinet..........	F	Sr.	31	13	12	25	30
Brad Parsons	F	Jr.	30	14	10	24	22
Shane Campbell	F	Sr.	29	16	7	23	82
George Parros	F	So.	31	7	10	17	38
David Schneider.......	D	Jr.	23	8	7	15	22
Ethan Doyle.............	F	Sr.	30	5	9	14	46
Neil McCann	D	So.	29	2	9	11	28
Josh Roberts	F	Jr.	28	2	8	10	18
Steve Slaton...........	D	Fr.	28	2	8	10	36
Matthew Maglione ...	D	Fr.	30	4	5	9	12
David Del Monte	F	Jr.	27	3	6	9	24
Chris Owen	F	Fr.	30	1	7	8	14
David Bennett	D	Jr.	31	0	7	7	26
Scott Prime.............	F	So.	20	3	2	5	6
Thomas Colclough...	F	Fr.	18	1	3	4	10
S. Fouladgar-Mercer .	F	Fr.	23	1	1	2	0
Drew Morrison	F	Fr.	9	0	2	2	4
Trevor Beaney	D	So.	26	0	2	2	12
Peter Zavodny.........	D	Sr.	9	1	0	1	12
Dan Hursh	F	Fr.	12	1	0	1	4
Hugh McKee	D	Fr.	1	0	0	0	0
Ryan Kraliz.............	F	Jr.	4	0	0	0	0
Nate Nomeland	G	So.	9	0	0	0	0
Jason Dillow	D	Sr.	15	0	0	0	2
Marc Hounjet	F	Fr.	17	0	0	0	12
Dave Stathos...........	G	Jr.	26	0	0	0	6

GOALTENDING

	Games	Min.	W	L	T	Goals	SO	Avg.
Dave Stathos	26	1432	8	13	4	73	0	3.06
Nate Nomeland ..	9	453	2	3	1	27	1	3.57

RENSSELAER POLYTECHNIC INSTITUTE ENGINEERS

SCORING

	Pos.	Class	Games	G	A	Pts.	PIM
Matt Murley	F	Jr.	34	24	18	42	34
Jim Henkel..............	F	Jr.	34	11	19	30	44
Marc Cavosie	F	So.	28	13	16	29	47
Carson Butterwick....	F	So.	28	9	20	29	36
Jim Vickers	D	Jr.	34	8	20	28	28
Nolan Graham..........	F	So.	29	11	14	25	26
Ryan Shields...........	F	Fr.	34	5	8	13	16
Conrad Barnes	F	Fr.	33	4	9	13	20
Andrew McPherson .	F	Jr.	31	5	6	11	34
Danny Eberly...........	D	So.	28	3	8	11	51
Eric Cavosie	F	So.	30	1	10	11	20
M. Hammarstrom	F	Fr.	33	2	7	9	6
Ben Barr	F	Fr.	32	4	4	8	29
Scott Basiuk............	D	Fr.	28	3	5	8	41
Steve Munn.............	D	Jr.	33	2	5	7	68
Hamish Cunning	D	Jr.	29	0	4	4	14
Francois Senez........	D	So.	21	0	3	3	14
Chris Migliore	F	Jr.	30	2	0	2	54
Steve Collova	D	Fr.	16	0	2	2	2
Josh Budish	F	Fr.	14	0	1	1	4
Jim Palmer	G	Jr.	1	0	0	0	0
Kevin Kurk	G	Fr.	10	0	0	0	2
Nathan Marsters	G	Fr.	28	0	0	0	0
Glenn Coupal	D	Sr.	31	0	0	0	26

GOALTENDING

	Games	Min.	W	L	T	Goals	SO	Avg.
Jim Palmer	1	3	0	0	0	0	0	0.00
Nathan Marsters ..	28	1631	14	13	1	64	4	2.35
Kevin Kurk	10	424	3	2	1	23	0	3.26

ST. LAWRENCE SAINTS

SCORING

	Pos.	Class	Games	G	A	Pts.	PIM
Mike Gellard	F	Sr.	37	19	38	57	14
Erik Anderson	F	Sr.	32	17	34	51	4
Russ Bartlett	F	Jr.	37	18	25	43	20
Alan Fyfe	F	Sr.	36	16	23	39	22
Matt Desrosiers	D	Sr.	37	7	25	32	22
Blair Clarance.........	F	So.	34	11	9	20	48
Robin Carruthers	F	Jr.	34	6	12	18	24
Ray DiLauro	D	Jr.	34	3	11	14	28
Jim Lorentz.............	F	So.	37	6	7	13	24
Charlie Daniels	F	Jr.	34	5	5	10	8
Jack O'Brien	F	Jr.	23	4	3	7	4
Josh LeRoy	D	GR	37	2	5	7	26
Allie Skelly	F	So.	26	2	4	6	14
Rich Peverley	F	Fr.	29	2	4	6	4
Kevin Veneruzzo......	D	Sr.	35	2	3	5	30
Ryan Glenn	D	Fr.	37	3	1	4	34
Andy Marchetti........	F	Sr.	30	2	2	4	8
Ziga Petac	F	Fr.	14	2	1	3	2
Jeremy Symington....	G	Sr.	27	0	2	2	0
Sean Muir	F	Jr.	34	0	2	2	26
Tony Maci	D	Fr.	7	0	1	1	10
Jeremy Cormier	D	Fr.	9	0	1	1	6
Mike Muir	F	Jr.	29	0	1	1	21
Tim Hall	G	So.	2	0	0	0	0
Russ Mazgut...........	F	So.	4	0	0	0	2
Sean Coakley	G	Sr.	15	0	0	0	0

COLLEGE HOCKEY *ECAC*

GOALTENDING

	Games	Min.	W	L	T	Goals	SO	Avg.
Tim Hall	2	9	0	0	0	0	0	0.00
J. Symington	27	1474	16	8	0	72	3	2.93
Sean Coakley	15	784	4	5	4	46	1	3.52

UNION SKATING DUTCHMEN

SCORING

	Pos.	Class	Games	G	A	Pts.	PIM
Jeff Wilson	F	Jr.	34	12	10	22	18
Charles Simard	D	Jr.	31	7	14	21	64
Clark Jones	F	Sr.	34	2	19	21	20
Kris Goodjohn	F	So.	34	7	13	20	32
Jason Ralph	F	Sr.	34	13	6	19	28
Jeff Hutchins	F	Jr.	31	9	10	19	58
Randy Dagenais	D	So.	31	3	14	17	12
Nathan Gillies	F	So.	25	5	9	14	8
Bryan Yackel	F	Sr.	32	5	7	12	49
Alex Todd	D	Sr.	28	6	5	11	74
Jordy Federko	F	So.	23	5	5	10	4
Jason Kean	D	So.	32	2	7	9	59
Doug Christiansen	D	Jr.	28	6	2	8	32
Seamus Galligan	F	Jr.	22	3	5	8	12
Drew Taylor	F	Jr.	27	2	6	8	6
Paul Kilfcy	D	Sr.	33	1	5	6	32
Brent Booth	D	Fr.	31	0	5	5	22
Ales Havlik	D	Jr.	20	0	3	3	16
P.J. Byrne	D	Fr.	11	0	2	2	10
Glenn Sanders	F	Fr.	14	0	2	2	0
Bryant Westerman	F	Sr.	24	0	2	2	64
Kurt Goodjohn	D	Fr.	27	0	2	2	8
Kyle Loney	G	Fr.	1	0	1	1	0
Marc Wise	G	So.	7	0	1	1	0
Frederic Cyr	D	Jr.	4	0	0	0	6
Brandon Snee	G	Jr.	33	0	0	0	2

GOALTENDING

	Games	Min.	W	L	T	Goals	SO	Avg.
Kyle Loney	1	5	0	0	0	0	0	0.00
Brandon Snee	33	1849	12	17	4	96	1	3.11
Marc Wise	7	191	0	1	0	13	0	4.08

VERMONT CATAMOUNTS

SCORING

	Pos.	Class	Games	G	A	Pts.	PIM
J.F. Caudron	F	Sr.	34	16	21	37	22
Jeff Miles	F	Fr.	34	8	23	31	14
Graham Mink	F	Jr.	32	17	12	29	52
Patrick Sharp	F	Fr.	34	12	15	27	36
Bryson Busniuk	F	So.	34	11	11	22	20
Ryan Cox	F	Jr.	34	10	11	21	34
Andreas Moborg	D	Sr.	28	7	14	21	12
John Longo	F	So.	34	5	12	17	16
Martin Wilde	D	Sr.	33	3	13	16	32
Jerry Gernander	F	Sr.	34	3	13	16	32
Ryan Miller	F	So.	23	6	6	12	22
Mike Torney	F	Sr.	27	4	7	11	38

	Pos.	Class	Games	G	A	Pts.	PIM
Jim Gernander	D	Sr.	34	2	8	10	18
J.F. Gamelin	F	So.	27	6	2	8	18
Chris Hills	F	Jr.	32	1	6	7	33
Billy Kelly	F	Fr.	24	2	4	6	10
Thomas Hajek	D	So.	34	0	5	5	12
Oriel McHugh	D	Fr.	32	3	1	4	22
Dustin Corbett	D	Fr.	16	0	2	2	16
Mark Gouett	D	Jr.	24	0	1	1	25
Andrew Allen	G	Sr.	24	0	1	1	0
Mike Erensen	D	Fr.	1	0	0	0	0
Tim Peters	G	Jr.	4	0	0	0	2
David Liptak	F	So.	7	0	0	0	0
Shawn Conschafter	G	So.	10	0	0	0	0

GOALTENDING

	Games	Min.	W	L	T	Goals	SO	Avg.
S. Conschafter	10	539	4	5	0	23	0	2.56
Andrew Allen	24	1340	9	10	2	64	1	2.87
Tim Peters	4	239	1	3	0	18	0	4.52

YALE BULLDOGS

SCORING

	Pos.	Class	Games	G	A	Pts.	PIM
Jeff Hamilton	F	Sr.	31	23	32	55	39
Ben Stafford	F	Sr.	31	14	32	46	16
Nick Deschenes	F	So.	31	17	20	37	22
Luke Earl	F	Jr.	27	14	13	27	4
Jeff Dwyer	D	Fr.	31	3	18	21	16
Evan Wax	F	So.	30	7	13	20	6
Jason Noe	F	Jr.	29	6	6	12	24
Adam Sauve	F	Sr.	26	5	7	12	12
Joe Dart	D	Sr.	31	2	10	12	28
Spencer Rodgers	F	Jr.	28	4	4	8	20
Lee Jelenic	F	Jr.	28	2	6	8	52
Bryan Freeman	D	So.	31	0	8	8	22
Stacey Bauman	D	So.	30	0	6	6	28
Ryan Steeves	F	Fr.	23	3	2	5	10
Denis Nam	F	So.	24	1	3	4	2
Peter Toomey	F	Sr.	16	2	1	3	0
Vin Hellemeyer	F	Fr.	16	1	2	3	2
Gabe Polsky	F	Jr.	16	0	3	3	2
John Gauger	D	Sr.	20	1	1	2	52
Nathan Murphy	F	Fr.	15	0	2	2	6
Greg Boucher	D	So.	6	0	1	1	0
Robert Mutter	D	Jr.	26	0	1	1	12
Chris O'Connell	G	So.	1	0	0	0	0
David Sproule	D	Jr.	2	0	0	0	0
Peter Dobrowolski	G	Fr.	4	0	0	0	0
Nate Berry	D	Fr.	5	0	0	0	6
Mike Klema	F	Fr.	5	0	0	0	0
Dan Lombard	G	Jr.	29	0	0	0	2

GOALTENDING

	Games	Min.	W	L	T	Goals	SO	Avg.
Chris O'Connell	1	7	0	0	0	0	0	0.00
P. Dobrowolski	4	136	0	1	1	8	0	3.54
Dan Lombard	29	1725	14	15	0	105	1	3.65

HOCKEY EAST

FINAL STANDINGS

Team	G	W	L	T	Pts.	GF	GA
Boston Col. (33-8-2)....	24	17	5	2	36	103	57
Maine (20-12-7)..........	24	12	7	5	29	70	62
Providence (22-13-5)...	24	13	8	3	29	76	71
New Hamp. (21-12-6)..	24	11	8	5	27	61	47
Lowell (19-16-3)..........	24	10	11	3	23	67	66
Boston U. (14-20-3)	24	9	12	3	21	66	77
Northeastern (13-19-4).	24	7	13	4	18	58	73
Merrimack (14-20-4) ...	24	7	14	3	17	60	86
Mass. (8-22-4).............	24	7	15	2	16	53	81

Overall record in parentheses.

PLAYOFF RESULTS

QUARTERFINALS

Maine 2, Northeastern 1
Maine 6, Northeastern 3
(Maine won series, 2-0)

New Hampshire 4, Lowell 2
Lowell 2, New Hampshire 1
Lowell 2, New Hampshire 1
(Lowell won series, 2-1)

Providence 6, Boston University 3
Boston University 2, Providence 1
Providence 4, Boston University 3 (2OT)
(Providence won series, 2-1)

Boston College 1, Merrimack 0
Boston College 5, Merrimack 1
(Boston College won series, 2-0)

SEMIFINALS

Providence 4, Maine 3
Boston College 5, Lowell 1

CHAMPIONSHIP GAME

Boston College 5, Providence 3

ALL-STAR TEAM

First team	Pos.	Second team
Ty Conklin, N. Hampshire	G	Nolan Schaefer, Providence
Bobby Allen, Boston College	D	Jim Fahey, Northeastern
Ron Hainsey, Lowell	D	Matt Libby, Providence
Brian Gionta, Boston College	F	Anthony Aquino, Merrimack
Carl Corazzini, Boston Univ.	F	Chuck Kobasew, Boston Col.
Devin Rask, Providence	F	Krys Kolanos, Boston Col.

AWARD WINNERS

Player of the year: Brian Gionta, Boston College
Rookie of the year: Chuck Kobasew, Boston College
Coach of the year: Paul Pooley, Providence
Leading scorer: Brian Gionta, Boston College
Playoff MVP: Chuck Kobasew, Boston College

INDIVIDUAL LEADERS

Goals: Brian Gionta, Boston College (33)
Assists: Graig Mischler, Northeastern (38)
Points: Brian Gionta, Boston College (54)
Penalty minutes: Brooks Orpik, Boston College (124)
Goaltending average: Ty Conklin, New Hampshire (2.05)

TOP SCORERS

	Games	G	A	Pts.
Brian Gionta, Boston College.............	43	33	21	54
Devin Rask, Providence.....................	39	23	28	51
Krys Kolanos, Boston College	41	25	25	50
Chuck Kobasew, Boston College.......	43	27	22	49
Anthony Aquino, Merrimack.............	38	17	25	42
Graig Mischler, Northeastern.............	36	10	32	42
Darren Haydar, New Hampshire........	39	18	23	41
Ben Eaves, Boston College	41	13	26	39
Peter Fregoe, Providence	40	16	21	37
Ed McGrane, Lowell..........................	38	17	20	37

INDIVIDUAL STATISTICS

BOSTON COLLEGE EAGLES

SCORING

	Pos.	Class	Games	G	A	Pts.	PIM
Brian Gionta.............	F	Sr.	43	33	21	54	47
Krys Kolanos............	F	So.	41	25	25	50	54
Chuck Kobasew	F	Fr.	43	27	22	49	38
Ben Eaves	F	Fr.	41	13	26	39	12
Jeff Giuliano.............	F	Jr.	43	14	21	35	28
Mike Lephart............	F	Sr.	42	15	19	34	46
Tony Voce	F	Fr.	42	12	14	26	40
Ales Dolinar	F	Jr.	42	7	16	23	33
J.D. Forrest	D	Fr.	38	6	17	23	42
Marty Hughes	D	Sr.	41	5	18	23	41
Bobby Allen..............	D	Sr.	42	5	18	23	30
Rob Scuderi	D	Sr.	43	4	19	23	42
Brooks Orpik............	D	Jr.	40	0	20	20	124
Brett Peterson..........	D	Fr.	39	1	6	7	34
Ty Hennes	F	Fr.	40	2	4	6	10
Bill Cass	D	So.	38	0	6	6	58
Mark McLennan	F	Sr.	37	3	2	5	4
A.J. Walker	F	So.	20	2	0	2	0
Justin Dziama	F	Fr.	28	1	1	2	36
Joe Schuman............	D	Fr.	10	0	1	1	8

	Pos.	Class	Games	G	A	Pts.	PIM
Anthony D'Arpino	D	So.	4	0	0	0	0
Dan Sullivan.............	D	Sr.	2	0	0	0	0
Tom Egan.................	G	So.	1	0	0	0	0
Tim Kelleher.............	G	So.	5	0	0	0	0
Scott Clemmensen...	G	Sr.	39	0	0	0	0

GOALTENDING

	Games	Min.	W	L	T	Goals	SO	Avg.
Tom Egan..........	1	3	0	0	0	0	0	0.00
S. Clemmensen..	39	2312	30	7	2	82	3	2.13
Tim Kelleher.......	5	269	3	1	0	13	0	2.90

BOSTON UNIVERSITY TERRIERS

SCORING

	Pos.	Class	Games	G	A	Pts.	PIM
Carl Corazzini	F	Sr.	34	16	20	36	48
Brian Collins	F	So.	37	14	16	30	16
Mike Pandolfo..........	F	Jr.	37	16	13	29	30
Dan Cavanaugh	F	Jr.	35	7	21	28	41
Freddy Meyer...........	D	So.	28	6	13	19	82
Jack Baker	F	Jr.	28	9	9	18	51
Mike Bussoli	D	So.	37	3	14	17	52
Nick Gillis.................	F	Sr.	35	7	7	14	16

	Pos.	Class	Games	G	A	Pts.	PIM
John Sabo	F	So.	35	6	8	14	58
Pat Aufiero	D	Jr.	34	5	8	13	30
John Cronin	D	So.	37	2	11	13	36
Chris Dyment	D	Jr.	37	1	10	11	38
Gregg Johnson	F	Fr.	35	5	5	10	20
Mark Mullen	F	Fr.	31	2	8	10	18
Frantisk Skladany	F	Fr.	35	4	5	9	4
Ken Magowan	F	Fr.	34	5	1	6	22
Stephen Greeley	F	Fr.	22	1	2	3	16
Scott Perry	F	Sr.	23	0	3	3	8
Keith Emery	D	Sr.	17	0	3	3	8
Jason Tapp	G	Jr.	23	0	2	2	6
Colin Sheen	D	Sr.	29	0	1	1	28
Ryan Priem	F	So.	22	0	1	1	14
Sean Fields	G	Fr.	16	0	0	0	4
Mike DiMella	F	Jr.	1	0	0	0	0
Andy Warren	G	Fr.	2	0	0	0	0

GOALTENDING

	Games	Min.	W	L	T	Goals	SO	Avg.
Sean Fields	16	949	6	8	1	40	1	2.53
Jason Tapp	23	1301	8	12	2	73	0	3.37
Andy Warren	2	8	0	0	0	1	0	7.76

LOWELL RIVER HAWKS

SCORING

	Pos.	Class	Games	G	A	Pts.	PIM
Ed McGrane	F	So.	38	17	20	37	6
Ron Hainsey	D	So.	33	10	26	36	51
Brad Rooney	F	Sr.	38	13	21	34	52
Laurent Meunier	F	Fr.	35	10	24	34	54
Kyle Kidney	F	Sr.	37	10	18	28	88
Yorick Treille	F	Jr.	31	10	14	24	35
Tom Rouleau	F	Jr.	38	10	10	20	71
Geoff Schomogyi	F	So.	36	5	10	15	31
Dan Fontas	F	Jr.	38	6	8	14	40
Jeff Boulanger	F	Sr.	30	5	5	10	70
Peter Hay	F	Fr.	19	6	3	9	14
Darryl Green	D	Fr.	32	3	6	9	16
Mark Concannon	F	So.	19	2	7	9	6
Chris Gustafson	D	Jr.	38	2	6	8	36
Jerramie Domish	D	Fr.	31	3	4	7	68
Ken Farrell	D	So.	22	2	5	7	8
Josh Reed	D	So.	17	1	6	7	22
Kevin Kotyluk	D	Jr.	14	3	2	5	41
Nicholas Carso	F	Sr.	24	1	4	5	8
Stephen Slonina	F	So.	34	2	2	4	50
R.J. Tolan	D	Jr.	31	2	1	3	30
Anders Strome	F	Fr.	21	1	1	2	8
Josh Allison	D	Jr.	29	0	2	2	29
Jimi St. John	G	Jr.	26	0	1	1	6
Chris Davidson	G	Fr.	3	0	0	0	0
Cam McCormick	G	So.	11	0	0	0	0

GOALTENDING

	Games	Min.	W	L	T	Goals	SO	Avg.
Chris Davidson	3	138	1	1	0	4	1	1.73
Jimi St. John	26	1532	15	10	1	65	0	2.55
Cam McCormick	11	615	3	5	2	32	1	3.12

MAINE BLACK BEARS

SCORING

	Pos.	Class	Games	G	A	Pts.	PIM
Martin Kariya	F	So.	39	12	24	36	10
Michael Schutte	D	So.	38	15	10	25	20
Niko Dimitrakos	F	Jr.	29	11	14	25	43
Matthias Trattnig	F	Sr.	37	11	13	24	51
Chris Heisten	F	So.	33	5	19	24	28
Robert Liscak	F	So.	39	11	9	20	36
Lucas Lawson	F	So.	39	9	11	20	16
Dan Kerluke	F	Sr.	39	9	9	18	28
Doug Janik	D	Jr.	39	3	15	18	52

	Pos.	Class	Games	G	A	Pts.	PIM
Tom Reimann	F	So.	38	5	12	17	12
Peter Metcalf	D	Jr.	31	5	9	14	44
Francis Nault	D	Fr.	31	2	11	13	18
Todd Jackson	F	Fr.	39	4	8	12	8
Kevin Clauson	D	Sr.	39	2	8	10	24
Brendan Donovan	F	Fr.	15	2	8	10	16
A.J. Begg	D	Sr.	39	2	5	7	72
Eric Turgeon	D	Jr.	33	2	3	5	14
Don Richardson	F	Jr.	16	0	4	4	2
Gray Shaneberger	F	So.	25	3	0	3	10
Cliff Loya	D	So.	36	1	2	3	28
Mike Mantenuto	F	Fr.	14	2	0	2	8
Cameron Lyall	F	Fr.	12	0	1	1	0
Matt Yeats	G	So.	33	0	1	1	0
Steve Wright	G	Fr.	1	0	0	0	0
Trapper Clark	G	So.	2	0	0	0	0
Mike Morrison	G	Jr.	10	0	0	0	0

GOALTENDING

	Games	Min.	W	L	T	Goals	SO	Avg.
Steve Wright	1	0	0	0	0	0	0	0.00
Mike Morrison	10	490	2	3	3	16	0	1.96
Matt Yeats	33	1897	18	9	4	76	2	2.40
Trapper Clark	2	16	0	0	0	2	0	7.47

MASSACHUSETTS MINUTEMEN

SCORING

	Pos.	Class	Games	G	A	Pts.	PIM
Tim Turner	F	So.	32	16	10	26	28
Jeff Turner	F	Sr.	34	5	19	24	24
Martin Miljko	F	Jr.	31	12	10	22	36
Jimmy Callahan	F	So.	32	3	15	18	28
Brad Nizwantowski	F	So.	29	6	10	16	34
Kris Wallis	F	Sr.	33	7	8	15	18
Samuli Jalkanen	D	So.	33	1	13	14	40
Thomas Pock	F	Fr.	33	6	6	12	59
Darcy King	F	Jr.	25	4	7	11	6
Scott Horvath	F	Fr.	31	6	4	10	18
Jay Shaw	F	Sr.	30	2	6	8	40
Toni Soderholm	D	Jr.	24	1	7	8	23
R.J. Gates	F	Sr.	30	3	4	7	43
Mike Warner	F	Fr.	34	4	1	5	14
Luke Duplessis	D	Jr.	30	1	4	5	69
J.R. Zavisza	F	So.	25	1	1	2	14
Justin Shaw	D	Jr.	11	0	2	2	18
Joey Culgin	D	So.	18	0	2	2	18
Kelly Sickavish	D	Fr.	27	0	2	2	26
Nick Stephens	D	Sr.	16	0	2	2	20
Anthony Scaparotti	F	So.	3	0	1	1	2
Nick Kuiper	D	Fr.	13	0	1	1	2
Markus Helanen	G	Sr.	25	0	1	1	2
Jedd Crumb	F	Jr.	7	0	1	1	0
Randy Drohan	D	Jr.	31	0	1	1	55
Jeff Timmons	F	Fr.	1	0	0	0	0
Mike Johnson	G	Jr.	16	0	0	0	0

GOALTENDING

	Games	Min.	W	L	T	Goals	SO	Avg.
Markus Helanen	25	1318	6	15	1	72	3	3.28
Mike Johnson	16	739	2	7	3	47	0	3.81

MERRIMACK WARRIORS

SCORING

	Pos.	Class	Games	G	A	Pts.	PIM
Anthony Aquino	F	So.	38	17	25	42	22
Nick Parillo	F	Jr.	38	16	13	29	36
Marco Rosa	D	Fr.	33	6	18	24	22
John Pyliotis	F	Sr.	37	7	16	23	52
Stephen Moon	D	Sr.	38	5	17	22	32
Ryan Kiley	F	Jr.	38	11	7	18	72
Joey Gray	F	Sr.	35	7	7	14	64
Vincent Clevenger	F	Sr.	38	6	7	13	36

	Pos.	Class	Games	G	A	Pts.	PIM
Ron Mongeau	F	Sr.	38	3	9	12	44
Tony Johnson	D	Fr.	28	2	8	10	25
Alex Sikatchev	F	So.	34	2	7	9	12
Luke Smith	F	So.	37	3	5	8	8
Nick Cammarata	F	So.	28	3	3	6	33
Jeff State	D	Fr.	35	1	2	3	58
Greg Lauze	D	Fr.	31	0	3	3	6
Eric Pederson	D	Fr.	28	1	1	2	16
Brad Mills	D	Jr.	17	1	1	2	6
Lou Eyster	F	Fr.	35	0	2	2	12
Tim Foster	D	Jr.	33	0	2	2	18
Jayson Philbin	F	Sr.	14	1	0	1	8
Darren Clarke	D	Fr.	7	0	1	1	6
Sean Ober	F	Fr.	5	0	0	0	4
Joe Exter	G	So.	25	0	0	0	2
Tim Reidy	F	Fr.	12	0	0	0	0
Tom Welby	G	Sr.	17	0	0	0	8
Mark Ferullo	D	Jr.	1	0	0	0	0
Jason Wolfe	G	Jr.	2	0	0	0	0

GOALTENDING

	Games	Min.	W	L	T	Goals	SO	Avg.
Tom Welby	17	867	3	8	3	44	1	3.04
Joe Exter	25	1384	11	12	1	71	2	3.08
Jason Wolfe	2	45	0	0	0	3	0	4.04

NEW HAMPSHIRE WILDCATS

SCORING

	Pos.	Class	Games	G	A	Pts.	PIM
Darren Haydar	F	Jr.	39	18	23	41	38
Lanny Gare	F	So.	39	11	20	31	49
Colin Hemingway	F	So.	37	9	17	26	16
Garrett Stafford	D	So.	37	5	21	26	44
David Busch	F	Jr.	39	9	15	24	10
Matt Swain	F	Sr.	32	14	9	23	14
Jim Abbott	F	So.	33	10	12	22	52
Corey-Joe Ficek	F	Sr.	39	7	15	22	36
Nathan Martz	F	Fr.	37	5	14	19	20
Joshua Prudden	F	So.	37	8	8	16	28
Johnny Rogers	F	Sr.	39	6	8	14	16
Sean Austin	D	Sr.	38	4	10	14	45
Eric Lind	D	Sr.	39	4	9	13	30
Jeff Haydar	F	Sr.	39	3	10	13	46
Kevin Truelson	D	So.	32	3	9	12	22
Mark White	D	Sr.	39	3	5	8	38
Mick Mounsey	D	Fr.	37	1	4	5	20
Mike Lubesnick	D	Fr.	34	1	3	4	14
Steve Saviano	F	Fr.	16	1	1	2	2
Travis Banga	F	Fr.	13	0	2	2	6
Tim Horst	D	Fr.	8	0	0	0	14
Michael Ayers	G	Fr.	5	0	0	0	0
Matt Carney	G	So.	6	0	0	0	0
Ty Conklin	G	Sr.	34	0	0	0	0

GOALTENDING

	Games	Min.	W	L	T	Goals	SO	Avg.
Ty Conklin	34	2048	17	12	5	70	4	2.05
Matt Carney	6	299	4	0	1	12	0	2.41
Michael Ayers	5	26	0	0	0	2	0	4.68

NORTHEASTERN HUSKIES

SCORING

	Pos.	Class	Games	G	A	Pts.	PIM
Graig Mischler	F	Sr.	36	10	32	42	34
Mike Ryan	F	So.	33	17	12	29	52
Willie Levesque	F	Jr.	35	13	16	29	62

	Pos.	Class	Games	G	A	Pts.	PIM
Jim Fahey	D	Jr.	36	4	23	27	48
Mike Jozefowicz	D	Sr.	34	3	17	20	14
Chris Lynch	F	Jr.	36	12	6	18	50
Scott Selig	F	Fr.	35	7	8	15	34
Joe Mastronardi	F	So.	34	6	9	15	46
Trevor Reschny	F	Fr.	36	6	7	13	28
John Peterman	D	Sr.	35	4	6	10	58
Brian Cummings	F	Sr.	36	3	6	9	44
Eric Ortlip	F	Fr.	30	4	4	8	20
Sean MacDonald	F	Sr.	29	3	5	8	4
Ryan Dudgeon	F	Fr.	18	3	2	5	18
Arik Engbrecht	D	Jr.	21	1	4	5	20
Rich Spiller	F	Jr.	27	1	3	4	36
Kevin Welch	F	Sr.	21	2	1	3	30
Brian Sullivan	D	So.	32	1	2	3	37
Leon Hayward	F	Jr.	31	1	2	3	2
Joe Mancuso	D	Jr.	15	0	3	3	2
Matt Keating	F	Sr.	22	0	2	2	34
Ryan Zoller	F	Jr.	3	1	0	1	4
Mike Gilhooly	G	So.	27	0	1	1	0
Brian Tudrick	F	Fr.	12	0	0	0	6
Rahim Mawji	F	Fr.	2	0	0	0	0
Matt Coates	G	So.	1	0	0	0	0
Jason Braun	G	Jr.	13	0	0	0	0

GOALTENDING

	Games	Min.	W	L	T	Goals	SO	Avg.
Mike Gilhooly	27	1543	8	14	4	81	1	3.15
Matt Coates	1	19	0	0	0	1	0	3.20
Jason Braun	13	622	5	5	0	37	0	3.57

PROVIDENCE FRIARS

SCORING

	Pos.	Class	Games	G	A	Pts.	PIM
Devin Rask	F	So.	39	23	28	51	41
Peter Fregoe	F	Jr.	40	16	21	37	18
Matt Libby	D	Sr.	39	10	20	30	26
Drew Omicioli	F	Jr.	29	12	15	27	42
Marc Suderman	F	Jr.	40	7	19	26	10
Jon DiSalvatore	F	So.	36	9	16	25	29
Jay Leach	D	Sr.	40	4	21	25	104
Regan Kelly	D	Fr.	36	4	21	25	58
J.J. Picinic	F	Sr.	40	12	5	17	16
Adam Lee	F	Jr.	37	7	10	17	22
Doug Wright	F	So.	29	3	10	13	26
Michael Lucci	F	So.	36	7	4	11	50
Cody Loughlean	F	Fr.	39	5	6	11	30
Shawn Weiman	D	So.	27	2	9	11	28
Peter Zingoni	F	Fr.	28	2	6	8	38
Stephen Wood	D	Fr.	36	3	4	7	68
Heath Gordon	F	Sr.	12	1	3	4	14
Mike Robinson	F	Sr.	23	1	2	3	14
Dominic Torretti	D	Fr.	30	0	3	3	22
John Luszcz	F	Jr.	21	1	1	2	22
Jason Platt	D	Fr.	26	0	2	2	12
Jonathan Goodwin	F	Fr.	11	1	0	1	2
Cole Gendreau	F	Sr.	27	1	0	1	24
Nolan Schaefer	G	So.	25	0	1	1	2
Matt Curran	G	So.	1	0	0	0	0
Boyd Ballard	G	Sr.	16	0	0	0	2

GOALTENDING

	Games	Min.	W	L	T	Goals	SO	Avg.
Matt Curran	1	1	0	0	0	0	0	0.00
Nolan Schaefer	25	1529	15	8	2	63	3	2.47
Boyd Ballard	16	926	7	5	3	42	1	2.72

COLLEGE HOCKEY *Hockey East*

WESTERN COLLEGIATE HOCKEY ASSOCIATION

2000-01 SEASON

FINAL STANDINGS

Team	G	W	L	T	Pts.	GF	GA
N. Dakota (29-8-9)	28	18	4	6	42	115	80
St. Cloud St. (31-9-1)	28	20	8	0	40	111	69
Minnesota (27-13-2)	28	18	8	2	38	107	70
Colorado C. (27-13-1)	28	17	11	0	34	106	81
Wisconsin (22-15-4)	28	14	10	4	32	81	86
Denver (19-15-4)	28	14	11	3	31	84	78
Mankato St. (19-18-1)	28	13	14	1	27	91	99
Mich. Tech (8-24-4)	28	6	19	3	15	69	105
A'ka-Anch. (7-24-5)	28	4	20	4	12	61	104
M.-Duluth (7-28-4)	28	3	22	3	9	68	121

Overall record in parentheses.

PLAYOFF RESULTS

FIRST ROUND

Wisconsin 6, Denver 4
Wisconsin 6, Denver 2
(Wisconsin won series, 2-0)
Colorado College 3, Mankato State 0
Colorado College 7, Mankato State 3
(Colorado College won series, 2-0)
St. Cloud State 5, Alaska-Anchorage 1
St. Cloud State 8, Alaska-Anchorage 2
(St. Cloud State won series, 2-0)
Minnesota 7, Michigan Tech 2
Minnesota 3, Michigan Tech 1
(Minnesota won series, 2-0)
Minnesota-Duluth 3, North Dakota 2
North Dakota 6, Minnesota-Duluth 2
North Dakota 4, Minnesota-Duluth 0
(North Dakota won series, 2-1)

SUDDEN-DEATH QUARTERFINAL

Colorado College 4, Wisconsin 3

SEMIFINALS

North Dakota 2, Colorado College 1
St. Cloud State 3, Minnesota 0

CONSOLATION GAME

Colorado College 5, Minnesota 4

FINALS

St. Cloud State 6, North Dakota 5 (OT)

ALL-STAR TEAMS

First team	Pos.	Second team
Scott Meyer, St. Cloud State	G	Wade Dubielewicz, Denver
Jordan Leopold, Minnesota	D	Paul Manning, Colo. College
Travis Roche, North Dakota	D	Duvie Westcott, St. Cloud St.
Mark Cullen, Colo. College	F	Ryan Bayda, North Dakota
Bryan Lundbohm, N. Dakota	F	Dany Heatley, Wisconsin
Jeff Panzer, North Dakota	F	Erik Westrum, Minnesota

AWARD WINNERS

Player of the year: Jeff Panzer, North Dakota
Rookie of the year: Peter Sejna, Colorado College
Coach of the year: Dean Blais, North Dakota
Leading scorer: Jeff Panzer, North Dakota
Playoff MVP: Tyler Arnason, St. Cloud State

INDIVIDUAL LEADERS

Goals: Bryan Lundbohm, North Dakota (32)
Assists: Jeff Panzer, North Dakota (55)
Points: Jeff Panzer, North Dakota (81)
Penalty minutes: Matt DeMarchi, Minnesota (149)
Goaltending average: Colin Zulianello, Colorado College (2.21)

TOP SCORERS

	Games	G	A	Pts.
Jeff Panzer, North Dakota	46	26	55	81
Bryan Lundbohm, North Dakota	46	32	37	69
Erik Westrum, Minnesota	42	26	35	61
Ryan Bayda, North Dakota	46	25	34	59
Peter Sejna, Colorado College	41	29	29	58
Dany Heatley, Wisconsin	39	24	33	57
Tyler Arnason, St. Cloud State	41	28	28	56
Mark Cullen, Colorado College	31	20	33	53
Brandon Sampair, St. Cloud State	40	12	38	50
Jordan Leopold, Minnesota	42	12	37	49
Travis Roche, North Dakota	46	11	38	49

INDIVIDUAL STATISTICS

ALASKA-ANCHORAGE SEAWOLVES

SCORING

	Pos.	Class	Games	G	A	Pts.	PIM
Mike Scott	F	Jr.	36	8	15	23	46
Steve Cygan	F	Jr.	36	9	10	19	18
Matt Shasby	D	So.	35	4	14	18	32
Jesse Unklesbay	F	So.	35	9	8	17	31
Gregg Zaporzan	F	Jr.	26	8	9	17	20
Pete Talafous	F	Fr.	32	8	8	16	54
Dallas Steward	F	Fr.	33	4	10	14	10
Chris Sikich	D	Sr.	36	6	7	13	10
Joe Garvin	F	So.	35	4	8	12	25
Petr Chytka	F	So.	33	5	3	8	24
Dan Gilkerson	F	So.	35	5	3	8	12
Reggie Simon	F	Sr.	32	3	5	8	30
Corey Hessler	D	Jr.	31	4	2	6	43
Vladimir Novak	F	Fr.	35	3	3	6	15
Steve Ludwig	D	Sr.	13	0	6	6	4
Steve Suihkonen	D	So.	26	0	6	6	6
Morgan Roach	F	So.	22	1	4	5	2
Tyler Schnell	D	Fr.	22	1	3	4	10
Eric Lawson	D	Jr.	20	0	2	2	2
Mark Leitner	D	Sr.	36	0	2	2	14
Kurt Johnson	G	So.	1	0	0	0	0
Jade Galbraith	F	Fr.	3	0	0	0	0
Corey Strachan	G	So.	3	0	0	0	0
Kevin Reiter	G	Fr.	5	0	0	0	0
Jeremy Downs	D	Fr.	15	0	0	0	10
Jace Digel	F	Fr.	21	0	0	0	12
Chris King	G	Fr.	32	0	0	0	0

– 400 –

GOALTENDING

	Games	Min.	W	L	T	Goals	SO	Avg.
Chris King	32	1855	7	20	5	99	0	3.20
Kurt Johnson	1	60	0	1	0	5	0	5.00
Kevin Reiter	5	173	0	1	0	16	0	5.55
Corey Strachan	3	94	0	2	0	11	0	7.01

COLORADO COLLEGE TIGERS
SCORING

	Pos.	Class	Games	G	A	Pts.	PIM
Peter Sejna	F	Fr.	41	29	29	58	10
Mark Cullen	F	Jr.	31	20	33	53	26
Alex Kim	F	Jr.	41	17	21	38	53
Justin Morrison	F	Sr.	41	21	14	35	42
Noah Clarke	F	So.	41	12	20	32	22
Paul Manning	D	Sr.	34	2	28	30	48
Tom Preissing	D	So.	33	6	18	24	26
Joe Cullen	F	So.	34	8	12	20	38
Trent Clark	F	Jr.	40	6	13	19	27
Chris Hartsburg	F	Jr.	41	8	7	15	38
Mike Stuart	D	Jr.	33	1	13	14	36
Jesse Heerema	F	Jr.	31	8	5	13	18
Mike Colgan	D	Sr.	41	1	12	13	20
Andrew Canzanello	D	Fr.	37	3	9	12	26
Colin Stuart	F	Fr.	41	2	7	9	26
Shaun Winkler	F	Jr.	41	1	7	8	6
Brent Voorhees	D	Sr.	24	2	4	6	10
Tyler Liebel	F	Fr.	39	3	2	5	18
Jason Jozsa	D	So.	30	0	4	4	14
Reid Goolsby	F	Fr.	29	0	2	2	12
Jeff Sanger	G	Jr.	26	0	1	1	4
Sean Cromarty	F	Fr.	3	0	0	0	8
John Van Pelt	D	Fr.	12	0	0	0	0
Colin Zulianello	G	Sr.	17	0	0	0	2

GOALTENDING

	Games	Min.	W	L	T	Goals	SO	Avg.
Colin Zulianello	17	950	9	7	1	35	0	2.21
Jeff Sanger	26	1539	18	6	0	69	3	2.69

DENVER PIONEERS
SCORING

	Pos.	Class	Games	G	A	Pts.	PIM
Chris Paradise	F	Jr.	38	17	16	33	50
Kelly Popadynetz	F	Sr.	37	11	20	31	39
Bjorn Engstrom	F	Sr.	38	14	15	29	22
Connor James	F	Fr.	38	8	19	27	14
Matt Weber	F	So.	33	14	9	23	16
Ryan Caldwell	D	Fr.	36	3	20	23	76
Kevin Doell	F	So.	36	9	10	19	26
Jesse Cook	D	Jr.	37	2	15	17	22
Greg Barber	F	Fr.	35	7	8	15	22
Lukas Dora	F	Fr.	34	6	6	12	43
Bryan Vines	D	Jr.	38	3	7	10	20
Judd Stauss	D	Sr.	38	2	8	10	30
David Neale	F	Jr.	36	6	3	9	38
Greg Keith	F	Fr.	38	3	5	8	66
Aaron MacKenzie	D	So.	37	2	6	8	45
J.J. Hartmann	F	So.	18	2	5	7	6
Jordan Bianchin	F	So.	27	2	4	6	34
Max Bull	F	Fr.	33	2	4	6	18
Erik Adams	D	Jr.	36	1	4	5	24
Bryce Wallnutt	F	Sr.	13	2	1	3	6
Wade Dubielewicz	G	So.	29	0	2	2	2
Matt Laatsch	D	Fr.	1	0	0	0	0
Neil Phippen	D	Sr.	3	0	0	0	0
Jason Grahame	D	So.	4	0	0	0	0
Adam Berkhoel	G	Fr.	15	0	0	0	0

GOALTENDING

	Games	Min.	W	L	T	Goals	SO	Avg.
W. Dubielewicz	29	1542	12	9	3	59	2	2.30
Adam Berkhoel	15	745	7	6	1	38	1	3.06

MANKATO STATE MAVERICKS
SCORING

	Pos.	Class	Games	G	A	Pts.	PIM
Jesse Rooney	F	Sr.	38	22	13	35	32
Nate Mauer	F	Jr.	35	14	16	30	58
Jerry Cunningham	F	So.	32	8	19	27	20
Tim Jackman	F	Fr.	37	11	14	25	92
T.J. Guidarelli	F	Sr.	31	6	18	24	37
B.J. Abel	F	So.	38	11	12	23	36
Ben Christopherson	D	Sr.	38	5	18	23	72
Josh Kern	F	Jr.	35	7	13	20	69
Joe Bourne	D	So.	38	6	13	19	28
Peter Holoien	F	Sr.	33	7	10	17	18
Cole Bassett	F	Fr.	36	8	7	15	32
Ryan Severson	F	Sr.	32	7	6	13	24
Andy Hedlund	D	Jr.	38	6	6	12	64
Tyler Baines	F	Sr.	31	3	7	10	36
Justin Martin	F	Jr.	36	2	7	9	6
Dana Sorensen	F	Fr.	12	4	3	7	6
Peter Runkel	D	So.	37	0	6	6	66
Jon Bushy	D	Sr.	36	1	4	5	53
Shane Joseph	F	Fr.	16	0	5	5	2
Aaron Forsythe	D	Fr.	23	0	4	4	18
Matt Paluczak	D	Fr.	12	0	3	3	25
B.J. Anderson	F	Jr.	7	0	2	2	0
Todd Kelzenberg	G	Jr.	13	0	1	1	0
Eric Pateman	G	Jr.	29	0	1	1	2
Dwight Hirst	F	So.	2	0	0	0	0
Micah Wouters	F	Fr.	4	0	0	0	2
Nate Metcalf	D	Fr.	7	0	0	0	0

GOALTENDING

	Games	Min.	W	L	T	Goals	SO	Avg.
Eric Pateman	29	1693	15	12	1	97	1	3.44
Todd Kelzenberg	13	590	4	6	0	36	0	3.66

MICHIGAN TECH HUSKIES
SCORING

	Pos.	Class	Games	G	A	Pts.	PIM
Matt Ulwelling	F	Sr.	36	8	21	29	32
Brad Patterson	F	Jr.	36	6	16	22	20
Paul Cabana	F	Jr.	35	15	6	21	41
Jarrett Weinberger	F	Sr.	36	12	8	20	34
Brett Engelhardt	F	Fr.	35	6	10	16	73
Mat Snesrud	D	Sr.	32	5	11	16	28
Justin Brown	D	Fr.	36	3	13	16	28
Chris Durno	F	So.	35	9	6	15	46
Tim Laurila	D	Jr.	33	3	11	14	63
Clint Way	D	Sr.	36	2	12	14	36
Tab Lardner	F	Sr.	34	5	8	13	56
Frank Werner	F	Fr.	33	4	5	9	16
Tom Kaiman	D	Jr.	32	2	5	7	53
Jaron Doetzel	F	Jr.	36	3	3	6	14
John Pittis	F	Fr.	30	2	4	6	23
Jeff Keiver	F	So.	34	1	5	6	22
Tony DeLorenzo	F	Fr.	16	1	4	5	0
Bob Rangus	F	Fr.	10	2	2	4	2
Chuck Fabry	F	So.	13	1	1	2	4
Greg Amadio	D	So.	31	1	1	2	95
Adrian Fure	D	Sr.	16	0	2	2	6
Jason Moilanen	G	Sr.	5	0	1	1	0
Brian Rogers	G	So.	34	0	1	1	0
Ryan Lenton	D	Fr.	13	0	0	0	0

GOALTENDING

	Games	Min.	W	L	T	Goals	SO	Avg.
Jason Moilanen	5	181	0	1	1	10	0	3.31
Brian Rogers	34	2018	8	23	3	124	0	3.69

COLLEGE HOCKEY WCHA

MINNESOTA GOLDEN GOPHERS

SCORING

	Pos.	Class	Games	G	A	Pts.	PIM
Erik Westrum	F	Sr.	42	26	35	61	84
Jordan Leopold	D	Jr.	42	12	37	49	38
John Pohl	F	Jr.	38	19	26	45	24
Jeff Taffe	F	So.	38	12	23	35	56
Grant Potulny	F	Fr.	42	22	11	33	38
Troy Riddle	F	Fr.	38	16	14	30	49
Aaron Miskovich	F	Sr.	41	12	12	24	41
Matt Koalska	F	Fr.	42	10	14	24	36
Dylan Mills	D	Sr.	42	2	21	23	56
Paul Martin	D	Fr.	38	3	17	20	8
Nick Anthony	F	So.	34	5	12	17	30
Stuart Senden	F	Sr.	34	7	6	13	30
Matt DeMarchi	D	So.	39	4	9	13	149
Pat O'Leary	F	Jr.	38	5	4	9	44
Ben Tharp	F	So.	38	4	4	8	34
Nick Angell	D	Jr.	38	3	5	8	26
Jon Waibel	F	Fr.	42	1	7	8	34
Erik Wendell	F	Jr.	33	5	2	7	38
Matt Leimbek	F	Sr.	23	3	2	5	6
Joey Martin	D	Fr.	18	0	2	2	2
Pete Samargia	G	So.	5	0	1	1	0
Erik Young	G	So.	1	0	0	0	0
Chad Roberg	F	So.	6	0	0	0	0
Mark Nenovich	D	Jr.	9	0	0	0	4
Adam Hauser	G	Jr.	40	0	0	0	24

GOALTENDING

	Games	Min.	W	L	T	Goals	SO	Avg.
Erik Young	1	6	0	0	0	0	0	0.00
Pete Samargia	5	169	1	1	0	6	0	2.13
Adam Hauser	40	2366	26	12	2	101	3	2.56

MINNESOTA-DULUTH BULLDOGS

SCORING

	Pos.	Class	Games	G	A	Pts.	PIM
Tom Nelson	F	Jr.	38	16	25	41	61
Nate Anderson	F	Jr.	39	16	14	30	50
Andy Reierson	D	Jr.	39	7	15	22	18
Judd Medak	F	Jr.	30	7	14	21	44
Jon Francisco	F	So.	38	9	11	20	50
Beau Geisler	D	So.	39	2	18	20	26
Mark Carlson	F	Jr.	39	9	10	19	6
Drew Otten	F	So.	37	9	9	18	54
Mark Gunderson	F	Sr.	38	8	10	18	28
Derek Derow	F	Sr.	30	5	7	12	10
Junior Lessard	F	Fr.	36	4	8	12	12
Jesse Fibiger	D	Sr.	37	0	8	8	56
Matt Mathias	F	So.	31	4	3	7	20
Ryan Homstol	F	Sr.	39	2	4	6	50
Jay Hardwick	D	Fr.	32	1	2	3	20
Tyler Williamson	D	Fr.	23	0	3	3	4
Nick Anderson	F	Fr.	3	2	0	2	2
Jerrid Reinholz	F	Fr.	25	1	1	2	6
Craig Pierce	D	Sr.	16	0	2	2	16
Michael Miskovich	F	So.	14	1	0	1	8
Craig Weller	D	Fr.	6	0	1	1	0
Chad Kolar	F	Fr.	16	0	1	1	6
Adam Coole	G	Fr.	17	0	1	1	2
Ryan Coole	D	Sr.	37	0	1	1	46
Jason Gregoire	G	So.	1	0	0	0	0
Jim Murphy	F	Fr.	3	0	0	0	0
Steve Rodberg	D	So.	17	0	0	0	14
Rob Anderson	G	So.	28	0	0	0	4

GOALTENDING

	Games	Min.	W	L	T	Goals	SO	Avg.
Rob Anderson	28	1546	6	17	3	98	0	3.80
Adam Coole	17	744	1	10	1	53	0	4.27
Jason Gregoire	1	60	0	1	0	8	0	8.00

NORTH DAKOTA FIGHTING SIOUX

SCORING

	Pos.	Class	Games	G	A	Pts.	PIM
Jeff Panzer	F	Sr.	46	26	55	81	28
Bryan Lundbohm	F	Jr.	46	32	37	69	38
Ryan Bayda	F	So.	46	25	34	59	48
Travis Roche	D	So.	46	11	38	49	42
Wes Dorey	F	Sr.	46	17	20	37	32
Jason Notermann	F	So.	45	11	17	28	45
Kevin Spiewak	F	So.	46	7	21	28	38
Chad Mazurak	D	Jr.	46	7	19	26	68
Tim Skarperud	F	So.	46	10	14	24	22
Aaron Schneekloth	D	Jr.	46	6	14	20	36
David Lundbohm	F	Fr.	39	9	10	19	26
Trevor Hammer	D	Sr.	44	2	8	10	28
David Hale	D	Fr.	44	4	5	9	79
Paul Murphy	D	Jr.	32	1	7	8	6
Pat O'Leary	F	Fr.	33	4	3	7	29
Quinn Fylling	F	Fr.	42	4	3	7	25
Chris Leinweber	D	So.	43	1	6	7	32
Tyler Palmiscno	F	Fr.	29	3	2	5	6
Adrian Hasbargen	D	Jr.	25	2	2	4	14
Ryan Hale	F	Fr.	8	1	1	2	10
Karl Goehring	G	Sr.	30	0	2	2	0
Derrick Byfuglien	D	Fr.	6	0	1	1	2
Ryan Sofie	G	Fr.	1	0	0	0	0
Nate Wright	D	Fr.	1	0	0	0	2
Mike Possin	F	Jr.	6	0	0	0	4
Jeff Yurecko	F	So.	15	0	0	0	16
Andy Kollar	G	Jr.	19	0	0	0	2

GOALTENDING

	Games	Min.	W	L	T	Goals	SO	Avg.
Karl Goehring	30	1661	16	6	6	66	3	2.38
Andy Kollar	19	1126	13	2	3	50	1	2.66
Ryan Sofie	1	30	0	0	0	2	0	4.02

ST. CLOUD STATE HUSKIES

SCORING

	Pos.	Class	Games	G	A	Pts.	PIM
Tyler Arnason	F	Jr.	41	28	28	56	14
Brandon Sampair	F	Sr.	40	12	38	50	10
Mark Hartigan	F	Jr.	40	27	21	48	20
Jon Cullen	F	So.	41	14	26	40	12
Joe Motzko	F	So.	41	17	20	37	54
Duvie Westcott	D	Jr.	38	10	24	34	114
Nate DiCasmirro	F	Jr.	32	9	20	29	26
Keith Anderson	F	Sr.	41	8	18	26	28
Ryan Malone	F	So.	36	7	18	25	52
Derek Eastman	D	So.	38	7	17	24	39
Matt Hendricks	F	Fr.	36	3	9	12	23
Ritchie Larson	D	So.	39	5	6	11	28
Chris Purslow	F	So.	32	8	2	10	24
Jeff Finger	D	Fr.	41	4	5	9	84
Andy Lundbohm	F	Fr.	20	3	2	5	6
Colin Peters	D	Fr.	34	0	5	5	8
Scott Meyer	G	Sr.	36	0	4	4	16
Mike Walsh	F	So.	24	2	1	3	19
Brian Gaffaney	F	Sr.	32	2	1	3	44
Ryan LeMere	D	Fr.	36	0	3	3	64
Lee Brooks	F	Jr.	20	0	2	2	14
Brian Schuster	F	Fr.	9	1	0	1	12
Ryan Johnson	D	Fr.	10	1	0	1	4
Dean Weasler	G	Jr.	4	0	0	0	2
Jake Moreland	G	So.	4	0	0	0	0
Joel Peterson	D	Fr.	17	0	0	0	4

GOALTENDING

	Games	Min.	W	L	T	Goals	SO	Avg.
Dean Weasler	4	192	3	0	0	6	1	1.88
Scott Meyer	36	2096	25	8	1	78	2	2.23
Jake Moreland	4	189	3	1	0	8	1	2.53

WISCONSIN BADGERS
SCORING

	Pos.	Class	Games	G	A	Pts.	PIM
Dany Heatley	F	So.	39	24	33	57	74
Matt Murray	F	Jr.	41	13	16	29	75
Kent Davyduke	F	Jr.	37	11	18	29	51
Andy Wheeler	F	Jr.	38	9	16	25	32
Matt Hussey	F	Jr.	40	9	11	20	24
Matt Doman	F	Jr.	41	9	10	19	66
Jeff Dessner	D	Sr.	39	7	12	19	58
David Hukalo	F	Jr.	38	6	13	19	34
Alex Brooks	D	Sr.	41	3	16	19	76
Dan Boeser	D	Fr.	41	4	13	17	2
Brad Winchester	F	So.	41	7	9	16	71
Rene Bourque	F	Fr.	32	10	5	15	18
Dave Hergert	F	Jr.	40	7	7	14	4
Erik Jensen	F	So.	39	6	7	13	57
Kevin Granato	F	Sr.	31	5	5	10	22
Brian Fahey	D	So.	38	1	5	6	16
John Eichelberger	F	Fr.	25	0	5	5	2
Mark Jackson	D	So.	31	0	5	5	30
Rob Vega	D	Jr.	31	2	1	3	16
Jon Krall	D	Fr.	24	0	3	3	24
Mike Cerniglia	F	Sr.	5	0	2	2	0
Jake Heisler	F	Fr.	5	0	1	1	0
Rick Spooner	D	Sr.	1	0	0	0	0
Scott Kabotoff	G	So.	4	0	0	0	0
Graham Melanson	G	Sr.	41	0	0	0	6

GOALTENDING

	Games	Min.	W	L	T	Goals	SO	Avg.
G. Melanson	41	2446	22	15	4	125	3	3.07
Scott Kabotoff	4	46	0	0	0	3	0	3.94

COLLEGE HOCKEY *WCHA*

CANADIAN INTERUNIVERSITY ATHLETIC UNION

GENERAL INFORMATION

The Canadian Interuniversity Athletic Union is an alliance of three Canadian college leagues—the Atlantic Universities Athletic Association, Canada West University Athletic Association and Ontario Universities Athletic Association. After the regular season, the three leagues compete in an elimination tournament to decide the CIAU national champion. The award and trophy winners are based on regular-season play.

2001 NATIONAL CHAMPIONSHIPS

PLAYOFF STANDINGS

POOL A

Team (League)	W	L	Pts.	GF	GA
St. Francis Xavier (AUS)	2	1	4	14	10
Western Ontario (OUA)	1	1	2	7	8
Alberta (CWUAA)	0	2	0	6	10

POOL B

Team (League)	W	L	Pts.	GF	GA
Trois-Rivieres (OUA)	3	0	6	21	9
Wilfrid Laurier (OUA)	1	1	2	7	12
St. Thomas (CWUAA)	0	2	0	3	9

RESULTS

ROUND-ROBIN POOL PLAY

THURSDAY, MARCH 22

Trois-Rivieres 6, St. Thomas 1
St. Francis Xavier 5, Western Ontario 2

FRIDAY, MARCH 23

Western Ontario 5, Alberta 3
Wilfrid Laurier 3, St. Thomas 2

SATURDAY, MARCH 24

St. Francis Xavier 5, Alberta 3
Trois-Rivieres 10, Wilfrid Laurier 4

FINAL

SUNDAY, MARCH 25

Trois-Rivieres 5, St. Francis Xavier 4 (2OT)

ALL-TOURNAMENT TEAM

Player	Pos.	College
Luc Belanger	G	Trois-Rivieres
Dominic Auger	D	St. Francis
Sebastien Tremblay	D	Trois-Rivieres
Jeff Ambrosio	F	Wilfrid Laurier
Dean Stock	F	St. Francis
Alexandre Tremblay	F	Trois-Rivieres

Tournament Most Valuable Player: Alexandre Tremblay, T.-R.

2000-01 AWARD WINNERS

CIAU ALL-CANADIAN TEAM

Pos.	Player
G	Luc Belanger, Trois-Rivieres
	Clayton Pool, Alberta
D	Steve Gallace, St. Mary's
	Mike Garrow, Alberta
	Rob Maric, Western Ontario
	Ryan Marsh, Alberta
F	Yanick Evola, St. Francis Xavier
	Marc Gaudet, Manitoba
	Russ Hewson, Alberta
	Jason Sands, St. Thomas
	Alexandre Tremblay, Trois-Rivieres
	Mike Williams, York

TROPHY WINNERS

Player of the year: Russ Hewson, Alberta
Rookie of the year: Alexandre Tremblay, Trois-Rivieres
Most sportsmanlike player: Mike Williams, York
Scholastic player of the year: Mike Williams, York
Coach of the year: Rob Daum, Alberta

TOP SCORERS

	Games	G	A	Pts.
Russ Hewson, Alberta	28	21	35	56
Alexandre Tremblay, Trois-Rivieres	24	29	24	53
Kris Knoblauch, Alberta	28	24	26	50
Jean-Philippe Pare, Trois-Rivieres	24	16	32	48
Marc Gaudet, Manitoba	28	18	29	47
Shaun Fairweather, Western Ontario	23	20	22	42
Dan Bassi, Brock	23	18	24	42
Kent Nobes, Brock	23	23	18	41
Jeremy Stasiuk, Saskatchewan	27	23	18	41
Greg Davis, McGill	22	21	20	41
Chad Spurr, Prince Edward Island	24	16	25	41
Ryan Wade, Alberta	28	15	26	41
Jason Sands, St. Thomas	26	13	28	41

TOP GOALTENDERS

	Games	Min.	GA	Avg.
Luc Belanger, Trois-Rivieres	18	1039	33	1.91
Clayton Pool, Alberta	22	1332	47	2.12
Jarrett Rose, Western Ontario	14	821	30	2.19
Jamie Bruno, Toronto	13	732	29	2.38
Chad Marshall, Wilfrid Laurier	23	1343	58	2.59

COLLEGE HOCKEY *CIAU*

CANADIAN COLLEGES

ATLANTIC UNIVERSITIES SPORTS, 2000-01 SEASON

FINAL STANDINGS

Team (Overall)	G	W	L	T	Pts.	GF	GA
St. F'cis Xavier (25-13-3)	28	17	18	3	37	115	83
St. Thomas (22-12-4)	28	16	8	4	36	110	94
Dalhousie (19-15-1)	28	15	12	1	31	111	104
New Brunswick (16-16-5)	28	13	10	5	31	101	102
Acadia (12-19-4)	28	11	13	4	26	75	86
St. Mary's (13-18-3)	28	11	14	3	25	106	99
Moncton (7-18-4)	27	7	16	4	18	107	127
P. Edward Island (8-17-2)	27	8	17	2	18	84	114

PLAYOFF RESULTS

QUARTERFINALS

Dalhousie 2, St. Mary's 1
Dalhousie 2, St. Mary's 1

Acadia 5, New Brunswick 1
New Brunswick 4, Acadia 3
New Brunswick 3, Acadia 1

SEMIFINALS

St. Thomas 7, Dalhousie 2
Dalhousie 3, St. Thomas 1
St. Thomas 4, Dalhousie 1

N. Bruns. 4, St. F'cis Xavier 1
St. F'cis Xavier 5, N. Bruns. 4
St. F. X. 5, N. Bruns. 4 (2OT)

LEAGUE FINALS

St. Thomas 6, St. Francis Xavier 3
St. Francis Xavier 9, St. Thomas 1
St. Thomas 2, St. Francis Xavier 1 (OT)

ALL-STAR TEAMS

First team	Pos.	Second team
Greg Hewitt, St. Thomas	G	Gene Chiarello, N. Brunswick
Dominique Auger, St.F.X.	D	Martin Latulippe, Moncton
Steve Gallace, St. Mary's	D	Greg Minard, New Brunswick
Yanick Evola, St.F.X.	F	Marty Johnson, Dalhousie
Jason Sands, St. Thomas	F	Chris Pittman, Dalhousie
Chad Spurr, P. Edward Is.	F	Ryan Walsh, New Brunswick

AWARD WINNERS

Most Valuable Player: Jason Sands, St. Thomas
Rookie of the year: Chad Spurr, Prince Edward Island
Most sportsmanlike player: Paul Andrea, St. Francis Xavier
Coach of the year: Fabian Joseph, Dalhousie
Leading scorer: Jason Sands, St. Thomas
Chad Spurr, Prince Edward Island

INDIVIDUAL LEADERS

Goals: Ryan Walsh, New Brunswick (21)
Assists: Yanick Evola, St. Francis Xavier (28)
Jason Sands, St. Thomas (28)
Points: Jason Sands, St. Thomas (41)
Chad Spurr, Prince Edward Island (41)
Penalty minutes: Samuel Gagnon, Moncton (123)
Goaltending average: Greg Hewitt, St. Thomas (3.04)

TOP SCORERS

	Games	G	A	Pts.
Chad Spurr, Prince Edward Island	24	16	25	41
Jason Sands, St. Thomas	26	13	28	41
Yanick Evola, St. Francis Xavier	25	12	28	40
Marty Johnson, Dalhousie	25	14	24	38
Jim Midgley, St. Mary's	28	10	27	37
Chris Stanley, Dalhousie	28	19	17	36
Ryan Walsh, New Brunswick	28	21	13	34
Carl Prudhomme, Moncton	26	16	17	33
Brett Gibson, St. Mary's	27	15	18	33
Dan Tudin, Dalhousie	26	10	23	33

TOP GOALTENDERS

	Games	Min.	GA	Avg.
Greg Hewitt, St. Thomas	26	1047	53	3.04
Nick Foley, St. Mary's	28	886	45	3.05
David Haun, St. Francis Xavier	28	1139	59	3.11
Pat Perrigan, Dalhousie	14	651	35	3.22
Mark Cairns, Acadia	26	1131	62	3.29

FINAL STANDINGS

EAST DIVISION

Team (Overall)	G	W	L	T	Pts.	GF	GA
Manitoba (23-16-4)	28	17	8	3	37	117	87
Sask. (21-15-4)	28	14	10	4	32	104	97
Regina (15-19-5)	28	9	14	5	23	94	108
Brandon (4-29-3)	28	4	21	3	11	91	185

WEST DIVISION

Team (Overall)	G	W	L	T	Pts.	GF	GA
Alberta (40-3-2)	28	25	1	2	52	146	57
Calgary (17-21-4)	28	13	12	3	29	121	100
Lethbridge (20-18-3)	28	11	14	3	25	100	105
Brit. Columbia (9-22-4)	28	6	19	3	15	74	108

PLAYOFF RESULTS

EAST DIVISION SEMIFINALS
Saskatchewan 6, Regina 2
Saskatchewan 6, Regina 4

WEST DIVISION SEMIFINALS
Lethbridge 3, Calgary 1
Calgary 4, Lethbridge 3 (OT)
Calgary 5, Lethbridge 4

EAST DIVISION FINALS
Saskatchewan 5, Manitoba 3
Manitoba 4, Saskatchewan 3
Manitoba 2, Saskatchewan 0

WEST DIVISION FINALS
Alberta 4, Calgary 0
Alberta 8, Calgary 0

LEAGUE FINALS
Alberta 5, Manitoba 1
Alberta 3, Manitoba 1

ALL-STAR TEAMS

First team	Pos.	Second team
Clayton Pool, Alberta	G	Tim Winters, Manitoba
Mike Garrow, Alberta	D	Jeff Henkelman, Sask.
Ryan Marsh, Alberta	D	Barrett Labossiere, Manitoba
Russ Hewson, Alberta	F	Jeremy Stasiuk, Sask.
Kris Knoblauch, Alberta	F	Ryan Wade, Alberta
Marc Gaudet, Manitoba	F	Ron Grimard, Calgary

AWARD WINNERS

Most Valuable Player: Russ Hewson, Alberta
Rookie of the year: Jeff Zorn, Alberta
Most sportsmanlike player: Kris Knoblauch, Alberta
Coach of the year: Rob Daum, Alberta
Leading scorer: Russ Hewson, Alberta

INDIVIDUAL LEADERS

Goals: Colin Embley, Calgary (27)
Assists: Russ Hewson, Alberta (35)
Points: Russ Hewson, Alberta (56)
Penalty minutes: Jeremy Stasiuk, Saskatchewan (101)
Goaltending average: Clayton Pool, Alberta (2.12)

TOP SCORERS

	Games	G	A	Pts.
Russ Hewson, Alberta	28	21	35	56
Kris Knoblauch, Alberta	28	24	26	50
Marc Gaudet, Manitoba	28	18	29	47
Jeremy Stasiuk, Saskatchewan	27	23	18	41
Ryan Wade, Alberta	28	15	26	41
Colin Embley, Calgary	28	27	13	40
Matt Holmes, Calgary	28	12	26	38
Alex Argyriou, Brandon	28	14	22	36
Ron Grimard, Calgary	21	17	16	33
Kevin Marsh, Alberta	28	13	20	33

TOP GOALTENDERS

	Games	Min.	GA	Avg.
Clayton Pool, Alberta	22	1332	47	2.12
Tim Winters, Manitoba	27	1493	74	2.97
Steve Nelson, Saskatchewan	22	1191	60	3.02
Robert Filc, British Columbia	19	1095	58	3.18
Andy Houthuys, Lethbridge	16	866	52	3.60

FINAL STANDINGS

FAR EAST DIVISION

Team (Overall)	G	W	L	T	Pts.	GF	GA
Trois-Rivieres (33-1-2)	24	21	1	2	44	130	46
Concordia (14-14-5)	24	10	9	5	25	83	82
McGill (13-15-3)	24	10	11	3	23	81	90
Ottawa (9-20-2)	24	6	16	2	14	75	89

MID EAST DIVISION

Team (Overall)	G	W	L	T	Pts.	GF	GA
Toronto (18-17-1)	24	13	10	1	27	90	77
Queen's (9-21-3)..........	24	6	16	2	14	75	108
Royal Military (9-24-0)	24	5	19	0	10	58	112

MID WEST DIVISION

Team (Overall)	G	W	L	T	Pts.	GF	GA
York (20-11-3)	24	15	6	3	33	107	92
Guelph (19-16-2)	24	11	11	2	24	85	100
Brock (11-19-3)	24	11	11	2	24	115	114
Ryerson (4-27-0).........	24	4	20	0	8	70	140

FAR WEST DIVISION

Team (Overall)	G	W	L	T	Pts.	GF	GA
W. Ontario (28-10-1) ...	24	21	3	0	42	145	59
Waterloo (20-21-2)......	24	15	7	2	32	102	75
W. Laurier (18-18-4)....	24	9	11	4	22	69	69
Windsor (9-19-2)..........	24	8	14	2	18	82	114

PLAYOFF RESULTS

FAR EAST DIVISION SEMIFINALS
Concordia 2, McGill 1
Concordia 3, McGill 2 (OT)

FAR EAST DIVISION FINALS
Trois-Rivieres 2, Concordia 1
Trois-Rivieres 8, Concordia 2

MID EAST DIVISION SEMIFINALS
Royal Mil. Col. 3, Queen's 2
Royal Mil. Col. 5, Queen's 0

MID EAST DIVISION FINALS
Toronto 10, Royal Mil. Col. 0
Royal Mil. Col. 5, Toronto 2
Toronto 4, Royal Mil. Col. 1

MID WEST DIVISION SEMIFINALS
Guelph 2, Brock 1
Guelph 5, Brock 4

MID WEST DIVISION FINALS
York 5, Guelph 2
York 5, Guelph 3

FAR WEST DIVISION SEMIFINALS
Waterloo 3, W. Laurier 2 (OT)
Wilfrid Laurier 4, Windsor 3
Waterloo 5, Wilfrid Laurier 3

FAR WEST DIVISION FINALS
W. Ontario 3, Waterloo 2
W. Ontario 5, Waterloo 2

LEAGUE SEMIFINALS
W. Ontario 7, York 3
Trois-Rivieres 4, Toronto 1

LEAGUE FINALS
Trois-Rivieres 4, W. Ontario 3

ALL-STAR TEAMS

First team	Pos.	Second team
Luc Belanger, T.-R.	G	Chad Marshall, Wilf. Laurier
Rob Maric, Waterloo	D	Karl Castonguay, Concordia
Daniel McLean, McGill	D	Ryan McKie, W. Ontario
Alexandre Tremblay, T.-R.	F	Jeff Petrie, W. Ontario
Greg Davis, McGill	F	Jean-Philippe Pare, T.-R.
Mike Williams, York	F	Darren Mortier, W. Ontario

AWARD WINNERS

Most Valuable Player: Alexandre Tremblay, Trois-Rivieres
Rookie of the year: Alexandre Tremblay, Trois-Rivieres
Most sportsmanlike player: Mike Williams, York
Coach of the year: Clarke Singer, Western Ontario
Leading scorer: Alexandre Tremblay, Trois-Rivieres

INDIVIDUAL LEADERS

Goals: Alexandre Tremblay, Trois-Rivieres (29)
Assists: Jean-Philippe Pare, Trois-Rivieres (32)
Points: Alexandre Tremblay, Trois-Rivieres (53)
Penalty minutes: David Anthony, Ryerson (105)
Goaltending average: Luc Belanger, Trois-Rivieres (1.91)

TOP SCORERS

	Games	G	A	Pts.
Alexandre Tremblay, Trois-Rivieres ...	24	29	24	53
Jean-Philippe Pare, Trois-Rivieres...	24	16	32	48
Shaun Fairweather, Western Ontario.	23	20	22	42
Dan Bassi, Brock	23	18	24	42
Kent Nobes, Brock.............................	23	23	18	41
Greg Davis, McGill	22	21	20	41
Brett Turner, Waterloo	24	19	20	39
Mike Williams, York...........................	23	13	25	38
Joe Forte, Brock	21	14	23	37
Dave Burgess, McGill	24	10	27	37

TOP GOALTENDERS

	Games	Min.	GA	Avg.
Luc Belanger, Trois-Rivieres..............	18	1039	33	1.91
Jarrett Rose, Western Ontario...........	14	821	30	2.19
Jamie Bruno, Toronto........................	13	732	29	2.38
Chad Marshall, Wilfrid Laurier...........	23	1343	58	2.59
Denver England, Western Ontario	10	643	28	2.61

COLLEGE HOCKEY *Canadian Colleges*

INDEX OF TEAMS

NHL, MINOR LEAGUES, MAJOR JUNIOR LEAGUES

Acadie-Bathurst (QMJHL) . 354
Adirondack (UHL) 319
Albany (AHL) 256
Amarillo (Cent.HL) 308
Anaheim (NHL). 5
Arkansas (ECHL). 288
Asheville (UHL) 319
Atlanta (NHL) 8
Atlantic City (ECHL) 288
Augusta (ECHL) 288
Austin (Cent.HL) 308
Baie-Comeau (QMJHL) . . . 354
Barrie (OHL) 337
Baton Rouge (ECHL). 288
Belleville (OHL). 337
Binghamton (UHL) 319
Bossier (Cent.HL) 308
Boston (NHL) 11
Brampton (OHL) 337
Brandon (WHL). 369
Bridgeport (AHL) 256
Buffalo (NHL) 14
Calgary (NHL). 17
Calgary (WHL) 369
Cape Breton (QMJHL) 354
Carolina (NHL) 20
Charlotte (ECHL) 288
Chicago (AHL) 256
Chicago (NHL) 23
Chicoutimi (QMJHL) 354
Cincinnati (AHL) 256
Cincinnati (ECHL) 288
Cleveland (AHL) 256
Colorado (NHL) 26
Columbia (ECHL) 288
Columbus (ECHL) 288
Columbus (NHL). 29
Corpus Christi (Cent.HL) . 308
Dallas (NHL). 32
Dayton (ECHL) 288
Detroit (NHL) 35
Drummondville (QMJHL) . 354
Edmonton (NHL). 38

Elmira (UHL). 319
El Paso (Cent.HL) 308
Erie (OHL) 337
Flint (UHL) 319
Florida (ECHL) 288
Florida (NHL) 41
Fort Wayne (UHL) 319
Fort Worth (Cent.HL) 308
Grand Rapids (AHL) 256
Greensboro (ECHL) 289
Greensville (ECHL) 289
Guelph (OHL) 337
Halifax (QMJHL) 354
Hamilton (AHL) 256
Hartford (AHL) 256
Hershey (AHL) 256
Houston (AHL) 257
Hull (QMJHL) 354
Indianapolis (Cent.HL) . . . 308
Johnstown (ECHL) 289
Kalamazoo (UHL) 319
Kamloops (WHL) 369
Kelowna (WHL) 369
Kingston (OHL). 337
Kitchener (OHL) 337
Knoxville (UHL) 319
Kootenay (WHL) 369
Lethbridge (WHL) 369
London (OHL). 337
Los Angeles (NHL) 44
Louisiana (ECHL) 289
Lowell (AHL). 257
Lubbock (Cent.HL) 308
Macon (ECHL) 289
Manchester (AHL). 257
Manitoba (AHL) 257
Medicine Hat (WHL) 369
Memphis (Cent.HL). 308
Milwaukee (AHL) 257
Minnesota (NHL) 47
Mississauga (OHL) 337
Mississippi (ECHL) 289
Missouri (UHL). 319

Mobile (ECHL) 289
Moncton (QMJHL) 354
Montreal (NHL). 50
Montreal (QMJHL) 354
Moose Jaw (WHL) 369
Muskegon (UHL) 320
Nashville (NHL) 53
New Haven (UHL) 320
New Mexico (Cent.HL) . . 308
New Orleans (ECHL) 289
New Jersey (NHL). 56
New York Islanders (NHL). . 59
New York Rangers (NHL) . . 62
Norfolk (AHL) 257
North Bay (OHL) 337
Odessa (Cent.HL) 309
Oklahoma City (Cent.HL). . 309
Oshawa (OHL) 337
Ottawa (NHL). 65
Ottawa (OHL) 337
Owen Sound (OHL). 337
Pee Dee (ECHL) 289
Pensacola (ECHL) 289
Peoria (ECHL). 289
Peterborough (OHL) 337
Philadelphia (AHL) 257
Philadelphia (NHL) 68
Phoenix (NHL) 71
Pittsburgh (NHL) 74
Plymouth (OHL) 337
Port Huron (UHL) 320
Portland (AHL) 257
Portland (WHL). 369
Prince Albert (WHL) 369
Prince George (WHL) . . . 369
Providence (AHL) 257
Quad City (UHL) 320
Quebec (AHL) 257
Quebec (QMJHL) 354
Reading (ECHL) 289
Red Deer (WHL) 369
Regina (WHL). 369
Richmond (ECHL) 289

Rimouski (QMJHL) 354
Roanoke (ECHL) 290
Rochester (AHL) 257
Rockford (UHL) 320
Rouyn-Noranda (QMJHL) . 354
Saint John (AHL) 257
St. John's (AHL) 257
St. Louis (NHL). 77
San Angelo (Cent.HL) 309
San Antonio (Cent.HL) . . . 309
San Jose (NHL) 80
Sarnia (OHL). 337
Saskatoon (WHL) 369
Sault Ste. Marie (OHL) . . . 337
Scranton (AHL). 258
Seattle (WHL). 369
Shawinigan (QMJHL) 354
Sherbrooke (QMJHL) 354
Shreveport (Cent.HL) 308
South Carolina (ECHL) . . . 290
Spokane (WHL) 369
Springfield (AHL) 258
Sudbury (OHL) 337
Swift Current (WHL) 369
Syracuse (AHL). 258
Tampa Bay (NHL) 83
Toledo (ECHL). 290
Toronto (NHL) 86
Toronto (OHL). 337
Trenton (ECHL) 290
Tri-City (WHL) 369
Tulsa (Cent.HL) 309
Utah (AHL) 258
Val d'Or (QMJHL) 354
Vancouver (NHL) 89
Victoriaville (QMJHL) 354
Washington (NHL) 92
Wheeling (ECHL) 290
Wichita (Cent.HL) 309
Wilkes-Barre (AHL) 258
Windsor (OHL) 337
Worcester (AHL) 258

COLLEGE TEAMS

Acadia (AUS) 405
Alaska-Anch. (WCHA) 400
Alaska-F'banks (CCHA) . . . 389
Alberta (CWUAA) 406
Boston College (H.East) . . 397
Boston Univ. (H.East) 397
Bowling Green St. (CCHA) . 389
Brandon (CWUAA) 406
Brit. Columbia (CWUAA) . . 406
Brock (OUA) 407
Brown (ECAC). 393
Calgary (CWUAA) 406
Clarkson (ECAC) 393
Colgate (ECAC) 393
Colo. College (WCHA) 400
Concordia (OUA). 407
Cornell (ECAC) 393
Dalhousie (AUS) 405
Dartmouth (ECAC) 393

Denver (WCHA) 400
Ferris State (CCHA). 389
Guelph (OUA) 407
Harvard (ECAC) 393
Lake Superior St. (CCHA) . 389
Lethbridge (CWUAA). 406
Lowell (H.East) 397
Maine (H.East) 397
Manitoba (CWUAA). 406
Mankato State (WCHA) . . . 400
Massachusetts (H.East). . . 397
McGill (OUA) 407
Merrimack (H.East). 397
Miami of Ohio (CCHA). . . . 389
Michigan (CCHA) 389
Michigan State (CCHA) . . . 389
Michigan Tech (WCHA) . . . 400
Minnesota (WCHA) 400
Min.-Duluth (WCHA). 400

Moncton (AUS). 405
Nebraska-Omaha (CCHA) . 389
New Brunswick (AUS). . . . 405
New Hampshire (H.East) . . 397
North Dakota (WCHA) 400
Northeastern (H.East) 397
N. Michigan (CCHA) 389
Notre Dame (CCHA) 389
Ohio State (CCHA) 389
Ottawa (OUA) 407
Prince Edward Is. (AUS) . . 405
Princeton (ECAC) 393
Providence (H.East) 397
Quebec at T.-Riv. (OUA) . . 407
Queen's (OUA) 407
Regina (CWUAA) 406
Rensselaer (ECAC) 393
Royal Military (OUA) 407
Ryerson Poly. Inst. (OUA) . . 407

St. Cloud State (WCHA) . . . 400
St. Francis Xavier (AUS) . . 405
St. Lawrence (ECAC). 393
St. Mary's (AUS) 405
St. Thomas (AUS) 405
Saskatchewan (CWUAA) . . 406
Toronto (OUA) 407
Union (ECAC) 393
Vermont (ECAC) 393
Waterloo (OUA) 407
Western Michigan (CCHA). . 389
Western Ontario (OUA) . . . 407
Wilfrid Laurier (OUA) 407
Windsor (OUA) 407
Wisconsin (WCHA) 400
Yale (ECAC) 393
York (OUA). 407

INDEX OF TEAMS